D0989783

No Longer Property of
Phillips Memorial Library

BASEBALL RECORDS REGISTRY

Dedicated to the Society for American Baseball Research
and the spirit of cooperation it fosters

For Reference Only
Not For Circulation

BASEBALL RECORDS REGISTRY

*The Best and Worst
Single-Day Performances
and the Stories Behind Them*

by JOSEPH J. DITTMAR

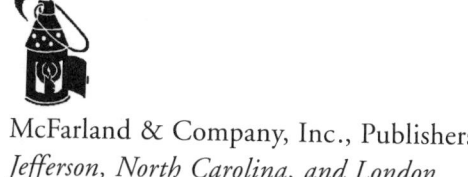

McFarland & Company, Inc., Publishers
Jefferson, North Carolina, and London

Phillips Memorial
Library
Providence College

REF
GV
877
D 576
1997

Front Cover: Seattle Mariners' southpaw Randy Johnson. *Back Cover:* Slick fielding shortstop Eddie Joost of the Cincinnati Reds seemed to be in the middle of every play on May 7, 1941, accepting a record-setting 19 chances (both photographs courtesy National Baseball Library and Archive, Cooperstown, New York).

ACKNOWLEDGMENTS: A book of this size would not have been possible without the help of many knowledgeable and dedicated baseball researchers. Foremost among them are members of the Society for American Baseball Research, especially Lyle Spatz and Jim "Snuffy" Smith, who have tirelessly served as editors and cheerleaders during the past six years, offering ideas and encouragement. Frank Phelps also assisted in the early stages. Indispensable, too, were the hours spent in libraries and the pounds of photocopies provided from distant cities by SABR members Bob Bluthardt, Jim Moore, Jim Nitz, John O'Malley, Bob Richardson, John Schwartz, Mike Selleck, David Stephan, Mark Strang, Bob Tiemann, Rich Topp, Jim Weigand, and Walt Wilson. Many of the more tedious details could not have been resolved without the National Baseball Library staff, and particularly Senior Research Associate Bill Deane, who staunchly verified data contained in the official league records. David W. Smith generously offered invaluable research materials from his remarkable Retrosheet project. Latter-day statistical data were provided by Gary Gillette, president of the Baseball Workshop. For years the late Ed Doyle added charm as well as information from his scrapbooks and treasure chest of personal remembrances. David Vincent extracted season home run totals from the Tattersall/McConnell home run log, and Marc Okkonen graciously provided his outstanding artwork of several turn-of-the-century ballparks. Confusing scoring plays in several games were clarified by rules experts Dennis Bingham and Allen Lewis. Frank Williams lent his expertise with several pitchers' won-lost records, and Norman Macht offered much help regarding the Red Barrett masterpiece.

Photographs on pages 282 and 291 are courtesy of *The Cininnati Enquirer*; photograph on page 555 courtesy of *Toronto Star Syndicate*; photograph on page 577 courtesy of John Kuntz; all others are courtesy of the National Baseball Library and Archive, Cooperstown, New York.

Wherever possible, baseball cartoons have been interspersed with the game descriptions. These delightful highlight summaries once graced most newspapers' sports pages and were an integral part of game coverage. Sadly, they have virtually disappeared over time. A debt of gratitude is owed to those artists for this often neglected contribution to baseball history, and to their newspapers for allowing their resurrection. Fifteen newspapers, most now extinct, are cited throughout this collection.

British Library Cataloguing-in-Publication data are available

Library of Congress Cataloguing-in-Publication Data

Dittmar, Joe.
    Baseball records registry : the best and worst single-day
performances and the stories behind them / by Joseph J. Dittmar.
      p.   cm.
    Includes bibliographical references and index.
    ISBN 0-7864-0293-8 (case binding : 50# alkaline paper) ∞
    1. Baseball—Records—United States.   2. Baseball—United States—
History.   I. Title.
GV877.D576   1997
796.357'0973—dc21   97-1472
                                    CIP

©1997 Joseph J. Dittmar. All rights reserved

No part of this book, specifically including the table of contents and index, may be reproduced or transmitted in any form or by any means, electronic or mechanical, including photocopying or recording, or by any information storage and retrieval system, without permission in writing from the publisher.

Manufactured in the United States of America

McFarland & Company, Inc., Publishers
  Box 611, Jefferson, North Carolina 28640

TABLE OF CONTENTS

INTRODUCTION

Baseball Records Registry is an accurate and comprehensive account of baseball's benchmark games. Want to know the record for the most runs scored to overcome defeat, the most home runs allowed by a winning pitcher, or the most men left on base in a single game? You'll find it here — not simply a listing, but the circumstances surrounding each record and details of the plays that produced it.

Many of baseball's records are widely celebrated, such as Roger Clemens' 20 strikeouts or the many players who have hit four home runs in one game. Those marks, of course, are described in this anthology. But readers will discover that not all records are cause for celebration when they learn how catcher Steve O'Neill endured eight stolen bases in one inning, or how Roy Patterson was abandoned on the mound one humiliating day to face no fewer than 57 batters during a nine-inning pummelling.

Readers will also find that the surrounding circumstances are often as fascinating as the records themselves. Consider that the last man to make six errors in a single contest did so because he was playing out of position, or that the major factor accounting for 23 doubles being hit in a game was an overflow of 8,000 patrons milling about an outfield, reducing the playing field to schoolboy dimensions.

A comprehensive index offers easy access to players, umpires, teams, and events. Want to know in which record-setting games your favorite player was involved? Or are you interested only in stolen base records? The index offers easy reference to either domain.

The chronological arrangement of this book is purposeful, tracing the evolution not only of the record-setting events, but of the game itself — the style of play, the reporting, the strategies, the scoring rules, and the interaction among fans, managers, and owners. The ambience of the era was oftentimes as instrumental in the establishment of the record as were the players' performances.

Omitted from this work are accounts of multi-game, accumulated statistics and streaks. Thus there is no treatment of DiMaggio's 56-game hitting streak or Hank Aaron's 715th home run. Those events are not within the scope of this work and have been well documented elsewhere. Rather, each individual game, or in a few cases a doubleheader (and one tripleheader), stands alone as the pinnacle of some single-day achievement or the nadir of failure and embarrassment.

The ground rules of *Baseball Records Registry* also eliminate World Series, League Championship, and nineteenth-century games. The author appreciates the rich history of the National Pastime prior to the turn of the century but feels that many incongruities make reasonable comparisons between the nineteenth and twentieth centuries impossible. The fair-foul and the foul-strike rules, the vacillating number of balls for a walk or strikes for an out, underhand pitching, flat bats, the general lack of gloves, etc., all make correlation most difficult. True, a case could be made for launching this collection with games played in 1893, when the pitcher's delivery point reached its present distance. But the turn of the century was when baseball and the significant playing/scoring rules attained a degree of stability. Thus all records in this book, unless otherwise noted, pertain to twentieth-century accomplishments. A nineteenth-century treatment of similar material would make a welcome supplement to this work.

The timing of this publication corresponds with a turbulent period in baseball history. With labor strife temporarily assuaged, baseball record books are now about to fall under attack. The advent of inter-league play in 1997 looms to disrupt the established inventory of American and National League records, so that this work contains a final analysis of traditional records as compiled by the separate leagues.

THE BOXSCORES

The common thread that binds these games over the 96-year period is that standard of baseball reporting, the boxscore. Great pains have been taken to present the reader with accurate, greatly detailed, and balanced versions of these miniature accounting sheets. To that end, the author has relied heavily on the reporting of multiple hometown newspapers, they being generally more descriptive and accurate than wire service renditions, although both *The Sporting News* and *Sporting Life* were included in the investigations.

The earliest known boxscores of the nineteenth century simply contained runs scored and outs made; as the decades passed, at-bats, hits, fielding, and pitching data were gradually added. Turn-of-the-century boxscores contained satisfying fielding information for each player, but they excluded certain statistics that modern readers have come to expect. Games played prior to 1912 in the National League and prior to 1913 in the American League had neither earned runs nor RBIs listed in newspapers or charted in the official records. It wasn't until 1920 that RBIs were first officially logged for both leagues. Thus, for earned runs and RBIs, a meticulous analysis of multiple newspaper accounts was undertaken in order to piece together the necessary information. Fortunately for baseball historians, with a plethora of early

newspapers competing for circulation and baseball occupying such an important place in America's leisure time, the sport was afforded wonderfully detailed reporting. Many newspapers carried play-by-play descriptions of the home team's games, some on the front pages. Thus in compiling this book it was possible not only to glean earned runs and RBIs but also to discover such details as which batters struck out, who got caught stealing, the innings in which substitutes appeared, or who hit into and who fielded the double plays.

Pitching statistics for all games earlier than 1970 were verified through the official day-by-day league records. This contributed a degree of certainty to the number of team at-bats, hits, and left-on-base as well as to which batter made the final out for each side. Although this may seem like an unnecessary step to readers of modern boxscores, in baseball's adolescence, hometown newspapers often varied in their reporting of such information, and wire services were even more unreliable. Whenever multiple hometown newspaper accounts did not balance with play-by-play descriptions and the aforementioned official league pitching records, another tactic was followed. The official league record for each and every player who participated in such a game was researched and then combined to produce a balanced boxscore. Such games are noted with a "DBD" (day-by-day records) reference in the "Sources" section of the boxscore. Obviously, official league records, especially those that were recorded, tabulated and transferred manually, are also fallible. But because they have been supplemented where necessary, the reader holds in his hands the most accurate boxscore possible with the technology and information now available.

The "Sources" section of each boxscore also notes the newspapers that supplied information about each particular game. The names of these newspapers were provided so that readers wishing to verify the details here presented may readily do so, and so that future researchers who wish to expand their knowledge of a particular record will know what sources have already been examined.

For games beginning in the late 1940s, Dave Smith's Retrosheet collection was used wherever possible. This outstanding collection of old score books from announcers, writers and team officials helped to offset the more superficial baseball reporting that had begun by that time. The Retrosheet collection proved to be an invaluable source of accuracy as did its modern day counterpart, The Baseball Workshop. For example, as recently as 1989, newspaper boxscores from both the hometown and the wire services omitted a player from the boxscore who was a late-inning defensive replacement. The Baseball Workshop exposed that omission.

A word about notations of "AL" and "NL": When a city with both an American League and a National League team faced another city with two teams, the designation "AL" or "NL" was used to indicate which teams were playing (for instance, "Philadelphia AL vs. New York"). If a city with two teams faced a city with only one team, the designation is unnecessary and has been omitted (for instance, "Philadelphia vs. Cincinnati").

UNEXPECTED TREASURES

Personally, this effort has been an education and a joy. Collecting information has carried me briefly to libraries in Chicago, Cleveland, Dallas, Detroit, New York, Philadelphia and Pittsburgh, and frequently led me on overnight trips to the National Baseball Library in Cooperstown and to the Library of Congress in Washington D.C. I've had the pleasure of meeting and corresponding with SABR members and baseball experts from across the country, exchanging research and sharing some of the delights and frustrations of poring over miles of microfilm in hopes of finding needed morsels of information.

The least expected but perhaps the most exciting aspect of my journey concerned the record claims themselves. Little did I realize six years ago that baseball's annals would be anything less than perfect. After all, many ardent researchers have contributed to them. But alas, like many human efforts, those collections harbored an unexpected degree of inaccuracy. Particularly suspect were many of the benchmarks established prior to 1920, a time when the baseball public was not consumed with statistics as it is today. Some of the errors have been perpetuated for decades, leaking into general baseball literature and tainting one publication after another. Appendix C describes several dozen of these errors and the alterations necessary to maintain the integrity of baseball records. They are of three general types: 1) records established in older games that were never noted, 2) old claims about events that simply never happened, and 3) new discoveries that exceed past claims. The reasons for the inaccuracies include shoddy newspaper reporting, typographical errors, information taken out of context, and less than thorough research, particularly the reliance on a single wire-service source. One or two sources are rarely enough to make any seasoned baseball researcher content, so each of these discoveries has been verified through multiple primary sources including several hometown newspapers along with the official league records. For games of the first few decades, as many as a dozen newspapers from the towns of the two combatants were explored.

Baseball records are a dynamic lot, subject to change not only through the accomplishments of modern players, but also through the application of improved research techniques to the achievements of the past. It should be expected that future researchers will continue to exhume new information, thereby upgrading the veracity of baseball record books.

JOE DITTMAR
March 1, 1997

BOXSCORE LEGEND

>	Team's Last Batter in the game
2B	Doubles
3B	Triples
A	Assists
AB	Official At-Bats
ATTENDANCE	In event of conflicting attendance figures, an average was calculated and rounded
BALANCE	This mathematical formula "proves" the statistics, putting them in balance to account for each and every plate appearance made in a single game.
BB	Bases on balls: allowed by pitchers, credited to batters, (I) after batter's name indicates intentional walk when known
BBWS	Baseball Workshop (listed as a "Source"). An organization dedicated to scoring games pitch-by-pitch; their data were utilized with games beginning in 1984.
BK	Balk
BP	Batters facing pitchers (includes *all* plate appearances)
CI	Catcher's interference or any defensive interference allowing a batter to reach base
CS	Runner caught stealing (when known)
DBD	*Day-By-Day* (listed as a "Source"). Indicates that official league records for each player were researched for these games.
DP	Double plays, fielders followed by the (batter) when known
E	Errors
ER	Earned runs allowed
H	Hits, made by batters, allowed by pitchers
HP	Hit by pitch, pitcher followed by (batter); also in "balance" proof of box-score
HR	Home Runs; in parentheses is that player's total at game's conclusion
I	RBIs; also see BB
ICI	*Information Concepts Incorporated* (listed as a "Source"). Indicates that these daily records (housed in the National Baseball Library) for each player were researched.
IP	Innings pitched, .1 = one-third of an inning; .2 = two-thirds of an inning
L,1-2	This pitcher took the loss; his record *after* this game was 1 Win–2 Losses
OB	Left on Base
OUT	in BALANCE, number of outs made by a team in the game
p9	Pitcher entered game in ninth inning
PB	Passed Ball
ph3,rf	This player pinch-hit in third inning then played right field

5

PK	Runners picked off base
PO	Putouts
R	Runs, scored by batters, allowed by pitchers
Retrosheet	Archival Play-By-Play Accounts taken from reporters, announcers, or team officals' scorebooks
SB	Stolen Base
SF	Sacrifice Fly (when known)
SH	Sacrifice Hit
SO	Strikeouts made by pitchers (in boxscore); by batters (in summary)
SOURCES	Details of game were culled predominantly from these. The first newspaper (alphabetically) from a particular city has that city name spelled out. All other newspapers from that city have the city name omitted, for example, *Detroit Free Press*, *News*, and *Tribune* are three separate Detroit newspapers.
TIME	In event of conflicting game times, hometown majority took precedence.
W,4-3	This pitcher got the victory; his record *after* the game was 4 wins, 3 loses
WP	Wild Pitch

THE REGISTRY

He Who Laughs Last, Laughs Best

1. Team Scores Ten Runs in the Bottom of the Ninth

MILWAUKEE   at   DETROIT
(Brewers, 13)   (Tigers, 14)

Thursday, April 25, 1901, Bennett Park

Baseball fans in the city of Detroit buzzed with excitement over their entry into the brash new "major" league. For both the Tigers and their guests, the Milwaukee Brewers, this day marked both franchises' very first game in the American League as it is known

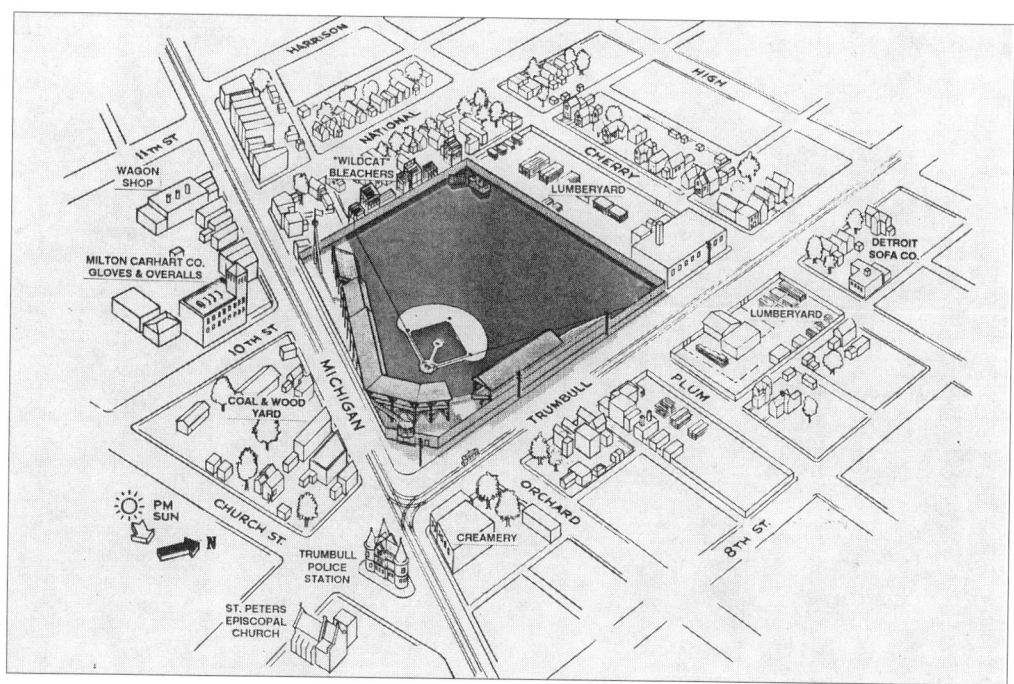

Bennett Park — Detroit (courtesy of Marc Okkonen).

7

today. The scene of the action was Bennett Park, named after Charlie Bennett, a local favorite and catcher for the Detroit Wolverines more than a decade earlier. Charlie's career had ended abruptly when he lost both legs in a train accident. Nevertheless, he was in attendance to catch the ceremonial first ball.

Bennett Park was a typical turn-of-the-century ballpark. Built on a former haymarket, the playing surface was lumpy at best, and cobblestones frequently surfaced, creating a fielding adventure. Flags were flown from a modest wooden grandstand that extended from first to third base. Seating capacity was slightly over 8,000, and it was understood that any excess attendance for special events would gather along the fringes of the outfield. This day was just such an event, and the standing-room-only crowd proved instrumental in the outcome of the contest.

The celebration began with a parade to the park by both teams, city officials, invited guests, and about 500 members of the Elks. The procession enabled the fans to get a glimpse of their new heroes, and the hometown ball club displayed fresh red overcoats

and caps emblazoned with little red tigers. By the time the clubs reached the field it was engulfed in humanity, 10,023 paid, surpassing by thousands the previous record turnout for a baseball game in Detroit. Players of both teams then gathered around the batting area to exchange flowers and trophies while on home plate sat a dog named "Oom Paul," Detroit's mascot.

Oom Paul's reputation was quickly placed in jeopardy as the Brewers jumped off to a 7-0 lead after just three innings. The home club sabotaged its own efforts by committing five errors to that point. After six innings, Milwaukee manager Hugh Duffy felt comfortable enough with a 7–3 lead to relieve starter Pink Hawley and give Pete Dowling some work. In retrospect, it was a disastrous move as Dowling was ruthlessly pummeled in his two innings of work.

Milwaukee had entered the last half of the ninth with a very comfortable 13–4 advantage. But then disaster struck as the Tigers pushed across ten runs for the win, hammering Dowling for two singles and four doubles in the frame before registering an out.

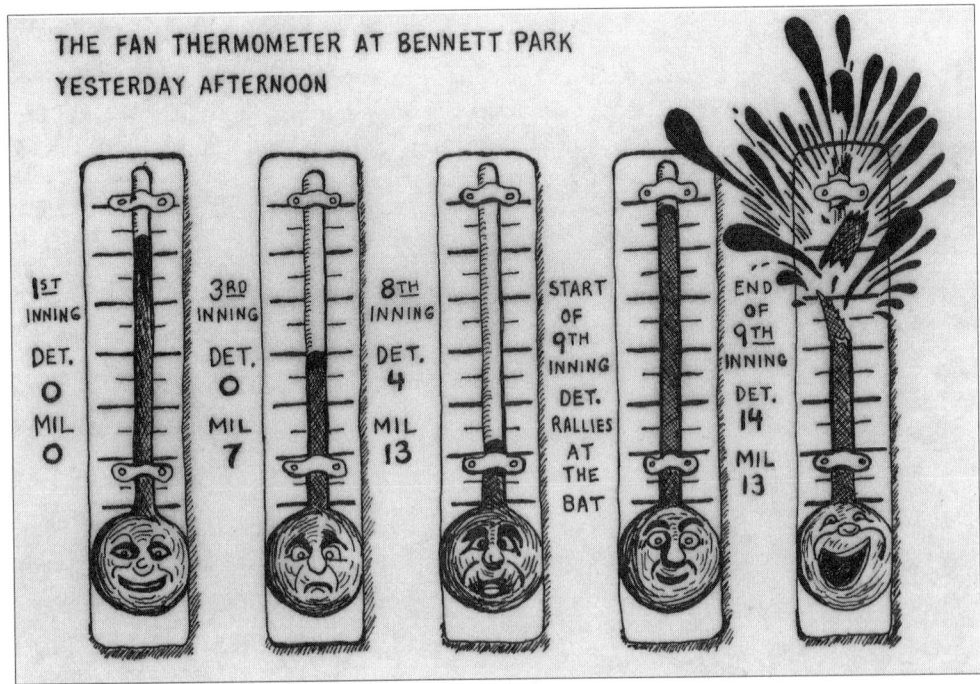

THE FAN THERMOMETER AT BENNETT PARK
YESTERDAY AFTERNOON

1ST INNING	3RD INNING	8TH INNING	START OF 9TH INNING	END OF 9TH INNING
DET. 0	DET. 0	DET. 4	DET. RALLIES AT THE BAT	DET. 14
MIL 0	MIL 7	MIL 13		MIL 13

The Detroit News *depicted the hometown crowd sentiment as the game progressed (reprinted with permission of* The Detroit News*).*

Hero Dillon was carried around the field (National Baseball Library & Archive, Cooperstown, N.Y.).

Although neither the ten runs they scored in the bottom of the ninth nor the ten-run deficit from which they emerged remain records, the tenacity displayed by the Tigers certainly fed the baseball torch burning in the new major league city.

Following is a play-by-play of Detroit's miraculous deliverance:

• Doc Casey led off the ninth with a ground-rule double into the crowd standing in left field.

• Jimmy Barrett beat out a slow roller to third baseman Jimmy Burke.

• Kid Gleason singled to center, knocking in Casey.

• Ducky Holmes doubled home Barrett as the fervor of the crowd waxed. With each positive Tiger move they thundered their approval, unnerving Brewer hurler Dowling.

• Pop Dillon followed suit with another double, his third of the day, sending Gleason and Holmes across the dish.

• Kid Elberfeld sent still another double into the crowd in right center enabling Dillon to score. The Tigers were then just four runs down, and the first out had yet to be made. This brought Brewer manager

Hugh Duffy in from his center field position, and he ordered Dowling from the box in favor of Bert Husting. But Bert had not warmed up, and his first toss was a wild one, sending Elberfeld to third.

• Doc Nance grounded to short for Detroit's first out of the inning. At this point the frenzied crowd, which had begun to encroach on the outfielders, was making further play almost impossible. To avoid any notion of a forfeit, the Tiger players ran onto the field and pushed the throng back. Although this provided Husting an opportunity to thoroughly warm up, it didn't help Milwaukee's cause.

• Fritz Buelow, the eighth Tiger batter to appear this inning, walked. Then, according to the *Detroit Free Press*, "hats were being thrown in the air, coats were flying, and everyone was yelling themselves hoarse."

• Emil Frisk fueled the frenzy by singling to left, knocking in Elberfeld.

• Doc Casey appeared at the plate for the second time in the inning and beat out a bunt, filling the bases.

• Barrett disappointed and silenced the crowd temporarily when he was called out on strikes by home plate umpire Jack Sheridan, a dauntless call to say the least. There were then two outs, and the Tigers still trailed by three runs.

• Gleason then hit a sharp grounder to Burke who could have ended the game with a clean grab. But he fumbled it, keeping Detroit's hopes alive as Buelow scored on the misplay.

• Holmes beat out another slow roller to Burke on which Frisk scored. It was then 13–12.

• Dillon delivered the coup de grâce by doubling into the crowd. It was his fourth two-bagger of the game as Casey scored, and Gleason followed with the winning run. Not for twelve years would another major leaguer hit four doubles in a single game.

With Dillon's double, the delirious crowd surged onto the field, everyone trying to pat their hero on the back. Surrounded by hundreds, Pop couldn't escape. Finally, he was hoisted onto the fans' shoulders and paraded in triumph around the grounds.

Milwaukee Brewers	AB	R	H	I	PO	A	E
Irv Waldron rf	5	1	0	0	0	0	0
Billy Gilbert 2b	6	1	3	0	1	4	0
>Bill Hallman lf	5	1	0	0	4	0	1
John Anderson 1b	4	1	2	0	11	1	0
Wid Conroy ss	5	4	4	3	2	3	1
Hugh Duffy cf	4	2	1	1	2	0	0
Jimmy Burke 3b	5	2	3	4	2	2	2
Tom Leahy c	4	1	1	1	4	2	0
Pink Hawley p	3	0	1	2	0	2	0
Pete Dowling p7	1	0	1	0	0	1	0
Bert Husting p9	0	0	0	0	0	0	0
	42	13	16	11	*26	15	4

Detroit Tigers	AB	R	H	I	PO	A	E
Doc Casey 3b	6	3	2	0	1	4	0
Jimmy Barrett cf	5	1	1	0	2	0	0
Kid Gleason 2b	6	2	3	2	2	2	1
Ducky Holmes rf	6	2	2	2	0	0	1
>Pop Dillon 1b	6	3	4	5	9	1	1
Kid Elberfeld ss	4	1	2	2	5	5	3
Doc Nance lf	5	0	1	1	3	0	1
Fritz Buelow c	4	1	1	0	5	5	0
Roscoe Miller p	0	0	0	0	0	0	0
Emil Frisk p3	5	1	3	1	0	5	0
	47	14	19	13	27	22	7

Milwaukee	IP	H	R	ER	BB	SO
Hawley	6	5	3	2	1	0
Dowling	2	10	7	7	1	3
Husting L,0–1	.2	4	4	0	1	1
	*8.2	19	14	9	3	4

Detroit	IP	H	R	ER	BB	SO
Miller	2.1	6	7	4	1	0
Frisk W,1–0	6.2	10	6	6	3	2
	9	16	13	10	4	2

* *Two outs when winning run scored.*

Milwaukee	0	2	5	0	0	0	3	3	0	-13
Detroit	0	0	0	2	1	0	0	1	10	-14

OB: Milwaukee 8, Detroit 10
2B: Conroy, Duffy, Burke, Casey,
   Gleason, Dillon 4, Elberfeld 2
SB: Casey, Gleason
SO: Casey, Elberfeld, Holmes,
   Barrett, Hallman, Burke
BB: Waldron, Anderson, Duffy, Hawley
   Barrett, Elberfeld, Buelow
SH: Hallman, Leahy
WP: Dowling, Husting, Frisk

PB: Leahy
TIME: 2:35
ATTENDANCE: 10,023
UMPIRES: Jack Sheridan, Alfred
   Mannasseau
SOURCES: Detroit Evening News, Free-
   Press, Journal, Tribune; Milwaukee
   Journal, Sentinel; Sporting News

BALANCE	OUT	+R	+OB	=BP	=AB	+BB	+SH	+HB	+CI
Milwaukee	27	13	8	48	42	4	2	0	0
Detroit	26	14	10	50	47	3	0	0	0

Boston Explosion Buries Athletics

2. Team Scores Nineteen Runs in Consecutive Innings

BOSTON, AL   at   PHILADELPHIA
(Pilgrims, 23)   (Athletics, 12)

Thursday, May 2, 1901, Columbia Park

The Boston Pilgrims, fresh off a 14–1 drubbing by the Philadelphia Athletics, turned the tables on Connie Mack's squad and mauled them 23–12. In the process, the Pilgrims scored nine runs in the second inning followed by ten in the third. The *19*

Collins (left) and Parent led the Pilgrims' assault.

tallies in two consecutive frames remains a mark unsurpassed in modern baseball annals, although it was matched 52 years later (see 6-18-53).

The Pilgrims commenced rather innocuously by scoring two runs in the top of the first off 23-year-old rookie right-hander Pete Loos. Loos was a local boy who had impressed Mack in an exhibition game against the Athletics. Now, with three of Philadelphia's four starters experiencing a rash of physical problems, Mack was in desperate need of a warm body to send to the mound. Thus Loos entered his first major league game.

Newspapers of the day surmised that the rookie's nerves got the best of him in the second inning as the first four Pilgrims were issued free passes on only 16 pitches. Boston batters soon learned to keep their bats on their shoulders and, with each pitch, the crowd roared their disapproval. When Loos finally went 2–0 to the fifth batter, Tommy Dowd, Mack rescued the rookie and sent veteran Bill Bernhard to the hill. As Pete returned to the bench, little did he realize that he had pitched for the last time in the major leagues. With Bernhard on the mound, Boston switched tactics and, instead of waiting for walks, began to clobber the ball. Here's how those two record-setting innings unfolded:

• As noted, Loos walked Freddy Parent, Hobe Ferris, Lou Criger, and Ted Lewis before throwing two balls to Dowd.

• Bernhard completed Dowd's walk, then got Charlie Jones to lift a high fly to left. Fred Ketchum, who had a reputation as an atrocious fielder, came in too far for the ball, jumped, but came up empty handed. As the ball rolled to the distant left field wall, all three base runners scored and Jones arrived at third. This so incensed Bernhard that he simply lobbed the ball to the plate from this point on.

• Chick Stahl popped out to third baseman Lave Cross, but captain Jimmy Collins knocked home Jones with a single.

• Buck Freeman walked, and Parent, up for the second time, doubled home both runners.

• Ferris bounced meekly to Bernhard who tossed to first baseman Socks Seybold for the second out.

• After Criger doubled home Parent, Lewis mercifully popped out to Bernhard.

Thirteen batters had stepped to the plate, and the nine-run buffeting was precipitated by only three hits coupled with six walks and an error. The Pilgrims then led 11–2, but that was only the beginning; the next inning witnessed an even more torrid Boston offense.

• Dowd led off the third inning with his third consecutive walk.

• After Jones flied out to right, Stahl tripled home Dowd.

• Both Collins and Freeman followed with singles, Collins getting an RBI.

• Parent tripled both of his teammates across the plate and scored himself on Ferris' single.

• Criger tripled home Ferris.

• After Lewis bounced out third to first, Dowd singled home Criger.

• Jones redeemed himself for making the first out of the inning by doubling Dowd to third.

• Stahl grounded to Fultz who bobbled the ball so badly, both Dowd and Jones scored.

• Collins continued the onslaught by doubling home Stahl.

• Freeman, the fourteenth batter, compassionately popped out to Powers.

In sum, during the third frame, Boston had scored ten runs on nine hits, a walk, and another error. Their two-inning massacre totals were: 27 batters, 19 runs, 12 hits, seven free passes, and two crucial Philadelphia errors. Understandably, the Pilgrims were so tired they didn't score again until they caught their breath in the ninth when they notched another pair. Substitutes were mostly a myth in 1901, especially in Boston where only nine fielders and five pitchers participated in more than ten games throughout the season.

Boston Pilgrims	AB	R	H	I	PO	A	E
>Tommy Dowd lf	4	3	2	2	0	0	0
Charlie Jones rf	6	3	1	0	1	0	1
Chick Stahl cf	6	3	2	2	3	0	0
Jimmy Collins 3b	6	2	4	4	5	3	0
Buck Freeman 1b	5	2	1	0	12	0	1
Freddy Parent ss	5	4	4	5	2	2	1
Hobe Ferris 2b	5	2	3	1	1	5	0
Lou Criger c	5	2	3	2	3	0	1
Ted Lewis p	4	2	1	2	0	2	0
	46	23	21	18	27	12	4

Phila Athletics	AB	R	H	I	PO	A	E
Jack Hayden rf	6	2	3	2	3	0	0
>Phil Geier cf	6	1	1	0	4	0	0
Dave Fultz ss	5	2	2	0	2	4	1
Nap Lajoie 2b	5	3	4	4	2	0	0
Socks Seybold 1b	5	2	3	3	12	1	0
Lave Cross 3b	5	1	3	2	2	2	0
Fred Ketchum lf	5	0	0	0	0	0	1
Mike Powers c	5	1	1	0	1	2	1
Pete Loos p	0	0	0	0	0	1	0
Bill Bernhard p2	5	0	2	0	1	4	0
	47	12	19	11	27	14	3

Boston	IP	H	R	ER	BB	SO
Lewis W,1-0	9	19	12	11	0	2

Philadelphia	IP	H	R	ER	BB	SO
Loos L,0-1	1	2	7	7	6	0
Bernhard	8	19	16	10	2	0
	9	21	23	17	8	0

Boston	2	9	10		0	0	0		0	0	2		-23
Phila.	2	0	2		1	2	0		0	0	5		-12

OB: Boston 5, Philadelphia 8
2B: Dowd 2, Jones, Collins, Parent 2, Criger, Lewis, Hayden, Lajoie, Seybold, Cross, Powers, Bernhard
3B: Stahl, Parent, Criger
HR: Lajoie(1)
SB: Dowd, Geier, Lajoie 2
SO: Seybold, Powers
BB: Dowd 3, Freeman, Parent, Ferris, Criger, Lewis
SH: Lewis

PB: Criger 2
TIME: 2:05
ATTENDANCE: 2,841
UMPIRE: John Haskell
SOURCES: Boston Globe, Herald, Post; Philadelphia North American, Evening Bulletin, Evening Telegraph, Inquirer, Item, Press, Public-Ledger, Record, Times

---

BALANCE	OUT+R+OB=BP=AB+BB+SH+HP+CI
Boston	27	23	5	55	46	8	1	0	0
Philadelphia	27	12	8	47	47	0	0	0	0

Boston also established two other twentieth-century, major league standards in this game, although to date, neither is listed in certain record books. All *nine Pilgrims scored two or more runs*, a mark which has been tied by several teams but never surpassed. Four Athletics also crossed the plate two or more times for a *two-team total of 13* (still the AL mark).

Patterson Runs the Gauntlet

3. Pitcher Faces 57 Batters, Allows 53 Official At-Bats

CHICAGO   at   MILWAUKEE
(White Sox, 7)   (Brewers, 21)

Sunday, May 5, 1901, Lloyd Street Park

Roy Patterson was an excellent young hurler. Showing great promise in 1900, he went 17–6 with four shutouts for Charles Comiskey's Chicago club. Much success was expected of him again in 1901, and Roy obliged with 20 wins. But this was one game in which the "Boy Wonder," as he was nicknamed, would rather have not participated.

This was the inaugural season for the American League as a major league, and the Chicago White Sox, under player/manager Clark Griffith, were tied for first place with Detroit at 7–3. The Milwaukee Brewers, meanwhile, had gotten off to a poor start at 3–7. Just ten days earlier, on opening day, they had been embarrassed in Detroit by blowing a nine-run lead in the bottom of the ninth. The Brewers were ready to try anything to get their season on track, so in desperation they invoked an unusual privilege. In baseball's early days, the home team had its choice of whether to bat first or last. Conventional wisdom dictated last, but this day Milwaukee chose to bat first. This drew giggles and jeers from the overflow hometown crowd and looked futile when Chicago jumped out to a 4–1 lead after three innings. Milwaukee starter Bert Husting had dished out seven free passes during this time, and the huge crowd called loudly for his removal from the hill. After Husting walked the bases loaded to start the fourth, Brewers player/manager Hugh Duffy complied by bringing on Bill Reidy. Reidy performed admirably, allowing the Sox just one hit in the rest of the game.

Patterson — the boy wondered about his career this day.

Held to only two hits in the first three innings by Patterson, the Brewers broke open the game with eight runs in their half of the fourth, one of which came on the team's first home run of the year. For accomplishing this feat, shortstop Wid Conroy won two new hats from a local manufacturer. Milwaukee continued to pile on the runs at Patterson's expense, taking advantage of shoddy fielding by the Sox while blasting several ground-rule doubles into the crowd encroaching from the outfield. Just why Chicago's manager Griffith kept Patterson in the box was not explained, although *The Evening Wisconsin* described some heavy betting action among the crowd. By the time the blood had stopped flowing, the Brewers had exonerated themselves in front of the hometown fans by winning 21–7, and Chicago's Roy Patterson had established two records that would still be on the books 95 years later. The Boy Wonder had *faced a total of 57 batters in the game and allowed 53 official at-bats.* His 25 hits and 21 runs allowed, while noteworthy, were later exceeded by others on several occasions.

Patterson and his manager Griffith did lead the White Sox to the American League pennant this year, winning 44 games between them. Thanks in part to this contest, however, Patterson allowed opposing batsmen an astounding 345 hits by year's end but still finished second in this abashed category. Iron Man McGinnity of Baltimore yielded 412!

Milwaukee Brewers	AB	R	H	I	PO	A	E
Irv Waldron rf	7	4	4	3	3	0	0
Billy Gilbert 2b	7	3	5	4	6	5	0
>Bill Hallman lf	7	3	5	2	2	0	0
John Anderson 1b	5	3	3	4	9	0	1
Wid Conroy ss	6	2	2	3	2	2	0
Hugh Duffy cf	6	2	3	1	3	0	0
Jimmy Burke 3b	5	2	1	1	0	2	0
Joe Connor c	4	2	1	1	2	1	0
Bert Husting p	2	0	0	0	0	2	0
Bill Reidy p4	4	0	1	0	0	1	0
	53	21	25	19	27	13	1

Chicago White Sox	AB	R	H	I	PO	A	E
Dummy Hoy cf	2	1	0	0	3	0	1
Fielder Jones rf	2	0	0	0	1	0	0
Sam Mertes 2b	3	0	0	2	1	3	0
Frank Isbell 1b	4	1	0	1	12	1	1
Fred Hartman 3b	5	0	0	0	0	3	1
Frank Shugart ss	4	2	0	0	2	2	2
>Herm McFarland lf	2	1	1	0	4	0	1
Billy Sullivan c	4	1	2	3	4	0	1
Roy Patterson p	3	1	0	1	0	2	0
	29	7	3	7	27	11	7

Milwaukee	IP	H	R	ER	BB	SO
Husting	3	2	6	6	10	1
Reidy W,1-2	6	1	1	0	4	0
	9	3	7	6	14	1

Chicago	IP	H	R	ER	BB	SO
Patterson L,2-2	9	25	21	13	2	2

Milwaukee	0	1	0	8	3	6	0	3	0	-21
Chicago	0	4	0	2	0	0	1	0	0	- 7

OB: Milwaukee 9, Chicago 9
DP: Gilbert-Anderson (Jones)
      Hartman-Isbell-Sullivan
2B: Waldron 2, Gilbert, Anderson 3,
      Sullivan
3B: Gilbert
HR: Conroy (2)
SB: Anderson 2, Isbell
BB: Anderson, Burke, Hoy 3, Jones 3,
      Mertes 2, Isbell, Shugart,
      McFarland 3, Patterson

SH: Connor 2
PB: Connor
TIME: 2:20
ATTENDANCE: 7,500
UMPIRE: Tommy Connolly
SOURCES: Evening Wisconsin; Milwaukee
   Daily News, Journal, Sentinel;
   Chicago Chronicle, Inter-Ocean,
   Tribune

BALANCE	OUT	+R	+OB	=BP	=AB	+BB	+SH	+HP	+CI
Milwaukee	27	21	9	57	53	2	2	0	0
Chicago	27	7	9	43	29	14	0	0	0

"A Game of Baseball Ain't Ever Over Until It's Over"

4. Team Scores Nine Runs in the Ninth Inning with Two Outs, Bases Empty

WASHINGTON   at   CLEVELAND
(Senators, 13)   (Blues, 14)

Thursday, May 23, 1901, League Park

Baseball's early answer to the oracle of Delphi, Rube Waddell, once fashioned the headline for this game. In probably the most remarkable comeback in baseball history, the Cleveland Blues (later Indians) defeated the Washington Senators 14–13. Not that the final score was so unusual, but in the bottom of the ninth with two outs and nobody on, the Senators were leading comfortably, 13–5. Most of Cleveland's League Park fans had departed, and the batboys had even begun packing equipment. The die-hard hometown patrons who remained, did

so merely to scoff. They got their chance right away as Blues pitcher Bill Hoffer, in a token of surrender, led off the bottom of the ninth. One of the epithets heard from the stands was directed at Hoffer. "Win your own game, Hoffer. Hit her out and run around nine times, then you'll win."* Hoffer struck out. Ollie Pickering then grounded out. The Senators were only one out away from an easy win, but it never came.

With two outs, trailing by eight runs and the bases empty, here's what happened:

Casey Patten (left) couldn't hold an eight-run lead. Lee (right) couldn't hold back the tide.

---

*"Never too late to win," Cleveland Plain Dealer, 24 May 1901, p. 8, col. 1.

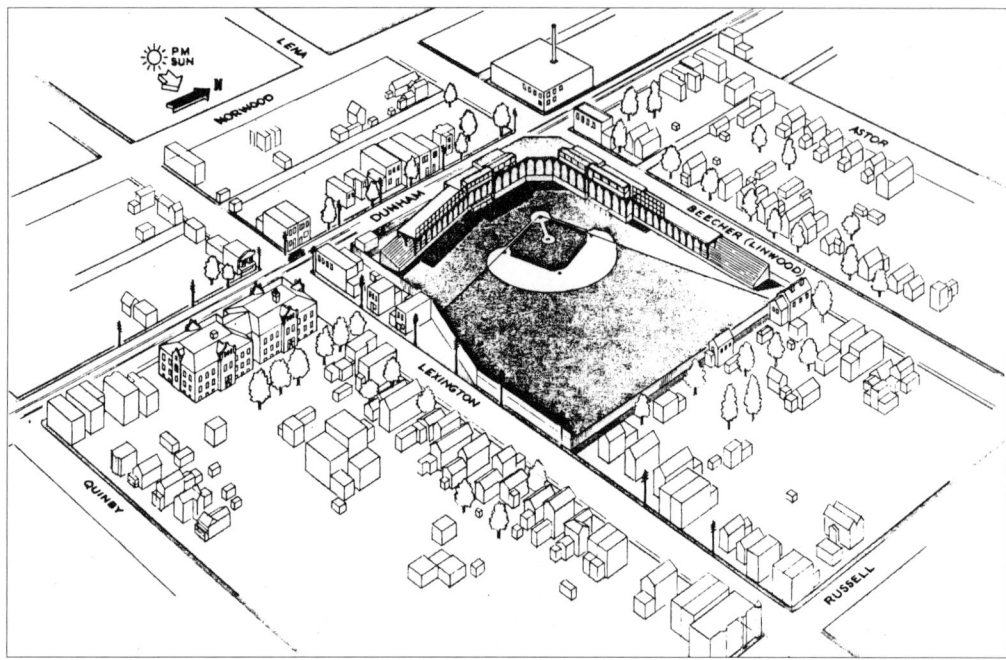

League Park, Cleveland, scene of one of the greatest comebacks in baseball history (courtesy of Marc Okkonen).

• At 5:13 p.m., Jack McCarthy singled to right as the remaining spectators became agitated at the seemingly useless delay.

• Bill Bradley also singled, further aggravating those who wished to complete their scorecards.

• When first baseman Candy LaChance swung and missed at two bad pitches, it looked like it was finally dinner time. But then Candy singled to center, driving home McCarthy.

• Washington's Casey Patten then hit Bob Wood with a pitch to load the bases.

• Frank Scheibeck doubled, clearing the bases and making it 13–9.

• Frank Genins singled home Scheibeck. It was then 13–10. At this point Washington captain, Bill Everett, called time and demanded that the surging crowd be herded away from the playing area and back into the stands.

• When Patten got behind (2–1) in the count to Truck Eagan, Watty Lee was called in to stem the tide but completed the walk.

• Erve Beck, pinch-hitting for Hoffer, sent a ball deep to left. Pop Foster, with his back to the wall and standing on tip-toes, had the ball just glance off his glove for a double, knocking in Cleveland's 11th and 12th runs. By then the crowd was hysterical and the Blues trailed by just a solitary marker.

• When Pickering got his only hit of the game, a single just out of the reach of shortstop Clingman, pandemonium erupted. The Blues had tied it! The few remaining fans swarmed onto the field, tossing hats, umbrellas, canes and cushions into the air "as if a cyclone had struck that part of the landscape."* For a time the game was in danger of being forfeited. Finally, the field was cleared.

• A passed ball enabled Pickering to take second, and McCarthy's second single of the inning handcuffed left fielder Foster. While he momentarily fumbled it, Pickering delivered the coup de grâce by scoring the winning run. It was only 5:28 p.m., having taken but 15 minutes to render this deliverance.

*"Never too late to win," Cleveland Plain Dealer, 24 May 1901, p. 8, col. 1.

The frantic crowd swarmed over the field, hoisted the Cleveland players to their shoulders, and carried them to the dressing room. One strike away from defeat, this Cleveland club wrote a story that ranks with the great escapes of all time. *Nine runs in the ninth after two outs and no runners aboard remains a major league record*, although there have been more runs scored under similar circumstances in another inning (see 8-08-54).

An unlikely hero in this game was Frank Scheibeck, who led his team with four hits and four RBIs. Frank had the lowest season batting average (.213) of any regular in the league, and after this year, played only three more games in his career.

A fitting epilogue transpired the following day. On May 24, Cleveland carried a 5–0 lead into the top of the ninth, whereupon the Senators turned the tables and scored five runs to tie it. After the Blues failed to score in the bottom of the ninth, the game was called a tie because of darkness.

Washington Senators	AB	R	H	I	PO	A	E
John Farrell cf	6	1	0	3	0	0	0
>Sam Dungan rf	6	0	1	2	1	0	0
Joe Quinn 2b	5	1	2	2	3	2	0
Pop Foster lf	5	1	3	0	2	0	1
Bill Everett 1b	3	1	0	0	12	1	0
Mike Grady c	4	2	2	2	4	0	1
Billy Clingman ss	4	2	2	0	3	7	0
Bill Coughlin 3b	3	3	2	0	0	0	0
Casey Patten p	4	2	2	1	1	2	0
Watty Lee p9	0	0	0	0	0	0	0
	40	13	14	10	*26	12	2

Cleveland Blues	AB	R	H	I	PO	A	E
Ollie Pickering rf	6	1	1	1	0	0	0
>Jack McCarthy lf	5	2	2	0	6	0	0
Bill Bradley 3b	5	2	4	1	2	2	2
Candy LaChance 1b	5	1	3	2	12	0	0
Bob Wood c	4	1	1	0	2	0	1
Frank Scheibeck ss	5	2	4	4	0	1	1
Frank Genins cf	4	1	1	1	4	0	0
Truck Eagan 2b	4	2	1	0	0	5	0
Bill Hoffer p	4	1	1	1	1	4	0
Erve Beck ph9	1	1	1	2	0	0	0
	43	14	19	12	27	12	4

Washington	IP	H	R	ER	BB	SO
Patten	8.2	16	11	7	3	3
Lee L,4-2	0	3	3	3	0	0
	*8.2	19	14	10	3	3

Cleveland	IP	H	R	ER	BB	SO
Hoffer W,2-4	9	14	13	6	3	0

* *Two outs when winning run scored*

Washington	0 5 0	1 3 0	2 0 2	-13
Cleveland	0 0 0	0 4 0	0 1 9	-14

OB: Washington 7, Cleveland 7
DP: Clingman-Quinn-Everett (Genins)
2B: Coughlin, Scheibeck, Beck
3B: Dungan
SB: Grady, Clingman
SO: Pickering, Scheibeck, Hoffer
BB: Everett, Grady, Coughlin, McCarthy, Genins, Eagan

SH: Everett, Clingman, Coughlin, Patten
HP: By Patten (Wood)
PB: Grady
TIME: 2:00
ATTENDANCE: 1,620
UMPIRE: Joe Cantillon
SOURCES: Cleveland Leader, Plain Dealer, Press; Washington Post, Star

---

BALANCE	OUT+R+OB=BP=AB+BB+SH+HP+CI
Washington	27 13 7 47 40 3 4 0 0
Cleveland	26 14 7 47 43 3 0 1 0

Nine in the Ninth, Again

5. Team Scores Nine Runs in the Ninth Inning with Two Outs, Bases Empty; Pitcher Allows Ten Consecutive Hits

BOSTON   at   MILWAUKEE
(Pilgrims, 13)   (Brewers, 2)

Sunday, June 2, 1901, Lloyd Street Park

Less than two weeks earlier (see 5-23-01), the Cleveland Blues set a seemingly unattainable record when they scored nine runs in the ninth inning after there were two outs and not a soul on base. It's easy to understand why this feat might occur just once again in the next 95 years. But little would anyone expect it to happen so soon. With the celebration barely ended in Cleveland, the American League's Boston Pilgrims performed a miracle of their own in Milwaukee, although of lesser consequence. This time the inconceivable rally didn't affect the outcome. Nevertheless, it takes its place in the all-time register for the *most runs scored in the ninth inning after two outs and no runners on base.*

This was just the first season of play for the newly declared "major" league, and at the time of this contest, only the aforementioned Cleveland club had a worse record than the Milwaukee Brewers. Milwaukee did in fact finish in the cellar, and before the 1902 season, the franchise was moved to St. Louis.

This day's game saw some fireworks even before the record-tying ninth frame. In the fifth inning, with the game still tied 2–2, Boston's Tommy Dowd stole second base. But when he overslid the bag, umpire John Haskell called him out. The Pilgrims' player-manager Jimmy Collins raced onto the field to protest the call and was joined by teammate Buck Freeman. While Collins argued, Freeman jostled the arbiter, resulting in both players being ejected. Because Boston had so few players on the bench (only nine non-pitchers appeared in more than ten games all

year), the two were replaced with a pair of pitchers, Nig Cuppy and Ben Beville. Having lost their two best hitters, things didn't look promising for Boston. But in the sixth inning, Milwaukee's Bill Reidy couldn't find the plate and walked four batters. Interspersed was a crucial error by substitute shortstop Bill Friel resulting in two unearned runs, giving the Pilgrims a lead they would never relinquish.

As was the case in many games played in baseball's early days, the crowd played a vital role in the establishment of this benchmark performance. Typically, this day's standing-room-only crowd overflowed into the outfield

Bill Reidy in less turbulent times.

periphery, contributing not only to the game's 11 doubles but actually keeping Boston's ninth inning alive when it should have ended. After the first two visitors had made routine outs, Ben Beville lofted a lazy fly to left which Bill Hallman would have easily caught for the third out. But there was such a congregation there that Hallman couldn't reach the ball and it fell into the masses for a ground-rule double. That was the beginning of the Pilgrims' nine-run rally.

Although it was not instrumental in the victory, Boston's record-tying ninth frame unfolded as follows:

• Both Chick Stahl and Nig Cuppy led off with routine outs.

• Ben Beville doubled into the overflow crowd in left.

• Freddie Parent homered over the left field fence.

• Hobe Ferris singled.

• Ossee Schreckengost doubled.

• Cy Young, the league's winningest pitcher, singled.

• Tommy Dowd singled.

• Charlie Hemphill also singled.

• Stahl, up for the second time, doubled.

• Cuppy, the pitcher playing left field, also doubled.

• Beville doubled for the second time in the inning.

• Parent finally ended the melee with an out.

Milwaukee pitcher Bill Reidy, abandoned on the mound for the entire rally, *surrendered ten consecutive hits*, a major league record which still survives, although it is now shared with Pittsburgh's Heinie Meine, who was equally molested by Brooklyn on June 23, 1930.

So often the most unlikely characters are embroiled in record-setting performances. Such was the case for "Candy Ben" Beville, a pitcher filling in at first base who was the main offensive weapon in this historic inning. It is remarkable that his two ninth-inning doubles were the *only hits in his entire one-year career!*

Boston Pilgrims	AB	R	H	I	PO	A	E
Tommy Dowd lf,3b5	4	2	4	1	1	0	0
Charlie Hemphill rf	5	2	1	1	0	0	0
Chick Stahl cf	5	1	3	2	1	0	0
Jimmy Collins 3b	2	0	0	0	2	2	0
Nig Cuppy lf5	4	1	2	2	0	0	0
Buck Freeman 1b	2	0	1	1	6	0	0
Ben Beville 1b5	3	2	2	1	5	0	1
>Freddy Parent ss	5	1	1	2	1	3	0
Hobe Ferris 2b	5	1	1	0	2	5	2
Ossee Schreckengost c	4	2	2	0	8	0	1
Cy Young p	5	1	1	2	1	6	0
	44	13	18	12	27	16	4

Milwaukee Brewers	AB	R	H	I	PO	A	E
>Irv Waldron cf	5	0	0	0	1	0	0
Billy Gilbert 2b	4	1	1	0	2	5	0
Bill Hallman lf	4	0	2	1	1	0	0
John Anderson 1b	4	0	0	0	14	0	0
Bill Friel ss	3	0	0	0	3	3	1
Hugh Duffy cf	4	0	1	0	2	0	0
Jimmy Burke 3b	4	0	0	0	1	4	0
Tom Leahy c	4	1	1	0	3	2	0
Bill Reidy p	2	0	1	1	0	2	0
Billy Maloney ph9	1	0	0	0	0	0	0
	35	2	6	2	27	16	1

Boston	IP	H	R	ER	BB	SO
Young W,6-3	9	6	2	1	2	7

Milwaukee	IP	H	R	ER	BB	SO
Reidy L,4-4	9	18	13	11	5	2

Boston	1	0	1	0	0	2	0	0	9	-13
Milwaukee	1	1	0	0	0	0	0	0	0	- 2

OB: Boston 11, Milwaukee 8
2B: Stahl 2, Hallman 2, Beville 2, Schreckengost 2, Cuppy 2, Leahy
3B: Gilbert
HR: Parent (1)
SB: Dowd 2, Anderson
BB: Dowd, Hemphill, Stahl, Beville, Schreckengost, Friel, Reidy
SH: Parent

HP: By Reidy (Dowd)
TIME: 1:50
ATTENDANCE: 8,500
UMPIRE: Jack Haskell
SOURCES: Boston Globe, Herald, Post; Evening Wisconsin; Milwaukee Daily News, Journal; Sporting Life

BALANCE	OUT	+R	+OB	=BP	=AB	+BB	+SH	+HP	+CI
Boston	27	13	11	51	44	5	1	1	0
Milwaukee	27	2	8	37	35	2	0	0	0

Fans Swarm the Playing Field

6. Team Gets 31 Hits in a Nine-Inning Game; Teams Combine for 36 Singles and 101 At-Bats

NEW YORK   at   CINCINNATI
(Giants, 25)   (Reds, 13)

Sunday, June 9, 1901, League Park

New York and Cincinnati were the two top teams in the National League this Sunday, and the weather was glorious, attracting patrons from as far away as 70 miles. It was the largest crowd in years in Cincinnati, and as was the custom of the day, the overflow crowd was herded into the vast outfield. But even that didn't provide sufficient space, so thousands more were positioned between the grandstand and the playing field. Extra seats of every description were provided at the last minute in an effort to keep the crowd at bay as the players abandoned their normal bench positions and sat along the foul lines. Happy were the faces of those fans who planted themselves in the satin finished sofas; three-legged stools; silk divans; desk, rocking, and parlor chairs that littered foul territory. Even outside the park there was a capacity crowd stationed atop roofs, freight cars, and telephone poles.

Part of the throng traveled from Muncie, Indiana, home of Cincinnati's Amos Rusie, "The Hoosier Thunderbolt." Rusie had pitched over 3,500 innings for the Giants a decade earlier, winning 233 games, but injured his arm in 1898 and hadn't won a game since. Now with the Reds, the hometown fans hoped for his revival. Kip Selbach, formerly a Red but now playing for the visitors, attracted a large delegation from his home town of Columbus, Ohio. As he approached the plate for his first at-bat, play was halted while he was presented a bouquet of roses and a new bat. Kip then proceeded to smack the first of his six hits in leading

New York to a *record-setting 31 hit attack*. It is still *the most hits by one team in a nine-inning game* (although tied 8-28-92). Not surprisingly, the Giants also became the first modern team to have three batters in their lineup garner five or more hits. In addition, the two teams combined for benchmarks that still stand with *36 singles and 101 at-bats*. The 101 at-bats is a newly discovered standard that should soon find its way into the record books.

Instrumental in these records was the crowd, which in essence reduced the playing

Al "Kip" Selbach — a lifetime .293 hitter.

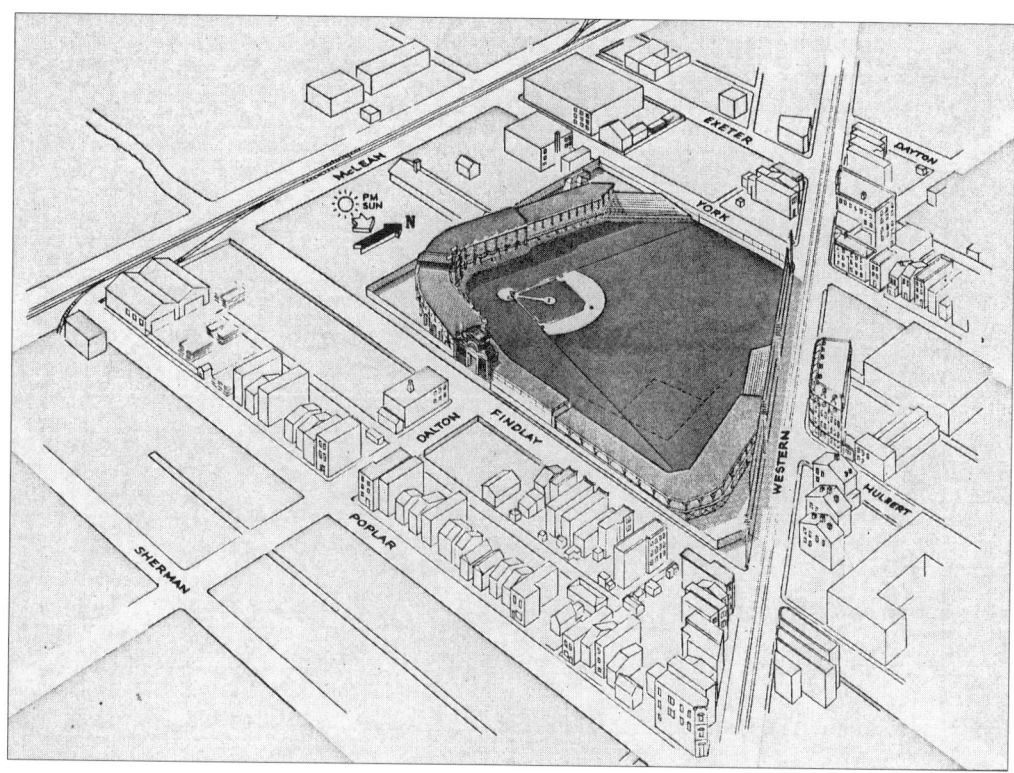

Drawing showing the park in 1902. In 1901 home plate was located in the right-field corner. The original grandstand was left in place (courtesy of Marc Okkonen).

area to schoolboy dimensions. Before the game had even begun, noted *The Cincinnati Commercial Tribune,* "the crowd had formed a circle about a hundred feet behind the infield." Because of this, the "ground rule" was installed, making balls hit into the masses, doubles. Fourteen times the rule was invoked. Of course, foul balls popped behind the plate or along the foul lines also went into the crowd untouched by fielders. This put an additional premium on outs and gave distinct advantages to the hitters.

As the game progressed, the crowd encroached, forcing play into an ever decreasing area. Outfielders nearly became infielders, and the few police were unable to stem the tide. Patrons in the stands, seeing the score out of hand, turned to frivolity to occupy themselves. Numerous "cushion fights" erupted, generally pitting customers in the grandstand against patrons on the field. Chairs were knocked over, pads were flying everywhere, hats were crushed, and when

there was a pause, one could observe wayward cushions hanging from the rafters and fences.

Finally, by the last of the ninth, the mob in the outfield had surged almost to second base. Perhaps they were unaware of what had happened in Cleveland a few weeks earlier (see 5-23-01). With Harry Steinfeldt at the plate and two men on base, umpire Emslie made one last effort to complete the game. He walked toward second base in an attempt to halt the mounting wave of humanity. But by the time he got there, he was completely enveloped by several thousand fans, making further play impossible. As a matter of fact, the players also became trapped in a blanket of humanity. A *Cincinnati Enquirer* reporter described it from the grandstand: "When play stopped, the park was covered with fans, and the players could only be [distinguished] by their caps." Emslie was forced to declare the game a forfeit. His announcement also signaled the onslaught of the grand finale

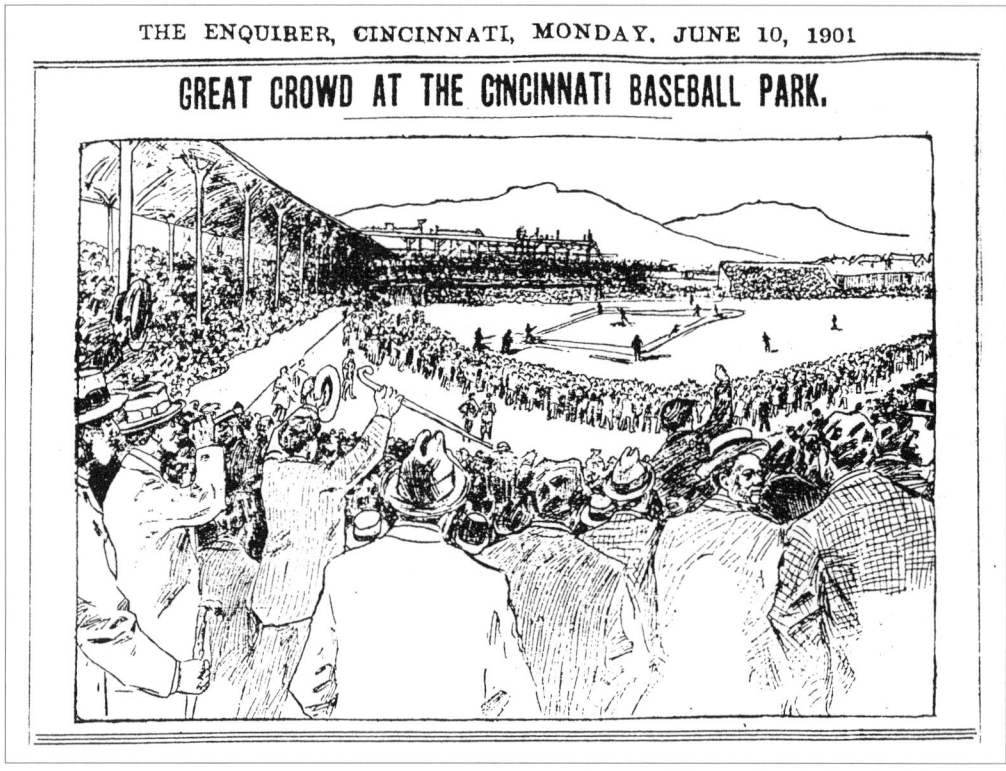

THE ENQUIRER, CINCINNATI, MONDAY, JUNE 10, 1901

GREAT CROWD AT THE CINCINNATI BASEBALL PARK.

Scene from the game as depicted in The Cincinnati Enquirer *(reprinted with permission of* The Cincinnati Enquirer*).*

cushion fight. Four or five thousand of the stuffed pads filled the air for another ten minutes as the players fought their way to the clubhouse. Note that despite 49 hits and 38 runs scored in this game, less than 2½ hours was required for completion.

New York Giants	AB	R	H	I	PO	A	E
Geo. Van Haltren cf	7	5	5	2	2	0	0
Kip Selbach lf	7	4	6	2	2	0	1
Sammy Strang 2b	7	2	2	3	1	5	0
Charlie Hickman rf	6	5	5	2	0	0	0
George Davis ss	6	2	4	2	5	6	1
>John Ganzel 1b	7	1	3	2	11	0	0
Charlie Buelow 3b	6	2	1	1	2	2	1
John Warner c	5	2	2	2	3	1	0
Bill Phyle p	6	2	3	2	0	2	1
	57	25	31	18	26	*16	4

Cincinnati Reds	AB	R	H	I	PO	A	E
Algie McBride cf	5	1	0	0	1	0	0
Dick Harley lf	6	3	3	0	1	0	2
Jake Beckley 1b	4	3	4	2	10	0	0
>Sam Crawford rf	6	3	4	3	3	0	0
Harry Steinfeldt 2b	5	1	2	2	4	8	1
Charlie Irwin 3b	4	0	1	1	0	2	1
Maggie Magoon ss	5	1	3	0	4	2	0
Bill Bergen c	5	1	0	0	4	2	0
Bill Phillips p	0	0	0	0	0	0	1
Amos Rusie p4	3	0	1	1	0	2	0
Barney McFadden p9	1	0	0	0	0	0	0
	44	13	18	9	27	16	5

New York	IP	H	R	ER	BB	SO
Phyle W,5-0	*8.2	18	13	9	5	3

Cincinnati	IP	H	R	ER	BB	SO
Phillips L,6-3	3	11	10	8	0	1
Rusie	5	15	10	8	1	0
McFadden	1	5	5	2	1	0
	9	31	25	18	2	1

* Game forfeited to NY with two out in last of ninth due to encroaching crowd.

New York   4 0 6   3 0 0   2 5 5   -25
Cincinnati   0 0 4   0 0 0   6 2 1   -13

OB: New York 8, Cincinnati 10
DP: Strang-Davis-Ganzel
    Phyle-Davis-Ganzel
2B: Van Haltren 2, Selbach 2, Irwin,
    Hickman 2, Davis 3, Buelow,
    Beckley 2, Steinfeldt
SB: Davis, Crawford
SO: Steinfeldt, Bergen, Rusie,
    Van Haltren
BB: Hickman, Warner, McBride, Irwin,
    Beckley 2, Phillips
SH: Davis

WP: Phyle
PB: Warner
TIME: 2:15
ATTENDANCE: 17,280
UMPIRE: Bob Emslie
SOURCES: Cincinnati Enquirer, Com-
    mercial Tribune, Post, Times, Star;
    ICI; New York Herald, Press, Sun,
    Times, Tribune, World; Sporting
    Life; Sporting News

BALANCE	OUT	+R	+OB	=BP	=AB	+BB	+SH	+HP	+CI
New York	27	25	8	60	57	2	1	0	0
Cincinnati	26	13	10	49	44	5	0	0	0

Pitiful Pitching Performance Precipitates Parker's Packing

7. Pitcher Allows 26 Hits, 21 Runs and 48 Official At-Bats in Eight Innings

CINCINNATI   at   BROOKLYN
(Reds, 3)   (Superbas, 21)

Friday, June 21, 1901, Washington Park

Harley "Doc" Parker was a marginal, major league talent. Hurling from 1893 to 1896 for the National League Chicago Colts, he compiled a record of 5–7 with a 5.29 ERA. Doc then departed from the major leagues. But in 1901 the Cincinnati Reds were desperate for pitching help and, after losing nine straight games, resurrected Parker from

Bill Dahlen—four RBIs

Willie Keeler—five hits

Louisville of the Western Association. He should have stayed there because his first major league outing in five years was a disaster. Never before had Brooklyn witnessed such a massacre. So bad a battering did Brooklyn bestow on the hapless Harley that even today his name still appears in the all-time baseball ledger. In just eight innings, Doc established a modern *major league record by allowing 26 hits and a National League record of 21 runs.* Every home town player who lifted a bat hit safely. Led by "Wee Willie" Keeler who had five hits, Brooklyn scored in each of the first seven frames until they were too tired to run the bases. *The Brooklyn Eagle* reported that by the eighth inning they simply "allowed themselves to be retired without attempting to run out the hits, which were fielded slowly and painfully by the tired and weary Cincinnatis [sic]." In a post-game interview, Parker remarked, "I

didn't expect to get out and win hands down the first time… The next time that I get into the box, I hope to give a better account of myself." It would be difficult to imagine one giving a worse account of oneself, but Doc was never given that opportunity. The following day it was reported that Cincinnati released Parker, and he never again pitched in the major leagues.

His records, however, live in infamy. The *21 runs-allowed* were later surpassed by a Detroit pitcher (see 5-18-12) but *remain the National League mark. The 26 hits-permitted* has also been tied twice (see 5-18-12 & 9-11-36) but *never surpassed in a nine-inning game. Forty-eight official at-bats allowed by one pitcher* also established a National League record, although it lasted only 72 hours. As bizarre as this performance was, it was superseded in one aspect by a teammate only three days later (see 6-24-01).

Cincinnati Reds	AB	R	H	I	PO	A	E
Johnny Dobbs cf	4	0	1	0	1	0	0
Dick Harley lf	4	1	3	0	2	1	0
Jake Beckley 1b	4	0	1	0	9	1	0
Sam Crawford rf	3	1	0	0	3	0	0
Maggie Magoon ss	4	0	1	2	2	5	3
Harry Steinfeldt 2b	3	1	0	0	3	7	2
>Charlie Irwin 3b	4	0	1	0	0	1	0
Heinie Peitz c	3	0	0	0	3	0	0
Doc Parker p	3	0	0	0	1	1	0
	32	3	7	2	24	16	5

Brooklyn Superbas	AB	R	H	I	PO	A	E
Willie Keeler rf	5	5	5	1	0	0	0
Cozy Dolan rf7	1	0	1	1	0	0	0
Jimmy Scheckard lf	5	3	3	3	9	0	0
Tom Daly 2b	6	2	2	3	5	2	0
Bill Dahlen ss	6	3	4	4	2	2	0
Tom McCreery cf	5	0	1	1	2	0	0
Duke Farrell 1b	6	3	3	1	4	1	1
>Frank Gatins 3b	5	1	1	1	0	0	0
Deacon McGuire c	4	2	3	3	4	0	1
Brickyard Kennedy p	5	2	3	1	1	1	0
	48	21	26	19	27	6	2

Cincinnati	IP	H	R	ER	BB	SO
Parker L,0-1	8	26	21	14	2	0

Brooklyn	IP	H	R	ER	BB	SO
Kennedy W,1-2	9	7	3	2	2	3

```
Cincinnati   0 1 2   0 0 0   0 0 0   - 3
Brooklyn     1 1 4   1 7 1   6 0 x   -21
```

OB: Cincinnati 4, Brooklyn 7
DP: Parker-Steinfeldt-Beckley
      Steinfeldt-Beckley
      Daly-Farrell
2B: Keeler, Sheckard, Dahlen 2,
      McGuire
HR: Keeler (1)
SB: Harley, Crawford, Keeler, Daly,
      Sheckard 2, Farrell, McGuire
BB: Crawford, Steinfeldt, Sheckard,
      McGuire

SH: McCreery, Gatins
WP: Parker
TIME: 1:48
ATTENDANCE: 1,900
UMPIRE: Frank Dwyer
SOURCES: Brooklyn Eagle, Standard
   Union; Cincinnati Enquirer; New
   York Herald, Sun, Times, Tribune,
   World; Sporting News

BALANCE	OUT+R+OB=BP=AB+BB+SH+HP+CI
	OUT	R	OB	BP	AB	BB	SH	HP	CI
Cincinnati	27	3	4	34	32	2	0	0	0
Brooklyn	24	21	7	52	48	2	2	0	0

Phillips Joins Teammate Parker in Recordbooks

8. Pitcher Faces 55 Batters, Allows 49 Official At-Bats

CINCINNATI   at   PHILADELPHIA
(Reds, 1)   (Phillies, 19)

Monday, June 24, 1901, Philadelphia Park

Cincinnati's first year manager Bid McPhee had a very strong stomach. Either that or he was a disciple of the Marquis de Sade. Just three days earlier, McPhee watched as one of his pitchers, Harley "Doc" Parker, was dismembered by Brooklyn (see 6-21-01). By the time the bleeding had stopped, Parker needed an undertaker more than a doctor. On this day, a coroner was needed in Philadelphia as Bill Phillips, another member of McPhee's pathetic pitching corps, was the sacrificial lamb in the second game of a doubleheader.

The Reds' staff in 1901 allowed more hits and earned runs than any other club in the league. The team also made the most errors, and this game exemplified the worst that Cincinnati had to offer. With the ink barely dry on Parker's record book entry, teammate Phillips, aided by nine* errors, allowed 22 hits, 19 runs, and surpassed Parker by allowing Philadelphia to *amass 49 official at-bats*. To this day, Phillips and Parker stand first and second in the National League for having allowed the most official at-bats in a nine-inning game. Phillips also *faced a total of 55 batters, the most ever in a nine-inning National League game.*

Unlike Doc Parker's fleeting career, however, Bill Phillips survived his waterloo and pitched a few more productive years. Manager McPhee's fate more closely paralleled Parker's. Despite a sterling playing career, Bid did not shine as a manager. He was relieved of his duties after 65 games the following season and never again managed in the major leagues.

Cincinnati had been shut out, 8–0, in the

Bill Phillips: Bludgeoned in Philadelphia

first game of this day's doubleheader and had lost 12 of their last 13 contests. So lackluster was their play in this second game that Philadelphia's Monte Cross actually stole third when Phillips attempted a pickoff of Doc White at first.

Cincinnati's only run of the day came in the fifth inning when, with Bill Bergen on first and Charlie Irwin on third, Bergen feigned a steal of second. Philadelphia's backstop, Klondike Douglass, threw down to Monte Cross who became slightly confused as whether to tag Bergen or to make a play on Irwin. As a result, Irwin beat Cross' peg

Newspapers varied in their error totals for Cincinnati. No official league records remain from the 1901 American League season.

Elmer Flick knocked in five runs.

home, and Bergen waltzed into second for a double steal.*

Phillies rookie Doc White, who later starred for the Chicago White Sox, pitched a strong game and was also Philadelphia's batting hero, with four hits including an inside-the-park home run. His 1901 supporting cast represented a strange combination of hitting talents. Ed Delahanty, Douglass, Elmer Flick, Roy Thomas, and Harry Wolverton all batted over .300 while Cross and Billy Hallman each hit under .200. Hughie Jennings, the only Quaker to take the collar this day, hit .275.

This was the consensus as reported by six Philadelphia newspapers. A seventh, The Philadelphia Inquirer, *reported that Irwin scored on a sacrifice fly by Phillips. Such were the vagaries of turn-of-the-century baseball reporting.*

SECOND GAME

Cincinnati Reds	AB	R	H	I	PO	A	E
Johnny Dobbs cf	4	0	0	0	1	0	0
Dick Harley lf	4	0	0	0	1	1	1
Jake Beckley 1b	4	0	1	0	9	1	1
Sam Crawford rf	4	0	0	0	1	0	3
Maggie Magoon ss	3	0	0	0	3	3	1
>Harry Steinfeldt 2b	4	0	0	0	1	3	1
Charlie Irwin 3b	2	1	2	0	2	4	0
Bill Bergen c	3	0	1	0	5	0	0
Bill Phillips p	3	0	1	0	1	2	2
	31	1	5	0	24	14	9

Phila Phillies	AB	R	H	I	PO	A	E
>Roy Thomas cf	6	2	3	2	3	0	0
Billy Hallman 2b	5	2	2	3	2	4	0
Ed Delahanty lf	6	2	3	1	0	0	0
Elmer Flick rf	5	3	3	5	2	0	0
Harry Wolverton 3b	6	1	2	1	1	2	0
Hughie Jennings 1b	5	1	0	0	11	0	0
Klondike Douglass c	6	2	3	0	6	1	0
Monte Cross ss	4	3	2	0	1	2	0
Doc White p	6	3	4	2	1	4	0
	49	19	22	14	27	13	0

Cincinnati	IP	H	R	ER	BB	SO
Phillips L,6-6	8	22	19	10	4	4

Philadelphia	IP	H	R	ER	BB	SO
White W,5-7	9	5	1	1	1	7

Cincinnati	0 0 0	0 1 0	0 0 0	- 1
Philadelphia	3 2 0	6 3 0	5 0 x	-19

OB: Cincinnati 5, Philadelphia 12
2B: Hallman, Flick, Wolverton, Cross
      Douglass
3B: Flick
HR: White (1)
SB: Irwin, Bergen, Douglass, Cross
SO: Dobbs 2, Harley, Steinfeldt 2,
      Beckley 2, Thomas, Wolverton,
      Jennings 2
BB: Magoon, Flick, Jennings, Cross 2
SH: Thomas, Hallman
HP: Irwin

WP: Phillips
TIME: 1:50
ATTENDANCE: 5,048
UMPIRE: Elmer Cunningham
SOURCES: Cincinnati Enquirer,
      Commercial Tribune; Philadelphia
      Evening Telegraph, Inquirer, North
      American, Press, Public Ledger,
      Record, Times; Sporting Life;
      Sporting News

BALANCE	OUT+R+OB=BP=AB+BB+SH+HP+CI
Cincinnati	27 1 5 33 31 1 0 1 0
Philadelphia	24 19 12 55 49 4 2 0 0

Jack Gets Ripped

9. Pitcher Allows 24 Hits in Seven Innings; Greatest Margin of Victory in Shutout

CLEVELAND   at   DETROIT
(Blues, 0)   (Tigers, 21)

Sunday, September 15, 1901, Burns Park

It would be safe to say that Jack Bracken, Cleveland's 20-year-old rookie right-hander, did not have his best "stuff" this day. Bracken had joined a besieged (53–71) Blues staff a month earlier and blended right in

with his 3–6 log and a 4.38 ERA. It was this game, however, that would distinguish Jack in the minds of baseball historians for generations to come. In it, Bracken was heartlessly hacked to pieces by the host Tigers who

gathered no fewer than 24 hits in just seven innings. Umpire John Haskell then mercifully called the game because of what *The Detroit Free Press* contended was "to prevent the Tigers from making more runs." Bracken himself had grown so disgusted with his handiwork in the sixth inning that he started to walk off the field, but captain Candy LaChance called him back and insisted that he finish his task, or "take his medicine," as contemporary reporters described it. By that time, it was already 17–0 with little hope for a three-inning miracle. Haskell's shortsightedness, however, probably cost Bracken a singular ranking in baseball annals, robbing him of an opportunity to surpass Harley Parker (see 6-21-01), and later Aloysius Travers (5-18-12) and Horace Lisenbee (9-11-36) who

each allowed 26 hits in a regulation-length game. Each of the aforementioned had the unfair advantage of facing the opposition for eight frames.

The Tigers also established a major league benchmark for the *greatest margin of victory in a shutout— 21.* Despite batting in only seven innings, that standard endured for 74 years (see 9-16-75).

Bracken finished the season on September 27 with a 6.21 ERA and a 4–8 ledger. He then found more appropriate employment, leaving the major league diamond forever. Alas, Jack left few, if any, photographic images of himself for baseball historians, as he was not with the club when team pictures were snapped in the spring of 1901 nor in the spring of 1902.

Cleveland Blues	AB	R	H	I	PO	A	E
>Ollie Pickering cf	4	0	1	0	1	0	0
Tom Donovan rf	3	0	1	0	1	1	0
Erve Beck 2b	3	0	0	0	2	7	0
Candy LaChance 1b	3	0	1	0	11	1	0
Bill Bradley 3b	3	0	1	0	2	2	0
Zaza Harvey lf	3	0	0	0	0	0	0
Jim McGuire ss	3	0	0	0	3	2	1
Joe Connor c	2	0	1	0	1	1	0
Jack Bracken p	3	0	1	0	0	1	0
	27	0	6	0	21	15	1

Detroit Tigers	AB	R	H	I	PO	A	E
Jimmy Barrett cf	3	4	2	2	3	0	0
Ducky Holmes rf	4	3	3	1	2	0	0
Sport McAllister 3b	5	2	3	7	1	0	1
>Kid Gleason 2b	6	1	3	1	2	0	0
Kid Elberfeld ss	4	0	1	1	3	2	0
Fritz Buelow c7	1	1	1	2	0	0	0
Doc Nance lf	5	3	2	1	1	1	0
Pop Dillon 1b	5	1	4	1	6	0	0
Al Shaw c,ss7	5	4	3	2	3	0	1
Ed Siever p	4	2	2	2	0	4	1
	42	21	24	20	21	7	3

Cleveland	IP	H	R	ER	BB	SO
Bracken L,3-7	7	24	21	16	3	1

Detroit	IP	H	R	ER	BB	SO
Siever W,15-14	7	6	0	0	1	2

Cleveland	0 0 0	0 0 0	0	- 0
Detroit	2 0 2	4 3 6	4	-21

OB: Cleveland 7, Detroit 7
DP: Siever-Elberfeld-Dillon
    Nance-Elberfeld (Beck fly ball)
    LaChance-McGuire-LaChance
2B: Barrett, Holmes, McAllister 2,
    Buelow, Dillon, Shaw, Siever
HR: McAllister(3)
SB: Barrett
SO: Pickering, Harvey, McAllister
BB: Connor, Barrett 2, Holmes

SH: Holmes, Siever
HP: By Bracken (Barrett, McAllister)
WP: Bracken
PB: Connor 2
TIME: 1:50
ATTENDANCE: 4,100
UMPIRES: John Haskell, Bill Hart
SOURCES: Cleveland Plain Dealer,
    Press; Detroit Free Press, News

BALANCE	OUT+R+OB=BP+AB+BB+SH+HP+CI
Cleveland	21 0 7 28 27 1 0 0 0
Detroit	21 21 7 49 42 3 2 2 0

Opposite: *Jimmy Barrett reached base six times on two hits, two walks, once hit by a pitch, and once on a force out.*

This was the final game of the season played in Detroit. Readers may note that it was staged in Burns Park, not on the Tigers' usual home field of Bennett Park. It seems that strict "blue laws" prohibited baseball from being played within the city limits on Sundays, so those games had to be held in neighboring Springwells Township, just beyond city limits. The park was named after Tiger president George Burns.

Merle Mauled in the Sixth

10. Pitcher Faces 16 Batters, Allows 12 Hits in One Inning

PHILADELPHIA, AL   at   BOSTON
(Athletics, 22)   (Pilgrims, 9)

Tuesday, July 8, 1902, Huntington Avenue Grounds

Around the turn of the century, pitchers usually finished what they started. This contest was very unusual because by the sixth inning, a half-dozen hurlers had seen action. By then, it had become clear to Boston Pilgrims' manager Jimmy Collins that his team was going to lose, so Jimmy decided not to waste another moundsman.

Not only had Boston starter Gary Prentiss been mistreated by the Philadelphia Athletics, even the venerable Cy Young was abused. The A's had scored eight runs in the first three innings. That set the stage for Merle "Doc" Adkins to try to stem the tide. But Connie Mack's boys were in a hitting frenzy, and no one could stop them. *The Boston Journal* reported that the Pilgrim infielders were "in danger of their lives and the outfielders were running about with their tongues out... Quakers indeed!" The reporter further noted, "They were sandbaggers of the more villainous type, without conscience and without mercy." In one inning alone, the sixth, Philadelphia combined 12 hits with a walk and two Boston errors to tally 12 runs. Topsy Hartsel, Lave Cross, and Danny Murphy each collected two singles. Harry Davis doubled and homered (a grand slam). Socks Seybold singled and tripled, and Rube Waddell and Monte Cross each contributed

a single. But it was Doc Adkins' martyrdom that remains in the record books. Doc *faced no less than 16 batters in that one inning* and *allowed 12 hits*, both standards yet to be surpassed. Adkins possessed quite a stocky build (5'10", 220 pounds), and *The Boston Post* noted that Pilgrim manager Collins left "the fat boy [on the hill] to take his medicine." Eventually, both teams became exhausted in the heat of the day, the Athletics from running around the bases, and the Pilgrims from chasing the ball. Adkins lasted just one more season in the major leagues, finishing with a lifetime 1–1 record in a total of only six games.

The star of the day was a youngster by the name of Danny Murphy who had just been called up from Norwich of the Connecticut League. Murphy had played some games for the New York Giants in 1900 and 1901, so he was not a rookie. But this was his first game in the majors in 1902 and his first ever in the American League. Actually, Danny arrived late for the game. He missed the first inning but dressed just in time to bat for teammate Lou Castro leading off the second frame. His single drove starter Prentiss to the showers, and his next plate appearance produced a home run, sending Cy Young to the same destination. Not only did Murphy smash six

Recordholder: Merle "Doc" Adkins

clean hits, but he also fielded 12 chances flawlessly. (Although the wire services reported Murphy committing two errors, three home town newspapers, the *Globe*, *Herald*, and *Journal* each recorded none. The *Journal* even described his fielding as "superb" and "without an error.") Four Boston and four Philadelphia newspapers all lauded Murphy, expressing bewilderment over the Giants releasing him. Danny became a regular for Connie Mack and over the next ten

years contributed to several championship teams.

Rube Waddell picked up a shoddy victory in this game. With his team leading 9–6, he was summoned to smother a Boston rally in the bottom on the fifth and faced but three batters. Rube then singled and scored in the Athletics' 12-run sixth inning. After that, Manager Mack considered Waddell's expertise superfluous and saved him to start the following day's game.

Phila Athletics	AB	R	H	I	PO	A	E
Topsy Hartsel lf	6	3	4	1	2	1	0
Dave Fultz cf	6	4	3	1	2	1	0
>Harry Davis 1b	6	3	3	6	8	0	1
Lave Cross 3b	6	3	4	4	2	1	0
Socks Seybold rf	6	3	3	2	0	0	0
Lou Castro 2b	0	0	0	0	0	0	0
Danny Murphy ph2,2b	6	3	6	6	5	7	0
Monte Cross ss	5	1	1	0	6	4	0
Mike Powers c	3	0	0	0	2	0	0
Os. Schreckengost c5	3	1	1	0	0	0	0
Bert Husting p	3	0	1	1	0	0	1
Rube Waddell p5	1	1	1	1	0	0	0
Snake Wiltse p6	2	0	0	0	0	0	0
	53	22	27	22	27	14	2

Philadelphia	IP	H	R	ER	BB	SO
Husting	4	8	6	6	0	0
Waddell W,3-1	1	0	0	0	0	1
Wiltse	4	10	3	2	1	0
	9	18	9	8	1	1

Philadelphia	2	2	4	1 0 12	0 1 0	-22
Boston	0	1	1	0 4 0	1 2 0	- 9

OB: Philadelphia 8, Boston 9
DP: Dougherty-Ferris-LaChance
    M.Cross-Davis (Adkins)
    Ferris-Parent-LaChance
2B: Fultz, Davis, L.Cross, Seybold
3B: Seybold, Stahl 2, Ferris
HR: Davis(3), Murphy(1), Collins(5)
SB: M.Cross
SO: Powers 2, Criger
BB: Hartsel, Fultz, M.Cross,
    LaChance
SH: Davis

Boston Pilgrims	AB	R	H	I	PO	A	E
Patsy Dougherty lf	4	1	2	0	3	1	0
Jimmy Collins 3b	5	3	2	2	0	4	1
Chick Stahl cf	3	1	3	1	1	0	1
Harry Gleason cf6	2	1	1	0	1	0	1
Buck Freeman rf	5	1	2	2	1	0	0
Freddy Parent ss	5	2	3	0	2	3	1
Candy LaChance 1b	4	0	1	0	12	0	0
Hobe Ferris 2b	5	0	2	2	3	4	2
Lou Criger c	5	0	2	1	4	2	0
Gary Prentiss p	0	0	0	0	0	1	0
Cy Young p2	1	0	0	0	0	0	1
> Doc Adkins p4	4	0	0	0	0	4	0
	43	9	18	8	27	19	7

Boston	IP	H	R	ER	BB	SO
Prentiss L,2-2	1	4	3	2	0	0
Young	1	7	5	5	0	1
Adkins	7	16	14	5	3	1
	9	27	22	12	3	2

HP: Dougherty
PB: Criger
TIME: 2:02
ATTENDANCE: 3,631
UMPIRE: Tommy Connolly
SOURCES: Boston Globe, Herald,
    Journal, Post; Philadelphia
    Inquirer, North American, Press,
    Public Ledger, Record;
    Sporting News

BALANCE	OUT	+ R	+ OB	= BP	= AB	+ BB	+ SH	+ HP	+ CI
Philadelphia	27	22	8	57	53	3	1	0	0
Boston	27	9	9	45	43	1	0	1	0

Opposite: *The* Boston Herald *put Murphy on a pedestal and Prentiss, Young, and Adkins in an ambulance (reprinted with permission of the* Boston Herald*).*

11. Team Makes 14 Successful Bunts in One Game

WASHINGTON   at   CLEVELAND
(Senators, 6)   (Blues, 7)

Tuesday, August 5, 1902, League Park

In baseball's early days, before the advent of the lively ball, bunts were common fare. Low scoring games often relied on the bunt for either a sacrifice or a hit, but this day's game left even the veterans shaking their heads.

Otto Hess, Cleveland's 23-year-old, rookie left-hander, had made his major league debut only two days earlier. In this, just his second outing, Washington was quick to detect a peculiar weakness in his game. Otto pitched well but became extremely rattled each time he was forced to field a bunt. The Senators exploited this deficiency by dropping *14 bunts, believed to be the major league record for one team in a game.* Each attempt was successful in one way or another. Three precipitated errors by Hess, four turned into hits, and seven were scored as sacrifices.

The real hero of this game was Cleveland's diminutive shortstop Johnny Gochnauer. He doubled in the tying runs in the bottom of the eighth, then doubled again and scored the game winner in the bottom of the tenth. Johnny's valiant efforts came after breaking his finger in the third inning. It was then that "Big Ed" Delahanty drove a blistering line drive toward left center. Gochnauer leaped and deflected the ball with his primitive glove, but the drive had such force that it broke the little finger of his left hand. With Johnny in obvious pain, Jack Thoney was sent from the dugout to take his

Otto Hess had trouble fielding bunts.

place. Fortunately for the Blues, Gochnauer refused to leave the field.

Otto Hess eventually rectified his fielding problem and went on to a mediocre career as a part-time outfielder, part-time pitcher. He reached his zenith in 1906 when he won 20 games with a 1.83 ERA. Gochnauer was less successful, lasting but three years in the majors, while compiling a .187 lifetime batting average.

Washington Senators	AB	R	H	I	PO	A	E
Jimmy Ryan cf	4	1	2	1	3	0	0
Jack Doyle 2b	5	1	1	0	1	2	2
Ed Delahanty 1b	5	1	2	0	12	0	0
Bill Keister rf	2	0	1	2	1	0	0
Bill Coughlin 3b	5	0	0	0	2	2	1
Watty Lee lf	5	1	2	0	1	0	0
Bones Ely ss	1	1	1	0	3	4	1
Boileryard Clarke c	4	1	1	0	5	0	0
>Casey Patten p	2	0	0	1	0	4	1
	33	6	10	4	*28	12	5

Cleveland Blues	AB	R	H	I	PO	A	E
Harry Bay cf	4	1	1	1	0	0	1
Bill Bradley 3b	5	0	1	3	3	4	0
Nap Lajoie 2b	5	0	0	0	4	3	1
Charlie Hickman 1b	4	0	1	0	17	2	1
Elmer Flick rf	5	1	0	0	1	0	0
Jack McCarthy lf	5	1	1	0	1	0	0
Johnny Gochnauer ss	5	1	2	2	0	5	0
>Bob Wood c	5	1	1	0	4	3	0
Otto Hess p	2	2	1	0	0	4	3
	40	7	8	6	30	21	6

WASHINGTON	IP	H	R	ER	BB	SO
Patten L,10-12	*9.1	8	7	4	3	3

One out when winning run scored

CLEVELAND	IP	H	R	ER	BB	SO
Hess W,1-1	10	10	6	3	3	3

Washington   3 0 0   2 0 1   0 0 0   0   - 6
Cleveland   0 0 2   0 0 0   2 2 0   1   - 7

OB: Washington 9, Cleveland 9
DP: Hickman-Wood-Hickman (Doyle)
     Bradley-Lajoie-Hickman
2B: Delahanty, Keister, McCarthy,
     Gochnauer 2, Wood
3B: Bradley
SB: Bay, Lajoie
SO: Keister, Coughlin, Patten, Hess,
     Bay, Bradley
BB: Keister, Ely 2, Bay, Hess 2

SH: Keister 2, Ely 2, Clarke,
    Patten 2
HP: By Patten (Hickman)
    By Hess (Ryan, Patten)
WP: Hess
TIME: 1:55
ATTENDANCE: 2,094
UMPIRE: Silk O'Loughlin
SOURCES: Cleveland Leader, Plain
    Dealer, Press; Washington Post, Star

BALANCE	OUT+R+OB=BP=AB+BB+SH+HP+CI							
Washington	30	6	9	45	33	3	7	2	0
Cleveland	28	7	9	44	40	3	0	1	0

Dreyfuss Refunds Patron's Money

12. Catcher Allows Six Passed Balls in One Game

CINCINNATI   at   PITTSBURGH
(Reds, 2)   (Pirates, 11)

Saturday, October 4, 1902, Exposition Park

It was a cold, cloudy Saturday in Pittsburgh, and 24 hours of rain had turned Exposition Park into a swamp; only the batters box and pitchers mound had been covered with canvas. The hometown Pirates had long since clinched the National League pennant, running away from second place Brooklyn by 27.5 games, the largest margin by any modern pennant winner. Visiting Cincinnati had no chance to improve their fourth position in the standing, and the entire affair probably should have been canceled. However, Barney Dreyfuss, Pittsburgh's owner, wanted to see his club establish a new, single-season, team-victory record. This was the Pirates last game of the season and they needed it for their 103rd win.

According to the rules at the time, the captain of the home team decided if the playing field was fit for competition, and

Barney Dreyfuss (coutesy of Pittsburgh Pirates Baseball Club).

Pittsburgh Captain Fred Clarke ruled such, despite protests from the Reds. So in an effort to express their contempt, the Reds decided to turn the "game" into a burlesque.

To begin, Cincinnati fielded a masquerade lineup. Thirty-five-year-old first baseman, and the team's leading home run hitter, Jake Beckley, started as pitcher for the only time in his career. Rube Vickers, a rookie pitcher, was Beckley's catcher, although *The Cincinnati Enquirer* mentioned that, "As a backstop, Vickers couldn't catch cold in a linen duster in Manitoba on Christmas Day." Outfielder Cy Seymour was stationed at third base and later pitched for the only time this season. Mike Donlin, another outfielder, played shortstop and also finished on the mound. Noodles Hahn, a 23-game winner and best hurler on the staff, was positioned at first base. Second baseman Jack Morrissey and third baseman Harry Steinfeldt began their only games of the year in the outfield. Only shortstop Tommy Corcoran, who guarded

second base, and player-manager Joe Kelley, who roamed center field, were remotely familiar with their defensive positions.

As dreadful as the lineup was, the play was even worse. In the second inning, Cy Seymour feigned exhaustion and had a glass of water brought to him at third base. Beckley left the pitchers mound to join his teammate in the refreshment. Corcoran, Steinfeldt, Kelley and Morrison all wore their warmup coats during the game while Kelley, Donlin, and Seymour smoked cigarettes in the field. New uniform styles were also tried by the Reds. Donlin wore the brim of his cap over his ear, and Seymour pulled one of his stockings down over his shoe. Rube Vickers didn't exert himself at all behind the plate and established the *all-time record for passed balls in a game with six* despite catching only four innings!* Rube put on a show whenever a ball got by him by slowly walking after it, pausing, then very deliberately pulling a handkerchief from his pocket to loudly blow his nose. He was much more aggressive, however, when it came to fielding bunts. At times, Vickers and Seymour actually wrestled in the field to gain control of bunted balls. *The Pittsburgh Leader* also noted, "The outfielders walked after long drives as if they were working by the hour, frequently making wide detours in order to avoid wetting their shoes in the ponds of water that dotted sections of the outer gardens." The foul play culminated in manager Joe Kelley's appearance at the plate smoking a cigarette. Umpire Hank O'Day demanded that Kelley discard the smoldering cylinder but Joe protested, claiming there was nothing in the rules to prohibit the act. He puffed smoke profusely as several pitches whizzed by him until Pirate catcher Zimmer wrestled it out of his possession.

These shenanigans so infuriated Pirate owner Dreyfuss that he sent employees through the stands announcing that all patron monies would be refunded at the box office after the game, and that the Reds would not get a cent for their efforts. When

---

Six passed balls in one game has since been tied twice—by Gino Petralli of Texas on August 30, 1987, and by Jerry Goff of Houston on May 12, 1996.

The "game" as seen through the eyes of a Pittsburgh Press *cartoonist.*

Cincinnati Reds	AB	R	H	I	PO	A	E
Mike Donlin ss,p8	5	1	1	0	1	1	0
Jake Beckley p,1b5	4	0	2	1	7	2	0
>Joe Kelley cf,3b5	5	0	1	0	0	0	0
Cy Seymour 3b,p5,ss8	4	0	1	0	1	3	0
Tommy Corcoran 2b	4	0	0	0	2	5	0
Harry Steinfeldt rf	4	1	1	0	1	1	1
Jack Morrissey lf	4	0	2	0	2	0	0
Rube Vickers c	1	0	1	1	0	1	1
Heinie Peitz c5	3	0	0	0	3	1	0
Noodles Hahn 1b,cf5	3	0	0	0	7	0	0
	37	2	9	2	24	14	2

Pittsburgh Pirates	AB	R	H	I	PO	A	E
Ginger Beaumont cf	4	2	2	0	0	0	0
Fred Clarke lf	4	2	2	4	2	2	1
Tommy Leach 3b	5	0	0	0	0	1	1
Honus Wagner ss	5	2	1	0	4	3	2
Kitty Bransfield 1b	5	1	3	3	9	0	0
Jimmy Sebring rf	5	0	2	1	4	1	0
>Claude Ritchey 2b	4	1	0	0	2	3	1
Chief Zimmer c	4	1	2	1	6	0	0
Deacon Phillippe p	3	2	2	1	0	2	0
	39	11	14	10	27	12	5

Cincinnati	IP	H	R	ER	BB	SO
Beckley L,0-1	4	9	8	4	1	2
Seymour	3	4	3	3	3	3
Donlin	1	1	0	0	0	0
	8	14	11	7	4	5

Pittsburgh	IP	H	R	ER	BB	SO
Phillippe W,20-9	9	9	2	1	2	5

Cincinnati	0 1 0	0 1 0	0 0 0	- 2
Pittsburgh	3 4 0	1 0 0	3 0 x	-11

OB: Cincinnati 10, Pittsburgh 8
DP: Ritchey-Wagner-Bransfield
       Sebring-Ritchey-Wagner (Kelley)
       Steinfeldt-Peitz (Ritchey)
2B: Beckley, Bransfield, Sebring,
       Phillippe
3B: Clarke, Wagner, Bransfield
HR: Clarke(3)
SB: Donlin
SO: Beckley, Hahn 2, Donlin, Kelley,
       Clarke, Phillippe, Beaumont,
       Leach, Wagner

BB: Beckley, Hahn, Beaumont, Clarke,
       Ritchey, Phillippe
WP: Seymour
PB: Vickers 6
TIME: 1:30
ATTENDANCE: 900
UMPIRE: Hank O' Day
SOURCES: Cincinnati Enquirer,
       Commercial Tribune; Pittsburgh
       Dispatch, Gazette, Leader, Post,
       Press

BALANCE	OUT+R+OB=BP=AB+BB+SH+HP+CI

BALANCE	OUT	R	OB	BP	AB	BB	SH	HP	CI
Cincinnati	27	2	10	39	37	2	0	0	0
Pittsburgh	24	11	8	43	39	4	0	0	0

Barney confronted Kelley, threatening to file a complaint with the league office, Joe only laughed and responded, "If you had furnished us rubber suits we would have played your team, but under the circumstances, I think that the way the team is lined up, it is the best mud team in the world."* Ironically, by the time the farce was ended, it was the Pirates who had committed the most errors.

Although quite amusing, this burlesque was not novel. Just a week earlier, the St. Louis Browns "entertained" the Chicago White Sox in similar fashion. Then, the Sox battery traded positions each inning while most of the St. Louis fielders took turns at "pitching." No records, however, were established in that farce.

An Abundance of Assists

13. Teams Record 43 Assists in One Nine-Inning Game

NEW YORK   at   BROOKLYN
(Giants, 2)   (Superbas, 1)

Tuesday, April 21, 1903, Washington Park

It was opening day in Brooklyn, 1903. The usual festivities included a parade of the hometown players from the dressing room to the field for a flag raising cermony as the capacity crowd sung the Star Spangled Banner. Mrs. Charles Ebbets, in the absence of the mayor, threw out the first ball, and despite the fact that the Giants and the Superbas had already opened the season on April 17 at the Polo Grounds, this was Brooklyn's first chance to show their enthusiasm for the local club. Many of the nearly 17,000 in attendance, however, had come from across the river, dividing patron allegiance and leaving little in the way of even standing room.

This day's pitchers, New York's Christy Mathewson and Brooklyn's Henry Schmidt, were the same pair that christened the campaign in New York. Then, Schmidt emerged victorious over the Giants and Mathewson. This day would be different. (Only two National League rookie pitchers in the 20th-

century have been opening day starters — Schmidt and the Phillies' Al Gerheauser in 1943).

Typical of the dead-ball era, this was a low scoring affair. The home team took the lead in the very first inning. Sammy Strang led off with a walk, was safe at second on an error, stole third, and scored on Ed Householder's ground single through short. That's the way it stood until the sixth when the Giants retaliated with George Browne's walk, stolen base, and a single by George Van Haltren. The game winner tallied in the final frame as Dan McGann singled, Billy Lauder and Billy Gilbert both walked, and John Warner put the Giants in the lead with a single. Lauder also tried to score but was thrown out at the plate. In the bottom of the ninth, despite urging by a hometown band playing "Come Home Bill Bailey, Come Home," the Superbas could do nothing with Mathewson and went down in order to end

---

"Kelley Made a Farce of the Game," Commercial Tribune, 5 October, 1902.

The 1903 Superbas. The top row shows Schmidt (second from left) and Jacklitsch (fourth from left).

the game. The same band then played "Ain't It a Shame?"

It was an exciting game for the boisterous crowd, but no one realized at the time that it would eventually take its place in the all-time ledger as the game that witnessed the *most assists by both teams in a nine-inning game*— *43*. This is now merely the National League mark because an American League game (see 5-27-09) later surpassed it. Some record books list different games in which 45 and 44 assists were made by both clubs. Official league records, however, do not support those claims.

No mention was made in newspaper descriptions of the profusion of assists, but only five balls were caught in the outfield. More instrumental were the numerous rundowns and fluke balls hit back at pitcher Schmidt. Several times, hard shots caromed off him, only to be fielded by teammates. In the second frame, the Giants' Bresnahan was run down between third and home, affording

several assists. And in the third inning, Brooklyn's Strang got himself caught in rundown between third and home, changing direction at least five times before being tagged out by Mathewson. In addition to throwing out several attempted base stealers, Brooklyn backstop Fred Jacklitsch was involved in at least two rundowns, precipitating *seven assists which tied the existing ML record for a catcher*. Battery mate Schmidt had eight assists, the high watermark of his career.

Having been discovered in the Pacific Coast League by Superbas manager Ned Hanlon, Henry Schmidt was a 29-year-old rookie at the time of this game. He finished the 1903 campaign with a 22-13 log, five shutouts, and was Brooklyn's finest pitcher. But in 1904, he returned his contract with a note that simply read, "I do not like living in the East and will not report." Schmidt remained adamant in his feelings and never again hurled in the major leagues.

New York Giants	AB	R	H	I	PO	A	E
George Browne rf	3	1	1	0	0	0	0
Geo. Van Haltren cf	4	0	1	1	2	0	0
Dan McGann 1b	4	1	2	0	14	0	0
Roger Bresnahan lf	2	0	0	0	1	0	0
Charlie Babb ss	3	0	1	0	1	6	0
Billy Lauder 3b	2	0	0	0	1	4	1
Billy Gilbert 2b	3	0	0	0	1	3	2
>John Warner c	4	0	2	1	6	3	0
Christy Mathewson p	2	0	1	0	1	3	0
	27	2	8	2	27	19	3

Brooklyn Superbas	AB	R	H	I	PO	A	E
Sammy Strang 3b	3	1	1	0	1	1	0
Judge McCredie rf	4	0	0	0	1	0	0
Jimmy Sheckard lf	4	0	0	0	0	1	0
Ed Householder cf	4	0	1	1	1	0	0
Jack Doyle 1b	4	0	0	0	15	0	0
>Bill Dahlen ss	3	0	0	0	4	4	0
Tim Flood 2b	3	0	1	0	3	3	0
Fred Jacklitsch c	3	0	0	0	2	7	0
Henry Schmidt p	3	0	0	0	0	8	0
	31	1	3	1	27	24	0

New York	IP	H	R	ER	BB	SO
Mathewson W,1-1	9	3	1	0	2	5

Brooklyn	IP	H	R	ER	BB	SO
Schmidt L,1-1	9	8	2	2	5	2

New York	0 0 0	0 0 1	0 0 1	- 2
Brooklyn	1 0 0	0 0 0	0 0 0	- 1

OB: New York 6, Brooklyn 5
DP: Jacklitsch-Dahlen
     Warner-Gilbert
SB: Browne, Bresnahan, Lauder,
     Strang, Sheckard 2
CS: Van Haltren, McGann
BB: Browne, Bresnahan, Babb, Lauder,
     Gilbert, Strang, Dahlen

SH: Bresnahan, Lauder, Mathewson
TIME: 1:55
ATTENDANCE: 16,500
UMPIRE: Augie Moran
SOURCES: Brooklyn Eagle; DBD; New
     York American, Herald, Times,
     Tribune, Sun, World

BALANCE	OUT+R+OB=BP=AB+BB+SH+HP+CI
New York	27 2 6 35 27 5 3 0 0
Brooklyn	27 1 5 33 31 2 0 0 0

A Comedy of Errors

14. Teams Make 18 Errors in One Game

DETROIT   at   CHICAGO
(Tigers, 9)   (White Sox, 10)

Wednesday, May 6, 1903, South Side Park

Chicago's South Side Park was a pitcher's paradise, one of the most difficult arenas in which to score runs. During the White Sox nine years of occupation (1901–1909), teams combined to average just over seven runs per game, and only 65 home runs were hit there by all teams. But there were ways to score other than by long hits.

During this time period, unearned runs were nearly as plentiful as those earned. Games were conducted on cloudy days without auxiliary lighting, playing surfaces were

often lumpy or wet, and fielder's gloves weren't the lavish devices they are today. Those mitts in Cooperstown were actually used for scooping up ground balls and snaring line drives.

A glance through the record books will illustrate that most of the modern-day records for fielding inadequacy were established around the turn of the century. On this day, the White Sox took their place among the dregs when they *committed 12 errors, tying the record for a nine-inning game.*

Detroit Tigers	AB	R	H	I	PO	A	E
>Jimmy Barrett cf	4	2	0	0	2	0	0
Kid Elberfeld 3b	3	2	1	0	1	0	0
Sam Crawford lf	3	2	0	0	2	0	0
Charlie Carr 1b	5	1	1	1	9	0	1
Doc Gessler rf	5	0	1	2	1	0	0
Heinie Smith 2b	5	0	3	1	3	2	2
Joe Yeager ss	3	0	0	0	1	7	2
Fritz Buelow c	3	1	0	0	6	3	0
Alex Jones p	3	1	0	0	0	2	0
Mal Eason p6	2	0	0	0	0	0	1
	36	9	6	4	*25	14	6

Chicago White Sox	AB	R	H	I	PO	A	E
Cozy Dolan 1b	5	1	1	0	12	0	1
Fielder Jones cf	4	2	2	0	0	0	0
Danny Green rf	4	2	3	1	0	0	1
Bill Hallman lf	2	2	0	0	3	0	0
Frank Isbell 3b	5	3	1	2	0	8	3
>Tom Daly 2b	3	0	0	1	3	0	0
Lee Tannehill ss	4	0	2	2	5	3	4
Ed McFarland c	3	0	0	0	3	0	0
Patsy Flaherty p	4	0	1	0	1	3	3
	34	10	10	6	27	14	12

Detroit	IP	H	R	ER	BB	SO
Jones	5	8	7	5	5	4
Eason L,1-2	3.1	2	3	1	3	2
	*8.1	10	10	6	8	6

Chicago	IP	H	R	ER	BB	SO
Flaherty W,4-1	9	6	9	0	3	1

* One out when winning run scored.

Detroit	2 2 0	2 0 0	0 3 0	- 9
Chicago	0 0 0	2 5 0	0 0 3	-10

OB: Detroit 10, Chicago 7
DP: Buelow-Carr
   Yeager-Smith-Carr (McFarland)
   Tannehill-unassisted
2B: Isbell, Gessler
SB: Daly, Smith
SO: Gessler, Dolan, Daly 2, Isbell
   Flaherty 2
BB: Barrett, Yeager, Buelow, Daly 2,
   Green, Hallman 3, F.Jones,
   McFarland
SH: Barrett, Elberfeld, Crawford 2,
   Yeager, Buelow

HP: By Flaherty (Elberfeld)
WP: Jones, Flaherty
PB: McFarland
TIME: 2:10
ATTENDANCE: 2,400
UMPIRE: Jack Sheridan
SOURCES: Chicago Chronicle, Daily
   News, Inter-Ocean, Record-Herald,
   Tribune; Detroit Free Press, News;
   Sporting Life

BALANCE	OUT+R+OB=BP=AB+BB+SH+HP+CI
Detroit	27 9 10 46 36 3 6 1 0
Chicago	25 10 7 42 34 8 0 0 0

Their opponents were the Detroit Tigers who had established the benchmark just two years earlier. This day, the Tigers contributed six errors of their own to help set the *two-team, all-time record for a nine-inning game at 18.* There was no special factor involved in this absurdity other than a cold front which blew in from Lake Michigan. The game had begun amid 70-degree temperatures, but between the fourth and fifth innings, the frosty wind had registered a drop of 20 degrees. By then, however, Chicago had committed more than half their total errors.

Appropriately, the game was decided in the bottom of the ninth on two Detroit errors. Trailing 9–7, Chicago's Fielder Jones led off with a single. Danny Green also sin-gled, and Bill Hallman drew his third free pass of the day, loading the sacks with nobody out. Frank Isbell then forced Hallman at second on a ground out which enabled Jones to cross the plate. That made it 9–8, one out, with Isbell and Green at first and third respectively. Tom Daly then blooped a fly ball down the line in right field. Tiger first sacker, Charlie Carr gave chase and caught up to the teaser but dropped it, enabling Green to score the tying run. Carr, still thinking he had a play on the batter, then wheeled and threw wildly toward first where pitcher Eason had covered on the play. Eason chased down the wild heave and looked up to see Isbell, now rounding third, make a move toward home. Attempting to

Lee Tannehill led the error parade.

cut off the winning run, Eason himself made a wild toss toward the plate — but into the players bench — enabling Isbell to waltz home. It was a fitting ending to a ludicrous game.

Patsy Flaherty, Chicago's winning left–hander, seemed to do everything he could to give the Tigers the game. He walked three batters, hit one, threw two wild pitches, and committed three errors of his own. Although this day's victory left him with an attractive 4–1 record, by season's end Patsy managed to lead the league in losses with 25.

Lee Tannehill, Chicago's rookie shortstop, led all fielders with four blunders. It's ironic that he would humble himself in this note-worthy game because Lee went on to have a distinguished fielding career. Weak at the plate, Tannehill survived 12 years in the majors because of his glove. This season he led the league in double plays and the follow-ing season was switched to third base, where he led in assists four of the next five years.

It should be pointed out that there is some disagreement concerning this record perfor-mance. Official league records for the Ameri-can League prior to 1905 are not known to exist, therefore historians can only recon-struct details from newspaper accounts of the day. However, newspapers usually relied on their own reporters' scoresheets so that for the same game there could, and often were, many different interpretations. This is espe-cially true in matters of judgement such as the distinction between an error and a hit. Even with a detailed play–by–play account, judgements were made on questionable plays that may or may not have agreed with the scorer who was deemed "official." The above version was gleaned from a combination of sources, and while both the *Chicago Inter Ocean* and the *Sporting Life* reported 18 errors, most other newspapers reported only 14 or 15. Unfortunately, there is little hope that this discrepancy will ever be definitively resolved.

Crowd Cheers O'Neill Despite Six Errors

15. Player Makes Six Errors in One Game

ST. LOUIS, AL   at   BOSTON
(Browns, 5)   (Pilgrims, 3)

Saturday, May 21, 1904, Huntington Avenue Grounds

The St. Louis Browns were being enter-tained by the Boston Pilgrims at the Hunt-ington Avenue Grounds. First place Boston had been playing terrific ball, starting the season at 19–8, while the Browns stood in sixth at 12–14. The Pilgrims, however, had to play this afternoon's game without the services of their regular shortstop, Freddie Parent, out with an injured leg. Parent, referred to by the *Boston Globe* as "the king of shortstops," missed only two games all year, but his absence figured prominently in the outcome of this one. As Boston was

lacking in substitutes, using only 13 position players and five pitchers throughout the entire season, Parent's position was filled by Bill O'Neill, who normally played in the outfield.

The game lasted 13 innings with both hurlers throwing well enough to win. St. Louis, however, had a secret weapon — Boston's O'Neill. In the opening frame, the first three Browns to make contact, hit the ball to O'Neill. Bill muffed each one. In the second inning, Bill erred on the fourth con-secutive ball hit in his direction and was well

Bill O'Neill still holds a dubious fielding record.

on his way to a very ignominious record. Yet when he appeared at the plate for the first time, the crowd cheered him encouragingly. O'Neill appropriately responded with a strikeout. It wasn't until the seventh inning that he finally played an opportunity cleanly, for which the crowd again cheered him. By this time, the purpose of the cheering was somewhat ambiguous, as the *Boston Post* noted that bets were being made on each ball hit in O'Neill's direction. The uncertainty of what he'd do kept everyone on the edge of his seat. In the ninth, Bill again displayed his incompetence, this time with a poor throw to first for his fifth error of the game. He was then on the verge of doing something unique. Not since 1890, when many players still fielded bare-handed, had anyone committed six errors in a single contest.

The game continued into extra innings tied at 3–3. It was time again for St. Louis to unleash its secret weapon. In the 13th, after two outs, O'Neill (who did wear a mitt) juggled an easy grounder for his record-setting *sixth error in a game*. This blunder was fatal as it allowed the Browns to score two unanswered runs and garner the victory. St. Louis pitcher Harry Howell knocked in the game winning run with a triple to left. To date, no other major league player has ever committed six errors in a single game. Ironically, Freddie Parent watched this travesty from the bench where he flawlessly fielded a foul ball.

St. Louis Browns	AB	R	H	I	PO	A	E
Jesse Burkett lf	7	1	5	2	3	0	0
>Snags Heidrick cf	7	1	1	0	4	0	1
Charlie Hemphill rf	5	0	0	0	3	1	0
Bobby Wallace ss	6	0	1	0	5	3	0
Tom Jones 1b	6	0	0	0	11	0	0
Hunter Hill 3b	6	0	1	0	1	1	0
Dick Padden 2b	6	1	1	0	1	1	0
Mike Kahoe c	5	1	0	0	10	1	0
Harry Howell p	6	1	2	1	1	6	0
	54	5	11	3	39	13	1

Boston Pilgrims	AB	R	H	I	PO	A	E
Patsy Dougherty lf	5	0	0	0	2	0	0
Jimmy Collins 3b	6	0	1	0	4	4	0
>Chick Stahl cf	6	0	1	0	0	0	0
Buck Freeman rf	5	1	2	0	2	0	0
Bill O'Neill ss	5	1	1	0	1	4	6
Candy LaChance 1b	5	0	0	0	15	1	0
Hobe Ferris 2b	4	1	2	0	4	5	1
Lou Criger c	4	0	1	3	10	0	0
Jesse Tannehill p	5	0	0	0	1	3	0
	45	3	8	3	39	17	7

St. Louis	IP	H	R	ER	BB	SO
Howell W,4-4	13	8	3	3	3	9

Boston	IP	H	R	ER	BB	SO
Tannehill L,5-2	13	11	5	1	1	7

```
StL   2 0 0   1 0 0   0 0 0   0 0 0    2   -5
Bos   0 0 0   3 0 0   0 0 0   0 0 0    0   -3
```

OB: St. Louis 12, Boston 6
DP: Ferris-LaChance (Hill)
     Kahoe-Wallace (O'Neill)
2B: Collins, Ferris
3B: Howell, Criger
SB: Stahl, Hemphill, Hill, Wallace
SO: Burkett, Heidrick 3, Jones,
     Padden, Howell, Freeman 2,
     O'Neill 2, Stahl, LaChance,
     Criger, Tannehill 2

BB: Hemphill, Dougherty, Ferris,
     Criger
SH: Kahoe
TIME: 2:40
ATTENDANCE: 10,641
UMPIRE: Tommy Connolly
SOURCES: Boston Globe, Herald, Post;
     St.Louis Globe-Democrat

BALANCE	OUT+R+OB=BP=AB+BB+SH+HP+CI							
St. Louis	39	5	12	56	54	1	1	0	0
Boston	39	3	6	48	45	3	0	0	0

Bruising Doubleheader Befalls Chance

16. Player Gets Hit by Four Pitches During Doubleheader

CHICAGO   at   CINCINNATI
(Cubs, 4, 5)   (Reds, 7, 2)

Monday, May 30, 1904, League Park

Hit batsmen didn't always cause the turmoil that they do in today's game. Decades ago, many batters actually tried to get plunked in order to give their teams an additional base runner. In the twentieth-century, however, no one has ever gotten hit more than three times in one day except the Chicago Hall of Famer, Frank "Husk" Chance.

Chance was an aggressive player as well as a team leader, attributes which carried him to a successful managerial career and later into the Hall of Fame. As a player, Husk never performed for an entire season simply because his rugged style often precipitated injury. His batting stance of crowding the plate made him the recipient of many wayward pitches, and on this day Frank reached the summit of victimization.

The Cubs, or Colts as some newspapers termed them, were in Cincinnati for an

Chance was often "beaned."

important Decoration Day, morning-afternoon doubleheader. Only two percentage points separated the third place Reds from the Cubs, who were tied with New York for first. The skies were gray throughout the day, and a steady rain fell by the late innings of the second game. In the morning game, Chance, playing first base and batting third, appeared at the plate in the top of the first inning. The Reds Jack Harper, ace of the staff, unleashed a high inside fastball which caught Chance in the left cheek, just below his eye (one newspaper reported impact on the temple). He crumbled to the ground as Cub teammates rushed to his aid. The *Chicago Daily News* reported that Chance was knocked unconscious, although *The Cincinnati Enquirer* disagreed. Regardless, Frank was on the ground for several minutes as blood streamed from a two inch gash on his face. Refusing to leave the contest and still dazed, he was helped to first and was eventually left on base as the inning ended.

In his next plate appearance, in the fourth, Frank avoided bodily contact as he popped out to first. In the seventh, Chance led off the inning and again was drilled by Harper. Reports varied as to the point of contact, but all newspapers agreed it was not damaging. It was in vain, however, because again Chicago failed to score. The ninth inning arrived with the Reds comfortably ahead 7–0, and just to be sure Chance had gotten the message, Harper hit him for the third time. There was no report of rushing the mound or threatening bat-waving. Instead, Chance went to first and soon scored on a grand slam by Davy Jones, making the final tally of the first game a more respectable, 7–4.

As was the custom, the ballpark emptied after the morning game. When the two teams resumed confrontation for the 3 o'clock portion of the twin bill, over 13,000 more fans paid their way to see if their Reds could hold on to first place. On the hill for the Reds was left-hander Win Kellum. When Chance stepped to the plate in the top of the first, he had a teammate on third with one out. With first base open, Kellum proceeded to drill Husk in the ribs. Again, there was not one report of any confrontation. Frank simply took his base on what was the record-setting *fourth time in a doubleheader* that he had been *hit by a pitch*. This time he did score on Jimmy Slagle's triple. In the third inning, Chance singled and was caught stealing. He fouled out to Donlin in the sixth inning after nearly being hit for a fifth time, walked in the eighth, and flied out to Seymour for Chicago's last out in the ninth. No other major leaguer to date has duplicated Husk's misfortune.

Although certain record books have recorded that Chance was hit *five* times on this day, that is inaccurate. Three hometown newspapers specified in their game details that the number was *four*. *The Cincinnati Times-Star* quoted, "Chance was hit four times by the pitchers on Monday — three in the morning and once in the afternoon." The *Cincinnati Commercial Tribune* stated, "He felt three raps off Harper's speed in the morning game, and Kellum hit him on the arm in the afternoon." *The Cincinnati Enquirer* reported, "In the forenoon he was given a base three times because he was hit... In the afternoon game Kellum hit Chance fairly in the short ribs, and on another occasion, narrowly missed him." Even more clearly, *The Chicago Daily News* play-by-play description confirms just four occasions.

An interesting anecdote relating to the afternoon game was described in *The Cincinnati Enquirer*. It seems that Chicago's Bob Wicker was a rather deliberate worker, which was not well appreciated by the Cincinnati fans. During the seventh inning, the packed house, in unison, began counting aloud each time the ball was returned by the catcher. "1-2-3-4..., they counted with the precision of a boxing referee." The newspaper was aghast to report that sometimes the count reached 15 before Wicker again delivered his next pitch. By today's standards, that could almost be termed a "quick-pitch."

MORNING GAME

Chicago Cubs	AB	R	H	I	PO	A	E	Cincinnati Reds	AB	R	H	I	PO	A	E
Otto Williams cf	4	0	1	0	0	0	0	Miller Huggins 2b	4	1	2	0	5	4	0
Doc Casey 3b	4	1	1	0	0	3	0	Mike Donlin lf	5	2	1	2	2	0	0
Frank Chance 1b	1	1	0	0	7	0	0	>Joe Kelley 1b	5	1	2	1	15	0	0
Jimmy Slagle lf	2	1	0	0	1	0	0	Cy Seymour cf	4	1	2	1	1	0	0
Davy Jones rf	4	1	1	4	1	0	0	Cozy Dolan rf	4	1	3	1	0	0	0
Johnny Evers 2b	4	0	1	0	2	2	0	Tommy Corcoran ss	4	0	0	1	1	3	0
Jack O'Neill c	3	0	0	0	10	1	0	Orville Woodruff 3b	4	0	1	0	0	4	0
>Joe Tinker ss	4	0	1	0	3	3	0	Heinie Peitz c	2	1	2	1	3	4	0
Carl Lundgren p	3	0	0	0	0	2	0	Jack Harper p	4	0	0	0	0	2	0
	29	4	5	4	24	11	0		36	7	13	7	27	17	0

Chicago	IP	H	R	ER	BB	SO
Lundgren L,5-3	8	13	7	7	3	8

Chicago	0 0 0	0 0 0	0 0 4	- 4
Cincinnati	0 1 0	0 3 3	0 0 x	- 7

OB: Chicago 4, Cincinnati 8
DP: Woodruff-Huggins-Kelley
  (Lundgren)
2B: Peitz
3B: Donlin
HR: Jones
CS: Williams, Donlin
SO: Williams, Jones, O'Neill, Tinker
  Huggins, Donlin, Seymour, ...

Cincinnati	IP	H	R	ER	BB	SO
Harper W,7-0	9	5	4	4	2	4

SO: ... Corcoran, Harper 4
BB: Slagle 2, Huggins, Peitz 2
HP: By Harper (Chance 3, O'Neill)
WP: Lundgren, Harper
TIME: 1:55
ATTENDANCE: 3,810
UMPIRES: Gus Moran, Charles Zimmer

BALANCE	OUT+R+OB=BP=AB+BB+SH+HP+CI
Chicago	27 4 4 35 29 2 0 4 0
Cincinn	24 7 8 39 36 3 0 0 0

AFTERNOON GAME

Chicago Cubs	AB	R	H	I	PO	A	E
Otto Williams cf	5	0	1	0	4	0	0
Doc Casey 3b	5	1	2	0	3	2	1
>Frank Chance 1b	3	1	1	0	6	3	0
Jimmy Slagle lf	4	0	2	2	2	0	0
Davy Jones rf	1	1	0	0	0	0	0
Johnny Evers 2b	3	1	0	0	2	2	0
Jack O'Neill c	4	0	0	0	8	2	0
Joe Tinker ss	4	1	1	2	2	0	0
Bob Wicker p	4	0	1	1	0	2	0
	33	5	8	5	27	11	1

Cincinnati Reds	AB	R	H	I	PO	A	E
Miller Huggins 2b	4	0	1	0	4	3	1
Mike Donlin lf	4	0	0	0	3	1	1
Joe Kelley 1b	4	1	2	1	7	0	0
>Cy Seymour cf	5	0	2	0	3	0	0
Cozy Dolan rf	2	0	1	0	0	0	0
Tommy Corcoran ss	4	0	0	0	4	1	1
Orville Woodruff 3b	4	1	1	0	2	3	0
Admiral Schlei c	4	0	1	0	4	1	1
Win Kellum p	3	0	1	0	0	2	0
Heinie Peitz ph9	1	0	1	0	0	0	0
Fred Odwell pr9	0	0	0	0	0	0	0
	35	2	10	1	27	11	4

Chicago	IP	H	R	ER	BB	SO
Wicker W,5-0	9	10	2	2	4	3

Chicago	2 0 0	0 0 0	0 0 3	- 5
Cincinnati	0 0 0	0 0 0	0 1 1	- 2

OB: Chicago 7, Cincinnati 11
3B: Kelley 2, Slagle, Tinker
SB: Casey, Evers, Schlei, Dolan,
  Kellum
CS: Seymour, Chance
SO: O'Neill, Dolan, Schlei, Kellum
BB: Chance, Jones, Huggins, Donlin,
  Kelley, Dolan
SH: Jones, Evers, Dolan

Cincinnati	IP	H	R	ER	BB	SO
Kellum L,6-2	9	8	5	3	2	1

HP: By Kellum (Chance, Jones)
TIME: 2:00
ATTENDANCE: 12,177
UMPIRES: Charles Zimmer, Gus Moran
SOURCES: Chicago Chronicle, Daily
  News, Tribune; Cincinnati Enquirer,
  Times Star, Post, Commercial Tribune

BALANCE	OUT+R+OB=BP=AB+BB+SH+HP+CI
Chicago	27 5 7 39 33 2 2 2 0
Cincinnati	27 2 11 40 35 4 1 0 0

The Coombs-Harris Marathon

17. Pitcher Faces 89 Batters and Strikes Out 18 in 24-Inning Game

PHILADELPHIA, AL   at   BOSTON
(Athletics, 4)   (Red Sox, 1)

Saturday, September 1, 1906, Huntington Avenue Grounds

The weather couldn't have been more glorious, and two games were promised the hometown Boston fans. Instead, they got only one, but what a game it was. Patrons saw more than the 18 innings they expected, 24 to be exact, in one of the most thrilling and well played games to date in major league history. Numerous scoring opportunities were squelched by scintillating pitching, and 212 fielding chances were offered with only three errors, a noteworthy feat during this era.

Expecting to see two games, many fans had taken their time arriving at the ballpark. After all seats had been claimed, the contest had to be halted several times to corral excess patrons behind outfield ropes, particularly in right field where a ground-rule triple was invoked. These triples provided numerous thrills and eventually led to the Philadelphia victory.

Several major league records were established this day. Prior to the contest, the longest major league game had lasted a mere 20 innings. This day's *24-inning match* remained the major league record for 14 years (see 5-01-20) and *was not exceeded in the American League for 74 years* (see 5-09-84). Equally remarkable was the fact that both starting hurlers went the distance. Philadelphia's Jack Coombs, just a few months removed from Colby College, Maine, impressed the overflow crowd with his precocious

This was the most famous of Jack Coombs' 158 career wins.

poise and ability. Jack *struck out 18 Red Sox; no hurler struck out more until 1962* (see 9-12-62). Twenty-four-year-old Joe Harris toiled for the home club. Despite losing his first 14 games of the season, Joe matched Coombs in effectiveness for 23 innings. Both hurlers remain *AL record holders for facing the most batters in one game* (Coombs 89, Harris 87). Each pitched through the gauntlet of the entire opposing lineup nearly 10 times.

The Athletics drew first blood by scoring an unearned run in the third frame. After Mike Powers fanned, Coombs singled and stole second. Topsy Hartzel then bounced out to Harris. When Moose Grimshaw next booted Bris Lord's grounder, Coombs scooted home. Boston drew even in the sixth when Freddy Parent tripled with one out and was driven home by Chick Stahl's single.

That was the extent of the scoring for the next 17 innings although there were ample opportunities.

• In the eighth, each team got a runner to second with two outs, but Lord grounded out for Philadelphia and Parent struck out for Boston.

• In the tenth, Philadelphia's Monte Cross opened by drawing a base on balls and was sacrificed to second by Jack Knight. But Joe Harris fanned Powers and got Coombs on a pop up to first.

• With two outs in the 11th, the Athletics' Ossie Schreckengost pinch-hit for Harry Davis and tripled into the crowd, but Harris got Socks Seybold on a bouncer back to the box.

• Philadelphia repeated their two-out threat in the 12th when Jack Knight also tripled. Harris was again equal to the task by retiring Powers on a fly ball to right.

• Boston also threatened in the 12th. Stahl singled and was sacrificed by Hobe Ferris. After Coombs struck out Jack Huey, manager Connie Mack ordered Grimshaw walked. The strategy paid off when Coombs also fanned Red Morgan.

• Opportunity knocked again for the Red Sox in the 14th as Parent led off with a double. But Coombs turned it up a notch by fanning Stahl and Ferris, and inducing Huey to ground out.

• Both clubs put runners in scoring position in the 15th. For Philadelphia, with one out Knight tripled in his second consecutive plate appearance. But Powers flied out to shallow center, and Coombs grounded out. Grimshaw led off for Boston in the bottom half of the inning and was safe on Monte Cross' throwing error. After Morgan sacrificed, manager Mack ordered pinch hitter Buck Freeman intentionally walked. Freeman became incensed at the strategy, and after three straight wide ones, jumped across the plate to swing at the fourth offering. For his impetuousness, Buck was declared out, possibly cost his club the game, and drew the ire of the Boston press. Coombs then took control by striking out Harris. That marked the third inning in which the youngster had slammed the door on a Boston threat with a strikeout.

• Coombs again shined in the 18th. After Harris fouled out, Jack Hayden walked. Parent singled, sending Hayden to third. Connie Mack then displayed extraordinary confidence in his rookie hurler by ordering Stahl walked, loading the bases. With the infield drawn to double play depth, Coombs responded, fanning both Ferris and Huey.

• The 19th inning again tested Coombs. Grimshaw led off and was safe on second baseman Danny Murphy's error. Morgan sacrificed, but Lou Criger flied out to center and Harris struck out. Coombs had again extinguished the threat with a strikeout.

• In the 20th after two were out, Knight singled for Philadelphia and stole second. Powers, however, fanned.

After that, neither team had a batter reach second base until the fateful 24th. Then, after Coombs struck out, Hartzel singled and stole second. Lord also struck out, and with two strikes on Schreckengost, the inning once more appeared fruitless for Philadelphia. But the famine was broken when Schreckengost singled home Hartzel, and both Socks Seybold and Murphy followed with triples. In the bottom of the frame Boston expired with merely a whimper — a single by Grimshaw.

The marathon had provided many heroes. Coombs and Harris have already been applauded. In addition, Mike Powers was a

Mike Powers set two records in this game.

tower of strength behind the plate for the Athletics, establishing two records. To date, no backstop has caught more *innings in a game without an error.* Also, Powers accepted *more chances (25) than any catcher in a major league game.* (Contemporary record books list 26 chances for Powers, but official league records and several of the cited sources relate 25.) In addition, Powers threw out five runners attempting to steal, including two in the seventh inning. Finally Tim Hurst, as the customary lone umpire, must be given considerable recognition for calling every ball, strike, and out during the four hour and forty-seven minute duration. Remarkably, not one negative comment concerning his work could be found in the newspapers cited.

Jack Coombs went on to an outstanding career, winning 158 games while losing only 110 and led the Athletics to their pennants in 1910 and 1911 by winning 59 games. Joe Harris finished a significantly less brilliant career after only three seasons, compiling an insufferable 3–30 lifetime record. Harris still owns both the worst winning percentage (.091) and the fewest wins of any 20th-century pitcher who threw more than 300 lifetime innings.

STAHL'S "CHICKS" YANKED OFF PERCH IN 24TH

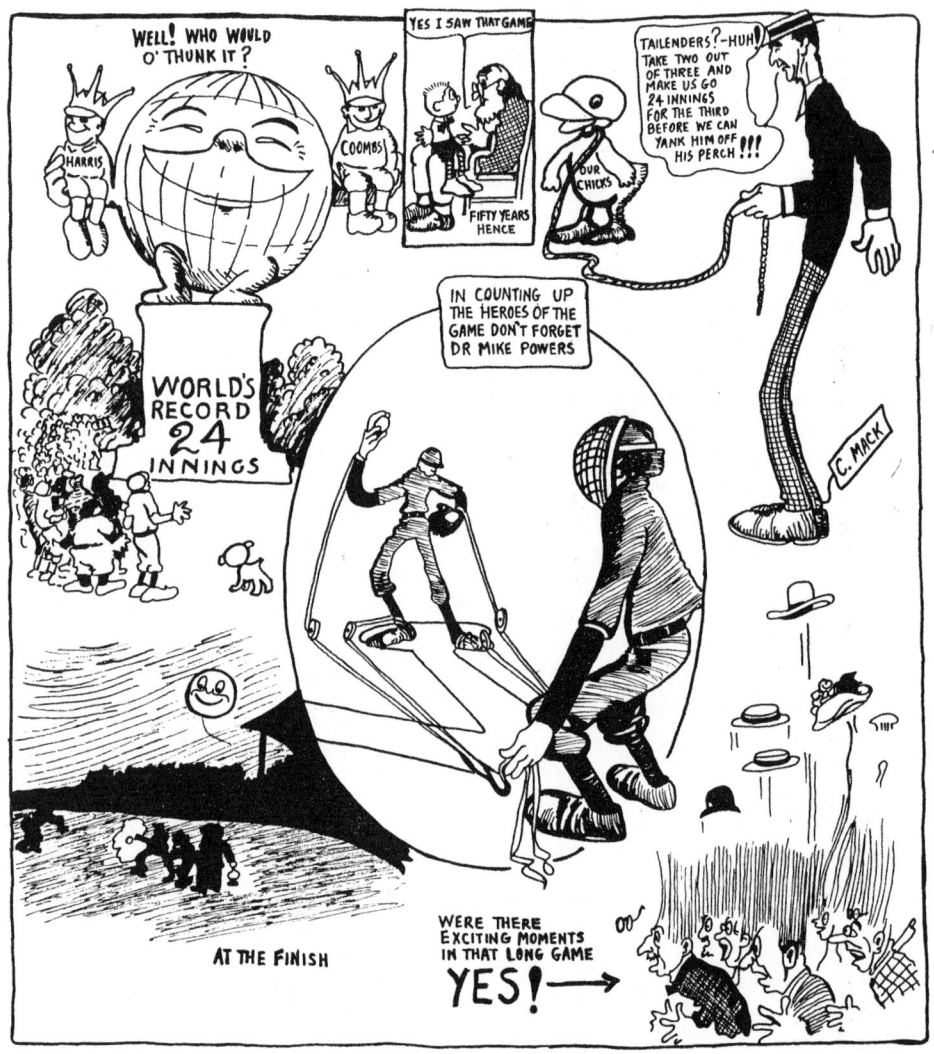

Highlights of the game as portrayed by the Boston Herald *(reprinted with permission of the* Boston Herald*).*

Phila Athletics	AB	R	H	I	PO	A	E		Boston Red Sox	AB	R	H	I	PO	A	E
Topsy Hartzel lf	10	1	2	0	2	1	0		Jack Hayden rf	9	0	2	0	7	0	0
Bris Lord cf	9	0	1	0	6	0	0		Freddy Parent ss	10	1	4	0	6	9	0
Harry Davis 1b	4	0	0	0	12	1	0		Chick Stahl cf	7	0	2	1	5	0	0
Schreckengost ph11,1b	6	1	2	1	16	0	0		Hobe Ferris 2b	9	0	1	0	5	9	0
Socks Seybold rf	10	1	1	1	4	0	0		Jack Hoey lf	10	0	2	0	4	0	0
Danny Murphy 2b	9	0	2	1	3	7	1		Moose Grimshaw 1b	8	0	2	0	25	2	0
>Monte Cross ss	9	0	1	0	9	3	1		Red Morgan 3b	7	0	0	0	2	3	0
Jack Knight 3b	7	0	5	0	1	4	0		Bill Carrigan c	5	0	1	0	6	2	1
Mike Powers c	9	0	1	0	18	7	0		Buck Freeman ph15	1	0	0	0	0	0	0
Jack Coombs p	9	1	1	0	1	10	0		> Lou Criger c16	4	0	0	0	11	1	0
	82	4	16	3	72	33	2		Joe Harris p	9	0	1	0	1	6	0
										79	1	15	1	72	32	1

Philadelphia	IP	H	R	ER	BB	SO		Boston	IP	H	R	ER	BB	SO
Coombs W,6-7	24	15	1	1	6	18		Harris L,2-18	24	16	4	3	2	14

Philadelphia	0 0 1	0 0 0	0 0 0	0 0 0	0 0 0	0 0 0	0 0 0	0 0 3	- 4
Boston	0 0 0	0 0 1	0 0 0	0 0 0	0 0 0	0 0 0	0 0 0	0 0 0	- 1

OB: Philadelphia 11, Boston 16
DP: Ferris-Parent-Grimshaw (Cross)
    Cross-Murphy-Davis (Ferris)
2B: Ferris, Parent
3B: Parent, Schreckengost, Murphy,
    Knight 2, Seybold
SB: Hartzel, Lord, Cross, Knight,
    Combs 2, Stahl
CS: Murphy, Knight 2, Hayden,
    Hoey, Grimshaw, Morgan 2
SO: Hartzel 3, Lord 2, Davis,
    Murphy, Cross 3, Knight,
    Powers 2, Coombs, Hayden 2,
    Parent 2, Stahl, Ferris 4,
    Huey 2, Morgan 2, Freeman,
    Harris 4

BB: Cross, Knight, Hayden, Morgan,
    Stahl 2(1I), Grimshaw 2(2I)
SH: Lord, Knight, Ferris, Morgan 2
HP: By Coombs(Stahl), by Harris
    (Murphy)
TIME: 4:47
ATTENDANCE: 18,084
UMPIRE: Tim Hurst
SOURCES: Boston Globe, Herald; DBD;
    North American, Philadelphia Even-
    ing Telegraph, Inquirer, Press

BALANCE	OUT	+	R	+	OB	=	BP	+	AB	+	BB	+	SH	+	HP	+	CI
Philadelphia	72		4		11		87		82		2		2		1		0
Boston	72		1		16		89		79		6		3		1		0

Rickey's Wounded Wing Enables Senators to Run Wild

18. Catcher Allows 13 Stolen Bases in One Game

WASHINGTON   at   NEW YORK
(Senators, 16)   (Highlanders, 5)

Friday, June 28, 1907, Hilltop Park

Wesley Branch Rickey etched a place for himself in baseball annals long before his signing of Jackie Robinson. Rickey, who began his major league career in 1905 as a backup catcher for the St. Louis Browns, possessed a strong throwing arm at the start of his career but mysteriously injured his shoulder prior to reporting to the Highlanders (later Yankees) in 1907. Highlander manager Clark Griffith knew that Rickey couldn't throw, but when first string catcher Red Kleinow also got hurt, Branch was pressed into emergency action. It didn't take long for the last place Senators to discover and exploit the weakness.

In the very first inning, Rickey attempted to throw a runner out at second, and the ball wound up in right field where Willie Keeler fielded it. After that, as Rickey later recalled in a biography by Arthur Mann,* he never made another throw, and the Senators ran to second as soon as they got on. On the contrary, newspapers of the day reported that Rickey did make several more attempts, once apparently nipping Jim Delahanty at third. Jim, however, was called safe by umpire Tim Hurst. Other throws sailed over the heads or out of the reach of second sacker Jimmy Williams and shortstop Kid Elberfeld. New York hurler Lew Brockett contributed to the mayhem with a slow delivery, enabling the base runners to get excellent jumps. Twice the visitors worked a double-steal, from first to second and from third to home.

Reaching base was little trouble for the Senators. *The New York Sun* reported that "the Washingtons thumped the ball until it was lopsided," reaching two New York

*Arthur Mann, Branch Rickey (Boston: Houghton Mifflin, 1957), 49.

hurlers for a total of nine walks and 20 base hits. Perhaps this logjam of base runners prevented further embarrassment, for *The Sun* also reported that the Senators only stopped long enough to catch their breath between bases. This day's record of *13, is the most bases ever stolen off one catcher in a game.* In addition, Rickey suffered the ignomity of striking out with the bases loaded to end the Highlander's biggest offensive inning. This was the last year that Branch ever caught in the majors, although he did pinch-hit a few times seven years later.

Fortunately for Rickey, his later brilliant baseball career as a pioneer in breaking the color barrier, developer of minor league systems, equipment innovator, and astute judge of talent far overshadowed this devastation. "The Mahatma" was aptly nicknamed and entered the Hall of Fame in 1967.

Branch Rickey

Washington Senators	AB	R	H	I	PO	A	E
Otis Clymer lf	5	2	3	1	1	0	0
>Bob Ganley rf	5	1	2	1	0	0	0
Jim Delahanty 3b	6	3	2	3	0	2	0
John Anderson 1b	4	3	3	0	6	0	0
Charlie Jones cf	5	2	3	3	5	0	0
Nig Perrine 2b	4	1	1	1	4	3	0
Dave Altizer ss	5	3	2	3	3	2	0
Mike Heydon c	6	0	2	1	8	0	0
Long Tom Hughes p	5	1	2	1	0	2	0
	45	16	20	14	27	9	0

New York Highlanders	AB	R	H	I	PO	A	E
Danny Hoffman cf	5	0	1	0	0	0	0
Willie Keeler rf	5	0	1	1	3	0	1
Kid Elberfeld ss	4	1	2	1	2	3	0
Hal Chase 1b	5	1	2	1	10	0	1
Frank LaPorte 3b	5	0	2	2	0	4	0
Jimmy Williams 2b	5	0	1	0	5	3	0
>Wid Conroy lf	3	1	1	0	2	0	0
Branch Rickey c	3	1	0	0	5	2	1
Earl Moore p	0	0	0	0	0	2	0
Lew Brockett p2	4	1	2	0	0	2	0
	39	5	12	5	27	16	3

Washington	IP	H	R	ER	BB	SO
Hughes W,3-5	9	12	5	5	4	7

New York	IP	H	R	ER	BB	SO
Moore L,2-3	1	5	4	4	0	0
Brockett	8	15	12	11	9	4
	9	20	16	15	9	4

Washington   4 1 1   3 0 2   1 0 4   -16
New York   0 0 0   0 2 0   3 0 0   - 5

OB: Washington 13, New York 11
2B: Chase, Williams
3B: Clymer, Jones
HR: Altizer(2)
SB: Chase, Clymer, Ganley 3, Heydon,
      Delahanty 2, Anderson 2, Jones 2
      Altizer 2
BB: Clymer, Ganley, Jones, Perrine 2
      Anderson 2, Altizer, Hughes, ...

BB: ... Elberfeld, Conroy 2, Rickey
SH: Clymer, Ganley
TIME: 2:20
ATTENDANCE: 2,000
UMPIRES: John Stafford(H), Tim Hurst
SOURCES: New York American, Herald,
    Sun, Times, Tribune, World;
    Washington Evening Star, Post

BALANCE	OUT+R+OB=BP=AB+BB+SH+HP+CI							
Washington	27	16	13	56	45	9	2	0	0
New York	27	5	11	43	39	4	0	0	0

Hooks Wilts the Phillies

19. Pitcher Throws Ten-Inning, No-Hit Victory

PHILADELPHIA, NL　　at　　NEW YORK
(Phillies, 0)　　　　　　　　　(Giants, 1)

Saturday, July 4, 1908, Polo Grounds

Prior to this date, no pitcher had ever *won a no-hitter of more than nine innings*. There had been over 50 no-hitters thrown since the birth of the National League in 1876, and even some of more than nine innings. But each time a hurler ventured into extra innings the result was either a no-decision or a loss. For example, in 1884, Sam Kimber of Brooklyn in the American Association, hurled ten no-hit innings only to have the game called on account of darkness. And in 1906, Brooklyn's Harry McIntire tossed 10 & 2/3 innings before allowing a hit but eventually lost in the 13th inning. On this day, however, destiny was on the side of George "Hooks" Wiltse.

Wiltse pitched 11 of his 12 major league seasons with the New York Giants. This, his fifth year, was his finest. Working in the shadow of Christy Mathewson, Hooks amassed 23 victories in 1908, and this game represented the highlight of his season.

Pitching in the first game of a morning-afternoon, Independence Day doubleheader at the Polo Grounds, Wiltse was untouch-

Hooks Wiltse was almost perfect for ten innings.

able. From the sixth inning on, the 7,000 home town fans cheered madly as Hooks returned to the dugout after each inning. Later in the contest, they erupted after each out. His teammates encouraged him from the field, and according to *The New York World,* "mopped him with wet towels between innings." Hooks took not only a no-hitter, but also a perfect game, into the ninth. Then, with two men out, up to the plate stepped opposing moundsman George McQuillan. The crowd was in a frenzy as McQuillan fouled off the first offering. Next came a called strike, then a ball. The fourth pitch appeared to everyone to be a third strike — everyone that is, except umpire Charles "Cy" Rigler. Despite vigorous objection by catcher Bresnahan and right fielder Mike Donlin, who had rushed in from his defensive position, Rigler held firm. As play continued, the very next pitch hit McQuillan on the arm, destroying the perfect game and sending groans of disappointment through the stands and unprintable epithets at Rigler. Wiltse then retired the 28th

batter, Eddie Grant, but the 0–0 contest was yet to be decided. Hooks was still vulnerable to the curse of the extra-inning no-hitter.

In the bottom of the tenth, the Philadelphia defense cracked behind McQuillan. Art Devlin led off with a single. On Spike Shannon's attempted sacrifice bunt, Grant tossed the ball over the head of first baseman Kitty Bransfield, enabling Devlin to reach third base and Shannon second. Al Bridwell then hit a grounder to shortstop Ernie Courtney. In his haste to nip Devlin at the plate, Courtney kicked the ball out of his own glove, allowing Devlin to glide home with the game winner, and Wiltse made history with his no-hit, extra-inning victory.

Phila Phillies	AB	R	H	I	PO	A	E
Eddie Grant 3b	4	0	0	0	3	4	1
Otto Knabe 2b	4	0	0	0	1	4	0
John Titus rf	4	0	0	0	1	0	0
>Sherry Magee lf	4	0	0	0	2	0	0
Kitty Bransfield 1b	3	0	0	0	14	0	0
Ossie Osborn cf	3	0	0	0	2	0	0
Mickey Doolan ss	1	0	0	0	2	2	0
Ernie Courtney ss4	2	0	0	0	1	3	1
Red Dooin c	3	0	0	0	1	1	1
George McQuillan p	2	0	0	0	0	3	0
	30	0	0	0	27	17	3

New York Giants	AB	R	H	I	PO	A	E
Fred Tenney 1b	4	0	2	0	14	1	0
Larry Doyle 2b	3	0	0	0	0	1	0
Roger Bresnahan c	4	0	0	0	5	1	0
Mike Donlin rf	3	0	1	0	4	0	0
Cy Seymour cf	4	0	1	0	0	0	0
Art Devlin 3b	4	1	2	0	0	0	0
Spike Shannon lf	2	0	0	0	3	0	0
>Al Bridwell ss	4	0	2	0	3	7	0
Hooks Wiltse p	2	0	0	0	1	4	0
	30	1	8	0	30	14	0

Philadelphia	IP	H	R	ER	BB	SO
McQuillan L,11-9	9	8	1	0	0	1

New York	IP	H	R	ER	BB	SO
Wiltse W,10-8	10	0	0	0	0	5

Philadelphia	0 0 0	0 0 0	0 0 0	0	- 0
New York	0 0 0	0 0 0	0 0 0	1	- 1

OB: Philadelphia 1, New York 7
DP: Knabe-Bransfield (Tenney)
     Grant-Bransfield (Bresnahan)
SB: Donlin
SH: Doyle, Shannon 2, Wiltse
HP: By Wiltse (McQuillan),
     by McQuillan (Donlin)
TIME: 1:40

ATTENDANCE: 7,000
UMPIRE: Cy Rigler
SOURCES: New York American, Herald,
     Sun, Tribune, Times, World; Phila-
     delphia Inquirer, North American,
     Public Ledger, Record

BALANCE	OUT	+R	+OB	=BP	=AB	+BB	+SH	+HP	+CI
Philadelphia	30	0	1	31	30	0	0	1	0
New York	27	1	7	35	30	0	4	1	0

20. Pitcher Throws a Doubleheader Shutout

CHICAGO   at   BROOKLYN
(Cubs, 5,3)   (Superbas, 0,0)

Saturday, September 26, 1908, Washington Park

With less than two weeks remaining in the regular season, three teams were struggling fiercely for the National League pennant. On this morning, here's how those three clubs stacked up:

	W	L	Pct	GB
New York	88	52	.629	.5
Chicago	91	54	.628	
Pittsburgh	91	55	.623	.5

The Cubs were being hosted by Brooklyn who was out of the race, but the Washington Park fans turned out in droves. Exactly who they came to cheer is questionable. One newspaper, in the same paragraph, first described the crowd as cheering for the Cubs, hoping the crosstown rival Giants wouldn't take the pennant. A few sentences later, the same reporter told how the Brooklynites cheered when the Giants-Reds scores were posted, showing the Giants winning the first game of their doubleheader. At any rate, there was a packed house in Brooklyn, and the bipartisan crowd was raucous.

In the first game of this Brooklyn-Chicago doubleheader, 25-year-old "Big Ed" Reulbach took the hill for the Cubs. The tall right-hander had already won his 20th game of the season, having beaten Brooklyn seven times in seven

attempts. To make matters even more grim for the home team, Big Ed was on a streak of pitching 12 consecutive scoreless innings. A sometimes wild, fastball pitcher, Reulbach had it all together in this game, allowing just five Brooklyn hits and one walk while striking out seven. In the fifth inning, Ed faced his only serious trouble when the first two hitters singled; but two infield pop-ups and a

"Big Ed," a 6-foot, 1-inch, 190-pounder, recorded a 182–106 lifetime log.

Reulbach posted four of Chicago's last eight victories.

hurler, for Reulbach had turned on the adrenalin and pitched even better in the nightcap. In the second game, Brooklyn could muster only three hits and an intentional walk. Again, there was only one precarious inning for Big Ed—the seventh. With the Cubs clinging to a 1–0 lead, Brooklyn's Tom Catterson led off with a single to left-center. Reulbach then fumbled Harry Lumley's sacrifice bunt, putting two on with none out. Johnny Kling, the Cubs backstop who also had a terrific day at the plate, then dampened Brooklyn's rally by throwing a bullet to shortstop Joe Tinker, catching Catterson napping. John Hummel fanned, but Reulbach wild-pitched Lumley to second. After Tim Jordan, the league's leading home run hitter was intentionally walked, Reulbach then slammed the door on Brooklyn by inducing Al Burch to tap weakly to third for an inning ending force out. That was the closest Brooklyn came to scoring all day.

ground out smothered the fire. No Brooklyn runner reached third during the game as the Cubs prevailed, 5–0.

During the intermission, Reulbach asked his manager Frank Chance if he could also pitch the second game. "You've had enough" responded Chance, "… remember that these games mean a great deal to us for we can ill afford to lose another contest this season with New York still in the lead."* But Reulbach pleaded, assuring his manager that he was capable. Chance thought it over and reasoned that, if successful, the remainder of his staff would be that much better rested for an important upcoming series with Cincinnati. Then too, as Reulbach argued, Chance could always bring in a reliever if necessary and be no worse off.

The following day, it was difficult to tell who was happier, Chance or his young

According to the *New York Herald*, Brooklyn owner Charles Ebbets summed up the day's events when he said, "Judging by the results of the afternoon, Brooklyn would probably not have made a hit or gotten to first base in the third game. I am delighted that no third game was scheduled."*

Reulbach followed this outing with a shutout over Cincinnati on October 1, his fourth in succession. In all, he posted four of Chicago's final eight victories and finished at 24–7. The Cubs, in a thrilling pennant race, did triumph by one game over both the Giants and the Pirates, and they concluded a brilliant season by beating Detroit four games to one in the World Series.

"Reulbach Pitches a Double No Run Game in One Afternoon," New York Herald, 27 September, 1908.

MORNING GAME

Chicago Cubs	AB	R	H	I	PO	A	E
Jack Hayden rf	4	0	0	1	2	0	0
Johnny Evers 2b	4	1	3	1	2	3	0
>Wildfire Schulte lf	4	0	0	0	1	0	0
Frank Chance 1b	4	0	0	0	8	0	0
Harry Steinfeldt 3b	4	1	2	1	1	1	0
Solly Hofman cf	4	0	1	1	2	0	0
Joe Tinker ss	4	1	1	0	2	3	0
Johnny Kling c	4	2	3	1	9	1	0
Ed Reulbach p	2	0	0	0	0	1	0
	34	5	10	5	27	9	0

Brooklyn Superbas	AB	R	H	I	PO	A	E
Tom Catterson lf	4	0	0	0	4	0	0
Harry Lumley rf	4	0	0	0	2	0	0
John Hummel 2b	4	0	1	0	2	1	1
Tim Jordan 1b	3	0	0	0	9	1	0
>Al Burch cf	4	0	0	0	3	0	0
Tommy McMillan ss	3	0	1	0	1	0	2
Tommy Sheehan 3b	3	0	1	0	0	2	1
Joe Dunn c	3	0	2	0	5	1	0
Kaiser Wilhelm p	3	0	0	0	1	5	0
	31	0	5	0	27	10	4

Chicago	IP	H	R	ER	BB	SO
Reulbach W,21-7	9	5	0	0	1	7

Brooklyn	IP	H	R	ER	BB	SO
Wilhelm L,14-22	9	10	5	4	1	5

Chicago   0 0 0   0 1 0   1 2 1   - 5
Brooklyn   0 0 0   0 0 0   0 0 0   - 0

OB: Chicago 7, Brooklyn 5
2B: Kling, Evers
SB: Steinfeldt
CS: Steinfeldt, Burch
SO: Schulte 3, Reulbach 2, Hummel,
     Catterson, Burch 2, McMillan,
     Dunn, Wilhelm

BB: Reulbach, Jordan
SH: Hayden, Evers, Schulte, Reulbach
PB: Dunn
TIME: 1:40
ATTENDANCE: 15,000
UMPIRES: Brick Owens, Bob Emslie

BALANCE	OUT+R+OB=BP=AB+BB+SH+HP+CI

	OUT	R	OB	BP	AB	BB	SH	HP	CI
Chicago	27	5	7	39	34	1	4	0	0
Brooklyn	27	0	5	32	31	1	0	0	0

AFTERNOON GAME

Chicago Cubs	AB	R	H	I	PO	A	E
Jack Hayden rf	4	1	1	0	3	0	0
Johnny Evers 2b	4	0	1	1	1	1	0
Wildfire Schulte lf	2	0	1	0	3	0	0
Frank Chance 1b	4	0	0	0	9	0	0
>Harry Steinfeldt 3b	4	0	0	0	1	1	0
Solly Hofman cf	3	0	0	0	1	0	0
Joe Tinker ss	3	0	0	0	3	5	0
Johnny Kling c	3	1	2	0	6	1	0
Ed Reulbach p	1	1	0	0	0	2	1
	28	3	5	1	27	10	1

Brooklyn Superbas	AB	R	H	I	PO	A	E
Tom Catterson lf	4	0	1	0	5	0	0
Harry Lumley rf	4	0	2	0	2	0	0
>John Hummel 2b	4	0	0	0	4	1	0
Tim Jordan 1b	2	0	0	0	7	0	0
Al Burch cf	3	0	0	0	2	0	0
Tommy McMillan ss	3	0	0	0	2	2	1
Tommy Sheehan 3b	3	0	0	0	1	2	0
Joe Dunn c	3	0	0	0	3	3	2
Jim Pastorius p	2	0	0	0	1	3	0
Harry Pattee ph9	1	0	0	0	0	0	0
	29	0	3	0	27	11	3

Chicago	IP	H	R	ER	BB	SO
Reulbach W,22-7	9	3	0	0	1	4

Brooklyn	IP	H	R	ER	BB	SO
Pastorius L,3-20	9	5	3	1	3	2

Chicago   0 0 1   0 0 0   0 2 0   - 3
Brooklyn   0 0 0   0 0 0   0 0 0   - 0

OB: Chicago 2, Brooklyn 3
DP: Reulbach-Tinker-Chance (Hummel)
     McMillan-Hummel-Jordan
     (Reulbach)
SB: Schulte
CS: Hayden, Schulte
SO: Hayden, Hofman, Hummel, Dunn,
     McMillan, Pattee
BB: Schulte 2, Reulbach, Jordan(I)

SH: Reulbach
WP: Pastorius, Reulbach
TIME: 1:12
ATTENDANCE: 15,000
UMPIRES: Bob Emslie, Brick Owens
SOURCES: Chicago Daily News, Inter-
     Ocean; New York Tribune, Sun,
     Times, Herald, World

BALANCE	OUT+R+OB=BP=AB+BB+SH+HP+CI

	OUT	R	OB	BP	AB	BB	SH	HP	CI
Chicago	27	3	2	32	28	3	1	0	0
Brooklyn	27	0	3	30	29	1	0	0	0

Inconspicuous Assistance

21. Teams Combine for 44 Assists in Nine-Inning Game

CLEVELAND   at   ST. LOUIS
(Naps, 5)   (Browns, 2)

Thursday, May 27, 1909, Sportsman's Park

A scan of this game's boxscore fails to disclose the sensational offensive numbers one might expect in a record-setting game. Closer examination of the defensive half of the balance sheet, however, reveals an assist total never before, nor since, seen in twentieth-century major-league baseball. This day a fielding benchmark was established — a *two-team total of 44 assists in a nine-inning game* as the Cleveland Naps (named after their player/manager Nap Lajoie) conquered the St. Louis Browns, 5–2.

This is a standard that has been clouded in error for decades. Previous record books claimed the mark in this catagory was 45, set in an American League game between New York and Chicago on August 21, 1905. How-ever, examination of official league records provides a total of only 41 for that game. Next, two National League contests laid claim to 44 combined assists — Brooklyn vs. New York on April 21, 1903, and New York vs. Cincinnati on May 15, 1909. Neither of these claims can also withstand comparison to official league data, the former revealing 43 and the latter 42. This day's game, on the other hand, while not previously listed in record books, does in fact stand up to the scrutiny of official league records.

The game itself offered little toward the pennant race. With little over a month gone in the season, both squads were already in the second division, which is where they finished. A highlight was perhaps the matchup of two

Joss (left) and Pelty induced many ground balls and also led their teams in assists.

good pitchers. Barney Pelty was the only Browns hurler in 1909 not to have a losing record, and Addie Joss, although in the twilight of a tragedy-shortened career, was still extremely effective with a 1.71 ERA. This day, the two hurlers had the batters beating the ball into the turf. For Joss this was not unusual. Of the eight games during 1909 in which Cleveland accumulated 20 or more assists, Joss pitched five of them. For Pelty on the other hand, this was his only game in which St. Louis garnered 20 or more assists. Only six balls were caught by Browns outfielders; none by the Naps. On the other hand, Roy Hartzell, St. Louis right fielder, harvested two of the record total assists by throwing out runners on the basepaths. Both Pelty and Joss did plenty of fielding themselves, mostly on poorly placed sacrifice-bunt

attempts. (Neither pitcher tallied more assists in a game all season.) There was also one rundown that amassed several assists, that being in Cleveland's half of the third inning. Then, with Lajoie on first and Wilbur Good on third, Nap was caught napping. Pelty had him picked off by throwing to first baseman Tom Jones. But Lajoie broke for second, and Good, thinking the play would follow his manager, broke for home. Jones wisely threw to catcher Jim Stephens, who along with third baseman Hobe Ferris, successfully engaged Good in a rundown. No details were available, however, of the number of assists credited during this play. Although there was no mention of a record-setting performance in newspapers of the day, this game set the assist standard for the balance of the century.

Cleveland Naps	AB	R	H	I	PO	A	E
Wilbur Good rf	5	2	3	2	0	0	0
Bill Bradley 3b	5	0	2	1	0	1	0
Terry Turner ss	5	0	0	0	3	6	0
>Nap Lajoie 2b	5	0	2	1	3	5	1
Bill Hinchman cf	4	1	1	0	0	0	0
George Stovall 1b	2	0	0	0	18	0	0
Ted Easterly c	4	0	2	1	3	3	0
Bris Lord lf	3	2	2	0	0	0	0
Addie Joss p	3	0	1	0	0	7	0
	36	5	13	5	27	22	1

Cleveland	IP	H	R	ER	BB	SO
Joss W,3-2	9	7	2	1	0	2

Cleveland	1 0 1		0 0 0		1 2 0		- 5	
St. Louis	0 0 0		1 1 0		0 0 0		- 2	

OB: Cleveland 8, St. Louis 3
DP: Williams-Wallace-Jones
    Easterly-Turner (McAleese SO)
    Bradley-Lajoie-Stovall(Williams)
3B: Good
SB: Lord
CS: Hartzell, Jones
SO: Jones, McAleese, ?
BB: Stovall, Lord

St. Louis Browns	AB	R	H	I	PO	A	E
Roy Hartzell rf	4	0	1	0	1	2	0
Art Griggs lf	4	1	1	0	3	0	0
Hobe Ferris 3b	4	0	1	0	2	2	2
Bobby Wallace ss	4	0	1	1	2	4	0
>Jimmy Williams 2b	4	0	0	0	2	2	0
Tom Jones 1b	3	1	1	0	12	3	0
John McAleese cf	2	0	0	0	2	0	0
Jim Stephens c	3	0	2	1	2	3	0
Barney Pelty p	3	0	0	0	1	6	1
	31	2	7	2	27	22	3

St. Louis	IP	H	R	ER	BB	SO
Pelty L,3-2	9	13	5	4	2	1

SH: McAleese, Joss, Stovall
WP: Joss
TIME: 1:48
ATTENDANCE: 3,500
UMPIRES: Tommy Connolly, John Kerin
SOURCES: Cleveland Leader, Plain
    Dealer, Press; DBD; St.Louis Globe-
    Democrat, Post-Dispatch

BALANCE	OUT	+	R	+	OB	=	BP	=	AB	+	BB	+	SH	+	HP	+	CI
Cleveland	27		5		8		40		36		2		2		0		0
St.Louis	27		2		3		32		31		0		1		0		0

A Titanic Pitching Duel

22. Pitcher Throws 18-Inning Shutout

WASHINGTON   at   DETROIT
(Nationals, 0)   (Tigers, 0)

Friday, July 16, 1909, Bennett Park

Summers served the Nationals a bushel of goose eggs.

When Washington invaded Detroit for a four game series in mid-July, 1909, there wasn't much to get excited about. The Tigers were at the summit of the American League standings while the Nationals* were solidly entrenched in the basement. And, although Washington could score in only one of the four games, their futility contributed to the establishment of a duration record that still stands. In this the final contest of the series, the two teams played an 18-inning scoreless game, and Detroit's Oron Edgar Summers, "Kickapoo Ed", went the distance. It was the *first time in the twentieth century that a hurler tossed an 18-inning white-wash.* (Amazingly, this feat later would be duplicated twice — see 5-15-18 & 7-02-33.) At 6:45 p.m., home plate umpire John Kerin called the game on account of darkness, much to the chagrin of both players and spectators. Everyone but Kerin felt there was plenty of daylight remaining.

There were several

*The Washington Post *was now referring to the team as the Nationals. They were formerly referred to as the Senators.*

scoring opportunities for each club throughout the contest. For Washington:

• They had two hits in the same inning only once, the first. Then, with one down, Clyde Milan bunted safely and Jack Lelivelt singled, but Summers got Bob Unglaub on a long fly, and struck out Jiggs Donohue.

• In the third, Dolly Gray led off with a two-bagger but was doubled off second on George Browne's liner to Donie Bush.

• In the ninth, Browne opened with a walk and Milan again bunted safely. After Lelivelt flew out, Unglaub stroked a blooper into right for which first baseman Claude Rossman lunged, caught, and tagged first to double off Milan.

• Speed Kelly was safe on a Bush throwing error to lead off the 13th. George McBride followed with a single to center. Here, Summers got lucky as his next pitch got away from battery mate Oscar Stanage. Kelly thought he could advance, but Stanage recovered in time to catch him in a rundown between second and third. Gabby Street then grounded out, and Bob Groom fanned.

• Summers strengthened over the last five innings, allowing only three base runners on two errors and a walk. All came with two outs, however.

The Tigers could do nothing with Washington's rookie hurler Dolly Gray, getting just a leadoff single and one walk in eight innings. But thanks in part to six free passes by reliever Groom, they had more serious scoring opportunities than did the Nationals:

• Gray had pitched brilliantly through the first eight frames. But with a 3–1 count to Matty McIntyre leading off the ninth, Dolly staggered from the mound in great pain, apparently having torn a muscle in his side. In stepped Groom who completed the walk. Bush was safe on a Donohue error, Sam Crawford sacrificed both runners, and with Ty Cobb up, things looked bleak for Washington. But Ty bounced to Groom who caught McIntyre at the plate, and then Rossman fanned.

• Germany Schaefer singled in the tenth and worked his way to third base with two outs but died there.

• McIntyre walked to start the 11th, but neither Crawford nor Cobb could deliver after Bush had sacrificed.

• There were two outs in the 12th after both George Moriarty and Stanage had walked, but Summers couldn't deliver the victorious blow.

• In the 15th, Stanage led off with a single to center and was removed for a pinch runner, Red Killefer. Summers then bunted to Groom who, hurrying his throw to catch Killefer at second, tossed the ball into center field. Killefer took third; Summers was safe at first. McIntyre was then intentionally passed to load the bases and create a force play at the plate. With the bases jammed, no outs, and the meat of the Tiger lineup on its way, the outcome looked grim for Washington. But the next batter, Donie Bush, popped out to third baseman Kelly. Then, Crawford topped a two-strike pitch toward first base as Killefer sprinted toward home with the potential game winner. Groom fielded it and made a desperate toss to his battery mate. It was a very close play at the plate, but Street, thinking Killefer had beaten the play and seeing umpire Kerin give the safe signal, began walking toward the bench, followed by his teammates. The Tiger base runners also began walking toward the clubhouse. But umpire Kerin remained at the plate, beckoning the players. One of them returned to ask, "What's the matter?" "Runner's out," replied Kerin. Amid much shouting and confusion, both teams stormed back onto the field, surrounding Kerin and demanding an explanation. The umpire explained that he had made a mistake, thinking there were only two base runners and that a tag play was in order. Killefer was really out on the force at home. Almost simultaneously, both teams realized that the inning, and the game, was not yet over. Crawford started back toward first as Washington second baseman Unglaub grabbed the ball from teammate Street's hand. Unglaub chased Crawford as the fans screamed and howled. The other Detroit runners also scrambled back to their bases, each avoiding a tag by a National. Once all the base runners and fielders were back in position, the balance of the Tigers again surrounded Kerin for a few more minutes of dispute. After the commotion was settled, there were still only two outs, the bags were still loaded, and Ty Cobb was the next hitter. Groom struck him out, ending one of the most bizarre half-innings in baseball history.

Summers pitched superbly, issuing two walks (one intentional) and allowing just seven hits, only one of which came in the last 12 innings. In essence, he tossed a double-header shutout. The Nationals' Dolly Gray and Bob Groom, both rookies, combined to better Summers in one pitching department,

for they surrendered only six hits through the 18 innings despite a combined 7–22 won–lost record at the time.

In 1909, tied games were not suspended but instead were replayed in their entirety. Thus on August 22, the two clubs replayed this contest with Detroit winning 3–1; George Mullin prevailing over Walter Johnson.

Kickapoo Ed Summers had a fine career (68–45, 2.42 ERA) albeit cut short by arm miseries. In 1912, he retired after just five major league campaigns.

Washington Nationals	AB	R	H	I	PO	A	E
George Browne lf	6	0	1	0	1	0	0
Clyde Milan cf	7	0	2	0	4	0	0
Jack Lelivelt rf	7	0	1	0	3	0	0
Bob Unglaub 2b	7	0	0	0	1	6	0
Jiggs Donohue 1b	6	0	0	0	27	1	2
Speed Kelly 3b	6	0	0	0	2	3	0
Orth Collins ph17	1	0	0	0	0	0	0
Wid Conroy 3b17	0	0	0	0	0	0	0
George McBride ss	7	0	1	0	5	7	1
Gabby Street c	7	0	1	0	11	4	0
Dolly Gray p	3	0	1	0	0	3	0
> Bob Groom p9	4	0	0	0	0	8	1
	61	0	7	0	54	32	4

Detroit Tigers	AB	R	H	I	PO	A	E
Matty McIntyre lf	5	0	1	0	6	0	0
Donie Bush ss	5	0	0	0	3	5	2
Sam Crawford cf	7	0	0	0	4	0	0
Ty Cobb rf	7	0	0	0	3	0	0
Claude Rossman 1b	8	0	1	0	24	2	0
>George Moriarty 3b	7	0	1	0	0	6	0
Germany Schaefer 2b	7	0	2	0	2	4	2
Oscar Stanage c	4	0	1	0	8	3	0
Red Killefer pr15	0	0	0	0	0	0	0
Boss Schmidt c16	1	0	0	0	3	0	0
Ed Summers p	7	0	0	0	1	4	1
	58	0	6	0	54	24	5

Washington	IP	H	R	ER	BB	SO
Gray 2-9	8	1	0	0	1	0
Groom 5-13	10	5	0	0	6	8
	18	6	0	0	7	8

Detroit	IP	H	R	ER	BB	SO
Summers 10-5	18	7	0	0	2	10

Washington	0	0	0		0	0	0		0 0 0
Detroit	0	0	0		0	0	0		0 0 0

	0	0	0	0	0	0	0	0	– 0
	0	0	0	0	0	0	0	0	– 0

OB: Washington 9, Detroit 15
DP: Bush unassisted (Browne)
    Rossman unassisted (Unglaub)
    Unglaub-Donohue-Kelly
2B: Gray
SB: Cobb, Unglaub, Moriarty, McBride
CS: Browne, Lelivelt
SO: Browne, Milan, Gray 2, Groom 3,
    Lelivelt 2, Donohue, McIntyre,
    Bush, Cobb, Rossman 2, Moriarty,
    Schmidt, Stanage
BB: Browne, Donohue(I), McIntyre 3
    (1I), Cobb, Moriarty, ...

BB: Stanage 2 (1I)
SH: Bush 3, Crawford
TIME: 3:15
ATTENDANCE: 3,078
UMPIRES: John Kerin, Jack Sheridan
SOURCES: Detroit Free Press, Journal,
    Times, News; DBD; Sporting Life;
    Washington Evening Star, Post

BALANCE	OUT	+	R	+	OB	=	BP	=	AB	+	BB	+	SH	+	HP	+	CI
Washington	54		0		9		63		61		2		0		0		0
Detroit	54		0		15		69		58		7		4		0		0
----

23. Catcher Throws Out
Six Runners Attempting to Steal

ST. LOUIS   at   BROOKLYN
(Cardinals, 9)   (Superbas, 1)

Monday, August 23, 1909, Washington Park

In 1909, Brooklyn backstop Bill Bergen had a terrific season in the field. Not only did he accumulate 202 assists, good enough for ninth best all-time for catchers, but he also established a modern single-game record. Only one catcher since has been able to equal his mark of *throwing out six base runners attempting to steal in a nine-inning contest.* (The Athletics Wally Schang matched the feat on May 12, 1915.)

Bergen's heroics were witnessed by the hometown fans in Washington Park, Brooklyn, during the second game of a Monday doubleheader. The accomplishment was no fluke as Bill had given notice that his arm was a lethal weapon while still in the minor leagues. There, Bergen once retired a bases loaded situation by picking off all three base runners. This day also presented plenty of opportunities. St. Louis collected 15 hits and six walks as the fans screamed for the removal of Brooklyn hurler Jimmy Pastorius before he had even thrown a half-dozen pitches. Pastorius was having a terrible season, but the Superbas pitching staff was riddled with injuries. Manager Harry Lumley needed a complete game effort from his hurler.

Bergen had been sidelined with a split finger and was a bit rusty when Jap Barbeau, the game's first batter, walked and stole second. After that the Brooklyn catcher was deadly, throwing out six of the next seven base stealers. Apparently unaffected by Bergen's sharpshooting, the Cardinals nevertheless emerged victorious in a 9–1 rout. Also unimpressed were the visiting sportswriters. Although providing much detail of the game,

mention of Bergen's heroics was conspicuously absent from all five of the St. Louis newspapers cited.

Bergen's day of sharpshooting evolved as follows:

• In the second inning, with one out, Barbeau was caught stealing second, Bergen to shortstop McElveen. Rube Ellis then walked and also tried his luck at larceny but was also gunned down, Bergen to second baseman Alperman.

• After Jack Bliss and Ed Konetchy had both singled to open the third frame, "Bliss was caught off second on Bergen's fast throw to Alperman."* According to *Total Baseball*, (third edition, page 2316), "caught stealing" statistics were not defined in scoring rules until 1951. Historically, when new scoring rules are first stated, they apply to all previous games. This situation, although not the typical caught stealing assist, nevertheless fulfills the new rule's requirements, and as such, should be accepted as Bergen's third victim.

• With one out in the fourth inning, Alan Storke was nailed at second while attempting to steal, Bergen to Alperman.

• Bliss found himself on first with two outs in the sixth. For the second time he tested Bergen's arm and failed, Bergen to Alperman.

• Bergen caught his sixth thief in the seventh inning. With one out, Steve Evans singled but was doubled up by Bergen's throw to Alperman as Joe Delahanty fanned.

Perhaps it was the 9–1 St. Louis lead, but despite Bergen's lethal accuracy, the intrepid

---

*"*Dodgers Win First Game, 7–0; Lose Second, 9–1,*" New York Evening Telegram, *23 August 1909.*

Bergen: rifle arm, rubber bat (George Brace photo).

Konetchy again tested the backstop in the top of the ninth. With one gone, Ed walked and then successfully stole second. Between successful thefts in the first and the ninth, six Cardinals had been thrown out by Bergen. Bill did have the last laugh, however. In the bottom of the ninth, with two down and the game hopelessly lost, Bergen walked, and yes, stole second!

As adept as Bergen was afield, he was pathetically anemic on offense. Pitchers must have loved to see him step to the plate. Bill's record leaves little room for argument that he was the worst batter in the history of major league baseball. Hitting less than most of his battery mates, Bergen assembled an astonishing 11-year, lifetime batting average of .170 (516/3028) and a career on-base percentage of less than .200! No other batter in the history of modern baseball with more than 2500 at-bats has hit under .210 lifetime. Bergen fell short of that by a solid 40 points! On this day however, Bill showed everyone why he remained so long on a major league roster.

SECOND GAME

St. Louis Cardinals	AB	R	H	I	PO	A	E
Jap Barbeau 3b	3	1	1	1	1	1	0
Rube Ellis lf	4	1	1	0	3	0	0
Jack Bliss c	3	1	2	1	5	1	1
Ed Konetchy 1b	4	2	3	2	8	2	0
Steve Evans rf	4	2	3	3	1	0	0
>Joe Delahanty 2b	4	0	1	2	3	3	0
Howard Murphy cf	3	1	1	0	2	0	0
Alan Storke ss	4	0	1	0	3	3	0
Fred Beebe p	4	1	2	0	1	0	0
	33	9	15	9	27	10	1

Brooklyn Superbas	AB	R	H	I	PO	A	E
Al Burch cf	4	0	2	0	2	0	0
>Wally Clement lf	5	1	2	0	2	0	0
Ed Lennox 3b	4	0	2	0	0	0	0
Pryor McElveen ss	4	0	1	0	4	1	0
Whitey Alperman 2b	4	0	0	0	6	2	0
John Hummel 1b	4	0	1	0	5	0	0
George Hunter rf	4	0	0	0	1	0	0
Bill Bergen c	3	0	1	0	7	7	1
Jim Pastorius p	3	0	0	0	0	1	0
Tim Jordan ph9	1	0	0	0	0	0	0
	36	1	9	0	27	11	1

St. Louis	IP	H	R	ER	BB	SO
Beebe W,13-14	9	9	1	1	2	5

Brooklyn	IP	H	R	ER	BB	SO
Pastorius L,1-9	9	15	9	9	6	5

```
St. Louis    4 0 0   0 3 1   0 1 0   - 9
Brooklyn     1 0 0   0 0 0   0 0 0   - 1
```

OB: St. Louis 6, Brooklyn 10
DP: Bergen-Alperman (Delahanty S.O.)
2B: Barbeau, Evans
3B: Evans
SB: Barbeau, Konetchy, Bergen, Burch
CS: Barbeau, Ellis, Bliss 2, Storke, Evans
SO: Barbeau, Bliss, Delahanty, Storke, Beebe, Alperman, Hunter 2, Bergen, Pastorius
BB: Barbeau, Ellis, Bliss, Konetchy, Evans, Murphy, Burch, Bergen
SH: Barbeau, Bliss

SF: Delahanty
WP: Beebe
PB: Bergen
TIME: 1:47
ATTENDANCE: 2,500
UMPIRE: Bill Klem
SOURCES: Brooklyn Eagle, Standard Union; New York American, Evening Telegram, Herald, Press, Sun, Tribune, World; St. Louis Globe-Democrat, Post-Dispatch, Republic, Star, Times; Sporting Life

BALANCE	OUT	+	R	+	OB	=	BP	+	AB	+	BB	+	SH	+	HP	+	CI
St. Louis	27		9		6		42		33		6		3		0		0
Brooklyn	27		1		10		38		36		2		0		0		0

Bergen's sharpshooting mark has long been reported erroneously in baseball record books. The accepted claim to date has been for *seven* base runners thrown out by him in this contest. However, meticulous examination of 15 newspapers (see SOURCES section of boxscore) confirms that only *six* Cardinals were caught by Bergen.

Two other claims of six runners caught stealing were also investigated. On May 12, 1915, Wally Schang of the Philadelphia Athletics did tie Bergen's mark by nailing six

St. Louis Browns. Especially impressive was the fact that Schang was only a part-time backstop, having played more games at third base and more in the outfield than behind the plate. Less than six weeks later, on June 18, 1915, the same Athletics were again tested by the Chicago White Sox with identical results. In that game, with Wally Schang out with an injury, three different Athletics took a turn at nailing Sox base runners. Jack Lapp caught four, Wickey McAvoy one, and Ira Thomas one.

Dr. Jekyll and Mr. Hyde

24. Pitcher Walks Seven Consecutive Batters, Eight in One Inning

WASHINGTON   at   CHICAGO
(Nationals, 4)   (White Sox, 6)

Saturday, August 28, 1909, South Side Park

Dolly Gray, 5–19 in 1909

Washington's 30-year-old, rookie left-hander, William "Dolly" Gray, pitched a one-hitter this day but lost, 6–4. It was the first game of the doubleheader and the reason he lost was not because his teammates fumbled the ball; they made not one error. The problem was Dolly's control, as he gave the Chicago fans his rendition of a Dr. Jekyll-Mr. Hyde performance. In the first, third, seventh and eighth innings, Dr. Jekyll retired the side in order. One base on balls was all the White Sox could muster in each of the fourth, fifth and sixth innings. But in the second inning, Mr. Hyde transformed a brilliant pitching performance into a nightmare. Dolly lost all contact with home plate and *set two major league records when he walked eight batters, seven of them in succession*, while giving the home team six runs. *The Washington Star* reported, "It looked like a military drill. Each batsman went to the plate and stayed just long enough to permit Gray to write out his pass and then sedately marched to first, while someone would just as sedately walk in from third. It's a

WALSH, P.   SMITH, P.   WHITE, P.   SCOTT, P.   BURNS, P.

OWENS, C.   PAYNE, C   CHICAGO BASE BALL CLUB OF AMERICAN THE LEAGUE   ISBELL, 1ST. B.   PURTELL, 2ND B.

Wm. SULLIVAN, MGR. & C.
1909

ATZ, 2ND B.   TANNEHILL, 3RD B.

PARENT, S.S.   GEO. DAVIS, S.S.   ALTIZER, O.F.   Sporting Life PHILADELPHIA.   DOUGHERTY, O.F.   HAHN, O.F.

The walking White Sox of 1909

fact that the players sat on the bags waiting for the next man to push them along." Things were so bad that, after Gray issued his sixth straight pass, teammate and second baseman Germany Schaefer visited the mound to suggest that Gray switch positions with him. And, when Patsy Dougherty headed for the plate for the second time in the inning, Chicago manager Billy Sullivan pleaded with him to go without a bat. Here are the particulars of Gray's Waterloo:

• Dougherty led off with a ground single past Unglaub (the only Sox hit of the day).

• Isbell sacrificed him to second (Gray to Unglaub).

• Then Tannehill, Atz, Owens, Scott, Altizer, Parent and Cole walked consecutively.

• Dougherty grounded out (Shaefer to Unglaub), Altizer scoring.

• Isbell, the only man who hadn't reached

base in the inning, then walked, again loading the bases.

• Tannehill grounded to Killefer for an unassisted force out to mercifully end the suffering.

Examining this scene today might cause the reader to ask why the manager stayed with his rookie so long. One can only speculate, but in 1909, the Nationals (formerly Senators) were the doormat of the league. Despite Walter Johnson, the staff allowed more hits, walks, and runs than any other club. But in line with the strategy of the day, the hurlers still finished 99 of the 156 games started. Relief was usually a drink of cold water. As a team, Washington finished last, 20 games out of seventh, so skipper Joe Cantillon was accustomed to incompetence. Perhaps he was desperate just for a warm body to take the mound each day. After

all, Dolly Gray was the third best pitcher he had, finishing the season with a 9–19 slate.

The reader should also be made aware that 81 years later someone almost relieved Dolly Gray of his record. The would-be savior appeared in a Yankee uniform as another rookie by the name of Steve Adkins. Making his major league debut on September 13, 1990, Steve warmed up for his brush with immortality by issuing three free passes in his very first inning. But that was only the beginning, for after getting the first batter to fly out opening the second inning, Steve got serious and walked the next five batters. Stump Merrill, Yankees pilot, apparently unaware of Adkins' lifetime opportunity, heartlessly yanked the youngster from the hill while possibly only two batters away from the all-time record.

FIRST GAME

Washington Nationals	AB	R	H	I	PO	A	E
George Browne rf	5	0	1	1	1	0	0
>Germany Schaefer 2b	5	0	2	1	0	2	0
Bob Unglaub 1b	4	0	0	0	15	0	0
Jack Lelivelt cf	3	1	3	0	4	0	0
Clyde Milan lf	3	1	0	0	0	0	0
Red Killefer 3b	3	0	0	0	1	2	0
George McBride ss	4	0	2	2	2	4	0
Gabby Street c	4	1	1	0	1	1	0
Dolly Gray p	3	1	0	0	0	5	0
Jack Slattery ph9	1	0	0	0	0	0	0
	35	4	9	4	24	14	0

Chicago White Sox	AB	R	H	I	PO	A	E
Dave Altizer rf	2	1	0	1	2	0	0
Freddy Parent ss	3	0	0	1	1	4	2
Willis Cole cf	3	0	0	1	2	0	0
Patsy Dougherty lf	3	1	1	1	1	0	0
Frank Isbell 1b	2	0	0	0	13	0	1
Lee Tannehill 3b	3	1	0	0	2	4	0
Jake Atz 2b	3	1	0	0	2	5	0
>Frank Owens c	3	1	0	1	4	0	0
Jim Scott p	1	1	0	1	0	2	0
	23	6	1	6	27	15	3

Washington	IP	H	R	ER	BB	SO
Gray L,3-13	8	1	6	6	11	1

Chicago	IP	H	R	ER	BB	SO
Scott W,9-8	9	9	4	2	2	2

Washington   0 2 0   0 0 0   2 0 0 - 4
Chicago   0 6 0   0 0 0   0 0 x - 6

OB: Chicago 5, Washington 7
DP: Atz-Parent-Isbell (Unglaub)
     Tannehill unassisted (Killefer)
2B: McBride, Lelivelt, Browne
SB: Lelivelt, Dougherty, Schaefer
CS: Altizer
SO: Scott, Gray, Unglaub
BB: Lelivelt, Milan, Altizer 2, Atz,
     Parent, Cole, Dougherty, Isbell,

BB: ... Tannehill, Owens, Scott 2
SH: Killefer, Isbell
TIME: 1:45
ATTENDANCE: 6,800
UMPIRE: Billy Evans
SOURCES: Chicago Daily News;
     Washington Post, Star

BALANCE	OUT+R+OB=BP=AB+BB+SH+HP+CI								
Washington	27	4	7	38	35	2	1	0	0
Chicago	24	6	5	35	23	11	1	0	0

Much Ado About Nothing

25. Player Goes to the Plate Six Times Without an Official At-Bat

ST. LOUIS, NL   at   PHILADELPHIA
(Cardinals, 10)   (Phillies, 5)

Wednesday, June 1, 1910, Philadelphia Park

When the name Miller Huggins is mentioned, one thinks of the manager who feuded with Babe Ruth and molded the Yankee juggernaut of the 1920's. But before managing, Miller was a scrappy second baseman and an excellent leadoff batter for both the Reds and the Cardinals. He usually appeared among the league leaders in bases on balls and averaged about 30 stolen bases per season throughout his 13-year playing career. This day personified his presence on the playing field. For the first time in the twentieth century, a player *went to the plate six times without registering an official at-bat*. As peculiar as this record feat seems, it was later duplicated twice (see 6-13-34 and 6-16-38).

Only 800 fans appeared on this chilly, dreary day in Philadelphia Park. Coupled with the uninviting weather, the home team had been playing dreadful baseball. The Phillies, tied for first place only two weeks

earlier, had just dropped 13 of their last 14 games, including eight in a row. Management was furious with the team, particularly the pitchers who were accused of not being in good playing condition and/or loafing on the diamond. Immediately following this game, their ninth consecutive loss, feathers were sent flying. George McQuillan, the starting pitcher, was fined $250 and suspended indefinitely without pay. Moundsman Frank Scanlon was released outright, and Patsy Flaherty was returned to the minors. What precipitated the furor was another wretched team pitching performance resulting in another blown lead and game. The Phillies had jumped out to a 4–0 lead after just three innings, were tied, regained the lead going into the ninth, then lost convincingly, 10–5.

Huggins walked in the first, third and fifth innings but failed to score. In the sixth, he hit a sacrifice fly, knocking in St. Louis'

St. Louis Cardinals	AB	R	H	I	PO	A	E
Miller Huggins 2b	0	1	0	2	2	1	1
Rube Ellis lf	5	1	0	1	3	0	0
Rebel Oakes cf	5	0	2	3	4	0	0
Elmer Zacher rf	5	1	1	1	1	0	0
>Steve Evans 1b	4	1	1	0	13	0	0
Ed Phelps c	4	2	4	1	2	1	0
Rudy Hulswitt ss	2	1	1	0	1	3	0
Frank Betcher 3b	3	0	0	0	1	4	0
Mike Mowrey ph9	0	0	0	0	0	0	0
Roger Bresnahan pr9	0	1	0	0	0	0	0
Arnold Hauser 3b9	0	0	0	0	0	1	0
Bob Harmon p	0	0	0	0	0	0	0
Frank Corridon p2	4	1	2	0	0	3	0
Johnny Lush ph9	1	1	1	1	0	0	0
Slim Sallee p9	0	0	0	0	0	0	0
	33	10	12	9	27	13	1

Philadelphia Phillies	AB	R	H	I	PO	A	E
John Titus rf	2	1	0	0	2	0	1
Joe Ward ph9	1	0	0	0	0	0	0
Johnny Bates cf	3	2	2	0	3	0	0
Eddie Grant 3b	1	1	0	0	2	1	0
>Sherry Magee lf	3	1	0	1	2	0	0
Kitty Bransfield 1b	4	0	2	2	10	0	0
Otto Knabe 2b	3	0	0	1	3	3	0
Mickey Doolan ss	4	0	2	0	2	3	1
Pat Moran c	3	0	0	0	3	2	0
George McQuillan p	2	0	0	0	0	1	0
Lew Moren p6	2	0	0	0	0	2	0
Patsy Flaherty p9	0	0	0	0	0	1	0
	28	5	6	4	27	13	2

Huggins' stature and batting style were conducive to getting on base.

St. Louis	IP	H	R	ER	BB	SO
Harmon	1	2	2	2	2	0
Corridon W,3-2	7	3	3	2	4	1
Sallee	1	1	0	0	0	0
	9	6	5	4	6	1

Philadelphia	IP	H	R	ER	BB	SO
McQuillan	5	6	4	4	6	2
Moren L,4-3	3.1	5	5	5	4	0
Flaherty	.2	1	1	0	1	0
	9	12	10	9	11	2

St.Louis   0 0 0   1 1 2   0 0 6   -10
Philadelphia 2 0 2   0 0 0   1 0 0   - 5

OB: St.Louis 13, Philadelphia 8
DP: McQuillan-Knabe-Bransfield
    Knabe-Bransfield (Ellis)
    Knabe-Doolan-Bransfield
SB: Zacher, Bates, Bransfield
CS: Knabe
SO: Corridon, Ellis, Titus
BB: Huggins 4, Ellis, Oakes, Zacher,
    Evans, Hulswitt 3, Titus 2,
    Bates, Grant 2, Magee
SH: Grant 2, Moran, Huggins
SF: Knabe, Huggins

HP: By McQuillan (Phelps), by Moren
    (Betcher, Evans, Mowrey), by
    Corridon (Bates, Magee)
TIME: 2:02
ATTENDANCE: 800
UMPIRES: Bill Brennan(H), Hank O'Day
SOURCES: Philadelphia Inquirer, Even-
    ing Item, Evening Times, North
    American, Press, Evening Public
    Ledger, Public Ledger, Record; St.
    Louis Globe-Democrat,Post-Dispatch

BALANCE	OUT	+R	+OB	=BP	=AB	+BB	+SH	+HP	+CI
St. Louis	27	10	13	50	33	11	2	4	0
Philadelphia	27	5	8	40	28	6	4	2	0

fourth and tying run. In the eighth he again sacrificed. In the final frame, he walked with the bases loaded, pushed over the lead run, and eventually scored. Ed Phelps, Cardinals catcher, was considered the batting hero. Along with being hit by a pitch, Ed had four hits in as many at-bats. All 18 hits in the contest were singles.

By October, the Phillies managed to turn their season around somewhat, finishing in fourth place. The Cardinals, however, played poorly the rest of the year and finished in seventh position, 40 games out of first.

Miller Huggins again led the league in walks this year with 116, and George McQuillan did return to the rotation although he was traded to Cincinnati in February of 1911.

The Equalizer

26. Teams Play to a Near-Perfect Tie

PITTSBURGH   at   BROOKLYN
(Pirates, 8)   (Superbas, 8)

Saturday, August 13, 1910, Washington Park

Since the turn of the century, there have been almost 800 major league games that have ended in a tie. Most of these occurred in the first two decades when runs were scarce, and contests were low scoring affairs. The live ball era of the 1920's, with its wide-open games, made the likelihood of a stalemate more remote, and by the 1940's, stadium lights began to render "game called on account of darkness" even less commonplace. That left deadlocked games mostly in the hands of the Sunday Blue Laws and community curfews which gradually faded in the 1960's. But, of all the games that ended in a tie, there's never been one quite like the doubleheader nightcap played this day in Brooklyn.

Brooklyn's Superbas, also referred to as Dodgers by some of the press, were hosting the Pittsburgh Pirates. The Pirates were still in the pennant race, only six games behind the Cubs, but the Superbas were languishing in sixth, playing less than .500 ball. After Pittsburgh took the first game of the doubleheader, 3–2 in 13 innings, the teams battled back and forth in the second game. The lead switched hands several times but when dark-

ness fell, the two were deadlocked, 8–8. The newspapers of the day made no special mention of this tie. As noted, they were commonplace. Only years later, after statistical gurus had time to survey years of boxscores, did this one stand out.

Given all the parameters and variables in a major league game, this was as close to a *perfect tie* that any statistician could hope for. Not only did each team score eight runs, they each had 38 at-bats, 13 hits, 27 putouts, 13 assists, five RBIs, two errors, one double, three walks, five strikeouts and a passed ball. Each squad designated two pitchers who combined to allow a total of seven earned runs. Until the bottom of the ninth, when Brooklyn commissioned a pinch runner, each team had used ten players. *The New York Herald* even commented on four hair-raising catches, by Tommy Leach and Fred Clarke of the Pirates and by Zack Wheat and Jack Dalton of the Superbas.

If the reader would like to stretch his or her imagination, even more obscure similarities could be made. The second baseman, shortstop and right fielder from each team

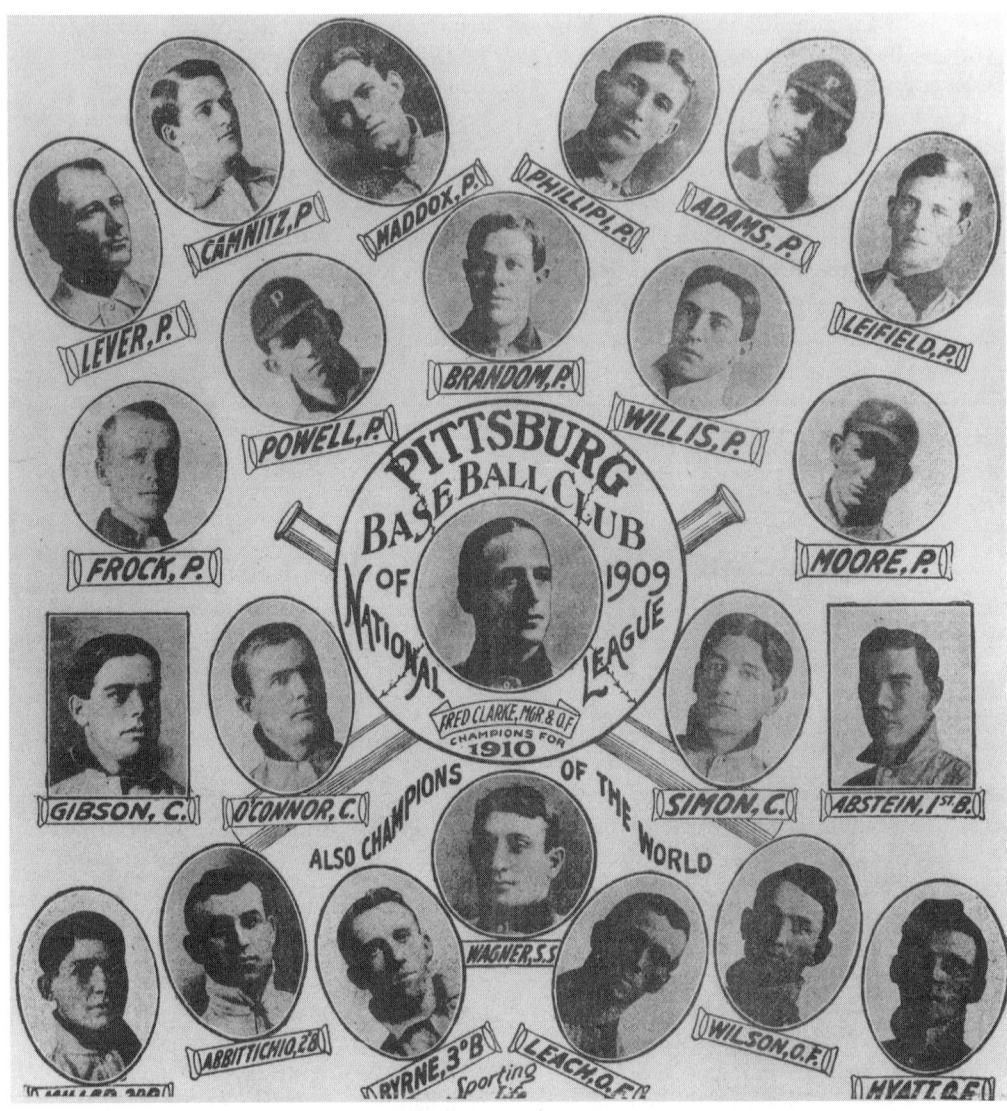

The Pirates of 1910

got two hits; both second basemen scored two runs. Each catcher had four at-bats, no runs scored, one hit, and one assist. Each third base-man scored one run; each center fielder had two putouts. Each first baseman scored one run, and so forth, and so on, ad nauseam.

SECOND GAME

Pittsburgh Pirates	AB	R	H	I	PO	A	E	Brooklyn Superbas	AB	R	H	I	PO	A	E
Bobby Byrne 3b	4	1	0	0	1	0	0	Bill Davidson cf	5	1	0	0	2	0	0
Tommy Leach cf	5	2	2	0	2	1	1	Jake Daubert 1b	4	1	3	0	10	0	2
Fred Clarke lf	4	1	2	1	5	0	0	Zack Wheat lf	5	0	1	1	2	0	0
Honus Wagner ss	5	0	2	0	4	2	0	John Hummel 2b	3	2	2	0	3	2	0
Dots Miller 2b	4	2	2	0	0	3	0	Jack Dalton rf	5	2	2	1	1	1	0
Jack Flynn 1b	4	1	2	2	8	1	0	Ed Lennox 3b	4	1	1	1	2	2	0

Pittsburgh Pirates	AB	R	H	I	PO	A	E
Owen Wilson rf	5	1	2	2	1	1	1
>George Gibson c	4	0	1	0	5	1	0
Howie Camnitz p	3	0	0	0	1	0	0
Sam Leever p5	0	0	0	0	0	4	0
	38	8	13	5	27	13	2

Brooklyn Superbas	AB	R	H	I	PO	A	E
Al Burch pr9	0	0	0	0	0	0	0
>Pryor McElveen ss	4	0	2	2	1	4	0
Tex Erwin c	4	0	1	0	6	1	0
Nap Rucker p	2	0	0	0	0	1	0
Rube Dessau p6	2	1	1	0	0	2	0
	38	8	13	5	27	13	2

Pittsburgh	IP	H	R	ER	BB	SO
Camnitz	4.1	7	6	6	2	5
Leever	4.2	6	2	1	1	0
	9	13	8	7	3	5

Brooklyn	IP	H	R	ER	BB	SO
Rucker	5	11	7	7	1	3
Dessau	4	2	1	0	2	2
	9	13	8	7	3	5

Pittsburgh	0 1 1	0 5 1	0 0 0	- 8
Brooklyn	0 0 0	3 3 0	0 2 0	- 8

OB: Pittsburgh 9, Brooklyn 8
DP: Leever-Wagner-Flynn (McElveen)
2B: Clarke, Dalton
3B: Miller 2, Dalton
HR: Wilson(2)
SB: Hummel
CS: Wagner
SO: Wagner, Flynn, Wilson 2, Camnitz
    Wheat, Dalton, McElveen, Erwin,
    Rucker
BB: Byrne, Flynn, Leever, Daubert,
    Hummel, Lennox
SH: Clarke, Miller

SF: McElveen
HP: by Camnitz (Hummel);
    by Rucker (Gibson)
PB: Gibson, Erwin
TIME: 2:05
ATTENDANCE: 16,000
UMPIRES: Bill Brennan, Hank O'Day
SOURCES: Brooklyn Daily Eagle,
    Standard Union; New York Herald,
    Sun, Times, Tribune, World;
    Pittsburgh Leader, Post, Press,
    Gazette Times

BALANCE	OUT	+	R	+	OB	=	BP	=	AB	+	BB	+	SH	+	HP	+	CI
Pittsburgh	27		8		9		44		38		3		2		1		0
Brooklyn	27		8		8		43		38		3		1		1		0

Giants Explode in the First

27. Team Scores Seven Runs Before Making Their First Out

ST. LOUIS, NL   at   NEW YORK
(Cardinals, 5)   (Giants, 19)

Saturday, May 13, 1911, Hilltop Park

About a month before this game, Giants owner John T. Brush lost his ballpark to a massive fire, so while the Polo Grounds was being rebuilt, the club temporarily played their home games at the Yankees' arena, Hilltop Park. On this day, the John McGraw-led Giants generated an inferno of their own by scorching the Cardinals for *seven runs before they made their first out of the game.* This record endured for 37 years (see 8-13-48).

Slim Sallee, Cardinal left-hander, had had particular good fortune hurling against the Giants, so much so that New York manager John McGraw opted to oppose him with his ace, Christy Mathewson. Christy had an easy time of it in the top of the first, facing just

As a New York Herald *cartoonist saw the game.*

three batters. Then came the Giants turn at bat, and here's what transpired:

• Josh Devore led off with a single to center.

• Larry Doyle singled to right, sending Devore to third. Josh wasn't about to stop there until McGraw, coaching third, grabbed him around the neck and wrestled him back to the bag. "You've been reading about Ty Cobb scoring from first on a short single, and you think you can do it," reprimanded McGraw.*

• Fred Snodgrass tripled to the center field fence scoring both Devore and Doyle.

• Red Murray drew a base on balls.

• With a 1–0 count on Fred Merkle, Sallee was relieved by Bob Harmon, the ace of the Cardinals staff. Merkle greeted the new hurler with an inside-the-park home run to right-center field, knocking in three more runs.

• Al Bridwell, the potential first out, was safe when shortstop Arnold Hauser juggled his grounder.

• Art Devlin drew a pass.

• Chief Meyers singled to center, scoring Bridwell and sending Devlin to second.

• Christy Mathewson joined the fun by poking a single to right, knocking in Devlin and putting Meyers on third.

• Devore, up for the second time, tapped an easy one back to the mound. Harmon saw Meyers coming halfway down the third base line and engaged him in a rundown, but Chief managed to escape, loading the sacks.

• Doyle granted the first out by flying to Rube Ellis in left, precipitating derisive cheers. At this point, the record seven runs had already been scored.

• Snodgrass walked, forcing home Meyers.

• Murray was hit by a pitch, forcing in Mathewson and sending Harmon to the showers. Grover Lowdermilk then became the third Cardinal pitcher of the inning.

• Merkle, for the second time in the frame, greeted a reliever with three RBIs, this time by doubling down the third base line. Fred thus became the first major leaguer to

---

Giants Swamp the St. Louis Club, 19–5," New York Herald, 13 May 1911.

Murray contributed without an at-bat.

harvest six RBIs in the first inning of a game. *No batter in the twentieth-century has driven home more runs in a single inning.*

• Bridwell singled, sending Merkle to third. The two then pulled off a double steal with Merkle scoring the 13th run of the inning.

• By this time, the crowd was tiring of the run scoring even though it was all being done by their hometown heroes. They now cheered when Devlin struck out.

• With Meyers batting, Lowdermilk wild-pitched Bridwell to third before registering an inning-ending strikeout.

As could be expected, the balance of the game took on a meaningless dimension while the Giants made wholesale substitutions.

And, with the lopsided lead, Mathewson's skills were no longer needed. This gave McGraw a chance to view his young strikeout artist, Rube Marquard. Rube took the hill to begin the second inning and proceeded to *fan 14 Cardinals in his eight-inning relief role.* To this day, Marquard's feat remains the record by a left-hander. (Only Walter Johnson ever struck out more in relief.)

In many facets, baseball scoring rules were considerably different in 1911. No more demonstrative of this is the fact that Mathewson was officially credited with the victory in this game despite pitching just one inning. Scoring rules were not so different, however, to account for this game being carried in record books as having witnessed ten runs scored by the Giants before they made their first out. All of the cited sources disagree with this claim. As described, "only" seven runs scored *before* the first out was registered even though the first ten runners did score. A later game (see 8-13-48) now stands as the record for the most runs scored before a team made its first out of a game.

St. Louis Cardinals	AB	R	H	I	PO	A	E
Miller Huggins 2b	4	2	2	0	1	5	0
Arnold Hauser ss	5	0	2	0	1	1	1
Rube Ellis lf	5	1	2	1	1	0	1
Ed Konetchy 1b	4	1	3	4	9	0	0
>Otto McIver rf	4	0	1	0	0	1	1
Mike Mowrey 3b	4	0	1	0	1	3	0
Rebel Oakes cf	4	0	1	0	2	0	0
Roger Bresnahan c	0	0	0	0	2	0	0
Jack Bliss c2	4	1	1	0	7	2	0
Slim Sallee p	0	0	0	0	0	0	0
Bob Harmon p1	0	0	0	0	0	0	0
Lou Lowdermilk p1	3	0	0	0	0	3	0
	37	5	13	5	24	15	3

New York Giants	AB	R	H	I	PO	A	E
Josh Devore rf	5	2	1	0	0	1	0
Larry Doyle 2b	5	2	1	0	3	2	0
Doc Crandall 2b7	1	0	0	0	1	0	0
>Fred Snodgrass cf	4	3	1	3	0	0	0
Red Murray lf	0	2	0	1	0	0	0
Beals Becker lf2	2	0	0	0	0	0	1
Fred Merkle 1b	2	2	2	7	2	0	0
Hank Gowdy 1b3	0	1	0	0	6	0	0
Al Bridwell ss	4	2	3	2	0	2	0
Art Devlin 3b	1	1	0	0	0	0	0
Art Fletcher 3b2	3	1	2	2	0	3	1
Chief Meyers c	2	1	1	1	1	0	0
Grover Hartley c2	1	0	0	1	14	1	0
Christy Mathewson p	1	1	1	1	0	0	0
Rube Marquard p2	4	1	0	0	0	1	0
	35	19	12	18	27	10	2

St. Louis	IP	H	R	ER	BB	SO
Sallee L,2-2	0	3	4	4	1	0
Harmon	.1	3	8	7	2	0
Lowdermilk	7.2	6	7	7	8	6
	8	12	19	18	11	6

New York	IP	H	R	ER	BB	SO
Mathewson W,5-1	1	1	0	0	0	1
Marquard	8	12	5	3	3	14
	9	13	5	3	3	15

St. Louis   0 0 2   0 0 0   3 0 0 - 5
New York   13 3 0   0 2 0   1 0 x -19

OB: St.Louis 9, New York 5
DP: Doyle-Merkle (Hauser)
      Fletcher-Doyle-Merkle
2B: Merkle
3B: Konetchy, Snodgrass, Fletcher 2
HR: Merkle(2)
SB: Merkle, Bridwell, Hartley,
      Becker 2, Crandall
CS: Becker, Gowdy
BB: Huggins, McIver, Lowdermilk,
      Devore, Snodgrass 2, Murray,
      Becker, Merkle, Gowdy 2, Devlin,
      Bridwell, Hartley

SF: Hartley
HP: By Harmon (Murray),
      by Marquard (Konetchy)
WP: Lowdermilk
PB: Bresnahan
TIME: 2:20
ATTENDANCE: 18,000
UMPIRES: Bill Brennan, Hank O'Day
SOURCES: New York American, Herald,
      Sun, Tribune, World; St.Louis
      Globe-Democrat, Post Dispatch

BALANCE	OUT	+R	+OB	=BP	=AB	+BB	+SH	+HP	+CI
St. Louis	27	5	9	41	37	3	0	1	0
New York	24	19	5	48	35	11	1	1	0

Pirates Stumble to Assist Record

28. Team Makes 28 Assists in One Nine-Inning Game

NEW YORK   at   PITTSBURGH
(Giants, 9)   (Pirates, 4)

Wednesday, June 7, 1911, Forbes Field

Pittsburgh newspapers bemoaned the sloppy play of the hometown club. They had every reason to, for the Pirates committed no fewer than seven errors in this game as well as a number of other misplays that didn't appear in the boxscore. *The Pittsburgh Post* called it a "blunderfest." The result was another Pirate loss, but also an unexpected team record, for on this day the Pirates *collected 28 assists, the most by any twentieth-century team in a nine-inning game.*

Several factors were instrumental in amassing this benchmark:

First, Pirate errors actually contributed to the record performance in that they afforded multiple opportunities for the fielders to gain assists. For example, in the fifth inning, both Bobby Byrne and Claude Hendrix scooped ground balls and threw to first baseman Bill McKechnie who dropped each one. Both fielders were properly credited with assists even though no putouts were made.

Second, some unusual plays also helped the Pirates accumulate assists. In the third frame, the Giants' Art Fletcher was thrown out running from first to third on Fred Snodgrass' single. Center fielder Tommy Leach had thrown home to catcher Mike Simon too late to catch another runner, but Simon pegged on to third, nipping Fletcher. Later in the same inning, Leach fielded Fred Merkle's single and again threw home attempting to intercept Snodgrass. This time, pitcher Babe Adams cut off the throw and tossed to Honus Wagner, who threw to McKechnie to ambush Merkle in a rundown. In the fifth inning, Snodgrass got himself caught in a rundown between third and home in which Hendrix, Simon, and Byrne were all credited with assists.

Third, and perhaps most instrumental,

The Pittsburgh Dispatch *expressed the fans' disgust.*

Carey's home run as The Pittsburgh Dispatch *saw it.*

was the pitching of rookie right-hander, Claude Hendrix. Claude, a 22-year-old spitballer, was brought into his first major league game to relieve a shell-shocked Babe Adams. Adams had given up five runs in the third inning. Hendrix pitched superbly, allowing just three hits over the final six innings. Only four batted balls (three singles and a muffed fly) reached the outfield. The Giants did manage to score four runs off him in the fifth inning but without a hit. The damage was done with a walk, three errors, and a passed ball; all the runs being unearned. Such was the quality of play on the Pirates part.

The shabby play by both teams also provided some levity. Jack Flynn, normally a first baseman, was rushed into service in the fourth inning when Pirate outfielder Tommy Leach injured his leg. Flynn was not a good fielding first sacker. In the outfield, he was downright dangerous. After camping under a lazy fly in his first inning of service, Jack allowed the ball to slip through his hands, nearly knocking himself out. As he abjectly looked on, center fielder Owen Wilson chased down the ball. This was the first and last major league game that Jack Flynn spent in the outfield.

The Giants augmented the improprieties with five errors of their own, the most ludicrous of which provided Pittsburgh's Max Carey with a home run. In the ninth inning, Carey sent a long fly to right-center field. Both Red Murray and Fred Snodgrass raced after it, Murray having the better angle. Red just missed making the catch but ran another 30 feet before he could stop. Snodgrass stopped within a few feet of where the ball bounced but thought Murray had made the catch. Murray assumed that Snodgrass had fielded the sphere. Meanwhile Carey, amid howls of the spectators, raced around the bases and crossed the plate before Al Bridwell, the shortstop, finally retrieved the ball.

While their 28 assists remain the major league mark, the Pirates were no strangers to rundowns and fielding ground balls. Six weeks earlier, they had collected 26 assists. And before this season was concluded, official records show they had gathered 20 or more assists in seven different contests.

Hendrix was victimized by shoddy fielding.

New York Giants	AB	R	H	I	PO	A	E
Josh Devore lf	3	1	1	0	1	0	0
Beals Becker ph6,lf	2	0	0	0	1	0	0
Art Fletcher 2b	4	1	2	1	3	1	0
>Fred Snodgrass cf	4	1	1	2	2	0	0
Red Murray rf	3	2	2	1	1	0	0
Fred Merkle 1b	4	1	1	1	8	1	0
Al Bridwell ss	4	1	0	0	5	1	3
Art Devlin 3b	4	1	3	1	0	1	2
Chief Meyers c	4	1	0	0	6	1	0
Louis Drucke p	4	0	0	0	0	5	0
	36	9	10	6	27	10	5

Pittsburgh Pirates	AB	R	H	I	PO	A	E
Max Carey lf	4	2	2	1	0	0	0
Bobby Byrne 3b	4	0	2	1	4	3	1
Bill McKechnie 1b	5	0	2	0	12	0	2
Honus Wagner ss	5	1	0	0	3	8	1
Dots Miller 2b	5	0	0	0	3	2	2
Tommy Leach cf	0	1	0	0	0	2	0
Jack Flynn rf4	4	0	1	0	0	0	1
>Owen Wilson rf,cf4	5	0	1	1	0	0	0
Mike Simon c	3	0	0	0	3	5	0
Babe Adams p	1	0	0	0	0	1	0
Claude Hendrix p4	3	0	0	0	2	7	0
	39	4	8	3	27	28	7

New York	IP	H	R	ER	BB	SO
Drucke W,3-1	9	8	4	3	3	3

Pittsburgh	IP	H	R	ER	BB	SO
Adams L,8-4	3	7	5	3	0	1
Hendrix	6	3	4	0	1	1
	9	10	9	3	1	2

New York	0 0 5	0 4 0	0 0 0	- 9
Pittsburgh	0 1 0	0 0 0	0 1 2	- 4

OB: New York 3, Pittsburgh 12
DP: Wagner-Miller (Bridwell)
2B: Devlin
3B: Carey
HR: Carey(1)
SB: Becker, Snodgrass, Murray, Leach
CS: Fletcher 2, Snodgrass, Merkle,
    McKechnie
SO: Drucke 2, Flynn, Simon, Hendrix
BB: Murray, Carey, Byrne, Leach
SH: Snodgrass

HP: By Adams (Fletcher),
    by Drucke (Simon)
PB: Simon
TIME: 2:10
ATTENDANCE: 6,300
UMPIRES: William Finneran, Cy Rigler
SOURCES: Homestead Daily Messenger;
    DBD; New York American, Times;
    Pittsburgh Gazette Times, Leader,
    Post, Press, Sun Telegraph

BALANCE	OUT+R+OB=BP+AB+BB+SH+HP+CI
New York	27 9 3 39 36 1 1 1 0
Pittsburgh	27 4 12 43 39 3 0 1 0

Tiger Perseverance Pays Off

29. Team Overcomes 12-Run Deficit to Win

CHICAGO   at   DETROIT
(White Sox, 15)   (Tigers, 16)

Sunday, June 18, 1911, Bennett Park

Chicago's Doc White was on easy street. His White Sox teammates had built him a 13–1 lead halfway through the game, sending many of the original 10,111 patrons home.

Those who remained, did so to jeer their locals.

The Sox had routed Detroit starter Ed Summers in the very first inning by scoring

Cobb (left) and Crawford (right) pose here with Joe Jackson.

seven runs on five hits and three walks. Matty McIntyre led the initial attack with a pair of singles and two RBIs. The Tigers countered with a token run in the second frame, but Chicago piled on three more in each of the fourth and fifth innings. White was coasting with a twelve-run lead.

Then things started to unravel for Doc. The Tigers chipped away with four runs in their half of the fifth and three in the sixth. Hugh Duffy, Chicago's manager, was hesitant about pulling his 32-year-old starter because of the easy victory his teammates had seemingly presented him. But the contest, then standing at 13–8, was quickly becoming competitive.

Duffy allowed White to bat leading off the visitors' seventh, and Doc obliged by singling and scoring the first of two additional Chicago runs, making it 15–8. They were the last runs the White Sox scored. Not wishing to further test his fortune, Duffy replaced White with Fred Olmstead who succeeded in taming the Tigers in the home seventh.

Meanwhile, Clarence Mitchell, a 20-year-old Detroit rookie, had shut down the Sox in the visitors' eighth. In the home half of the eighth, Clarence got his first career hit when he singled off the third base bag and eventually scored as did Joe Casey, Donie Bush, Ty Cobb and Sam Crawford. The entire rally was made up of five singles and two walks. With the score then 15–13, future Hall-of-Famer Ed Walsh, whom the *Detroit Free Press* referred to as "the imperial guard of Duffy's army," was summoned to stem the tide. "Big Ed" rewarded his manager by fanning pinch hitter Biff Schaller to end the inning.

Mitchell retired the Sox in order in the top of the ninth and was lifted for a pinch hitter, Chick Lathers, in the bottom of the frame. Detroit had but three outs remaining and Walsh began by striking out Lathers. But Davey Jones singled, and Bush doubled him around to third. That brought to the plate Ty Cobb, who already had four hits and four RBIs on the day. Ty was probably not walked because on deck was the previous year's American League RBI leader, Sam Crawford.

On a 2–1 pitch, the speedy Cobb chopped a high bouncer toward third, presenting Chicago's Harry Lord with a nearly impossible play. Lord didn't have much time to decide and chose to try to catch Ty at first. His hurried throw and Cobb arrived almost simultaneously, both in the dirt. Ty had started to slide about ten feet in front of the

Chicago White Sox	AB	R	H	I	PO	A	E
Matty McIntyre rf	5	4	4	2	1	0	0
Harry Lord 3b	6	2	4	3	0	4	1
Nixey Callahan lf	5	1	1	2	2	0	0
Ping Bodie cf	4	1	1	1	1	0	0
>Rollie Zeider ss	5	2	0	0	2	7	0
Shano Collins 1b	4	0	0	0	11	0	0
Lee Tannehill 2b	4	1	2	0	4	4	0
Freddie Payne c	5	2	2	2	4	0	1
Doc White p	3	2	2	1	0	1	0
Fred Olmstead p7	1	0	0	0	0	0	0
Ed Walsh p8	0	0	0	0	0	0	0
	42	15	16	11	*25	16	2

Detroit Tigers	AB	R	H	I	PO	A	E
Delos Drake lf	4	1	0	0	2	0	0
Davy Jones ph8,lf	1	1	1	0	0	0	0
Donie Bush ss	5	3	1	2	2	1	1
Ty Cobb cf	6	3	5	5	1	0	1
>Sam Crawford rf	5	2	3	3	1	0	0
Jim Delahanty 1b	4	0	1	3	11	0	0
George Moriarty 3b	5	1	1	1	0	0	0
Charley O'Leary 2b	5	1	3	0	2	5	0
Oscar Stanage c	3	1	1	0	3	2	2
Joe Casey c6	1	1	1	0	4	0	0
Biff Shaller ph8	1	0	0	0	0	0	0
Boss Schmidt c9	0	0	0	0	1	0	0
Ed Summers p	0	0	0	0	0	1	0
Ralph Works p1	1	0	1	1	0	1	0
George Mullin ph5	1	0	1	0	0	0	0
Bill Covington p6	1	1	1	0	0	0	0
Clarence Mitchell p8	1	1	1	0	0	1	0
Chick Lathers ph9	1	0	0	0	0	0	0
	45	16	21	15	27	11	4

Chicago	IP	H	R	ER	BB	SO
White	6	12	8	8	1	2
Olmstead	1.2	5	5	5	2	0
Walsh L,8-7	.2	4	3	3	0	2
	*8.1	21	16	16	3	4

Detroit	IP	H	R	ER	BB	SO
Summers	.1	4	7	4	2	0
Works	4.2	5	6	4	4	2
Covington	2	5	2	2	0	3
Mitchell W,1-0	2	2	0	0	0	2
	9	16	15	10	6	7

One out when winning run scored.

Chicago	7 0 0	3 3 0	2 0 0	–15
Detroit	0 1 0	0 4 3	0 5 3	–16

OB: Chicago 8, Detroit 8
DP: Zeider-Tannehill-Collins
2B: Bush, Crawford
3B: Cobb, Crawford, Lord, Payne
SB: Lord, Callahan, Zeider 2
CS: Bodie
SO: Bodie 2, Payne, Zeider, Collins, Olmstead, Callahan, Bush, Stanage, Schaller, Lathers
BB: McIntyre, Bodie 2, Zeider, White, Tannehill, Jones, Bush, Crawford

SH: Callahan, Collins
HP: By Olmstead (Delahanty)
WP: Works, White
TIME: 2:24
ATTENDANCE: 10,111
UMPIRES: Fred Perrine, Bill Dinneen
SOURCES: Chicago Daily News, Inter-Ocean, Record Herald, Tribune; Detroit Free Press, Journal, News, Times

BALANCE	OUT+R+OB=BP=AB+BB+SH+HP+CI
Chicago	27 15 8 50 42 6 2 0 0
Detroit	25 16 8 49 45 3 0 1 0

bag, kicking up a dust storm and actually colliding with first baseman Shano Collins. Collins lost the ball in the confusion, and as the ball rolled into foul territory, Ty raced to second while both Jones and Bush scored. Cobb, now hatless, pants torn, and dirt covered, danced around the keystone sack, deriding Walsh and the White Sox. The game was tied, 15–15.

Still with only one out, Sam Crawford stepped to the plate. Walsh's first pitch to "Wahoo Sam" was a fast ball on the outside edge of the plate, but umpire Perrine called it a ball. Walsh was furious while Cobb danced and taunted more loudly. Next came a called strike and another ball. With a 2–1 count, Crawford then blistered Walsh's next offering over the head of center fielder Ping Bodie to the deepest part of the park. Cobb easily scored the game winner as Crawford was given credit for a double. And, *for the first time in the twentieth century, a team had overcome a 12-run deficit to emerge victorious*. The same crowd that had jeered in the first inning then madly poured onto the field and carried their heroes, Cobb and Crawford, to the clubhouse.

Yankees Steal Fifteen Bases

30. Team Steals 15 Bases on 20 Attempts in One Game

ST. LOUIS, AL　　at　　NEW YORK
(Browns, 12)　　　　　　(Yankees, 18)

Thursday, September 28, 1911, Hilltop Park

On a chilly autumn day in New York, the Yankees hosted the Browns in what the *New York Tribune* called a "travesty on baseball." The contest meant little in the standings with New York in fourth place and the Browns buried in the basement, already having lost 103 games. Perhaps the Yankee base runners simply were trying to keep warm as they ran almost at will on three different pitchers and two catchers. Their *15 stolen bases in one game* is still the all-time mark for team pilferage.

Base runners were plentiful in this burlesque, for in addition to collecting 13 hits, the Yankees were issued a like number of free passes. The Browns were given seven walks to complement their 12 hits. Shoddy fielding registered six errors for each club, enabling four runners to score; two more scored on wild pitches and one on a passed ball. In all, 30 runs were scored on "only" 24 hits.

After stealing only one base in the first inning, the Yankees erupted in the second. It was then that they frustrated the Browns' battery of Earl Hamilton and Jim Stephens by stealing six more. Catcher Stephens' throws were poor, but even when they were accurate, shortstop Ed Hallinan and second baseman Allie Moulton dropped them. Hal Chase also stole home during the frame. When the inning concluded, Stephens was mercifully replaced by veteran Nig Clarke, but the abuse continued. So bold and reckless were the New Yorkers, that in addition to the 15 successful thieves, five others were caught in the act, one at home plate. *Twenty stolen base attempts by one team is also a major league mark* although this effort has never been noted in baseball record books.

The pilferage reached ludicrous proportions in the eighth inning when, according to the *New York Times*, Roy Hartzell drew a pass and continued running toward second base. On a very close play, he was ruled safe. This so incensed Browns' shortstop Hallinan,

that he argued the decision until he was ejected from the contest. (The *New York Evening Telegram* disagreed with the *Times* by stating that Hallinan reached first on a single rather than a walk.)

St. Louis accumulated 21 assists in the fracas, thanks in part to a strange play in the third inning. Browns' pitcher, Elmer Brown, in a bluff pickoff move toward second base, caught the Yankees' Jack Warhop off third, and in the ensuing run-

down, six Browns (including the left fielder) touched the ball before Warhop was tagged out.

The *New York Times* was particularly harsh on the Browns, summing up their performance by calling them "a minor league team masquerading in major league livery." The Yankees themselves, however, equaled the Browns' error total in this game, and the following season finished beneath the Browns, dead last.

St. Louis Browns	AB	R	H	I	PO	A	E
Allie Moulton 2b	4	2	1	1	0	2	1
Burt Shotton cf	4	1	1	1	3	0	0
>Willie Hogan lf	5	2	0	1	0	1	0
Frank LaPorte 3b	3	1	2	2	1	3	0
Pete Compton rf	5	1	2	1	2	0	1
Joe Kutina 1b	5	1	2	2	8	0	0
Ed Hallinan ss	3	0	0	0	6	5	1
Bobby Wallace ss8	1	0	0	0	1	0	0
Jim Stephens c	1	0	0	0	0	1	1
Nig Clarke c3	3	1	0	0	3	5	2
Earl Hamilton p	1	0	0	0	0	1	0
Elmer Brown p3	2	1	1	0	0	1	0
Red Nelson p5	2	2	2	2	0	2	0
	39	12	11	10	24	21	6

New York Yankees	AB	R	H	I	PO	A	E
Bert Daniels rf	4	3	3	1	2	0	1
>Cozy Dolan 3b	4	3	2	0	2	0	0
Hal Chase cf	4	3	2	2	3	0	0
Birdie Cree lf	2	2	1	2	3	0	0
Jack Knight 1b	3	1	1	1	10	1	1
Roy Hartzell ss	4	2	1	0	3	5	0
Harry Curry 2b	4	2	1	0	1	1	3
Bob Williams c	5	2	1	2	3	3	1
Jack Warhop p	1	0	0	0	0	0	0
Jack Quinn p4	2	0	1	1	0	2	0
	33	18	13	9	27	12	6

St. Louis	IP	H	R	ER	BB	SO
Hamilton L,4-12	2	6	7	6	3	0
Brown	2	1	4	1	5	0
Nelson	4	6	7	4	5	2
	8	13	18	11	13	2

New York	IP	H	R	ER	BB	SO
Warhop	3.1	2	6	3	6	1
Quinn W,8-9	5.2	9	6	4	1	4
	9	11	12	7	7	5

```
St. Louis    0 0 4    4 0 0    0 1 3    -12
New York     3 4 1    3 0 2    2 3 x    -18
```

OB: St. Louis 9, New York 5
2B: Kutina, Nelson
3B: Williams
SB: Daniels 3, Dolan 3, Chase 4, Cree 4, Hartzell
CS: Shotton, Knight, Hartzell, Curry, Cree, Dolan
SO: Knight, Williams, Shotton 2, Hamilton, Brown, Hogan
BB: Daniels 2, Dolan 2, Chase, Cree 3, Knight 2, Hartzell, Curry, Warhop, Moulton 2, Shotton 2, Hogan, LaPorte, Clarke

SF: Quinn, LaPorte
HP: By Warhop (Hallinan)
WP: Nelson 2, Hamilton
PB: Williams, Clarke
TIME: 2:15
ATTENDANCE: 1,000
UMPIRES: Silk O'Loughlin, Rip Egan
SOURCES: New York American, Evening Telegram, Herald, Press, Sun, Times, Tribune, World; Sporting Life; St Louis Globe-Democrat, Post-Dispatch, Republic, Times

----

BALANCE	OUT	+R	+OB	=	BP	= AB	+BB	+SH	+HP	+CI
St. Louis	27	12	9		48	39	7	1	1	0
New York	24	18	5		47	33	13	1	0	0

Opposite: Birdie Cree contributed four stolen bases to the record.

Following is a summary of the Yankee
track meet:

INNING	SUCCESSFUL THIEF (base stolen)	APPREHENDED THIEF (base)
1	Chase (3)	Knight (2)
2	Daniels (2), Daniels (3) & Dolan (2), Chase (2), Chase (H) & Cree (2)	—
3	—	—
4	Dolan (2), Dolan (3), Cree (2)	Curry (2), Hartzell (2)
5	—	—
6	Cree (2)	—
7	Daniels (2), Chase (3), Cree (2)	Dolan (H), Cree (3)
8	Hartzell (2)	—

Cobb Attack Sets the Stage

31. Pitcher Allows 24 Runs, 26 Hits and 6 Triples in One Game

DETROIT   at   PHILADELPHIA
(Tigers, 2)   (Athletics, 24)

Saturday, May 18, 1912, Shibe Park

The volatile Ty Cobb not only fought
with opposing players, teammates, and
umpires, but with fans as well. As the result
of one such incident in 1912, there unfolded a
series of events which included Ty's suspension, a player walkout, a postponed game,
and a major league game in which a ludicrous band of sandlotters donned Tiger uniforms.

In the Cobb era, patrons sat much closer
to the playing arena than they do today,
making verbal assaults all the more pronounced. Then too, there was little law-
enforcement presence in most parks, creating
an ambiance conducive to abuse. Such was
the scene during a game in New York on May
15, 1912. The Tigers and Yankees were
engaged in the last of a three game series, and
nerves were frayed. The fans had been riding
Cobb mercilessly, Ty himself often exchanging barbs with them. The major offender this

day was singled out as Claude Lucker, who
through vile language, had been questioning
Cobb's ancestry. Lucker was seated just a few
rows behind third base, close to the Tiger
dugout. His epithets were absorbed by Cobb
on each trip to and from the bench. Midway
through the game, Ty walked over to the
New York dugout and warned manager Harry
Wolverton of the Yankees. "There's going to
be trouble if this fellow isn't stopped."* Cobb
also repeated the warning at a box occupied
by New York club officials, but all he got
were shrugs. Finally he could stand it no
longer and, followed by several bat-wielding
teammates, stormed into the stands after
Lucker. Newspapers varied in their description of the fracas, but most agreed that Cobb
badly pummelled the tormentor with his fists,
knocked him to the ground, then kicked and
spiked him. Lucker's defenders claimed that
he was not the culprit and that Cobb's act

---

*Ty Cobb, with Al Stump, My Life in Baseball, the True Record, Garden City, NY, Doubleday & Co., Inc., 1961, 132.

was a cowardly one insofar as Lucker had lost one hand and three fingers of the other in an industrial accident. Cobb was ejected from the game.

The following day, while Detroit was rained out of a game in Philadelphia, Cobb was indefinitely suspended by American League President Ban Johnson. Sentiment of the players and the press was divided between Ty and the ignoble patron. Players throughout the league had also been subjected to similar abuse, and although many hated Cobb, they were now in support of his position.

On May 17, the "Cobb-less" Tigers engaged and prevailed over the Athletics, 6–3. After the game, however, the united players wired a telegram to Ban Johnson and told manager Hughie Jennings that unless Cobb was reinstated, they refused to ever play for the Tigers again. Meanwhile, Ban Johnson had threatened Detroit owner Frank Navin with a $5,000 per day fine and possible loss of his franchise should the Tigers forfeit any games.

By May 18, the 20,000 fans who packed Shibe Park weren't sure what to expect, nor was Navin. The Tigers dressed for the game and took some warm-up practice, but about an hour before the scheduled start of the game, one of the Tigers asked the umpire if Cobb's suspension had been lifted. A negative response triggered an exodus by all the

Above: *Travers warming up for his only major league game.* Below: The Philadelphia Record *summarized the events.*

Tigers, making Navin's worst nightmare a real possibility.

Meanwhile, steps had been taken to assist the Tigers should they have had to face the specter of a forfeit. William T. Nolan, a Philadelphia sportswriter, had reportedly been asked by Connie Mack to round up a group of local players to take the place of the Tigers so there'd be no forfeit. The plan was for the sandlotters to get dressed and merely walk onto the field. The game would then be called off but not officially forfeited, saving Navin's franchise and the huge fine.

Aloysius S. Travers, student and assistant manager of the St. Joseph's College baseball team at the time, was a friend and classmate of Nolan's son, John. Al Travers knew most of the local ballplayers. John visited Travers a few hours before the game and told Al that his father wanted Travers to gather 10 to 12 fellows from the neighborhood to take the place of the Tigers should they walk out. Travers hurried to the local sandlot, gathered some boys and led them to Shibe Park where Mr. Nolan escorted them to the Detroit locker room. There they waited to possibly don Tiger uniforms.

Eventually, led by Cobb, the striking Tigers did parade into the locker room and turned over their uniforms to the sandlotters. George Mullin, Tiger hurler, gave his flannels to Travers and told the youngster, "you can steal everything, but don't steal the glove."* Being the recruiter, Travers was also afforded the privilege of constructing the misfits' lineup. Al nominated himself for the third batting spot, and he elected to pitch because that commanded a $25 stipend while each of the other fielding positions afforded just $10. The sandlotters were also shocked to learn that Connie Mack had changed his mind, and that they would actually have to play the scheduled game against the Athletics.

What manager Hughie Jennings fielded was a sorry looking bunch. For some, it was the chance of a lifetime; for several others, it was a re-birth. In addition to the youngsters, several Tiger scouts and coaches also entered

the fray. Forty-one-year-old Joe Sugden had played 12 years in the majors but not once since 1905. Deacon McGuire, now 48, had caught his first major league game 28 years earlier. Even manager Jennings, at 43, sent himself to the plate for the first time in three years. This band of Tiger imposters managed to score but two unearned runs in the fifth inning when Sugden and McGuire both garnered their only hits of the game, each singling. Boardwalk Brown next hit Pat Meany, loading the bases with just one out. The Athletics' catcher, Jack Lapp, then tried to pick off Meany but threw the ball into right field, allowing both of the ancients to tally.

Seeing this buffoonery develop, hundreds of fans demanded their money back but were rebuffed. Instead, they were forced to sit through a record-setting devastation, as were the protesting players who did some heckling of their own from the grandstand. No further demonstrations erupted, however.

Aloysius Travers, the 20-year-old designated Tiger hurler for the day, later became a Jesuit priest and taught at St. Joseph's College Prep in Philadelphia. His faith this day was severely tested as his teammates contributed seven errors to the debacle. Travers remains the modern day, *major league record holder for most runs (24) allowed in a game as well as for the most triples (6) allowed.* The six triples have been recorded erroneously as only five in modern record books. This is probably due to the fact that most out-of-town newspapers showed only five. However, the hometown Philadelphia newspapers, and more importantly the official league records, all credit the Athletics with six triples.

Travers also tied the mark (see 6-21-01) for *most hits (26) allowed in a nine-inning contest.* This was the only game of his major league career as it was for Jim McGarr, Ed Irvin, Dan McGarvey, Bill Leinhauser, John (Smith) Coffey, Pat Meaney, and Hap Ward. Billy Maharg, a former lightweight boxer, somehow managed another cameo appearance for the Phillies in 1916 and was later implicated in the Black Sox scandal.

On Sunday, May 19, the day following

---

* *"Hero Recalls 1912 Baseball Strike."* New York Times, *19 May, 1962, p. 20.*

this baseball parody, the Tigers and Athletics were not scheduled to play. They were to resume engagement on Monday. By then, Ban Johnson had arrived in town, and after an early meeting with A's owner Ben Shibe, managers Connie Mack and Hughie Jennings, the scheduled game was postponed. Johnson was not about to back down, however. The postponement was simply to enable Detroit to assemble a more competitive squad and give Tiger president, Frank Navin, additional time to arrive in Philadelphia. The league was prepared to ban and blacklist all the strikers. News reports of the day carried rumors of other teams threatening to join in

the strike, but these were generally denied by the players.

Navin did finally join his team later on May 20 and immediately spoke with Cobb, then the entire team. At that team meeting, Cobb thanked his mates for their support but said he didn't want them to jeopardize their careers as ballplayers by continuing to refuse to play. Navin offered to pay any fines levied by the league, and the players reluctantly agreed to end their strike. Cobb himself, however, was to remain under suspension.

All of the American League club owners met in Philadelphia on May 21 to decide the fate of Cobb and the strikers. It was decided

Detroit Tigers	AB	R	H	I	PO	A	E
Jim McGarr 2b	4	0	0	0	1	3	0
Billy Maharg 3b	1	0	0	0	0	2	0
Ed Irvin ph3,3b,c7	3	0	2	0	0	1	1
Al Travers p	3	0	0	0	0	7	0
Hughie Jennings ph9	1	0	0	0	0	0	0
Dan McGarvey lf	3	0	0	0	1	1	1
Bill Leinhauser cf	4	0	0	0	0	1	0
>Joe Sugden 1b	4	1	1	0	13	3	1
Deacon McGuire c	2	1	1	0	2	3	2
John Coffey 3b7	0	0	0	0	2	1	0
Pat Meaney ss	2	0	0	0	3	2	1
Hap Ward rf	2	0	0	0	2	0	0
	29	2	4	0	24	24	7

Detroit	IP	H	R	ER	BB	SO
Travers L,0-1	8	26	24	14	7	1

Philadelphia Athletics	AB	R	H	I	PO	A	E
Harl Maggert lf	4	2	3	-	0	0	0
Amos Strunk cf	6	3	4	-	0	0	0
Eddie Collins 2b	6	4	5	-	0	1	0
Frank Baker 3b	5	3	2	-	0	0	0
Danny Murphy rf	3	4	2	-	1	0	0
Stuffy McInnis 1b	6	2	4	-	7	1	0
>Jack Barry ss	4	2	2	-	3	1	0
Jack Lapp c	4	1	1	-	16	1	1
Jack Coombs p	1	0	0	-	0	1	0
Boardwalk Brown p4	3	2	2	-	0	2	0
Herb Pennock p7	1	1	1	-	0	1	0
	43	24	26	—	27	8	1

Philadelphia	IP	H	R	ER	BB	SO
Coombs W,2-1	3	0	0	0	1	3
Brown	3	3	2	0	0	5
Pennock	3	1	0	0	1	7
	9	4	2	0	2	15

Detroit	0 0 0	0 2 0	0 0 0	- 2
Philadelphia	3 0 3	0 8 4	4 2 x	-24

OB: Detroit 4, Philadelphia 4
DP: Meaney-Coffey
2B: Maggert, Strunk, Barry, Pennock
3B: Irvin 2, McInnis, Strunk, Baker, Murphy, Brown, Maggert
SB: McGarvey, Collins 5, McInnis 2, Baker, Murphy 2
CS: McGuire
SO: McGarr 4, Leinhauser 3, Ward 2, Irvin, Travers, Meaney 2, Coffey, Jennings, Brown
BB: Ward, McGuire, Maggert 2, Baker, Murphy 3, Barry

SH: Lapp
SF: Barry
HP: By Brown (Meaney), by Pennock (McGarvey)
TIME: 1:45
ATTENDANCE: 20,000
UMPIRES: Bill Dinneen, Fred Perrine
SOURCES: Detroit Free Press, News; New York Times; Philadelphia Evening Bulletin, Evening Telegraph, Evening Times, Inquirer, North American, Record

---

BALANCE	OUT+R+OB=BP=AB+BB+SH+HP+CI
Detroit	27 2 4 33 29 2 0 2 0
Philadelphia	24 24 4 52 43 7 2 0 0

---

to fine each of the striking players $100 and to continue Cobb's suspension. Meanwhile, the bona fide Tigers traveled to Washington where they defeated the Senators, 2–0. Finally, on May 26, Johnson lifted Cobb's suspension and fined him $50 for his part in the controversy.

Although this affair fell short of the formation of anything resembling a players union, it did test the strength of the owners and the league president. It also ultimately produced some positive results, for security was tightened throughout the league, affording more protection for the players from abusive fans.

Historical note: Cobb was not the first twentieth-century player to be suspended for using his fists on a spectator. In 1910, Art Devlin pummelled a fan during a game in Brooklyn and was suspended for more than a week while several teammate accomplices were fined. However, no player strike ensued from this incident.

A Festival of Hitting and Running

32. Teams Score 17 Runs in the Ninth Inning

NEW YORK, NL   at   BOSTON
(Giants, 21)   (Braves, 12)

Thursday, June 20, 1912, Walpole Street Grounds

Kling watched the conclusion from the bench.

The appearance of 2,700 fans at South End Grounds in Boston for this game was a testimony to team loyalty. The Braves were mired in last place, 24 games behind the front-running, visiting Giants. Their pitching staff had given up the most hits in the league, and their batters had struck out more than any other team. The outcome of this contest was not surprising. The details of defeat were.

Johnny Kling, player-manager for the Braves, elected right-hander Buster Brown to start the game. Giants manager, John McGraw, countered with Hooks Wiltse. Wiltse pitched well for eight innings before he was given the rest of the day off. Boston's Buster Brown, however, lasted only 1⅔ innings, followed by Ed Donnelly who was knocked out after another 1⅓. By this time it was already 9–0 in favor of the Giants. Kling, the starting

Devore stole four bases — two in the ninth.

The Braves were determined to make the final score look respectable, and Shore was equal to the task. A walk, a Shore error, seven singles, and a home run, tallied ten runs for the home team, making the final score a more palatable 21–12. *The two-team, 17 ninth-inning runs is a modern major league record.* The Giants also tied another major league standard when *thirteen teammates each scored at least one run.*

Lost among the orgy of run scoring was another baserunning feat. The Giants at this time were a base-stealing machine. The year before, in 1911, they had established the modern, team stolen base mark with 347. This year, they again led the league with 319 thefts, and six different players had 30 or more. (Only one other team had over 200.) Among their 319, they tied the National League record of 17 steals of home. In this game, the Giants stole nine bases, and the two teams combined for a total of 14. For years, record books have reported this game with 16 stolen bases, 11 for the Giants and five for the Braves. But a check through the official, daily league records shows that the Giants stole "only" nine bases. Contributing to the frivolous base running was the fact that the first-string catchers on both sides retired early. Actually, the third-string backstops on each team eventually made their way into the game. Boston's Gil Whitehouse, only 18 years old, made his major league debut in the fourth inning and labored nervously the rest of the way. Gil was assessed with a passed ball, several errors on close plays at the plate, and struck out in each of his three plate appearances.

Ernie Shore, the Giants' battered rookie pitcher, was never given another chance by McGraw. His career was not over, however, for this was the same Ernie Shore who gained

catcher at 37 years of age, felt he too had all his aged bones could handle and watched the rest of the action from the dugout. The Gothamites continued to pound away, and after eight innings, they led 14–2. Although 16 runs were already scored by the two teams, the ninth inning output was about to exceed the first eight combined.

Brad Hogg had labored since the fourth inning for the Braves, and manager Kling could see no reason to waste another hurler in this rout. So, although the Giants again rallied in the top of the ninth, Hogg was left to finish. (It was Hogg's last major league game for several years.) Before completing their turn at bat, the New Yorkers added another seven runs to their total, making it 21–2. McGraw then cleared his bench, giving every splinter-picker some action. All others were sent to the clubhouse save 21-year-old rookie pitcher, Ernie Shore. McGraw wanted to get his first look at the big college kid; the view was a nightmare.

immortality on June 23, 1917, while twirling for the Red Sox. That was the game in which Babe Ruth, as the starting pitcher, walked the first batter then was ejected for protesting. Shore relieved, and after the runner was thrown out attempting to steal, he retired the next 26 batters.

Another not-so-famous participant in this game deserves a special note. Charles "Buster" Brown, Boston starter this day, was credited with his seventh loss of the campaign, giving him a 50–95 lifetime log. Buster piled on a few more losses before the season closed and then ended his career in 1913 at 51–105. Thus Brown forged the worst lifetime winning percentage (.327) in this century for any hurler with more than 150 decisions.

New York Giants	AB	R	H	I	PO	A	E
Fred Snodgrass cf,1b8	4	2	1	2	2	1	0
Larry Doyle 2b	4	2	3	1	2	0	0
Tillie Shafer pr6,2b	2	2	1	2	0	0	0
Fred Merkle 1b	3	3	2	2	2	1	0
George Burns cf8	1	1	0	0	3	0	0
Red Murray lf	4	1	1	2	2	0	0
Moose McCormick lf8	1	1	1	2	0	0	0
Beals Becker rf	1	1	1	1	1	0	0
Josh Devore rf4	3	0	2	2	1	0	1
Buck Herzog 3b	2	2	0	1	0	2	0
Heinie Groh 3b8	1	0	0	0	1	1	0
Chief Meyers c	2	1	2	1	2	1	0
Art Wilson pr3,c	4	2	1	0	5	1	0
Grover Hartley c9	0	0	0	0	2	0	0
>Art Fletcher ss	5	2	2	1	2	1	0
Hooks Wiltse p	5	1	3	1	2	1	0
Ernie Shore p9	0	0	0	0	0	0	1
	42	21	20	18	27	9	2

Boston Braves	AB	R	H	I	PO	A	E
Ed McDonald 3b	4	1	2	2	2	2	1
Vin Campbell cf	4	1	1	0	5	2	0
Bill Sweeney 2b	5	1	1	2	2	1	0
Jay Kirke lf	5	2	1	1	6	0	0
Doc Miller rf	5	3	4	2	1	0	0
Ben Houser 1b	5	2	3	4	4	1	0
>Frank O'Rourke ss	5	1	1	1	2	2	0
Johnny Kling c	1	0	0	0	1	1	0
Gil Whitehouse c4	3	0	0	0	4	0	2
C. Buster Brown p	0	0	0	0	0	0	0
Ed Donnelly p2	0	0	0	0	0	0	0
Brad Hogg p4	4	1	1	0	0	1	1
	41	12	14	12	27	10	4

New York	IP	H	R	ER	BB	SO
Wiltse W,4-2	8	6	2	2	1	6
Shore	1	8	10	3	1	1
	9	14	12	5	2	7

Boston	IP	H	R	ER	BB	SO
C. Brown L,3-7	1.2	3	4	4	3	1
Donnelly	1.1	5	5	1	0	0
Hogg	6	12	12	7	5	4
	9	20	21	12	8	5

New York	2 2 5	2 0 1	2 0 7	-21
Boston	0 0 0	0 0 0	1 1 10	-12

OB: New York 5, Boston 4
2B: Wiltse, Miller, Doyle, Houser, Shafer
3B: McDonald
HR: Merkle(3), Doyle(7), Miller(2),
　　Houser(3)
SB: McDonald 2, Becker, Devore 4,
　　Shafer, Wiltse, Herzog, Kirke,
　　Snodgrass, Campbell, Sweeney
SO: Murray 2, Groh, Wilson, Hartley,
　　McDonald 2, Kirke, Miller,
　　Whitehouse 3
BB: Snodgrass 2, Merkle, Burns,
　　Becker, Devore, Herzog 2,
　　McDonald, Campbell

SF: Fletcher, Herzog, Murray
WP: Wiltse
PB: Whitehouse
BK: Donnelly
TIME: 2:20
ATTENDANCE: 2,700
UMPIRES: Bill Brennan, Bob Emslie
SOURCES: Boston Globe, Herald, Post;
　　New York Herald, Sun, Times,
　　Tribune, World

BALANCE	OUT+R+OB=BP=AB+BB+SH+HP+CI							
New York	27	21	5	53	42	8	3	0	0
Boston	27	12	4	43	41	2	0	0	0

DEBUNKING DEVORE

It has been reported in more than one contemporary source that the fine New York base stealer, Josh Devore, once stole four bases in the same inning. This astounding performance supposedly occurred in the ninth inning of this contest, and most of the claims include the necessary fact that Devore batted twice in the frame. As with many of baseball's repeated record claims, this one is purely fictional.

According to play-by-play found in the *Boston Globe*, only 11 Giants batted in that ninth inning, and Devore was the eighth man up. He did single, stole second and third, but was left stranded as both Heinie Groh and Art Wilson fanned, and Art Fletcher flied to center. Devore did steal four bases in this game as most daily newspapers reported, but not in the same inning.

Collins Steals Six Bases

33. Player Steals Six Bases in One Game

PHILADELPHIA   at   DETROIT
(Athletics, 9)   (Tigers, 7)

Wednesday, September 11, 1912, Navin Field

In a game marred by frequent arguments, an attack on an umpire, and the ejection of three players, 25-year-old Eddie Collins *stole six bases*, establishing a record that no other player would duplicate for nearly 80 years.

The fireworks began in the third inning of a 2–2 game when Ty Cobb stepped to the plate with two outs and teammate Donie Bush on second base. With first base open, the Athletics decided to intentionally walk the "The Peach." Such strategy was held as ignoble by some in 1912, so most clubs had secret codes or signs for such activity. For the Athletics, the signal was rather obvious as the normally sphinx-like manager Connie Mack would lean forward on the bench and yell, "Play ball," to his pitcher. After one very wide offering, Cobb sensed the strategy. On the second pitch, Ty stepped over the plate and lined a single to left, scoring Bush. However, home plate umpire Tommy Connolly

courageously invoked the rarely used "foul strike" rule.* Cobb was called out for stepping across home plate, and the run was disallowed. This decision induced the wrath of the hometown patrons and a charge toward the plate by most of the Tigers. One of the grandstand patrons did more than hoot. A bottle was hurled in Connolly's direction, landing close enough to bounce up and hit the arbiter in the mouth. Momentarily stunned, Connolly recovered and ejected Detroit manager Hughie Jennings for excessive arguing. Cobb then refused to take the field and sat sulking in the dugout in protest. After nearly five minutes, Ty was finally cajoled by teammates into resuming his fielding position.

Tiger protestations were not over, however. Several innings later Detroit coach Ossie Vitt was banished for his continued dissent over the Cobb ruling. Donie Bush too

*The Detroit Free Press, *September 12, 1912, p.16—described the "foul strike" rule as a violation of Rule 50 of the Playing Code. "A foul strike is a batted ball by the batsman when either or both feet is upon the ground outside the lines of the batsman's position." Section 4 of Rule 51 says: "The batsman is out if he makes a foul strike as defined in Rule 50."*

Athletics' Sparkplug—Eddie Collins

The game's excessive squabbling merely served as a distraction from the Athletics' victory and the record-setting performance of Collins. All of Collins' thefts came at the expense of rookie catcher Brad Kocher and fifth-year hurler Joe Lake. The *Detroit Times* placed most of the blame for the Athletics' liberties on pitcher Lake, reporting his windup took so much time that often his batterymate didn't even bother to throw. The *Detroit Free Press* was even less charitable when it described Lake's effort as "stupid, slovenly, and an inefficient article of pitching." They also questioned the work of base path umpire Bertie Hart, wondering how the "unfortunate arbiter could find his way around without a little dog to lead him."

was ejected in the seventh inning for arguing a call on a close play at first.

The game was a cakewalk for Philadelphia until Detroit rallied in the home ninth and nearly tied the game. After Duke Houck was knocked out of the game, Stan Coveleski was beckoned to end the contest. But Stan walked the tying run, and the only batter he faced, on four pitches. That hurriedly brought the veteran Eddie Plank to the mound. Plank wild pitched the two base runners into scoring position before inducing Bobby Veach to end the game by grounding out.

Following is a log of Collins' offensive efforts with his stolen base count in parentheses:

• In the first inning, he grounded out, Baldy Louden to Eddie Onslow.

• In the third, Eddie singled to left, stole second (1), reached third on a fielder's choice, and was left on base.

• In the fourth, he reached base on Louden's error, stole second (2) and went to third on catcher Kocher's errant throw. With Frank Baker on first, Collins then stole home (3) as part of a double steal.

• In the sixth, Collins singled, stole

second (4) and third (5) but was left on base.

• In the eighth, Collins singled, stole second (6) and reached third on a passed ball. With Frank Baker on first and two outs, they attempted a double steal. Eddie scored, and his run counted, but because Baker was tagged out at second, Collins was not given credit for his seventh stolen base of the game. His run scored on a fielder's choice.

In the following day's edition of *The Detroit News*, sportswriter H. G. Salsinger defended Cobb's tactic of stepping over the plate while attempting to thwart an inten-

tional pass. Salsinger contended that people came to the ball park to see men like Cobb, Collins, Speaker, and Jackson hit the ball, and when a pitcher purposely walked a heavy hitter he was unsportsmanlike and unfair to the people who support the game. In such cases, the batter should have some way of protecting his team such as by stepping over the plate.

Despite the speed and daring of both Cobb (61 steals) and Collins (63 steals), neither led the league this year in stolen bases. That honor went to the Senators' Clyde "Deerfoot" Milan, who pilfered 88 sacks.

Philadelphia Athletics	AB	R	H	I	PO	A	E
Eddie Murphy rf	5	2	3	2	4	0	0
Harl Maggert cf	5	1	1	0	2	0	0
Eddie Collins 2b	5	2	3	1	2	3	0
Frank Baker 3b	3	0	0	0	0	6	0
Stuffy McInnis 1b	4	1	1	0	11	0	0
Jimmy Walsh lf	5	1	3	0	3	0	0
Jack Barry ss	4	1	1	0	0	3	0
>Ben Egan c	3	1	2	1	4	0	1
Duke Houck p	3	0	0	0	1	1	1
Stan Coveleski p9	0	0	0	0	0	0	0
Eddie Plank p9	0	0	0	0	0	0	0
	37	9	14	4	27	13	2

Detroit Tigers	AB	R	H	I	PO	A	E
Donie Bush ss	1	1	0	0	1	4	1
Charlie Deal 3b8	1	1	1	1	0	1	0
Red Corriden 3b,ss8	4	1	2	0	1	1	1
Sam Crawford rf	3	0	0	2	2	0	0
Ty Cobb cf	4	0	2	0	1	0	0
>Bobby Veach lf	4	1	2	1	1	0	0
Baldy Louden 2b	3	1	1	0	3	7	1
Eddie Onslow 1b	4	1	1	0	12	1	1
Brad Kocher c	4	0	1	1	6	5	1
Joe Lake p	3	0	0	0	0	2	1
Davy Jones ph9	1	1	1	1	0	0	0
	32	7	11	6	27	21	6

Philadelphia	IP	H	R	ER	BB	SO
Houck W,6-7	8.1	10	7	6	4	2
Coveleski	0	0	0	0	1	0
Plank	.2	1	0	0	0	0
	9	11	7	6	5	2

Detroit	IP	H	R	ER	BB	SO
Lake L,9-17	9	14	9	5	6	4

Philadelphia	0	1	1		4	1	0	1 1 0	- 9
Detroit	2	0	0		1	0	0	0 0 4	- 7

OB: Philadelphia 8, Detroit 7
DP: Barry-Collins-McInnis (Crawford)
2B: Walsh, Kocher, Louden
SB: Murphy, Maggert(2), Collins(6), Baker, McInnis, Cobb(2), Louden
CS: Cobb, Baker
SO: Egan, Houck(2), Kocher(2), McInnis
BB: Baker(2), McInnis, Barry, Louden Egan(2), Bush(3), Corriden
SH: Houck
SF: Crawford(2), Veach

HP: By Houck (Cobb)
WP: Houck, Plank
PB: Egan
TIME: 2:32
ATTENDANCE: 4,342
UMPIRES: Tommy Connolly, Bertie Hart
SOURCES: Detroit Free Press, Journal, News, Times; Philadelphia Evening Telegraph, Inquirer, Press, Record

BALANCE	OUT	+R	+OB	=BP	=AB	+BB	+SH	+HP	+CI
Philadelphia	27	9	8	44	37	6	1	0	0
Detroit	27	7	7	41	32	5	3	1	0

Collins Again Steals Six

34. Player Steals
Six Bases in One Game

PHILADELPHIA, AL   at   ST. LOUIS
(Athletics, 8)   (Browns, 2)

Sunday, September 22, 1912, Sportsman's Park

Just 11 days earlier, Eddie Collins had set a modern major league record by stealing six bases in one game. Now, with the season waning, Eddie repeated his recent effort by stealing six more bases in the first game of a doubleheader against the Browns. It was another day of crime that would have made even Willie Sutton proud. This time Collins victimized two pitchers and two catchers.

Eddie got on base all five times he batted, four times with hits and once on a fielder's choice. After that, fortune came into play, because every time he stood on first base he could look down toward second and see an empty bag; there were never any teammates to blockade his path. Here's how his day progressed:

• In the opening frame, Collins forced Murphy at second base, stole second (1) and was later himself forced at third.

• Leading off the third inning, Eddie beat out a bunt, was sacrificed to second, and scored on Doc Shanley's fielding error.

• After Harl Maggert had led off with a double, Collins beat out another bunt in the fifth. He then stole second (2) and scored on Stuffy McInnis' double.

• With one out in the seventh round, he

Collins ran wild again.

singled to left, stole second (3) and went to third on Walt Alexander's low throw into center field. With McInnis on first, Collins then stole home (4) on the front end of a double steal.

• In the eighth frame, with Murphy on second and one out, Collins singled to center. Eddie stole second (5) and third (6) but was left on base as the inning ended.

Collins was also on deck in the ninth when Maggert flied out to Gus Williams ending the game. It took 79 years before another player could repeat this effort (see 6-16-91). In the second game of the double-header, Collins reached first base only once but did not steal.

For Browns catcher Jim "Little Nemo" Stephens this stolen base business was a recurring nightmare. Less than a year earlier the five-foot, six-inch backstop was behind the plate in the most prolific stolen base game of the century (see 9-28-11).

FIRST GAME

Philadelphia Athletics	AB	R	H	I	PO	A	E
Eddie Murphy rf	5	1	1	0	1	0	0
>Harl Maggert cf	6	0	1	0	2	0	0
Eddie Collins 2b	5	3	4	1	1	1	1
Jack Barry ss	3	0	0	0	4	6	1
Stuffy McInnis 1b	3	1	1	1	10	1	0
Jimmy Walsh lf	4	2	1	0	3	0	0
Joe Mathes 3b	4	0	1	0	0	0	1
Jack Lapp c	4	1	3	3	6	2	0
Eddie Plank p	3	0	1	0	0	1	0
	37	8	13	5	27	11	3

St. Louis Browns	AB	R	H	I	PO	A	E
Burt Shotton cf	4	0	0	1	2	0	0
Gus Williams rf	3	0	0	0	1	0	0
Willie Hogan lf	4	0	1	0	1	0	0
Del Pratt 2b	4	0	2	0	1	2	0
Eddie Miller 1b	4	1	0	0	10	0	1
Jimmy Austin 3b	4	0	1	1	1	1	0
Doc Shanley ss	1	0	0	0	3	0	1
Bobby Wallace ss5	2	0	0	0	0	3	0
Jim Stephens c	1	0	0	0	3	0	0
> Walt Alexander c5	3	1	2	0	5	2	2
Mack Allison p	1	0	0	0	0	3	0
George Stovall ph5	0	0	0	0	0	0	0
Buddy Napier p6	0	0	0	0	0	1	0
Bunny Brief ph8	1	0	0	0	0	0	0
Roy Mitchell p9	0	0	0	0	0	1	0
	32	2	6	2	27	13	4

Philadelphia	IP	H	R	ER	BB	SO
Plank W,26-5	9	6	2	0	3	6

St. Louis	IP	H	R	ER	BB	SO
Allison L,6-14	5	7	3	2	1	3
Napier	3	5	4	4	4	2
Mitchell	1	1	1	0	0	1
	9	13	8	6	5	6

Philadelphia	0 1 1	0 1 0	3 1 1	- 8
St. Louis	0 0 0	0 1 0	0 1 0	- 2

OB: Philadelphia 12, St. Louis 6
2B: Murphy, Maggert, McInnis, Walsh, Plank
SB: Collins 6, McInnis 3
CS: Barry
SO: Barry, Mathes 3, Plank 2, Hogan, Williams 2, Miller, Alexander, Allison
BB: Murphy, McInnis 2, Walsh, Lapp, Williams, Wallace, Stovall(I)
SH: Barry, Plank 2

HP: By Allison (Barry), by Napier (Mathes)
PB: Lapp
TIME: 2:00
ATTENDANCE: 12,000
UMPIRES: Bill Dinneen, Joe O'Brien
SOURCES: Philadelphia Evening Times, Inquirer, North American, Press, Public Ledger, Record; New York Times; St. Louis Globe-Democrat, Post-Dispatch

---

BALANCE	OUT+R+OB=BP=AB+BB+SH+HP+CI
Philadelphia	27 8 12 47 37 5 3 2 0
St. Louis	27 2 6 35 32 3 0 0 0

McAllister   Williams   Mitchell   Stone   Flanagan   Balenti   Pratt   Hamilton

Middle Row: Compton, Johnston, Leverenz, Weilman, Stovall, Shotton
Bottom Row: Brief, Lavan, Alexander, Austin, Rodgers, Baumgardner

ST. LOUIS AMERICANS

Dwight Stone: top row, fourth from the left

Stone Stymies the Yankees

35. Team Leaves 15 Runners on Base in Shutout Loss

NEW YORK, AL   at   ST. LOUIS
(Yankees, 0)   (Browns, 7)

Thursday, May 22, 1913, Sportsman's Park

St. Louis Browns rookie Dwight Stone would last just two years in the major leagues. He was a mediocre pitcher at best, yet thanks to just the right amount of wildness and luck, his name still appears in the all-time record book. On this day Dwight was constantly in hot water and was so erratic that in the fifth inning, despite working on a shutout, acting manager Lou Criger became worried enough to send teammate Walt Leverenz to the bullpen to begin warming up.

The visiting New York Yankees had multiple opportunities to break into the scoring column but continued to come up short. Six

New York Yankees	AB	R	H	I	PO	A	E
Bert Daniels rf	4	0	1	0	2	0	0
Harry Wolter cf	2	0	1	0	1	1	0
Roy Hartzell 2b	5	0	0	0	2	2	0
Birdie Cree lf	4	0	0	0	2	0	0
Hal Chase 1b	3	0	1	0	7	0	0
>Ed Sweeney c	4	0	1	0	5	3	0
Ezra Midkiff 3b	4	0	1	0	1	0	0
Bill McKechnie ss	2	0	0	0	4	1	2
Ed Klepfer p	1	0	0	0	0	1	0
George Clark p6	2	0	1	0	0	2	1
	31	0	6	0	24	10	3

St. Louis Browns	AB	R	H	I	PO	A	E
Burt Shotton cf	4	2	2	1	3	0	0
>Johnny Johnston lf	4	1	1	0	1	0	0
Gus Williams rf	3	0	1	1	0	0	0
Del Pratt 2b	4	1	2	1	3	3	0
Bunny Brief 1b	3	0	1	2	12	0	0
Jimmy Austin 3b	3	1	1	0	0	0	0
Bobby Wallace ss	2	2	1	0	2	7	0
Bill McAllester c	2	0	0	0	6	0	1
Dwight Stone p	4	0	1	1	0	3	0
	29	7	10	6	27	13	1

New York	IP	H	R	ER	BB	SO
Klepfer L,0-1	5.1	9	5	5	5	2
Clark	2.2	1	2	1	1	2
	8	10	7	6	6	4

St. Louis	IP	H	R	ER	BB	SO
Stone W,1-2	9	6	0	0	7	4

New York	0 0 0	0 0 0	0 0 0	- 0
St. Louis	0 0 1	0 3 1	0 2 x	- 7

OB: New York 15, St. Louis 7
DP: Hartzell-McKechnie-Chase
      Wolter-Sweeney (Johnston)
      Pratt-Wallace-Brief (Sweeney)
2B: Johnston, Shotton, Clark, Wolter
      Midkiff
3B: Brief
SB: Daniels, Wallace, Cree
BB: Wolter 2, McKechnie 2, Chase 2,
      Cree, Shotton, Williams, Austin,
      Wallace, McAllester 2
SH: Brief, Johnston, Daniels, Wallace

HP: By Stone (Wolter, Sweeney,
      Klepfer)
WP: Stone
TIME: 2:15
ATTENDANCE: ?
UMPIRES: George Hildebrand and
      Tommy Connolly
SOURCES: New York Times; St. Louis
      Globe-Democrat, Post Dispatch,
      Republic, Star

BALANCE	OUT	+R	+OB	=BP	=AB	+BB	+SH	+HP	+CI
New York	27	0	15	42	31	7	1	3	0
St. Louis	24	7	7	38	29	6	3	0	0

Phillips Memorial
Library
Providence College

hits, seven walks, three hit-batsmen, and a Browns error went for naught as the New Yorkers established a *modern major league record of 15 base-runners left stranded in a nine-inning shutout game.* This record of futility was later tied (see 7-29-31 and 8-1-41) and eventually surpassed (see 5-24-94).

After allowing just two hits over the first four innings, Stone began living on the edge:

• In the fifth, he walked Bill McKechnie and hit both Ed Klepfer and Harry Wolter to load the sacks with just one out. A force out at home and a breathtaking catch by Burt Shotton in deep center field ended that threat, leaving the bases loaded.

• In the seventh, Yankee relief pitcher George Clark led off with his first major league hit, a double. Bert Daniels grounded out and Wolter walked, but Stone came through by getting Roy Hartzell to ground out and fanning Birdie Cree for the third out.

• In the eighth, Hal Chase led off with a single but was wiped out by a double play. The next batter, Ezra Midkiff then smashed a long double to right. McKechnie walked, but Clark fouled out, ending the inning with two more left on base.

• Stone started the ninth by retiring Daniels. But Wolter doubled and went to third on a wild pitch. After Hartzell was retired, Cree walked and stole second. Chase then popped up the potential game ending out, but catcher Bill McAllester dropped the ball in foul territory. Given a new life, Chase proceeded to walk, again loading the bases. Jeff "Ed" Sweeney then harmlessly popped up to second baseman Del Pratt to end the suspense and inscribe Stone's name in baseball's record book.

Stone finished this season with a 2–6 log. The following year, his last in the majors, he was equally unsuccessful while compiling an 8–14 record for Kansas City in the Federal League. This day's mound opponent, Ed Klepfer, was making his first major league start after several relief stints, and this game represented Ed's only decision of the year. He finished his career in 1919, compiling a 22–17 lifetime ledger.

Yankees Get Pummeled

36. Six Teammates Hit by Pitch in One Game

NEW YORK	at	WASHINGTON
(Yankees, 9)		(Nationals, 3)

Friday, June 20, 1913, Griffith Stadium

On this date, the cellar-dwelling Yankees (15–39) were being welcomed by the Washington Nationals (31–26) for a doubleheader in Griffith Stadium. Washington was hoping to use this six-game series to launch their drive into the pennant race but, much to the chagrin of Senator fandom, the tail-enders swept both ends of the twin bill. In the second game of the doubleheader, the New Yorkers, although victorious, established an unenviable record when *six of their batters were plunked* by Washington pitchers, *the most hit-batsmen on one club in this century.* It's a record that has yet to be surpassed.

There were no extenuating circumstances such as a wet field or raw recruits pitching. The culprits all had previously seen major league action, and it was a hot, dry day in Washington. Simply, the Nationals' hurlers were wild.

Bert Daniels was hit in each of the first three innings.

Our Pennant Dreams Are Given a Jolt by the Yankees

The Washington Times *expressed considerable disgust with the doubleheader loss.*

The transgressions began in the very first frame when the Yankees' Bert Daniels led off against Bert Gallia. Gallia was wild and hit Daniels in the ribs. Harry Wolter then singled before Birdie Cree absorbed a pitch on the leg to fill the sacks. Gallia then hit Gossett, forcing in New York's first run. That made three hit-batsmen of the first four batters. Washington manager Clark Griffith had seen enough and sent moundsman Joe Engel to the rescue. Engel didn't hit anyone else in this inning but gave up two singles to send off New York with a 4–0 lead.

In the second inning, Engel became infected with the homicidal impulse and beaned leadoff batter Daniels. Daniels was not seriously hurt although this was the second time he had led off an inning, and the

second time he had been hit by a pitched ball. After an error and a sacrifice, Dick Gossett stepped to the plate. He too had been hit in the first inning, and like Daniels, was again drilled with a pitch, this time on the arm. The inning ended after two more singles, the second of which led to a rare double play. With Gossett on second and Roy Hartzell on first, Roger Peckinpaugh lashed a single to right. Danny Moeller came up quickly with the ball and fired a strike to catcher Rip Williams. Gossett, seeing the accurate throw, retreated toward third, but Williams tossed to third baseman Frank LaPorte to nip him. Meanwhile Hartzell, thinking Gossett would score, had taken a wide turn around second. LaPorte relayed to second baseman Morgan who tagged

Hartzell, completing the twin-killing. The Yankees had then been hit-by-pitches five times in the first two innings, yet there was no incidence of altercation.

The third frame began with a Babe Borton double, an out, and an Al Schulz RBI-single. Then, up stepped Bert Daniels, who had been abused by two different pitchers in each of his first two plate appearances. Now, he faced the third Washington hurler, Tom Hughes. Hughes followed his teammates' example and also drilled Daniels, although this time in the chest. The inning ended when Gossett, who

twice had been hit by a pitch, fanned. There were no further incidents in the game.

In all the sources checked for this game, there wasn't any mention of "bad blood," a fight, or retaliation. The New York pitchers didn't hit a batter the entire game. Instead, four of the Yankee hit-batsmen scored as the club used this doubleheader victory to help claw their way out of the basement by season's end. And, Bert Daniels lived to play one more major league season.

Note: There were no hit batsmen in the first game.

SECOND GAME

New York Yankees	AB	R	H	I	PO	A	E
>Bert Daniels rf	2	3	1	0	5	0	0
Harry Wolter cf	5	2	1	0	2	0	0
Birdie Cree lf	3	1	3	1	0	0	0
Dick Gossett c	3	1	0	1	3	0	0
Roy Hartzell 3b	5	0	3	2	2	1	0
Roger Peckinpaugh ss	5	0	1	0	3	5	1
Babe Borton 1b	5	1	3	2	9	1	0
Claud Derrick 2b	5	0	1	1	3	4	0
Al Schulz p	4	1	1	1	0	1	0
	37	9	14	8	27	12	1

Washington Nationals	AB	R	H	I	PO	A	E
>Danny Moeller rf	4	0	0	0	1	1	1
Ray Morgan 2b	2	1	0	0	2	3	0
Clyde Milan cf	4	0	1	0	3	1	0
Chick Gandil 1b	4	0	2	1	8	1	0
Frank LaPorte 3b	4	0	0	0	2	2	0
Howard Shanks lf	4	0	1	0	3	0	0
George McBride ss	1	0	0	0	2	0	0
Joe Gedeon ss5	2	2	1	0	1	1	0
Rip Williams c	4	0	1	0	5	1	0
Bert Gallia p	0	0	0	0	0	0	0
Joe Engel p1	0	0	0	0	0	1	1
Long Tom Hughes p3	3	0	1	1	0	2	0
Walter Johnson ph9	0	0	0	1	0	0	0
	32	3	7	3	27	13	2

New York	IP	H	R	ER	BB	SO
Schulz W,2-7	9	7	3	3	4	2

Washington	IP	H	R	ER	BB	SO
Gallia L,0-3	0	1	4	4	0	0
Engel	1.1	3	2	2	0	0
Hughes	7.2	10	3	2	1	2
	9	14	9	8	1	2

New York	4 2 2	0 1 0	0 0 0	- 9
Washington	1 0 0	0 1 0	0 0 1	- 3

OB: New York 10, Washington 7
DP: Derrick-Peckinpaugh-Borton
    Derrick-Borton
    Schulz-Derrick-Borton
    Moeller-Williams-LaPorte-Morgan
2B: Cree, Borton, Schulz, Williams
3B: Gedeon, Hughes
SB: Daniels, Hartzell
SO: Gossett, Peckinpaugh, Moeller 2
BB: Schulz, Moeller, Morgan 2,
    Gedeon
SH: Daniels, Cree

SF: Johnson
HP: By Gallia (Daniels, Cree,
    Gossett), by Engel (Daniels,
    Gossett), by Hughes (Daniels)
TIME: 1:55
ATTENDANCE: 8,000
UMPIRES: Ed McGreevy, Tom Connolly
SOURCES: DBD; New York American,
    Times; Washington Evening Star,
    Herald, Post, Times

BALANCE	OUT+R+OB=BP=AB+BB+SH+HP+CI
New York	27 9 10 46 37 1 2 6 0
Washington	27 3 7 37 32 4 1 0 0

----

37. Pitcher Walks 15 in Less Than Eight Innings

PHILADELPHIA   at   DETROIT
(Athletics, 16)   (Tigers, 9)

Saturday, July 12, 1913, Navin Field

In an era when baseball games usually were completed in less than two hours, this day's contest tried the patience of Tiger fans. Not only were they forced to witness a three hour rout of the home club; they also had to sit through a 23-walk performance by the two pitching staffs. Leading this pitiful exhibition was the Athletics' Carroll "Boardwalk" Brown.

Boardwalk Brown acquired his nickname when Connie Mack's scouts discovered him pitching on the sandlots surrounding Atlantic City, New Jersey. On this day, Boardwalk gave new meaning to that moniker by hosting his own walking parade, for *in only 7⅔ innings, Brown issued 15 free passes*, the most by any hurler in any game since the turn of the century to that time.

In Detroit this day, a swirling wind gave the outfielders plenty of trouble. Those same gusts were a major concern for Boardwalk Brown, who just couldn't locate home plate. Under normal conditions, a performance such as Brown's would have provided an express ticket to the showers. But thanks to his teammates' offensive firepower, and the Tigers' atrocious fielding, the Athletics jumped off to an early lead which they never relinquished. This enabled manager Mack to be even more patient than he normally was.

Detroit's rookie outfielder, Hugh High, had been providing the Tigers with some additional offense while Ty Cobb missed a week with an injured knee. So when Ty returned to action, Manager Hughie Jennings kept High in the lineup and moved Cobb, at his own request, to second base for the first time in his nine-year career. The move was

disastrous. Of five fielding chances, Ty misplayed three of them. Cobb got a putout in the opening frame when he tagged Frank Baker attempting to steal, and his first assist in the ninth when he also tossed out Baker on a ground ball. Mingled with his two successes, Ty booted three grounders. On another occasion he failed to cover the initial sack when first baseman Del Gainer fielded a Philadelphia bunt attempt, but was not assessed an error.

Cobb erred on the first play of the game, propelling the A's on their way to a three-run opening frame. Brown then retired the Tigers in the bottom half of the inning with only one hit and no walks. It was the only inning in which he did not allow a base on balls.

Brown was helped by some terrific Philadelphia fielding and terrible Detroit baserunning, and seemed to bear down in the critical situations. In both the sixth and seventh innings, he walked three men without being scored upon either time. Of his 15 walks, nine were issued after two were out, and only one of those scored. The Tigers left 17 runners on base including the bases loaded three times and two runners twice. They also ran themselves out of potential run scoring situations three times. In the third, Cobb was caught stealing home while Detroit was trailing 5–0. In the sixth, with the sacks jammed, Red McKee failed to exert himself trying to score on a sacrifice fly and was doubled at the plate. And finally in the ninth, Bobby Veach squelched a Tiger rally when he was caught stealing second.

Despite being labeled "the Boxman from Borneo" by *The Detroit News Tribune*,

Boardwalk Brown got caught in a Detroit whirlwind.

Boardwalk Brown was not such an uncivilized hurler in 1913. Discounting this debacle, Brown furnished a discreet 2.8 walks per nine innings. A 17–11 record this season was also his personal best during a five-year major league career.

Philadelphia Athletics	AB	R	H	I	PO	A	E
Eddie Murphy rf	5	2	1	0	1	0	0
Rube Oldring lf	6	2	2	0	2	0	0
Eddie Collins 2b	4	4	2	2	1	4	0
Frank Baker 3b	5	2	4	5	0	0	0
Stuffy McInnis 1b	5	2	1	0	8	0	0
Amos Strunk cf	5	1	1	2	3	1	0
Jack Barry ss	5	0	2	4	6	4	0

Detroit Tigers	AB	R	H	I	PO	A	E
Donie Bush ss	5	1	1	0	0	1	1
Ossie Vitt 3b	4	3	2	0	3	2	0
Sam Crawford rf	5	2	3	2	1	0	1
Ty Cobb 2b	3	2	2	1	1	1	3
Bobby Veach lf	4	0	1	1	3	0	2
Del Gainer 1b	4	1	1	1	9	1	0
Red McKee c	3	0	2	1	8	1	0

Philadelphia Athletics	AB	R	H	I	PO	A	E
>Jack Lapp c	5	2	1	0	6	1	0
Boardwalk Brown p	4	1	1	0	0	3	0
Eddie Plank p8	1	0	0	0	0	0	0
	45	16	15	13	27	13	0

Detroit Tigers	AB	R	H	I	PO	A	E
Henri Rondeau ph9	1	0	0	0	0	0	0
>Hugh High cf	3	0	1	2	1	0	0
Jean Dubuc p	2	0	0	0	1	4	0
Will House p7	0	0	0	0	0	2	0
Wally Pipp ph8	1	0	0	0	0	0	0
Oscar Stanage ph8	1	0	1	0	0	0	0
Les Hennessey pr8	0	0	0	0	0	0	0
Joe Lake p9	0	0	0	0	0	0	0
	36	9	14	8	27	12	7

Philadelphia	IP	H	R	ER	BB	SO
Brown W,10-4	7.2	10	5	5	15	3
Plank	1.1	4	4	4	1	2
	9	14	9	9	16	5

Detroit	IP	H	R	ER	BB	SO
Dubuc L,6-9	6	10	9	5	3	4
House	2	1	1	1	3	1
Lake	1	4	6	3	1	0
	9	15	16	9	7	5

Philadelphia 3 0 2 1 3 0 0 1 6 -16
Detroit   0 0 0 0 1 0 0 5 3 - 9

OB: Philadelphia 10, Detroit 17
DP: Strunk-Collins-Lapp (Vitt)
    Brown-Barry-McInnis (McKee)
    Collins-Barry-McInnis (Veach)
2B: Baker, Strunk, Vitt
3B: Barry, Crawford, McKee
SB: Collins, Cobb, Veach, Strunk
CS: Baker, Veach, Cobb
SO: Strunk, Lapp, Brown 3, Veach,
    Gainer, Rondeau, High 2
BB: Murphy, Collins 2, Barry, Lapp,
    McInnis, Strunk, Bush, Vitt 2,
    Crawford, Cobb 2, Veach 2, Dubuc

BB: Gainer 2, McKee 2, High 3
SF: Cobb
HP: By Dubuc (Baker)
WP: Plank
PB: McKee 2
TIME: 2:53
ATTENDANCE: 6,184
UMPIRES: George Hildebrand, Silk
    O'Loughlin
SOURCES: Detroit Free Press, News-
    Tribune; DBD; Philadelphia Evening
    Telegraph, Inquirer, Press, Record

BALANCE	OUT+R+OB=BP+AB+BB+SH+HP+CI
Philadelphia	27 16 10 53 45 7 0 1 0
Detroit	27 9 17 53 36 16 1 0 0

Giants Get Fourteen Hits But Can't Score

38. Team Gets 14 Hits in Shutout Loss

NEW YORK, NL   at   CHICAGO
(Giants, 0)   (Cubs, 7)

Sunday, September 14, 1913, West Side Grounds

A pair of pitchers, each looking for his 20th win, drew an overflow crowd in Chicago on a pleasant Sunday afternoon. Rube Marquard took the hill for John McGraw's visiting Giants, who were soon to clinch their third straight pennant. For the hometown Cubs, ace Larry Cheney was looking to lead his club, now 13 games out, to a possible runner-up position. Neither hurler threw particularly well, especially Cheney, who gave up 14 hits. But mixed with an ample dose of good fortune, Larry was able

Cheney achieved a miracle shutout.

to call on his reserve to escape one Giant rally after another and toss a very unlikely shutout. *It was the most hits allowed in a shutout victory* and has yet to be surpassed, although it was once duplicated (see 7-10-28).

The largest Cubs attendance of the season watched the Giants get hits in every inning except the ninth, yet only one of their runners ever reached third base. Reckless base running took its toll as four potential run-scoring rallies were squelched:

• Leading off the game for the Giants, Fred Snodgrass singled but was tossed out attempting to steal by catcher Jimmy Archer. Fred argued the call until he was banished by umpire Cy Rigler, setting in motion a series of substitutions and position switches by manager McGraw. Larry Doyle was the victim of the second out, but the third batter,

Art Fletcher, also singled. Like Snodgrass, Fletcher unsuccessfully tested Archer's throwing arm and was out attempting to steal.

• George Burns started the second frame with a sharp single to left but foolishly tried to stretch his hit into a double. Wildfire Schulte threw him out by 20 feet. Tillie Shafer then singled and Red Murray forced him at second. Chief Meyers rapped out the third single of the inning, sending Murray to second, but the stanza ended when Fred Merkle grounded out.

• The third inning resulted in more frustration for the New Yorkers. After Rube Marquard led off with another single, Moose McCormick flied out routinely. Doyle then garnered the seventh single for the Giants, sending Marquard to second. Next, Fletcher sent a sharp grounder to Red Corriden who fumbled it for the game's only error, loading the bases with just one out. Cheney, however, was equal to the task. Down on a swinging third strike went George Burns, followed by a called third strike on Shafer.

• Shafer opened the sixth with the Giants' tenth single of the contest. Just as he started to steal, Cheney threw to his first baseman, Vic Saier, who threw out Shafer at second. After Murray struck out, Meyers hit a long double, which would have scored Shafer. Merkle ended the frame with an out.

Player-manager Johnny Evers' name appears in the Chicago boxscore because he was on the field for the first pitch. After that, Cheney preferred that the ball in play be scuffed a little more and began rubbing it in the dirt around the mound. When umpire Rigler called a halt to the activity, Evers protested vehemently and was ejected.

New York Giants	AB	R	H	I	PO	A	E
Fred Snodgrass cf	1	0	1	0	0	0	0
Moose McCormick rf1	3	0	0	0	2	0	0
Art Fromme p7	0	0	0	0	0	3	0
Jim Thorpe ph9	1	0	0	0	0	0	0
>Larry Doyle 2b	5	0	2	0	4	0	0
Art Fletcher ss	4	0	2	0	1	1	0
George Burns lf	4	0	1	0	2	0	0
Tillie Shafer 3b,cf7	4	0	2	0	0	2	0
Red Murray rf,cf1,rf7	4	0	0	0	4	1	0
Chief Meyers c	4	0	3	0	2	3	0
Fred Merkle 1b	4	0	1	0	8	1	0
Rube Marquard p	2	0	1	0	0	1	0
Buck Herzog ph7,3b7	2	0	1	0	1	0	0
	38	0	14	0	24	12	0

Chicago Cubs	AB	R	H	I	PO	A	E
Tommy Leach cf	4	3	3	1	0	0	0
Johnny Evers 2b	0	0	0	0	0	0	0
Red Corriden 2b1	3	1	1	0	3	3	1
Wildfire Schulte lf	4	0	2	2	1	1	0
Art Phelan 3b	3	1	1	2	2	1	0
Vic Saier 1b	4	0	1	1	9	1	0
>Wilbur Good rf	4	0	1	1	3	0	0
Al Bridwell ss	2	0	0	0	3	3	0
Jimmy Archer c	3	1	2	0	6	2	0
Larry Cheney p	2	1	0	0	0	4	0
	29	7	11	7	27	15	1

New York	IP	H	R	ER	BB	SO
Marquard L,19-10	6	5	3	3	1	0
Fromme	2	6	4	4	1	0
	8	11	7	7	2	0

Chicago	IP	H	R	ER	BB	SO
Cheney W,20-12	9	14	0	0	0	4

New York	0 0 0	0 0 0	0 0 0	- 0
Chicago	1 0 0	0 0 2	0 4 x	- 7

OB: New York 11, Chicago 2
2B: Meyers, Leach, Schulte, Archer
CS: Snodgrass, Fletcher, Shafer, Saier
SO: Burns, Shafer, McCormick, Murray
BB: Phelan, Bridwell
SH: Corriden, Cheney

TIME: 2:00
ATTENDANCE: 22,000
UMPIRES: Cy Rigler, Bill Klem
SOURCES: Chicago Inter-Ocean, Record-Herald, Tribune; New York Times

BALANCE	OUT	+R	+OB	=BP	=AB	+BB	+SH	+HP	+CI
New York	27	0	11	38	38	0	0	0	0
Chicago	24	7	2	33	29	2	2	0	0

Frivolity—Johnson Pays the Price

39. Pitcher Loses
All-Time ERA Single Season Record

BOSTON   at   WASHINGTON
(Red Sox, 9)   (Nationals, 10)

Saturday, October 4, 1913, Griffith Stadium

Before this contest had even begun, there was an air of absurdity surrounding it. The day before, two of Boston's regular outfielders, Harry Hooper and Duffy Lewis, each took a turn on the mound for the only time in their careers. For the Nationals (formerly and later called Senators), pitchers Rex

Dawson and Doc Hedgpeth made the only major league appearances of their lives. Now facing the last game of the season, each team was already locked into its final league standing—host Washington in second, visiting Boston in fourth. The game meant little. *The Washington Evening Star* even predicted

Hooper left early.

Boston also contributed to the levity by starting outfielder Duffy Lewis at third base (the only occasion in 1,459 career games), and Charley "Sea Lion" Hall, a pitcher, at second base.

Before the game was concluded, Nationals players had switched positions within innings, stood with their backs to the batter, and on one occasion, all the Washington fielders stood huddled around second base while pitches were being thrown. Germany Schaefer, a noted clown, was right in his element. Although he was responsible for patrolling right field, he spent most of the game in the infield, between first and second. *The Washington Post* described his infrequent visits to the right-field garden with feigning sleep in the grass or perching atop a "bull sign." Outfielder Howard Shanks eventually occupied the shortstop position, catcher Eddie Ainsmith pitched and played second base, and backstop John Henry guarded first.

Griffith had been a seven-time, 20-game winner but hadn't pitched a full inning in the major leagues in four years. Nevertheless, amid a thunderous ovation, he took the hill in the eighth inning. Leading off, Boston's Wally Rehg lofted a hit over Walter Johnson's head in center field but was thrown out at the plate. Griffith, "The Old Fox," then retired the next two batters in routine fashion. Later, he placed himself in peril by occupying right field where he was not only hit on the head by a ball, but allowed an inside-the-park home run. No error was charged on either mishap.

Griffith's batterymate was Jack Ryan, just a month shy of his 45th birthday. Jack, now a coach, hadn't played regularly for ten years but quickly made himself at home by tagging out two runners at the plate attempting to stretch triples into home runs.

The first eight innings, however, were only a prelude to the rowdy ninth. With a 10–3 lead, the Nationals felt confident of victory,

the two teams would "go along and hustle for a few innings, but at the finish it will be turned into a farce. The players will be shifted about in various positions for which they were never intended and it is not unlikely that Griffith won't pitch for an inning or so." ("Griffith" was Clark Griffith, once a star 19th-century pitcher, now nearly 44, Washington's manager and part owner.)

The forecast was frighteningly accurate except that the Nationals didn't wait for a few serious innings. In the starting lineup for Washington were the following:

• Merito Acosta, a 17 year old outfielder.

• Walter "The Big Train" Johnson, 36 wins and 7 losses, starting in center field and batting fourth.

• Mutt Williams, in the first game of his career, on the mound.

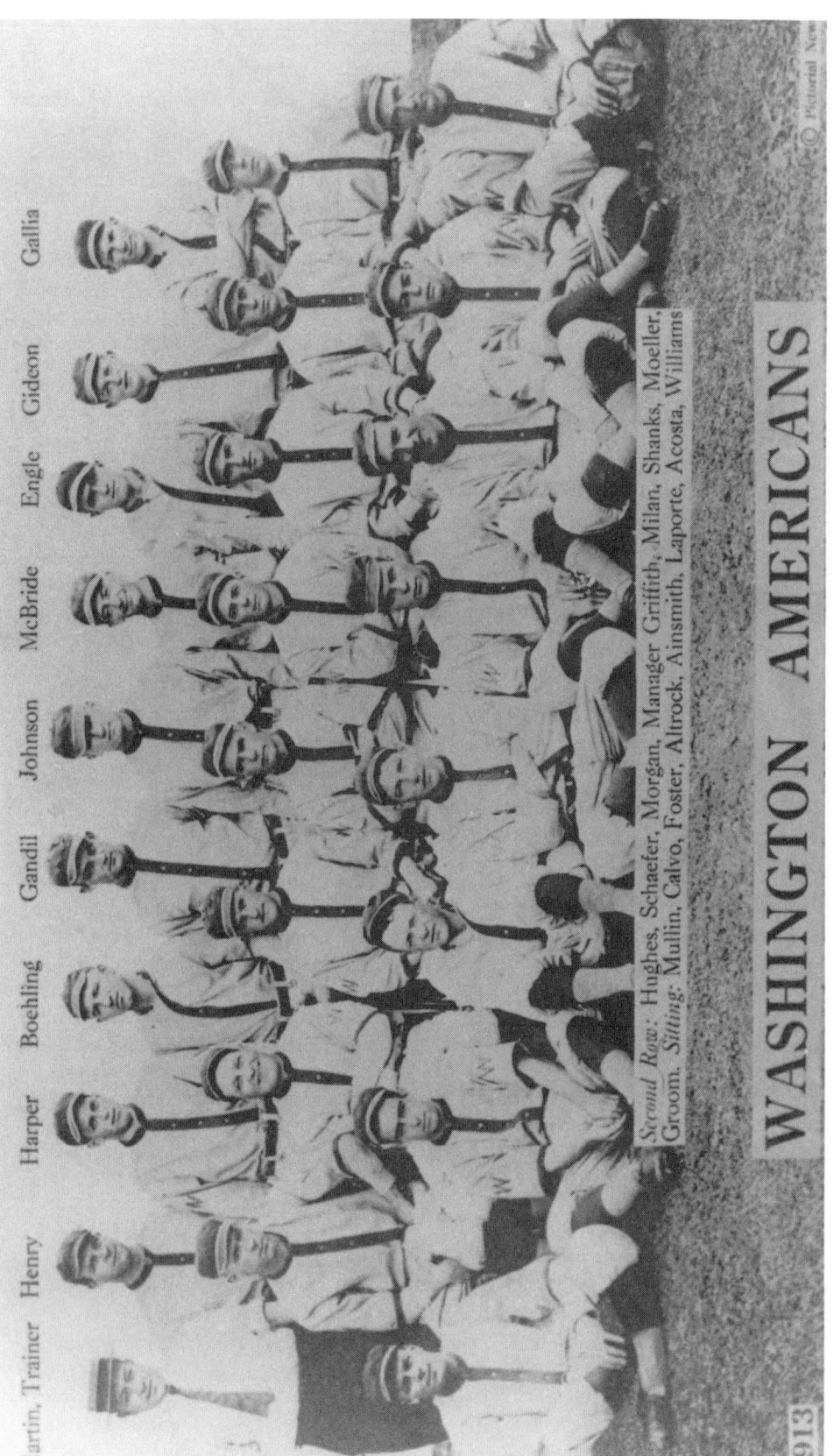

Martin, Trainer   Henry   Harper   Boehling   Gandill   Johnson   McBride   Engle   Gideon   Gallia

WASHINGTON AMERICANS

Second Row: Hughes, Schaefer, Morgan, Manager Griffith, Milan, Shanks, Moeller, Groom. Sitting: Mullin, Calvo, Foster, Altrock, Ainsmith, Laporte, Acosta, Williams

1913

© Pictorial News

The 1913 Washington Americans

so from right field walked Germany Schaefer to pitch the final frame. Schaefer's twirling career had spanned all of two-thirds of an inning the previous season. This year he was even less proficient — he didn't get anyone out. According to *The Boston Globe*, here's how the last half-inning unfolded:

• With Schaefer pitching, Boston's Duffy Lewis led off with a bunt single.

• Walter Johnson replaced Schaefer and lobbed in a few, allowing Clyde Engle (single) and Steve Yerkes (double) to fatten their batting averages, Yerkes getting two RBIs.

• Schaefer, seeing that The Big Train wasn't taking his task seriously, *returned* to the mound. He was greeted by Hal Janvrin's high drive off the right-field scoreboard. Before the aged Griffith could retrieve the ball, Janvrin had circled the bases with a two-run home run.

• Wally Snell then singled and stole his only base of the season. With this, Schaefer realized he didn't have his best "stuff" and relinquished the mound to *catcher* Ed Ainsmith who had been playing second base.

• Ainsmith, making the *only* pitching appearance of his 15-year career, served up triples to both "Pinch" Thomas (RBI) and Wally Rehg (RBI). Rehg, for the second time in the game, was thrown out at the plate trying to stretch his triple into a four-bagger. His run would have tied the "game."

• The situation then got somewhat serious as Boston trailed by only 10–9, and still there was just one out. To the rescue came 19-year-old Joe Gedeon who had *never* pitched, and would *never again* pitch in the major leagues. Gedeon was golden in his only major league appearance as he got Bill Mundy to fly out to Johnson in center.

• The next scheduled Boston batter was Harry Hooper, hitting in the third position. Harry was nowhere to be found, however, as he had gone to the showers at the start of the inning. So, up to the plate stepped the clean-up batter, Duffy Lewis. No one seemed to notice Hooper's absence as Lewis grounded out, Shanks to Williams, thus ending one of the most disgraceful half-innings in modern baseball history.

Scoring this game was a nightmare for all attending reporters. Of the Nationals, only Shanks, Ryan, A. Williams and Acosta played the same position for the entire ninth inning. (It is possible that Griffith moved to center for a batter or two.) In addition to the continual position switching of the players, the umpires, Tom Connolly and Bill Dinneen, were also drawn into the tomfoolery, permitting four outs in several innings. Even the "official" scorer lost his head. In the surviving official league records, there are painful omissions. Several Washington players did not have their batting statistics recorded, and only Boston's Fred Anderson

Washington Fielding Positions on October 4, 1913

Inn	P	C	1B	2B	3B	SS	LF	CF	RF
1	D.Williams	Henry	Gandil	Morgan	Foster	McBride	Acosta	Johnson	Moeller
2	D.Williams	Henry	Gandil	Morgan	Foster	McBride	Acosta	Johnson	Moeller
3	D.Williams	Henry	Gandil	Morgan	Foster	McBride	Acosta	Johnson	Moeller
4	D.Williams	Henry	A.Williams	Ainsmith	McBride	Shanks	Acosta	Johnson	Schaefer
					Shanks	McBride			
5	Bentley	A.Williams	Henry	Ainsmith	Gedeon	Shanks	Acosta	Johnson	Schaefer
6	Bentley	A.Williams	Henry	Ainsmith	Gedeon	Shanks	Acosta	Johnson	Schaefer
7	Engel	A.Williams	Henry	Ainsmith	Gedeon	Shanks	Acosta	Johnson	Schaefer
8	Griffith	Ryan	A.Williams	Ainsmith	Gedeon	Shanks	Acosta	Johnson	Schaefer
9; batter 1	Schaefer	Ryan	A.Williams	Ainsmith	Gedeon	Shanks	Acosta	Johnson	Griffith
9; batters 2&3	Johnson	Ryan	A.Williams	Ainsmith	Gedeon	Shanks	Acosta	Schaefer	Griffith
9; batters 4&5	Schaefer	Ryan	A.Williams	Ainsmith	Gedeon	Shanks	Acosta	Johnson	Griffith
9; batters 6&7	Ainsmith	Ryan	A.Williams	Schaefer	Gedeon	Shanks	Acosta	Johnson	Griffith
9; batters 8&9	Gedeon	Ryan	A.Williams	Schaefer	Ainsmith	Shanks	Acosta	Johnson	Griffith

Boston Red Sox	AB	R	H	I	PO	A	E
Wally Rehg lf	4	0	3	1	0	1	0
Bill Mundy 1b	5	0	0	0	12	2	1
*Harry Hooper cf	4	1	0	0	2	2	0
>Duffy Lewis 3b	4	1	3	0	2	2	0
Clyde Engle rf	4	2	4	1	0	0	0
Charley Hall 2b	1	0	0	0	0	2	0
Steve Yerkes 2b6	2	1	1	2	0	4	0
Hal Janvrin ss	3	2	2	4	2	3	0
Wally Snell c	4	1	1	0	6	2	0
Fred Anderson p	3	0	0	0	0	3	0
Pinch Thomas ph9	1	1	1	1	0	0	0
	35	9	15	9	24	21	1

Lewis batted last in Hooper's position. AB assigned to Hooper.

Washington Nationals	AB	R	H	I	PO	A	E
Merito Acosta lf	4	2	1	0	1	0	0
Danny Moeller rf	2	2	2	1	0	0	0
G. Schaefer rf,p,cf,2b	3	0	2	2	3	1	0
Eddie Foster 3b	3	1	2	1	1	0	0
> Joe Gedeon 3b,p	2	0	0	0	0	0	0
Walter Johnson cf,p,cf	3	2	2	1	2	2	0
Chick Gandil 1b	2	0	2	1	2	1	0
A. "Rip" Williams 1b,c	0	1	0	0	4	3	0
Ray Morgan 2b	2	0	0	0	3	0	0
E. Ainsmith 2b,p,3b	2	0	0	0	2	1	0
John Henry c,1b	3	1	2	1	3	2	0
Jack Ryan c	1	0	0	0	2	1	0
Geo. McBride ss,3b	2	0	2	1	2	2	0
Howard Shanks ss,3b	2	0	1	0	1	3	0
D. "Mutt" Williams p	2	1	1	0	1	2	1
Jack Bentley p	1	0	0	0	0	1	0
Joe Engel p	0	0	0	0	0	0	0
C. Griffith p,rf	1	0	1	1	0	1	0
	35	10	18	9	27	20	1

Boston	IP	H	R	ER	BB	SO
Anderson L,0-6	8	18	10	8	3	3

Washington	IP	H	R	ER	BB	SO
D. Williams W,1-0	4	5	3	2	2	1
Bentley	2	1	0	0	0	0
Engel	1	1	0	0	1	1
Griffith	1	1	0	0	0	0
Schaefer	0	3	3	3	0	0
Johnson	0	2	2	2	0	0
Ainsmith	.1	2	1	1	0	0
Gedeon	.2	0	0	0	0	0
	9	15	9	8	3	2

```
Boston        0 2 0   1 0 0   0 0 6   - 9
Washington    3 0 2   3 1 0   1 0 x   -10
```

OB: Boston 3, Washington 5
DP: Lewis-Mundy-Snell
    D. Williams-McBride-Gandil
2B: Yerkes, Johnson, Griffith
3B: Rehg 2, Thomas, Acosta, Foster, Henry 2
HR: Janvrin 2(3)
SB: Rehg, Lewis 2, Snell, Acosta, Moeller, Johnson 2, Gandil 2, Shanks, D.Williams
CS: Lewis
SO: C. Hall, Anderson, Johnson, Ainsmith 2

BB: Rehg, Hooper, Janvrin, Acosta,
    Johnson, A. Williams
SH: C. Hall, A. Williams
PB: Ryan
TIME: 1:50
ATTENDANCE: 8,000
UMPIRES: Tommy Connolly, Bill Dinneen
SOURCES: Boston Globe, Herald; DBD;
    Washington Evening Star, Herald,
    Post, Times

BALANCE	OUT	+R	+OB	=BP	=AB	+BB	+SH	+HP	+CI
Boston	27	9	3	39	35	3	1	0	0
Washington	24	10	5	39	35	3	1	0	0

and Washington's Joe Engel had their pitching totals registered. Also, because of this confusion and the lack of inning-by-inning detail, just playing positions are listed along-side each player in the boxscore. A separate table is shown with Washington players' fielding positions. It has been gleaned, piecemeal, from all of the listed sources.

Whether purposely or accidentally, Walter Johnson's pitching contributions to this fiasco were among those never recorded on the official sheets. Johnson was credited with a season 1.09 ERA, and that's the way it stood for decades. The record was his for having recorded the lowest single-season ERA for anyone pitching 300+ innings.

Many years later, however, this game's omission was discovered, and with both runners scoring that Johnson had faced, his 1913 ERA swelled to 1.14. That still would have been the single season record for pitchers hurling 300+ innings had it not been for a phenomenal season generations later by St. Louis Cardinals' ace Bob Gibson. Gibson bewildered the National League in 1968 with a 1.12 ERA. Thus, the Big Train was robbed of the all-time, single-season ERA record by his own horseplay.

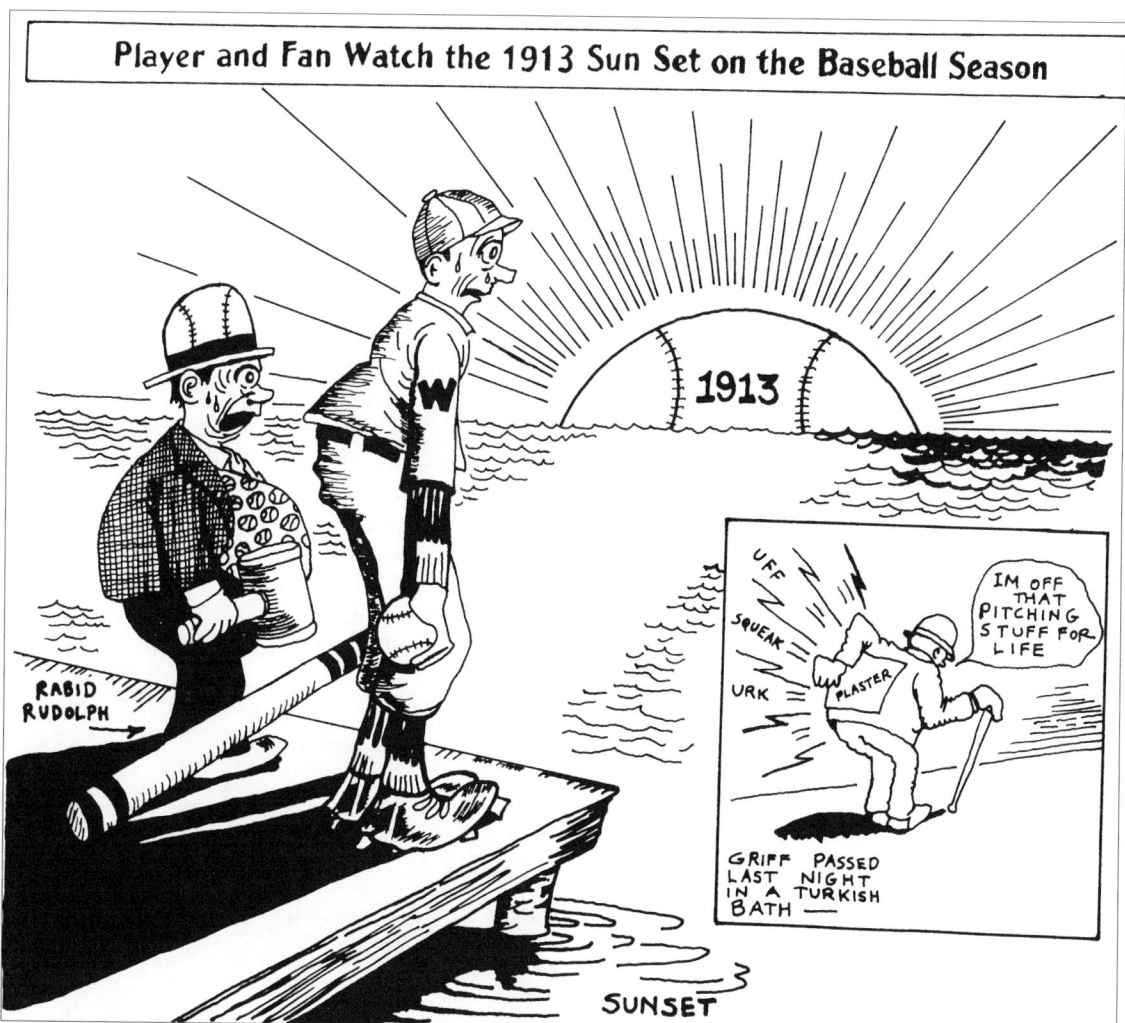

The Washington Times *expressed the sentiments of the fans, players, and Clarke Griffith.*

Doubleheader Futility

40. Teams Combine for 11 Hits in Doubleheader

DETROIT   at   ST. LOUIS
(Tigers, 2,0)   (Browns, 1,2)

Saturday, May 30, 1914, Sportsman's Park

St. Louis was brimming with professional baseball activity on this Memorial Day. The city's entrant in the newly formed Federal League, the Terriers, were entertaining the Kansas City Packers in a doubleheader at Handlan's Park. The same number of games were also scheduled for Sportsman's Park, where the Browns were hosting the Detroit Tigers. Both confrontations ended as splits, but the American League games provided a lasting record in futility, for *both clubs combined to collect a grand total of just 11 hits in the doubleheader, the all time record low.* This was the personification of dead-ball-era baseball.

In the opener, Detroit's Harry Coveleski took the hill for the visitors, while the Browns' Earl Hamilton defended the home turf. Both were good dead-ball hurlers, but neither was especially brilliant this year. They each had a commendable ERA of about 2.50 and allowed just under 8 hits per game. (Dutch Leonard this year had a 0.96 ERA and allowed just 5.5 hits per game). The contest was a pitchers duel right from the start, there being just one hit in the first four innings and five total safeties by the time the last out was made.

Coveleski pitched a brilliant one-hitter, allowing a solitary hit in the fifth inning by Tilly Walker. Walker opened that frame by ripping a double down the left field line and moving to third on John Leary's sacrifice. Buzzy Wares followed with a squeeze attempt, but Walker retreated, and amidst the confusion, Buzzy was safe on a close play at first. While the entire Tiger infield argued with first base umpire Bill Dinneen, Wares pilfered the unguarded middle sack, much to the delight of the hometown fans. With first

base then open, Coveleski purposely walked Sam Agnew. Next, pitcher Earl Hamilton watched a called third strike pass him by for the second out. When Ivon Howard rolled one to Moriarty at third, it looked as if Coveleski would escape unscathed, but George booted it. All hands were safe as Walker crossed the dish with the first run of the game. Jimmy Austin then ended the inning by popping out to second.

The Tigers finally reached Hamilton for two runs in the eighth. An error by Austin put Bobby Veach on first. After George Burns fouled out, Moriarty coaxed a pass, and both runners moved up on a passed ball. Oscar Stanage singled home Veach, and Coveleski did the same for Moriarty. All the runs in this game were unearned, and it ended with Detroit on top, 2–1.

The second encounter matched the Browns' ace, Carl Weilman, against the Tigers' fifth starter, Alex Main. Main was relieved after eight innings, but both he and his adversary

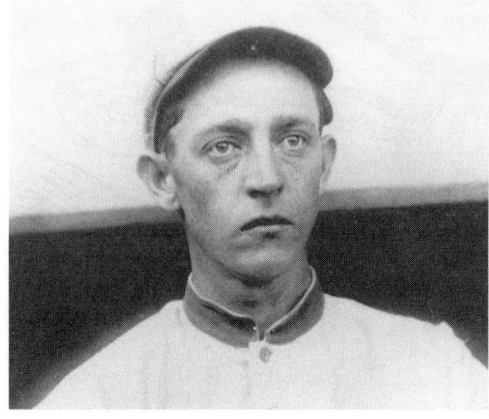

Clarence "Tilly" Walker, Browns' hero with a hit and run scored in each game.

pitched well. The Browns won this one, 2–0, with both runs scoring in the seventh. Again it was Tilly Walker who started the rally with a triple to right-center field. He scored moments later on a sacrifice fly by Leary. Wares next struck out but reached first when Stanage missed the ball. An aborted pick-off attempt sent him all the way to third, and he arrived home on a squeeze bunt by Frank Crossin. For the game, the Tigers and Browns could each muster just three safeties, bringing the grand total for both teams in the doubleheader to 11, the all-time record low. Contributing to the paucity of hits was the absence of Ty Cobb from the Detroit lineup. Cobb had suffered a cracked rib when hit by a pitch on May 18 and didn't return to action until June 5.

FIRST GAME

Detroit Tigers	AB	R	H	I	PO	A	E
Donie Bush ss	4	0	0	0	4	4	0
Marty Kavanagh 2b	4	0	0	0	2	2	0
Hugh High cf	3	0	1	0	1	0	0
Sam Crawford rf	4	0	0	0	1	0	0
Bobby Veach lf	4	1	1	0	3	0	0
>George Burns 1b	4	0	0	0	9	0	0
George Moriarty 3b	2	1	0	0	0	5	1
Oscar Stanage c	3	0	1	1	7	0	0
Harry Coveleski p	3	0	1	1	0	0	1
	31	2	4	2	27	11	2

St. Louis Browns	AB	R	H	I	PO	A	E
Ivon Howard cf	3	0	0	0	2	0	0
Jimmy Austin 3b	4	0	0	0	2	0	1
Del Pratt 2b	4	0	0	0	3	3	0
Gus Williams rf	3	0	0	0	1	0	0
Eddie Miller ph9	0	0	0	0	0	0	0
Tilly Walker lf	4	1	1	0	2	0	0
>John Leary 1b	3	0	0	0	10	1	0
Buzzy Wares ss	3	0	0	0	4	3	0
Sam Agnew c	2	0	0	0	3	1	0
Earl Hamilton p	3	0	0	0	0	1	0
	29	1	1	0	27	9	1

Detroit	IP	H	R	ER	BB	SO
Coveleski W,4-4	9	1	1	0	3	7

St. Louis	IP	H	R	ER	BB	SO
Hamilton L,6-5	9	4	2	0	1	2

Detroit 0 0 0 0 0 0 0 2 0 - 2
St.Louis 0 0 0 0 1 0 0 0 0 - 1

OB: Detroit 4, St. Louis 5
2B: Walker
SB: Wares
CS: Veach
BB: Moriarty, Howard, Agnew (I), Miller
SH: Leary

HP: By Hamilton (High)
PB: Agnew
TIME: 1:45
ATTENDANCE: 14,000
UMPIRES: Tommy Connolly, Bill Dinneen

BALANCE	OUT	+R	+OB	=BP	=AB	+BB	+SH	+HP	+CI
Detroit	27	2	4	33	31	1	0	1	0
St. Louis	27	1	5	33	29	3	1	0	0

SECOND GAME

Detroit Tigers	AB	R	H	I	PO	A	E
Donie Bush ss	4	0	0	0	2	3	0
Marty Kavanagh 2b	4	0	1	0	2	4	0
Hugh High cf	3	0	0	0	1	0	0
> Harry Heilmann ph9	1	0	0	0	0	0	0
Sam Crawford rf	3	0	2	0	1	0	0
Bobby Veach lf	3	0	0	0	0	0	0
George Burns 1b	3	0	0	0	13	1	0
George Moriarty 3b	3	0	0	0	1	2	0
Oscar Stanage c	3	0	0	0	2	1	1
Alex Main p	2	0	0	0	1	6	1
Jean Dubuc ph8	1	0	0	0	0	0	0
Mark Hall p8	0	0	0	0	1	0	0
	30	0	3	0	24	17	2

St. Louis Browns	AB	R	H	I	PO	A	E
Burt Shotton cf	3	0	1	0	3	0	0
Jimmy Austin 3b	3	0	0	0	1	2	0
Del Pratt 2b	4	0	0	0	0	2	1
>Gus Williams rf	4	0	0	0	2	0	0
Tilly Walker lf	1	1	1	0	2	0	0
John Leary 1b	2	0	1	1	12	1	0
Buzzy Wares ss	2	1	0	0	1	2	0
Frank Crossin c	1	0	0	1	5	0	0
Carl Weilman p	3	0	0	0	1	3	0
	23	2	3	2	27	10	1

Detroit	IP	H	R	ER	BB	SO
Main L,4-2	7	2	2	1	3	3
Hall	1	1	0	0	0	0
	8	3	2	1	3	3

St. Louis	IP	H	R	ER	BB	SO
Weilman W,4-2	9	3	0	0	0	5

Detroit	0 0 0	0 0 0	0 0 0	- 0
St. Louis	0 0 0	0 0 0	2 0 x	- 2

OB: Detroit 3, St. Louis 5
DP: Weilman-Austin-Leary (Burns)
2B: Leary
3B: Walker
SB: Pratt
BB: Shotton, Walker 2
SH: Austin, Wares, Crossin
SF: Leary
HP: By Main (Crossin)

WP: Main
TIME: 1:39
ATTENDANCE: 14,000
UMPIRES: Bill Dinneen, Tommy Connolly
SOURCES: Detroit Free Press,
   Tribune; St.Louis Globe-Democrat,
   Post-Dispatch, Republic

BALANCE	OUT	+ R	+ OB	= BP	= AB	+ BB	+ SH	+ HP	+ CI
Detroit	27	0	3	30	30	0	0	0	0
St. Louis	24	2	5	31	23	3	4	1	0

Terriers Wouldn't Die

41. Teams Score 15 Runs in 12th Inning

Brooklyn, FL   at   St. Louis
(Tiptops, 12)   (Terriers, 13)

Tuesday, June 16, 1914, Federal League Park

In 1914, the Federal League declared itself a "major league" and, waving lucrative contracts, wealthy businessmen-owners were able to lure many American and National leaguers into its fold. Most of the defectors, however, were past their primes, and coupled with the ample, green recruits on most rosters, some bizarre games emerged.

This day's contest progressed as just another average game — until the twelfth. The visiting Brooklyn Tiptops jumped on the St. Louis Terriers' Dave Davenport for three quick runs in the first, but St. Louis tied it in their half. That's all the scoring there was until the eighth inning as the 23-year-old Davenport and Brooklyn's Tom Seaton locked horns. Then the Tiptops scored a pair of runs on three hits, climaxed by Tex Westerzil's triple. The Terriers responded, bunching three hits and a walk in the bottom of the ninth to send the game into extra innings.

Thirty-seven-year-old, Terrier player-manager, Modecai "Three Finger" Brown, then installed himself on the mound to start the tenth. He handled the Tiptops easily until the twelfth, when the once great pitching arm was cruelly tested. After Brown struck out Claude Cooper, Art Griggs tripled, Danny Murphy and Solly Hofman singled, and Westerzil doubled. Eddie Gagnier singled, Grover Land sacrificed, Seaton homered, George Anderson singled, and Cooper doubled, giving the visitors a seven-run lead. Amazingly, despite the fireworks, Brown did not summon relief. So thrilled and confident were the Tiptops with their 12–5 margin, that Griggs ended the frame by purposely waving at three pitches.

But the Terriers weren't about to roll over, as twice before they had come from behind to knot the score. Jack Tobin led off the bottom of the twelfth with a home run. After Ward Miller grounded out, Fred Kommers,

The St. Louis Globe-Democrat *portrayed the twelfth frame.*

Armando Marsans (left) and Hugh Miller— Terriers batting heroes

Delos Drake, and Al Boucher each singled. Anderson dropped Al Bridwell's fly, and Mike Simon walked. Grover Hartley pinch-hit for his manager and beat out an infield roller. After Armando Marsans singled, Seaton was finally relieved by Duke Houck with the score 12–11. Houck faced only two hitters — Tobin singled, loading the bases, and Ward Miller walked, forcing in the tying run. Then with the sacks jammed and just one out, Brooklyn's Rudy Sommers was called upon to

quiet the hometown fans who were celebrating with a throwing frenzy. Bats, hats, coats, and anything that wasn't nailed down was being tossed about. Hugh Miller then batted for Kommers and knocked in the game-winning, eighth tally with a pinch-hit single. All totaled, *15 runners had crossed the plate* in this twelfth inning, *the most runs scored in an extra inning in a twentieth-century, major league game.*

Brooklyn Tiptops	AB	R	H	I	PO	A	E
George Anderson lf	7	2	2	0	2	0	2
Claude Cooper cf	6	1	1	1	0	0	0
>Art Griggs 1b	6	2	2	0	14	0	0
Danny Murphy rf	4	2	2	3	0	0	0
Solly Hofman 2b	5	2	4	1	5	7	0
Tex Westerzil 3b	6	1	2	2	2	3	1
Eddie Gagnier ss	6	1	1	2	1	5	0
Grover Land c	4	0	0	1	10	3	0
Tom Seaton p	6	1	3	2	0	5	0
Duke Houck p12	0	0	0	0	0	0	0
Rudy Sommers p12	0	0	0	0	0	0	0
	50	12	17	12	*34	23	3

St. Louis Terriers	AB	R	H	I	PO	A	E
Armando Marsans 2b	7	1	5	1	3	5	0
Jack Tobin rf	5	2	2	1	3	0	0
Ward Miller lf	5	0	3	3	1	0	0
Fred Kommers cf	5	2	1	0	1	0	0
> Hugh Miller ph12	1	0	1	1	0	0	0
Delos Drake 1b	6	2	1	0	15	0	1
Al Boucher 3b	6	1	2	2	0	0	0
Al Bridwell ss	5	2	2	1	0	5	0
Mike Simon c	5	1	0	1	12	1	0
Dave Davenport p	3	0	0	0	0	2	0
Doc Crandall ph9	1	0	1	1	0	0	0
Henry Chapman pr9	0	1	0	0	0	0	0
Mordecai Brown p10	1	0	0	0	1	0	1
Grover Hartley ph12	1	1	1	1	0	0	0
	51	13	19	12	36	13	2

Brooklyn	IP	H	R	ER	BB	SO
Seaton L,10-5	11.1	17	13	11	4	9
Houck	0	1	0	0	1	0
Sommers	0	1	0	0	0	0
	11.1	19	13	11	5	9

St. Louis	IP	H	R	ER	BB	SO
Davenport	9	8	5	5	4	8
Brown W,4-3	3	9	7	7	0	3
	12	17	12	12	4	11

* One out when winning run scored.

Brooklyn	3 0 0	0 0 0	0 2 0	0 0 7	-12
St Louis	3 0 0	0 0 0	0 0 2	0 0 8	-13

OB: Brooklyn 9, St.Louis 11
DP: Marsans-Drake
2B: Hofman, Bridwell, Westerzil, Cooper
3B: Westerzil, Griggs
HR: Murphy(4), Seaton(1), Tobin(4)
SB: Drake, Boucher, W.Miller, Land, Cooper
BB: Cooper, Murphy, Hofman, Land, Tobin, W.Miller, Kommers, Bridwell, Simon

SH: Griggs, Murphy, Tobin
SF: Land
HP: By Seaton (W.Miller)
WP: Brown
TIME: 2:55
ATTENDANCE: 300
UMPIRES: Ollie Anderson, Charles Van Sickle
SOURCES: ICI; New York Times, American; St. Louis Globe Democrat, Post-Dispatch, Republic

BALANCE	OUT+R+OB=BP=AB+BB+SH+HP+CI							
Brooklyn	36	12	9	57	50	4	3	0	0
St. Louis	34	13	11	58	51	5	1	1	0

Nunamaker Nails Three in One Inning

42. Catcher Throws Out
Three Runners in One Inning

NEW YORK   at   DETROIT
(Yankees, 1)   (Tigers, 4)

Monday, August 3, 1914, Navin Field

As a 25-year-old backup Yankee catcher, Les Nunamaker gave both past and future baseball backstops something to envy. Never before, nor since, has any catcher duplicated the work he did on this day in the seventh inning at Navin Field in Detroit.

Coasting along behind Harry Coveleski with a 4–0 lead, the Tigers threatened to pad their lead in the seventh inning. Hugh High, playing for an injured Ty Cobb, led off with a base on balls and advanced to second on Sam Crawford's single. With Bobby Veach batting, Nunamaker threw a strike to the keystone cushion, catching High, high and dry. Later in the count, Crawford tried to get himself into

Nunamaker toiled for the Red Sox, Yankees, Browns, and Indians.

scoring position by stealing second, but Nunamaker rifled another throw that caught Sam at second. Veach then singled. Bobby, himself no slouch on the basepaths, decided he would be the one to garner the Tigers' first stolen base of the day. Veach raced toward second but met the same fate as his comrades. Les Nunamaker thus had thrown out the side. It was the first and only time in modern baseball history that a *catcher threw out three runners on the basepaths in one inning.* Les went on to finish his unobtrusive career with a .268 batting average in 715 games over 12 major league seasons.

Nunamaker's feat has been described rather creatively in some present day accounts. Some record books claim that Les threw out three runners trying to steal even though High was picked off second. Rules of the day, however, were unclear on this distinction, so an argument could be made for three caught stealing. But, most descriptions mention the incident as having happened in the first or second inning when in fact it occurred in the seventh. Several accounts claim that all three of the victims singled; in reality, High had walked. Finally, most reports even list the wrong three baserunners. How this myriad of errors originated could not be determined from the six sources listed.

New York Yankees	AB	R	H	I	PO	A	E
Luke Boone 2b	3	0	0	0	3	3	0
Tom Daley lf	3	1	1	0	4	1	0
Doc Cook rf	2	0	1	0	0	0	0
Birdie Cree cf	4	0	1	1	2	0	0
Charlie Mullen 1b	3	0	0	0	7	0	0
Roger Peckinpaugh ss	4	0	0	0	5	1	0
Les Nunamaker c	4	0	2	0	0	3	0
Fritz Maisel 3b	4	0	1	0	3	2	0
King Cole p	2	0	0	0	0	4	0
> Ray Caldwell ph9	1	0	0	0	0	0	0
	30	1	6	1	24	14	0

Detroit Tigers	AB	R	H	I	PO	A	E
Donie Bush ss	4	0	1	0	1	4	0
George Moriarty 3b	4	0	1	0	2	4	0
Hugh High cf	3	0	1	0	2	0	0
Sam Crawford rf	4	0	1	0	2	0	0
Bobby Veach lf	4	1	3	0	1	0	0
Harry Heilmann 2b	2	2	1	0	4	2	0
George Burns 1b	3	1	2	0	11	0	0
>Del Baker c	3	0	1	1	4	0	0
Harry Coveleski p	3	0	1	2	0	2	0
	30	4	12	3	27	12	0

New York	IP	H	R	ER	BB	SO
Cole L,6-5	8	12	4	4	4	0

Detroit	IP	H	R	ER	BB	SO
Coveleski W,14-8	9	6	1	1	3	4

New York	0 0 0	0 0 0	0 1 0	- 1
Detroit	0 2 0	0 0 2	0 0 x	- 4

OB: New York 8, Detroit 7
DP: Coveleski-Moriarty-Burns (Cree)
SB: Nunamaker, Maisel
CS: Crawford, Veach
PK: High
2B: Burns
SO: Maisel 2, Cole, Mullen
BB: Boone, Cole, Mullen, Heilmann
    Baker, High, Burns

SH: Heilmann, Daley, Cook
HP: By Coveleski (Cook)
TIME: 1:30
ATTENDANCE: 2,407
UMPIRES: Billy Evans, Rip Egan
SOURCES: Detroit Free Press, Journal,
    News, Tribune; New York American,
    Times

BALANCE	OUT	+ R	+ OB	= BP	= AB	+ BB	+ SH	+ HP	+ CI
New York	27	1	8	36	30	3	2	1	0
Detroit	24	4	7	35	30	4	1	0	0

43. Seven Players Hit by Pitch in One Game

DETROIT　　at　　WASHINGTON
(Tigers, 11)　　　　　(Nationals, 0)

Monday, August 24, 1914, Griffith Stadium

On a rainy day in Washington, DC, the Detroit Tigers invaded Griffith Stadium for a doubleheader. The second game pitted Detroit's 24-year-old Hooks Dauss against the Senators' 20-year-old rookie, Jim Shaw.

George "Hooks" Dauss

With that kind of inexperience, coupled with a rain-slicked ball, it's not altogether surprising that this was the *first game of the twentieth century in which seven batsmen were hit by pitches.* (Record books have listed two earlier dates with seven hit-batsmen, but recent research has proven both those claims erroneous.)

Shaw began the hit parade when he uncorked a fastball into the shoulder of Detroit's George Burns in the second inning. Burns was obviously in pain but remained in the contest a few minutes longer, until he scored the Tigers' second run. Leading off the fifth, Red McKee was Shaw's next victim. McKee also came around to score and, with George Moriarty at third and Ty Cobb at second, Shaw was relieved by 19-year-old Jack Bentley. Bentley didn't have much opportunity to hit anybody, because with a three-ball count on his first batter, Sam Crawford, Moriarty promptly stole home as the ball eluded Senators' backstop Eddie Ainsmith. Cobb seeing this, also dashed for the plate but was thrown out. As Bentley covered home on the play, Cobb spiked the thumb of his pitching hand, forcing him out of the game. Interestingly, neither *The Detroit Tribune* nor *The Detroit Free Press* made any mention of a spiking and even went so far as to say that Bentley's exit was merely a delay tactic by Washington while hoping for a downpour. On an already soggy field, a deluge at that point would have cancelled the game and averted a Washington loss. (The Nationals couldn't have been very successful if they had been delaying the contest, as the 11–0 conclusion encompassed just one hour and 55 minutes.)

Bentley was replaced by the next execu-

tioner, 19-year-old Harry Harper. Facing Harper in the eighth inning, Detroit's Harry Heilmann, who had substituted for the hit-batsman George Burns, was himself hit by a pitch. Heilmann also eventually scored.

The 1914 Nationals had one of the youngest collections of pitchers ever assembled in major league baseball, with Walter Johnson as the dean of the staff at 26 years old. After him, the ages of the regular hurlers

SECOND GAME

Detroit Tigers	AB	R	H	I	PO	A	E
Donie Bush ss	5	1	1	1	3	4	0
George Moriarty 3b	5	3	3	1	0	2	0
Ty Cobb cf	4	2	3	0	2	0	0
Sam Crawford rf	2	0	0	2	2	0	0
Bobby Veach lf	5	1	2	1	0	0	0
Hugh High lf9	0	0	0	0	0	0	0
Marty Kavanagh 2b	4	1	1	1	2	3	0
George Burns 1b	0	1	0	0	2	0	0
Harry Heilmann 1b2	2	1	0	1	7	1	0
>Red McKee c	4	1	1	2	9	0	0
Hooks Dauss p	3	0	1	1	0	1	0
	34	11	12	10	27	11	0

Washington Nationals	AB	R	H	I	PO	A	E
Danny Moeller rf	4	0	3	0	2	0	0
Eddie Foster 3b	4	0	1	0	1	1	0
Mike Mitchell lf	2	0	0	0	1	0	0
Chick Gandil 1b	3	0	0	0	6	0	0
Ray Morgan 2b	3	0	0	0	4	1	0
>Howard Shanks cf	4	0	0	0	2	0	0
George McBride ss	3	0	0	0	5	3	0
Eddie Ainsmith c	1	0	0	0	1	2	0
Rip Williams c5	2	0	0	0	4	0	1
Jim Shaw p	1	0	0	0	0	3	0
Jack Bentley p5	0	0	0	0	1	0	0
Harry Harper p5	1	0	0	0	0	0	0
Wally Smith ph8	0	0	0	0	0	0	0
Jim Stevens p9	0	0	0	0	0	0	0
	28	0	4	0	27	10	1

Detroit	IP	H	R	ER	BB	SO
Dauss W,16-11	9	4	0	0	2	5

Washington	IP	H	R	ER	BB	SO
Shaw L,8-12	4.1	8	5	5	0	1
Bentley	.1	0	0	0	1	0
Harper	3.1	2	3	2	2	2
Stevens	1	2	3	3	0	0
	9	12	11	10	3	3

Detroit	1 1 0	0 3 0	0 3 3	–11
Washington	0 0 0	0 0 0	0 0 0	– 0

OB: Detroit 6, Washington 6
DP: Bush-Burns
    Heilmann-Bush (Mitchell)
    Bush-Kavanagh-Heilmann
2B: Dauss, Bush, Foster
3B: McKee
SB: Crawford 2, Cobb 2, Veach,
    Moriarty
CS: Cobb
SO: Kavanagh, Heilmann, McBride 2,
    Dauss, Foster, Ainsmith, Harper
BB: Crawford, Kavanagh, Dauss,
    Mitchell, W.Smith

SF: Crawford 2, Heilmann
HP: By Dauss (Mitchell, Gandil,
    Morgan), by Shaw (Burns, McKee)
    by Harper (Heilmann), by
    Stevens (Cobb)
WP: Dauss
TIME: 1:55
ATTENDANCE: ?
UMPIRES: Billy Evans, Rip Egan
SOURCES: Detroit Free Press, News,
    Tribune; Washington Evening Star,
    Herald, Post, Times

BALANCE	OUT	+	R	+	OB	=	BP	=	AB	+	BB	+	SH	+	HP	+	CI
Detroit	27		11		6		44		34		3		3		4		0
Washington	27		0		6		33		28		2		0		3		0

were 24, 23, 21, 20, and a pair of 19-year-olds. Shaw, Bentley and Harper were all rookie hurlers. But the fourth Senator pitcher to take the hill this day was not only a rookie, this was his very first major league game. Twenty-four-year-old Jim Stevens accepted the baton from his teammates and completed the new major league record by hitting the second batter he faced, Ty Cobb. That was the seventh player hit in the game, and like his battered teammates before him, Cobb also scored.

Tiger hurler Hooks Dauss was no seraph throughout this affair. He contributed his share of transgression by pummelling three Nationals. None of them scored, however, nor was there any report of altercation resulting from the blows. There was a scuffle of another sort when mid-way through the contest, a fight broke out among the spectators, and the limited number of police were having a difficult time attempting to quell the disturbance. It may be bewildering for modern day fans to envision what happened next, but led by Ty Cobb, a group of Tigers sprinted from their dugout and climbed into the bleachers to assist the lawmen. This was one method of settling such a problem in 1914; once order was restored, play continued.

This level of human target practice — seven hit-batsmen — did not occur again for almost 57 years (see 4-13-71 and 9-03-89).

Zabel Provides Longlasting Relief

44. Pitcher Records
Relief Outing of 18-Plus Innings

BROOKLYN   at   CHICAGO
(Robins, 3)   (Cubs, 4)

Thursday, June 17, 1915, West Side Park

George "Zip" Zabel, 24-year-old right-hander, this day worked the *longest relief outing in major league history—18⅓ innings*, while leading the Cubs to a hometown victory over Brooklyn. Zabel was called into action in the opening frame when, with two outs, Chicago starter Bert Humphries tried to stop a hard bouncer over the mound with his pitching hand. Humphries had his fingernail torn off on the attempt, thus setting the stage for Zabel's marathon performance. Zip took the mound with no warmup and quickly escaped by participating in a thwarted double-steal attempt by the Robins (as Brooklyn was then nicknamed).

From that point Zabel was masterful, employing a sweeping curve and active fastball to allow only nine hits and one intentional walk over the next 18 innings. Only twice, in the fifth and fifteenth, were the

Zabel retired 55 batters in relief.

Robins able to manage two hits in the same frame. And from the eighth through the fourteenth, no Robin hit safely. Some porous fielding enabled Brooklyn to dent the plate twice against Zabel, but both runs were unearned. The Cubs did provide some solid fielding support, particularly in the sixteenth. Then, with Hy Myers on first and one away, George Cutshaw drove a liner to deep center field. The Cubs' Cy Williams raced with his back to the infield, lunged, and made a sensational one-handed catch, turning a somersault in the process.

Zabel's adversary was Brooklyn ace Jeff Pfeffer, who also hurled a terrific game. Jeff was in constant peril, however, thanks in part to eight walks (four intentional) and four Brooklyn errors. The intentional walk strat-egy was successful in that no runs scored in any inning in which it was utilized. Eleven Chicago batters in extra innings had a chance to end the contest with a timely hit, but Pfeffer was equal to the task, stranding 18 Cubs.

The game was finally decided on another error in the bottom of the 19th. Bobby Fisher led off with a single. Wildfire Schulte then drove a deep fly to right which forced Casey Stengel back to the fence; Fisher tagged and went to second. Polly McLarry walked, but Vic Saier flied out to center for the second out. Cy Williams then sent a screaming grounder toward right on which Cutshaw made a nice pickup. The inning seemed over, but the second baseman slipped and threw high over first. Before the ball could be retrieved, Fisher raced home with the game winner.

Brooklyn Robins	AB	R	H	I	PO	A	E
Ollie O'Mara ss	8	1	1	0	7	3	0
Hy Myers cf	8	0	2	1	3	0	1
Jake Daubert 1b	8	1	1	0	18	1	0
George Cutshaw 2b	8	1	3	0	6	10	1
>Zack Wheat lf	7	0	2	1	5	0	0
Casey Stengel rf	6	0	1	0	4	0	2
Lew McCarty c	4	0	1	0	4	0	1
Otto Miller c10	3	0	1	1	6	1	0
Gus Getz 3b	6	0	0	0	2	4	0
Jeff Pfeffer p	7	0	0	0	1	5	0
	65	3	12	3	56	*24	5

Brooklyn	IP	H	R	ER	BB	SO
Pfeffer L,6-5	18.2	*13	4	2	8	6

* *Two out when winning run scored*

Brooklyn	1 0 0	0 0 0	0 1 0	0 0 0
Chicago	2 0 0	0 0 0	0 0 0	0 0 0

OB: Brooklyn 8, Chicago 18
DP: Getz-Cutshaw-Daubert (Fisher)
2B: Phelan, Bresnahan, Schulte, Myers, O'Mara
HR: Saier(6)
SB: Williams, Getz
CS: Cutshaw 2
SO: O'Mara, Cutshaw, Wheat, McCarty, Pfeffer 2, Fisher, McLarry, Williams, Bresnahan 3
BB: Stengel(I), McLarry 2, Saier 3(2I), Phelan 3(2I)

Chicago Cubs	AB	R	H	I	PO	A	E
Wilbur Good rf	9	1	1	0	1	0	0
Bobby Fisher ss	8	1	3	0	4	9	1
Wildfire Schulte lf	8	1	2	1	7	1	0
Polly McLarry 2b	7	0	0	0	6	5	1
Vic Saier 1b	6	1	1	1	20	1	0
>Cy Williams cf	9	0	2	1	4	0	0
Roger Bresnahan c	8	0	1	0	8	3	0
Art Phelan 3b	5	0	2	0	6	7	1
Bert Humphries p	0	0	0	0	0	0	0
Zip Zabel p1	7	0	1	0	1	7	0
	67	4	13	3	57	33	3

Chicago	IP	H	R	ER	BB	SO
Humphries	.2	2	1	1	0	0
Zabel W,5-4	18.1	10	2	0	1	6
	19	12	3	1	1	6

Chicago	0 0 1	0 0 0	0	- 3
	0 0 1	0 0 0	1	- 4

SH: Fisher, Zabel, Schulte, Getz, Wheat
TIME: 3:30
ATTENDANCE: ?
UMPIRES: Cy Rigler, Bill Hart
SOURCES: Chicago Daily Journal, Daily News, Tribune; DBD; New York American, World, Times

----
BALANCE	OUT+R+OB=BP=AB+BB+SH+HP+CI							
Brooklyn	57	3	8	68	65	1	2	0	0
Chicago	56	4	18	78	67	8	3	0	0

Wilder Then the Old March Hare

45. Pitcher Walks 16 in Nine Innings

NEW YORK, AL   at   PHILADELPHIA
(Yankees, 15)   (Athletics, 7)

Wednesday, June 23, 1915, Shibe Park

In 1914, no team won more games in the major leagues than the Philadelphia Athletics. That winter, however, Connie Mack's team dissolved. Whether because of money, aggressive recruiting by the Federal League, or rumors of certain players laying down in the World Series, Mack's club became a mere skeleton of its former self when the following season opened. Gone was the pitching tandem of Chief Bender and Eddie Plank (they defected to the Federal League); Eddie Collins had been sold to the White Sox, and Frank Baker had temporarily retired. Once the 1915 season began, Connie sold four more of his regulars — Eddie Murphy, Jack Barry, Bob Shawkey, and Herb Pennock. This upheaval spawned predictable results. The 1915 Athletics lost 109 games and finished in the cellar, 58½ games out.

In the spring of 1915, Mack thought he still had enough young talent both on the team and waiting on the sandlots to contend again. Through a close and informal network of friends, Mack had kept in touch with promising players, and now he gave many of them a chance to display their talents. Before the season ended, Connie afforded 27 hopefuls an opportunity to pitch for his club, the most until 1996 California fans watched 29 candidates.

One of those pitching prospects was a 24-year-old, rookie left-hander named Bruno "Boon" Haas. Haas had just finished pitching for four years at Worcester Academy in Massachusetts where, thanks in part to his wicked curve and impeccable control, he reportedly went undefeated. On this day, however, Bruno entered his name in the all-time ledgers in much less glory. Perhaps it was the nervousness of his first start in the major leagues, the 7,000 howling Philadelphia patrons, the atrocious fielding of his teammates, or as *The Philadelphia Press* reported, "…that he felt out of place on the eighteen-inch elevation at Shibe Park." (Rules of the day specified a 15" mound however.) For whatever reason, the *Philadelphia Evening Ledger* described Haas as "wilder than the old March hare," while he *walked 16 Yankees in a nine-inning game*, the most ever by one pitcher.

This was the second game of a doubleheader. Cap Crowell, another collegian, had made his major league debut with the A's in the first game, and now it was Haas' turn. On his way to a 15–7 thrashing, Bruno walked the following batters:

Inning	Batters Walked
1	Hugh High, Fritz Maisel
2	Jack Warhop, High
3	Birdie Cree
4	Roy Hartzell, Paddy Bauman, High
5	Cree, Les Nunamaker, Warhop
6	Maisel, Cree
7	Cree
8	—
9	Roger Peckinpaugh, Luke Boone

HAAS WAS TOO LIBERAL WITH HIS PASSES

The Philadelphia Press *noted the proceedings.*

As the bases on balls began to pile up, the crowd became aware of the rookie's chance for immortality and cheered for him to break the record. At the time, the most free passes issued in a game had been 15. The Shibe Park patrons were very aware of the mark because it was established by one of their own — Boardwalk Brown — just two years earlier. On this day, Brown himself witnessed the onslaught of his record from the visitors dugout, having been sold to the Yankees in 1914.

While the crowd cheered for more walks, Haas did his best to avert an ignominious place in the record books. Having issued 14 passes through the first seven innings, Bruno gained a measure of control and pitched a walk-free eighth. The ninth inning opened with an air of excitement. It was heightened

when, after retiring Hugh High, Haas walked Roger Peckinpaugh. After Fritz Maisel singled, Charlie Mullen hit a potential game-ending, double-play grounder. Maisel was out at second, but Mullen beat the relay to first, preserving Haas' chance for the record. Birdie Cree then tantalized the crowd by working Haas to a three-ball count before grounding to Owen Conway at third base. As *The Philadelphia Record* described it, "… and it looked as if it were all over. Conway saved the day by throwing wild to first." Roy Hartzell then singled and Luke Boone delivered the holy grail by gaining the 16th free pass. Imagine how the mortified Haas must have felt as the hometown fans cheered madly. And what of Boardwalk Brown? *The Philadelphia Record* noted: "Brown buried his face in his hands, overcome." The *Record* was

New York Yankees	AB	R	H	I	PO	A	E
Hugh High cf	3	1	2	1	2	0	0
Roger Peckinpaugh ss	5	3	2	2	3	5	1
Fritz Maisel 3b	4	2	2	1	0	2	0
Charlie Mullen 1b	5	1	0	0	12	0	0
Birdie Cree rf	2	1	0	0	2	1	1
Roy Hartzell lf	5	1	2	2	1	0	0
Paddy Baumann 2b	3	2	2	1	2	3	0
Luke Boone 2b8	1	1	1	0	2	2	0
>Les Nunamaker c	5	2	2	1	3	0	0
Jack Warhop p	3	1	0	1	0	2	0
	36	15	13	9	27	15	2

Philadelphia Athletics	AB	R	H	I	PO	A	E
Jimmy Walsh cf	5	1	1	0	1	0	0
Amos Strunk rf	5	2	3	1	2	1	0
Jack Lapp c	5	1	4	3	6	4	2
Rube Oldring lf	4	2	2	1	0	0	0
>Stuffy McInnis 1b	4	0	2	2	9	3	0
Owen Conway 3b	4	0	0	0	2	1	4
Lew Malone 2b	4	0	1	0	3	4	0
Larry Kopf ss	4	0	1	0	3	4	0
Bruno Haas p	4	1	1	0	1	3	1
	39	7	15	7	27	20	7

New York	IP	H	R	ER	BB	SO
Warhop W,5-4	9	15	7	5	1	1

Philadelphia	IP	H	R	ER	BB	SO
Haas L,0-1	9	13	15	8	16	4

New York	0 1 0	3 2 2	4 1 2	-15
Philadelphia	0 0 2	0 0 1	0 3 1	- 7

OB: New York 11, Philadelphia 7
DP: Peckinpaugh-Mullen (Haas)
     Peckinpaugh-Baumann-Mullen
2B: Oldring 2, Lapp
3B: Strunk
SB: Nunamaker, Baumann, Peckinpaugh,
     Oldring
SO: Peckinpaugh, Mullen, Hartzell,
     Warhop, Malone
BB: High 3, Peckinpaugh, Maisel 2,
     Cree 4, Hartzell, Baumann,
     Boone, Nunamaker, Warhop 2,
     Oldring

SH: Mullen
SF: McInnis
WP: Haas 3
TIME: 2:14
ATTENDANCE: 7,000
UMPIRES: Silk O'Loughlin, George
     Hildebrand
SOURCES: New York American, Times;
     Philadelphia Evening Ledger,
     Evening Telegraph, Inquirer, North
     American, Press, Record

BALANCE	OUT	+	R	+	OB	=	BP	=	AB	+	BB	+	SH	+	HP	+	CI
New York	27		15		11		53		36		16		1		0		0
Philadelphia	27		7		7		41		39		1		1		0		0

----

not clear, however, whether Brown's reaction was joy or sorrow.

After the game, Connie Mack was asked about his new recruit Haas, who had made three wild pitches in addition to the slew of walks. *The North American* reported that Connie was not alarmed and said, "The boy is in the majors to stick." Despite Mack's forecast, Bruno Haas pitched in just five more major league games, ending his career by allowing 28 walks and 23 hits in 14⅓ innings. Six years later, he reappeared as a half back for Akron in the newly formed National Football League.

Nationals Run Wild in First Inning

46. Team Steals Eight Bases in One Inning

WASHINGTON   at   CLEVELAND
(Nationals, 11)   (Indians, 4)

Monday, July 19, 1915, League Park

Only 622 fans paid to see the last place, hometown Indians this day, and most of them left after the first inning. The Indians had been playing uninspired ball, and if it hadn't been for a pathetic Athletics club this year, Cleveland surely would have finished last. As it was, when the final curtain was drawn, they finished seventh, 44.5 games behind the pennant-winning Red Sox.

This game was one of those laughers that was essentially won in the first half-inning. In it, the visiting Washington Nationals got only two hits but took advantage of four walks, four errors, and most notably, eight stolen bases, to jump out to a 6–0 lead which they never relinquished. It was the *first time in the twentieth-century that any major league team had stolen eight bases in one inning.* (Since then, it has been repeated only once — see 7-17-19.) Steve O'Neill, the victimized catcher, was normally a very fine glove man. He had led the league's catchers in

Steve O'Neill in a photo that looks as if it may have been taken during the game.

double plays the year before, and this season he would lead all backstops in assists. But on this day, according to the *Cleveland Plain Dealer*, "… pitcher [Rip] Hagerman and the infielders dozed and allowed the Nationals to run wild." Hagerman faced just five batters yet allowed five of the eight steals.

Leadoff hitter Danny Moeller started the proceedings by drawing a base on balls and stealing second. Eddie Foster popped out to short, but Clyde Milan walked, putting runners on first and second. Moeller and Milan then tried a double-steal, but because Moeller got such a big lead, catcher O'Neill threw to second. Milan was safe. Meanwhile, Moeller kept right on running around third and slid

safely home, stealing two bases on the same play. After Howard Shanks, the fourth batter, also walked, Milan stole third. The fans then expected another double steal, but Chick Gandil instead tripled to left-center, driving home his two mates. Gandil himself scored on Jack Graney's wild throw home.

That was all for Rip Hagerman; Sad Sam Jones entered the breach. Jones got Tom Connelly to fly out to Graney, but Eddie Ainsmith singled. A barrage of Cleveland errors then accompanied more of Washington's bold baserunning as Ainsmith stole second and took third on O'Neill's poor throw. After George McBride walked, he and Ainsmith succeeded in another double steal.

Washington Nationals	AB	R	H	I	PO	A	E
Danny Moeller rf	4	2	2	1	1	0	0
Eddie Foster 2b	3	0	1	2	4	1	1
Clyde Milan cf	3	2	2	0	3	0	0
Howard Shanks lf	3	1	0	0	3	0	0
Chick Gandil 1b	5	2	4	3	9	0	0
Tom Connelly 3b	3	0	0	1	1	2	0
Rip Williams ph9	1	1	0	0	0	0	0
Doug Neff 3b9	0	0	0	0	1	0	0
Eddie Ainsmith c	5	1	1	0	3	0	0
>George McBride ss	4	1	0	0	2	7	0
Walter Johnson p	3	1	1	0	0	0	0
Nick Altrock p7	1	0	0	0	0	0	0
	35	11	11	7	27	10	1

Cleveland Indians	AB	R	H	I	PO	A	E
Billy Southworth cf	5	1	1	0	8	0	1
>Ray Chapman ss	5	1	2	0	0	2	0
Jack Graney lf	3	1	1	1	4	0	1
Jay Kirke 1b	3	1	0	0	7	0	1
Elmer Smith rf	4	0	2	1	2	0	0
Walter Barbare 3b	4	0	0	0	2	1	0
Bill Wambsganss 2b	4	0	2	2	0	2	0
Steve O'Neill c	4	0	0	0	4	2	1
Rip Hagerman p	0	0	0	0	0	0	0
Sad Sam Jones p1	2	0	0	0	0	4	0
Tex Hoffman ph7	1	0	0	0	0	0	0
Fritz Coumbe p8	0	0	0	0	0	1	0
Jim Eschen ph9	1	0	1	0	0	0	0
	36	4	9	4	27	12	4

Washington	IP	H	R	ER	BB	SO
Johnson W,15-8	6	2	0	0	0	0
Altrock	3	7	4	3	1	2
	9	9	4	3	1	2

Cleveland	IP	H	R	ER	BB	SO
Hagerman L,4-9	.1	1	4	3	3	0
Jones	6.2	8	5	3	2	2
Coumbe	2	2	2	2	1	0
	9	11	11	8	6	2

Washington	6 0 0	1 0 1	1 0 2	-11
Cleveland	0 0 0	0 0 0	1 3 0	- 4

OB: Cleveland 7, Washington 6
2B: Chapman 2, Moeller, Gandil
3B: Moeller, Gandil 2
SB: Moeller 3, Milan 2, Ainsmith 2, McBride
SO: Connelly, McBride, Wambsganss, O'Neill
BB: Moeller, Milan 2, Shanks 2, McBride, Kirke
SF: Foster 2, Connelly, Graney

PB: O'Neill
BK: Hagerman
TIME: 1:33
ATTENDANCE: 622
UMPIRES: Ollie Chill, Billy Evans
SOURCES: Akron Beacon Journal;
    Cleveland Leader, Plain Dealer,
    Press; Columbus Ohio State Journl;
    Washington Herald, Post, Star

BALANCE	OUT+R+OB=BP=AB+BB+SH+HP+CI							
Washington	27	11	6	44	35	6	3	0	0
Cleveland	27	4	7	38	36	1	1	0	0

Ainsmith scored, and McBride took third on another throwing error, this time by first baseman Jay Kirke. Kirke's wild toss was retrieved by center fielder Billy Southworth, who in turn pegged wild to third, enabling McBride to tally. Walter Johnson ended the fiasco by flying out to right.

Walter Johnson was the workhorse of the Washington staff, and although he had given up only two hits through the first six innings,

manager Clark Griffith decided to give his ace some deserved time off. Griffith substituted with the comedian pitcher Nick Altrock, whose principal duty for the last three years had been coaching and entertaining the fans on the road with his amusing antics. It was Altrock's only game of the year on the playing field. His lack of activity was evident as he conceded a walk, seven hits, and four runs in his three innings of relief work.

Shibe Park Walk-A-Thon

47. Team Gets 18 Walks; Teams Get 30 Walks in Nine-Inning Game

DETROIT   at   PHILADELPHIA
(Tigers, 16)   (Athletics, 2)

Tuesday, May 9, 1916, Shibe Park

Less than a year before, Shibe Park fans had witnessed a Connie Mack recruit named Bruno Haas set the all-time, free-pass record by walking 16 Yankees in a nine-inning game. But that was mere child's play compared to this game's mound madness. This day the Shibe Park mound-virus infected five different hurlers, contributing to a *nine-inning game total of 30 bases on balls*. Not even an extra-inning game has ever produced more. For their part, the Tigers were handed *18 free passes, the most for any team in a twentieth-century, nine-inning contest.*

Carrying the base-on-balls pathogen was a stiff, cold wind that blew across the Philadelphia diamond. The organism was so infectious that before the first five innings were complete, 24 batters had been given free tickets to first base. The ultimate insult was borne by Tiger rookie hurler, George Cunningham. George started the contest but was relieved in the third frame while pitching a no-hitter and leading 9–0. Talk about destroying a young man's confidence; Cunningham had faced only twelve batters! After walking

Cunningham was yanked while tossing a no-hitter but picked up a win despite only 2⅓ innings of work.

Notes on the game by The Philadelphia Press.

six, Cunningham contaminated reliever Bernie Boland in the third inning. Bernie spread the blight by walking six more Athletics.

Starting for Mack's A's was the infamous, 29-year-old Jack Nabors, who entered the game with a 1–2 slate. Jack had already won his only game of the year (and career) and was saddled with this day's loss as well as another 17 before the season's end. Actually, Nabors, 1–25 lifetime, owns the worst career winning percentage of any pitcher with 20 or more decisions. (Some historians dispute his

Detroit Tigers	AB	R	H	I	PO	A	E
Donie Bush ss	2	3	0	0	1	2	0
Frank Fuller 2b6	1	0	0	0	0	2	0
>Ossie Vitt 3b	4	2	1	1	2	1	0
Ty Cobb cf	5	2	2	4	1	0	0
Sam Crawford rf	4	2	1	1	1	0	0
Harry Heilmann lf	5	2	3	3	5	0	0
George Burns 1b	4	1	2	2	11	0	0
Ralph Young 2b,ss6	4	1	0	1	4	7	0
Oscar Stanage c	4	1	1	1	2	0	0
Del Baker c8	1	0	0	0	0	0	0
George Cunningham p	1	1	1	1	0	0	0
Bernie Boland p3	1	1	1	1	0	0	0
	36	16	12	15	27	12	0

Philadelphia Athletics	AB	R	H	I	PO	A	E
Whitey Witt ss	4	0	0	0	3	3	2
Jimmy Walsh rf	2	1	0	0	0	1	1
Amos Strunk cf	3	0	0	0	4	1	0
Rube Oldring lf	0	0	0	0	2	1	0
Mike Murphy c3	3	0	0	0	5	1	0
>Nap Lajoie 2b	4	0	0	1	4	5	0
Stuffy McInnis 1b	3	1	1	0	6	2	0
Charlie Pick 3b	2	0	0	0	2	5	0
Wally Schang c	0	0	0	0	1	0	0
Carl Ray p3	3	0	0	0	0	1	0
Jack Nabors p	0	0	0	0	0	0	2
Harry Weaver p2	0	0	0	0	0	0	0
Bill Stellbauer ph2,lf3	4	0	2	1	0	0	0
	28	2	3	2	27	20	5

Detroit	IP	H	R	ER	BB	SO
Cunningham W,3-2	2.1	0	1	1	6	0
Boland	6.2	3	1	1	6	2
	9	3	2	2	12	2

Philadelphia	IP	H	R	ER	BB	SO
Nabors L,1-3	1	4	5	4	3	0
Weaver	1	2	4	4	3	0
Ray	7	6	7	4	12	3
	9	12	16	12	18	3

Detroit   1 8 0   0 6 1   0 0 0   -16
Philadelphia   0 0 1   0 0 0   0 1 0   - 2

OB: Detroit 13, Philadelphia 12
DP: Oldring-McInnis-Pick (Cobb)
    Young-Bush-Burns (Stellbauer)
    Strunk-McInnis
2B: Cobb 2, Cunningham, Heilmann,
    Stellbauer
3B: Stellbauer
SB: Young, Crawford
CS: Young
SO: Burns, Young, Stanage, Walsh,
    Ray
BB: Bush 3, Fuller, Vitt 3, Cobb,
    Crawford 2, Heilmann, Young 2,
    Stanage, Cunningham, Boland 3,
    Witt, Walsh 3, Strunk 2, Murphy

BB: ... Oldring, McInnis, Pick 2,
    Schang
SF: Lajoie, Burns 2
WP: Weaver
TIME: 2:28
ATTENDANCE: ?
UMPIRES: Silk O'Loughlin, Ollie
    Chill
SOURCES: Detroit Free Press, News;
    Philadelphia Evening Bulletin,
    Evening Ledger, Evening Telegraph,
    Inquirer, North American, Press,
    Record

BALANCE	OUT	+R	+OB	=BP	=AB	+BB	+SH	+HP	+CI
Detroit	27	16	13	56	36	18	2	0	0
Philadelphia	27	2	12	41	28	12	1	0	0

----

loss on April 28 this year at Washington saying it truely belongs to teammate Cap Crowell.)

Nabors lasted just one inning, contributing three free passes. He was replaced by another Mack hopeful named Harry Weaver. Harry pitched the second frame, permitting another three walks. Trailing 9–0 after the Tigers had finished with Nabors and Weaver, Mack dispatched Phil Ray for the mop-up work. Phil ably contributed to the record-setting, two-club performance by walking an even dozen in his seven innings of labor. All this generosity caused the sports writers to lament about the amount of time consumed by all the walks. Playing time was logged at 2:28.

This game was one in a series of four between the two clubs. By the time the series had ended, the two pitching staffs had issued a combined 85 bases on balls — the Athletics handed out 49 and the Tigers 36.

Kauff Caught Napping

48. Player Gets Picked Off First Base Thrice in One Game

NEW YORK, NL   at   BOSTON
(Giants, 12)   (Braves, 1)

Friday, May 26, 1916, Braves Field

Benny Kauff was known as the "Ty Cobb of the Federal League." In the two short years of the league's existence, he led it in both batting average and stolen bases. In this the following year, Benny joined the National League New York Giants in time to set a record yet to be duplicated.

Kauff was quite a showman. Fast talking

Kauff was a dandy.

in an attempted squeeze, he then was picked off first, again by Tyler.

• 7th inning — With two outs, he walked. When caught off first, Benny created a rundown while teammate Robertson scored. Again it was the losing pitcher Tyler who nabbed him.

• 9th inning — Kauff walked and had a chance to put this record completely out of reach for future generations but was *not* caught off first. He later scored a run.

Although clearly the leader at dozing around the first base sack, Benny was not alone in his embarrassment. In the fifth inning, Rabbit Maranville met the same fate.

Kauff's exciting lifestyle eventually led to his baseball demise. In 1920, Commissioner Landis banished him from the game for being implicated in a stolen car ring. Although Kauff was

and a smart dresser, he often wore gaudy jewelry and flashed a lush bankroll. But on this day, he entertained the Boston fans at Braves Field in a considerably less flamboyant manner when he became the first and only player known in this century to be *picked off first base three times in a game.* Here's how his day of infamy progressed:

• 1st inning — With the bases empty, Kauff lined out to Rabbit Maranville for the third out.

• 3rd inning — Benny walked with the bases loaded, driving in a run, then proceeded to end the rally and the inning by being picked off first by the Braves' pitcher Lefty Tyler.

• 5th inning — Safe on Red Smith's error

cleared of any criminal charges in court, his pleas for readmission into baseball were denied. At the age of 30, his major league career had ended.

Two other notes pertaining to this contest should be mentioned. This game represented the Giants' 14th consecutive road victory. They went on to win their 17th a few days later which remains the all-time, road winning streak. In September of this same year they won 26 in a row at home, also a record. Despite these two record streaks, however, the Giants could only finish in fourth with an 86–66 log. For the Giants this day, 31-year-old Sailor Stroud pitched seven innings of relief work, earning his last victory in the major leagues.

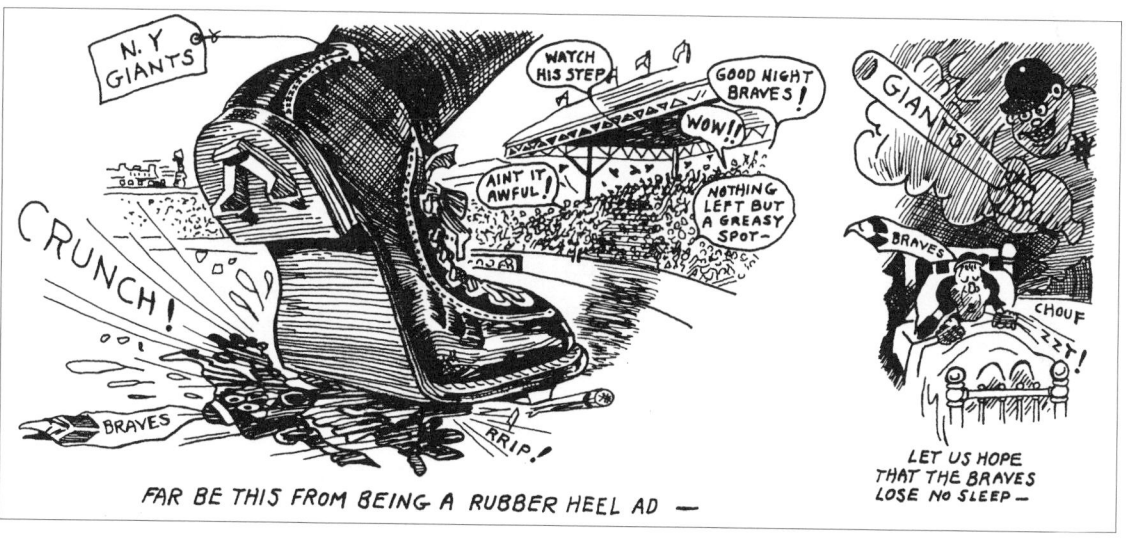

The Boston Post *did not consider Kauff's actions among the game highlights.*

New York Giants	AB	R	H	I	PO	A	E
George Burns lf	3	4	2	0	1	0	0
Dave Robertson rf	4	3	3	0	2	0	0
Edd Roush rf9	0	0	0	0	0	0	0
Larry Doyle 2b	2	2	2	4	2	3	1
Benny Kauff cf	2	1	0	1	4	0	0
Art Fletcher ss	3	2	2	2	4	5	0
Fred Merkle 1b	4	0	3	1	7	0	0
Bill McKechnie 3b	5	0	1	1	1	2	0
Bill Rariden c	3	0	0	0	3	0	0
George Kelly ph8	1	0	1	1	0	0	0
Red Dooin c8	1	0	0	0	3	0	0
Jeff Tesreau p	1	0	0	0	0	1	0
> Sailor Stroud p3	4	0	0	0	0	3	0
	33	12	14	10	27	14	1

Boston Braves	AB	R	H	I	PO	A	E
Rabbit Maranville ss	4	0	1	0	5	3	0
Johnny Evers 2b	3	0	0	0	2	2	0
Zip Collins lf	3	0	0	0	2	0	0
Joe Wilhoit rf	4	0	0	0	6	0	0
Ed Konetchy 1b	4	0	2	0	7	3	0
Red Smith 3b	3	0	1	0	0	1	1
Pete Compton cf	4	1	1	0	1	0	0
Hank Gowdy c	3	0	1	0	4	0	1
Walt Tragesser c7	1	0	0	0	0	0	0
>Lefty Tyler p	4	0	1	1	0	6	1
	33	1	7	1	27	15	3

New York	IP	H	R	ER	BB	SO
Tesreau	2	2	1	1	2	1
Stroud W,1-1	7	5	0	0	1	2
	9	7	1	1	3	3

Boston	IP	H	R	ER	BB	SO
Tyler L,3-1	9	14	12	9	6	4

New York	1 0 2	0 2 0	2 1 4	-12
Boston	0 1 0	0 0 0	0 0 0	- 1

OB: New York 6, Boston 8

DP: Simth-Evers-Konetchy (McKechnie)
    Doyle-Fletcher-Merkle (Konetchy)

2B: Fletcher, Gowdy, Konetchy, Burns
    Doyle

3B: Burns, Doyle

SB: Doyle

PK: Kauff 3, Maranville

BB: Burns 2, Doyle, Kauff 3, Evers,
    Collins, Smith

SH: Merkle, Robertson

SF: Doyle 2, Fletcher

HP: By Tyler (Fletcher)

WP: Tyler

TIME: 2:10

ATTENDANCE: 6,200

UMPIRES: Hank O'Day, Mal Eason

SOURCES: Boston Globe, Herald,
    Journal, Post; New York American,
    Times

BALANCE	OUT	+R	+OB	=BP	=AB	+BB	+SH	+HP	+CI
New York	27	12	6	45	33	6	5	1	0
Boston	27	1	8	36	33	3	0	0	0

Downpour Then Dusk Dictates Degeneracy

49. Teams Steal 14 Bases in Five-Inning Game

PITTSBURGH   at   ST. LOUIS
(Pirates, 9)   (Cardinals, 5)

Sunday, August 13, 1916, Robison Park

Dots Miller swiped two bases on the same pitch.

Robison Park in St. Louis was one of the last of the major league's old-time wooden ballparks. It had outlived its peers simply because its owners couldn't afford the state-of-the-art, concrete-and-steel construction that had swept the league. But despite a limited budget, the grounds crew had been afforded a canvas with which to cover the infield in the event of rain. That canvas was in place on the evening of August 12, but it proved woefully inadequate when faced with the heavy downpours that occurred throughout the night and into Sunday morning, August 13. So much rain fell that it flooded beneath the canvas, turning the infield into a quagmire. The scheduled doubleheader probably would have been called off had it not been for the 6,000 vociferous fans who had braved the elements and began demanding action around the two o'clock scheduled starting time. Umpires Ernest Quigley and Al Orth assuaged them by trying to get in both games, but it wasn't until an hour later that play could actually begin.

As batted balls skidded off the mud puddles, the Cardinals were able to assemble a major league, season-high 23 hits in defeating the visiting Pirates in the first game. The contest lasted 11 innings and consumed almost three hours, so the second game didn't begin until six P.M. Neither team wanted to play another game, but the umpires insisted.

After Pittsburgh jumped on "Mule" Watson for eight runs in the first two innings, the game took on new meaning. Then the Pirates

wanted to complete the contest before darkness fell. The Cardinals on the other hand, tried every delaying tactic they could imagine. Base runners tried to consume time by drawing throws from the pitchers, engaging the infielders in rundowns, and throws by the catcher, all while stealing bases. Despite shoes laden with the extra weight of mud, the Missourians stole at every opportunity. For example, in the bottom of the second, trailing 8–0, the Cards' Dots Miller singled. While Pittsburgh's Al Mamaux wound up with a sweeping double swing of his right arm, Miller departed for second base. Failing to draw any reaction, Dots continued to third. Catcher Bill Fischer also ignored the

SECOND GAME

Pittsburgh Pirates	AB	R	H	I	PO	A	E
Doug Baird 3b	1	2	0	0	0	1	1
Max Carey cf	2	2	1	0	4	0	0
Wildfire Schulte lf	3	2	2	1	1	0	0
Bill Hinchman rf	3	2	2	3	1	0	0
Doc Johnston 1b	3	1	1	2	4	0	0
Jack Farmer 2b	3	0	0	0	0	0	0
Alex McCarthy ss	3	0	2	0	0	0	0
Bill Fischer c	3	0	0	0	5	0	0
>Al Mamaux p	3	0	0	0	0	1	0
	24	9	8	6	15	2	1

St. Louis Cardinals	AB	R	H	I	PO	A	E
Jack Smith cf	3	1	1	0	0	0	0
Roy Corhan ss	0	1	0	0	1	2	2
Bob Bescher lf	3	0	0	0	3	0	0
Rogers Hornsby 3b	3	1	1	0	0	0	0
Owen Wilson rf	3	2	2	4	2	0	1
Dots Miller 1b	3	0	2	0	6	0	1
>Frank Snyder c	3	0	1	1	1	0	0
Bruno Betzel 2b	2	0	0	0	2	2	0
Milt Watson p	0	0	0	0	0	0	0
Joe Lotz p2	1	0	0	0	0	1	0
Tommy Long ph4	1	0	0	0	0	0	0
Hi Jasper p5	0	0	0	0	0	0	0
	22	5	7	5	15	5	4

Pittsburgh	IP	H	R	ER	BB	SO
Mamaux W,17-8	5*	7	5	4	3	5

St. Louis	IP	H	R	ER	BB	SO
Watson L,1-2	1.1	6	7	3	2	1
Lotz	2.2	1	2	1	1	0
Jasper	1	1	0	0	0	0
	5*	8	9	4	3	1

Pittsburgh	4 4 0	1 0	- 9
St. Louis	0 0 0	2 3	- 5

* Game called because of darkness.
OB: Pittsburgh 3, St. Louis 5
2B: Johnston
3B: Hinchman
HR: Wilson(3)
SB: Corhan 2, Hornsby 2, Miller 2, Wilson, Snyder 2, Carey 2, Smith 2, McCarthy
CS: Johnston
SO: Mamaux, Bescher, Snyder, Lotz, Hornsby, Miller

BB: Baird 2, Carey, Corhan 3
WP: Jasper
TIME: 1:00
ATTENDANCE: 6,500
UMPIRES: Ernest Quigley, Al Orth
SOURCES: Pittsburgh Gazette Times, Leader, Post, Press; St. Louis Globe-Democrat, Post Dispatch, Republic, Star, Times

BALANCE	OUT+R+OB=BP+AB+BB+SH+HP+CI
Pittsburgh	15 9 3 27 24 3 0 0 0
St. Louis	15 5 5 25 22 3 0 0 0

runner, allowing Miller to take third on the same pitch. A *St. Louis Times* reporter noted this was the first time he had ever seen the same runner steal two bases on one pitch. This burlesque base running didn't work because Pittsburgh ignored the attempts, allowing St. Louis to "steal" 11 bases in the darkness-shrouded, five-inning game. While scoring their runs early in the game, the Pirates themselves stole three bases, making the two-team total 14. As the modern record for stolen bases by both clubs in a nine-inning game is "only" 16, this day's five-inning total was quite significant. For many reasons, not the the least of which are ball-park lights and the modern disqualifier of "defensive indifference," it is improbable that today's fans will ever witness similar statistics.

Goose Eggs Galore

50. Teams Get No Hits in Nine Innings

CINCINNATI   at   CHICAGO
(Reds, 1)   (Cubs, 0)

Wednesday, May 2, 1917, Weeghman Park

Amid frigid temperatures brought on by an arctic breeze from Lake Michigan, only 2,500 Cub fans watched one of baseball's most celebrated games. In it, Cincinnati's Fred Toney and Chicago's Jim "Hippo" Vaughn locked horns for *nine innings of no-hit baseball*, the first and only time two hurlers performed at such a level in the major leagues. The record-setting contest was ultimately decided in the top of the tenth on the game's first hits and an error.

With the season in its infancy, the host Cubs entered this game in second place with a 10–7 log. The visiting Reds, 9–10 and in sixth place, were faltering and hadn't scored a run in 25 straight innings. On the mound were two of the National League's best.

Each hurler walked just two batters in the first nine innings and faced little danger of being scored upon. Actually, there were only three runners left on base for the entire ten innings, and only one got as far as second.

Larry Kopf ended the double no-hitter.

The Cubs gave Toney little trouble. In the second frame, after Fred Merkle had lined out to Heinie Groh, Cy Williams drew a walk. But Les Mann grounded out (4–3), and Art Wilson popped out to short. Then, in the fifth inning, Williams walked again. Mann lined out to left, and Wilson popped up to the right side of the infield. Thirty-nine-year-old Dave Shean cleverly allowed the ball to drop, forcing Williams at second (4–3) and narrowly missing a double play; but Charlie Deal flied out to center, ending the inning. That was the extent of Chicago baserunning for the entire game.

For the first nine innings, Vaughn likewise overpowered Cincinnati, facing just 27 batters, striking out ten, and allowing just one ball to leave the infield (Neale flied out in the first). Three Reds did reach base, but thanks to one caught stealing and two Cub double plays, the Reds through nine had left no base runners on. Heinie Groh led off the fourth with a walk, but Kopf hit into a double play

(4–3–6). Neale then reached first on Zeider's error but was caught stealing. Again leading off in the seventh, Groh worked a 1–1 count. When the next pitch was a called strike two, Heinie argued until he got himself evicted. Gus Getz ably coaxed the free pass, but again Kopf hit into a twin killing (1–4–3). Greasy Neale finished the frame by popping out to Wilson. That was the limit of excitement for the visitors until the tenth inning.

In the visitors half of the tenth, Getz fouled out to Wilson. Then Kopf, who hadn't gotten the ball out of the infield and had hit into two double plays, lined sharply to right for the first safety of the contest. *The Chicago Tribune* reported: "Fred Merkle made a desperate lunge to his right with one hand stretched out and perhaps came within a foot of the ball, but it was out of reach and the terrible suspense was broken." Neale then flied to center for out number two. Hal Chase, the next batter, also hadn't gotten a ball out of the infield all day but now sent a

Cincinnati Reds	AB	R	H	I	PO	A	E
Heinie Groh 3b	1	0	0	0	2	3	0
Gus Getz 3b7	1	0	0	0	2	1	0
Larry Kopf ss	4	1	1	0	1	4	0
Greasy Neale cf	4	0	0	0	1	0	0
Hal Chase 1b	4	0	0	0	12	0	0
>Jim Thorpe rf	4	0	1	1	1	0	0
Dave Shean 2b	3	0	0	0	3	1	0
Manuel Cueto lf	3	0	0	0	5	0	0
Emil Huhn c	3	0	0	0	3	0	0
Fred Toney p	3	0	0	0	0	1	0
	30	1	2	1	30	10	0

Chicago Cubs	AB	R	H	I	PO	A	E
Rollie Zeider ss	4	0	0	0	1	0	1
Harry Wolter rf	4	0	0	0	0	0	0
Larry Doyle 2b	4	0	0	0	4	4	0
Fred Merkle 1b	4	0	0	0	8	1	0
>Cy Williams cf	2	0	0	0	2	0	1
Les Mann lf	3	0	0	0	0	0	0
Art Wilson c	3	0	0	0	14	1	0
Charlie Deal 3b	3	0	0	0	1	0	0
Hippo Vaughn p	3	0	0	0	0	3	0
	30	0	0	0	30	9	2

Cincinnati	IP	H	R	ER	BB	SO
Toney W,5-1	10	0	0	0	2	3

Chicago	IP	H	R	ER	BB	SO
Vaughn L,3-2	10	2	1	0	2	10

```
Cincinnati  0 0 0   0 0 0   0 0 0   1   -1
Chicago     0 0 0   0 0 0   0 0 0   0   -0
```

OB: Cincinnati 1, Chicago 2
DP: Doyle-Merkle-Zeider (Kopf)
   Vaughn-Doyle-Merkle (Kopf)
SB: Chase
CS: Neale
SO: Groh, Chase, Thorpe 2, Shean 2,
   Cueto, Huhn, Toney 2, Doyle,
   Williams, Vaughn
BB: Groh, Getz, Williams 2

TIME: 1:45
ATTENDANCE: 2,500
UMPIRES: Al Orth, Cy Rigler
SOURCES: Chicago American, Daily
   Journal, Daily News, Tribune;
   Cincinnati Commercial Tribune,
   Enquirer

BALANCE	OUT+R+OB=BP=AB+BB+SH+HP+CI								
Cincinnati	30	1	1	32	30	2	0	0	0
Chicago	30	0	2	32	30	2	0	0	0

screaming, low liner straight at Cy Williams in center which should have ended the inning. Cy let it drop just above his shoe tops. *The Chicago Daily Journal* explained, "The official scorer gave Cy a juicy error, as he had the ball in both hands." Cub manager Fred Mitchell later claimed that the ball hit the ground a foot in front of Williams. Regardless, Kopf dashed to third, Chase stopped at first, and still there were two outs. Next up was Jim Thorpe, football and Olympic great. Thorpe had grounded out in the first before striking out twice looking. Chase stole second before Thorpe beat a ball into the muddy turf toward third. Both Vaughn and Wilson chased it as Thorpe sped toward first. Vaughn got to the ball first but realized he had little chance of getting Thorpe, so he hurriedly tossed to Wilson, trying to catch Kopf coming home from third. However, Wilson was still returning to the plate and had his back turned. Vaughn's toss hit Wilson on the shoulder and bounded away,

allowing Kopf to score easily. The ball rolled far enough that Chase too thought he could score and came barreling home. But Wilson retrieved the ball and tagged out Chase, ending the top half of the tenth. Thorpe, having gotten credit for an infield single, was the only Red left on base in the game.

The Cubs had just one more shot at Toney. Larry Doyle led off the bottom of the tenth by striking out. Fed Merkle next thrilled the faithful fans by sending a deep fly to left which forced Manuel Cueto against the left-field wall to make the catch. Cy Williams also nearly shattered Toney's glorious day when he sent a long fly toward right which landed foul by about a foot. Fred regained his composure and fanned Williams for the final out.

For Toney, this ten-inning no-hitter wasn't much to get excited about. In 1909, while hurling in the minors for Winchester in a Blue Grass League championship game, Fred won a 19-strikeout, 17-inning no-hitter, 1–0.

Bob Grooms the Sox

51. Team Records 23 At-Bats in Nine-Inning Game

CHICAGO   at   ST. LOUIS
(White Sox, 0)   (Browns, 3)

Sunday, May 6, 1917, Sportsman's Park

It was a quirk, a fluke, something that wouldn't be repeated for 44 years in major league baseball (see 5-9-61). A sparkling, no-hit performance by the St. Louis Browns' Bob Groom, was combined with several walks, sacrifices, caught stealing, and a double play to result in the Chicago White Sox *batting in all nine innings while recording just 23 official at-bats, the fewest ever.*

Groom was a 33-year-old, right-handed veteran of nine major league seasons. Usually a starter, Bob was occasionally called upon

in relief. On this day, he acted in both roles during a doubleheader.

As the 1917 season unfolded, the visiting White Sox, among the favored pennant contenders, ran into a temporary detour in St. Louis. The day before this doubleheader, the Browns' Ernie Koob was credited with hurling a no-hitter against this same Chicago club that would eventually lead the league in runs scored. Strangely, the Browns, who hadn't finished first in the division in eight years, were off to a good start with a 9–8

Groom hurled an unusual no-hitter.

When it was announced that Groom would start the second game, the crowd protested. Bob gave them even more to complain about when he walked the first batter of the game but quickly calmed the masses by getting Buck Weaver to hit into a double play and striking out Eddie Collins. He also walked Joe Jackson to lead off the second frame, but Joe was tossed out attempting to steal. In the fourth, Groom beaned Weaver. Buck too was trapped off first and thrown out at second base. Again in the sixth, Groom walked the lead off hitter, Swede Risberg, but retired the next three batters, making Risberg the only Chicago player left on base for the game. That was also the extent of Chicago base-runners.

log. It's understandable then, that despite cloudy, chilly conditions, an overflow crowd of 20,000 paid their way into Sportsman's Park, many standing in the outfield periphery.

The first game saw the White Sox jump out to a 2–0 lead before the Browns countered with five in the fourth. Chicago came back with two more in the sixth before Eddie Plank shut them down. St. Louis then summoned Bob Groom to hold their slim 5–4 lead over the last two frames. Although he was wild and walked three batters, Groom responded by pitching a hitless eighth and ninth innings. As they began game two, the ChiSox and Browns were then tied for second place with identical 10–8 records.

About the fourth inning, the same crowd that had protested when Groom initially took the mound, began cheering him. His inside fastballs kept the White Sox off balance, allowing his curves, changeups, and spitballs to set down the visitors. By the ninth inning, the crowd was on its feet; the noise was deafening. Groom had nearly tossed a no-hitter the year before against Cleveland, but it was broken up after two outs in the eighth. This day was different. When Liebold grounded out to Sisler unassisted for the final out, thousands stormed the field. Groom didn't even get as far as the foul line before the mob hoisted him on their shoulders and carried him to the dugout. *The St. Louis Globe-Democrat* noted that it was the first time

in many seasons that fans had shown such enthusiasm.

The St. Louis Star reported an extensive post-game interview with the day's hero. In it, Groom claimed that he was oblivious to the no-hitter until he returned to the "coop" (dugout) after the eighth inning, and a screaming fan made him aware of his chance for immortality. Groom hadn't been aware of his no-hitter, he said later, because the Sox had had four baserunners. Then in the ninth,

he felt that since good luck and good fielding had carried him that far, it would continue to do so. With two outs and two strikes on the game's last batter, catcher Hank Severeid came to the mound and said: "For the love of Mike, put everything you got on the ball now and don't lose this fellow." "Look for everything I own," answered Groom, and Nemo Leibold grounded out to Sisler. And Bob Groom had completed a very unusual no-hitter.

SECOND GAME

Chicago White Sox	AB	R	H	I	PO	A	E
>Nemo Leibold rf	3	0	0	0	1	0	0
Buck Weaver 3b	2	0	0	0	3	5	0
Eddie Collins 2b	3	0	0	0	2	0	0
Joe Jackson lf	2	0	0	0	1	0	0
Happy Felsch cf	3	0	0	0	1	0	0
Chick Gandil 1b	3	0	0	0	12	1	0
Swede Risberg ss	2	0	0	0	1	2	1
Ray Schalk c	2	0	0	0	3	2	0
Joe Benz p	2	0	0	0	0	3	0
Eddie Murphy ph9	1	0	0	0	0	0	0
	23	0	0	0	24	13	1

St. Louis Browns	AB	R	H	I	PO	A	E
Burt Shotton lf	4	0	0	0	1	0	0
Jimmy Austin 3b	4	0	2	0	1	1	0
George Sisler 1b	3	2	3	0	7	2	0
Baby Doll Jacobson rf	4	0	2	0	1	0	0
>Armando Marsans cf	4	0	0	0	4	0	0
Ernie Johnson 2b	3	1	1	1	1	0	0
Hank Severeid c	3	0	0	0	8	2	0
Doc Lavan ss	3	0	0	0	3	3	0
Bob Groom p	2	0	0	0	1	1	0
	30	3	8	1	27	9	0

Chicago	IP	H	R	ER	BB	SO
Benz L,0-1	8	8	3	3	0	1

St. Louis	IP	H	R	ER	BB	SO
Groom W,2-2	9	0	0	0	3	4

Chicago	0 0 0	0 0 0	0 0 0	- 0
St. Louis	1 1 0	0 0 0	0 1 x	- 3

OB: Chicago 1, St. Louis 5
DP: Severeid-Lavan-Sisler (Weaver)
2B: Jacobson, Johnson
SB: Sisler 2, Austin
CS: Jackson, Marsans, Weaver
SO: Leibold, Collins, Gandil, Benz, Jacobson
BB: Leibold, Jackson, Risberg
SH: Groom, Sisler, Schalk

HP: By Groom (Weaver)
TIME: 1:32
ATTENDANCE: 20,000
UMPIRES: Dick Nallin, Billy Evans
SOURCES: Chicago Tribune; St.Louis Globe-Democrat, Post Dispatch, Star, Times

BALANCE	OUT+R+OB=BP=AB+BB+SH+HP+CI
Chicago	27 0 1 28 23 3 1 1 0
St. Louis	24 3 5 32 30 0 2 0 0

Opposite: *Four of the five White Sox outfielders failed to hit Groom; (left to right) Nemo Leipold, Eddie Murphy, Shano Collins, Joe Jackson, and Happy Felsch.*

Johnson Outduels Williams

52. Pitcher Hurls 18-Inning Shutout

CHICAGO   at   WASHINGTON
(White Sox, 0)   (Nationals, 1)

Wednesday, May 15, 1918, Griffith Stadium

In a magnificent pitching encounter, Washington's Walter Johnson outlasted Chicago's Lefty Williams, *tying the record for having pitched the longest shutout— 18 innings* (see 7-16-09). Williams was superb, not permitting a base runner until there were two out in the seventh, then allowing only eight singles through the final 11 frames. Lefty's fastball must have been rising this day as the Nationals made 35 of their outs either by pop-ups or fly balls, including 15 of the first 21 batters. However, Johnson was equal to the challenge, and although he gave up 10 safeties, including two doubles, Walter struck out nine and allowed more than one base runner in only the first and fourteenth stanzas. As a result, each team had precious few scoring opportunities.

For the White Sox:

• Chicago knocked but was denied entry in the first when, with one out, both Eddie Murphy and Buck Weaver recorded infield singles. Some sharp fielding then saved Johnson as Chick Gandil bounced into a twin-killing.

• In the seventh, with one down, Murphy singled

Williams pitched superbly but lost.

Johnson helped his cause with a single.

the 14th, with two down, Nemo Leibold was safe on another infield hit, and Johnson walked his only batter of the day — Murphy. Johnson then got Weaver on a foul out to Eddie Ainsmith.

• Fred McMullin opened the 16th with a single and was sacrificed to second by Ray Schalk. But Johnson got Williams on a ground out and Leibold flied to Milan. (Williams had fanned in each of his first five at-bats.)

• The only Chicago player to reach third was Swede Risberg in the 18th. With one out, Risberg doubled, McMullin flied out, but Swede moved to third on a passed ball. Johnson then tried to walk Schalk so he could face Williams. With the count full, Schalk reached across the plate to hit a fourth wide one but grounded to Morgan.

The Nationals had even fewer threats:

• After two were out in the seventh, Clyde Milan singled to become the first National to reach base. He was moved to second on a walk to Howard Shanks, but Williams escaped any damage by getting Judge to fly out to Collins.

• There was serious trouble for Lefty in the eighth. Morgan was hit with a pitch, and moved to second on a single by Eddie Foster. Williams then speared Ainsmith's hot smash and forced Morgan at third. Johnson popped out, but Burt Shotton walked, loading the bases. Lefty got out of the jam when Doc Lavan flied out to Collins.

• In the twelfth, Washington put two men

and was sacrificed to second by Weaver; but Gandil grounded out to Joe Judge, and Ray Morgan tossed out Shano Collins.

• Murphy doubled in the 12th after one was gone, but Weaver and Gandil left him anchored there.

• Since the first inning, Chicago had not put two men on in the same frame. Now in

on after two were out. Judge singled and Morgan walked, but both were stranded when Foster flied out to Collins.

• With one down in the 17th, Milan and Shanks singled; but Judge forced Milan at third and Morgan popped out to first.

• The pitching classic was terminated in the bottom of the 18th. After Foster led off with an out, Ainsmith singled. Johnson (batting .312, 10–32) also singled, sending Ainsmith to third. Then, with an 0–2 count on Shotton, Williams heaved a wild pitch over the head of Schalk which rolled to the grandstand as Ainsmith romped home with the game winner. Lefty knew the game was over as soon as he released the ball; he didn't even cover home plate but rather walked straight to the clubhouse. It was a heartbreaking loss for the White Sox, who could have moved into second place had they won.

Noteworthy was the fact that although this was essentially a doubleheader and 139 chances were fielded, it remained an errorless game — rather uncommon in 1918. (Errors were still occurring at the lively rate of three per nine-inning game.) Also, despite rumblings that Walter Johnson had seen his finest days, the future Hall of Famer was in rare form. This game marked the 31st consecutive inning in which he had not allowed a run, and since April 28, he had permitted but three runs in 53⅔ innings. He finished the season at 23–13 and led the circuit in shutouts (8), strikeouts (162), and ERA (1.27).

Clark Griffith, a pitcher for 21 seasons and now veteran manager of the Nationals, called this the best extra-inning game he had ever seen — easy for him to say since his team emerged victorious. (Note that through 18 innings there were no substitutions.)

Chicago White Sox	AB	R	H	I	PO	A	E
Nemo Leibold lf	7	0	1	0	8	0	0
Eddie Murphy rf	6	0	3	0	5	0	0
Buck Weaver ss	6	0	2	0	1	4	0
Chick Gandil 1b	7	0	0	0	16	0	0
Shano Collins cf	7	0	0	0	9	0	0
Swede Risberg 2b	7	0	1	0	5	4	0
Fred McMullin 3b	7	0	2	0	4	4	0
>Ray Schalk c	6	0	1	0	4	0	0
Lefty Williams p	6	0	0	0	0	2	0
	59	0	10	0	52	14	0

Chicago	IP	H	R	ER	BB	SO
Williams L,5-2	17.1	8	1	1	2	3

Chicago	0 0 0		0 0 0		0 0 0
Washington	0 0 0		0 0 0		0 0 0

OB: Chicago 8, Washington 10
DP: Lavan-Morgan-Judge (Gandil)
2B: Murphy, Risberg
CS: McMullin, Weaver
SO: Leibold, Risberg 2, McMullin, Williams 5, Judge, Morgan, Johnson
BB: Murphy, Shanks, Morgan
SH: Weaver, Schalk
HP: By Williams (Morgan)
WP: Williams
PB: Ainsmith

Washington Nationals	AB	R	H	I	PO	A	E
Burt Shotton rf	7	0	1	0	0	0	0
Doc Lavan ss	7	0	0	0	4	6	0
Clyde Milan cf	7	0	2	0	3	0	0
Howard Shanks lf	6	0	1	0	10	0	0
Joe Judge 1b	7	0	1	0	22	1	0
Ray Morgan 2b	5	0	0	0	2	6	0
Eddie Foster 3b	7	0	1	0	0	3	0
Eddie Ainsmith c	7	1	1	0	12	2	0
>Walter Johnson p	7	0	1	0	1	1	0
	60	1	8	0	54	19	0

Washington	IP	H	R	ER	BB	SO
Johnson W,6-4	18	10	0	0	1	9

	0 0 0		0 0 0		- 0
	0 0 0		0 0 1		- 1

TIME: 2:47
ATTENDANCE: 1,700
UMPIRES: Brick Owens, George Hildebrand
SOURCES: Chicago Daily News, Herald-Examiner, Tribune; Washington Evening Star, Post, Times

BALANCE	OUT+R+OB=BP=AB+BB+SH+HP+CI
Chicago	54 0 8 62 59 1 2 0 0
Washington	52 1 10 63 60 2 0 1 0

Giants Win But Phillies Steal the Show

53. Team Steals
Eight Bases in Ninth Inning

NEW YORK, NL   at   PHILADELPHIA
(Giants, 10)   (Phillies, 5)

Monday, July 7, 1919, Baker Bowl

The Phillies were a horrid team in 1919. By the first week of July, they were already in last place, 21 games behind their league leading guests, the New York Giants. First year manager Jack Coombs, once a stellar hurler for the crosstown Athletics, was at wits' end watching his team's sloppy and uninspired play. Jack didn't fret much longer, however; he resigned the next day.

This Monday, in the first game of a doubleheader at the Philllies' Baker Bowl, things weren't much different. Dropped pop-ups, bad throws, failure to cover bases, and atrocious pitching enabled John McGraw's Giants to build a secure 10–2 lead entering the bottom of the ninth. In to mop-up for the McGrawmen was right-hander "Pol" Perritt;

Pol Perritt ignored the base runners.

his battery mate was reserve catcher Mike Gonzalez. The ambiance can best be described with one word — APATHY, at least on the part of the Giants. And, the Phillies were about to give their skipper a unique bon voyage present.

Irish Meusel led off the bottom of the ninth for the Quakers by grounding out to short. Fred Luderus walked, and while Perritt was pitching to the next hitter, Luderus continued to walk to second and then to third without so much as a throw from catcher Gonzalez. This represented two of Fred's six stolen bases for the entire season. "Possum" Whitted then flied to left for out number two. Ed Sicking next beat out a roller to third, driving in Luderus. Ed decided that he too could use a few extra stolen bases on his ledger, so he also walked around to third, getting two of his four steals for the year. Next up was Forrest "Hick" Cady, himself a backup catcher. Hick singled to left, driving home Sicking. While standing on first, Cady must have been trembling with excitement because he hadn't stolen a base in 4 years! Courageously, he too made it to both second and third without a throw, finally scoring when "Gavvy" Cravath singled off the short right-field wall. It was now 10–5, but the Giants apparently weren't worried because catcher Gonzalez still didn't throw to any base as Cravath strolled around to third. That made a total of *eight stolen bases in the inning* for the Phillies with only one intervening out. Amazingly, this was not the first time a team stole eight bases in one inning. Just four years earlier, the Senators pulled this stunt on the Cleveland Indians (see 7-19-15).

Who knows how much longer McGraw would have allowed this to go on had not the Phillies' Leo Callahan terminated the record proceedings by bouncing out to Perritt.

Just why the Giants stood by and watched this unilateral parade is uncertain, although it's likely they felt that they had an insurmountable lead. The whole affair was indeed a team effort, or lack thereof. First, Perritt took full windups, even with the runners on base. Second, Gonzalez was believed to have had a weak throwing arm. And finally, during none of these attempts did the Giant infielders make a move away from their normal fielding positions.

This benchmark is well cemented in the record books, for in 1920 baseball rules were revised such that a player would no longer be credited with a stolen base if the defensive team demonstrated indifference.

IN THE NINTH PERRITT KEPT WINDING-UP WITH MEN ON AND THE PHILLIES STARTED TO STEAL ALL THE BASES IN SIGHT.

How The Philadelphia Press *saw the ninth.*

FIRST GAME

New York Giants	AB	R	H	I	PO	A	E
George Burns lf	6	0	2	1	0	0	0
Ross Youngs rf	5	1	2	0	1	0	0
Art Fletcher ss	4	1	1	0	1	3	0
> Al Baird ss7	1	0	0	0	0	3	0
Larry Doyle 2b	4	2	2	1	3	5	0
Benny Kauff cf	4	2	2	0	2	0	0
Heinie Zimmerman 3b	5	2	3	2	1	0	0
Hal Chase 1b	5	1	3	4	13	0	2
Mike Gonzales c	5	1	2	0	6	0	0
Jesse Barnes p	4	0	1	0	0	1	0
Lee King ph9	1	0	0	0	0	0	0
Pol Perritt p9	0	0	0	0	0	1	0
	44	10	18	8	27	13	2

Philadelphia Phillies	AB	R	H	I	PO	A	E
>Leo Callahan rf	5	1	2	0	3	0	0
Harry Pearce 2b	4	0	0	0	3	3	0
Doug Baird 3b	3	0	1	1	0	4	1
John Cavanaugh 3b7	1	0	0	0	0	0	0
Irish Meusel cf	4	1	0	0	2	0	0
Fred Luderus 1b	3	1	2	0	12	0	0
Possum Whitted lf	4	0	0	0	2	0	0
Dave Bancroft ss	2	0	0	0	1	5	1
Eddie Sicking ph7,ss	2	1	1	1	0	1	0
Hick Cady c	4	1	1	1	4	0	0
Gene Packard p	0	0	0	0	0	0	0
Frank Woodward p3	1	0	0	0	0	0	0
Pat Murray p6	2	0	0	0	0	0	0
Gavvy Cravath ph9	1	0	1	1	0	0	0
	36	5	8	4	27	13	2

New York	IP	H	R	ER	BB	SO
Barnes W,11-4	8	5	2	1	0	6
Perritt	1	3	3	1	1	0
	9	8	5	2	1	6

Philadelphia	IP	H	R	ER	BB	SO
Packard L,3-5	2.1	6	5	4	0	0
Woodward	2.2	6	2	2	1	0
Murray	4	6	3	3	2	3
	9	18	10	9	3	3

New York	0 2 3	0 2 2	0 0 1	-10
Philadelphia	0 1 0	0 0 1	0 0 3	- 5

OB: New York 11, Philadelphia 5
DP: Doyle-Chase (Whitted)
    Bancroft-Luderus (Gonzales)
2B: Gonzales, Callahan
SB: Fletcher, Youngs, Kauff, Burns,
    Luderus 2, Sicking 2, Cady 2,
    Cravath 2
SO: Burns, Youngs, Fletcher, Cady,
    Cavanaugh, Bancroft, Whitted,
    Woodward, Murray

BB: Youngs, Doyle, Kauff, Luderus
HP: By Packard (Fletcher)
TIME: 2:00
ATTENDANCE: ?
UMPIRES: Cy Rigler, Bill Byron
SOURCES: New York Times; Philadel-
    phia Evening Bulletin, Inquirer,
    North American, Press, Public
    Ledger, Record

BALANCE	OUT	+ R	+ OB	= BP	= AB	+ BB	+ SH	+ HP	+ CI
New York	27	10	11	48	44	3	0	1	0
Philadelphia	27	5	5	37	36	1	0	0	0

Browns' Assists Not Enough

54. Team Records 27 Assists

PHILADELPHIA, AL   at   ST. LOUIS
(Athletics, 7)   (Browns, 4)

Saturday, August 16, 1919, Sportsmans Park

The Philadelphia Athletics had been the doormats of the league for the past four seasons, and this year was even worse. In 1919, Connie Mack's troops assembled one of the most pathetic records in modern baseball history, finishing at 36–104 (.257), 20 games out of seventh! It was fortunate, perhaps, that the season was abbreviated by the aftermath of the war, for the Athletics lost games at an even greater pace (8–33, .195) as the campaign waned. By this date, while Philadelphia was locked in the basement, the Browns were still in contention, only 7.5 games behind the league leading White Sox. In the first two games of a three game series, the Browns had taken advantage of the Athletics to inch closer to the league leaders; but the final game was a different story.

Philadelphia's Walt Kinney, one of Mack's

1919 stalwarts, not only pitched the visiting Athletics to victory but batted well enough to nearly win it singlehandedly. For the host Browns, Ernie Koob had been given one of his infrequent 1919 starting assignments, but the fans were calling for his head even before the second inning had concluded. In that frame, Koob allowed a walk, a single, and several hard hit balls before Kinney stepped to the plate with two gone. With an 0–2 count on the opposing moundsman, Koob offered a slow curve over the heart of the plate which Kinney rocketed into the right-field bleachers. Before the frame concluded, two more Athletics crossed the plate, and Koob crossed the threshold to the clubhouse. Kinney later knocked in another teammate with a double to lead his club to a 7–4 win.

Not mentioned in any of the sources cited

was the establishment of a new American League benchmark; for in this contest the Browns *reaped 27 assists, an AL mark which stands to this day.* Also not mentioned was the manner in which the Browns accomplished this feat. We do know that three pop-ups were caught by St. Louis infielders, and that two Philadelphia batters struck out. That accounts for five outs which under normal circumstances do not have assists associated with them. We also know that the Browns turned no double plays and had no outfield putouts.

The Browns' four errors were either botched pickups or wild throws — no plays that would have afforded an infielder an assist. The Athletics' Fred Thomas and Wickey McAvoy were each caught stealing by catcher Hank Severeid, and Joe Dugan was thrown out by center fielder Ken Williams while trying to stretch a single.

Although none of the newspapers of the day described any protracted rundowns or other occurrences that may have punctuated such a harvest, a play in the eighth inning may have accounted for several extra assists. With one out, Dugan on third and McAvoy on second, McAvoy stepped away from the sack. When Severeid threw down to Joe Gedeon at second, Dugan started for the plate, drawing the play. Most newspapers merely reported Dugan out at the plate, but both *The Philadelphia Inquirer* and *The Philadelphia Press* mentioned that Dugan was caught in a "run-up." No details could be found, however, of how many fielders participated.

Joe Gedeon spearheaded the Browns' assist record.

If one were to look to the pitchers for clues to this anomaly, there were no skilled sinkerball pitchers on the mound. Actually, the record number of assists was facilitated by a combination of three different hurlers who combined for a 4–19 season's slate — hardly what might be termed a successful pitching crew. In 1919, excluding this game, the greatest assist totals by the Browns were 21 and 20. In neither of those contests were Koob, Davenport, or Wright involved.

Philadelphia Athletics	AB	R	H	I	PO	A	E
Manny Kopp cf	4	1	0	0	2	0	0
Fred Thomas 3b	5	1	2	0	1	6	1
>Tilly Walker lf	4	0	1	1	2	0	0
George Burns rf	4	0	0	0	1	0	0
Whitey Witt 2b	3	1	1	0	1	2	0
Joe Dugan ss	4	1	2	0	1	0	0
Wickey McAvoy c	3	1	1	1	5	1	0
Dick Burrus 1b	3	1	0	0	13	1	0
Walt Kinney p	4	1	2	4	1	4	0
	34	7	9	6	27	14	1

St. Louis Browns	AB	R	H	I	PO	A	E
Jimmy Austin 3b	5	1	1	0	3	3	2
Joe Gedeon 2b	5	0	0	1	2	7	0
Baby Doll Jacobson rf	5	1	3	0	0	0	0
>George Sisler 1b	5	0	0	1	18	2	0
Ken Williams cf	3	0	1	1	0	1	0
Jack Tobin lf	4	0	1	0	0	0	0
Wally Gerber ss	2	1	0	0	1	6	2
Hank Severeid c	4	0	1	1	2	4	0
Ernie Koob p	0	0	0	0	1	1	0
Dave Davenport p2	2	0	0	0	0	2	0
Herman Bronkie ph7	0	0	0	0	0	0	0
Rasty Wright p8	0	0	0	0	0	1	0
Wally Mayer ph9	1	0	1	0	0	0	0
Earl Smith pr9	0	1	0	0	0	0	0
	36	4	8	4	27	27	4

Philadelphia	IP	H	R	ER	BB	SO
Kinney W,7-9	9	8	4	2	4	5

St. Louis	IP	H	R	ER	BB	SO
Koob L,2-1	1.2	4	5	3	1	0
Davenport	5.1	4	1	1	2	1
Wright	2	1	1	0	1	1
	9	9	7	4	4	2

Philadelphia	0 5 0	0 0 1	0 1 0	- 7
St.Louis	2 0 0	1 0 0	0 0 1	- 4

OB: Philadelphia 5, St. Louis 9
2B: Walker, Witt, Kinney, Severeid,
Mayer
HR: Kinney(1)
SB: Walker, Jacobson 2, Williams
CS: Thomas, McAvoy
SO: Walker, Dugan, Austin, Gedeon,
Williams 2, Davenport
BB: Kopp, Walker, Witt, Burrus,
Williams, Gerber 2, Bronkie

SH: McAvoy
PB: Severeid
TIME: 1:55
ATTENDANCE: 10,000
UMPIRES: Dick Nallin, Bill Dinneen
SOURCES: Philadelphia Evening Bul-
letin, Inquirer, North American,
Public Ledger, Press, Record; St.
Louis Globe-Democrat, Post-Dispatch

BALANCE	OUT+R+OB=BP=AB+BB+SH+HP+CI							
Philadelphia	27	7	5	39	34	4	1	0	0
St. Louis	27	4	9	40	36	4	0	0	0

Giants Flatten Phillies in Fast Finale

55. Teams Play Nine-Inning Game in 51 Minutes

PHILADELPHIA, NL   at   NEW YORK
(Phillies, 1)   (Giants, 6)

Sunday, September 28, 1919, Polo Grounds

In a tribute to the hometown Giants, almost 20,000 fans visited the Polo Grounds for the last day of the National League season. The doubleheader meant nothing in the standings as both teams were firmly entrenched in their respective positions.

The Giants had clinched second place, and the Phillies last. The press too was already thinking ahead as sports pages were replete with articles about the infamous, soon to be played, "Black Sox" World Series. The Giants and their guests also seemed to be looking ahead, because they *completed the first game in the record time of 51 minutes*. Amazing? Yes, especially considering the fact that the contest contained 18 hits, 7 runs, and an average sprinkling of walks and strike-outs.

No extraordinary efforts were observed to accelerate this contest until around the sixth inning when the players were noted running to and from their positions, urged on by umpire Klem.

Barnes needed just 51 minutes for his 25th win.

They were probably aware that a week earlier there had been a 55-minute game, leading to several innings this day in which the side was retired on five or six pitches. Both *The New York Tribune* and *The New York World* noted that there was an unusual amount of first-ball hitting. But in the ninth, the Phillies' Fred Luderus put the record at risk by singling to center with two outs. The next and last batter, Dave Bancroft, did taint the mark slightly when he swung halfheartedly, grounding to Larry Doyle for the last out.

There were also some outstanding fielding plays which hastened the outcome. In the ninth, great fielding plays by the Giants' Fletcher and Doyle retired the first two Phillies before Luderus singled. New York rookie Frank Frisch also contributed with some fine fielding around third base earlier in the game. On the other side of the ledger, Phillies rookie outfielder Bevo LeBourveau made a pair of great throws to the plate, nipping two Giant baserunners.

The oddest play of the day occurred in the first inning. When the Giants' Ross Youngs grounded to Bancroft, teammate George Burns was tagged out in a rundown between second and third base. On the same play, Youngs attempted to take second and was also caught, resulting in an unusual double play.

Of course, excellent pitching by New York's Jesse Barnes also helped speed matters along. Jesse threw only 64 pitches, which *The New York American* claimed was also a new major league record. And, Giant outfielders were called on to make only two putouts as Barnes collected his league-leading 25th victory. It was the best season of his career.

Luderus put the record in jeopardy.

FIRST GAME

Philadelphia Phillies	AB	R	H	I	PO	A	E
Bevo LeBourveau lf	4	0	0	0	2	2	0
Lena Blackburne 3b	4	1	1	0	2	2	0
Cy Williams cf	4	0	0	0	4	0	0
Irish Meusel rf	4	0	0	1	0	0	0
Fred Luderus 1b	4	0	2	0	10	1	0
>Dave Bancroft ss	4	0	1	0	1	4	0
Gene Paulette 2b	3	0	0	0	2	3	0
Jack Adams c	3	0	0	0	2	1	0
Lee Meadows p	3	0	1	0	1	2	0
	33	1	5	1	24	15	0

New York Giants	AB	R	H	I	PO	A	E
>George Burns lf	2	1	1	1	1	0	0
Ross Youngs rf	3	1	1	0	0	0	0
Benny Kauff cf	4	1	1	2	1	0	0
Larry Doyle 2b	4	1	2	0	3	8	0
Art Fletcher ss	4	0	2	0	3	7	1
Frankie Frisch 3b	4	0	1	1	1	3	0
George Kelly 1b	4	1	3	1	16	0	0
Earl Smith c	4	0	1	1	2	0	0
Jesse Barnes p	3	1	1	0	0	1	0
	32	6	13	6	27	19	1

Philadelphia	IP	H	R	ER	BB	SO
Meadows L,12-20	8	13	6	5	3	1

New York	IP	H	R	ER	BB	SO
Barnes W,25-9	9	5	1	0	0	2

| Philadelphia | 1 0 0 | 0 0 0 | 0 0 0 | – 1 |
| New York | 0 1 3 | 0 0 2 | 0 0 x | – 6 |

OB: Philadelphia 5, New York 7
DP: Bancroft-Blackburne
     Bancroft-Luderus-Paulette (Youngs)
2B: Blackburne, Burns, Youngs,
     Fletcher, Kelly, Barnes
SB: Burns
SO: Paulette, Meadows, Kelly
BB: Burns 2, Youngs
SH: Barnes

SF: Burns
TIME: 51 minutes
ATTENDANCE: 17,500
UMPIRE: Bill Klem
SOURCES: New York American, Herald,
    Sun, Times, Tribune, World; Phila-
    delphia Inquirer, Press, Record

BALANCE	OUT	+ R	+ OB	= BP	+ AB	+ BB	+ SH	+ HP	+ CI
Philadelphia	27	1	5	33	33	0	0	0	0
New York	24	6	7	37	32	3	2	0	0

A Diamond Epic

56. Numerous Records Fall in 26-Inning Game

BROOKLYN   at   BOSTON
(Robins, 1)   (Braves, 1)

Saturday, May 1, 1920, Braves Field

On a dreary, drizzling May Day in Boston, in front of only about 4,500 fans, one of baseball's most celebrated games unfolded. Around game time, the dripping, gray skies threatened the start of what evolved into *the longest major league game on record—a 26-inning*, 1–1 deadlock between the hometown Braves and the visiting Brooklyn Robins.

The rain halted before the first inning had ended and was not a factor thereafter. Later, darkness became the terminator, forcing play to be concluded after three hours and fifty minutes. Records galore fell by the wayside as hurlers Leon Cadore of Brooklyn and Joe Oeschger of Boston both went the distance in what amounted to nearly a tripleheader.

In addition to the number of innings played and pitched, several participants firmly entrenched themselves in baseball's record books with some mind-boggling statistics.

• Teammates Charles Pick and Norman Boeckel of the Braves each accumulated *11 official at-bats*, a figure that has since been equalled but never surpassed. Pick, however, remains the only player to accumulate as many at-bats without a hit.

• Leon Cadore *assisted on 12 outs*, tying the record for pitchers. He also *faced* the awesome *total of 96 batters* during the contest. No pitcher in the twentieth-century has ever faced more. One can only guess how many pitches he threw.

• Walter Holke, first baseman for the Braves, probably wore out his mitt with *42 putouts*. The most anyone else has ever had is 32.

Most of the team-records established in this contest have since been surpassed, but among those that still stand are:

• *Most team-fielding chances in a game—119, by Boston.*

• *Most outfield chances in a game—24, by Brooklyn*

• *Most assists by both teams—72*

Although this game was of more biblical proportion, Oeschger and Cadore had clashed 11 days earlier in an 11-inning, 1–0 prelude. Then, Cadore emerged victorious.

Joe Oeschger pitched 21 consecutive scoreless innings.

BROOKLYN'S SCORING THREATS

The Robins were the first to score. Leading off the fifth, Ernie Krueger walked and Cadore followed with a one-hopper back to Oeschger. It was a perfect double play ball, but Joe fumbled it, negating any chance of getting Krueger at second. He did recover in time, however, to nip Cadore at first. Ivy Olson next lined a single over shortstop, scoring Krueger. Ivy then moved to second on a wild pitch, but Oeschger fanned Bernie Neis, and Jimmy Johnston lined out to left. That was Brooklyn's run for the day.

There were no other Robin threats until the 17th frame when Zack Wheat led off with a single to right. After Wally Hood sacrificed, Ed Konetchy got an infield hit on a sizzling grounder which Rabbit Maranville was barely able to stop, saving a run. Chuck Ward then hit another grounder which Maranville scooped up and made a quick throw to third baseman Tony Boeckel in an attempt to catch Wheat off third. It failed, loading the bases with only one out. What happened next was called by *The Boston Herald*, "the greatest play ever staged on a Boston diamond." Rowdy Elliott grounded back to Oeschger who quickly pegged home for a force out on Wheat. Catcher Hank Gowdy then fired to first, attempting an inning-ending double play. But his toss was low and wide, pulling first baseman Walter Holke off the bag. Konetchy, running from second to third, saw this and streaked toward home with the lead run. Holke recovered and hurriedly fired off-line to Gowdy. Hank reached for the throw, turned blindly, and recklessly hurled himself across the plate, nipping Konetchy just a few feet from the plate. The odd 1–2–3–2 double play saved the game.

After that, Brooklyn could manage just

This day, despite the tie, Oeschger was the dominant pitcher. While Cadore faced more threatening rallies, Oeschger permitted just three runners to reach third base during the entire 26 innings. Amazingly, both hurlers seemed to strengthen as the day wore on. Cadore didn't allow a hit after a 20th-inning single. Oeschger, whom *The Boston Globe* called the "pride of the Braves and idol of Boston fandom," allowed no hits and only one base runner — on a walk — after the 17th frame. In essence, he nearly pitched a perfect game during the final nine innings!

Despite its length, the suspense as well as the many outstanding defensive plays kept the crowd on the edge of its seat. Following is a description of the game's scoring threats.

Leon Cadore faced 96 batters.

one more baserunner — a walk to Hood — over the last nine innings.

BOSTON'S SCORING THREATS

The Braves tallied their sole marker in the sixth. Les Mann led off with an easy bouncer back to Cadore for the first out, but Walton Cruise laced a triple to left-center. Holke next hit a Texas-leaguer into short left field on which Zack Wheat darted in and caught on the outer edge of the infield grass, nearly doubling Cruise off third. Tony Boeckel then delivered a clutch, two-out single that scored Cruise. Maranville followed with a double to right-center on which Boeckel tried to score. Hood's throw was off line, but Cadore intercepted and relayed to catcher Krueger who tagged the onrushing Boeckel. The play ended the inning with the game then tied.

In the eighth Mann opened with a single, and Cruise sacrificed him to second. Holke hit a scorcher back toward the box which would have scored the run had not Cadore batted it down. The third out was routine.

The Braves threatened seriously in the bottom of the ninth when Maranville started by singling to left. Lloyd Christenbury, pinch-hitting for Mickey O'Neil, beat out an attempted sacrifice bunt. Oeschger then sacrificed his mates, and Ray Powell was intentionally passed, filling the sacks with just one away. With the game on the line and the infield playing at double-play depth, Cadore induced Pick to hit a ground ball to second baseman Olson. Ivy ran toward first to meet the base runner, Powell; but Powell ran out of the base line trying to avoid a tag. Olson then threw to first to complete the game-saving double play.

Holke filled the scoresheet with 42 putouts.

Boston blew another golden opportunity in the 15th. Cruise started with a walk, and Holke attempted to sacrifice him to second. Third baseman Johnston tried to get the lead runner at second but failed, producing two on and none out.

Boeckel also bunted, but Elliott was on it in a hurry and fired to Johnston for a force out at third. Holke too was forced at third when Maranville grounded to Cadore, and

Gowdy ended the threat by flying out to right. When Mann was picked off first after singling in the 20th, it marked the last hit of the day for the home team.

Following this game, the Robins hopped a train back to Brooklyn for a Sunday game with the Phillies. Philadelphia won in 13 innings. Monday they traveled back to Boston and lost to the Braves in 19 innings. In three days, Brooklyn had played 58

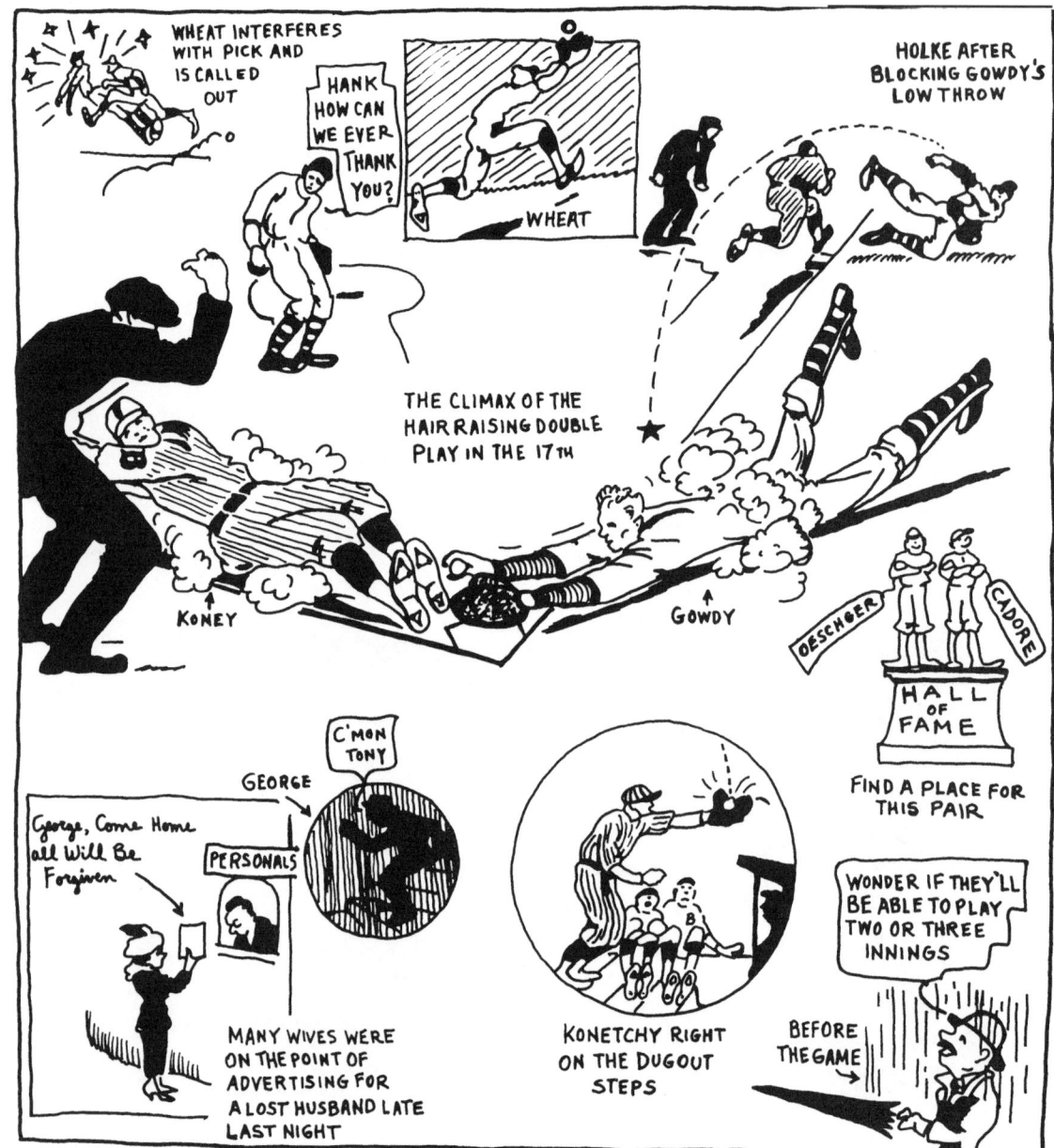

Highlights of the game. (Reprinted courtesy of The Boston Globe.)

innings and traveled back and forth from Boston to Brooklyn.

Joe Oeschger got off to a phenomenal start in 1920. Including this game, Joe had pitched in four games to date, throwing 55 innings and allowing just two earned runs. The rest of the season, however, he furnished earned runs at a 4.17 clip, closing with 15 wins, 13 losses, and an ERA of 3.46. Leon Cadore didn't fare much better, achieving a 15–14 log, with a 2.62 ERA.

The two teams re-played this game later in the season and Boston won it. But by season's end, the Braves had sunk to seventh place, 30 games behind the pennant winners, the Brooklyn Robins.

Brooklyn Robins	AB	R	H	I	PO	A	E
Ivy Olson 2b	10	0	1	1	5	8	1
Bernie Neis rf	10	0	1	0	9	0	0
Jimmy Johnston 3b	10	0	2	0	3	1	0
Zack Wheat lf	9	0	2	0	3	0	0
Hy Myers cf	2	0	1	0	2	0	0
Wally Hood pr4,cf	6	0	1	0	9	1	0
Ed Konetchy 1b	9	0	1	0	30	0	0
Chuck Ward ss	10	0	0	0	5	3	1
Ernie Krueger c	2	1	0	0	4	3	0
Rowdy Elliott c7	7	0	0	0	7	3	0
>Leon Cadore p	10	0	0	0	1	12	0
	85	1	9	1	78	31	2

Boston Braves	AB	R	H	I	PO	A	E
Ray Powell cf	7	0	1	0	8	0	0
Charlie Pick 2b	11	0	0	0	6	11	2
Les Mann lf	10	0	2	0	6	0	0
Walton Cruise rf	9	1	1	0	4	0	0
Walter Holke 1b	10	0	2	0	42	1	0
>Tony Boeckel 3b	11	0	3	1	1	7	0
Rabbit Maranville ss	10	0	3	0	1	9	0
Mickey O'Neil c	2	0	0	0	4	1	0
L. Christenbury ph9	1	0	1	0	0	0	0
Hank Gowdy c10	6	0	1	0	6	1	0
Joe Oeschger p	9	0	1	0	0	11	0
	86	1	15	1	78	41	2

Brooklyn	IP	H	R	ER	BB	SO
Cadore (2-1)	26	15	1	1	5	7

Boston	IP	H	R	ER	BB	SO
Oeschger (2-1)	26	9	1	1	4	7

```
Brooklyn  0 0 0   0 1 0   0 0 0   0 0 0   0 0 0   0 0 0   0 0 0   0 0 0   0 0   - 1
Boston    0 0 0   0 0 1   0 0 0   0 0 0   0 0 0   0 0 0   0 0 0   0 0 0   0 0   - 1
```

OB: Brooklyn 11, Boston 17
DP: Olson-Konetchy (Pick)
  Oeschger-Gowdy-Holke-Gowdy
  (Elliott)
2B: Maranville, Oeschger
3B: Cruise
SB: Myers, Hood
CS: Myers; Boeckel
PK: Neis, Hood; Mann
SO: Olson, Neis 2, Johnston, Hood,
  Elliott, Cadore; Pick, Mann,
  Cruise, Gowdy, Oeschger 3
BB: Wheat, Hood, Konetchy, Krueger;
  Powell 3, Mann, Cruise

SH: Hood; Powell, Cruise, Holke,
  O'Neil, Oeschger
WP: Oeschger
TIME: 3:50
ATTENDANCE: 4,500
UMPIRES: Barry McCormick, Bob Hart
SOURCES: Boston Globe, Herald, Post;
  New York American, Times;
  Retrosheet; DBD

BALANCE	OUT	+R	+OB	=BP	=AB	+BB	+SH	+HP	+CI
Brooklyn	78	1	11	90	85	4	1	0	0
Boston	78	1	17	96	86	5	5	0	0

The Major League's Last Tripleheader

57. Teams Play Tripleheader

CINCINNATI at PITTSBURGH
(Reds, 13,7,0) (Pirates, 4,3,6)

Saturday, October 2, 1920, Forbes Field

A contemptuous rain threatened to prematurely end the 1920 baseball season. With just a few regular season games remaining, precipitation had washed out all games in both leagues on September 30 and a few more on October 1. Playing their last four

games was important to Pittsburgh, for if they had won them all, and Cincinnati had lost theirs, the Pirates, rather than the Reds, would have finished third. In 1920, the first three teams shared in World Series money.

As fate would have it, the Reds were in

Pittsburgh at the time, probably hoping the rain would continue right through to the start of the World Series. They were in third place, 3.5 games ahead of the Pirates.

The Pirates, on the other hand, wanted desperately to play the entire scheduled series with the Reds. When both the September 30 and October 1 games were postponed, Pittsburgh owner Barney Dreyfuss sought special permission from league president John A. Heydler to play a tripleheader on October 2, at Forbes Field. Heydler consented. Playing three games in one day was not without precedent as Brooklyn had hosted Pittsburgh for three on September 1, 1890; and on September 7, 1896, Baltimore and Louisville clashed thrice. Nor was Dreyfuss' expectation of a sweep unrealistic. In the aforementioned tripleheaders, both Brooklyn and Baltimore swept their opponents.

The first game started at noon, in front of just a few hundred patrons. As the day wore on, however, thousands more made their way into the park. Although the temperatures were frigid, this was to be the last major league ball played in Pittsburgh in 1920. Pirate ace, Wilbur Cooper, pitched the first game. Wilbur was shooting for his 25th victory of the campaign, but the Reds jumped all over him for ten hits and eight runs in just over two innings. Cincinnati won in a landslide, 13–4, clinching third place. With both clubs then sapped of any incentive, the second and third games took on a farcical nature.

Game two saw multiple players manning alien fielding positions. Cincinnati backstop Ivy Wingo started at second base, and pitchers Rube Bressler, Dutch Ruether, Fritz Coumbe and Hod Eller saw action in right field, first base, center field and second base respectively. The Reds also prevailed in the second game, 7–3.

The third game witnessed still more shenanigans. Again, Wingo started at second base, pitchers Bressler in center, Eller at first, and Coumbe in right field. Mercifully, at 6 p.m., umpire Harrison called the game after six innings because of darkness. Pittsburgh finally won one, 6–0, snapping their day's two-game losing streak.

Clyde Barnhart had a one-day, three-game hit streak.

There were no obvious heroes this day although five players appeared in all three games — Barnhart, Tierney and Nicholson of the Pirates; Duncan and Rath of the Reds.

FIRST GAME

Cincinnati Reds	AB	R	H	I	PO	A	E
Morrie Rath 2b	4	1	1	0	2	5	0
Jake Daubert 1b	5	3	2	0	17	0	0
Heinie Groh 3b	6	1	2	3	0	4	0
>Edd Roush cf	6	0	2	1	1	0	0
Pat Duncan lf	5	2	2	0	3	0	0
Larry Kopf ss	5	2	3	3	1	4	2
Greasy Neale rf	4	1	1	1	0	0	0
Bill Rariden c	5	2	2	1	3	1	0
Ray Fisher p	4	1	3	2	0	4	0
	44	13	18	11	27	18	2

Pittsburgh Pirates	AB	R	H	I	PO	A	E
Carson Bigbee lf	5	0	1	0	4	0	0
Max Carey cf	5	0	2	0	3	0	0
>Cotton Tierney 2b	5	0	1	0	1	1	0
Billy Southworth rf	3	0	0	0	1	0	0
Clyde Barnhart 3b	4	2	2	0	2	2	0
Charlie Grimm 1b	3	1	1	0	11	1	0
Pie Traynor ss	4	0	1	0	2	6	2
Walter Schmidt c	4	1	0	0	3	3	0
Wilbur Cooper p	0	0	0	1	0	0	0
Whitey Glazner p	1	0	0	0	0	1	0
Fred Nicholson ph6	1	0	0	1	0	0	0
John Wisner p7	0	0	0	0	0	0	0
George Cutshaw ph9	1	0	0	0	0	0	0
	36	4	8	2	27	14	2

Cincinnati	IP	H	R	ER	BB	SO
Fisher W,10-11	9	8	4	1	3	3

Pittsburgh	IP	H	R	ER	BB	SO
Cooper L,24-15	2.1	10	8	7	0	0
Glazner	3.2	4	1	1	2	0
Wisner	3	4	4	4	1	1
	9	18	13	12	3	1

```
Cincinnati    1 1 6    1 0 0    0 0 4   -13
Pittsburgh    0 3 0    0 0 1    0 0 0   - 4
```

OB: Cincinnati 9, Pittsburgh 8
DP: Schmidt-Traynor-Grimm-Traynor
   (Rariden);
   Rath-Daubert (Tierney)
2B: Roush 2, Groh, Tierney, Barnhart
3B: Kopf 2, Daubert
SB: Duncan 3, Rariden, Fisher,
   Daubert, Groh
CS: Rath, Roush

SO: Neale, Carey, Traynor, Schmidt
BB: Rath 2, Fisher, Southworth,
   Grimm, Cooper
HP: By Cooper (Neale), by Wisner
   (Daubert)
TIME: 2:03
ATTENDANCE: 6,000
UMPIRES: Pete Harrison, Hank O'Day

```
BALANCE    OUT+R+OB=BP=AB+BB+SH+HP+CI
Cincinnati  27  13  9  49  44  3   0   2   0
Pittsburgh  27   4  8  39  36  3   0   0   0
```

SECOND GAME

Cincinnati Reds	AB	R	H	I	PO	A	E
Ivy Wingo 2b,c4	5	1	2	0	4	1	0
Rube Bressler rf	4	1	2	0	4	0	0
Dutch Ruether 1b	3	0	0	0	5	0	0
Morrie Rath 2b5	2	1	2	1	2	2	0
Pat Duncan lf	4	1	1	0	1	0	0
Eddie Sicking ss	5	0	2	2	0	2	0
Sam Crane 3b	5	1	1	1	1	4	0
Fritz Coumbe cf	5	1	0	0	1	0	0
Nick Allen c	1	0	1	0	1	0	0
> Hod Eller 2b4,1b5	4	1	3	2	8	0	1
Lynn Brenton p	4	0	0	0	0	7	0
	42	7	14	6	27	16	1

Pittsburgh Pirates	AB	R	H	I	PO	A	E
Carson Bigbee lf	2	1	0	0	1	0	0
Max Carey cf	4	0	0	0	3	1	0
Cotton Tierney ss	3	0	0	1	1	3	0
Fred Nicholson rf	4	2	3	0	0	0	0
Clyde Barnhart 3b	4	0	1	1	0	2	1
Possum Whitted 1b	4	0	1	1	7	3	0
>George Cutshaw 2b	4	0	0	0	5	2	2
Bill Haeffner c	3	0	0	0	9	1	0
Jimmy Zinn p	3	0	1	0	1	3	0
	31	3	6	3	27	15	3

Cincinnati	IP	H	R	ER	BB	SO
Brenton W,2-1	9	6	3	3	2	5

Pittsburgh	IP	H	R	ER	BB	SO
Zinn L,1-1	9	14	7	5	2	7

Cincinnati	0 0 0	0 0 0	7 0 0	– 7
Pittsburgh	1 0 0	1 0 0	0 0 1	– 3

OB: Cincinnati 10, Pittsburgh 4
DP: Brenton-Rath-Eller (Whitted)
2B: Bressler, Eller, Nicholson,
       Barnhart
3B: Whitted
SB: Duncan, Crane, Coumbe, Bigbee
CS: Nicholson
SO: Ruether, Duncan, Sicking, Coumbe
       Brenton 3, Bigbee, Whitted, …

SO: … Cutshaw 2, Haeffner
BB: Bressler, Duncan, Bigbee 2
SF: Tierney
WP: Zinn
TIME: 1:56
ATTENDANCE: 8,500
UMPIRES: Pete Harrison, Hank O'Day

BALANCE	OUT	+R	+OB	=BP	=AB	+BB	+SH	+HP	+CI
Cincinnati	27	7	10	44	42	2	0	0	0
Pittsburgh	27	3	4	34	31	2	1	0	0

THIRD GAME

Cincinnati Reds	AB	R	H	I	PO	A	E
Ivy Wingo 2b	2	0	0	0	2	2	0
Rube Bressler cf	3	0	0	0	1	0	1
>Hod Eller 1b	3	0	1	0	3	0	0
Pat Duncan lf	2	0	0	0	2	0	0
Eddie Sicking ss	2	0	0	0	0	1	0
Sam Crane 3b	2	0	1	0	1	0	0
Morrie Rath rf	0	0	0	0	0	0	0
Fritz Coumbe rf2	2	0	1	0	1	0	0
Bill Rariden c	2	0	0	0	8	1	0
Buddy Napier p	2	0	1	0	0	0	0
	20	0	4	0	18	4	1

Pittsburgh Pirates	AB	R	H	I	PO	A	E
Cotton Tierney 2b	4	1	2	2	1	8	0
>Pie Traynor ss	3	1	0	0	3	2	0
Clyde Barnhart 3b	3	0	1	0	0	1	0
Fred Nicholson lf	3	1	1	1	0	0	0
Cliff Lee cf	2	0	0	1	2	0	0
Charlie Grimm 1b	2	1	2	1	9	0	0
Jimmy Zinn rf	3	1	1	0	1	0	0
Bill Haeffner c	3	0	1	1	2	0	0
Johnny Morrison p	3	1	0	0	0	2	0
	26	6	8	6	18	13	0

Cincinnati	IP	H	R	ER	BB	SO
Napier L,4-2	6	8	6	2	1	8

Pittsburgh	IP	H	R	ER	BB	SO
Morrison W,1-0	6	4	0	0	1	2

Cincinnati	0 0 0	0 0 0	– 0
Pittsburgh	3 0 0	0 0 3	– 6

OB: Cincinnati 3, Pittsburgh 5
DP: Tierney-Traynor-Grimm (Eller)
       Morrison-Tierney-Grimm (Rariden)
2B: Nicholson, Tierney, Napier
SO: Bressler, Eller, Tierney, Zinn,
       Traynor, Nicholson, Haeffner 2,
       Morrison 2
BB: Wingo, Grimm
SF: Lee

HP: By Napier (Traynor)
TIME: 1:01
ATTENDANCE: 6,000
UMPIRES: Pete Harrison, Hank O'Day
SOURCES: Cincinnati Commercial
   Tribune, Enquirer; Pittsburgh
   Dispatch, Gazette Times, Post,
   Press

BALANCE	OUT	+R	+OB	=BP	=AB	+BB	+SH	+HP	+CI
Cincinnati	18	0	3	21	20	1	0	0	0
Pittsburgh	18	6	5	29	26	1	1	1	0

Rookie Clyde Barnhart, who had made his major league debut just ten days earlier, does remain, however, the only player in modern baseball history to produce a three-game hitting streak in the course of a single after-

noon. And, as if playing a tripleheader wasn't enough, that night the Pirates boarded a train to Chicago where they played the Cubs the following day in their season finale.

Flack and Heathcote Trade Uniforms

58. Players Traded
Between Doubleheader Games

ST. LOUIS, NL   at   CHICAGO
(Cardinals, 1,1)   (Cubs, 4,3)

Tuesday, May 30, 1922, Wrigley Field

When one thinks of baseball records and Wrigley Field, offensive fireworks are usually the main ingredient. This day was different. The Cubs did please the hometown fans by winning both ends of a Memorial Day, morning-afternoon doubleheader, but the unique aspect of the day was a player trade. Between games, the Cubs' Max Flack and the Cardinals' Cliff Heathcote were traded for one another, pulled on each other's uniform, and appeared in the second game for their former opponents. In modern times, it is the

Heathcote and Flack traded uniforms between games of a doubleheader.

first known instance of players playing on two different teams in one day.

Flack, one of the few remaining survivors of the Federal League, was an excellent leadoff batter and had been a better hitter of late than Heathcote. Max had hit .294, .302, and .301 in 1919, 1920, and 1921 respectively, while Cliff had finished at .279, .284, and .244. Neither was a power hitter. Heathcote, however, had dazzling speed and was eight years younger. But the real reason for the trade probably stemmed from a spring training incident. Then, Flack was beaned, after which he left the team, claiming that his skull had been fractured. Upon his return, he was fined for leaving training camp without permission. The fallout may have motivated Cub manager, Bill Killifer, to trade him.

Flack had lived just a few blocks from Wrigley Field and went home between games of the twin bill. Upon his return, he was shocked when manager Killifer told him, "Maxie boy, you're in the wrong clubhouse!" The veteran Flack took the trade philosophically, while Heathcote spent most of the intermission in the visitors' clubhouse where he wept.*

After the trade, Flack remained with the Cardinals for the three final years of his career. Heathcote played another eight seasons with the Cubs, before ending his playing days with the Reds and Phillies. The Cubs got more mileage out of Heathcote than the Cards did of Flack, although neither player was a vital producer for the balance of his career.

In retrospect, here's how the trade stacked up:

Max Flack 1914–1925	Before Trade	After Trade		Cliff Heathcote 1918–1932@	Before Trade	After Trade
# Seasons †	8.5	3.5		# Seasons †	4.5	10.5
Games	1071	340		Games	431	856
At-Bats	4030	1222		At-Bats	1492	2657
Bat. Avg.	.278	.278		Bat. Avg.	.270	.280

All numbers derived from Total Baseball, 2nd ed.
† Half season credited to each player during trade year
@ Heathcote played for Cincinnati and Philadelphia in 1931 and 1932. Only statistics compiled while playing for the Cubs are included.

MORNING GAME

St. Louis Cardinals	AB	R	H	I	PO	A	E
Jack Smith rf	4	0	0	0	2	0	1
Specs Toporcer ss	3	0	0	0	3	2	0
Milt Stock 3b	3	0	0	0	3	3	0
Rogers Hornsby 2b	3	0	2	0	2	3	0
Jack Fournier 1b	3	0	0	0	5	0	0
>Austin McHenry lf	4	1	1	0	2	0	0
Cliff Heathcote cf	3	0	0	0	1	0	0
Eddie Ainsmith c	3	0	1	1	6	1	0
Bill Sherdel p	1	0	0	0	0	0	0
Roy Walker p4	1	0	0	0	0	0	1
Joe Schultz ph8	1	0	0	0	0	0	0
Bill Bailey p8	0	0	0	0	0	0	0
	29	1	4	1	24	9	2

Chicago Cubs	AB	R	H	I	PO	A	E
Jigger Statz cf	4	0	1	0	3	0	0
Charlie Hollocher ss	4	1	3	0	1	2	0
Marty Krug 3b	3	1	2	0	4	3	0
Ray Grimes 1b	3	1	1	1	9	1	0
Max Flack rf	4	0	0	1	0	0	0
Zeb Terry 2b	4	1	2	1	2	1	0
Turner Barber lf	4	0	1	0	3	0	0
Bob O'Farrell c	2	0	0	0	4	2	0
>George Steuland p	4	0	1	1	1	0	0
	32	4	11	4	27	9	0

St. Louis	IP	H	R	ER	BB	SO
Sherdel L,7-3	3.2	6	3	3	2	1
Walker	3.1	5	1	0	0	3
Bailey	1	0	0	0	0	1

Chicago	IP	H	R	ER	BB	SO
Steuland W,1-0	9	4	1	1	4	4

*Gene Karst and Martin J. Jones, Who's Who in Professional Baseball (New Rochelle; Arlington House, 1973), 308, 423.

St. Louis	0 1 0	0 0 0	0 0 0	- 1
Chicago	0 0 0	3 1 0	0 0 x	- 4

OB: St. Louis 5, Chicago 8
DP: Hollocher-Terry-Grimes (Hornsby)
    O'Farrell-Krug (Heathcote-S.O.)
    Hornsby-Toporcer-Fournier(Terry)
2B: Hornsby, Krug, Grimes
SB: Barber
CS: Hollocher
SO: Stock, Fournier, McHenry, Flack,Heathcote,
    Grimes, O'Farrell, Stueland 2

BB: Toporcer, Stock, Hornsby,
    Fournier, O'Farrell 2(1-I)
SH: Krug, Grimes
TIME: 1:44
ATTENDANCE: 5,000
UMPIRES: Paul Sentelle, Barry
    McCormick

BALANCE	OUT	+	R	+	OB	=	BP	+	AB	+	BB	+	SH	+	HP	+	CI
St. Louis	27		1		5		33		29		4		0		0		0
Chicago	24		4		8		36		32		2		2		0		0

AFTERNOON GAME

St. Louis Cardinals	AB	R	H	I	PO	A	E
Max Flack rf	4	0	1	0	2	1	0
Specs Toporcer ss	4	0	1	0	1	4	1
Jack Smith cf	3	0	0	0	1	0	0
Rogers Hornsby 2b	3	0	0	0	2	2	0
Jack Fournier 1b	4	0	1	0	10	1	0
Austin McHenry lf	3	1	2	0	1	0	0
>Milt Stock 3b	4	0	2	1	1	1	0
Vern Clemons c	3	0	0	0	6	2	0
Bill Doak p	3	0	0	0	0	3	0
	31	1	7	1	24	14	1

Chicago Cubs	AB	R	H	I	PO	A	E
Jigger Statz cf	4	1	2	0	5	0	0
Charlie Hollocher ss	4	0	1	0	1	1	0
Marty Krug 3b	4	1	1	0	2	4	0
Ray Grimes 1b	2	1	0	1	8	0	0
Cliff Heathcote rf	4	0	2	0	2	0	0
Turner Barber lf	3	0	2	2	4	1	0
>Zeb Terry 2b	3	0	1	0	2	3	0
Bob O'Farrell c	3	0	0	0	3	2	0
Vic Aldridge p	3	0	0	0	0	1	0
	30	3	9	3	27	12	0

St. Louis	IP	H	R	ER	BB	SO
Doak L,7-2	8	9	3	3	2	6

Chicago	IP	H	R	ER	BB	SO
Aldridge W,6-3	9	7	1	1	3	3

St. Louis	0 1 0	0 0 0	0 0 0	- 0
Chicago	1 0 0	0 0 0	0 2 x	- 3

OB: St. Louis 6, Chicago 7
DP: Krug-Grimes (Doak)
CS: Smith, Grimes
SO: Hornsby, Stock, Doak, Hollocher,
    Barber, Terry, O'Farrell 2,
    Aldridge
BB: Smith, Hornsby, McHenry,
    Grimes 2(1-I)
SH: Barber, Terry
WP: Doak

TIME: 1:45
ATTENDANCE: 12,000
UMPIRES: Barry McCormick, Paul
    Sentelle
SOURCES: Chicago Daily Journal,
    Daily News, Tribune, Evening Post;
    DBD; St. Louis Globe Democrat,
    Post Dispatch

BALANCE	OUT	+	R	+	OB	=	BP	+	AB	+	BB	+	SH	+	HP	+	CI
St. Louis	27		1		6		34		31		3		0		0		0
Chicago	24		3		7		34		30		2		2		0		0

Pirate Pairs Pillage Phillies

59. Ten Teammates Get Two Hits in One Game

PITTSBURGH	at	PHILADELPHIA
(Pirates, 17)		(Phillies, 10)

Monday, August 7, 1922, Baker Bowl

The Pirates were hot! *The Philadelphia North American* described Pittsburgh's visit to

the Quaker City with: "The Pirate craft swung to its moorings here with the proud

Whitey Glazner picked up two hits and the victory.

Pittsburgh was even afforded a chance for its record-setting performance. This was the first game during the Pirates' two-week road trip in which their starting hurler had not gone the distance, and opportunistically, both Pittsburgh relievers chipped in with a pair of safeties.

Baker Bowl dimensions and ground rules also augmented the fusillade. Several of Pittsburgh's doubles were routine fly balls that found their way to the inviting right field wall, only 280 feet away. Also, each of the Phillies' three round-trippers bounced over the three-foot high, left-field wall — home runs by Baker Bowl standards. This was an era when defensive speed in the outfield and the ability to cut off balls in the gap could mean a lot more than just one base.

Pittsburgh's firepower was not a mirage. The following day they collected 46 hits in a doubleheader. For the year they led the league in runs, hits, triples, stolen bases, and batting average. The lowest batting average among the regulars belonged to future Hall of Famer Pie Traynor at .282, and even the four top bench-warmers combined for a .315 average. The Pirates, at this point in the season, were making a strong effort to move foward in the standings. Before this game they were in fourth place, 7.5 games out. But despite winning 60 percent of their remaining games, they still couldn't catch McGraw's Giants and finished tied for third, eight games out.

Offensively, the Quakers led the league in home runs but also in strikeouts which, when coupled with a pitching staff that allowed more earned runs than any other, precipitated a seventh place finish, 35.5 games out.

record of seven straight victories, ten out of twelve on its eastern voyage." To make matters worse for the home team, the Pirates had beaten the Phillies in all ten meetings thus far this season.

The Phillies didn't make it easy for the marauding Buccaneers, enticing the entire crew of invaders into the fray. They swabbed the decks with Pirate ace Wilbur Cooper, and five of their own mates smashed a pair of hits apiece. But by the time the cannons had stopped smoking, three Philadelphia hurlers had been forced to walk the plank as Pittsburgh recorded *ten individuals in their lineup who each contributed two hits*, a benchmark in team offense (later tied, see 9-2-25). Actually it was because of the Phillies' offense that

Pittsburgh Pirates	AB	R	H	I	PO	A	E
Rabbit Maranville ss	5	1	2	1	1	2	0
Max Carey cf	5	2	2	1	3	0	1
Carson Bigbee lf	6	3	2	0	0	0	0
Clyde Barnhart rf	2	1	1	2	0	0	0
Reb Russell ph4,rf	3	2	2	3	0	0	0
Cotton Tierney 2b	5	2	2	1	0	3	0
Pie Traynor 3b	6	1	2	2	5	3	0
Charlie Grimm 1b	5	2	2	4	9	0	0
>Walter Schmidt c	6	2	2	0	9	0	0
Wilbur Cooper p	1	0	1	1	0	0	0
Hal Carlson p3	2	0	2	0	0	0	0
Whitey Glazner p4	2	1	2	2	0	2	0
	48	17	22	17	27	10	1

Pittsburgh	IP	H	R	ER	BB	SO
Cooper	2.2	8	6	6	0	2
Carlson	.2	1	2	2	4	1
Glazner W,7-7	5.2	6	2	1	0	6
	9	15	10	9	4	9

Pittsburgh	2 1 1	8 0 0	0 4 1	-17		
Philadelphia	2 2 2	2 0 0	0 2 0	-10		

OB: Pittsburgh 9, Philadelphia 10
2B: Bigbee, Russell, Traynor, Grimm,
    Schmidt, Carlson, Rapp 3, Mokan,
    Williams
3B: Tierney
HR: Glazner(1), Walker(8), Smith(1),
    Lee (14)
CS: Tierney
SO: Maranville, Tierney, Grimm, Rapp
    Parkinson 2, Williams, Mokan,
    Smith, Lee, Henline, Hubbell

Philadelphia Phillies	AB	R	H	I	PO	A	E
Goldie Rapp 3b	5	4	4	0	0	0	0
>Frank Parkinson 2b	5	2	2	3	1	3	0
Cy Williams cf	5	0	2	1	5	0	0
Curt Walker rf	3	1	1	3	3	0	0
Johnny Mokan lf	4	0	2	0	4	0	0
Jimmy Smith ss	5	1	1	1	2	2	0
Cliff Lee 1b	5	1	2	1	6	1	1
Butch Henline c	5	0	1	0	5	1	0
Lefty Weinert p	1	1	0	0	0	0	0
John Singleton p4	0	0	0	0	0	1	1
Bill Hubbell p4	3	0	0	0	1	1	0
R.Wrightstone ph9	1	0	0	0	0	0	0
	42	10	15	9	27	9	2

Philadelphia	IP	H	R	ER	BB	SO
Weinert	3	7	5	3	2	3
Singleton L,1-9	.1	4	6	4	0	0
Hubbell	5.2	11	6	6	1	0
	9	22	17	13	3	3

BB: Carey, Russell, Tierney, Rapp,
    Parkinson, Walker, Mokan
SH: Maranville
SF: Grimm, Walker
TIME: 2:20
ATTENDANCE: ?
UMPIRES:Charlie Moran, Ernie Quigley
SOURCES: DBD; Philadelphia Inquirer,
    North American, Public Ledger,
    Record; Pittsburgh Dispatch,
    Gazette Times, Post, Press

BALANCE	OUT	+R	+OB	=BP	=AB	+BB	+SH	+HP	+CI
Pittsburgh	27	17	9	53	48	3	2	0	0
Philadelphia	27	10	10	47	42	4	1	0	0

The Granddaddy of All Slugfests

60. Teams Combine for 51 Hits and 49 Runs in Nine-Inning Game

PHILADELPHIA, NL   at   CHICAGO
(Phillies, 23)   (Cubs, 26)

Friday, August 25, 1922, Wrigley Field

Baseball's hitting records took on significant revision in the 1920s with the introduction of a livelier ball. In 1918, the best offenses were producing only 4.1 runs

Chicago's Charlie Hollocher (left) and Hack Miller (opposite) each had six RBI's.

Both Chicago and Philadelphia newspapers were replete with lists of 20th-century standards that were established or tied. Among them were:

• *Most plate appearances by one team in a nine-inning game—66 by the Phillies (still stands).*

• *Most plate appearances by both teams in a nine-inning game—125 (still stands).*

• *Most hits by both teams in a nine-inning game—51 (still stands)*

• *Most runs by one team in a game—26 by the Cubs (later surpassed)*

• *Most runs by both teams in a game of any length—49 (still stands)*

• *Most at-bats in one inning by one player—3 by Marty Callahan (later tied)*

• *Most team hits in one inning—11 by Cubs (tied existing major league record; later surpassed)*

• *Most runs by one team in one inning—14 by Cubs (tied existing major league record; later surpassed)*

• *Most times reached base safely in a nine-inning game—7 by Chicago's Cliff Heathcote (since tied).*

• *Most plate appearances in a nine-inning game—8 by Phillies teammates Russell Wrightstone and Frank Parkinson (later tied).*

• *Most teammates score one or more runs—13 by Phillies (tied existing major league record; still stands)*

• *Most players, both clubs, score one or more runs—22 (still stands)*

In addition, the two pitching staffs issued a combined 21 free passes (NL record was 23) and were battered for 76 total bases (possibly a record at the time). The fielders also contributed enormously to the turmoil by committing nine errors.

The contest began innocently enough with

per game, but by 1922 National and American League leaders both averaged *over 5.6 runs per game.* Even the least productive teams were now averaging 3.87 runs, quite an improvement in just four years. Never was the lively ball more evident than in this bloodbath, as many of the hitting and scoring marks set this day have yet to be challenged. Usually, games of this ilk played at Wrigley Field are, to a large degree, caused by strong winds blowing fly balls out of the park. None of the Chicago newspapers credited mother nature this day, although *The Chicago Herald Examiner* noted that there was a cool breeze from the west (blowing out toward right). All three home runs were hit by right-handed batters, two clearing the right field facade and the other the center field wall.

the Cubs leading 1–0 after one inning. The Phillies scored three runs in the top of the second to take the lead, but in the bottom half pitcher Jimmy Ring lost his composure after arguing with umpire Bob Hart about several pitches. The Cubs then mauled him for ten runs on six hits, three walks, and two errors. Ring had looked to the bench for relief during the onslaught, but Phillies manager Kaiser Wilhelm had no one warming up. Chicago's Tony Kauffman struck out twice that inning to help Ring survive. At the end of two, the Cubs led, 11–3.

The Phillies countered with a couple of runs in the top of the third, and Ring quieted the Cubs in the bottom of the frame. Philadelphia continued to chip away with another run in the top of the fourth making it 11–6, within reasonable range. But the Cubs blew the game open in their half of the fourth. Combining 11 hits, three walks, two Philadelphia errors, and a hit-batsman, Chicago tallied 14 times, sending Ring to the showers. Their lead was then seemingly insurmountable at 25–6. During the debacle, Marty Callaghan became the *first player of the century to bat three times in the same inning.*

The Phillies collected three more runs in the fifth, and the Cubs tallied their final run in the sixth, making it 26–9. That's how it stood until the eighth frame. Bill Killefer, the Windy City manager, then decided to give a few of his rookies some mop-up work. No team had ever overcome a 17-run deficit, especially with just two innings remaining, but the Phillies had not yet conceded defeat. They were about to participate in one of the most gallant comeback attempts in baseball history.

Nineteen-year-old Uel "Poss" Eubanks was the first Cub rookie to take the hill in the top of the eighth. Uel had nothing on his deliveries, and the visitors took advantage of him. Before he was mercifully relieved, he had given up eight runs while retiring just two batters. It was the last time Eubanks ever pitched in the major leagues. The next rookie to take the mound was "Big Ed" Morris. Ed was able to squelch the rally, halting the score at 26–17, still a fairly secure lead with just three outs needed for the win.

But the ninth brought further disaster for the Chicago newcomers. Morris couldn't get anyone out and allowed four more runs. It was then 26–21 and still there were no outs. To the rescue was sent Earnest "Tiny" Osborne, another rookie who supplied the hometown fans with further palpitations. He allowed the Phillies to score another pair of runs, making the score 26–23. Then, with two gone and the bases loaded, Osborne had to face Bevo Lebourveau, who had replaced Cy Williams earlier in the game. Bevo was hot, having singled in each of his three plate appearances, but Osborne struck him out to end the slugfest thriller. The three left on base for the Phillies brought their day's total to 16, giving some indication of the multiple opportunities they failed to exploit.

Despite this single-game outpouring, the Cubs finished fourth in runs scored, fifth in hits, and fifth in the final standings. The Phillies finished seventh in all three departments.

Philadelphia Phillies	AB	R	H	I	PO	A	E
Russ Wrightstone 3b	7	3	4	4	0	2	1
Frank Parkinson 2b	4	1	2	2	4	6	0
Cy Williams cf	3	1	0	0	2	0	1
> Bevo Lebourveau cf5	4	2	3	2	0	0	0
Curt Walker rf	6	2	4	1	2	0	1
Johnny Mokan lf	4	2	3	2	1	0	0
Art Fletcher ss	3	1	0	0	0	2	0
Jimmy Smith ss5	4	2	1	2	1	3	0
Roy Leslie 1b	1	1	0	1	4	0	0
Cliff Lee 1b4	4	4	3	0	6	0	1
Butch Henline c	2	1	2	0	4	0	0
Frank Withrow c5	4	1	2	3	0	0	0
Jimmy Ring p	2	0	1	1	0	1	0
Lefty Weinert p4	4	2	1	1	0	0	0
Goldie Rapp ph9	0	0	0	0	0	0	0
	52	23	26	19	24	14	4

Chicago Cubs	AB	R	H	I	PO	A	E
Cliff Heathcote cf	5	5	5	4	4	0	1
Charlie Hollocher ss	5	2	3	6	5	2	1
John Kelleher ss7	1	0	0	0	0	0	0
Zeb Terry 2b	5	2	2	2	2	2	0
Barney Friberg 2b7	1	0	1	0	0	0	0
Ray Grimes 1b	4	2	2	2	7	1	0
>Marty Callaghan rf	7	3	2	1	2	0	1
Hack Miller lf	5	3	4	6	1	0	0
Marty Krug 3b	5	4	4	1	1	1	1
Bob O'Farrell c	3	3	2	2	1	1	0
Gabby Hartnett c6	0	0	0	0	4	0	1
Tony Kaufmann p	2	0	0	0	0	1	0
Turner Barber ph4	1	2	0	0	0	0	0
George Stueland p5	1	0	0	0	0	0	0
George Maisel ph7	1	0	0	0	0	0	0
Uel Eubanks p8	0	0	0	0	0	1	0
Ed Morris p8	0	0	0	0	0	0	0
Tiny Osborne p9	0	0	0	0	0	0	0
	46	26	25	24	27	9	5

Philadelphia	IP	H	R	ER	BB	SO
Ring L,11-12	3.1	12	16	6	5	2
Weinert	4.2	13	10	5	5	2
	8	25	26	11	10	4

Chicago	IP	H	R	ER	BB	SO
Kaufmann W,7-8	4	9	6	3	3	0
Stueland	3	7	3	3	2	2
Eubanks	.2	3	8	4	3	0
Morris	.1	4	4	4	1	1
Osborne	1	3	2	2	2	3
	9	26	23	16	11	6

Philadelphia	0	3	2	1	3	0	0	8	6	-23
Chicago	1	10	0	14	0	1	0	0	x	-26

OB: Philadelphia 16, Chicago 9

DP: Smith-Parkinson-Lee (O'Farrell)
Smith-Parkinson-Lee (Grimes)
Wrightstone-Parkinson-Lee

2B: Parkinson, Walker, Mokan, Terry, Withrow, Heathcote 2, Hollocher, Friberg, Grimes, Krug 2

3B: Wrightstone, Walker

HR: Miller 2(11), O'Farrell(3)

SB: Weinert, Hollocher

CS: Williams

SO: Williams, LeBourveau, Withrow, Mokan, Weinert, Smith, Stueland, Callaghan, Kaufmann 2

BB: Wrightstone, Parkinson 3, Rapp, Williams, Mokan 3, Henline, Lee,

BB: Heathcote 2, Terry, Grimes 2, Miller, Krug, O'Farrell, Barber Hartnett

SH: Parkinson, Walker, O'Farrell

SF: Leslie, Hollocher

HP: By Weinert (Grimes)

WP: Stueland

TIME: 3:01

ATTENDANCE: 7,100

UMPIRES: Bob Hart, Cy Rigler

SOURCES: Chicago American, Daily Journal, Daily News, Herald-Examiner, Tribune; DBD; Philadelphia Inquirer, North American, Public Ledger, Record

---

BALANCE	OUT	+	R	+	OB	=	BP	=	AB	+	BB	+	SH	+	HP	+	CI
Philadelphia	27		23		16		66		52		11		3		0		0
Chicago	24		26		9		59		46		10		2		1		0

Philly Fusillade Wrecks Redbirds

61. Teams Record
79 Total Bases in Nine-Inning Game;
23 Different Players Hit Safely

ST. LOUIS, NL   at   PHILADELPHIA
(Cardinals, 14)   (Phillies, 20)

Friday, May 11, 1923, Baker Bowl

The ball wasn't the only thing Cy Williams hammered.

Earned run ratios swelled, and hitters fattened their batting averages as the Phillies and the Cardinals traded blows this day in Baker Bowl. Ranked as the best hitter's park in the National League since the turn of the century,* Baker Bowl presented batters with a right field wall only 280 feet from home plate, 35 feet closer than the present day "Green Monster" in Fenway Park, Boston. Then too, balls that bounced over the three-foot tall wall in left field were also considered home runs.

This was the last of a four game series between the two teams, and St. Louis was thoroughly enjoying Quaker City hospitality. The Cards had won the first three games while collecting 48 hits and 27 runs. The Phillies, on the other hand, had lost seven games in a row. As Cardinal bats continued to smoke, they collected 22 more hits in this game, including four home runs. But the Redbird pitchers swooned. The home team made their 18 hits count; aided by nine walks they scored 20 runs. Of course six Phillies' homers, all with men on base, helped immensely. That made for a *two-team total of ten home runs, the most in a major league game to date.* It took 27 years for two clubs to exceed this mark (see 6-23-50).

Total Baseball, 2nd ed., edited by John Thorn and Pete Palmer (New York: Warner Books, Inc., 1991), 2517–21.

St. Louis Cardinals	AB	R	H	I	PO	A	E
Jack Smith lf	6	3	3	2	2	0	0
Eddie Dyer rf	3	2	2	2	1	0	0
Les Mann ph6,rf	3	2	2	3	0	0	0
Specs Toporcer ss	5	1	1	1	4	2	0
Jim Bottomley 1b	6	1	4	1	6	2	0
>Milt Stock 3b	6	1	3	0	1	1	0
Hy Myers cf	5	0	1	1	2	0	1
Howard Freigau ss	3	0	1	2	3	2	1
Eddie Ainsmith c	3	1	1	0	4	1	0
Harry McCurdy ph8,c	1	0	0	0	0	1	0
Jesse Haines p	1	0	1	0	1	0	0
Bill Sherdel p3	1	1	1	2	0	2	0
Clyde Barfoot p5	0	0	0	0	0	0	0
Max Flack ph6	1	1	1	0	0	0	0
Johnny Stuart p6	0	0	0	0	0	0	0
Lou North p6	1	0	0	0	0	1	0
Ray Blades ph9	1	1	1	0	0	0	0
	46	14	22	14	24	12	2

Philadelphia Phillies	AB	R	H	I	PO	A	E
Johnny Mokan lf	4	3	3	7	2	0	0
Heinie Sand 3b	5	2	1	0	0	1	0
Cy Williams cf	5	4	3	7	5	0	0
>Curt Walker rf	4	2	1	0	0	1	0
Walter Holke 1b	4	1	1	0	7	1	0
Frank Parkinson 2b	5	1	3	5	3	6	0
Russ Wrightstone ss	4	3	2	0	7	2	0
Butch Henline c	3	3	2	0	2	1	0
Petie Behan p	1	1	1	1	1	0	0
Lefty Weinart p6	1	0	0	0	0	1	0
Lee Meadows p8	1	0	1	0	0	0	0
	37	20	18	20	27	13	0

St. Louis	IP	H	R	ER	BB	SO
Haines	2.1	3	4	4	2	0
Sherdel L,2-3	2	7	7	7	1	1
Barfoot	.2	2	1	1	0	0
Stuart	0	0	2	2	2	0
North	3	6	6	4	4	1
	8	18	20	18	9	2

Philadelphia	IP	H	R	ER	BB	SO
Behan W,1-1	5	10	8	8	3	0
Weinert	2.1	8	4	4	0	0
Meadows	1.2	4	2	2	0	2
	9	22	14	14	3	2

St. Louis   1 1 1   3 0 3   0 3 2   -14
Philadelphia   0 0 5   3 4 2   3 3 x   -20

OB: St. Louis 9, Philadelphia 5
DP: Wrightstone-Parkinson-Holke
2B: Smith, Bottomley, Stock, Blades,
     Flack, Mokan, Sand
3B: Stock
HR: Dyer(2), Mann 2(3), Sherdel(1),
     Mokan 2(4), Williams 3(12),
     Parkinson(2)
SB: Smith, Dyer, Mokan, Wrightstone
CS: Bottomley, Mokan 2
SO: Mann, Stock, Sand, Parkinson
BB: Toporcer, Freigau, Ainsmith ...

BB: Mokan 2, Sand, Williams, Walker 2,
     Wrightstone, Henline 2
SH: Holke, Behan 2
SF: Freigau
TIME: 2:20
ATTENDANCE: ?
UMPIRES: Bill Klem, Bob Hart
SOURCES: DBD; Philadelphia Inquirer,
     North American, Record; St. Louis
     Globe-Democrat, Post-Dispatch

BALANCE	OUT	+R	+OB	=BP	+AB	+BB	+SH	+HP	+CI
St. Louis	27	14	9	50	46	3	1	0	0
Philadelphia	24	20	5	49	37	9	3	0	0

Among the sources referenced, not a word was mentioned about two other new standards. *This game also established the all-time, total-base record at 79* as 12 players chipped in with one or more extra base hits. In addition, *23 different players hit safely.* No nine-inning game has ever surpassed either of these marks.

The Phillies onslaught was led by Fred "Cy" Williams. Cy had seven RBIs on three hits,

all home runs, that ran his season total to 12, tops in the major leagues. His third of the game came in the bottom of the eighth, so he didn't get another at-bat to try to become the first player in the twentieth-century to hit four homers in one game. He did, however, lead the league by season's end with 41 round-trippers, which was more than either the Braves, Red Sox or Senators teams had. He did this despite appearing in only 136 games.

Little Johnny Mokan, 5'7", 165 lbs., also smashed a double, a pair of four baggers, and drove home seven runs. This game represented a big part of Johnny's season as he accumulated only ten homers and 48 RBIs all year.

This was the fifth consecutive year that the Phillies led the National League in home runs. In all but one of those seasons, they also finished in the cellar. Perhaps having the highest team ERA each year had something to do with their futility.

Giants Score in All Nine Innings

62. Team Scores in Each of Nine Innings; Three Teammates Get Five Hits Apiece

NEW YORK, NL   at   PHILADELPHIA
(Giants, 22)   (Phillies, 8)

Friday, June 1, 1923, Baker Bowl

Upon first thought, it wouldn't seem to be so unusual. After all, there have been more than 100,000 major league games played. But this day's occurrence is more rare than a perfect game, an unassisted triple play, or a player hitting four home runs in a game. This was the first time since the turn of the century that a team had accomplished the trick, and it would take 41 seasons to be repeated. And, it's never been done in the entire history of the American League.

The setting was ideal. John McGraw's Giants were in first place, had led the league in scoring runs three of the last four seasons and would do so again this year. The Phillies were already mired in last place, sporting the most generous pitching staff in the major leagues. This season they would provide earned runs at a 5.34 clip. And then, this contest was conducted in the most conducive run scoring park in the major leagues.* Note that perhaps because of Baker Bowl's proclivity for run scoring, both managers waited until the seventh inning, with New York leading 18–7, to begin substitutions.

The New Yorkers weren't particular about whom they pounded. Four Philadelphia pitchers, who this year combined for a 6–30 won–lost record and a 6.45 ERA, were equally abused. And when the Giants weren't hitting, which wasn't often, the Phillies kept New York rallies alive with their shoddy fielding. Seven errors enriched the basepaths for the New Yorkers.

McGraw's squad hit safely in every frame although they collected only one in the third, fourth, and eighth. The third inning hit was combined with three walks for a score. The fourth inning hit was a mammoth home run into the center field bleachers by Jimmy O'Connell. In the eighth frame the Giants supplemented their solo hit with a walk, wild pitch, a sacrifice, and an error to tally a pair of runs. The closest that Philadelphia hurlers came to a shutout inning was the ninth when rookie Jim Bishop retired the first two batters. But then George Kelly tripled, and O'Connell doubled him home. That was Jimmy's fifth hit of the contest and enabled the Giants to *tie the modern major league record for most players (three) on one team with*

---

*Total Baseball, *2nd ed., edited by John Thorn and Pete Palmer (New York: Warner Books, Inc., 1991), 2517–21.*

Jimmy O'Connell—five hits and seven RBIs.

five or more hits. O'Connell also excelled in the field with eight putouts, including one for which he reached into the stands in left center to rob Curt Walker of a home run.

In addition to O'Connell, Ross Youngs also drove in seven runs. By strange twists of fate, both players had their playing careers tragically cut short.

O'Connell was a Pacific Coast League star who was purchased by the Giants in 1921 for $75,000, a considerable sum in those days. Left with the San Francisco Seals for a little more seasoning during 1922, Jimmy was brought up to the big time for 87 games in 1923. In 1924, he hit .317 in 52 games with the Giants before he became involved in a bribery scheme and was barred from baseball for life by Commissioner Landis.

Ross "Pep" Youngs was a favorite of McGraw. A slashing line-drive hitter, base stealer, and hustling fielder, Youngs established himself as a consistent contender for batting average, doubles, and on-base-percentage leader. At the age of 30, however, he died of Bright's disease, a terminal kidney disorder. In 1972, the Veterans Committee elected him to the Hall of Fame.

This game provided a major contribution for the 1923 Giants to lead both major leagues in hits and runs scored. They did succumb, however, to their cross-town rival, the Yankees, in the World Series.

New York Giants	AB	R	H	I	PO	A	E
Dave Bancroft ss	5	4	3	0	1	2	0
Travis Jackson ss7	1	0	0	0	0	1	0
Heinie Groh 3b	7	4	5	3	3	1	0
Frankie Frisch 2b	5	2	2	1	1	0	0
F. Maguire pr7,2b	1	1	0	0	2	1	1
Irish Meusel lf	3	2	1	1	0	0	0
Bill Cunningham lf7	1	0	0	0	1	0	0
Ross Youngs rf	6	3	5	7	1	0	0
George Kelly 1b	7	2	2	1	5	0	0
Jimmy O'Connell cf	6	3	5	7	8	0	0
Earl Smith c	5	0	0	0	3	1	0
Alex Gaston c7	0	1	0	0	2	0	0
Rosy Ryan p	1	0	0	0	0	1	0
> Claude Jonnard p2	4	0	0	0	0	0	0
	52	22	23	20	27	7	1

Philadelphia Phillies	AB	R	H	I	PO	A	E
>Johnny Mokan lf	4	2	2	0	1	0	1
Russ Wrightstone 3b	5	3	3	4	1	2	2
Cy Williams cf	4	0	2	1	3	0	0
Freddy Leach cf7	1	0	1	0	0	0	0
Curt Walker rf	4	0	2	2	1	0	0
Cottom Tierney 2b	5	0	0	0	3	4	0
Walter Holke 1b	5	1	3	0	8	0	1
Heinie Sand ss	3	2	1	0	2	3	2
Frank Parkinson ph9	1	0	0	0	0	0	0
Jimmie Wilson c	3	0	0	0	5	0	0
Mickey O'Brien c7	2	0	0	0	3	1	1
Ralph Head p	0	0	0	0	0	0	0
Petie Behan p2	1	0	0	0	0	0	0
Jesse Winters p5	1	0	0	0	0	0	0
Jim Bishop p7	1	0	0	0	0	2	0
Goldie Rapp ph9	1	0	1	0	0	0	0
	41	8	15	7	27	12	7

New York	IP	H	R	ER	BB	SO
Ryan	1.2	4	5	5	2	0
Jonnard W,3-1	7.1	11	3	3	2	4
	9	15	8	8	4	4

Philadelphia	IP	H	R	ER	BB	SO
Head L,1-6	1.2	6	6	5	2	0
Behan	2.1	4	2	2	5	2
Winters	2	8	10	8	0	3
Bishop	3	5	4	2	2	1
	9	23	22	17	9	6

New York	4 2 1	1 5 5	1 2 1	-22
Philadelphia	1 4 0	1 1 0	0 1 0	- 8

OB: New York 14, Philadelphia 11
DP: Sand-Tierney-Holke
      Maguire-Kelly
2B: Groh, Frisch, O'Connell 3, Williams, Walker, Holke 2
3B: Youngs, Kelly, Wrightstone
HR: O'Connell(4)
SB: Frisch, O'Connell
CS: Meusel
SO: Kelly 2, Jonnard 4, Williams, Holke, Sand 2
BB: Bancroft, Frisch, Smith, Youngs, Meusel 3, O'Connell, Jonnard, ...

BB: ... Mokan 2, Walker, Sand
SH: Jonnard, Behan
HP: By Bishop (Gaston)
WP: Winters, Bishop
PB: Smith, Wilson
TIME: 2:47
ATTENDANCE: ?
UMPIRES: Ernie Quigley, Cy Pfirman
SOURCES: DBD; New York Times; Philadelphia Inquirer, North American, Record

BALANCE	OUT+R+OB=BP=AB+BB+SH+HP+CI
New York	27 22 14 63 52 9 1 1 0
Philadelphia	27 8 11 46 41 4 1 0 0

O'Doul Victim of Chance

63. Pitcher Faces 16 Batters, Allows 13 Runs in One Inning

BOSTON   at   CLEVELAND
(Red Sox, 3)   (Indians, 27)

Saturday, July 7, 1923, Dunn Field

In 1929, Frank "Lefty" O'Doul set the National League record for most hits in a season with 254. His big-league career, however, began as a pitcher in 1919. By 1923 he was having serious second thoughts about his chosen vocation, and this day's game may have finally convinced Lefty to leave the rosin bag behind and turn to the lumber. (He later produced two batting titles along with a .349 lifetime average). His manager, Frank "The Peerless Leader" Chance, seemed to have a strange pitching philosophy — leave them in the box until they can't throw anymore. Except for the world champion Yankees, the Red Sox used fewer pitchers during the season than any other major league club, and those pitchers allowed more earned runs than any other staff in the American League.

On this day, in the first game of a doubleheader at Cleveland's Dunn Field (later called League Park), O'Doul epitomized that strategy when he was left on the mound to *face 16 batters and allow 13 runs in one inning.* The 16 batters-faced in one inning merely tied the record set 21 years earlier (see 7-8-02), but the 13 runs-allowed has never been matched in this century. Those 13 runs become even more absurd when one learns that they were all unearned. O'Doul actually would have escaped the inning unscathed had it not been for an error. It all happened in the bottom of the sixth with Lefty in his third inning of relief and the Sox trailing 11–2. Below are the gruesome details of O'Doul's infamous inning:

• Steve O'Neill walked but was forced out by Stan Coveleski.

• Charlie Jamieson, on a 23-game hitting streak and leading the league in hits, singled to right sending Coveleski to second.

• Joe Connolly flied out to Mike Menosky for the second out.

• Player-manager Tris Speaker walked to load

This game represented a highlight of Rube Lutzke's five year career.

O'Doul in happer times as a Brooklyn outfielder.

the sacks and set the stage for the crucial error.

• Joe Sewell next sent a fly ball to Ira Flagstead in right field, but Ira dropped it allowing Coveleski and Jamieson to score. Speaker went to third; Sewell stopped at first. (It had not been a good day for Flagstead because earlier in the contest, while playing shortstop, he made another error which cost his team three unearned runs.)

• Riggs Stephenson doubled off the right-field wall scoring Speaker, Sewell stopping at third. It was then 14–2.

• Rube Lutzke singled to right, knocking home both Sewell and Stephenson. Rube took second on the throw home.

• Frank Brower walked, as did O'Neill for the second time in the inning, loading the bases. Still, manager Chance refused to rescue his southpaw despite the fact that *The Boston Globe* reported that O'Doul constantly looked toward the dugout for help.

• Coveleski singled home Lutzke and Brower with O'Neill taking third. The score then read 18–2.

• O'Doul walked Jamieson, again loading the bases.

• Connolly singled home both O'Neill and Coveleski.

• With the game now a farce, Knode batted for Speaker and walked, filling the runways once again.

• Sewell continued the onslaught by singling, driving home Jamieson and Connolly, and sending Knode to third. It was then 22–2. Next, in a gesture that can only be labeled as callous brutality, Sewell stole second.

• Stephenson, the 16th batter of the inning, doubled to left scoring both Knode and Sewell. As a token of mercy or perhaps another of heartlessness, Stephenson also tried to steal but was thrown out, O'Doul to McMillan.

In the top of the seventh, O'Doul was still in the game and led off for Boston. He walked but was left stranded. In the bottom of the frame, relief finally came in the form of rookie Carl Stimson, who took the mound for the Red Sox. Perhaps O'Doul's arm had

finally worn out. (This game was an excellent example of how misleading ERAs can be, especially in earlier years when teams made ample errors. O'Doul pitched terribly but because of the early error, he was charged with no earned runs in the disasterous frame.)

It was curious strategy indeed that Cleveland attempted stolen bases with such an enormous lead. When Sewell stole in the sixth inning, the score was 22–2. Stephenson was caught in the same frame when the count read 24–2. In the following inning, Rube Lutzke stole second with his team still ahead 24–2, and later that same inning, O'Neill was caught with two outs and a 25–2 score. O'Neill's venture may have been an act of mercy as he hadn't a stolen base the entire season, and *The Boston Globe* mentioned that the crowd had a good laugh over this attempt. Steve, a lumbering catcher, had provided some levity earlier in the game as well. In the fourth inning, while O'Neill was on first, Coveleski was robbed of a clean single to right when his batterymate was thrown out at second. Aside from O'Neill's attempt, the others were probably serious, although Indian intentions were unclear from the game descriptions.

Manager Chance wasn't picking on only O'Doul, because before the season ended he heartlessly watched as another one of his hurlers also faced 16 batters in one inning (see 9-28-23).

By *scoring 13 runs after there were two outs*, Cleveland set a major league record that has yet to be surpassed.

This game established another standard when the Indians *tallied 27 runs, the most ever by a twentieth-century major league team up to that time* (later broken). The score could have been worse had it not been for the fact that the Indians grew tired and began taking extra chances on the bases, resulting in several careless outs. Three Indians were thrown out at home — Stephenson in the fifth inning, Brower in the seventh, and Sewell in the eighth.

Cleveland also *tied the American League record by scoring in each of the eight innings they batted.*

FIRST GAME

Boston Red Sox	AB	R	H	I	PO	A	E
Mike Menosky rf,lf4	5	0	2	0	3	1	0
Shano Collins cf	4	1	0	0	0	0	0
Ira Flagstead ss,rf4	5	0	1	0	0	4	2
George Burns 1b	4	1	1	1	4	1	0
Joe Harris lf	2	1	1	0	2	0	0
Pinky Pittinger 2b4	3	0	2	0	3	1	0
Howard Shanks 2b,ss4	4	0	2	1	4	3	0
>Norm McMillan 3b	5	0	3	0	4	2	1
Roxy Walters c	1	0	0	0	0	1	0
Dick Reichle ph4	1	0	0	0	0	0	0
Al DeVormer c4	2	0	1	0	4	0	0
Curt Fullerton p	1	0	0	0	0	0	1
Lefty O'Doul p4	1	0	0	0	0	3	0
Carl Stimson p7	1	0	0	0	0	1	0
	39	3	13	2	24	17	4

Cleveland Indians	AB	R	H	I	PO	A	E
Charlie Jamieson lf	6	4	3	3	5	0	0
Homer Summa rf	3	1	2	2	0	0	0
Connolly ph5,rf,cf7	3	2	1	2	1	0	0
Tris Speaker cf	3	3	3	2	2	0	0
Ray Knode ph6,1b	1	1	0	0	2	0	0
Joe Sewell ss	4	3	3	2	2	4	1
Riggs Stephenson 2b	5	2	3	5	3	5	0
Rube Lutzke 3b	5	3	4	6	1	2	1
>Frank Brower 1b,rf7	6	2	2	0	8	1	0
Glenn Myatt c	1	2	1	0	1	0	0
Steve O'Neill ph4,c	1	1	1	1	1	0	0
Stan Coveleski p	4	3	1	2	1	2	0
Dewey Metivier p7	1	0	0	0	0	0	0
	43	27	24	25	27	14	2

Boston	IP	H	R	ER	BB	SO
Fullerton L,0-3	3	7	8	3	4	0
O'Doul	3	11	16	3	8	0
Stimson	2	6	3	3	2	1
	8	24	27	9	14	1

Cleveland	IP	H	R	ER	BB	SO
Coveleski W,9-8	6	7	2	2	1	0
Metivier	3	6	1	1	3	1
	9	13	3	3	4	1

Boston	0 0 0	2 0 0	0 0 1	- 3
Cleveland	3 2 3	1 2 13	1 2 x	-27

OB: Boston 13, Cleveland 10
DP: Sewell-Brower (Collins)
    Lutzke-Brower (Reichle)
    Sewell-Stephenson-Knode (Shanks)
2B: Pittinger, Stephenson 3, Lutzke 2
3B: Jamieson, Brower
SB: Sewell 2, Lutzke, Brower
CS: Stephenson, O'Neill
SO: Stimson, Metivier
BB: Collins, Burns, Shanks, O'Doul,
    Jamieson, Connolly, Speaker 2,
    Knode, Sewell 2, Stephenson, ...

BB: Lutzke, Brower, Myatt, O'Neill 3
SH: Coveleski
SF: Stephenson, Lutzke
HP: By Fullerton (Sewell)
PB: DeVormer
TIME: 2:10
ATTENDANCE: 9,000
UMPIRES: Brick Owens, Tommy Connolly
SOURCES: Boston Globe, Herald, Post;
    Cleveland Plain Dealer

BALANCE	OUT+R+OB=BP=AB+BB+SH+HP+CI
Boston	27 3 13 43 39 4 0 0 0
Cleveland	24 27 10 61 43 14 3 1 0

Ehmke Also Victim of Chance

64. Pitcher Faces 16 Batters, Allows 11 Runs in One Inning

NEW YORK, AL   at   BOSTON
(Yankees, 24)   (Red Sox, 4)

Friday, September 28, 1923, Fenway Park

Howard Ehmke, side-arming ace of the Boston Red Sox, had won his 20th game of the season more than a week earlier. The Sox,

solidly entrenched in the cellar, were going nowhere, but their guests this day were the powerful New York Yankees, who had long

Neither Elmer Smith (left) nor Joe Dugan started this game, but each contributed three hits.

before clinched the American League crown. Taking the mound for the New Yorkers was their ace, Sad Sam Jones, also a twenty-game winner. Despite the disparity of the teams, the pitching matchup was enough to draw a respectable crowd, for everyone knew that both hurlers had recently thrown no-hitters.

On September 4, Jones threw a no-hitter against the Athletics in Philadelphia. Not to be outdone, Ehmke duplicated the feat in the Quaker City on September 7. Jones followed his no-hitter with a two-hitter on September 10. Ehmke topped him with a one-hitter on September 11. Although both pitchers then settled down into the realm of mere mortals, the Boston fans were ready for a pitchers duel. What they got was another debacle (see 7-7-23) thrust upon their home team.

Boston Manager Frank Chance habitually refused to relieve pitchers in mid-inning once a game got away from him. A few months earlier, he sadistically watched Lefty O'Doul get pummeled for 13 runs in a single inning (see 7-7-23). This day it was Ehmke's turn in the torture chamber. Howard tied his team-mate O'Doul and the modern major league record by *facing 16 batters in one inning*. Ehmke, however, allowed only 11 runs in his ordeal (compared to O'Doul's 13).

The Yankees in this game were led by Babe Ruth and catcher Wally Schang, both of whom had five hits. A 20-year-old ex-collegian named Henry Louis Gehrig, who was filling in for Wally Pipp, also made his presence felt. (Gehrig did not become a regular until 1925.) New York's *30 hits remained the American League record for a nine-inning game for 69 years (see 8-28-92).*

New York Yankees	AB	R	H	I	PO	A	E
Whitey Witt cf	4	3	2	0	1	0	0
Hinkey Haines cf6	2	1	0	1	2	0	0
Mike McNally 3b	1	1	1	0	0	0	0
Joe Dugan 3b2	5	2	3	2	2	0	0
Babe Ruth lf	6	4	5	3	5	0	0
Lou Gehrig 1b	7	3	4	4	5	1	2
Bob Meusel rf	2	0	0	0	0	0	0
Elmer Smith rf3	4	2	3	1	0	0	0
Aaron Ward 2b	3	2	1	1	3	2	0
Mike Gazella ph6,2b	2	1	1	1	2	0	0
Wally Schang c	6	2	5	5	2	1	0
Everett Scott ss	1	0	0	0	1	1	0
> Ernie Johnson ss1	6	2	2	2	4	1	0
Sad Sam Jones p	6	1	3	1	0	0	0
	55	24	30	21	27	6	2

New York	IP	H	R	ER	BB	SO
Jones W,21-8	9	11	4	4	1	1

New York	4	0	1		0	1	11		2	3	2	-24
Boston	0	0	0		3	0	0		0	1	0	- 4

OB: New York 11, Boston 9
DP: Schang-Scott
2B: Witt, Ruth 2, Gehrig 3, Smith,
Schang, Burns, Menosky, Shanks
HR: Ruth(38), Ward(10)
SB: Haines, Smith
CS: Picinich
SO: Gehrig, Meusel 2, Smith, Ward
Gazella, Jones, Donohue
BB: Witt, McNally, Ruth, Smith, Ward
Gazella, Donohue

Boston Red Sox	AB	R	H	I	PO	A	E
Johnny Mitchell ss	5	0	1	0	4	3	0
Val Picinich c	5	0	1	0	8	0	1
John Donohue rf	4	1	0	0	1	2	0
George Burns 1b	4	1	2	1	5	1	0
> Dick Reichle 1b7	1	0	0	0	2	0	0
Mike Menosky lf	4	1	1	2	2	0	0
Shano Collins cf	4	1	3	0	3	0	1
Howard Shanks 3b	4	0	1	1	1	2	0
Norm McMillan 2b	4	0	2	0	1	2	1
Howard Ehmke p	2	0	0	0	0	1	0
Joe Harris ph6	1	0	0	0	0	0	0
Clarence Blethen p7	1	0	0	0	0	0	0
	39	4	11	4	27	11	3

Boston	IP	H	R	ER	BB	SO
Ehmke L,20-17	6	21	17	16	4	6
Blethen	3	9	7	6	2	1
	9	30	24	22	6	7

SF: Schang
PB: Picinich
TIME: 1:54
ATTENDANCE: ?
UMPIRES: Tommy Connolly, Bill
Dinneen, Pants Rowland
SOURCES: Boston Globe, Herald;
DBD; New York American, Times

BALANCE	OUT+R+OB=BP=AB+BB+SH+HP+CI
New York	27 24 11 62 55 6 1 0 0
Boston	27 4 9 40 39 1 0 0 0

Kelly—A One-Man Wrecking Crew

65. Player Drives in All Eight of His Team's Runs

CINCINNATI   at   NEW YORK
(Reds, 6)   (Giants, 8)

Saturday, June 14, 1924, Polo Grounds

George "Highpockets" Kelly was both a consistent hitter and fielder for John McGraw's Giants during the decade of the 1920s, and this was his finest season. A future Hall of Famer, this was George's fourth of six consecutive campaigns in which he batted over .300. And for the second time, he also led the league in RBIs with 136. Not generally considered an extravagant home run hitter, Kelly nevertheless on this day became the first major leaguer to homer three times in one game—on two different occasions; rather unexpected for a player who had only three home runs thus far into the season. Before the year ended, however, George also set another National League record by hitting seven homers in six games, with at least one in each.

In this game, Kelly's most noteworthy accomplishment was the fact that he *knocked in all eight New York runs, the most by any player who drove in all of his team's runs in a game* (later surpassed). The eight RBIs also tied the existing National League record for most RBIs in a game (later surpassed).

Kelly's triad of long distance clouts all landed in the left field seats and enabled the Giants to creep back into a first-place tie with the Cubs. Following is a summary of Highpockets' plate appearances:

Inning	Pitcher	Score Before	Outs	Event	RBI	Score After
2	Sheehan	Cin 4, NY 0	0	HR puts Giants on board	1	Cin 4, NY 1
3	Sheehan	Cin 4, NY 1	2	Grand Slam gives NY lead	4	Cin 4, NY 5
5	Benton	Cin 4, NY 5	1	Intentional walk loads bases	0	Cin 4, NY 5
7	Benton	Cin 6, NY 5	0	Singles home tying run	1	Cin 6, NY 6
9	Donohue	Cin 6, NY 6	2	Two-run HR wins game	2	Cin 6, NY 8

Three times Kelly put his team ahead, the last time with a game-winning exclamation point. However, his third home run in the bottom of the ninth was clouded in controversy. It seems that the exuberant crowd stormed onto the field and mobbed their hero to the point where it was impossible for Kelly to continue around the bases. Despite a warning by first base umpire Ernie Quigley to touch all the bases, after rounding first George made a bee-line to the center field clubhouse with the crowd hot on his heels. Considerable debate ensued among the umpires and the official scorer as rules at the time were unclear about the necessity of a batter who hit a game winning homer to touch all the bases. Many of the fans milled around the press box after the end of play trying to ascertain how it would all be ruled. Umpire-in-Chief Hank O'Day said after the game that the official scorer had the right to credit Kelly with a home run as there was nothing in the scoring rules about touching all the bases if a batter drives the ball over the fence or into the stands in the ninth inning, winning the game. The umpires officially were interested only in the first run of the inning which settled the game in favor of the Giants. Ironically, this was the same highly respected arbiter who was behind the plate when Fred Merkle failed to touch second base during the

Kelly didn't bother to run out his third home run.

heated 1908 pennant race in this same stadium.

According to *The New York Times*, the matter wasn't finally settled until later that night when National League president, John A. Heydler, declared Kelly's act a home run. Heydler said that the wording of the "scoring rule" relating to hits-winning-games was faulty and in conflict with the "playing rules." He permitted Kelly's home run but condemned his act of not circling the bases and promised future supplementary scoring instructions requiring such a batter to touch every base in order to receive proper credit.

Cincinnati Reds	AB	R	H	I	PO	A	E
Curt Walker rf	5	1	2	1	5	0	0
Edd Roush cf	5	0	2	1	2	0	0
Rube Bressler 1b	4	0	0	0	7	0	0
>Pat Duncan lf	5	0	1	0	0	0	0
Babe Pinelli 3b	3	1	2	0	3	2	0
Ike Caveney ss	4	1	2	0	3	3	2
Hughie Critz 2b	4	1	1	1	2	5	1
Ivy Wingo c	4	1	1	0	4	4	0
Tom Sheehan p	2	1	1	2	0	0	0
Rube Benton p4	1	0	0	0	0	0	0
Pete Donohue p7	1	0	0	0	0	1	0
	38	6	12	5	26*	15	3

New York Giants	AB	R	H	I	PO	A	E
Ross Youngs rf	4	1	1	0	3	0	0
Frankie Frisch 2b	5	1	2	0	3	3	1
Hack Wilson lf,cf6	4	2	1	0	2	0	0
>George Kelly 1b	4	3	4	8	12	0	0
Jimmy O'Connell cf	2	0	0	0	2	1	0
Hank Gowdy ph5	1	0	0	0	0	0	0
Irish Meusel lf6	1	0	1	0	0	0	0
Travis Jackson ss	4	0	2	0	1	9	0
Heinie Groh 3b	4	0	0	0	1	2	0
Frank Snyder c	4	0	0	0	3	1	0
Virgil Barnes p	0	0	0	0	0	1	0
Joe Oeschger p3	2	1	1	0	0	0	0
Fred Lindstrom ph7	1	0	0	0	0	0	0
Claude Jonnard p8	0	0	0	0	0	0	0
Bill Terry ph8	1	0	0	0	0	0	0
Rosy Ryan p9	0	0	0	0	0	0	0
	37	8	12	8	27	17	1

Cincinnati	IP	H	R	ER	BB	SO
Sheehan	3	5	5	5	2	0
Benton	3.2	4	1	1	1	1
Donohue L,5-3	2	3	2	2	0	1
	8.2*	12	8	8	3	2

New York	IP	H	R	ER	BB	SO
Barnes	2	4	4	3	1	1
Oeschger	5	8	2	2	1	0
Jonnard	1	0	0	0	0	0
Ryan W,4-3	1	0	0	0	0	0
	9	12	6	5	2	1

* Two outs when winning run scored

Cincinnati	0 4 0	0 0 2	0 0 0	- 6
New York	0 1 4	0 0 0	1 0 2	- 8

OB: Cincinnati 7, New York 6
DP: Pinelli-Wingo-Bressler (Gowdy)
  Critz-Caveney-Bressler (Snyder)
  Snyder-Kelly-Jackson-Frisch
  (Caveney)
2B: Walker, Sheehan, Roush, Jackson
3B: Walker
HR: Kelly 3(6)
SB: Frisch
CS: Wilson, Youngs
SO: Duncan, Youngs, Wilson
BB: Bressler, Pinelli, Youngs,
  Wilson, Kelly(I)

WP: Benton
PB: Wingo
BK: Barnes
TIME: 1:55
ATTENDANCE: 22,500
UMPIRES: Hank O'Day, Ernie Quigley
  Cy Pfirman
SOURCES: Cincinnati Commercial
  Tribune, Enquirer; New York Times,
  Tribune, World

BALANCE	OUT+R+OB=BP=AB+BB+SH+HP+CI
Cincinnati	27 6 7 40 38 2 0 0 0
New York	26 8 6 40 37 3 0 0 0

Sunny Jim Shines

66. Player Drives in 12 Runs in One Game

ST. LOUIS   at   BROOKLYN
(Cardinals, 17)   (Robins, 3)

Tuesday, September 16, 1924, Ebbets Field

Late in the 1924 campaign, the Cardinals invaded Brooklyn hoping to play the "spoiler" role. St. Louis had long since dropped out of the pennant race; they were entrenched in sixth place, ten games behind the fifth place Cubs. The Robins (named after their manager Wilbert Robinson) on the other hand, were only one game from the top, looking up at their front-running neighbors, the Giants. Brooklyn needed this victory.

The Robins were spearheaded by the National League's second leading hitter, Zack Wheat, then at .375, and its number one home run hitter, Jack Fournier with 27. The Cardinal lineup countered with the omnipotent Rogers Hornsby who on this date was leading the league in batting average, slugging average, total bases, doubles, and walks, and was second in runs scored and home runs. Batting behind Hornsby was a 24-year-old, left-handed hitting first baseman by the name of Jim Bottomley. Nicknamed "Sunny Jim" for his refreshing disposition, Bottomley himself was no slouch at the plate. He had benefited from Hornsby's .507 on-base percentage all season but never to the extent as on this day. Supported not only by Hornsby but by the rest of his teammates as well, Bottomley parlayed six hits into *twelve RBIs, still the major league standard for a single game* (tied 9-07-93).

No matter what kind of streak a batter is on, it takes a fortuitous series of events to be able to knock in 12 runs in just six plate appearances. Bottomley was a fine hitter. In the 20th-century only he and Doc Cramer twice harvested six hits in a nine-inning game. But Jim needed plenty of teammates on base and conducive pitching each time he stepped to the plate. Indeed, every time he batted, there were runners on base, twelve in all, eight of them in scoring position. And the five hurlers he faced were not the finest, having won a combined total of 16 games with a 4.06 ERA for the 92–62 Robins. Nevertheless, Sunny Jim sparkled each time up. Here's how his day unfolded:

Inning	Outs	Pitcher	Runners	Event	RBIs
1	0	Ehrhardt	1st, 2nd, 3rd	Singled to center	2
2	2	Hollingsworth	1st, 2nd	Doubled down left field line	1
4	1	Decatur	1st, 2nd, 3rd	Homered over right field wall	4
6	1	Decatur	3rd	Homered over right field wall	2
7	1	Wilson	2nd, 3rd	Singled to right	2
9	0	Roberts	3rd	Singled down right field line	1

The game was laced with its share of strange plays and strategy, some of which may have contributed to the record-setting performance.* For example, Taylor Douthit stole second base in the sixth inning with the score 9–1. Could it have been that he was trying to get into scoring position for Bottomley's next at-bat? In the seventh frame

*Smith, David W., Sunny Jim Bottomley's Big Day, *SABR Research Exchange, Spring 1992.*

with the score 13–1, after Heinie Meuller singled, Douthit bunted and astonishingly was credited with a sacrifice when the pitcher threw late to second base. Stranger still was what followed. Hornsby, batting .423 on the morning of this game, also sacrificed, moving the two runners into scoring position for Bottomley, who then delivered two RBIs with a single.

Possibly interwoven with the Cardinal shenanigans was the fact that the previous single-game RBI record holder was none other than this day's Brooklyn manager, Wilbert Robinson. While playing for the National League's Baltimore Orioles on June 10, 1892, Robinson went seven for seven with 11 RBIs. Now, "Robbie" watched in horror as his pennant hopes dimmed, and Sunny Jim ravaged five of

Sunny Jim Bottomley—six hits and 12 RBIs.

his hurlers. One can't help but wonder if he was tempted to have Bottomley intentionally walked in the top of the ninth in order to preserve his own RBI record.

Another strange piece of strategy followed Bottomley's ninth inning plate appearance. At the time of this contest, in addition to his 11-RBI mark, Robinson was the only player ever to collect seven hits in a game.

After Bottomley's sixth hit and 12th RBI, he was inexplicably removed from the game for a pinch runner. There were no outs at the time and, although it was a long shot, there was a chance he may have reached the plate a second time in the frame. Unfortunately, there was no discussion of these strategies in newspaper coverage of the game.

St. Louis Cardinals	AB	R	H	I	PO	A	E
H. Mueller rf,1b9	3	3	2	1	3	0	0
Taylor Douthit cf	3	3	1	0	2	0	0
Rogers Hornsby 2b	4	2	2	0	2	2	0
Ray Blades pr9,2b	0	1	0	0	0	0	0
Jim Bottomley 1b	6	3	6	12	5	0	0
Jack Smith pr9,rf	0	0	0	0	1	0	0
Chick Hafey lf	6	1	2	2	5	1	0
Mike Gonzalez c	4	1	1	1	2	0	0
> Vern Clemons c6 .	2	0	0	0	1	0	0
Specs Toporcer 3b	1	0	0	0	0	0	0
Jimmy Cooney 3b1	4	0	1	1	0	0	0
Tommy Thevenow ss	5	0	0	0	5	4	0
Bill Sherdel p	4	3	3	0	1	0	0
Flint Rhem p9	0	0	0	0	0	0	0
	42	17	18	17	27	7	0

Brooklyn Robins	AB	R	H	I	PO	A	E
Andy High 2b	4	0	2	0	4	0	0
Johnny Mitchell ss	4	0	1	0	1	4	0
Zack Wheat lf	4	0	0	0	1	0	0
Jack Fournier 1b	2	1	0	0	5	1	1
Dick Loftus 1b7	1	0	1	0	3	0	0
Eddie Brown cf	4	0	1	0	5	0	0
Milt Stock 3b	3	1	1	0	1	1	0
Tommy Griffith rf	2	0	0	0	2	0	0
Hank DeBerry c	3	0	1	1	4	0	0
Rube Ehrhardt p	0	0	0	0	0	0	0
J. Hollingsworth p1	1	0	0	0	0	0	0
Art Decatur p4	0	0	0	0	1	1	0
Jimmy Johnston ph6	1	0	1	0	0	0	0
Tex Wilson p7	0	0	0	0	0	1	0
Zack Taylor ph8	1	1	1	0	0	0	0
Jim Roberts p9	0	0	0	0	0	1	0
> C. Hargreaves ph9	1	0	0	0	0	0	0
	31	3	9	1	27	9	1

Cardinals	IP	H	R	ER	BB	SO
Sherdel W,7-9	8	8	2	2	2	1
Rhem	1	1	1	0	3	0
	9	9	3	2	5	1

Robins	IP	H	R	ER	BB	SO
Ehrhardt L,5-2	0	4	4	4	1	0
Hollingsworth	3	2	3	3	3	2
Decatur	3	6	6	5	2	0
Wilson	2	4	3	3	0	1
Roberts	1	2	1	1	0	0
	9	18	17	16	6	3

St. Louis   4 1 0   4 0 4   2 1 1   -17
Brooklyn   0 1 0   0 0 0   0 1 1   - 3

OB: St. Louis 7, Brooklyn 6
DP: Thevenow-Hornsby (DeBerry)
    Thevenow-Hornsby-Bottomley (Mitchell)
    Mueller-unassisted (Brown)
2B: Bottomley, Sherdel
3B: Mueller, Hornsby, Hafey, Gonzalez
HR: Bottomley 2(14)
SB: Douthit, Cooney
SO: Douthit, Hornsby, Toporcer, Brown
BB: Mueller 3, Douthit, Hornsby (I), Sherdel,
    Fournier, Stock, DeBerry, Griffith 2

SH: Douthit 2, Hornsby
WP: Rehm, Decatur
PB: Clemons
TIME: 1:55
ATTENDANCE: 3,000
UMPIRES: Bill Klem, Frank Wilson
SOURCES: Brooklyn Daily Eagle; New York
    American, Times, Tribune, World; St. Louis
    Globe-Democrat, Post-Dispatch

BALANCE	OUT	+	R	+	OB	=	BP	=	AB	+	BB	+	SH	+	HP	+	CI
St. Louis	27		17		7		51		42		6		3		0		0
Brooklyn	27		3		6		36		31		5		0		0		0

Overflow Crowd Conducive to Triples

67. Team Hits Eight Triples in One Game; Teams Combine for Nine Triples

ST. LOUIS   at   PITTSBURGH
(Cardinals, 5)   (Pirates, 15)

Saturday, May 30, 1925, Forbes Field

Barney Dreyfuss, Pirates owner, was in the process of expanding his stadium. When Forbes Field was built in 1909, it had a seating capacity of 23,000; in 1915 that was

AFTERNOON GAME

St. Louis Cardinals	AB	R	H	I	PO	A	E
Ray Blades lf	4	1	1	0	2	0	0
Jack Smith rf	4	1	0	0	2	0	0
>Rogers Hornsby 2b	3	2	1	2	0	1	1
Jim Bottomley 1b	4	0	1	0	13	0	0
Les Bell 3b	4	0	2	1	1	6	1
Heinie Mueller cf	3	0	1	0	1	0	0
Jimmy Cooney ss	4	1	2	0	1	4	0
Bob O'Farrell c	4	0	1	1	4	2	0
Pea Ridge Day p	1	0	0	0	0	0	0
Eddie Dyer p3	2	0	0	0	0	2	0
Max Flack ph9	1	0	0	0	0	0	0
	34	5	9	4	24	15	2

Pittsburgh Pirates	AB	R	H	I	PO	A	E
Max Carey cf	5	0	2	0	5	1	0
Eddie Moore 2b	5	2	2	0	4	2	0
Kiki Cuyler rf	4	4	2	0	2	0	0
Clyde Barnhart lf	5	4	4	5	1	0	0
Pie Traynor 3b	4	2	3	2	3	2	1
Glenn Wright ss	5	2	3	3	0	4	0
George Grantham 1b	5	0	2	1	6	0	1
>Earl Smith c	5	1	1	1	6	1	0
Johnny Morrison p	4	0	0	0	0	2	0
	42	15	19	12	27	12	2

St. Louis	IP	H	R	ER	BB	SO
Day L,2-4	2	6	5	5	0	1
Dyer	6	13	10	6	0	1
	8	19	15	11	0	2

Pittsburgh	IP	H	R	ER	BB	SO
Morrison W,6-4	9	9	5	4	5	5

St. Louis	2 2 0		0 1 0		0 0 0		- 5
Pittsburgh	3 0 4		4 0 2		1 1 x		-15

OB: St. Louis 7, Pittsburgh 5
DP: Bell-Bottomley (E.Smith)
     Morrison-Traynor-Grantham(Mueller)
     Wright-Moore-Grantham (Cooney)
2B: Traynor 2
3B: O'Farrell, Carey 2, Moore, Cuyler,
     Barnhart 2, Traynor, Wright
HR: Hornsby(12), E.Smith(5)
SB: Blades, Traynor, Wright
SO: Blades, J. Smith, Bottomley, Day,
     Mueller, Moore, Morrison
BB: Blades, J. Smith, Hornsby 2, Mueller

SF: Traynor
HP: By Day (Cuyler)
TIME: 1:38
ATTENDANCE: 28,000
UMPIRES: Bob Hart, Peter McLaughlin,
     Cy Rigler
SOURCES: Pittsburgh Gazette Times,
     Post, Press; St.Louis Globe-
     Democrat, Post-Dispatch

BALANCE	OUT+R+OB=BP=AB+BB+SH+HP+CI
St. Louis	27 5 7 39 34 5 0 0 0
Pittsburgh	24 15 5 44 42 0 1 1 0

---

expanded to 25,000. Now, in 1925, new stands were being built in right field which would boost accommodations to 41,000. But at the time of this Memorial Day, morning-afternoon doubleheader, those new accommodations were not quite ready. So when 28,000 fans paid their way into the park in the afternoon, several thousand were ushered into the outfield. Those patrons became instrumental in the establishment of new major league record, one that has withstood the test of time.

Overflow crowds fringing the outfield were commonplace during baseball's expansion of the first few decades of the twentieth century. But while most ground rules invoked under such circumstances awarded two bases for balls hit into the outfield crowd, scorers this day granted three bases. Thus the Pirates hit *eight triples for a new, modern major league record which has never been equalled.* The Cardinals also contributed one three-bagger enabling the clubs to *tie the two-team standard of nine,* which also still stands. The fact that the home club out-tripled the visitors eight to one may have been an indicator of crowd cooperation. Hometown fans were known to allow balls hit by their club to disappear in the sea of humanity. Conversely, hits by opponents somehow caromed off legs and feet to quickly return to the field of play.

Of the nine triples in the contest, eight were of the ground rule variety, bouncing into the standees. The three-baggers of Eddie

Max Carey—two triples into the crowd.

Moore and Clyde Barnhart, as well as Max Carey's second triple, were stroked into left field; whereas that of Bob O'Farrell, Kiki Cuyler, Glenn Wright, Pie Traynor, and Carey's first three-bagger were lined to right. Only Clyde Barnhart's second triple could have been considered "normal"; his sharp drive skipped past center fielder Heinie Mueller. Not surprisingly, in the morning game, with the entire (18,000) audience seated, no triples were hit.

This doubleheader was also historically significant because of a managerial switch. Since 1919, when Branch Rickey had taken the reins in St. Louis, the Cardinals had been an example of mediocrity. For years Rickey had not been popular with either his players or the fans, and when the club started 1925 with a 13–24, last place position, president Sam Breadon decided a change was needed. Between games of this doubleheader, 29-year-old Rogers Hornsby was named player-manager of the team, a common money-saving tactic of the times. Hornsby joined Dave

Bancroft (Braves), George Sisler (Browns), Eddie Collins (White Sox), Tris Speaker (Indians), Ty Cobb (Tigers), and Stanley Harris (Senators) as baseball's 1925 double-duty personnel. Hornsby did help improve the Cardinals, piloting them out of the cellar this year and into a World's Championship the following season.

Mack's Greatest Comeback

68. Team Overcomes 12-Run Deficit to Win

CLEVELAND   at   PHILADELPHIA
(Indians, 15)   (Athletics, 17)

Monday, June 15, 1925, Shibe Park

Lamar was on a 16 game hitting streak.

By 1925, Connie Mack had seen a lot of baseball. Already he had played in 11 major league campaigns and managed in 27, but never had his team been involved in a comeback of this day's magnitude. Only one other time in baseball history (see 6-18-11) had a *club resurrected from a 12-run deficit to emerge victorious.* It has not been repeated since.

The Athletics had been in and out of first place for nearly five weeks but were now stumbling. On Friday they had been clobbered by the White Sox 15–1, and on Sunday they had been shut out on only five hits. They had their fans feeling anxious about the future.

This day, Jake Miller, Cleveland's rookie left-hander, was gunning for his third straight victory. The Indian hitters were on the warpath, pummeling five Philadelphia hurlers for 22 hits and 15 runs in the first seven rounds. The Athletics, meanwhile, could muster but ten scattered hits and four runs off the rookie hurler. Twice the Tribe fashioned 12-run leads —14–2 after five and a half innings, and 15–3 after batting in the top of the seventh. For Philadelphians, it appeared certain that the home team would slip back into a first place tie with Washington. The A's picked up a lone tally in the bottom of the seventh, making it 15–4. Then came the bottom of the eighth which witnessed a gruesome scalping of the Indians. Here's how the A's pulled victory from the deepest hole in major league history.

• Chuck Galloway innocently led off with a base on balls.

• Manager Mack could see no reason to waste a pinch hitter on Tom Glass, the fifth A's hurler in only his second major league game. Tom batted for himself and flied out to right.

• Max Bishop, sometimes called "Camera Eye" because of his affinity for walks, coaxed one of his specialties.

• Jimmy Dykes then ripped a line-drive triple toward the scoreboard in right center, driving both runners home. The score was then 15–6 with little cause for concern.

• Bill Lamar, on a 16-game hit streak,

Al Simmons homered in the eighth.

singled to center, knocking home Dykes. It was then 15–7.

• Cleveland player-manager Tris Speaker thought the heat had gotten to his rookie hurler and ordered By Speece to the hill. Speece was greeted by Al Simmons with a single which bounced strangely over the head of first baseman Ray Knode. *The Cleveland Plain Dealer* reported that this ball would have been an out had not the Shibe Park turf been in such deplorable condition.

• Frank Welch, who had earlier replaced an injured Bing Miller, also singled to right, scoring Lamar and making it 15–8.

• Connie Mack must have felt the game was still out of reach because he then allowed Charlie Berry to bat. Charlie had had his first major league at-bat only a few innings earlier but continued the onslaught with an RBI single. It was then 15–9.

• Speaker had seen enough of Speece and relieved him with Carl Yowell. It was like throwing kerosene on a fire. Yowell walked Jim Poole, also a rookie, loading the sacks.

• For the second time in the inning, Galloway batted. This time he lashed a single to left, driving home two mates. With the score then 15–11, Speaker had had enough of his marginal pitchers and brought on his ace, George Uhle. Uhle was a time-tested, dependable right-hander who would win his 100th major league game this year. *The Cleveland Plain Dealer* dubbed him "the flower of Mr. Speaker's casting corps."

• Tom Glass was the next scheduled hitter. Tom had made the only out in the inning when it didn't much matter. Now Mack knew he had enough momentum to catch the Tribe, so he sent Sammy Hale in to pinch hit. Uhle induced Hale to hit a sharp grounder to short, but it took a bad hop over Joe Sewell's head for another single and another run. It was then 15–12 as *The Cleveland Plain Dealer* again wailed about the field conditions.

• In a bizarre strategic move, Hale next sprinted toward second on an attempted steal. The ball and Sammy arrived simultaneously, but when the sphere hit the runner, Hale was declared safe.

• Next, Bishop singled to center, driving home Galloway and Hale. The A's then trailed by only one run, 15–14.

• Dykes sent a roller to short that had the potential of an inning-ending double play. Bishop was forced at second, but Dykes just beat the throw to first. That was the second out of the frame, after which Walt French entered the fray as a pinch runner for Dykes.

• Lamar was the next batter. Bill was having his finest season (he would finish at .356) and had four hits thus far in this game, but the strategy that followed would be hotly debated in most baseball circles. With the tying run (French) on first, two outs, and clean-up hitter Al Simmons on deck, Lamar was intentionally walked, sending the tying run into scoring position. To make the strategy even more debatable, as Simmons stepped to the plate, he was batting .385! In Cleveland's defense, Lamar batted left-handed, Simmons right-handed, and Uhle threw right-handed.

• Simmons didn't allow the fans nor the press much time to debate the wisdom of the strategy. Al drove Uhle's third pitch high and far. It went so high that it became only the second ball ever to land on the roof atop the upper deck in left. As Simmons rounded the bases, pandemonium erupted. Fans sailed straw hats and indiscriminate debris onto the field. Neighborhood rooftops that served as inexpensive bleachers had their construction severely tested as fans stomped their feet and jumped for joy. The A's players hooted, howled, slapped each other's backs, and tossed their bats about. Even the venerable Connie Mack himself, normally stoic, tossed his scorecard into the air and shook hands with most of the team members while his son Earle, the nominal captain, turned cartwheels in front of the bench.

• After everyone settled down, Welch flied out to right for the final out of the inning.

The Athletics had been ruthlessly efficient. The nine players who had gotten hits and the four players who walked, all scored. No one was left on base in the inning. Rube Walberg dismissed the Indians in the ninth with a pair of strikeouts and a pop up to give the A's a share of the all-time comeback record. For A's hurler Tom Glass this was a very special game, for it was his first and only major league victory as well as the last big-league game in which he ever pitched.

Cleveland Indians	AB	R	H	I	PO	A	E
Charlie Jamieson lf	6	2	5	3	2	0	0
Pat McNulty rf	1	0	0	0	0	0	0
Cliff Lee rf2	4	1	2	3	5	0	0
Tris Speaker cf	6	1	2	2	2	0	0
Joe Sewell ss	6	1	4	2	2	5	0
Glenn Myatt c	6	3	2	1	2	0	0
Freddie Spurgeon 2b	6	2	2	0	3	3	0
Rube Lutzke 3b	4	2	2	0	1	1	0
Ray Knode 1b	5	3	4	2	5	1	0
> Luke Sewell ph9	1	0	0	0	0	0	0
Jake Miller p	5	0	1	0	2	0	0
By Speece p8	0	0	0	0	0	0	0
Carl Yowell p8	0	0	0	0	0	0	0
George Uhle p8	0	0	0	0	0	0	0
	50	15	24	13	24	10	0

Philadelphia Athletics	AB	R	H	I	PO	A	E
Max Bishop 2b	4	1	2	2	1	2	0
Jimmy Dykes 3b	6	2	2	2	1	2	0
Walt French pr8	0	1	0	0	0	0	0
Bill Lamar lf	5	3	4	2	2	1	0
Al Simmons cf	6	2	3	3	7	0	0
Bing Miller rf	2	0	0	0	0	0	0
> Frank Welch rf4	3	1	1	2	1	0	0
Cy Perkins c	2	0	0	0	6	0	0
Charlie Berry c6	2	1	2	1	2	0	1
Mickey Cochrane c9	0	0	0	0	2	0	0
Jim Poole 1b	4	3	2	0	4	0	0
Chuck Galloway ss	3	2	2	3	1	0	1
Eddie Rommel p	0	0	0	0	0	0	0
Stan Baumgartner p2	0	0	0	0	0	0	0
Jimmie Foxx ph2	1	0	0	0	0	0	0
Fred Heimach p3	0	0	0	0	0	0	0
Art Stokes p4	0	0	0	0	0	2	0
Tom Glass p6	1	0	0	1	0	0	0
Sammy Hale ph8,3b	1	1	1	1	0	0	0
Rube Walberg p9	0	0	0	0	0	0	0
	40	17	19	17	27	7	2

Cleveland	IP	H	R	ER	BB	SO
Miller	7.1	12	8	8	6	1
Speece	0	3	3	3	0	0
Yowell	0	1	2	2	1	0
Uhle L,7-5	.2	3	4	4	1	0
	8	19	17	17	8	1

Philadelphia	IP	H	R	ER	BB	SO
Rommel	1.1	3	4	4	1	0
Baumgartner	.2	2	0	0	0	1
Heimach	1.1	6	4	4	0	1
Stokes	1.2	5	4	4	1	3
Glass W,1-0	3	7	3	2	0	1
Walberg	1	1	0	0	0	2
	9	24	15	14	2	8

Cleveland	0	4	2	2	4	2	1	0	0	-15
Philadelphia	0	1	1	0	0	1	1	13	x	-17

OB: Cleveland 11, Philadelphia 9
DP: J.Sewell-Knode (Foxx)
    J.Sewell-Spurgeon-Knode (Dykes)
2B: Jamieson, Lee, Speaker, Dykes,
    Lamar, Poole
3B: Lee, Dykes, Poole
HR: J.Sewell(1), Myatt(8), Simmons(11)
SB: Jamieson, Myatt, Spurgeon, Lutzke,
    Hale
SO: Lee, Myatt, Spurgeon, Lutzke 2,
    L.Sewell, J.Miller 2, B. Miller
BB: Lutzke 2, Bishop 2, Lamar(I),
    Perkins, Poole, Galloway 2, Stokes

SF: Lee, Glass
HP: By J.Miller (Welch)
WP: Rommel, Stokes
TIME: 3:00
ATTENDANCE: 8,000
UMPIRES: Brick Owens, Bill Dinneen,
    Pants Rowland
SOURCES: Cleveland Plain Dealer,
    Press; Philadelphia Evening Bull-
    etin, Inquirer, Public Ledger,
    Record

BALANCE	OUT	+	R	+	OB	=	BP	=	AB	+	BB	+	SH	+	HP	+	CI
Cleveland	27		15		11		53		50		2		1		0		0
Philadelphia	24		17		9		50		40		8		1		1		0

A Giant Offense

69. Team Records 58 At-Bats, Four Teammates Get Four Hits, Ten Get Two or More Hits

NEW YORK, NL   at   PHILADELPHIA
(Giants, 24)   (Phillies, 9)

Wednesday, September 2, 1925, Baker Bowl

Philadelphia's Baker Bowl, that hitters' Shangri-la, was the scene of this day's offensive carnage. John McGraw's visiting New York Giants entered the Quaker City ballyard eight games behind league leading Pittsburgh. The host Phillies, meanwhile, were struggling to avoid last place, at the time tied for that dishonor with the Cubs. Their pitching staff was impotent, the only one in the majors with a team ERA over 5.00. No Philadelphia starter had a winning record, and they led the league in hits and walks allowed. So it's not altogether surprising that the second game of this doubleheader resulted in a 24–9 pummelling.

Starting that second game was 31-year-old Art Decatur, whom the Phillies acquired earlier in the season by trading Bill Hubbell to Brooklyn. Decatur's 5.27 ERA was a perfect fit for the shabby Philadelphia staff; only two teammates with 65+ innings, had ERAs lower than Art's. Decatur's opposing moundsman this day was a rookie named Freddie Fitzsimmons, who had made his major league debut only a month earlier.

The game started innocently enough with the Giants leading 2–1 after two innings. Then a relentless New York attack began, driving not only Decatur from the hill but also his successors, Huck Betts, Ray Pierce, and Jack Knight. Finally, Hal Carlson lent some stability to the proceedings by quieting the New Yorkers in the last two innings. During the day's onslaught, *ten Giants collected two or more hits*, tying a twentieth-century record (see 8-07-22) which has not since been repeated. In addition, *four Giants each stroked four hits*, which remained the major league record for 33 years (see 5-13-58). With 30 hits, the New Yorkers fell just short of the all-time standard for hits by one team in a game (see 6-09-01). To accomplish all of this, New York needed *58 official at-bats*, which to this day also remains the benchmark for a nine-inning game.

Irish Meusel, who four years earlier had been traded by the Phillies to New York for

Irish Meusel led the attack with nine RBIs.

three players, led the Giant attack with four hits and nine runs batted in. [At this time only Jim Bottomley (see 9-16-24) had driven in more runs in one game.] Irish singled with two outs in the first and scored on Bill Terry's circuit clout. Terry's "blast," as well as Freddy Lindstrom's later in the game, was a line drive that bounced over the low left-field wall — a home run by 1925 standards in Baker Bowl. Leading off the third, Meusel struck out. With two outs in the fourth, he singled home Frankie Frisch from second. There were two outs again in the fifth when

Irish cleared the sacks with a double. In the sixth, Meusel got an RBI on a fielder's choice and later himself tallied. With two mates aboard and no outs in the seventh, the right-hander poked a home run over the nearby right-field wall. Finally, batting in his sixth consecutive frame during the eighth, Irish drove home his ninth run with a one-out sacrifice fly.

Among their 30 safeties, the Giants harvested at least two per frame except for the ninth when they went hitless. The following page summarizes their bounty:

SECOND GAME

New York Giants	AB	R	H	I	PO	A	E
Billy Southworth cf	6	4	4	2	2	0	0
Frankie Frisch 2b	7	3	4	2	3	4	0
Irish Meusel rf	6	3	4	9	5	0	0
Bill Terry 1b	6	1	3	2	12	0	0
George Kelly lf	6	4	2	1	2	0	0
Pip Koehler lf8	1	0	0	0	1	0	0
Freddy Lindstrom 3b	7	3	4	2	0	0	0
Travis Jackson ss	4	2	2	0	0	1	0
> Doc Farrell ph6,ss	3	0	2	2	0	1	0
Mickey Devine c	6	1	3	3	2	1	0
F. Fitzsimmons p	6	3	2	1	0	3	0
	58	24	30	24	27	10	0

Philadelphia Phillies	AB	R	H	I	PO	A	E
Heinie Sand ss	5	0	2	0	0	5	0
Freddy Leach cf	3	1	1	0	0	0	0
George Burns ph7,lf	2	0	0	0	0	0	0
Russ Wrightstone rf	3	0	1	2	0	0	0
Cy Williams rf8	1	2	1	1	0	0	0
George Harper lf	3	0	0	0	4	0	0
Johnny Mokan cf8	2	1	1	1	2	0	0
Chicken Hawks 1b	4	1	2	1	7	0	1
>Wally Kimmick 3b	5	1	2	0	3	5	0
Barney Friberg 2b	4	1	2	0	7	3	0
Lew Wendell c	2	0	0	2	4	1	0
Art Decatur p	1	1	1	0	0	0	0
Huck Betts p4	1	0	0	0	0	0	0
Ray Pierce p5	0	0	0	0	0	0	0
Jack Knight p6	0	0	0	0	0	0	1
Hal Carlson p7	2	1	1	2	0	0	0
	38	9	14	9	27	14	2

New York	IP	H	R	ER	BB	SO
Fitzsimmons W,4-2	9	14	9	9	2	2

Philadelphia	IP	H	R	ER	BB	SO
Decatur L,4-11	3.2	9	6	6	1	2
Betts	1	4	4	1	1	0
Pierce	.1	5	6	6	0	0
Knight	1.2	10	7	7	0	0
Carlson	2.1	2	1	1	0	3
	9	30	24	21	2	5

```
New York      2 0 2   2 4 9   4 1 0   -24
Philadelphia  1 0 1   1 0 0   0 5 1   - 9
```

OB: New York 10, Philadelphia 6
2B: Frisch 2, Meusel, Terry, Devine, Fitzsimmons, Wrightstone
HR: Meusel(19), Terry(9), Lindstrom (4), Williams(11), Mokan(6), Carlson(2)
CS: Friberg
SO: Meusel, Kelly, Koehler, Farrell, Fitzsimmons, Sand, Burns

BB: Southworth, Terry, Williams, Hawks
SF: Meusel, Wendell 2
TIME: 2:08
ATTENDANCE: ?
UMPIRES: Bill Klem, Barry McCormick
SOURCES: New York Times; Philadelphia Evening Bulletin, Inquirer, Ledger, Record; Retrosheet

BALANCE	OUT+R+OB=BP=AB+BB+SH+HP+CI
New York	27 24 10 61 58 2 1 0 0
Philadelphia	27 9 6 42 38 2 2 0 0

GIANTS' HITS, BY INNING, ON SEPTEMBER 2, 1925

Inning	Player (hit)	Total
1	Meusel (1b), Terry (HR)	2
2	Lindstrom (1b), Devine (1b)	2
3	Terry (1b), Lindstrom (HR)	2
4	Fitzsimmons (2b), Frisch (2b), Meusel (1b)	3
5	Jackson (1b), Fitzsimmons (1b), Southworth (1b), Meusel (2b)	4
6	Kelly (1b), Lindstrom (1b), Jackson (1b), Devine (2b), Southworth (1b), Frisch (1b), Terry (2b), Lindstrom (1b), Farrell (1b), Devine (1b)	10
7	Southworth (1b), Frisch (2b), Meusel (HR), Kelly (1b), Farrell (1b)	5
8	Southworth (1b), Frisch (1b)	2
9	None	**30**

Bequeathed a burgeoning lead, the rookie Fitzsimmons went the distance despite being buffeted by the Phillies for 14 hits, including three home runs in the eighth. Two of those blows cleared the inviting right-field wall. The other soared into the left-field bleachers.

Despite another month of play, neither team much improved its standing. The Giants still finished in second place, 8.5 behind the champion Pirates, and the Phillies avoided the basement by a slim half-game.

This Giant lineup was dotted with future managers and Hall of Famers. Billy Southworth, Frisch, Terry and Fitzsimmons later managed; and Frisch, Terry, George Kelly, Lindstrom, Travis Jackson, and manager McGraw have their plaques on display in Cooperstown.

Phils Get Pinched

70. Team Gets Six Pinch Hits in One Game

BROOKLYN   at   PHILADELPHIA
(Robins, 12)   (Phillies, 6)

Thursday, September 9, 1926, Baker Bowl

The day before this contest, Brooklyn had entered the last of the ninth leading Philadelphia 4–2 but eventually lost 8–4 on Cy Williams' game-winning grand slam. Now the Robins returned the favor. Trailing 6–3 in the top of the ninth, Brooklyn staged a dazzling rally, including nine hits and two walks to emerge with a 12–6 victory. That ninth inning also capped off a fortuitous day of managing for Brooklyn's Wilbert Robinson, who got maximum effort from his bench-warmers. Throughout the contest,

Robinson beckoned five pinch hitters and each one delivered successfully. As replacements, Dick Cox and Moose Clabaugh each batted twice in that explosive ninth, with Cox singling in each at bat. At the time there was no rule in place to interpret Cox's distinctive performance, and most scorers credited him with two pinch hits in the same inning, a feat that had occurred at least three previous times since the turn of the century. That questionable scoring meant that Brooklyn had collected *six pinch hits in the game, the standard that is listed in today's record books.* Regardless of the scoring decision, no researcher to date has found another team with more than five successful pinch hits in one game.

Prior to the final frame, the home club had been in complete control. Sixteen-game winner Hal Carlson had held Brooklyn at bay through the first eight innings on eight hits and three runs. Two of those markers had crossed the plate in the seventh when Robinson first engaged his posse of pinch-hitters. Then, following Johnny Butler's double, pinch hitters Zack Wheat, Jack Fournier, and Jerry Standaert all singled in succession. But the Phillies still held a 5–3 lead, an advantage which in Baker Bowl was precarious at best. Cy Williams, who had homered in his final at-bat a day earlier, supplied most of the Philadelphia offense. This day, Cy cleared the not-too-distant (280') right-field wall in the first and third innings. In the fourth inning, he whistled a streaking liner that boomed off the hulking tin barrier just a few feet foul before striking out. (Newspaper reporters were well aware that no twentieth-century player had yet deposited four consecutive home runs.) The Phillies added a single run in the bottom of the seventh to give themselves a 6–3 advantage.

Then came the fateful and record-setting ninth when 13 Robins stepped to the plate. Here's how it evolved:

• Johnny Butler opened with a double to left field.

• Dick Cox batted for Chick Fewster and singled to center, driving home Butler.

• Hank DeBerry, who had entered the

Dick Cox had two pinch-hit singles.

game in the seventh, popped out to third baseman Bob Rice for the first out.

• Manager Robinson was almost out of pinch hitters but summoned rookie "Moose" Clabaugh to bat for pitcher McWeeny. Despite hitting 62 homers in 121 games* in the East Texas League this year, Moose had yet to garner his first major league safety. However, Carlson was weakening rapidly, and Clabaugh smashed a ringing double off the right-center field wall sending Cox to third. With that, Carlson became a persona non grata and was replaced by Wayland Dean. Phillies fans knew this was perilous because by losing Carlson, they were losing the only mediocre hurler on the squad. Everyone else was downright pitiful.

• Dean, with a 4.90 ERA, lasted through

*Minor League Baseball Stars, *Revised edition, Society for American Baseball Research (Manhattan, KS: Ag Press, Inc., 1984), 35.*

only three hitters. Merwin Jacobson singled to center, knocking in Cox and Clabaugh with the tying runs. After walking both Max Carey and Gus Felix to load the bases, Dean too became an undesirable and was succeeded by Ed Baecht.

• Baecht threw about a dozen warm-up tosses but only two official ones. Babe Herman socked Ed's second offering to left, driving home two more Robins and giving the visitors an 8–6 lead. Baecht had faced just one batter before hitting the showers. (Somehow Baecht escaped this season with a 2–0 log despite a 6.11 ERA.)

• Ray "Lefty" Pierce was beckoned to relieve Baecht. Ray surprised the fans when, he induced Bill Marriott to hit into a fielder's choice ground-out for the second out.

• Hope was short lived, however, as Butler got his second hit of the inning, a single to left scoring Felix.

• Next was a history making at-bat. Cox stepped to the plate for the second time, having previously singled. When he again singled, it was scored as his second pinch hit of the inning and Brooklyn's sixth team pinch hit of the game. The hit also scored Marriott, making it 10–6.

• DeBerry, who had made the first out,

this time doubled, sending home both Butler and Cox. Pierce then followed his mound predecessors to the showers, and Lefty Taber, the fifth Phillies hurler of the inning, assumed the pitching burden. (To date, no NL club has ever used more pitchers in one inning. AL mark of six was established in 1983.)

• Clabaugh then also appeared for the second time in the inning as a pinch hitter. When he popped out to Friberg, the crowd erupted into a prolonged and derisive cheer.

Brooklyn hurler Doug McWeeny had lost six straight decisions, and his prospects for breaking the streak weren't rosy. He had entered the fray in relief of Burleigh Grimes trailing 5–3 and was still behind 6–3 when he exited. But Doug became the unforeseen beneficiary of Brooklyn's battering and received credit for the win.

By 1959 no less than 15 pinch hitters had registered two hits in an inning,[*] leading officials to question such scoring. A ruling was soon passed proclaiming that a pinch hitter can receive credit for only one pinch hit in a game. Should his team bat around, in his second plate appearance he is considered hitting for himself and as such is no longer a pinch hitter.

Brooklyn Robins	AB	R	H	I	PO	A	E
Merwin Jacobson rf	5	1	1	2	1	0	0
Max Carey cf	4	2	2	0	5	0	0
Gus Felix lf,2b9	4	1	0	0	0	1	0
Babe Herman 1b	5	0	3	3	12	0	0
Bill Marriott 3b	5	1	0	0	0	0	0
Johnny Butler ss	5	3	4	1	1	4	0
Sammy Bohne 2b	2	0	0	0	2	3	1
Zack Wheat ph7	1	0	1	0	0	0	0
Chick Fewster 2b7	0	1	0	0	0	0	0
Dick Cox ph9,lf	2	2	2	2	1	0	0
Charlie Hargreaves c	2	0	0	0	3	1	0
Jack Fournier ph7	1	0	1	1	0	0	0
Hank DeBerry c7	2	0	1	2	2	0	0
Burleigh Grimes p	2	0	0	0	0	0	0
Jerry Standaert ph7	1	0	1	1	0	0	0
Doug McWeeny p7	0	0	0	0	0	1	0
> Moose Clabaugh ph9	2	1	1	0	0	0	0
Dazzy Vance p9	0	0	0	0	0	0	0
	43	12	17	12	27	10	1

Philadelphia Phillies	AB	R	H	I	PO	A	E
Heinie Sand ss	4	1	1	0	2	4	0
Cy Williams rf	5	2	2	4	0	1	0
Johnny Mokan lf	5	0	1	0	2	0	0
Freddy Leach cf	5	2	4	0	3	0	1
>Russ Wrightstone 1b	4	0	1	1	11	0	0
Jimmie Wilson c	4	0	0	0	3	0	2
Barney Friberg 2b	3	0	1	1	2	2	0
Bob Rice 3b	4	0	0	0	4	1	0
Hal Carlson p	3	1	2	0	0	2	0
Wayland Dean p9	0	0	0	0	0	0	0
Ed Baecht p9	0	0	0	0	0	0	0
Ray Pierce p9	0	0	0	0	0	0	0
Lefty Taber p9	0	0	0	0	0	0	0
	37	6	12	6	27	10	3

*Leonard Gettelson, compiler, One for the Book (St. Louis: The Sporting News, 1959), p. 51.

Brooklyn	IP	H	R	ER	BB	SO
Grimes	6	10	5	5	1	2
McWeeny W,10-11	2	1	1	1	1	1
Vance	1	1	0	0	0	0
	9	12	6	6	2	3

Philadelphia	IP	H	R	ER	BB	SO
Carlson	8.1	12	6	5	0	1
Dean L,8-12	0	1	3	3	2	0
Baecht	0	1	0	0	0	0
Pierce	.1	3	3	3	0	0
Taber	.1	0	0	0	0	0
	9	17	12	11	2	1

Brooklyn	0 0 0	0 0 1	2 0 9	-12
Philadelphia	1 0 4	0 0 0	1 0 0	- 6

OB: Brooklyn 6, Philadelphia 8
2B: Butler 2, DeBerry, Standaert, Clabaugh, Mokan, Leach
3B: Leach
HR: Williams 2(16)
SO: Herman, Williams 2, Carlson
BB: Carey, Felix, Friberg, Carlson
SH: Sand
SF: Wrightstone

TIME: 2:10
ATTENDANCE: ?
UMPIRES: Peter McLaughlin, Beans
    Reardon, Ernie Quigley
SOURCES: Brooklyn Daily Eagle; DBD;
    New York Times; Philadelphia
    Inquirer, Public Ledger, Record

BALANCE	OUT	+R	+OB	=BP	=AB	+BB	+SH	+HP	+CI
Brooklyn	27	12	6	45	43	2	0	0	0
Philadelphia	27	6	8	41	37	2	2	0	0

A Swift Exit

71. Teams Play Doubleheader in Two Hours, Seven Minutes

NEW YORK, AL   at   ST. LOUIS
(Yankees, 1,2)   (Browns, 6,6)

Sunday, September 26, 1926, Sportsman's Park

It was an ideal situation for a record-setting performance — the last day of the regular season and both teams locked into their final standing. The Yankees had won a doubleheader the day before, thereby clinching the American League pennant, while the Browns were firmly entrenched in seventh place, eager to end the campaign. In addition, the weather was so cold and windy that New York manager Miller Huggins refused to don his baseball flannels, opting for warmer, civilian attire. All of the above prevailed upon the two clubs to complete the *fastest doubleheader ever played — two hours and seven minutes.*

The opening contest consumed one hour and twelve minutes while the nightcap lasted only 55 minutes. Nevertheless, there was no reported evidence of intentional distortion by the teams in order to achieve this lightning duet. Actually, in tuning up for the World Series, the Yankees stroked 19 hits in the two games while the Browns gathered 26, hardly what one might term "hurrying things along." There were several pitching changes during the afternoon, and in the eighth inning of the first game, the Browns batted around while scoring four runs. The opener was hastened, however, by eight double plays, six by the Browns.

Interwoven in the nightcap lineup were some old faces occupying unfamiliar positions for the Browns. Player-manager George Sisler, who had done some pitching early in his career, was urged by the patrons to take the mound for the last two innings of the season. Sisler did and pitched well. He didn't allow a hit and struck out Earle Combs, Bob Meusel, and Aaron Ward. Harry Rice, normally an outfielder, finished at shortstop; Wally Gerber, the usual shortstop, roamed center field; and outfielder Ken Williams occupied the keystone sack. Forty-six-year-old coach Jimmy Austin played in his only game of the year at third base, his bastion of a decade earlier. Jimmy delighted the hometown fans by stealing home in the eighth inning.

For the Yankees, Fred Merkle made his last appearance as a player, and Spencer Adams and Aaron Ward played their only games at third base. *The New York American* noted that Santa Claus wasn't present or he may have played too. Babe Ruth, leading the league in multiple offensive categories, took the day off after one plate appearance because of a minor leg injury suffered a day earlier.

This Yankee tune-up for the World Series was not fruitful. In the October festival, the

Sisler picked up a save in relief.

New Yorkers carried a three games to two lead back to Yankee Stadium, but the Cardinals, behind Pete Alexander, took games six and seven to wear baseball's championship crown.

FIRST GAME

New York Yankees	AB	R	H	I	PO	A	E
Earle Combs cf	4	0	0	0	2	0	0
Bob Meusel rf	3	0	2	0	1	0	0
Babe Ruth lf	1	0	0	0	1	0	0
Ben Paschal lf2	2	0	0	0	2	0	0
Lou Gehrig 1b	3	1	1	0	8	1	0
Tony Lazzeri 2b	4	0	1	0	2	6	2
Mark Koenig ss	4	0	3	1	4	2	0
Joe Dugan 3b	4	0	3	0	2	1	0
>Pat Collins c	4	0	0	0	1	0	0
Dutch Ruether p	2	0	0	0	1	1	0
Urban Shocker p6	0	0	0	0	0	0	0
	31	1	10	1	24	11	2

St. Louis Browns	AB	R	H	I	PO	A	E
Hershel Bennett lf	5	0	2	1	1	1	0
Harry Rice cf	5	1	3	1	4	0	0
>George Sisler 1b	5	1	1	1	14	0	0
Bing Miller rf	3	1	2	1	1	0	0
Marty McManus 2b	3	1	1	0	4	6	1
Pinky Hargrave c	4	1	2	1	1	1	0
Gene Robertson 3b	4	0	2	1	1	0	1
Wally Gerber ss	4	1	1	0	1	7	0
Chet Falk p	4	0	1	0	0	1	0
	37	6	15	6	27	16	2

New York	IP	H	R	ER	BB	SO
Ruether L,14-9	5	7	2	2	1	0
Shocker	3	8	4	2	0	1
	8	15	6	4	1	1

St. Louis	IP	H	R	ER	BB	SO
Falk W,4-4	9	10	1	1	3	1

New York	0 0 0	0 0 0	0 0 1	- 1
St.Louis	2 0 0	0 0 0	0 4 x	- 6

OB: New York 7, St. Louis 9
DP: Hargrave-Gerber (Ruth SO)
    Sisler unassisted
    Dugan-Lazzeri-Gehrig
    Gerber-McManus-Sisler
    Gerber-McManus-Sisler
    Gerber-McManus-Sisler
    Koenig-Gehrig
    Bennett-Gerber-McManus
2B: Miller, Robertson

3B: Sisler, McManus
CS: Meusel
SO: Ruth, Rice
BB: Meusel, Gehrig, Shocker, McManus
SH: Paschal
SF: Miller
TIME: 1:12
UMPIRES: Dick Nallin, Billy Evans, Harry Geisel

BALANCE	OUT+R+OB=BP=AB+BB+SH+HP+CI
New York	27 1 7 35 31 3 1 0 0
St. Louis	24 6 9 39 37 1 1 0 0

SECOND GAME

New York Yankees	AB	R	H	I	PO	A	E
Earle Combs rf	4	0	1	0	3	0	0
Bob Meusel cf	4	0	0	0	0	0	0
Ben Paschal lf	3	1	3	0	6	0	0
Lou Gehrig 1b	2	1	1	2	1	0	0
Fred Merkle 1b6	2	0	0	0	6	0	0
Tony Lazzeri 3b	1	0	1	0	0	0	0
Spencer Adams 3b2	2	0	0	0	1	2	0
Mike Gazella ss	4	0	1	0	3	2	0
>Aaron Ward 2b	4	0	1	0	1	1	0
Bill Skiff c	3	0	0	0	3	0	0
Bob Shawkey p	2	0	1	0	0	0	0
Sad Sam Jones p6	1	0	0	0	0	0	0
	32	2	9	2	24	5	0

St. Louis Browns	AB	R	H	I	PO	A	E
Hershel Bennett lf	4	1	1	0	3	0	0
Harry Rice cf,ss9	3	1	1	0	3	1	0
George Sisler 1b,p8	4	0	2	1	6	1	0
Bing Miller rf	3	0	0	1	4	0	0
Marty McManus 2b	4	1	2	0	1	3	0
Ken Williams 2b9	0	0	0	0	0	0	0
Pinky Hargrave c	3	0	0	0	1	0	0
Wally Schang ph8,c	1	1	1	1	4	0	0
Gene Robertson 3b	2	1	1	0	0	2	0
Jimmy Austin 3b6	2	1	1	1	1	1	0
Wally Gerber ss,cf9	3	0	1	0	2	0	0
Ernie Wingard p	3	0	1	1	1	3	0
> Cedric Durst 1b8	1	0	0	0	1	1	0
	33	6	11	5	27	12	0

New York	IP	H	R	ER	BB	SO
Shawkey L,8-7	5	7	3	3	1	1
Jones	3	4	3	3	0	0
	8	11	6	6	1	1

St. Louis	IP	H	R	ER	BB	SO
Wingard W,5-8	7	9	2	2	0	1
Sisler	2	0	0	0	2	3
	9	9	2	2	2	4

New York	2 0 0	0 0 0	0 0 0	- 2
St. Louis	2 0 0	1 0 0	0 3 x	- 6

OB: New York 5, St. Louis 6
DP: Robertson-McManus-Sisler
    Austin-Sisler
2B: Bennett, McManus, Robertson,
    Schang, Austin, Wingard
HR: Gehrig(16)
SB: Austin
SO: Combs, Meusel, Ward, Skiff,
    Hargrave
BB: Paschal, Adams, Rice
SH: Gerber

SF: Miller
WP: Sisler
TIME: 55 minutes
ATTENDANCE: 2,000
UMPIRES: Dick Nallin, Billy Evans,
    Harry Geisel
SOURCES: New York American, Times;
    St. Louis Globe-Democrat, Post-
    Dispatch, Star

BALANCE	OUT+R+OB=BP=AB+BB+SH+HP+CI
New York	27 2 5 34 32 2 0 0 0
St. Louis	24 6 6 36 33 1 2 0 0

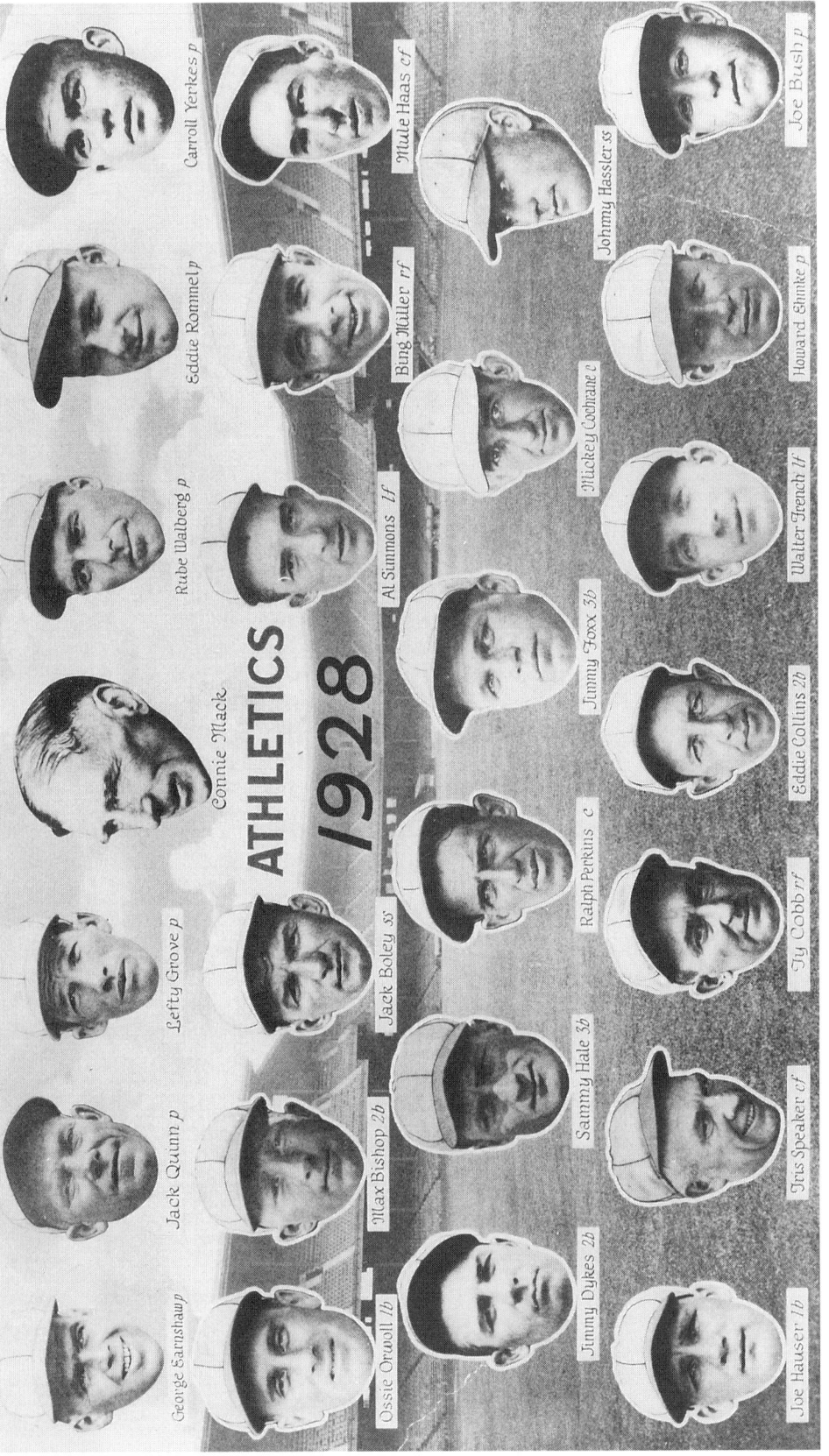

Carroll Yerkes p
Eddie Rommel p
Rube Walberg p
Connie Mack.
ATHLETICS
1928
Lefty Grove p
Jack Quinn p
George Earnshaw p

Mule Haas cf
Bing Miller rf
Al Simmons lf
Jack Boley ss
Max Bishop 2b
Ossie Orwoll 1b
Jimmy Dykes 2b

Johnny Hassler ss
Mickey Cochrane c
Jimmy Foxx 3b
Ralph Perkins c
Sammy Hale 3b

Joe Bush p
Howard Ehmke p
Walter French lf
Eddie Collins 2b
Ty Cobb rf
Tris Speaker cf
Joe Hauser 1b

The 1928 Philadelphia Athletics.

Hall of Fame Preview

72. One Game Features 17 Future Hall of Famers

NEW YORK, AL   at   PHILADELPHIA
(Yankees, 9)   (Athletics, 7)

Thursday, May 24, 1928, Shibe Park

In 1927 the New York Yankees overwhelmed the American League, winning the pennant by 19 games, and then swept Pittsburgh in the World Series. Led by the formidable duo of Ruth and Gehrig, the Yankees also boasted a stellar supporting cast including future Hall of Famers Earle Combs, Tony Lazzeri, Waite Hoyt, Herb Pennock, and Stan Coveleski. Many around the league expected more of the same in 1928, but there was a new kid on the block who was beginning to flex his muscles.

The Athletics, runners-up the previous year, were developing an awesome club of their own. To an already solid line-up, Connie Mack added outfielders Tris Speaker, Bing Miller, Mule Haas, pitcher "Big George" Earnshaw, and pitcher-first baseman Ossie Orwoll. Speaker was then 40 years old and had slowed considerably, but each of the others made their presence known. In addition, Jimmie* Foxx, not yet old enough to vote, was getting more and more playing time.

The 1928 season quickly developed into a two-team race. By the morning of May 24, here's how the American League stacked up:

AMERICAN LEAGUE

	W	L	Pct.	G.B.
New York	26	6	.813	....
Philadelphia	21	8	.742	3.5
Cleveland	21	15	.583	7.5
Boston	14	18	.437	12
St. Louis	15	20	.429	12.5
Chicago	13	22	.371	14.5
Detroit	14	24	.368	15
Washington	11	22	.333	15.5

Earlier in the season, the Yankees and the Athletics had each won two games on the other's turf. Philadelphians were excited about their pennant chances, so when New York invaded the Quaker City for a May 24 doubleheader, fans from far and wide flocked to Shibe Park. The first pitch was not scheduled until 1:30 p.m., but when the ticket windows were opened at 10:45 a.m., there were already thousands in line, some of whom had been there since daybreak. By noon, the "parking field" at 21st and Lehigh was jammed to capacity with 500 "motor cars" bearing identification from such places as New York, New Jersey, Maryland, Delaware, and Washington DC. Even had there been additional parking space, it would have been inaccessible, as newspaper photos attest to the mass of humanity that sealed off surrounding streets. There was an air of feverish expectancy throughout the neighborhood. The Yankees also arrived about noon and had to fight their way through the hostile partisans. Ruth especially was verbally confronted.

With the throng completely beyond police control, the entrance gates finally opened around 12:30. Ballpark reference sources put 1928 Shibe Park seating capacity between 27,500 and 33,600, and "largest attendance" figures around 38,000. Philadelphia newspapers of the next day, however, belie those claims. *The Philadelphia Public Ledger* reported paid attendance at nearly 42,000 and unpaid attendance inside the park — pass holders, wall scalers, etc.— adding at least another 2,000. Other newspaper estimates were similar. Despite the park's ample

---

Throughout his playing days, Foxx signed his name as both "Jimmy" and "Jimmie." Newspapers ususally used Jimmy, although baseball reference works use Jimmie.

New York Yankees, taken in September 1928. Left to right, front row — Tom Zachary, Cedric Durst, Leo Durocher, Bennett, Myles Thomas, Hank Johnson, Rosy Ryan; center row — Woods, Joe Dugan, Mike Gazella, O'Leary, Miller Huggins, Fletcher, Benny Bengough, Gene Robertson; back row — Babe Ruth, Tony Lazzeri, Bill Dickey, Pat Collins, George Pipgras, Ben Paschal, Mark Koenig, Al Shealy, ?, Johnny Grabowski, George Burns, Fred Heimach, Matthews, Lou Gehrig. (Missing are Herb Pennock, Waite Hoyt, and Earle Combs.)

capacity, still another 15,000–20,000 disappointed patrons (many holding scalped tickets) "retreated from the barricaded portals or lingered outside the concrete horseshoe to listen to the noises of the long and rapid-turning battletide."* It was the largest crowd to date in Philadelphia baseball history.

Inside the arena, the onrushing tide of spectators fought for every available vantage point. They clambered for positions in the aisles, atop the scoreboard, and perches on the steel girders. Some of the more athletic (*The Philadelphia Inquirer* said 3,000) patrons even risked a spider-like climb to the top of the sloping left-field roof. (Two days later it was reported that several wire cutters and sledgehammers had been left in the park by owners seeking entrance to their seating accommodations.) Remarkably, despite all lack of crowd control and caution, there were no injuries nor deaths reported.

To afford the reader a greater appreciation of the atmosphere within and around the ballpark as well as the flavorful 1928 style of baseball reporting, the following is excerpted from *The Philadelphia Inquirer* account of the game:

"Over the low [12'] wall in right field, rabid rooters scaled the barbed wire walls like doughboys in France when the word was given 'over the top.' Despite the efforts of the police, several ladders were smuggled into the vast throng of ten thousand which banked itself on Twentieth street. As if by pre-arranged signal, four of them were placed against the walls and the fans surged over them like Greeks over the Trojan battlements. Many, once they reached the top, were caught on the barbed wire, and their antics in extricating themselves kept the fans in riotous good humor.

"One rooter in jumping to the ground had his coat sleeve caught on a barb. As he slipped to earth the coat remained in the wire, much to the delight of the vast throng who followed the progress of the invasion with as much interest as they did the batting practice of the Yanks.

"Another less fortunate wall climber

caught his trouser leg in a steel prong and dangled in the air as the thousands roared. His belt, however, did not give way and companions pulled him back to safety.

"Even the white pole along the right field foul line, served as a practice ground for embryonic steeplejacks, and several of them, instead of dropping to earth [from] atop the wall, "shinnied" up to the top pavilion. Each successive climb was met with a vast cheer from the crowd until so many accomplished the goal that it became monotonous.

"The new score boards did double work, serving as a parking place for a hundred or more fans as well as flashing the progress of the game.

"The porch and top roofs of the houses on Twentieth street held five thousand more baseball bugs [fans], despite feeble efforts by the police to keep them off. On roofs two blocks away, fifty or more [fans] were sighted viewing the battle through field glasses. They must have had a good view of the tilt for in the sixth inning of the first game when a doubtful strike was called on Cobb, one threw his hat on the roof, stamped on it, shook his fist at [umpire] Van Graflan and then disappeared from sight over the sidewall."

The first game of the doubleheader was a landmark in baseball history, but not because of the pennant race. In the Philadelphia half of the boxscore were listed no fewer than seven future Hall of Famers—Ty Cobb, Tris Speaker, Mickey Cochrane, Al Simmons, Eddie Collins, Jimmie Foxx, and Lefty Grove. The Yankees sported their own cast of demigods—Earle Combs, Babe Ruth, Lou Gehrig, Tony Lazzeri, Waite Hoyt, and Leo Durocher (who gained fame as a manager). All totaled, Shibe Park fans were treated to a view of *13 future Hall of Fame players in one game.* In addition, both managers—Miller Huggins and Connie Mack, as well as umpires Tommy Connolly and Bill McGowan, are honored guests in Cooperstown.

The Athletics were on a five-game win streak, but the Yankees were not very gracious guests in the first game. Lefty Grove

---

*Bill Brandt, "75,000 Storm Park as Athletics Win and Lose to N.Y.," Philadelphia Public Ledger, 25 May 1928, front page, col. 1.

himself had won six straight but was mauled by the Bronx Bombers behind Tony Lazzeri's three hits and six RBIs. Grove was not in the game in the ninth when Lazzeri tripled with the bases loaded to clinch it. The A's stayed close the entire game, but a ninth-inning rally was extinguished when, with two outs and the tying runs at second and third, Ty Cobb sizzled a line drive seemingly headed toward center field. Reliever Hoyt was able to knock it down and beat Cobb with a toss to first, ending the thriller. Rookie Al Shealy was the winner, sporting a 6–0 record. Al faded quickly, however, and pitched only one more season, finishing with an 8–6 career log.

The second contest was more befitting hometown expectations. Rookie left-hander Ossie Orwoll stymied Babe Ruth and company on only six hits en route to a 5–2 payback leaving the two clubs in the same relative positions as when the day began. Both Cobb and Speaker, 41 and 40 years of age respectively, played well in both ends of the twin-bill.

FIRST GAME

New York Yankees	AB	R	H	I	PO	A	E
Earle Combs cf	4	2	3	0	1	0	0
Leo Durocher ss	4	1	1	0	1	4	1
Babe Ruth lf	4	1	1	2	1	0	0
Lou Gehrig 1b	5	2	1	1	16	0	0
Bob Meusel rf	3	2	2	0	1	0	0
Tony Lazzeri 2b	5	0	3	6	1	5	1
Joe Dugan 3b	5	0	0	0	0	4	0
>Pat Collins c	5	0	0	0	6	1	0
Al Shealy p	4	1	1	0	0	2	0
Wilcy Moore p8	0	0	0	0	0	0	0
Waite Hoyt p9	0	0	0	0	0	1	0
	39	9	12	9	27	17	2

Philadelphia Athletics	AB	R	H	I	PO	A	E
Max Bishop 2b	5	1	2	2	2	4	0
>*Ty Cobb* rf	6	1	3	0	2	0	0
Tris Speaker cf	4	1	2	1	2	0	0
Joe Hauser 1b	4	0	1	0	7	0	1
Mickey Cochrane c	5	2	2	0	9	1	0
Walt French lf	3	0	0	1	1	0	0
Al Simmons ph7	1	0	1	1	0	0	0
Ossie Orwoll pr7	0	0	0	0	0	0	0
Mule Haas lf8	0	1	0	0	0	0	0
Sammy Hale 3b	5	0	0	0	1	2	0
Joe Boley ss	3	0	0	0	3	0	1
Eddie Collins ph7	1	0	0	0	0	0	0
Jimmy Dykes ss8	0	0	0	0	0	0	0
Lefty Grove p	3	1	1	0	0	2	0
Jimmie Foxx ph8	1	0	0	0	0	0	0
Ike Powers p9	0	0	0	0	0	0	0
Howard Ehmke p9	0	0	0	0	0	0	0
Bing Miller ph9	0	0	0	0	0	0	0
Bullet Joe Bush pr9	0	0	0	0	0	0	0
	41	7	12	5	27	9	2

New York	IP	H	R	ER	BB	SO
Shealy W,6-0	7.1	11	5	4	3	4
Moore	1	1	2	2	2	1
Hoyt	.2	0	0	0	1	0
	9	12	7	6	6	5

Philadelphia	IP	H	R	ER	BB	SO
Grove L,6-2	8	10	6	6	3	8
Powers	0	1	1	1	0	0
Ehmke	1	1	2	2	1	2
	9	12	9	9	4	10

New York	0 0 2	0 0 1	3 0 3	– 9
Philadelphia	0 0 0	1 1 1	1 1 2	– 7

OB: New York 8, Philadelphia 13
DP: Hale-Bishop-Hauser (P.Collins)
2B: Combs 2, Meusel, Cobb 2
3B: Meusel, Lazzeri, Bishop, Cochrane
SB: Lazzeri, Cobb
SO: Durocher 2, Ruth 2, Gehrig, Dugan, P. Collins 2, Al Shealy 2, Hauser, Hale 2, Boley, Grove
BB: Combs, Durocher, Meusel 2, Bishop, Speaker, Hauser, Haas, Dykes, Miller

HP: By Powers (Ruth)
WP: Moore
TIME: 2:38
ATTENDANCE: 44,000 (42,000 paid)
UMPIRES: Roy Van Graflan, *Tommy Connolly*, *Bill McGowan*
SOURCES: New York Times; Philadelphia Evening Bulletin, Inquirer, Public Ledger, Record; Retrosheet

---

BALANCE	OUT+R+OB=BP=AB+BB+SH+HP+CI
New York	27 9 8 44 39 4 0 1 0
Philadelphia	27 7 13 47 41 6 0 0 0

Gaston Gifted with Goose Eggs

73. Pitcher Throws 14-Hit Shutout

CLEVELAND   at   WASHINGTON
(Indians, 0)   (Nationals, 9)

Tuesday, July 10, 1928, Griffith Stadium

Milt Gaston defied the odds.

Milt Gaston, journeyman hurler for the mediocre (36–44) Washington Nationals, this day maximized a combination of good fortune and good pitching in tying a major league record by *allowing 14 hits enroute to whitewashing* the Cleveland Indians. That tied the mark set by Larry Cheney on September 14, 1913. Gaston was no newcomer to this type of high-wire act, as he had previously shut out the Red Sox on 12 hits while pitching for the Browns in 1926.

In the second game of a doubleheader, Gaston was making his 14th start of the season, previously having completed only three games. Milt was in trouble the entire game, punctuated by the Indians loading the bases in both the first and last innings. He allowed hits in each frame including two in the first, sixth and eighth, and three in the ninth. Five Indians were stranded on third base including one with no outs, two with one out, and two with two outs. In six of the innings the Cleveland leadoff batter hit safely. Each time, however, Milt managed to wriggle out of the trap. Two double plays and some sensational fielding helped preserve his shutout.

The very first inning provided the hometown crowd

SECOND GAME

Cleveland Indians	AB	R	H	I	PO	A	E
Charlie Jamieson lf	2	0	2	0	1	0	0
George Gerken lf4	2	0	2	0	3	0	0
Carl Lind 2b	4	0	1	0	4	2	0
Sam Langford cf	4	0	1	0	3	0	0
Joe Sewell ss	4	0	1	0	0	0	1
Ed Montague ss7	1	0	1	0	0	0	0
Lew Fonseca 1b	2	0	2	0	2	1	0
> Bruce Caldwell 1b4	3	0	1	0	4	0	0
Homer Summa rf	4	0	1	0	3	0	0
Johnny Hodapp 3b	4	0	2	0	3	2	0
Glenn Myatt c	4	0	0	0	0	0	1
Jake Miller p	1	0	0	0	1	1	0
Emil Levsen p4	2	0	0	0	0	1	1
Martin Autrey ph9	1	0	0	0	0	0	0
	38	0	14	0	24	7	3

Washington Nationals	AB	R	H	I	PO	A	E
Sam Rice rf	2	1	1	2	1	0	0
Dick Spalding pr3,rf	2	0	1	0	1	0	0
Bucky Harris 2b	5	0	0	0	3	4	0
Red Barnes cf	3	2	1	0	4	0	0
>Joe Judge 1b	4	1	2	0	8	1	0
Bobby Reeves ss	2	1	1	2	3	3	0
Sammy West lf	4	1	2	0	4	0	0
Ossie Bluege 3b	4	2	2	1	2	1	0
Muddy Ruel c	3	1	2	0	1	0	0
Bennie Tate c5	1	0	0	0	0	0	0
Milt Gaston p	3	0	1	1	0	1	0
	33	9	13	6	27	10	0

Cleveland	IP	H	R	ER	BB	SO
Miller L,3-4	3	10	8	8	0	0
Levsen	5	3	1	1	2	0

Washington	IP	H	R	ER	BB	SO
Gaston W,3-7	9	14	0	0	2	2

```
Cleveland     0 0 0   0 0 0   0 0 0  -  0
Washington    0 5 3   1 0 0   0 0 x  -  9
```

OB: Cleveland 14, Washington 7
DP: Harris-Judge-Reeves (Myatt)
    Reeves-Harris-Judge (Summa)
    Hodapp-Lind-Caldwell (Harris)
2B: Gerken, Summa, Reeves, Ruel
3B: Fonseca, Judge
HR: Rice(2)
SB: Barnes, Bluege
SO: Langford, Levsen
BB: Gerken, Langford, Barnes 2
SH: Lind, Judge

SF: Reeves 2, Gaston
HP: By Miller (Rice)
PB: Tate
TIME: 1:49
ATTENDANCE: ?
UMPIRES: Brick Owens, Harry Geisel,
    Bick Campbell
SOURCES: Cleveland Plain Dealer,
    Press; Washington Evening Star,
    Herald, Post

BALANCE	OUT+R+OB=BP=AB+BB+SH+HP+CI							
Cleveland	27	0	14	41	38	2	1	0	0
Washington	24	9	7	40	33	2	4	1	0

with a preview of Gaston's day-long, Houdini–like performance. Charlie Jamieson got things started for the Indians with a single and was sacrificed to second. After Sam Langford walked, Joe Sewell popped out to second for out number two. Shortstop Bobby Reeves then made a terrific effort to stop Lew Fonseca's drive, holding him to an infield single which loaded the sacks. Gaston then induced Homer Summa to pop up to Reeves.

Johnny Hodapp led off the second with a single but was erased on a double play. Jamieson did the same leading off the third, but Gaston retired the next three in order.

Cleveland's best scoring opportunity occurred in the fourth when Fonseca led off with a triple. But both Summa and Hodapp fouled out to Ossie Bluege, and Sammy West made a fine catch of Glenn Myatt's fly.

With one down in the fifth, the Tribe seriously threatened when George Gerken doubled and took third on a passed ball. Fine fielding again saved Gaston as Reeves made a sensational stop and threw out Carl Lind. Langford then routinely flied out to West.

Joe Sewell led off the sixth with a single. After Bruce Caldwell flied out, Summa doubled, putting himself and Sewell in scoring position. Again Gaston escaped as Hodapp sent a shallow fly to center and Myatt grounded out.

In the seventh, after Levsen fanned, Gerken walked and Lind singled. Both were stranded, however, as Langford popped to center, and Sewell flied to right.

The eighth brought more frustration for the Indians. Caldwell opened with a single but was erased on a double play. Hodapp also singled, but Myatt popped out to short.

With little hope of winning, Cleveland

nevertheless again rallied in the ninth. After pinch hitter Martin Autrey grounded out, Gerken singled to center. Lind flied out, but Langford singled to left and Gerken stopped at second. Ed Montague then grounded a ball off the third base bag which was retrieved in time to keep Gerken from scoring. With the sacks loaded, Caldwell pounded a ball toward deep right-center field. Right fielder Dick Spalding darted after it and, with his back to the infield, speared the ball to end the contest.

Baker Bowl Bloodbath

74. Teams Record 73 Hits in Doubleheader; Four Teammates Score Four Runs Apiece, Nine Score Two or More Runs

ST. LOUIS, NL   at   PHILADELPHIA
(Cardinals, 6,28)   (Phillies, 10,6)

Saturday, July 6, 1929, Baker Bowl

Ah, Baker Bowl. The major-league hitter's paradise was this day once again the scene of a dazzling offensive eruption. Pitchers ran for cover, several before retiring a single batter, as the Cardinals and Phillies *collected 73 hits in a doubleheader*, establishing a modern-day benchmark that still stands. The two clubs also scored 50 runs, which tied the major league record at the time and still retains a share of the National League mark.

If one were to graph each season's National League runs scored, 1929 would show an abrupt upward spike. Nearly 15% more runs were scored this year than in any previous twentieth-century season. So lively was the ball, that this year's hometown Phillies averaged 11 hits per game and led the league with a team batting average of .309, and a team slugging percentage of .467. Their achilles heel, and it was a badly festered one, was a pitching staff with a ludicrous 6.13 ERA. Claude Willoughby, this day's second game starter, had the lowest

ERA on the staff at 5.00. Two of his relievers in that contest had double-digit ERAs.

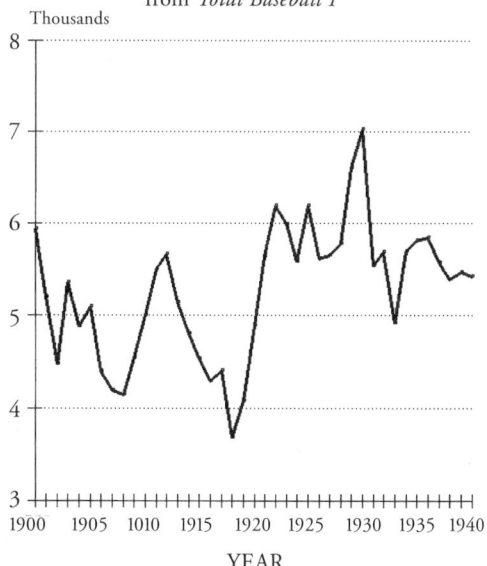

NATIONAL LEAGUE RUNS SCORED
from *Total Baseball I*

record, and nine Redbirds scored two or more, tying the modern major league mark. In both the first and fifth innings, 14 Cardinals batted and 10 scored. While the Phillies' 13 hits in the opener was enough for a victory, their 17 safeties in second game could manufacture only six runs in defeat.

Five years earlier, Jim Bottomley had collected 12 RBIs on six hits in one game. This day he again led the St. Louis offense with seven hits and 11 RBIs in the doubleheader as both he and teammate Chick Hafey poled grand slams in the nightcap. Also in the second game, Cardinal center fielder Taylor Douthit tied a major league record by stepping to the plate eight times, and teammate Fred Frankhouse emerged with a victory despite allowing 17 hits. The Phillies' Ray Benge was similarly bestowed with a win in the opening contest when he permitted six runs and 12 hits in just seven innings of work.

Fred Frankhouse (above) and Ray Benge (below) were awarded victories despite some paltry hurling.

The Cardinals took full advantage of Philadelphia's pathetic pitching corps. They needed it. St. Louis hadn't won a game in two weeks and had lost 10 straight entering this doubleheader. In the first game, the Missourians pummelled a pair of Philly flingers for 15 hits; it wasn't enough, however, as they went down to their 11th consecutive defeat, 10–6. But that was only a warm-up.

In the second game, the Cardinals simply massacred the Phillies. On 28 hits, St. Louis *scored 28 runs and established a new twentieth-century standard,* surpassing Cleveland's six-year-old mark (see 7-7-23). Every Cardinal hit safely and scored. *Four teammates scored four runs each, establishing another major league*

FIRST GAME

St. Louis Cardinals	AB	R	H	I	PO	A	E
Taylor Douthit cf	5	0	1	0	5	0	0
Andy High 3b	5	2	4	0	1	0	0
Frankie Frisch 2b	4	0	1	0	2	0	0
Carey Selph 2b8	1	0	0	0	0	0	0
Jim Bottomley 1b	5	2	3	4	5	0	0
Chick Hafey lf	5	1	1	0	2	0	0
Wally Roettger rf	3	1	1	0	3	0	0
Ernie Orsatti ph7	1	0	0	0	0	0	0
> Wattie Holm rf7	1	0	0	0	0	0	0
Earl Smith c	2	0	1	0	2	0	0
Eddie Delker pr6	0	0	0	0	0	0	0
Bubber Jonnard c6	1	0	0	0	3	0	0
Charlie Gelbert ss	4	0	3	2	1	3	0
Bill Sherdel p	3	0	0	0	0	1	0
Syl Johnson p7	1	0	0	0	0	0	0
	41	6	15	6	24	4	0

Philadelphia Phillies	AB	R	H	I	PO	A	E
>Denny Sothern cf	6	1	1	0	1	0	0
Lefty O'Doul lf	4	3	2	1	2	0	0
Fresco Thompson 2b	4	0	1	0	1	3	0
Don Hurst 1b	4	1	2	2	12	3	0
Pinky Whitney 3b	4	2	3	2	2	1	0
Chuck Klein rf	5	2	2	2	1	0	0
Tommy Thevenow ss	3	0	1	1	5	5	0
Walt Lerian c	2	0	1	0	3	0	0
Ray Benge p	3	0	0	0	0	1	0
Spud Davis ph7	0	0	0	0	0	0	0
Phil Collins pr7	0	1	0	0	0	0	0
Hal Elliott p8	1	0	0	0	0	1	0
	36	10	13	8	27	14	0

St. Louis	IP	H	R	ER	BB	SO
Sherdel L,6-8	6.1	13	10	10	7	4
Johnson	1.2	0	0	0	1	1
	8	13	10	10	8	5

Philadelphia	IP	H	R	ER	BB	SO
Benge W,7-8	7	12	6	6	1	2
Elliott	2	3	0	0	0	1
	9	15	6	6	1	3

```
St. Louis       0 0 0   4 0 0   2 0 0   -  6
Philadelphia    0 0 0   2 4 1   3 0 x   - 10
```

OB: St. Louis 9, Philadelphia 12
DP: Hurst-Thevenow-Hurst (High)
2B: High, O'Doul 2, Hurst, Klein, Lerian
HR: Bottomley 2(18), Whitney(7), Klein(21)
SO: Douthit, Hafey, Johnson, Elliot, Sothern, Thompson, Benge, Klein

BB: Smith, O'Doul, Hurst, Whitney, Thevenow, Lerian 3, Davis
SF: Thompson, Thevenow
WP: Sherdel
TIME: 2:22
UMPIRES: Cy Rigler, Beans Reardon, Bob Hart

BALANCE	OUT+R+OB=BP+AB+BB+SH+HP+CI
St. Louis	27 6 9 42 41 1 0 0 0
Philadelphia	24 10 12 46 36 8 2 0 0

SECOND GAME

St. Louis Cardinals	AB	R	H	I	PO	A	E
Taylor Douthit cf	6	4	5	2	2	0	0
Carey Selph 2b	2	1	2	1	1	3	0
> Eddie Delker 2b4	3	2	1	0	3	1	0
Andy High 3b	6	4	2	2	0	5	0
Jim Bottomley 1b	5	4	4	7	12	0	0
Chick Hafey lf	7	4	5	5	6	0	0
Wattie Holm rf	5	2	1	1	0	1	0
Jimmie Wilson c	6	2	2	4	3	1	0
Charlie Gelbert ss	6	3	2	1	0	3	0
Fred Frankhouse p	7	2	4	2	0	2	0
	53	28	28	25	27	16	0

Philadelphia Phillies	AB	R	H	I	PO	A	E
Denny Sothern cf	5	2	2	1	3	1	1
Lefty O'Doul lf	3	2	2	1	1	0	0
Chuck Klein rf	5	0	2	0	2	0	0
Don Hurst 1b	5	0	2	1	10	1	0
Pinky Whitney 3b	4	0	1	0	2	3	1
Fresco Thompson 2b	5	1	4	2	3	5	0
Tommy Thevenow ss	5	0	1	1	3	4	0
Spud Davis c	3	0	1	0	2	0	0
> George Susce c6	2	1	1	0	1	0	0
Claude Willoughby p	0	0	0	0	0	0	0
Elmer Miller p1	0	0	0	0	0	0	0
Luther Roy p1	2	0	0	0	0	0	0
June Green p5	1	0	1	0	0	2	0
	40	6	17	6	27	16	2

St. Louis	IP	H	R	ER	BB	SO
Frankhouse W,2-1	9	17	6	6	3	2

Philadelphia	IP	H	R	ER	BB	SO
Willoughby L,9-8	0	3	6	6	3	0
Miller	0	0	2	2	2	0
Roy	4.1	13	9	8	1	0
Green	4.2	12	11	11	3	1
	9	28	28	27	9	1

St. Louis   10 1 0   2 10 0   0 5 0   -28
Philadelphia   2 1 0   1 0 0   0 1 1   - 6

OB: St.Louis 10, Philadelphia 11
DP: Thevenow-Hurst
     High-Selph-Bottomley
     Gelbert-Delker-Bottomley
2B: Hafey 2, Gelbert 2, Thevenow,
     Susce, Green
3B: Selph
HR: Bottomley (19), Hafey (21),
     Sothern (4)
SO: Delker, Klein, Roy
BB: Douthit 2, Selph, Delker, Holm,
     Bottomley 2, Wilson, Gelbert,
     O'Doul, Whitney, Green
SH: Selph

SF: Holm, O'Doul
HP: By Green (High)
BK: Frankhouse
TIME: 2:28
ATTENDANCE: 15,000
UMPIRES: Beans Reardon, Bob Hart, Cy
     Rigler
SOURCES: Philadelphia Evening
     Bulletin, Evening Public Ledger,
     Inquirer, Public Ledger, Record;
     Sporting News; St. Louis Globe-
     Democrat

BALANCE   OUT+R+OB=BP=AB+BB+SH+HP+CI
St. Louis   27 28 10 65 53 9 2 1 0
Philadelphia 27   6 11 44 40 3 1 0 0

Tribe Saves Best for Last

75. Team Scores Nine Runs in the Ninth Inning with Two Outs

CLEVELAND   at   NEW YORK
(Indians, 14)   (Yankees, 6)

Sunday, August 4, 1929, Yankee Stadium

After being shut out in the first game of a doubleheader, the visiting Indians also trailed throughout the nightcap. In the top of the ninth the Yankees led 6–5, and Cleveland was down to their last out. Then, there erupted a rally the likes of which had not been witnessed in more than a quarter century and has not been seen since. After there were two outs, the Tribe proceeded to shatter three New York hurlers en route to scoring nine runs. Unlike two similar instances in 1901, however, Cleveland did not start their heroics with the bases empty — this rally began with a runner on first base. (Note:

more runs have been scored in an inning after two outs, but not in the **ninth** inning.)

Here's how that record-tying ninth developed for the Indians:

• Eddie Morgan was safe on Mark Koenig's fumble.

• Koenig then threw out Joe Sewell with Morgan taking second.

• Earl Averill beat out a hit down the third base line, but Morgan was tagged out when he overran third (Lary-Dickey-Koenig).

• Lew Fonseca was safe at first and Averill at second on Lyn Lary's error. (As this would

Lary bobbled Fonseca's grounder.

• Johnny Hodapp beat out a slow roller toward Koenig, scoring Averill with the tying run.

• Jackie Tavener hit the first ball out of the infield when he singled sharply to left, knocking home Fonseca and leaving the bases full.

• Glenn Myatt followed with single to center, scoring Falk and Hodapp, and sending Tavener to third.

• Indian relief pitcher Johnny Miljus also singled to center, driving home Tavener. Myatt stopped at second and that was the end for Heimach, who was relieved by Roy Sherid.

• When Yankee backstop Bill Dickey was charged with a passed ball, both runners moved ahead one base.

• Up for the second time in the inning, Morgan singled through the box, scoring Myatt.

• Joe Sewell hit his sixth home run of the year into the right field bleachers, driving home Miljus and Morgan ahead of himself.

• Averill ended the debauchery with a fly ball to center.

The Yankees were unable to recover from this stunning outburst as the Indians triumphed for the second time in the three game series and ninth time in 13 encounters thus far into the campaign. Neither club, however, was able to catch the runaway Philadelphia Athletics, who left their nearest pennant contender, the Yankees, 18 games behind. The Tribe finished third, 24 games out.

have been the third out of the inning, all subsequent runs were scored as unearned.) The Yankees' Wilcy Moore had pitched well, but southpaw Fred Heimach was then called on to face the left-handed swinging Bibb Falk.

• Falk walked, loading the bases.

SECOND GAME

Cleveland Indians	AB	R	H	I	PO	A	E
Eddie Morgan rf	6	2	3	2	0	0	1
Joe Sewell 3b	4	1	1	3	2	4	0
>Earl Averill cf	5	2	3	0	0	0	0
Lew Fonseca 1b	3	2	2	1	7	0	0
Bibb Falk lf	3	2	1	2	5	0	0
Johnny Hodapp 2b	5	1	2	2	2	2	0
Ray Gardner ss	3	0	1	0	3	4	0
Joe Hauser ph8	1	0	0	0	0	0	0
Jackie Tavener ss8	1	1	1	1	0	1	0
Luke Sewell c	3	0	0	0	5	0	0
Charlie Jamieson ph8	1	0	0	0	0	0	0
Glenn Myatt c8	1	1	1	2	3	0	0
Wes Ferrell p	2	1	1	0	0	1	0
Milt Schoffner p4	1	0	0	0	0	2	0
Dick Porter ph8	1	0	0	0	0	0	0
Johnny Miljus p8	1	1	1	1	0	0	0
	41	14	17	14	27	14	1

New York Yankees	AB	R	H	I	PO	A	E
Earle Combs cf	4	1	4	0	2	0	0
Gene Robertson 3b	3	1	2	2	1	1	0
Ben Paschal ph7	1	0	0	0	0	0	0
Lyn Lary 3b8	1	0	0	0	0	1	1
>Lou Gehrig 1b	5	0	0	0	15	0	1
Babe Ruth rf	4	0	2	0	1	1	0
Tony Lazzeri 2b	3	2	2	2	0	5	0
Cedric Durst lf	2	1	0	0	3	0	0
Bob Meusel ph4,lf	2	0	0	0	1	0	0
Bill Dickey c	5	0	3	1	0	1	0
Mark Koenig ss	3	1	1	0	4	5	1
Herb Pennock p	2	0	0	0	0	1	0
Wilcy Moore p5	1	0	0	0	0	1	0
Fred Heimach p9	0	0	0	0	0	0	0
Roy Sherid p9	0	0	0	0	0	0	0
Sammy Byrd ph9	1	0	0	0	0	0	0
	37	6	14	5	27	16	3

Cleveland	IP	H	R	ER	BB	SO
Ferrell	3.1	10	5	1	1	1
Shoffner	3.2	2	1	1	5	2
Miljus W,7-8	2	2	0	0	1	1
	9	14	6	2	7	4

New York	IP	H	R	ER	BB	SO
Pennock	4.2	9	5	5	2	0
Moore L,5-2	4	2	2	0	1	0
Heimach	0	4	5	0	1	0
Sherid	.1	2	2	0	0	0
	9	17	14	5	4	0

```
Cleveland    0 0 2    0 3 0    0 0 9    -14
New York     0 1 2    2 0 1    0 0 0    - 6
```

OB: Cleveland 7, New York 15
DP: Koenig-Gehrig (J.Sewell)
    J.Sewell-Gardner-Fonseca (Moore)
2B: Combs 2, Ruth
3B: Falk, Ferrell
HR: J.Sewell(6), Lazzeri(12)
SO: Ruth, Meusel, Koenig, Pennock
BB: J.Sewell, Averill, Falk 2, Ruth,
    Robertson, Gehrig, Lazzeri,
    Meusel, Koenig 2
SH: J.Sewell, Fonseca, Combs, Moore

SF: Fonseca, Combs, Lazzeri
PB: Dickey
TIME: 2:48
ATTENDANCE: 55,000
UMPIRES: George Moriarty, Roy Van-
    Gaflan, Bill McGowan
SOURCES: Cleveland Plain Dealer, Press;
    New York American, Evening-Post, Herald
    Tribune, Sun, Times, World

BALANCE	OUT+R+OB=BP=AB+BB+SH+HP+CI							
Cleveland	27	14	7	48	41	4	3	0	0
New York	27	6	15	48	37	7	4	0	0

Benton Battered in Triumph

76. Pitcher Allows Six Home Runs in Victory

NEW YORK, NL   at   CHICAGO
(Giants, 14)   (Cubs, 12)

Monday, May 12, 1930, Wrigley Field

In the history of modern major league baseball there have been five occasions when a pitcher has allowed six home runs in one game. Amazingly, in two of these contests, the victims actually emerged with a pitching victory! The first of these anomalies occurred in Chicago's Wrigley Field on a blustery day in May.

John McGraw's Giants were holding first place by a slim half-game over their hosts, Joe McCarthy's Cubs. This was 1930, the National League high watermark for offensive fireworks, and both the Giants and Cubs were contributing their shares. Each team this year batted over .300 and averaged more than six runs-scored per game. So it wasn't altogether shocking that after five innings, with help from a southwest gale, the McGrawmen had scored 14 runs. The fact that the score was 14–0, however, concerned the Windy City fans.

Larry Benton was breezing along for the Giants, confident of his first win of the season. He himself had contributed to the debauchery with a wind-blown home run. Meanwhile, in the Cubs locker room, smelling salts were being administered to the first two Chicago hurlers, Sheriff Blake and Bill

The 14-run lead was unsafe in Benton's hands.

McAfee (who had made a very inauspicious major league debut). Alas, unbeknownst to Benton, his Armageddon was soon about to begin.

In the fifth inning, Cliff Heathcote innocently got the Cubs on the board with a solo circuit blast. In the sixth, after Hack Wilson and Gabby Hartnett walked, Clyde Beck delivered a more substantial tremor in the form of a three-run homer. That made the score 14–4, still a very comfortable lead for the Giants. But in the seventh inning a major quake erupted. Heathcote led off with his second round-tripper. Kiki Cuyler grounded out, but Wilson and Charlie Grimm each hammered one into the center field bleachers near the scoreboard. Les Bell flied to left for out number two. Benton then fanned Hartnett, apparently ending the inning at 14–7, but catcher Shanty Hogan dropped the third strike and threw wildly to first, permitting Hartnett to run all the way to second base. That brought up Clyde Beck, who had homered the previous inning. Clyde repeated his effort, crushing one into the left center field bleachers, making it 14–9. McGraw had seen enough and deported Benton to the showers having given up six home runs while still leading. The Giants hung on, although reliever Joe Heving made it even more excit-

ing by allowing three additional runs and putting the tying runs on base with just one out in the bottom of the ninth. Joe Genewich relieved and slammed the door on the Cubs by inducing Heathcote to hit into a game-ending double play.

For Larry Benton, this game represented a piece of immortality. His six-home-run victory would be duplicated only one more time in the next 65 years. And, although he had won 25 games for McGraw just two years earlier, this was his last victory in a Giant uniform. Nine days later, on May 21, he was traded to Cincinnati.

New York Giants	AB	R	H	I	PO	A	E
Freddy Leach lf	6	1	1	3	1	0	0
Freddy Lindstrom 3b	4	2	3	0	1	1	0
Bill Terry 1b	6	1	1	0	7	0	0
Mel Ott rf	4	2	2	3	2	0	0
Pat Crawford 2b	5	1	0	0	3	3	0
Travis Jackson ss	6	1	0	1	5	4	0
Andy Reese cf	6	2	2	1	1	0	0
>Shanty Hogan c	5	2	3	1	7	0	2
Larry Benton p	4	2	3	3	0	0	0
Joe Heving p7	0	0	0	0	0	0	0
Joe Genewich p9	0	0	0	0	0	0	0
	46	14	15	12	27	8	2

Chicago Cubs	AB	R	H	I	PO	A	E
Woody English ss	6	1	2	1	0	3	1
>Cliff Heathcote rf	4	2	2	2	1	0	0
Kiki Cuyler lf	5	0	1	1	1	0	0
Hack Wilson cf	2	2	1	1	5	0	1
Charlie Grimm 1b	5	1	1	1	7	3	0
Les Bell 3b	5	1	1	0	0	0	1
Gabby Hartnett c	4	3	1	0	10	0	0
Clyde Beck 2b	5	2	3	5	1	3	1
Sheriff Blake p	1	0	1	0	1	0	0
Bill McAfee p3	0	0	0	0	0	0	0
Bud Teachout p3	3	0	1	0	1	1	0
Riggs Stephenson ph9	1	0	1	1	0	0	0
	41	12	15	12	27	10	4

New York	IP	H	R	ER	BB	SO
Benton W,1-2	6.2	9	9	8	5	6
Heving	1.2	6	3	3	1	2
Genewich	.2	0	0	0	0	0
	9	15	12	11	6	8

Chicago	IP	H	R	ER	BB	SO
Blake L,3-3	2.2	7	8	7	5	3
McAfee	0	3	5	3	0	0
Teachout	6.1	5	1	1	2	5
	9	15	14	11	7	8

New York 0 6 7   0 1 0   0 0 0   -14
Chicago   0 0 0   0 1 3   5 1 2   -12

OB: New York 12, Chicago 8
DP: Jackson-Crawford-Terry (Wilson)
    Crawford-Jackson-Terry (Heathcote)
2B: Reese, Lindstrom 2, English,
    Hartnett
HR: Leach (3), Benton (1), Ott (4),
    Heathcote 2(5), Beck 2(3),
    Wilson (8), Grimm (1)
SB: Heathcote
SO: Leach, Terry 3, Ott, Jackson,
    Reese, Benton, English 2, Bell 2
    Cuyler, Hartnett, Beck, Teachout

BB: Lindstrom 2, Ott 2, Crawford,
    Hogan (I), Benton, Heathcote 2,
    Wilson 3, Hartnett
WP: McAfee, Teachout
TIME: 2:26
ATTENDANCE: 13,500
UMPIRES: Bill Klem, Lou Jorda, Ted
    McGrew
SOURCES: Chicago Daily News, Herald-
    Examiner, Tribune; New York Times

BALANCE	OUT	+R	+OB	=BP	+AB	+BB	+SH	+HP	+CI
New York	27	14	12	53	46	7	0	0	0
Chicago	27	12	8	47	41	6	0	0	0

Bishop Walks Eight Times in Doubleheader

77. Player Records Eight Walks in Doubleheader

NEW YORK, AL   at   PHILADELPHIA
(Yankees, 7,1)   (Athletics, 15,4)

Wednesday, May 21, 1930, Shibe Park

Bishop turned his back on Yankee offerings.

Philadelphia fans usually packed the home park any time Babe Ruth came to town, some to heckle, others to admire. Such was the case this day when the Athletics hosted the Yankees in a Wednesday afternoon doubleheader. Philadelphia newspapers varied in their attendance figures, reporting between 25,000 and 30,000 for the two games. Whatever the actual number, those who witnessed these two games saw several tape measure home runs as well as a new major league record established.

The defending World Champion A's were just a game behind front running Washington. The Yankees were in third place but had won three in a row and seven of their last eight.

In the first game, the Bambino put on a home run exhibition. He blasted three round-trippers in a regular season game for the first time in his career. The second blast was said to be the longest ever hit in the Quaker City to date, clearing the first row of houses beyond the right-field wall. Jimmie Foxx also thrilled the crowd in the opener by smashing one onto the left-field rooftop as well as socking a 468-foot triple to dead center. That blast also would have been a four-bagger if Al Simmons had not clogged the basepaths waiting to see if Earle

FIRST GAME

New York Yankees	AB	R	H	I	PO	A	E
Earle Combs cf	4	1	0	0	4	0	0
>Lyn Larry ss	5	2	1	0	2	2	1
Babe Ruth lf	4	3	3	6	1	0	0
Tony Lazzeri 2b	4	0	1	0	2	3	1
Lou Gehrig 1b	4	0	0	0	8	0	0
Bill Dickey c	3	0	2	0	4	0	1
Benny Bengough c7	1	0	1	0	0	0	0
Dusty Cooke rf	3	0	1	0	1	0	0
Sammy Byrd rf8	1	0	0	0	0	0	0
Ben Chapman 3b	4	1	2	1	2	3	0
Red Ruffing p	2	0	1	0	0	1	0
Roy Sherid p5	1	0	0	0	0	1	0
Hank Johnson p7	0	0	0	0	0	0	0
Foster Edwards p8	0	0	0	0	0	0	0
Bubbles Hargrave ph9	1	0	0	0	0	0	0
	37	7	12	7	24	10	3

Philadelphia Athletics	AB	R	H	I	PO	A	E
Max Bishop 2b	1	2	0	1	2	4	0
Mule Haas cf	6	1	1	1	2	1	0
Jimmy Dykes 3b	6	1	1	1	2	1	0
Al Simmons lf	4	2	3	3	0	0	0
>Jimmie Foxx 1b	5	4	3	3	10	0	0
Bing Miller rf	4	0	2	1	3	0	0
Wally Schang c	3	1	1	1	5	2	0
Cy Perkins c8	1	0	1	1	2	0	0
Joe Boley ss	5	2	2	1	1	3	0
George Earnshaw p	1	0	0	0	0	1	0
Doc Cramer ph4	1	0	0	0	0	0	0
Jack Quinn p5	1	0	0	0	0	1	0
Spence Harris ph7	0	1	0	0	0	0	0
Lefty Grove p8	0	1	0	0	0	0	0
	38	15	14	13	27	13	0

New York	IP	H	R	ER	BB	SO
Ruffing	4	7	4	3	3	2
Sherid L,0-3	2	1	2	2	4	1
Johnson	1	5	7	4	2	0
Edwards	1	1	2	2	2	0
	8	14	15	11	11	3

Philadelphia	IP	H	R	ER	BB	SO
Earnshaw	4	7	6	6	1	5
Quinn W,3-2	3	1	0	0	0	1
Grove	2	4	1	1	0	2
	9	12	7	7	1	8

New York	2 0 3	1 0 0	0 1 0	- 7
Philadelphia	0 0 0	2 2 0	9 2 x	-15

OB: New York 4, Philadelphia 11
DP: Chapman-Lazzeri
2B: Dickey, Simmons 2, Chapman
3B: Foxx
HR: Ruth 3(9), Chapman (2), Foxx (8)
BB: Combs, Bishop 5, Simmons, Foxx,
　　Miller, Schang, Harris, Grove

SF: Simmons
WP: Johnson, Edwards
TIME: 2:41
UMPIRES: Dick Nallin, Harry Geisel,
　　Bill Dinneen

BALANCE	OUT+R+OB=BP=AB+BB+SH+HP+CI
New York	27 7 4 38 37 1 0 0 0
Philadelphia	24 15 11 50 38 11 1 0 0

SECOND GAME

New York Yankees	AB	R	H	I	PO	A	E
>Earle Combs cf	4	0	1	0	2	0	0
Lyn Larry ss	3	0	1	0	1	3	0
Babe Ruth lf	4	0	1	0	2	0	0
Tony Lazzeri 2b	4	0	0	0	0	3	0
Lou Gehrig 1b	3	1	1	0	14	0	0
Bubbles Hargrave c	4	0	0	0	3	0	0
Sammy Byrd rf	4	0	1	1	3	0	0
Ben Chapman 3b	3	0	0	0	2	0	0
Lefty Gomez p	2	0	0	0	0	4	0
Red Ruffing ph7	1	0	0	0	0	0	0
Lou McEvoy p7	0	0	0	0	0	1	0
Mark Koenig ph9	1	0	0	0	0	0	0
	33	1	5	1	27	11	0

Philadelphia Athletics	AB	R	H	I	PO	A	E
Max Bishop 2b	2	0	0	0	1	4	0
Mule Haas cf	5	1	2	1	2	0	0
>Jimmy Dykes 3b	5	1	1	1	2	0	0
Al Simmons lf	4	1	1	2	4	0	0
Jimmie Foxx 1b	2	0	1	0	5	0	1
Bing Miller rf	4	0	1	0	3	0	0
Cy Perkins c	4	0	0	0	8	0	0
Joe Boley ss	3	0	2	0	2	1	1
Rube Walberg p	4	1	1	0	0	1	0
	33	4	9	4	27	6	2

"Mickey Cochrane SAYS:

One of the features of the ball game was the fact that Max Bishop walked no less than eight times in both games. How he looks them over so closely is a mystery to everyone.

Summing up the Yankee attack only takes two words—Babe Ruth—the homer hammerer tied the [modern] world's record for home runs in the first game by blasting three of his copyrighted smacks out of the park. He drove in six of the seven runs in the first game.

A few of the observations from Mickey Cochrane's column in The Public Ledger.

New York	IP	H	R	ER	BB	SO
Gomez L,2-2	6	7	3	3	5	2
McEvoy	2	2	1	1	1	0
	8	9	4	4	6	2

Philadelphia	IP	H	R	ER	BB	SO
Walberg W,6-2	9	5	1	1	3	6

New York	0 0 0	0 0 0	1 0 0	– 1
Philadelphia	2 0 1	0 0 0	0 1 x	– 4

OB: New York 9, Philadelphia 11
DP: Bishop-Boley-Foxx
2B: Haas 2, Boley 2, Gehrig
HR: Simmons (6), Dykes (2)
BB: Combs, Gehrig, Chapman, Foxx 2, Bishop 3, Boley
HP: By Walberg (Lary)
WP: McEvoy
TIME: 1:49

ATTENDANCE: 30,000
UMPIRES: Harry Geisel, Bill Dinneen,
    Dick Nallin
SOURCES: New York Times; Philadelphia Evening
    Bulletin, Evening Public Ledger, Inquirer, Public
    Ledger, Record

BALANCE	OUT	+R	+OB	=BP	+AB	+BB	+SH	+HP	+CI
New York	27	1	9	37	33	3	0	1	0
Philadelphia	24	4	11	39	33	6	0	0	0

Combs would shag it down. And, Simmons himself got into the long-ball act by bouncing one over the left field pavilion in the nightcap.

But the record established this day was not by a slugger. Max Bishop had hit only 15 career home runs in six prior seasons, but Max had an uncanny eye for the strike zone. Nicknamed "Camera Eye," Bishop had led the league in free passes the year before even though he played in only 129 games. In this day's opening game, he walked five times; in the second game, three times. Although seven others had previously walked five times in one game, it was the *first occasion that any player had ever walked eight times in one day.* And to date, no one has yet to match Bishop's feat other than himself. (Remarkably, Bishop tied his own record four years later, see 7-8-34.) The closest anyone else has come is six walks in one day. Ironically, the only time Bishop failed to coax a free pass in the first game was during Philadelphia's biggest inning. In their nine-run seventh, Max grounded out.

Despite the absence of two of the A's future Hall of Famers, the Mackmen prevailed, sweeping the doubleheader.

Mickey Cochrane, with his ankle in a cast, watched the fireworks from a box seat. Connie Mack was at home recovering from the extraction of a few molars, leaving the club in the able hands of team captain Eddie Collins.

A Unique Mack Attack

78. Team Collects Two Triple-Steals in One Game

PHILADELPHIA   at   CLEVELAND
(Athletics, 14)   (Indians, 1)

Friday, July 25, 1930, League Park

Connie Mack's Athletics were the class of the league on the morning of July 25, 1930. The reigning World Champions led the Senators by four games and were 15–6 on their current western road trip. Their success was the result of quite an arsenal of weapons. In addition to veterans Al Simmons (who was leading the league at .393), Mickey Cochrane (.373), and Bing Miller (.303), the Mackmen also had a 22-year-old youngster named Jimmie Foxx. The kid on this date already had 26 home runs and 102 RBIs to accompany his .343 batting average. The pitching staff wasn't too shabby either. Lefty Grove was leading the league in strikeouts and winning percentage with a 13–4 slate. He was ably supported by George Earnshaw (13–6), Roy Mahaffey (8–4), Rube Walberg (9–6), Eddie Rommel (6–3) and 46-year-old Jack Quinn (8–5). As if the offense and pitching weren't enough, the A's were also leading the league in fielding percentage. But on this day the Mackmen incorporated a unique method of demolition. For the first time in modern baseball history, a team pulled off *two triple-steals in a single game*. To date, this feat has never been repeated.

In the very first inning, wildness of Indians pitcher Pete Jablonowski set the stage for the first triple-theft. Among other action, Al Simmons had walked, Bing Miller had beaten out an infield hit and Dib Williams

also had walked, loading the bases with two outs. With Jimmy Dykes batting, Simmons dashed for home and slid safely across before the ball even reached Tribe catcher Joe Sprinz. At the same time, Miller went to third and Williams to second.

Then, in the fourth inning, amid a six run uprising, the A's again scalped the Indians. This time the victim was a young relief pitcher named Milt Shoffner. With two outs, Foxx on first, Simmons on second, and Miller at bat, Cochrane — who had been on third — made a dash for the dish. Again it wasn't even close, as each runner was credited with a stolen base. The young Shoffner was so upset that he then surrendered an inside-the-park home run to the hitter, Miller.

Another peculiarity of this game may be noticed in the boxscore. All 11 of the A's assists came from the arms of just two players, second baseman Max Bishop and shortstop Dib Williams.

You won't find Pete Jablonowski, today's Cleveland starter, in the baseball encyclopedias. After toiling rather unsuccessfully (17–19) for four different teams in six years, Pete was banished to the minors. When he emerged a few years later he was no longer Pete Jablonowski but instead Pete *Appleton*. His entire career pitching record is now listed under his new name.

Foxx (left) and Cochrane (center) each participated in one triple steal. Simmons (right) was involved in both.

Philadelphia Athletics	AB	R	H	I	PO	A	E
Max Bishop 2b	3	2	1	1	2	6	1
Mule Haas cf	2	3	0	0	2	0	0
Doc Cramer cf6	2	0	1	0	1	0	0
Mickey Cochrane c	6	1	0	0	2	0	0
Cy Perkins c9	0	0	0	0	1	0	0
>Al Simmons lf	5	3	2	3	2	0	0
Jimmie Foxx 1b	3	2	1	0	13	0	0
Bing Miller rf	5	3	4	4	1	0	0
Dib Williams ss	3	0	1	0	3	5	1
Jimmy Dykes 3b	4	0	2	3	0	0	0
Lefty Grove p	3	0	0	0	0	0	0
	36	14	12	11	27	11	2

Cleveland Indians	AB	R	H	I	PO	A	E
Bob Seeds lf	4	1	1	0	3	0	1
Dick Porter rf	4	0	2	0	1	0	0
Eddie Morgan 1b	3	0	1	1	12	0	0
Johnny Hodapp 2b	3	0	0	0	2	3	0
Ray Gardner 2b7	1	0	0	0	0	0	0
Earl Averill cf	4	0	2	0	2	0	0
Joe Sewell 3b	2	0	0	0	1	1	1
Ed Montague ss7	2	0	0	0	0	0	0
>Joe Sprinz c	4	0	0	0	4	1	0
Jonah Goldman ss,3b7	3	0	0	0	2	5	0
Pete Jablonowski p	1	0	0	0	0	2	0
Milt Shoffner p4	1	0	0	0	0	1	0
Belve Bean p6	1	0	0	0	0	2	0
	33	1	6	1	27	15	2

Philadelphia	IP	H	R	ER	BB	SO
Grove W,14-4	9	6	1	1	0	2

Cleveland	IP	H	R	ER	BB	SO
Jablonowski L,4-5	3.1	3	6	5	6	1
Shoffner	2	5	6	6	4	0
Bean	3.2	4	2	2	0	2
	9	12	14	13	10	3

Philadelphia	3 1 0	6 0 2	0 2 0	-14
Cleveland	0 0 0	0 0 0	0 1 0	- 1

OB: Philadelphia 8, Cleveland 6
DP: Hodapp-Goldman-Morgan (Williams)
      Bishop-Williams-Foxx (Hodapp)
2B: Porter, Dykes 2, Williams, Morgan
HR: Bishop(9), Miller(8), Simmons(24)
SB: Miller 2, Simmons 2, Williams,
      Cochrane, Foxx
SO: Grove 3, Shoffner, Montague
BB: Bishop 3, Haas 2, Simmons, Dykes
      Foxx 2(1I), Williams

SH: Grove 2
SF: Williams, Morgan
TIME: 2:08
ATTENDANCE: ?
UMPIRES: Bill McGowan, Brick Owens,
      Bick Campbell
SOURCES: Cleveland Plain Dealer,
      Press; Philadelphia Evening
      Bulletin, Inquirer, Record

BALANCE	OUT+R+OB=BP=AB+BB+SH+HP+CI
Philadelphia	27 14 8 49 36 10 3 0 0
Cleveland	27 1 6 34 33 0 1 0 0

Longest "Strikeout-Less" Game

79. Teams Play 12-Inning Game Without Striking Out

CHICAGO, AL   at   ST. LOUIS
(White Sox, 10)   (Browns, 8)

Tuesday, July 7, 1931, Sportsman's Park

Simons was the hero with three of his 12 career RBIs.

In one of baseball's more statistically bizarre games, the St. Louis Browns and Chicago White Sox played a *twelve-inning contest in which neither team recorded a strikeout,* the longest such occurrence in baseball annals. Making this even more unexpected is the fact that strikeouts were plentiful in the American League this season. Actually, 1931 witnessed the second highest strikeout total in the American League in 13 years. In addition, the Browns this season led the league in batter strikeouts.

Otherwise a rather ordinary contest, this game was marked by comebacks, strategic maneuvers, and blown opportunities. After squandering three leads, the White Sox finally prevailed with two runs in the top of

Chicago White Sox	AB	R	H	I	PO	A	E
Lu Blue 1b	5	2	3	1	13	0	0
Mel Simons cf	6	2	3	3	9	0	0
Carl Reynolds rf	5	1	1	2	1	1	0
>Lew Fonseca lf	5	1	1	0	7	0	0
Luke Appling ss	5	1	1	2	2	6	0
John Kerr 2b	5	0	0	1	3	5	0
Irv Jeffries 3b	5	0	1	1	1	2	2
Frank Grube c	5	1	1	0	0	0	0
Tommy Thomas p	3	1	1	0	0	1	0
Red Faber p8	1	0	0	0	0	1	0
Hal McKain p12	0	0	0	0	0	0	0
Johnny Watwood ph12	1	1	1	0	0	0	0
	46	10	13	10	36	16	2

Chicago	IP	H	R	ER	BB	SO
Thomas	7.1	9	7	6	3	0
Faber W,3-4	3.2	3	1	1	3	0
McKain	1	1	0	0	0	0
	12	13	8	7	6	0

St. Louis Browns	AB	R	H	I	PO	A	E
Fred Schulte cf	5	2	2	3	5	0	0
Oscar Melillo 2b	6	0	3	0	2	3	0
Goose Goslin lf	5	0	1	0	4	1	0
Red Kress 3b,ss9	6	0	1	0	3	5	0
Rick Ferrell c	6	1	2	0	1	0	0
Tom Jenkins rf	4	1	1	2	1	0	0
Earl McNeely ph10,rf	1	0	0	0	0	0	0
Jack Burns 1b	4	0	1	0	18	0	0
Jim Levey ss	2	2	0	0	2	3	0
Lin Storti ph8,3b	3	0	0	0	0	0	1
Lefty Stewart p	3	1	1	1	0	3	0
> Chad Kimsey ph9,p	2	1	1	1	0	2	0
	47	8	13	7	36	17	1

St. Louis	IP	H	R	ER	BB	SO
Stewart	9	10	8	8	1	0
Kimsey L,2-6	3	3	2	1	0	0
	12	13	10	9	1	0

Chicago   0 1 0   0 4 0   0 3 0   0 0 2   -10
St. Louis 0 0 2   0 1 0   2 2 1   0 0 0   - 8

OB: Chicago 3, St. Louis 10
DP: Jeffries-Kerr-Blue (Kress)
    Kimsey-Kress-Burns (Reynolds)
2B: Fonseca, Stewart, Mellilo, Burns
3B: Reynolds, Appling
HR: Schulte 2(4), Jenkins(2),
    Kimsey(2)
BB: Blue, Schulte, Goslin(I), Burns,
    Jenkins, Levey, Kimsey(I)
SH: Reynolds, Fonseca, Burns

WP: Thomas
TIME: 2:24
ATTENDANCE: 2,500
UMPIRES: George Hildebrand, George
    Moriarty, Bick Campbell
SOURCES: Chicago Daily News, Herald-
    Examiner, Tribune; St.Louis Globe-
    Democrat, Post-Dispatch

BALANCE	OUT+R+OB=BP=AB+BB+SH+HP+CI						
Chicago	36	10	3	49	46	1	2	0	0
St. Louis	36	8	10	54	47	6	1	0	0
----

the twelfth on a single by Mel Simons. The Browns, on the other hand, were unable to exploit multiple game-winning situations. In three of the last four innings, St. Louis had runners in scoring position with only one out but failed to capitalize.

The Browns did give the hometown fans something to cheer about by coming back three times to either tie or take the lead, highlighted by a pinch-hit home run in the bottom of the ninth. St. Louis reliever Chad Kimsey threw right-handed but batted left. A lifetime .282 hitter, Kimsey had fashioned the highest batting average on the Browns a year earlier (24/70–.343). When manager Bill Killefer sent him to the plate to pinch hit opening the home half of the ninth, he responded with a game-tying home run off

aging Chicago right-hander Red Faber. Faber was still toiling for the Sox on Kimsey's next plate appearance in the bottom of the tenth. With two outs and a runner on second, Kimsey was intentionally walked even though the next batter, Fred Schulte, had already hit two home runs. Schulte was a right-handed batter, however, and the strategy paid off as he popped out.

Although Chicago did not have the fewest strikeouts in the American League this year, they did put together an impressive string of making contact with pitches. Including the game of a day earlier with the Browns and the game a day later with the Indians, the White Sox batters struck out only three times in 32 innings.

St. Louis's Kimsey tied it in the ninth but lost it to Chicago in the 12th.

Baker Bowl Batting Practice

80. Team Records
58 At-Bats in One Game

NEW YORK, NL   at   PHILADELPHIA
(Giants, 23)   (Phillies, 5)

Saturday, July 11, 1931, Baker Bowl

When the Giants invaded the City of Brotherly Love for a doubleheader on this date, their hosts were in a very generous mood. Actually, the first game resulted in little more than batting practice for New York as they amassed 28 hits and tied the modern major-league record of *58 at-bats in a nine-inning game*. The carnage was not altogether shocking because the Phillies pitching staff not only had the highest ERA in the league, but the New Yorkers were second in team batting at .293. In the Giants' starting lineup, sporting .300+ averages, were Bill Hunnefield (.326), Freddy Leach (.303), Chick Fullis (.392), Bill Terry (.339), Johnny Vergez (.304), and Shanty Hogan (.336). On the hill for the home club was Jumbo Jim Elliott, the staff ace who wound up the season with a 4.27 ERA.

The visitors jumped all over Jumbo Jim early. The left-hander got through the first inning allowing only one run, but the second frame was a different story. Then, the visitors blasted both Elliott and his relief, Dutch Schesler, for six more tallies, and by the time the Phillies came to bat in their half of the fourth, they were already trailing 16–0. Although the Phillies tallied single runs in five of the last six frames, the contest grew even more lopsided as the Giants added seven more, making the final count 23–5.

This game nearly tied several other major league records. The Giants scored in every inning but the fifth; only the Giants of 1923 had scored in all nine. The two clubs also combined for 99 official at-bats, which is an impressive total but not a benchmark, even though it is listed as such in some record books. The all-time standard of 101 was

Freddy Leach led the onslaught with five hits. Note the sunglasses screwed into his cap visor.

established by New York and Cincinnati 30 years earlier (see 6-9-01).

The Phillies did show great resiliency this day when they bounced back to win the nightcap 6–5 on a ninth-inning rally.

FIRST GAME

New York Giants	AB	R	H	I	PO	A	E
Bill Hunnefield 2b	6	3	4	3	1	1	0
Doc Marshall 2b7	1	0	0	0	2	1	1
Freddy Leach lf	7	4	5	3	3	0	0
Chick Fullis cf	7	1	1	1	2	0	0
Bill Terry 1b	5	2	2	4	4	1	0
Sam Leslie 1b7	2	2	2	1	2	0	0
>Mel Ott rf	7	2	3	2	3	1	0
Travis Jackson ss	6	2	3	2	1	5	0
Johnny Vergez 3b	5	3	3	2	1	1	0
Shanty Hogan c	6	2	3	2	6	0	0
Clarence Mitchell p	6	2	2	0	2	1	0
Hal Schumacher p9	0	0	0	0	0	0	0
	58	23	28	20	27	11	1

Philadelphia Phillies	AB	R	H	I	PO	A	E
Fred Brickell cf	3	0	0	0	2	0	0
Hal Lee cf7	2	1	2	0	2	0	0
Bobby Stevens ss	3	0	1	0	0	4	2
Chuck Klein lf	5	2	3	2	5	0	0
Buzz Arlett rf	5	1	3	1	3	0	1
Pinkey Whitney 3b	5	0	1	0	1	2	0
Spud Davis c	1	0	1	0	1	0	0
Gene O'Connell c4	3	0	1	0	2	0	0
Clise Dudley ph9	1	0	0	0	0	0	0
Don Hurst 1b	4	1	2	2	8	0	0
>Barney Friberg 2b	5	0	0	0	3	3	1
Jumbo Jim Elliott p	0	0	0	0	0	0	0
Dutch Schesler p2	4	0	0	0	0	0	0
	41	5	14	5	27	9	4

New York	IP	H	R	ER	BB	SO
Mitchell W,9-5	8	12	4	4	2	5
Schumacher	1	2	1	1	1	1
	9	14	5	5	3	6

Philadelphia	IP	H	R	ER	BB	SO
Elliott L,11-8	1	6	7	4	0	0
Schesler	8	22	16	14	0	1
	9	28	23	18	0	1

New York   1 6 7   2 0 3   1 2 1   -23
Philadelphia 0 0 0   1 0 1   1 1 1   - 5

OB: New York 9, Philadelphia 12
DP: Ott-Mitchell
2B: Fullis, Jackson 2, Leach 2,
    Hogan, Arlett, Klein, Leslie,
    Lee 2
HR: Leach(4), Terry(5), Ott(12),
    Hurst(4), Leslie(3), Klein(22)
SO: Vergez, Stevens, Arlett 2,
    Whitney, O'Connell, Schesler
BB: Stevens 2, Hurst

HP: By Schesler (Vergez)
TIME: 3:21
ATTENDANCE: 16,500
UMPIRES: Charlie Moran, Jim Scott,
    Ernie Quigley
SOURCES: New York American, Times;
    Philadelphia Inquirer, Public
    Ledger, Record

BALANCE	OUT	+R	+OB	=BP	=AB	+BB	+SH	+HP	+CI
New York	27	23	9	59	58	0	0	1	0
Philadelphia	27	5	12	44	41	3	0	0	0

Red Sea Causes Double Trouble

81. Teams Combine for 23 Doubles in One Game

CHICAGO, NL   at   ST. LOUIS
(Cubs, 13)   (Cardinals, 17)

Sunday, July 12, 1931, Sportsman's Park

The conduct and supervision of fans sixty years ago were vastly different from what we now expect, and so often crowd behavior led to some unusual baseball games (see 5-30-25). Such was the case on this day in St. Louis, when in the second game of a doubleheader, *two teams combined for 23 doubles*, a record that has yet to be approached.

Locked in a tight pennant race, the Cubs came into town for a twin-bill in fourth place, only six games behind the league leading Cardinals. It was a sweltering hot, cloudy, humid day in St. Louis, but the weather wasn't the only thing steaming. Added to the long-standing rivalry between these two clubs was an incident that had occurred in Chicago only five days earlier when bitter feelings resulted from Cub-inflicted Cardinal spike wounds. This day's encounter held the potential for a real grudge match. *The St. Louis Post-Dispatch* even referred to the visitors as "the hated Cubs."

The main gates were opened at nine

o'clock, and long before noon all reserved seats in the park were occupied. Other spectators jammed the aisles. Ropes were then stretched around the outfield from foul line to foul line, 30 feet from the walls, and the bleacher gates were opened. The invading hordes surged into the park, and when they sensed there were no police to corral them behind the ropes, they flooded the playing field like swarming bees. This happened at the same time the Cubs were engaged in fielding practice, and it didn't take long for several enterprising patrons to storm the infield and join the visitors in their practice glove work. Soon there were hundreds of transgressors scrambling for batted balls which were immediately claimed as souvenirs. When the pseudo-infielders had consumed all of the Cubs' spare balls, they turned their attention to the player benches, cramming around both dugouts, peering at the players and exchanging unpleasantries with the Cubs. *The St. Louis Globe-Democrat*

A St. Louis Globe-Democrat *photo shows part of the crowd during the first game when there was still some semblance of order and control. (Photo courtesy of St. Louis Mercantile Library.)*

estimated that there were at least 8,000 customers on the field, including children and infants being carried by their mothers.

With rain a distinct threat but refunds anathema to any owner, Cardinal president Sam Breadon roused the umpires, grounds crew, ushers, players, coaches, and all available policeman to clear the infield in preparation of starting the contests. Evacuating the infield went fairly smoothly, but the outfield was another story. There were so many fans without seats that they formed a sea of Redbird partisans covering most of the outfield, and attempts to back them up to the walls was like playing with quicksilver. When pressure was applied in the middle, both ends surged forward; if pressure was applied to the ends, the center bulged forward. Finally, the crowd-control element decided it was hopeless and opted simply to begin the first game. The few hundred fearless patrons who had climbed to the pavilion roof had a bird's-eye view of the throng standing on the field in fair territory starting about 70 feet behind first base, extending into center field not more than 150 feet behind second, and around to left field about 100 feet behind third base. In foul territory, the crowd bulged in huge wads in front of both dugouts, blocking players' views and forcing box seat holders to stand in order to see any of the action. Angry patrons yelled at Breadon, asking him why he allowed so many into the park. His defense was that there were often many tourists from far away cities, and he didn't like to disappoint them. (A heart of gold.)

When all the receipts were tallied, a new St. Louis attendance record was established, or more appropriately, the old record was crushed. More than 11,000 fans were without seats. (Although the Browns also played in Sportsman's Park, all the previous attendance records had been established during Cardinal games.)

SPORTSMAN'S PARK ATTENDANCE RECORDS AS OF 7-12-31*

Attendance	Date	Opponents
45,715	July 12, 1931	Cubs at Cardinals
39,960	October 7, 1926 (W.S.)	Yankees at Cardinals
38,284	May 20, 1928	Giants at Cardinals
34,000	Seating capacity in 1931	

*Martin J. Haley, "45,715 See Fighting Cardinals and Cubs Split Doubleheader," St. Louis Globe-Democrat, 13 July, 1931, Front page, col. 6-7.

The games themselves were as ludicrous as the preliminary affairs. The overwhelming crowd had necessitated special ground rules calling for a "double" whenever a ball was hit into it. Several times during each contest there were delays to push the throng back under the threat of forfeiture. Ordinary fly balls, as well as some ground balls, miraculously transformed into two-base blows as fans fought among themselves and with the outfielders whenever a prospective souvenir approached. On a few occasions, the Redbird sea was parted to allow one of their own outfielders to sneak through to make a catch. *The St. Louis Post-Dispatch* reporter felt that of the 32 "doubles" hit in the two games, all but five or six would have been easily caught fly balls.

The second game, in which this all-time doubles record was established, was even more outlandish than the first. The Cubs sent six hurlers into the maelstrom who combined to allow 21 hits and 17 runs. While there had been "only" nine doubles awarded in the opener, the nightcap provided a two-team total of 23. By the time the second game had begun, fans had moved to just about wherever they wanted. There was then as much room behind the right-field mob as in front of it, and the outfielders were forced to play just beyond the infield.

Hundreds placed themselves in great danger to view the action, occupying the front of the backstop (scene of foul tips and wild pitches)

Three of Gus Mancuso's four hits were doubles.

as well as along the first and third-base foul lines. Instead of fear, these intrepid observers heartily flung themselves in front of balls traveling at blinding speeds in order to carry home a souvenir. Fortunately, no such viewer was wounded, although one patron was badly injured when pushed over the railing from his upper-deck grandstand seat.

SECOND GAME

Chicago Cubs	AB	R	H	I	PO	A	E
Footsie Blair 2b	6	3	3	4	2	2	1
Woody English ss	6	1	3	2	2	5	1
Kiki Cuyler rf	3	0	0	0	1	0	0
>Hack Wilson lf	6	0	1	0	1	0	0
Rogers Hornsby 3b	4	1	2	0	1	1	0
Danny Taylor cf	4	1	0	0	1	0	1
Charlie Grimm 1b	5	2	1	0	8	0	0
Gabby Hartnett c	5	3	5	1	8	1	0
Pat Malone p	0	1	0	0	0	0	0
Guy Bush p4	0	0	0	0	0	0	0
Les Bell ph4	1	1	1	2	0	0	0
Ed Baecht p5	0	0	0	0	0	0	0
Charlie Root p5	0	0	0	0	0	0	0
Les Sweetland ph6	1	0	0	0	0	0	0
Sheriff Blake p6	0	0	0	0	0	1	0
Lon Warneke p8	0	0	0	0	0	0	0
Riggs Stephenson ph9	1	0	0	0	0	0	0
	42	13	16	9	24	10	3

St. Louis Cardinals	AB	R	H	I	PO	A	E
Sparky Adams ss	4	3	1	0	2	3	4
George Watkins rf	5	3	1	1	0	0	0
Frankie Frisch 2b	5	3	3	1	1	5	0
Ripper Collins 1b	6	2	4	4	8	0	0
Chick Hafey lf	5	2	3	3	0	0	0
Pepper Martin cf	6	1	3	3	3	1	0
Andy High 3b	4	1	1	1	0	0	0
Gus Mancuso c	5	1	4	2	13	1	0
Flint Rhem p	1	0	0	0	0	1	1
Ernie Orsatti ph4	2	1	1	1	0	0	0
Allyn Stout p5	0	0	0	0	0	0	0
> Paul Derringer p5	3	0	0	0	0	0	0
	46	17	21	16	27	11	5

Chicago	IP	H	R	ER	BB	SO
Malone	3.1	10	7	4	0	3
Bush	.2	3	3	3	1	0
Baecht L,2-3	0	0	2	2	2	0
Root	1	2	1	1	0	0
Blake	2	6	4	4	3	3
Warneke	1	0	0	0	1	0
	8	21	17	14	7	6

St. Louis	IP	H	R	ER	BB	SO
Rhem	4	7	6	3	3	5
Stout	0	2	4	3	1	0
Derringer W,10-3	5	7	3	3	1	6
	9	16	13	9	5	11

Chicago	2 0 0	4 4 1	0 0 2	-13
St. Louis	3 0 0	7 3 2	0 2 x	-17

OB: Chicago 9, St. Louis 13
DP: Martin-Mancuso (D.Taylor)
    Frisch-Adams-Collins
    English-Grimm
2B: Blair 2, English 3, Hornsby,
    Hartnett 3, Bell, Watkins.
    Frisch 2, Collins 3, Hafey 2,
    High, Mancuso 3, Orsatti
HR: Blair(1)
SO: Blair 3, English, Cuyler 2,
    Wilson 3, Taylor, Grimm, Hafey,
    Watkins, Frisch, Rhem,
    Derringer 2
BB: Cuyler 2, Hornsby, D.Taylor, ...

BB: ... Malone, Adams 2, Watkins,
    Hafey, Frisch, High, Mancuso
SH: Cuyler, Malone
HP: By Root(High)
WP: Blake, Stout, Derringer 2
TIME: 2:44
ATTENDANCE: 45,715
UMPIRES: Cy Pfirman, Cy Rigler,
    Robert Clarke
SOURCES: Chicago Herald-Examiner,
    Tribune; St. Louis Globe-Democrat,
    Post-Dispatch, Star

BALANCE	OUT	+R	+OB	=BP	=AB	+BB	+SH	+HP	+CI
Chicago	27	13	9	49	42	5	2	0	0
St. Louis	24	17	13	54	46	7	0	1	0

Ferrell Fortunate in Shutout

82. Team Leaves 15 Runners on Base in Shutout Loss

CLEVELAND   at   WASHINGTON
(Indians, 6)   (Senators, 0)

Wednesday, July 29, 1931, Griffith Stadium

Players on losing teams often bemoan the fact that the opposing pitcher had "nothing" on his pitches. Never was that story more appropriate than on this day when the Washington Senators knocked around Cleveland ace Wes Ferrell for ten hits to complement

Cronin (above) got on base four times but couldn't score on Ferrell (opposite).

their five walks. Ferrell did have "something," however, when he most needed it as all the runners perished, and Washington tied a modern major league record by *stranding 15 base runners in a shutout loss.* (This standard was later surpassed, see 5-24-94.)

The Senators had base runners in every inning but couldn't get a clutch hit when they needed it. They left the sacks full in the third inning, two players on in the second, fourth, fifth, and seventh, and a lone runner on in the first, sixth, eighth, and ninth. Joe Cronin, a future Hall of Famer, was stranded each of the four times he reached base. As a batter, first baseman Joe Kuhel left six runners on base, four of them in scoring position.

The Senators' best scoring opportunities came in the third and seventh frames. In the third, Washington loaded the bases with only one out but Sammy West popped out to short, and Joe Kuhel flied to right. In the seventh, with runners at first and third and one out, Kuhel popped out to third and Ossie Bluege grounded into a force out.

Washington's Fred Marberry, who through a series of starting and relief appearances had won nine consecutive games, was this day's loser. The Indians' Joe Vosmik provided all the offense that Ferrell needed when he clouted a titanic, three-run homer into the left center field bleachers in the opening frame.

Wes Ferrell went on to compile a fine 22–12 log with 27 complete games in 1931, and this contest represented one of his two shutouts.

Cleveland Indians	AB	R	H	I	PO	A	E
Dick Porter rf	3	0	1	1	1	0	0
Johnny Burnett 2b	5	1	1	1	3	6	0
Earl Averill cf	5	0	2	1	2	0	0
>Eddie Morgan 1b	5	1	1	0	12	1	0
Joe Vosmik lf	4	1	2	3	2	0	0
Willie Kamm 3b	4	0	1	0	1	0	0
Luke Sewell c	4	0	1	0	2	0	0
Ed Montague ss	3	2	0	0	3	3	0
Wes Ferrell p	4	1	2	0	1	2	0
	37	6	11	6	27	12	0

Washington Senators	AB	R	H	I	PO	A	E
Buddy Myer 2b	3	0	0	0	1	6	0
Sam Rice rf	5	0	1	0	1	0	0
Heinie Manush lf	4	0	1	0	2	0	0
Joe Cronin ss	3	0	2	0	2	2	0
Sammy West cf	5	0	1	0	2	0	0
>Joe Kuhel 1b	5	0	1	0	14	0	0
Ossie Bluege 3b	4	0	2	0	1	1	0
Roy Spencer c	4	0	1	0	4	0	0
Firpo Marberry p	1	0	0	0	0	1	0
Joe Judge ph4	1	0	0	0	0	0	0
Bump Hadley p5	1	0	1	0	0	2	0
Pinky Hargrave ph8	1	0	0	0	0	0	0
Lloyd Brown p9	0	0	0	0	0	0	0
	37	0	10	0	27	12	0

Cleveland	IP	H	R	ER	BB	SO
Ferrell W,14-9	9	10	0	0	5	1

Washington	IP	H	R	ER	BB	SO
Marberry L,10-2	4	6	5	5	2	1
Hadley	4	2	0	0	1	2
Brown	1	3	1	1	0	0
	9	11	6	6	3	3

Cleveland	3 1 0	1 0 0	0 0 1	- 6
Washington	0 0 0	0 0 0	0 0 0	- 0

OB: Cleveland 7, Washington 15
DP: Cronin-Myer-Kuhel (Morgan)
2B: Rice
3B: Vosmik
HR: Vosmik(5)
SO: Morgan, Kamm, Montague, Hargrave
BB: Porter 2, Montague, Myer 2,
    Manush, Cronin 2

TIME: 2:01
ATTENDANCE: ?
UMPIRES: Harry Geisel, George
    Moriarty, Brick Owens
SOURCES: Cleveland Plain Dealer,
    Press; Washington Post, Star

BALANCE	OUT+R+OB=BP=AB+BB+SH+HP+CI
Cleveland	27	6	7	40	37	3	0	0	0
Washington	27	0	15	42	37	5	0	0	0

The Washington Evening Star *pictured the results of Ferrell's work. The escapee bird represented two straight Senator wins.*

Larruping Lou Laces Four

83. Player Hits Four Consecutive Home Runs; Teams Combine for 77 Total Bases, 41 Extra Bases

NEW YORK, AL   at   PHILADELPHIA
(Yankees, 20)   (Athletics, 13)

Friday, June 3, 1932, Shibe Park

Not since the nineteenth century had a major league player hit four home runs in a game. Bobby Lowe of the Boston Nationals was the first to accomplish the feat in 1894 (his were consecutive) and the Phillies' Ed Delahanty (not consecutive) tied the mark in

Gehrig posed with Bobby Lowe shortly after his historic day.

1896, but no American Leaguer had ever swatted four in a single contest. All that changed on this day when 28-year-old Lou Gehrig *lashed a quartet of consecutive round-trippers* in his first four plate appearances to lead the Yankees over the world champion Athletics. Lou then had two more opportunities to hit number five with the crowd encouraging him, but a ground out and a long fly out completed his day. Gehrig also became the first batter to hit three or more home runs in a game four times.

The A's, winners of three straight pennants, had lost their edge in domination of the league. One of the reasons was the mysterious, erratic hurling of George "Moose" Earnshaw. George had been one of Connie Mack's "horses" from 1929 to 1931 but was now mysteriously slipping. When asked by a reporter about his hurler's performance in this game, Mack confessed: "I don't know what is wrong with him. He gives up a home run, then strikes out the side. I can't figure him out."* This game was a prime example. George was staked to an 8–4 lead by his heavy-hitting teammates after four innings, but despite eight strikeouts, he had to be relieved after the fifth. Four more members of the staff that a year earlier had led the league in winning percentage, shutouts, earned run average, and complete games followed Earnshaw, and all were promptly pummelled.

When asked about Gehrig's performance, Connie Mack responded, rather placidly, "He was hittin' 'em today, yes indeed."† Here's what Connie witnessed:

• Gehrig began his pyrotechnics in the first inning when with two outs and Jack Saltzgaver on first, he drove an Earnshaw pitch into the upper deck of the center field bleachers, giving the New Yorkers a 2–0 lead. This was his only home run of the day with any teammates on base.

• Lou led off the fourth with another home run off Earnshaw, this time over the right field wall (which at the time was 12 feet tall).

• In the fifth frame, Earnshaw was shat-

tered. Earle Combs led off with a homer, followed by Jack Saltzgaver's out and a four-ply blast by Babe Ruth. Gehrig followed suit with another tape measure shot into the center field upper deck.

• Facing Roy Mahaffey, Lou led off the seventh with another homer. This one narrowly missed being a foul ball as it just curved around the right field foul pole on its exodus from the park. When questioned about his fourth at-bat Gehrig said: "I didn't feel special. I just thought to myself, 'Gehrig you're up to bat. Try and get a hit.' And I swung. I'll admit when that fourth homer began to curve foul, I felt a gulp in my throat, but I swallowed it when the ball went over fair."†

• In the eighth, Lou grounded out, Max Bishop to Jimmie Foxx.

• Gehrig came to the plate again in the ninth as the fans were cheering for him to hit another one. Lou almost obliged as he sent a long fly ball toward the flagpole in deep center field. Al Simmons, who had been moved to center after Bing Miller entered the game in the ninth, had to make a running one-handed circus catch to retire the record breaker. Most reporters felt that Gehrig may have circled the bases had the ball fallen in front of the 468 foot marker. Later, Gehrig was reported as lamenting: "Say, why'd they move that guy Simmons to center in the ninth? I might've had another hit if he hadn't pulled that high powered catch."† (Scoring rules of the day precluded Lou from being credited with a sacrifice on this play, yet he was given an RBI when a runner tagged and scored from third.)

In addition to Gehrig, there was another Yankee hero in this game. Thanks to a ninth-inning grand slam, Tony Lazzeri matched Gehrig's RBI total and did him one better in the hit department. Tony also hit for the cycle.

As reported in most newspapers, several other records were established in this slugfest. The Yankees' deluge of *seven home runs tied the existing major league single-team, single-game standard* (since surpassed). Their *50*

---

*Al Horwits, "Earnshaw Sad Puzzle to Mack," Evening Public Ledger, 4 June 1932, p. 13, col. 8.
†Cy Peterman, "Gehrig's 4 Homers Tie 36 Yr. Mark As Yanks Get 50 Bases on 23 Hits," Philadelphia Evening Bulletin, 4 June 1932, p. 15, col. 1–2.

total bases established a new major league benchmark (since surpassed) as did the *two-team total of 77 which remains the American League mark* to this day. In addition, the two teams combined for a rather obscure major league standard, i.e., *most extra bases on long hits, game, both clubs — 41.* This standard was surpassed on May 28, 1995.

Despite all the jubilation afforded Gehrig and his teammates for their spectacular accom-plishments, New Yorkers were forced to divide their emotions with news of a sadder note. Jux-taposed with the Yankees' triumph were head-lines relating the sudden retirement of the Giants' institution, John McGraw. McGraw had been ill for some time, to the point where he was unable to accompany his team on road trips. June 3, 1932 was the day he chose to resign after 30 years at the helm, and the team announced Bill Terry as the new pilot.

New York Yankees	AB	R	H	I	PO	A	E
Earle Combs cf	5	2	3	1	3	0	0
Jack Saltzgaver 2b	4	1	1	1	3	2	0
Babe Ruth lf	5	2	2	1	3	0	1
Myril Hoag pr,lf9	0	1	0	0	1	0	0
Lou Gehrig 1b	6	4	4	6	7	0	1
Ben Chapman rf	5	3	2	1	4	0	0
Bill Dickey c	4	2	2	1	5	0	0
Tony Lazzeri 3b	6	3	5	6	0	1	0
>Frankie Crosetti ss	6	1	2	2	0	5	2
Johnny Allen p	2	0	0	0	1	0	1
Gordon Rhodes p4	1	0	1	0	0	0	0
Jumbo Brown p6	1	0	0	0	0	1	0
Lefty Gomez p8	1	1	1	0	0	0	0
	46	20	23	19	27	9	5

Philadelphia Athletics	AB	R	H	I	PO	A	E
Max Bishop 2b	4	2	2	0	3	2	0
Doc Cramer cf	5	1	1	3	1	0	0
Oscar Roettger ph8	1	0	0	0	0	0	0
Bing Miller lf9	0	0	0	0	0	0	0
Mickey Cochrane c	5	1	1	2	10	2	0
Dib Williams ph9	1	0	0	0	0	0	0
Al Simmons lf,cf9	4	2	0	0	2	0	0
Jimmie Foxx 1b	3	3	2	1	8	0	0
>Ed Coleman rf	6	2	2	3	2	1	0
Eric McNair ss	5	1	3	2	1	2	0
Jimmy Dykes 3b	4	1	1	0	0	1	0
George Earnshaw p	2	0	0	0	0	2	1
Mule Haas ph5	1	0	1	0	0	0	0
Roy Mahaffey p6	0	0	0	0	0	0	0
Rube Walberg p7	0	0	0	0	0	0	0
Lew Krausse p8	0	0	0	0	0	0	0
Ed Madjeski ph8	1	0	0	0	0	0	0
Eddie Rommel p9	0	0	0	0	0	1	0
	42	13	13	11	27	11	1

New York	IP	H	R	ER	BB	SO
Allen	3.2	7	8	4	5	2
Rhodes	1.1	1	2	2	2	0
Brown W,1-1	2	3	2	1	1	0
Gomez	2	2	1	1	0	1
	9	13	13	8	8	3

Philadelphia	IP	H	R	ER	BB	SO
Earnshaw	5	8	7	6	2	8
Mahaffey L,4-3	1	6	4	4	0	0
Walberg	1	2	1	1	1	1
Krausse	1	4	2	2	0	0
Rommel	1	3	6	6	3	0
	9	23	20	19	6	9

New York	2 0 0	2 3 2	3 2 6	-20
Philadelphia	2 0 0	6 0 2	0 2 1	-13

OB: New York 6, Philadelphia 11
DP: Cochrane-McNair
   Bishop-Foxx (Ruth)
   Coleman-Cochrane
2B: Lazzeri, McNair, Ruth, Coleman
3B: Bishop, Cramer, Chapman, Foxx, Lazzeri
HR: Gehrig 4(11), Cochrane(10), Combs(5),
   Ruth(15), Lazzeri(3), Foxx(19)
SB: Lazzeri
CS: Dickey
SO: Saltzgaver 2, Ruth, Lazzeri,
   Crosetti 2, Allen 2, Brown,
   Williams, Simmons, Foxx

BB: Combs, Saltzgaver, Ruth, Chapman Dickey 2,
   Bishop, Simmons 2, Foxx 3, Dykes, Mahaffey
SH: Bishop, Saltzgaver
WP: Rhodes
TIME: 2:55
ATTENDANCE: 5,000
UMPIRES: Harry Geisel, Bill McGowan, Roy
   Van Graflan
SOURCES: DBD; New York Times; Philadelphia
   Evening Bulletin, Evening Public Ledger, Inquirer,
   Public Ledger, Record

BALANCE	OUT	+R	+OB	=BP	=AB	+BB	+SH	+HP	+CI
New York	27	20	6	53	46	6	1	0	0
Philadelphia	27	13	11	51	42	8	1	0	0

Burnett's Nine Hits Not Enough

84. Player Gets
Nine Hits in 18-Inning Game;
Team Gets 33 Hits; Teams Combine for 58 Hits

PHILADELPHIA   at   CLEVELAND
(Athletics, 18)   (Indians, 17)

Sunday, July 10, 1932, League Park

At first glance, you'd think it was a boxscore misprint. But when the hit column is tabulated, it confirms that Cleveland shortstop Johnny Burnett did indeed gather *nine hits in one major league game.* No other player has stroked as many as eight.

Inning	Burnett's AB
1	Singled
2	Singled
4	Singled
5	Doubled
7	Singled
7	Struck out
9	Singled
11	Doubled
13	Singled
16	Singled
17	Flied out

The occasion was a bizarre but thrilling, 18-inning, Sunday single game in Cleveland's League Park. Sunday professional baseball was not yet permitted in Pennsylvania, so the Athletics, despite being in the midst of a home stand, traveled to Cleveland for this single game. Remember, this was prior to the existence of a players union, and one-day road trips were not rare. (Sometimes, major league clubs even played local or minor league nines on their "off" days.)

Eddie Rommel—a relief endurance record.

Nine of Johnny Burnett's 521 lifetime hits came in this game. Entering the contest, he was hitting .298 (64/215).

Burnett's heroics led the Indians in a *33-hit attack, still the most by any major league team in a single game.* Unfortunately for the Tribe it wasn't enough, because the A's parlayed 25 hits of their own to squeak out an 18–17 win. The *two-club total of 58 hits also remains the major league benchmark for one game.* And, although they were later surpassed, two other standards were recorded in this game. The 24 runners left on base by the Indians exceeded what was then listed as the major league record, and the 35 runs scored by the two teams was a new American League record.

When the Athletics traveled to Cleveland this day, manager Connie Mack took with him only two pitchers, 20-year-old Lew Krausse and 34-year-old Eddie Rommel. Three successive doubleheaders, on July 7, 8, and 9, had drained the regulars, so Krausse was to get the start, and Rommel was the emergency backup. (Eddie had just pitched three innings on Friday and two more on Saturday.) Rommel had been an A's workhorse from 1920 through 1926, working as both a starter and reliever, twice leading the league in victories. But the innings had taken their toll on the veteran and this would be Eddie's last season in the majors as a player. (He later umpired in the American League.)

The A's jumped out to a 2–0 lead in the top of the first, but the Indians countered with three in their half on an Earl Averill home run. Mack let Krausse bat in the top of the second but then decided that Lew would better serve the team by watching the balance of the game from the dugout. Rommel was summoned to pitch in the bottom of the second. To say that Eddie didn't have his best "stuff" would be an understatement, as he was mauled for 20 hits during the following eight regulation innings! Miraculously, he didn't lose because his teammates were also knocking the cover off the ball and making spectacular fielding plays. Because there was no relief on the bench, Rommel labored on until Philadelphia finally scored an unanswered run in the 18th. By then, he had established several astonishing records. His *17 innings of relief work* still stand as the American League record, and the *29 hits he allowed* is the most by any pitcher, starter or reliever, in one game, in the twentieth-century. Statistics on the number of pitches he threw are not known to exist, although we do know from official records that Rommel faced 87 batters. Allowing for his nine walks and seven strikeouts, a conservative estimate would credit him with at least 300 pitches. Probably most astounding of all is the fact that Rommel won the game! It was his last major league victory.

The 10,000 spectators were treated to three ties and six lead changes during the afternoon. No margin was safe nor situation secure as the Indians overcame a five-run deficit in the seventh, and the Athletics scored 16 of their 18 runs after two were retired. Five times, it looked as if Cleveland had the game won, but each time Philadelphia eluded the grim reaper.

• With two out and none on in the top of the ninth, the Tribe led 14–13. Jimmy Dykes then sent a routine grounder toward first baseman Eddie Morgan for an apparent game-ending play. But Morgan booted it, giving the A's life. Al Simmons followed with a walk, which brought to the plate the feared Jimmie Foxx. Foxx had already hit two homers in the game, becoming the first player ever to deposit two in the same game into the distant (374 feet) left-field bleachers of League Park.* Jimmie now slashed a double to left, scoring both Athletic runners and giving his team the lead once again.

• In the bottom of the ninth, trailing 15–14, Willie Kamm led off with a double to left, but Wes Ferrell fanned and Dick Porter flied out to left. Burnett, who already had five hits, stroked an infield single over second, enabling Kamm to score and tie the game. Averill also singled, sending Burnett to third with the winning run, and took second unmolested on the next pitch. Again, the A's were on the brink of defeat, and the home crowd was about to celebrate when Joe Vosmik sent a low liner toward the right field line. But right fielder Mule Haas was not

---

*Franklin Lewis, "Here's Game, Mack Tells Tribe, but A's Tire in 18th Win," Cleveland Press, 11 July 1932, p. 16, col. 7–8.

about to concede and raced to his left, lunged, speared the ball, somersaulted, and stood up with the ball in his glove, saving the game for Philadelphia.

• The Indians had another terrific opportunity to send the fans home for dinner in the 11th. After Ferrell flied out to left, Porter walked. Burnett continued his torrid hitting with a double off the right field screen (only 290 feet from home plate*), Porter stopping at third. Averill was intentionally walked, loading the bases with only one out. Vosmik,

however, grounded sharply to Dib Williams at second, who threw home to Ed Madjeski forcing Porter; Madjeski relayed to first to get Averill. The A's had again escaped defeat.

• Morgan opened the bottom of the 12th with a double to center. After Glenn Myatt flied out to right, Bill Cissell lined a single to left. Thinking third baseman Dykes might spear the ball, Morgan hesitated and it cost him dearly. Dykes' relay from Simmons was on the money and nailed Morgan at the plate. Cissell took second on the play

Philadelphia Athletics	AB	R	H	I	PO	A	E
Mule Haas rf	9	3	2	0	7	1	0
Doc Cramer cf	8	2	2	1	5	0	0
Jimmy Dykes 3b	10	2	3	4	0	7	0
Al Simmons lf	9	4	5	2	1	1	0
Jimmie Foxx 1b	9	4	6	8	19	2	0
>Eric McNair ss	10	0	2	1	6	3	0
Johnnie Heving c	4	0	0	0	1	0	0
Ed Madjeski c7	5	0	0	0	9	1	0
Dib Williams 2b	8	1	2	0	5	9	0
Lew Krausse p	1	0	0	0	0	1	0
Eddie Rommel p2	7	2	3	1	1	5	1
	80	18	25	17	54	30	1

Philadelphia	IP	H	R	ER	BB	SO
Krausse	1	4	3	3	1	0
Rommel W,1-0	17	29	14	13	9	7
	18	33	17	16	10	7

Cleveland Indians	AB	R	H	I	PO	A	E
Dick Porter rf	10	3	3	2	3	0	0
Johnny Burnett ss	11	4	9	2	5	5	1
Earl Averill cf	9	3	5	4	4	1	0
Joe Vosmik lf	10	2	2	1	8	1	0
>Eddie Morgan 1b	11	1	5	4	15	0	1
Glenn Myatt c	7	2	1	0	10	1	0
Bill Cissell 2b	9	1	4	3	4	5	2
Willie Kamm 3b	7	1	2	0	5	6	0
Clint Brown p	4	0	2	0	0	3	1
Willis Hudlin p7	0	0	0	0	0	0	0
Wes Ferrell p7	5	0	0	0	0	0	0
	83	17	33	16	54	22	5

Cleveland	IP	H	R	ER	BB	SO
Brown	6.2	13	8	7	1	3
Hudlin	0	0	2	2	2	0
Ferrell L,16-6	11.1	12	8	6	4	7
	18	25	18	15	7	10

Philadelphia	2 0 1		2 0 1		7 0 2	
Cleveland	3 0 0		3 1 1		6 0 1	

	0 0 0	0 0 0	2 0 1	- 18
	0 0 0	0 0 0	2 0 0	- 17

OB: Philadelphia 15, Cleveland 24
DP: Williams-McNair-Foxx (Vosmik)
     Burnett-Cissell-Morgan (Heving)
     Williams-Madjeski-Foxx (Vosmik)
     Kamm-Cissell-Morgan (McNair)
2B: Haas, Dykes, Foxx, McNair,
     Porter, Burnett 2, Vosmik,
     Morgan 2, Myatt, Cissell, Kamm
3B: Williams
HR: Foxx 3(33), Averill(16)
SB: Cissell
SO: Haas, Cramer 2, Simmons,
     Madjeski 2, Williams, Krausse,
     Rommel 2, Burnett, Averill,
     Morgan 3, Ferrell 2
BB: Haas, Cramer 2, Simmons, Foxx,
     Williams, Rommel, Porter, ...

BB: ... Averill 2, Vosmik, Myatt 3,
     Cissell, Kamm 2
SH: Kamm, Ferrell
WP: Rommel 2
TIME: 4:05
ATTENDANCE: 10,000
UMPIRES: George Hildebrand, Brick
     Owens
SOURCES: Cleveland Plain Dealer,
     Press; Philadelphia Evening Bulle-
     tin, Inquirer, Public Ledger,
     Record

BALANCE	OUT+R+OB=BP=AB+BB+SH+HP+CI
Philadelphia	54 18 15 87 80 7 0 0 0
Cleveland	54 17 24 95 83 10 2 0 0

----

*Philip J. Lowrey, Green Cathedrals (Reading, MA: Addison-Wesley Publ. Co., 1992), 143.

but Kamm grounded out, ending another threat.

• After six consecutive scoreless innings, the Athletics finally broke through in the 16th frame on Foxx's third home run into the concrete bleachers in left. The two-run shot gave the A's a 17–15 lead, but the Indians still had three outs. In the home half of the inning, Porter led off with a double to center, and Burnett continued his offensive habit with a single (hit number nine). Porter stopped at third but scored when Averill flied to right. Both Vosmik and Morgan singled, driving home Burnett with the tying run, and still there was only one away with Indians on first and second. Myatt next forced Morgan with Vosmik taking third. Cissell then sent shrieks through the faithful with a deep fly to

right which looked like it would hit the wall. But, once again, Haas was there to leap high and make a one-handed, game-saving catch.

In the final frame the Athletics were again fortunate, and this time it left them victorious. After the first two batters were retired, Foxx singled to left. Eric McNair also singled to left, but the ball took a high hop over Vosmik's head and rolled to the wall, permitting Foxx to score from first with the lead run. McNair was out trying to stretch his hit into a triple. The Indians went down without a whimper in their half with both Averill and Morgan fanning.

Following this marathon, the two teams packed their bags and traveled back to Philadelphia for a next-day doubleheader. Cleveland won both ends, 9–8 and 12–7.

Thurston Thrashed in Triumph

85. Pitcher Allows
Six Home Runs in Victory

BROOKLYN	at	NEW YORK
(Dodgers, 18)		(Giants, 9)

Saturday, August 13, 1932, Polo Grounds

Sloppy Thurston was in a generous mood.

Only two years earlier, Larry Benton of the Giants became the first pitcher in modern major-league history to allow six home runs in a game yet escape victorious (see 5-12-30). On this day, however, the tables were turned on the Gothamites as, for the second and most recent occasion, a hurler was *assaulted for a half-dozen circuit clouts and still won his game.*

By 1932, Hollis J. "Sloppy" Thurston was a journeyman hurler for the Dodgers. He had once won 20 games for the White Sox but was now in the twilight of his nine-year career. Hollis' sobriquet was a misnomer he inherited from his father. Sloppy was a meticulous dresser as well as a colorful performer who on this day carved a permanent place for himself in baseball's all-time ledger.

Approximately 48,000 fans assembled in New York's Polo Grounds for a doubleheader, although the majority were of Brooklyn persuasion. The Dodgers, under pilot Max Carey, were very much in the pennant race, just a few games behind the Cubs. And, they had just won 16 of their last 20 games. The Giants, on the other hand, were struggling to maintain first division status under their new player-manager of two months, Bill Terry.

The Dodgers swept the twin bill, although it was the opening game which is now carried in the record books. In it, Brooklyn scored all 18 of their runs in three consecutive innings, i.e. the 4th, 5th and 6th. Lefty O'Doul, the league's leading hitter, got four successive singles in those three innings. Hack Wilson in the same three rounds got a

FIRST GAME

Brooklyn Dodgers	AB	R	H	I	PO	A	E
Danny Taylor cf	5	2	1	3	7	0	0
Joe Stripp 3b	5	0	1	2	0	0	0
Gordon Slade pr6,3b	1	0	0	0	1	3	0
Lefty O'Doul lf	5	3	4	1	1	0	0
Johnny Frederick lf8	1	0	1	0	0	0	0
Hack Wilson rf	5	3	3	3	1	0	0
Max Rosenfeld rf6	1	0	0	0	1	0	0
>Tony Cuccinello 2b	6	3	3	3	3	2	0
Glenn Wright ss	4	1	2	1	1	2	3
Bud Clancy 1b	5	1	3	1	12	0	0
Al Lopez c	4	3	2	2	0	0	0
Val Picinich c6	1	0	0	0	0	0	0
Sloppy Thurston p	5	2	4	2	0	3	0
	48	18	24	18	27	10	3

New York Giants	AB	R	H	I	PO	A	E
Jo-Jo Moore lf	5	0	0	0	0	1	0
Hughie Critz 2b	5	0	0	0	6	5	1
Bill Terry 1b	5	4	4	3	8	0	1
Mel Ott rf	5	3	3	2	5	0	0
>Freddy Lindstrom cf	5	2	2	2	4	0	0
Shanty Hogan c	3	0	0	0	1	0	0
Bob O'Farrell c7	1	0	1	1	1	0	0
Gil English 3b	4	0	1	0	1	3	0
Doc Marshall ss	4	0	0	1	1	4	0
Jim Mooney p	1	0	0	0	0	1	0
Dolf Luque p4	0	0	0	0	0	0	0
Chick Fullis ph4	1	0	0	0	0	0	0
Hal Schumacher p5	0	0	0	0	0	0	1
Hi Bell p5	0	0	0	0	0	0	0
Sam Gibson p6	1	0	1	0	0	2	0
Sam Leslie ph8	1	0	0	0	0	0	0
F. Fitzsimmons p9	0	0	0	0	0	0	0
	41	9	12	9	27	16	3

Brooklyn	IP	H	R	ER	BB	SO
Thurston W,10-5	9	12	9	8	0	0

New York	IP	H	R	ER	BB	SO
Mooney L,5-8	3.1	7	5	4	1	0
Luque	.2	1	0	0	0	0
Schumacher	.2	4	5	1	0	0
Bell	1	8	8	6	0	0
Gibson	2.1	3	0	0	0	0
Fitzsimmons	1	1	0	0	0	0
	9	24	18	11	1	0

Brooklyn	0	0	0	5	7	6	0	0	0	-18
New York	0	0	0	3	1	0	0	3	2	- 9

OB: Brooklyn 5, New York 5
DP: English-Critz-Terry (Stripp)
   Marshall-Critz-Terry (Taylor)
   English-Critz-Terry (Slade)
   Marshall-Critz-Terry (Cuccinello)
2B: Lopez, Thurston, Cuccinello
3B: Wilson
HR: Cuccinello(8), Taylor(8), Wilson
   (20), Ott 2(24), Lindstrom(13),
   Terry 3(22)
BB: Wright

HP: By Bell (Taylor)
WP: Luque
TIME: 2:15
ATTENDANCE: 48,000
UMPIRES: Dolly Stark, George
   Magerkurth, Cy Rigler
SOURCES: Brooklyn Eagle; New York
   Herald-Tribune, Times, World-
   Telegram

BALANCE	OUT+R+OB=BP=AB+BB+SH+HP+CI
Brooklyn	27 18 5 50 48 1 0 1 0
New York	27 9 5 41 41 0 0 0 0

triple, single and his 20th home run. Even the celebrated Thurston gathered two singles and a double during the triad. But the Giants fought back valiantly. In their half of the 4th inning, trailing 5–0, Terry, Mel Ott and Freddy Lindstrom hit home runs on three consecutive pitches. Before the game ended, Terry collected two more and Ott one more, making a total of six round-trippers for the losers. Thurston persevered for the duration, tying Larry Benton's two-year-old record. Some might say he even surpassed Benton in that

Sloppy also pitched a complete game. Notice that despite all the extra-base swinging, there was nary a strikeout recorded by either side.

Since Thurston's "achievement," three other pitchers have attempted imitation with only partial success. Alphonse "Tommy" Thomas of the 1936 Browns, Wayman "Bill" Kerksieck of the 1939 Phillies, and George Caster of the 1940 Athletics, were each able to bestow six home runs on their opponents in one game, but all fell short in garnering a victory.

Cecil's Debut a Hit

86. Player Gets Five Hits in Debut

CLEVELAND   at   WASHINGTON
(Indians, 10)   (Senators, 11)

Tuesday, May 16, 1933, Griffith Stadium

Only one game separated the third place Washington Senators from the league leading Cleveland Indians. A Washington win, coupled with a loss by the second place Yankees, would have meant first place residence for the Senators. But because of a light drizzle at game time, only about 1,000 fans turned out to witness a record breaking inaugural by a 19-year-old third baseman.

Washington's Cecil Travis, just called up from the Chattanooga farm club to spell the injured Ossie Bluege, *rapped out five hits in his first major league game.* To date, no other major leaguer has duplicated this performance. Travis had been leading the Southern Association with a .452 batting average before incurring a spike wound on his right hand. Subsequently, despite dropping over 100 points from his average, he was still needed by the Senators. This day, Cecil connected safely in his first four plate appearances, singling in the second, third, fourth, and sixth innings before reaching safely on an error in the eighth. He singled again in the tenth, enabling him to reach base in each of

his first six major league at-bats. In the twelfth, Travis grounded sharply back to Indian hurler Mel Harder who had to make a difficult play to retire the talented rookie.

The youngster also excelled in the field, handling five chances with a flair. The game's very first batter, Dick Porter, and later Earl Averill, both tested the rookie with excellent bunts. Each time Travis was equal to the task, making bare-handed pickups and accurate throws to first.

The contest itself was a thriller, as the Senators blew a 7–1 lead and then triumphed in the bottom of the twelfth on a bases-loaded single by first baseman Joe Kuhel. Washington was an offensive-minded club but had been hampered by pitching inefficiency, averaging three hurlers per game since opening day. Because there were only eight pitchers on the staff, all arms earned their pay. This day, six of the eight were pressed into action. Only Al Thomas, who had been married that morning and was not with the club, and Earl Whitehill, who was warming up in the bullpen at the conclusion, did not

The Washington Evening Star summary of the game (clockwise from the right): The Indians were knocked out of first place; Cecil Travis, along with others, was highly touted by owner "uncle" Clark Griffith prior to the season; Joe Kuhel had finally supplanted a Senators' insitution at first base, Joe Judge, who had been released in January.

enter the fray. Things were so desperate that after the game, as reported by *The Washington Evening Star*, Senator pilot Joe Cronin had asked for a volunteer to pitch the following day.

The *11 pitchers used by the two teams, set a new American League mark* (later surpassed). And, by *three Senators* (Travis, Kuhel, and Luke Sewell) *each gathering five hits, the club tied a major league standard*

Cecil Travis loudly announced his debut.

yet to be exceeded. Also noteworthy is the fact that only three of the 121 batters struck out.

After this auspicious start, Travis cooled considerably, collecting only eight more hits in 36 additional at-bats, and Bluege soon regained his health. (Travis did, however, take over third base the following season.) Washington's 27 hits were an ominous message to the rest of the league. By year's end, they led the majors in hits and batting average, which was enough to overcome the erratic pitching staff and carry the Senators to the American League pennant.

Cleveland Indians	AB	R	H	I	PO	A	E
Dick Porter rf	6	2	2	2	5	0	0
J. Burnett ss,2b10	7	0	2	2	1	1	0
>Earl Averill cf	6	1	1	1	5	0	0
Bill Cissell 2b	6	1	1	0	2	1	1
B. Knickerbocker ss10	0	0	0	0	0	0	0
Eddie Morgan 1b	5	2	1	0	9	1	0
Willie Kamm 3b	6	1	1	2	5	3	0
Joe Vosmik lf	5	1	4	3	3	1	1
Roy Spencer c	6	1	3	0	3	0	0
Belve Bean p	1	0	0	0	0	0	0
Sarge Connally p3	1	1	1	0	0	1	0
Wes Ferrell ph6	1	0	0	0	0	0	0
Howard Craghead p6	0	0	0	0	1	0	0
Mike Powers ph7	1	0	0	0	0	0	0
Clint Brown p7	0	0	0	0	0	0	0
Mel Harder p8	2	0	0	0	0	2	0
	53	10	16	10	34	10	2

Washington Senators	AB	R	H	I	PO	A	E
>Joe Kuhel 1b	8	1	5	5	11	0	0
Heinie Manush lf	6	1	2	0	5	0	0
Goose Goslin rf	5	0	2	0	2	0	1
Joe Cronin ss	7	0	2	1	4	3	2
Fred Schulte cf	7	1	1	0	7	0	0
Cecil Travis 3b	7	3	5	0	1	4	0
Buddy Myer 2b	6	2	3	1	3	3	0
Luke Sewell c	7	2	5	2	3	1	0
Lefty Stewart p	2	1	1	1	0	2	0
Bobby Burke p6	0	0	0	0	0	0	0
Monty Weaver p7	0	0	0	0	0	0	0
Jack Russell p8	0	0	0	0	0	0	0
Dave Harris ph8	1	0	0	0	0	0	0
Bill McAfee p9	0	0	0	0	0	0	0
Sam Rice ph10	1	0	1	0	0	0	0
General Crowder p11	0	0	0	0	0	0	0
Ossie Bluege ph12	0	0	0	0	0	0	0
John Kerr pr12	0	0	0	0	0	0	0
	57	11	27	10	36	13	3

Cleveland	IP	H	R	ER	BB	SO
Bean	2.2	8	6	6	0	0
Connally	2.1	5	2	2	1	1
Craghead	1	2	0	0	0	0
Brown	1.1	3	1	0	1	0
Harder L,3-4	4	9	2	2	2	0
	11.1	27	11	10	4	1

Washington	IP	H	R	ER	BB	SO
Stewart	5.2	11	6	6	0	0
Burke	1	1	1	0	0	0
Weaver	1	4	3	3	2	0
Russell	.1	0	0	0	0	0
McAfee	2	0	0	0	0	1
Crowder W,5-2	2	0	0	0	0	1
	12	16	10	9	2	2

```
Cleveland    0 1 0   0 2 3   1 3 0   0 0 0   -10
Washington   0 3 4   0 1 0   0 1 1   0 0 1   -11
```

OB: Cleveland 11, Washington 19
2B: Cissell, Connally, Vosmik
3B: Kuhel, Porter, Morgan
HR: Kuhel(3)
CS: Burnett
SO: Cissell, Harder, Stewart
BB: Porter, Morgan, Goslin 2 (1I),
     Stewart, Bluege (I)
SH: Weaver, Myer, Manush

HP: By Stewart(Vosmik); By McAfee
    (Averill)
TIME: 3:34
ATTENDANCE: 1,000
UMPIRES: Roy Van Gaflan, Brick Owens
SOURCES: Cleveland Plain Dealer,
    Press; New York Times; Washington
    Evening Star, Post

BALANCE	OUT+R+OB=BP=AB+BB+SH+HP+CI
Cleveland	36 10 11 57 53 2 0 2 0
Washington	34 11 19 64 57 4 3 0 0

Hubbell's 18-Inning Whitewash

87. Pitcher Throws 18-Inning Shutout

ST. LOUIS, NL	at	NEW YORK
(Cardinals, 0)		(Giants, 1)

Sunday, July 2, 1933, Polo Grounds

While Giant hitters languished in 1933 (finishing sixth in team batting at .263), the pitching staff cultivated the league's lowest ERA and most shutouts, carrying the club to the summit of the National League. The backbone of that staff was future Hall-of-Famer Carl Hubbell. Nicknamed "King Carl" or "The Mealticket," Hubbell was at his finest this day when in the first game of a doubleheader he pitched a four-hour, *18-inning shutout. This tied the modern record for the longest shutout game by one pitcher* (see also 7-16-09 and 5-15-18).

The Giants and the Cardinals were one-two in the standings on the morning of July 2, with only 3.5 games separating the teams. St. Louis had just beaten the league leaders in two of the last three games and were looking forward to this twin-bill to further tighten the gap. New Yorkers turned out in droves to witness the action, 50,000 of them, forming the largest crowd in the National League this season. The Giants, as usual, didn't do much hitting but rode the wings of Hubbell and Roy Parmelee to win both games by 1–0 scores, quite a feat considering the Cardinals led the league in both runs scored and RBIs this year.

Hubbell's game was a real masterpiece — he pitched 12 perfect innings, allowed only six hits (four of them the infield variety), walked none, and permitted only one runner to reach third. Carl retired the first 12 batters, later sent 19 straight to the bench, and disposed of ten more near the end of the game. His mound opponent, Tex Carleton, also pitched a magnificent game. But Carleton, pitching on only two day's rest, deservedly tired after 16 shutout frames and was relieved by Jesse Haines. The Giants reached Haines in the bottom of the 18th when Jo-Jo Moore led off with a walk and was sacrificed to second by Gus Mancuso. Travis Jackson, pinch hitting for Blondy Ryan, was

Hubbell tied the record for the longest shutout.

then intentionally walked. Hubbell's grounder forced Jackson out at second, with Moore taking third. Hughie Critz then singled home Moore with the game winning run. In addition to delivering the deathblow, second baseman Critz narrowly missed a modern record by assisting on 12 fielding plays. The mark of 13 set in 1919 still exists.

An interesting story accompanied the second game of this doubleheader which will afford the reader some insight into baseball vagaries of the era. Because the Cardinals wanted so much to keep pace with the Giants, they sent their ace — Dizzy Dean — to the mound with only one day's rest. Dean responded with a five-hitter but lost.

Hubbell's performance was not an anomaly. He proceeded to win 23 games including 10 shutouts, compiled a 1.66 ERA, hurled 46.1 consecutive scoreless innings, and walked only 47 batters in 309 innings. And if that wasn't enough, he beat the Senators twice in the World Series and was named the National League's Most Valuable Player.

FIRST GAME

St. Louis Cardinals	AB	R	H	I	PO	A	E
Pepper Martin 3b	7	0	0	0	3	6	0
Frankie Frisch 2b	7	0	0	0	7	5	0
Ernie Orsatti cf	7	0	1	0	0	0	0
Ripper Collins 1b	7	0	2	0	15	5	0
>Joe Medwick lf	7	0	1	0	7	0	0
Ethan Allen rf	6	0	0	0	4	0	0
Jimmie Wilson c	6	0	2	0	11	1	0
Leo Durocher ss	3	0	0	0	3	4	1
Rogers Hornsby ph11	1	0	0	0	0	0	0
Gordon Slade ss11	1	0	0	0	1	2	0
Tex Carleton p	4	0	0	0	2	3	0
Bob O'Farrell ph17	1	0	0	0	0	0	0
Jesse Haines p17	0	0	0	0	0	2	0
	57	0	6	0	53	28	1

New York Giants	AB	R	H	I	PO	A	E
>Hughie Critz 2b	9	0	3	1	4	12	0
Lefty O'Doul lf	4	0	1	0	0	0	0
Bernie James pr11	0	0	0	0	0	0	0
Kiddo Davis cf12	2	0	0	0	2	0	0
Bill Terry 1b	6	0	2	0	26	1	0
Mel Ott rf	6	0	0	0	2	0	0
Johnny Vergez 3b	5	0	0	0	3	1	0
Jo-Jo Moore cf,lf12	7	1	0	0	3	0	0
Gus Mancuso c	7	0	1	0	13	1	0
Blondy Ryan ss	6	0	2	0	0	5	0
Travis Jackson ph18	0	0	0	0	0	0	0
Carl Hubbell p	7	0	1	0	1	7	0
	59	1	10	1	54	27	0

St. Louis	IP	H	R	ER	BB	SO
Carleton	16	8	0	0	7	7
Haines L,2-3	1.2	2	1	1	3	1
	17.2	10	1	1	10	8

New York	IP	H	R	ER	BB	SO
Hubbell W,11-5	18	6	0	0	0	12

St. Louis	0 0 0		0 0 0		0 0 0		0 0 0	– 0
New York	0 0 0		0 0 0		0 0 0		0 0 1	– 1

OB: St. Louis 5, New York 19
DP: Ryan-Critz-Terry (Medwick)
2B: Orsatti, Collins
3B: Terry
SO: Martin 2, Frisch, Orsatti 2, Collins, Medwick, Wilson, Durocher, Carleton 2, O'Farrell Critz, O'Doul, Terry, Vergez 3, Moore, Ryan
BB: O'Doul, Terry, Ott 2(2I), Moore, Vergez 3, Ryan, Jackson (I)
SH: Slade, Carleton, Davis, Terry, Mancuso, Hubbell

TIME: 4:03
ATTENDANCE: 50,000
UMPIRES: Bill Klem, Cy Pfirman, George Barr
SOURCES: New York American, Post, Times, World-Telegram; St. Louis Globe-Democrat, Post-Dispatch

BALANCE	OUT+R+OB=BP=AB+BB+SH+HP+CI
St. Louis	54 0 5 59 57 0 2 0 0
New York	53 1 19 73 59 10 4 0 0

Goslin Cooks His Own Goose

88. Player Hits into Four Double Plays

CLEVELAND   at   DETROIT
(Indians, 1)   (Tigers, 4)

Saturday, April 28, 1934, Navin Field

Goslin was a .316 lifetime hitter.

Future Hall-of-Famer Goose Goslin had been traded to Detroit during the off-season and was now leading the Tigers to their position atop the American League. After his new team's first seven games, he was hitting .345 and batting cleanup in an explosive lineup. But this day Goose experienced one of the more embarrassing days in major league history when, in front of the home-town fans, he *grounded into four double plays in a single game*. To make matters worse, he also made a crucial error enabling Cleveland to score its only run, thereby destroying his own pitcher's shutout.

Goslin's humiliation began in the very first inning when, with one out and teammates Charlie Gehringer on third and Mickey Cochrane on first, he smashed a hard grounder to Indians first baseman Hal Trosky. Trosky stepped on first and threw to short-stop Bill Knickerbocker who tagged a sliding Cochrane for the double play.

In the top of the third inning the Tigers' Tommy Bridges was breezing along, having routinely retired the first two batters. Cleveland's Earl Averill then lifted a high fly to left. Goose coasted under it and dropped the ball for a two-base muff. Joe Vosmik followed with a double, driving home Averill with the Indians' only run of the game. In the bottom half of the frame, with the Indians' Mel Harder still on the hill, Goslin again stepped to the plate with a chance to redeem himself. Gehringer and

Cochrane were again at first and third with one away. This time, Goose drove a hard grounder to second baseman Eddie Moore. Moore tossed to Knickerbocker who threw over to Trosky, completing another double play.

By the fifth, Thornton Lee had replaced Harder on the mound for Cleveland. That didn't change things for Goslin, however. Again with one out, and Gehringer the base runner at first, Goose grounded sharply to Trosky, who touched first and threw to second. Knickerbocker applied the tag to Gehringer, ending the inning.

With Lloyd Brown on the slab for the

Indians in the eighth, Charlie Gehringer hit his fourth single of the day. But again Gehringer would not score because Goslin was to follow. This time, Goose tapped back to the box. Brown wheeled and threw to Knickerbocker who threw on to Trosky, completing the fourth inglorious twin-killing on Goslin.

Withstanding Goslin's day of ignominy, the Tigers did go on to win the American League pennant by seven games over the Yankees. Goose was also able to put this day behind him and finished with a .305 batting average, 100 RBIs, and 106 runs scored.

Cleveland Indians	AB	R	H	I	PO	A	E
Sam Rice rf	4	0	0	0	3	0	0
Frankie Pytlak c	4	0	1	0	1	1	0
Earl Averill cf	4	1	1	0	3	0	0
Joe Vosmik lf	4	0	3	1	2	0	0
Hal Trosky 1b	4	0	0	0	8	2	1
Willie Kamm 3b	3	0	0	0	0	2	0
> Odell Hale ph9	1	0	0	0	0	0	0
Eddie Moore 2b	2	0	0	0	3	3	0
Bill Knickerbocker ss	3	0	0	0	4	2	0
Mel Harder p	1	0	0	0	0	0	0
Clint Brown p4	0	0	0	0	0	0	0
Dick Porter ph5	1	0	0	0	0	0	0
Thornton Lee p5	0	0	0	0	0	0	0
Dutch Holland ph8	1	0	0	0	0	0	0
Lloyd Brown p8	0	0	0	0	0	1	0
	32	1	5	1	24	11	1

Detroit Tigers	AB	R	H	I	PO	A	E
Billy Rogell ss	3	1	0	0	1	1	0
Charlie Gehringer 2b	4	0	4	1	1	4	0
Mickey Cochrane c	4	0	2	1	7	0	0
>Goose Goslin lf	4	0	0	0	2	0	1
Gee Walker rf	3	1	0	0	3	0	0
Hank Greenberg 1b	3	1	1	0	8	0	1
Pete Fox cf	3	0	2	2	2	0	0
Marv Owen 3b	2	1	0	0	3	2	0
Tommy Bridges p	2	0	0	0	0	1	0
	28	4	9	4	27	8	2

Cleveland	IP	H	R	ER	BB	SO
Harder L,0-1	3	6	4	3	2	0
C. Brown	1	1	0	0	0	1
Lee	3	1	0	0	0	0
L. Brown	1	1	0	0	0	0
	8	9	4	3	2	1

Detroit	IP	H	R	ER	BB	SO
Bridges W,1-0	9	5	1	0	1	7

Cleveland	0 0 1		0 0 0		0 0 0		-	1
Detroit	0 0 2		2 0 0		0 0 x		-	4

OB: Cleveland 5, Detroit 3
DP: Owen unassisted (Trosky)
    Trosky-Knickerbocker (Goslin)
    Trosky-Knickerbocker (Goslin)
    Moore-Knickerbocker-Trosky (Goslin)
    Owen-Gehringer-Greenberg (Vosmik)
    L. Brown-Knickerbocker-Trosky (Goslin)
2B: Vosmik, Greenberg
CS: Fox
SO: Owen, Harder, Trosky, Moore, Porter,
    Pytlak, Knickerbocker, Holland

BB: Moore, Rogell, Owen
SH: Bridges
TIME: 1:59
ATTENDANCE: 14,000
UMPIRES: Harry Geisel, George
    Moriarty
SOURCES: Cleveland Plain Dealer;
    Detroit Free Press, News, Times

BALANCE	OUT	+R	+OB	=BP	=AB	+BB	+SH	+HP	+CI
Cleveland	27	1	5	33	32	1	0	0	0
Detroit	24	4	3	31	28	2	1	0	0

More Ado Over Nothing

89. Player Goes to the Plate Six Times Without an Official At-Bat

BOSTON, NL   at   ST. LOUIS
(Braves, 9)   (Cardinals, 0)

Wednesday, June 13, 1934, Sportsman's Park

Bill Urbanski, a not-so-famous shortstop for the Boston Braves, this day carved a place for himself in baseball history. Only once before had a *batter stepped to the plate six times in a game without registering an official at-bat* (see 6-01-10). Bill tied that mark this day by gathering four bases on balls and two sacrifice hits.

Urbanski led off the game with a walk and repeated his success in the third frame. In the fourth and sixth rounds he sacrificed, and walked again in both the seventh and ninth innings. Despite his proclivity for reaching base, Bill scored only one time, in the third. In addition to his offensive contributions, Urbanski also excelled afield. His leaping snare of a line drive in the seventh helped preserve the Boston shutout.

Urbanski didn't make his major league debut until he was 28 years old and then played six solid (if unspectacular) seasons, all with the Braves. This year was his finest, and on this date he was the league's fifth leading hitter (.357). Bill finished the year with 177 base hits, 104 runs scored, and a .293 batting average. In 1937, he incurred an ankle injury early in the season which failed to respond to treatment, forcing his retirement.

Bill Urbanski

Boston Braves	AB	R	H	I	PO	A	E
Bill Urbanski ss	0	1	0	0	2	3	0
>Marty McManus 3b	6	2	2	1	0	0	0
Buck Jordan 1b	4	2	3	2	12	0	1
Wally Berger cf	4	0	2	2	1	0	0
Randy Moore rf	5	0	0	0	3	0	0
Hal Lee lf	5	0	1	1	3	0	0
Pinky Whitney 2b	4	2	1	0	3	3	0
Shanty Hogan c	5	0	2	0	3	0	0
Fred Frankhouse p	4	2	2	2	0	5	0
	37	9	13	8	27	11	1

St. Louis Cardinals	AB	R	H	I	PO	A	E
Pepper Martin 3b	4	0	0	0	0	1	0
Jack Rothrock rf	4	0	1	0	0	0	0
Frankie Frisch 2b	3	0	0	0	5	3	1
B. Whitehead 2b7	1	0	1	0	3	2	0
Joe Medwick lf	4	0	2	0	2	0	0
Ripper Collins 1b	4	0	0	0	6	2	0
Bill DeLancey c	3	0	0	0	4	1	0
Ernie Orsatti cf	4	0	0	0	3	0	0
Leo Durocher ss	4	0	1	0	4	4	4
Wild Bill Hallahan p	0	0	0	0	0	0	0
Spud Davis ph3	0	0	0	0	0	0	0
Tex Carleton pr3	0	0	0	0	0	0	0
Jesse Haines p4	1	0	1	0	0	1	0
Buster Mills ph7	1	0	0	0	0	0	0
Jim Winford p8	0	0	0	0	0	2	0
> Pat Crawford ph9	1	0	0	0	0	0	0
	34	0	6	0	27	16	5

Boston	IP	H	R	ER	BB	SO
Frankhouse W,9-2	9	6	0	0	2	3

St. Louis	IP	H	R	ER	BB	SO
Hallahan L,2-6	3	6	3	3	3	3
Haines	4	6	5	4	2	0
Winford	2	1	1	0	1	0
	9	13	9	7	6	3

Boston	0 0 3	1 0 3	1 0 1	- 9
St. Louis	0 0 0	0 0 0	0 0 0	- 0

OB: Boston 11, St. Louis 9
DP: Frisch-Durocher-Collins(McManus)
   Whitehead-Durocher-Collins
   Winford-Whitehead-Collins(McManus)
2B: Berger, Jordan, McManus
SO: Moore, Whitney, Frankhouse,
   Martin, DeLancey, Orsatti
BB: Urbanski 4, Jordan, Whitney,
   DeLancey, Davis
SH: Urbanski 2, Frankhouse

HP: By Winford (Berger)
WP: Frankhouse, Haines
TIME: 2:17
ATTENDANCE: 2,400
UMPIRES: Ernie Quigley, Beans
   Reardon
SOURCES: Boston Globe, Post; St.
   Louis Globe-Democrat, Post-Dispatch

BALANCE	OUT	+	R	+	OB	=	BP	=	AB	+	BB	+	SH	+	HP	+	CI
Boston	27		9		11		47		37		6		3		1		0
St. Louis	27		0		9		36		34		2		0		0		0

Max Gets Another Free Ride into Record Books

90. Player Draws Eight Walks in Doubleheader

PHILADELPHIA, AL   at   BOSTON
(Athletics, 4,2)   (Red Sox, 7,7)

Sunday, July 8, 1934, Fenway Park

In an article in *The Philadelphia Inquirer* written by Connie Mack in 1932, the Tall Tactician named the most adept leadoff batters he had ever seen in professional base-ball. As the best, he nominated John McGraw, followed by Billy Hamilton and

Jesse Burkett. But of players then still active in the game, Connie felt none were more skilled at getting on base than Max "Camera Eye" Bishop. At the time the article was written, Bishop was consistently accumulating seasons of .400+ on-base percentages for the Athletics. Encyclopedic reconstructions of the era's on-base averages put Bishop in the rare company of Ruth, Foxx, and Gehrig; but there was one category in which Max stood alone. By walking eight times in a doubleheader in 1930, Bishop had achieved a record untouched by any of the aforementioned demigods.

Then on December 12, 1933, Max was traded to the Red Sox, where he continued to engage his uncanny judgement. In this his first season in Boston, despite hitting only .261, Bishop amassed a .445 on-base average punctuated by this game. For the second time in his career, Max *walked eight times in a doubleheader.* To this day, he remains the only individual to accomplish this feat.

Bishop walked four times in each contest as Boston swept the twin bill. The Athletics out-hit the Sox, but the Philadelphia pitching staff provided the margin of victory — for Boston. A's hurlers were the most generous in the league, issuing 4.66 walks per nine innings. But on this day they outdid themselves. In the opener, Bill Dietrich handed out nine walks, costing himself the game. In addition to providing Boston with ample base runners, he forced home two runs — one on a bases loaded walk, and another when he

Max did it again.

drilled a Boston batter in the ribs with the sacks full.

The nightcap provided more of the same. This time, two Athletics hurlers provided seven walks. The only bright spot for Philadelphia was that Jimmie Foxx and Bob Johnson emerged from the doubleheader as the number one and two home-run leaders in the major leagues.

The first contest provided some levity for those scoring the game when in the seventh inning, Boston's Hank Johnson pitched to Bob Johnson, who hit a fly ball which was caught by Roy Johnson.

FIRST GAME

Philadelphia Athletics	AB	R	H	I	PO	A	E
Eric McNair ss	5	0	1	0	2	3	1
Doc Cramer cf	5	0	2	0	2	0	0
Bob Johnson lf	4	1	1	1	4	0	0
Jimmie Foxx 1b	4	2	3	2	7	1	0
Pinky Higgins 3b	4	0	1	0	0	2	0
>Bing Miller rf	4	1	1	0	1	0	0
Rabbit Warstler 2b	3	0	0	1	2	5	1
Charlie Berry c	3	0	2	0	5	1	0
Bill Dietrich p	4	0	1	0	1	1	0
	36	4	12	6	24	13	2

Boston Red Sox	AB	R	H	I	PO	A	E
Max Bishop 2b	1	1	0	1	2	1	0
Bill Werber 3b	4	1	1	1	1	1	1
Eddie Morgan 1b	4	1	1	1	7	2	0
Roy Johnson lf	5	0	1	3	3	0	0
>Carl Reynolds cf	4	0	0	0	0	0	0
Dick Porter rf	4	0	1	0	0	0	0
Rick Ferrell c	2	2	1	0	7	2	0
Lyn Lary ss	1	1	0	0	4	3	0
Hank Johnson p	4	1	2	1	3	1	0
	29	7	7	7	27	10	1

Philadelphia	IP	H	R	ER	BB	SO
Dietrich L,2-6	8	7	7	5	9	3

Philadelphia	0 0 0	0 0 1	1 0 2	- 4
Boston	0 1 0	0 1 1	0 4 x	- 7

OB: Philadelphia 11, Boston 10
DP: McNair-Warstler-Foxx (Ferrell)
    H. Johnson-Morgan
    Bishop-Lary-Morgan (Miller)
2B: Morgan, H. Johnson
3B: Miller
HR: B. Johnson(25), Foxx 2(26)
SB: Warstler

Boston	IP	H	R	ER	BB	SO
H. Johnson W,4-4	9	12	4	4	5	7

BB: B.Johnson, Foxx, Higgins, Berry,
    Warstler, Bishop 4, Lary 2,
    Reynolds, Ferrell 2
SH: Miller, Werber, Lary
HP: By Dietrich (Morgan)
TIME: 2:21
UMPIRES: Bill Summers, Brick Owens

BALANCE	OUT+R+OB=BP=AB+BB+SH+HP+CI
Philadelphia	27	4	11	42	36	5	1	0	0
Boston	24	7	10	41	29	9	2	1	0

SECOND GAME

Philadelphia Athletics	AB	R	H	I	PO	A	E
Eric McNair ss	4	0	0	0	0	2	0
Doc Cramer cf	4	0	1	1	1	1	0
Bob Johnson lf	4	1	1	0	1	0	0
Jimmie Foxx 1b	4	0	2	1	8	1	1
Pinky Higgins 3b	4	0	2	0	2	2	1
Bing Miller rf	4	0	0	0	4	0	0
Rabbit Warstler 2b	4	0	0	0	3	5	0
Charlie Berry c	4	1	2	0	3	1	0
Johnny Marcum p	2	0	0	0	2	0	0
Al Benton p7	0	0	0	0	0	1	0
> Charlie Moss ph9	1	0	0	0	0	0	0
	35	2	8	2	24	13	2

Boston Red Sox	AB	R	H	I	PO	A	E
Max Bishop 2b	1	2	0	0	2	2	0
Bill Werber 3b	5	2	2	0	0	2	0
>Eddie Morgan 1b	5	2	3	0	10	0	0
Roy Johnson lf	4	1	2	4	2	0	0
Carl Reynolds cf	3	0	0	2	6	0	0
Dick Porter rf	3	0	1	1	0	0	0
Rick Ferrell c	4	0	1	0	5	0	0
Lyn Lary ss	3	0	1	0	2	5	0
Fritz Ostermueller p	4	0	0	0	0	2	0
	32	7	10	7	27	11	0

Philadelphia	IP	H	R	ER	BB	SO
Marcum L,3-7	6	9	7	6	4	2

Philadelphia	0 0 0	1 1 0	0 0 0	- 2
Boston	4 0 1	0 0 0	2 0 x	- 7

OB: Philadelphia 7, Boston 8
DP: Higgins-Warstler-Foxx
2B: B. Johnson, Morgan 2, R. Johnson,
    Porter
SB: R. Johnson, Porter, Lary
BB: Marcum, Bishop 4, Reynolds,
    Porter, Lary

Boston	IP	H	R	ER	BB	SO
Ostermueller W,7-8	9	8	2	2	1	1

TIME: 1:55
ATTENDANCE: 24,018
UMPIRES: Brick Owens, Bill Summers
SOURCES: Boston Globe, Herald;
    Philadelphia Inquirer, Record

BALANCE	OUT+R+OB=BP=AB+BB+SH+HP+CI
Philadelphia	27	2	7	36	35	1	0	0	0
Boston	24	7	8	39	32	7	0	0	0

Ott Scores Six Times

91. Player Scores Six Runs in a Nine-Inning Game

NEW YORK, NL   at   PHILADELPHIA
(Giants, 21)   (Phillies, 4)

Saturday, August 4, 1934, Baker Bowl

By 1934, Mel Ott had already established hero-status for himself. A favorite of the New York fans as well as manager John McGraw, the reserved Ott was an excellent right fielder who had led the National League in various offensive categories including home runs, slugging percentage, and bases on balls. After leading his team to a World Series championship a year earlier, fans had come to expect outstanding performances from "Master Melvin." But on this day, in the second game of a doubleheader, Philadelphia patrons saw him do something that had never been done in twentieth-century, major-league baseball when Mel *scored six runs in a nine-inning game.*

Of course this record required plenty of cooperation from his teammates, but Ott made it all possible by getting on base each of the six times he stepped to the plate. Mel scored in the first inning after doubling. In the third and fourth, he required no help

whatsoever when he added two home runs to his league-leading total. A walk provided his scoring opportunity in the seventh. The final frame saw the Giants score 11 runs, a new ninth-inning, major league mark (later surpassed). Ott batted twice during the upheaval, singling and being hit by a pitch, and scored both times.

Reggie Grabowski, the fourth Philadelphia hurler, labored in vain to smother the fury of that ninth-inning, New York attack. Reggie seriously threatened the all-time standards for pitching futility in a single inning by facing 15 batters (ML record 16) and allowing 11 runs (NL mark 12). He did manage to etch his name in baseball annals by becoming the *first hurler to surrender 10 singles in one frame.* Ott, meanwhile, was not only the first to score six runs in a game, but ten years later became the next player to perform this feat (see 4-30-44).

SECOND GAME

New York Giants	AB	R	H	I	PO	A	E
Hughie Critz 2b	6	2	2	1	1	6	0
Travis Jackson ss	5	2	1	2	5	2	0
Bill Terry 1b	6	3	3	1	10	1	1
Mel Ott rf	4	6	4	4	0	0	0
Hank Leiber cf	6	3	4	3	2	0	0
Phil Weintraub lf	6	2	3	3	3	0	0
Gus Mancuso c	6	1	4	4	4	0	0
>Johnny Vergez 3b	6	1	1	0	1	2	0
Hi Bell p	1	0	0	0	0	0	0
Hal Schumacher p1	4	1	1	1	1	3	0
	50	21	23	19	27	14	1

Philadelphia Phillies	AB	R	H	I	PO	A	E
Dick Bartell ss	5	1	2	0	2	1	0
Lou Chiozza 2b	5	0	0	0	1	6	0
>Ethan Allen lf	5	0	2	0	2	0	1
Johnny Moore rf	4	2	2	1	1	0	1
Dolph Camilli 1b	4	1	2	1	11	2	0
Kiddo Davis cf	4	0	2	0	4	0	0
Bucky Walters 3b	4	0	1	0	1	1	0
Jimmie Wilson c	4	0	2	2	3	1	0
Snipe Hansen p	0	0	0	0	0	0	0
Euel Moore p1	2	0	1	0	0	0	0
Syl Johnson p4	1	0	0	0	1	1	0
Andy High ph8	1	0	0	0	0	0	0
Reggie Grabowski p9	0	0	0	0	1	0	0
	39	4	14	4	27	12	2

The 5'9" Ott packed a lot of power.

New York	IP	H	R	ER	BB	SO
Bell	.2	5	2	2	0	0
Schumacher W,17-5	8.1	9	2	2	0	2
	9	14	4	4	0	2

Philadelphia	IP	H	R	ER	BB	SO
Hansen L,3-6	.1	3	4	4	1	0
E. Moore	3.1	8	5	5	0	0
Johnson	4.1	1	1	0	1	1
Grabowski	1	11	11	10	0	1
	9	23	21	19	2	2

```
New York       5 0 1   3 0 0   1 0 11   -21
Philadelphia   2 0 2   0 0 0   0 0 0    - 4
```

OB: Philadelphia 8, New York 5
DP: Vergez-Critz-Terry
    Critz-Jackson-Terry
2B: Ott, Weintraub, Leiber 2, Wilson,
    J.Moore
HR: Ott 2(28), Jackson(14)
BB: Jackson, Ott
HP: By Grabowski (Ott)

TIME: 2:18
ATTENDANCE: 16,000
UMPIRES: Cy Pfirman, Ziggy Sears,
    George Magerkurth
SOURCES: New York Times;
    Philadelphia Inquirer, Record

BALANCE	OUT	+R	+OB	=BP	=AB	+BB	+SH	+HP	+CI
New York	27	21	5	53	50	2	0	1	0
Philadelphia	27	4	8	39	39	0	0	0	0

Stranded on the South Side

92. Teams Leave 30 Runners on Base in One Game

NEW YORK, AL   at   CHICAGO
(Yankees, 13)   (White Sox, 10)

Tuesday, August 27, 1935, Comiskey Park

In a game that could be called anything but a credit to the national pastime, the Yankees and White Sox attained a new record for futility when the *two teams combined to strand 30 baserunners in a nine-inning contest.* It was the first time since the turn of century that two clubs had so united. Subsequently, two other contests have matched this ignominious total.

On Chicago's south side, home of the White Sox, sandlot pitching, bush-league fielding, and Sunday-picnic baserunning would have sent most of the 18,000 patrons home had it not been only the first game of a doubleheader. The fans were inclined to be forgiving as this was the third of four successive doubleheaders in which the two clubs met.

Leaving teammates marooned was nothing new for either team. In the first game of the doubleheader the day before, New York left 17 and Chicago 19 in a 15-inning contest. This day, although the bases were left loaded just twice, each team stranded runners in all but one inning. Future Hall of Famer, Al Simmons, despite a ninth-inning, three-run homer when the game was safely lost, failed to advance or score a total of nine base runners during his first five plate appearances. Rip Radcliff was a close second with seven. The game ended when George Washington flied out to left; appropriately, there were two Sox on base at the time.

A summary of the left-on-base follows:

Ben Chapman failed to advance only one base runner while leading his team's offense.

LEFT ON BASE BY INNING

Inning	1	2	3	4	5	6	7	8	9	Total
New York	2	1	3	2	1	2	2	2	0	15
Chicago	2	2	2	0	3	1	1	2	2	15

New York Yankees	AB	R	H	I	PO	A	E
>Jesse Hill lf	5	2	2	0	1	0	0
Red Rolfe 3b	6	1	2	1	1	2	0
Ben Chapman cf	5	3	3	2	2	0	0
Lou Gehrig 1b	5	2	3	2	10	2	0
George Selkirk rf	5	0	1	3	3	0	0
Bill Dickey c	5	1	3	2	3	2	0
Jack Saltzgaver 2b	4	1	1	0	4	3	2
Blondy Ryan ss	6	1	2	2	3	5	0
Pat Malone p	1	0	0	0	0	0	0
Vito Tamulis p3	4	2	1	0	0	2	1
Johnny Murphy p9	0	0	0	0	0	0	0
	46	13	18	12	27	16	3

Chicago White Sox	AB	R	H	I	PO	A	E
Rip Radcliff lf	5	1	0	0	1	0	0
Al Simmons cf	6	1	1	3	3	0	1
Tony Piet 2b	6	1	2	2	1	5	0
Luke Appling ss	5	1	2	0	2	3	0
Zeke Bonura 1b	6	0	2	0	12	2	0
Jimmy Dykes 3b	3	2	2	0	1	2	1
Marty Hopkins 3b9	0	0	0	0	0	0	0
Jocko Conlan rf	2	1	1	1	0	0	0
Jackie Hayes ph8	1	0	0	1	0	0	0
Mule Haas rf9	0	0	0	0	2	0	0
> George Washington ph9	1	0	0	0	0	0	0
Luke Sewell c	5	1	3	2	5	1	0
Sad Sam Jones p	1	1	1	0	0	2	0
Carl Fischer p6	0	0	0	0	0	0	0
Whit Wyatt p7	2	1	2	0	0	2	0
	43	10	16	9	27	17	2

New York	IP	H	R	ER	BB	SO
Malone	2.1	7	5	5	2	2
Tamulis W,8-5	5.2	8	5	3	3	0
Murphy	1	1	0	0	1	0
	9	16	10	8	6	2

Chicago	IP	H	R	ER	BB	SO
Jones L,5-5	5.1	10	6	3	4	1
Fischer	1.1	5	4	4	3	0
Wyatt	2.1	3	3	1	1	2
	9	18	13	8	8	3

New York	0 0 0	3 1 3	3 3 0	-13
Chicago	0 3 2	0 0 1	0 1 3	-10

OB: New York 15, Chicago 15

2B: Chapman, Dickey, Malone, Jones

3B: Rolfe, Dickey, Ryan, Conlan, Wyatt

HR: Simmons(15)

SB: Hill, Chapman, Gehrig

SO: Hill, Saltzgaver, Malone, Bonura, Simmons

BB: Hill, Chapman, Gehrig, Selkirk, Dickey, Saltzgaver 2, Tamulis, Radcliff, Appling, Dykes, Hopkins, Jones 2

SH: Hill, Conlan 2

HP: By Malone(Dykes)

WP: Malone, Wyatt

TIME: 3:16

ATTENDANCE: 18,000

UMPIRES: Charles Donnelly, Bill Summers, Bill Dinneen

SOURCES: Chicago American, Daily News, Daily Times, Tribune; New York Times

BALANCE	OUT+R+OB=BP=AB+BB+SH+HP+CI
New York	27 13 15 55 46 8 1 0 0
Chicago	27 10 15 52 43 6 2 1 0

Lazzeri's Grandest Day

93. Player Hits Two Grand Slams in One Game, Drives in 15 Runs in Consecutive Games

NEW YORK, AL   at   PHILADELPHIA
(Yankees, 25)   (Athletics, 2)

Sunday, May 24, 1936, Shibe Park

By 1936, Tony Lazzeri and Lou Gehrig were the last remnants of the Yankee juggernaut of the late 1920s. "Murderer's Row" now had been ably replaced by the likes of Dickey, DiMaggio, Selkirk, Crosetti, and Rolfe. As the 32-year-old Lazzeri had struggled through a pair of sub-par years, pundits were anticipating his demise. Stepping aside for the younger players, he was now batting eighth but was about to have a season like the Lazzeri of old.

Entering this contest, Tony was in the midst of a torrid hitting streak which began on May 21, in Detroit, with a home run. The Yankees were idle on May 22 but came to Philadelphia for a doubleheader on Saturday, May 23. In those two games he had four hits and five RBIs, three of the hits being home runs. Now, a day later, Tony experienced the greatest offensive explosion of his career by smashing three more home runs, two with the bases full, and *driving in the still existing, American League record of 11 runs.* Coupled with the second game of the day before, Lazzeri had then *driven in 15 runs in two games, which remains the major league mark.* Tony's *two grand slams in a one game were also a major league first* in 1936. In addition, he barely missed a fourth home run which would have made him only the second player

Lazzeri capped off a dazzling week.

Then Philadelphia pitching and Tony Lazzeri came to the fore. While the most generous staff in the league (4.7 walks per game) outdid themselves by issuing 16 free passes and providing fertile ground for run production, Lazzeri's day of glory unfolded as follows:

• George Turbeville opened the second inning by walking Bill Dickey, Ben Chapman, and George Selkirk. Lazzeri then homered for his first grand slam of the day. (Philadelphia newspapers are in stark contrast as to where this ball landed. *The Philadelphia Inquirer* reported "lower deck in left" while the *Record* noted "dropped a fly in 20th St.." The right field wall ran along 20th Street.)

• Next in a long line of Philadelphia hopeful hurlers, Bill Dietrich, fanned Lazzeri in the third.

• While his teammates piled on five more runs in the fourth frame, Lazzeri could only coax a walk out of Dietrich.

• In the fifth, Red Bullock, the third A's hurler, loaded the bases. Bullock then turned the mound duties over to Herman Fink, and Lazzeri greeted him with a blast into the upper deck of the center field bleachers for grand slam number two. By this time the Philadelphia fans had grown weary of their moundsmen and began derisive cheering and littering the field after each New York accomplishment.

• Lazzeri's third homer came when he led off the seventh. This shot, off Woody Upchurch, sailed into the second tier of seats in left field.

• Scribes estimated that Tony's triple in the eighth was his hardest hit ball of the day. This blast missed by about 12 inches from leaving the park in straight-away center and

to do so in this century (see 6-3-32). Lazzeri's three round-trippers also brought his total to seven in four games, six in three games, as well as five in two games. All three combinations still share a place in baseball annals.

In this game, the dreary (10–13) Athletics startled the first-place Yankees by jumping out to a 2–0 lead in the opening stanza.

was hit with such force that he was unable to circle the bases. Lazzeri had to be content with a triple, but both base runners scored, giving him 11 RBIs to that point.

• The slaughter ended when Selkirk fanned with two outs and a runner on in the ninth. Lazzeri was on deck.

This debacle also culminated a lusty slugging streak for the entire New York team.

Including this game, the last three with Philadelphia resulted in the Yankees amassing 13 homers, 107 total bases, 52 runs, and 49 hits. In concluding its description of the bombardment, the *Evening Public Ledger* gave the A's flingers this advice — "don't forget to DUCK."

Herman Fink, who surrendered Lazzeri's first slam, was laboring in the second season of a three-year career. He left the big league

New York Yankees	AB	R	H	I	PO	A	E
Frankie Crosetti ss	6	2	2	3	3	5	0
Red Rolfe 3b	4	2	0	0	3	2	0
Joe DiMaggio lf	7	2	3	3	2	0	0
Lou Gehrig 1b	4	3	2	1	6	0	0
Jack Saltzgaver 1b	1	0	0	0	4	0	0
Bill Dickey c	5	3	2	3	3	0	1
Art Jorgens c	1	0	0	0	0	0	0
Ben Chapman cf	2	4	2	0	2	0	0
>George Selkirk rf	5	3	1	2	2	0	0
Tony Lazzeri 2b	5	4	4	11	2	1	0
Monte Pearson p	5	2	3	2	0	1	0
	45	25	19	25	27	9	1

Philadelphia Athletics	AB	R	H	I	PO	A	E
Lou Finney 1b	3	1	2	0	5	0	0
Chubby Dean 1b	1	0	1	0	0	0	0
Rabbit Warstler 2b	2	1	1	0	3	3	0
Rusty Peters ss	1	0	0	0	1	0	0
Wally Moses cf	4	0	0	0	4	0	0
George Puccinelli rf	3	0	1	0	1	0	0
Pinky Higgins 3b	4	0	1	1	3	1	0
Bob Johnson lf	2	0	0	0	1	0	0
Emil Mailho lf	2	0	0	0	2	0	0
S. Newsome ss,2b	4	0	0	0	1	3	0
Charlie Berry c	4	0	0	0	6	0	0
George Turbeville p	0	0	0	0	0	1	0
Bill Dietrich p2	1	0	1	0	0	0	0
Al Niemiec ph4	0	0	0	0	0	0	0
Red Bullock p5	0	0	0	0	0	0	0
Herman Fink p5	0	0	0	0	0	0	0
Woody Upchurch p6	1	0	0	0	0	0	0
> Frankie Hayes ph9	1	0	0	0	0	0	0
	33	2	7	1	27	8	0

New York	IP	H	R	ER	BB	SO
Pearson W,6-1	9	7	2	2	3	3

Philadelphia	IP	H	R	ER	BB	SO
Turbeville L,1-4	1.1	1	5	5	5	0
Dietrich	2.2	6	5	5	5	3
Bullock	.1	1	5	5	4	0
Fink	.2	3	2	2	0	0
Upchurch	4	8	8	8	2	2
	9	19	25	25	16	5

New York   0 5 0   5 6 1   2 6 0   -25
Philadelphia 2 0 0   0 0 0   0 0 0   - 2

OB: New York 9, Philadelphia 7
DP: Newsome-Warstler-Finney
    Crosetti-Gehrig
2B: DiMaggio, Chapman 2, Dean
3B: Dickey 2, Lazzeri
HR: Lazzeri 3(8), DiMaggio(3),
    Crosetti 2(4)
BB: Crosetti, Rolfe 3, Gehrig 2,
    Dickey, Chapman 5, Selkirk 2,
    Lazzeri, Pearson, Warstler,
    Puccinelli, Niemiec

WP: Pearson, Bullock 2
PB: Berry
TIME: 2:34
ATTENDANCE: 8,000
UMPIRES: Bill Summers, Charles
    Johnston
SOURCES: New York Times; Philadelphia
    Evening Bulletin, Evening Public
    Ledger, Inquirer, Record

BALANCE	OUT+R+OB=BP=AB+BB+SH+HP+CI
	OUT	R	OB	BP	AB	BB	SH	HP	CI
New York	27	25	9	61	45	16	0	0	0
Philadelphia	27	2	7	36	33	3	0	0	0

diamond with a 10–20 lifetime log and a 5.22 ERA.

Deceptively cloaked as a pitcher, the Athletics' Woody Upchurch became the ultimate sacrificial lamb during the three games. Woody started the first game of Saturday's doubleheader, giving up three runs while retiring only four batters. Undaunted, he returned for the last two innings of the nightcap, whereupon he was clobbered for six more runs. Hoping for a show of mercy on this the Christian Sabbath, Upchurch again

took the hill as the last of five A's hurlers. Because the game had long before been decided, Woody was permitted to pitch untethered for the last four innings and surrendered eight more runs. It was enough to start a lad thinking about a new career, which is exactly what he did, for this was Upchurch's final appearance in the major leagues. Woody retired without a victory but mustered an ample 7.42 ERA.

On the positive side, it may be noted that the Athletics played errorless ball and no one was injured.

Klein Clouts Four in Forbes

94. Player Hits Four Home Runs in Ten-Inning Game

PHILADELPHIA   at   PITTSBURGH
(Phillies, 9)   (Pirates, 6)

Friday, July 10, 1936, Forbes Field

Klein had his greatest day in Pittsburgh.

Chuck Klein began amassing Hall of Fame statistics with the Phillies in 1928. During the next six seasons, he won one triple crown and led the league on multiple occasions in each of the following: runs, hits, doubles, home runs, RBIs, and slugging percentage. Then on November 21, 1933, he was traded to the Cubs for three journeymen players and $65,000. Unhappy and with his production significantly diminished, he was traded back to Philadelphia on May 21 of 1936. It didn't take long for Chuck to recapture his old stroke, for on this day the 31-year-old climaxed an excellent career by *blasting four home runs in one game*, becoming the first modern National Leaguer to do so. Klein also remains the oldest player to connect for four homers in one game.

Unlike many of Klein's heroics, this feat did not take place in Baker Bowl; rather, the Phillies were being

Philadelphia Phillies	AB	R	H	I	PO	A	E
Ernie Sulik cf	5	1	1	0	5	0	0
Johnny Moore lf	5	1	1	0	1	0	0
Chuck Klein rf	5	4	4	6	5	0	0
Dolph Camilli 1b	4	2	1	0	10	1	0
Bill Atwood c	4	0	1	0	2	0	0
J. Wilson pr10,c	0	1	0	0	0	0	0
Lou Chiozza 3b	5	0	2	1	1	1	0
Leo Norris ss	4	0	1	2	3	4	2
>Chile Gomez 2b	5	0	0	0	3	2	0
Claude Passeau p	4	0	1	0	0	0	0
Bucky Walters p9	0	0	0	0	0	1	0
	41	9	12	9	30	9	2

Pittsburgh Pirates	AB	R	H	I	PO	A	E
Woody Jensen lf	4	1	1	0	3	0	0
Lloyd Waner cf	4	1	1	1	4	0	1
Paul Waner rf	4	2	2	1	1	0	0
Arky Vaughan ss	5	0	1	1	2	2	2
Gus Suhr 1b	4	0	2	1	13	1	0
Bill Brubaker 3b	5	0	0	0	1	1	0
Pep Young 2b	3	0	1	0	1	5	1
> C. Lavagetto ph9,2b	1	1	0	0	1	1	0
Al Todd c	2	0	0	0	3	0	0
Tom Padden c6	2	1	0	0	1	0	0
Jim Weaver p	1	0	0	0	0	2	0
Red Lucas ph5	1	0	0	0	0	0	0
Mace Brown p6	1	0	0	0	0	2	0
Fred Schulte ph9	1	0	1	1	0	0	0
Hal Finney pr9	0	0	0	0	0	0	0
Bill Swift p10	0	0	0	0	0	0	0
	38	6	9	5	30	14	4

Philadelphia	IP	H	R	ER	BB	SO
Passeau	8.2	8	6	4	2	2
Walters W,6-8	1.3	1	0	0	3	0
	10	9	6	4	5	2

Pittsburgh	IP	H	R	ER	BB	SO
Weaver	5	6	5	4	1	2
Brown	4	2	1	1	0	1
Swift L,8-6	1	4	3	2	0	0
	10	12	9	7	1	3

Philadelphia   4 0 0   0 1 0   1 0 0   3   - 9
Pittsburgh   0 0 0   1 0 3   0 0 2   0   - 6

OB: Philadelphia 5, Pittsburgh 7
DP: Chiozza-Gomez-Camilli (Lucas)
     Camilli-Norris-Camilli (Vaughan)
     Vaughan-Lavagetto-Suhr (Gomez)
     Walters-Gomez-Camilli (Brubaker)
2B: Camilli
3B: Suhr
HR: Klein 4(14)
SO: Chiozza, Passeau 2, Todd, Weaver
BB: Camilli, Jensen, L.Waner, P.Waner,
     Suhr, Lavagetto

SH: Atwood, Norris
TIME: 2:15
ATTENDANCE: 2,500 (paid)
UMPIRES: Ziggy Sears, Bill Klem,
   Lee Ballanfant
SOURCES: Philadelphia Inquirer,
   Record; Pittsburgh Post-Gazette,
   Press

BALANCE	OUT+R+OB+BP=AB+BB+SH+HP+CI							
Philadelphia	30	9	5	44	41	1	2	0	0
Pittsburgh	30	6	7	43	38	5	0	0	0

hosted by the Pittsburgh Pirates. In 1936, Forbes Field, home of the Pirates, sported a 300-foot, right-field foul line ending with a nine-and-one-half foot concrete wall, capped by an additional 18 feet of wire mesh. This inviting distance quickly sloped to 375 feet in right-center field. Because Klein was a strong pull hitter, these dimensions took on signifcant importance.

Indeed, all four of Klein's home runs were hit to right field, although none found the minimum distance. *The Philadelphia Record* estimated that each blast traveled in the 350-foot range except his third, which covered closer to 400 feet. None were of the "Ruthian" variety, i.e., high towering blasts that nearly disappeared from sight; Chuck's four this day were of the line drive type.

• In the opening stanza, Klein provided his team with a promising 3–0 lead when he homered off Pirate starter Jim Weaver with none out and two mates aboard. It was to be his only homer of the day with any teammates on base.

• Right-hander Weaver narrowly escaped the same fate in the second inning when,

The not-so-famous Hal Finney.

with two outs, Klein sent a line drive toward the right-field foul pole. Paul Waner, shifted toward the line, was able to race to the base of the pole, leap, and haul down the missile just barely in foul grounds.

• Klein again faced Weaver in the fifth frame, this time as the first hitter of the inning. With another stroke of his hot bat, Chuck again deposited the ball into the right field bleachers and increased the Phillies lead to 5–1.

• By the time Klein batted again in the seventh, the Pirates had rallied and made it a tight, 5–4 contest. Another right-hander, Mace Brown, had assumed the mound duties for the home club. Now there were two outs, but Mace met a similar fate as his predecessor when Klein lined one over the screen in right center, landing about 400 feet from home plate. That gave the Phillies a small cushion at 6–4.

• Klein was well aware of his brush with

glory as he knelt on deck with two out in the top of the ninth. Alas, teammate Johnny Moore grounded out to first, and with the Phillies leading by two, it appeared Chuck had seen his last at-bat. Claude Passeau was finishing strong, having faced only six Pirates in the past two innings and having retired the first two batters in the bottom of the ninth. However, fate was on the side of Chuck Klein. Passeau next walked pinch hitter Cookie Lavagetto, but backup catcher Tom Padden sent a routine, potential game-ending roller toward shortstop Leo Norris. Norris fumbled it and all hands were safe. Fred Schulte pinch hit for Brown and singled, knocking home Lavagetto and sending Padden to third. Bucky Walters then relieved Passeau, and Hal Finney ran for Schulte. Walters walked Woody Jensen, loading the bases, and also Lloyd Waner, forcing over the tying run. It looked bleak for the Phils as Paul Waner, the National League's leading hitter at .355, stepped to the plate. Walters called on all his reserve and induced Waner to ground out to second. The game had been tied 6–6, and Chuck Klein would lead off the top of the tenth.

• Throughout the sultry afternoon, storm clouds had been brewing. By the time the tenth stanza was about to begin, and Bill Swift took the mound for the Pirates, a dramatic symphony of falling rain and clapping thunder escorted Klein to the plate. With lightning streaking around the ballpark, Swift made his first delivery. Klein couldn't wait and rocketed that first pitch into the right field corner, well over the screen but barely inside the foul pole. Remindful of a later day scene from the movie "The Natural," Chuck rounded the bases amid thunder, lightning, and a stiffening rain. It was the only run the Phillies needed although they did tack on another pair, making it 9–6. The Pirates did not succumb easily, however, as the first two Pirates reached base in the bottom of the tenth. But then Bill Brubaker grounded into a snappy double play, and Johnny Moore made a sensational, diving catch of Lavagetto's fly in shallow left to cap off Klein's day of glory.

Hal Finney, the Pirate pinch runner for Fred Schulte in the ninth, was busy this year constructing a little known claim to infamy. For four years, Finney had served as a second and third-string backstop for Pittsburgh and batted a respectable .240 (46 for 192). But this year, Hal compiled a record of futility unparalleled in major league annals when he batted 35 times without getting a hit. He did get on base, however, just as he did in this game — as a pinch runner, and scored three times in 21 games. Other players have batted more often in a single season without a hit, but they were all pitchers. Finney's impotence this year dwarfs his nearest non-pitcher competitor, Larry Littleton of the 1981 Cleveland Indians, who went 0 for 23.

Lisenbee's Landmark Lashing

95. Pitcher Allows 26 Hits in Eight Innings; Three Teammates Get Five Hits Apiece

PHILADELPHIA, AL   at   CHICAGO
(Athletics, 2)   (White Sox, 17)

Friday, September 11, 1936, Comiskey Park

Philadelphia faithful suffered miserably in 1936 as both the Phillies and the Athletics each lost 100 games and claimed the cellar as their residence. Pitching was the key to both

Lisenbee — abandoned on the mound.

clubs' wretched performances. But while the Phillies' staff led their league in allowing earned runs, it was the Athletics who were especially horrendous. This year, the A's became one of two staffs who, for the first time in the century, permitted more than six earned runs per game. (The Browns also allowed more than six.) Of the 19 warm bodies sent to the hill by manager Connie Mack throughout the season, only three emerged with earned run averages lower than 5.00, and one of that trio labored only two innings.

Horace "Hod" Lisenbee was an integral part of that pathetic pitching corps. After an auspicious rookie year in 1927, when he went 18–9 for the Washington Senators and beat the Yankees five times, Hod's career spiraled downward. In seven additional seasons, laboring for three other teams, he won just 19 more games while losing 49. But no game could have been more devastating to his self-esteem than the one played on this day. Left on the mound to absorb an unmerciful pounding from the bats of the White Sox, Lisenbee engraved his name in baseball ledgers by *allowing 26 hits in a nine-inning game.* (Actually, Chicago accumulated their 26 hits in only eight frames.) No pitcher

since has equalled this ignominy, although Hod merely tied the mark set by two others (see 6-21-01 and 5-18-12).

Lisenbee did show flashes of competence at times. For example, in the second and fourth innings he retired the Sox in order. On the other hand, he allowed four hits in the first, two in the third, six in the fifth, four in the sixth, six in the seventh, and four in the eighth. Hod had been touched for 20 hits in his last four innings of work, and Mack obviously had no intentions of relieving him. Had this game been played in Philadelphia, Lisenbee would probably now hold this record singularly as Chicago would have batted in the ninth.

The primary benefactors of Lisenbee's flogging were Mike Kreevich, Zeke Bonura, and Luke Appling, who each harvested five hits. That *tied the mark for most players on one team collecting five or more hits in a nine-inning game (3).* No other trio since has accomplished this feat.

Perhaps this game was also the persuader that finally convinced Lisenbee (or his manager) that he should begin thinking about another profession. Nevertheless, he stayed with the club long enough to add one more loss to his final 1936 log (1–7). Hod did depart the majors after this season but pitched in the minors for several years (including a seven inning no-hitter in 1944). Then in 1945, after an eight year, major-league hiatus, Lisenbee resurfaced as a 46-year-old to pitch in 31 games for the Reds.

While this game signaled the end for Lisenbee, it heralded the debut of a rookie named Lester Henry Rock for the White Sox. Playing for the Bentonville Mustangs of the Arkansas-Missouri League (class D), Rock had been an all-star and won the batting crown by .0007. In this game he appeared at the plate for the first and only time in his major league career, and was miraculously credited with an RBI despite hitting into a doubleplay. (The RBI exclusion for hitting into a doubleplay was not put into the scoring rules until 1939.) *The Chicago Herald-Examiner* referred to the rookie as "Les 'Plymouth' Rock, budding first-sacker from Bentonville, Arkansas."

Philadelphia Athletics	AB	R	H	I	PO	A	E
Lou Finney 1b	4	0	0	0	9	0	0
Wally Moses cf	3	1	1	0	3	0	0
Hugh Luby 2b	4	0	0	0	0	7	0
Bob Johnson lf	3	0	0	0	1	2	0
Pinky Higgins 3b	4	0	3	0	5	2	0
George Puccinelli rf	3	1	0	0	1	0	0
Frankie Hayes c	3	0	1	0	2	0	0
Charlie Moss c8	0	0	0	1	0	0	0
>Rusty Peters ss	4	0	1	1	3	3	1
Hod Lisenbee p	2	0	0	0	0	0	0
	30	2	6	2	24	14	1

Chicago White Sox	AB	R	H	I	PO	A	E
Rip Radcliff lf	6	4	4	0	1	0	0
Mike Kreevich rf	6	4	5	3	3	0	0
Larry Rosenthal cf	4	3	2	1	2	0	0
Zeke Bonura 1b	5	3	5	3	6	0	0
Les Rock 1b8	1	0	0	1	0	0	0
Luke Appling ss	6	0	5	3	3	2	0
>Jackie Hayes 2b	5	2	3	3	4	4	0
Tony Piet 3b	5	0	1	1	0	1	0
Luke Sewell c	4	0	0	0	6	2	0
Merv Shea c7	0	0	0	0	2	0	0
Monty Stratton p	5	1	1	1	0	1	0
	47	17	26	16	27	10	0

Philadelphia	IP	H	R	ER	BB	SO
Lisenbee L,1-6	8	26	17	14	4	1

Chicago	IP	H	R	ER	BB	SO
Stratton W,4-6	9	6	2	2	5	6

Philadelphia	0 0 0		0 1 0		0 0 1		– 2		
Chicago	4 0 0		0 4 3		4 2 x		–17		

OB: Philadelphia 6, Chicago 10
DP: Sewell-Hayes (Moses)
    Hayes-Appling-Bonura (Finney)
    Luby-Peters-Finney (Rock)
2B: Radcliff 2, Kreevich 2, Hayes
3B: Kreevich
HR: Hayes(4), Stratton(1)
SO: Luby, Johnson, Peters 2, Piet, Lisenbee 2,
BB: Moses, Johnson, Puccinelli, Moss, Lisenbee,
    Rosenthal 2, Hayes, Shea

WP: Lisenbee
TIME: 1:57
ATTENDANCE: 14,000
UMPIRES: Bill Dinneen, Bill Summers,
    Steve Basil
SOURCES: Chicago Daily Times, Herald-
    Examiner, Tribune; Philadelphia
    Inquirer, Record

BALANCE	OUT+R+OB=BP=AB+BB+SH+HP+CI

	OUT	R	OB	BP	AB	BB	SH	HP	CI
Philadelphia	27	2	6	35	30	5	0	0	0
Chicago	24	17	10	51	47	4	0	0	0

Almada Scores Nine Times

96. Player Scores
Nine Runs in Doubleheader

WASHINGTON   at   ST. LOUIS
(Nationals, 16,15)   (Browns, 10,5)

Sunday, July 25, 1937, Sportsman's Park

Mel Almada, in his fifth major league season, had been traded six weeks earlier to Washington from the Red Sox as part of a multi-player deal. The left-handed native of Mexico flourished with his new team, leading off and hitting .309 for the Nationals. This day was one of his finest, when during a Sunday doubleheader, Mel *scored nine times* to establish a major league record that has yet to be repeated in a single day's work. Mel's five counters in the nightcap merely tied the existing American League mark.

Thanks to some lusty hitting by his teammates, Almada scored each time he reached base during the doubleheader. While generating 31 runs, Washington stroked 40 hits at the expense of the most generous staff in the league. Six different Nationals collected four or more safeties during the day, led by Buddy Lewis, who had eight hits and two walks. It was the second time in two afternoons that the Browns lost a doubleheader to Washington.

Almada scored his four runs in the opener by the fifth inning. In the nightcap, Mel scored in the first, second, sixth, eighth, and ninth frames.

Washington's trouncing of the Browns tarnished a planned tribute to St. Louis manager Jim Bottomley. "Sunny Jim" had shined for 14 of his 16 major league seasons in St. Louis, mostly with the Cardinals. Now as player-manager of the Browns, the hometown fans honored him with gifts and flowers after the fifth inning of the first game. What they should have given him were a few good pitchers, for despite averaging more than five runs per game and fielding efficiently, the Browns were struggling to avoid breathing basement air. Alas, Jim could work no miracles, and by season's end the hapless St. Louis hurlers had given up an average of 11.5 hits and 6.00 earned runs per game, solidifying their last place finish. Washington finished sixth.

Mel Almada was traded the following year

Mel Almada — the only player in the 20th century to score nine runs in a doubleheader.

to the Browns for Sammy West. A year later he was sold for $25,000 to Brooklyn, where he ended his seven-year career at the age of only 26 with 706 hits and a .284 lifetime batting average.

FIRST GAME

Washington Nationals	AB	R	H	I	PO	A	E
Mel Almada cf	5	4	3	1	6	0	2
Buddy Lewis 3b	6	3	5	3	1	2	0
Cecil Travis ss	6	2	2	2	1	1	0
Al Simmons lf	6	2	2	1	2	0	0
>John Stone rf	6	1	1	1	0	0	0
Joe Kuhel 1b	4	2	4	4	10	2	0
Buddy Myer 2b	5	0	2	2	3	3	0
Rick Ferrell c	5	1	2	1	3	2	0
Wes Ferrell p	5	1	2	0	1	2	0
	48	16	23	15	27	12	2

St. Louis Browns	AB	R	H	I	PO	A	E
Harry Davis 1b	4	1	1	0	9	0	0
Sammy West cf	5	1	1	4	5	0	0
Joe Vosmik lf	4	2	3	0	4	1	0
Harlond Clift 3b	1	0	1	0	0	0	0
Nig Lipscomb 3b3,2b4	4	1	1	0	0	4	0
Beau Bell rf,3b4	5	2	3	3	2	2	0
Bill Knickerbocker ss	4	0	0	0	2	3	0
Rollie Hemsley c	2	1	1	0	1	0	0
Bill Strickland p4	2	0	1	0	0	1	0
Jim Bottomley ph9	1	0	0	1	0	0	0
Tom Carey 2b	1	1	1	0	1	1	0
Ben Huffman ph3,c	4	0	1	1	1	0	0
Lou Koupal p	0	0	0	0	0	0	0
Bill Trotter p2	0	1	0	0	0	0	1
Jack Knott p3	0	0	0	0	0	0	0
Russ Van Atta p3	0	0	0	0	0	0	0
> Ethan Allen rf4	4	0	0	0	2	0	0
	41	10	14	9	27	12	1

Washington	IP	H	R	ER	BB	SO
W. Ferrell W,8-11	9	14	10	9	4	4

St. Louis	IP	H	R	ER	BB	SO
Koupal L,1-3	1.1	8	6	6	0	0
Trotter	.2	5	5	4	1	0
Knott	.1	1	1	1	0	0
Van Atta	.2	2	1	1	1	1
Strickland	6	7	3	3	0	1
	9	23	16	15	2	2

```
Washington   3 4 6   0 2 1   0 0 0   -16
St. Louis    0 4 2   0 0 0   2 0 2   -10
```

OB: Washington 7, St. Louis 8
DP: Lipscomb-Knickerbocker-Davis
  Vosmik-Davis
2B: Almada, Lewis, Simmons, Kuhel,
  Myer, Davis, Carey
3B: Stone
HR: West(6), Kuhel(5), Almada(3),
  Bell(10)
SB: Almada, Kuhel

SO: Travis, Stone, Knickerbocker,
  Vosmik, Lipscomb, Strickland
BB: Almada, Kuhel, Davis, Vosmik,
  Knickerbocker, Trotter
TIME: 2:22
UMPIRES: Bill Dinneen, Lou Kolls,
  Charles Johnston

BALANCE	OUT+R+OB=BP=AB+BB+SH+HP+CI								
Washington	27	16	7	50	48	2	0	0	0
St. Louis	27	10	8	45	41	4	0	0	0

SECOND GAME

Washington Nationals	AB	R	H	I	PO	A	E
Mel Almada cf	4	5	3	0	6	0	0
Buddy Lewis 3b	4	4	3	1	2	1	0
Cecil Travis ss	6	2	2	4	2	5	0
>Al Simmons lf	6	2	3	4	2	0	0
John Stone rf	5	1	4	4	0	0	0
Joe Kuhel 1b	4	1	1	0	7	1	0
Buddy Myer 2b	4	0	1	2	4	3	1
Wally Millies c	5	0	0	0	3	0	0
Jimmy DeShong p	5	0	0	0	1	0	0
	43	15	17	15	27	10	1

St. Louis Browns	AB	R	H	I	PO	A	E
Harry Davis 1b	5	1	1	1	13	1	0
>Sammy West cf	6	1	3	0	3	0	0
Joe Vosmik lf	3	1	1	0	1	0	0
Beau Bell 3b	5	1	2	2	1	1	0
Ethan Allen rf	4	0	1	0	2	0	1
Bill Knickerbocker ss	4	0	1	1	3	1	0
Rollie Hemsley c	5	0	1	0	4	0	0
Nig Lipscomb 2b	4	0	1	0	0	5	0
Jim Walkup p	3	0	1	0	0	2	0
Ben Huffman ph8	1	1	0	0	0	0	0
Chief Hogsett p9	0	0	0	0	0	0	0
Tommy Heath ph9	0	0	0	0	0	0	0
	40	5	12	4	27	10	1

Washington	IP	H	R	ER	BB	SO
DeShong W,10-8	9	12	5	4	6	2

St. Louis	IP	H	R	ER	BB	SO
Walkup L,6-8	8	16	14	14	5	3
Hogsett	1	1	1	1	1	1
	9	17	15	15	6	4

```
Washington   3 3 0   1 0 3   0 4 1   -15
St. Louis    2 0 0   1 0 0   0 2 0   - 5
```

OB: Washington 7, St. Louis 15
DP: Davis unassisted
2B: Almada, Lewis, Simmons, Stone, Kuhel,
  West
3B: Simmons
HR: Stone(3)
SB: Almada
SO: Kuhel 2, Millies, DeShong, Lipscomb, Walkup
BB: Almada 2, Lewis 2, Kuhel, Myer, Davis,
  Vosmik 2, Allen, Heath, Knickerbocker

HP: By DeShong (Lipscomb)
WP: DeShong, Walkup
TIME: 2:08
ATTENDANCE: 8,148
UMPIRES: Lou Kollis, Charles Johnston,
  Bill Dinneen
SOURCES: St. Louis Globe-Democrat,
  Post-Dispatch; Washington Star, Times

BALANCE	OUT+R+OB=BP=AB+BB+SH+HP+CI								
Washington	27	15	7	49	43	6	0	0	0
St. Louis	27	5	15	47	40	6	0	1	0

Tigers Twice Maul Browns

97. Team Scores 36 Runs in Doubleheader

ST. LOUIS   at   DETROIT
(Browns, 1,7)   (Tigers, 16,20)

Saturday, August 14, 1937, Navin Field

Offensively, the Tigers of 1937 were man-eaters. Led by batting champion Charlie Gehringer, they topped the American League in hits and batting average, with five of their starting eight hitting over .300. First baseman Hank Greenberg led the majors in runs-batted-in with 183, while backstop Rudy York homered every 10.7 times at bat, by far the best frequency in either league. On this day, in front of 29,000 hometown fans in Navin Field, Detroit had all pistons firing when they amassed a *major league record 36 runs in a doubleheader*. It's a mark that still stands. The hapless victims of this attack were the St. Louis Browns, owners of a porcine team-ERA of 6.00 for the season.

Compared to the Tiger offense, the Detroit pitching staff behaved like a bunch of pussycats. When ace "Schoolboy" Rowe went down early in the season with an ailing wing, so went the Motor City hopes. Detroit optimism further faded when player-manager Mickey Cochrane suffered a cracked skull in a May 25 beaning. Cochrane never caught another major league game. Despite these tribulations, the

offense and the best defense in the league carried the Tigers to a second place finish.

This doubleheader had several heroes. Detroit hurler Eldon "Submarine" Auker –batted only .198 this season but led the first game offense with two home runs and five RBIs while tossing a four-hitter. Gee Walker and Pete Fox each totaled seven hits in the two games as did Charlie Gehringer, who

went seven for eight. For Browns fans there wasn't much to cheer about save perhaps Gerald "Nig" Lipscomb. A rookie utility infielder, Nig was beckoned to mop-up both debacles and performed as well as, if not better than, any of the presumed moundsmen despite being reached for a pair of home runs by Auker. Nig was no stranger to the mound. He had frequently pitched batting practice, which is exactly what this day turned out to be. This doubleheader represented two of his three pitching appearances in a one-year, major league career.

The Detroit Free Press added a bit of tongue-in-cheek humor to their game description. On August 7 and 10, the Tigers had run into some eighth-inning misfortune and blown each game. It was enough to make the hometown fans think that particular frame carried some sort of jinx. This doubleheader confirmed those suspicions when the Bengals scored in every possible inning of each game except the eighth.

Fox (opposite) and Walker (above) each contributed seven hits to the debacle.

FIRST GAME

St. Louis Browns	AB	R	H	I	PO	A	E	Detroit Tigers	AB	R	H	I	PO	A	E
Harry Davis 1b	3	0	2	0	8	0	0	Gee Walker cf,lf7	5	2	4	1	2	0	0
Sammy West cf	2	0	0	0	2	0	0	Pete Fox rf	6	1	4	1	1	0	0
Ethan Allen cf6	2	0	0	0	2	0	0	Charlie Gehringer 2b	3	2	2	0	5	4	0
Harlond Clift 3b	3	1	1	0	3	5	0	Hank Greenberg 1b	5	3	2	2	15	1	0
Joe Vosmik lf	4	0	0	0	1	0	0	Rudy York c	4	0	2	1	2	1	0
Beau Bell rf	3	0	1	1	2	1	0	> Birdie Tebbetts c7	2	0	0	0	1	0	0
>Bill Knickerbocker ss	3	0	0	0	2	2	0	Goose Goslin lf	1	1	0	1	0	0	0
Tom Carey 2b	3	0	0	0	3	2	0	Chet Laabs cf7	0	1	0	0	0	0	0
Tommy Heath c	2	0	0	0	0	1	0	Marv Owen 3b	4	2	1	2	0	3	0
Ben Huffman c6	1	0	0	0	1	0	0	Billy Rogell ss	3	2	1	3	0	2	0
Lou Koupal p	1	0	0	0	0	0	0	Charlie Gelbert ss7	1	0	0	0	0	1	0
Bill Strickland p3	1	0	0	0	0	0	0	Eldon Auker p	4	2	2	5	1	5	0
Nig Lipscomb p5	1	0	0	0	0	0	0		38	16	18	16	27	17	0
	29	1	4	1	24	11	0								

St. Louis	IP	H	R	ER	BB	SO
Koupal L,3-5	2.2	7	7	7	5	0
Strickland	1.1	5	5	5	4	0
Lipscomb	4	6	4	4	2	1
	8	18	16	16	11	1

Detroit	IP	H	R	ER	BB	SO
Auker W,9-7	9	4	1	1	4	2

St. Louis	0 0 0	0 0 1	0 0 0	- 1
Detroit	1 1 5	1 4 1	3 0 x	-16

OB: St. Louis 5, Detroit 10
DP: Rogell-Gehringer-Greenberg
    Cliff-Carey-Davis
    Knickerbocker-Carey-Davis (Greenberg)
    Owen-Gehringer-Greenberg
2B: Walker, Greenberg, Clift, Bell
3B: Rogell
HR: Auker 2(3)

BB: Davis, Clift, Bell, Knickerbocker
    Walker, Gehringer 3, Greenberg,
    Goslin 3(21), Laabs, Owen, Rogell
SH: Auker
TIME: 2:02
UMPIRES: Bill Summers, Steve Basil, Harry Geisel

BALANCE	OUT+R+OB=BP=AB+BB+SH+HP+CI
St. Louis	27 1 5 33 29 4 0 0 0
Detroit	24 16 10 50 38 11 1 0 0

SECOND GAME

St. Louis Browns	AB	R	H	I	PO	A	E
Harry Davis 1b	3	1	0	0	11	2	0
Sammy West cf	2	0	0	0	1	0	0
Ethan Allen cf4	2	1	1	2	1	0	0
Harlond Clift 3b	5	1	2	3	3	5	0
Joe Vosmik lf	5	0	1	0	1	0	0
Beau Bell rf	4	1	1	1	2	0	0
>Bill Knickerbocker ss	5	1	1	0	0	1	0
Rollie Hemsley c	3	1	1	0	2	1	1
Tom Carey 2b	3	0	1	0	2	1	0
Bill Trotter p	1	0	0	0	1	0	0
Ed Baecht p3	1	0	0	0	0	0	0
Nig Lipscomb p5	2	1	2	0	0	0	0
	36	7	10	6	24	10	1

Detroit Tigers	AB	R	H	I	PO	A	E
Gee Walker cf	5	2	3	4	0	0	0
Jo-Jo White cf7	1	0	0	0	2	0	0
Pete Fox rf	5	4	3	1	2	0	0
Charlie Gehringer 2b	5	3	5	6	2	5	0
Hank Greenberg 1b	5	3	2	1	11	0	0
Rudy York c	3	2	1	2	4	1	0
Birdie Tebbetts c6	2	0	0	0	1	0	0
Goose Goslin lf	4	1	2	3	2	0	0
Chet Laabs lf6	2	0	0	0	0	0	0
Marv Owen 3b	4	2	2	0	1	1	0
>Billy Rogell ss	5	1	2	1	2	3	0
Boots Poffenberger p	4	2	2	1	0	3	0
	45	20	22	19	27	13	0

St. Louis	IP	H	R	ER	BB	SO
Trotter L,0-3	2	9	10	10	2	0
Baecht	2.1	7	6	6	3	1
Lipscomb	3.2	6	4	2	1	0
	8	22	20	18	6	1

Detroit	IP	H	R	ER	BB	SO
Poffenberger W, 8-2	9	10	7	7	6	3

St. Louis	0 1 0	0 0 0	0 0 6	- 7
Detroit	4 6 1	2 3 1	3 0 x	-20

OB: St. Louis 8, Detroit 9
DP: Rogell-Gehringer-Greenberg
2B: Greenberg 2, Poffenberger, Gehringer,
    Fox
3B: Clift
HR: Gehringer 2(11), York (17), Goslin (4),
    Walker (12), Fox (8), Clift (21), Bell (12)
BB: Davis 2, Allen, Bell, Hemsley, Carey,
    Fox, Gehringer, Greenberg, York,
    Owen 2

SH: Poffenberger
HP: By Trotter (Rogell)
PB: York 2
TIME: 2:20
ATTENDANCE: 29,000
UMPIRES: Steve Basil, Harry Geisel, Bill Summers
SOURCES: Detroit Free Press, News, Times; New York
    Times; St. Louis Globe-Democrat, Post-Dispatch

BALANCE	OUT+R+OB=BP=AB+BB+SH+HP+CI
St. Louis	27 7 8 42 36 6 0 0 0
Detroit	24 20 9 53 45 6 1 1 0

Kelleher's Devastating Departure

98. Pitcher Faces
16 Batters in One Inning

PHILADELPHIA, NL   at   CHICAGO
(Phillies, 2)   (Cubs, 21)

Thursday, May 5, 1938, Wrigley Field

Hal Kelleher's career was just about over before this game began. A Philadelphia native, Hal had made an auspicious debut with the hometown Phillies in September of 1935 by tossing a shutout at the Reds. But since then, Kelleher had labored in mediocrity, mostly as a reliever, and his 6.00+ ERA was not the style of performance that instilled confidence in his manager or the fans. Now relegated primarily to mop-up work, Hal failed miserably even in that role on this day when he set a *new National League record by allowing 12 runs in one inning* and *tied the major league mark by facing 16 batters before retiring the side.*

Although the Cubs were in second place in the season's infancy, this game with the woeful, last place Phillies provided little attraction. Only 1,314 patrons paid to watch.

It didn't take long for the expected outcome to develop. Chicago jumped on three Philadelphia hurlers in the very first inning to take a 4–0 lead. Phillies starter Wayne LaMaster had to leave the game after hurting his arm with a 2–1 count on Stan Hack, the first Cub batter. The situation went downhill from there as the staff that issued the most walks and had the league's highest ERA, demonstrated their forte. Tommy Reis replaced LaMaster and completed Hack's base on balls. Reis also walked Billy Herman, who along with Hack moved up a base on Ripper Collins' sacrifice. After Frank Demaree was purposely passed, Joe Marty singled home two runs. Reis was then permitted to throw two more balls to Augie Galan before being relieved by Pete Sivess. Sivess completed the walk, again filling the bases, but surprised the Cubs by fanning Tony Lazzeri. The inning

got back on track when Sivess walked Gabby Hartnett, forcing home the third run. Chicago pitcher Al Epperly was the next batter, and he too was walked, forcing over yet another tally. Hack mercifully ended the frame by grounding out. Such was the modus operandi of the Philadelphia pitching staff.

The Cubs added a total of five more runs in the fifth, sixth and seventh by combining only six hits with a liberal infusion of walks. With the score then 9–1, and the game hopelessly lost, the stage was set for Hal Kelleher's captivating, one-inning performance.

• Herman opened with a single into short right field.

• Collins walked on four pitches.

Hal Kelleher went out with a flurry.

Philadelphia Phillies	AB	R	H	I	PO	A	E
>Emmett Mueller 2b	3	0	0	0	3	3	0
Chuck Klein rf	3	0	2	0	3	0	0
Hal Kelleher p8	0	0	0	0	0	0	0
Hersh Martin cf	4	0	0	0	0	0	0
Earl Browne 1b	3	0	0	0	9	1	0
George Scharein ss	4	0	2	0	1	2	0
Pinky Whitney 3b	4	1	0	0	1	4	0
Morrie Arnovich lf	4	0	1	0	2	0	1
Bill Atwood c	3	0	0	1	2	0	0
Cap Clark c7	0	1	0	0	2	0	0
Wayne LaMaster p	0	0	0	0	0	0	0
Tommy Reis p1	0	0	0	0	1	0	0
Pete Sivess p1	2	0	0	0	0	1	0
Art Rebel ph8,rf	2	0	1	1	0	0	0
	32	2	6	2	24	11	1

Chicago Cubs	AB	R	H	I	PO	A	E
Stan Hack 3b	5	2	3	2	2	1	0
Billy Herman 2b	3	3	1	0	1	5	0
Ripper Collins 1b	5	3	2	2	11	2	0
Frank Demaree rf	5	1	1	1	2	0	0
Joe Marty cf	6	4	4	4	2	0	0
Augie Galan lf	4	3	3	4	2	0	0
Coaker Triplett lf9	0	0	0	0	0	0	0
Tony Lazzeri ss	4	1	0	0	3	4	0
Bobby Mattick ph8,ss	1	0	1	1	0	0	0
Gabby Hartnett c	3	2	2	3	4	0	0
> Ken O'Dea ph8,c	1	0	0	0	0	0	0
Al Epperly p	3	2	1	3	0	1	0
	40	21	18	20	27	13	0

Philadelphia	IP	H	R	ER	BB	SO
LaMaster L,0-3	0	0	1	1	1	0
Reis	.1	1	3	3	3	0
Sivess	6.2	7	5	5	6	1
Kelleher	1	10	12	12	3	1
	8	18	21	21	13	2

Chicago	IP	H	R	ER	BB	SO
Epperly W,1-0	9	6	2	2	5	4

Philadelphia   0 1 0   0 0 0   0 0 1   - 2
Chicago   4 0 0   0 1 2   2 12 x   -21

OB: Philadelphia 8, Chicago 8
DP: Collins-Lazzeri-Collins (Martin)
     Whitney-Mueller-Browne (Lazzeri)
     Sivess-Mueller-Browne (Demaree)
2B: Klein, Hack, Marty, Hartnett
3B: Hack, Galan, Hartnett
HR: Collins(4), Galan(3)
SO: Martin, Browne, Whitney,
     Arnovich, Demaree, Lazzeri
BB: Mueller 2, Klein, Browne, Hack,
     Clark, Herman 3, Collins, ...

BB: ... Galan 2, Demaree(I), Lazzeri,
     Hartnett 2, Epperly 2
WP: Sivess, Epperly
TIME: 2:19
ATTENDANCE: 1,314
UMPIRES: George Magerkurth, George Parker,
     Charlie Moran
SOURCES: Chicago American, Daily News, Herald-
     Examiner, Tribune; Philadelphia Inquirer

BALANCE	OUT+R+OB=BP+AB+BB+SH+HP+CI								
Philadelphia	27	2	8	37	32	5	0	0	0
Chicago	24	21	8	53	40	13	0	0	0

• Demaree singled to center, driving in Herman.

• Marty grounded to deep short forcing Demaree, but Collins scored on the play.

• Galan singled to right, sending Marty to third.

• Lazzeri walked to load the bases.

• Hartnett doubled to right, knocking in both Marty and Galan.

• Epperly singled home Lazzeri and Hartnett, and continued to third on Morrie Arnovich's error.

• Hack singled to right, scoring Epperly.

• Herman, up for the second time, walked.

• Collins singled to center, scoring Hack and sending Herman to third.

• Demaree shocked the crowd by fanning.

• Marty restored the tempo with a single to center, driving in Herman and sending Collins to third.

• Galan drove both his teammates home with a triple into the right field corner.

• Bobby Mattick batted for Lazzeri and beat out a slow roller toward second. Galan scored on the play.

• Ken O'Dea, the 16th batter, stepped in for Hartnett and fouled out to catcher Cap Clark.

For Hal Kelleher, this was the coup de

grâce. Battered once again, he was encouraged to seek employment elsewhere and never again hurled in the major leagues. The Cubs went on to the National League crown but lost four straight to the Yankees in the World Series. The Phillies, even without Kelleher, finished in the basement for the first of five consecutive seasons.

Al Epperly, this day's winning pitcher, had a most unusual major league career. This was Al's rookie year and his only major league complete game. He finished 1938 with a 2–0 log, then disappeared from the scene until 1950 when he appeared, without a decision, in five games for the Dodgers.

Bob Bashes Browns

99. Player Drives in All Eight of His Team's Runs

ST. LOUIS, AL   at   PHILADELPHIA
(Browns, 3)   (Athletics, 8)

Sunday, June 12, 1938, Shibe Park

Indian Bob supplied all the A's runs.

On an otherwise dreary Philadelphia Athletics club of 1938, "Indian Bob" Johnson shined. Although the A's were to finish last in the American League, Connie Mack's troops had not yet hit their stride. Entering this day's doubleheader, they still held sixth place as Johnson paced the team in runs, home runs, RBIs, batting average, and slugging average.

Though the Philadelphia squad was indeed woeful, they faced stiff competition for last place from their guests of this day, the St. Louis Browns. In 1937, the Browns had inherited the basement from the A's, who had claimed the "honor" in 1935 and 1936. In each of the three years, the other club finished as the closest neighbor, in seventh place. Without the influx of new players that is now provided by free agency, the two teams were once again doomed to inferiority in 1938.

Entering this day's doubleheader, Bob Johnson had been in a long-ball hitting streak, having hit eight homers in his last 14 games. As did most of the league, Bob also had been hitting Browns pitching very well. In the first two games of this series, he had had seven hits in nine trips to the plate, including two home runs. Now Johnson was about to face Browns starter Jim Walkup, who already owned an 0–6 log for the season. As the first game progressed, Bob continued his torrid streak with three hits, including two more home runs, in four official at-bats and a share of the major league record when he *knocked in all eight of his team's runs* (later surpassed). His two homers, numbers 14 and 15, also moved him into second place in that category behind Jimmie Foxx.

Johnson's eight RBIs came with three swings. In the opening frame, with one out, Lou Finney doubled and stopped at third on Mule Haas's single. Frankie Hayes then walked for the first of four times, loading the sacks. Walkup's first pitch to Johnson was rocketed into the upper deck in left field for a grand slam, giving the A's all the runs they would need. In the third inning, Finney

again started a rally with a single, Hayes walked, and Johnson then singled home Finney. Bob's last three RBIs came in the seventh after Haas had doubled to left and Hayes had again walked. At that point, Julio Bonetti was called upon to relieve Walkup. Johnson greeted Bonetti with a titanic, three-run blast that bounced over the roof above the left field bleachers giving him his 6th, 7th, and 8th RBIs.

Indian Bob played 150 games in the outfield this year; this was one of only three in which he was stationed at second base. Johnson finished the season with 30 homers, 113 RBIs, and a .313 batting average, but it wasn't enough to avert another last place finish for the Athletics. As was customary, the Browns finished seventh.

FIRST GAME

St. Louis Browns	AB	R	H	I	PO	A	E
>Buster Mills lf	4	0	0	0	3	0	0
George McQuinn 1b	4	0	2	0	11	3	0
Red Kress ss	4	0	0	0	2	3	0
Harlond Clift 3b	3	2	2	1	0	2	0
Sammy West cf	4	0	0	0	0	0	0
Beau Bell rf	3	1	1	0	1	0	0
Billy Sullivan c	4	0	1	1	5	1	0
Don Heffner 2b	4	0	1	1	2	4	0
Jim Walkup p	3	0	0	0	0	1	0
Julio Bonetti p7	0	0	0	0	0	0	0
Mike Mazzera ph9	1	0	0	0	0	0	0
	34	3	7	3	24	14	0

Philadelphia Athletics	AB	R	H	I	PO	A	E
Wally Moses rf	4	0	0	0	5	0	0
Lou Finney 1b	4	2	2	0	13	0	0
>Mule Haas cf	5	2	2	0	2	0	0
Frankie Hayes c	0	2	0	0	2	0	0
Bob Johnson 2b	4	2	3	8	4	2	2
Sam Chapman lf	4	0	1	0	1	0	0
Ace Parker 3b	4	0	1	0	0	2	0
Wayne Ambler ss	4	0	0	0	0	6	0
Buck Ross p	3	0	2	0	0	1	0
	32	8	11	8	27	11	2

St. Louis Browns	IP	H	R	ER	BB	SO
Walkup L,0-7	6	9	7	7	6	2
Bonetti	2	2	1	1	0	1
	8	11	8	8	6	3

Philadelphia Athletics	IP	H	R	ER	BB	SO
Ross W,3-1	9	7	3	3	3	2

St. Louis	0 0 0	1 0 0	0 0 2	– 3
Philadelphia	4 0 1	0 0 0	3 0 x	– 8

OB: St. Louis 7, Philadelphia 7
DP: Parker-Johnson-Finney
   McQuinn-Kress-McQuinn
2B: Finney, Haas
HR: Johnson 2(15), Clift(4)
BB: Mills, Clift, Bell, Hayes 4,
   Finney, Moses
SH: Ross
WP: Walkup

TIME: 2:29
ATTENDANCE: 25,851
UMPIRES: Louis Kolls, George
   Moriarty
SOURCES: Philadelphia Inquirer,
   Record; St. Louis Globe-Democrat,
   Post-Dispatch

BALANCE	OUT+R+OB=BP=AB+BB+SH+HP+CI							
St. Louis	27	3	7	37	34	3	0	0	0
Philadelphia	24	8	7	39	32	6	1	0	0

Foxx Trots Six Times

100. Player Draws Six Walks in Nine-Inning Game

BOSTON, AL   at   ST. LOUIS
(Red Sox, 12)   (Browns, 8)

Thursday, June 16, 1938, Sportsman's Park

Boston's Jimmie "The Beast" Foxx had been terrorizing American League pitchers for over a decade, and this year was no different. After only 49 games, he had already hit 19 home runs — three more than his nearest major league rival, Rudy York; and gathered 71 RBIs — far exceeding Earl Averill's 52. Not quite as lofty in the batting average department, Foxx stood a mere fifth in the majors at .351. It's no wonder that opponents hated to see him step to the plate. Perhaps it was fear, or simply inept hurling of the Browns pitching staff, but on this day no one wanted to give Jimmie anything to hit. In *six plate appearances, Foxx walked each time*. That broke the mark of five set by the Athletics' Max Bishop in 1930 and established a twentieth-century major league record that has yet to be repeated in a nine-inning game. (Both Miller Huggins and Bill Urbanski previously had stepped to the plate six times without an official at-bat, but their days each included sacrifices.)

Boston arrived at the ballpark this day only two games out of first and having beaten their hosts in seven of eight encounters. (A day earlier, Foxx had had a double, home run, two RBIs, and no walks against the Browns.) The Browns, meanwhile, were in familiar territory — the basement. The opposing moundsmen, 25-year-old Red Sox rookie Charlie Wagner, and the Browns' 26-year-old veteran

Les Tietje, struck little fear in the hearts of batters. Wagner was starting his fourth major league game and was already encumbered with a 7.78 ERA. Tietje, toiling in his sixth and final major league campaign, was busily adding to his lifetime 5.11 ERA. Due to some lusty hitting and a see-saw battle, neither hurler was around for the conclusion nor involved in the decision. On a peculiar note, Harlond Clift, Browns third sacker and cleanup hitter, matched Foxx walk for walk his first four times up before he popped out.

Prior to the game, Foxx complained that his sinus was bothering him so much that he couldn't see well and suggested that he'd like to take the afternoon off. But manager Joe Cronin needed his big slugger to keep pace in the pennant race. So Jimmie played anyway, and obviously his sight was quite good.

Apparently unaware of his historic opportunity, Foxx put the record in jeopardy during his last plate appearance. With two men out in the top of the ninth, runners at second and third, and a 3–0 count, Jimmie swung viciously at reliever Russ Van Atta's next offering but missed. The following delivery sent him to first for the sixth time. The Browns' strategy of offering Jimmie little to swing at was fairly successful as he was left on base four of the six times. Below is a summary of Foxx's plate appearances.

JIMMIE FOXX WALKS SIX TIMES ON JUNE 16, 1938

Inning	Pitcher	Score Bos–StL	Runners on these bases	Outs	Foxx as a baserunner	Notes
1	Tietje	0–0	Second	2	forced out	Semi-intentional BB
3	Tietje	3–1	None on	0	LOB	
4	Tietje	5–1	None on	2	LOB	
7	Linke	5–6	None on	0	Scored	
8	Linke	7–6	Second	1	Scored	Intentional BB
9	Van Atta	10–6	Second, Third	2	LOB	

Foxx walked in each of his six plate appearances.

The day following this run-scoring exhibition, Boston traveled to Chicago where Foxx again led the Red Sox to a 5–1 victory. In that game he had two singles but only one walk.

By season's end, The Beast had badly bruised American League pitching. Jimmie not only won the batting crown (.349), but also led both major leagues in slugging (.704) and on-base (.462) percentages, total bases (398), and RBIs (175). In addition, he tied Hank Greenberg for the league lead in walks with 119.

Boston Red Sox	AB	R	H	I	PO	A	E
Doc Cramer cf	6	1	1	1	1	0	0
Joe Vosmik lf	5	3	4	1	0	0	0
Ben Chapman rf	6	3	3	2	1	1	0
Jimmie Foxx 1b	0	2	0	0	9	0	0
Joe Cronin ss	6	2	4	4	5	4	0
>Pinky Higgins 3b	6	0	1	2	1	0	0
Eric McNair 2b	4	0	1	0	6	5	0
Johnny Peacock c	5	0	1	1	4	1	0
Charlie Wagner p	2	1	1	0	0	0	0
Archie McKain p5	0	0	0	0	0	0	0
Emerson Dickman p5	1	0	0	0	0	0	0
Johnny Marcum p6	2	0	1	0	0	1	0
	43	12	17	11	27	12	0

St. Louis Browns	AB	R	H	I	PO	A	E
>Buster Mills lf	6	1	1	0	3	0	0
George McQuinn 1b	5	0	3	2	9	0	0
Red Kress ss	4	0	1	0	3	6	1
Harlond Clift 3b	1	2	0	1	2	1	0
Mike Mazzera cf	2	1	2	0	1	0	0
Ethan Allen ph5,cf	2	1	1	0	2	0	0
Beau Bell rf	5	1	1	2	4	0	0
Billy Sullivan c	5	0	1	1	1	0	0
Don Heffner 2b	5	1	2	1	2	3	0
Les Tietje p	2	0	0	0	0	0	0
Roy Hughes ph6	1	1	1	0	0	0	0
Ed Linke p7	0	0	0	0	0	0	0
Ed Cole p8	0	0	0	0	0	0	0
Tommy Heath ph8	1	0	1	0	0	0	0
Russ Van Atta p9	0	0	0	0	0	0	0
Glenn McQuillen ph9	1	0	1	1	0	0	0
	40	8	15	8	27	10	1

Boston	IP	H	R	ER	BB	SO
Wagner	4.2	6	3	3	3	1
McKain	0	0	0	0	1	0
Dickman	.2	4	3	3	2	0
Marcum W,4-4	3.2	5	2	2	0	2
	9	15	8	8	6	3

St. Louis	IP	H	R	ER	BB	SO
Tietje	6	9	5	4	4	0
Linke W,1-4	1.1	5	5	5	2	1
Cole	.2	1	0	0	0	0
VanAtta	1	2	2	2	2	0
	9	17	12	11	8	1

Boston   1 2 0   2 0 0   2 3 2   -12
St. Louis 0 1 0   2 0 3   0 0 2   - 8

OB: Boston 12, St. Louis 11
DP: Heffner-Kress-McQuinn
    Cronin-McNair-Foxx (Allen)
2B: Cramer, Kress, Chapman, Cronin 2,
    McQuillen
SB: Chapman
BB: Vosmik, Foxx 6, McNair, Kress,
    Clift 4, Allen

WP: Linke
TIME: 2:40
ATTENDANCE: 1,028 (paid)
UMPIRES: Harry Geisel, Steve Basil
SOURCES: Boston Globe, Herald, Post; St. Louis
    Globe-Democrat, Post-Dispatch; New York Times

BALANCE	OUT+R+OB=BP=AB+BB+SH+HP+CI
Boston	27 12 12 51 43 8 0 0 0
St. Louis	27 8 11 46 40 6 0 0 0

Peaches Creamed by Giants

101. Team Hits Five Two-Out Home Runs in One Inning

CINCINNATI at NEW YORK
(Reds, 3) (Giants, 17)

Tuesday, June 6, 1939, Polo Grounds

The Giants had led the league in home runs the previous year and were on schedule to retain their laurels in 1939. This one game, however, surpassed even their wildest long-ball expectations as a strong northwest breeze converted innocuous pop flies to right field

Peaches Davis — creamed in the fourth.

into circuit trips around the bases. New York was thus able to:

1) Tie the existing major league record of seven home runs in a game (later surpassed).

2) Set a *new major league record for home runs in an inning with five* (since tied).

3) Tie the existing record of three consecutive home runs in an inning (later surpassed).

First-place Cincinnati invaded the Polo Grounds to meet the sixth-place Giants. On the hill for the Reds was Johnny Vander Meer, who had pitched consecutive no-hitters a year earlier but was now struggling with an inflated ERA and a 3–2 slate. The home team jumped on him early with six singles, sending Johnny to the showers after just two-thirds of an inning. As it turned out, he was

more fortunate than his successors. "Peaches" Davis, first out of the bullpen, caused little excitement by allowing homers in the second and third innings to Jo-Jo Moore and Mel Ott respectively. At this juncture the score read 6–0, still a reasonable game. Peaches then retired the first two batters in the bottom of the fourth before the Giants exploded in an orgy of circuit blasts. Here's what happened next:

• **Harry Danning** homered into the right field upper deck.

• Mel Ott walked and Zeke Bonura singled to right.

• **Frank Demaree** then lifted a wind-blown fly ball to right which landed among the paying customers.

• Wesley Livengood, formally the batting practice pitcher, was summoned to relieve Davis. Wesley was right in his element. After walking Tony Lazzeri he served a gopher ball to the unlikely **Burgess Whitehead**, who hit only two home runs all season. (Whitehead finished his career with 17 home runs in 3,316 at-bats.)

• Next up was opposing pitcher **Manny Salvo**, who would go on to accumulate a .129 lifetime batting average. Manny's eyes must have lit up when he saw the offerings of Livengood, for he buffeted a shot that caromed off the outfield fence. Right fielder Ival Goodman played it so poorly that Salvo circled the bases for the only home run of his career.

• For the second time in the inning, **Jo-Jo Moore** stepped to the plate. Probably a little embarrassed that he had made an out earlier in the frame, Jo-Jo redeemed himself with a blast into the upper deck.

Salvo collected the victory as well as his only career home run.

That made the total *five home runs in one inning, all after there were two outs*. It was a new record that has yet to be matched. (The closest any other team has come is three home runs after two outs.)

The Reds did, however, get the last laugh as they went on to win the National League pennant, riding the arms of MVP Bucky Walters and Paul Derringer, while first baseman Frank McCormick led the league in hits and runs-batted-in.

The Cincinnati Enquirer *lamented the efforts of their pitching staff.*

Cincinnati Reds	AB	R	H	I	PO	A	E
Bill Werber 3b	5	1	4	0	0	3	0
Lonny Frey 2b	4	1	2	0	0	5	0
>Ival Goodman rf	4	0	0	0	3	0	0
Frank McCormick 1b	4	1	2	1	10	0	0
Ernie Lombardi c	2	0	0	0	2	1	0
Wil Hershberger c5	2	0	1	0	3	0	0
Harry Craft cf	2	0	0	0	1	0	0
F. Bordagaray cf5	2	0	1	0	0	0	0
Wally Berger lf	1	0	0	0	1	1	0
Lee Gamble lf5	3	0	0	0	0	0	0
Billy Myers ss	4	0	0	0	4	2	0
Johnny Vander Meer p	0	0	0	0	0	0	0
Peaches Davis p1	1	0	0	0	0	1	0
Wes Livengood p4	0	0	0	0	0	0	0
Lew Riggs ph5	1	0	0	0	0	0	0
Junior Thompson p5	1	0	1	0	0	1	0
Les Scarsella ph9	1	0	0	0	0	0	0
	37	3	11	1	24	14	0

New York Giants	AB	R	H	I	PO	A	E
>Jo-Jo Moore lf	6	3	3	2	1	0	0
Billy Jurges ss	4	1	1	0	1	2	0
Harry Danning c	5	2	2	2	7	2	0
Mel Ott rf	3	3	2	2	2	0	0
Zeke Bonura 1b	4	3	3	1	10	0	0
Frank Demaree cf	4	2	3	4	5	0	0
Tony Lazzeri 3b	4	1	2	2	0	1	0
Burgess Whitehead 2b	5	1	2	2	1	3	0
Manny Salvo p	5	1	2	2	0	4	0
	40	17	20	17	27	12	0

Cincinnati	IP	H	R	ER	BB	SO
Vander Meer L,3-3	.2	6	3	3	0	0
Davis	3	8	7	7	1	1
Livengood	.1	3	4	4	2	1
Thompson	4	3	3	3	2	2
	8	20	17	17	5	4

New York	IP	H	R	ER	BB	SO
Salvo W,3-3	9	11	3	3	2	5

Cincinnati	0 0 0	0 0 3	0 0 0	- 3
New York	3 1 2	8 3 0	0 0 x	-17

OB: Cincinnati 9, New York 5
DP: Frey-Myers-McCormick (Whitehead)
    Salvo-Danning-Bonura (McCormick)
2B: Bonura, McCormick, Salvo, Frey
HR: Moore 2(2), Ott(9), Danning(6),
    Demaree(2), Whitehead(1), Salvo(1)
CS: Ott
BB: Frey, Goodman, Jurges, Ott 2,
    Demaree, Lazzeri

SF: Bonura
TIME: 2:33
ATTENDANCE: 7,405
UMPIRES: George Magerkurth, Bill Stewart
SOURCES: Cincinnati Enquirer; New York
    Herald-Tribune, Post, Times, World-
    Telegram

BALANCE	OUT	+R	+OB	=BP	=AB	+BB	+SH	+HP	+CI
Cincinnati	27	3	9	39	37	2	0	0	0
New York	24	17	5	46	40	5	1	0	0

A New Murderer's Row

102. Team Records
98 At-Bats, 13 Home Runs and
87 Total Bases in Doubleheader

NEW YORK, AL   at   PHILADELPHIA
(Yankees, 23,10)   (Athletics, 2,0)

Wednesday, June 28, 1939, Shibe Park

Sensational headlines and photos of a battered and bloodied pugilist, "Two-ton" Tony

Galento, dominated the nation's sports pages
on June 29, 1939, describing how Joe Louis

Babe Dahlgren (right), playing in place of the immortal Lou Gehrig (left), had three home runs in the double-header.

had successfully defended his heavyweight title with a fourth round technical knockout. Elsewhere, in considerably smaller type size, was the story of a flogging of another sort — the Yankees had invaded Philadelphia. Without a referee to stop an obvious mismatch, the New Yorkers slugged their helpless sparring partners in a doubleheader thrashing of

the Athletics by scores of 23–2 and 10–0. Included in the carnage were several new major league records:

• The Yankees clubbed *eight home runs* in the first game, a *new single-game major league standard* (since surpassed).

• They then followed with five additional circuit clouts in the nightcap, setting another mark of *13 home runs by one team in a double-header* (still stands).

• By gathering *53 total bases* in the opener, the Yankees established an additional major league record (since surpassed).

• Although it wasn't mentioned in newspapers of the day, the New Yorkers also *totaled 87 bases in the doubleheader*, which remains the major league benchmark.

Throughout the day, it made little difference who was on the mound for the Athletics as the Yankees indiscriminately rocketed balls into the stands. Each of the five Philadelphia hurlers allowed at least one circuit blast, and each Yankee starter, other than the pitchers and Red Rolfe, contributed to the long-ball mayhem. (Rolfe donated five hits.)

In the opening encounter, Bill Dickey hit one over the right field wall in the second inning, but the A's tied it in their half. That was the last time during the day, however, there was even a hint of competitiveness. In the next frame, after there were two outs, the New Yorkers harvested five runs thanks to homers by Joe DiMaggio, George Selkirk, and Babe Dahlgren. In the fourth, DiMaggio again connected, as did Joe Gordon. Tommy Henrich opened the sixth with a circuit blast, and Dahlgren hammered another in the seventh. Philadelphia fans, at first forlorn, became spellbound and then delighted as souvenirs were deposited throughout the neighborhood.

The Yankees showed no signs of exhaustion

FIRST GAME

New York Yankees	AB	R	H	I	PO	A	E
Frankie Crosetti ss	6	1	2	0	4	7	0
Red Rolfe 3b	7	2	4	1	0	1	1
Tommy Henrich rf	7	3	3	4	2	0	0
Joe DiMaggio cf	5	4	3	3	4	0	0
Bill Dickey c	5	4	3	1	2	0	0
Buddy Rosar c7	1	0	0	0	0	0	0
George Selkirk lf	7	3	4	5	3	0	0
>Joe Gordon 2b	7	3	3	3	2	5	0
Babe Dahlgren 1b	6	2	4	5	10	1	0
Monte Pearson p	5	1	1	0	0	1	0
	56	23	27	22	27	15	1

Philadelphia Athletics	AB	R	H	I	PO	A	E
Dario Lodigiani 3b	4	0	1	0	1	6	1
Wayne Ambler ss	3	0	0	0	0	1	0
> Skeeter Newsome ss5	2	0	1	0	0	5	0
Dee Miles rf	3	1	0	0	4	0	0
Bob Johnson cf	4	0	1	0	2	1	0
Frankie Hayes c	3	0	1	1	2	0	0
Sam Chapman 1b	3	1	1	0	11	0	1
Eric Tipton lf	4	0	1	0	3	0	0
Sep Gantenbein 2b	3	0	0	0	4	2	1
Lynn Nelson p	1	0	1	1	0	0	0
Bill Beckman p3	0	0	0	0	0	0	0
Bob Joyce p4	2	0	0	0	0	0	0
Bill Nagel ph9	1	0	0	0	0	0	0
	33	2	7	2	27	15	3

New York	IP	H	R	ER	BB	SO
Pearson W,7-1	9	7	2	2	4	2

Philadelphia	IP	H	R	ER	BB	SO
Nelson L,5-3	2.2	9	6	4	1	1
Beckman	1	7	8	8	1	0
Joyce	5.1	11	9	7	3	0
	9	27	23	19	5	1

New York	0 1 5	9 0 4	4 0 0	–23
Philadelphia	0 1 1	0 0 0	0 0 0	– 2

OB: New York 11, Philadelphia 9
DP: Gordon-Crosetti-Dahlgren (Tipton)
2B: Chapman, Johnson, Henrich, Selkirk
3B: Lodigiani
HR: DiMaggio 2(5), Dahlgren 2(6), Dickey(10), Selkirk(12), Gordon(9), Henrich(7)
SB: Selkirk, Dahlgren, Gordon
SO: Gordon, Hayes, Joyce

BB: Crosetti, DiMaggio 2, Dickey, Pearson, Lodigiani, Miles, Chapman, Gantenbein
SF: Hayes
PB: Hayes 2
TIME: 2:27
UMPIRES: John Quinn, Bill McGowan, George Pipgras

BALANCE	OUT	+R	+OB	=BP	=AB	+BB	+SH	+HP	+CI
New York	27	23	11	61	56	5	0	0	0
Philadelphia	27	2	9	38	33	4	1	0	0

SECOND GAME

New York Yankees	AB	R	H	I	PO	A	E
Frankie Crosetti ss	6	1	3	1	2	0	0
Red Rolfe 3b	6	1	1	0	0	1	0
>Tommy Henrich rf	4	1	1	0	4	0	0
Joe DiMaggio cf	5	2	2	2	4	0	0
Bill Dickey c	4	0	1	1	3	0	0
George Selkirk lf	3	1	0	0	5	0	0
Joe Gordon 2b	5	3	3	4	2	3	0
Babe Dahlgren 1b	4	1	3	2	6	2	0
Lefty Gomez p	5	0	2	0	1	0	0
	42	10	16	10	27	6	0

Philadelphia Athletics	AB	R	H	I	PO	A	E
Dario Lodigiani 3b	3	0	0	0	4	1	0
Wayne Ambler ss	4	0	0	0	3	0	0
Dee Miles rf	4	0	0	0	2	0	0
>Bob Johnson cf	4	0	1	0	4	0	0
Earle Brucker c	3	0	0	0	2	0	0
Sam Chapman 1b	3	0	0	0	5	0	0
Eric Tipton lf	3	0	0	0	4	0	0
Sep Gantenbein 2b	3	0	1	0	3	2	0
George Caster p	1	0	0	0	0	0	0
Chubby Dean p6	2	0	1	0	0	2	0
	30	0	3	0	27	5	0

New York	IP	H	R	ER	BB	SO
Gomez W,6-2	9	3	0	0	1	2

Philadelphia	IP	H	R	ER	BB	SO
Caster L,5-8	5	9	7	7	4	1
Dean	4	7	3	3	1	0
	9	16	10	10	5	1

New York	5 0 0	0 2 0	0 1 2	-10
Philadelphia	0 0 0	0 0 0	0 0 0	- 0

OB: New York 11, Philadelphia 4
2B: Dahlgren, Gordon, Crosetti
HR: Crosetti(3), Gordon 2(11),
    DiMaggio(6), Dahlgren(7)
BB: Henrich 2, Selkirk 2, Dahlgren,
    Lodigiani
SH: Dickey
TIME: 1:40

ATTENDANCE: 21,612
UMPIRES: Bill McGowan, John Quinn,
    George Pipgras
SOURCES: New York Times, Herald-Tribune,
    World Telegram; Philadelphia Inquirer,
    Evening Bulletin,Record

BALANCE	OUT+R+OB=BP=AB+BB+SH+HP+CI
New York	27 10 11 48 42 5 1 0 0
Philadelphia	27 0 4 31 30 1 0 0 0

----

after their opening game slugging as Frankie Crosetti led off the second contest with a drive into the left field seats. Before the frame had ended, Gordon had joined him in long-ball hitting, and New York had a 5–0 lead. In the fifth stanza, DiMaggio hit his third of the day and Gordon his second. Dahlgren ended the massacre in the ninth with the Yankees' 13th home run of the doubleheader.

The 1939 Yankees were quietly being compared with the 1927 edition. Now, despite the absence of names like Ruth, Gehrig, Lazzeri, Combs, and Meusel, many argued that this club was superior, especially after this day. Connie Mack was quoted as saying after the doubleheader: "That should convince all those who have doubted my appraisal of this Yankee club as the greatest. Has anybody ever seen the like?"* The Bronx Bombers went on to win the American League pennant by 17 games over second place Boston and led the circuit in runs, home runs, runs batted in, walks, and slugging average. This season would be the first of four American League crowns in five years.

Philadelphia fans this day witnessed another rare display when Connie Mack left the dugout and walked onto the field prior to the start of the second game. The occasion was to greet Yankee captain Lou Gehrig, who had approached the plate to deliver his team's lineup. Mack shook hands with the great first baseman, whose career recently had ended abruptly. The 21,612 fans continued to cheer as Gehrig returned to the dugout, wiping tears from his eyes.

*"Daniel" (a World-Telegram Staff Correspondent), "Yanks Set 5 More Records," New York World-Telegram, 29 June 1939, Sports page 1, col. 1.

Tabor's Two Too Much

103. Teams Combine for 54 Runs in Doubleheader; Player Hits Two Grand Slams in One Game

BOSTON, AL   at   PHILADELPHIA
(Red Sox, 17,18)   (Athletics, 7,12)

Tuesday, July 4, 1939, Shibe Park

While Lou Gehrig gave his famous farewell speech in Yankee Stadium, there was a dazzling Independence Day celebration in Shibe Park, but the pyrotechnics were supplied for the most part by visitors from Boston. In an old-fashioned, swashbuckling slugfest, the rowdy Red Sox twice dumped the Athletics, 17–7 and 18–12. Not only was it the *most runs ever scored in a doubleheader by two teams*, but the second game also provided an individual mark of lasting fame.

The Boston brigade demonstrated their league-leading hitting prowess by roping 35 hits, including ten home runs, in the two games. Led by rookie third baseman Jim "Rawhide" Tabor, they amassed seven circuit clouts in the opener and three in the nightcap. Tabor, himself, tied two major league standards. After depositing a circuit clout in the opener, Jim returned to clout three in the nightcap. That *equalled the major league mark of four homers in a doubleheader* (later surpassed). In addition, *two* of his vesper-game *homers came with the bases loaded*, enabling him to match the standard set by Tony Lazzeri in this same park three years earlier (see 5-24-36).

Tabor joined another Boston rookie by the name of Ted Williams in homering in the first game. Then in the nightcap, Jim stroked his next home run, a grand slam, in the third inning off George Caster. That drive into the left-field upper deck gave Boston an 8–3 advantage. The seventh-place Athletics, however, roared back with seven runs of their own in the bottom of the frame to recapture

the lead. After further scoring by both sides, the game became tied 11–11 after five. In the sixth Tabor again found himself at the plate with the sacks full, now facing Lynn Nelson. This time, Jim lashed a drive that rattled off the left-center field fence, about 405 feet from home plate. As his teammates raced around the bases, the ball took an unexpected carom back toward the infield, allowing Tabor to also score standing up. It was a little less glamorous but far more exciting than Jim's initial grand slam. It also demoralized the Athletics, who were retired with barely a whimper the rest of the game. Tabor then capped his day of glory with a solo shot, also off Nelson, into the upper deck in left center in the eighth. All totaled, Rawhide drove home nine runs in this game, falling slightly short of Lazzeri's AL record of 11. Jim may have equalled or bettered that mark too, but he was walked once, and on another occasion was ordered to bunt.

Tabor never approached the class of his rookie teammate Williams but turned in nine respectable big league campaigns. He retired in 1947 with 1021 hits, 104 home runs, 598 RBIs, and a .270 career batting average.

Making his major league debut for the Athletics this day was the son of Hall of Famer Eddie Collins. Eddie Collins Jr. pinch-hit in the opener and then entered the second game as a pinch runner, finishing in left field. The Philadelphia fans gave him a rousing ovation which was as much a tribute to his father as it was of their hopes for his future success. At the time, Eddie Sr. was the general manager of the visiting Red Sox.

Jim Tabor—two grand slams.

FIRST GAME

Boston Red Sox	AB	R	H	I	PO	A	E
Bobby Doerr 2b	6	4	4	3	1	1	0
Tom Carey 2b8	0	0	0	0	1	1	0
Doc Cramer cf	6	1	2	2	3	0	0
Jimmie Foxx 1b	6	4	2	0	5	0	0
Ted Williams rf	4	3	2	4	5	0	0
>Joe Cronin ss	6	1	2	3	2	2	0
Lou Finney lf	5	0	2	2	1	0	0
Jim Tabor 3b	5	2	3	2	2	2	0
Gene Desautels c	5	0	1	0	7	0	0
Emerson Dickman p	3	1	1	0	0	1	0
Joe Heving p5	1	1	1	0	0	0	0
	47	17	20	16	27	7	0

Philadelphia Athletics	AB	R	H	I	PO	A	E
Sep Gantenbein 2b	4	0	2	0	2	1	1
Wayne Ambler ss	1	0	0	0	0	1	0
Wally Moses ph3	1	0	1	1	0	0	0
Skeeter Newsome ss4	3	0	1	0	0	1	0
Dick Siebert 1b	4	1	1	1	9	1	0
Bob Johnson lf	4	1	1	2	1	0	0
Eric Tipton lf8	1	0	0	0	0	0	0
Frankie Hayes c	4	1	1	1	4	0	0
Sam Chapman cf	5	1	2	1	5	1	0
Dee Miles rf	5	1	2	0	1	0	0
>Dario Lodigiano 3b	5	1	3	0	5	0	1
Cotton Pippen p	0	0	0	0	0	2	0
Buck Ross p3	3	1	1	1	0	0	0
Eddie Collins ph7	1	0	0	0	0	0	0
Chubby Dean p8	0	0	0	0	0	0	0
	41	7	15	7	27	7	2

Boston	IP	H	R	ER	BB	SO
Dickman	4	9	6	6	0	5
Heving W,4-3	5	6	1	1	1	0
	9	15	7	7	1	5

Philadelphia	IP	H	R	ER	BB	SO
Pippen L,1-6	2.2	9	10	4	0	0
Ross	4.1	9	6	6	2	2
Dean	2	2	1	1	0	1
	9	20	17	11	2	3

```
Boston          4 0 6    0 0 3    3 1 0    -17
Philadelphia    0 0 3    1 3 0    0 0 0    - 7
```

OB: Boston 6, Philadelphia 10
2B: Williams, Doerr, Cramer, Tabor,
    Newsome
HR: Williams(12), Chapman(10),
    Doerr(6), Johnson(12), Hayes(6),
    Cronin(9), Tabor(4)
SO: Cronin 2, Desautels, Johnson,
    Hayes 2, Chapman, Miles

BB: Williams 2, Hayes
SH: Siebert, Heving
HP: By Dickman (Gantenbein)
TIME: 2:31
UMPIRES: Bill Grieve, Bill Summers,
    Lou Kolis

```
BALANCE        OUT+R+OB=BP=AB+BB+SH+HP+CI
Boston         27  17 6  50  47  2   1  0  0
Philadelphia   27   7 10 44  41  1   1  1  0
```

SECOND GAME

Boston Red Sox	AB	R	H	I	PO	A	E
Bobby Doerr 2b	6	1	2	0	3	5	0
Doc Cramer cf	6	2	2	0	1	0	0
Jimmie Foxx 1b	4	3	2	3	13	2	0
Ted Williams rf	4	2	1	0	3	0	0
Joe Cronin ss	3	1	1	1	2	4	0
>Lou Finney lf	5	3	2	0	2	0	1
Jim Tabor 3b	4	5	3	9	0	4	0
Johnny Peacock c	5	1	2	3	2	0	0
Woody Rich p	0	0	0	0	0	0	0
Jack Wilson p1	2	0	0	0	0	0	0
Monty Weaver p3	0	0	0	0	0	0	0
Gene Desautels ph5	1	0	0	1	0	0	0
Denny Galehouse p5	2	0	0	0	1	1	1
	42	18	15	17	27	16	2

Philadelphia Athletics	AB	R	H	I	PO	A	E
Sep Gantenbein 2b	5	1	2	2	4	1	0
Wayne Ambler ss	5	1	2	2	1	3	1
> Wally Moses ph9	1	0	0	0	0	0	0
Dick Siebert 1b	4	2	1	0	4	2	1
Bob Johnson lf	2	1	2	2	1	0	0
Eddie Collins pr3,lf	3	1	1	0	5	0	0
Earle Brucker c	4	1	2	2	5	1	0
Sam Chapman cf	5	1	0	1	3	0	0
Dee Miles rf	4	1	3	1	2	0	0
Bill Nagel 3b	4	2	1	0	1	1	0
George Caster p	1	0	0	0	1	1	0
Chubby Dean p4	2	1	1	1	0	1	0
Lynn Nelson p6	2	0	0	0	0	0	0
	42	12	15	11	27	10	2

Boston	IP	H	R	ER	BB	SO
Rich	.1	4	3	3	0	0
Wilson	2	6	7	6	1	0
Weaver	1.2	3	1	1	2	1
Galehouse W,2-3	5	2	1	1	1	1
	9	15	12	11	4	2

Philadelphia	IP	H	R	ER	BB	SO
Caster	3	7	8	8	3	1
Dean L,2-6	2	3	5	4	3	0
Nelson	4	5	5	5	2	3
	9	15	18	17	8	4

Boston	0 2 6	0 3 4	0 1 2	-18
Philadelphia	3 0 7	1 0 0	0 0 1	-12

OB: Boston 6, Philadelphia 8

DP: Brucker-Gantenbein-Siebert-Gantenbein
Cronin-Doerr-Foxx
Cronin-Foxx

2B: Cronin, Siebert, Brucker 2,
Nagel, Peacock 2, Williams,
Miles, Cramer

HR: Tabor 3(7)

SB: Collins

CS: Doerr

SO: Foxx, Finney, Galehouse 2,
Ambler, Chapman

BB: Foxx 2, Williams 2, Cronin 2,
Finney, Tabor, Gantenbein,
Siebert, Brucker, Miles

SH: Cronin, Nagel

PB: Peacock

TIME: 2:30

ATTENDANCE: 25,000 (22,030 paid)

UMPIRES: Bill Summers, Lou Kolis,
Bill Grieve

SOURCES: Boston Globe, Herald, Post; Philadelphia Evening Bulletin, Inquirer, Record

----

BALANCE	OUT	+R	+OB	=BP	+AB	+BB	+SH	+HP	+CI
Boston	27	18	6	51	42	8	1	0	0
Philadelphia	27	12	8	47	42	4	1	0	0

Reds Turn Joost Loose

104. Player Accepts 19 Fielding Chances in Nine-Inning Game

CINCINNATI   at   NEW YORK
(Reds, 1)   (Giants, 0)

Wednesday, May 7, 1941, Polo Grounds

It's not often that defense shows itself in a boxscore, but Eddie Joost tallied some numbers on this day that distort a casual glance at the game's accounting sheet. Joost had seen limited action at second, third, and short during his first four years in the major leagues. This, his fifth season, represented his first full-time duty playing shortstop. His manager, "Deacon" Bill McKechnie, said after this game that Joost was the best shortstop in the league — pretty strong words in the face of Pee Wee Reese, Marty Marion and Arky Vaughan. But no one could discredit the record-setting game Joost had at the Polo Grounds when he *accepted 19 fielding chances in a nine-inning game*. Other than a first baseman or a catcher (who gets a putout for

every strikeout), it was the most chances accepted by any fielder in a nine-inning game since the turn of the century. (Shortstop Daniel Richardson of Washington also accepted 19 chances on June 20, 1892.)

Two veteran hurlers faced each other on this day — Cincinnati's "Bucky" Walters, a hero in the previous World Series, and the Giants' "Prince Hal" Schumacher. Both had good movement on their pitches as only two fly balls were fielded in the outfield all day, one by each club, *tying the major league mark for fewest outfield chances in a game.* That meant there was plenty of work for the infielders, and Joost got the lion's share. In addition to partaking in all four of the Reds' double plays, Eddie rang up ten assists, nine

The Cincinnati Enquirer *extolled the home club's victory.*

putouts, and stole the only base in the game. Ironically, he also committed the game's only error while throwing to first base in the seventh inning on an attempted double play. The only run of the game was scored by Ernie "The Schnozz" Lombardi when he blasted the first pitch of the second inning into the left-field upper deck.

Despite today's heroics, Joost finished as the season's leader neither in shortstop putouts nor assists. Those honors went to Reese and Marion respectively. Nor were the Reds able to defend their 1940 World Series title, finishing 12 games out. The Giants were also no threat, closing 25.5 games behind the league leading Dodgers.

Joost seemed to be in the middle of every play.

Cincinnati Reds	AB	R	H	I	PO	A	E
Bill Werber 3b	4	0	0	0	1	1	0
Lonny Frey 2b	4	0	1	0	4	6	0
Ival Goodman rf	2	0	1	0	0	0	0
Mike McCormick lf7	1	0	0	0	0	0	0
>Frank McCormick 1b	4	0	0	0	10	0	0
Ernie Lombardi c	2	1	1	1	2	0	0
Harry Craft cf	3	0	0	0	1	0	0
Eddie Joost ss	3	0	1	0	9	10	1
Jim Gleeson lf,rf7	3	0	0	0	0	0	0
Bucky Walters p	3	0	1	0	0	3	0
	29	1	5	1	27	20	1

New York Giants	AB	R	H	I	PO	A	E
Jo-Jo Moore lf	4	0	1	0	1	0	0
Burgess Whitehead 2b	4	0	1	0	4	6	0
Babe Young 1b	3	0	2	0	14	0	0
Harry Danning c	4	0	1	0	4	0	0
Mel Ott rf	2	0	0	0	0	0	0
Billy Jurges ss	4	0	1	0	3	4	0
Frank Demaree cf	4	0	1	0	0	0	0
>Joe Orengo 3b	3	0	0	0	1	5	0
Hal Schumacher p	2	0	0	0	0	1	0
	30	0	7	0	27	16	0

Cincinnati	IP	H	R	ER	BB	SO
Walters W,4-1	9	7	0	0	5	2

New York	IP	H	R	ER	BB	SO
Schumacher L,2-2	9	5	1	1	2	4

Cincinnati	0 1 0	0 0 0	0 0 0	- 1
New York	0 0 0	0 0 0	0 0 0	- 0

OB: Cincinnati 3, New York 8
DP: Walters-Joost-McCormick (Whitehead)
   Joost-Frey-McCormick (Orengo)
   Joost-McCormick (Whitehead)
   Walters-Joost-McCormick (Jurges)
   Orengo-Whitehead-Young(F. McCormick)
   Whitehead-Young (Frey)
   Jurges-Whitehead-Young (Craft)
HR: Lombardi(2)
SB: Joost
BB: Goodman, Lombardi, Young, Ott 2,
   Orengo, Schumacher

SO: Werber, M. McCormick, Craft,
   Gleeson, Danning, Orengo
WP: Schumacher
TIME: 1:40
ATTENDANCE: 4,950
UMPIRES: Lee Ballanfant, Al Barlick,
   Babe Pinelli
SOURCES: Cincinnati Enquirer; New
   York Herald-Tribune, Post, Times,
   World-Telegram

BALANCE	OUT	+R	+OB	=BP	=AB	+BB	+SH	+HP	+CI
Cincinnati	27	1	3	31	29	2	0	0	0
New York	27	0	8	35	30	5	0	0	0

Goofy Fools the Browns

105. Pitcher Walks 11 in Shutout Victory; Team Leaves 15 Runners on Base in Shutout Loss

ST. LOUIS, AL   at   NEW YORK
(Browns, 0)   (Yankees, 9)

Friday, August 1, 1941, Yankee Stadium

On this date, the St. Louis Browns were in seventh place, just a few percentage points out of the basement. And having lost 13 of 15 to their opponents, the first place Yankees, this day's outcome was no surprise. It was the manner in which the Browns went down in defeat that opened the record books for a few new entries.

The Yankees' Lefty "Goofy" Gomez wasn't very sharp this "ladies day" in New York, but

"Goofy" Gomez flirted with danger throughout the game.

had earlier tossed a five-inning shutout, also at the Browns.) Although St. Louis managed only five hits, Goofy uncorked one wild pitch and distributed no less than *11 walks, the most ever in a nine-inning shutout.* Four of those free passes were issued to Roy Cullenbine, who garnered 121 during the season. Only Ted Williams had more.

The Browns left runners on base in every inning. However, it was in the ninth that Gomez not only painted the finishing touches on his record game but almost squandered it as well. After retiring the first two batters, he lost touch with the plate, walking the bases loaded. The next batter, Chet Laabs, then took three straight balls, lending some measure of suspense to an otherwise customary Yankee victory. Lefty's next two servings were called strikes, and Laabs fouled off another pair before sending a towering fly to DiMaggio in center field.

St. Louis also tied another major league record when they left 15 runners on base. It was the third time in the twentieth century that a team had *stranded 15 runners on the base paths while being shut out.* Following is a summary of how Gomez hoodwinked the Browns:

he had just enough on his pitches when he needed it to whitewash the Browns for his first nine-inning shutout of the season. (Lefty

Inning	1	2	3	4	5	6	7	8	9	Total
# of Browns Walks	2	1	1	0	3	0	0	1	3	11
# of Browns LOB	3	1	2	1	2	1	1	1	3	15

Fifteen runners left on base while being shut out remained the major league benchmark for 53 years. On September 24, 1994, the St. Louis Cardinals stranded 16.

Gomez was once asked to what he attributed his frequent good fortune. Lefty replied: "Clean living and a fast outfield." This game may have represented one of those instances.

Joe DiMaggio, hot on the heels of his amazing 56-game hitting streak, used this contest to mark the 15th game of a new streak. (Joe had then hit in 71 of his last 72 games.) Johnny Berardino, the Browns shortstop this day, had a much more successful career after baseball as Dr. Steve Hardy in the famous soap opera "General Hospital." By then, he had dropped the second "r" from the spelling of his surname.

St. Louis Browns	AB	R	H	I	PO	A	E
Don Heffner 2b	4	0	1	0	0	5	0
Johnny Lucadello 2b7	1	0	0	0	1	1	0
Harlond Clift 3b	4	0	1	0	1	1	0
George McQuinn 1b	4	0	0	0	11	0	0
Walt Judnich cf	2	0	1	0	0	0	0
Bobby Estalella rf7	0	0	0	0	0	0	0
Roy Cullenbine lf	1	0	0	0	0	0	0
>Chet Laabs rf,cf7	5	0	0	0	4	0	1
Johnny Berardino ss	3	0	1	0	3	5	0
Bob Swift c	3	0	1	0	4	0	0
Eldon Auker p	1	0	0	0	0	3	0
Alan Strange ph4	1	0	0	0	0	0	0
Maury Newlin p4	2	0	0	0	0	1	0
	31	0	5	0	24	16	1

New York Yankees	AB	R	H	I	PO	A	E
Johnny Sturm 1b	5	0	0	0	3	1	0
Red Rolfe 3b	4	2	1	0	1	0	0
Tommy Henrich rf	5	3	4	3	2	0	0
Joe DiMaggio cf	4	2	2	1	4	0	0
Charlie Keller lf	4	1	2	1	5	0	0
>Bill Dickey c	5	0	2	2	8	0	0
Joe Gordon 2b	4	1	2	0	1	0	0
Phil Rizzuto ss	4	0	1	1	3	2	1
Lefty Gomez p	2	0	0	0	0	1	0
	37	9	14	8	27	4	1

St. Louis	IP	H	R	ER	BB	SO
Auker L,8-12	3	8	6	6	2	2
Newlin	5	6	3	1	3	0
	8	14	9	7	5	2

New York	IP	H	R	ER	BB	SO
Gomez W,10-3	9	5	0	0	11	4

St. Louis	0 0 0		0 0 0		0 0 0		- 0
New York	3 0 3		0 1 2		0 0 x		- 9

OB: St. Louis 15, New York 9
DP: Auker-Berardino-McQuinn (Dickey)
  Sturm-Rizzuto-Sturm (McQuinn)
  Gomez-Rizzuto-Sturm (Newlin)
2B: DiMaggio, Keller
3B: Dickey, Gordon
HR: Henrich 2(21)
SO: McQuinn, Cullenbine, Laabs,
  Swift, Rizzuto, Gomez
BB: Clift, McQuinn, Judnich 2,
  Estalella, Cullenbine 4, Swift,
  Berardino, Rolfe, DiMaggio, ...

BB: ... Keller, Gomez 2
WP: Gomez
TIME: 2:20
ATTENDANCE: 8,730 (5,858 paid, 2,872 ladies)
UMPIRES: Bill McGowan, John Quinn, and Bill Grieve
SOURCES: New York Herald-Tribune, Post, Sun, Times; St. Louis Globe-Democrat, Post-Dispatch

BALANCE	OUT	+R	+OB	=BP	=AB	+BB	+SH	+HP	+CI
St. Louis	27	0	15	42	31	11	0	0	0
New York	24	9	9	42	37	5	0	0	0

Pitcher Socks Three Home Runs

106. Pitcher Hits Three Home Runs in One Game

CHICAGO, NL   at   BOSTON
(Cubs, 5)   (Braves, 6)

Wednesday, May 13, 1942, Braves Field

Right-handed knuckle-baller Jim Tobin had been a pretty fair hitter, entering the season with a lifetime .249 (89/357) batting average. But this day's offensive effort engraved his name in baseball annals. In three successive plate appearances, Tobin lofted the ball over the left-field wall to become *the only pitcher in the twentieth-century to amass three circuit blasts in one game.*

Jim's outburst was not altogether astonishing as he entered this game with his team's best batting average (.348), having connected safely eight times in 23 at-bats, including two home runs. Just a day earlier Tobin had homered as a pinch hitter, so that by this day's conclusion, he had sent the ball out of the park four times in his last five plate appearances. His streak was barely

Tobin's knuckler, as well as his bat, leveled the Cubs.

Chicago Cubs	AB	R	H	I	PO	A	E
>Charlie Gilbert cf	4	0	0	0	3	0	0
Lennie Merullo ss	4	1	0	0	3	3	0
Stan Hack 3b	4	1	1	0	1	2	0
Bill Nicholson rf	4	1	2	3	3	0	0
Lou Novikoff lf	4	0	0	0	2	0	0
Lou Stringer 2b	3	0	0	0	1	3	0
Phil Cavaretta 1b	3	1	0	0	9	0	0
Clyde McCullough c	4	1	1	0	2	1	0
Jake Mooty p	3	0	0	0	0	1	1
Hi Bithorn p7	0	0	0	0	0	1	0
Rip Russell ph9	1	0	1	1	0	0	0
	34	5	5	3	24	11	1

Boston Braves	AB	R	H	I	PO	A	E
>Johnny Cooney 1b	5	0	1	0	11	0	0
Tommy Holmes cf	3	0	1	0	2	1	0
Eddie Miller ss	4	1	1	1	3	3	2
Nanny Fernandez 3b	3	0	0	0	3	2	1
Ernie Lombardi c	2	1	1	1	1	0	0
Phil Masi c5	2	0	0	0	1	0	0
Max West lf	3	0	1	0	0	0	0
Paul Waner rf	3	1	1	0	3	0	0
Sibby Sisti 2b	4	0	0	0	3	2	0
Jim Tobin p	4	3	3	4	0	5	1
	33	6	9	6	27	13	4

Chicago	IP	H	R	ER	BB	SO
Mooty	6.2	7	4	4	4	1
Bithorn L,0-3	1.1	2	2	2	0	1
	8	9	6	6	4	2

Boston	IP	H	R	ER	BB	SO
Tobin W,5-3	9	5	5	3	3	0

Chicago	0 0 2	0 0 2	0 0 1	- 5
Boston	0 0 0	1 1 0	2 2 x	- 6

OB: Chicago 5, Boston 7
2B: Russell
HR: Nicholson(3), Lombardi(5),
   Miller(3), Tobin 3(5)
SB: McCullough, Merullo
CS: Holmes
SO: West, Sisti
BB: Gilbert, Stringer, Cavaretta,
   Holmes, Fernandez, West, Waner

TIME: 1:56
ATTENDANCE: 3,448
UMPIRES: Lee Ballanfant, Al Barlick,
   Babe Pinelli
SOURCES: Boston Herald, Post; Chicago
   Daily News, Herald-Examiner, Sun,
   Times, Tribune

BALANCE	OUT+R+OB=BP=AB+BB+SH+HP+CI
Chicago	27 5 5 37 34 3 0 0 0
Boston	24 6 7 37 33 4 0 0 0

interrupted by his initial time at bat. Then, Jim lofted a deep fly to right that forced Bill Nicholson against the wall to make the catch. But the next three times up, Tobin gave no one any chance to catch his drives.

• Leading off the fifth, with his team trailing 2–1, Tobin hit his longest homer of the day beyond the bleachers and into the freight yards that fringed the Charles River. The staggering blow came off Chicago starter Jake Mooty.

• Jim again led off the seventh inning against Mooty with similar results, only this blast merely landed in the bleacher seats. The blow brought Boston to within one run, 4–3.

• Two were down in the eighth when Tobin again stepped to the plate. By this time the score was tied at four. There were two outs, Hi Bithorn was on the hill for Chicago, and Boston's Paul Waner was on

second. While pandemonium reigned in the stands over the possibility of another Tobin home run, time was called as Cubs manager Jimmie Wilson walked to the mound to discuss strategy, being joined by catcher Clyde McCullough and third baseman Stan Hack. The meeting lasted a few minutes and, scorning an intentional pass, McCullough returned to his position and said to Tobin: "We've got you now. We just had a meeting and we know how to pitch to you!"* Maybe they knew how, but Bithorn couldn't execute. With a 2–1 count, Tobin completed his trilogy.

Tobin's dazzling performance was not unheralded. Once while playing for Oakland in the Pacific Coast League, Jim drove home seven runs on a home run and a double in the same inning — both with the bases loaded!

After his three-home-run day, reporters

asked Jim for his comments and a comparison to his minor league achievement. "This was really it. This was the day. I've never had such a thrill in my life."* Mrs. Tobin witnessed her husband's heroics but may have questioned his comments.

Tobin slacked off considerably after this game, finishing the season with only one more home run and a .246 batting average. More importantly, the knuckler stopped fooling batters. Although Jim led the league in complete games (28) and innings pitched (288), his 12–21 log with a 3.97 ERA did little to help Boston avoid a seventh place finish. Tobin's six home runs this year were his personal best. He retired with 17 round-trippers and a .230 lifetime average to complement his 105–112 record and 3.44 ERA in nine campaigns.

*Gerry Hern, "Tobin Content to Remain a Pitcher," Boston Post, 14 May 1942, p. 16, col. 1.

Yanks Establish Twin-Killing Standard

107. Team Turns
Seven Double Plays in One Game

NEW YORK, AL   at   PHILADELPHIA
(Yankees, 11)   (Athletics, 2)

Friday Night, August 14, 1942, Shibe Park

Gordon was the middle-man on three of the double plays.

As World War II raged on, teams throughout the league began losing key players to the draft. The Yankees, however, remained essentially intact, and 1942 saw them persist as the dominant force in the American League. They were especially strong defensively. Up the middle they fielded Joe DiMaggio in center field, Phil Rizzuto at short, Joe Gordon at second, and Bill Dickey behind the plate. Sterling defense coupled with an aging and erratic Lefty Gomez pro-vided the circumstances for some record-setting fielding. In this game, Gomez supplied plenty of base runners, and the infield sparkled to produce *seven double plays, the most ever recorded by one team in a nine inning game.* The previous mark of six had been accomplished on a half-dozen occasions.

The 33-year-old Gomez was on his way out to pasture. (After this season he would pitch in only one more major league game.) On this night in Philadelphia's Shibe Park he

Rizzuto started two of the double plays.

New York Yankees	AB	R	H	I	PO	A	E
Buddy Hassett 1b	4	2	2	1	8	0	0
Red Rolfe 3b	4	2	2	0	4	2	1
>Tommy Henrich rf	6	1	1	4	0	0	0
Joe DiMaggio cf	5	2	2	0	1	0	0
Charlie Keller lf	5	1	3	2	0	0	0
Joe Gordon 2b	4	1	1	0	6	4	0
Bill Dickey c	5	1	3	2	4	3	0
Phil Rizzuto ss	5	0	0	1	4	4	0
Lefty Gomez p	3	0	0	0	0	0	0
Johnny Murphy p7	2	1	1	0	0	2	0
	43	11	15	10	27	15	1

Philadelphia Athletics	AB	R	H	I	PO	A	E
Mike Kreevich cf	2	0	0	0	3	0	0
Elmer Valo rf	3	1	1	0	2	0	0
Pete Suder 3b	3	1	1	0	2	3	1
Bob Johnson lf	4	0	2	2	1	0	1
Dick Siebert 1b	4	0	1	0	6	1	0
B. Knickerbocker 2b	4	0	0	0	0	2	0
>Eric McNair ss	3	0	1	0	3	1	0
Bob Swift c	2	0	1	0	10	0	0
Phil Marchildon p	1	0	0	0	0	0	0
Dee Miles pr5	0	0	0	0	0	0	0
Bob Harris p6	1	0	0	0	0	2	0
	27	2	7	2	27	9	2

New York	IP	H	R	ER	BB	SO
Gomez W,6-4	6	4	2	2	7	4
Murphy	3	3	0	0	0	0
	9	7	2	2	7	4

Philadelphia	IP	H	R	ER	BB	SO
Marchildon L,13-10	5	9	7	7	2	6
Harris	4	6	4	3	2	0
	9	15	11	10	4	6

New York   3 0 0   0 4 1   0 1 2   -11
Philadelphia 1 0 0   0 0 1   0 0 0   - 2

OB: New York 10, Philadelphia 5
DP: Dickey-Rolfe (Suder S.O.)
    Dickey-Rizzuto (Valo S.O.)
    Gordon-Rizzuto-Hassett (Kreevich)
    Rizzuto-Gordon-Hassett (Knickerbocker)
    Murphy-Rizzuto-Hassett (Harris)
    Rolfe-Gordon-Hassett (Johnson)
    Rizzuto-Gordon-Hassett (Knickerbocker)
2B: Rolfe, DiMaggio, Johnson,
    Murphy, Hassett, Dickey
3B: Keller
HR: Henrich(12)

BB: Hassett 2, Rolfe, Gordon, Valo,
    Kreevich 2, Suder, McNair,
    Swift, Marchildon
SH: Rolfe
PB: Swift
TIME: 2:15
ATTENDANCE: 17,956
UMPIRES: Bill Grieve, Joe Rue, Cal Hubbard
SOURCES: New York Times, World-Tribune; Phila-
    delphia Evening Bulletin, Inquirer, Record

BALANCE	OUT+R+OB=BP=AB+BB+SH+HP+CI
New York	27 11 10 48 43 4 1 0 0
Philadelphia	27 2 5 34 27 7 0 0 0

was especially wild, walking seven in just six innings of work. His fielders were equal to the task, however, bailing him out with four twin-killings. Johnny Murphy relieved Gomez in the seventh, and he too was the recipient of a two-ply execution in each inning he pitched. Here's how it all transpired:

• First inning—When A's Pete Suder struck out, Bill Dickey threw to Red Rolfe, catching Mike Kreevich trying to steal third.

• Third inning—After walking, Kreevich was again thrown out attempting to steal, this time at second after Elmer Valo fanned, Dickey to Phil Rizzuto.

• Fifth inning—Gomez was working on the edge of disaster. After retiring Bill Knickerbocker, he walked Eric McNair, Bob

Swift and Phil Marchildon in succession. Dee Miles then was sent in to pinch run for Marchildon. Kreevich next grounded to Gordon, who threw to Rizzuto, who threw on to Buddy Hassett, ending the threat.

• Sixth inning—After Dick Siebert had singled, Knickerbocker grounded to Rizzuto. This double play went Rizzuto to Gordon to Hassett.

• Seventh inning—After Bob Swift had singled, Bob Harris bounced to opposing pitcher Murphy who threw to Rizzuto, who threw on to Hassett.

• Eighth inning—With Valo on first after singling, Bob Johnson grounded to Red Rolfe, who threw to Gordon at second, who threw on to Hassett.

• Ninth inning—Ironically, it was shabby

fielding that set up the record seventh double play. Siebert led off and reached base on an error by Rolfe, but Knickerbocker sent a sharp grounder to Rizzuto. Phil flipped to Gordon, who threw to Hassett. So smooth and quick was this play that Knickerbocker was out before he got within ten feet of first.

New York's seven double plays gave them 150 thus far into the season. They finished with 190, narrowly missing their own major league single-season mark of 194 set a year earlier (since surpassed). This game was also New York's first night victory in Philadelphia; in three previous contests, the home team had emerged victorious. For Vernon "Lefty" Gomez, this was not only his last victory in a Yankee uniform but in the major leagues as well.

Thirty Left Marooned

108. Teams Leave 30 Runners on Base in One Game

NEW YORK, NL   at   PHILADELPHIA
(Giants, 10)   (Phillies, 6)

Sunday, July 18, 1943, Shibe Park

On this date both the Phillies (35–43) and their guests, the Giants (31–47), were playing a dispassionate brand of baseball. Not much changed by season's end when New York finished in the basement with Philadelphia, their nearest competitor. Pitching skills of the two teams reflected their placements. The Giants' staff was last in team ERA and allowed more hits than any other in the league; closest in each category was the Phillies corps. These attributes generated a proclivity for opposition baserunners throughout the season, so when the two teams met, there was superb opportunity for runs to be scored and logjams on the basepaths. Runs-scored there

Jimmy Wasdell hit safely three times but couldn't get home.

were in this game, the first of a doubleheader, but the claim to fame was provided by those baserunners who never crossed the plate. With the Giants providing 17 left-on-base and the Phillies 13, *the two clubs tied a major league mark (30) for futility in a nine-inning contest* (see 8-27-35).

During the first five innings alone, the Giants had collected ten hits, four walks, and one reached first on an error; but through it all, they could tally only three times and trailed the Phillies. The game was decided in the sixth when the New Yorkers batted around and scored four times. The rally,

capped by a wild heave by second baseman Danny Murtaugh, enabled the New Yorkers to score their sixth and seventh runs.

Just to settle any argument that the Phillies simply had a bad game, they stranded another dozen in the nightcap to reach the quarter-century mark in that department for the day. (The Giants stranded only six in the vesper game.)

During the war years, sports reporting was frequently diminished. This game was indicative, for despite consulting 11 newspapers from the cities of the participating teams, details of the action were scant.

FIRST GAME

New York Giants	AB	R	H	I	PO	A	E
Johnny Rucker cf	4	2	2	1	1	0	0
Mickey Witek 2b	6	0	3	1	3	3	0
Joe Medwick lf	6	1	3	1	3	0	0
Mel Ott rf	5	1	1	1	5	0	0
Ernie Lombardi c	5	2	2	1	4	0	0
Buster Maynard 3b	4	3	2	0	1	4	0
Billy Jurges ss	5	0	2	1	1	4	0
Joe Orengo 1b	4	1	3	2	9	0	0
Carl Hubbell p	1	0	1	0	0	0	0
Harry Feldman p4	0	0	0	0	0	0	0
Sid Gordon ph5	1	0	0	0	0	0	0
> Bill Lohrman p5	3	0	0	1	0	0	0
	44	10	19	9	27	11	0

Philadelphia Phillies	AB	R	H	I	PO	A	E
>Danny Murtaugh 2b	5	2	1	0	4	3	2
Ron Northey rf	5	1	3	3	2	1	0
Coaker Triplett lf	4	0	1	1	1	0	0
Jimmy Wasdell cf	5	0	3	1	3	0	0
Babe Dahlgren 1b	4	0	1	0	7	1	0
Pinky May 3b	4	0	0	0	0	2	0
Glen Stewart ss	3	0	0	0	0	3	0
Schoolboy Rowe ph7	1	0	0	0	0	0	0
Charlie Brewster ss8	1	1	1	0	2	1	0
Mickey Livingston c	4	1	3	0	7	0	0
Al Gerheauser p	2	1	1	0	0	0	0
Newt Kimball p5	1	0	0	0	0	0	0
Tex Kraus p6	1	0	0	0	1	1	0
Buster Adams ph9	1	0	1	1	0	0	0
	41	6	15	6	27	12	2

New York	IP	H	R	ER	BB	SO
Hubbell	3.2	7	4	4	3	2
Feldman	.1	0	0	0	0	0
Lohrman W,5-5	5	8	2	2	1	2
	9	15	6	6	4	4

Philadelphia	IP	H	R	ER	BB	SO
Gerheauser	4.1	10	3	2	3	0
Kimball L,1-5	1	3	4	3	2	1
Kraus	3.2	6	3	3	2	1
	9	19	10	8	7	2

New York	1 0 1	0 1 4	0 3 0	-10
Philadelphia	0 0 1	3 0 0	0 1 1	- 6

OB: New York 17, Philadelphia 13
DP: Jurges-Witek-Orengo
2B: Murtaugh, Livingston, Northey 2, Lombardi
SB: Maynard
SO: Gordon, Lohrman, Livingston, Stewart, Gerheauser, Triplett
BB: Rucker 2, Maynard, Lombardi, Ott, Orengo 2, Murtaugh, May, Triplett, Livingston
SH: Hubbell, Maynard, Jurges
HP: By Lohrman (Dahlgren)

WP: Hubbell, Kimball
TIME: 2:37
ATTENDANCE: 14,589
UMPIRES: Babe Pinelli, Al Barlick
SOURCES: New York Daily Mirror, Daily News, Herald-Tribune, Journal American, Post, Sun, Times; Philadelphia Daily News, Evening Bulletin, Inquirer, Record

BALANCE	OUT	+	R	+	OB	=	BP	=	AB	+	BB	+	SH	+	HP	+	CI
New York	27		10		17		54		44		7		3		0		0
Philadelphia	27		6		13		46		41		4		0		1		0

Giants Feast on Dodger Wildness

109. Team Drives in
26 Runs, Draws 17 Walks;
Player Scores Six Runs, Draws Five Walks

BROOKLYN   at   NEW YORK
(Dodgers, 8)   (Giants, 26)

Sunday, April 30, 1944, Polo Grounds

The weather was lovely, and New York's first doubleheader of the season lured an overflow crowd to the Polo Grounds for an interborough rivalry with the hated Dodgers. More than 58,000 entered the stadium and another 20,000 were turned away disappointed. Only one other time, in 1936, had greater masses jammed into the horseshoe shelter of Coogan's Bluff. Those who did arrive before the gates were closed at 1:55 P.M. witnessed several record performances as well as a vintage display by the irascible Brooklyn manager Leo Durocher.

Opposing moundsmen in the first game were cousins Cliff and Rube Melton. By baseball standards of the day, each man was a veritable behemoth, standing 6'5" and weighing over 200 pounds. Their skills, unfortunately, did not match their physical dimensions, and the clansmen were considered journeymen pitchers at best. Although Cliff had won 20 games seven years earlier, his skills had eroded; and Rube would never approach such a level of success.

The Dodgers jumped out to a 2–0 lead off Cliff, but the Giants responded with three of their own off Rube in the opening round. When it came time for Rube to bat in the top of the second, Durocher lifted his starter in favor of a pinch hitter. Rube departed having faced just eight batters and was eventually saddled with the loss.

By most gauges, the Dodgers had the worst pitching staff in the majors in 1944 — the highest ERA, the most walks, and the second-most hits. A major contributor was Les Webber, who next toed the rubber to open the home half of the second. True to form, Les faced six Giants, even got one out, but gave up a hit and walked four straight. Durocher was fuming and called Chink Zachary into the fray. Zachary followed suit by walking the only two Giants he faced, exiting with the Giants leading 7–2.

The next Brooklyn victim was Fritz Ostermueller, who concluded the second inning with no further damage. However, Fritz joined the party in the third frame when he allowed four more Giant runs on two hits and a pair of walks. Fritz was mercifully sent to the showers for a pinch hitter in the top of the fourth when the Dodgers rallied for five runs. In doing so, Brooklyn sent Cliff Melton to join his cousin in the clubhouse; he had been unable to enjoy the fruits of an 11–2 lead.

The Giants rebuilt their nine-run advantage by scoring five times in the bottom of the fourth off the fifth Dodger hurler, Tommy Warren. The score stood at 16–7 until the sixth, when Durocher had seen enough. Perhaps it was an attempt to get his team fired up or simply his penchant for the spotlight, but then Leo began arguing with the home plate umpire Beans Reardon. As Reardon attempted to whisk dirt off home plate, Durocher kicked more on. He then turned his attention to first base umpire Tom Dunn, who had less patience than his comrade and banished the feisty pilot. As Durocher made the long walk to the center field clubhouse, he and the field around him became decorated with fruits, vegetables, and bottles.

The Giants infield knocked in 16 runs — (left to right) Weintraub (11), Hausman (2), Kerr (1), and Luby (2).

Tommy Warren was abandoned on the mound the rest of the game, giving up eight more runs in the bottom of the eighth to conclude the scoring at 26–8. After the game, when scribes sorted through the record books, here's what they uncovered:

- *The Giants had set a new major-league standard for runs-batted-in for a game — 26.*
- *Three New Yorkers scored five or more runs, a mark yet to be surpassed.*
- *They tied the National League marks of 17 walks in a game, as well as six straight.*
- *Mel Ott tied his own ML benchmark by*

scoring six runs, and his NL record by walking five times. This day, Ott also added to his NL lifetime records by scoring his 1700th run and knocking in his 1700th run.

Phil Weintraub almost inked his name in baseball annals by driving home 11 runs, one shy of the NL and ML marks of 12 (see 9-16-24). Having spent most of his professional days in the minors, this was the part-time outfielder/first baseman's greatest game on a major-league diamond. His first six plate appearances produced two walks, two doubles, a triple, and a home run. In his last at-bat, there were two Giants aboard when he lashed a line drive which was caught. In five previous big-league seasons, Weintraub had accumulated just 109 RBIs in 924 at-bats. Sundays, however, were magical for Phil,

dating back to his minor league days. While playing for Rochester in 1936, Weintraub had been having such success (24 for 50) on the Christian Sabbath that by July his teammates had nicknamed him "Sunday Punch."

FIRST GAME

Brooklyn Dodgers	AB	R	H	I	PO	A	E
F. Bordagaray rf,lf7	5	2	1	1	2	0	0
Dixie Walker lf	4	1	2	0	3	0	1
Paul Waner rf7	1	0	1	0	1	0	0
Luis Olmo 2b	5	0	1	2	3	2	1
Augie Galan cf	4	0	1	1	2	0	0
Lloyd Waner cf7	1	0	0	0	0	0	0
Howie Schultz 1b	4	2	3	2	6	0	0
Bill Hart ss	3	1	1	0	3	0	0
>Bobby Bragan 3b	5	1	0	0	0	3	0
Mickey Owen c	2	1	2	1	3	1	0
Roy Jarvis c7	1	0	0	0	1	0	0
Rube Melton p	0	0	0	0	0	0	0
Whit Wyatt ph2	1	0	0	0	0	0	0
Les Webber p2	0	0	0	0	0	0	0
Chink Zachary p2	0	0	0	0	0	0	0
F. Ostermueller p2	0	0	0	0	0	0	0
Clancy Smyres ph4	1	0	0	0	0	0	0
Tommy Warren p4	2	0	0	0	0	0	0
	39	8	12	7	24	6	2

New York Giants	AB	R	H	I	PO	A	E
Johnny Rucker cf	7	3	2	0	3	0	0
George Hausmann 2b	5	2	1	2	1	3	0
Mel Ott rf	2	6	2	1	2	0	0
Joe Medwick lf	4	5	2	1	0	0	0
Phil Weintraub 1b	5	5	4	11	11	1	0
>Ernie Lombardi c	5	1	3	7	5	0	0
Hugh Luby 3b	4	0	1	2	0	0	0
Buddy Kerr ss	5	2	1	1	5	3	1
Cliff Melton p	2	0	0	0	0	2	1
Harry Feldman p4	3	2	2	1	0	1	0
	42	26	18	26	27	10	2

Brooklyn	IP	H	R	ER	BB	SO
R. Melton L,0-1	1	2	3	3	3	1
Webber	.1	1	4	4	4	1
Zachary	0	0	0	0	2	0
Ostermueller	1.2	2	4	4	2	1
Warren	5	13	15	11	6	2
	8	18	26	11	17	5

New York	IP	H	R	ER	BB	SO
C. Melton	3.1	7	7	3	0	2
Feldman W,1-1	5.2	5	1	1	4	3
	9	12	8	4	4	5

Brooklyn	2 0 0	5 0 0	1 0 0	- 8
New York	3 4 4	5 0 2	0 8 x	-26

OB: Brooklyn 8, New York 10
DP: Feldman-Kerr-Weintraub (Bragan) Hausmann-Kerr-Weintraub (Warren)
2B: Weintraub 2, Owen, Rucker, Lombardi 2, P. Waner, Feldman, Hausmann, Medwick
3B: Rucker, Weintraub
HR: Schultz 2(4), Kerr(1), Weintraub(1)
SB: Schultz, Hart, Ott
SO: Bordagaray, Hart, Bragan 2, Jarvis, Rucker 2, Hausmann, Kerr, Melton

BB: Schultz, Hart 2, Owen, Hausmann, Ott 5, Lombardi 2, Weintraub 2, Medwick 3, Luby 2, Kerr, Feldman
SH: Hausmann
WP: R. Melton, Warren, C. Melton
TIME: 2:58
ATTENDANCE: 58,068 (52,037 paid)
UMPIRES: Beans Reardon, Tom Dunn, Larry Goetz
SOURCES: New York Herald-Tribune, Post, Times, World-Telegram

---

BALANCE	OUT+R+OB=BP=AB+BB+SH+HP+CI
Brooklyn	27 8 8 43 39 4 0 0 0
New York	24 26 10 60 42 17 1 0 0

Red's Frugality Frustrates Reds

110. Pitcher Throws 58 Pitches in Nine-Inning Shutout; Teams Complete Night Game in 1 Hour, 15 Minutes

BOSTON   at   CINCINNATI
(Braves, 2)   (Reds, 0)

Thursday Night, August 10, 1944, Crosley Field

Charles "Red" Barrett was a red-headed, right-handed hurler toiling in just his second full major-league season. An eccentric personality with average pitching talent, Red excelled in the arena of building team morale with his constant clowning and joking. The Cincinnati Reds didn't find him too funny this day, however, when Barrett threw only *58 pitches over nine innings* for a shutout victory. As far as baseball historians know, this is the *fewest number of pitches ever thrown in a nine-inning game.* Throughout the contest, Barrett didn't fall behind in the count to a single batter,* surrendered just two singles, and neither walked nor struck out anyone. When the *game was completed in only one hour and fifteen minutes*, it also established the still-standing mark as the *fastest night game in major league history.*

A Reds castoff, Barrett out-pitched his more publicized opponent, Bucky Walters. Only two Cincinnati players reached first safely — Gee Walker singled with two out in the first, and Eddie Miller singled to lead off the sixth. Miller was the only Red who got as far as second. Barrett induced 13 ground outs, five fly balls, three pop-ups in fair territory, four foul outs, and two line-drive outs.

The Boston victory resulted from two tainted runs. Butch Nieman opened the second frame with sharp grounder that scooted through Woody Williams' legs. Frank Grayson, official scorer this night, charitably accorded a single on the play. Two infield outs moved Butch to third from whence he

scored on a Damon Phillips single. Boston scored their second run when, with one out in the fifth, Phillips doubled over center fielder Gee Walker's head. Whitey Wietelmann then lifted a high fly to deep right field which dropped for a three-base error, as

Barrett thrived on working quickly.

---

* *"Braves Put Whitewash on Reds, 2–0,"* Boston Post, *11 August 1944, p. 10, col. 5.*

Cincinnati's Tony Criscola tripped and fell while ascending the outfield terrace.

In recent years, Barrett's performance was clouded in mystery. His 58-pitch legacy had been passed down through the record books, but its source documentation became lost, leading some historians to question its plausibility. During research for this chapter, the evidence was re-discovered. In his column the day after the contest, *Cincinnati Times-Star* reporter Frank Grayson wrote: "[Barrett] pitched just 58 balls in the course of the game." Making the claim all the more believable is the fact that Grayson also served as the official scorer that night.

Barrett's teammate, Damon Phillips, remembered him as the fastest working pitcher he ever played behind. In a letter written to the author, Phillips related that the less time Red spent between pitches, the bet-ter he pitched: "The catcher knew that when he returned a pitch to Red that he wanted a sign for the next pitch as soon as the ball reached Red's glove. As an infielder it was great to play behind him because there was no wasted time and the fielders had to stay ready for action. He had pin-point control and could throw strikes with consistency."

Barrett broke into the majors with Cincinnati before joining the Braves in 1943. Then, on May 23, 1945, Red was shipped to the Cardinals where for one partial season he enjoyed brilliant success, recording 21 wins against only 9 losses. Combining his efforts in both Boston and St. Louis, Red led the league in wins (23), complete games (24), and innings pitched (285). After that, he returned to mediocrity and finished his career back in Boston with a 69–69 lifetime log.

Boston Braves	AB	R	H	I	PO	A	E
Max Macon lf	4	0	0	0	3	0	0
Tommy Holmes cf	4	0	2	0	2	0	0
Chuck Workman 3b	3	0	0	0	0	2	0
Butch Nieman rf	4	1	1	0	1	0	0
Stew Hofferth c	4	0	0	0	2	0	0
Buck Etchison 1b	3	0	0	0	14	2	0
Damon Phillips ss	4	1	3	1	1	2	0
>Whitey Wietelmann 2b	4	0	0	0	2	4	0
Red Barrett p	3	0	0	0	2	2	0
	33	2	6	1	27	12	0

Cincinnati Reds	AB	R	H	I	PO	A	E
Woody Williams 2b	4	0	0	0	0	4	0
>Tony Criscola rf	4	0	0	0	2	0	1
Gee Walker cf	3	0	1	0	6	0	0
Frank McCormick 1b	3	0	0	0	12	1	0
Ray Mueller c	3	0	0	0	1	1	0
Eric Tipton lf	3	0	0	0	1	0	0
Steve Mesner 3b	3	0	0	0	1	1	0
Eddie Miller ss	3	0	1	0	3	2	0
Bucky Walters p	2	0	0	0	1	3	0
Estel Crabtree ph9	1	0	0	0	0	0	0
	29	0	2	0	27	12	1

Boston	IP	H	R	ER	BB	SO
Barrett W,7-11	9	2	0	0	0	0

Cincinnati	IP	H	R	ER	BB	SO
Walters L,16-6	9	6	2	1	1	1

Boston	0 1 0	0 1 0	0 0 0	- 2
Cincinnati	0 0 0	0 0 0	0 0 0	- 0

OB: Boston 6, Cincinnati 2
2B: Phillips, Holmes
SO: Barrett
BB: Etchison
SH: Workman
TIME: 1:15
ATTENDANCE: 7,783

UMPIRES: Jocko Conlan, George Barr, Ziggy Sears
SOURCES: Boston Globe, Herald, Post, Record; Cincinnati Enquirer, Post, Times-Star; Dayton Daily Herald, Daily News

----

BALANCE	OUT	+	R	+	OB	-	BP	=	AB	+	BB	+	SH	+	HP	+	CI
Boston	27		2		6		35		33		1		1		0		0
Cincinnati	27		0		2		29		29		0		0		0		0

Indians Win Unassisted

111. Team Records No Assists in Nine-Inning Game

NEW YORK   at   CLEVELAND
(Yankees, 2)   (Indians, 4)

Wednesday, July 4, 1945, League Park

In the first game of an Independence Day doubleheader, the host Cleveland Indians provided an aberration that had never before been seen in major-league history when they *fielded in all nine innings without getting a single assist.* (The St. Louis Browns had not had an assist in a 1943 game but fielded only eight innings.) This standard has been tied twice since (see 6-25-89 and 9-11-95).

Fifteen drives were pulled down by Tribe outfielders. Catcher Frankie Hayes caught two pop ups, the infielders snared six air balls, and pitcher Steve Gromek fanned four.

The Yankees even scored both of their runs on fly balls. Bud Metheny opened the seventh with a single. Cleveland outfielders Felix Mackiewicz and Paul O'Dea then gifted New York's Russ Derry with a single as they permitted a routine fly to drop between them.Two batters later, Bill Drescher lofted one deep enough for Metheny to score the first visitor's run. (Rules of the day credited Drescher with an RBI but no sacrifice.) The second Yankee tally also resulted from a fly ball — this one into the seats by Derry in the ninth.

It was a strange game in other ways as well. Thanks to ample walks, the Indians needed but two hits in scoring all four of their runs. With two outs in the second, Hayes walked and scored on Mackiewicz's double. In the fourth inning, Cleveland tallied three more runs on a like number of walks followed by Al Cihocki's double and pitcher Gromek's sacrifice bunt.

The side-arming Gromek provided the Tribe with excellent hurling throughout the season, finishing third in the league in wins at 19–9, and second only to Hal Newhouser in winning percentage. He was 5–0 against the Yankees this year, and only twice in a total of 30 starts did he fail to pitch at least six innings. Steve had a propensity for retiring batters on fly balls, a dangerous habit for a hurler in League Park with its 290-foot right field wall. Nevertheless, while the rest of the Cleveland staff was supported with well over 11 assists per game, Gromek needed his fielders for less than nine.

Gromek had the Yankees swinging under the ball.

FIRST GAME

New York Yankees	AB	R	H	I	PO	A	E
Snuffy Stirnweiss 2b	3	0	0	0	3	6	0
Frankie Crosetti ss	4	0	0	0	1	2	0
Hersh Martin lf	4	0	1	0	1	0	0
Nick Etten 1b	4	0	0	0	12	1	0
Bud Metheny rf	4	1	2	0	0	0	0
Russ Derry cf	4	1	3	1	3	0	0
Oscar Grimes 3b	4	0	0	0	0	2	0
Bill Drescher c	4	0	1	1	3	1	0
Hank Borowy p	2	0	1	0	1	1	0
Mike Milosevich ph7	1	0	0	0	0	0	0
Ken Holcombe p7	0	0	0	0	0	0	0
> Tuck Stainback ph9	1	0	0	0	0	0	0
	35	2	8	2	24	13	0

Cleveland Indians	AB	R	H	I	PO	A	E
Dutch Meyer 2b	4	0	0	0	2	0	0
Mickey Rocco 1b	4	0	0	0	2	0	0
Paul O'Dea rf	4	0	0	0	3	0	0
Jeff Heath lf	2	1	1	0	8	0	0
>Lou Boudreau ss	3	0	1	0	1	0	0
Frankie Hayes c	1	2	0	0	6	0	0
Felix Mackiewicz cf	2	1	1	1	4	0	0
Al Cihocki 3b	3	0	1	2	1	0	0
Steve Gromek p	2	0	1	1	0	0	0
	25	4	5	4	27	0	0

New York	IP	H	R	ER	BB	SO
Borowy L,9-5	6	4	4	4	5	1
Holcombe	2	1	0	0	0	1
	8	5	4	4	5	2

Cleveland	IP	H	R	ER	BB	SO
Gromek W,9-4	9	8	2	2	1	4

New York	0 0 0	0 0 0	1 0 1	– 2
Cleveland	0 1 0	3 0 0	0 0 x	– 4

OB: New York 7, Cleveland 4
DP: Crosetti-Stirnweiss-Etten (Mackiewicz)
2B: Mackiewicz, Cihocki, Gromek
HR: Derry(6)
CS: Heath
SO: Stirnweiss, Derry, Grimes, Stainback, Meyer, Cihocki
BB: Stirnweiss, Heath 2, Hayes 2, Mackiewicz
SH: Boudreau, Gromek

TIME: 1:45
ATTENDANCE: 24,625
UMPIRES: Jim Boyer, Red Jones, Bill Summers
SOURCES: Cleveland Plain Dealer, Press; DBD; New York Daily News; Herald-Tribune, Times; Sporting News

BALANCE	OUT+R+OB=BP=AB+BB+SH+HP+CI							
New York	27	2	7	36	35	1	0	0	0
Cleveland	24	4	4	32	25	5	2	0	0

Boudreau Gets Shifty with Williams

112. Player Gets Five Extra-Base Hits in One Game

CLEVELAND   at   BOSTON
(Indians, 10,4)   (Red Sox, 11,6)

Sunday, July 14, 1946, Fenway Park

On this date the Boston Red Sox were enjoying one of their greatest seasons. Riding the wave of a .712 winning percentage, they were leading their arch-rivals, the second place Yankees, by nine games. The Cleveland Indians, meanwhile, were in sixth place, struggling to exit the second division. As a near capacity crowd of 31,984 packed

Boudreau barked out shift signals to his fielders.

Fenway Park for the Sunday doubleheader, two future Hall of Famers were about to occupy center stage in a memorable baseball drama.

Ted Williams, "The Splendid Splinter," was only five days removed from a prolific All-Star Game played in this same Fenway Park. In leading his team to a 12–0 thrashing of the National League, Ted collected a walk, two singles, and two home runs while scoring four times and driving home five. One of those homers was the much celebrated blast off Rip Sewell's looping "eephus" pitch.

The extraordinary had become expected of Williams, and the first game of this day's doubleheader provided more of the same. When Ted, a dead pull-hitter, stepped to the plate for the first time, he faced an expected unorthodox Cleveland defense. For some time, the Indians had been stationing their first baseman, second baseman, and shortstop all between first and second base whenever Williams batted. Despite the inviting open space on the left side of the infield, Ted had refused to hit or bunt in that direction. The strategy worked for Cleveland as Williams sent a line drive toward what would have been the hole between first and second. But with three infielders jammed between the sacks, second baseman Jack Conway had little trouble snaring the scorcher. Despite the shift, it was the only time Williams was retired in this game.

By the time Ted batted again in the third, the Indians had forged a 5–0 lead, but the Sox had loaded the bases. Williams rendered the shift moot as he plastered Steve Gromek's second pitch, a fastball, over the Cleveland bullpen, bringing his team to within a run. When Ted led off the fifth facing Don Black, the Tribe was leading by an 8–6 margin. This time he clobbered a first-pitch change-up beyond the Boston bullpen, again pulling his team to within one run. In the seventh, Williams singled and scored his third run, cutting the Indians' lead to 10–8. That's how it stood when, in the eighth, Ted stepped to the plate with two outs and two mates aboard. Joe Berry, the third Cleveland hurler, started Ted with two wide ones and then tried to sneak a curve ball over the plate. Williams got around on it quickly and pulled the ball into the right field seats just inside the foul marker for his third homer of the game. It also gave Boston an 11–10 lead which endured the final frame.

Williams' three home runs and eight RBIs overshadowed a remarkable offensive performance by Cleveland's player-manager Lou Boudreau. Lou provided his club with plenty of offense beginning in the first inning when he clouted a three-run home run. In his next four plate appearances he doubled each time, resulting in a day's production of five extra-base hits, four RBIs and three runs scored.

The five extra-base hits set a modern major-league, single-game mark (since tied many times). It wasn't enough, however, to offset The Splendid Splinter.

While Boudreau's hitting heroics were confined to the opener, his revolutionary strategy in the vesper game etched itself in baseball memories and books forever. Williams led off the second inning facing the unorthodox defense he had come to expect. Nonetheless, he blistered a line drive off first baseman Jimmy Wasdell's glove into the right-field corner for a double and eventually scored. Boudreau must have been frustrated and desperate, just the type of mood that precipitates extraordinary creativity. How could they get this guy out?

As Williams approached the plate the following inning, there was commotion on the field as well as in the stands. The fans and the Red Sox players including Williams were laughing, but Boudreau was dead serious as he began moving his fielders into an even more exaggerated shift than most fans had ever seen. Now the third baseman, Ken Keltner, was stationed to the right of second base on the edge of the outfield grass. Shortstop Boudreau also played on the outfield fringe, midway between first and second. First baseman Wasdell was positioned in the outfield grass about six feet from the right-field foul line and about 35 feet behind the bag. Second baseman Jack Conway became an extra right fielder playing shallow and about 25 feet off the line. Right and center fielders Hank Edwards and Pat Seerey stood on the lip of the right and right-center field warning track. That left one man, left fielder George Case, to cover all the territory to the left of second base in both the infield and outfield! Case played what might be called "deep shortstop." Several newspapers termed it the "C" (for Cleveland) formation.

Williams could have easily singled, or perhaps even doubled, simply by pushing a ball to the left side of the diamond. But Ted spurned hitting or bunting to left, and Cleveland's strategy paid off as he grounded out to Boudreau on the first pitch from Red Embree. In the sixth inning, the exaggerated shift was again installed but for naught as Ted walked on four straight pitches. During this at-bat Williams toyed with his opponents by threatening to bunt. For his final plate appearance in the seventh frame, the Indians reverted to their standard shift because at the time there were Red Sox on first and second. The exaggerated shift would have promoted a double steal. Ted negated the effects of any shift by walking for his 97th time in the season.

After the game, Boudreau declared: "It's no gag. What can you do with a guy like that? I never saw Babe Ruth, but he couldn't have been any tougher. Williams doesn't bunt or hit to left very well, and I figure he's got to hit the ball out of the park against that lineup [his shift]."*

Ted Williams was not the first batsman to face such a defensive alignment. Another player named Williams, Cy Williams, while with the Phillies during the 1920s, was also confronted with such extremes. Like his later namesake, Cy also was a thinly built, extreme pull-hitter. Bill McKechnie, current Cincinnati manager, recalled that when Cy came to bat, the defensive team simply forgot that third base and left field existed. "The first baseman and right fielder hugged the line. The second baseman moved close to first base and the center fielder pulled over into normal rightfield. The shortstop played where the second baseman normally stands and the left fielder moved into the center fielder's spot. The third baseman played like the shortstop usually does for a left-handed, right-field hitter."†

Boston continued on a path to their first American League title in 28 years, finishing 17 games ahead of the third-place Yankees and 12 in front of the runner-up Tigers. Alas, they lost by one run in the seventh game of the World Series to the St. Louis Cardinals who also employed a version of the "Boudreau Shift." Williams was five for 25 in that series.

*Frank Gibbons, "Tribe's 'Shift' Halts Williams, But Too Late," Cleveland Press, 14 July 1946, p. 18, col. 4.
†Jack Maloney, "Lou Lines Up 'C' Formation," The Sporting News, 24 July 1946, p. 5, col. 5.

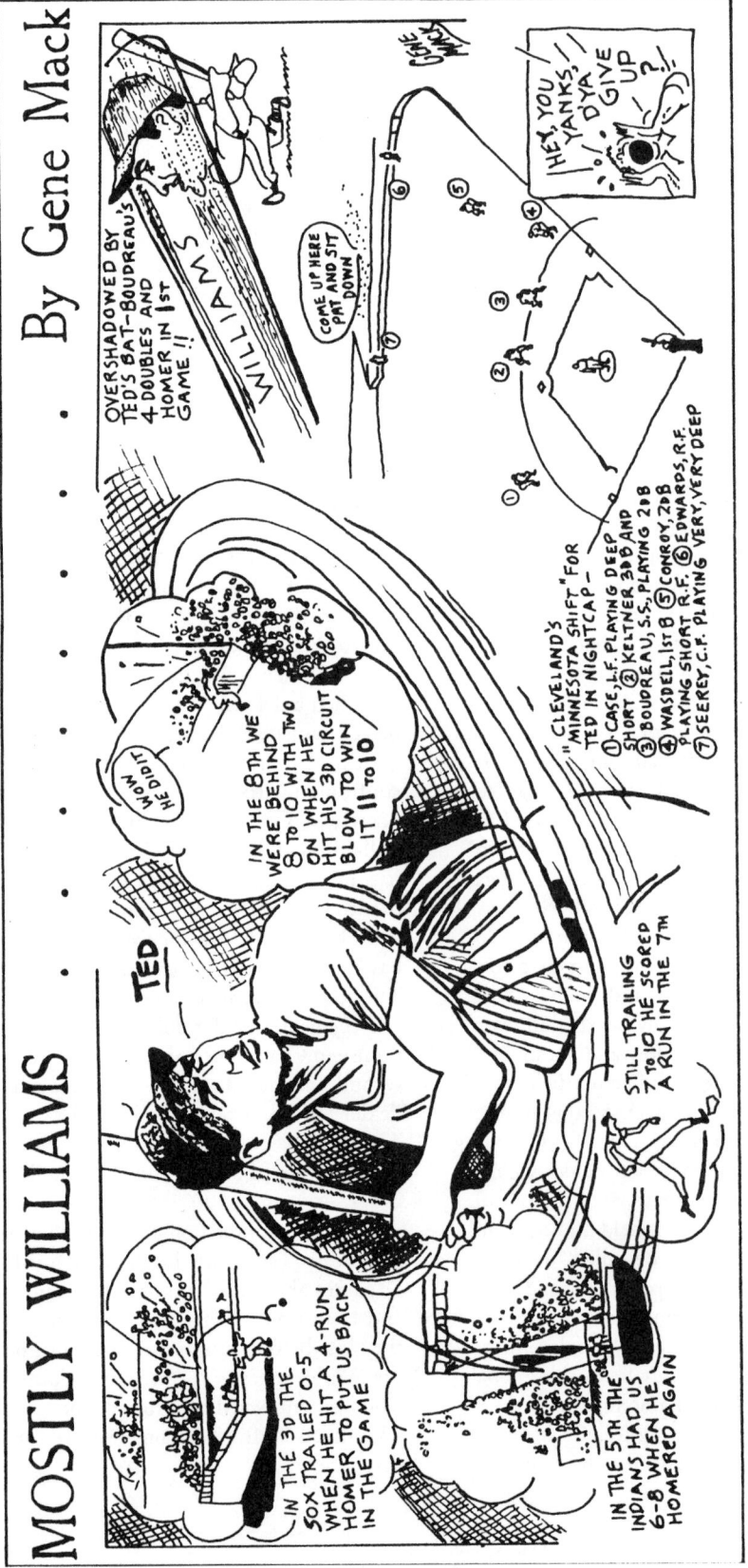

Famed illustrator Gene Mack portrayed the highlights in the Boston Globe (reprinted courtesy of the Boston Globe).

FIRST GAME

Cleveland Indians	AB	R	H	I	PO	A	E
George Case lf	6	1	2	1	3	0	0
Jack Conway 2b	6	0	2	0	5	2	0
Pat Seerey cf	3	2	2	0	0	0	0
>Hank Edwards rf	6	1	1	1	5	0	0
Lou Boudreau ss	5	3	5	4	0	3	1
Ken Keltner 3b	3	1	2	3	1	3	0
Jimmy Wasdell 1b	5	0	1	0	5	1	2
Jim Hegan c	5	2	2	0	5	0	0
Steve Gromek p	2	0	0	0	0	0	0
Don Black p3	2	0	1	1	0	2	0
Joe Berry p7	0	0	0	0	0	0	0
F. Mackiewicz ph9	1	0	0	0	0	0	0
	44	10	18	10	24	11	3

Boston Red Sox	AB	R	H	I	PO	A	E
Leon Culberson rf	5	2	3	0	0	0	0
Johnny Pesky ss	4	2	0	0	1	7	0
Dom DiMaggio cf	5	0	1	0	2	0	0
Ted Williams lf	5	4	4	8	2	0	0
Bobby Doerr 2b	5	1	4	0	6	3	0
>Rudy York 1b	5	0	1	1	11	1	0
Rip Russell 3b	4	0	0	0	1	2	0
Roy Partee c	4	2	3	0	2	0	0
Hal Wagner c9	0	0	0	0	1	0	0
Joe Dobson p	0	0	0	0	0	0	0
Clem Dreisewerd p1	1	0	0	0	0	3	0
Jim Bagby p5	1	0	0	0	1	0	0
Johnny Lazor ph8	1	0	0	0	0	0	0
Tex Hughson p9	0	0	0	0	0	1	0
	40	11	16	9	27	17	0

Cleveland	IP	H	R	ER	BB	SO
Gromek	2.2	6	5	5	1	3
Black	3.1	7	3	2	0	0
Berry L,1-2	2	3	3	0	0	1
	8	16	11	7	1	4

Boston	IP	H	R	ER	BB	SO
Dobson	.2	4	4	4	1	0
Dreisewerd	4	7	4	4	1	1
Bagby W,3-3	3.1	5	2	2	3	1
Hughson	1	2	0	0	0	1
	9	18	10	10	5	3

Cleveland	4 0 1	0 3 1	1 0 0	-10
Boston	0 0 5	1 1 0	1 3 x	-11

OB: Cleveland 12, Boston 7
DP: Wasdell-Conway-Wasdell (York)
    Boudreau-Conway-Wasdell (York)
    Pesky-Doerr-York (Hegan)
2B: Case, Boudreau 4, Hegan, Black, York,
    DiMaggio
3B: Hegan, Conway
HR: Boudreau(5), Keltner(8), Williams 3(26)
SB: Pesky

SO: Case, Gromek, Mackiewicz, Doerr,
    DiMaggio, York, Dreisewerd
BB: Seerey 3, Keltner 2, Pesky
SH: Dreisewerd
TIME: 2:32
UMPIRES: Eddie Rommel, Jim Boyer,
    Bill Grieve

BALANCE	OUT	+	R	+	OB	=	BP	=	AB	+	BB	+	SH	+	HP	+	CI
Cleveland	27		10		12		49		44		5		0		0		0
Boston	24		11		7		42		40		1		1		0		0

SECOND GAME

Cleveland Indians	AB	R	H	I	PO	A	E
George Case lf	5	2	2	1	0	0	0
Jack Conway 2b	1	1	0	0	1	5	0
Pat Seerey cf	4	0	1	0	2	0	0
Hank Edwards rf	5	1	2	1	3	0	0
Lou Boudreau ss	4	0	1	1	3	4	0
>Ken Keltner 3b	4	0	0	0	1	3	0
Jimmy Wasdell 1b	3	0	1	0	12	0	0
Sherm Lollar c	3	0	0	2	2	0	0
Tom Jordan ph8,c	1	0	1	1	0	0	0
Red Embree p	2	0	0	0	0	0	0
Gene Woodling ph7	1	0	0	0	0	0	0
Bob Lemon p7	0	0	0	0	0	3	0
Dutch Meyer ph8	1	0	0	0	0	0	0
Charlie Gassaway p9	0	0	0	0	0	0	0
	34	4	8	4	24	15	0

Boston Red Sox	AB	R	H	I	PO	A	E
Leon Culberson rf	3	0	1	0	0	0	0
Tom McBride ph7,rf	0	0	0	0	1	0	0
Johnny Pesky ss	4	0	2	0	2	2	0
Dom DiMaggio cf	4	0	1	1	5	0	0
Ted Williams lf	2	2	1	0	1	0	0
Bobby Doerr 2b	3	2	1	0	2	1	0
Rudy York 1b	3	1	2	2	2	0	0
Rip Russell 3b	4	0	1	1	3	1	0
>Hal Wagner c	4	0	0	1	11	0	0
Bill Zuber p	2	1	0	0	0	0	0
Boo Ferriss p8	0	0	0	0	0	0	0
	29	6	9	5	27	4	0

Cleveland	IP	H	R	ER	BB	SO
Embree L,6-7	6	7	5	5	3	1
Lemon	1	2	1	1	2	0
Gassaway	1	0	0	0	0	0
	8	9	6	6	5	1

Boston	IP	H	R	ER	BB	SO
Zuber W,2-1	7.2	5	3	3	7	7
Ferriss	1.1	3	1	1	1	3
	9	8	4	4	8	10

```
Cleveland    0 0 1   0 0 0    1 1 1   - 4
Boston       0 3 0   0 0 2    1 0 x   - 6
```

OB: Cleveland 11, Boston 5
DP: Conway-Boudreau-Wasdell(DiMaggio)
    Keltner-Conway-Wasdell(Russell)
    Russell-Doerr-York(Seerey)
2B: Edwards, Russell, Williams
HR: Case(1)
SB: Case, Conway
SO: Seerey 2, Edwards 2, Keltner 2, Lollar,
    Embree, Woodling, Meyer, Pesky
BB: Conway 4, Seerey, Boudreau, Keltner,
    Wasdell, Williams 2, Doerr, York, Zuber

SH: McBride
TIME: 2:12
ATTENDANCE: 31,581 (paid)
UMPIRES: Jim Boyer, Bill Grieve
    Eddie Rommel
SOURCES: Boston Globe, Herald, Post;
    Cleveland Plain Dealer, Press;
    Sporting News

BALANCE	OUT	+R	+OB	=BP	=AB	+BB	+SH	+HP	+CI
Cleveland	27	4	11	42	34	8	0	0	0
Boston	24	6	5	35	29	5	1	0	0

York's Yeomanly Yield

113. Player Hits Two Grand Slams in One Game

BOSTON, AL   at   ST. LOUIS
(Red Sox, 13)   (Browns, 6)

Saturday Night, July 27, 1946, Sportsman's Park

As a 1937 rookie, Rudy York stormed through the American League at a .307 clip, amassing 35 home runs and 103 RBIs. Foremost within that season was a turbulent month of August in which he smashed 18 home runs and drove in 49, both of which remain single-month, major-league standards. The following season, he set another benchmark (which has since been tied) by hammering three grand slams in a single month (May). Rudy enjoyed nine productive years in Detroit but when an aging Hank Greenberg, who was returning from war duty, had to be moved back to his former first-base position, York became expendable. He was then traded to the Red Sox on January 3, 1946, for shortstop Eddie Lake. York

continued his offensive productivity in Boston which culminated on this day as he *became the third major leaguer to smash two grand slams in a single game*. This was to be his only full season with Boston, and despite considerable productivity (17 HR, 117 RBI, .279), he was again traded the following year to the White Sox.

York's day of glory with the Red Sox got off to a blazing start. In the very first inning, after Johnny Pesky had doubled with one out, Ted Williams was purposely passed, setting up a possible double play. York foiled the strategy by doubling off Bob Muncrief, driving home both mates. The next inning, the bases became filled on singles by Wally Moses, Pesky, and another walk to Williams.

York enjoyed the St. Louis hospitality.

score. Trouble again brewed for the Browns' hurler in the seventh, when after Moses had singled, Pesky doubled for the second time. Amid a serenade of boos from the St. Louis fans, Williams was again intentionally walked, loading the sacks. York next ripped a terrific drive into the left field seats near the scoreboard's west light tower, at least 50 feet farther than his first clout. (That blow gave York 84 RBIs on the season.) By the fifth inning then, Rudy had driven home ten runs and was in an ideal position to shatter the all-time standard of 12 RBIs set by Jim Bottomley 22 years earlier. Both of York's remaining plate

York then deposited reliever Tex Shirley's 1–1 pitch into the left field seats, about 400 feet away, for his first grand slam of the day. Shirley walked York in the fourth after Williams had doubled, but the Sox failed to

appearances did come with teammates aboard, but in the seventh he fanned, and in the ninth he grounded into a double play. Below is a summary of York's day of grandeur.

Inning	1	2	4	5	7	9
Outs	1	1	0	1	2	1
Baserunners	Pesky 2nd Williams 1st	Moses 3rd Pesky 2nd Williams 1st	Williams 2nd	Moses 3rd Pesky 2nd Williams 1st	Williams 1st	Pesky 2nd Williams 1st
Pitcher	Muncrief	Shirley	Shirley	Shirley	Ferens	Kinder
York's AB	Double	Home Run	Walk	Home Run	Struck Out	GIDP
Yield	2 RBIs	4 RBIs	—	4 RBIs	—	—

Boston Red Sox	AB	R	H	I	PO	A	E
Wally Moses rf	6	2	2	0	1	0	0
Johnny Pesky ss	5	3	3	1	2	2	0
Ted Williams lf	2	3	2	0	0	0	0
Catfish Metkovich lf	0	0	0	0	2	0	0
>Rudy York 1b	5	3	3	10	10	0	0
Bobby Doerr 2b	4	1	1	1	3	4	0
Dom DiMaggio cf	5	0	0	0	5	0	0
Rip Russell 3b	5	0	2	0	1	4	0
Hal Wagner c	4	1	2	0	3	0	0
Charlie Wagner p	3	0	0	0	0	1	0
Earl Johnson p7	1	0	0	0	0	0	0
	40	13	15	12	27	11	0

St. Louis Browns	AB	R	H	I	PO	A	E
Chuck Stevens 1b	3	0	0	0	9	0	0
Johnny Berardino 2b	3	0	0	0	1	2	1
Bob Dillinger 3b7	0	0	0	0	0	0	0
Vern Stephens ss	3	1	1	0	1	2	0
Johnny Lucadello 2b7	2	0	1	0	1	1	0
>Jeff Heath lf	4	2	1	2	0	0	0
Al Zarilla rf	3	2	2	1	0	0	0
Walt Judnich cf	3	1	2	3	1	0	0
Frank Mancuso c	2	0	0	0	5	0	0
Hank Helf c6	2	0	0	0	6	1	0
Mark Christman 3b,ss7	4	0	0	0	3	4	0
Bob Muncrief p	0	0	0	0	0	1	0
Tex Shirley p2	1	0	1	0	0	0	0
Stan Ferens p5	1	0	0	0	0	0	0
Glenn McQuillen ph7	1	0	0	0	0	0	0
Ellis Kinder p8	0	0	0	0	0	0	0
Babe Dahlgren ph9	1	0	0	0	0	0	0
	33	6	8	6	27	11	1

Boston	IP	H	R	ER	BB	SO
Wagner W,1-0	6.1	7	6	6	5	2
Johnson	2.2	1	0	0	2	1
	9	8	6	6	7	3

St. Louis	IP	H	R	ER	BB	SO
Muncrief L,2-6	1.1	6	7	6	1	1
Shirley	3	7	6	6	4	4
Ferens	2.2	1	0	0	0	3
Kinder	2	1	0	0	3	4
	9	15	13	12	8	12

Boston	4 5 0	0 4 0	0 0 0	-13
St. Louis	0 0 0	3 0 3	0 0 0	- 6

OB: Boston 9, St. Louis 7

DP: Pesky-Doerr-York (Berardino)
Russell-Doerr-York (Christman)
Christman-Lucadello-Stevens (York)

2B: Pesky 2, York, Williams, Russell

3B: Doerr

HR: York 2(13), Heath(7), Zarilla(2), Judnich(12)

SO: Moses 2, Doerr 2, DiMaggio 2, York, Russell, Wagner 3, Johnson, Stevens, Judnich, McQuillen

BB: Pesky, Williams 4(2I), York, …

BB: ... Doerr, H.Wagner, Stevens 2, Dillinger 2, Heath, Zarilla, Judnich

SH: C. Wagner

TIME: 2:22

ATTENDANCE: 13,669

UMPIRES: Bill Summers, Joe Paparella, Red Jones

SOURCES: Boston Globe, Herald, Post; St. Louis Globe-Democrat, Post-Dispatch

BALANCE	OUT+R+OB=BP=AB+BB+SH+HP+CI							
Boston	27	13	9	49	40	8	1	0	0
St. Louis	27	6	7	40	33	7	0	0	0

A Walk on the Wild Side

114. Team Draws 18 Walks in One Game

BOSTON   at   CLEVELAND
(Red Sox, 4)   (Indians, 13)

Thursday Night, May 20, 1948, Municipal Stadium

After only 21 games into the 1948 season, the Cleveland Indians (15–6) had established

themselves as a pennant contender, holding a slim half-game lead over the second place

Philadelphia Athletics. Cleveland's guests this day, the Boston Red Sox (11–13), had yet to hit their stride and were languishing in the second division. The Indians needed a win to solidify their prestigious standing, and the hometown fans turned out in droves to supply encouragement. Not only did they see their team prevail, but they also witnessed one of the more bizarre games in major league history as Boston hurlers *issued 18 bases on balls*, tying a 32-year-old major league record (see 5-09-16). In that 1916 game, however, the Athletics issued 18 walks to the Tigers over nine innings. This day's game deserves special recognition in that Boston dispensed their 18 free passes in only eight frames.

Starting for the Sox was left-handed journeyman Mickey Harris. Mickey had not been especially wild in his four previous major league seasons, walking 152 batters in 535 innings (about 2.5 per 9 innings). But Harris was decisively out of control this day in walk-ing seven batters in only 1⅓ innings. By the time he was relieved by a 19-year-old rookie named Mickey McDermott, also a lefty, the Tribe already led 7–0.

McDermott, a gangling fireballer who was as wild as he was fast, once fanned 25 hitters in a seven-inning, semi-pro game (his catcher dropped four third strikes). McDermott ably continued the burlesque by pitching the final 6⅔ innings, contributing a wild pitch and 11 free passes to the walk-a-thon. After the game, Cleveland player-manager Lou Boudreau claimed he wasn't aware of his team's opportunity to establish a new major-league mark. Had he been, he claimed, he would not have swung at a 3–2 delivery (fly out) to conclude Cleveland's batting in the last of the eighth. Boudreau felt the pitch would have been ball four. One other Cleveland batter, Pat Seerey, felt he also deserved another walk in the eighth when a full-count, high and outside offering was called a third strike rather than ball four.

CLEVELAND BATTERS WHO WALKED, BY INNING, ON MAY 20, 1948

Inning	1st	2nd	3rd	4th	5th	6th	7th	8th
Cleveland Batters Walked	Clark Boudreau Gordon Seerey	Lemon Boudreau(I) Gordon(I)	Clark	Keltner Seerey(I) Hegan Lemon	Robinson	Seerey Tucker	Robinson	Keltner Tucker

Boston's generosity was drenched with irony, for during the 1946, 1947 and 1948 seasons they allowed the second fewest number of bases on balls in the American League. Only the Detroit staff was more miserly in the walk department. This single contest represented 3% of all the walks issued by the Red Sox during the entire season.

Several boxscore anomalies resulted from this rash of free passes. Note that Cleveland's Bob Lemon, Jim Hegan and Ken Keltner each received RBIs without the benefit of a hit. In 1948, according to the on-again, off-again sacrifice fly rule, Keltner was given an RBI courtesy of a fly ball, but no sacrifice fly was credited. And, both Hegan and Lemon walked with the sacks filled in the fourth to garner their RBIs. A game total of three Cleveland runners were forced across the plate on bases loaded walks. Every Indian walked at least twice except Hegan, who was busy striking out (three times) while demonstrating the patience to walk but once. Pat Seerey led the parade with three free passes as six Indians scored after having been walked.

One might question the wisdom of Boston manager Joe McCarthy who, despite both of his hurlers' erratic twirling, ordered the bases filled via intentional walks on three different occasions. Harris was the principal victim of this strategy. After having passed five Indians before he had retired a like number, Mickey was twice ordered to walk the high wire in the second frame alone. In that inning both batters who were intentionally passed not only loaded the sacks, but they both eventually scored. McDermott was also ordered to

Southpaw Harris started the burlesque by walking seven.

fill the bases with an intentional walk in the fourth. Seerey was the recipient, and he too scored.

It was also a long night for home plate umpire Ed Hurley. As noted in the *Cleveland Press*, McDermott and his battery mate Birdie Tebbetts complained continually about the ball and strike calls, stimulating a foul mood around home plate.

After a dismal 14–28 record on Memorial Day, the Red Sox sprinted to the finish line, concluding with an identical record (96–58) as the Indians. It was the first time two clubs tied for laurels in an American League regular season. In a dramatic one-game playoff, player-manager Lou Boudreau led the Tribe into the World Series where they vanquished the Braves in six games.

Boston Red Sox	AB	R	H	I	PO	A	E
Dom DiMaggio cf	5	0	1	2	0	1	0
Wally Moses rf	4	0	1	0	2	0	1
Ted Williams lf	5	0	1	2	1	0	0
>Vern Stephens ss	5	0	1	0	3	2	0
Bobby Doerr 2b	2	0	0	0	4	3	0
Billy Goodman 3b	4	0	2	0	0	3	1
Jake Jones 1b	4	0	0	0	5	0	0
Birdie Tebbetts c	2	2	0	0	9	1	0
Mickey Harris p	0	0	0	0	0	1	0
Mickey McDermott p2	4	2	2	0	0	2	0
	35	4	8	4	24	13	2

Cleveland Indians	AB	R	H	I	PO	A	E
Thurman Tucker cf	4	2	2	0	1	0	0
Allie Clark lf	3	1	2	3	1	0	0
>Lou Boudreau ss	4	2	1	1	0	2	0
Eddie Robinson 1b	3	1	1	2	15	1	0
Joe Gordon 2b	3	2	1	1	1	5	0
Ken Keltner 3b	3	1	0	1	0	4	0
Pat Seerey rf	2	1	1	2	2	0	0
Jim Hegan c	4	1	0	1	6	0	0
Bob Lemon p	3	2	0	1	1	2	0
	29	13	8	12	27	14	0

Boston	IP	H	R	ER	BB	SO
Harris L,1-3	1.1	4	7	7	7	1
McDermott	6.2	4	6	4	11	6
	8	8	13	11	18	7

Cleveland	IP	H	R	ER	BB	SO
Lemon W,4-2	9	8	4	4	5	6

```
Boston       0 0 2   2 0 0   0 0 0   - 4
Cleveland    2 5 0   2 1 1   0 2 x   -13
```

OB: Boston 9, Cleveland 11
DP: Goodman-Doerr-Jones (Keltner)
      Doerr-Stephens-Jones (Gordon)
2B: Robinson, McDermott, Goodman
HR: Boudreau(3)
CS: Boudreau
SO: D. DiMaggio, Moses, Williams,
      Jones 3, Tucker 2, Gordon,
      Seerey, Hegan 3
BB: Moses, Doerr 2, Tebbetts 2,
      Tucker 2, Clark 2, Boudreau 2(1I)
      Robinson 2, Gordon 2(1I), …

BB: … Keltner 2, Seerey 3(1I),
      Hegan, Lemon 2
SH: Clark
WP: McDermott
TIME: 2:33
ATTENDANCE: 43,158
UMPIRES: Ed Hurley, Bill Grieve,
      Charlie Berry
SOURCES: Boston Globe, Herald, Post;
      Cleveland Plain Dealer, Press

BALANCE	OUT	+R	+OB	=BP	=AB	+BB	+SH	+HP	+CI
Boston	27	4	9	40	35	5	0	0	0
Cleveland	24	13	11	48	29	18	1	0	0

Pat Sears the A's

115. Player Hits Four
Home Runs in 11-Inning Game

CHICAGO, AL   at   PHILADELPHIA
(White Sox, 12)   (Athletics, 11)

Sunday, July 18, 1948, Shibe Park

Pat Seerey, a slugging, right-handed hitting heavyweight, had joined Chicago via a trade with Cleveland on June 2 of this year. Affectionately referred to by the Chicago Press as "Fat Pat,"* "Mr. Five by Five,"† and "the portly member of the White Sox ensemble,"§ the 25-year-old Seerey had opened some eyes with an astonishing strikeout ratio while still with the Indians. In his first full season, 1944, Pat led the league by fanning

*John Hoffman, "Pat's 4 homers give Sox 12–11 win," Chicago Sun-Times, 19 July 1948, p. 60, col. 3
†"Sox Seerey Hits Four Homers," Chicago Herald-Examiner, 19 July 1948, Sports section, p. 1, col. 1.
§Irving Vaughan, "4 Homers by Seerey take 1st, 12 to 11," Chicago Tribune, 19 July 1948, Sports section, p. 1, col. 8.

A ball's-eye view of Seerey as depicted in The Evening Bulletin.

99 times in only 342 official at-bats. This was the same season in which the Yankees' Nick Etten had led the league in homers (22) while striking out only 29 times. Seerey followed with similar futility during his next two seasons, again leading the league despite playing less than full time. Before the days of Gorman Thomas, Dave Kingman, and Rob Deer, Pat was a strikeout artist ahead of his time. But the 1948 Sox were desperate for power. As a team, they had hit only 53 circuit blasts a year earlier, and had said goodbye to their leading long-ball hitter, Rudy York, whose skills were quickly dissipating. Thus Seerey was inserted into the lineup, usually in the clean-up position. This day, in the first game of a doubleheader, Pat did just that—clean up. In addition to smashing a game-winning circuit clout, he drove in seven runs and became only the fifth man in major league history to hit four home runs in a game.

Seerey's heroics took just eight pitches. His first, second, and fourth homers were launched on the first pitch, while his third round-tripper came on a 2–2 count. Each was a titanic blast. Here's how Pat's record-tying day unfolded:

• Against A's starter Carl Scheib, Pat struck out leading off the second inning.

• In the fourth, with nobody on, Seerey rocketed Scheib's first delivery out of the stadium, clearing the left-field roof. The ball touched nothing from the time it hit the bat until it landed on Somerset Street reminding Philadelphia fans of a bygone Jimmie Foxx era.

• Pat's second blast, in the fifth frame, also came off Scheib's initial offering. This one bounced on top of the left-field tar paper before disappearing from sight. Teammate Don Kolloway had been on third after tripling.

• By the time Seerey again stepped to the plate in the sixth, Scheib had been relieved by Bob Savage. Pat became the eighth and final batter that Savage faced. With two mates aboard and a 2–2 count, Seerey parked the next ball again on the left-field roof, sending Savage off to join Scheib. This blast didn't have quite the impetus of his first two blows and bounced back onto the playing field.

• Seerey then came to bat in the seventh against Charlie Harris and fouled out to catcher Mike Guerra. Harris became the first A's hurler to escape Seerey's home run touch.

• With the score knotted at 11–11 in the ninth, Joe Coleman, fourth Philadelphia hurler of the day, wisely walked Seerey.

• After two were down in the top of the eleventh and the score still tied at 11, Seerey found a Lou Brissie offering to his liking and

Free-swinging Pat Seerey

lofted it into the upper deck seats in left. It was his shortest hit of the day, but nevertheless, the game winner.

This had not been the first time that Seerey electrified fans with a long ball demonstration. While with Cleveland in a 1945 game at Yankee Stadium, Pat had launched three home runs and a triple. But the strikeouts always came back to haunt him, and then Indians coach, Rogers Hornsby, gave up while attempting to turn him into an efficient slugger.

In the second game this day's doubleheader, called after five because of a Pennsylvania curfew law, Seerey was 0 for 2. Six days later, Pat struck a less glorious note when he became the first major leaguer to strike out seven times in a doubleheader.

FIRST GAME

Chicago White Sox	AB	R	H	I	PO	A	E
Don Kolloway 2b	7	2	5	3	5	2	0
Tony Lupien 1b	7	1	1	0	8	2	0
Luke Appling 3b	7	1	3	1	2	5	0
Pat Seerey lf	6	4	4	7	3	0	0
Aaron Robinson c	6	0	3	0	4	1	0
>Taffy Wright rf	6	0	2	0	0	0	0
Dave Philley cf	6	1	2	0	5	0	0
Cass Michaels ss	6	3	4	0	6	3	1
Frank Papish p	0	0	0	0	0	1	0
Glen Moulder p2	1	0	0	0	0	0	0
Ralph Hodgin ph4	1	0	0	0	0	0	0
Earl Caldwell p4	0	0	0	0	0	0	0
Floyd Baker ph6	1	0	0	1	0	0	0
Howie Judson p6	3	0	0	0	0	0	0
Marino Pieretti p11	0	0	0	0	0	0	0
	57	12	24	12	33	14	1

Philadelphia Athletics	AB	R	H	I	PO	A	E
Eddie Joost ss	7	4	4	5	1	2	0
Barney McCosky lf	2	2	1	1	3	1	0
Don White cf	4	1	2	0	2	0	0
Lou Brissie p10	0	0	0	0	0	0	0
Sam Chapman ph11	0	0	0	0	0	0	0
Billy DeMars pr11	0	0	0	0	0	0	0
>Ferris Fain 1b	5	0	0	2	13	0	0
Hank Majeski 3b	5	0	1	1	0	3	0
Elmer Valo rf	3	0	1	0	4	0	0
Buddy Rosar c	3	0	0	0	5	0	0
Mike Guerra c5	3	0	0	0	3	0	0
Pete Suder 2b	5	2	1	0	2	1	0
Carl Scheib p	1	1	0	0	0	4	0
Bob Savage p5	1	0	0	0	0	0	0
Charlie Harris p6	1	1	1	0	0	0	1
Joe Coleman p8	0	0	0	0	0	0	0
Ray Coleman ph9,cf	2	0	1	0	0	0	0
	42	11	12	9	33	11	1

Chicago	IP	H	R	ER	BB	SO
Papish	1	3	5	4	4	0
Moulder	2	0	0	0	0	1
Caldwell	2	4	2	2	1	1
Judson W,2-3	5.2	5	4	4	7	2
Pieretti	.1	0	0	0	0	0
	11	12	11	10	12	4

Philadephia	IP	H	R	ER	BB	SO
Scheib	4.2	9	4	4	1	2
Savage	1	5	5	5	1	0
Harris	1.2	4	2	1	0	0
J. Coleman	1.2	2	0	0	1	1
Brissie L,9-7	2	4	1	1	0	1
	11	24	12	11	3	4

Chicago   0 0 1   1 2 5   2 0 0   0 1   –12
Philadelphia 1 4 0   1 1 0   4 0 0   0 0   –11

OB: Chicago 15, Philadelphia 14
DP: McCosky-Rosar (fly ball-Hodgin)
    Kolloway-Michaels-Lupien(Majeski)
2B: Robinson, Wright, Kolloway, Philley,
    Joost 2, Majeski
3B: Kolloway
HR: Seerey 4(11), Joost(13)
SB: Appling
SO: Lupien, Seerey, Judson 2, Rosar, Majeski 2, Suder
BB: Seerey, Robinson, Wright, Suder, McCosky 4,
    Chapman, Fain 2, Majeski, Valo 2, Scheib

SH: McCosky, White 2
HP: By Papish (Valo)
WP: Papish, Moulder, Savage
BK: Judson
TIME: 3:44
ATTENDANCE: 17,296
UMPIRES: Eddie Hurley, Charlie Berry, Bill Grieve
SOURCES: Chicago Herald-Examiner, Sun-Times,
    Tribune; Philadelphia Evening Bulletin, Inquirer

BALANCE	OUT+R+OB=BP=AB+BB+SH+HP+CI
Chicago	33 12 15 60 57 3 0 0 0
Philadelphia	33 11 14 58 42 12 3 1 0

Indian Massacre

116. Fourteen Teammates Get at Least One Hit in Nine-Inning Game

CLEVELAND   at   ST. LOUIS
(Indians, 26)   (Browns, 3)

Thursday, August 12, 1948, Sportsman's Park

Although the residents of St. Louis lived on the western limits of baseball civilization, Indian attacks had become just a nightmare of the past, that is until the 1948 version arrived.

The American League entry on the Mississippi sported a history of exploitation. Rarely finishing in the first division since their 1902 inaugural campaign, the Browns were closing out a half-century of incompetence before their move to Baltimore. This was a classic Browns club, one that would etch its name into the record books several times over the next few years as the victim of massacres. This day was just such a case as rookie southpaw Gene Bearden both pitched and batted his tribe to one of the most lopsided victories in baseball annals, 26–3. In the process, *14 different Indians contributed hits, the most teammates to do so in modern baseball history.* Even the substitutes, who were liberally inserted in the sixth inning, feasted on Browns pitching. Every Indian who stepped to the plate hit safely. This was a St. Louis staff that had been a major source of nourishment for American League batting averages,

leading the circuit in hits, walks, and earned runs allowed in both 1947 and 1948.

The record setter was the second game of a doubleheader. The Browns actually won the opener, 8–4, to climb within percentage points of sixth place, but success was fleeting.

Bearden was staked to a nine-run lead before throwing his first pitch.

The nightcap was decided in the very first inning when the Indians forced three different St. Louis hurlers to run the gauntlet while scoring nine times. After that it was simply a matter of how many and by how much. The Indians continued to pound away, totalling 27 hits and 25 runs through the first seven frames. With two innings left to bat, they had an excellent opportunity to shatter two other modern records — the Giants' 31 hits (see 6-09-01) and the Cardinals' 28 runs scored (see 7-06-29). But the Browns' Karl Drews, freshly claimed on waivers from the Yankees, muffed their smoking bats, allowing just two hits and one run over the final two stanzas.

Cleveland's bountiful hit harvest was no fluke, for in 1948 they led the major leagues in that department, averaging nearly 10 hits per game. That offensive fire power, coupled with the pitching of Bearden, Lemon, and Feller, carried them to their last World's Championship to date.

SECOND GAME

Cleveland Indians	AB	R	H	I	PO	A	E
Dale Mitchell lf	6	3	3	2	0	0	0
Walt Judnich rf6	1	1	1	1	2	0	0
Hal Peck rf,lf6	6	4	4	3	3	0	0
Lou Boudreau ss	5	2	3	4	2	3	0
Eddie Robinson 1b	7	2	2	2	9	0	0
Joe Gordon 2b	3	1	3	1	0	2	0
Bob Kennedy pr6,2b	2	2	1	0	2	2	0
Larry Doby cf	5	2	1	2	5	0	0
Thurman Tucker cf6	2	0	1	0	0	0	0
Ken Keltner 3b	5	1	1	2	0	0	0
> Allie Clark 3b6	2	0	1	1	1	1	0
Jim Hegan c	4	4	3	1	2	0	0
Joe Tipton c6	1	0	1	1	1	1	0
Gene Bearden p	6	4	4	4	0	3	0
Bob Feller p8	0	0	0	0	0	0	0
	55	26	29	24	27	12	0

St. Louis Browns	AB	R	H	I	PO	A	E
Bob Dillinger 3b	3	0	0	0	1	1	0
Paul Lehner cf	3	0	0	0	5	0	0
Jerry Priddy 2b	2	0	0	0	1	1	0
Andy Anderson 2b5	2	1	1	0	0	2	1
Don Lund lf	4	2	2	0	4	0	0
Hank Arft 1b	3	0	2	0	8	0	0
Dick Kokos rf	4	0	1	3	1	0	0
Roy Partee c	3	0	1	0	4	0	0
Al Zarilla ph9	1	0	0	0	0	0	0
Eddie Pellagrini ss	0	0	0	0	0	0	0
Sam Dente ss2	4	0	0	0	3	4	0
Fred Sanford p	0	0	0	0	0	0	0
Frank Biscan p1	0	0	0	0	0	0	0
Al Widmar p1	1	0	0	0	0	0	0
Bryan Stephens p4	1	0	0	0	0	0	0
Karl Drews p8	1	0	0	0	0	1	0
> Joe Schultz ph9	1	0	0	0	0	0	0
	33	3	7	3	27	9	1

Cleveland	IP	H	R	ER	BB	SO
Bearden W,11-3	7	4	1	1	2	2
Feller	2	3	2	2	1	0
	9	7	3	3	3	2

St. Louis	IP	H	R	ER	BB	SO
Sanford L,8-14	.2	5	5	5	0	1
Biscan	0	3	4	4	1	0
Widmar	2.2	9	6	5	1	2
Stephens	3.2	10	10	8	4	1
Drews	2	2	1	1	0	0
	9	29	26	23	6	4

Cleveland	9 0 4	2 4 3	3 1 0	-26
St. Louis	0 0 0	1 0 0	0 0 2	- 3

OB: Cleveland 8, St. Louis 6
DP: Dente-Priddy-Arft (Keltner)
    Dente-Arft (Clark)
2B: Peck 2, Keltner, Arft, Hegan, Mitchell
3B: Robinson
HR: Bearden(2), Doby(9), Hegan(12), Judnich(2)
SB: Mitchell, Peck, Doby, Hegan
SO: Robinson, Doby, Hegan, Bearden, Kokos, Widmar
BB: Peck, Boudreau 2, Gordon 2, ...

BB: ... Hegan(I), Dillinger, Lehner, Arft
WP: Widmar, Stephens
PB: Partee
TIME: 2:23
ATTENDANCE: 12,877 (11,727 paid)
UMPIRES: Eddie Rommel, Art Passarella, Johnny Stevens
SOURCES: Cleveland Plain Dealer, Press; St. Louis Globe-Democrat, Post-Dispatch

---

BALANCE	OUT+R+OB=BP+AB+BB+SH+HP+CI
Cleveland	27 26 8 61 55 6 0 0 0
St. Louis	27 3 6 36 33 3 0 0 0

---

117. Team Scores Nine Runs Before Making Their First Out

NEW YORK, NL   at   PHILADELPHIA
(Giants, 7)   (Blue Jays, 12)

Friday Night, August 13, 1948, Shibe Park

The Philadelphia National League franchise was undergoing a metamorphosis. In November of 1943, the club had been purchased by the Carpenter family, who sought to transform the doormat that had finished in either seventh or eighth place, twenty-four of their last twenty-nine seasons including 15 of the last 16. To help the Quaker City patrons forget this ugly past, Bob Carpenter initiated a contest to rename the team. The winning sobriquet, the "Blue Jays," was a tough sell, however, and the fans resisted. As the years passed, the press continued to use both Blue Jays and Phillies interchangeably, often within the same sentence. Such was the case in 1948 when the Blue Jays established a *new major league record by scoring nine runs in the first inning before they made their first out*. It's a mark that still stands although it is generally ignored in modern record books.

Carpenter did more than just attempt to change his team's name. One of his initial moves after acquiring the club was to hire family friend and former pitching great, Herb Pennock, to serve as the club's first real general manager. Under Pennock, the farm system began developing quality minor league players. By 1948, as the use of the new nickname waned, the farm system began bearing fruit. This was the rookie season for the likes of Richie Ashburn, Curt Simmons, and Robin Roberts. Although technically not a rookie, Granny Hamner also played in his first full major league season. However, the team that would win the pennant two years later still had some rough edges.

For the season, the club scored the fewest runs per game in the league, and three different managers took the helm during the campaign. This was also an unlikely day for the Jays to establish such a record. It was Friday the 13th, they were in a run-scoring slump, had just lost five straight games, and came to bat in the bottom of the first already trailing, 3–0. Then, an astonishing nine runs scored before anyone made an out. Here's how it unfolded:

• Richie Ashburn led off with a single to center.

• Granny Hamner showed some power when he tripled off the scoreboard in right-center driving home Ashburn.

• Johnny Blatnik knocked in Hamner with a single to center.

• Dick Sisler also singled to right, moving Blatnik to second.

• Bert Haas then blooped a dinky fly into right for a single on which the runners had to hold temporarily, so the bases were then full. With that, New York manager Leo Durocher had enough of his starter Ray Poat and called in rookie Alex Konikowski.

• Eddie Miller greeted Konikowski with a three-run double over the third base bag. That made six straight hits for the Blue Jays.

• Del Ennis, one for his last 27, next hit a roller to shortstop Buddy Kerr who fumbled it, and all hands were safe. All three Philadelphia newspapers as well as the wire services reported this as an error on Kerr. (Coupled with the description of another error on Buddy in the eighth, newspaper boxscores the next day showed a "2" alongside his name in the error column.) But Buddy must have taken the official scorer to dinner that night, because a search of league records will bear testimony to the fact that not only was Ennis

Ashburn made two fabulous catches in addition to scoring three runs.

credited with a hit on this play, but Kerr was charged with no errors in the game.

• Konikowski then issued a free pass to Seminick and one for himself to the showers. The bases were again loaded as Andy Hansen assumed the mound duties for the Giants.

• Nineteen-year-old Curt Simmons helped his own cause by singling to left, driving in both Miller and Ennis. When Bobby Thomson misplayed the ball, Seminick also tallied, and Simmons scampered all the way to third.

• Ashburn, up for the second time in the

New York Giants	AB	R	H	I	PO	A	E
Bill Rigney 2b	5	1	3	2	3	4	0
Whitey Lockman cf	5	1	0	1	5	0	0
Sid Gordon 3b	5	0	1	0	1	1	0
Johnny Mize 1b	4	1	2	1	8	0	0
Willard Marshall rf	4	1	2	1	1	0	0
Walker Cooper c	1	0	0	1	0	0	0
> Wes Westrum c2	4	0	1	0	2	2	0
Bobby Thomson lf	4	1	0	0	2	0	1
Buddy Kerr ss	3	1	1	1	2	4	0
Ray Poat p	0	0	0	0	0	0	0
Alex Konikowski p1	0	0	0	0	0	0	0
Andy Hansen p1	1	0	0	0	0	1	0
Lucky Lohrke ph4	1	0	0	0	0	0	0
Ken Trinkle p4	0	0	0	0	0	0	0
Les Layton ph6	0	1	0	0	0	0	0
Monte Kennedy p6	0	0	0	0	0	0	0
Dave Koslo p6	0	0	0	0	0	0	0
	37	7	10	7	24	12	1

Philadelphia Blue Jays	AB	R	H	I	PO	A	E
Richie Ashburn cf	4	3	3	1	4	0	0
Granny Hamner 2b	4	1	3	1	4	1	0
Johnny Blatnik lf	5	1	2	2	0	0	0
>Dick Sisler 1b	5	1	3	1	11	0	0
Bert Haas 3b	4	1	1	0	0	2	0
Eddie Miller ss	4	1	2	3	0	5	0
Del Ennis rf	4	1	2	0	2	0	0
Andy Seminick c	3	1	0	0	6	0	0
Curt Simmons p	2	1	1	2	0	1	1
Monk Dubiel p6	1	1	0	0	0	0	0
	36	12	17	10	27	9	1

New York	IP	H	R	ER	BB	SO
Poat L,10-7	0	5	5	5	0	0
Konikowski	0	2	3	3	1	0
Hansen	3	3	2	2	0	0
Trinkle	2	2	0	0	0	1
Kennedy	0	0	1	1	2	0
Koslo	3	5	1	1	0	1
	8	17	12	12	3	2

Philadelphia	IP	H	R	ER	BB	SO
Simmons W,6-11	5.1	9	7	5	3	3
Dubiel	3.2	1	0	0	2	2
	9	10	7	5	5	5

New York   3 0 0   0 0 4   0 0 0   - 7
Philadelphia 10 0 0   0 0 1   0 1 x   -12

OB: New York 8, Philadelphia 4
DP: Miller-Hamner-Sisler (Lohrke)
     Gordon-Mize
     Kerr-Rigney-Mize (Blatnik)
     Westrum-Kerr
2B: Miller, Ashburn
3B: Hamner
BB: Mize, Marshall, Koslo, Layton,
     Kerr, Ashburn, Seminick, Simmons
SO: Westrum 2, Kerr 2, Hansen,
     Sisler, Haas

SH: Hamner
WP: Kennedy
TIME: 2:26
ATTENDANCE: 13,112
UMPIRES: Bill Stewart, Butch Henline
     Jocko Conlan
SOURCES: DBD; New York Herald-
     Tribune, Times; Philadelphia
     Bulletin, Daily News, Inquirer

BALANCE	OUT+R+OB=BP=AB+BB+SH+HP+CI							
New York	27	7	8	42	37	5	0	0	0
Philadelphia	24	12	4	40	36	3	1	0	0

----

inning, drove a long double to left-center, scoring Simmons with the ninth run.

• Hamner tried to bunt his way on but was thrown out by Hansen. This was the first out of the frame, but as Ashburn made third on the play, Granny was given credit for a sacrifice. (Perhaps he too accompanied Kerr and the official scorer to dinner.)

• Blatnik sent a fly to left that was too shallow for any advance by Ashburn. That was out number two.

• Sisler then smoked a sizzler toward second. Bill Rigney was able to knock it down but couldn't make a play as Ashburn scored the tenth run. Sisler was credited with a hit.

• Haas mercifully ended the carnage by flying out to center, but not before the Blue

Jays had scored more runs in the first inning of this game than they had in their last five games combined.

Despite the apparent gift, Simmons couldn't hold the Giants and had to be relieved in the sixth by Monk Dubiel. Monk closed the books on the New Yorkers by allowing just one hit over the last 3.2 innings. Simmons was credited with the victory, however, and left immediately after the game for two weeks of National Guard duty.

Another Walk on the Wild Side

118. Team Draws 11 Walks in One Inning; Four Teammates Draw Two Walks Apiece in One Inning

WASHINGTON   at   NEW YORK
(Senators, 5)   (Yankees, 20)

Sunday, September 11, 1949, Yankee Stadium

In 1949, when the Senators and Yankees locked horns, fans witnessed the two wildest pitching staffs in the major leagues. The New York squad was the most generous, issuing 5.27 free passes per nine innings; Washington conferred 4.99. In the first game of a doubleheader this day, however, it was the Senators who excelled in charitable contributions by bestowing 17 bases-on-balls on their hosts, including *11 in one inning for a new major league mark.* (The previous record had been "only" eight.) *Four diferent Yankees collected two free tickets in the frame for another major league mark.* The 17 total walks in a single game donated by the Senator staff also narrowly missed the all-time mark of 18 (see 5-09-16 & 5-20-48). The Senators were well on their way to obliterating the mark of 18 walks when they had issued 13 after only three innings. But Washington's Buzz Dozier, who shocked the huge crowd by laboring behind sun glasses, belied his appearances and restored some sense of stability to the fray by walking only four Yankees over the final five frames.

The bizarre fifty-minute, home-team half of the third saw 18 Yankees appear at the plate. Here's how that record-setting pageant progressed (walk number in parenthesis):

• Phil Rizzuto led off with a free pass (1).
• Cliff Mapes also strolled (2).
• Bobby Brown doubled down the right-field line, scoring both Rizzuto and Mapes.
• Joe DiMaggio grounded to Eddie Yost, whose throw bounced off Joe's shoulder into right field for a three base error. Brown scored on the play.
• Yogi Berra then looped a double into center sending DiMaggio home and starter Paul Calvert to the showers.
• Charlie Keller welcomed reliever Dick Welteroth by walking (3).
• Joe Collins also walked (4) loading the sacks.
• Jerry Coleman accepted more of Welteroth's generosity when he too walked (5) to force home Berra.
• Allie Reynolds couldn't wait for another free pass and instead singled to left scoring Keller and Collins. Coleman stopped at second. On the play, left fielder Bud Stewart and shortstop Sam Dente collided heavily, both being forced to leave the game. Stewart had to be carried off on a stretcher.
• When play resumed, Jerry Coleman was

Pitcher Buzz Dozier (right) slowed the record pace for walks. Buzz is chatting here with bullpen coach Joe Fitzgerald.

FIRST GAME

Washington Senators	AB	R	H	I	PO	A	E
Sherry Robertson 2b	1	0	0	0	0	1	0
Al Kozar 2b1	4	0	1	1	3	4	0
Gil Coan cf	5	2	1	0	3	0	0
Bud Stewart lf	2	0	2	0	0	0	0
Clyde Vollmer lf3	3	0	0	0	2	0	0
Eddie Robinson 1b	5	1	2	2	6	0	0
Buddy Lewis rf	4	0	0	0	0	0	0
>Eddie Yost 3b	4	0	1	0	3	0	1
Sam Dente ss	1	0	0	0	0	0	0
Mark Christman ss3	2	0	1	1	3	4	0
Jake Early c	2	1	0	0	4	2	0
Paul Calvert p	1	0	0	0	0	0	0
Dick Welteroth p3	0	0	0	0	0	0	0
Julio Gonzalez p3	0	0	0	0	0	0	0
Buzz Dozier p3	2	0	0	0	0	0	0
Roberto Ortiz ph9	1	1	1	0	0	0	0
	37	5	9	4	24	11	1

New York Yankees	AB	R	H	I	PO	A	E
Phil Rizzuto ss	5	2	3	1	2	0	1
>Cliff Mapes rf,cf7	5	3	1	0	4	0	0
Bobby Brown 3b	5	4	4	5	1	3	0
Joe DiMaggio cf	3	2	1	2	2	0	0
Gene Woodling rf	0	1	0	0	0	0	0
Yogi Berra c	3	2	2	2	2	0	0
Charlie Silvera c5	1	1	0	0	5	1	0
Charlie Keller lf	4	1	2	3	1	0	0
Joe Collins 1b	4	1	0	2	9	0	1
Jerry Coleman 2b	2	0	1	2	1	4	0
S. Stirnweiss 2b6	1	1	0	0	0	0	0
Allie Reynolds p	5	2	2	1	0	2	0
Spec Shea p8	1	0	1	0	0	0	0
	39	20	17	18	27	10	2

Washington	IP	H	R	ER	BB	SO
Calvert L,6-15	2	3	5	4	4	3
Welteroth	.1	2	5	4	4	0
Gonzalez	.1	0	2	0	4	0
Dozier	5.1	12	8	8	5	1
	8	17	20	16	17	4

New York	IP	H	R	ER	BB	SO
Reynolds W,16-4	7	5	0	0	1	4
Shea	2	4	5	2	4	3
	9	9	5	2	5	7

Washington	0	0	0	0	0	0	0	1	4	-	5
New York	0	0	12	2	0	3	2	1	x	-	20

OB: Washington 10, New York 12
DP: Kozar-Christman-Robinson (Silvera)
2B: Brown 2, Berra
3B: DiMaggio
HR: Robinson(17)
SB: Rizzuto
CS: Yost
PK: Coleman
SO: Coan, Vollmer, Lewis 3, Dozier,
    Yost, Keller, Collins 2, Reynolds
BB: Lewis, Yost, Christman, Early 2,
    Rizzuto 2, Mapes 2, Woodling 2, ...

BB: ... DiMaggio, Brown, Berra,
    Silvera, Keller 2, Collins 2,
    Coleman 2, Stirnweiss
TIME: 3:02
ATTENDANCE: 41,800 (paid)
UMPIRES: Art Passarella, Eddie
    Rommel, Jim Boyer, Johnny Stevens
SOURCES: New York Herald-Tribune,
    Sun, Times, World-Telegram;
    Retrosheet; Washington Post

BALANCE	OUT+R+OB=BP=AB+BB+SH+HP+CI

	OUT	R	OB	BP	AB	BB	SH	HP	CI
Washington	27	5	10	42	37	5	0	0	0
New York	24	20	12	56	39	17	0	0	0

trapped off second and tagged out in a run-down (Early-Christman-Yost). Reynolds took second on the play.

• Rizzuto singled to left, sending Reynolds to third.

• Mapes walked (6) for the second time in the stanza, loading the bases and sending Welteroth to the locker room. Julio Gonzalez was called upon to halt the recklessness.

• Brown watched four bad ones (7) from Gonzalez, forcing Reynolds home.

• DiMaggio made the second out by flying out to Clyde Vollmer in left, scoring Rizzuto and sending Mapes to third.

• Berra walked (8) to re-load the bases.

• Keller also walked (9), forcing home Mapes.

• Collins followed with still another free pass (10) to bring home Brown. That was all for Gonzalez, who was replaced by Buzz Dozier.

• Coleman walked (11), forcing home Berra.

• Reynolds ended the extravaganza by popping out to Eddie Robinson at first.

Browns' Pitchers Showcased

119. Team Uses Nine Pitchers in Nine-Inning Game

CHICAGO, AL   at   ST. LOUIS
(White Sox, 4)   (Browns, 3)

Sunday, October 2, 1949, Sportsman's Park

It was blatant showmanship, pure and simple. In a pre-planned attempt to give their fans something to remember, the St. Louis Browns established a yet-to-be-broken major league record by *using nine different pitchers in a nine-inning game.* Each hurler toed the rubber for one full inning.

This was the last day of the regular season

Roy Sievers, one of the few bright spots in the Browns lineup, was on his way to American League Rookie-of-the-Year honors.

and the White Sox were being entertained by the Browns. Chicago, however, didn't need nine hurlers and circus conditions to be entertained in St. Louis; any one pitcher would have sufficed. The Browns "pitching" corps, to use the term lightly, was again the most wretched in the league. This was the fourth consecutive campaign in which they led the league in hits and earned runs allowed.

Despite laboring only one inning each, eight of the nine St. Louis hurlers still allowed a batter to hit safely as the Sox won an unusually close game (for the Browns) by a 4–3 score. Al Papai was the only Browns hurler to escape unscathed. As the hometown fans had also come to expect, only one of the Chicago runs was earned. (In addition to turning the fewest double plays, the Browns committed the most errors and had the lowest fielding percentage in the circuit.)

FIRST GAME

Chicago White Sox	AB	R	H	I	PO	A	E
Dave Philley rf	5	1	1	0	1	0	0
Bill Higdon cf	5	0	2	1	2	0	0
Cass Michaels 2b	4	1	2	0	2	5	0
>Gus Zernial lf	5	0	1	0	0	0	0
John Ostrowski 3b	4	1	1	0	0	2	0
Charlie Kress 1b	4	0	2	0	12	2	0
Eddie Malone c	3	1	0	0	4	1	0
Floyd Baker ss	4	0	2	3	4	3	0
Bill Wight p	4	0	2	0	2	2	0
Eddie Kleiman p9	0	0	0	0	0	0	0
	38	4	13	4	27	15	0

St. Louis Browns	AB	R	H	I	PO	A	E
Bob Dillinger 3b	5	0	3	0	1	2	0
Paul Lehner 1b	5	0	0	0	11	0	0
Whitey Platt lf	4	2	1	0	2	0	0
Roy Sievers cf	5	1	5	2	0	0	0
Les Moss c	3	0	2	1	4	1	0
Red Embree p8	0	0	0	0	0	0	0
Dick Starr p9	1	0	0	0	0	0	0
Dick Kokos rf	4	0	0	0	2	0	0
>Owen Friend 2b	5	0	0	0	3	5	0
John Sullivan ss	3	0	2	0	2	4	0
Ned Garver p	0	0	0	0	0	0	0
Joe Ostrowski p2	0	0	0	0	0	0	0
Cliff Fannin p3	1	0	0	0	0	0	0
Tom Ferrick p4	0	0	0	0	0	0	0
Karl Drews p5	1	0	0	0	0	0	0
Bill Kennedy p6	0	0	0	0	0	0	0
Andy Anderson ph6	1	0	0	0	0	0	0
Al Papai p7	0	0	0	0	0	0	0
Sherm Lollar c8	0	0	0	0	2	0	0
	38	3	13	3	27	12	0

Chicago	IP	H	R	ER	BB	SO
Wight W,15-13	8	12	3	3	4	3
Kleiman	1	1	0	0	0	0
	9	13	3	3	4	3

St. Louis	IP	H	R	ER	BB	SO
Garver	1	1	0	0	0	0
Ostrowski	1	1	0	0	0	0
Fannin	1	3	1	1	0	0
Ferrick	1	1	0	0	0	1
Drews	1	1	0	0	0	0
Kennedy L,4-11	1	2	3	3	1	3
Papai	1	0	0	0	0	0
Embree	1	2	0	0	0	1
Starr	1	2	0	0	1	0
	9	13	4	4	2	5

```
Chicago      0 0 1   0 0 3   0 0 0  - 4
St. Louis    0 0 1   0 0 0   2 0 0  - 3
```

OB: Chicago 9, St. Louis 13
DP: Baker-Michaels-Kress (Lehner)
    Sullivan-Friend-Dillinger-Lollar (Malone)
2B: Higdon 2, Baker
HR: Sievers(16)
SB: Dillinger
CS: Ostrowski
SO: Zernial, Ostrowski, Malone, Kress,
    Wight, Sullivan, Drews, Anderson

BB: Michaels, Malone, Platt, Moss, Kokos,
    Sullivan
SH: Lollar
WP: Kennedy
TIME: 2:08
ATTENDANCE: 10,196 (9,849 paid)
UMPIRES: Jim Boyer, Bill McKinley
SOURCES: Chicago Sun-Times, Tribune; St. Louis
    Globe-Democrat, Post-Dispatch

BALANCE	OUT	+	R	+	OB	=	BP	=	AB	+	BB	+	SH	+	HP	+	CI
Chicago	27		4		9		40		38		2		0		0		0
St. Louis	27		3		13		43		38		4		1		0		0

Of the parade of pitchers, a Browns spokesman explained it as "our means of giving the fans a last look at them for the season." The fans may have been happier to see them on a train to another city.

Ironically, in the second game of this day's doubleheader, a St. Louis rookie right-hander named Ed Albrecht made his major league debut and did what the nine veteran hurlers could not — he won. Ed's eleventh-hour victory made him one of only two Browns pitchers with winning records (reliever Tom Ferrick was 6–4). Albrecht, however, quickly became infected with the Browns syndrome as that was his only major-league victory.

The Boston Massacre

120. Team Scores 29 Runs, Totals 60 Bases, Wins by 25 Runs

ST. LOUIS, AL   at   BOSTON
(Browns, 4)   (Red Sox, 29)

Thursday, June 8, 1950, Fenway Park

Like a more famous incident of 180 years earlier, Bostonians were again captivated by a revolution — but this time it was a scoring revolution. During their current home stand, the Red Sox had tallied 55 runs in the past five games. Remarkably, this amounted to

A Boston Herald *artist depicted a badly beaten Browns manager — Zack Taylor (reprinted with permission of the* Boston Herald*).*

mere batting practice for what was about to unfold. The visiting St. Louis Browns never should have stepped off the train.

Like many other clubs in 1950, Boston had had particular success against the woeful (5.20 ERA) St. Louis staff. During an earlier series, the Sox had scored 33 times in four games. Now, with Boston in full, run-scoring gear, the Browns' inept staff was especially vulnerable. In the first game of the series, on

Veteran Zarilla collected five hits.

Ferrick was called upon to stop the deluge.

June 7, the Red Sox erupted for 23 hits in crushing St. Louis 20–4. After that game, St. Louis outfielder Dick Kokos finally determined Boston's secret to success. "The way they make outfielders chase the ball, you can't catch your breath when it's your turn to bat."* But the worst was yet to come.

As the *St. Louis Post-Dispatch* went to press on the afternoon of June 8, the sports page headline screamed: "Red Sox Step Up Slugging; 22 Runs in First 5 Innings." And before it ended, the "Boston Massacre" had taken on another meaning as the Sox slugged their way to a 29–4 victory. It was not only the *most runs scored in a game in this century by one team,* but it was also the *largest margin of victory.*

The June 8 encounter also established several other twentieth-century marks that have withstood the test of time:

• *Most Runs-Batted-In, One Team, One Game*—29. *Most Runs-Batted-In, One Team, Consecutive Games*—49

• *Most Total Bases, One Team, One Game*—60. *Most Total Bases, One Team, Consecutive Games*—102

• *Most Runs Scored, One Team, Consecutive Games*—49

• *Most Hits, One Team, Consecutive Games*—51

• *Most Teammates Scoring Three or More Runs, One Game*—7

• *Most Teammates Scoring Four or More Runs, One Game*—4 (tied ML mark)

In addition, this travesty exhibited some other noteworthy performances. Clyde Vollmer, Boston's leadoff batter, became the first (and only to date) major leaguer to step to the plate eight times in a game in which his team batted in only eight frames. (Others have done this, but they were on visiting teams which batted in the ninth.) Red Sox outfielder Al Zarilla tied two major league records by punching four doubles in the game and two in one inning. He narrowly missed a fifth in his last at-bat when he forced the Browns' Roy Sievers against the wall in deep center for an out. Strangely, Zarilla had no RBIs. Bobby Doerr had one of the finest offensive days in his Hall-of-Fame career, stroking three home runs and driving

*Hy Hurwitz, "Sox Break 5 Major Records in 29–4 Rout of Browns," Boston Globe, 9 June 1950, Sports section, first page, col. 3–4.

in eight. Boston batted around four times in their eight turns at bat, and in the fourth inning when the Sox batted around for the third straight time, Ted Williams made two of the three outs. Finally, Boston hurler Chuck Stobbs walked in each of his first four plate appearances before twice singling.

Even the umpires were aghast at the play of the Browns. "Did you ever see anything like it?" Cal Hubbard exclaimed. "It was a disgrace," added Eddie Rommel. "Why the

St. Louis pitching was terrible. I've been around the American League 35 years, and I never saw or heard of a pitcher getting four walks in a game as Stobbs did, and two of them in one inning." Joe Paparella remarked: "I can't understand it. The Red Sox were swinging from their heels, and those Brownie pitchers kept trying to throw the ball by them."*

In 1994, this author spoke with Tom Ferrick, the last of the St. Louis pitchers on that fateful day, and the only one not scored

St. Louis Browns	AB	R	H	I	PO	A	E
Don Lenhardt lf	4	2	2	0	4	0	0
Dick Kokos rf	4	1	2	1	2	0	1
Sherm Lollar c	3	0	1	0	0	0	0
Les Moss c6	1	0	0	0	2	0	0
Roy Sievers cf	4	0	1	2	3	0	0
>Hank Arft 1b	3	0	1	1	5	0	0
Owen Friend 2b	4	0	1	0	5	0	0
Tom Upton ss	3	0	0	0	1	5	0
Leo Thomas 3b	3	1	0	0	2	3	0
Cliff Fannin p	0	0	0	0	0	0	0
Ned Garver ph3	1	0	0	0	0	0	0
Cuddles Marshall p3	1	0	0	0	0	0	0
Sid Schacht p4	2	0	0	0	0	0	0
Tom Ferrick p8	0	0	0	0	0	0	0
	33	4	8	4	24	8	1

Boston Red Sox	AB	R	H	I	PO	A	E
>Clyde Vollmer cf	7	1	1	2	5	0	0
Johnny Pesky 3b	7	3	5	2	0	1	0
Ted Williams lf	5	3	2	5	4	0	0
Vern Stephens ss	6	4	3	3	5	3	0
Walt Dropo 1b	6	5	4	7	5	1	0
Al Zarilla rf	7	4	5	0	0	0	0
Bobby Doerr 2b	6	4	4	8	2	1	0
Matt Batts c	6	2	2	2	6	0	0
Chuck Stobbs p	3	3	2	0	0	0	0
	53	29	28	29	27	6	0

St. Louis	IP	H	R	ER	BB	SO
Fannin L,1-3	2	7	8	8	4	0
Marshall	1.2	7	9	9	5	0
Schacht	3.2	13	12	9	2	2
Ferrick	.2	1	0	0	0	0
	8	28	29	26	11	2

Boston	IP	H	R	ER	BB	SO
Stobbs W,4-1	9	8	4	4	7	5

```
St. Louis   0 0 3   0 0 0   0 0 1   - 4
Boston      0 8 5   7 2 0   2 5 x   -29
```

OB: St. Louis 10, Boston 11
DP: Dropo unassisted
    Doerr-Stephens-Dropo (Schacht)
2B: Zarilla 4, Batts, Arft, Vollmer,
    Stephens, Pesky 2
3B: Stephens
HR: Williams 2(16), Dropo 2(14),
    Doerr 3(6)
SO: Kokos, Friend 2, Garver,
    Marshall, Batts, Stobbs

BB: Lenhardt, Kokos, Moss, Sievers, Arft, Upton,
    Thomas, Vollmer, Williams 2, Stephens, Dropo,
    Doerr, Batts, Stobbs 4
HP: By Stobbs (Arft)
TIME: 2:42
ATTENDANCE: 5,105
UMPIRES: Cal Hubbard, Eddie Rommel, Joe Paparella
SOURCES: Boston Globe, Herald; St. Louis
    Globe-Democrat, Post-Dispatch

BALANCE	OUT+R+OB=BP=AB+BB+SH+HP+CI							
St.Louis	27	4	10	41	33	7	0	1	0
Boston	24	29	11	64	53	11	0	0	0

*Hy Hurwitz, "Sox Break 5 Major Records in 29–4 Rout of Browns," Boston Globe, 9 June 1950, Sports section, first page, col. 3–4.

upon. The Browns were losing by more than 20 runs in the bottom of the eighth, said Tom, when a call came to the bullpen for him to quickly warm up. Ferrick was bewildered over this strategy and questioned his manager after the game. Taylor replied that he thought the record for runs scored was 30, and he desperately wanted to avoid the ignominy of breaking that mark.

Imagine how Browns ace Ned Garver felt when his name was announced as the starting pitcher for the third and final game of this series. Garver performed admirably (relatively speaking), allowing the Sox "only" seven runs through seven innings and left trailing 7–6. His teammates then turned the tables on the Red Sox and rallied for a 12–7 victory. Boston's seven runs, however, were still enough to *set a new three-game, run-scoring standard of 56.*

Bronx Bombers Blitzed in Briggs

121. Teams Hit
11 Home Runs in One Game

NEW YORK   at   DETROIT
(Yankees, 9)   (Tigers, 10)

Friday Night, June 23, 1950, Briggs Stadium

It was a matchup of the best two teams in the American League with Detroit holding a narrow, one-game lead over New York. Motor City fans turned out in droves, over 51,000 or twice the season's average, to see their heroes defend the slim margin over the defending world champions. They knew it wouldn't be easy as the Tigers were about to face the menacing figure of pitcher Tommy Byrne, who held a commanding 11–2 lifetime mark against Detroit and had already beaten them on three occasions this season. Detroit countered with their best pitcher to date, Ted Gray, owner of a 7–2 log.

Things looked bleak for the hometown rooters as the Bronx Bombers jumped off to a 6–0 runaway after three and a half innings on the strength of four circuit clouts. In the process, the Yankees drove the shell-shocked starter, Gray, to the showers. But in the bottom of the fourth, the Tigers answered the challenge with eight tallies on four home runs of their own, taking an 8–6 lead. Among the four was a grand slam by relief pitcher

Dizzy Trout and a titanic, two-run blast by Vic Wertz that bounced on the roof, 125 feet above the 370-foot mark in right-center.

The Yankees, however, weren't about to roll over. DiMaggio hit a solo shot in the seventh, and Henrich pinch-hit a two-run homer in the eighth to enable New York to recapture a 9–8 lead. Each club made three more outs without crossing the plate, bringing on the last half-inning.

Briggs Stadium was vibrating with solicitous anticipation as Tiger hitters chose their lumber in the last of the ninth. George Kell, the league's leading hitter at .375, opened by fouling out, but Wertz raised passions by doubling to left center. That brought to the plate Hoot Evers whose earlier homer had been his first base hit in four games. Hoot sparked pandemonium when he smashed a drive off the fence at the 415-foot mark in right center. While DiMaggio and Bauer chased the carom, Evers circled the bases with the heroic game winner amid 51,000 delirious Tiger fans.

Dizzy Trout connected for a grand slam.

This two-team, home run barrage established several major league records. This was the *first time that two clubs combined to hit 11 home runs in a single game*, a mark that lasted until 1995. It was also the *first time in the American League that nine different players connected for home runs in one game*. No game has ever had more players do so, although this mark has been tied many times since. And finally, this contest represents the *most runs scored in a game (19), all coming by way of the home run*. Following is a summary of this game's record-setting home run assault:

HR Hitter	Inning	Outs	Men On	Pitcher
Bauer (NY)	1st	1	Rizzuto (1st)	Gray
Bauer (NY)	3rd	2	None	Gray
Berra (NY)	3rd	2	DiMaggio (2nd)	Gray
Coleman (NY)	4th	0	None	Gray
Trout (Det)	4th	1	Groth (3rd) Kolloway (2nd) Swift (1st)	Byrne
Priddy (Det)	4th	2	None	Byrne
Wertz (Det)	4th	2	Kell (1st)	Sanford
Evers (Det)	4th	2	None	Sanford
DiMaggio (NY)	7th	2	None	Trout
Henrich (NY)	8th	1	Johnson (1st)	Trout
Evers (Det)	9th	1	Wertz (2nd)	Page

New York Yankees	AB	R	H	I	PO	A	E
Phil Rizzuto ss	4	1	2	0	1	2	0
Cliff Mapes rf	2	0	0	0	0	0	0
Gene Woodling lf5	2	0	0	0	0	0	0
Hank Bauer lf,rf5	5	2	2	3	2	0	0
Joe DiMaggio cf	5	2	2	1	1	0	0
Yogi Berra c	4	1	1	2	5	1	0
>Johnny Mize 1b	5	0	1	0	11	0	0
Billy Johnson 3b	4	1	1	0	2	2	0
Jerry Coleman 2b	3	1	2	1	3	5	0
Tommy Henrich ph8	1	1	1	2	0	0	0
Joe Page p8	0	0	0	0	0	0	0
Tommy Byrne p	1	0	0	0	0	0	0
Fred Sanford p4	0	0	0	0	0	0	0
Tom Ferrick p4	1	0	0	0	0	3	0
Bobby Brown ph8	1	0	1	0	0	0	0
Billy Martin 2b8	0	0	0	0	0	1	0
	38	9	13	9	25*	14	0

Detroit Tigers	AB	R	H	I	PO	A	E
Johnny Lipon ss	5	0	2	0	2	1	0
Jerry Priddy 2b	5	1	2	1	3	3	0
George Kell 3b	4	1	2	0	0	5	0
Vic Wertz rf	5	2	2	2	2	0	0
>Hoot Evers lf	5	2	2	3	2	0	0
Johnny Groth cf	4	1	1	0	1	0	0
Don Kolloway 1b	4	1	1	0	12	1	0
Bob Swift c	1	1	0	0	5	0	0
Pat Mullin ph8	1	0	0	0	0	0	0
Aaron Robinson c9	0	0	0	0	0	0	0
Ted Gray p	0	0	0	0	0	0	0
Dizzy Trout p4	2	1	1	4	0	0	0
Paul Calvert p8	0	0	0	0	0	0	0
Fred Hutchinson p8	1	0	0	0	0	0	0
	37	10	13	10	27	10	0

New York	IP	H	R	ER	BB	SO
Byrne	3.2	5	5	5	4	1
Sanford	0	3	3	3	0	0
Ferrick	3.1	2	0	0	0	1
Page L,3-5	1.1	3	2	2	0	1
	8.1*	13	10	10	4	3

* One out when winning run scored

Detroit	IP	H	R	ER	BB	SO
Gray	3	8	6	6	1	1
Trout	4.1	3	3	3	1	4
Calvert	0	2	0	0	0	0
Hutchinson W,8-4	1.2	0	0	0	0	0
	9	13	9	9	2	5

New York	2 0 3	1 0 0	1 2 0	- 9
Detroit	0 0 0	8 0 0	0 0 2	-10

OB: New York 6, Detroit 6
2B: DiMaggio, Mize, Wertz
HR: Bauer 2(4), Berra(7), Coleman(4),
     DiMaggio(14), Henrich(5), Trout(1),
     Priddy(3), Wertz(10), Evers 2(12)
CS: Priddy
SO: Bauer, DiMaggio, Mize 2, Coleman,
     Priddy, Wertz, Trout
BB: Berra, Byrne, Kell, Swift 2, Gray

SH: Mapes, Rizzuto
TIME: 2:41
ATTENDANCE: 51,400
UMPIRES: Cal Hubbard, Eddie Rommel,
   Jim Honochick, Joe Paparella
SOURCES: Detroit Free Press, News;
   New York Times

BALANCE	OUT+R+OB=BP=AB+BB+SH+HP+CI
New York	27 9 6 42 38 2 2 0 0
Detroit	25 10 6 41 37 4 0 0 0

Many observers, including the Detroit News *cartoonist, felt the 1950 "Spalding sphere" was a rabbit ball (reprinted with permission of* The Detroit News*).*

Hodges Hits Four Homers

122. Player Hits Four Home Runs, Totals 17 Bases in Nine-Inning Game

BOSTON   at   BROOKLYN
(Braves, 3)   (Dodgers, 19)

Thursday Night, August 31, 1950, Ebbets Field

As the three-quarter moon shined on a warm, muggy Ebbets Field this night, it brought with it stardust for the Dodgers' slugging first baseman Gil Hodges. Gil became the *first National Leaguer since the turn of the century to blast four home runs in a nine-inning game.* He joined Bobby Lowe (1894), Ed Delahanty (1896), and Lou

Gehrig (1932) as the nine-inning achievers. Chuck Klein (1936) and Pat Seerey (1948) performed the virtuoso in extra innings. Hodges was also the first to achieve the feat in a night game.

In addition, the 26-year-old singled in the seventh, giving him *a game total of 17 bases, a twentieth-century record (later surpassed).*

Hodges was en route to a 32-home-run season.

frame with mates Robinson and Furillo on and none out. This blast was also deposited in the lower left-field seats.

• The only hurler to retire Hodges all night was Mickey Haefner. In the fourth, Furillo, Hodges and Campanella each grounded out. Hodges was retired, third to first.

• In the sixth, after Furillo had singled with no outs, Gil whacked his third circuit clout, this time off Bob Hall. The ball landed in the same vicinity as the first two.

• With one out in the seventh, Hodges faced Johnny Antonelli. He singled and later scored.

• Antonelli served up home run number four in the eighth inning with one out; Furillo was again aboard, this time via a fielder's choice. This was Gil's longest homer, traveling into the upper deck of the left-field seats.

When Hodges hit his third home run of the game, it also gave the Dodgers the distinction of becoming the first club to have three players hit three homers in one game in a single season. Duke Snider and Roy Campanella had each hit three in games earlier in the year.

In the locker room after the game, Hodges said this night was the biggest baseball thrill of his life, made bigger because his wife was in the stands. After hitting homers off a Spahn fastball, a Roy change-up, and a Hall fastball, Hodges said: "I was really swinging for it when I realized I had a chance at the record. The pay-off was a curve that didn't break. No doubt of that one. It felt like an upper-decker... when it left my bat."*

Coincidentally, both Lowe and Delahanty also singled in their quartet-homer games. Hodges' single was questionable, however. His seventh inning bouncer (New York papers referred to it as a liner) to Bob Elliott was fielded cleanly, but the throw pulled first baseman Earl Torgeson off the bag.

Hodges also became the first to bang his homers off four *different* hurlers.

• His first came off future Hall of Famer Warren Spahn in the second inning with no outs, driving home Carl Furillo who had led off with a single. The blow landed in the lower deck of the left-field seats.

• Norm Roy was his victim in the third

*Associated Press, "Curve That Didn't Break Made 4th Homer Possible—Hodges," Boston Globe, 1 September 1950, p. 26, col. 3–4.

Boston Braves	AB	R	H	I	PO	A	E
Roy Hartsfield 2b	5	0	1	0	4	1	3
Sam Jethroe cf	5	0	0	0	1	0	0
>Earl Torgeson 1b	4	1	1	0	7	0	0
Bob Elliott 3b	3	0	1	0	1	4	0
Walker Cooper c	3	0	0	0	3	0	0
Del Crandall c7	1	1	0	0	2	0	1
Sid Gordon lf	4	1	3	2	4	0	0
Willard Marshall rf	4	0	2	1	1	0	0
Buddy Kerr ss	3	0	0	0	1	4	0
Warren Spahn p	1	0	0	0	0	0	0
Norm Roy p3	0	0	0	0	0	1	0
Mickey Haefner p3	0	0	0	0	0	0	0
Pete Reiser ph5	1	0	0	0	0	0	0
Bob Hall p5	0	0	0	0	0	1	0
Johnny Antonelli p6	1	0	0	0	0	0	0
Tommy Holmes ph9	1	0	0	0	0	0	0
	36	3	8	3	24	11	4

Brooklyn Dodgers	AB	R	H	I	PO	A	E
Tommy Brown lf	4	0	1	2	1	0	0
Pee Wee Reese ss	5	1	2	3	1	4	1
Duke Snider cf	5	1	1	3	4	0	0
Jackie Robinson 2b	5	1	1	0	2	1	0
Bobby Morgan 3b9	0	0	0	0	0	1	0
Carl Furillo rf	5	4	2	0	1	0	0
Gil Hodges 1b	6	5	5	9	7	1	0
Roy Campanella c	4	2	2	0	4	0	0
Bruce Edwards c8	1	1	1	0	2	0	0
Billy Cox 3b,2b9	5	3	2	0	3	3	0
>Carl Erskine p	5	1	4	0	2	0	0
	45	19	21	17	27	10	1

Boston	IP	H	R	ER	BB	SO
Spahn L,16-15	2	7	5	5	1	2
Roy	.1	3	3	3	0	0
Haefner	1.2	1	2	2	1	0
Hall	1.2	6	4	4	3	1
Antonelli	2.1	4	5	4	2	2
	8	21	19	18	7	5

Brooklyn	IP	H	R	ER	BB	SO
Erskine W,2-3	9	8	3	3	3	6

Boston	0 1 0	0 0 0	0 2 0	- 3
Brooklyn	0 3 7	0 0 4	3 2 x	-19

OB: Boston 9, Brooklyn 11

2B: Reese, Marshall 2

HR: Hodges 4(23), Gordon (24), Snider (24)

SO: Hartsfield, Jethroe 3, Reiser, Torgeson, Brown, Reese 2, Snider 2

BB: Torgeson, Elliott, Kerr, Brown 2, Reese, Snider, Robinson, Furillo, Campanella

SH: Cox

HP: By Antonelli (Erskine)

TIME: 3:03

ATTENDANCE: 14,226

UMPIRES: Jocko Conlin, Artie Gore, Bill Stewart

SOURCES: Boston Globe, Herald, Post; New York Herald-Tribune, Times, World-Telegram; Retrosheet

BALANCE	OUT+R+OB=BP=AB+BB+SH+HP+CI
Boston	27 3 9 39 36 3 0 0 0
Brooklyn	24 19 11 54 45 7 1 1 0

Brooklyn Blast-Off

123. Team Scores 15 Runs in First Inning; 19 Consecutive Batters Safely Reach Base

CINCINNATI   at   BROOKLYN
(Reds, 1)   (Dodgers, 19)

Wednesday Night, May 21, 1952, Ebbets Field

The 1952 Brooklyn Dodgers were a powerhouse, leading the National League in runs scored, home runs, RBIs, slugging average, walks, and stolen bases. Early in the campaign, they gave the league notice of their firepower when they crushed the

Cincinnati Reds in unusual fashion. On this date, the Dodgers utilized ten hits, seven walks, and two hit batsmen to score 15 runs in the very first inning. In doing so, they established a host of modern team records including:

• *Most runs scored in one inning—15* (remains NL mark)

• *Most runs scored in the first inning—15* (remains modern mark)

• *Most runs scored after two outs—12* (retains share of NL mark)

• *Most batters in one inning—21* (remains NL mark)

• *Most runs-batted-in in one inning—15* (remains NL mark)

• *Most consecutive batters to reach base safely—19* (remains ML mark)

During the 59-minute, half-inning marathon, Pee Wee Reese became the first batter since the turn of the century to reach base safely three times in one inning. In addition, each Dodger except Gil Hodges (who walked twice), got at least one hit, scored at least one run, and drove home another during the frame. Following are the stormy details of Brooklyn's tumultuous take-off with the running score in parenthesis. On the mound for Cincinnati was a side-winding right-hander and former 20-game winner, Ewell Blackwell.

Bobby Morgan accounted for all the Dodger runs after the first.

• Billy Cox innocently grounded out, Bobby Adams to Ted Kluszewski.

• Reese walked.

• On a full count, Duke Snider homered over the right-field scoreboard (2–0).

• Jackie Robinson, leading the National League in hitting, looped a Texas-league double into left.

• After working a full count, Andy Pafko walked. Pafko at the time was tied for the major league home run lead with eight.

• George Shuba, filling in for Carl Furillo who was in the midst of a 1 for 38 slump, singled home Robinson (3–0) with Pafko stopping at second. That was all for Black-well, whose once great fastball was conspicuous by its absence. "He was throwing basketballs,"* said Duke Snider. Bud Byerly then took the mound.

• On an aborted hit-and-run play with Hodges batting, Pafko was thrown out at third, Dixie Howell to Bobby Adams. Shuba took second on the fielder's choice, but there were then two down in the inning. It was, however, the only out Byerly would record.

• Hodges eventually walked.

• Catcher Rube Walker was playing in place of future Hall-of-Famer Roy Campanella. According to Dodgers' statistician Allan Roth, Campy had a lifetime average of only .065 when facing Blackwell. So the left-handed swinging Walker got a rare start.

*Bill Roeder, "Everything Broken But Gil's Slump," New York World-Telegram and Sun, 22 May 1952, p. 24, col. 4.

Left-hander Chris Van Cuyk won just two more games in his major league career.

Rube singled home Shuba (4–0) and Hodges went to third.

• Brooklyn pitcher Chris Van Cuyk, the beneficiary of this outburst, contributed an RBI single (5–0) to left scoring Hodges. Walker stopped at second.

• Cox then batted for the second time and singled to left. That scored Walker (6–0), and Van Cuyk held at second.

• Reese also singled to left, knocking home Van Cuyk (7–0); Cox stopped at second. That sent Byerly to the showers without having retired a batter (just a baserunner). Herm Wehmeier was the next pitching victim.

• Wehmeier walked Snider, filling the bases.

• Robinson was hit by a pitch, forcing home Cox (8–0).

• Pafko then singled to left, driving home Reese and Snider (10–0). Robinson held at second. That forced Wehmeier to the locker room without having retired a single batter. He was relieved by Frank Smith, the fourth Red hurler.

• Smith perpetuated the farce by walking Shuba to load the sacks and then also walked Hodges to force home Robinson (11–0).

• Walker's grounder took a bad hop over the head of Grady Hatton for a single. That sent home Pafko and Shuba (13–0) and moved Hodges to third.

• Van Cuyk again singled, this time through the box, scoring Hodges (14–0) and sending Walker to second.

• Cox stepped to the plate for the third time and was hit by a pitch on his left elbow which again loaded the bases. Bobby Morgan ran for Cox and later in the game belted a pair of two run homers.

• Reese walked, forcing home Walker (15–0).

• Snider mercifully ended the 59-minute debacle by watching a third strike go by.

The half inning had taken so long that Ewell Blackwell, Cincinnati starter, showered and returned to the team hotel only to find that the Dodgers were still at bat in the first inning. During the interminable rally, Dodgers' hurler Van Cuyk twice went to the bullpen to keep his arm warm.

Despite an inning that lasted nearly an hour, the rest of the game progressed swiftly. Total game time was only two hours and 26 minutes. After the opening round the only other scoring came via the home run route — a pair of two-run shots by Brooklyn's Morgan and a solo clout by Cincinnati's Howell that broke the shutout. Van Cuyk not only disposed of the Reds on 99 pitches, but also contributed four hits of his own which was one more than he had had in his previous two big-league seasons combined.

Cincinnati manager Luke Sewell was hesitant to give the Dodgers much credit or afford his club much compassion. "It wasn't so much Brooklyn's great hitting as it was our rotten pitching. Why, I'm a catcher and out of shape. But I'll bet $500 I can go out there right now and they can't get 15 runs off me."* Sewell lasted just a few more months as a major league manager, and Blackwell was soon traded to the New York Yankees where a sore shoulder and an ailing kidney ended his career.

*Associated Press, "It Could Be Worse, Luke! Think of Those 1883 Cubs!," The Cincinnati Enquirer, 23 May 1952, p. 28, col. 5.

Cincinnati Reds	AB	R	H	I	PO	A	E
Grady Hatton 2b	1	0	0	0	0	0	0
Johnny Temple 2b3	3	0	0	0	1	3	0
Bobby Adams 3b	1	0	0	0	2	1	0
Eddie Kazak 3b4	3	0	0	0	0	0	0
Ted Kluszewski 1b	1	0	0	0	1	0	0
Johnny Wyrostek 1b4	3	0	1	0	8	0	0
>Joe Adcock lf	4	0	0	0	1	0	0
Wally Westlake cf	3	0	1	0	2	0	0
Bob Borkowski rf	3	0	0	0	2	0	0
Dixie Howell c	3	1	2	1	4	2	0
Roy McMillan ss	1	0	1	0	0	0	0
Eddie Pellagrini ss4	2	0	0	0	3	2	0
Ewell Blackwell p	0	0	0	0	0	0	0
Bud Byerly p1	0	0	0	0	0	0	0
Herm Wehmeier p1	0	0	0	0	0	0	0
Frank Smith p1	1	0	0	0	0	1	0
Wally Post ph6	1	0	0	0	0	0	0
Joe Nuxhall p6	1	0	0	0	0	1	0
	31	1	5	1	24	10	0

Brooklyn Dodgers	AB	R	H	I	PO	A	E
Billy Cox 3b	2	1	1	1	0	0	0
Bobby Morgan pr1,3b	3	2	2	4	1	3	0
Pee Wee Reese ss	3	2	2	2	0	3	0
Duke Snider cf	4	2	2	2	2	0	0
Dick Williams cf7	1	0	0	0	1	0	0
Jackie Robinson 2b	1	2	1	1	0	0	0
Rocky Bridges 2b3	3	0	0	0	3	3	0
Andy Pafko rf	4	1	1	2	1	0	1
Carl Furillo rf7	1	0	0	0	0	0	0
>George Shuba lf	5	2	2	1	4	0	0
Gil Hodges 1b	2	2	0	1	9	0	0
Rube Walker c	5	2	2	3	6	0	0
Chris Van Cuyk p	5	3	4	2	0	2	0
	39	19	17	19	27	11	1

Cincinnati	IP	H	R	ER	BB	SO
Blackwell L,1-6	.1	3	4	4	2	0
Byerly	.1	4	5	5	1	0
Wehmeier	0	1	3	3	1	0
Smith	4.1	8	7	7	6	2
Nuxhall	3	1	0	0	0	3
	8	17	19	19	10	5

Brooklyn	IP	H	R	ER	BB	SO
Van Cuyk W,3-2	9	5	1	1	0	5

Cincinnati	0 0 0	0 1 0	0 0 0	- 1
Brooklyn	15 0 2	0 2 0	0 0 x	-19

OB: Cincinnati 3, Brooklyn 8
DP: Reese-Bridges-Hodges (Temple)
    Pellagrini-Temple-Wyrostek (Bridges)
    Morgan-Bridges-Hodges (Pellagrini)
2B: Robinson, Shuba, Reese
HR: Snider(4), Morgan 2(2), Howell(1)
CS: Pafko
SO: Hatton, Kluszewski, Wyrostek,
    Smith, Post, Reese, Williams,
    Snider, Furillo, Hodges
BB: Reese 3, Snider, Robinson, Furillo,
    Shuba, Hodges 3

HP: By Wehmeier (Robinson); by
    Smith (Cox)
TIME: 2:26
ATTENDANCE: 11,850
UMPIRES: Larry Goetz, Frank
    Dascoli, Frank Secory, Lon
    Warneke
SOURCES: Cincinnati Enquirer;
    New York Herald-Tribune,
    Times, World-Telegram & Sun,
    Retrosheet

BALANCE	OUT	+R	+OB	+BP	=AB	+BB	+SH	+HP	+CI
Cincinnati	27	1	3	31	31	0	0	0	0
Brooklyn	24	19	8	51	39	10	0	2	0

Redbirds' Remarkable Recovery

124. Team Overcomes 11-Run Deficit to Win

ST. LOUIS, NL   at   NEW YORK
(Cardinals, 14)   (Giants, 12)

Sunday, June 15, 1952, Polo Grounds

Enos Slaughter led the resurrection with five RBIs.

The New York Giants, winners of the 1951 pennant race on Bobby Thomson's storybook home run, this day became the victims of a miracle of a different sort. After jumping off to an 11–0 lead after three innings, the New Yorkers watched in disbelief as the Cardinals rallied for 14 runs of their own in forging *the National League's greatest comeback victory*, 14–12. (Still retains a share of the NL mark.)

The Giants trailed the league leading Dodgers by 3.5 games, but were looking to make up some ground in their doubleheader with the visiting Cardinals. Despite blistering heat, the largest National League crowd of the year, 41,899, paid to see a twin bill. The hometown assembly saw their heroes bat around and erupt for five runs in the second inning. They batted around again in the third, tallying six more times. Homers by Hank Thompson and

Westrum homered early and then was rested.

Wes Westrum led the assault. Giant fans then felt assured of an easy win; manager Leo Durocher included. Considering the heat, Durocher decided to rest two of his veterans, Westrum and Bob Elliott, for the nightcap. The Giants felt particularly comfortable because they also had their pitching ace, Sal "The Barber" Maglie, on the mound. Maglie

was making his fourth bid for a league-leading win number ten and was understandably confident. "With that big a lead, I was sure we had this one stowed away," said the Barber in the clubhouse, "so I just let up. Then I couldn't get going again."*

The Cardinals obviously were not as impressed with New York's 11–0 lead. Manager Eddie Stanky thought about giving some of his veteran regulars a rest but later related: "Something inside me told me not to make the changes, though. Call it a silly hunch, call it anything, but the rally we put on then became the greatest I've ever seen."† The Redbirds gladly accepted Maglie's relaxed deliveries and erupted in the fifth. Tommy Glaviano led off with a circuit smash, then came four singles and a walk. It was still only 11–4, and with two outs Maglie needed only one more to be eligible for his elusive tenth victory. But Enos Slaughter sent "The Barber" to his shop, with a three-run homer, and Hoyt Wilhelm was beckoned to extinguish the St. Louis merrymaking.

Three more Giant hurlers followed Wilhelm, and each was stroked for additional hits and runs. St. Louis tallied three in the seventh to close within one run. In the eighth, the Redbirds finally forged ahead on a pair of runs including a solo homer by shortstop Solly Hemus. Just for insurance, Hemus blasted another circuit clout in the ninth, this one a two-run shot into the right field upper deck.

By the time New York batted in the bottom of the ninth, they were demoralized, embarrassed, and trailing 14–11. But the Cardinals left the door open.

After Hank Thompson fanned, and pinch hitter Bill Howerton lined out to first, both Don Mueller and Alvin Dark walked. Another pinch hitter, Bill Rigney, grounded toward third but was safe on Tommy

*John Drebinger, "Giants Gain Split with Cards on Westrum's Homer," *New York Times, 16 June 1952, p. 22, col. 1.*
†Bob Broeg, "Cards Clip 'Barber' Maglie After Giants Lead by 11–0," *St. Louis Post-Dispatch, 16 June 1952, Sports section, p. 1, col. 2–3.*

Glaviano's error loading the bases. Another grounder by pinch hitter Sal Yvars was also bobbled, this time by Hemus, enabling New York's 12th run to cross the plate. Now with the bases loaded the huge crowd was on their feet and screaming for one more hit. The ex-citement ended when the next batter, Davey Williams, fouled out to catcher Del Rice.

After intermission the Giants rebounded to win the nightcap, 3–0. Although New York collected only five hits, Westrum won it with a three run home run.

FIRST GAME

St. Louis Cardinals	AB	R	H	I	PO	A	E
Solly Hemus ss	5	3	2	3	3	1	1
Red Schoendienst 2b	6	1	2	0	1	0	0
>Stan Musial cf,lf5	6	2	2	2	1	1	0
Dick Sisler 1b	5	2	2	1	11	0	0
Peanuts Lowrey lf,cf5	4	1	1	0	5	0	0
Enos Slaughter rf	5	2	3	5	2	0	0
Tommy Glaviano 3b	5	1	2	2	0	5	2
Del Rice c	5	1	3	0	4	0	0
Joe Presko p	0	0	0	0	0	0	0
Jack Crimian p2	1	0	0	0	0	0	0
Bill Werle p3	2	1	1	0	0	1	0
Hal Rice ph7	1	0	0	1	0	0	0
Eddie Yuhas p7	0	0	0	0	0	1	0
Willard Schmidt p9	0	0	0	0	0	0	0
	45	14	18	14	27	9	3

New York Giants	AB	R	H	I	PO	A	E
>Davey Williams 2b	6	0	3	1	2	4	1
Whitey Lockman 1b	5	0	3	3	10	0	1
Bobby Thomson 3b	5	0	0	0	0	3	0
Hank Thompson cf	4	2	1	1	5	0	0
Bob Elliott lf	2	1	0	0	0	0	0
Chuck Diering lf4	1	0	0	0	3	0	0
Bill Howerton ph9	1	0	0	0	0	0	0
Don Mueller rf	4	3	2	1	3	0	0
Alvin Dark ss	4	2	2	2	1	1	0
Wes Westrum c	2	2	2	3	1	0	0
Ray Noble c4	2	0	0	0	2	1	0
Bill Rigney ph9	1	0	0	0	0	0	0
Sal Maglie p	1	2	1	0	0	1	1
Hoyt Wilhelm p5	1	0	0	0	0	0	0
George Spencer p7	0	0	0	0	0	0	0
Max Lanier p8	0	0	0	0	0	0	0
George Wilson ph8	1	0	0	0	0	0	0
Monte Kennedy p9	0	0	0	0	0	0	0
Sal Yvars ph9	1	0	0	0	0	0	0
	41	12	14	11	27	10	3

St. Louis	IP	H	R	ER	BB	SO
Presko	1.2	6	5	4	1	0
Crimian	.1	7	6	6	1	0
Werle	4	0	0	0	0	3
Yuhas W,3-2	2.2	1	1	0	2	0
Schmidt	.1	0	0	0	0	0
	9	14	12	10	4	3

New York	IP	H	R	ER	BB	SO
Maglie	4.2	9	7	7	1	1
Wilhelm	1.2	4	3	1	0	1
Spencer	.2	1	1	1	0	0
Lanier L,1-4	1	2	1	1	1	0
Kennedy	1	2	2	2	0	0
	9	18	14	12	2	2

St. Louis	0 0 0	0 7 0	3 2 2	-14
New York	0 5 6	0 0 0	0 0 1	-12

OB: St. Louis 7, New York 7
DP: Williams-Dark-Lockman (Musial)
  Hemus-Sisler (Lockman)
2B: Slaughter
3B: D. Rice
HR: Slaughter(5), Thompson(5), Westrum(10),
  Glaviano(2), Hemus 2(6)
SO: Hemus, Crimian, Thomson, Dark, Thompson
BB: Hemus, Lowrey, Thompson, Dark, Mueller,
  Elliott

SH: Maglie, Yuhas
TIME: 3:22
ATTENDANCE: 41,899
UMPIRES: Tom Gorman, Augie Donatelli
  Lee Ballanfant, Al Barlick
SOURCES: New York Herald-Tribune,
  Times; St.Louis Globe-Democrat,
  Post-Dispatch; Retrosheet

BALANCE	OUT+R+OB=BP=AB+BB+SH+HP+CI
St. Louis	27 14 7 48 45 2 1 0 0
New York	27 12 7 46 41 4 1 0 0

Bubba Bushwacked

125. Team Scores Seven Runs in Ninth Inning After Bases Empty, Two Outs

CHICAGO   at   CINCINNATI
(Cubs, 9)   (Reds, 8)

Sunday, June 29, 1952, Crosley Field

On a 100-degree day, Cincinnati right-hander Emory "Bubba" Church was coasting along behind an 8–2 lead after eight innings. With the Cubs having been able to manage only eight hits and no walks, he was comfortably in control of this game. To start the ninth, Church retired Cub leadoff batter Toby Atwell on a ground out and then struck out Bob Addis. He was only one out away from his first victory of the season, but Chicago then mounted *the greatest ninth-inning, bases-empty, two-out rally in National League history when they scored seven runs* and hung on to win 9–8. It was the most runs the Cubs had scored in one inning since April 30 when they routed the same Bubba Church, then of the Phillies.

Here's how that miraculous rally developed (with running score in parentheses):

• Bill Serena doubled.
• Roy Smalley walked.
• Gene Hermanski, pinch hitting for Joe Hatten, singled to drive home Serena (3–8) and send Smalley to third.
• Eddie Miksis then bunted toward third. Cincinnati's Ed Kazak hurriedly tried for a play at the plate but threw wildly allowing Smalley to score (4–8).
• That was all for Bubba Church, who was relieved by Frank Smith. The first thing the ace reliever did was to hit Hal Jeffcoat with a pitch loading the bases.
• Dee Fondy's third hit of the game was a single, driving home Hermanski and Miksis (6–8). Fondy was then lifted for a pinch runner, Randy Jackson.
• Hank Sauer lashed a screaming line drive off the left-field wall for a double, scoring Jeffcoat (7–8). Jackson held at third.

• With left-handed hitting Toby Atwell due up, a frantic Cincinnati manager Luke Sewell summoned the ace of his staff, lefty Ken Raffensberger. Cub manager Phil Cavarretta countered with a right-handed pinch hitter Bruce Edwards. The chess game continued with Edwards being intentionally walked to fill the bases. The Reds were still looking for that elusive third out.

• Left-handed swinging Bob Addis was the next scheduled hitter, so Cavarretta sent to the plate the right-handed, former Red, Johnny Pramesa. Pramesa crowned the magnificent comeback when he singled to right, driving in Jackson and Sauer (9–8). It was the first lead the Cubs enjoyed since the first half-inning.

• Serena, who had begun the rally with a double, now ended it with a weak pop out.

Dutch Leonard then ably retired the demoralized Reds in the bottom of the ninth to sew up the victory.

Cincinnati could not have felt very secure in the second game even though they carried a 9–1 advantage into the ninth. But lightning was not to strike twice on the same day, and they emerged with a split of the double-header.

The Reds were a team prone to two-out cataclysms. Only five weeks earlier in Brooklyn, trailing the Dodgers 3–0 in the bottom of the first, the Reds took an hour to register the third out. Meanwhile the Dodgers had scored 12, two-out runs (see 5-21-52).

Church had his finest seasons while pitching for the Phillies in 1950 and 1951 before being traded to Cincinnati. Sportscaster Gene Kelly is getting acquainted.

FIRST GAME

Chicago Cubs	AB	R	H	I	PO	A	E	Cincinnati Reds	AB	R	H	I	PO	A	E
Eddie Miksis 2b	5	1	1	0	4	2	0	Cal Abrams cf	1	1	1	0	0	0	0
Hal Jeffcoat cf	4	1	0	0	4	1	0	B. Borkowski cf3,lf7	3	1	1	0	2	0	0
Dee Fondy 1b	5	2	3	3	5	0	0	Bobby Adams 3b	3	3	3	1	2	2	0
Randy Jackson pr9	0	1	0	0	0	0	0	Eddie Kazak 3b8	1	0	0	0	1	1	1
Phil Cavarretta 1b9	0	0	0	0	0	0	0	Grady Hatton 2b	4	1	1	0	3	2	0
Hank Sauer lf	5	1	1	1	4	0	0	Ted Kluszewski 1b	3	1	1	1	3	0	0
Toby Atwell c	4	0	2	1	2	0	0	Wally Westlake cf7	1	0	0	0	3	0	0
Bruce Edwards ph9,c	0	0	0	0	0	0	0	Willard Marshall rf	4	0	2	2	0	0	0
Bob Addis rf	4	0	1	0	2	0	0	Joe Adcock lf,1b7	5	0	2	2	6	0	0
Johnny Pramesa ph9	1	0	1	2	0	0	0	>Andy Seminick c	5	1	1	0	7	0	0
Dutch Leonard p9	0	0	0	0	0	1	0	Roy McMillan ss	4	0	2	0	0	4	0
>Bill Serena 3b	5	1	2	0	4	5	0	Bubba Church p	4	0	1	1	0	1	0
Roy Smalley ss	3	1	1	0	2	2	1	Frank Smith p9	0	0	0	0	0	0	0
Johnny Klippstein p	2	0	0	0	0	0	0	Ken Raffensberger p	0	0	0	0	0	0	0
Willie Ramsdell p5	0	0	0	0	0	0	0		38	8	15	7	27	10	1

Chicago Cubs	AB	R	H	I	PO	A	E
Tommy Brown ph7	1	0	0	0	0	0	0
Bob Schultz p7	0	0	0	0	0	0	0
Joe Hatten p8	0	0	0	0	0	0	0
G. Hermanski ph9,rf	1	1	1	1	0	0	0
	40	9	13	8	27	11	1

Chicago	IP	H	R	ER	BB	SO
Klippstein	4.1	9	6	6	1	0
Ramsdell	1.2	2	0	0	0	0
Schultz	1	4	2	2	1	1
Hatten W,4-4	1	0	0	0	0	0
Leonard	1	0	0	0	1	0
	9	15	8	8	3	1

Cincinnati	IP	H	R	ER	BB	SO
Church	8.2	10	6	3	1	4
Smith L,7-6	0	2	3	0	0	0
Raffensberger	.1	1	0	0	1	0
	9	13	9	3	2	4

Chicago	1 0 0	1 0 0	0 0 7	- 9
Cincinnati	2 1 0	0 3 0	1 1 0	- 8

OB: Chicago 7, Cincinnati 8
DP: McMillan-Hatten-Kluszewski (Jeffcoat)
   Senena-Miksis
2B: Serena 2, Fondy, Adams, Sauer
HR: Fondy(5)
SO: Sauer, Addis, Serena, Klippstein,
   Westlake
BB: Edwards(I), Smalley, Abrams,
   Adams, Westlake
SH: Hatten, Marshall

HP: By Smith (Jeffcoat)
TIME: 2:22
ATTENDANCE: 13,622
UMPIRES: Tom Gorman, Augie
   Donatelli, Lee Ballanfant, Al Barlick
SOURCES: Cincinnati Enquirer;
   Chicago Herald-American, Sun-Times,
   Tribune

BALANCE	OUT+R+OB=BP+AB+BB+SH+HP+CI							
Chicago	27	9	7	43	40	2	0	1	0
Cincinnati	27	8	8	43	38	3	2	0	0

Bosox Single-Inning Rampage

126. Team Scores 17 Runs in One Inning; Player Gets Three Hits in One Inning; Player Scores Three Runs in One Inning

DETROIT   at   BOSTON
(Tigers, 3)   (Red Sox, 23)

Thursday, June 18, 1953, Fenway Park

This year, the Red Sox were not what one might consider an offensive menace, having averaged just four runs per game. (By season's end they finished fifth in team hits and sixth in runs scored, averaging 4.29 runs per game.) So on Wednesday, June 17, statisticians were shocked when the Sox erupted for 21 hits in defeating the Tigers 17–1. In retro-spect, that was merely a prelude to Thursday's action when Boston *scored 17 runs in the seventh inning, the largest half-inning outburst in modern major-league history.* (Previous record was 15; see 5-21-52.) During the avalanche, several other benchmarks made their way into baseball's modern-day record book including:

Sammy White scored three of his season's 59 runs in one inning.

standard had been 2, by many players. White is the only player this century to score three.

In addition, two other marks were equalled:

• *Most times at bat in one inning—3 by Sammy White, Gene Stephens, Tommy Umphlett, John Lipon, and George Kell.* This mark had been shared by 14 big leaguers.

• *Most runs scored in consecutive innings—19.* Only one other club scored 19 runs in consecutive innings (see 5-02-01).

For those with sadistic inclinations, following are the details of the Detroit devastation. (The runs scored are portrayed in parentheses.)

• Sammy White led off against Detroit's Steve Gromek with a single to right.

• Gene Stephens also singled to right with White taking third.

• After Stephens stole second, Tommy Umphlett singled to left, scoring both White (1) and Stephens (2).

• Out number one was registered when Johnny Lipon went down swinging.

• George Kell doubled off the left-field wall sending Umphlett to third.

• Billy Goodman walked, loading the bases.

• Jimmy Piersall singled to right driving home Umphlett (3) and Kell (4).

• Dick Gernert homered into the left-field screen scoring Goodman (5) and Piersall (6) ahead of himself (7).

• Boston reliever, Ellis Kinder, singled to right.

• White, up for the second time, walked,

• *Most team hits in one inning—14*; the previous mark had been 12, by three teams. The BoSox' 14 remains the AL mark to date.

• *Most runs-batted-in by one team in one inning—17*; previous record of 14 had been established by the Red Sox in 1948. Boston's 17 remains the ML record to date.

• *Most batters facing pitchers in one inning—23*; previous mark of 19 had been shared by two clubs. The Sox' 23 remains the ML standard.

• *Most hits by one player in one inning—3 by Gene Stephens*; the previous record had been 2, by many players. Stephens is the only player in this century to collect three.

• *Most runs scored by one player in one inning—3 by Sammy White*; the previous

Gene Stephens, an unlikely record breaker, had been filling in for Korean War pilot Ted Williams.

and Dick Weik replaced Steve Gromek on the mound for the Tigers. Weik made an immediate contribution with a wild pitch, advancing both runners.

• Stephens doubled into short right, scoring both Kinder (8) and White (9).

• Umphlett walked.

• Lipon, who had made the first out of the inning, now singled to left, driving home Stephens (10).

• Kell lined out to Don Lund in left for out number two.

• Goodman singled to center, scoring Umphlett (11). Ted Lepcio ran for Goodman, and Earl Harrist replaced Weik on the hill.

• Al Zarilla pinch hit for Piersall and walked.

• Gernert also walked, forcing home Lipon (12).

• Kinder singled to center for his second hit of the inning while driving in Lepcio (13) and Zarilla (14).

• White, up for the third time, also singled to center scoring Gernert (15).

• Stephens singled to right for his third hit of the frame, knocking in Kinder (16).

• Umphlett singled to center, scoring White for the third time (17).

• Lipon walked, filling the bases.

• Kell, who had made the second out, flied out to Lund again, ending the extravaganza. Lund had his back to the wall as he made the catch.

During the 48 minute procession, the Red Sox had scored 17 runs on 14 hits and six bases on balls. Amazingly, all the runs were earned, for although the Tigers made five errors in the game, none were committed in this record-setting stanza.

As is the case with many of baseball's mind-boggling benchmarks, rationality simply can't explain the events. For example, Boston's record-breaking Gene Stephens, who collected three hits in the famous inning, entered the game with 34 hits in 162 at bats (.210). Sammy White, a .265 hitter, scored three runs in the frame. Teammate and relief ace Ellis Kinder, possessor of a lifetime .142 batting average and who had gone hitless in 32 consecutive at-bats the year before, singled twice in the seventh stanza. Five years earlier, he also had gathered two hits in a 14-run Boston inning. When reminded of this, Ellis cracked: "This stuff is getting to be old hat."*

Detroit hurler Ned Garver was saddled with the loss although he was clearly his club's "best" pitcher this day. For teammates Steve Gromek and Dick Weik this game represented a case of very bad timing. Only three days earlier, both pitchers had been sitting on the bench of the second-place Cleveland Indians as members of a contender with an excellent pitching staff. Now with last-place Detroit, they were battling the St. Louis Browns to escape from the basement. This had been their first appearances as members of their new team. Ironically, the Tiger mauling this day actually brought them a half game closer to the Browns who were busy losing a doubleheader to the Yankees.

*Gerry Moore, "Sox Set 11 New Marks,...," Boston Post, 19 June 1953, p. 26, col. 3.

Detroit Tigers	AB	R	H	I	PO	A	E
Harvey Kuenn ss	4	0	1	0	1	0	1
Johnny Pesky 2b	3	0	0	0	2	0	1
Ray Boone 3b	3	1	0	0	4	2	1
Bob Nieman rf	3	0	1	0	1	0	2
Jim Delsing cf	3	1	1	1	0	0	0
Walt Dropo 1b	4	1	3	2	7	0	0
Matt Batts c	4	0	1	0	6	0	0
Don Lund lf	4	0	0	0	3	0	0
Ned Garver p	1	0	0	0	0	3	0
Steve Gromek p6	1	0	0	0	0	1	0
Dick Weik p7	0	0	0	0	0	0	0
Earl Harrist p7	0	0	0	0	0	0	0
> Pat Mullin ph9	1	0	0	0	0	0	0
	31	3	7	3	24	6	5

Boston Red Sox	AB	R	H	I	PO	A	E
Billy Goodman 2b	4	2	4	2	5	1	0
Ted Lepcio pr7,2b	1	2	1	0	3	1	0
Jimmy Piersall rf	5	1	2	3	1	0	0
Al Zarilla ph7,rf	1	1	1	0	0	0	0
Dick Gernert 1b	5	2	2	4	5	2	0
Floyd Baker 3b	3	0	1	0	1	0	0
Ellis Kinder p6	4	2	2	2	0	3	0
Sammy White c	6	4	4	2	5	0	0
>Gene Stephens lf	6	3	3	3	3	0	0
Tommy Umphlett cf	5	2	3	3	2	1	0
Johnny Lipon ss	4	3	2	3	2	5	0
Marv Grissom p	1	0	0	0	0	1	0
Hersh Freeman p4	1	0	1	0	0	0	0
George Kell 3b6	4	1	1	0	0	1	0
	50	23	27	22	27	15	0

Detroit	IP	H	R	ER	BB	SO
Garver L,5-6	5.1	10	5	4	2	3
Gromek	1	7	9	9	3	2
Weik	.1	3	4	4	1	0
Harrist	1.1	7	5	5	3	1
	8	27	23	22	9	6

Boston	IP	H	R	ER	BB	SO
Grissom	3	0	0	0	2	1
Freeman	2	2	2	2	1	0
Kinder W,4-1	4	5	1	1	1	1
	9	7	3	3	4	2

Detroit	0 0 0	2 0 1	0 0 0	- 3
Boston	0 3 0	0 0 2	17 1 x	-23

OB: Detroit 6, Boston 13
DP: Kell-Lepcio-Gernert (Lund)
2B: Kell, Stephens
HR: Dropo(5), Gernert(12)
SB: Stephens
SO: Dropo, Gromek, Piersall, Lipon,
    Gernert 2, Kinder 2
BB: Pesky, Boone, Delsing, Garver,
    Goodman, Zarilla, White, Lipon 2,
    Gernert 2, Stephens, Umphlett

SH: Goodman, Nieman
WP: Weik
TIME: 3:03
ATTENDANCE: 3,101 (paid)
UMPIRES: Ed Hurley, Hank Soar, Eddie
    Rommel, Charlie Berry
SOURCES:Boston Herald, Post; Detroit
    Free Press, News; Retrosheet

BALANCE	OUT	+	R	+	OB	=	BP	=	AB	+	BB	+	SH	+	HP	+	CI
Detroit	27		3		6		36		31		4		1		0		0
Boston	24		23		13		60		50		9		1		0		0

Braves Blast Twelve Home Runs

127. Team Hits Eight Home Runs in One Game, 12 in Doubleheader

MILWAUKEE   at   PITTSBURGH
(Braves, 19,4)   (Pirates, 4,5)

Sunday, August 30, 1953, Forbes Field

In 1953 Milwaukee baseball fans were reunited with major league baseball, accepting with open arms the 1952, seventh-place Boston Braves. (In 1901, the Milwaukee Brewers had been charter members of the newborn American League but survived only

Jim Pendleton had his greatest offensive game.

which had never been seen in the National League. In the opener, the visitors pounded *eight home runs, which was more than any NL team had ever hit in a single game.* (To date, no NL club has ever hit more.) But that wasn't all. In the nightcap, the Braves returned to clout four more round trippers, establishing a *NL doubleheader mark (12) that has yet to be surpassed.* (The Yankees hold the major league standard of 13; see 6-28-39.)

Leading the long-ball parade were Mathews and 29-year-old rookie Jim Pendleton. Jim, filling in for an injured Andy Pafko, had only one circuit clout in 142 previous at-bats yet blasted a trio in the curtain raiser. Mathews hit two in the opener and one in the second. Eddie, only 21-years-old, brought his season's total to 43 including 28 on the road, breaking Ralph Kiner's league mark of 25. Joining in the merrymaking were Johnny Logan, Del Crandall and Jack Dittmer in the first contest; and Logan, Sid Gordon and Joe Adcock in the closer. Adcock's was an inside-the-park shot, his second such round-tripper during the season.

Milwaukee's outburst was a demonstration of their pent-up talents. They had scored only four runs in two games with the Giants before invading the Forbes Field health resort, and the pitiful Pirate pitchers were just what the doctor ordered for the benumbed Brave bats. Pittsburgh hurlers had allowed 82 hits, 11 homers, and 50 runs in their last six games. And, despite the Pirate offense having averaged six runs scored per game over the past seven outings, they had lost every one. Milwaukee took full advantage of their hosts' generosity.

one season before evolving into the St. Louis Browns.) The change in scenery and the support of 1.8 million fans worked wonders for the Braves. Coupled with some shrewd trades (for Joe Adcock and Andy Pafko), the return of Johnny Antonelli and Del Crandall from military service, and the emergence of rookie Bob Buhl and sophomore Eddie Mathews, the Braves made a swift ascent to second place. Mathews, in particular, burgeoned into a slugging superstar with 47 homers, 135 RBIs and a .302 batting average.

At no time during the Braves inaugural mid-west campaign did their newly found offensive power shine more than on this day. As ungrateful guests of the last-place Pirates for a Sunday doubleheader, Milwaukee erupted in a long-ball display the likes of

FIRST GAME

Milwaukee Braves	AB	R	H	I	PO	A	E
Billy Bruton cf	5	2	2	0	3	0	1
Johnny Logan ss	6	1	2	4	1	3	0
Sibby Sisti pr8,ss	0	1	0	0	0	2	0
Eddie Mathews 3b	5	2	2	4	2	0	0
Harry Hanebrink 3b8	0	0	0	0	0	1	0
Joe Adcock 1b	5	1	3	0	5	0	0
George Crowe 1b8	0	0	0	0	4	0	0
Del Crandall c	5	2	2	1	5	0	0
Ebba St. Clair c8	0	0	0	0	1	1	0
Jim Pendleton rf	5	5	4	5	3	0	1
Sid Gordon lf	1	2	1	0	1	0	0
Bob Thorpe pr6,lf	2	0	0	0	1	0	0
Jack Dittmer 2b	5	2	3	4	1	2	0
Mel Roach 2b8	1	0	0	0	0	0	0
>Johnny Antonelli p	5	1	1	1	0	0	0
	45	19	20	19	27	9	2

Pittsburgh Pirates	AB	R	H	I	PO	A	E
Carlos Bernier lf	5	0	0	0	4	0	0
>Danny O'Connell 3b	5	0	1	0	2	2	0
Cal Abrams rf	4	0	1	0	2	0	1
Frank Thomas cf	4	0	0	0	2	1	0
Johnny O'Brien 2b	4	1	0	0	3	4	0
Eddie O'Brien ss	4	1	2	0	2	3	0
Preston Ward 1b	4	1	1	0	8	0	0
Mike Sandlock c	2	1	1	0	3	1	0
Vic Janowicz ph7,c	2	0	0	0	1	0	0
Johnny Lindell p	1	0	1	1	0	0	0
Bob Hall p4	0	0	0	0	0	0	1
Eddie Pellagrini ph5	1	0	0	0	0	0	0
Jim Waugh p6	0	0	0	0	0	0	0
Dick Cole ph7	1	0	1	1	0	0	0
Roger Bowman p8	0	0	0	0	0	0	0
Nick Koback ph9	1	0	1	0	0	0	0
	38	4	9	2	27	11	2

Milwaukee	IP	H	R	ER	BB	SO
Antonelli W,11-9	9	9	4	2	0	6

Pittsburgh	IP	H	R	ER	BB	SO
Lindell L,5-16	3	6	5	5	4	2
Hall	2	5	4	1	1	1
Waugh	2	5	6	6	2	0
Bowman	2	4	4	4	1	1
	9	20	19	16	8	4

Milwaukee	0 1 1	3 4 2	4 4 0	-19
Pittsburgh	0 0 1	0 0 0	2 1 0	- 4

OB: Milwaukee 8, Pittsburgh 7
DP: Dittmer-Logan-Adcock (Abrams)
2B: Sandlock, Dittmer
3B: Bruton, Koback
HR: Mathews 2(42), Pendleton 3(4),
    Logan(9), Crandall(13), Dittmer(7)
CS: Crandall
SO: Logan, Adcock, Antonelli 2,
    O'Connell, Abrams 2, Thomas, ...

SO: ... E. O'Brien 2
BB: Bruton, Mathews, Adcock,
    Crandall, Pendleton, Gordon 3
SH: Antonelli
TIME: 2:41
UMPIRES: Babe Pinelli, Dusty Boggess,
    Bill Engeln, Bill Stewart

BALANCE	OUT+R+OB=BP=AB+BB+SH+HP+CI

	OUT	R	OB	BP	AB	BB	SH	HP	CI
Milwaukee	27	19	8	54	45	8	1	0	0
Pittsburgh	27	4	7	38	38	0	0	0	0

SECOND GAME

Milwaukee Braves	AB	R	H	I	PO	A	E
Billy Bruton cf	3	1	1	0	1	0	0
Del Crandall ph7	1	0	0	1	0	0	0
Bob Thorpe rf7	1	0	1	0	0	0	0
Johnny Logan ss	5	2	3	2	2	5	0
>Eddie Mathews 3b	5	2	2	3	4	1	1
Joe Adcock 1b	4	1	1	2	8	0	0
Walker Cooper c	4	0	0	0	5	0	0
Jim Pendleton rf,cf7	4	1	1	0	2	0	0
Sid Gordon lf	4	2	2	1	1	0	0
Jack Dittmer 2b	4	2	1	0	4	5	0
Bob Buhl p	1	0	0	0	0	1	0
Don Liddle p6	1	0	0	0	0	0	0
	37	11	12	9	27	12	1

Pittsburgh Pirates	AB	R	H	I	PO	A	E
Cal Abrams rf	3	1	0	0	2	0	0
Danny O'Connell 3b	5	1	2	0	2	3	0
Hal Rice lf	4	0	3	1	1	0	0
Frank Thomas cf	5	0	0	0	3	0	0
Preston Ward 1b	4	0	0	0	10	3	1
Toby Atwell c	4	1	3	0	3	0	0
Johnny O'Brien 2b	5	1	3	2	4	3	0
>Eddie O'Brien ss	4	0	1	0	2	4	1
Paul LaPalme p	3	1	1	0	0	3	0
Johnny Hetki p7	0	0	0	0	0	0	0
Carlos Bernier ph8	1	0	0	0	0	0	0
Bob Friend p9	0	0	0	0	0	0	0
	38	5	13	3	27	16	2

Milwaukee	IP	H	R	ER	BB	SO
Buhl	5	9	5	4	4	2
Liddle W,6-4	4	4	0	0	2	3
	9	13	5	4	6	5

Pittsburgh	IP	H	R	ER	BB	SO
LaPalme L,6-15	6.2	9	9	4	0	1
Hetki	1.1	2	2	1	0	0
Friend	1	1	0	0	0	0
	9	12	11	5	0	1

Milwaukee	1 0 3	0 0 0	6 1 0	-11
Pittsburgh	2 1 0	0 2 0	0 0 0	- 5

OB: Milwaukee 1, Pittsburgh 12
DP: Dittmer-Logan-Adcock (Atwell)
    Logan-Dittmer-Adcock (J.O'Brien)
    E. O'Brien-J. O'Brien-Ward
3B: Logan
HR: Logan(10), Mathews(43), J. O'Brien (2),
    Adcock(15), Gordon(18)
SO: Logan, Abrams, Thomas, Ward, LaPalme,
    Bernier
BB: Abrams 2, Rice, Ward, Atwell, E. O'Brien

SH: Buhl, Liddle
WP: LaPalme
TIME: 2:15
ATTENDANCE: 9,458
UMPIRES: Dusty Boggess, Bill Engeln,
    Bill Stewart, Babe Pinelli
SOURCES: Milwaukee Journal, Sentinel;
    Pittsburgh Post-Gazette, Press

BALANCE	OUT+R+OB=BP=AB+BB+SH+HP+CI
Milwaukee	27 11 1 39 37 0 2 0 0
Pittsburgh	27 5 12 44 38 6 0 0 0

Musial's Five-Home-Run Doubleheader

128. Player Hits Five
Home Runs in Doubleheader

NEW YORK	at	ST. LOUIS
(Giants, 6,9)		(Cardinals, 10,7)

Sunday, May 2, 1954, Busch Stadium

Every baseball fan knew that Stan "The Man" Musial was already one of the all-time greats. His slashing, line-drive hitting style had secured six league batting titles, earned him the Most Valuable Player Award three times, and enabled him to carry a .345 life-time average into the 1954 campaign. Although Stan had hit more than 30 home runs in a season three times, he was not known as a powerful, Ralph Kiner–calibre slugger. Actually, he had never hit more than two home runs in any big-league game; but on this day Musial surprised and delighted the 26,662 home-town fans. In perhaps his greatest offensive day, Stan drove in nine runs while connecting for a *new major-league mark*

of five home runs in a doubleheader. He also established a *National League standard of 21 total bases in a twin bill* which was later exceeded (see 8-01-72).

Musial's achievement was unexpected in more ways than one. Stan was normally a slow starter, but following this doubleheader he was batting .400 and had eight homers in his team's first 16 games. In addition, because of some pre-game rain, there had been no batting practice this day. Said Musial: "Funny thing, as a general rule, when we don't have batting practice, I don't hit too well."*

Giants southpaw Johnny Antonelli started the first game having pitched 15 straight

*Jack Rice, "Stan Taxes Memory—Can't Recall 'Day Like This'," St. Louis Globe-Democrat, 3 May 1954, first Sports page, col. 7.

"The Man" made boys of Giants pitching.

scoreless innings, but he had a lot of trouble with the Cardinals' left-handed swingers. Wally Moon opened the home half of the first with a 400-foot home run to left-center, and before Antonelli was relieved in the fifth, Musial had hit a pair, and rookie Tom Alston also had connected for one. Musial's third blast to reach the roof of the right-field pavilion in the opener was off Jim Hearn in the eighth. It proved to be the game winner.

The nightcap featured two more home runs and three more RBIs by Musial although they came in a losing cause. By the time Stan stepped to the plate to lead off the ninth, the fans were delirious for more. With the crowd cheering and urging their hero to hit

his sixth homer, Musial became overanxious and popped up to first baseman Whitey Lockman. After the game, Stan explained: "Jansen got me out on a bad pitch, a high fastball inside. Yeah, I was going for one that time."*

The details of Stan's big day follow:

FIRST GAME:

• First Inning — Walked by Johnny Antonelli.

• Third Inning — Hit a home run onto the roof of the right-field pavilion. It came off an Antonelli change-up with nobody on base.

• Fifth Inning — Hit another home run onto the roof of the right-field pavilion off

Bob Broeg, "Musial's Five Homers in Doubleheader a New Major League Record," St. Louis Post-Dispatch, p. 4C, col. 1.

Antonelli. This one came on a fast ball with Red Schoendienst on base.

• Sixth Inning — Singled to right off Jim Hearn.

• Eighth Inning — Hit his third homer onto the roof of the right-field pavilion with Moon and Schoendienst on base. It came off a Hearn slider.

SECOND GAME:

• First Inning — Walked by Don Liddle and later scored.

• Third Inning — Flied out to deep center (410 feet) off Liddle.

• Fifth Inning — Hit a home run over the right-field pavilion off a Hoyt Wilhelm curve. Schoendienst was on base.

• Seventh Inning — Hit another home run

over the same pavilion off a Wilhelm knuckle ball. Nobody was on base.

• Ninth Inning — Popped out to Lockman against Larry Jansen.

Overshadowed by Musial's heroics was the Giants' Don Mueller, who had six hits in the twin bill. Mueller, incidentally, was the last player to hit five home runs in two consecutive games, although not in a doubleheader. He did it on September 1–2, 1951.

Musial finished the season with his typical barrage of offensive statistics —.330 batting average, 35 home runs, 126 RBIs, and a .433 on-base average. He also led the league with 41 doubles and 120 runs scored. He didn't get much help, however, as the Cardinals finished sixth, 25 games behind the world champion Giants.

FIRST GAME

New York Giants	AB	R	H	I	PO	A	E
Davey Williams 2b	4	1	1	0	2	1	0
Alvin Dark ss	4	0	1	0	0	2	1
Hank Thompson 3b	4	1	1	1	1	4	1
Monte Irvin lf	3	2	2	2	2	0	0
Don Mueller rf	4	0	1	1	0	0	0
Willie Mays cf	3	0	0	0	2	0	0
Whitey Lockman 1b	4	1	1	1	9	1	0
Wes Westrum c	4	1	2	1	7	2	0
Johnny Antonelli p	2	0	0	0	1	1	0
Jim Hearn p5	0	0	0	0	0	0	0
Mario Picone p8	0	0	0	0	0	0	0
> Bobby Hofman ph9	1	0	0	0	0.	0	0
	33	6	9	6	24	11	2

St. Louis Cardinals	AB	R	H	I	PO	A	E
Wally Moon cf	5	2	2	1	2	0	0
Red Schoendienst 2b	3	3	0	0	3	3	0
Stan Musial rf	4	3	4	6	4	0	0
Ray Jablonski 3b	5	0	1	0	0	2	0
Rip Repulski lf	5	1	2	0	2	0	0
Tom Alston 1b	4	1	4	2	8	1	0
Alex Grammas ss	2	0	0	0	1	1	0
> Solly Hemus ph5,ss	3	0	1	1	0	0	0
Del Rice c	3	0	0	0	6	1	0
Gerry Staley p	1	0	0	0	1	2	0
Peanuts Lowrey ph5	1	0	0	0	0	0	0
Al Brazle p6	1	0	0	0	0	0	0
	37	10	14	10	27	10	0

New York	IP	H	R	ER	BB	SO
Antonelli	4	6	6	5	3	4
Hearn L,0-2	3.1	8	4	4	2	2
Picone	.2	0	0	0	0	0
	8	14	10	9	5	6

St. Louis	IP	H	R	ER	BB	SO
Staley	5	7	5	5	0	3
Brazle W,1-0	4	2	1	1	2	3
	9	9	6	6	2	6

```
New York   0 0 0   3 2 1   0 0 0   - 6
St. Louis  2 0 1   1 2 0   0 4 x   -10
```

OB: New York 3, St. Louis 9
DP: Schoendienst-Grammas-Alston(Mays)
    Jablonski-Schoendienst-Alston (Thompson)
2B: Thompson, Irvin, Repulski
HR: Moon(3), Musial 3(6), Alston(3),
    Lockman(3), Westrum(1), Irvin(4)
CS: Alston
SO: Thompson 2, Irvin, Antonelli 2, Hofman,
    Repulski 2, Grammas, Rice 2, Lowrey

BB: Irvin, Mays, Schoendienst 2,
    Musial, Alston, Rice
SH: Staley, Hearn
TIME: 2:48
UMPIRES: Augie Donatelli, Lee
    Ballanfant, Al Barlick, Lon Warneke

BALANCE	OUT	+	R	+	OB	=	BP	=	AB	+	BB	+	SH	+	HP	+	CI
New York	27		6		3		36		33		2		1		0		0
St. Louis	24		10		9		43		37		5		1		0		0

SECOND GAME

New York	AB	R	H	I	PO	A	E
Whitey Lockman 1b	2	1	0	0	10	1	0
Alvin Dark ss	5	0	0	0	2	1	0
Hank Thompson 3b	4	1	1	0	0	2	0
Monte Irvin lf	4	1	1	0	0	0	0
Don Mueller rf	5	3	5	2	2	0	0
Willie Mays cf	4	0	1	3	6	0	0
Ebba St. Claire c	4	1	2	0	3	1	0
Joey Amalfitano pr9	0	0	0	0	0	0	0
Wes Westrum c9	0	0	0	0	1	0	0
Ron Samford 2b	1	0	0	0	0	1	0
Dusty Rhodes ph4	1	1	1	0	0	0	0
Hoyt Wilhelm p4	2	0	0	0	0	1	0
Larry Jansen p7	1	0	1	1	0	2	0
Don Liddle p	1	0	0	0	1	0	0
Bill Taylor ph4	0	0	0	0	0	0	0
> Bobby Hofman ph4,2b	4	1	1	3	2	3	0
	38	9	13	9	27	12	0

St. Louis	AB	R	H	I	PO	A	E
Wally Moon cf	4	0	1	0	2	0	0
Red Schoendienst 2b	5	2	2	0	2	2	0
Stan Musial rf	4	3	2	3	4	1	0
Ray Jablonski 3b	5	1	3	1	1	0	0
>Rip Repulski lf	4	1	0	0	3	0	0
Tom Alston 1b	2	0	1	3	7	0	0
Alex Grammas ss	3	0	0	0	2	3	0
Tom Poholsky p7	0	0	0	0	0	1	0
Peanuts Lowrey ph7	0	0	0	0	0	0	0
Cot Deal p8	0	0	0	0	0	0	0
Bill Sarni c	2	0	0	0	2	0	0
Solly Hemus ph6	2	0	0	0	0	0	0
Joe Presko p	1	0	0	0	0	1	0
Royce Lint p4	0	0	0	0	0	0	0
Mel Wright P4	1	0	0	0	0	0	0
Joe Frazier ph6	1	0	1	0	0	0	0
Stu Miller pr6	0	0	0	0	0	0	0
Del Rice c7	1	0	0	0	4	0	0
	35	7	10	7	27	8	0

New York	IP	H	R	ER	BB	SO
Liddle	3	3	3	3	3	0
Wilhelm	3	6	4	4	0	3
Jansen W,1-0	3	1	0	0	2	2
	9	10	7	7	5	5

St. Louis	IP	H	R	ER	BB	SO
Presko	3.1	4	3	3	3	0
Lint L,1-1	.1	3	5	5	2	0
Wright	2.1	4	0	0	0	1
Poholsky	1	0	0	0	0	1
Deal	2	2	1	1	0	2
	9	13	9	9	5	4

New York   0 0 0   8 0 0   0 0 1   - 9
St. Louis   3 0 0   0 3 0   1 0 0   - 7

OB: New York 9, St. Louis 7
DP: Thompson-Hofman-Lockman(Repulski)
     Jansen-Dark-Lockman(Schoendienst)
2B: Schoendienst, Alston, Mueller,
     Thompson
3B: Mueller, Schoendienst
HR: Hofman(1), Musial 2(8),
     Jablonski(4)
SB: Jablonski
SO: Lockman, Mays, St. Claire,
     Wilhelm Moon, Repulski 2,
     Grammas, Rice
BB: Lockman 3, Thompson, Irvin,
     Musial, Repulski, Alston 2,
     Lowrey

SF: Mays
HP: By Liddle (Moon),
     by Deal (St.Claire)
TIME: 2:58
ATTENDANCE: 26,662
UMPIRES: Lee Ballanfant, Al
     Barlick, Lon Warneke, Augie
     Donatelli
SOURCES: New York Times; St.
     Louis Globe-Democrat, Post-
     Dispatch

BALANCE	OUT	+R	+OB	=BP	=AB	+BB	+SH	+HP	+CI
New York	27	9	9	45	38	5	1	1	0
St. Louis	27	7	7	41	35	5	0	1	0

Indians Attack Quickly

129. Team Scores Eight Runs
Before Making Their First Out

BALTIMORE   at   CLEVELAND
(Orioles, 3)   (Indians, 11)

Tuesday Night, July 6, 1954, Municipal Stadium

This was the Indians' greatest regular season. Winners of 54 of 77 games (a .701 winning percentage), Cleveland already had reduced the American League race to three teams. Only New York and Chicago were within 20 games of the first-place Tribe. Most of the thrust was being provided by a pitching staff that was fashioning the lowest American-league team ERA in 36 years. This day, however, it was the offense that registered its mark in baseball annals when the Indians *scored eight runs before making their first out of the game.* It was, and still is, the most runs ever scored to start an American League contest. (The Phillies hold the major-league record — see 8-13-48.)

Glynn led off with his fourth homer in two games.

Recently moved from St. Louis, where they had been known as the Browns, the Orioles were trying to upgrade their bottom-dwelling image. To date, they held sixth place, 3.5 games out of fourth. Taking the mound for the visitors was their ace Joe Coleman, but Cleveland wasted little time in flexing their first-place muscles. Here's how that record-setting, opening round progressed amid a light, wind-blown drizzle:

• Bill Glynn led off with his fifth home run of the campaign, a 400-foot blast to right center (1–0).

• Bobby Avila, the American League's leading batter, singled.

• Larry Doby followed suit, sending Avila to third. Doby took second on right fielder Cal Abrams' wild throw into third.

• Al Rosen, the Tribe clean-up hitter, was walked intentionally, loading the sacks.

• Wally Westlake promptly unloaded them with a three-run triple (4–0) to right center on a ball that could have been caught (according to *The Baltimore Sun* reporter).

• Dave Philley walked.

• George Strickland, batting .228, drove Westlake home (5–0) and Philley to third on a single to right. That was enough for Baltimore manager Jimmy Dykes whose prayers for heavier rain failed. Coleman was whisked to the clubhouse and replaced with Mike Blyzka. Blyzka rode in from the center-field bullpen in Cleveland's sparkling-red roadster. It was the only bright spot in the Orioles' evening.

• The red-hot Indians scarcely noticed the change as Jim Hegan resumed the assault by singling to center. Philley tromped home (6–0) and Strickland stopped at second.

• A burly Early Wynn beat out a bunt to pack the sacks again.

• Glynn appeared for the second time and singled to right, scoring Strickland and Hegan (8–0). A winded Wynn stopped at second.

• Avila ended the streak by flying out to right for the first out.

• Doby got things back on track with a single to center, scoring Wynn (9–0) and sending Glynn to second.

• Rosen walked again, filling the bases.

• Westlake stalled the rally when he popped up to first base for the second out.

• Philley continued the Indian massacre by singling to center, driving in Glynn and

Doby with the 10th and 11th runs. Rosen went to third on the hit. Philley then poured salt in the gaping wound by stealing second.

• Strickland, the 16th batter, compassionately grounded out to Jim Brideweser.

Wynn's baserunning didn't catch up to him until the eighth. Working on a no-hitter through seven, Early then yielded five hits and three runs over the final two frames to garner his 10th victory.

The Indians played even better baseball in the second half of the season and finished with a 111–43 regular season log. Alas, they were upset in the World Series by the New York Giants who swept them.

Baltimore Orioles	AB	R	H	I	PO	A	E
Cal Abrams rf	3	0	0	0	2	0	1
Dick Kryhoski 1b	4	0	0	0	8	2	1
Chuck Diering cf	3	0	0	0	3	0	0
Vern Stephens 3b	3	0	0	0	0	1	0
Bob Kennedy 3b	1	1	1	0	0	1	0
Gil Coan lf	4	1	1	0	1	0	0
Clint Courtney c	3	1	1	1	4	0	0
Bobby Young 2b	4	0	1	1	2	3	0
Jim Brideweser ss	4	0	1	1	2	3	0
Joe Coleman p	0	0	0	0	0	0	0
Mike Blyzka p1	2	0	0	0	1	0	0
Eddie Waitkus ph8	1	0	0	0	0	0	0
Howie Fox p1	0	0	0	0	1	1	0
> Jim Fridley ph9	1	0	0	0	0	0	0
	33	3	5	3	24	11	2

Cleveland Indians	AB	R	H	I	PO	A	E
Billy Glynn 1b	4	2	3	3	13	0	0
Bobby Avila 2b	5	1	2	0	1	5	0
Larry Doby cf	5	2	2	1	3	0	0
Al Rosen 3b	2	1	1	0	1	1	0
Wally Westlake lf	5	1	1	3	2	0	0
Dave Philley rf	4	1	2	2	0	0	0
George Strickland ss	5	1	1	1	1	3	1
>Jim Hegan c	4	1	1	1	6	0	0
Early Wynn p	4	1	1	0	0	0	0
	38	11	14	11	27	9	1

Baltimore	IP	H	R	ER	BB	SO
Coleman L,9-7	0	5	7	7	2	0
Blyzka	7	9	4	4	4	4
Fox	1	0	0	0	0	0
	8	14	11	11	6	4

Cleveland	IP	H	R	ER	BB	SO
Wynn W,10-6	9	5	3	3	3	4

Baltimore	0 0 0	0 0 0	0 1 2	– 3
Cleveland	11 0 0	0 0 0	0 0 x	–11

OB: Baltimore 6, Cleveland 9
2B: Rosen
3B: Westlake, Brideweser
HR: Glynn(5)
SB: Philley
SO: Stephens, Abrams, Waitkus, Brideweser, Strickland, Doby 2, Westlake
BB: Abrams, Diering, Courtney, Glynn Rosen 3(2I), Philley, Hegan

TIME: 2:00
ATTENDANCE: 11,442
UMPIRES: John Stevens, Eddie Rommel, Larry Napp, Red Flaherty
SOURCES: Baltimore Sun; Cleveland Plain Dealer, Press; Retrosheet

BALANCE	OUT+R+OB=BP=AB+BB+SH+HP+CI							
Baltimore	27	3	6	36	33	3	0	0	0
Cleveland	24	11	9	44	38	6	0	0	0

130. Player Totals 18 Bases, 13 Extra Bases in One Game

MILWAUKEE   at   BROOKLYN
(Braves, 15)   (Dodgers, 7)

Saturday, July 31, 1954, Ebbets Field

Adcock demonstrated two-fisted power in Brooklyn.

however, richly rewarded for their loyalty as they witnessed an offensive extravaganza led by their strapping first baseman. Adcock batted five times, collecting four home runs and a double for *18 total bases and 13 extra bases, thereby establishing two new major-league standards that still stand.* In addition, five other records were tied:

• Four home runs in one game tied the major-league benchmark previously accomplished by four players since 1900.

• Five extra-base hits tied the ML standard.

• Five home runs in two consecutive games also tied the ML mark.

• The Braves' 13 extra-base hits tied the NL record (later surpassed).

• The two clubs' 10 home runs also tied the NL mark (later surpassed).

Adcock, as yet, had not been considered a slugger, collecting only 64 home runs in 2,088 previous major-league at-bats. This day's quartet increased his season total to 19, one more than he had hit the entire previous year. "I never hit more than two in one game before, not even in the minors" said Joe in a post-game interview. Maybe it was the new bat. Having broken his last bat in his final plate appearance Friday night, Joe had borrowed reserve catcher Charlie White's lumber. "I don't know why I happened to choose Charlie's bat. It was so heavy that I could

Milwaukee's 6'4", 220-pound first baseman, Joe Adcock, entered this game hitting .314 with 15 home runs. One of those round trippers had come in Brooklyn on Friday night complementing a single and a double. Joe had had particular success with Dodger pitchers, hitting .383 (18 for 48) against them this year, and over .400 in Ebbets Field. His success had New York writers jestfully dubbing the park "Adcock's Alley." Due in part to Adcock's exploits, the Braves were on an eight-game win streak and had prevailed in eight of 11 encounters with Brooklyn prior to this game.

This was a torrid day in Brooklyn, 95-degree heat with high humidity; not a pleasant vacation for the 475 excursioning Milwaukeeans in attendance. They were,

Palica surrendered a double and a home run.

Milwaukee Braves	AB	R	H	I	PO	A	E
Billy Bruton cf	6	0	4	1	4	0	0
>Danny O'Connell 2b	5	0	0	0	4	4	0
Eddie Mathews 3b	4	3	2	2	3	2	0
Hank Aaron lf	5	2	2	0	0	0	0
Joe Adcock 1b	5	5	5	7	11	0	0
Andy Pafko rf	4	2	3	2	0	0	0
Jim Pendleton rf7	1	1	0	0	0	0	0
Johnny Logan ss	2	1	1	1	1	1	0
Roy Smalley ss6	2	1	1	0	0	1	0
Del Crandall c	4	0	0	0	2	1	0
Sammy Calderone c7	1	0	1	0	2	0	0
Jim Wilson p	1	0	0	0	0	0	0
Lew Burdette p2	3	0	0	0	0	4	0
Bob Buhl p8	0	0	0	0	0	0	0
Dave Jolly p8	1	0	0	0	0	0	0
	44	15	19	13	27	13	0

Brooklyn Dodgers	AB	R	H	I	PO	A	E
Junior Gilliam 2b	4	1	4	0	3	1	0
Pee Wee Reese ss	3	0	1	0	1	2	0
Don Zimmer ss6	1	0	0	0	1	1	0
Duke Snider cf	4	0	1	1	0	0	0
George Shuba lf8	1	0	0	0	0	0	0
Gil Hodges 1b	5	1	1	1	7	0	0
Sandy Amoros lf,cf8	5	2	3	0	6	0	0
Jackie Robinson 3b	0	0	0	0	0	0	0
Don Hoak 3b6	2	1	1	2	0	1	1
Carl Furillo rf	5	1	2	1	3	0	0
>Rube Walker c	5	1	1	2	6	1	0
Don Newcombe p	0	0	0	0	0	0	0
Clem Labine p2	0	0	0	0	0	0	0
Walt Moryn ph2	1	0	0	0	0	0	0
Erv Palica p3	0	0	0	0	0	0	0
Pete Wojey p5	1	0	0	0	0	1	0
Johnny Podres p8	2	0	2	0	0	1	0
	39	7	16	7	27	8	1

Milwaukee	IP	H	R	ER	BB	SO
Wilson	1	5	1	1	0	0
Burdette W,10-11	6.1	8	5	5	2	3
Buhl	0	2	0	0	0	0
Jolly	1.2	1	1	1	1	1
	9	16	7	7	3	4

Brooklyn	IP	H	R	ER	BB	SO
Newcombe L,6-6	1	4	4	4	0	0
Labine	1	1	0	0	0	0
Palica	2.1	5	5	5	2	1
Wojey	2.2	4	3	3	0	3
Podres	2	5	3	1	0	1
	9	19	15	13	2	5

Milwaukee	1 3 2	0 3 0	3 0 3	-15
Brooklyn	1 0 0	0 0 1	0 4 1	- 7

OB: Milwaukee 5, Brooklyn 10
DP: Mathews-O'Connell-Adcock (Hodges)
    O'Connell-Logan-Adcock (Moryn)
    Zimmer-Gilliam-Hodges(Jolly)
2B: Gilliam, Pafko, Bruton 3, Aaron,
    Amoros, Adcock
3B: Amoros
HR: Mathews 2(27), Adcock 4(19),
    Hoak(5), Pafko(12), Hodges(28),
    Walker(2)
SO: O'Connell, Mathews, Smalley,
    Crandall 2, Snider, Hodges,
    Furillo, Walker

BB: Mathews, Logan, Gilliam, Zimmer, Robinson
SH: O'Connell
SF: Hoak
HP: By Wilson (Robinson)
WP: Podres
TIME: 2:53
ATTENDANCE: 12,263
UMPIRES: Dusty Boggess, Bill Engeln, Bill
    Stewart, Al Barlick
SOURCES: Milwaukee Journal, Sentinel; New
    York Herald-Tribune, Times; Retrosheet

BALANCE	OUT+R+OB=BP=AB+BB+SH+HP+CI
Milwaukee	27 15 5 47 44 2 1 0 0
Brooklyn	27 7 10 44 39 3 1 1 0

hardly lift it the first time I went to bat. I hit a home run though, so I kept on using it."* (Adcock later recanted this bat tale.)†

All four home runs were deposited into the lower left-center field seats, although his blast in the fifth bounced off the upper-deck facade. The gopher balls were delivered by four different pitchers, and according to *The New York Times*, the 26-year-old's heroics required just seven pitches. Two homers and the double greeted first offerings; the other two homers came off second pitches.

*Bob Wolf, "Borrowed Weapon Smashes Dodgers Into Submission," Milwaukee Journal, *1 August 1954, Part 3, p. 1, col. 1.*
†Bill James, The Baseball Book 1990 *(New York: Villard Books, 1990), 186.*

Newspapers varied slightly on what type of pitches were blasted, but according to *The Milwaukee Journal*:

2nd Inning—As the first batter, Adcock knocked Don Newcombe's first pitch fastball into the seats.

3rd Inning—With nobody on, Joe smashed Erv Palica's first pitch, a curve, for a double off the top of the wall in left center. Adcock later claimed this was the hardest ball he hit that day.

5th Inning—Palica's slider, with two runners on, bounced off the upper deck facade.

7th Inning—With one on, Pete Wojey hung a curve for Adcock's third homer.

9th Inning—Leading off, Joe tomahawked a high, 1–0 fastball from Johnny Podres.

The Dodger hurlers were frustrated by Adcock's hitting prowess and in his first at-bat the following day, Joe dodged two inside pitches from Brooklyn's Russ Meyer before doubling. On his next trip to the plate, Adcock was drilled in the head by a Clem Labine fastball, forcing him to be carried off the field. Fortunately, Adcock had been wearing the newly fashioned "batting helmet,"

which probably saved his life. The controversial tactic seemed to be the only way the Dodgers could stop him, and Joe still keeps the dented helmet as a trophy.

On September 11, the Dodgers' Don Newcombe sent another fastball in the direction of Adcock's head. This time Joe used his arm to protect himself, suffering a wrist injury that sidelined him for the balance of the campaign. Coupled with an injury to Hank Aaron a week earlier, the Braves were thus effectively eliminated from the 1954 pennant race (won by the Giants).

Adcock got a late start playing baseball. He hadn't played in an organized baseball game until his freshman year at Louisiana State University which he attended on a basketball scholarship. Five years later, he was playing for the Cincinnati Reds. In 1953, Joe was traded to Milwaukee for Rocky Bridges and cash as part of a four-way deal. Despite several broken bones and multiple seasons in platoon situations, Adcock finished his career with 336 home runs and a .277 batting average. Joe spent the twilight of his career in the American League and eventually managed the Cleveland Indians in 1967.

Lightning Strikes for a Third Time

131. Team Scores 12 Runs in One Inning with Bases Empty, Two Outs

CINCINNATI   at   BROOKLYN
(Reds, 7)   (Dodgers, 20)   •

Sunday, August 8, 1954, Ebbets Field

During a two-year period in the early 1950s, the Cincinnati Reds were a team susceptible to violent offensive eruptions. Facing the Dodgers in Brooklyn on May 21, 1952, the Reds were victims of a major-league record 15 first-inning runs. Then on June 29 of the same year, the Reds hosted the Chicago Cubs in a doubleheader. In the

ninth inning of the first game, with two outs and the bases empty, Cincinnati led 8–2. The Cubs then proceeded to humiliate the Reds in front of the home crowd by rallying for seven runs and holding on for the upset. Now, in 1954, Cincinnati was again the quarry in Brooklyn where they were bludgeoned in the bottom of the eighth as the

Hoak enjoyed the grand-slam serving by Smith.

Dodgers crossed the plate 13 times, 12 of which came after the bases were empty and there were two outs. The *12 runs scored after two were down and the bases empty* established a major-league standard that endures in baseball annals. Making the situation even more pathetic for the vanquished Reds was the fact that a timely error made all 12 of those runs unearned.

For non–Cincinnati fans who can stomach the details:

• Howie Judson opened the inning on the mound for the Reds, and Gil Hodges led off for the Dodgers with a triple to right-center field.

• Carl Furillo flied to right with Hodges scoring.

• Jim Gilliam grounded out, second to first, for out number two.

• With the pitcher on deck, Judson fell behind Roy Campanella 3–0 and was ordered to issue an intentional pass.

• Clem Labine, hitting .050, was the delighted recipient of a walk from Judson. (Labine reached base only five times in 34 plate appearances this year and scored but two runs, both in this contest.)

• The bases became jammed when Don Hoak also looked at four bad pitches, leaving the Reds still seeking that elusive third out.

• Next, Pee Wee Reese sent a sharp grounder toward third baseman Chuck Harmon, but the ball went right through him enabling both Campanella and Labine to score. Hoak went to third and Reese took second on a throw to the plate. That brought southpaw Jackie Collum from the bullpen to face the left-swinging Duke Snider.

• Collum stoked the rally flames by walking Snider to re-load the bases.

• On a 3–2 pitch the runners were moving as Jackie Robinson lashed a long single off the right-field wall. All three runners scored and Sandy Amoros pinch-ran for Robinson.

• Hodges appeared at the plate for the second time and lined a double to left.

• Furillo singled both mates home.

• Gilliam was nicked by a pitch.

• Campanella singled home Furillo with Gilliam stopping at second.

• For the second time in the frame, Labine was issued a free pass, loading the sacks and sending Collum to the showers.

• Cincinnati manager Birdie Tebbetts was losing faith in his bullpen, so he sent his sixth hurler, Frank Smith, directly from the dugout to the mound. Birdie could be excused for his indiscretion because he wasn't with the Reds in 1952; but calling on Frank Smith in such a situation was akin to pouring gasoline on a fire. In both of the aforementioned Cincinnati debacles, Frank had contributed lustily. Combined, Smith had faced 30 batters, allowed six walks, ten hits, ten runs, and hit one batter. This occasion would be little different.

• Smith warmed up by going to a full count on Hoak before Don blasted a grand slam into the upper left-field stands. It was then 20–5.

• Showing not the least sympathy, Reese walked.

• Equally calloused, Snider singled.

• Amoros, who had pinch-run for Robinson, also walked. Compassion then finally arrived for Smith, not from the Dodgers but from his manager, who summoned Art Fowler to the hill.

• Once more Hodges stepped to the plate, this time with a chance for his third extra-base hit of the inning. Gil unloaded a towering fly to deep center. With his

back to the fence, Gus Bell made a leaping catch to mercifully terminate the Reds' misery.

Hoping for a miracle of their own, the Reds gamely rallied for two runs in the ninth to make the final count 20–7.

Despite Frank Smith's intriguing penchant for occupying the mound at inopportune times, his 1954 pitching record was quite respectable. Frank won five, saved 20, and compiled a 2.67 ERA for a Cincinnati club that breathed the air of fifth place.

Meanwhile the Dodgers, with an impressive offensive team, couldn't equalize New York's pitching and settled for second place, five games behind the world champion Giants.

Cincinnati Reds	AB	R	H	I	PO	A	E
Bobby Adams 2b	4	1	1	1	4	2	0
Nino Escalara cf,lf7	4	2	2	0	2	0	0
Lloyd Merriman lf	3	0	1	0	0	0	0
Gus Bell ph7,cf	2	1	1	0	2	0	0
Ted Kluszewski 1b	4	2	3	2	6	0	0
Wally Post rf	3	0	2	1	3	0	0
>Chuck Harmon 3b	4	0	1	3	1	3	1
Roy McMillan ss	3	0	0	0	2	3	0
Bob Borkowski ph8	1	0	0	0	0	0	0
Rocky Bridges ss8	0	0	0	0	0	0	0
Hobie Landrith c	3	1	1	0	4	1	0
Fred Baczewski p	2	0	0	0	0	0	0
Karl Drews p5	0	0	0	0	0	0	0
Ed Bailey ph7	1	0	0	0	0	0	0
Harry Perkowski p7	0	0	0	0	0	0	0
Jim Greengrass ph8	1	0	0	0	0	0	0
Howie Judson p8	0	0	0	0	0	0	0
Jackie Collum p8	0	0	0	0	0	0	0
Frank Smith p8	0	0	0	0	0	0	0
Art Fowler p8	0	0	0	0	0	0	0
	35	7	12	7	24	9	1

Brooklyn Dodgers	AB	R	H	I	PO	A	E
Don Hoak 3b	4	3	2	4	1	0	0
Pee Wee Reese ss	5	1	2	1	2	5	0
Duke Snider cf	4	1	1	0	0	0	1
Jackie Robinson lf	4	1	1	3	3	0	0
Sandy Amoros pr8,lf	0	1	0	0	1	0	0
>Gil Hodges 1b	6	4	4	0	10	1	0
Carl Furillo rf	4	2	3	4	2	0	0
Jim Gilliam 2b	4	2	1	3	1	4	0
Roy Campanella c	3	3	2	2	6	0	0
Carl Erskine p	3	0	0	0	1	1	0
Clem Labine p8	0	2	0	0	0	1	0
	37	20	16	17	27	12	1

Cincinnati	IP	H	R	ER	BB	SO
Baczewski	4	5	3	3	3	1
Drews L,2-3	2	4	4	4	1	2
Perkowski	1	0	0	0	0	0
Judson	.2	1	5	1	3	0
Collum	0	4	7	0	2	0
Smith	0	2	1	0	2	0
Fowler	.1	0	0	0	0	0
	8	16	20	8	11	3

Brooklyn	IP	H	R	ER	BB	SO
Erskine W,14-10	7.1	9	5	5	4	5
Labine	1.2	3	2	2	0	0
	9	12	7	7	4	5

| Cincinnati | 1 0 2 | 0 0 0 | 1 1 2 | - 7 |
| Brooklyn | 1 0 0 | 2 0 4 | 0 13 x | -20 |

OB: Cincinnati 8, Brooklyn 6
DP: Adams-McMillan-Kluszewski (Gilliam)
   Gilliam-Reese-Hodges (McMillan)
   Reese-Gilliam-Hodges(Greengrass)
   Harmon-Kluszewski (Robinson)
2B: Kluszewski, Hodges
3B: Escalara, Hodges
HR: Campanella(17), Gilliam(11), Hoak(6)
SO: Escalara 2, Merriman, Baczewski,
   Harmon, Reese, Snider, Erskine
BB: Escalara, Kluszewski, Landrith,
   Post, Hoak 2, Snider 2, Labine 2,
   Robinson 2, Campanella 2, Reese

SF: Adams, Harmon, Furillo, Post
HP: By Collum (Gilliam)
WP: Erskine
TIME: 2:57
ATTENDANCE: 10,884
UMPIRES: Tom Gorman, Augie
   Donatelli, Jocko Conlan, Art
   Gore
SOURCES: Cincinnati Enquirer;
   New York Herald-Tribune, Times,
   World-Telegram; Retrosheet

BALANCE	OUT	+R	+OB	=BP	=AB	+BB	+SH	+HP	+CI
Cincinnati	27	7	8	42	35	4	3	0	0
Brooklyn	24	20	6	50	37	11	1	1	0

Peak Attendance

132. Crowd of 86,563 Attends Game

NEW YORK   at   CLEVELAND
(Yankees, 1,2)   (Indians, 4,3)

Sunday, September 12, 1954, Municipal Stadium

The day certainly called for a celebration. After three consecutive years of finishing as runners-up behind New York, Cleveland was poised for their first pennant in six years, and just their second since 1920. Especially gratifying was the fact that their closest competitors this season were the Yankees, this day's guests. Since the Indians' 1948 championship, the Yankees had dominated both the American and the National League, winning five straight world's championships.

With only a dozen remaining regular-season games, the Tribe now led second-place New York by 6.5 games. For the Yankees to retain any notion of their former lofty status, they needed to sweep this doubleheader; not an impossible task considering they led the season series 11–9. On the other hand, Cleveland fans saw the twin-bill as the world champions' last gasp and came to savor their demise. Cleveland's heroes were led by eventual league leaders Bobby Avila (.341) and Larry Doby (32 HRs, 126 RBIs), plus Al

Rosen (.300, 24 HRs, 102 RBIs) and a terrific pitching staff. That corps included Bob Lemon, Early Wynn. Mike Garcia, Art Houtemann, Bob Feller, Hal Newhouser, Don Mossi, and Ray Narleski. Lemon and Wynn finished with eight of their team's 11 victories over New York this season.

In 1954, no baseball park's capacity exceeded that of Municipal Stadium, boasting accommodations for 73,811. This day saw those provisions pushed beyond the limit as bright warm weather helped encourage an avalanche of humanity to descend upon the 23-year-old structure. By the time the turnstiles had stopped clicking, 84,587 avid supporters had paid their money, and another 1,976 had entered via complimentary passes. *Those 86,563 total attendees represent the largest crowd to have ever witnessed a major-league baseball game.* (The previous regular season "paid" attendance record had also been attained in Municipal Stadium on June 20, 1948.) Many of the participants in this

Avila's best season helped Cleveland to the pennant.

walkways. The three sections of green bleacher seats normally reserved for a hitter's background were reduced by one-half. Remarkably, still other hopefuls were turned away at the gates, which closed after the seventh inning of the opener rather than the customary fifth frame of the nightcap. As mind numbing as this throng was, *The Cleveland Press* expected that these figures would be exceeded by upcoming World Series turnouts. (They weren't.)

Crowds of this size also led to some astonishing food consumption. The Berlo Vending Company, which handled the concessions, estimated that five tons, or approximately 100,000 wieners, were consumed in addition to about 85,000 bottles of beer.

Cleveland won both ends of the twin bill, virtually clinching the pennant. It was the first time this year the Yankees had been so swept and was especially satisfying for the Indians to beat their old nemesis Allie Reynolds in the

milestone were uncomfortable, however, over 12,000 being without seats. Fans packed the aisles, stood 10–11 rows deep behind the wire outfield fences, and 3–5 rows deep in the

FIRST GAME

New York Yankees	AB	R	H	I	PO	A	E	Cleveland Indians	AB	R	H	I	PO	A	E
Gil McDougald 2b	4	0	1	0	2	3	0	Al Smith lf	5	2	1	0	3	0	0
Joe Collins 1b	4	0	1	0	10	2	0	Bobby Avila 2b	4	1	2	1	3	4	1
Mickey Mantle cf	4	1	1	0	2	0	0	>Larry Doby cf	4	0	1	0	2	0	0
Yogi Berra c	3	0	2	0	6	1	0	Al Rosen 3b	3	0	2	2	0	1	0
Irv Noren lf	3	0	0	1	1	0	0	Vic Wertz 1b	3	0	0	0	9	0	0
Enos Slaughter rf	4	0	0	0	1	0	1	Billy Glynn pr7,1b	0	0	0	0	2	0	0
Andy Carey 3b	3	0	1	0	0	3	0	Dave Philley rf	2	0	0	0	2	0	0
Willie Miranda ss	3	0	0	0	1	4	1	George Strickland ss	4	0	1	0	1	1	0
> Hank Bauer ph9	1	0	0	0	0	0	0	Jim Hegan c	4	1	1	0	5	1	0
Whitey Ford p	1	0	0	0	0	1	0	Bob Lemon p	2	0	0	0	0	4	0
Eddie Robinson ph7	1	0	0	0	0	0	0		31	4	8	3	27	11	1
Allie Reynolds p7	0	0	0	0	1	0	0								
	31	1	6	1	24	14	2								

New York	IP	H	R	ER	BB	SO
Ford	6	5	1	1	4	4
Reynolds L,11-4	2	3	3	2	3	1
	8	8	4	3	7	5

Cleveland	IP	H	R	ER	BB	SO
Lemon W,22-6	9	6	1	1	2	5

New York   0 0 0   0 0 1   0 0 0   - 1
Cleveland   0 0 0   0 1 0   2 1 x   - 4

OB: New York 7, Cleveland 11
DP: McDougald-Miranda-Collins (Strickland)
2B: Mantle, Rosen
SO: Mantle 3, Noren, Slaughter, Doby,
    Wertz 3, Strickland
BB: Berra, Carey, Avila, Doby, Rosen,
    Wertz, Philley 2, Lemon

SH: Ford, Lemon
SF: Noren
TIME: 2:40
UMPIRES: Eddie Rommel, Joe Paparella,
    Jim Honochick, Red Flaherty

BALANCE	OUT	+R	+OB	=BP	=AB	+BB	+SH	+HP	+CI
New York	27	1	7	35	31	2	2	0	0
Cleveland	24	4	11	39	31	7	1	0	0

SECOND GAME

New York Yankees	AB	R	H	I	PO	A	E
Hank Bauer rf	4	0	1	0	0	0	0
Andy Carey 3b	2	1	1	0	3	2	0
Enos Slaughter ph9	1	0	0	0	0	0	0
Mickey Mantle cf	3	0	0	0	1	0	0
>Yogi Berra c	4	1	1	2	4	1	0
Eddie Robinson 1b	3	0	0	0	8	0	0
Irv Noren lf	2	0	0	0	5	0	0
Gil McDougald 2b	3	0	0	0	2	0	0
Phil Rizzuto ss	3	0	0	0	1	3	0
Tommy Byrne p	3	0	0	0	0	2	0
	28	2	3	2	24	8	0

Cleveland Indians	AB	R	H	I	PO	A	E
Al Smith lf	2	1	2	0	1	0	0
Bobby Avila 2b	4	1	3	1	3	1	0
Larry Doby cf	1	0	0	0	0	0	0
Wally Westlake cf2	3	0	1	2	1	0	0
Hank Majeski 3b	4	0	0	0	3	2	0
Vic Wertz 1b	3	0	0	0	4	2	0
Al Rosen ph8	0	0	0	0	0	0	0
Billy Glynn pr8	0	0	0	0	0	0	0
Dave Philley rf	4	0	0	0	2	0	0
>George Strickland ss	4	0	0	0	0	0	0
Jim Hegan c	3	0	0	0	12	1	0
Early Wynn p	3	1	1	0	1	1	0
	31	3	7	3	27	7	0

New York	IP	H	R	ER	BB	SO
Byrne L,1-1	8	7	3	3	3	5

Cleveland	IP	H	R	ER	BB	SO
Wynn W,21-11	9	3	2	2	2	12

New York   2 0 0   0 0 0   0 0 0   - 2
Cleveland   0 0 0   0 3 0   0 0 x   - 3

OB: New York 2, Cleveland 7
2B: Carey, Westlake
HR: Berra
SB: Glynn
SO: Bauer 2, Slaughter, Mantle 3,
    Berra, Robinson 2, McDougald,
    Rizzuto, Byrne, Westlake, Wertz,
    Philley, Hegan, Wynn
BB: Mantle, Noren, Smith 2, Rosen

SH: Carey
TIME: 2:09
ATTENDANCE: 86,563 (84,587 paid)
UMPIRES: Joe Papparella, Jim Honochick,
    Red Flaherty, Eddie Rommel
SOURCES: Cleveland Plain Dealer, Press;
    New York Times

BALANCE	OUT	+R	+OB	=BP	=AB	+BB	+SH	+HP	+CI
New York	27	2	2	31	28	2	1	0	0
Cleveland	24	3	7	34	31	3	0	0	0
----

opener. Because of superb Cleveland pitching, most baseball mavens then predicted a World's Championship for the Indians regardless of who prevailed in the still-contested National League race. Alas, the Giants made quick work of Cleveland in a four-game World Series sweep, thanks in large part to some Dusty Rhodes heroics and a much publicized over-the-shoulder catch by Willie Mays.

Chisox Maul A's

133. Team Scores 29 Runs in Nine-Inning Game

CHICAGO   at   KANSAS CITY
(White Sox, 29)   (Athletics, 6)

Saturday, April 23, 1955, Municipal Stadium

This was the inaugural season in Kansas City for the transplanted Athletics from Philadelphia. Not since 1886 had this Midwest town hosted major-league baseball, and after this debacle, Kansas City learned why Philadelphia fans had avoided the team in Connie Mack Stadium. New owner Arnold Johnson brought with him the worst pitching staff in the majors, and the change in scenery did nothing to alter their standard of performance. Having suffered the most hits and earned runs in both leagues in 1954, the much abused corps added the most-walks-allowed to their 1955 credentials. This day's game served as a showcase for that flagrant incompetence as the White Sox harvested 29 hits and six walks in crushing the A's 29–6.

Remarkably, although several records were tied by Chicago, no new benchmarks were established:

• 29 runs scored tied the modern standard set by Boston (see 6-8-50).

• 7 ChiSox had three or more hits in the game tying the AL mark (see 6-28-39).

• 29 hits fell one shy of the AL record.

• 55 total bases were five short of ML high (see 6-8-50).

• 7 home runs missed the old standard by one (see 8-30-53).

• Sherm Lollar tied a ML mark by hitting safely twice in two separate innings. Oddly, the four hits came off four different hurlers.

• 35 runs scored by the two teams fell one shy of the AL standard.

Sherman Lollar — two hits in each of two innings.

Chicago entered the game with a team batting average of .252, sixth best in the AL, but wasted little time in taking advantage of Kansas City pitching. Abetted by a stiff breeze blowing toward left field, the White Sox scored four in the first inning highlighted by a Bob Nieman three-run homer. The A's countered with three of their own in the bottom of the frame, but that was as close as the game ever got.

Lollar got two hits in the second including a lead-off home run. Also, Nieman singled home a pair in the seven-run frame as the Sox began to forge their insurmountable lead.

Nieman homered again in the third inning for two more runs, giving him seven RBIs with just one-third of the game consumed. With six more offensive innings in front of him, Bob was in an excellent position to shatter Bottomley's 12-RBI mark. But in the sixth, after walking in a 17–6 game, Bob was replaced to give his

Nellie Fox (left) and Minnie Minoso. Before today, Minnie had only three runs scored and four RBIs in his first seven games.

ailing leg a rest. Also during the sixth inning, Lollar collected two more hits, both singles.

While still in the eighth, with 29 runs in the books, the White Sox had another

Chicago White Sox	AB	R	H	I	PO	A	E
Chico Carrasquel ss	6	5	5	0	0	1	0
Nellie Fox 2b	5	2	1	1	2	2	0
Minnie Minoso lf	6	5	4	5	3	0	0
George Kell 3b	5	2	2	2	0	2	1
Stan Jok pr6,3b	1	1	0	1	1	1	0
Bob Nieman rf	4	3	3	7	1	0	0
Ed McGhee pr6,cf	1	1	0	0	0	0	0
Walt Dropo 1b	7	3	3	3	6	0	0
Jim Rivera cf,rf6	7	1	3	2	4	0	0
Sherm Lollar c	6	4	5	5	10	0	0
Jack Harshman p	5	2	3	2	0	1	0
> Harry Dorish p8	1	0	0	0	0	1	0
	54	29	29	28	27	8	1

Kansas City A's	AB	R	H	I	PO	A	E
Vic Power 1b	5	2	1	1	6	1	0
>Spook Jacobs 2b	3	1	0	0	2	2	0
Jim Finigan 3b	4	2	2	1	3	3	1
Gus Zernial lf	4	0	0	0	3	0	1
Bill Renna rf	3	1	2	4	1	0	0
Bill Wilson cf	3	0	0	0	4	0	1
Joe DeMaestri ss	3	0	0	0	0	1	0
Jack Littrell ss8	1	0	0	0	0	0	0
Joe Astroth c	3	0	1	0	7	1	0
Eric MacKenzie c8	1	0	0	0	0	0	0
Bobby Shantz p	0	0	0	0	1	1	0
Lee Wheat p2	0	0	0	0	0	0	0
Bill Stewart ph2	1	0	0	0	0	0	0
Bob Trice p3	0	0	0	0	0	1	0
Moe Burtschy p4	1	0	0	0	0	0	0
Bob Spicer p6	1	0	0	0	0	0	0
Ozzie Van Brabant p8	0	0	0	0	0	0	0
Elmer Valo ph9	1	0	0	0	0	0	0
	34	6	6	6	27	10	3

Chicago	IP	H	R	ER	BB	SO
Harshman W,2-0	7	6	6	5	3	7
Dorish	2	0	0	0	1	2
	9	6	6	5	4	9

Kansas City	IP	H	R	ER	BB	SO
Shantz L,0-2	1.2	7	9	8	1	0
Wheat	.1	3	2	2	1	0
Trice	1.1	5	5	4	0	0
Burtschy	2.1	7	6	6	1	1
Spicer	1.2	4	5	5	2	1
Van Brabant	1.2	3	2	2	1	1
	9	29	29	27	6	3

```
Chicago       4 7 3   2 0 6   3 4 0   -29
Kansas City   3 0 2   0 1 0   0 0 0   - 6
```

OB: Chicago 7, Kansas City 5
2B: Finnigan 2, Rivera 2, Minoso,
     Astroth, Kell, Fox
HR: Nieman 2(5), Harshman(1),
     Renna(2), Power(2), Dropo(2),
     Lollar 2(2), Minoso(1)
SB: Minoso
SO: Dropo 2, Harshman, Power 2,
     Zernial 2, Wilson, Littrell,
     Astroth, Stewart, Burtschy
BB: Carrasquel, Minoso(I), Nieman,
     McGhee, Lollar, Harshman, ...

BB: ... Jacobs 2, Renna, Wilson
SF: Fox, Jok
HP: By Spicer (Fox)
WP: Shantz
TIME: 3:08
ATTENDANCE: 18,338
UMPIRES: Eddie Rommel, Joe Paparella,
    Jim Honochick, Frank Umont
SOURCES: Chicago American, Daily News,
    Tribune, Sun-Times; Kansas City Star

BALANCE	OUT	+ R	+ OB	= BP	= AB	+ BB	+ SH	+ HP	+ CI
Chicago	27	29	7	63	54	6	2	1	0
Kansas City	27	6	5	38	34	4	0	0	0

scoring opportunity. With two outs, in a bewildering piece of baserunning, Minnie Minoso stole second. Ed McGhee then walked, but Walt Dropo struck out to end the inning. That left the Sox three more outs to break most of the aforementioned tied records. However, Ozzie Van Brabant, the sixth Athletics pitcher, was uncooperative and retired Chicago in order in the top of the ninth. It was the only inning the Sox failed to get so much as a base runner. Earlier damage by Chicago had been narrowly averted when

long drives by both Dropo and Jim Rivera sailed foul by only a few feet.

Chicago's Jack Harshman, a converted first baseman, not only pitched his team to victory but also contributed mightily with the bat. Jack provided three hits, including the longest home run of the day and the only one of nine that traveled over the right field fence. The Sox' 29 hits raised the team batting average from .252 to .306, and their seven home runs doubled their season's total to date.

Giants-Cubs Marathon Topples Records

134. Teams Use 14 Pinch Hitters, Issue 11 Intentional Walks in 17-Inning Game

NEW YORK, NL   at   CHICAGO
(Giants, 6)   (Cubs, 5)

Wednesday, May 2, 1956, Wrigley Field

A sparse Chicago crowd watched 17 innings, 48 players, and five hours and 13 minutes elapse before a winner was decided

this day at Wrigley Field. Along the way, records galore fell:

• The Giants *used 25 players*, and the *two*

Daryl Spencer — batting hero

The hero of the game was Giants rookie second baseman, Daryl Spencer. Daryl had two singles, a triple, a home run, and knocked in the game-winning tally with a sacrifice fly in the 17th inning. By the end of the day, he was also fourth in the National League in runs-batted-in. Another New York rookie, pitcher Joe Margoneri, received credit for his first major league victory in front of only 2,389 weary but die-hard Chicagoans. This was the cellar-dwelling Cubs' seventh consecutive defeat.

Hoak's sixth strikeout carried added ignominy. He was at the plate with the tying run at second and two outs in the bottom of the 17th — a perfect opportunity to redeem himself. Don had a 2–1 count when Margoneri was relieved by Ruben Gomez. Hoak worked it to 3–2 before watching the called third-strike zip by. He also watched the game end and his name become etched in baseball's austere registers. This wasn't a game in which he simply faced an overpowering pitcher; his six strikeouts came against six different hurlers! Later in the clubhouse, Hoak was inconsolable, spending nearly a half hour sitting in front of his locker, hands covering his head.

By the time of Hoak's final strikeout, the Giants had only two men left on their bench. Jim Hearn, who had pitched the day before, and Ray Monzant, who was nursing a sore shoulder. The Cubs, on the other hand, still had a veritable army available — nine men. The *two clubs also tied the major league record by engaging six catchers.*

The 11 intentional walks were the result of lavish managerial strategy. For example, in the 17th, Alvin Dark doubled after there was one away. Jim Brosnan then wild pitched him to third, so Cub manager Stan Hack ordered both Willie Mays and Dusty Rhodes walked to establish a double play possibility.

clubs combined for 48, both new, major league standards on this date. (Since then, both have been surpassed; see 9-19-72 and 9-2-86.)

• Chicago's Don Hoak earned the dubious distinction of *striking out six times,* establishing a National League benchmark and tying the major league mark set 43 years earlier.

• New York tied the National League mark by *using eight pitchers* in the marathon (later exceeded; see 4-20-86).

• The two managers matched wits, each sending seven pinch hitters to the plate. The *two-team total of 14 is still the major league standard,* although it has been tied twice.

• Not reported in the newspapers of the day was another new record *for intentional bases on balls.* New York hurlers issued four, while Chicago dispensed seven for a *two club total of 11* (record still stands).

• In addition, the time of the game, 5:13, fell just short of the existing summit of 5:19 set 16 years earlier.

Don Hoak — saw better days

Hack may have taken the idea from Giants manager Bill Rigney who, in a similar situation in the ninth, directed walks to Walt Moryn and Ernie Banks. The New York media described Rigney's maneuvers as "out-Stengeling" his American League counterpart.

For the record, Mays, Westrum, and Banks were each intentionally passed twice. Rhodes, Mueller, Thompson, Moryn, and Landrith were each gifted once.

Brosnan not only lost this game, but thanks to the excessive managerial manipulation, all four of the walks on his slate were ordered from the bench. In addition to Brosnan, Jim Davis was commanded to walk two, Russ Meyer one, Margoneri one, Hoyt Wilhelm two, and Al Worthington one. The maze of player orchestration also must have made Whitey Lockman feel like a man without a country as he journeyed between left field and first base throughout the game.

New York Giants	AB	R	H	I	PO	A	E
Whitey Lockman lf,	8	0	2	0	4	1	1
1b10,1f11,1b15							
Alvin Dark ss	8	1	3	1	3	2	0
Willie Mays cf	6	1	0	0	3	0	0
Bob Lennon rf,lf10	5	0	0	0	1	0	0
Bobby Hofman ph11,1b	2	0	0	0	4	1	0
Dusty Rhodes ph15,lf	1	0	0	0	1	0	0
Daryl Spencer 2b	7	2	4	3	5	3	0
>Foster Castleman 3b	8	0	4	1	2	3	1
Gail Harris 1b	4	0	1	0	9	2	0
Don Mueller ph10,rf	2	0	0	0	0	0	0
Ray Katt c	2	0	0	0	4	0	0
George Wilson ph6	1	0	0	0	0	0	0
Wes Westrum c6	1	0	0	0	12	1	1
Hank Thompson ph16	0	0	0	0	0	0	0
Jim Mangan c16	0	0	0	0	2	0	0
Al Worthington p	2	1	1	0	0	0	0
Don Liddle p5	2	1	1	0	1	2	0
Hoyt Wilhelm p8	0	0	0	0	0	0	0
Steve Ridzik p9	1	0	0	0	0	1	0
W. Terwilliger ph12	1	0	0	0	0	0	0
Marv Grissom p12	0	0	0	0	0	1	0
Windy McCall p13	1	0	0	0	0	0	0
J. Antonelli ph16	1	0	0	0	0	0	0
Joe Margoneri p16	0	0	0	0	0	1	1
Ruben Gomez p17	0	0	0	0	0	0	0
	63	6	16	5	51	18	4

Chicago Cubs	AB	R	H	I	PO	A	E
>Don Hoak 3b	7	0	1	0	1	3	0
Solly Drake cf	8	1	2	1	6	0	0
Dee Fondy 1b	7	1	3	0	13	1	1
Ernie Banks ss	5	1	2	2	5	1	0
Walt Moryn rf	7	0	2	0	4	0	0
Jim King lf	3	0	0	0	2	0	0
Monte Irvin ph7,lf	5	0	0	0	3	0	0
Gene Baker 2b	8	2	4	1	5	5	0
Hobie Landrith c	2	0	0	0	6	1	0
Eddie Miksis ph8	1	0	1	0	0	0	0
Elvin Tappe c9	0	0	0	0	2	0	0
Gale Wade ph10	0	0	0	0	0	0	0
Harry Chiti c11	2	0	0	0	4	0	0
Russ Meyer p	2	0	0	0	0	3	0
Frank Kellert ph8	1	0	0	0	0	0	0
Turk Lown p9	0	0	0	0	0	1	0
Jim Davis p10	1	0	0	0	0	1	0
Pete Whisenant ph13	0	0	0	0	0	0	0
V. Vallentinetti p14	0	0	0	0	0	0	0
Owen Friend ph15	1	0	0	0	0	0	0
Jim Brosnan p16	0	0	0	0	0	1	0
C. McCullough ph17	1	0	1	0	0	0	0
Richie Myers pr17	0	0	0	0	0	0	0
	61	5	16	4	51	17	1

New York	IP	H	R	ER	BB	SO
Worthington	4	9	4	4	3	1
Liddle	3	3	1	0	1	4
Wilhelm	1.1	1	0	0	2	1
Ridzik	2.2	0	0	0	1	4
Grissom	1.2	0	0	0	1	1
McCall	2.1	2	0	0	0	3
Margoneri W,1-0	1.2	1	0	0	1	1
Gomez	.1	0	0	0	0	1
	17	16	5	4	9	16

Chicago	IP	H	R	ER	BB	SO
Meyer	8	10	5	4	1	5
Lown	1.1	1	0	0	1	2
Davis	3.2	3	0	0	3	3
Valentinetti	2	0	0	0	1	0
Brosnan L,0-1	2	2	1	1	4	1
	17	16	6	5	10	11

```
New York   0 1 1   0 0 2   1 0 0      0 0 0   0 0 0   0 1   - 6
Chicago    1 0 0   1 2 0   0 1 0      0 0 0   0 0 0   0 0   - 5
```

OB: New York 21, Chicago 17
DP: Harris-unassisted (King)
   Dark-Spencer-Harris (Kellert)
2B: Baker, Dark 2, Castleman 2,
   McCullough
3B: Spencer, Harris
HR: Drake(2), Baker(1), Banks(4),
   Spencer(3)
SB: Moryn
CS: Lockman, Banks
BB: Dark, Mays 2 (2I), Rhodes (I),
   Spencer, Mueller (I), Westrum
   3 (2I), Thompson (I); Hoak,
   Banks 3 (2I), Moryn (I), Meyer,
   Landrith (I), Wade, Whisenant
SO: Lockman 2, Mays, Lennon 2,
   Hofman, Spencer, Harris, Wilson
   Worthington, Terwilliger; Banks
   Hoak 6, Drake 2, Moryn, Irvin 2,

SO: ... King, Baker, Chiti, Friend
SH: Lockman, Mueller, Hoak, Chiti,
   Fondy
SF: Castleman, Spencer
HP: By Meyer (Mays)
WP: Wilhelm, Davis, Brosnan
PB: Chiti
TIME: 5:13
ATTENDANCE: 2,389
UMPIRES: Tom Gorman, Hal Dixon,
   Babe Pinelli, Dusty Boggess
SOURCES: Chicago Sun-Times, Tribune;
   DBD; New York Herald-Tribune, Times,
   World-Telegram; Sporting News

BALANCE	OUT+R+OB=BP+AB+BB+SH+HP+CI							
New York	51	6	21	78	63	10	4	1	0
Chicago	51	5	17	73	61	9	3	0	0

Gone with the Wind

135. Teams Combine for 15 Home Runs in Doubleheader

MILWAUKEE	at	CHICAGO
(Braves, 9,11)		(Cubs, 10,8)

Wednesday, May 30, 1956, Wrigley Field

Due to a paucity of talent, the Chicago Cubs hadn't breathed first division air in nine Septembers, and with this season barely under way, the story looked much the same. Already in the cellar, 10½ games out, the pathetic Cubs were forced to entertain the Milwaukee Braves, a persistent contender since departing Boston for the 1953 cam-

paign. The Braves were riding the crest of first place and sporting the NL's stingiest ERA at 2.84. All bets were off for this doubleheader, however, because a generous tail wind was gusting toward the outfield. Historically, under such Wrigley Field conditions, run scoring had proven both liberal and unpredictable. This day would be no different. By the time the final out was made, the two teams had each won one game and had *combined for 15 home runs, a new major league mark which still stands.*

It didn't take long for the tone of the day to be set. Starting for Chicago was Russ "The Mad Monk" Meyer, who relished the nickname bestowed on him for his explosive temper. Monk retired the first two Braves before his weakness was swiftly and perilously exploited. Eddie Mathews deposited Meyer's second pitch among the right-field bleacher patrons. Meyer's very next offering resulted in a similar blast by Hank Aaron. Bobby Thomson then made the Braves the 36th club to hit three consecutive home runs with a blast into the left-field seats. The Mad Monk was visibly shaken as the next batter, Billy Bruton, cautiously took his position in the batter's box. Meyer's first pitch, aimed at Bruton's head, narrowly missed its target. But Monk's second delivery found its mark and caromed off the rim of Bruton's batting helmet in the vicinity of his ear. Bruton stood, stared, and directed several obscene descriptives toward Meyer, who answered by inviting Billy to the mound. Bruton sprinted toward the mound, and just as he and Meyer met with fists flying, Milwaukee manager and third base coach, Charlie Grimm, tackled The Mad Monk. Soon confusion reigned. Meyer kicked and flailed his spikes while Bruton kicked back, forming the nucleus of action surrounded by umpires and opposing benches which had emptied. Both bleeding combatants were ejected and, while Bruton was unable to play in the nightcap, Meyer did return for more.

Staked to a 3–0 lead in the opener, Milwaukee starter Bob Buhl faltered, and the game continued with a steady shuffle of relievers and more home runs. First game long ball hitting can be summarized as follows:

Inning	Batter		Pitcher	Runners On	Hit To
1	Eddie Mathews	Mil	Russ Meyer	None	Right
1	Hank Aaron	Mil	Russ Meyer	None	Right
1	Bobby Thomson	Mil	Russ Meyer	None	Left
1	Gene Baker	Chi	Bob Buhl	Eddie Miksis	Left
2	Turk Lown	Chi	Bob Buhl	Hobie Landrith	Left
3	Bobby Thomson	Mil	Turk Lown	None	Left
6	Joe Adcock	Mil	Turk Lown	Jack Dittmer	Center
6	Hobie Landrith	Chi	Dave Jolly	Pete Whisenant	Right
6	Dee Fondy	Chi	Dave Jolly	Gene Baker	Left-center

The second game brought similar destruction to each pitcher's ERA. Both starters lost their temporary abuse-exempt status in the second inning when the scoring and home run hitting began once again. Noteworthy is the fact that each of the opening game starters, Buhl and Meyer, were called into second-game action. Neither had thrown many pitches before shameful first-game exits, so their respective managers hoped they could contribute positively to second-game results. Unfortunately, each added to his day's record of futility by being mauled for a second time. Buhl was again a gopher-ball victim and Meyer was roundly booed by the hometown Cub fans.

Inning	Batter		Pitcher	Runners On	Hit To
2	Bobby Thomson	Mil	Warren Hacker	None	Left
4	Hank Aaron	Mil	Warren Hacker	None	Left
6	Eddie Mathews	Mil	Warren Hacker	None	Right
6	Bobby Thomson	Mil	Warren Hacker	Hank Aaron	Left
8	Harry Chiti	Chi	Bob Buhl	Monte Irvin	Left
9	Ernie Banks	Chi	Ernie Johnson	None	Left

Leading Milwaukee's 1956 offensive production were (left to right) Hank Aaron, Eddie Mathews, and Joe Adcock.

FIRST GAME

Milwaukee Braves	AB	R	H	I	PO	A	E
Danny O'Connell 2b	2	0	0	0	1	4	0
Joe Adcock ph6	1	1	1	2	0	0	0
Dave Jolly p6	0	0	0	0	0	0	0
Chuck Tanner ph7	1	0	0	0	0	0	0
Lou Sleater p8	1	0	1	0	0	0	0
Johnny Logan ss	5	1	0	0	1	0	0
Eddie Mathews 3b	5	2	4	2	2	0	0
Hank Aaron rf	5	1	2	2	2	0	0
>Bobby Thomson lf,cf1	4	2	3	2	4	0	0
Billy Bruton cf	0	0	0	0	0	0	0
Andy Pafko lf1	4	0	1	1	1	0	0
Frank Torre 1b	3	0	2	0	6	1	0
Del Rice c	2	0	0	0	1	1	0
Wes Covington ph5	1	0	0	0	0	0	0
Del Crandall c5	2	0	0	0	5	0	0
Bob Buhl p	1	0	0	0	0	0	0
Red Murff p2	0	0	0	0	0	1	0
Jim Pendleton ph4	1	0	0	0	0	0	0
Ernie Johnson p4	0	0	0	0	0	0	0
Jack Dittmer 2b6	2	2	2	0	1	0	0
	40	9	16	9	24	7	0

Chicago Cubs	AB	R	H	I	PO	A	E
Eddie Miksis 3b	5	1	1	0	3	1	0
Gene Baker 2b	4	2	1	2	4	2	0
>Dee Fondy 1b	5	1	2	2	3	2	0
Ernie Banks ss	4	2	2	0	2	2	0
Walt Moryn rf	2	0	0	1	3	0	0
Monte Irvin lf	4	0	1	0	1	0	0
Pete Whisenant cf	3	1	2	1	1	1	0
Hobie Landrith c	4	2	2	2	9	0	0
Russ Meyer p	0	0	0	0	0	0	0
Turk Lown p1	2	1	1	2	1	0	0
Jim Davis p6	0	0	0	0	0	0	0
Jim King ph6	1	0	0	0	0	0	0
Vito Valentinetti p7	1	0	0	0	0	0	0
Jim Brosnan p8	0	0	0	0	0	0	0
	35	10	12	10	27	8	0

Milwaukee	IP	H	R	ER	BB	SO
Buhl	1.1	5	5	5	0	0
Murff	1.2	3	1	1	0	0
Johnson	2	0	0	0	1	2
Jolly L,2-1	1	3	4	4	1	1
Sleater	2	1	0	0	1	2
	8	12	10	10	3	5

Chicago	IP	H	R	ER	BB	SO
Meyer	.2	3	3	3	0	0
Lown	4.1	5	4	4	6	6
Davis	1	2	1	1	1	0
Valentinetti	1	4	0	0	0	0
Brosnan W,1-3	2	2	1	1	1	3
	9	16	9	9	8	9

Milwaukee	3 0 1	0 0 4	0 0 1	- 9
Chicago	3 2 1	0 0 4	0 0 x	-10

OB: Milwaukee 14, Chicago 5
DP: Banks-Baker-Fondy (Logan)
3B: Banks, Whisenant
HR: Mathews(6), Aaron(5), Thomson 2
 (6), Baker(2), Lown(1), Adcock(3),
 Landrith(1), Fondy(2)
SO: Logan, Mathews, Aaron, Thomson,
 Pafko, Rice, Covington, Buhl,
 Pendleton, Banks, Landrith, Lown,
 King, Valentinetti
BB: O'Connell, Logan, Mathews, ...

BB: ... Thomson 2, Torre 2, Dittmer,
 Baker, Moryn, Whisenant
SF: Moryn, Aaron
HP: By Meyer (Bruton)
PB: Landrith
TIME: 3:19
ATTENDANCE: 25,000(estimated)
UMPIRES: Bill Engeln, Vic Delmore,
 Jocko Conlan, Augie Donatelli

BALANCE	OUT+R+OB=BP=AB+BB+SH+HP+CI
Milwaukee	27 9 14 50 40 8 1 1 0
Chicago	24 10 5 39 35 3 1 0 0

SECOND GAME

Milwaukee Braves	AB	R	H	I	PO	A	E
Jack Dittmer 2b	4	1	2	0	2	2	0
Johnny Logan ss	4	1	0	0	1	3	0
Eddie Mathews 3b	3	2	1	1	2	2	0
Hank Aaron rf	5	3	2	3	1	0	0
Bobby Thomson cf	5	3	3	5	2	0	0
>Chuck Tanner lf	5	1	2	0	1	0	0
Frank Torre 1b	4	0	3	1	14	0	0
Del Crandall c	4	0	0	0	4	0	0
Ray Crone p	4	0	0	0	0	4	0
Bob Buhl p8	0	0	0	0	0	0	0
Ernie Johnson p8	0	0	0	0	0	1	0
	38	11	13	10	27	12	0

Chicago Cubs	AB	R	H	I	PO	A	E
Eddie Miksis 3b	5	0	1	0	1	1	0
Gene Baker 2b	5	0	0	0	2	3	1
Dee Fondy 1b	5	0	2	1	7	0	0
Ernie Banks ss	4	2	1	1	4	5	0
Walt Moryn rf	5	2	2	0	3	1	0
Monte Irvin lf	5	1	2	1	2	0	0
>Pete Whisenant cf	5	2	2	3	4	1	0
Harry Chiti c	3	2	3	3	4	0	1
Warren Hacker p	2	0	0	0	0	0	0
Russ Meyer p6	0	0	0	0	0	0	0
Sam Jones p7	0	0	0	0	0	0	0
Jim King ph7	0	0	0	0	0	0	0
Jim Hughes p8	0	0	0	0	0	0	0
Hobie Landrith ph8	0	0	0	0	0	0	0
Jim Davis p9	0	0	0	0	0	0	0
	39	9	13	9	27	11	2

Milwaukee	IP	H	R	ER	BB	SO
Crone W,4-1	7	10	7	7	3	2
Buhl	.1	1	1	1	1	0
Johnson	1.2	2	1	1	0	0
	9	13	9	9	4	2

Chicago	IP	H	R	ER	BB	SO
Hacker L,0-5	5	7	6	4	1	2
Meyer	1	3	4	4	1	0
Jones	1	3	1	1	0	2
Hughes	1	0	0	0	1	0
Davis	1	0	0	0	0	0
	9	13	11	9	3	4

| Milwaukee | 0 1 0 | 1 0 4 | 5 0 0 | –11 |
| Chicago | 0 1 0 | 3 0 0 | 1 3 1 | – 9 |

OB: Milwaukee 4, Chicago 7
DP: Baker-Banks-Fondy (Logan)
2B: Whisenant, Aaron, Moryn
3B: Irvin, Chiti
HR: Banks (12), Chiti (3), Aaron (6)
    Mathews (7), Thomson 2(8)
SO: Crandall, Crone 3, Moryn, Irvin
BB: Dittmer, Mathews 2, Banks, Chiti,
    King, Landrith

SH: Logan
PB: Crandall
TIME: 2:32
ATTENDANCE: 29,113
UMPIRES: Vic Delmore, Jocko Conlan,
    Augie Donatelli, Bill Engeln
SOURCES: Chicago American, Sun-Times,
    Tribune; Milwaukee Journal, Sentinel

BALANCE	OUT+R+OB=BP+AB+BB+SH+HP+CI
Milwaukee	27 11 4 42 38 3 1 0 0
Chicago	27 9 7 43 39 4 0 0 0

The reader may note several peculiarities among the day's four-ply swats. Seven of the nine Braves homers were solo shots, while five of the six Cubs blasts came with one teammate aboard. None of the 15 round trippers accounted for more than two runs.

While this outburst was transpiring in Chicago, another historic long-ball event was occurring in New York, where 24-year-old Mickey Mantle came within 18 inches of being the first major leaguer to hit a home run out of Yankee Stadium. Also, later this season, these same Milwaukee Braves established a then major-league record by hitting two or more home runs in each of eight consecutive games.

Frustration in Fenway

136. Team Leaves 20 Runners on Base in Nine-Inning Game

NEW YORK   at   BOSTON
(Yankees, 7)   (Red Sox, 13)

Friday Night, September 21, 1956, Fenway Park

On a clear but frosty night in Boston, the visiting Yankees' bats were warm, stroking 15 hits, including five by Moose Skowron and a prodigious 480-foot home run by Mickey Mantle. With men on base, however, those same war clubs turned cold as the New Yorkers *stranded a major-league record 20 men left on base*, shattering the former mark of 18 that had been shared by 13 clubs. Ironically, this standard of futility unparalleled in major-league annals came one jubilant day after the Yankees had clinched the pennant. And, the record wasn't set at the expense of a lineup of second-stringers while the regulars rested for the upcoming World Series. Despite fatigue and a well deserved rest, both Mantle and Yogi Berra had insisted on playing; Berra being stationed in the outfield for the first time since 1948.

New York stranded runners in every inning. Following is a summary of that Yankee record performance. Numbers in parentheses represent standard fielding positions, and I=inning, H=hits, W=walks, R=runs, L=left on base, U=unassisted.

I	H	W	R	L	Last out of inning
1	3	1	3	3	With the bases loaded and two out, pitcher Bob Turley grounded out (1-3).
2	3	0	1	2	There were runners at the corners and two outs when Elston Howard popped out to second.
3	2	0	0	2	With runners at first and second and none out, Turley struck out, Jerry Lumpe grounded out (5-3), as did Enos Slaughter (3U).
4	0	4	1	3	With the bases loaded and two out, pinch hitter Irv Noren flied out to left.
5	1	0	0	1	Two were out and a runner on first when Yogi Berra grounded out (3U).
6	2	1	0	3	Bases were loaded with two outs when Lumpe was retired.
7	1	2	2	2	Jerry Coleman flied out to deep right with runners at the corners and two outs.
8	1	1	0	2	With runners at the corners and one out, Mantle flied out to right, and Siebern was called out on strikes.
9	2	0	0	2	After the first two batters had singled, Tommy Carroll and Coleman each struck out, and George Wilson flied out to left.

Billy Klaus led the Sox attack with five RBIs.

The most discouraged Yankees were Howard, who failed to advance or drive home seven teammates, and Lumpe who stranded six.

On the brighter side, when Jimmy Piersall hit into his second double play of the contest, it marked the 200th twin-killing of the season for the Yankees, a new club record. In addition, Mantle's titanic blast gave the Yankees 183 HR and a new American League team home run mark. (They finished with 190.) The clout to center field, on a 3–2 pitch from Frank Sullivan, missed by a foot from leaving the park. Mickey also became the first American Leaguer in 18 years to hit more than 50 round trippers in a single season.

Although New York had already clinched the pennant, an ample crowd turned out to watch an important individual drama unfold.

Mickey Mantle was in the midst of a phenomenal offensive season and threatening to become only the second triple-crown winner in the past 20 years. Standing in his path was Ted Williams, the last man to attain such levels in both 1942 and 1947. After this game, Mantle's average stood at .3524 as compared to Williams' .356, but Ted faced an opponent even more formidable than Mantle — official at-bats. In 1956, league rules demanded 400 official at-bats to qualify for the batting crown. Walks, of course, are not counted as official at-bats. Bases on balls were, however, an integral part of Williams' game. Throughout his career, he had developed a keen eye and refused to swing at balls outside the strike zone. Then too, pitchers were often encouraged to walk long-ball hitting, .344 lifetime hitters. (Only Babe Ruth drew more lifetime walks than Williams.) Despite over 90 walks this season, Ted still needed 24 more official at-bats in the seven remaining Sox games, but five of those contests were scheduled against New York. Yankee pitchers thus were in a position to control the batting champion, for even if they didn't intentionally walk Williams, they weren't about to give him many fat pitches. Mantle did win the triple crown this year although batting title requirements were changed in 1957 to include all plate appearances.

Williams met a similar fate in 1954 when he finished with the highest batting average, but because of a league-leading 136 walks, he amassed only 386 official at-bats and was not awarded the crown.

New York Yankees	AB	R	H	I	PO	A	E
Jerry Lumpe ss	6	1	0	0	1	2	1
Enos Slaughter rf	4	1	1	0	1	0	0
Mickey McDermott p6	1	1	1	0	0	1	0
Mickey Mantle cf	5	3	3	2	0	1	0
Yogi Berra lf	3	0	1	1	1	2	0
Norm Siebern lf6	2	0	0	0	2	0	0
Moose Skowron 1b	6	1	5	1	9	0	0
Elston Howard c	6	0	1	0	3	0	0
Andy Carey 3b	1	0	1	1	0	2	0
Billy Hunter pr3,3b	0	0	0	0	0	0	0
Joe Collins ph6	1	0	0	0	0	0	0
Tommy Carroll 3b6	1	0	0	0	0	1	0
Jerry Coleman 2b	4	0	2	1	6	5	0
Bob Turley p	2	0	0	0	0	0	0
Sonny Dixon p3	0	0	0	0	0	0	0
Irv Noren ph4	1	0	0	0	0	0	0
Tom Morgan p4	0	0	0	0	0	0	0
Jim Coates p5	0	0	0	0	0	1	0
> George Wilson ph6,rf	1	0	0	0	1	0	0
	44	7	15	6	24	15	1

Boston Red Sox	AB	R	H	I	PO	A	E
Milt Bolling 3b	3	3	1	0	1	2	1
Billy Klaus ss	5	2	2	5	0	1	2
Ted Williams lf	4	2	2	1	2	0	0
Gene Stephens pr8,lf	0	1	0	0	1	0	0
Mickey Vernon 1b	3	0	1	2	7	0	0
Norm Zauchin pr6,1b	1	0	1	0	1	0	0
Jackie Jensen rf	3	1	1	2	1	0	0
>Jimmy Piersall cf	5	0	1	3	6	0	0
Ted Lepcio 2b	3	1	1	0	2	2	0
Sammy White c	4	1	2	0	6	1	0
Frank Sullivan p	0	0	0	0	0	1	0
Faye Throneberry ph3	1	1	1	0	0	0	0
George Susce p4	2	1	1	0	0	1	0
Ike Delock p8	0	0	0	0	0	0	0
	34	13	14	13	27	8	3

New York	IP	H	R	ER	BB	SO
Turley L,8-4	2.2	7	6	6	2	1
Dixon	.1	0	0	0	0	0
Morgan	1	3	3	2	2	0
Coates	1	1	3	3	2	0
McDermott	3	3	1	1	1	0
	8	14	13	12	7	1

Boston	IP	H	R	ER	BB	SO
Sullivan	3	8	4	2	1	2
Susce W,2-4	4	4	3	2	8	1
Delock	2	3	0	0	0	3
	9	15	7	4	9	6

| New York | 3 1 0 | 1 0 0 | 2 0 0 | - 7 |
| Boston | 0 0 6 | 3 3 0 | 0 1 x | -13 |

OB: New York 20, Boston 5
DP: Carey-Coleman-Skowron (Piersall)
    McDermott-Coleman-Skowron (Piersall)
2B: Slaughter, Berra, Piersall, Vernon, Skowron
3B: Klaus
HR: Mantle(51)
SO: Siebern, Skowron, Howard, Turley,
    Carroll, Coleman, Bolling
BB: McDermott, Mantle, Berra, Hunter, Carroll,
    Coleman 2, Wilson 2, Bolling 2, Williams,
    Vernon, Jensen 2, Susce

SF: Carey
HP: By Coates (Lepcio)
TIME: 3:23
ATTENDANCE: 24,616
UMPIRES: John Rice, Hank Soar, Red
    Flaherty, Bill Summers
SOURCES: Boston Globe, Herald, Post;
    New York Times; Retrosheet

BALANCE	OUT	+ R	+ OB	= BP	= AB	+ BB	+ SH	+ HP	+ CI
New York	27	7	20	54	44	9	1	0	0
Boston	24	13	5	42	34	7	0	1	0

Slaughterhouse Five

137. Five Teammates Get Four or More Hits in Nine-Inning Game

SAN FRANCISCO   at   LOS ANGELES
(Giants, 16)   (Dodgers, 9)

Tuesday, May 13, 1958, Memorial Coliseum

In 1958, Los Angeles fans got their first look at major league baseball, and with the season barely one month old, they also saw a significant major league record established. For the first and only time this century, *five different players from one team each collected four or more hits in a nine-inning game.* Unfortunately, it was the hometown Dodgers who were on the receiving end of this battering, and the perpetrators were none other than their cross-continent traveling companions and arch rivals, the San Francisco Giants.

The Dodgers had not taken well to their migration. Despite the ludicrous 251-foot left-field fence, the team batting average slipped, and the club scored fewer runs than they had the season before in Brooklyn. The pitching staff suffered even more from the jet lag. Whereas in 1957 the Dodger staff had the best ERA (3.35) in the National League, they now were the dregs (4.47). This day demonstrated why.

Willie Mays showed the West Coast fans what all the cheering had been about in the Polo Grounds. At the expense of the woeful Dodger staff, Willie was in the midst of a torrid streak, having collected seven hits, five HRs and 11 RBIs in his last 12 at-bats. This day was little different as he led the Giants' assault with a walk, stolen base, and five hits, including two triples and two 400-foot home runs. Mays set the tempo in the opening frame after he was forced to hit the deck by a Don Newcombe fastball. Two pitches later, Willie blasted his first homer. Daryl Spencer, Bob Schmidt, Danny O'Connell and 20-year-old Orlando Cepeda also contributed four hits apiece in a 26-hit assault.

Although they had won the pennant only two years earlier, the Dodgers were now 9–17 and looking up at the rest the National League. Club president Walter O'Malley offered several explanations. First, all-star catcher Roy Campanella had been rendered a quadriplegic in an off-season automobile accident. "Campy" had been a team leader

Bob Schmidt— one of five Giants to Harvest four or more hits.

and experienced handler of the pitching staff. Second, the team was trying too hard to make a good impression on the vast throngs that were coming to the park (attendance had more than doubled over the first 21 dates in Brooklyn). And third, the club was having trouble adjusting to the unorthodox dimensions of the park.

By season's end, things didn't get much better for the Dodgers. They finished in seventh place, just two games above the last place Phillies who remarkably led the league in base hits. The Giants, meanwhile, finished third, 12 games behind the pennant winning Milwaukee Braves.

San Francisco Giants	AB	R	H	I	PO	A	E
Jim Davenport 3b	5	2	2	0	0	4	1
>Don Taussig rf	7	1	1	0	1	0	0
Willie Mays cf	5	4	5	4	3	0	0
Hank Sauer lf	3	2	0	1	0	0	0
W. Kirkland pr5,lf	1	0	1	1	0	0	0
Orlando Cepeda 1b	6	3	4	2	11	2	0
Daryl Spencer ss	6	4	4	6	3	3	1
Bob Schmidt c	6	0	4	1	5	0	0
Danny O'Connell 2b	5	0	4	1	3	3	0
Mike McCormick p	1	0	0	0	0	0	0
Ray Monzant p1	0	0	0	0	0	2	0
Jim King ph3	0	0	0	0	0	0	0
Andre Rogers ph3	1	0	1	0	0	0	0
Al Worthington p3	3	0	0	0	0	0	0
Jim Finigan ph9	1	0	0	0	0	0	0
Marv Grissom p9	0	0	0	0	1	0	0
	50	16	26	16	27	14	2

Los Angeles Dodgers	AB	R	H	I	PO	A	E
Jim Gilliam lf	4	1	0	0	1	0	0
>Gino Cimoli cf	5	2	2	0	1	0	0
Charley Neal 2b	5	2	2	4	1	2	0
Carl Furillo rf	4	1	2	3	2	0	0
Johnny Podres pr6	0	0	0	0	0	0	0
Elmer Valo rf7	1	0	1	0	0	0	0
Gil Hodges 1b	5	2	3	1	10	1	0
Dick Gray 3b	4	0	0	0	2	3	2
Don Zimmer ss	4	0	0	0	5	2	0
Joe Pignatano c	4	0	1	0	5	1	0
Don Newcombe p	0	1	0	0	0	1	0
Fred Kipp p3	1	0	0	0	0	1	0
Ed Roebuck p4	0	0	0	0	0	0	0
Duke Snider ph5	1	0	0	1	0	0	0
Sandy Koufax p6	0	0	0	0	0	0	0
Norm Larker ph7	1	0	0	0	0	0	0
Danny McDevitt p8	0	0	0	0	0	1	0
Johnny Roseboro ph9	1	0	0	0	0	0	0
	40	9	11	9	27	12	2

San Francisco	IP	H	R	ER	BB	SO
McCormick	.1	2	3	3	1	1
Monzant	1.2	2	3	3	1	0
Worthington W,3-1	6	6	3	3	2	2
Grissom	1	1	0	0	1	1
	9	11	9	9	5	4

Los Angeles	IP	H	R	ER	BB	SO
Newcombe	2.1	7	7	4	1	3
Kipp L,1-3	.2	3	3	3	1	0
Roebuck	2	7	3	3	1	1
Koufax	2	4	2	2	2	1
McDevitt	2	5	1	1	0	0
	9	26	16	13	5	5

San Francisco   5 2 0   4 2 1   1 1 0   -16
Los Angeles   3 3 1   0 1 0   0 1 0   - 9

OB: San Francisco 13, Los Angeles 11
DP: Hodges-Gray-Zimmer (Worthington)
    Neal-Hodges (Cepeda)
    Neal-Zimmer (Spencer)
2B: Spencer, Schmidt, Davenport
3B: Spencer, Mays 2
HR: Mays 2(8), Furillo(4), Neal 2(6),
    Hodges(4), Spencer 2(8),
    Cepeda(9)
SB: Mays
CS: Mays
SO: Davenport, Taussig, Sauer, Cepeda,
    Schmidt, Cimoli, Neal 2, Hodges

BB: Davenport 2, Mays, Sauer, Kirkland
    Gilliam 2, Gray, Zimmer, Newcombe
SH: O'Connell
HP: By McCormick (Cimoli),
    by Worthington (Pignatano)
TIME: 3:16
ATTENDANCE: 13,417 (10,507 paid)
UMPIRES: Ken Burkhart, Dusty Boggess,
    Ed Sudol, Tom Gorman
SOURCES: Los Angeles Times; Retrosheet;
    San Francisco Chronicle, Examiner

BALANCE	OUT	+R	+OB	=BP	=AB	+BB	+SH	+HP	+CI
San Francisco	27	16	13	56	50	5	1	0	0
Los Angeles	27	9	11	47	40	5	0	2	0

Baseball's Loaves-and-Fishes Miracle

138. Team Scores 11 Runs in One Inning on One Hit

CHICAGO   at   KANSAS CITY
(White Sox, 20)   (Athletics, 6)

Wednesday Night, April 22, 1959

The Chicago White Sox were a team that knew how to use miracles. Despite carrying the yoke of "the hitless wonders," the Sox had finished in second place in each of the past two campaigns. The 1958 season was especially serendipitous when they hit the fewest home runs and outscored their opponents by a total of only 19 runs yet finished as runners-up to the Yankees. Scribes had joked for years that a typical Chicago rally consisted of a walk, stolen base, sacrifice, and wild pitch.

This season was little different. Although they had the best base-stealing team in the majors, Chicago was again on pace to hit the fewest home runs. Management was concerned enough with their punchless attack that they opened negotiations with Washington in an effort to acquire slugger Roy

Callison got the only hit in the 11-run inning.

Torgeson got an RBI and a run scored without an official at-bat.

Sievers. In addition, manager Al Lopez had become so exasperated that he routed his team out of bed this Wednesday morning to command a two-hour batting practice session.

The Sox responded later in the night with a 16-hit attack against the Athletics, but it wasn't the hits that drew the headlines. Rather, Chicago demonstrated a new level of efficiency in scoring runs *without* hits. After falling behind 6–1, the Sox stormed back to take an 8–6 lead after six innings. At that point they already had gathered 11 hits and three walks. Then came the miraculous seventh when Kansas City pitching and fielding generosity afforded the Sox an astonishing *eleven runs on only one hit.* Here's how that frame unfolded (runs scored in parentheses):

• Right-hander Tom Gorman took the mound for the Athletics. Chicago's Ray Boone was safe when his grounder to shortstop Joe DeMaestri was thrown wild.

• In typical ChiSox style, Al Smith attempted to sacrifice but was safe when third baseman Hal Smith fumbled the pick up.

• Johnny Callison then collected the only hit of the inning when he singled to right scoring Boone (1). Right fielder Roger Maris mishandled the hit enabling Smith (2) to also score and Callison to move around to third.

• Luis Aparicio walked and promptly stole second. (It was one of 56 steals for Luis.)

• Chicago relief pitcher Bob Shaw was also given a free pass, loading the bases. That was all for the A's Gorman, who was replaced by Mark Freeman.

• Earl Torgeson pinch-hit for Sammy Esposito (who had earlier pinch-run for Billy Goodman). Earl also walked and collected an RBI as Callison (3) strolled home.

• Nellie Fox walked and forced home teammate Aparicio (4).

• Jim Landis made the first out when he bounced back to Freeman, forcing Shaw at the plate.

Chicago White Sox	AB	R	H	I	PO	A	E
Billy Goodman 3b	3	1	2	0	0	0	0
S. Esposito pr5,3b	0	1	0	0	2	0	0
Earl Torgeson ph7	0	1	0	1	0	0	0
Bubba Phillips 3b7	1	0	0	1	0	0	0
Nellie Fox 2b	5	1	4	5	0	3	0
Jim Landis cf	6	1	1	0	5	0	0
>Sherm Lollar c	5	2	2	1	8	0	0
Norm Cash 1b	1	1	0	0	5	0	0
Ray Boone 1b5	2	2	0	2	3	1	0
Jim Rivera rf	2	1	2	1	0	0	0
Al Smith rf5	2	2	0	1	1	0	0
Johnny Callison lf	4	1	1	2	0	0	0
Lou Skizas pr7,lf	1	1	0	0	2	0	0
Luis Aparicio ss	4	4	3	4	0	4	0
Early Wynn p	0	0	0	0	0	0	0
Bob Shaw p2	4	1	1	0	1	3	0
	40	20	16	18	27	11	0

Kansas City A's	AB	R	H	I	PO	A	E
Bill Tuttle cf	4	1	1	0	5	1	0
Whitey Herzog lf	4	1	1	1	3	0	0
Hector Lopez 2b	5	0	2	1	2	4	1
>Roger Maris rf	5	1	2	3	2	0	1
Kent Hadley 1b	3	0	0	0	8	0	0
Hal Smith 3b	4	0	0	0	1	1	1
Frank House c	3	1	0	0	6	0	0
Joe DeMaestri ss	4	1	1	0	2	2	1
Ned Garver p	1	1	1	1	0	0	0
Bud Daley p4	1	0	0	0	0	2	0
Russ Meyer p6	0	0	0	0	0	0	0
Preston Ward ph6	1	0	1	0	0	0	0
Tom Gorman p7	0	0	0	0	0	0	0
Mark Freeman p7	0	0	0	0	0	1	0
George Brunet p7	0	0	0	0	0	3	0
Harry Simpson ph9	1	0	0	0	0	0	0
	36	6	9	6	27	14	4

Chicago	IP	H	R	ER	BB	SO
Wynn	1.2	6	6	6	2	2
Shaw W,1-0	7.1	3	0	0	2	6
	9	9	6	6	4	8

Kansas City	IP	H	R	ER	BB	SO
Garver	3.2	6	5	2	1	0
Daley L,0-2	1.2	5	3	3	2	0
Meyer	.2	0	0	0	0	1
Gorman	0	1	6	2	3	0
Freeman	.1	0	2	0	2	0
Brunet	2.2	4	4	1	5	4
	9	16	20	8	13	5

Chicago	0	1	1		3	1	2		11 0 1		-20
Kansas City	1	5	0		0	0	0		0 0 0		- 6

OB: Chicago 11, Kansas City 7
2B: Lollar 2, Rivera, Goodman, Fox, Maris, Ward
HR: Maris(3), Aparicio(2)
SB: Tuttle, Aparicio
SO: Landis, Lollar, Boone, Skizas, Shaw, Lopez, Maris, Hadley 2, H. Smith 2, DeMaestri, Daley
BB: Esposito, Torgeson, Phillips, Fox 2, Lollar 2(1I), Cash, Boone, A. Smith, Aparicio 2, Shaw, Tuttle, Herzog, Hadley, House

SH: Landis, A.Smith, Shaw
SF: Boone
HP: By Brunet (Callison)
TIME: 3:12
ATTENDANCE: 7,446
UMPIRES: John Rice, Eddie Rommel, Larry Napp, Johnny Stevens
SOURCES: Chicago American, Daily News, Sun-Times, Tribune; Retrosheet

BALANCE	OUT+R+OB=BP=AB+BB+SH+HP+CI							
Chicago	27	20	11	58	40	13	4	1	0
KansasCity	27	6	7	40	36	4	0	0	0

• Sherman Lollar got the game back on track by walking and forcing home Torgeson (5).

• A's manager Harry Craft then beckoned left-hander George Brunet to take the hill, but Brunet resumed the charity and walked Boone, bringing home Fox (6).

• Smith also walked, scoring Landis (7).

• Callison broke the monotony by *not* walking. Instead, Johnny was hit on the wrist

by a pitch, bringing in Lollar (8). Lou Skizas ran for Callison.

• Back in the swing of things, Brunet walked Aparicio sending Boone home (9). That was the eighth free pass issued by Athletics hurlers this inning.

• Shaw must have felt compassion for his Kansas City counterpart and struck out for the second out.

• After that temporary break in decorum,

Brunet walked Bubba Phillips, scoring Smith (10). Phillips had been pinch-hitting for Torgeson who earlier in the frame had "pinch-walked" for Esposito.

• Nellie Fox walked for the second time in the inning and harvested his second RBI without touching the ball as Skizas (11) trotted home.

• Landis mercifully ended the carnage by grounding out, Brunet to first baseman Kent Hadley. It was the second out of the inning made by Landis, both on grounders back to the pitcher.

There you have it—11 runs on one hit, three errors, 10 walks, and one hit-batsman. The Sox left the sacks filled and hit only one ball past the pitcher's mound. Nine of the runs were forced in by walks, and only two of the 11 runs were earned during the 45-minute half-inning. The 10 walks fell only one short of the all-time single-inning mark (see 9-11-49). And, Chicago's biggest offensive guns were two of their smallest players — Luis Aparicio who had three hits including a three-run home run, and Nellie Fox who collected four hits and five RBIs. Six Sox scored runs and four got RBIs without getting a hit. Approaching the plate in the leadoff position for Chicago was a particularly bizarre experience. Sammy Esposito pinch-ran for Billy Goodman in the fifth and scored. Sammy did step to the plate in the sixth but walked. When he was scheduled to hit in the seventh, left-handed hitting Earl Torgeson pinch-hit for him and walked. Torgeson thereby collected an RBI and later in the inning himself scored. But when the Sox batted around and Earl was again scheduled to bat, left-hander Brunet was on the hill. Thus, right-handed Bubba Phillips pinch-hit for Torgeson and also walked and collected an RBI. (Phillips later blemished his record by grounding out in the ninth.)

The miracle in Kansas City served as a portent of things to come. Chicago finished the season sixth in hits, sixth in runs scored, and eighth (last) in homers yet captured the AL flag, their first in 40 years. Kansas City finished in seventh place, and their pitching staff allowed more hits than any other in the circuit.

Harvey's Perfect Defeat

139. Pitcher Throws
12 Perfect Innings But Loses

PITTSBURGH　　at　　MILWAUKEE
(Pirates, 0)　　　　　　　(Braves, 1)

Tuesday Night, May 26, 1959, County Stadium

The baseball world had witnessed nine-inning, perfect games before. Since the birth of the National League in 1876, six hurlers (seven if you count Ernie Shore's 1917 classic) had mowed down all 27 batters they faced. Several pitchers even retired more than 27 straight in a single game. Waite Hoyt in a 1919 game retired 34 consecutive Yankees between the second and thirteenth innings. But no pitcher had ever started and carried a perfect game beyond the ninth frame, that is until this night when Pittsburgh's Harvey Haddix was untouchable for 12 innings.

Harvey "The Kitten" Haddix was a 155-pound, 33-year-old left-hander now toiling for his fourth major league club. While with the Cardinals in 1953 he had posted 20 victories including a league leading six shutouts, but since then his career had eroded into one little better than mediocre. With his innings-pitched falling, the Kitten concluded the 1958 campaign with an 83–68 lifetime log and a 3.66 ERA. But the Pirates were hoping another experienced starter like Haddix would boost them from their 1958 second place landing. Thus in January of 1959, Harvey was acquired in a multi-player deal with Cincinnati.

Haddix had been giving the Pirates just about what they had expected. Eight games into the season, he had a 3–2 mark with 44 innings pitched and had allowed 46 hits and 10 walks. This night nobody expected a flawless outing, especially against the first place Milwaukee Braves who had led the league in hitting a year earlier and now featured seven regulars batting over .300. As Harvey warmed up before the game, he felt his fastball lacked its usual speed, and his curve wasn't breaking the way he liked. To make matters worse, he was fighting a cold but told Pirate manager Danny Murtaugh that he would do the best he could for as long as possible. The best he could do was a masterpiece, a game that many claim is the greatest pitching performance of all time.

On the cold and threatening evening, Milwaukee manager Fred Haney had stacked his lineup with seven right-handed bats. But Haddix had his fastball and slider working to perfection, bewildering the first 36 Braves who stepped to the plate. Outstanding control enabled him to stay ahead of every batter until the twelfth when Andy Pafko worked him to a 2–0 count before bouncing back to the mound. Later, his catcher Smokey Burgess claimed: "Harvey had the greatest stuff he ever had and pinpoint control of all four pitches, his fastball, curve, slider, and change up."* Haddix struck out eight, five swinging and three called, all by the end of the ninth frame.

Very few batted balls even threatened to fall safely. In the third, Johnny Logan lined a ball that was snared with a short leap by shortstop Dick Schofield. In the eleventh, Del Crandall lined to Bill Virdon who made a fine catch in short center field. In the twelfth, third baseman Don Hoak, who would later wear the label of "goat," made a great stop of Lew Burdette's bounder to his left and threw him out. Even rain, which began to fall lightly in the seventh, couldn't deter Haddix. The partisan crowd of 19,194 recognized the brilliance unfolding before their eyes and gave Harvey a standing ovation after the ninth and each frame thereafter.

The game ended in the bottom of the thirteenth. Felix Mantilla led off for the Braves with a routine bounder to Hoak. Don fielded the ball cleanly (as he had done six times earlier), took his time before throwing, but bounced it in front of first baseman Rocky Nelson who failed to come up with the toss. There were scattered cheers from the stands when the scorer's decision of an error was announced. (Both Haddix and Burgess thought they had Mantilla struck out before the ground ball.) Eddie Mathews then sacrificed Mantilla to second (Haddix to Mazeroski). Hank Aaron, the league's leading hitter, was intentionally walked to get to the slow-footed Joe Adcock. Adcock hadn't hit the ball out of the infield all night. With a count of one ball and no strikes, Joe unloaded a low liner over the right-center field fence just out of the reach of a frantically leaping Virdon. In the haze of a fine mist, mass confusion transpired. Mantilla scored, but Aaron, not realizing the ball had left the park and thinking the game was over, ran past second and then across the pitcher's mound toward the dugout. Adcock had been running with his head down, passed Aaron and rounded third. Under instructions from an equally confused coaching staff, both runners then returned to the basepaths retracing their steps. Frank Dascoli, chief of the umpire crew, ruled that Adcock was out for having passed Aaron between second and third but because Aaron retraced his steps and crossed the plate, his run counted — or that's what some thought. The *Pittsburgh Post-Gazette*, the *Milwaukee Sentinel*, and wire services reported a final score of 2–0.

*Jack Hernon, "Haddix Had His Glory...," Pittsburgh Post-Gazette, 28 May 1959, p. 21, col. 2.

Haddix — the only pitcher to retire 36 straight in a game.

Interviewed after the marathon, an exhausted but gracious Haddix could only lament, " I just wanted to keep them from scoring, that's all I was interested in. But we just didn't get that run I needed... I was pitching Adcock about the same way all night and that last time didn't get away with it. The slider was up too high and we lost." Harvey admitted that he tired in the last few innings. "You could see it, couldn't you? They were getting the ball up in the air a little more than I wanted them to."*

The Pirates had several opportunities to win it for Haddix. In the third, three hits yielded no runs because of a base running blunder by Roman Mejias, who tried to go from first to third on an infield hit off the leg of Burdette. They got two hits in the ninth but again failed to push across a run when Bob Skinner lined out with runners at the corners. Milwaukee and Burdette were tenacious and remained in contention by also turning three doubleplays. Perhaps Haddix should have been grateful to Roman

But the *Pittsburgh Press* and the *Milwaukee Journal* claimed the winning tally was 1–0. The confusion was resolved the following day by National League president Warren Giles who ruled that since Adcock had passed Aaron, his hit could only be a double. That made Aaron's run superfluous and the official score should be registered as 1–0.

Mejias and the impotent Pirate lineup. After all, if they had scored early, Harvey would have pitched just another nine-inning perfect game.

In later years, rumors swirled that would make Haddix's masterpiece even more astonishing. Bob Buhl, who sat in the Milwaukee bullpen that night, divulged in a

*Jack Hernon, "Adcock Spoils No-Hit Effort in Thirteenth," Pittsburgh Post-Gazette, *27 May 1959, p. 32, col. 6.*

Pittsburgh Pirates	AB	R	H	I	PO	A	E
Dick Schofield ss	6	0	3	0	2	4	0
>Bill Virdon cf	6	0	1	0	8	0	0
Smokey Burgess c	5	0	0	0	8	0	0
Rocky Nelson 1b	5	0	2	0	14	0	0
Bob Skinner lf	5	0	1	0	4	0	0
Bill Mazeroski 2b	5	0	1	0	1	1	0
Don Hoak 3b	5	0	2	0	0	6	1
Roman Mejias rf	3	0	1	0	1	0	0
Dick Stuart ph10	1	0	0	0	0	0	0
Joe Christopher rf10	1	0	0	0	0	0	0
Harvey Haddix p	5	0	1	0	0	2	0
	47	0	12	0	38*	13	1

Milwaukee Braves	AB	R	H	I	PO	A	E
Johnny O'Brien 2b	3	0	0	0	3	5	0
Del Rice ph10	1	0	0	0	0	0	0
Felix Mantilla 2b11	1	1	0	0	1	2	0
Eddie Mathews 3b	4	0	0	0	2	3	0
Hank Aaron rf	4	0	0	0	1	0	0
>Joe Adcock 1b	5	0	1	1	17	3	0
Wes Covington lf	4	0	0	0	4	0	0
Del Crandall c	4	0	0	0	2	1	0
Andy Pafko cf	4	0	0	0	6	0	0
Johnny Logan ss	4	0	0	0	2	5	0
Lew Burdette p	4	0	0	0	1	3	0
	38	1	1	1	39	22	0

Pittsburgh	IP	H	R	ER	BB	SO
Haddix L,3-3	12.2	1	1	0	0	8

Milwaukee	IP	H	R	ER	BB	SO
Burdette W,8-2	13	12	0	0	0	2

| Pittsburgh | 000 | 000 | 000 | 000 | 0 | - 0 |
| Milwaukee | 000 | 000 | 000 | 000 | 1 | - 1 |

* two out when winning run scored
OB: Pittsburgh 8, Milwaukee 1
DP: Adcock-Logan-Adcock (Skinner)
   Mathews-O'Brien-Adcock (Haddix)
   Adcock-Logan (Burgess)
2B: Adcock
SO: Mazeroski, Hoak, O'Brien,
   Mathews, Adcock 2, Pafko,
   Burdette 3
BB: Aaron (I)
SH: Mathews

TIME: 2:54
ATTENDANCE: 19,194
UMPIRES: Vinnie Smith, Frank Dascoli,
   Frank Secory, Hal Dixon
SOURCES: DBD; Milwaukee Journal, Sentinel;
   Pittsburgh Post-Gazette, Press; Retrosheet

BALANCE	OUT+R+OB=BP=AB+BB+SH+HP+CI							
Pittsburgh	39	0	8	47	47	0	0	0	0
Milwaukee	38	1	1	40	38	1	1	0	0

1993 interview that the Braves had been stealing the signs of Pirate catcher Burgess the entire evening and relaying them to the hitters.

"Smokey couldn't bend over very far when he caught, so with binoculars, you could pick up every sign," said Buhl. "We used a towel system in the bullpen to signal the hitters. Most of our guys took the signs, others thought it would foul them up if they knew what was coming." [Towel on the shoulder meant a fastball; towel moving around signaled a breaking ball.]

"You have to understand that Harvey had such marvelous movement and changes of speed that night that it didn't matter if the hitter knew what was coming or not. If we signaled a fastball, Harvey was often taking a little off the fastball so that it didn't look like one at all."†

The batting hero, Joe Adcock, said he was one of the players who didn't partake of the sign stealing. "I don't know anything about anybody stealing signs that night," said Joe with a chuckle. "... I never wanted to know what was coming. It would have thrown me off and made me think too much. But then again, there were obviously a lot of guys who wanted to know."†

The Kitten completed the season with a 12–12 log while the Pirates landed in fourth, nine games out. He went on to pitch four more years with Pittsburgh and two with Baltimore finishing his career with a 136–113 won–lost record and a 3.63 ERA.

†Steve Stout, "The Greatest Game Ever Pitched," The National Pastime, Number 14 (1994), 4.

Rocky Rips the Orioles

140. Player Hits
Four Home Runs in One Game

CLEVELAND   at   BALTIMORE
(Indians, 11)   (Orioles, 8)

Wednesday Night, June 10, 1959, Memorial Stadium

Rocky Colavito, 25-year-old, streak-hitting slugger of the Cleveland Indians, this night became the eighth batter in major league history to *hit four home runs in a single game.* He also became just the third to do so consecutively (following Bobby Lowe and Lou Gehrig) in leading the Tribe over the Orioles 11–8.

Colavito's feat was surprising from several aspects. First, he had been mired in a 3 for 28 slump and had hit only three circuit clouts in the last three weeks. Fickle fans had feasted on trade rumors stirred by manager Joe Gordon and general manager Frank Lane. Second, although Rocky had hit 87 homers during the past three seasons, he had never hit more than two in any one game. Third, Baltimore's cavernous Memorial Stadium was the most difficult major-league arena in which to hit home runs. In each of the previous five seasons of its occupation by the Orioles, fewer round-trippers had been hit there than in any other park,* even by visiting clubs. No *player* had ever hit more than two in a game there, and in 1956 when Mickey Mantle hit 52 home runs, none left Memorial Stadium.

Colavito began his record-tying day rather harmlessly by walking in the first inning off Baltimore starter Jerry Walker. At the time there were two outs and Tito Francona was on first, having singled.

Walker was still on the hill in the third and walked lead-off batter Vic Power. After Tito Francona popped out, Colavito deposited a slider into the bleachers about

360 feet away, just inside the left field foul pole.

Baltimore reliever Arnold Portocarrero was Colavito's next victim in the fifth. After Francona led off and struck out, Rocky hit his mightiest shot — an estimated 425 foot rocket into the left field stands. According to Colavito, it came on a "slider or curve, inside and up a little bit."†

Portocarrero was exploited again in the sixth. With two outs and Francona on second, Arnold delivered a sinking fastball down and away. Colavito drove it on a line more than 400 feet over the left-center field fence.

The final blow came off Baltimore reliever Ernie Johnson. Johnson hadn't allowed a home run in 30 innings worked this season,

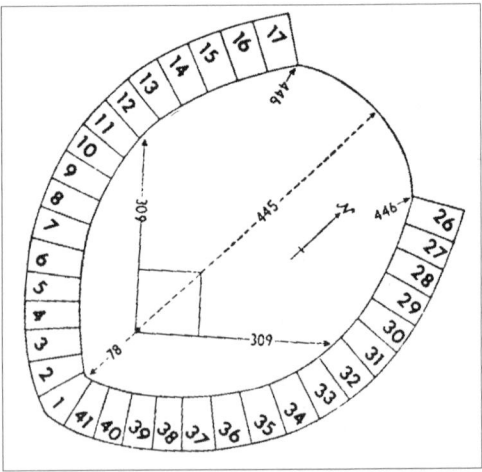

Field dimensions in 1959.

*Jim Weigand, Home Runs by Park 1950–1959 (Barberton, Ohio, 1993), 33–62.
†Harry Jones, "Just Swung for Hits, Says Rocky," Cleveland Plain Dealer, 11 June 1959, p. 33, col. 8.

Colavito had been a fan favorite in Cleveland.

but the Cleveland slugger picked out a fast ball, "up and in," and roped it into the same spot as homer number two.

Colavito finished 1959 with 42 home runs and 111 RBIs although a late season slump dragged his batting average down to .257. During the off season, he and Frank Lane struggled through some difficult contract negotiations. Then, just two days before the 1960 opener, Cleveland fans were stunned when it was announced that Rocky had been traded to the Tigers for 1959 batting champion Harvey Kuenn.

Cleveland Indians	AB	R	H	I	PO	A	E
Woodie Held ss	5	1	1	0	5	1	0
Vic Power 1b	4	1	0	0	4	1	0
Tito Francona cf	5	2	2	1	2	0	0
Rocky Colavito rf	4	5	4	6	3	0	0
Minnie Minoso lf	5	1	3	3	1	0	0
Willie Jones 3b	3	0	0	0	1	1	0
Geo. Strickland 3b5	2	0	1	0	1	1	0
>Dick Brown c	4	0	1	0	7	1	0
Billy Martin 2b	3	1	1	1	3	0	0
Ray Webster ph7,2b	1	0	0	0	0	0	0
Gary Bell p	3	0	0	0	0	1	0
Mike Garcia p7	1	0	0	0	0	0	0
	40	11	13	11	27	6	0

Baltimore Orioles	AB	R	H	I	PO	A	E
Albie Pearson cf	3	1	2	0	5	0	0
Al Pilarcik rf	5	1	1	2	2	0	0
Gene Woodling lf	5	1	3	1	3	0	0
Gus Triandos c	2	0	1	1	5	0	0
Joe Ginsberg c7	1	1	0	0	0	0	0
Bob Hale 1b	3	0	0	0	5	0	0
George Zuverink p6	0	0	0	0	0	0	0
Bob Boyd ph7	1	0	0	0	0	0	0
Ernie Johnson p8	0	0	0	0	0	0	0
Bob Nieman ph9	1	1	1	0	0	0	0
Billy Klaus 3b	5	0	2	4	0	1	0
>Chico Carrasquel ss	5	0	0	0	2	3	0
Billy Gardner 2b	4	1	1	0	1	5	0
Jerry Walker p	1	1	1	0	0	0	0
A. Portocarrero p3	1	0	0	0	0	0	0
Whitey Lockman 1b6	1	1	0	0	4	0	0
	38	8	12	8	27	9	0

Cleveland	IP	H	R	ER	BB	SO
Bell W,5-5	6.1	8	7	7	4	3
Garcia	2.2	4	1	1	0	3
	9	12	8	8	4	6

Baltimore	IP	H	R	ER	BB	SO
Walker L,4-3	2.1	4	6	6	2	1
Portocarrero	3.1	7	4	4	1	3
Zuverink	1.1	0	0	0	0	0
Johnson	2	2	1	1	0	0
	9	13	11	11	3	4

Cleveland	3 1 2	0 1 3	0 0 1	-11
Baltimore	1 2 0	0 0 0	4 0 1	- 8

OB: Cleveland 5, Baltimore 8
2B: Brown, Held, Francona, Klaus, Nieman
HR: Minoso(7), Colavito 4(18), Martin(7)
SB: Minoso
SO: Held, Francona, Jones, Bell, Triandos, Ginsberg,
    Carrasquel, Klaus, Gardner, Portocarrero
BB: Power, Colavito, Brown, Pearson 2, Ginsberg,
    Lockman
SF: Triandos

TIME: 2:54
ATTENDANCE: 15,883
UMPIRES: Bill Summers, Bill McKinley
    Hank Soar, Nestor Chylak
SOURCES: Baltimore Sun; Cleveland
    Plain Dealer, Press; Retrosheet

BALANCE	OUT+R+OB=BP=AB+BB+SH+HP+CI
Cleveland	27 11 5 43 40 3 0 0 0
Baltimore	27 8 8 43 38 4 1 0 0

Alston Empties His Bench

141. Team Uses Nine Pinch Hitters in Nine-Inning Game

LOS ANGELES   at   ST. LOUIS
(Dodgers, 10)   (Cardinals, 11)

Tuesday Night, September 22, 1959, Busch Stadium

On a night when the Chicago White Sox clinched their first pennant in 40 years, the National League race was boiling to a climax. With only five games remaining for each club, the Dodgers and Braves were locked in a first-place tie, and the Giants were hovering just one game back. Every pitch, swing, defensive play, and managerial call was crucial as evidenced by intense analysis in newspapers of the day.

With the Dodgers playing in St. Louis this night, skipper Walter Alston reached deep into his hat of magic tricks in an attempt to keep his team atop the league standings. After blowing two leads, the Los Angeles pilot made a desperate comeback attempt by *using nine pinch hitters in a nine-inning game*

for a new major league benchmark. This standard has since been tied once (see 9-21-93).

This contest held promise of being a pitcher's duel. St. Louis right-hander Larry Jackson had had particular success against Los Angeles, and the Dodgers' often-wild left-hander, Sandy Koufax, was beginning to show signs of future greatness, having struck out 18 batters in a game one month earlier. Neither hurler, however, made it out of the first inning. The Dodgers jumped out to a 3–0 lead in the opening round, and the Cardinals countered with four on a grand slam by Hal Smith. One in the second and two in the third restored the Dodger lead at 6–4. But in the home half of the third, a seven-hit

Alston piloted his team to the World's Championship.

Frank "Hondo" Howard crushed his second career home run.

barrage, including Curt Flood's home run, enabled the Cards to regain the advantage, 9–6. It was during this rally that the score-board trumpeted a Milwaukee victory over Pittsburgh, twisting the knife in the hearts of the Dodgers.

Alston then accelerated his parade of pinch-hitting assignments. With Jackson having been relieved by left-hander Marshall Bridges in the first inning, and the Dodgers now trailing, Alston moved toward a right-handed lineup. Don Demeter pinch-hit for Duke Snider, Carl Furillo for Norm Larker, and Joe Pignatano for John Roseboro. Pig-natano himself was later pinch-hit for by Ron Fairly when the Cardinals switched back to a right-hander, Lindy McDaniel.

In the ninth, Rip Repulski pinch-hit for Norm Sherry, the third-string Dodger back-stop. Had Los Angeles then been able to tie the game, an interesting situation would have developed behind the plate because no other Dodger had caught a game that year. The other four Dodger pinch-hitters were: Chuck Essegian, Sandy Amoros, and rookies Tommy Davis and Frank Howard. For Davis, later two-time batting champion, this was his first major-league at-bat. Howard almost did send the game into overtime when he unloaded a 400-foot, line drive, three-run homer in the top of the ninth to bring Los Angeles to within one run. Of the nine Dodger pinch-hitters, five failed to produce, but Pignatano walked, Repulski singled, Essegian doubled, and Howard homered.

Although the Dodgers lost this game and fell behind by one game with only four to play, they did prevail in a thrilling pennant race. The Giants faded by losing three of their last four, and the Braves and Dodgers finished with identical 86–68 logs, forcing a three game playoff. It took only two games for the Dodgers to march on to the World Series, and six to claim the World's Champi-onship.

Los Angeles Dodgers	AB	R	H	I	PO	A	E
>Jim Gilliam 3b	5	1	1	0	1	1	1
Charlie Neal 2b	5	1	2	0	3	2	0
Wally Moon lf	5	1	3	0	2	0	0
Duke Snider cf	1	0	0	1	0	0	0
Don Demeter ph5,cf	3	0	0	0	3	0	0
Norm Larker rf	2	1	2	2	0	1	0
Carl Furillo ph5,rf	2	0	0	0	0	1	1
Gil Hodges 1b	4	2	2	2	5	2	0
Maury Wills ss	4	0	0	0	2	4	0
John Roseboro c	2	0	0	0	4	0	0
Joe Pignatano ph6,c	0	1	0	0	2	0	0
Ron Fairly ph8	1	0	0	0	0	0	0
Norm Sherry c8	0	0	0	0	1	0	0
Rip Repulski ph9	1	1	1	0	0	0	0
Sandy Koufax p	0	0	0	0	0	1	0
Chuck Churn p1	1	1	1	0	0	0	0
Clem Labine p3	0	0	0	0	0	0	0
Tommy Davis ph4	1	0	0	0	0	0	0
Stan Williams p4	0	0	0	0	0	0	0
Chuck Essegian ph6	1	0	1	1	0	0	0
Fred Kipp p6	0	0	0	0	0	1	0
Sandy Amoros ph8	1	0	0	0	0	0	0
Danny McDevitt p8	0	0	0	0	1	0	0
Frank Howard ph9	1	1	1	3	0	0	0
	40	10	14	9	24	13	2

St. Louis Cardinals	AB	R	H	I	PO	A	E
>Don Blasingame 2b	5	1	3	0	3	4	0
Cunningham 1b,rf4,1b8	3	2	1	1	6	1	1
Gino Cimoli rf,lf4	4	0	2	2	3	0	0
Ken Boyer 3b	3	2	1	0	1	4	0
Gene Oliver lf	1	1	1	0	0	0	0
Stan Musial ph3,1b	3	1	1	0	5	0	0
Lindy McDaniel p8	0	0	0	0	0	0	0
Hal Smith c	4	1	1	4	7	0	0
Curt Flood cf	5	1	1	3	0	0	0
Alex Grammas ss	4	1	2	0	1	3	0
Larry Jackson p	0	0	0	0	0	0	0
Marshall Bridges p1	3	1	1	0	1	0	0
Duke Carmel rf8	1	0	0	0	0	0	0
	36	11	14	10	27	12	1

Los Angeles	IP	H	R	ER	BB	SO
Koufax	.2	2	4	4	2	0
Churn L,3-2	2	6	5	5	0	2
Labine	.1	2	0	0	0	0
Williams	2	1	2	1	3	1
Kipp	2	2	0	0	3	1
McDevitt	1	1	0	0	0	1
	8	14	11	10	8	5

St. Louis	IP	H	R	ER	BB	SO
Jackson	0	4	3	3	1	0
Bridges W,6-3	7	5	4	4	4	5
McDaniel	2	5	3	3	1	1
	9	14	10	10	6	6

Los Angeles	3 1 2	0 0 1	0 0 3	-10
St. Louis	4 0 5	0 2 0	0 0 x	-11

OB: Los Angeles 9, St. Louis 11
DP: Boyer-Blasingame-Cunningham (Hodges)
   Grammas-Cunningham (Neal)
2B: Churn, Essegian, Grammas, Cimoli
HR: Smith(13), Hodges(24), Flood(7),
   Howard(1)
SO: Neal, Snider, Demeter, Hodges,
   Wills, Davis, Cimoli, Boyer,
   Flood, Grammas, Carmel
BB: Gilliam, Snider, Furillo, Hodges,
   Wills(I), Pignatano, Blasingame, ...

BB: ... Cunningham 2(1I), Boyer 2(1I),
   Musial, Smith, Grammas
SH: Bridges, Cimoli
TIME: 3:03
ATTENDANCE: 12,732
UMPIRES: Al Barlick, Dusty Boggess, Stan Landes,
   Shag Crawford
SOURCES: Los Angeles Times; New York Times;
   Retrosheet; St. Louis Globe-Democrat, Post-Dispatch

BALANCE	OUT+R+OB=BP=AB+BB+SH+HP+CI
Los Angeles	27 10 9 46 40 6 0 0 0
St. Louis	24 11 11 46 36 8 2 0 0

Orioles Again Rudely Awakened

142. Team Scores Eight Runs Before Making Their First Out

BALTIMORE   at   NEW YORK
(Yankees, 15)   (Orioles, 9)

Sunday, April 24, 1960, Yankee Stadium

Howard entered the game with just two singles in his last 18 at bats.

It's not often that a baseball game is virtually over before a team can even record a putout. On August 13, 1948, Philadelphia scored nine times against the Giants before any Phillie was retired, establishing the all-time major league standard. (A frequently reported mark of 10 runs by the 1911 Giants is erroneous.) The American League version of this benchmark is eight tallies, registered by Cleveland against the Baltimore (see 7-6-54). Now six years later, Baltimore was again victimized, this time in New York as the Yankees *notched eight runs before making their first out.*

The Orioles scored a run in the top of the first before New York batted. Jack Fisher was the unfortunate starter for Baltimore as the Yankee parade then began (run numbers in parentheses):

• Bobby Richardson led off with a single to center.

• Hector Lopez singled to right with Richardson stopping at second.

• Mickey Mantle walked, loading the bases.

• Yogi Berra singled for two RBIs (2) and sent Mantle to third.

• Bill Skowron singled to right, scoring Mantle (3) and sending Berra to third.

• Gil McDougald doubled to left to drive home Berra (4) and send Skowron to third.

• Gordon Jones replaced Fisher but promptly served a gopher ball to Elston Howard. The shot into the right-field stands scored Skowron and McDougald in front of him (7).

• Jones was equally generous with Tony Kubek. Kubek's round tripper also landed in the right-field stands (8) and enabled the Yankees to tie the AL record.

• Jones then regained his composure and struck out Jim Coates, got Richardson on a fly ball to center, and Lopez on a bouncer to second.

The Yankees scored four more times in the bottom of the second and coasted into the eighth with a 12–1 advantage. Over the final two frames, Baltimore did some record-making of their own when two unlikely candidates each blasted grand slam home runs. Neither Billy Klaus nor Albie Pearson had started the contest, yet their hitting accomplishments equalled an often-tied major league mark of two grand slams in a game by one team. For Klaus and Pearson this was also their finest day of 1960, for each player drove in a total of six runs and hit only this one home run during the entire season!

Baltimore Orioles	AB	R	H	I
Marv Breeding 2b	2	0	0	0
Billy Klaus ph5,2b	3	1	1	4
Al Pilarcik cf	5	2	2	1
>Jackie Brandt rf	4	1	0	0
Gene Woodling lf	0	0	0	0
Albie Pearson lf3	3	1	1	4
Jim Gentile 1b	4	0	0	0
Brooks Robinson 3b	4	1	1	0
Gus Triandos c	3	0	0	0
John Anderson p7	0	0	0	0
Johnny Powers ph9	0	1	0	0
Ron Hansen ss	3	1	1	0
Jack Fisher p	0	0	0	0
Gordon Jones p1	0	0	0	0
Bob Boyd ph3	1	0	0	0
Steve Barber p3	0	0	0	0
Clint Courtney c7	1	1	0	0
	33	9	6	9

New York Yankees	AB	R	H	I
Bobby Richardson 2b	5	1	1	0
Hector Lopez lf	3	2	1	0
Clete Boyer 3b9	0	0	0	0
Mickey Mantle cf	3	2	1	0
Ken Hunt cf7	0	0	0	0
Yogi Berra rf	4	2	3	3
Elmer Valo rf7	0	1	0	0
Bill Skowron 1b	5	2	2	2
Gil McDougald 3b	4	1	1	1
Andy Carey 3b8,lf9	1	0	0	1
Elston Howard c	5	2	3	5
>Tony Kubek ss	4	2	2	3
Jim Coates p	2	0	0	0
Johnny James p9	0	0	0	0
	36	15	14	15

Baltimore	IP	H	R	ER	BB	SO
Fisher L,1-2	0	5	6	6	1	0
Jones	2	6	6	6	0	2
Barber	4	1	0	0	1	3
Anderson	2	2	3	3	3	1
	8	14	15	15	5	6

New York	IP	H	R	ER	BB	SO
Coates W,2-0	8	4	5	5	4	2
James	1	2	4	4	1	1
	9	6	9	9	5	3

Baltimore	1 0 0	0 0 0	0 4 4	– 9
New York	8 4 0	0 0 0	0 3 x	–15

OB: Baltimore 3, New York 5
2B: McDougald, Berra, Robinson
3B: Mantle, Hansen, Howard 2
HR: Pilarcik(1), Pearson(1), Klaus(1), Kubek 2(2), Howard(1)
SO: Breeding, Brandt 2, Mantle, Skowron, Howard 2, Coates 2
BB: Brandt, Woodling, Powers, Hansen, Barber, Lopez 2, Mantle, Valo, Kubek

SH: Coates 2, Hunt
HP: By James (Courtney)
WP: Barber
TIME: 3:00
ATTENDANCE: 19,460
UMPIRES: Frank Umont, Cal Drummond, Charlie Berry, Larry Napp
SOURCES: Baltimore Sun; New York Daily News, Times, Herald-Tribune; Retrosheet

BALANCE	OUT+R+OB=BP=AB+BB+SH+HP+CI
Baltimore	27 9 3 39 33 5 0 1 0
New York	24 15 5 44 36 5 3 0 0

Mays Is Marvelous

143. Player Hits Four Home Runs
in One Game

SAN FRANCISCO   at   MILWAUKEE
(Giants, 14)   (Braves, 4)

Sunday, April 30, 1961, County Stadium

One of baseball's Hall-of-Fame elite, Willie Mays, played many spectacular games in his career, but he called this "easily the greatest day I ever had."* He said it even surpassed his 1954 World Series performance with his celebrated over-the-head catch in deep center field. What he was referring to was his *record-tying four home runs* and eight RBIs in leading the Giants to a 14–4 victory over the Milwaukee Braves.

Mays thus became the ninth player in major-league history to accomplish the feat. In addition to the nineteenth-century's Bobby Lowe and Ed Delahanty; Lou Gehrig, Chuck Klein, Pat Seerey, Gil Hodges, Joe Adcock, and Rocky Colavito also achieved the standard.

Willie's greatest day came as a surprise to everyone including himself. Despite his prodigious home run power, to this point in his career Mays had never hit as many as three round-trippers in one game. And, after the Braves' Warren Spahn had no-hit the Giants on Friday night, Mays went hitless again on Saturday, leaving him 0 for 7 in the series. Willie had complained that he wasn't seeing the ball well and that his bat felt "heavy." Several teammates had even offered him their lumber. But when this game began, everything seemed to fall into place.

Each of Mays' blasts left no doubt it would leave the park as not one traveled less than 400 feet. All were hit to left and left-center. Here's how Willie's day unfolded:

WILLIE MAYS ON APRIL 30, 1961

Inning	Pitcher	Runners	Pitch†	Event	Result
1	Burdette	None	fastball	420' HR	SF 1 — ML 0
3	Burdette	Davenport(1st)	sinker	400' HR	SF 4 — ML 3
5	Drabowsky	None	—	lined out to center	—
6	Morehead	Davenport (1st) Hiller (2nd)	slider	450' HR	SF 11 — ML 3
8	McMahon	Davenport (3rd)	slider	430' HR	SF 14 — ML 4

†*According to the Braves' pitching chart. Mays' opinion was: sinker, sinker, slider, slider.*

Willie was to be the fifth Giants batter in the top of the ninth, and when Jose Pagan led off with a single it looked as if he might get another long-ball opportunity. To avoid a double play, Billy Loes sacrificed. Chuck Hiller, who already had three hits, next grounded out, short to first. As Jim Davenport approached the plate and Mays the on-deck circle, the Milwaukee crowd cheered, hoping to see Willie bat one more time. Alas, Davenport also grounded out, second to first, foiling any chance for a fifth

*UPI, "Mays, 0 for 7 Against Braves, Feared Slump Would Continue," New York Times, *1 May 1961, Sports section, p. 1, col. 3.*

San Francisco Giants	AB	R	H	I
Chuck Hiller 2b	6	2	3	1
>Jim Davenport 3b	4	3	1	1
Willie Mays cf	5	4	4	8
Willie McCovey 1b	3	0	0	0
Jim Marshall 1b8	0	0	0	0
Orlando Cepeda lf	5	1	1	1
Matty Alou lf8	0	0	0	0
Felipe Alou rf	4	1	1	1
Ed Bailey c	4	0	0	0
Jose Pagan ss	5	3	4	2
Billy Loes p	3	0	0	0
	39	14	14	14

Milwaukee Braves	AB	R	H	I
Roy McMillan ss	4	1	1	0
Frank Bolling 2b	4	1	2	0
Eddie Mathews 3b	4	0	1	0
Hank Aaron cf	4	2	2	4
Mel Roach lf	4	0	1	0
Joe Adcock 1b	4	0	0	0
Charlie Lau c	3	0	1	0
Don McMahon p8	0	0	0	0
George Brunet p9	0	0	0	0
Lee Maye ph9	0	0	0	0
>John DeMerit rf	4	0	0	0
Lew Burdette p	1	0	0	0
Carl Willey p4	0	0	0	0
Moe Drabowsky p5	0	0	0	0
Billy Martin ph5	1	0	0	0
Seth Morehead p6	0	0	0	0
Ken MacKenzie p7	0	0	0	0
Johnny Logan ph7	1	0	0	0
Hawk Taylor c8	0	0	0	0
	34	4	8	4

San Francisco	IP	H	R	ER	BB	SO
Loes W,2-1	9	8	4	4	1	3

Milwaukee	IP	H	R	ER	BB	SO
Burdette L,1-1	3	5	5	5	0	0
Willey	1	3	2	2	0	0
Drabowsky	1	0	0	0	1	0
Morehead	1	2	4	4	1	1
MacKenzie	1	0	0	0	0	1
McMahon	1	3	3	3	2	0
Brunet	1	1	0	0	0	0
	9	14	14	14	4	2

San Francisco	1 0 3	3 0 4	0 3 0	-14
Milwaukee	3 0 0	0 0 1	0 0 0	- 4

OB: San Francisco 6, Milwaukee 4
E: Mathews
DP: Davenport-Hiller-Marshall(DeMerit)
    Burdette-McMillan-Adcock(Davenport)
    Bolling-McMillan-Adcock(Pagan)
2B: Hiller 2
3B: Davenport
HR: Mays 4(6), Pagan 2(2), Cepeda(3),
    F. Alou(2), Aaron 2(3)
SO: Cepeda, Bailey; Adcock, Burdette, Logan
BB: Davenport, McCovey 2, F. Alou; Maye

SH: Loes 2
HP: By Burdette (Davenport)
    by MacKenzie (Bailey)
TIME: 2:40
ATTENDANCE: 13,114
UMPIRES: Chris Pelekoudas, Al
    Forman, Jocko Conlan, Ken Burkhart
SOURCES: Milwaukee Journal; New York
    Times; Retrosheet

BALANCE	OUT+	R+	OB=	BP+	AB+	BB+	SH+	HP+CI
San Francisco	27	14	6	47	39	4	2	2	0
Milwaukee	27	4	4	35	34	1	0	0	0

homer by the 29-year-old Mays as the fans lustily booed.

In the clubhouse, Mays was asked about that possible fifth home run. "To tell the truth, I don't think I would have hit any-thing. You see, I started to think about it when it was announced over the public address, and I know I'd be pressing trying to go for another one."[*]

Mays' circuit clouts led an *eight-homer*

*Lou Chapman, "Mays at Best," Milwaukee Sentinel, 1 May 1961, part 2, p. 5, col. 2.

Mays called this his greatest day.

Giant offense which tied the existing single-team, one-game major league mark. With the help of two home runs by the Braves' Henry Aaron, the *two clubs also tied the NL home run standard (10) for a single game.* Both marks have since been surpassed.

A day earlier, the Giants also had rapped five home runs, giving them a *two-game total of 13. That set a new NL record and tied the ML mark that still stands.*

Although the Giants finished third in 1961, Mays went on to complete another superb season by harvesting 40 home runs, 123 RBIs, a .308 batting average, and leading the league in runs scored with 129.

Diamond Jim Sparkles

144. Player Hits Grand Slams in Consecutive Innings

BALTIMORE   at   MINNESOTA
(Orioles, 13)   (Twins, 5)

Tuesday, May 9, 1961, Metropolitan Stadium

There is some dispute over how Jim Gentile earned the nickname "Diamond Jim." Some claim it was due to his penchant for flashy custom cars while others say he was so tagged for his enormous untapped talent, i.e. a diamond in the rough. In any case, both characteristics befit him. The 6' 4", 215-pound Gentile began his big-league career in the Dodger organization but couldn't dislodge Gil Hodges from the initial sack. After languishing for eight years, Jim was finally acquired in 1960 by Baltimore where he began to demonstrate the marvelous ability that had been predicted of him.

Gentile made an immediate impact with the Orioles. His 28 HRs, 98 RBIs, and a .292 batting average earned him an all-star berth. He followed that with a monstrous campaign in 1961 when his 46 HRs, 141 RBIs, and .302 average not only repeated his all-star selection but ranked him third in the MVP voting. It was early in this season that he gained baseball immortality by becoming the *first player to hit grand slam home runs in consecutive plate appearances or in consecutive innings*. Gentile also became the fourth

major leaguer to hit two in one game, joining Tony Lazzeri, Rudy York, and Jim Tabor.

It happened in Metropolitan Stadium where Jim had batted many times while in the minors with St. Paul. There the fans remembered his incidents of thrown batting

A talented but temperamental slugger.

Gentile began his major league career in the Dodger organization.

helmets, failures to run out routine ground balls, and arguments with managers. Nevertheless, before the game, a clubhouse boy erected a sign over his locker that read: "Welcome Home Diamond Jim." When Gentile stepped to the plate for the first time, the Orioles had loaded the bases on a walk to Whitey Herzog, a double by Jackie Brandt, and a walk to Brooks Robinson. Minnesota starter Pedro Ramos was in an especially generous groove, having allowed seven circuit smacks in six appearances, and no less than 13 men had been on base when his pitches left the park. Diamond Jim then rocketed a Ramos 0–2 offering 425 feet over the center field fence for his eighth home run of the young season. In the second frame, after one out, Chuck Estrada singled and Herzog again walked chasing Ramos from the mound. Reliever Paul Giel threw wild to second on Brandt's tap with Estrada scoring and Herzog taking third. Brooks Robinson also walked again filling the bases. Jim then tore into the first pitch and sent the same trio home with his second grand slam, this one 370 feet into the right field stands. At this point, Gentile was poised to shatter Jim Bottomley's mark of 12 RBIs set in 1924.

Gentile next appeared at the plate in the fourth inning with one out and Brandt on first. But this time, he was given nothing worthy of hitting and walked. In the sixth, he struck out swinging with Robinson on second. In the eighth, with Brandt on third and one out, Gentile popped into shallow left. Shortstop Zoilo Versalles made a nice catch going away which enabled Brandt to hustle home and afforded Gentile a sacrifice fly for his ninth RBI. The RBI gave him the AL lead with 30. Jim was lifted by manager Paul Richards during wholesale lineup changes in the bottom of the eighth.

After the game, Gentile exposed his temperament when he told a reporter: "I thought the only way I'd get into the record book was by breaking water coolers or something."*

Bill Hengen, "Roaming Around," Minneapolis Star, 10 May 1961, section D, p. 2, col. 1.

Diamond Jim was rewarded for his offensive outburst by being benched the next night, a normal occurrence when Baltimore faced a left-handed pitcher.

Gentile's skills were fleeting. After his titanic 1961 season, he never again batted over .251, and his petty rages soon made him a persona non grata. Later stops in Kansas City, Houston, and Cleveland failed to revive his career, which ended with the 1966 campaign.

Baltimore Orioles	AB	R	H	I
Whitey Herzog rf	2	2	1	0
> Earl Robinson ph8,rf	2	1	1	0
Jackie Brandt cf	5	3	3	0
Russ Snyder cf8	0	0	0	0
Brooks Robinson 3b	2	2	1	1
Jim Gentile 1b	3	2	2	9
Jim Busby lf8	0	0	0	0
Dick Williams lf	5	0	0	0
Gordon Jones p8	0	0	0	0
Gus Triandos c	4	1	1	0
Jerry Adair pr9,ss	0	0	0	0
Ron Hansen ss	5	1	1	2
Frank Zupo c9	0	0	0	0
Marv Breeding 2b	5	0	0	0
Chuck Estrada p	4	1	1	0
Walt Dropo 1b8	0	0	0	0
	37	13	11	12

Minnesota Twins	AB	R	H	I
Zoilo Versalles ss	4	0	3	0
Lenny Green cf	3	0	1	0
Bill Pleis p5	0	0	0	0
Reno Bertoia ph6	1	0	0	0
Chuck Stobbs p7	0	0	0	0
Jim Lemon ph8	1	0	0	0
Ray Moore p9	0	0	0	0
Dan Dobbek lf,cf5	4	0	0	0
Harmon Killebrew 3b	4	1	1	1
Don Mincher 1b	3	1	0	0
Earl Battey c	1	0	0	0
Don Lee p3	0	0	0	0
> Elmer Valo ph4,lf	3	0	0	0
Bob Allison rf	4	2	3	3
Billy Gardner 2b	4	0	0	0
Pedro Ramos p	0	0	0	0
Paul Giel p2	0	0	0	0
Hal Naragon ph2,c	4	1	2	1
	36	5	10	5

Baltimore	IP	H	R	ER	BB	SO
Estrada W,2-1	7	7	3	3	5	8
Jones	2	1	1	1	0	1
	9	8	4	4	5	9

Minnesota	IP	H	R	ER	BB	SO
Ramos L,2-2	1.1	3	6	6	3	1
Giel	.2	1	3	2	1	0
Lee	2	1	0	0	1	2
Pleis	2	3	2	2	1	3
Stobbs	2	2	2	2	0	1
Moore	1	1	0	0	1	1
	9	11	13	12	7	8

Baltimore	4 5 0	0 2 0	0 2 0	-13
Minnesota	0 0 0	3 0 0	0 1 1	- 5

OB: Baltimore 6, Minnesota 10
E: Giel
DP: Hansen-Gentile (Valo)
2B: Brandt 2, Green, Herzog, B. Robinson, Triandos
HR: Gentile 2(9), Allison 2(5), Naragon(2), Hansen(3), Killebrew(6)
SO: Herzog, E. Robinson, Gentile, Williams, Hansen 2, Estrada 2, Green, Bertoia, Dobbek 2, Battey, Killebrew, Mincher 2, Naragon

BB: Herzog 2, B. Robinson 2, Gentile, Triandos, Dropo, Versalles, Killebrew, Mincher 2, Valo
SF: B. Robinson, Gentile
HP: By Estrada (Dobbek)
WP: Estrada 2
TIME: 3:10
ATTENDANCE: 4,514
UMPIRES: Ed Runge, Sam Carrigan, Cal Drummond, Joe Paparella
SOURCES: Baltimore Sun; Minneapolis Star; Retrosheet; Washington Post

BALANCE	OUT	+R	+OB	=BP	=AB	+BB	+SH	+HP	+CI
Baltimore	27	13	6	46	37	7	2	0	0
Minnesota	27	5	10	42	36	5	0	1	0

Herb's Final Score

145. Team Records 23 At-Bats in Nine-Inning Game

CLEVELAND   at   CHICAGO
(Indians, 2)   (White Sox, 4)

Tuesday Night, May 9, 1961, Comiskey Park

Herb Score had been ticketed for greatness. After a stellar rookie performance in 1955, which included a league-leading 245 strikeouts and a 16–10 log, scribes were comparing him to greats of the past. Score confirmed the praises with a 20–9 mark and another league-leading 263 strikeouts in 1956. But 1957 was barely under way when tragedy arose. Pitching on May 7, Herb was struck in the eye by a line drive off the bat of Gil McDougald and remained out of action the rest of the season. Returning the following year, he could not recapture his old effectiveness, nor could he do so in 1959. Score was eventually traded to the White Sox

in 1960 where he finished with a 5–10 ledger. This was to be his first start of 1961.

Facing Score this chilly night was Cleveland ace Jim Perry. Both hurlers combatted wildness to keep the contest a low scoring affair. Perry allowed only four hits, but in typical Chicago style the Sox massaged them into a like number of runs. In the first, they put together a single, walk, hit batsman, and sacrifice fly by Jim Landis to break into the scoring column. Another sacrifice fly, this one by Al Smith, put the second Chicago run on the board in the fourth. Landis then became the batting hero with a game-winning, two-run homer in the bottom of the eighth breaking a 2–2 deadlock.

Cleveland likewise parlayed two runs, neither with the benefit of a hit. In the second frame the Indians worked their magic with a walk, balk, and two sacrifices to put over their initial tally. They scored without a hit again in the fourth on two walks and two sacrifices.

In addition to ten walks, the feature of the game was the number of sacrifices harvested by the two teams — seven in all, five by Cleveland. As the Indians walked and were sacrificed, putouts accumulated without official at bats, so that by the game's conclusion, they had amassed only *23 at-bats, tying the all-time standard for the fewest in nine innings* (see also 5-6-17). Chicago also helped matters with one double play.

This record-tying performance was completely overlooked by the press which focused on the complete-game, two-hit victory by Herb Score. After the game, Score told a reporter: "I know that I'm a better pitcher than I have been. I have had control trouble

Landis supplied most of the offense.

Cleveland Indians	AB	R	H	I
Johnny Temple 2b	4	0	1	0
Tito Francona lf	3	0	0	0
Jimmy Piersall cf	3	1	1	0
Woodie Held ss	2	1	0	0
Willie Kirkland rf	2	0	0	0
Vic Power 1b	2	0	0	2
>Bubba Phillips 3b	4	0	0	0
Johnny Romano c	1	0	0	0
Jim Perry p	2	0	0	0
	23	2	2	2

Chicago White Sox	AB	R	H	I
Luis Aparicio ss	3	0	0	0
Nellie Fox 2b	3	1	1	0
Minnie Minoso lf	3	0	0	0
Roy Sievers 1b	2	1	1	0
Jim Landis cf	3	2	2	3
J.C. Martin 3b	4	0	0	0
>Al Smith rf	3	0	0	1
Sherm Lollar c	2	0	0	0
Herb Score p	3	0	0	0
	26	4	4	4

Cleveland	IP	H	R	ER	BB	SO
Perry L,2-2	8	4	4	4	4	4

Chicago	IP	H	R	ER	BB	SO
Score W,1-0	9	2	2	2	6	5

Cleveland	0 1 0	1 0 0	0 0 0	- 2
Chicago	1 0 0	1 0 0	0 2 x	- 4

OB: Cleveland 5, Chicago 6
E: Phillips, Held
DP: Sievers-Lollar-Martin (Held)
     Temple-Held-Power (Landis)
2B: Landis
HR: Landis(4)
SO: Francona, Piersall, Power, Perry,
     Romano, Minoso, Lollar, Score 2
BB: Piersall, Held 2, Kirkland, Romano 2,
     Fox, Minoso, Sievers, Lollar
SH: Perry, Kirkland, Francona
SF: Landis, Power 2, Smith

HP: By Perry (Sievers, Aparicio)
WP: Score
BK: Score
TIME: 2:22
ATTENDANCE: 10,311
UMPIRES: Nestor Chylak, Al Smith,
     Bill McKinley, Hank Soar
SOURCES: Chicago American, Daily News,
     Sun-Times, Tribune; Cleveland Plain
     Dealer, Press; Retrosheet

BALANCE	OUT+R+OB=BP=AB+BB+SH+HP+CI
Cleveland	27	2	5	34	23	6	5	0	0
Chicago	24	4	6	34	26	4	2	2	0

this Spring, but I think I've solved that problem. I'm sure I can help the team from here on."* Sox manager Al Lopez, who had shown great patience with Score over the past two seasons, also reflected optimism when he said: "I think he has found himself now."† Sadly, both forecasts were woefully inaccurate as this was Herb's final major-league victory.

*Wendell Smith, "Gamble Pays as Sox End Streak," Chicago American, 10 May 1961, p. 25, col. 8.
†Ibid.

Cheney Fans 21

146. Pitcher Strikes Out
21 Batters in 16-Inning Game

WASHINGTON   at   BALTIMORE
(Senators, 2)   (Orioles, 1)

Wednesday Night, September 12, 1962, Memorial Stadium

Phenomenal baseball records are often achieved by the most unlikely individuals. How many fans would remember Zip Zabel, Johnny Burnett, Phil Weintraub, Tony Cloninger, or Cesar Gutierrez had it not been for their one radiant day on the

Tom Cheney — holder of a 19–29 lifetime log.

innings), and Jack Coombs and Warren Spahn (in extra innings) had fanned as many as 18.

Tom Cheney had passed through St. Louis and Pittsburgh before settling in the nation's capital. The six foot, 180 pound right-hander had demonstrated infrequent and erratic mound mastery. For example, thus far this season he had completed only three games in 20 starts, but each was a shut-out. Nor was Tom known as a strikeout artist, for on this night he struck out more batters than he had in all of 1961.

The game began inauspiciously for the 27-year-old as he fanned no Orioles in the opening frame and only one in the second. The pace quickened as he then fanned 16 over the next nine innings, and the modern strikeout mark of 18 fell in the 14th as Baltimore's Dick Hall went down swinging. A new all-time standard of 20 was set in the 15th inning at the expense of Russ Snyder, and with two outs in the 16th, pinch-hitter Dick Williams watched a third strike go by to end the game and give Cheney his 21st marker. Each Baltimore starter fanned except Boog Powell; with Snyder, Gentile, Nicholson, Breeding and Hall each being victimized three times.

diamond (see index for each man's day in the sun). Included in this list certainly must be Tom Cheney, winner of only 19 games during his eight major-league seasons. But on one September night Cheney set the baseball world on its heels by *fanning 21 batters in a single game*, establishing a benchmark which still stands.

Prior to Cheney's heroics, no hurler had struck out more than 18 in any one game since the turn of the century, regardless of the number of innings pitched. Before the birth of the American League, Charlie Sweeney and Hugh Daily had each struck out 19. But since 1901, only Feller and Koufax (in nine

Cheney did more than simply strike out batters. His 228 pitches were reached for just ten safeties, and he held the Orioles hitless from the eighth until the 16th when Nicholson singled. Tom used a variety of pitches including a fastball, slider, and knuckler, but it was his curveball that most baffled Baltimore. Marv Breeding said after the game that Cheney had the best stuff he had seen all year. Brooks Robinson agreed.

Bud Zipfel won the game for Washington with one of his ten lifetime homers.

In July of 1963, with an 8–9 record and a 2.71 ERA, Cheney suffered a severe elbow injury which cut short his major-league career. Comeback attempts in 1964 and again in 1966 proved unsuccessful.

Washington Senators	AB	R	H	I
John Kennedy ss	6	0	1	0
Ron Stillwell 2b	3	1	1	0
Jim King ph10	1	0	1	0
Chuck Cottier 2b10	2	0	0	0
Chuck Hinton rf	7	0	1	0
Bud Zipfel 1b	7	1	3	2
Ken Retzer c	7	0	0	0
Claude Osteen pr16	0	0	0	0
Bob Schmidt c16	0	0	0	0
Joe Hicks cf	5	0	1	0
Johnny Schaive ph16	1	0	0	0
Jimmy Piersall cf16	0	0	0	0
Don Lock lf	7	0	1	0
Eddie Brinkman 3b	5	0	1	0
>Tom Cheney p	6	0	0	0
	57	2	10	2

Baltimore Orioles	AB	R	H	I
Jerry Adair ss	6	0	2	0
Russ Snyder rf	7	0	2	0
Brooks Robinson 3b	5	0	1	0
Jim Gentile 1b	7	0	1	0
Boog Powell lf	6	0	1	0
Dave Nicholson cf	7	0	1	0
Hobie Landrith c	6	0	0	0
Jackie Brandt ph16	1	0	0	0
Marv Breeding 2b	6	1	1	0
> Dick Williams ph16	1	0	0	0
Milt Pappas p	2	0	0	0
Charlie Lau ph7	1	0	1	1
Dick Hall p8	3	0	0	0
Billy Hoeft p16	0	0	0	0
Wes Stock p16	0	0	0	0
	58	1	10	1

Washington	IP	H	R	ER	BB	SO
Cheney W,6-8	16	10	1	1	4	21

Baltimore	IP	H	R	ER	BB	SO
Pappas	7	4	1	1	3	4
Hall L,6-6	8.1	5	1	1	1	4
Hoeft	.1	1	0	0	0	0
Stock	.1	0	0	0	1	0
	16	10	2	2	5	8

Washington	1 0 0	0 0 0	0 0 0	0 0 0	0 0 0	1	- 2
Baltimore	0 0 0	0 0 0	1 0 0	0 0 0	0 0 0	0	- 1

OB: Washington 13, Baltimore 13
E: Adair, Breeding
2B: Hinton, Snyder, Adair, Gentile, Hicks, Breeding
HR: Zipfel(6)
SB: Adair
CS: Kennedy
SO: Kennedy 2, Zipfel 2, Hicks, Lock, Cheney, Adair, Snyder 3, Robinson, Gentile 3, Nicholson 3, Landrith, Breeding 3, Williams, Pappas 2, Hall 3
BB: Kennedy, Stillwell, Hicks, Brinkman 2, Adair, Robinson 2, Powell

SH: Cheney
WP: Cheney
BK: Pappas
TIME: 3:59
ATTENDANCE: 4,098
UMPIRES: Bill McKinley, Nestor Chylak, Frank Umont, Bob Stewart
SOURCES: Baltimore Sun; Washington Post; New York Times; Retrosheet

BALANCE	OUT+R+OB=BP=AB+BB+SH+HP+CI
Washington	48 2 13 63 57 5 1 0 0
Baltimore	48 1 13 62 58 4 0 0 0

Triple Indignity

147. Team Loses 120th Game in One Season

NEW YORK, NL   at   CHICAGO
(Mets, 1)   (Cubs, 5)

Sunday, September 30, 1962, Wrigley Field

Joe Pignatano ended his career in exotic fashion.

The inaugural campaign of the 1962 New York Mets was insufferable, establishing its perpetrators as one of the worst teams in baseball history. Their 210 errors was the most by a major league club in 14 years. And with 119 losses already in the books, they approached the final day of the season with longing, only to stumble upon one last triple-pronged humiliation.

First, New York lost to the Cubs 5–1 for their *120th defeat, the most by any club in the twentieth century.* Finishing the season just as they had begun was easy, as Mets starter Bill Hunter gave up a single in the second inning and then walked the next three batters. Later, New York reliever Craig Anderson wild-pitched another run home, showing the Chicago fans exactly why the home team did not finish in last place. The defeat left the Mets a quarantined 60.5 games off the pace, 18 games behind their ninth-place hosts, and 40 games below .500. Had the season been fun? "I would have to say no to that one," said manager Casey Stengel. "It was a rough season for me. I had to get used to losing all over again."*

Second, the Mets killed their most promising rally in the eighth inning by hitting into a triple play. Sammy Drake opened with a pinch single and stopped at second when Richie Ashburn also singled. Joe Pignatano then hit a broken-bat looper behind, and to the right of, second base. The runners thought it would be a single, but Cubs second sacker Ken Hubbs dashed back onto the grass and made a leaping glove-hand stab of the ball. Hubbs tossed to Ernie Banks at first, and Banks threw on to Andre Rodgers at second completing the triple killing.

Third, this was an embarrassing bit of baserunning for Ashburn and Drake, even if they were Mets. Perhaps it was the culmination of a year's frustration, or the dread of having to return to New York in 1963, but none of the triple play accomplices (Drake, Ashburn, and Pignatano) ever played in another major league game. Ashburn, who had been stationed at second base for only the second time in his career, left the game prematurely and never played another major-league inning!

*Louis Effrat, "The Mets Long Season Ends with Their 120th Defeat, 5–1," New York Times, 1 October 1962, p. 43, col. 7–8.

If it hadn't been for the reporters, only 3,960 witnesses could have described the misadventure as the Cubs attracted a paltry 609,802 paying customers for the entire season.

New York Mets	AB	R	H	I
Richie Ashburn 2b	4	0	1	0
Ken MacKenzie p8	0	0	0	0
Choo Choo Coleman c	3	0	0	0
Joe Pignatano c7	1	0	0	0
Joe Christopher rf	4	0	0	0
Frank Thomas lf	3	1	2	1
Marv Throneberry 1b	2	0	0	0
Ed Kranepool 1b8	1	0	0	0
>Felix Mantilla 3b	4	0	1	0
Jim Hickman cf	3	0	0	0
Elio Chacon ss	2	0	0	0
Willard Hunter p	0	0	0	0
Ray Daviault p2	1	0	0	0
Sammy Taylor ph5	1	0	0	0
Craig Anderson p5	0	0	0	0
Sammy Drake ph8,2b	1	0	1	0
	30	1	5	1

Chicago Cubs	AB	R	H	I
>Ken Hubbs 2b	4	0	1	0
Ron Santo 3b	4	1	1	0
Billy Williams lf	4	1	0	0
Ernie Banks 1b	4	1	0	0
George Altman rf	3	2	3	1
Nelson Mathews cf	2	0	2	2
Andre Rodgers ss	3	0	0	0
Cuno Barragan c	3	0	0	1
Bob Buhl p	4	0	0	0
	31	5	7	4

New York	IP	H	R	ER	BB	SO
Hunter L,1-6	1	1	1	1	4	0
Daviault	3	3	1	1	1	2
Anderson	3	3	3	0	1	1
MacKenzie	1	0	0	0	0	1
	8	7	5	2	6	4

Chicago	IP	H	R	ER	BB	SO
Buhl W,12-13	9	5	1	1	3	6

```
New York   0 0 0   1 0 0   0 0 0   - 1
Chicago    0 1 1   0 1 0   2 0 x   - 5
```

OB: New York 5, Chicago 8
E: Christopher, Mantilla, Ashburn
DP: Ashburn-Throneberry
TP: Hubbs-Banks-Rodgers(Pignatano)
2B: Mantilla, Mathews
HR: Thomas(34)
SB: Santo, Altman
SO: Ashburn, Coleman, Christopher, Kranepool, Chacon, Daviault, Barragan, Buhl 3
BB: Thomas, Throneberry, Chacon, Hubbs, Altman, Mathews 2, Rodgers, Barragan

WP: Anderson
TIME: 2:16
ATTENDANCE: 3,960
UMPIRES: Frank Secory, Tony Venzon, Paul Pryor, Augie Donatelli
SOURCES: Chicago American, Daily News, Sun-Times, Tribune; New York Herald-Tribune, Times

BALANCE	OUT+R+OB=BP=AB+BB+SH+HP+CI

BALANCE	OUT	+	R	+	OB	=	BP	=	AB	+	BB	+	SH	+	HP	+	CI
New York	27		1		5		33		30		3		0		0		0
Chicago	24		5		8		37		31		6		0		0		0

Paul Mauled

148. Pitcher Allows
Four Consecutive Home Runs

LOS ANGELES   at   CLEVELAND
(Angels, 5)   (Indians, 9)

Wednesday Night, July 31, 1963, Municipal Stadium

Foytack was later able to laugh about his day in Cleveland.

After Paul Foytack compiled a 58–51 log as a starter with Detroit in the 1950s, his pitching career turned south. By this year his skills had eroded to the point that, as a reliever, he was traded to the Los Angeles Angels.

There was little chance that Paul ever would have seen his name in baseball annals were it not for the second game of a double-header on this date. (The only category in which he had ever led the league was walks-allowed.) Foytack had taken the mound in relief with the Angels trailing 5–1 in the fifth. After allowing only one Indian safety in his initial relief frame, he began the sixth by retiring the first two batters. Then the roof caved in as *Paul served home run balls to the next four Indians in succession.* To date he is the only pitcher to suffer such indignity.

Woodie Held was the third batter in the

sixth. He picked out a low inside fastball and hammered it into the left-field seats giving the Tribe a 6–1 advantage. Next up was Cleveland starter Pedro Ramos. Ramos, a .155 lifetime hitter, had just one hit in 1963 prior to this game but jumped on a high curve and deposited it over the fence in left. Remarkably, it was his second circuit clout of the contest. Tito Francona followed in the Cleveland batting order, and he pulled a high outside fastball into the right-field stands. By now, the fans were delirious, and the center field fireworks launcher was falling behind in his work. Rookie Larry Brown was the next hitter. Larry had yet to hit his first major-league homer but pounced on a slider that cut the heart of plate and sent it over the left field fence. That was all the patience that Angels' manager Bill Rigney could offer. But as he finally made his way toward the mound, he was roundly booed by the Cleveland fans. Foytack, meanwhile, got a standing ovation as he walked toward the dugout. The cheers reverted to boos when the next Cleveland hitter, Willie Kirkland, singled to break the long-ball streak.

The four consecutive home runs established a new American League mark and tied the National League standard set by the Milwaukee Braves on June 8, 1961. Milwaukee's outburst, however, was easier to comprehend. The rocket launchers were all terrific sluggers — Eddie Mathews, Hank Aaron, Joe Adcock, and Frank Thomas. And, they accomplished their outburst off two different hurlers.

Later interviewed, Foytack was asked why he hadn't decked Brown rather than throw a ball over the heart of the plate. He replied that he *was* trying to knock Brown down on the 2–0 count but had no idea where his pitches were going. Brown, meanwhile, thought he'd be knocked down on the first pitch; then on the second pitch. By the third pitch he didn't know what to expect. That's when he got the perfect one that was intended as the brushback. Francona also thought he'd have had to hit the dust but got a juicy offering instead.

For Ramos, this game represented a career high not only in home runs, but also in strikeouts. He fanned 15 Angels but wasn't around for the ending. When he tired in the ninth, Gary Bell terminated a threat by inducing Lee Thomas to ground into a game-ending double play.

SECOND GAME

Los Angeles Angels	AB	R	H	I
Albie Pearson cf	4	1	3	0
Jim Fregosi ss	5	1	1	1
>Lee Thomas 1b	5	1	1	2
Leon Wagner lf	4	1	2	2
Billy Moran 2b	4	0	1	0
Bob Rodgers c	2	0	1	0
Hank Foiles c7	1	0	0	0
Felix Torres 3b	4	0	1	0
Ken Hunt rf	4	1	1	0
Eli Grba p	1	0	0	0
Don Lee p3	0	0	0	0
Frank Kostro ph5	1	0	0	0
Paul Foytack p5	0	0	0	0
Jack Spring p6	0	0	0	0
Bob Sadowski ph7	1	0	0	0
Julio Navarro p7	0	0	0	0
Joe Koppe ph9	1	0	0	0
	37	5	11	5

Cleveland Indians	AB	R	H	I
Tito Francona lf	4	2	3	1
Larry Brown ss	5	2	2	1
>Willie Kirkland cf	4	1	1	0
Max Alvis 3b	2	0	0	0
Jerry Kindall 2b5	2	0	2	0
Fred Whitfield 1b	4	1	1	4
Joe Azcue c	4	0	1	0
Al Luplow rf	4	0	0	0
Woodie Held 2b,3b5	4	1	1	1
Pedro Ramos p	4	2	2	2
Gary Bell p9	0	0	0	0
	37	9	13	9

Los Angeles	IP	H	R	ER	BB	SO
Grba L,1-2	2.1	4	4	4	1	1
Lee	1.2	2	1	1	0	1
Foytack	1.2	5	4	4	0	1
Spring	.1	2	0	0	0	0
Navarro	2	0	0	0	1	2
	8	13	9	9	2	5

Cleveland	IP	H	R	ER	BB	SO
Ramos W,5-4	8.1	11	5	5	2	15
Bell	.2	0	0	0	0	0
	9	11	5	5	2	15

```
Los Angeles   1 0 0   0 0 0   4 0 0  - 5
Cleveland     0 0 5   0 0 4   0 0 x  - 9
```

OB: Los Angeles 7, Cleveland 6
E: Fregosi, Moran, Held
DP: Fregosi-Moran-Thomas (Brown)
     Kindall-Brown-Whitfield (Thomas)
2B: Azcue, Fregosi
HR: Thomas(9), Ramos 2(2), Held(11),
     Whitfield(9), Francona(7),
     Brown(1), Wagner(21)
SO: Fregosi 2, Wagner, Moran 3, Foiles,
     Torres 3, Hunt 3, Koppe, Kostro,
     Kirkland, Alvis, Azcue 2, Held

BB: Pearson, Rodgers, Francona,
     Kirkland
TIME: 2:42
ATTENDANCE: 7,288
UMPIRES: Hank Soar, Bob Stewart, Al
     Salerno, Ed Runge
SOURCES: Cleveland Plain Dealer,
     Press; Los Angeles Times;
     Retrosheet

BALANCE	OUT	+R	+OB	=BP	=AB	+BB	+SH	+HP	+CI
Los Angeles	27	5	7	39	37	2	0	0	0
Cleveland	24	9	6	39	37	2	0	0	0

How the rally sounded to a Cleveland Press *cartoonist.*

A Family Affair

149. Three Brothers Bat Consecutively in Same Inning

SAN FRANCISCO   at   NEW YORK
(Giants, 2)   (Mets, 4)

Tuesday Night, September 10, 1963, Polo Grounds

No fewer than 17 families have sent three or more brothers into major league combat. There were five Delahanty brothers, four O'Neill's, and 15 other trios of siblings to appear in big league games. But only once, it is believed, have *three brothers all played on*

Left to right: Jesus, Matty, and Felipe all batted in the eighth.

the same team, in the same game, and batted consecutively in the same inning — in ascending order of age!

The San Francisco Giants' organization had nurtured a family of talented outfielders from the Dominican Republic by the name of Alou. Felipe, a right-handed batter, was the first Alou brother to emerge in 1958 when he appeared in 75 games. Left-handed Matty broke in two years later, and Jesus, a right-hander, made his major-league debut in this very game.

Felipe was a part-time outfielder until 1961 when his batting average and playing time took on substance. Previously, he had found his path blocked by the likes of Willie Mays, Willie Kirkland, and Orlando Cepeda, but later Felipe joined forces with Mays, Cepeda, Willie McCovey and Harvey Kuenn to form one of the more potent offenses of the early 1960s. Felipe's career later peaked with the Braves with whom he twice led the National League in hits.

At 5'9", 160 pounds, Matty was the smallest of the kinsman but assembled the highest lifetime batting average (.307). Matty made his debut in September of 1960 but ran into the same obstacles as brother Felipe and never became a regular with the Giants. Not until he was traded to the Pirates and was afforded an opportunity to play regularly did Matty's talents blossom. In 1966, he was crowned the NL batting champ with a .342 average, and in 1969 he led the circuit with 231 hits.

Jesus was the youngest and largest (6'2", 195 lbs.) of the brothers. When called up from Tacoma on this date, Jesus saw a formidable logjam of outfielders in brother Felipe, Mays, McCovey, Kuenn, and brother Matty. But after Felipe was soon traded, Jesus saw considerable playing time. As were his two older brothers, Jesus was also traded after six seasons in San Francisco and then spent several productive campaigns in Houston.

The historic game occurred as the waning season bloated rosters, the Mets were secure cellar tenants, and the Giants clung precariously to fourth place. San Francisco needed this win and used five pitchers and three pinch hitters in a vain attempt to escape defeat.

It was in the top of the eighth that Giants manager Alvin Dark called on the Dominicans. Trailing 3–0, Jesus pinch-hit for shortstop Jose Pagan and grounded out to short. Matty then swung for pitcher Bob Garibaldi and fanned. Felipe, the starting leadoff batter, also grounded out, tapping to Mets

pitcher Carl Willey. It was an embarrassing exhibition for the Alous as none of them hit the ball out of the infield. Dark had said before the game that he had hoped the Giants would have gotten a 10-run lead so he could use all three Alous in the same outfield. But simply batting in the same inning of the same game was enough to produce a unique mark in baseball annals.

San Francisco Giants	AB	R	H	I
Felipe Alou rf	4	0	0	0
Chuck Hiller 2b	4	0	1	0
Willie McCovey lf	4	1	3	1
Willie Mays cf	4	0	0	0
Orlando Cepeda 1b	4	1	1	1
>Tom Haller c	4	0	1	0
Jim Davenport 3b	3	0	0	0
Jose Pagan ss	2	0	0	0
Jesus Alou ph8	1	0	0	0
Ernie Bowman ss8	0	0	0	0
Billy O'Dell p	0	0	0	0
Gaylord Perry p2	1	0	0	0
Norm Larker ph5	1	0	0	0
Jack Fisher p5	0	0	0	0
Bob Garibaldi p5	0	0	0	0
Matty Alou ph8	1	0	0	0
Ron Herbel p8	0	0	0	0
	33	2	6	2

New York Mets	AB	R	H	I
Joe Christopher rf	3	0	1	0
Pumpsie Green 3b	3	2	2	0
Ron Hunt 2b	3	1	2	1
>Jim Hickman lf	5	1	2	2
Tim Harkness 1b	4	0	2	1
Dick Smith cf	3	0	2	0
Chris Cannizzaro c	2	0	0	0
Duke Carmel ph5	0	0	0	0
Choo Choo Coleman c6	1	0	0	0
Al Moran ss	4	0	0	0
Carl Willey p	3	0	0	0
	31	4	11	4

San Francisco	IP	H	R	ER	BB	SO
O'Dell L,12-8	1.1	5	2	2	2	2
Perry	2.2	0	0	0	2	2
Fisher	0	2	1	0	0	0
Garibaldi	3	3	0	0	1	1
Herbel	1	1	1	1	1	1
	8	11	4	3	6	6

New York	IP	H	R	ER	BB	SO
Willey W,9-12	9	6	2	2	0	3

San Francisco	0 0 0	0 0 0	0 0 2	– 2
New York	2 0 0	0 1 0	0 1 x	– 4

OB: San Francisco 4, New York 12
E: F. Alou
DP: Garibaldi-Haller-Cepeda (Moran)
2B: Harkness, Hunt
HR: Hickman(16), McCovey(38), Cepeda(29)
SB: Smith
SO: F. Alou, Cepeda, Davenport, Green, Cannizzaro 2, Willey 3
BB: Green 2, Hunt, Smith, Carmel(I), Willey

SH: Christopher
HP: By O'Dell (Christopher); by Garibaldi (Hunt)
WP: Herbel
TIME: 2:45
ATTENDANCE: 14,945 (paid)
UMPIRES: Doug Harvey, Al Barlick, Lee Weyer, Ed Vargo
SOURCES: New York Times; Retrosheet; San Francisco Examiner, Chronicle

BALANCE	OUT+R+OB=BP=AB+BB+SH+HP+CI
San Francisco	27 2 4 33 33 0 0 0 0
New York	24 4 12 40 31 6 1 2 0

New Kids on the Block

150. Team Fields All-Rookie Lineup

NEW YORK   at   HOUSTON
(Mets, 10)   (Colt .45's, 3)

Friday Night, September 27, 1963, Colts Stadium

The Houston Colt .45's, in only their second major-league season, were safely entrenched in ninth place with only three games remaining to be played. Their opponents, the New York Mets, were the other NL sophomore expansion team which had already locked up the cellar position. Now, in a previously publicized, novel publicity stunt designed to attract some attention to a meaningless series, Colt's manager Harry Craft orchestrated the *first all-rookie lineup in baseball annals*. It was a success in conception but a failure in execution as New York won handily, and Houston fans and players alike found that it was a long way from the minors to the majors, even at the low levels of expansion.

The average age of the Houston starters was 19 years and four months, and only Jimmy Wynn and Aaron Pointer were old enough to vote (at the time — 21 years of age). Houston pitcher Jay Dahl was a 17-year-old southpaw who had graduated from Bloomington (California) High School in June, making him the youngest NL hurler to start a game since 15-year-old Joe Nuxhall made his wartime debut with the Redlegs in 1944. It was short-lived glory for Dahl, however. He never pitched again from a major league mound.

Five of the Colt's were in their first year of professional baseball, and four made this their first major-league game. Those four were Dahl; Joe Hoerner, an elder statesman at 26; Danny Coombs at 21; and Sonny

Jim Wynn (left) and Rusty Staub

Jackson at 19. Five others — Joe Morgan, Aaron Pointer, Glenn Vaughan, Jerry Grote, and Mike White — had made their major league debuts within the past week. Even the substitutes were rookies as 16 greenhorns made their way into the boxscore before third year veteran Carl Warwick appeared as a pinch hitter in the eighth. And, when the rookie pitchers got into trouble it was first

baseman Rusty Staub who walked over to give them a comforting word, as befitting a veteran of 19. Ironically for Dick Drott, the oldest and last of the Colt .45's to enter the game, this was his last appearance in a major league contest.

Preceding each of the Houston player names in the boxscore is their age at the time of the game.

New York Mets	AB	R	H	I
Joe Christopher rf	4	0	1	1
Dick Smith cf	5	1	1	0
Ron Hunt 2b	5	1	1	1
Ted Schreiber 2b9	0	0	0	0
Frank Thomas lf	5	1	2	0
Rod Kanehl lf9	0	0	0	0
Jim Hickman 3b	5	1	3	1
Tim Harkness 1b	5	2	1	0
Ed Kranepool 1b9	0	0	0	0
Chris Cannizzaro c	4	2	1	2
Al Moran ss	5	2	3	2
>Al Jackson p	5	0	2	1
	43	10	15	8

	Houston Colt .45s	AB	R	H	I
(19)	Sonny Jackson ss	3	0	0	0
(21)	Ernie Fazio 3b6	1	1	0	0
(20)	Joe Morgan 2b	5	0	2	1
(21)	Jimmy Wynn cf	4	0	2	0
(19)	Rusty Staub 1b	5	1	2	1
(21)	Aaron Pointer rf	5	0	1	0
(19)	>Brock Davis lf	5	0	1	1
(19)	Glenn Vaughan 3b,ss6	4	0	2	0
(20)	Jerry Grote c	3	0	1	0
(20)	Dave Adlesh c7	1	0	0	0
(17)	Jay Dahl p	0	0	0	0
(21)	Danny Coombs p3	0	0	0	0
(26)	Johnny Weekly ph3	0	0	0	0
(26)	Joe Hoerner p4	1	1	0	0
(24)	Mike White ph6	1	0	0	0
(25)	Jim Dickson p7	0	0	0	0
(26)	Carl Warwick ph8	1	0	0	0
(27)	Dick Drott p9	0	0	0	0
		39	3	11	3

New York	IP	H	R	ER	BB	SO
Jackson W,13-17	9	11	3	3	3	8

Houston	IP	H	R	ER	BB	SO
Dahl L,0-1	2.2	7	7	5	0	0
Coombs	.1	3	1	1	0	0
Hoerner	3	2	0	0	0	2
Dickson	2	1	1	0	1	0
Drott	1	2	1	1	0	0
	9	15	10	7	1	2

New York 0 3 5   0 0 0   1 0 1   -10
Houston   0 0 0   1 1 0   0 0 1   - 3

OB: New York 8, Houston 12
E: Davis 2, S. Jackson, Harkness, Hickman
2B: Hunt, Hickman, Harkness
3B: Morgan
SO: Hunt, Harkness, S. Jackson, Morgan, Staub, Pointer, Davis, Grote 2, Adlesh
BB: Christopher, Fazio, Wynn, Weekly

SF: Cannizzaro
WP: Dahl, Drott
TIME: 2:39
ATTENDANCE: 6,907 (5,802 paid)
UMPIRES: Frank Walsh, Ken Burkhart, Paul Pryor, Frank Secory
SOURCES: Houston Chronicle, Post; New York Times; Retrosheet

BALANCE	OUT	+R	+OB	=BP	=AB	+BB	+SH	+HP	+CI
New York	27	10	8	45	43	1	1	0	0
Houston	27	3	12	42	39	3	0	0	0

An Interminable Doubleheader

151. Teams Amass 234 At-Bats in 32-Inning Doubleheader Lasting Nine Hours, 52 Minutes

SAN FRANCISCO   at   NEW YORK
(Giants, 5,8)   (Mets, 3,6)

Sunday, May 31, 1964, Shea Stadium

When the huge throng sat down for the 1:05 start of a doubleheader, little did they realize that many wouldn't return home until the next day. Those who stayed until the bitter end witnessed endurance, performance, and attendance records tumble through nine innings of a first game and 23 frames of the nightcap. The *32 innings-played established a major league mark for a doubleheader* as did the *9 hours and 52 minutes of play*. Furthermore, the *second game alone encompassed 7 hours and 23 minutes for a new National League standard*. All three marks still stand.

A series of less glamorous standards were also set in the category of official at-bats. For the *first time in modern baseball history, player(s) accumulated 14 at-bats in a doubleheader*— Joe Christopher, Jim Hickman, Ed Kranepool, Roy McMillan, and Frank Thomas for the Mets, and Jesus Alou for the Giants. (Alou has heretofore been omitted from the record books.) The *Mets alone amassed 119 official at-bats on the day, and the two clubs combined for 234 at-bats*. All of the above at-bat records remain in baseball annals.

Although 57,037 paid their way into the park, less than 10,000 remained at 11:25 P.M. when the action ceased. The first game belonged to the Giants' Juan Marichal who subdued the Mets on eight hits and no walks, running his record to 8–1. The nightcap featured multiple blown scoring opportunities and 33 runners left on base. Del Crandall finally drove home the game's winning tally with his two out, pinch hit double in the top of the 23rd, and the home club went down

without a whimper in the bottom of the frame giving San Francisco a sweep.

In addition to endurance records, the largest crowd to date this season also saw a triple-play in the 14th inning of the second contest. After Jesus Alou singled, Willie Mays walked. Orlando Cepeda then lined to Met's shortstop Roy McMillan, who stepped on second to retire Alou, then threw to first baseman Ed Kranepool to get Mays.

The crowd also saw Mays play shortstop for three innings, Cepeda steal home, and 12 pitchers share in *two strikeout records—36 in an extra-inning game by both clubs (remains*

Cisco deserved a batter fate.

NL mark) and 47 by both clubs in a double-header (later surpassed). Two pitchers, Galen Cisco of the Mets and Gaylord Perry of the Giants, each pitched an entire game in relief, and both catchers, Tom Haller of the Giants and Chris Cannizzaro of the Mets, lasted the entire seven hours and 23 minutes.

Stories surrounding the games were also numerous. The Harry M. Stevens, Inc. caterers reported that fans consumed about two tons of hot dogs and hamburgers. Shortages were reported, however, and when one concessionaire in the right-field stands ran out of hot dogs, he gave away the buns free. Thirsty gourmets complained that the beer ran out while amateur pugilists entertained themselves with numerous confrontations. And after the 22nd inning, television broadcaster Lindsey Nelson announced that this was the longest game ever televised in living color. (The only longer games occurred in 1945, 1920, and 1906.)

FIRST GAME

San Francisco Giants	AB	R	H	I
Harvey Kuenn lf	5	0	3	1
Matty Alou pr9,lf	0	0	0	0
>Del Crandall c	4	0	0	0
Willie Mays cf	3	1	1	0
Jim Ray Hart 3b	4	1	1	0
Orlando Cepeda 1b	4	2	3	1
Jim Davenport 2b	3	0	1	1
Jesus Alou rf	4	1	2	1
Gil Garrido ss	3	0	1	0
Juan Marichal p	4	0	0	0
	34	5	12	4

New York Mets	AB	R	H	I
Rod Kanehl 2b	4	0	1	0
Roy McMillan ss	4	0	0	0
Jesse Gonder c	4	0	0	0
Frank Thomas lf	4	0	1	0
Dick Smith pr8,lf	0	0	0	0
Joe Christopher rf	4	1	1	0
Ed Kranepool 1b	4	1	1	0
Jim Hickman cf	4	1	2	3
Charley Smith 3b	3	0	2	0
Al Jackson p	1	0	0	0
Tom Sturdivant p6	0	0	0	0
George Altman ph7	1	0	0	0
Larry Bearnarth p8	0	0	0	0
> Johnny Stephenson ph9	1	0	0	0
	34	3	8	3

San Francisco	IP	H	R	ER	BB	SO
Marichal W,8-1	9	8	3	3	0	7

New York	IP	H	R	ER	BB	SO
Jackson L,3-7	5	8	4	4	1	3
Sturdivant	2	2	0	0	0	0
Bearnarth	2	2	1	1	0	1
	9	12	5	5	1	4

San Francisco	0 0 0	1 0 3	0 0 1	- 5
New York	0 3 0	0 0 0	0 0 0	- 3

OB: San Francisco 6, New York 6
E: Hickman, Hart
DP: Garrido-Davenport-Cepeda(McMillan)
    McMillan-Kranepool (Garrido)
2B: Cepeda, C. Smith
HR: Hickman(3)
SB: Cepeda
CS: Mays
SO: Kuenn, Hart 2, Marichal, Gonder,
    Thomas, Hickman, C. Smith,
    Jackson, Altman, Stephenson
BB: Mays

SH: Crandall, Jackson, Garrido
SF: Davenport
HP: By Marichal (C. Smith)
TIME: 2:29
ATTENDANCE: 55,000 (estimated)
UMPIRES: Ken Burkhart, Ed Sudol,
    Paul Pryor, Frank Secory
SOURCES: New York Times; San
    Francisco Chronicle, Examiner;
    Retrosheet

BALANCE	OUT	+R	+OB	=BP	=AB	+BB	+SH	+HP	+CI
San Francisco	27	5	6	38	34	1	3	0	0
New York	27	3	6	36	34	0	1	1	0

SECOND GAME

San Francisco Giants	AB	R	H	I		New York Mets	AB	R	H	I
Harvey Kuenn lf	5	1	0	0		Rod Kanehl 2b	1	0	0	0
Gaylord Perry p13	3	0	0	0		Jesse Gonder ph2	1	0	0	0
Del Crandall ph23	1	0	1	1	>	Amado Samuel 2b3	7	0	2	0
Bob Hendley p23	0	0	0	0		Roy McMillan ss	10	1	2	0
Jesus Alou rf	10	1	4	2		Frank Thomas lf	10	1	2	0
>W. Mays cf,ss10,cf13	10	1	1	1		Joe Christopher rf	10	2	4	3
Orlando Cepeda 1b	9	1	3	0		Ed Kranepool 1b	10	1	3	1
Tom Haller c	10	1	4	1		Jim Hickman cf	10	1	2	0
Chuck Hiller 2b	8	1	1	1		Charlie Smith 3b	9	0	4	1
Jim Ray Hart 3b	4	0	1	1		Chris Cannizzaro c	9	0	1	1
M. Alou ph10,cf,lf13	6	0	0	0		Bill Wakefield p	0	0	0	0
Gil Garrido ss	3	0	0	0		George Altman ph2	0	0	0	0
Willie McCovey ph8	1	0	0	0		Al Jackson pr2	0	0	0	0
Jim Davenport ss8,	4	1	1	1		Craig Anderson p3	0	0	0	0
3b10,ss13						Tom Sturdivant p3	0	0	0	0
Bobby Bolin p	2	0	1	0		Dick Smith ph5	1	0	0	0
Ken MacKenzie p7	0	0	0	0		Frank Lary p6	0	0	0	0
Bob Shaw p7	0	0	0	0		Hawk Taylor ph7	1	0	0	0
Duke Snider ph9	1	0	0	0		Larry Bearnarth p8	3	0	0	0
Ron Herbel p9	0	0	0	0		Galen Cisco p15	2	0	0	0
Cap Peterson ph13,3b	4	1	0	0		John Stephenson ph23	1	0	0	0
	81	8	17	8			85	6	20	6

San Francisco	IP	H	R	ER	BB	SO		New York	IP	H	R	ER	BB	SO
Bolin	6.2	8	6	5	2	7		Wakefield	2	2	2	2	2	1
MacKenzie	0	1	0	0	0	0		Anderson	.1	4	4	4	0	0
Shaw	1.1	1	0	0	0	1		Sturdivant	2.2	3	0	0	1	2
Herbel	4	3	0	0	0	3		Lary	2	0	0	0	0	2
Perry W,3-1	10	7	0	0	1	9		Bearnarth	7	3	0	0	4	4
Hendley	1	0	0	0	0	2		Cisco L,2-5	9	5	2	2	2	5
	23	20	6	5	3	22			23	17	8	8	9	14

San Francisco	2 0 4	0 0 0	0 0 0	0 0 0	0 0 0	0 0 0	0 0 0	0 2	- 8
New York	0 1 0	0 0 2	3 0 0	0 0 0	0 0 0	0 0 0	0 0 0	0 0	- 6

OB: San Francisco 16, New York 16
E: Garrido, Haller, Cepeda, Cisco
DP: Perry-Davenport-Cepeda (Cisco)
  Davenport-Cepeda (Kranepool)
  Christopher-Kranepool (Hiller)
TP: McMillan-Kranepool (Cepeda)
2B: J. Alou, Kranepool, Cepeda, Crandall
3B: Kranepool, Haller, Davenport
HR: Christopher(3)
CS: J. Alou, C. Smith
SO: Kuenn 2, Perry, J. Alou, Mays 2,
  Cepeda 2, Hiller, Garrido, McCovey,
  Davenport, Peterson, Bolin, Kanehl,
  Samuel, Thomas, McMillan 2,
  Christopher, Cisco, Kranepool 2,
  Hickman 4, C. Smith 2, Cannizzaro 3,
  Taylor, Bearnarth 2, Stephenson

BB: Kuenn 2, J. Alou, Mays, Hiller,
  Davenport 2, Bolin, Peterson(I),
  Samuel, Cannizzaro, Altman(I)
SH: Herbel, Hiller, C. Smith, Cisco
HP: By Shaw (Samuel); by Cisco (Cepeda)
PB: Cannizzaro
TIME: 7:23
ATTENDANCE: 57,037
UMPIRES: Ed Sudol, Paul Pryor, Frank
  Secory, Ken Burkhart
SOURCES: New York Times; Retrosheet;
  San Francisco Chronicle, Examiner

BALANCE	OUT+R+OB=BP=AB+BB+SH+HP+CI
San Francisco	69 8 16 93 81 9 2 1 0
New York	69 6 16 91 85 3 2 1 0

Economy of Effort

152. Team Records 19 At-Bats in Nine-Inning Game; Teams Combine for 46 At-Bats

KANSAS CITY   at   BALTIMORE
(Athletics, 0)   (Orioles, 1)

Saturday Night, September 12, 1964, Memorial Stadium

The first column of any modern boxscore indicates each player's official at-bats or ABs, but these numbers often exclude some very important aspects of the game. For example, walks, sacrifices, sacrifice flies, hit-batsmen, and catcher's interference are not officially recorded as at-bats, yet a team's total ABs will vary depending on the number of these as well as on the more obvious hits, errors, and double plays. Boxscore readers normally see team at-bats total between 25 and 40, and never had a club in a nine-inning game recorded fewer than 20 at-bats. But on this date, behind a freak combination of events as well as a superb pitching performance, the Baltimore Orioles needed *only 19 official at-bats* to prevail over the Kansas City Athletics.

So often in record-setting games the impetus is provided by unlikely candidates. This game's main participants were a couple of rookies. Kansas City furnished 24-year-old left-hander Bob Meyer who, despite his first year status, was already toiling for his third major league club. Bob would eventually go on to win a lifetime total of two games. Defending the home turf was a

Orsino's hit led to the game's only run.

20-year-old southpaw named Frank Bertaina; this game provided him with his only win of the season. But for a little over two hours, both neophytes pitched superbly, each allowing just one hit, although both experienced control problems.

Kansas City, with a .243 team batting average, was the first to threaten to score in the fifth. Doc Edwards opened with a double, Ed Charles fanned, and Dick Green walked. Meyer bunted both runners along, but Bert Campaneris fouled out.

Baltimore, batting .246, nearly broke the scoring ice in the seventh. Sam Bowens led off with a walk, was bunt sacrificed to second, and moved to third on Jerry Adair's ground out. With Orsino batting, a short passed ball eluded catcher Edwards enough to entice Bowens to score. But Doc recovered quickly and tossed to Meyer who tagged out the sliding Bowens. This was a half-inning with only one at bat.

The game was decided in the bottom of the eighth when second-string catcher John Orsino led off with a double. It was Baltimore's only hit. Pinch runner Bob Saverine hustled to third on Bertaina's sacrifice bunt, and Jackie Brandt drove him home with a sacrifice fly. Appropriately, the only run of the game thus scored with only one official at-bat.

In addition to the Orioles' single-club mark, Kansas City accumulated a modest total of 27 at-bats. The combatants thus also produced the *two-team record for fewest at-bats in a nine inning game — 46.*

Kansas City Athletics	AB	R	H	I
Bert Campaneris lf	4	0	0	0
Jose Tartabull lf8	0	0	0	0
Wayne Causey ss	3	0	0	0
Rocky Colavito rf	3	0	0	0
Jim Gentile 1b	3	0	0	0
Nelson Mathews cf	4	0	0	0
>Doc Edwards c	4	0	1	0
Ed Charles 3b	3	0	0	0
Dick Green 2b	2	0	0	0
Bob Meyer p	1	0	0	0
	27	0	1	0

Baltimore Orioles	AB	R	H	I
Jackie Brandt cf,lf9	3	0	0	1
>Luis Aparicio ss	3	0	0	0
Boog Powell lf	2	0	0	0
Lenny Green cf9	0	0	0	0
Brooks Robinson 3b	2	0	0	0
Sam Bowens rf	2	0	0	0
Bob Johnson 1b	1	0	0	0
Norm Siebern 1b9	0	0	0	0
Jerry Adair 2b	3	0	0	0
John Orsino c	2	0	1	0
Bob Saverine pr8	0	1	0	0
Dick Brown c9	0	0	0	0
Frank Bertaina p	1	0	0	0
	19	1	1	1

Kansas City	IP	H	R	ER	BB	SO
Meyer L,2-6	8	1	1	1	6	4

Baltimore	IP	H	R	ER	BB	SO
Bertaina W,1-0	9	1	0	0	5	7

Kansas City	0 0 0	0 0 0	0 0 0	- 0
Baltimore	0 0 0	0 0 0	0 1 x	- 1

OB: Kansas City 6, Baltimore 4

E: Charles

DP: D. Green-Causey-Gentile (Robinson)

2B: Edwards, Orsino

SB: Colavito, Aparicio

SO: Gentile, Mathews, Edwards, Charles 2, D. Green, Meyer, Powell, Bowens, Johnson, Adair

BB: Causey, Colavito, Gentile, D. Green, Meyer, Aparicio, Powell, Robinson, Bowens, Johnson, Orsino

SH: Meyer, Bertaina 2, Johnson

SF: Brandt

TIME: 2:04

ATTENDANCE: 12,898 (8,301 paid)

UMPIRES: Bill Haller, Eddie Hurley, Sam Carrigan, Red Flaherty

SOURCES: Baltimore Sun; Kansas City Star; Retrosheet; Washington Post

BALANCE	OUT+R+OB=BP=AB+BB+SH+HP+CI
Kansas City	27 0 6 33 27 5 1 0 0
Baltimore	24 1 4 29 19 6 4 0 0

Cards Completely Frame Cubs

153. Team Scores in Each of Nine Innings

ST. LOUIS   at   CHICAGO
(Cardinals, 15)   (Cubs, 2)

Sunday, September 13, 1964, Wrigley Field

Cub fans who turned out to honor the soon-to-retire umpire Jocko Conlan, witnessed much more than a touching pre-game ceremony. The game itself was one that would not soon be forgotten. For the first time in 41 years, a major league team *scored in every frame of a nine-inning game*, as the visiting St. Louis Cardinals trounced the Chicago Cubs, 15–2.

Although one may consider this feat more likely than pitching a perfect game or an individual hitting two grand slams in one game, this has not been the case in major league history. Since the turn of the century there have been at least a dozen perfect games, and seven players have homered with the bases loaded twice in one game, but there have been only two teams to score in all nine innings. The only other club, the 1923 Giants, turned the trick against the Phillies (see 6-01-23). Several other teams have scored in every inning in which they batted, but because they were the winning home team, they didn't bat in the bottom of the ninth.

St. Louis battered five of the six Cub hurlers for 18 hits including three home runs. Round-trippers by Julian Javier in the second and Mike Shannon in the sixth posted the lone Cardinal markers in those

two frames. Lou Brock's blast came while leading off a two-run fourth, and every starter hit safely except pitcher Curt Simmons. Except for the eighth and ninth innings, the Cardinals scored with either none or one out. Not only did they hit safely in every frame, but they also left base runners in all but the seventh.

St. Louis was also helped considerably by

Dick Groat sparked the Cardinal attack.

porous Chicago fielding. Seven errors resulted in four unearned runs and gave St. Louis plenty of extra scoring opportunities. Chicago's final, ninth-inning error was crucial in the record-setting performance. In the top of the ninth, Dal Maxvill opened by

flying out to right. Ken Boyer next lifted a routine pop up, but second baseman Ron Campbell dropped it. Bill White then singled Boyer to third, and a sacrifice fly by Mike Shannon sent the Cardinals into baseball annals.

St. Louis Cardinals	AB	R	H	I
Curt Flood cf	5	2	3	1
Lou Brock lf	6	2	2	1
Dick Groat ss	5	2	4	3
Dal Maxvill pr7,ss	1	1	0	0
Ken Boyer 3b	5	2	2	2
Bill White 1b	5	1	1	1
Mike Shannon rf	5	1	2	4
>Julian Javier 2b	6	2	3	1
Bob Uecker c	4	1	1	0
Curt Simmons p	4	1	0	0
Ray Washburn p9	0	0	0	0
	46	15	18	13

Chicago Cubs	AB	R	H	I
Joey Amalfitano 2b	3	1	1	0
Sterling Slaughter p7	0	0	0	0
John Flavin p7	0	0	0	0
Jimmy Stewart ph8	1	0	0	0
Lee Gregory p9	0	0	0	0
Ellis Burton rf	5	0	1	1
Billy Williams lf	4	0	0	0
Ron Santo 3b	4	0	1	1
>Ernie Banks 1b	3	0	0	0
Billy Cowan cf	4	0	0	0
Andre Rodgers ss	3	1	3	0
Ron Campbell 2b7	1	0	1	0
Jimmy Schaffer c	3	0	1	0
Dick Ellsworth p	1	0	0	0
Freddie Burdette p4	0	0	0	0
Leo Burke ph4	1	0	0	0
Don Elston p5	0	0	0	0
Don Kessinger ph,ss7	2	0	0	0
	35	2	8	2

St. Louis	IP	H	R	ER	BB	SO
Simmons W,15-9	8	8	2	2	5	7
Washburn	1	0	0	0	1	0
	9	8	2	2	6	7

Chicago	IP	H	R	ER	BB	SO
Ellsworth L,14-15	3.2	7	7	6	2	2
F. Burdette	.1	0	0	0	0	0
Elston	2	4	3	1	0	1
Slaughter	0	4	3	3	0	0
Flavin	2	2	1	1	0	3
Gregory	1	1	1	0	0	0
	9	18	15	11	2	6

St. Louis   2 1 2   2 2 1   3 1 1   -15
Chicago   1 0 0   0 0 1   0 0 0   - 2

OB: St. Louis 10, Chicago 12
E: Brock, Ellsworth, Santo, Elston
     Rodgers, Campbell, Amalfitano 2
DP: Santo-Campbell-Banks (Shannon)
2B: Brock, Javier 2, Groat, Santo,
     Rodgers
HR: Javier(11), Brock(12), Shannon(5)
SO: Brock 2, White, Uecker 2, Simmons,
     Santo, Cowan 2, Schaffer, Burke,
     Ellsworth, Kessinger
BB: Boyer, Uecker, Amalfitano, Santo,
     Williams, Banks 2, Schaffer

SH: White, Simmons, Flood
SF: Shannon
TIME: 2:46
ATTENDANCE: 11,606
UMPIRES: Lee Weyer, Doug Harvey,
   Jocko Conlan, Tony Venzon
SOURCES: Chicago American, Daily
   News, Sun-Times, Tribune; Retro-
   sheet; Sporting News; St.Louis
   Globe-Democrat, Post-Dispatch

BALANCE	OUT	+R	+OB	=BP	=AB	+BB	+SH	+HP	+CI
St. Louis	27	15	10	52	46	2	4	0	0
Chicago	27	2	12	41	35	6	0	0	0

Maloney Wildly Effective

154. Pitcher Throws Second Ten-Inning No-Hitter in One Season

CINCINNATI   at   CHICAGO
(Reds, 1)   (Cubs, 0)

Thursday, August 19, 1965, Wrigley Field

It had been a banner season for Jim Maloney. In April he tossed a one-hitter against the Braves, and in June he tossed 10 hitless innings against the Mets only to allow two hits and lose in the eleventh. Now, facing the Cubs in the first game of a doubleheader, Jim nailed down his first official no-hitter and became the *first modern major-leaguer to hurl no-hit ball for 10 or more innings twice in the same season.*

Chicago did not submit without a struggle due primarily to Maloney's wildness. The 6'2", 200-pounder threw 187 pitches, including 14 full counts. Jim walked 10 Cubs, hit one, and although he didn't allow a ball to be hit out of the infield until the eighth, he was in constant trouble:

• After walking the bases loaded in the third inning, the 25-year-old escaped by getting Billy Williams to ground out, second to first.

• In the fourth, Ron Santo threatened to extinguish the no-hitter when he hit a sharp ground ball which shortstop Leo Cardenas was able to reach and

It was the second time this season that Maloney hurled 10 hitless innings.

throw to first for the second out. Maloney then walked the next two hitters before retiring Don Kessinger on a called third strike.

• Larry Jackson walked to open the eighth, was sacrificed to second, and advanced to third on a long fly by Doug Clemens. The wind snuffed the drive, enabling center fielder Vada Pinson to make the catch. Then, after intentionally walking Billy Williams, Maloney struck out Ernie Banks swinging.

• Maloney loaded the bases again in the ninth on two walks and a hit batter, but Don Landrum popped out to Cardenas to end the threat.

• The tenth opened for the Cubs with a familiar base on balls to Clemens. But Williams flied out, and Banks hit the first pitch into a game-ending double play.

Maloney retired the Cubs in order five times, struck out the side in the fifth, and had at least one strikeout in every frame but the tenth. His 12 strikeouts ran his season's total to 178 in 186 innings. Reds outfielders logged only three putouts.

The Cincinnati flame-thrower got all the offensive support he needed from Cardenas, who rapped a drive off the left-field foul pole in the top of the tenth. It spoiled an outstanding effort by Chicago's Larry Jackson, who threw only 109 pitches in the same ten innings.

FIRST GAME

Cincinnati Reds	AB	R	H	I
Tommy Harper lf	5	0	1	0
>Pete Rose 2b	5	0	1	0
Vada Pinson cf	3	0	2	0
Frank Robinson rf	4	0	2	0
Gordy Coleman 1b	4	0	0	0
Marty Keough 1b10	0	0	0	0
Deron Johnson 3b	4	0	0	0
Johnny Edwards c	4	0	0	0
Leo Cardenas ss	4	1	1	1
Jim Maloney p	4	0	2	0
	37	1	9	1

Chicago Cubs	AB	R	H	I
Don Landrum cf	4	0	0	0
Doug Clemens lf	3	0	0	0
Billy Williams rf	4	0	0	0
>Ernie Banks 1b	5	0	0	0
Ron Santo 3b	3	0	0	0
Ed Bailey c	2	0	0	0
Glenn Beckert 2b	2	0	0	0
Don Kessinger ss	2	0	0	0
Jimmy Stewart ph9,ss	1	0	0	0
Larry Jackson p	2	0	0	0
	28	0	0	0

Cincinnati	IP	H	R	ER	BB	SO
Maloney W,14-6	10	0	0	0	10	12

Chicago	IP	H	R	ER	BB	SO
Jackson L,11-15	10	9	1	1	0	5

Cincinnati 0 0 0   0 0 0   0 0 0   1 - 1
Chicago   0 0 0   0 0 0   0 0 0   0 - 0

OB: Cincinnati 7, Chicago 10
E: Banks
DP: Cardenas-Rose-Keough (Banks)
     Kessinger-Banks (Coleman)
3B: Robinson
HR: Cardenas(9)
SO: Harper 2, Johnson, Edwards, Maloney, Landrum 2, Clemens 2, Banks, Santo, Bailey, Beckert, Kessinger 2, Jackson 2
BB: Clemens 2, Williams(I), Bailey 2, Beckert 2, Kessinger, Jackson 2

SH: Pinson, Landrum
HP: By Maloney (Santo)
TIME: 2:51
ATTENDANCE: 11,342
UMPIRES: Mel Steiner, Al Barlick, Augie Donatelli, Stan Landes
SOURCES: Chicago American, Daily News, Sun Times, Tribune; Cincinnati Enquirer; Retrosheet

BALANCE	OUT+R+OB=BP=AB+BB+SH+HP+CI								
Cincinnati	30	1	7	38	37	0	1	0	0
Chicago	30	0	10	40	28	10	1	1	0

Campy Plays Them All

155. Player Takes All Nine Fielding Positions in One Game

CALIFORNIA   at   KANSAS CITY
(Angels, 5)   (Athletics, 3)

Wednesday Night, September 8, 1965, Municipal Stadium

Charles Finley, promotor, showman, and owner of the Kansas City Athletics, had been struggling to maintain fan interest and attendance during a 51–87 season. Having had some success earlier in the season with promotions for "Farmer's Night," "Automotive Industry Night," and "Sportsman Night," Finley now devised "Campy Campaneris Night." The promotion was intended to honor the most popular Kansas City player of the time — the versatile Bert Campaneris — and proved to be a financial success although the theatrics cost the last place A's yet another defeat.

The 23-year-old Campaneris had most often been stationed at shortstop, but had also played third base and outfield. In only his second major league season, the fans' favorite was also his team's current leader in runs, hits, doubles, triples, and stolen bases. Finley's plan was to have Campaneris further demonstrate his all-purpose ability by *playing one inning at each fielding position including pitcher.* As the game unfolded here's how Campaneris performed:

1st: Campy started the game at his familiar shortstop position and handled no fielding chances. In the bottom of the frame he walked and scored the A's first run.

2nd: He moved to second base and assisted on a pickoff of Ed Kirkpatrick (1–3–4–1–6).

3rd: Bert had no fielding chances while playing third base. Leading off the home half, he grounded out (1–3).

4th: Playing left field, Campy caught a Jose Cardenal fly ball.

5th: Caught a fly ball in center field off the bat of Paul Schaal.

6th: In right field, he dropped a Jim Fregosi fly ball which enabled Albie Pearson to score California's second run. Bert failed to redeem himself as he went down swinging to lead off the bottom half of the inning.

7th: As a first baseman, caught Schaal's fair pop up.

8th: Campaneris took the mound and
— got Cardenal on a pop up to second.
— walked Pearson on four pitches.
— walked Fregosi on four pitches.
— on an 0–2 delivery, Joe Adcock singled home Pearson.
— struck out Bobby Knoop (called), and catcher Billy Bryan threw out Fregosi attempting to steal third.
As the second A's batter, he grounded out (6–3).

9th: Campaneris went behind the plate and
— Kirkpatrick singled and stole second.
— Tom Egan walked.
— Schaal lined out to center and Kirkpatrick went to third after the catch.
— Dean Chance struck out swinging.
— With Cardenal at the plate, the Angels attempted a double steal. Campaneris threw to Dick Green at second who stepped up and made a quick return to the plate. Campy had the ball in plenty of time to get Kirkpatrick who decided to try to jar the ball loose by coming in hard standing up. A violent collision sent Campaneris to the ground, but he hung on to the ball for the third out. Campy jumped up and a short shoving match with Kirkpatrick ensued for which Ed was fervently booed the

balance of the evening. Campaneris, meanwhile, was sent to the hospital for X-rays which proved negative.

A Kansas City rally in the bottom of the ninth tied the contest at three — two runs coming on singles by Wayne Causey, Jim Landis, Ken Harrelson, and Dick Green.

The Angels finally prevailed in the 13th on K.C. reliever John O'Donohue's wildness. After he walked Knoop, Kirkpatrick bunted, but the pitcher's throw to second was late. Bob Rodgers followed with another bunt which O'Donohue threw past third allowing Knoop to score. A second run scored on Cardenal's sacrifice fly.

Campaneris' dropped fly ball in the sixth and his pitching wildness in the eighth had cost his team the game in regulation. He was probably just as happy the publicity stunt had ended. During the next 16 seasons, aside from three games in the outfield, Campy never manned a fielding position other than shortstop.

Campy's demonstration probably cost the A's the game.

California Angels	AB	R	H	I
Jose Cardenal cf	6	0	0	1
>Albie Pearson lf	5	2	1	0
Jim Fregosi ss	5	1	1	0
Joe Adcock 1b	4	0	2	2
Marcelino Lopez pr8	0	0	0	0
Vic Power 1b8	0	0	0	0
Willie Smith ph10	1	0	0	0
Charlie Dees 1b10	1	0	0	0
Bobby Knoop 2b	3	1	1	0
Ed Kirkpatrick rf	5	0	2	0
Tom Egan c	2	0	0	0
Bob Rodgers c10	2	1	0	0
Paul Schaal 3b	5	0	1	0
Dean Chance p	4	0	0	0
Bob Lee p9	1	0	0	0
Merritt Ranew ph13	1	0	0	0
Jim Coates p13	0	0	0	0
	45	5	8	3

Kansas City Athletics	AB	R	H	I
Bert Campaneris ss,2b2,3b3, lf4,cf5,rf6,1b7,p8,c9	3	1	0	0
Rene Lachemann c10	2	0	2	0
J. Tartabull lf,rf4,lf5	4	0	0	0
Wayne Causey 2b,ss2	5	1	2	0
Ed Charles 3b,2b3,3b4	6	0	1	1
Jim Landis cf,rf5,cf6	5	1	1	0
Billy Bryan c	3	0	1	0
Aurelio Monteagudo p9	0	0	0	0
Ken Harrelson ph9	1	0	1	1
Fred Talbot pr9	0	0	0	0
John Wyatt p10	0	0	0	0
Tommie Reynolds ph11	1	0	0	0
John O'Donoghue p12	0	0	0	0
Diego Segui p13	0	0	0	0
Johnny Blanchard ph13	1	0	0	0
Randy Schwartz 1b	2	0	0	0
Mike Hershberger rf7	0	0	0	0
> Larry Stahl ph7,rf8	3	0	0	0
Lu Clinton rf	1	0	0	0
Dick Green 2b4	4	0	1	1
Dick Joyce p	2	0	0	0
Don Mossi p7	0	0	0	0
Jim Dickson p7	0	0	0	0
Santiago Rosario 1b8	3	0	0	0
	46	3	9	3

California	IP	H	R	ER	BB	SO
Chance	8.1	5	3	3	2	6
Lee W,9-6	3.2	4	0	0	2	2
Coates	1	0	0	0	0	0
	13	9	3	3	4	8

Kansas City	IP	H	R	ER	BB	SO
Joyce	6	5	2	1	1	2
Mossi	.1	0	0	0	0	0
Dickson	.2	0	0	0	1	1
Campaneris	1	1	1	1	2	1
Monteagudo	1	1	0	0	1	1
Wyatt	2	1	0	0	2	0
O'Donoghue L,8-18	1	0	2	0	1	0
Segui	1	0	0	0	1	0
	13	8	5	2	9	5

California   000   101   010   000   2   - 5
Kansas City   100   000   002   000   0   - 3

OB: California 12, Kansas City 10
E: Campaneris, Causey, O'Donoghue
DP: Bryan-Charles (Knoop SO)
2B: Adcock, Bryan, Charles
SB: Campaneris, Tartabull, Kirkpatrick
CS: Fregosi, Kirkpatrick
PK: Kirkpatrick
SO: Knoop, Chance 4, Campaneris,
     Landis, Schwartz 2, Stahl,
     Green 2, Joyce
BB: Pearson 2, Fregosi, Knoop 3,
     Egan 2, Schaal, Campaneris,
     Tartabull, Causey, Stahl

SH: Tartabull, Kirkpatrick
SF: Cardenal
HP: By Chance (Landis)
WP: Dickson
PB: Egan
TIME: 4:14
ATTENDANCE: 21,576
UMPIRES: Cal Drummond, Bill Kinnamon,
     Johnny Stevens, Larry Napp
SOURCES: Kansas City Star, Times;
     Los Angeles Times; Retrosheet

BALANCE	OUT+R+OB=BP=AB+BB+SH+HP+CI
California	39 5 12 56 45 9 2 0 0
Kansas City	39 3 10 52 46 4 1 1 0

FIELDING POSITIONS, BY INNING,
OF THE KANSAS CITY ATHLETICS, SEPTEMBER 8, 1965

Pos	P	C	1	2	3	S	L	C	R
1	Joyce	Bryan	Schwartz	Causey	Charles	**Campaneris**	Tartabull	Landis	Clinton
2	Joyce	Bryan	Schwartz	**Campaneris**	Charles	Causey	Tartabull	Landis	Clinton
3	Joyce	Bryan	Schwartz	Charles	**Campaneris**	Causey	Tartabull	Landis	Clinton
4	Joyce	Bryan	Schwartz	Green	Charles	Causey	**Campaneris**	Landis	Tartabull
5	Joyce	Bryan	Schwartz	Green	Charles	Causey	Tartabull	**Campaneris**	Landis
6	Joyce	Bryan	Schwartz	Green	Charles	Causey	Tartabull	Landis	**Campaneris**
7	Mossi/Dickson	Bryan	**Campaneris**	Green	Charles	Causey	Tartabull	Landis	Hershberger
8	**Campaneris**	Bryan	Rosario	Green	Charles	Causey	Tartabull	Landis	Stahl
9	Monteagudo	**Campaneris**	Rosario	Green	Charles	Causey	Tartabull	Landis	Stahl
10	Wyatt	Lachemann	Rosario	Green	Charles	Causey	Tartabull	Landis	Stahl
11	Wyatt	Lachemann	Rosario	Green	Charles	Causey	Tartabull	Landis	Stahl
12	O'Donoghue	Lachemann	Rosario	Green	Charles	Causey	Tartabull	Landis	Stahl
13	Segui	Lachemann	Rosario	Green	Charles	Causey	Tartabull	Landis	Stahl

Perfect and Nearly Perfect

156. Teams Combine for One Hit in Nine-Inning Game

CHICAGO   at   LOS ANGELES
(Cubs, 0)   (Dodgers, 1)

Thursday Night, September 9, 1965, Dodger Stadium

Sandy Koufax had already thrown three no-hitters in his illustrious career, but in none of them was he challenged as he was this night. In this his fourth no-hitter, the Dodger flame-thrower kicked in the booster rockets and allowed not even a single base runner for his first perfect game. Perfect indeed was exactly what he had to be, because his mound opponent, the Cubs' Bob Hendley, pitched almost as superbly. Hendley allowed only one hit and one walk while being collared with the loss on an unearned run. By combining their performances, this contest still stands as the mark for the *fewest hits (1) by both clubs in a nine-inning game as well as for the fewest men left on base by both clubs (1) in a nine-inning game.* As far as double-sided pitching excellence is concerned, this game can only be compared with the double no-hitter of May 2, 1917 in which Jim Vaughn and Fred Toney each completed nine frames without permitting a hit (see entry for that game).

In 1965, Koufax was at the pinnacle of his game. This would be the fourth of five consecutive seasons in which the left-hander led the league in ERA; the third of five in which he led in strikeouts; and the sixth in a row in which he held opponents to the lowest batting average. National Leaguers this year had an on-base-percentage of an infinitesimal .228 against Koufax, and in every National League city, batters hoped they would miss him in a three game series. It was shocking when he lost.

Bob Hendley, on the other hand, was not the type of hurler one would expect to be involved in such a colossal pitcher's duel. In this, his fifth major-league campaign, Bob

had never had a winning season and was the possessor of a 37–42 lifetime log. His opponents' on-base-percentage was perennially well over .300, and no one shuddered when he led the Cubs into town. But through this game, he and Koufax are now inexorably linked in the record books, although previously the most they had in common was that they were each 6'2" left-handers.

The contest progressed through four frames with neither team able to reach base. Then in the home half of the fifth, Lou Johnson led off with a walk. (Hendley later told a reporter that both he and his catcher, Chris Krug, thought they had struck out Johnson on the 3–2 pitch.) Next, Ron Fairly bunted Johnson to second (the out went Hendley to Ernie Banks). Johnson then attempted to steal third, and a wild throw into left field by Krug enabled him to score. Thus the Dodgers scored without a hit.

The only other offense, and only hit of the day, was provided again by Johnson in the seventh. With two outs, the former Cub blooped a double just out of the reach of first baseman Banks but was left stranded. Given the circumstances, this game could have ended as a double no-hitter.

The Cubs risked possible criticism by starting two players who were making their major league debut in the midst of a pennant race. Outfielders Byron Browne and Don Young received a baptism by fire(baller Koufax). Of course, Chicago was not involved in the race, and vice president John Holland said, "We couldn't care less who wins the pennant…we should be entitled to play them [Browne & Young] as we

Koufax was perfect.

see fit."* Actually, the pair played well. Young made a great catch about 400 feet from home plate, and Browne hit the hardest drive of the night off Koufax — a line drive to center in the second inning that Willie Davis caught waist-high.

Koufax was impeccable. Only one batter — Billy Williams in the seventh — saw the count reach three balls. After going 3–0 to Williams, Koufax threw three straight strikes,

the last of which was softly lifted into left field. Back in the first inning, Glenn Beckert smashed a line drive down the left-field line that landed foul by inches. The only other threat to perfection came in the sixth when shortstop Maury Wills threw Krug's grounder into the dirt, but first baseman Wes Parker scooped it for the out.

Sandy strengthened as the game progressed, striking out the last six Cub batters,

Bob Hunter, "Koufax's 'Golden Hour' Perks Up Dodgers," Chicago American, 10 September 1965, Sports section, p. 1, col. 6.

each amid escalating, thunderous roars from the 29,139 fans. In the eighth frame, he rocketed a called third strike past Ron Santo and retired Banks and Browne swinging. The first batter in the ninth, Krug, went down swinging. Then pinch hitter Joey Amalfitano fanned on just three pitches. The game concluded with another pinch hitter, Harvey Kuenn, who swung and missed at a 2–2 offering. As an ear-splitting din erupted, Koufax danced off the mound and into the arms of his teammates. His game total of 14 whiffs marked the 18th time this season he had reached double figures and ran his season's total to 332, only 16 shy of Bob Feller's existing mark. (Koufax went on to fan 382, the major league record until Nolan Ryan's 383 in 1973.) Feeding the Cubs a diet of 113 fastballs and curves, Koufax registered his

fourth no-hitter in successive seasons, making him the first major leaguer to reach that plateau. (Larry Corcoran, Cy Young, and Bob Feller each had registered three no-hitters.)

After the game, several of the Cub players extolled Koufax's effort. Ernie Banks said, "The man was just great. It was beautiful. The first five innings he was getting the curve ball over real good. Then he got tremendous momentum… he just kept throwing the ball right on through. And throwing strikes."*

Third baseman Ron Santo said that Sandy threw him four curves in a row early in the contest. But that changed later. "I never saw him throw as hard as he did the last time I was up. He threw one ball right past me, and I was waiting for it. This guy could drive you to drink."†

Chicago Cubs	AB	R	H	I
Don Young cf	3	0	0	0
Glenn Beckert 2b	3	0	0	0
Billy Williams rf	3	0	0	0
Ron Santo 3b	3	0	0	0
Ernie Banks 1b	3	0	0	0
Byron Browne lf	3	0	0	0
Chris Krug c	3	0	0	0
Don Kessinger ss	2	0	0	0
Joey Amalfitano ph9	1	0	0	0
Bob Hendley p	2	0	0	0
> Harvey Kuenn ph9	1	0	0	0
	27	0	0	0

Los Angeles Dodgers	AB	R	H	I
Maury Wills ss	3	0	0	0
Jim Gilliam 3b	3	0	0	0
John Kennedy 3b8	0	0	0	0
Willie Davis cf	3	0	0	0
Lou Johnson lf	2	1	1	0
Ron Fairly rf	2	0	0	0
Jim Lefebvre 2b	3	0	0	0
Dick Tracewski 2b9	0	0	0	0
Wes Parker 1b	3	0	0	0
>Jeff Torborg c	3	0	0	0
Sandy Koufax p	2	0	0	0
	24	1	1	0

Chicago	IP	H	R	ER	BB	SO
Hendley L,2-3	8	1	1	0	1	3

Los Angeles	IP	H	R	ER	BB	SO
Koufax W,22-7	9	0	0	0	0	14

Chicago   0 0 0   0 0 0   0 0 0   - 0
Los Angeles 0 0 0   0 1 0   0 0 x   - 1

OB: Chicago 0, Los Angeles 1
E: Krug
2B: Johnson
SB: Johnson
SO: Young, Beckert, Williams 2, Santo, Banks 3, Browne, Krug, Amalfitano, Hendley 2, Kuenn, Lefebvre 2, Koufax
BB: Johnson

SH: Fairly
TIME: 1:43
ATTENDANCE: 29,139
UMPIRES: Ed Vargo, Chris Pelekoudas, Bill Jackowski, Paul Pryor
SOURCES: Chicago American, Daily News, Sun-Times, Tribune; Los Angeles Herald-Examiner, Times; Retrosheet

BALANCE	OUT+R+OB=BP=AB+BB+SH+HP+CI
Chicago	27 0 0 27 27 0 0 0 0
Los Angeles	24 1 1 26 24 1 1 0 0

*Charles Maher, "Even Koufax Admits Game 'Nearly Perfect'," Los Angeles Times, 10 September 1965, part III, p. 4, col. 1.
†Ibid.

Tony Twice Grand

157. Pitcher Hits Two Grand Slams, Drives in Nine Runs

ATLANTA   at   SAN FRANCISCO
(Braves, 17)   (Giants, 3)

Sunday, July 3, 1966, Candlestick Park

On a sun-drenched afternoon in San Francisco, the Atlanta Braves' Tony Cloninger shattered several batting marks for pitchers when he *clouted two grand-slam homers and drove home nine runs.* The 25-year-old right-hander became the first National Leaguer and fifth major leaguer to slam two home runs with the bases loaded in the same game, joining Tony Lazzeri, Jim Tabor, Rudy York, and Jim Gentile of the American League. Cloninger's nine RBIs also broke Vic Raschi's major-league mark of seven in a game for a pitcher.

Of late, the 6'2", 200 pounder had been an offensive powerhouse. In his four previous starts he had driven home nine mates, including five in a multi-homer game against the Mets. His five-game total of 18 RBIs even surpassed several of his teammates' season totals.

This contest was practically over as soon as it began as Cloninger connected for his first grand slam in the opening frame, capping a seven-run Braves' rally. Tony's heroics came with two outs and a full count off the Giants' left-handed starter Joe Gibbon. The blow cleared the center-field fence near the 410-foot sign.

Facing right-hander Bob Priddy in the third inning with one out and one on, Cloninger grounded out, third to first.

In the fourth, the bases were again loaded with two outs when Tony stepped to the plate. This time, left-hander Ray Sadecki was the Cloninger grand slam victim on an 0–1 count, the ball being lined over the right-field fence.

Tony was on deck in the fifth when there

Cloninger pitched 779 innings between 1964 and 1966.

were two men on, two outs, and the number eight batter, Denis Menke, at the plate. The crowd, hoping to see Cloninger get an opportunity to become the first major leaguer hit three grand slams in a game, implored the home team to walk him. When Menke swung and grounded into a force out the crowd booed him for being so inconsiderate.

Cloninger flied out to left while leading off the sixth, and completed his RBI total in the eighth by singling home Woody Woodward with one out.

This game climaxed Cloninger's career as both his batting and pitching prowess quickly faded. Following this outburst, Tony was used as a pinch-hitter six times before the season ended, but the best he could do was coax one base-on-balls; and over the balance of the campaign he amassed just four more RBIs in 55 at-bats. His pitching decline was equally precipitous. Having won 43 games (43–25) over the past two seasons, including 24 in 1965, shoulder and eye problems contributed to a disappointing 37–49 log for the remainder of his career.

Atlanta Braves	AB	R	H	I
Felipe Alou 1b	3	0	0	0
Mike de la Hoz 3b5	2	0	0	0
Mack Jones cf	6	1	3	0
Hank Aaron rf	4	2	1	1
Gary Geiger rf5	2	1	1	1
Rico Carty lf	4	3	3	1
John Herrnstein lf5	1	0	0	0
Joe Torre c	6	2	3	3
Frank Bolling 2b	5	2	2	2
>Woody Woodward ss	6	2	4	0
Denis Menke 3b,1b5	3	2	0	0
Tony Cloninger p	5	2	3	9
	47	17	20	17

San Francisco Giants	AB	R	H	I
Jesus Alou rf	4	0	1	0
Tom Haller c,1b3	3	1	1	1
Willie Mays cf	1	1	0	0
Don Landrum cf5	2	0	0	0
Willie McCovey 1b	1	0	0	0
Dick Dietz c3	3	0	0	0
Jim Ray Hart 3b	3	0	1	0
Ozzie Virgil 3b7	1	0	0	0
Len Gabrielson lf	4	0	1	1
Jim Davenport ss	1	0	0	0
Don Mason 2b4	3	0	0	0
Hal Lanier 2b,ss4	4	0	2	0
Joe Gibbon p	0	0	0	0
Bob Priddy p1	0	0	0	0
Ray Sadecki p3	3	1	1	1
> Cap Peterson ph9	1	0	0	0
	34	3	7	3

Atlanta	IP	H	R	ER	BB	SO
Cloninger	9	7	3	3	2	5

San Francisco	IP	H	R	ER	BB	SO
Gibbon L,3-5	.2	5	5	5	0	0
Priddy	2	4	3	3	2	0
Sadecki	6.1	11	9	5	2	4
	9	20	17	13	4	4

Atlanta	7 1 0	5 1 0	0 1 2	-17
San Francisco	0 0 0	1 1 0	0 1 0	- 3

OB: Atlanta 8, San Francisco 6
E: Cloninger, Hart, Lanier, Gabrielson
DP: Woodward-Bolling-F.Alou (Mays) Virgil-Mason-Haller (de la Hoz)
2B: Woodward 2, M.Jones, Geiger
HR: Torre(19), Cloninger 2(4), Carty(3), Aaron(25), Sadecki(2), Haller(16)
SO: M. Jones 2, Geiger, Woodward, Dietz, Landrum, McCovey, Virgil, Sadecki
BB: F. Alou, Carty, Menke 2, Haller, Mays

SF: Bolling
WP: Cloninger, Sadecki
TIME: 2:42
ATTENDANCE: 27,002
UMPIRES: Doug Harvey, Harry Wendelstedt, Shag Crawford, Ed Vargo
SOURCES: Atlanta Constitution; San Francisco Chronicle, Examiner; Retrosheet

BALANCE	OUT	+R	+OB	=BP	=AB	+BB	+SH	+HP	+CI
Atlanta	27	17	8	52	47	4	1	0	0
San Francisco	27	3	6	36	34	2	0	0	0

Barber Trimmed

158. Pitchers Combine to Lose Nine-Inning No-Hitter; Team Has 14 Baserunners, No Hits

DETROIT   at   BALTIMORE
(Tigers, 2)   (Orioles, 1)

Sunday, April 30, 1967, Memorial Stadium

In one of the strangest games in baseball history, the Detroit Tigers overcame a no-hitter and defeated the Baltimore Orioles 2–1. Making the contest even more unusual was the fact that two Oriole hurlers combined for the no-hitter.

Throughout baseball annals, several pitchers had tossed no-hitters for nine frames only to lose in extra innings. There had even been a game in 1956 where three Cincinnati hurlers tossed a combined no-hitter but lost in the tenth. But as of 1967, only one moundsman (Ken Johnson in 1964) had ever lost a nine-inning no-hitter. This day's game thus marked baseball's *first combined no-hitter lost in nine innings.* In addition, this contest also stands as *the no-hitter of any length in which the most opposing runners reached base safely—14.*

Starting for the Orioles in the first game of a doubleheader was 28-year-old left-hander Steve Barber. In his eighth major league season, Steve had already claimed a one-hit victory only two weeks earlier. (That hit had come with one out in the ninth by Jim Fregosi of the California Angels.) But this day was another story. Barber was exceedingly wild, walking 10 and hitting a pair. Two other Tigers reached base safely on errors as the visitors put at least one runner on base in each inning except the fifth. In one of the most bizarre baseball statistics, Detroit's Mickey Stanley, Bill Freehan, and Norm Cash each reached base three times during the no-hitter. Stanley walked three times, Freehan walked twice and was hit by a pitch, and Cash walked twice and was safe on an error. Don Wert reached base twice, once on an error and once via a free pass.

Despite the glut of baserunners, none were able to cross the plate until there were two outs in the ninth. Barber walked the first two batters, Norm Cash and Ray Oyler. (Oyler had tried to sacrifice, but the Oriole moundsman wouldn't give him anything to bunt.) Dick Tracewski ran for Cash as Earl Wilson sacrificed the runners along. Willie Horton then was announced as a pinch-hitter for Dick McAuliffe, and Oriole's skipper Hank Bauer strode to the mound. Bauer let his pitcher know that he was worried about his wildness and implored him not to walk Horton. Barber responded by saying, "If you

Barber gained fame despite the loss.

think it's bad in there [dugout], you ought to be out here."* Horton fouled out.

Jake Wood then ran for Oyler. The next batter, Mickey Stanley, faced a 1–2 count and Barber was just one pitch away from victory. But the left-hander then unleashed a wild pitch that bounced three feet in front of rookie substitute catcher Larry Haney enabling Tracewski to score the tying run and Wood to take third. After completing a walk to Stanley, Barber was replaced by Stu Miller despite having his no-hitter still intact. The

hometown fans showed their appreciation of Barber's effort with a standing ovation. Wert then bid for the first Detroit hit when he smacked a sharp ground ball toward second. Shortstop Luis Aparicio went far to his left, fielded it and flipped backhanded to rookie Mark Belanger who dropped it for an error, allowing the second run to score. Belanger, playing second, had just entered the contest as a pinch runner in the bottom of the eighth. Al Kaline, the league's leading hitter and in the midst of a 13–game hitting streak,

FIRST GAME

Detroit Tigers	AB	R	H	I
Dick McAuliffe 2b	3	0	0	0
Willie Horton ph9	1	0	0	0
Jerry Lumpe 2b9	0	0	0	0
Mickey Stanley cf	2	0	0	0
Don Wert 3b	3	0	0	0
>Al Kaline rf	4	0	0	0
Jim Northrup lf	4	0	0	0
Bill Freehan c	1	0	0	0
Norm Cash 1b	1	0	0	0
Dick Tracewski pr9,ss	0	1	0	0
Ray Oyler ss	2	0	0	0
Jake Wood pr9,1b	0	1	0	0
Earl Wilson p	3	0	0	0
Fred Gladding p9	0	0	0	0
	24	2	0	0

Baltimore Orioles	AB	R	H	I
Luis Aparicio ss	3	0	0	1
Russ Snyder cf	4	0	0	0
Frank Robinson rf	4	0	1	0
Brooks Robinson 3b	3	0	0	0
>Mike Epstein 1b	4	0	0	0
Curt Blefary lf	2	1	0	0
Woodie Held 2b	2	0	0	0
Larry Haney c9	0	0	0	0
Andy Etchebarren c	2	0	1	0
Charley Lau ph8	0	0	0	0
Mark Belanger pr8,2b	0	0	0	0
Steve Barber p	1	0	0	0
Stu Miller p9	0	0	0	0
	25	1	2	1

Detroit	IP	H	R	ER	BB	SO
Wilson W,2-2	8	2	1	1	4	4
Gladding	1	0	0	0	0	1
	9	2	1	1	4	5

Baltimore	IP	H	R	ER	BB	SO
Barber L,2-1	8.2	0	2	1	10	3
S. Miller	.1	0	0	0	0	0
	9	0	2	1	10	3

```
Detroit    0 0 0   0 0 0   0 0 2   – 2
Baltimore  0 0 0   0 0 0   0 1 0   – 1
```

OB: Detroit 11, Baltimore 4
E: Kaline, Barber, Belanger
DP: Cash-Oyler (Blefary)
    Aparicio-Held-Epstein (Kaline)
SB: Freehan, F. Robinson
SO: Stanley, Cash, Oyler, Epstein 3,
    Etchebarren, Barber
BB: Stanley 3, Kaline(I), Freehan 2,
    Wert, Cash 2, Oyler, Lau(I),
    B. Robinson, Blefary, Barber
SH: Cash, Oyler, Wert, Wilson,
    Barber, Held

SF: Aparicio
HP: By Barber (McAuliffe, Freehan)
WP: Barber
TIME: 2:38
ATTENDANCE: 26,884
UMPIRES: Bill Valentine, Marty
    Springstead, Johnny Stevens,
    Bob Stewart
SOURCES: Baltimore Sun; Detroit Free
    Press, News; Retrosheet

BALANCE	OUT+R+OB=BP=AB+BB+SH+HP+CI							
Detroit	27	2	11	40	24	10	4	2	0
Baltimore	27	1	4	32	25	4	3	0	0

*Jack Saylor, "'I Can't Complain,' Says Barber," Detroit Free Press, 1 May 1967, Section D, p. 1, col. 7–8.

ended the inning by grounding into a force play. The Tigers, however, had scored two runs without a hit and without a ball leaving the infield.

The lone Oriole run also had come without benefit of a hit. In the home eighth, Curt Blefary walked and Woodie Held sacrificed him to second. Charley Lau was intentionally passed, but Earl Wilson also walked Steve Barber, filling the bases. Aparicio then lifted a fly to medium right field. Kaline, owner of one of the best arms in baseball, made the catch and fired plate-ward. The throw was wide, and Blefary scored easily.

After the game, the imperturbable Barber spoke with amazing detachment. "In all honesty, I didn't deserve a no hitter. I have no great pride in my performance; it was not a work of art. They probably didn't get a hit because I didn't throw anything close enough to the plate. The wild pitch was a changeup

that got away from me; Haney didn't have a chance of stopping it."*

Barber's wildness also resulted in an excessive expenditure of energy. "I don't know how many pitches I threw today — 300 I think. I was tired from the fifth inning on."† Despite his exhaustion, Steve had allowed only one ball to be hit beyond the infield, that being Oyler's drive to the warning track in the second frame.

Barber's brush with fame was one of his last baseball highlights. His career had been on the downswing and, before the season ended, he was traded to the Yankees. Over the following seven seasons, he packed his bags another five times before retiring in 1974.

Earl Wilson, the overlooked winner in this pitcher's duel, went on to have his finest campaign, posting a 22–11 log and a 3.27 ERA.

*Associated Press, "Steve Stays Unruffled in Calamity," Detroit Free Press, 1 May 1967, Section C, p. 1, col. 4.
†Jack Saylor, "'I Can't Complain,' says Barber." Detroit Free Press, 1 May, 1967, Section D, p. 2, col. 7–8.

Seven Birds Blast Home Runs

159. Seven Teammates Hit Home Run in Same Game

BALTIMORE   at   BOSTON
(Orioles, 12)   (Red Sox, 8)

Wednesday Night, May 17, 1967, Fenway Park

With a stiff wind blowing straight out toward Fenway Park's "Green Monster," pitchers knew they were in for a long evening. That was particularly bad news for a collapsing Red Sox' staff which had just relinquished 44 runs in the past five games and ten homers in the past 28 innings. Before this game ended, seven different Orioles and two Red Sox belted balls out of the park. It was the *first time in baseball annals that seven teammates homered in the same game*, and the sixth occasion that nine different players

clobbered circuit clouts in one contest. Although both marks have since been tied, neither has been surpassed. The combined 10 home runs by both clubs fell short, by one, of tying the major-league standard.

With the exception of the first two Oriole hitters, each position in the batting order accounted for a round-tripper. Paul Blair connected in the first frame; Brooks Robinson in the second; and Frank Robinson in the fourth. Four of the long balls came in the seventh inning when Baltimore batted around

Etchebarren contributed a three-run shot.

and sealed the victory off the bats of Andy Etchebarren, Sam Bowens, Boog Powell, and Dave Johnson. Strangely, despite the offensive eruption, none of the seven Baltimore sluggers connected for a second homer. (At the time, eight homers would have tied the major league record for home runs by one team.) Nevertheless, the explosion constituted an Oriole single-game home run mark (7) as well as a new total-bases (38) standard. The Baltimore outburst was particularly unusual in that the team hit only 138 homers all year, meaning this game accounted for more than five percent of their entire season's total.

For Boston, Don Demeter and Carl Yastrzemski were the long-ball contributors. "Yaz" was the lone player to blister two four-baggers. His second circuit-clout was the last of the game and came in the bottom of the seventh. Yastrzemski was also on his way to a triple-crown and MVP season, leading Boston through a thrilling pennant race and into the seventh game of the World Series.

Baltimore Orioles	AB	R	H	I
Mark Belanger ss	3	1	1	0
Curt Blefary lf	4	0	0	0
Paul Blair cf	5	1	1	1
Frank Robinson rf	4	2	3	2
Brooks Robinson 3b	3	2	1	1
Boog Powell 1b	5	2	3	3
Dave Johnson 2b	3	2	2	1
Woodie Held 2b8	1	0	0	0
>Andy Etchebarren c	5	1	1	3
Jim Palmer p	0	0	0	0
Bill Dillman p2	2	0	1	0
Sam Bowens ph7	1	1	1	1
Eddie Fisher p7	0	0	0	0
Moe Drabowsky p7	1	0	1	0
	37	12	15	12

Boston Red Sox	AB	R	H	I
Reggie Smith cf	5	2	2	0
Mike Andrews 2b	4	0	1	0
Carl Yastrzemski lf	4	3	2	4
>George Scott 1b	5	1	3	0
Don Demeter rf	4	1	1	3
Rico Petrocelli ss	4	1	2	0
Joe Foy 3b	4	0	0	0
Mike Ryan c	3	0	2	1
Dennis Bennett p	1	0	0	0
Galen Cisco p4	2	0	0	0
Bill Landis p7	0	0	0	0
Don McMahon p8	0	0	0	0
Dalton Jones ph8	1	0	0	0
Dan Osinski p9	0	0	0	0
	37	8	13	8

Baltimore	IP	H	R	ER	BB	SO
Palmer	1	4	3	3	1	1
Dillman	5	5	3	2	1	4
Fisher	.2	4	2	2	0	0
Drabowsky	2.1	0	0	0	0	3
	9	13	8	7	2	8

Boston	IP	H	R	ER	BB	SO
Bennett	3.1	5	3	3	1	2
Cisco	2.2	5	5	5	1	1
Landis	1	3	4	4	1	1
McMahon	1	1	0	0	0	1
Osinski	1	1	0	0	1	1
	9	15	12	12	4	6

Baltimore	1 1 0	1 0 0	9 0 0	-12
Boston	3 0 0	1 2 0	2 0 0	- 8

OB: Baltimore 5, Boston 5
E: Johnson
DP: Dillman-Belanger-Powell (Bennett)
  Petrocelli-Andrews-Scott (Blair)
  Andrews-Petrocelli-Scott (Etchebarren)
  Petrocelli-Andrews-Scott (B. Robinson)
2B: Belanger, F. Robinson
HR: Blair(2), Demeter, B. Robinson(4), F. Robinson(8),
  Yastrzemski 2(7), Etchebarren(2), Bowens(1),
  Powell(2), Johnson(2)
CS: Demeter
SO: Belanger, Blair 2, F. Robinson, Johnson, Held,
  Smith, Andrews 2, Demeter, Foy 3, Ryan

BB: Blefary, F. Robinson, B. Robinson (I),
  Johnson, Yastrzemski, Ryan
SH: Belanger 2, Andrews
HP: By Bennett (B. Robinson)
WP: Fisher
TIME: 2:43
ATTENDANCE: 8,714
UMPIRES: Johnny Stevens, Bob Stewart,
  Bill Valentine, Marty Springstead
SOURCES: Baltimore Sun; Boston Globe,
  Herald; Retrosheet

BALANCE	OUT	+ R	+ OB	= BP	= AB	+ BB	+ SH	+ HP	+ CI
Baltimore	27	12	5	44	37	4	2	1	0
Boston	27	8	5	40	37	2	1	0	0

24 Innings—One Run

160. Teams Score One Run in 24 Innings

NEW YORK   at   HOUSTON
(Mets, 0)   (Astros, 1)

Monday Night, April 15, 1968, Astrodome

Only once had more innings been played in a major-league game (see 5-01-20), but never had fewer runs been scored in a completed contest. In this *the longest shutout in baseball history*, the Houston Astros finally crossed the plate in the 24th inning to wrench victory from the New York Mets. Tragically, after the six hours and six minutes of combat, the outcome was decided on an error. At the time, this contest also represented the most innings ever played in a night game (since surpassed).

Houston and New York, both expansion clubs of 1962, had been perennial bottom dwellers during the first six years of their existence. And, in each season except 1966, one of the two had scored the fewest runs in the league with the other not far off the pace. So it's little wonder that if two teams ever threatened a scoreless infinity, it would be the Astros and Mets.

Al Weis was subbing for sore-armed Bud Harrelson.

Taking the mound for New York was the previous season's rookie-of-the-year, Tom Seaver. Calling it the best game he'd pitched in his young career, Tom walked no one and allowed just two hits over ten frames. Don Wilson started for Houston, went nine innings, and permitted only five hits and three walks. Following the two starters was a parade of 11 relievers, seven Mets and four Astros. As the innings wore on, pitchers looked more and more like Walter Johnson, and it became apparent that short of a negotiated truce, the only way this contest would end was through a mistake.

There were plenty of baserunners as the two teams combined for 22 hits and 12 walks. But when it counted, no one could deliver the coup de grâce as each club squandered multiple scoring opportunities:

• With one out in the second, Houston's Hal King doubled to left and was wild-pitched to third. On Bob Aspromonte's grounder to second King tried to score, but the throw beat him to the plate. The 200-pound baserunner crashed into Mets catcher Jerry Grote who emerged from a cloud of dust holding the ball for the putout.

• New York's Ed Kranepool led off the seventh with a single and was sacrificed to second by Ed Charles. Grote flied out and Seaver walked, but Al Weis ended the frame by grounding out to first.

Rohr was victimized.

- In the ninth, the Mets put runners on first and second with two outs, but Seaver tapped back to the pitcher.
- After Charles struck out to open the 12th, the Mets loaded the bases when Grote singled (pinch hitter Phil Lintz popped out to second) and Weis and Ken Boswell also singled. But Tommie Agee grounded out, second to first.
- Houston also threatened in the 12th. After singling, Ron Davis was sacrificed to second. Jimmy Wynn was intentionally passed, but Rusty Staub fouled out to Grote, and King struck out.
- Again in the 13th the Astros put two on with one out. Pinch hitter Ivan Murrell flied to right, and Davis popped out to second.
- Charles opened the New York 17th with a double and was sacrificed to third by Grote. Pinch hitter Bud Harrelson then failed to execute a suicide squeeze by fouling off three bunt attempts. Weis ended the threat by grounding out to short.
- Davis and Norm Miller fanned to open the Houston 19th. Wynn and Staub then singled, but King flied out to right.
- The Mets also threatened in the 19th. Leading off, Cleon Jones singled and was sacrificed to second. After Charles was intentionally passed, both runners pulled a double steal. Jim Ray then retired the next two hitters, Grote and Danny Frisella, on swinging third strikes.
- In the 22nd, New York got Grote to second with two outs, but Weis grounded out third to first.
- The Astros also threatened in their half of the 22nd. Wynn struck out and Staub walked. King's grounder to short enabled Staub to reach second, but after Aspromonte was intentionally passed, Julio Gotay fanned.

The marathon of impotence finally ended in the last of the 24th. Norm Miller, unsuccessful in seven official at-bats, led off with a single and was balked to second by Les Rohr. After Jimmy Wynn (1 for 8) was intentionally walked, Rusty Staub advanced the runners by grounding out to second. John Bateman,

pinch hit for Hal King and was purposely passed, loading the bases. Next, Bob Aspromonte took two balls, fouled one off and then sent a sharp grounder toward Mets shortstop Al Weis. Weis had played brilliantly all night but wasn't quite the man he'd been six hours earlier. Al didn't bend quickly enough for the grounder, and it zipped through his legs into left field enabling Miller to trot home with the game winning tally. It was Houston's first run after 35 consecutive scoreless frames and the first run Mets pitchers had allowed after 38 consecutive scoreless innings.

"I just plain blew it," was all Weis could say of the missed potential double-play ball. Al had been substituting for a sore-armed Bud Harrelson. Aspromonte, the equally exhausted "batting hero," later said: "The bat felt like it weighed eight and a half pounds when I carried it to the plate."[*]

The frustrating night was shared by all the Mets but especially Ron Swoboda and Tommie Agee. Swoboda went down swinging five times; Agee struck out swinging three times and was called out once. Each went 0 for 10, narrowly avoiding an ignominious addition to the record books. Seven players previously had accumulated an 0 for 11 in extra-inning games.

Swoboda was also involved in some unusual strategy in the 16th inning. Houston's Hector Torres led off with a bunt single. With a sacrifice in order, Mets manager Gil Hodges ordered left fielder Swoboda into the infield. Astros pitcher Jim Ray negated the strategy when he tried to bunt three times and struck out. Swoboda then returned to his outfield position as Ron Davis also struck out and Norm Miller flied out.

Displays of tenacity and stamina could be found both on the field and in the stands. Not only did opposing catchers Grote and King both catch all 24 innings during the six hour marathon, but about 5,000 fans were still present at the 1:37 A.M. conclusion. An hour earlier, as they stood before Houston came to bat, the scoreboard flashed: "21st Inning Stretch."

---

[*]John Wilson, "Astros Defeat Mets in 24th," Houston Chronicle, 16 April 1968, Section 4, p. 1, col. 7.

New York Mets	AB	R	H	I
Al Weis ss	9	0	1	0
Ken Boswell 2b	10	0	1	0
Tommie Agee cf	10	0	0	0
Ron Swoboda rf	10	0	0	0
Art Shamsky lf	4	0	2	0
Cleon Jones pr9,lf	6	0	1	0
Ed Kranepool 1b	8	0	2	0
Jerry Buchek 3b	2	0	0	0
> Ed Charles 3b7	6	0	1	0
Jerry Grote c	7	0	2	0
Tom Seaver p	3	0	1	0
Ron Taylor p11	0	0	0	0
Phil Linz ph12	1	0	0	0
Cal Koonce p12	0	0	0	0
Bill Short p12	0	0	0	0
Dick Selma p13	0	0	0	0
Don Bosch ph14	1	0	0	0
Al Jackson p14	0	0	0	0
Bud Harrelson ph17	1	0	0	0
Danny Frisella p17	1	0	0	0
Don Cardwell ph22	0	0	0	0
Les Rohr p22	0	0	0	0
	79	0	11	0

Houston Astros	AB	R	H	I
Ron Davis cf	10	0	1	0
Norm Miller rf	8	1	1	0
Jimmy Wynn lf	8	0	1	0
Rusty Staub 1b	9	0	2	0
Hal King c	9	0	1	0
John Bateman ph24	0	0	0	0
>Bob Aspromonte 3b	9	0	0	0
Julio Gotay 2b	9	0	2	0
Hector Torres ss	8	0	3	0
Don Wilson p	2	0	0	0
Lee Thomas ph9	1	0	0	0
John Buzhardt p10	0	0	0	0
Doug Rader ph11	1	0	0	0
Danny Coombs p12	0	0	0	0
Ivan Murrell ph13	1	0	0	0
Jim Ray p14	2	0	0	0
Wade Blasingame p21	2	0	0	0
	79	1	11	0

New York	IP	H	R	ER	BB	SO
Seaver	10	2	0	0	0	3
Taylor	1	1	0	0	0	1
Koonce	.1	1	0	0	0	0
Short	1	1	0	0	2	1
Selma	.2	0	0	0	0	0
Jackson	3	1	0	0	0	4
Frisella	5	4	0	0	1	4
Rohr L,0-1	2.1	1	1	0	4	2
	23.1	11	1	0	7	15

Houston	IP	H	R	ER	BB	SO
Wilson	9	5	0	0	3	5
Buzhardt	2	0	0	0	0	1
Coombs	2	3	0	0	0	2
Ray	7	2	0	0	1	11
Blasingame W,1-0	4	1	0	0	1	1
	24	11	0	0	5	20

New York	0 0 0	0 0 0	0 0 0	0 0 0	0 0 0	0 0 0	0 0 0	0 0 0	- 0
Houston	0 0 0	0 0 0	0 0 0	0 0 0	0 0 0	0 0 0	0 0 0	0 0 1	- 1

OB: New York 16, Houston 16
E: Wilson, Weis
DP: Torres-Gotay-Staub (Charles)
    Grote-Weis (Torres strikeout)
2B: King, Charles
SB: Jones, Charles
CS: Gotay, Miller
SO: Weis, Boswell 3, Agee 4, Jones, Swoboda 5,
    Charles, Grote, Seaver, Bosch, Harrelson,
    Frisella; Davis 3, Miller 2, Wynn 2, King 2,
    Aspromonte 2, Gotay, Torres, Ray 2
BB: Weis, Kranepool, Charles(I), Grote(I), Seaver;
    Miller, Wynn 2(both I), Staub, Torres,
    Bateman(I), Aspromonte(I)

SH: Buchek, Miller, Grote, Kranepool, Cardwell
WP: Seaver, Wilson, Rohr
BK: Rohr
TIME: 6:06
ATTENDANCE: 14,219
UMPIRES: Ed Sudol, Lee Weyer, Bill
    Williams, Tom Gorman
SOURCES: Houston Chronicle, Post;
    New York Times; Retrosheet

BALANCE	OUT+R+OB=BP=AB+BB+SH+HP+CI								
New York	72	0	16	88	79	5	4	0	0
Houston	70	1	16	87	79	7	1	0	0

Leonhard Tames the Tigers

161. Team Records 23 At-Bats in Nine-Inning Game

DETROIT   at   BALTIMORE
(Tigers, 0)   (Orioles, 4)

Monday Night, May 6, 1968, Memorial Stadium

The 1968 baseball season is often described as the "Year of the Pitcher." Plummeting batting averages, a rise in low scoring games, 335 shutouts, and an abundance of outstanding individual pitching performances underscored a growing imbalance between pitchers and batters. Thus was the scene set for Baltimore's 26-year-old rookie right-hander Dave Leonhard, proud possessor of one lifetime major league victory, to enter baseball annals.

Leonhard pitched the sixth successive complete game by an Oriole as well as a one-hitter. In doing so, Dave allowed the Detroit Tigers *only 23 official at-bats in nine innings* which tied a major-league mark accomplished twice previously (see 5-6-17 & 5-9-61).

The Oriole rookie was facing a club that had missed the World Series by only one game a year earlier. This season Detroit would come back with a vengeance, leading the league in runs, home runs, RBIs, slugging, and not stop until they had won a World's Championship. In early season play,

however, the Orioles were floating atop the American League, having won seven straight and 12 of 14. Presently, they were a game and a half in front of the second-place visiting Tigers.

To bat in nine frames with only 23 official

In six seasons, Leonhard was 16–14.

Detroit Tigers	AB	R	H	I
Dick McAuliffe 2b	3	0	0	0
Mickey Stanley 1b	4	0	0	0
Al Kaline rf	2	0	0	0
Willie Horton lf	3	0	0	0
>Bill Freehan c	2	0	0	0
Jim Northrup cf	3	0	1	0
Don Wert 3b	2	0	0	0
Dick Tracewski ss	2	0	0	0
Eddie Mathews ph8	1	0	0	0
Ray Oyler ss8	0	0	0	0
Joe Sparma p	1	0	0	0
Tom Matchick ph6	0	0	0	0
Pat Dobson p6	0	0	0	0
Norm Cash ph8	0	0	0	0
Les Cain p8	0	0	0	0
	23	0	1	0

Baltimore Orioles	AB	R	H	I
Paul Blair cf	4	0	1	0
Curt Motton lf	3	0	0	0
Curt Blefary c	4	1	2	0
Brooks Robinson 3b	4	1	1	0
Boog Powell 1b	4	1	1	0
>Dave Johnson 2b	4	1	3	1
Dave May rf	3	0	2	2
Mark Belanger ss	3	0	1	0
Dave Leonhard p	2	0	0	0
	31	4	11	3

Detroit	IP	H	R	ER	BB	SO
Sparma L,1-3	5	7	3	3	1	3
Dobson	2	3	1	1	0	3
Cain	1	1	0	0	0	0
	8	11	4	4	1	6

Baltimore	IP	H	R	ER	BB	SO
Leonhard W,2-0	9	1	0	0	7	6

Detroit	0 0 0	0 0 0	0 0 0	- 0
Baltimore	0 1 0	2 0 1	0 0 x	- 4

OB: Detroit 5, Baltimore 5
E: Stanley
DP: Leonhard-Johnson-Powell(Horton SO)
   Belanger-Johnson-Powell(Freehan)
   Johnson-Belanger-Powell(Northrup)
   McAuliffe-Stanley(May)
   Oyler-McAuliffe(Robinson)
2B: Johnson, Blefary
SB: McAuliffe
CS: Stanley, Kaline, Northrup, May,
   Motton
SO: McAuliffe, Stanley, Horton 2,
   Tracewski, Sparma; Blair, Motton,
   Robinson, Powell 2, Leonhard

BB: McAuliffe, Kaline 2, Horton,
   Freehan, Matchick, Cash; Motton
SH: Leonhard
HP: By Leonhard (Wert, Freehan)
PB: Blefary
BK: Dobson
TIME: 2:28
ATTENDANCE: 8,000
UMPIRES: Marty Springstead, Red
   Flaherty, Bob Stewart, Lou DiMuro
SOURCES: Baltimore Sun; New York
   Times; Retrosheet; Washington Post

BALANCE	OUT+R+OB=BP=AB+BB+SH+HP+CI
Detroit	27 0 5 32 23 7 0 2 0
Baltimore	24 4 5 33 31 1 1 0 0

at-bats requires a very peculiar set of circumstances:

• First, the offensive team must be limited to very few hits because every hit adds another official at-bat. Leonhard took care of that by allowing only one hit — a two-out seventh-inning single by Jim Northrup.

• Second, the defensive team must make no errors as this too affords the offensive team another player to step to the plate. The Orioles fielded perfectly behind Leonhard.

• Third, the offensive team must be provided with plenty of base runners without recording at-bats, i.e., through walks or hit batsmen. Dave supplied the Tigers with a horn-of-plenty by walking seven and hitting two.

• And fourth, many of those base runners must somehow account for outs. This requirement was fulfilled by three Baltimore double plays, three Tigers caught stealing, and one retired in a rundown. The Orioles' Curt Blefary, whom many remember as an outfielder, did some catching later in his career. During this game he pegged out three of four attempted base stealers.

• Another factor which could come into play, although it did not in this game, is that of sacrifice hits. Any sacrifice hit provides an out without an official at-bat.

Wildness was Leonhard's earmark this game. But despite a batter being walked or hit in every frame, the Tigers managed only one hit off him. Dave's lack of control was also exacerbated by a new controversial spitball rule. Umpire Bob Stewart twice called automatic "balls" when Leonhard put his fingers to his mouth, and Marty Springstead once did the same claiming that Dave rubbed the back of his hand across his mouth. In addition to his seven walks, Leonhard hit both Don Wert and Bill Freehan.

Two major threats confronted Leonhard's shutout. In the sixth Dick McAuliffe hoisted a delivery into the right-field seats that hooked foul by inches. The next batter, Mickey Stanley, nearly cracked the no-hitter when he chipped a looping liner on which first baseman Boog Powell made a leaping backhanded catch while running to his right.

The second threat came in the seventh when Al Kaline led off with a free pass. A passed ball sent him to second, but Willie Horton struck out, and Freehan popped out. Jim Northrup next lined a 1–2 fastball

through the shortstop hole for the Tigers' first hit. Left fielder Curt Motton charged and fielded it as a one-hopper, holding Kaline to third. Leonhard then induced Wert to ground out, third to first.

Leonhard took a strange path to the major leagues. A mediocre hurler in both high school (2–2) and at Johns Hopkins University (3–3), Dave graduated and became a high school history teacher. He wasn't big (about 150 pounds) and he didn't throw fast, but a casual meeting with an old sandlot coach persuaded him to play in an Orioles rookie league after school let out in the summer of 1963. From there Leonhard worked his way through a series of low-minor league towns, nearly quitting on several occasions. He finally pitched for Baltimore in September of 1967, but after a terrible spring training the following year, Dave was shipped back to the minors. With Oriole relievers becoming overworked early in the season, Dave was again recalled. This time he pitched well and stayed with the club through 1972. Aside from this game's oddity, however, Leonhard left baseball fans little with which to remember him. He pitched his entire major league career in Baltimore, mostly in relief. Shoulder problems finally extinguished his major league career after six seasons. Leonhard's lifetime totals include a 16–14 won–lost log and a 3.15 ERA.

Northrup Rips Two Grand Slams

162. Player Hits Grand Slams in Consecutive Innings

DETROIT   at   CLEVELAND
(Tigers, 14)   (Indians, 3)

Monday Night, June 24, 1968, Municipal Stadium

In this the "Year of the Pitcher" (see description of 5-5-68), offensive fireworks were few and far between. The season was so dominated by hurlers that baseball's rulesmakers, in order to increase run production, lowered pitching mounds the following

The second-place Indians had just won three of five from the front-running Tigers, but here's what the Cleveland Press *thought of this night's trouncing.*

led the Tigers in hits, doubles, RBIs, and was an integral part of the club's 1968 World's Championship. The two slams were his second and third of the season.

While etching his name in baseball annals, Northrup made victims of Cleveland right-hander Eddie Fisher and left-hander Bill Rohr. After striking out with the bases loaded in the opening frame, Jim repeated his futility in the third with one mate aboard. But in the fifth, with one out and the sacks again jammed, Northrup connected with Fisher's first offering, a knuckleball. The blast arched over the 390-foot sign in right-center and gave Detroit a 7–2 lead. When the first three Tigers reached base in the sixth, it again brought Northrup to the plate. This time, the 28-year-old drove the first pitch from Rohr, a stomach-high fastball, over the right field wall just inside the foul pole. On his last plate appearance, leading off the eighth, Northrup was issued a base on balls.

Northrup's second slam left the Indians hopelessly trailing 14–2. So when the seventh inning began, it was Cleveland first baseman Willie Smith who took the mound. Smith, who had been filling in for an injured Tony Horton, provided the Tribe

season from 15 inches to ten. One of the year's few hitting eruptions came off the bat of Detroit outfielder Jim Northrup when he *twice connected for circuit clouts with the bases loaded in the same game* tying the major-league mark previously shared by Tony Lazzeri, Jim Tabor, Rudy York, Tony Cloninger, and Jim Gentile. Northrup and Gentile launched their slams in consecutive innings.

Swinging from the left side, Northrup was enjoying the first of three peak seasons as he

Northrup hit 153 career home runs.

with their most effective pitching of the night, allowing just one hit and one walk over the final three frames. Smith's unusual career took him through five major-league clubs, spanned nine seasons and 691 games, 29 of which saw him on a mound.

Detroit's victory was marred by the beaning of their all-star third baseman Don Wert. A Hal Kurtz fastball shattered Wert's batting helmet in the sixth inning and he was carried from the field on a stretcher. After a brief hospital stay, he returned to action.

Northrup hit another grand slam on June 29 against the White Sox, giving him another major league record of three in one week. His heroics this day also made a winner out of right-hander Denny McLain, who was on his way to a 31-win season.

Detroit Tigers	AB	R	H	I
Dick McAullife 2b	5	1	1	2
Dick Tracewski ss,3b6	5	1	1	1
Mickey Stanley cf	4	1	1	0
>Bill Freehan 1b	5	2	2	2
Willie Horton lf	1	1	1	0
Wayne Comer pr6,lf	1	1	0	0
Don Wert 3b	2	0	0	0
Ray Oyler pr6,ss	1	1	0	0
Jim Northrup rf	4	2	2	8
Jim Price c	4	3	2	1
Denny McLain p	5	1	1	0
	37	14	11	14

Cleveland Indians	AB	R	H	I
Billy Harris 2b,3b8	4	1	1	0
Russ Snyder rf	3	0	0	1
Jimmie Hall cf	4	1	1	0
Lee Maye lf	3	1	2	1
Ken Suarez c7	1	0	1	0
Duke Sims c,1b7	4	0	2	1
Willie Smith 1b,p7	4	0	0	0
Larry Brown ss	4	0	1	0
Max Alvis 3b	3	0	1	0
Dave Nelson 2b8	1	0	0	0
Mike Paul p	1	0	0	0
Eddie Fisher p5	0	0	0	0
Hal Kurtz p5	1	0	0	0
Billy Rohr p6	0	0	0	0
> Tommy Harper lf7	2	0	0	0
	35	3	9	3

Detroit	IP	H	R	ER	BB	SO
McLain W,13-2	9	9	3	3	0	8

Cleveland	IP	H	R	ER	BB	SO
Paul L,0-4	4	2	4	4	6	5
Fisher	.1	4	5	5	1	1
Kurtz	.2	2	3	3	0	0
Rohr	1	2	2	2	1	0
Smith	3	1	0	0	1	0
	9	11	14	14	9	6

| Detroit | 2 0 0 | 1 6 5 | 0 0 0 | -14 |
| Cleveland | 1 0 0 | 1 0 0 | 0 1 0 | - 3 |

OB: Detroit 8, Cleveland 6
E: Hall
DP: Harris-Brown-Smith (Tracewski)
2B: Hall, Maye, Freehan, Price, W. Horton, Brown
3B: Harris
HR: Price(1), Northrup 2(10)
SO: Stanley, Wert, Northrup 2, McLain 2, Harris 2, Snyder, Hall, Smith, Alvis, Nelson, Kurtz
BB: McAuliffe, Tracewski, Stanley, W. Horton 3(2I), Wert, Northrup, Price

SH: Stanley
SF: Snyder
HP: By Kurtz (Freehan, Wert)
TIME: 2:39
ATTENDANCE: 12,808
UMPIRES: Lou DiMuro, Marty Springstead, Red Flaherty, Bob Stewart
SOURCES: Cleveland Plain Dealer, Press; New York Times; Retrosheet

BALANCE	OUT	+R	+OB	=BP	=AB	+BB	+SH	+HP	+CI
Detroit	27	14	8	49	37	9	1	2	0
Cleveland	27	3	6	36	35	0	1	0	0

Bonds' Grand Inaugural

163. Player Hits Grand Slam in Debut

LOS ANGELES   at   SAN FRANCISCO
(Dodgers, 0)   (Giants, 9)

Tuesday Night, June 25, 1968, Candlestick Park

Bobby Bonds had impressed the Giants in spring training of 1968, but because he had not played above the Class-A minor league level, management felt he needed a little more seasoning. Shipped to Phoenix of the Pacific Coast League, the 22-year-old continued to excel by hitting .367. Now, with Willie McCovey the only Giant batting over .300, San Francisco needed more offense. Installed in right field, Bonds became the *first player since the turn of the century to hit a grand slam in his first major-league game.* (The Phillies Bill Duggleby had done it in 1898.)

Bobby began his inaugural game inauspiciously when he grounded out to lead off the third. In the fifth, with mates at the corners and no outs, he was hit on the shoulder by Claude Osteen. But in the sixth, with one out and the bases loaded, Bobby slammed John Purdin's first pitch ten rows deep into the left field seats for his first major-league hit.

"I can't say I was nervous," said Bonds. "It was a different kind of feeling. I guess you would say I was in a daze. When I went up to the plate, I made up my mind that I was

Bobby Bonds broke in with a bang.

going to hit my pitch. The first one he threw, was it. I was lucky."*

The big swing made Bonds an instant hero with Candlestick fans, and when he appeared at the plate in the eighth he was greeted with a standing ovation. Even after he then took a called third strike, he received another standing ovation.

This grand-slam home run business was becoming old hat for Bobby. In five similar situations while in the PCL this year, he had hit three grand slams. "But," he added on a post-game TV interview, "this has to be the biggest one."†

The rookie's heroics overshadowed the 122-pitch masterpiece by Giant hurler Ray Sadecki. Sadecki allowed just two weak hits — a bloop double by Claude Osteen and an infield single by Willie Davis — while registering his fourth shutout of the young season.

Bonds continued his exciting career, hitting home runs, stealing bases, and striking out. In 14 campaigns, serving eight different clubs, Bobby hit 332 home runs, stole 461 bases, and struck out 1757 times. He was an electrifying player who could often dominate games.

Los Angeles Dodgers	AB	R	H	I
Willie Davis cf	4	0	1	0
Paul Popovich ss	3	0	0	0
Ted Savage lf	4	0	0	0
Ken Boyer 3b	4	0	0	0
>Jim Lefebvre 2b	4	0	0	0
Ron Fairly rf	3	0	0	0
Tom Haller c	3	0	0	0
Wes Parker 1b	2	0	0	0
Claude Osteen p	2	0	1	0
John Purdin p6	0	0	0	0
Bob Bailey ph8	1	0	0	0
Mudcat Grant p8	0	0	0	0
	30	0	2	0

Los Angeles	IP	H	R	ER	BB	SO
Osteen L,6-10	5	6	5	5	3	1
Purdin	2	3	4	4	2	4
Grant	1	0	0	0	0	1
	8	9	9	9	5	6

Los Angeles	0 0 0	0 0 0	0 0 0	- 0
San Francisco	0 0 0	0 1 6	2 0 x	- 9

OB: Los Angeles 5, San Francisco 3
E: Hart, Lanier
DP: Parker-Popovich-Parker (McCovey)
    Popovich-Parker (J.Alou)
    Lefebvre-Popovich-Parker (Lanier)
2B: Osteen, Alou, Hart
HR: Bonds(1)
SO: Davis, Savage, Boyer, Lefebvre 2, Fairly 2, Haller 2, Osteen; McCovey, Hiatt 2, Bonds, Lanier, Sadecki
BB: Popovich, Parker; Hunt, McCovey 2(1I), Mays, Hart

San Francisco Giants	AB	R	H	I
Ron Hunt 2b	3	2	2	0
Jesus Alou lf,rf9	4	1	3	0
Willie McCovey 1b	2	1	0	0
Willie Mays cf	3	2	0	1
Ty Cline lf9	0	0	0	0
Jim Ray Hart 3b	3	2	2	3
Jack Hiatt c	4	0	1	0
Bobby Bonds rf,cf9	3	1	1	4
Hal Lanier ss	4	0	0	0
>Ray Sadecki p	4	0	0	0
	30	9	9	8

San Francisco	IP	H	R	ER	BB	SO
Sadecki W,8-9	9	2	0	0	2	10

HP: By Osteen (Bonds)
PB: Haller
TIME: 2:21
ATTENDANCE: 17,075
UMPIRES: Bob Engel, Al Barlick, Stan Landes, Ed Vargo
SOURCES: Los Angeles Times; Retrosheet; San Francisco Chronicle, Examiner

BALANCE	OUT+R+OB=BP=AB+BB+SH+HP+CI
Los Angeles	27 0 5 32 30 2 0 0 0
San Francisco	24 9 3 36 30 5 0 1 0

*Dan Hafner, "Giant Rookie Rips L.A. with Slam," Los Angeles Times, 26 June 1968, part III, p. 1, col. 8.
†Al Corona, "Grand Slams Habitual with Bonds," San Francisco Examiner, 26 June 1968, p. 52, col. 4.

The Blass-Williams Affair

164. Player Gets
All Four of His Team's Hits

PITTSBURGH   at   CHICAGO
(Pirates, 9)   (Cubs, 2)

Friday, September 5, 1969, Wrigley Field

At this late date in the campaign, the Cubs found themselves in an unusual position — atop the National League, Eastern Division. Although their lead had waned during the past few weeks, they still held a four game edge over the New York Mets. In third place were the visiting Pittsburgh Pirates who had lost 13 straight in Wrigley Field dating back to July 5, 1967.

The Cubs featured a well balanced team.

Blass had one home run in 546 major league at-bats.

Ferguson Jenkins, Bill Hands, and Ken Holtzman could hold their own with the three top arms of any staff. The offense was led by Billy Williams, Ron Santo, Ernie Banks, Glenn Beckert, Don Kessinger, and Jim Hickman. Williams led the team in hits and runs scored while Beckert had the highest batting average, and Santo outstripped his teammates in home runs and RBIs.

The Pirates, meanwhile, were predominately an offensive club led by Roberto Clemente, Willie Stargell, and Matty Alou. Their best moundsman was 27-year-old right-hander Steve Blass who, despite carrying a 4.56 ERA, was 13–8 prior to this contest. Steve was in his fifth major-league season and had finished 18–6 a year earlier.

The game that unfolded this chilly day in Wrigley Field was one that tested the limits of baseball probability and irony. Blass pitched a strong game, allowing only four hits, two walks, and two runs as the Pirates won 9–2 and further tightened the pennant race. What was so bizarre was the fact that *one player*, Billy Williams, *got all four of Chicago's hits, scored both the runs, and drove home both the runs.* (Don Kessinger was issued both of Blass's free passes.) Only once before had one player accounted for as many of his team's only hits — on August 1, 1903, Norman "Kid" Elberfeld had all four of his teams hits. The irony was that Blass, a .172 lifetime hitter, not only matched Williams in hits (4) but also slugged his first major-league home run.

"Seven-hundred and 13 to go," Blass said, referring to the number of additional home runs he needed to tie Babe Ruth's lifetime mark. Steve also recalled that when he had struck his last mighty blow, he had been playing for the Dodgers — the Canaan, Connecticut, Little League Dodgers.*

Williams couldn't understand his teammates' dilemma with Blass. Billy had been in an 0 for 11 slump but doubled to left-center in both the first and the fourth on fastballs. In the sixth he lined a change-up onto the right-field catwalk for a home run, and in the ninth, blasted a slider into the right-center field bleachers for his second round-tripper.

Blass, meanwhile, was confused as to how to pitch to Williams, lamenting that he had thrown him the same offerings as the rest of the Cubs. "Billy's invited me out to his house

Williams got all of his team's hits, runs, and RBIs.

Pittsburgh Pirates	AB	R	H	I
Matty Alou cf	4	0	0	0
Gene Alley 2b	5	1	1	0
>Willie Stargell lf	4	0	0	0
Roberto Clemente rf	3	3	1	0
Manny Sanguillen c	5	1	1	2
Al Oliver 1b	5	0	1	2
Jose Pagan 3b	5	1	3	1
Freddie Patek ss	3	1	1	0
Steve Blass p	5	2	4	3
	39	9	12	8

Chicago Cubs	AB	R	H	I
Don Kessinger ss	2	0	0	0
Glenn Beckert 2b	4	0	0	0
Billy Williams lf	4	2	4	2
Ernie Banks 1b	4	0	0	0
Jim Hickman rf	4	0	0	0
>Randy Hundley c	4	0	0	0
Paul Popovich 3b	3	0	0	0
Oscar Gamble cf	3	0	0	0
Ken Holtzman p	1	0	0	0
Al Spangler ph5	1	0	0	0
Ted Abernathy p6	0	0	0	0
Hank Aguirre p8	0	0	0	0
Willie Smith ph8	1	0	0	0
Don Nottebart p9	0	0	0	0
	31	2	4	2

Pittsburgh	IP	H	R	ER	BB	SO
Blass W,14-8	9	4	2	2	2	7

Chicago	IP	H	R	ER	BB	SO
Holtzman L,16-9	5	7	6	6	3	2
Abernathy	2.2	3	3	1	4	0
Aguirre	.1	1	0	0	0	0
Nottebart	1	1	0	0	1	1
	9	12	9	7	8	3

*Bill Christine, "Blass King for a Day as Pirates Club Cubs, 9–2," Pittsburgh Press, 6 September 1969, p. 8, col. 1.

| Pittsburgh | 0 4 0 | 0 2 0 | 0 3 0 | - 9 |
| Chicago | 0 0 0 | 0 0 1 | 0 0 1 | - 2 |

OB: Pittsburgh 12, Chicago 4
E: Abernathy
2B: Pagan, Williams 2
HR: Blass(1), Sanguillen(4), Williams 2(17)
SO: Alou, Stargell, Blass; Banks, Hickman 2, Hundley, Gamble, Holtzman, Smith
BB: Alou, Alley, Stargell 2(21), Clemente 2, Patek 2(11); Kessinger 2

SH: Alou
WP: Abernathy
TIME: 2:20
ATTENDANCE: 10,411
UMPIRES: Harry Wendelstedt, Ken Burkhart, Ed Sudol, Lee Weyer
SOURCES: Chicago Daily News, Sun-Times, Tribune; Pittsburgh Post-Gazette, Press; Retrosheet

BALANCE	OUT	+R	+OB	=BP	=AB	+BB	+SH	+HP	+CI
Pittsburgh	27	9	12	48	39	8	1	0	0
Chicago	27	2	4	33	31	2	0	0	0

for the rest of our stay here," said Blass. "I guess he doesn't want anything to happen to me!"*

Steve's three-run homer in the second frame came off Ken Holtzman who had pitched a no-hitter against the Braves a few weeks earlier. The day's hero followed his home run with three singles but fanned in the ninth when Don Nottebart got him to lunge at a breaking pitch. Blass lost his bat on the swing but later remarked that at least the bat landed fair.

The Cubs played this game without the services of their captain, Ron Santo, who was nursing an aching right knee. He had injured it three nights earlier while sliding into third base in Cincinnati.

Perhaps this game was a portent of things to come, for the Cubs thereafter went into a nosedive. While Chicago could muster only 8 wins against 16 losses by season's end, the Miracle Mets went 22–5 and won the pennant handily.

*Edward Press, "Great Day for Blass...and Billy," Chicago Tribune, 6 September 1969, Sports section, p. 5, col. 1.

Gordon Rolls Out Royal Reserves

165. Team Uses 27 Players in Nine-Inning Game

KANSAS CITY   at   CALIFORNIA
(Royals, 4)   (Angels, 11)

Wednesday Night, September 10, 1969, Anaheim Stadium

This record-setting game is a story of managerial excess as 27 Kansas City Royals saw action while being defeated by the California Angels 11–4. It remains the mark for the *most players used by one team in a nine-inning game*. At the time, 27 also represented the most players used by one team in a game of any length although the extra-inning

standard has since been exceeded (see 9-19-72).

The pilot of this scorers' nightmare was Joe Gordon, who had returned to the major-league managerial ranks after a seven-year hiatus. Joe had previously managed in Cleveland (1958–1960), Detroit (1960), and Kansas City (1961) with dubious success, then

Kansas City Royals	AB	R	H	I
Pat Kelly rf	4	1	1	1
Mike Fiore 1b	3	0	1	3
Fran Healy ph8,c	1	0	0	0
Lou Piniella lf	2	0	0	0
Scott Northey cf6	1	0	0	0
Joe Foy 3b	3	0	1	0
Dave Morehead p4	0	0	0	0
Joe Keough cf5,lf6	2	0	1	0
Bob Oliver cf	4	0	1	0
Chris Zachary p7	0	0	0	0
George Spriggs ph9	0	0	0	0
Jim Rooker pr9	0	0	0	0
Jerry Adair 2b	3	1	2	0
Juan Rios pr5,ss	1	0	0	0
> Billy Harris ph9	1	0	0	0
Buck Martinez c	2	1	1	0
Jim Campanis c6	1	0	0	0
Chuck Harrison 1b8	0	0	0	0
Jackie Hernandez ss	1	0	0	0
Luis Alcaraz ph5,2b	2	0	0	0
Bill Butler p	1	0	0	0
Al Fitzmorris p2	0	0	0	0
Ed Kirkpatrick ph3	1	0	0	0
Don O'Riley p3	0	0	0	0
Paul Schaal 3b4	1	0	0	0
Steve Jones p5	0	0	0	0
Fred Rico 3b7	0	1	0	0
	34	4	8	4

California Angels	AB	R	H	I
Sandy Alomar 2b	5	1	2	1
Jay Johnstone cf	5	3	2	0
Jim Fregosi ss	4	2	2	0
Marty Perez ss9	0	0	0	0
Rick Reichardt lf	6	1	1	2
Bubba Morton rf	2	0	2	5
> Bill Voss rf3	4	0	1	1
Aurelio Rodriguez 3b	4	1	3	0
Jim Spencer 1b	4	0	1	0
Joe Azcue c	4	1	2	0
Andy Messersmith p	3	2	1	1
	41	11	17	10

Kansas City	IP	H	R	ER	BB	SO
Butler L,7-10	1.1	3	3	3	2	0
Fitzmorris	.2	2	3	3	2	1
O'Riley	1.2	5	3	2	2	0
Morehead	1	1	1	1	2	0
Jones	1.1	2	0	0	1	2
Zachary	2	4	1	1	0	1
	8	17	11	10	9	4

California	IP	H	R	ER	BB	SO
Messersmith W,14-9	9	8	4	4	7	8

Kansas City	0 3 0	0 0 0	0 1 0	- 4
California	2 4 2	1 1 0	0 1 x	-11

OB: Kansas City 11, California 15
E: Piniella
DP: Fregosi-Alomar-Spencer (Oliver)
2B: Adair, Fiore, Morton, Voss, Azcue, Kelly
SO: Fiore, Healy, Northey, Oliver, Adair, Harris, Butler, Schaal; Fregosi, Reichardt, Spencer, Azcue
BB: Kelly, Fiore, Piniella 2, Martinez, Hernandez, Rico; Alomar, Johnstone, Fregosi 2, Rodriguez, Spencer, Azcue, Messersmith 2

HP: By Messersmith (Spriggs)
WP: Fitzmorris, O'Riley, Morehead
PB: Azcue
TIME: 3:09
ATTENDANCE: 7,018 (6,009 paid)
UMPIRES: Frank Umont, Ron Luciano, Bill Haller, Jim Honochick
SOURCES: Kansas City Times; Los Angeles Times; Retrosheet

BALANCE	OUT+R+OB=BP=AB+BB+SH+HP+CI							
Kansas City	27	4	11	42	34	7	0	1	0
California	24	11	15	50	41	9	0	0	0

became a scout and hitting instructor for the Los Angeles (AL) franchise. With the major-league expansion of 1969, Joe received yet another managerial opportunity.

There were few Californians who witnessed this historic event as many of the 6,009 paying faithful began leaving after the fourth inning of the slow moving contest. The Angels' attendance had averaged just over 10,000 per game, but with the season waning and the cellar only a few games in the distance, there was little to cheer for. The visiting Royals as well were struggling to avoid breathing last place air.

California starter Andy Messersmith faced a cavalcade of 20 *different* batters in this game which may be another record, although nothing of its kind is contained in contemporary tomes. Of those 20, 18 stepped to the plate more than a dozen times during the season, but only Lou Piniella hit over .275, and none of the Royals hit more than 14 home runs. California was even more impotent as no Angel hit over .270 nor hit more than 13 round trippers. California bats also succumbed to a pitiful .230 team batting average.

Gordon was once an acrobatic second baseman who could now turn his lineup upside-down.

Tom Is Terrific

166. Pitcher Strikes Out Ten Consecutive Batters

SAN DIEGO   at   NEW YORK
(Padres, 1)   (Mets, 2)

Wednesday, April 22, 1970, Shea Stadium

Just before this game, Tom Seaver accepted the Cy Young Award as the outstanding pitcher of the National League for 1969, when he went 25–7 with a 2.21 ERA. The 25-year-old right-hander was at the top of his game, having won his last ten decisions in 1969 and having added two more thus far in 1970. On this day Seaver continued his domination of National League batters as he struck out 19 Padres, including the last ten consecutively while garnering his 13th straight victory. The *19 whiffs tied the major-league mark* set a season earlier by Steve Carlton; but the *ten straight strikeouts put Seaver*

San Diego Padres	AB	R	H	I
Jose Arcia ss	3	0	0	0
Ivan Murrell ph8	1	0	0	0
Dave Roberts p8	0	0	0	0
Van Kelly 3b	4	0	0	0
Cito Gaston cf	4	0	0	0
>Al Ferrara lf	3	1	1	1
Nate Colbert 1b	3	0	0	0
Dave Campbell 2b	3	0	1	0
Jerry Morales rf	3	0	0	0
Bob Barton c	2	0	0	0
Mike Corkins p	2	0	0	0
Ramon Webster ph8	1	0	0	0
Ron Slocum ss8	0	0	0	0
	29	1	2	1

New York Mets	AB	R	H	I
Tommie Agee cf	3	1	1	0
Bud Harrelson ss	3	1	2	1
Ken Boswell 2b	4	0	1	1
Cleon Jones lf	4	0	0	0
>Art Shamsky rf	2	0	0	0
Ron Swoboda ph8,rf	1	0	0	0
Joe Foy 3b	2	0	0	0
Ed Kranepool 1b	2	0	0	0
Jerry Grote c	3	0	0	0
Tom Seaver p	3	0	0	0
	27	2	4	2

San Diego	IP	H	R	ER	BB	SO
Corkins L,0-2	7	4	2	2	5	5
Roberts	1	0	0	0	0	2
	8	4	2	2	5	7

New York	IP	H	R	ER	BB	SO
Seaver W,3-0	9	2	1	1	2	19

San Diego	0 1 0	0 0 0	0 0 0	- 1
New York	1 0 1	0 0 0	0 0 x	- 2

OB: San Diego 3, New York 6
2B: Boswell
3B: Harrelson
HR: Ferrara
SB: Agee
CS: Harrelson
SO: Murrell, Kelly 3, Gaston 3, Ferrara 2,
    Colbert, Campbell, Morales 3, Barton 2,
    Corkins 2, Webster; Agee 2, Boswell,
    Jones 2, Grote, Seaver

BB: Ferrara, Barton; Agee, Harrelson
    Shamsky(I), Foy, Kranepool
TIME: 2:14
ATTENDANCE: 14,197
UMPIRES: Harry Wendelstedt, Tony
    Venzon, Frank Secory, Bob Engel
SOURCES: New York Times; Retrosheet;
    San Diego Union

BALANCE	OUT+R+OB=BP=AB+BB+SH+HP+CI
San Diego	27 1 3 31 29 2 0 0 0
New York	24 2 6 32 27 5 0 0 0

TOM SEAVER'S STRIKEOUTS BY INNING, APRIL 22, 1970

Inning:	1st	2nd	3rd	4th	5th	6th	7th	8th	9th
1st out			c-Corkins	c-Gaston	s-Barton		s-Colbert	c-Barton	s-Kelly
2nd out	c-Kelly				c-Corkins		c-Campbell	s-Webster	c-Gaston
3rd out	s-Gaston	s-Morales	c-Kelly	c-Morales		c-Ferrara	c-Morales	s-Murrell	s-Ferrara

s = swinging; c = called

in a class by himself. Previously, the most any hurler had fanned in succession was eight (shared by four pitchers). Unlike Carlton's effort, however, Seaver won his game and also pitched in the daylight.

Seaver's masterpiece consisted of 136 pitches — 81 fastballs, 34 sliders, 19 curves, and two changeups. All the San Diego baserunners came in the first four frames. Al Ferrara touched him for a solo home run in the second, Bob Barton walked in the third, Ferrara walked and Dave Campbell singled in the fourth. "Actually he wasn't that strong in the early innings," said catcher Jerry Grote. "He just kept building up as the game went on. The cool weather helped and by the end of the game he was stronger than ever."*

The Cy Young Award winner struck out

Joseph Durso, "Seaver Strikes Out 19,...," New York Times, 23 April 1970, p. 48, col. 1.

Beginning in 1970, Seaver led the league in strikeouts five out of seven seasons.

each Padre batter at least once except Jose Arcia, who ironically was lifted for a pinch hitter in the eighth. Both San Diego pinch hitters were among the eight who went down swinging; 11 others were caught looking.

Despite Seaver's dominance, his teammates' paltry offensive support kept the contest suspenseful. Mindful of Carlton's 19-strikeout losing performance, and holding just a one-run lead, Seaver never felt at ease. "I was still worried I'd make a mistake and Ferrara [Padres' last batter] might hit it out," Seaver said. "But when I got two strikes on him, I thought I might never get this close

again so I might as well go for it."* Seaver went for it and got it.

At times it seemed that Seaver was merely playing catch with Grote, who also set a record for backstops. Grote caught one foul pop fly in addition to the strikeouts for a *total of 20 putouts and a new standard for a nine-inning game* (tied twice; see 4-29-86 and 9-18-96).

Coming off his Cy Young Award season, Seaver's 1970 record (18–12) is seemingly inferior. His individual performance, however, was arguably equal to his previous campaign. This season he led the league in strikeouts (283) and ERA (2.82).

*Joseph Durso, "Seaver Strikes Out 19,...," New York Times, *23 April 1970, p. 48, col. 1.*

Charitable Stottlemyre Stifles Senators

167. Pitcher Walks 11 in Eight-Plus Shutout Innings

WASHINGTON   at   NEW YORK
(Senators, 0)   (Yankees, 2)

Thursday Night, May 21, 1970, Yankee Stadium

Stottlemyre was 15–13 this year for the runner-up Yankees.

The Yankees' Mel Stottlemyre was in a very magnanimous mood this day, or more likely — very wild. Nevertheless, his benevolence went unappreciated as he *shut out the Washington Senators despite issuing 11 free passes*. That tied the major-league record established by fellow Yankee Lefty Gomez in 1941. Unlike Gomez, however, Stottlemyre wasn't around at the finish and needed relief to accomplish his altruistic endeavor.

A year earlier, Stottlemyre had allowed only 2.88 walks per nine innings, and this season, excluding this game, he issued just 2.50 passes per game. So the sudden generosity was anomalous.

Besides the 11 walks there were two wild pitches and a passed ball giving Washington plenty of scoring opportunities:

• In the opening frame, after the first two Senators were retired, Washington jammed the basepaths before Aurelio Rodriguez grounded out to second.

• Washington got two singles and a walk in the fourth inning but failed to score — in large part due to baserunner Bernie Allen being hit by a batted ball.

• Two free passes and a single were wasted in the fifth, the same inning in which Thurman Munson nailed Ed Stroud trying to steal.

• In the ninth, Yankee skipper Ralph Houk could stand Stottlemyre's wildness no longer. After retiring Del Unser, Stottlemyre gave up a single to Stroud, walked pinch hitter Jim French and then Frank Howard. It was too close a contest to afford the Yankee hurler a chance for a complete game, so Houck called on left-hander Steve Hamilton. With nine pitches, Hamilton fanned Mike Epstein and Allen, both of whom batted from the left side, to wrap up the New York victory.

The Yankees got all the runs they needed in the fifth inning off the Senators' rookie Dick Such, who was making his first big league start. Such allowed only two hits, but one of them was a circuit blast by Danny Cater following a lead-off walk to Roy White

in the fifth. The low liner into the left-field seats came on a 1–1 count and gave Cater a team-leading 31 RBIs.

Washington stranded a total of 14 baserunners, narrowly avoiding the ignominy of tying the mark for futility in that category. Several clubs had marooned 15 in shutout losses.

After leading the league with 24 complete games a year earlier, Stottlemyre had yet to finish anything he started this season, although this 141-pitch adventure marked his fourth straight triumph.

Washington Senators	AB	R	H	I
Ed Stroud cf	4	0	1	0
Lee Maye lf	4	0	2	0
Horacio Pina p7	0	0	0	0
Jim French ph9	0	0	0	0
Frank Howard rf	2	0	0	0
Mike Epstein 1b	4	0	1	0
>Bernie Allen 2b	3	0	0	0
Aurelio Rodriguez 3b	4	0	1	0
Eddie Brinkman ss	2	0	1	0
Johnny Roseboro ph8,c	0	0	0	0
Paul Casanova c	3	0	0	0
Rick Reichardt ph8*	1	0	0	0
Wayne Comer ph8*	0	0	0	0
Tim Cullen ss8	0	0	0	0
Dick Such p	2	0	0	0
Del Unser ph7,lf	1	0	0	0
	30	0	6	0

New York Yankees	AB	R	H	I
>Horace Clarke 2b	4	0	1	0
Curt Blefary rf	3	0	0	0
Jim Lyttle rf	0	0	0	0
Bobby Murcer cf	3	0	0	0
Roy White lf	1	1	0	0
Danny Cater 1b	3	1	1	2
Thurman Munson c	2	0	0	0
Gene Michael ss	2	0	0	0
Jerry Kenney 3b	3	0	1	0
Mel Stottlemyre p	3	0	0	0
Steve Hamilton p9	0	0	0	0
	24	2	3	2

Washington	IP	H	R	ER	BB	SO
Such L,1-2	6	2	2	2	3	3
Pina	2	1	0	0	1	1
	8	3	2	2	4	4

New York	IP	H	R	ER	BB	SO
Stottlemyre W,4-3	8.1	6	0	0	11	6
Hamilton S,3	.2	0	0	0	0	2
	9	6	0	0	11	8

* After Reichardt was ejected, Comer
  completed his strikeout.

Washington 0 0 0   0 0 0   0 0 0   - 0
New York   0 0 0   0 2 0   0 0 x   - 2

OB: Washington 14, New York 2
DP: Casanova-Epstein (Munson SO)
    Casanova-Epstein (Stottlemyre pop-up)
HR: Cater
SB: Maye, Munson
CS: Maye, Stroud
PK: White, Clarke
SO: Howard 2, Epstein 3, Allen,
    Casanova, Reichardt; Blefary,
    Murcer, Munson, Stottlemyre

BB: Stroud, French, Howard 3, Unser,
     Allen 2, Brinkman, Roseboro,
     Epstein; White 2, Munson, Michael
WP: Stottlemyre 2
PB: Munson
TIME: 2:32
ATTENDANCE: 9,254
UMPIRES: Art Frantz, Nestor Chylak,
     Johnny Stevens, Don Denkinger
SOURCES: New York Times, Daily News;
     Retrosheet; Washington Post

BALANCE	OUT+R+OB=BP=AB+BB+SH+HP+CI								
Washington	27	0	14	41	30	11	0	0	0
New York	24	2	2	28	24	4	0	0	0

Indians Render to Cesar

168. Player Gets Seven Consecutive Hits in One Game

DETROIT   at   CLEVELAND
(Tigers, 9)   (Indians, 8)

Sunday, June 21, 1970, Municipal Stadium

As noted elsewhere in this anthology, the true romance of baseball records is the unexpected and improbable nature of such events. Nowhere do those characteristics manifest themselves more strongly than in the second game of this day's doubleheader as Cesar "Cocoa" Gutierrez,[*] batting .218, *became the first modern major-league player to get seven consecutive hits in one game.* Cocoa also did it with only seven plate appearances; he made no outs before or after; he had no walks, sacrifices, nor was he hit by a pitch.

Three other batters had previously harvested seven or more hits in a game but all under different circumstances. Wilbert Robinson smacked six singles and one double in seven at-bats of an 1892 nine-inning game, the year before the pitcher's distance was settled at 60 feet, 6 inches. In 1932, during an 18-inning contest, Johnny Burnett roped two doubles and seven singles in 11 at-bats; and Rocky Colavito collected one triple and six singles in 10 at-bats during a 22-inning match in 1962.

Cocoa Gutierrez—a lifetime .235 hitter.

[*]*Whereas both* The Baseball Encyclopedia *(9th edition) and* Total Baseball *(3rd edition) spell Gutierrez' nickname as "Coca," contemporary Detroit newspapers printed it as "Cocoa." He reportedly received the moniker because he climbed coconut trees in Venezuela as a child.*

Thus Gutierrez became the first to compile a perfect seven-for-seven under today's diamond dimensions. Coincidentally, the 27-year-old also wore number seven on his uniform.

Gutierrez, a right-handed batter, was ticketed to be the Tiger's regular shortstop this season, but atrocious batting forced manager Mayo Smith to demote him to the bench in favor of Ken Szotkiewicz. The Detroit skipper was obliged to reconsider his strategy when Szotkiewicz, who batted from the left side, filled in with 6 hits in 46 at bats (.130) coupled with 21 strikeouts. For the past several days the two had been platooned, and Szotkiewicz played the first game of the doubleheader. It would be his last start for quite some time.

The morning of June 21st brought a cold rain to Cleveland with temperatures hovering around the 50 degree mark. But the weather could neither dampen nor chill the bat of Gutierrez, proud owner of 58 lifetime major-league hits. Once installed in the nightcap, Cocoa hit safely off each of the five Cleveland hurlers.

• Cesar looped a singled to center in the first frame off Cleveland starter Rick Austin and later scored on a fielder's choice. This was the major-league debut of Austin.

• In the third, with Austin still serving them up, Gutierrez lined a single to left and scored on an Al Kaline home run.

• Cocoa opened the fifth with a grounder deep into the hole between third and short off reliever Denny Higgins. Shortstop Jack Heidemann gloved the ball but couldn't get enough on his throw to nip the Venezuelan. Cocoa was left stranded.

• Leading off again in the seventh against Higgins, Cesar doubled down the left field line, eventually scoring on Jim Northrup's circuit clout.

• On the tail end of an eighth inning rally, Gutierrez lined a single over the second baseman's head, driving home Gates Brown. The blow came at the expense of Cleveland's third hurler Fred Lasher. Cocoa was then forced out at second.

• In the tenth, facing Dick Ellsworth with two outs and Don Wert on first, Cesar grounded a ball up the middle. Shortstop Heidemann dove and got his glove on the ball but couldn't hold it. In desperation Heidemann picked it up and tossed to second, attempting to get a force out on Wert. All hands were safe, but for the third straight time Cocoa was later forced out at second.

• Gutierrez was nervous as he approached the plate in the twelfth. He knew he already had six straight hits, and coach Wally Moses had told him that he needed one more to tie a record. Phil Hennigan was now on the mound for Cleveland, and he delivered a pitch that Cesar lined back toward the hurler's feet. Hennigan got his glove on the ball, but by the time he scrambled for it and threw to first, Gutierrez had touched the bag for his seventh consecutive safety. Perhaps fearing a repeat of his last two force outs, Cesar then made his only mistake of the day as he was cut down attempting to steal second.

Al Kaline, who batted behind Gutierrez, was carrying a lifetime .302 average into this game and already had amassed over 2,500 hits. Kaline, however, hadn't even had five hits in a game until earlier in this his 18th season. Gutierrez, on the other hand, had never had more than three hits in a game (three times) prior to his seven-hit outbreak.

Gutierrez had originally signed with the Pirates in 1961 but never made it to the big time. After brief trials with the San Francisco Giants in 1967 and again in 1969, he was sold to the Tigers. Appearing in 135 contests this season, which was far more than the combined total of the rest of his career, Cocoa rapped out 101 hits in 415 at-bats for a .243 batting average. Seldom did the five-foot, nine-inch shortstop fail to get his swings as he walked only 18 times.

The following season the Tigers changed managers as well as shortstops, and Cesar was afforded only 37 at-bats. New Detroit manager Billy Martin preferred Eddie Brinkman at shortstop, making 1971 the last season that Cesar Gutierrez would wear a major-league uniform. During his final season, Gutierrez had seven hits.

SECOND GAME

Detroit Tigers	AB	R	H	I
Mickey Stanley cf	6	1	2	1
Cesar Gutierrez ss	7	3	7	1
Al Kaline 1b	6	1	1	2
>Willie Horton lf	6	1	3	0
Jim Northrup rf	5	2	2	5
Elliott Maddox 3b	6	0	0	0
Ike Brown 2b	3	0	0	0
Gates Brown ph8	1	1	1	0
Bill Freehan c8	1	0	0	0
Jim Price c	1	0	0	0
Norm Cash ph8	1	0	0	0
John Hiller p8	0	0	0	0
Don Wert ph10	1	0	1	0
Tom Timmerman p10	1	0	0	0
Mike Kilkenny p	0	0	0	0
Daryl Patterson p1	2	0	0	0
Rus Nagelson ph6	1	0	0	0
Fred Scherman p6	0	0	0	0
Dick McAuliffe ph8,2b	3	0	0	0
	51	9	17	9

Cleveland Indians	AB	R	H	I
>Jack Heidemann ss	5	1	1	1
Eddie Leon 2b	5	1	1	0
Ted Uhlaender cf	6	2	3	1
Ray Fosse c	6	1	2	0
Tony Horton 1b	5	1	4	5
Roy Foster lf	4	0	0	0
Fred Lasher p8	0	0	0	0
Rich Rollins ph9	1	0	0	0
Dick Ellsworth p10	0	0	0	0
Lou Klimchock ph11	1	0	0	0
Phil Hennigan p12	0	0	0	0
Chuck Hinton rf	6	1	3	1
Graig Nettles 3b	3	1	3	0
Rick Austin p	1	0	0	0
Denny Higgins p3	1	0	0	0
Vada Pinson rf8	3	0	0	0
	47	8	17	8

Detroit	IP	H	R	ER	BB	SO
Kilkenny	.2	5	5	5	1	2
Patterson	4.1	4	2	2	1	3
Scherman	2	2	1	1	0	0
Hiller	2	2	0	0	1	1
Timmerman W,1-1	3	4	0	0	2	1
	12	17	8	8	5	7

Cleveland	IP	H	R	ER	BB	SO
Austin	2.1	5	5	5	2	3
Higgins	4.2	4	2	2	2	5
Lasher	2	3	1	1	1	1
Ellsworth	2	3	0	0	1	0
Hennigan L,4-3	1	2	1	1	1	0
	12	17	9	9	7	9

Detroit   1 0 4   0 0 0   2 1 0   0 0 1   - 9
Cleveland   5 1 0   0 1 1   0 0 0   0 0 0   - 8

OB: Detroit 13, Cleveland 11
E: T. Horton
DP: Kaline-Gutierrez-Kaline (Pinson)
     Fosse-Heidemann-Leon (Patterson)
2B: T. Horton, Fosse, Gutierrez,
     G. Brown
HR: T. Horton(9), Northrup 2(13),
     Stanley(3)
CS: Gutierrez
SO: Kaline 2, Northrup, Maddox,
     I. Brown 2, Price, Patterson,
     McAuliffe; Heidemann, Fosse,
     Foster, Hinton, Austin, Higgins,
     Pinson

BB: Stanley, Kaline, W. Horton,
     Northrup, Freehan(I), Price 2;
     Heidemann, Leon, Nettles 3
SH: Higgins
SF: T. Horton, Heidemann
WP: Scherman
PB: Price
TIME: 4:00
ATTENDANCE: 23,904
UMPIRES: Marty Springstead, Larry
     Barnett, Larry Napp, John Rice
SOURCES: Cleveland Plain Dealer,
     Press; Detroit Free Press, News;
     Retrosheet

BALANCE	OUT	+R	+OB	=BP	=AB	+BB	+SH	+HP	+CI
Detroit	36	9	13	58	51	7	0	0	0
Cleveland	36	8	11	55	47	5	3	0	0

Robinson Frankly Grand

169. Player Hits
Two Grand Slams in One Game

BALTIMORE   at   WASHINGTON
(Orioles, 12)   (Senators, 2)

Friday Night, June 26, 1970, R. F. Kennedy Stadium

Future Hall-of-Famer Frank Robinson had already left an indelible mark in baseball annals by winning the National League Rookie of the Year honors in 1956, the MVP award in both the National (1961) and American (1966) League, and the Triple Crown (1966) while with Baltimore. This day he added his name to the record books one more time when he *hit two grand slam home runs in the same game* as the Orioles whipped the Senators 12–2. The 34-year-old slugger thus became the seventh batter to drive home eight runs with two swings of the bat and the third player to do so in back-to-back innings.

Robinson was a doubtful starter, having been bothered by an aching back incurred while making a leaping, game-saving catch in the 13th inning at Boston the night before. (That play robbed Reggie Smith of a home run.) The pain was so severe that even after taking a pain-killing injection before his at-bat in the 14th, Frank could only bunt. After then staying awake most of the night with his sick son, Robinson was a tired as well as an aching ballplayer.

Travails aside, Robinson lined out to second base in the first inning. In the third frame, he walked. With Washington right-hander Joe Coleman on the mound in the fifth inning, Baltimore's Mark Belanger led off by popping out to short. Dave McNally

Frank Robinson finished his career in 1976 with 586 home runs.

Baltimore Orioles	AB	R	H	I
Don Buford lf	5	3	4	3
>Paul Blair cf	4	2	1	0
Frank Robinson rf	4	2	2	8
Boog Powell 1b	4	1	2	0
Brooks Robinson 3b	4	0	1	0
Dave Johnson 2b	5	1	0	0
Elrod Hendricks c	5	0	1	0
Mark Belanger ss	4	1	1	1
Dave McNally p	2	2	0	0
	37	12	12	12

Washington Senators	AB	R	H	I
Eddie Brinkman ss	3	0	1	0
Wayne Comer cf	4	0	1	0
Frank Howard lf	4	0	0	0
Rick Reichardt rf	2	2	2	2
Aurelio Rodriguez 3b	3	0	0	0
Del Unser pr9	0	0	0	0
Mike Epstein 1b	4	0	1	0
Paul Casanova c	4	0	1	0
>Tim Cullen 2b	4	0	0	0
Joe Coleman p	1	0	1	0
Joe Grzenda p5	0	0	0	0
Dick Nen ph6	1	0	0	0
Jim Shellenback p7	0	0	0	0
Ed Stroud ph8	1	0	0	0
Horacio Pina p9	0	0	0	0
	31	2	7	2

Baltimore	IP	H	R	ER	BB	SO
McNally W,11-5	9	7	2	2	2	4

Washington	IP	H	R	ER	BB	SO
Coleman L,5-6	4.1	6	5	5	5	5
Grzenda	1.2	3	5	5	2	0
Shellenback	2	0	0	0	1	1
Pina	1	3	2	2	2	0
	9	12	12	12	10	6

```
Baltimore    0 0 1   0 4 5   0 0 2   -12
Washington   0 0 0   0 0 0   1 0 1   - 2
```

OB: Baltimore 8, Washington 6
DP: Belanger-Johnson(Howard-line drive)
    B. Robinson-Johnson-Powell (Brinkman)
    B. Robinson-Johnson-Powell (Rodriguez)
    Epstein-Brinkman-Epstein (Hendricks)
2B: Blair, Powell 2, Epstein
HR: Buford(8), F. Robinson 2(14),
    Reichardt 2(8)
SO: Blair, B. Robinson, Johnson,
    Belanger, McNally 2; Howard 3,
    Casanova

BB: Buford, Blair 2, F. Robinson,
    Powell, B.Robinson, Belanger,
    McNally 3; Brinkman, Reichardt
HP: By McNally(Reichardt, Rodriguez)
TIME: 2:33
ATTENDANCE: 13,194
UMPIRES: Art Frantz, Nestor Chylak,
    Russ Goetz, Don Denkinger
SOURCES: Baltimore Sun; Retrosheet;
    Washington Post

BALANCE	OUT	+ R	+ OB	= BP	= AB	+ BB	+ SH	+ HP	+ CI
Baltimore	27	12	8	47	37	10	0	0	0
Washington	27	2	6	35	31	2	0	2	0

then walked, Don Buford singled, and Paul Blair also walked. That brought to the plate Robinson, who had yet to hit his first American League grand slam after belting five while in Cincinnati. (Frank had been traded to Baltimore in 1965 for Milt Pappas.) Robinson then drove a 2–2 pitch 390 feet over the stands to the base of the scoreboard in right field for his inaugural AL slam.

The following inning, Robinson repeated his heroics with the same three runners on base although the Senator hurler was now a left-hander, Joe Grzenda. Elrod Hendricks

led off with a single but was forced out by Belanger. McNally walked, and Buford again singled, driving home Belanger. As in the previous frame, Blair walked again, loading the sacks for Robinson. Frank kept the re-run accurate by homering, only this time the blast came off a 2–0 offering and landed in the upper stands of left-center, a distance measured at 462 feet.

In the eighth, with two outs and no one on base, Robinson hit a sharp grounder up the middle. Eddie Brinkman, Washington shortstop, made a successful diving stab, jumped to his feet and made a perfect peg to first for an out.

The former two-time MVP outfielder was again on deck in the ninth with the bases loaded. But Blair flied to right for the Orioles' 27th out, disappointing the Washington fans who had hoped to see yet another slam.

After his grand performance, Robinson was rather subdued. "I'm just basically happy about it because it contributed to a win. I'm not jumping up and down, if you know what I mean. I'm just happy about tonight, about the runs, about the win."*

The Orioles went on to win their second of three consecutive AL championships, although it was Baltimore's Boog Powell who won this year's AL MVP. Washington finished in an all-too-familiar last place. By 1972 the franchise was shipped off to Texas.

*Jim Elliott, "Frank's Bat Lifts Birds to 12–2 Win," The Baltimore Sun, 27 June 1970, section B, p. 3, col. 5.

An Absence of Malice?

170. Seven Players Hit by Pitch in One Game

MINNESOTA   at   KANSAS CITY
(Twins, 3)   (Royals, 5)

Tuesday Night, April 13, 1971, Municipal Stadium

There was hardly a safe place to hide as batters dodged pitches all night long. *Seven unlucky victims did get plunked, however, tying the twentieth-century major-league record* which had stood alone since 1914 (see 8-24-14). (The listing in modern record books of seven batters hit-by-pitches on August 1, 1903, is erroneous. There were only six hit in the second game that day.)

As impossible as it may seem to present day baseball fans, this day's seven hit-batsmen resulted in no fights, no charging of the mound, and no warnings issued by the umpires. Both sides felt the infractions were completely unintentional. "I don't think anyone was deliberately throwing at the hitters," said Minnesota manager Bill Rigney. "It was just a cool night (61 degrees) and everybody was a little stiff after Monday's game (80 degrees).† Royals skipper Bob Lemon concurred. "If you check the boxscore you'd probably think we had a shooting gallery. I don't think anybody threw at anybody."§ Both sides as well as umpire Larry Barnett pointed out that no one was hit on the head.

A scoresheet of the game, however, provides suspicious details of the hit-batter situations. No batter was hit by a pitch until the sixth inning when a sudden rash of wildness broke out (or "bruisarama," as *The Kansas City Star & Times* called it). From that point to the game's conclusion, the teams engaged in human target practice, exchanging one hit-batter every half-inning.

• Leading off the Minnesota sixth, trailing 3–2, Harmon Killebrew flied out to center. Rich Reese then became the first victim of Tom Burgmeier but was quickly erased on a double play.

• In the bottom half of the frame Kansas City's first batter, Lou Piniella, was hit by

†Dan Stoneking, "Twin Relievers Ready for West," The Minneapolis Star, 14 April 1971, section F, p. 1, col. 7.
§Sid Bordman, "Twins a Big Hit and Lose, Too," Kansas City Star & Times, 14 April 1971, section D, p. 6, col. 3.

Tom Burgmeier started the hit parade.

Stan Williams. Lou was then gunned down attempting to steal second.

• The seventh opened with the Twins' Leo

Cardenas becoming Burgmeier's second quarry. Cardenas was eventually left on base as Minnesota failed to score.

• Not until the fifth Royals batter had appeared in the home half of the seventh was the reciprocity brought up to date. With two outs and runners on first and second, Amos Otis received an 0–2 curveball on the foot. Piniella followed with a two-run single, but Otis was left stranded.

• When Reese stepped to the plate in the eighth, Killebrew was on first with one away. Jim York was the Royals' pitcher who this time "accidentally" hit Reese. Killebrew was later driven home by Cardenas, but Reese was left on base.

• The bottom of the eighth saw two of the first three Royals retired. Then, with Paul Schaal on first, Gail Hopkins was pummeled with a pitch. Both men were left, however, as Freddie Patek flied out.

• Minnesota had one more opportunity to bat in the ninth. With the Royals' Ted Abernathy on the hill, rookie pinch hitter Steve Braun was sent to lead off. Abernathy immediately hit Braun, but although Rod Carew

Minnesota Twins	AB	R	H	I
Cesar Tovar lf	4	0	0	0
Rod Carew 2b	5	0	1	0
Tony Oliva rf	5	1	1	1
>Harmon Killebrew 3b	5	1	2	0
Rich Reese 1b	2	1	1	0
Jim Holt cf	4	0	1	0
Leo Cardenas ss	1	0	1	2
George Mitterwald c	3	0	1	0
Paul Ratliff ph8,c	1	0	0	0
Steve Barber p	2	0	0	0
Stan Williams p5	0	0	0	0
Rick Renick ph7	0	0	0	0
Paul Powell pr7	0	0	0	0
Ron Perranoski p7	0	0	0	0
Steve Braun ph9	0	0	0	0
	32	3	8	3

Kansas City Royals	AB	R	H	I
>Freddie Patek ss	4	0	0	1
Joe Keough rf	3	0	0	1
Carl Taylor ph7,rf	0	1	0	0
Amos Otis cf	3	0	0	0
Lou Piniella lf	3	0	1	2
Ed Kirkpatrick c	3	0	0	0
Bob Oliver 1b	2	1	1	0
Tom Burgmeier p6	1	0	1	0
Jim York p7	0	0	0	0
Ted Abernathy p8	1	0	0	0
Cookie Rojas 2b	2	1	0	0
Paul Schaal 3b	3	2	1	1
Mike Hedlund p	1	0	0	0
Gail Hopkins ph5,1b	1	0	0	0
	27	5	4	5

Minnesota	IP	H	R	ER	BB	SO
Barber	4.1	1	2	2	2	2
Williams L,0-1	1.2	2	1	1	2	0
Perranoski	2	1	2	2	3	1
	8	4	5	5	7	3

Kansas City	IP	H	R	ER	BB	SO
Hedlund W,2-0	5	5	2	2	1	2
Burgmeier	1.1	0	0	0	1	0
York	1.1	2	1	1	1	0
Abernathy S,2	1.1	1	0	0	0	1
	9	8	3	3	3	3

Minnesota   1 0 0   1 0 0   0 1 0   - 3
Kansas City   0 0 0   0 3 0   2 0 x   - 5

OB: Minnesota 10, Kansas City 8
DP: Burgmeier-Rojas-Patek-Hopkins (Holt)
     Rojas-Patek-Hopkins (Carew)
2B: Schaal
HR: Oliva(2)
CS: Piniella
SO: Killebrew 2, Reese; Otis, Kirkpatrick,
     Abernathy
BB: Tovar, Cardenas, Renick; Patek, Taylor,
     Kirkpatrick, Rojas 2, Schaal,
     Hopkins(I)
SF: Cardenas

HP: By Burgmeier (Reese, Cardenas), by S.Williams
     (Piniella), by Perranoski (Otis, Hopkins), by
     Abernathy(Braun), by York(Reese)
TIME: 2:45
ATTENDANCE: 6,740
UMPIRES: Merlyn Anthony, George
     Maloney, Hank Soar, Larry Barnett
SOURCES: Kansas City Star & Times;
     Minneapolis Star; Retrosheet;
     St. Paul Pioneer Press

BALANCE	OUT	+R	+OB	=BP	=AB	+BB	+SH	+HP	+CI
Minnesota	27	3	10	40	32	3	1	4	0
Kansas City	24	5	8	37	27	7	0	3	0

Rich Reese was victimized twice.

later singled, Steve was left stranded as the Royals prevailed 5–3. The Twins did, however, "win" the hit-batsmen contest 4–3.

The only hurlers who didn't impose pain on the batters were the game's starters — Mike Hedlund of Kansas City and Steve L. Barber of Minnesota. The right-handed Barber was making his first major-league start after relieving in 18 games the previous season. This was not the same Steve (D.) Barber, a left-hander, who had won 20 games for the Orioles in 1963. This 23-year-old Minnesota Barber labored in just 22 major league games over two seasons, winning but one.

All Wise

171. Pitcher Throws No-Hitter, Hits Two Home Runs

PHILADELPHIA   at   CINCINNATI
(Phillies, 4)   (Reds, 0)

Wednesday Night, June 23, 1971, Riverfront Stadium

It was a one-man show this night in Cincinnati as Philadelphia's Rick Wise pitched and batted his way into the record books, becoming the *first (and only, to date) to hurl a no-hitter while also stroking two home runs*. The 25-year-old right-hander also narrowly missed a perfect game, walking only one of the 28 Reds he faced. And, his performance was particularly impressive when considering the offensive arsenal of the opposition. Although in an off year, this was the "Big Red Machine" that dominated the National League West in the early 1970s. Strange indeed was the fact that these Reds had also been no-hit three weeks earlier by Ken Holtzman, making them the fourth club in the last 50 years to be no-hit twice in a season.

This was not Wise's first brush with no-hit fame. His first encounter had come on the day of his initial major league victory — June 21, 1964. That was the day Jim Bunning had hurled his perfect game against the Mets in the opening game of a doubleheader. An 18-year-old Wise won the nightcap after tossing a perfect 4⅓ innings. Several years later, in 1968, Rick hurled a one-hitter against the Dodgers.

This day, the only blemish on Rick's otherwise perfect day was the result of a sixth inning walk to Dave Concepcion. After Tommy Helms had grounded out, Concepcion looked at three balls, a called strike, and finally a high fastball for the free pass. Wise then disposed of pinch hitter Bernie Carbo as well as Pete Rose. Rose was also the final out in a game which balanced the bespectacled Wise's lifetime record at 66–66.

Although Wise needed only 95 pitches (62 strikes) to complete his no-hitter, seven different Reds took him to a three-ball count. Five others went down on his first offering. Among his offerings, Rick threw 56 fastballs and 39 breaking pitches. Wise hadn't felt exceptional while warming up, and by his own account, Rick felt he had pitched much better a few weeks earlier in San Francisco on June 6, when he won the first game of a doubleheader 1–0.

Despite being hitless in 30 trips to the plate during 1966, Wise had been considered an average hitting moundsman, registering a .212 lifetime average prior to this season. This day the 6'2", 200-pounder slammed his first round-tripper over the left-field fence in the fifth inning after Roger Freed had doubled. With the Cincinnati fans affording a standing ovation, he connected again leading

Wise was traded the following year for Steve Carlton.

off the eighth against reliever Clay Carroll. It came on a 2–0 offering and was his ninth career home run. Rick had previously homered twice this season and, before it ended, he would again homer twice in one game. He concluded his career in 1982 with 15 circuit clouts.

Several nice fielding plays also aided Wise's record-setting performance. The Reds' first batter, Pete Rose, hit a bouncer between third and short, but Larry Bowa made a fine play to throw him out. Leading off the third, Tommy Helms hit a hard shot toward third. Rookie John Vukovich went to his knees to backhand the ball and threw on to first. Wise himself made a fine play on Helms leading off the sixth. Tommy hit a high chopper over the mound on which Rick nimbly backed up and jumped to retrieve, then threw to first for the out.

Wise's masterpiece was filled with drama, especially in the ninth as the Cincinnati crowd stood and cheered him. The Reds' first batter that frame was Jimmy Stewart, a pesky left-handed hitting utility player. Batting for Concepcion, Stewart worked the count full and started toward first after the next pitch, but umpire Jerry Dale raised his right arm signaling the third strike. Next, another lefty, Ty Cline, fouled off three straight 2–2 pitches before bouncing toward right. First baseman Deron Johnson went for the ball, so Wise had to hustle to first. Second baseman Terry Harmon fielded it and threw to Wise who was almost past the bag, but umpire Tom Gorman signaled the second out. That brought to the plate the perennial hitting-machine Pete Rose. Pete worked the count full while fouling off two pitches, then softly lined a ball toward third which Vukovich caught cleanly.

Wise may also be remembered as the player who was later traded for Steve Carlton. Although not of Hall of Fame calibre, Wise performed admirably for 18 major-league seasons, finishing with a 188–181 lifetime log and a career 3.69 ERA.

Philadelphia Phillies	AB	R	H	I
Terry Harmon 2b	4	0	0	0
Larry Bowa ss	4	0	0	0
Tim McCarver c	3	0	2	0
Deron Johnson 1b	2	0	0	0
Joe Lis lf	2	1	0	0
Ron Stone lf7	1	0	0	0
Willie Montanez cf	4	0	1	0
Roger Freed rf	4	1	1	1
John Vukovich 3b	4	0	1	0
>Rick Wise p	4	2	2	3
	32	4	7	4

Cincinnati Reds	AB	R	H	I
>Pete Rose rf	4	0	0	0
George Foster cf	3	0	0	0
Lee May 1b	3	0	0	0
Johnny Bench c	3	0	0	0
Tony Perez 3b	3	0	0	0
Hal McRae lf	3	0	0	0
Wayne Granger p9	0	0	0	0
Tommy Helms 2b	3	0	0	0
Dave Concepcion ss	1	0	0	0
Jimmy Stewart ph9	1	0	0	0
Ross Grimsley p	1	0	0	0
Bernie Carbo ph6	1	0	0	0
Clay Carroll p7	0	0	0	0
Ty Cline lf9	1	0	0	0
	27	0	0	0

Philadelphia	IP	H	R	ER	BB	SO
Wise W,8-4	9	0	0	0	1	3

Cincinnati	IP	H	R	ER	BB	SO
Grimsley L,4-3	6	4	3	3	2	1
Carroll	2	2	1	1	1	1
Granger	1	1	0	0	0	0
	9	7	4	4	3	2

Philadelphia	0 1 0	0 2 0	0 1 0	- 4
Cincinnati	0 0 0	0 0 0	0 0 0	- 0

OB: Philadelphia 5, Cincinnati 1
DP: Helms-May-Concepcion (Montanez)
    Bench-Helms-May (Lis SO)
2B: Montanez, Freed
HR: Wise 2(4)
CS: McCarver
SO: Freed, Vukovich; Foster, May,
    Stewart
BB: McCarver, Johnson 2; Concepcion

HP: By Grimsley (Lis)
TIME: 1:53
ATTENDANCE: 19,069 (13,329 paid)
UMPIRES: Jerry Dale, Tom Gorman,
    Chris Pelekoudas, Doug Harvey
SOURCES: Cincinnati Enquirer; Phila-
    delphia Inquirer; Retrosheet

BALANCE	OUT+R+OB=BP=AB+BB+SH+HP+CI
Philadelphia	27 4 5 36 32 3 0 1 0
Cincinnati	27 0 1 28 27 1 0 0 0

A Breezy Night by the Bay

172. Teams Combine for 43 Strikeouts in 20-Inning Game; Player Strikes Out Six Times in One Game

CALIFORNIA   at   OAKLAND
(Angels, 0)   (Athletics, 1)

Saturday Night, July 9, 1971, Oakland Coliseum

Maybe the lights were weak, the balls lopsided or rubbed with darker clay. Whatever the reason, batters just couldn't seem to make contact this night as the California Angels and the Oakland Athletics *combined for 43 strikeouts, setting a new standard for offensive*

STRIKEOUTS PER INNING, JULY 9, 1971

S = swinging; C = called; B = third strike bunt attempt
Letter in parentheses following batter name is first letter of pitcher's last name

Inning	California Batters			Oakland Batters	
1	C-Conigliaro (B)				
2	S-Cowan (B)			S-Blue (M)	
3	C-May (B)				
4	S-Conigliaro (B)	S-Cowan (B)		S-Duncan (M)	C-Brown (M)
5				S-Green (M)	
6	B-May (B)	S-Berry (B)	S-Conigliaro (B)	S-Rudi (M)	
7	S-Cowan (B)	S-McMullen (B)	C-O'Brien (B)	S-Brown (M)	
8	S-Moses (B)			B-Green (M)	S-Rudi (M)
9	S-Cowan (B)			S-Duncan (M)	S-Tenace (M)
10	S-Moses (B)	C-May (B)		C-Blue (M)	
11	S-Conigliaro (B)	S-Cowan (B)			
12	S-McMullen (F)			S-Duncan (M)	S-LaRussa (M)
13					
14					
15					
16	S-Berry (F)				
17	S-Cowan (F)	S-McMullen (F)	S-Spencer (F)	S-Blefary (F)	
18	S-O'Brien (F)	S-Alomar (F)		C-Hegan (Q)	
19	B-Conigliaro (L)	S-Spencer (K)		S-Davis (Q)	
20				S-Hunter (Q)	
	S=20; C=4; B=2			S=13; C=3; B=1	

California Angels	AB	R	H	I	Oakland Athletics	AB	R	H	I
Sandy Alomar 2b	8	0	2	0	>Angel Mangual cf,rf10	8	0	3	1
Ken Berry cf	8	0	2	0	Joe Rudi lf	8	0	0	0
Tony Conigliaro rf	8	0	0	0	Reggie Jackson rf	3	0	0	0
Tommie Reynolds rf19	0	0	0	0	Blue Moon Odom pr9	0	0	0	0
Billy Cowan lf	8	0	0	0	Rick Monday cf10	4	0	0	0
Ken McMullen 3b	8	0	2	0	Tommy Davis 1b,2b15	8	0	2	0
Jim Spencer 1b	8	0	2	0	Sal Bando 3b	4	0	0	0
Syd O'Brien ss	8	0	0	0	Dave Duncan c	5	0	0	0
Jerry Moses c	4	0	1	0	Curt Blefary ph14,c	1	1	0	0
Mickey Rivers ph13	1	0	0	0	Larry Brown ss	3	0	0	0
John Stephenson c13	3	0	0	0	Gene Tenace ph9	1	0	0	0
Rudy May p	4	0	1	0	Tony LaRussa ss10	1	0	0	0
Roger Repoz ph13	0	0	0	0	Mike Epstein ph14,1b	3	0	0	0
Eddie Fisher p13	1	0	0	0	Dick Green 2b,ss15	8	0	2	0
Tony Gonzalez ph18	1	0	1	0	Vida Blue p	3	0	0	0
> Mel Queen p18	1	0	0	0	Rollie Fingers p12	2	0	0	0
	71	0	11	0	Mike Hegan ph18	1	0	0	0
					Bob Locker p19	0	0	0	0
					Darold Knowles p19	0	0	0	0
					Catfish Hunter ph20	1	0	0	0
						64	1	7	1

California	IP	H	R	ER	BB	SO
May	12	3	0	0	6	13
Fisher	5	2	0	0	2	1
Queen L,1-2	2.2	2	1	1	0	3
	19.2	7	1	1	8	17

Oakland	IP	H	R	ER	BB	SO
Blue	11	7	0	0	0	17
Fingers	7	2	0	0	1	7
Locker	.2	2	0	0	0	1
Knowles W,3-4	1.1	0	0	0	0	1
	20	11	0	0	1	26

California	0 0 0	0 0 0	0 0 0	0 0 0	0 0 0	0 0 0	0 0	- 0
Oakland	0 0 0	0 0 0	0 0 0	0 0 0	0 0 0	0 0 0	0 1	- 1

OB: California 12, Oakland 13
E: O'Brien
DP: May-O'Brien-Spencer (Jackson)
2B: Moses
SB: Alomar, Jackson, Davis
CS: Mangual, Monday
SO: Alomar, Berry 2, Conigliaro 5,
   Cowan 6, McMullen 3, Spencer 2,
   O'Brien 2, Moses 2, May 3; Davis,
   Duncan 3, Blefary, Brown 2,
   Rudi 2, Tenace, LaRussa, Green 2,
   Blue 2, Hegan, Hunter
BB: Repoz; Mangual, Jackson, Bando 4, Blefary, Blue

HP: By Queen (Blefary)
WP: Blue
TIME: 5:05
ATTENDANCE: 22,938
UMPIRES: Merlyn Anthony, George Maloney, Hank
   Soar, Larry Barnett
SOURCES: Los Angeles Times; New York Times;
   Retrosheet

BALANCE	OUT+R+OB=BP=AB+BB+SH+HP+CI
California	60 0 12 72 71 1 0 0 0
Oakland	59 1 13 73 64 8 0 1 0

impotence. True, the game was an extensive 20-inning affair, and both starters (Rudy May and Vida Blue) were adept at striking out batters, but this exhibition obliterated the previous two-team mark which had stood at a mere 36.

The Angels were the more prolific contributors, fanning no less than *26 times which remains the benchmark for most strikeouts by one club in a game of any length.* Billy Cowan, who had been a strikeout savant throughout his career, led the record onslaught with *six whiffs,* all swinging. Although he had been leading the club in batting (.328) prior to the game, Billy thus joined an ignoble group in baseball annals, as *no batter has ever struck out more times in a game.* Teammate Tony Conigliaro was the runner-up with five, although one of his was of the "called" variety. Hitting just .222, Conigliaro was so frustrated after this game that he announced his retirement from baseball. Tony had been battling a pinched nerve in his neck as well as the damaged retina incurred from a beaning several years earlier. He did, however, return four years later in an unsuccessful comeback attempt.

Each member of both starting nines fanned at least once except Oakland's Angel Mangual, Sal Bando (who walked four times), and Reggie Jackson — ironically the lifetime major-league strikeout leader.

This game was even exceptional for Billy Cowan, who struck out once every four times at-bat during his eight year career.

Someone struck out in every frame except the 13th, 14th, and 15th. Twice Blue struck out the side—in the sixth and seventh, and Oakland reliever Rollie Fingers retired the Angels on strikes in the 17th.

The frequent breezes contributed to yet another record—*the longest American League game before a run was scored—20 innings*. Nine batters (5 Angels and 4 A's) struck out with runners in scoring position before Angel Mangual broke the spell. Mangual singled with two out in the bottom of the 20th to drive home Curt Blefary who had been hit by a pitch leading off the final frame. After Mike Epstein popped out, Dick Green's single moved Blefary to second. It looked like another wasted opportunity as pinch hitter Catfish Hunter struck out for the second out before Mangual delivered the game winning blow just under the wire. The teams couldn't have played another inning this night because a league curfew law prohibited starting any inning after 12:59 A.M. The game ended at 1:05.

A Heckler's Delight

173. Teams Combine to Use 18 Pitchers, Walk 30 Batters in 20-Inning Game

WASHINGTON   at   CLEVELAND
(Senators, 8)   (Indians, 6)

Started: Tuesday Night, September 14, 1971, Municipal Stadium
Finished: Monday Night, September 20, 1971, J. F. Kennedy Stadium

From start to finish this contest took seven days, two different umpiring crews, and 48 players to complete. The game concluded more than 350 miles from where it started, and the visiting club finished the game on their home turf as the Washington Senators defeated the Cleveland Indians 8–6 in 20 innings. In the process, three new major league standards were established.

It started innocently enough on the evening of September 14 as the second half of a doubleheader in Cleveland. Two pathetic clubs, both already more than 30 games off the pace, and neither of whom one would expect any record-setting performance, struggled to avoid a basement finish. After 16 frames of a 5–5 tie, the skirmish was thwarted by a league curfew rule that forbad an inning to begin after 12:59 A.M. Because the Senators had to leave town and were not scheduled to return this season, the outcome had to be settled the following week in Washington when the two teams would next meet. Few tears were shed on the shores of Lake Erie as the night's paid attendance of 2,639 had dwindled to about 100 by curfew. A *Cleveland Press* reporter facetiously claimed that you could hear a player bend over. Everybody was on stage as fans yelled to one another and taunted the players. For those who were apparently just too tired to go home, it became a "heckler's delight."

Those first 16 innings had set a reckless pace for both pitching staffs. Cleveland had watched eight different Washington hurlers take the mound while Senator batters had faced seven Indians. Six of those 15 moundsmen had labored less than an inning and there had already been 22 free passes issued.

The game was then resumed in Washington

Catcher Dick Billings was Washington's batting hero.

the following week as a preliminary to the regularly scheduled game. As with their Cleveland brethren, Senator fans demonstrated similar enthusiasm by stampeding 1,743 through the turnstiles, the lowest total to date in the American League. Actually, that figure was the total paid attendance for the entire night. When the suspended game began at 6:30 P.M. an actual count tallied 333 persons and two clusters of relaxed vendors. *The Washington Post* reported that one woman seated in the upper deck behind home plate had plenty of room to stretch out with three empty sections on each side of her. An adjoining column in the newspaper described an upcoming owners meeting to decide the fate of the Senators. (They moved to Texas the following season.)

Each hoping to pick up an easy victory, two aging war horses faced off in the suspended game — Denny McLain for Washington and Sam McDowell for Cleveland. (McLain was also announced to pitch the regularly scheduled game.) Despite playing in Washington and wearing their home white uniforms, the Senators were nevertheless the visitors and batted first. For three additional innings, neither club could cross the plate.

Then in the top of the 20th, the Indians' defense collapsed behind McDowell.

Elliott Maddox led off for Washington by walking. Lenny Randle attempted to sacrifice him along, but Chris Chambliss tried for the force out at second and was late. Next, Toby Harrah grounded to second, but the ball squirted through Kurt Bevacqua for an error; Maddox scored and Randle went to third. Dave Nelson was credited with a single when Stanley fell down while fielding his grounder; Randle scored and Harrah took second. McLain sacrificed both runners along and Del Unser was walked intentionally, loading the bases. Tommy McCraw also walked forcing home Harrah. Steve Mingori then replaced McDowell and got Don Mincher to line into a double play. Washington had scored three times to take an 8–5 lead.

Cleveland then batted in the bottom of the 20th. Bevacqua grounded out and Stanley flied out; but Ray Fosse, Eddie Leon, and Ted Uhlaender all singled to tally one run. When Vada Pinson fanned to end the six-hour marathon, the two teams had *combined for four runs in the 20th frame, tying the major league mark for that inning.*

The final four innings produced an additional eight free passes, making a *total of 30 walks in an extra-inning game for a new major league standard.* This event, however, has yet to be included in some record books. (Detroit and Philadelphia also issued 30 walks, although in a *nine*-inning contest — see 5-09-16.)

Thanks in part to those 30 bases on balls and the 29 hits, the two clubs also stranded 42 base runners. The *25 left-on-base by Washington was another new major league mark* although it too was not recognized at the time and is still ignored by record keepers. (Presently, the Senators' 25 LOB maintains a share of only the A.L. record.)

The reckless pace of pitcher usage first established in Cleveland slowed in Washington although three additional bodies made their way to the mound. Thus, a *game total of 18 hurlers remains the major league benchmark for a single game.* It has been equalled once, in 1995.

Steve Mingori was the 18th pitcher to enter the game.

Washington Senators	AB	R	H	I
Del Unser cf,rf9	10	1	2	0
Tommy McCraw lf	8	0	0	1
>Don Mincher 1b	9	0	0	0
Dick Billings c	10	2	3	3
Bernie Allen 3b	5	0	2	0
Elliott Maddox cf9	2	1	0	0
Larry Biittner rf	4	0	1	1
Lenny Randle 2b9	4	1	0	0
Toby Harrah ss	7	1	3	0
Tim Cullen 2b	1	1	0	0
Frank Howard ph8	1	0	0	0
Dave Nelson 2b8,3b9	4	0	1	1
Pete Broberg p	2	0	1	0
Joe Grzenda p7	0	0	0	0
Horacio Pina p7	0	0	0	0
Denny Riddleberger p7	0	0	0	0
Casey Cox p7	0	0	0	0
Jeff Burroughs ph9	0	1	0	0
Paul Lindblad p9	1	0	0	0
Jim Shellenback p11	2	0	1	0
Paul Casanova ph16	0	0	0	0
Mike Thompson p16	0	0	0	0
Denny McLain p17	1	0	0	0
	71	8	14	6

Cleveland Indians	AB	R	H	I
Ted Uhlaender rf	10	1	2	1
>Vada Pinson cf	9	1	3	1
Roy Foster lf	6	1	0	0
Graig Nettles 3b	6	0	2	4
Chris Chambliss 1b	8	0	2	0
John Lowenstein 2b	3	0	0	0
Curt Bevacqua ph7,2b	5	0	1	0
Lou Camilli ss	4	0	0	0
Chuck Hinton ph10	1	0	0	0
Fred Stanley ss11	4	0	0	0
Ken Suarez c	2	0	1	0
Ray Fosse ph7,c	4	2	1	0
Steve Dunning p	2	0	0	0
Frank Baker ph7	1	1	1	0
Ed Farmer p8	1	0	0	0
Phil Hennigan p9	0	0	0	0
Ray Lamb p9	0	0	0	0
Ted Ford ph10	1	0	0	0
Steve Hargan p11	1	0	0	0
Gomer Hodge ph15	1	0	1	0
Mark Ballinger p16	0	0	0	0
Mike Paul p16	0	0	0	0
Sam McDowell p17	1	0	0	0
Steve Mingori p20	0	0	0	0
Eddie Leon ph20	1	0	1	0
	71	6	15	6

Washington	IP	H	R	ER	BB	SO
Broberg	6.1	6	3	3	3	6
Grzenda	.1	1	1	1	0	0
Pina	0	0	1	1	1	0
Riddleberger	0	1	0	0	1	0
Cox	1.1	0	0	0	0	0
Lindblad	2	1	0	0	2	1
Shellenback	5	3	0	0	2	3
Thompson	1	0	0	0	0	1
McLain W,10-20	4	3	1	1	2	3
	20	15	6	6	11	14

Cleveland	IP	H	R	ER	BB	SO
Dunning	7	5	2	2	5	3
Farmer	1	1	1	1	2	1
Hennigan	.2	4	2	2	0	1
Lamb	1.1	0	0	0	0	0
Hargan	5	3	0	0	3	1
Ballinger	.2	0	0	0	2	1
Paul	.1	0	0	0	1	0
McDowell L,12-16	3.1	1	3	2	6	2
Mingori	.2	0	0	0	0	0
	20	14	8	7	19	9

Washington	0 0 0	1 1 0	0 0 3	0 0 0	0 0 0	0 0 0	0 3	- 8
Cleveland	1 0 0	0 0 0	4 0 0	0 0 0	0 0 0	0 0 0	0 1	- 6

At the game's completion neither team had any position players available, and the Senators had only two pitchers left on their roster — Dick Bosman and Bill Gogolewski.

Cleveland disappointed the handful of Washington fans who were present for the night's finale. The Tribe prevailed 3–1, collaring McLain with his 21st defeat. The Senators got the last laugh, however, ultimately finishing in 5th place (of six), 38.5 games out. The Indians, meanwhile, plummeted to 6th, 43 games behind the division champion Orioles.

OB: Washington 25, Cleveland 17
E: Billings, McDowell
DP: Shellenback-Harrah-Mincher(Nettles)
Chambliss-Stanley (Mincher)
2B: Nettles 2, Broberg, Allen, Pinson
HR: Billings(6)
SB: Pinson 2, Nettles, Harrah 2,
Maddox
CS: McCraw, Lowenstein
SO: Unser, Mincher 2, Billings,
Biittner, Randle, Cullen, Howard,
Shellenback; Uhlaender, Pinson 3,
Foster 2, Nettles, Chambliss 2,
Camilli, Stanley 2, Suarez,
Dunning
BB: Unser(I), McCraw 3, Mincher 2,
Maddox 3, Biittner, Nelson 2(1I),
Cullen 2, Harrah 3, Burroughs, ...

BB: ... Cassanova; Pinson, Foster 3(1I),
Nettles 3, Chambliss, Fosse 3(2I)
SH: Broberg, Bevacqua, Randle, McLain
WP: Broberg 2
PB: Billings, Suarez
TIME: 6:15
ATTENDANCE: (on 7-14) 2,639
(on 7-20) 1,743
UMPIRES: (7-14) Jim Evans, Hank Soar,
Larry Barnett, George Maloney;
(7-21) Jerry Neudecker, Russ
Goetz, Dave Phillips, Larry Napp
SOURCES: Cleveland Plain Dealer,
Press; Retrosheet; Washington Post

BALANCE	OUT	+	R	+	OB	=	BP	=	AB	+	BB	+	SH	+	HP	+	CI
Washington	60		8		25		93		71		19		3		0		0
Cleveland	60		6		17		83		71		11		1		0		0

A Midsummer Night's Dream

174. Player Hits Five Home Runs, Drives in 13 Runs, Totals 22 Bases in Doubleheader

SAN DIEGO   at   ATLANTA
(Padres, 9,11)   (Braves, 0,7)

Tuesday Night, August 1, 1972, Fulton County Stadium

This night in Atlanta, the Padres' Nate Colbert had a very productive bat. As players, fans, and umpires marveled, Nate demolished Braves' pitching in both ends of a doubleheader, smashing five home runs and driving home 13, while leading his club to 9–0 and 11–7 victories. Colbert's *five home runs tied the major league doubleheader mark and his 13 RBIs established a new one.* In addition, Colbert had two singles for a *total of 22 bases and another major league doubleheader record.*

Eighteen years earlier, as an eight-year-old St. Louis fan, Colbert sat in the bleachers at Sportsman's Park and watched his boyhood idol, Stan Musial, clout five round trippers in a doubleheader (see 5-2-54). "I remember that I was in Busch Stadium the afternoon Musial hit five homers in a doubleheader," said the 6'2", 215-pound first baseman. "I never thought anyone would ever equal that record, certainly not me."[*]

Perhaps no one else ever thought of Colbert as a record breaker either, but he was a one-man gang on an otherwise pitiful San Diego club. Even before this doubleheader, Nate had more than twice the number of RBIs, and four times as many home runs as any of the other last-place Padres.

[*]Phil Collier, "Colbert Belts 5 HRs as Padres Win Pair," San Diego Union, 2 August 1972, section C, p. 7, col. 3.

FIRST GAME

San Diego Padres	AB	R	H	I
Derrel Thomas ss	5	0	1	0
Dave Roberts 3b	2	2	0	0
Larry Stahl lf	2	2	1	0
Jerry Morales lf5	2	0	0	0
Nate Colbert 1b	5	3	4	5
Cito Gaston rf	4	2	2	2
Enzo Hernandez rf7	1	0	0	0
>Garry Jestadt 2b	4	0	0	0
Johnnie Jeter cf	4	0	1	1
Joe Goddard c	3	0	0	0
Clay Kirby p	4	0	0	0
	36	9	9	8

Atlanta Braves	AB	R	H	I
Dusty Baker cf	4	0	0	0
George Stone p8	0	0	0	0
Ralph Garr lf	3	0	1	0
Oscar Brown lf8	1	0	1	0
Hank Aaron 1b	2	0	0	0
Paul Casanova c6	2	0	0	0
Earl Williams c,1b6	3	0	2	0
Mike Lum rf	3	0	0	0
Darrell Evans 3b	4	0	0	0
Felix Millan 2b	4	0	1	0
Marty Perez ss	2	0	1	0
> Larvell Blanks ss6	2	0	1	0
Ron Schueler p	0	0	0	0
Mike McQueen p3	2	0	0	0
Sonny Jackson ph7,cf	1	0	0	0
	33	0	7	0

San Diego	IP	H	R	ER	BB	SO
Kirby W,8-11	9	7	0	0	2	7

Atlanta	IP	H	R	ER	BB	SO
Schueler L,4-5	2	3	6	6	4	1
McQueen	5	6	3	3	2	4
Stone	2	0	0	0	0	1
	9	9	9	9	6	6

```
San Diego    3 0 4    0 0 0    2 0 0   - 9
Atlanta      0 0 0    0 0 0    0 0 0   - 0
```

OB: San Diego 6, Atlanta 8
E: Kirby
DP: Thomas-Jestadt-Colbert(Williams)
2B: Williams, Perez, Gaston, Blanks
3B: Jeter
HR: Colbert 2(27), Gaston(5)
SO: Roberts, Stahl, Colbert, Gaston,
     Jeter, Kirby; Baker 2, Aaron,
     Casanova, Evans, McQueen, Jackson

BB: Roberts 3, Stahl, Jestadt,
     Goddard; Williams, Lum
WP: McQueen 2
TIME: 2:32
UMPIRES: Augie Donatelli, Stan Landes,
     Satch Davidson, Bruce Froemming

BALANCE	OUT+R+OB=BP=AB+BB+SH+HP+CI
San Diego	27 9 6 42 36 6 0 0 0
Atlanta	27 0 8 35 33 2 0 0 0

This day, the 26-year-old wasted no time in his assault on the Braves.

• In the top of the first, facing right-hander Ron Schueler, Nate blasted a mammoth 430-foot drive into the left-field lower deck driving home Dave Roberts and Larry Stahl who had both walked.

• By the third frame, left-hander Mike McQueen had replaced Schueler for Atlanta. Following another walk to Roberts and Stahl's single, Colbert singled to drive home Roberts. Nate then scored on Cito Gaston's home run.

• Facing McQueen again in the seventh, Colbert led off with a prodigious 450-foot blast deep to left center for his second round tripper and fifth run batted in. That gave San Diego a 9–0 lead which is how the contest ended.

• The nightcap offered no respite for Braves pitchers. Colbert walked against starter Tom Kelley and scored in the first as the Padres jumped off to a 2–0 lead.

• Right-hander Pat Jarvis was on the hill in the second inning with the bases loaded when Colbert next appeared at the plate. Nate slashed a low liner that cleared the left-field fence for a grand slam, giving the Padres

Colbert was a three-time All-Star for the Padres.

a 7–0 lead. It scored Derrel Thomas who had walked, Roberts who had singled, and Stahl who had walked.

• By the seventh frame another right-hander, Jim Hardin, was on the mound for the Braves. With one out, Stahl singled and Colbert sent a slicing line drive over the right-field fence for two more San Diego runs. That made it 9–1.

• The Braves rallied to close the gap to 9–7 going into the ninth. There were two Padres out and Colbert was on deck when Stahl singled. Nate took advantage of his additional at bat and lined an insurance home run over the left-field fence for his final two RBIs. By this time everyone, including Colbert, was dazed. "I was shocked," said Nate. "When I went by the second base

SECOND GAME

San Diego Padres	AB	R	H	I
Derrel Thomas ss	4	1	0	0
Dave Roberts 3b	5	1	2	1
Larry Stahl lf	3	4	2	0
Nate Colbert 1b	4	4	3	8
>Cito Gaston rf	5	0	1	1
Curt Blefary c	3	0	1	0
Johnnie Jeter cf	4	0	0	0
Fred Stanley 2b	4	0	0	0
Ed Acosta p	2	1	0	0
Mike Corkins p7	1	0	0	0
Mark Schaeffer p8	0	0	0	0
Al Severinsen p9	0	0	0	0
	35	11	9	10

Atlanta Braves	AB	R	H	I
Dusty Baker cf	4	0	2	2
Ralph Garr lf	4	0	1	1
Hank Aaron 1b	5	0	1	0
Earl Williams c	3	0	0	0
Paul Casanova c?	2	0	0	0
Mike Lum rf	4	2	3	0
>Darrell Evans 3b	4	2	2	2
Felix Millan 2b	2	0	0	0
Larvell Blanks 2b?	2	1	1	0
Marty Perez ss	3	1	2	1
Tom Kelley p	0	0	0	0
Pat Jarvis p2	1	0	0	0
Sonny Jackson ph5	1	0	1	0
Jim Hardin p6	0	0	0	0
Oscar Brown ph7	1	1	1	0
Joe Hoerner p8	0	0	0	0
Gil Garrido ph8	1	0	0	0
Cecil Upshaw p9	0	0	0	0
	37	7	14	6

San Diego	IP	H	R	ER	BB	SO
Acosta W,3-5	6	9	5	5	2	3
Corkins	1.2	3	2	2	2	1
Schaeffer	.1	0	0	0	0	0
Severinsen S,1	1	2	0	0	0	0
	9	14	7	7	4	4

Atlanta	IP	H	R	ER	BB	SO
Kelley L,5-7	1.1	1	4	3	5	1
Jarvis	3.2	4	3	3	1	3
Hardin	2	2	2	2	0	1
Hoerner	1	0	0	0	0	1
Upshaw	1	2	2	2	0	0
	9	9	11	10	6	6

San Diego	2 5 0	0 0 0	2 0 2	-11
Atlanta	0 0 0	1 0 0	4 2 0	- 7

OB: San Diego 3, Atlanta 8
E: Kelley, Perez, Garr
DP: Roberts-Stanley-Colbert (Millan)
  Perez-Millan-Aaron (Stahl)
  Thomas-Stanley-Colbert (Baker)
2B: Blefary, Evans, Lum 2
HR: Colbert 3(30), Evans(15)
SO: Thomas, Jeter 2, Acosta 2, Corkins;
  Williams, Evans, Jarvis, Garrido
BB: Thomas, Stahl 2, Colbert, Blefary,
  Acosta; Baker, Lum, Evans, Perez

SF: Garr
WP: Acosta, Corkins
BK: Acosta
TIME: 2:52
ATTENDANCE: 5,784
UMPIRES: Stan Landes, Satch Davidson,
  Bruce Froemming, Augie Donatelli
SOURCES: Atlanta Constitution,
  Journal; New York Times; San Diego
  Union

BALANCE	OUT+R+OB=BP=AB+BB+SH+HP+CI
San Diego	27 11 3 41 35 6 0 0 0
Atlanta	27 7 8 42 37 4 1 0 0

umpire [Bruce Froemming] I said, 'I don't believe that,' and he looked at me and said, 'I don't believe it either'."*

Froemming and Colbert weren't the only incredulous ones. Cito Gaston, who followed Colbert in the batting order, was shocked for quite a different reason. "I'm surprised I'm not in a hospital,"† said Gaston, fully expect-

*Ron Hudspeth, "Colbert Raps McLain Theory," Atlanta Journal, 2 August, 1972, section D, p. 6, col. 2.
†Collier, "Colbert Belts 5 HRs as Padres Win Pair."

ing to have been the victim of knockdown pitches after each of Colbert's homers.

Strangely, Colbert himself never became a pitching target and Braves coach Eddie Mathews explained why. "Nate hit the homers off five different pitchers. If he had hit more than one off any single pitcher, he would have been knocked down, and I'm sure he's pro enough to realize that."*

Hank Aaron, who watched both slugfests from first base, felt Colbert was one of the strongest ballplayers in the league. "If you noticed, every home run he hit tonight he swung very easy. You don't have to swing hard to hit home runs."† Braves coach Eddie Mathews concurred. "He didn't swing hard at all. I thought sure he had cork in his bat."§

*Hudspeth, "Colbert Raps McLain Theory," p. 1.
†Ibid.
§Ibid.

During the twin bill, the Padres scored in seven different innings, and Colbert was involved each time. Nate scored in all seven of those frames, had RBIs in six, and homered in five. The brilliant spree also vaulted Colbert into the major league lead in both home runs (30) and RBIs (82).

The campaign ended for Colbert with 38 home runs and 111 RBIs, neither of which led the league, and for the Padres, who finished in last place in the NL West for the fourth straight year since their entrance into the league. This season also represented the summit of Colbert's career. After an All-Star selection in 1973, back problems dissolved his skills, and three years later he disappeared from major league diamonds.

Beckert Beaches a Dozen Mates

175. Player Leaves 12 Runners Stranded on Base in One Game

NEW YORK, NL   at   CHICAGO
(Mets, 5)   (Cubs, 18)

Saturday, September 16, 1972, Wrigley Field

It's only been within the past few years that boxscore epicures have been treated to the "lo" statistic in certain newspapers, designating the number of runners left on base or not advanced by the batter. Game totals higher than eight for individuals are rarely seen, but more than 20 years ago the Cubs' Glenn Beckert established what might well be the all-time standard in this newly recognized category of futility. In an 18–5 blowout victory which included 16 Chicago hits and 15 walks, each Cub starter reached base at least three times or drove home at least three runs — each, that is, except Beckert. Amid his

team's merrymaking, Glenn had a miserable day, being meekly retired in each of his six plate appearances. Twice he even made two outs in the same inning. In the final tally, Beckert *failed to advance 12 Cub baserunners*, nine of whom were in scoring position. His futility was imposed by five different Met hurlers.

Glenn's opportunities would leave RBI-men drooling. Twice he left the bases loaded; on two other occasions he failed with two mates aboard; another time he stranded a runner on second; and once a runner on first. It should be pointed out that although this is

Glenn Beckert was a lifetime .283 hitter.

Hendricks was walked by five different pitchers.

not yet a certified record category, it may one day be so considered. It always will be reserved for a dismal batting performance by an individual amidst an offensive festival by his teammates.

This was also a wretched day for Mets ace Tom Seaver, who failed to go the distance in his fifth straight start. The future Hall of Famer was pummeled for six hits and issued five free passes in only 2⅓ innings. Tom realized it just wasn't his day when in the third inning, after walking the bases loaded, he served an 0–2 gopher ball to opposing moundsman Burt Hooton. It was Hooton's first major league round-tripper. Perhaps the 20-mile-per-hour south wind encouraged Chicago, for their 18 runs were also the most ever scored against the Mets in their 11-year

history and the most scored in the National League thus far this year.

Chicago had at least two base runners in each of the eight frames in which they batted and a game total of 33. Thanks in part to Beckert, 15 of them were left stranded. The Cubs twice batted around, sending a game total of 57 batters to the plate, or an average of over seven per stanza. (The record is 66 over nine innings.) And, of the generous 15 total walks issued to the home club, Elrod Hendricks was the recipient of five (consecutive). Although Hendricks played only 17 of his 711 career games in the senior circuit, this one enabled him to tie the modern National League mark for walks in a nine-inning game. The major league record belongs to Jimmie Foxx with a half-dozen (see 6-16-38).

BECKERT'S DAY OF FUTILITY — SEPTEMBER 16, 1972

Inning	First	Third	Third	Fifth	Seventh	Seventh
Outs	2	0	2	1	0	2
NY Pitcher	Seaver	Seaver	Strom	Webb	Rauch	Frisella
Runner on 1st	Monday	Monday		Monday		Monday
Runner on 2nd	Santo	Santo	Monday		Monday	Fanzone
Runner on 3rd	Hickman		Santo			Bourque
Beckert's AB	Flied out to center	Fouled out to catcher	Flied out to right	Flied out to center	Fouled out to third	Hit into 5–4 force out

This game also serves as an example of the sometimes ludicrous assignment of the "save" statistic. It should be noted that Bill Bonham was liberally bequeathed a "save" by virtue of the fact that he finished the game, pitched three or more effective innings, and preserved his team's lead. Lost within baseball's encyclopedic deluge of statistics is the fact that he entered this contest in the sixth frame with his club leading 13–3.

New York Mets	AB	R	H	I
Tommie Agee cf	5	0	1	1
Ken Boswell 2b	4	0	1	1
Willie Mays 1b	4	0	1	0
Jim Beauchamp lf7	1	0	0	0
>Cleon Jones rf	4	1	0	0
John Milner lf	4	0	0	0
Danny Frisella p7	0	0	0	0
Wayne Garrett 3b	2	1	1	0
Duffy Dyer c	4	1	1	1
Bud Harrelson ss	4	1	2	1
Lute Barnes pr8,ss	0	0	0	0
Tom Seaver p	1	0	0	0
Brent Strom p3	0	0	0	0
Bill Sudakis ph5	1	1	1	0
Hank Webb p5	0	0	0	0
Ed Kranepool ph6	1	0	1	0
Bob Rauch p6	0	0	0	0
Jim Fregosi 1b7	1	0	0	0
	36	5	9	4

Chicago Cubs	AB	R	H	I
Don Kessinger ss	4	3	3	0
Dave Rosello ss5	2	1	1	3
Jose Cardenal rf	5	2	3	5
Pete LaCock pr7,rf	1	1	0	0
Billy Williams lf	6	1	1	3
> Billy North cf8	1	0	0	0
Jim Hickman 1b	3	1	1	0
Pat Bourque pr7,1b	0	0	0	0
Ron Santo 3b	3	1	1	0
Carmen Fanzone ph7,3b	0	0	0	0
Rick Monday cf	3	2	3	2
Jim Tyrone lf8	0	0	0	0
Glenn Beckert 2b	6	0	0	0
Elrod Hendricks c	1	3	0	0
Burt Hooton p	3	2	2	4
Bill Bonham p6	2	1	2	1
	40	18	16	18

New York	IP	H	R	ER	BB	SO
Seaver L,17-12	2.1	6	8	8	5	1
Strom	1.2	4	5	5	3	1
Webb	1	1	0	0	1	1
Rauch	1.2	5	5	5	5	1
Frisella	1.1	1	0	0	1	3
	8	17	18	18	15	7

Chicago	IP	H	R	ER	BB	SO
Hooton W,10-13	5.1	6	5	4	3	5
Bonham S,3	3.2	3	0	0	0	2
	9	9	5	4	3	7

New York	0 1 0	0 1 3	0 0 0	- 5
Chicago	1 3 7	2 0 0	5 0 x	-18

OB: New York 8, Chicago 15
E: Jones, Mays, Monday
2B: Kessinger, Dyer, Monday 2
HR: Williams(31), Hooton(1), Cardenal 2(17), Rosello(1)
SO: Agee, Boswell, Mays, Jones, Garrett, Seaver, Fregosi; Kessinger, LaCock, Williams 2, North, Hickman, Hooton
BB: Jones, Garrett 2; Kessinger, Hickman 3, Santo 2, Fanzone, Monday 3, Hendricks 5(2I)

SH: Hooton
SF: Cardenal, Boswell
WP: Seaver, Rauch
PB: Hendricks
TIME: 3:06
ATTENDANCE: 20,192
UMPIRES: Nick Colosi, Andy Olsen, Tom Gorman, Chris Pelekoudas
SOURCES: Chicago Sun-Times, Today, Tribune; New York Times; Retrosheet

BALANCE	OUT+R+OB=BP=AB+BB+SH+HP+CI							
New York	27	5	8	40	36	3	1	0	0
Chicago	24	18	15	57	40	15	2	0	0

Oakland Bench Emptied

176. Team Uses Ten Pinch Hitters, Six Second Basemen and 30 Players in 15-Inning Game

CHICAGO   at   OAKLAND
(White Sox, 8)   (Athletics, 7)

Tuesday Night, September 19, 1972, Alameda County Coliseum

When the Chicago White Sox visited the Oakland Athletics this night the two were engaged in a dogfight over the league lead with Oakland holding a five-game edge. Each team needed this victory, and managers Dick Williams of Oakland and Chuck Tanner of Chicago knew how to pull all the strings in order to do so. Although both starting pitchers lasted at least four innings, Williams started juggling the rest of his lineup in the second frame. And before the dramatic conclusion, Oakland had sent *ten pinch hitters,*

Rookie Jorge Orta, product of the Mexican League, hit the game-winning home run. Orta collected 1,619 hits in 16 major-league seasons.

six second basemen, and 30 players onto the diamond — all three, new major league marks that can still be found in baseball record books.

In addition, there were several two-team records set in this 15-inning game. Chicago sent four pinch hitters into the fray, giving the *two teams a total of 14 and tying the major league standard as well as setting a new one in the American League.* Tanner also dispatched two men to play second base for a *two-team mark of eight, which is not only the record for most second basemen in a contest but is also the most players to field any position in a game* (excepting pitchers). The 51 total players (since exceeded) created a bewildering box-score that was incomplete in every source cited. Only by weaving strands from each was a comprehensive account made possible.

As in many record-setting situations, ludicrous circumstances surround the event, and this game was no exception. Four of the six second basemen employed by the A's never even stepped to the plate. Dal Maxvill, Ted Kubiak, Dick Green, and Tim Cullen were each denied an offensive opportunity although collectively they handled seven fielding chances flawlessly. Gene Tenace, who spent most of his career either behind the plate or around first base, was also called upon to spend five innings playing second. Gene must have been surprised to find himself the pivot man on an Oakland double play in the tenth inning. Larry Haney, normally a catcher, was probably even more astonished when he too was recruited to man the keystone position for the only time during his 12-year career. Larry successfully avoided any defensive involvement during his stint in the top of the 15th.

As the night's struggle wore on, manager Williams tested the depths of his bench. Catfish Hunter, a good hitting pitcher, successfully appeared as a pinch hitter in the 14th when he bunt-singled for Allan "The Panamanian Express" Lewis. Lewis, employed primarily as a pinch runner for six seasons, had six hits in 29 lifetime at bats (but also 44 stolen bases).

True desperation on the part of the A's came to light in the bottom of the 15th. Having allowed the go-ahead run in the visitors' half of the frame, Oakland then placed runners on first and second with two outs. Scheduled to bat was reliever Gary Waslewski, who had gotten his last major league hit two years earlier and carried a life-time average of .045 (4 for 89). Williams needed another batter and scanned the bench for a warm body. To his chagrin all he could find was another pitcher, 19-game winner Ken Holtzman who was scheduled to pitch the following night. Holtzman was hitting just .190 at the time but his 16 base hits were 16 more than Waslewski had. So to the plate walked Holtzman to face the fire-balling rookie Goose Gossage. The results were pre-dictable — Holtzman struck out (on four fast-balls) to end the game. Later, Williams was asked why he pinch hit with a pitcher in such a crucial situation. "There are several reasons I used Holtzman," said Williams. "To begin with, he was the last player I had."*

The dramatic game was earmarked by numerous two-out, clutch hits. Chicago scored three in the first after there were two outs on RBI-singles by Mike Andrews, Ed Spiezio, and Ed Herrmann. Herrmann then homered leading off the fourth to give the Sox a 4–0 advantage.

Oakland struck back with three runs in the home half of the fifth; Joe Rudi's two-out, two-run double followed by Matty Alou's single made it 4–3.

The White Sox padded their lead to 5–3 in the top of the ninth on an 0-2 count,

Alvarado hit his final career homer in the ninth.

two-out homer by Luis Alvarado (who had been in a 1 for 35 slump). But Rudi again came through with a two-out, two-run hit, a single, in the bottom half to send it into extra innings.

Oakland wasted several golden opportuni-ties to win it in extra innings. First, in the 10th, Reggie Jackson led off with a double but died on second.

The Sox wasted a chance to take the lead in the top of the 12th. They loaded the bases with one out and their number three and four hitters next to bat. But Dick Allen bounced out on a check swing, and Carlos May popped out.

Chicago regained the lead in the top of the 13th on Alvarado's two-out, two-run single. There were no outs yet plenty of high drama when Dave Duncan tied it at 7–7 with a two-run homer in the bottom of the frame.

In the bottom of the 14th, the Athletics blew their second golden opportunity to end the fray when they loaded the bases with only one out. Power-hitting Duncan surprisingly was then ordered to squeeze bunt but missed an outside pitch, and two A's wound up on third base for the second out. Dave was then intentionally walked re-loading the bases, but Haney grounded out to first.

Finally, with one out in the top of the 15th, the Sox scored without retaliation. Jorge Orta, one of the eight second basemen in the game, hit his second career home run which proved to be the game winner. It was about 2:40 A.M., Chicago time, when the ball sailed over the right-center field fence, 390 feet from the plate. Like his teammate Alvarado before him, Orta's clout came on an 0–2 offering.

The A's got two singles with only one out in the home half of the 15th but succumbed to the 21-year-old Gossage. After fouling off six pitches, Jackson popped out to short. On four offerings, Holtzman struck out.

Chicago White Sox	AB	R	H	I
Pat Kelly rf	6	0	0	0
Jim Lyttle cf	4	1	1	0
Bud Bradford ph10,cf	2	0	0	0
Dick Allen 1b	6	0	1	0
Carlos May lf	6	1	1	0
Mike Andrews 2b	4	1	1	1
Jorge Orta 2b9	2	2	1	1
Ed Spiezio 3b	6	1	2	1
>Ed Herrmann c	7	1	3	2
Rich Morales ss	2	0	0	0
Tony Muser ph6	0	0	0	0
Rick Reichardt ph6	1	0	0	0
Luis Alvarado ss6	2	1	2	3
Tom Bradley p	2	0	0	0
Terry Forster p5	1	0	1	0
Cy Acosta p10	0	0	0	0
Walt Williams ph12	1	0	0	0
Dave Lemonds p12	0	0	0	0
Moe Drabowsky p12	1	0	0	0
Vicente Romo p13	0	0	0	0
Goose Gossage p13	0	0	0	0
	53	8	13	8

Oakland Athletics	AB	R	H	I
Bert Campaneris ss	8	2	3	0
Joe Rudi lf	7	1	4	4
Matty Alou rf,1b9	8	0	2	1
Reggie Jackson cf	8	0	1	0
Mike Epstein 1b	3	0	0	0
Allan Lewis pr8,rf	2	0	0	0
Catfish Hunter ph14	1	0	1	0
Gary Waslewski p15	0	0	0	0
> Ken Holtzman ph15	1	0	0	0
Ge. Tenace c,2b10,rf15	5	0	0	0
Sal Bando 3b	5	2	4	0
Dal Maxvill 2b	0	0	0	0
Don Mincher ph2	1	0	0	0
Ted Kubiak 2b3	0	0	0	0
Gonzalo Marquez ph5	1	1	1	0
Dick Green 2b6	0	0	0	0
Angel Mangual ph6	1	0	0	0
Tim Cullen 2b7	0	0	0	0
Dave Duncan ph9,c	3	1	1	2
Blue Moon Odom p	1	0	0	0
Mike Hegan ph5	1	0	0	0
Bob Locker p6	0	0	0	0
Darold Knowles p6	0	0	0	0
George Hendrick ph7	1	0	0	0
Rollie Fingers p8	0	0	0	0
Brant Alyea ph9	0	0	0	0
Vida Blue pr9	0	0	0	0
Dave Hamilton p10	1	0	0	0
Joe Horlen p12	1	0	0	0
Larry Haney ph14,2b	1	0	0	0
	60	7	17	7

Chicago	IP	H	R	ER	BB	SO
Bradley	4.2	5	3	3	1	3
Forster	4.2	6	2	2	2	5
Acosta	1.2	0	0	0	2	2
Lemonds	.1	0	0	0	0	1
Drabowsky	.2	1	1	1	0	0
Romo	.2	1	1	1	0	0
Gossage W,5-0	2.1	4	0	0	2	2
	15	17	7	7	7	13

Oakland	IP	H	R	ER	BB	SO
Odom	5	7	4	4	1	3
Locker	.2	2	0	0	0	0
Knowles	1.1	0	0	0	1	1
Fingers	2	2	1	1	0	3
Hamilton	2.1	0	0	0	3	1
Horlen	2.2	1	2	1	1	0
Waslewski L,0-3	1	1	1	1	0	0
	15	13	8	7	6	8

Chicago	3 0 0	1 0 0	0 0 1	0 0 0	2 0 1	– 8
Oakland	0 0 0	0 3 0	0 0 2	0 0 0	2 0 0	– 7

OB: Chicago 8, Oakland 16
E: M. Alou, Alvarado
DP: Epstein-Odom (Spiezio pop up)
        Jackson-Tenace (Reichardt fly)
        Campaneris-Cullen-Epstein(Kelly)
        Campaneris-Tenace-M.Alou (May)
2B: Rudi, Campaneris, R. Jackson
HR: Herrmann(10), Alvarado(4),
        Duncan(19), Orta(2)
SB: Campaneris, Alvarado
CS: Campaneris
SO: Kelly 2, Lyttle, Bradford,
        Allen 2, Andrews, Morales;
        Alou 3, Jackson 3, Lewis,
        Holtzman, Tenace 2, Duncan 2,
        Hamilton

BB: Bradford, Allen, May, Orta, Alvarado,
        Forster; Rudi, Epstein, Tenace,
        Bando 2(1I), Duncan(I), Alyea
SH: Spiezio, Tenace
HP: By Hamilton (Kelly)
PB: Herrmann
TIME: 4:51
ATTENDANCE: 9,594
UMPIRES: Larry Napp, Art Frantz, Merlyn
        Anthony, George Maloney
SOURCES: Chicago Daily News, Sun-Times, Today,
        Tribune; Retrosheet; San Francisco Examiner

BALANCE	OUT	+	R	+	OB	=	BP	=	AB	+	BB	+	SH	+	HP	+	CI
Chicago	45		8		8		61		53		6		1		1		0
Oakland	45		7		16		68		60		7		1		0		0

A Night to Remember

177. Teams Leave 45 Runners on Base, Record 175 At-Bats in 25-Inning Game

ST. LOUIS   at   NEW YORK
(Cardinals, 4)   (Mets, 3)

Wednesday Night, September 11, 1974, Shea Stadium

In a contest that ended the day after it began, the St. Louis Cardinals defeated the New York Mets in a titanic, 25-inning struggle, 4–3. In the process seven new major league and four new National League standards were established, and one major league mark was tied. Many of those marks remain in today's record books.

The following chart lists the multitude of records established or tied at the time of this contest. "ML" reflects a new major league record, and "NL" designates a new National League benchmark. Those that have yet to be exceeded are in bold; others indicate no record was initiated.

RECORDS SET OR TIED ON SEPTEMBER 11, 1974

Performance	One-Team Mark	Two-Team Mark
Longest Night Game (innings)		**25 – new ML**
Longest Night Game (time)		7:04 – new ML
Most Official At-Bats (team)	**89 – new NL (Mets)**	**175 – new ML**
Most Official At-Bats (individual)	**11 – tied ML – D. Schneck (Mets)**	
Most Plate Appearances (team)	**103 – new NL (Mets)**	**202 – new ML**
Most Plate Appearances (individual)	**12 – new ML – F. Millan & J. Milner (Mets)**	
Longest Errorless game, 2B (individual)	**25 inn – new ML – F. Millan (Mets) & T. Sizemore (Cards)**	
Most Runners Left on Base		**45 – new ML**
Most Players Used	26 – new NL (Cardinals)	50 – new NL

Sudol manned the plate in all three Met marathons.

McBride raced home with the game winner.

Contemporary newspapers also listed another record tied in this game which in fact was not a record in the first place. Reports claimed that the seven intentional walks bestowed upon the two clubs tied the existing major league standard. This author, however, discovered a game played 18 seasons earlier in which 11 intentional walks were issued (see 5-2-56).

Only one major league game has ever lasted more innings, that being a 26-inning occasion in 1920 (see 5-1-20). That game encompassed just three hours and 50 minutes. By comparison, this staggering affair, which ended at 3:12 A.M. Thursday morning, consumed more than seven hours.

This marathon may even have gone longer had not New York's Hank Webb, the 13th hurler in the game, made a wild throw enabling the speedy Bake McBride to score from first. McBride had led off the 25th with an innocent infield single. With the hit-and-run sign on, Bake broke for second, only too early. Webb had him picked off but threw wildly past first baseman John Milner. (It was later learned that Webb had balked, and in such a case, McBride was on his own once he

passed second base.) McBride sped around the diamond and didn't even see third base coach Vern Benson's halt signal. Because there were no outs, Benson didn't want to risk a play at the plate, but McBride sailed home and scored when Mets catcher Ron Hodges fumbled Milner's throw. That lone tally was all the Cardinals needed as the Mets then failed to cross the plate for the 20th straight inning.

Prior to McBride's heroics there was little offensive action. After each club scored single runs in the first, Cleon Jones' two-run home run in the fifth gave the Mets a 3–1 lead which they carried into the ninth. Jerry Koosman then struck out two of the first three batters and was one out away from a regulation-length victory. But Ken Reitz signaled the start of the marathon when he hammered a Cardinal two-run homer to tie it. That was all the scoring for the next 15 innings.

Each team did have multiple scoring opportunities in overtime. In both the 16th and 17th, the Cardinals had two on with only one out but failed to score. In the 20th, St. Louis got their first two batters on, and in the 24th they left the bases loaded. The Mets stranded two baserunners in the 10th, 12th, 14th, and 22nd. They also left the bases loaded in the 23rd and 24th.

Although playing more than 20 innings was a novelty for the Cardinals, for the Mets it was becoming old hat. In 1964, they battled San Francisco for 23 innings, and in 1968 they clashed with Houston for 24 frames. This night's misfortune gave them a perfect record in over-20-inning games, 0–3.

Pity this night's home plate umpire, Ed Sudol, who remembered that he also had called every pitch in the other two Mets marathons as well. "My legs feel like a couple of lead posts," said Sudol, who didn't sit down the entire time. "The players kept coming up and asking, 'How're you standing?' and I didn't know what to say, because I didn't know how I was standing."* Sudol was also the victim of at least four foul tips.

St. Louis Cardinals	AB	R	H	I
Lou Brock lf	9	0	1	0
Danny Godby lf19	2	0	0	0
Ted Sizemore 2b	10	1	1	0
Reggie Smith rf	8	0	1	0
Joe Torre 1b	9	0	2	1
Ted Simmons c	3	0	1	0
Larry Herndon pr9	0	1	0	0
Marc Hill c9	1	0	0	0
Rich Scheinblum ph13	1	0	0	0
Dick Billings c13	5	0	1	0
Bake McBride cf	10	1	4	0
Ken Reitz 3b	10	1	4	2
Mike Tyson ss	2	0	0	0
Keith Hernandez ph12	1	0	0	0
Rich Folkers p12	0	0	0	0
Jose Cruz ph14	1	0	0	0
Ray Bare p14	0	0	0	0
Claude Osteen p14	4	0	0	0
Sonny Siebert p23	1	0	0	0
Bob Forsch p	1	0	0	0
Luis Melendez ph7	1	0	0	0
Mike Garman p7	0	0	0	0
Ron Hunt ph9	1	0	0	0
Al Hrabosky p9	0	0	0	0
Jim Dwyer ph12	0	0	0	0
> Jack Heidemann ss12	6	0	3	0
	86	4	18	3

New York Mets	AB	R	H	I
Bud Harrelson ss	7	0	0	0
Ken Boswell 3b17	4	0	0	0
Felix Millan 2b	10	1	4	0
Cleon Jones lf	9	2	3	2
Hank Webb p25	0	0	0	0
Brock Pemberton ph25	1	0	1	0
>John Milner 1b	10	0	2	1
Wayne Garrett 3b,ss17	10	0	0	0
Dave Schneck cf,rf9	11	0	2	0
Benny Ayala rf	2	0	1	0
Don Hahn ph9,cf	6	0	0	0
Jim Gosger lf25	0	0	0	0
Duffy Dyer c	9	0	2	0
Bruce Boisclair pr23	0	0	0	0
Ron Hodges c24	0	0	0	0
Jerry Koosman p	2	0	0	0
Ted Martinez ph9	1	0	0	0
Harry Parker p10	0	0	0	0
Ed Kranepool ph12	1	0	0	0
Bob Miller p13	0	0	0	0
George Theodore ph13	1	0	0	0
Bob Apodaca p14	1	0	0	0
Jerry Cram p17	3	0	1	0
Rusty Staub ph24,rf25	1	0	0	0
	89	3	16	3

St. Louis	IP	H	R	ER	BB	SO
Forsch	6	5	3	2	4	3
Garman	2	0	0	0	0	2
Hrabosky	3	2	0	0	0	3
Folkers	2	3	0	0	1	2
Bare	.1	0	0	0	1	0
Osteen	9.1	4	0	0	2	5
Siebert W,8-8	2.1	2	0	0	3	1
	25	16	3	2	11	16

New York	IP	H	R	ER	BB	SO
Koosman	9	5	3	3	4	5
Parker	3	2	0	0	0	0
Miller	1	1	0	0	1	1
Apodaca	3	2	0	0	1	1
Cram	8	7	0	0	2	4
Webb L,0-1	1	1	1	0	0	1
	25	18	4	3	8	12

*Neal Russo, "Cards Shade Mets in 25 Innings," St. Louis Post-Dispatch, 12 September 1974, Sports section, p. 1, col. 5–6.

St. Louis	1 0 0	0 0 0	0 0 2	0 0 0	0 0 0	0 0 0	0 0 0	0 0 0	1	– 4
New York	1 0 0	0 2 0	0 0 0	0 0 0	0 0 0	0 0 0	0 0 0	0 0 0	0	– 3

OB: St. Louis 20, New York 25
E: Tyson, Schneck, Dyer, Osteen, Webb, Hodges
DP: Sizemore-Torre-Tyson (Koosman) Millan-Milner (Simmons liner) Garrett-Millan-Milner(Sizemore)
2B: Milner, Schneck 2
HR: Jones(13)
SB: McBride(2nd)
CS: Brock(2nd)
PK: R.Smith(2nd)
SO: Brock 3, R.Smith, Torre 2, Billings, McBride, Tyson 2, Melendez, Osteen; Jones, Milner 3, Garrett 4, Schneck 3, Ayala 2, Hahn, Apodaca, Cram
BB: Sizemore, Smith 3(2I), Simmons, Torre, Reitz(I), Tyson; Millan, Harrelson, Jones(I), Milner 2(1I), Garrett, Ayala, Hahn(I), Dyer 2, Gosger(I)

CI: Torre reached on catcher's interference by Dyer in the 20th.
SH: Koosman, Forsch, Millan, McBride, Jones
HP: By Koosman(Tyson), by Parker(Dwyer)
WP: Forsch, Koosman, Cram
PB: Simmons
BK: Webb
TIME: 7:04
ATTENDANCE: 13,460
UMPIRES: Ed Sudol, Lee Weyer, Bob Engel, Frank Pulli
SOURCES: New York Times; Retrosheet; St. Louis Globe-Democrat, Post-Dispatch

BALANCE	OUT	+	R	+	OB	=	BP	=	AB	+	BB	+	SH	+	HP	+	CI
St. Louis	75		4		20		99		86		8		2		2		1
New York	75		3		25		103		89		11		3		0		0

Relief pitchers on both teams performed superbly. St. Louis hurler Claude Osteen twirled 9⅓ scoreless innings, prompting teammate Alan Foster to question whether Claude should get credit for a shutout.

The approximately 1,000 diehards who saw this contest to its ugly conclusion witnessed five sweepings of the infield and 15 dozen balls put into play. St. Louis first baseman Joe Torre contradicted most of the other participants when he later said that this was the fastest 25-inning game he had ever played in.

Ruhle Frustrates Royals

178. Team Leaves 15 Runners on Base in Shutout Loss

KANSAS CITY at DETROIT
(Royals, 0) (Tigers, 5)

Monday Night, May 12, 1975, Tiger Stadium

Tiger rookie hurler Vern Ruhle pitched on borrowed time this night, but despite permitting 12 baserunners in 7⅓ innings, he managed to keep Kansas City from crossing the plate. Three additional Royals reached base against reliever John Hiller, marking the

fourth occasion in major league history that a team left 15 baserunners stranded while being shut out.

Ruhle was in constant peril right from the start of this wind-whipped, 40-degree night. In the first three frames alone, Kansas City

Ruhle fashioned a 67–88 lifetime log over 13 seasons.

left seven runners marooned. With two visitors on and two out in the first, the 24-year-old right-hander induced Harmon Killebrew to ground out. He did the same to George Brett with the sacks loaded in the second. In the third, the Royals got two of their first three batters on base before Vada Pinson hit into a force out, and Cookie Rojas lined out to short. Meanwhile, the Tigers scored a pair in the third on a two-out single by Willie Horton.

In the fourth, the Royals went down in order for the only time in the game. They stranded a lone runner in the fifth, sixth, and seventh, with the sixth being especially discouraging after Pinson had led off with a double.

While the Royals were being stymied, Detroit rookie Leon Roberts gave his club a commanding 5–0 lead in the home half of the sixth with a three-run home run into an empty upper deck in left.

Killebrew led off the Kansas City eighth by lining out to left. But when Pinson singled and Rojas walked, Tiger manager Ralph Houk called on his ace reliever Hiller. The rally was extinguished as Al Cowens hit into a force out and Buck Martinez fanned. The Royals had then left a dozen base runners through eight.

The drama continued into the ninth as Jim Wohlford gained life on a Gary Sutherland error and Brett doubled him to third. Hiller then struck out Hal McCrae and got John Mayberry on a tapper back to the mound. When Killebrew walked, the shutout remained in grave danger, but Hiller fanned pinch hitter Amos Otis to end the game and preserve the shutout.

The Houdini–like performance of Ruhle and Hiller ran the Royals' left-on-base total to 230 after 31 games, a number much lamented by the Kansas City press.

Kansas City Royals	AB	R	H	I
Jim Wohlford rf	4	0	0	0
George Brett 3b	5	0	1	0
Hal McRae lf	5	0	3	0
John Mayberry 1b	5	0	2	0
Harmon Killebrew dh	3	0	0	0
Marty Pattin pr9	0	0	0	0
Vada Pinson cf	4	0	2	0
> Amos Otis ph9	1	0	0	0
Cookie Rojas 2b	2	0	0	0
Freddie Patek ss	2	0	1	0
Tony Solaita ph8	0	0	0	0
Al Cowens ph8	1	0	0	0
Frank White ss8	0	0	0	0
Buck Martinez c	4	0	0	0
	36	0	9	0

Detroit Tigers	AB	R	H	I
Ron LeFlore cf	3	1	0	0
Gary Sutherland 2b	4	0	0	0
Willie Horton dh	4	0	1	2
Nate Colbert 1b	3	1	1	0
Bill Freehan c	4	1	2	0
Leon Roberts rf	3	1	1	3
>Mickey Stanley lf	4	0	1	0
Tom Veryzer ss	2	1	1	0
Aurelio Rodriguez 3b	2	0	0	0
	29	5	7	5

Kansas City	IP	H	R	ER	BB	SO
D. Leonard L,0-1	5.1	6	5	5	3	6
Steve Mingori	2.2	1	0	0	0	3
	8	7	5	5	3	9

Detroit	IP	H	R	ER	BB	SO
V. Ruhle W,2-1	7.1	8	0	0	4	0
John Hiller	1.2	1	0	0	1	3
	9	9	0	0	5	3

Kansas City	0 0 0	0 0 0	0 0 0	– 0
Detroit	0 0 2	0 0 3	0 0 x	– 5

OB: Kansas City 15, Detroit 5
E: Sutherland
2B: Colbert, Pinson, G. Brett
HR: L. Roberts(3)
CS: L. Roberts
SO: McRae, Otis, Martinez; LeFlore 3,
    Sutherland, Colbert, L. Roberts,
    Stanley, Veryzer, Rodriguez
BB: Wohlford, Killebrew 2, Rojas 2;
    LeFlore, Colbert, L. Roberts

SH: Rodriguez, Patek
HP: By Leonard (Veryzer)
TIME: 2:39
ATTENDANCE: 7,002
UMPIRES: Ron Luciano, Armando
    Rodriguez, Bill Haller, Rich Garcia
SOURCES: Detroit Free Press, News;
    Kansas City Times; New York Times;
    Retrosheet

BALANCE	OUT	+R	+OB	=BP	=AB	+BB	+SH	+HP	+CI
Kansas City	27	0	15	42	36	5	1	0	0
Detroit	24	5	5	34	29	3	1	1	0

Torre Grounds into the Record Books

179. Player Hits into Four Double Plays in One Game

HOUSTON   at   NEW YORK
(Astros, 6)   (Mets, 2)

Monday Night, July 21, 1975, Shea Stadium

Being a former MVP and batting champion doesn't insulate a ballplayer from embarrassing himself on the playing field. As each sunrise affords fresh opportunity for either celebration or mortification, yesterday's heroes sometimes fall swiftly from grace. Such was the case this day for the Mets' Joe Torre.

Three years removed from celebrity status while playing for the Cardinals, Torre had been traded to New York. Now, in this his first season as a Met, Joe etched his name in baseball annals when he became the *charter member of the National League to hit into four double plays in a single game.* Torre's humiliating achievement had been attained by only one other major leaguer — Goose Goslin (see 4-28-34). Although contemporary newspapers reported that Mike Kreevich had also accomplished the feat, later research has disproved this claim.

Torre had begun his career as a catcher and typically didn't run well. As he aged, Joe abandoned the tools of ignorance while any amount of speed he may have had abandoned him. To date in his 15-year career, Torre had stolen just 22 bases while being caught 26 times. But the 35-year-old could still sting the ball, making him a double play threat anytime there was a teammate on first with fewer than two outs.

Ken Forsch was the Houston hurler this day. Prior to the game, Forsch had analyzed the New York lineup and decided how he would pitch to Torre. "With Torre, I just felt I should throw him speed pitches. He waits real good for curves and off-speed stuff, so [catcher] Cliff Johnson and I decided it

Ken Forsch plied impeccable strategy.

Torre's career spanned 18 seasons from 1960–1977.

would be best not to give him any extra time to adjust. It seemed best to give him something with some speed but that would also break down so he would hit them on the ground."*

Forsch's strategy worked to perfection as Torre snuffed out one Met rally after another:

• Houston jumped out to a 2–0 lead in the top of the first. In the Mets half, Del Unser flied out and then Felix Millan singled. That brought Torre to the plate, and he promptly began his assault on the record book by bouncing one back to Forsch. Ken tossed to Larry Milbourne at second who in turn threw to Bob Watson for the twin killing.

• Joe next appeared at the plate in the third with Houston leading 5–1. With one out, Unser and Millan were aboard via singles. This time a grounder to short started the action — Roger Metzger to Milbourne to Watson — and killed the rally.

• When Millan led off the Mets' sixth with his third straight single, the Astros held a 6–1 advantage. But Torre again squelched the offense, sending Millan sprawling at second as he grounded to Milbourne. The play went Milbourne to Metzger to Watson.

• Trailing 6–2, the Mets launched their final rally in the eighth when both Unser and Millan singled with no outs. That brought Torre to the plate with a chance to break the league mark. Obligingly, Joe bounced another grounder to short. Metzger threw to Milbourne who threw to Watson, and 20 previous National Leaguers who had hit into three double plays were thus liberated from the halls of infamy.

Felix Millan wasn't too thrilled about the proceedings as he had singled in all four of his plate appearances but was later waived out at second on each of Torre's ground balls.

Later interviewed, Torre reflected: "It

---

*Chuck Myers, "Forsch, Howard star in Astro win," Houston Post, *22 July 1975*, p. 1D, col. 7–8.

would have been fun if we had won... I'll just tell the kids I hit four bullets," and anticipating the wrath of the New York fans Joe added, "Tom Seaver said he'd hide me in his trunk to get me out of here."*

Torre hit into 18 additional twin killings this season, but they took place in 17 other games. He also didn't attempt any stolen bases.

Houston Astros	AB	R	H	I
Wilbur Howard cf	5	2	3	1
Greg Gross rf	5	1	2	0
>Enos Cabell lf	5	0	0	2
Bob Watson 1b	4	1	1	1
Cliff Johnson c	4	0	2	0
Doug Rader 3b	4	1	1	0
Roger Metzger ss	3	0	2	2
Larry Milbourne 2b	4	1	1	0
Ken Forsch p	3	0	0	0
	37	6	12	6

New York Mets	AB	R	H	I
Del Unser cf	4	0	2	0
Felix Millan 2b	4	0	4	0
Joe Torre 3b	4	0	0	0
Rusty Staub rf	3	1	1	1
Dave Kingman lf	4	1	1	1
Ed Kranepool 1b	4	0	1	0
Jerry Grote c	4	0	2	0
>Mike Phillips ss	4	0	0	0
George Stone p	0	0	0	0
Ken Sanders p3	1	0	0	0
Jack Heidemann ph5	1	0	0	0
Hank Webb p6	0	0	0	0
John Milner ph7	1	0	0	0
Rick Baldwin p8	0	0	0	0
	34	2	11	2

Houston	IP	H	R	ER	BB	SO
Forsch W,4-7	9	11	2	2	1	2

New York	IP	H	R	ER	BB	SO
Stone L,2-2	2.2	8	5	5	0	1
Sanders	2.1	2	1	1	1	0
Webb	2	0	0	0	0	2
Baldwin	2	2	0	0	0	1
	9	12	6	6	1	4

Houston	2 1 2	1 0 0	0 0 0	- 6
New York	0 1 0	0 0 0	1 0 0	- 2

OB: Houston 6, New York 6
E: Phillips, Torre
DP: Forsch-Milbourne-Watson (Torre)
Metzger-Milbourne-Watson (Torre)
Milbourne-Metzger-Watson (Torre)
Metzger-Milbourne-Watson (Torre)
Phillips-Millan-Kranepool(Cabell)
2B: Howard
3B: Metzger
HR: Staub(12), Kingman(19)
CS: Metzger

SO: Howard, Rader, Forsch 2;
Phillips 2
BB: Metzger; Staub
SH: Forsch
TIME: 1:59
ATTENDANCE: 13,414
UMPIRES: Andy Olsen, Terry Tata, Ed
Sudol, Bill Williams
SOURCES: Houston Post; New York
Times; Retrosheet

BALANCE	OUT+R+OB=BP=AB+BB+SH+HP+CI
Houston	27 6 6 39 37 1 1 0 0
New York	27 2 6 35 34 1 0 0 0

*Joseph Durso, "Torre Hits Into 4 Double Plays," New York Times, 22 July 1975, p. 25, col. 6–7.

Rennie Nets Seven Safeties

180. Player Gets
Seven Hits in Nine-Inning Game;
Team Scores 22 Runs in Shutout Victory

PITTSBURGH   at   CHICAGO
(Pirates, 22)   (Cubs, 0)

Tuesday, September 16, 1975, Wrigley Field

You'd have to have been around when Chester Arthur was president to have seen a major league baseball debacle of more devastating proportion. That was in 1883 when Providence routed Philadelphia 28–0. But since the turn of the century, there's *never been a more lopsided shutout than the 22–0 affair* that the Pirates inflicted on the Cubs this day.

Leading Pittsburgh's 24-hit parade was Rennie Stennett, a right-handed batter playing in his fifth season of an 11-year career. Contemporary newsmen called him the best fielding second baseman of the day, but it was for his bat that he'll forever be remembered. During the course of the slaughter, the 24-year-old Panamanian accomplished something that no other player in this century had — he *collected seven hits in a nine inning game.* (Johnny Burnett, Rocky Colavito, and Cesar Gutierrez had previously harvested seven hits in extra inning ventures.) In addition, Rennie's safeties came in seven consecutive plate appearances. Only one other player in history had ever gone seven for seven in nine innings, that being Wilbert Robinson in 1892. Stennett also *tied another major league mark by twice hitting safely two times in an inning.* Only three others had done that in a game since 1900 (Max Carey, Johnny Hodapp, and Sherm Lollar).

Batting .278, Stennett led off the game against right-hander Rick Reuschel with a double to right and later scored as the Pirates batted around. Still in the first inning, Rennie

stepped to the plate for a second time now facing right-handed reliever Tom Dettore. This time he lined a single to right driving home Frank Taveras. The next Pirate grounded out to first, moving Stennett to second, where umpire Dutch Rennert turned uncanny prophet and astonishingly forecast the record assault. "I think you're going to get seven hits today," said Rennert!* (Several other cited sources conflict with this claim.) Rennie again scored on a Willie Stargell single.

In the third, again facing Dettore, Stennett

Rennie Stennett compiled a .274 lifetime average.

---

*Joe Goddard, "Bucs Bat Cubs into Infamy," Chicago Sun-Times, 17 September 1975, Sports section, p. 1.

Pittsburgh Pirates	AB	R	H	I
Rennie Stennett 2b	7	5	7	2
W. Randolph pr8,2b	0	0	0	0
Richie Hebner 3b	7	3	2	3
Al Oliver cf	4	2	1	1
Miguel Dilone cf8	1	0	0	0
Willie Stargell 1b	4	2	3	3
Bob Robertson 1b5	3	1	1	0
Dave Parker rf	4	3	2	5
Richie Zisk lf	5	2	2	1
Manny Sanguillen c	5	2	2	1
> Ken Brett p8	1	0	0	0
Ramon Hernandez p9	0	0	0	0
Frank Taveras ss	6	1	3	3
John Candelaria p	5	1	1	2
Ed Ott ph8	1	0	0	0
	53	22	24	21

Chicago Cubs	AB	R	H	I
Don Kessinger 3b	3	0	0	0
Ron Dunn 3b7	1	0	0	0
Jim Tyrone lf	4	0	0	0
Jerry Morales cf	3	0	0	0
> Pete LaCock rf7	1	0	0	0
Jose Cardenal rf	2	0	1	0
Vic Harris cf7	1	0	0	0
Andre Thornton 1b	3	0	1	0
Paul Reuschel p8	0	0	0	0
Manny Trillo 2b	2	0	0	0
Rob Sperring 2b6	1	0	0	0
George Mitterwald c	3	0	0	0
Dave Rosello ss	3	0	1	0
Rick Reuschel p	0	0	0	0
Tom Dettore p1	1	0	0	0
Oscar Zamora p5	0	0	0	0
Tim Hosley ph5	1	0	0	0
Buddy Schultz p6	0	0	0	0
Champ Summers ph8	1	0	0	0
	30	0	3	0

Pittsburgh	IP	H	R	ER	BB	SO
Candelaria W,8-5	7	3	0	0	0	5
Brett	1	0	0	0	0	2
Hernandez	1	0	0	0	0	0
	9	3	0	0	0	7

Chicago	IP	H	R	ER	BB	SO
R. Reuschel L,10-16	.1	6	8	8	2	0
Dettore	3.2	7	8	7	2	1
Zamora	1	4	2	2	0	2
Schultz	2	6	4	2	1	2
P. Reuschel	2	1	0	0	1	0
	9	24	22	19	6	5

Pittsburgh	9 0 2	1 6 2	2 0 0	-22
Chicago	0 0 0	0 0 0	0 0 0	- 0

OB: Pittsburgh 12, Chicago 3
E: Dettore, Rosello, Dunn
2B: Stennett 2
3B: Stennett
HR: Hebner(15), Parker(24)
SO: Hebner 2, Oliver, Zisk,
 Candelaria; Kessinger, Morales,
 Cardenal, Trillo, Mitterwald,
 Rosello, Dettore
BB: Oliver 2, Parker, Zisk 2,
 Sanguillen

SF: Parker
HP: By Dettore (Parker)
WP: Dettore
TIME: 2:35
ATTENDANCE: 4,932
UMPIRES: Harry Wendelstedt, Bob
 Engel, Dutch Rennert, Doug Harvey
SOURCES: Chicago Daily News, Sun-
 Times, Tribune; Pittsburgh Post-
 Gazette, Press; Retrosheet

BALANCE	OUT+R+OB=BP=AB+BB+SH+HP+CI
Pittsburgh	27 22 12 61 53 6 1 1 0
Chicago	27 0 3 30 30 0 0 0 0

----

lined a single to center and scored on Richie Hebner's home run.

Stennett led off the fifth with a line-drive double to left and scored his fourth run on Al Oliver's single. Again Pittsburgh batted around, sending Dettore to join Reuschel in the locker room. With Stennett batting for

the second time in the frame, right-hander Oscar Zamora was now on the hill. Rennie singled to right for his fifth hit of the game and his second of the inning, marking the second inning in which he had hit safely twice. He was stranded, however, as Hebner fanned for the third out.

Leading off the seventh, Stennett was facing his fourth pitcher, Buddy Schultz, the first left-hander to labor for Chicago this day. It made no difference to Stennett as he singled to center for his sixth straight hit. He later scored his fifth run on Dave Parker's single.

The Pirate second baseman batted once more in the eighth when he faced right-hander Paul Reuschel, brother of Chicago's starter Rick. With two outs and nobody on Rennie floated a soft liner to right that looked as if it may have been caught. Right fielder Champ Summers started in to attempt a difficult catch, thought better of it and stopped, the ball bounding over his head. Stennett, despite a heavily taped ankle, skirted around to third base for his seventh hit. Pirate manager Danny Murtaugh had wanted to rest Stennett earlier but, because of the streak, kept him in. With the modern record secure, amid a standing ovation, pinch runner Willie Randolph was sent in as a replacement. It seemed like the sensible move to make, but rabid statisticians may have felt differently. Before the Pirate ninth had ended, Stennett's leadoff position missed by only three more batters of making an eighth plate appearance.

Records were unfamiliar to Stennett, and he later said he wasn't aware of what the major league mark was until a fan yelled to him after the game. "When I came up in the eighth inning, I was thinking about [Bill of the Cubs] Madlock's record. I knew he has six and I wanted to break that record. That's all I knew, I don't read the record book."*

Stennett had collected his seven safeties off five different pitchers including a pair of brothers, and the Pirates had gleaned 24 team hits, the most in the NL this season. Lamentably, the 24 hits broke the season's mark of 23, previously collected from the maligned Cub staff.

The incredulity of Stennett's accomplishment was perhaps best described by Pirate coach Don Leppert. "You can't go seven for seven," Leppert said after the game. "They could have a batting practice pitcher up there against you and you just couldn't get seven straight hits."† Don's judgement was somewhat faulty. Of the 14,000+ major leaguers to date, three have gotten seven straight hits in one game.

*Bob Smith, "Blazing Bucs Enter Inferno," Pittsburgh Press, 17 September 1975, p. 65, col. 2–3.
†Tom Fitzpatrick, "Suddenly Stennett Becomes the Hero," Chicago Sun Times, 17 September 1975, p. 143.

A Formidable Foursome

181. Four Pitchers Combine to Throw No-Hitter

CALIFORNIA   at   OAKLAND
(Angels, 0)   (Athletics, 5)

Sunday, September 28, 1975, Oakland Coliseum

Throughout baseball history, there had never been a combined, complete-game no-hitter tossed by more than two teammates. In 1956, three Cincinnati Reds joined forces to flirt with the honor but eventually lost both the no-hitter and the game in extra innings. But this day, due to extenuating circumstances, no fewer than *four Oakland Athletic pitchers were engaged in a season-ending no-hitter.*

Lindblad wasn't aware of the historical significance.

and watch me some football — Mean Joe Greene and the boys."* Blue allowed the only California base runners on two walks and an error by Bert Campaneris. One of the walks was erased on a double play.

As promised, despite wirling no-hit ball for five innings, Blue was replaced in the sixth by right-hander Glenn Abbott. "I hated to go in then," said Abbott. "I was conscious of the no-hitter and just wanted to do my best. I didn't want to be the goat and be booed."† But before Glenn threw his first pitch, the Oakland fans were indeed booing, albeit at the removal of Blue.

Abbott was asked to toss only one inning before he too was relieved by Paul Lindblad. Oblivious to the possible magnitude of the situation, Lindblad later said, "I wasn't aware of the no-hitter. I was just concerned about pitching an inning and getting out of there."§ It was during Abbott's stint that the Angels came closest to breaking the no-hitter. Oakland third baseman Sal Bando fielded Jerry Remy's routine grounder cleanly but had difficulty getting the ball out of his glove. His throw barely beat Remy to first.

At this point, Dark had fully intended to start the eighth with 20-year-old Mike Norris, then quickly relieve with Rollie Fingers who needed 1⅔ scoreless innings to bring his season's ERA below 3.00. But with the no-hitter developing, Dark decided to start the inning with the veteran Fingers. Rollie had been the Oakland closer over the past five seasons.

Unlike Lindblad, Fingers was excited and well aware of the occasion. He even had some extra incentive to maintain the goose eggs.

A week earlier, the Athletics had clinched their fifth consecutive American League West championship. Manager Al Dark, who last season had also piloted the A's to the World's Championship, was now busy making preparations for the pending American League playoffs. For the past week he had been working his starters just five innings per outing and most relievers one inning, hoping to keep them sharp without overtaxing their arms. So entering this game, 21-game winner Vida Blue (who had tossed a no-hitter by himself in 1970) knew he would be pitching an abbreviated game. "I knew I was only going to go five," said the left-hander in the clubhouse. "Besides, I wanted to get in here

*Glenn Schwarz, "4-Hurler 'No-No' Caps a Fine Season for Awesome A's," San Francisco Examiner, 29 September 1975, p. 45, col. 2–4.
†Ibid.
§Ibid.

Fingers had 10 wins and 24 saves in 1975.

Holtzman, a starter, provided little encouragement as he clutched his throat in a choke sign every time Fingers glanced over to the dugout.

After the game, there was much reflection concerning Dark's pitching changes, but most agreed with his strategy. "I would have done the same thing," said California manager Dick Williams. "Alvin has to get these guys prepared for the playoffs. Vida had to get his work in, that's all. And who's to say he's going to get the no-hitter anyway? I was embarrassed and humiliated watching four pitchers do that to my club. But I can understand why they all got in."†

The A's also won the game on the strength of Reggie Jackson's two home runs. The blasts, numbers 35 and 36, enabled Jackson to share in the home run crown with Milwaukee's George Scott and provided Blue with his 22nd victory.

Dark's preparation

"The only thing that was on my mind was the $5 bet I made with Kenny [Holtzman]," said Fingers. "I bet him I would finish the no-hitter."*

proved fruitless, however. Oakland, who had won the last three World Series, this year was swept by the Red Sox in the American League playoffs.

---

*Glenn Schwarz, "4-Hurler 'No-No' caps a fine season for awesome A's," San Francisco Examiner, 29 September 1975, p. 45, col. 2–4.
†Ibid. p. 43, col. 2.

California Angels	AB	R	H	I
Jerry Remy 2b	4	0	0	0
Dave Chalk 3b	2	0	0	0
> Mickey Rivers ph9	1	0	0	0
Lee Stanton cf	3	0	0	0
John Balaz rf	3	0	0	0
Bruce Bochte 1b	3	0	0	0
Ron Jackson lf	2	0	0	0
Morris Nettles ph8,lf	1	0	0	0
Paul Dade dh	1	0	0	0
Dan Briggs ph8,dh	1	0	0	0
Bob Allietta c	3	0	0	0
Ike Hampton ss	2	0	0	0
Dave Collins ph9	1	0	0	0
	27	0	0	0

Oakland Athletics	AB	R	H	I
>Billy North cf	4	0	1	0
Claudell Washington lf	4	2	1	0
Gene Tenace c,1b7	3	1	0	0
Reggie Jackson rf	4	2	2	3
Sal Bando 3b	4	0	2	2
Billy Williams dh	4	0	0	0
Joe Rudi 1b	1	0	0	0
Jim Holt ph3,1b	1	0	0	0
Tommy Harper ph6	1	0	0	0
Ray Fosse c7	0	0	0	0
Bert Campaneris ss	3	0	1	0
Don Hopkins pr6	0	0	0	0
Ted Martinez 2b7	1	0	0	0
Phil Garner 2b	3	0	1	0
Dal Maxvill ss7	1	0	1	0
	34	5	9	5

California	IP	H	R	ER	BB	SO
Gary Ross L,0-1	5	6	3	3	1	4
Sid Monge	2	2	2	2	1	1
Joe Pactwa	1	1	0	0	1	0
	8	9	5	5	3	5

Oakland	IP	H	R	ER	BB	SO
Vida Blue W,22-11	5	0	0	0	2	2
Glenn Abbott	1	0	0	0	0	0
Paul Lindblad	1	0	0	0	0	1
Rollie Fingers	2	0	0	0	0	2
	9	0	0	0	2	5

California	0 0 0	0 0 0	0 0 0	- 0
Oakland	2 0 1	0 0 0	2 0 x	- 5

OB: California 2, Oakland 8
E: Campaneris, Hampton
DP: Bando-Garner-Rudi (Stanton)
2B: Bando
HR: Reggie Jackson 2(36)
SB: Bando, Stanton, Hopkins
SO: Balaz, Briggs, Hampton, Collins,
     Ro. Jackson; Re. Jackson, Tenace,
     Bando, Campaneris, Garner

BB: Chalk, Dade; North, Tenace, Fosse
TIME: 1:59
ATTENDANCE: 22,131
UMPIRES: Bill Kunkel, Dave Phillips,
    Lou DiMuro (only three umpires!)
SOURCES: Los Angeles Times; New York
    Times; Retrosheet; San Francisco
    Examiner

BALANCE	OUT	+R	+OB	=BP	=AB	+BB	+SH	+HP	+CI
California	27	0	2	29	27	2	0	0	0
Oakland	24	5	8	37	34	3	0	0	0

Gone with the Wind

182. Player Hits Four Consecutive Home Runs in One Game; Team Overcomes 11-Run Deficit to Win

PHILADELPHIA   at   CHICAGO
(Phillies, 18)   (Cubs, 16)

Saturday, April 17, 1976, Wrigley Field

Shortly after this game began, Phillies fans realized that nothing short of divine intervention could save their heroes from the jaws of defeat. After only two innings the Cubs led 7–1, and then it got worse. The third inning provided Chicago with five additional tallies, making it 12–1, as television sets were turned off in disgust throughout the Philadelphia area. But gradually the gods smiled on the oppressed, and nearly four hours after it had begun, Mike Schmidt and company had facilitated a Philadelphia miracle. After trailing by 11 runs, the Phillies had come back to win in the tenth, 18–16, thereby *tying the National League record for the biggest run deficit to overcome for victory*. In the process, Schmidt joined an elite group of sluggers by *belting four home runs in the game* and became the first National Leaguer of the century to connect for four *consecutive* round trippers in a game. (Bobby Lowe had accomplished the feat 1894, as had American Leaguers Lou Gehrig and Rocky Colavito.)

After the team finished second in the NL East in 1975, Philadelphia fans would be happy with nothing less than a divisional championship this season. But both the team and Schmidt got off to a slow start. The Phillies dropped their first three games, and Schmidt, the major league home run champ for the past two years, was batting just .167 with one extra-base hit and nine strikeouts. Ironically, the 26-year-old had just been dropped to sixth in the batting order. "I don't think it made any difference where I hit," said Mike afterward. "The game got out of hand so early I think it gave everybody a chance to relax."* Not only was Schmidt batting out of his normal sequence, but he also had his most productive day in the major leagues while using teammate Tony Taylor's lighter bat.

After Schmidt led off the second by flying out to deep center, Garry Maddox gave the Phillies a nominal 1–0 lead on a solo home run. The Cubs then came back with a vengeance. Both Steve Swisher and Rick Monday also took advantage of Wrigley's 20-mile-an-hour wind by homering in a seven-run retort. The 7–1 Cub advantage came at the expense of the Phillies' ace, Steve Carlton.

Chicago piled on five more runs in the third thanks to four hits, a walk, and two hit-batsmen. After only three innings it was 12–1, and three Philadelphia hurlers had already seen their ERAs grossly inflated.

The Phillies scrounged out a meager run in the fourth, but Chicago balanced the scales with one of their own on Monday's second circuit blast. (Schmidt had singled leading off the frame but was erased on a fielder's choice.)

In the fifth, Schmidt got into the act, sending his first home run of the day onto Waveland Avenue. It came off a Rick Reuschel curveball with two outs and Jay Johnstone aboard. That closed the abyss slightly to 13–4, and just as importantly, Chicago did not retaliate.

Philadelphia chipped away with three more runs in the seventh. Larry Bowa's single, Jay Johnstone's triple, Greg Luzinski's sacrifice, and Schmidt's second homer to left did the damage. Mike's solo blast on a low fastball victimized Reuschel with two outs and made it 13–7.

Right-hander Mike Garman replaced Reuschel on the mound for the Cubs to start the eighth. Garman never got out of the inning as the Phillies pounded him for four hits, a walk, and five runs, including Schmidt's third consecutive home run. This one came off another low fastball with two outs and two mates aboard. It was Mike's longest clout of the day, landing high in the center field bleachers and testing the memory of old-timers who couldn't recall the last player to reach that frontier. Darold Knowles was called upon to end the madness, which he did, temporarily. The Cubs, however, had squandered their early 11-run lead and now held a slim 13–12 margin.

The ninth brought still more pain for the Cub faithful. After Bob Boone tied it with a leadoff homer, Bobby Tolan's single, Bowa's triple, and Johnstone's squeeze bunt gave Philadelphia a 15–13 advantage. Chicago had seen their once towering lead completely wiped out and were now in jeopardy of losing.

In the bottom of the ninth the Phillies' sixth hurler of the game, Tug McGraw, was working in his second inning of relief. After the first batter flied out to right, Tug needed just two outs to salt away this colossal comeback. But the Cubs finally responded as Jerry

*Ray Kelly, "Schmidt Ties Record with 4 Homers," The Philadelphia Sunday Bulletin, *18 April 1976, Section 2, p. 1, col. 5.*

Before today, Schmidt had never hit more than two home runs in a major league game.

Morales singled, Andre Thornton doubled, and Swisher singled them both home, sending the struggle into extra innings.

Knowles started the tenth by walking the leadoff batter, Dick Allen, and the Cubs brought in Paul Reuschel (Rick's brother) to face Schmidt. Paul delivered a high, inside fastball that Schmidt lined into the center field bleachers for his fourth consecutive home run to give the Phillies a 17–15 lead. Tim McCarver then singled, Boone doubled, and Dave Cash delivered a sacrifice fly to tack

on the Phillies' 18th tally.

It took two more Philadelphia pitchers to retire the Cubs in the bottom of the tenth, but not before another Chicago run scored on a pair of doubles. Tommy Underwood allowed two-baggers by pinch hitter Mike Adams and Bill Madlock, but when the tying run came to the plate in the person of Morales, the Phillies brought on starter Jim Lonborg. In his only relief appearance of the season, Lonborg threw one pitch and got Morales on a ground ball to third, ending one of baseball history's wildest contests.

"Considering the wind, I knew it was going to be a whoop-de-do kind of a game," said Cubs manager Jim Marshall. "I did think an 11-run lead was enough, but that Mike Schmidt never stopped coming at us."* Schmidt became the tenth batter in history, eighth in this century, to club four home runs in one game.

Phillies reliever McGraw blew a victory opportunity in the ninth but gained a reprieve when his club rallied once more in the tenth. Afterward, he feigned credit for Schmidt's heroics. "Smitty never would have done it without me,"† said Tug, referring to the two runs he allowed in the ninth, sending the game into overtime and thus providing Schmidt with anther time at bat.

The Phillies' bounty of 24 hits was the most they'd harvested in a game since 1922 when they collected 26 against none other than the Cubs. Meanwhile, Chicago pounded out 19 hits of their own at the expense of eight Philadelphia hurlers.

MIKE SCHMIDT IN WRIGLEY FIELD ON APRIL 17, 1976

Inn	Outs	Runners (base)	Pitcher	Pitch	Result	Score After
2	0	None	R. Reuschel		Flied deep to center	P0—C0
4	0	None	R. Reuschel		Singled to left	P1—C12
5	2	Johnstone (3rd)	R. Reuschel	Curveball	Homered to left	P4—C13
7	2	None	R. Reuschel	Low fastball, outside strike	Solo homer to left	P7—C13
8	2	Bowa (3rd) Allen (1st)	Garman	Low fastball, outside strike	Towering homer to deep center	P12—C13
10	0	Allen (1st)	P. Reuschel	Fastball, high and inside	Line-drive homer to center	P17—C15

*Ray Kelly, "Schmidt Ties Record with 4 Homers," The Philadelphia Sunday Bulletin, *18 April 1976, Section 2, p. 3, col. 5.*
†Allen Lewis, "Schmidt Hits 4 Home Runs," The Philadelphia Inquirer, *18 April 1976, section D, p. 3, col. 1.*

Philadelphia Phillies	AB	R	H	I
Dave Cash 2b	6	1	2	2
>Larry Bowa ss	6	3	3	1
Jay Johnstone rf	5	2	4	2
Greg Luzinski lf	5	0	1	1
Ollie Brown lf9	0	0	0	0
Dick Allen 1b	5	2	1	2
Mike Schmidt 3b	6	4	5	8
Garry Maddox cf	5	2	2	1
Tug McGraw p8	0	0	0	0
Tim McCarver ph10	1	1	1	0
Tom Underwood p10	0	0	0	0
Jim Lonborg p10	0	0	0	0
Bob Boone c	6	1	3	1
Steve Carlton p	1	0	0	0
Ron Schueler p2	0	0	0	0
Gene Garber p3	0	0	0	0
Tommy Hutton ph4	0	0	0	0
Ron Reed p4	0	0	0	0
Jerry Martin ph6	1	0	0	0
Wayne Twitchell p6	0	0	0	0
Bobby Tolan ph8,cf	3	2	2	0
	50	18	24	18

Chicago Cubs	AB	R	H	I
Rick Monday cf	6	3	4	4
Jose Cardenal lf	5	1	1	0
Champ Summers lf7	0	0	0	0
George Mitterwald ph8	1	0	0	0
Joe Wallis lf9	1	0	0	0
Bill Madlock 3b	7	2	3	3
>Jerry Morales rf	5	2	1	0
Andre Thornton 1b	4	3	1	1
Manny Trillo 2b	5	0	2	3
Steve Swisher c	6	1	3	4
Dave Rosello ss	4	1	2	1
Mick Kelleher ss	2	0	1	0
Rick Reuschel p	1	2	0	0
Mike Garman p8	0	0	0	0
Darold Knowles p8	0	0	0	0
Paul Reuschel p10	0	0	0	0
Buddy Schultz p10	0	0	0	0
Mike Adams ph10	1	1	1	0
	48	16	19	16

Philadelphia	IP	H	R	ER	BB	SO
Carlton	1.2	7	7	7	2	1
Schueler	.2	3	3	3	0	0
Garber	.2	2	2	2	1	1
Reed	2	1	1	1	1	1
Twitchell	2	0	0	0	1	1
McGraw W,1-1	2	4	2	2	1	2
Underwood	.2	2	1	1	0	1
Lonborg S,1	.1	0	0	0	0	0
	10	19	16	16	6	7

Chicago	IP	H	R	ER	BB	SO
R. Reuschel	7	14	7	7	1	4
Garman	.2	4	5	5	1	1
Knowles L,1-1	1.1	3	4	4	0	0
P. Reuschel	0	3	2	2	1	0
Schultz	1	0	0	0	0	0
	10	24	18	18	3	5

Philadelphia   0 1 0   1 2 0   3 5 3   3   -18
Chicago   0 7 5   1 0 0   0 0 2   1   -16

OB: Philadelphia 8, Chicago 12
DP: Trillo-Rosello-Thornton (Allen)
    Schmidt-Cash-Allen (Swisher)
2B: Cardenal, Madlock 2, Thornton,
    Boone, Adams
3B: Johnstone, Bowa
HR: Maddox(1), Swisher(1), Boone(1),
    Monday 2(3), Schmidt 4(5),
SO: Luzinski, Allen 2, Boone,
    Carlton; Mitterwald, Madlock 2,
    Trillo, Swisher 2, Wallis
BB: Bowa, Allen, Hutton; R. Reuschel,
    Morales 2(1I), Thornton, Trillo,
    Knowles

SH: R. Reuschel, Johnstone
SF: Luzinski, Cash
HP: By Schueler (R. Reuschel), by
    Garber (Thornton), by Twitchell
    Monday
BK: Schultz
TIME: 3:42
ATTENDANCE: 28,287
UMPIRES: Andy Olsen, Satch Davidson,
    Dutch Rennert, Ed Vargo
SOURCES: Chicago Tribune; Phila-
    delphia Inquirer, Sunday Bulletin;
    Retrosheet

BALANCE	OUT+R+OB=BP=AB+BB+SH+HP+CI							
Philadelphia	30	18	8	56	50	3	3	0	0
Chicago	30	16	12	58	48	6	1	3	0

Strife Breeds a Benchmark

183. Teams Use 45 Players in Nine-Inning Game

MONTREAL	at	CHICAGO
(Expos, 10)		(Cubs, 8)

Tuesday, September 5, 1978, Wrigley Field

United they stand; divided they fall. All season long the Cubs had played in harmony under manager Herman Franks, and despite one of the weakest pitching staffs in the league, they had maneuvered themselves into the thick of the pennant race. As September dawned, however, the arms began to crumble, and so too did team morale. Chicago had been comfortably holding third place behind the Pirates and the front-running Phillies, and Windy City fans were hoping for a dash to the flag. But after two straight losses to the fourth-place Expos, the Cubs were in danger of sinking deeper into the standings.

Franks was now under intense pressure from the fans, the media, and his players to re-direct the club toward the pennant. Sniping also had begun through the newspapers between Franks and Montreal skipper Dick Williams, who implied that he had been outfoxing Franks throughout the series. Some of the Cub players thought Herman was making too many moves. One even said his strategy was bordering on panic. Strain showed in Franks' reaction when he told the

press: "Tell 'em to get someone out for a change."[*]

Off the record, players had plenty of further criticism for their skipper:

• The pitchers felt spooked — one mistake and they thought they'd be yanked from the game.

• Many of those who had gotten the Cubs to this juncture felt they were now being benched in favor of younger players.

• Lineup changes were too drastic after a loss.

• Reliable pinch hitters were being used too early in games.

• Overemphasis was placed on playing righty-lefty percentages.

Mike Vail, the seldom-used outfielder with the team's best batting average, was not afraid to speak *on* the record. "How come every team in the National League respects me but this team?"[†] he asked. Then too, Bobby Murcer, the highest-paid Cub in history, wasn't playing during the September stretch.

Most of the complaints the Cubs had of their manager were demonstrated in the third game of this Montreal series as Franks used 24 Cubs in a desperate attempt to win. His adversary, Williams, almost matched him move for move by using 21 Expos, including eight pitchers. The resulting *two-team total of 45 participants remains the most ever used in a nine-inning game.* Noteworthy is the fact that this mark was established in one day, for many such records are set in games that are continued months after they've begun,

MORNING OF SEPTEMBER 5, 1978 NATIONAL LEAGUE EAST

	W	L	GB
Philadelphia	73	63	—
Pittsburgh	72	64	1
Chicago	69	68	4.5
Montreal	65	73	9
St. Louis	60	78	14
New York	55	83	19

[*]*Joe Goddard, "Cub players say Franks is to blame,"* The Chicago Sun-Times, *6 September 1978, p. 134, col. 1–2.*
[†]*Ibid. p. 132, col. 1–2.*

thereby taking advantage of a fresh infusion of players.

The Cubs' staff was so overworked that Donnie Moore, a middle reliever, was called upon to start his first and only game of the season. Chicago gave him a 3–0 lead, but Donnie couldn't get past the fifth inning and left trailing 4–3. The Cub offense then scored five in the bottom of the fifth to give their staff another advantage, 8–4. But a tired relief corps, punctuated by an erratic Bruce Sutter, allowed Montreal to crawl back into it and eventually win 10–8. Sutter, Chicago's relief ace, had temporarily lost touch with his sinker and had allowed 15 earned runs in his last 15 innings pitched.

The National League East standings were no different a month later with Montreal finishing in fourth, looking up at Chicago, Pittsburgh, and the division champs, Philadelphia. Both Franks and Williams returned to pilot their clubs the following season, although Franks was replaced late in the campaign.

Herman Franks wasn't smiling this day as he emptied his bench in defeat.

Montreal Expos	AB	R	H	I
Dave Cash 2b	5	1	1	1
Pepe Frias 2b8	0	0	0	0
Del Unser rf	2	0	0	0
Sammy Mejias ph7,rf	2	0	0	0
Andre Dawson cf	4	1	1	0
Tony Perez 1b	5	0	1	1
Warren Cromartie lf	4	2	2	0
>Gary Carter c	5	2	3	1
Larry Parrish 3b	4	2	2	3
Chris Speier ss	4	1	1	1
Woodie Fryman p	0	0	0	0
Gerry Pirtie p2	0	0	0	0
Ed Herrmann ph3	1	0	0	0
Randy Miller p3	0	0	0	0
Ellis Valentine ph5	1	1	1	2
Bill Atkinson p5	0	0	0	0
Wayne Twitchell p5	1	0	0	0
Tommy Hutton ph8	1	0	0	0
Darold Knowles p8	0	0	0	0
Stan Bahnsen p9	0	0	0	0
Mike Garman p9	0	0	0	0
	39	10	12	9

Chicago Cubs	AB	R	H	I
Ivan DeJesus ss	2	0	0	0
Mick Kelleher ss3	0	0	0	0
Bobby Murcer ph5	1	0	0	0
Dave Roberts p6	1	0	0	0
Manny Seoane p8	0	0	0	0
Bruce Sutter p8	0	0	0	0
Willie Hernandez p9	0	0	0	0
> Bill Buckner ph9	1	0	0	0
Rodney Scott 3b,ss6	2	0	0	1
Rudy Meoli 3b8	0	0	0	0
Ed Putman ph8,3b	1	0	0	0
Larry Biittner 1b	5	0	0	0
Dave Kingman lf	5	2	3	1
Manny Trillo 2b	5	2	2	1
Gene Clines rf	4	1	1	1
Jerry White cf	3	1	2	1
Larry Cox c	2	0	1	0
Dave Rader c6	2	1	2	0
Mike Vail ph9	1	0	1	0
Donnie Moore p	1	0	0	1
Lynn McGlothen p5	0	0	0	0
Scot Thompson ph5	0	1	0	0
Mike Sember 3b6,ss8	1	0	0	0
Greg Gross ph9	0	0	0	0
	37	8	12	6

Montreal	IP	H	R	ER	BB	SO
Fryman	1	5	3	3	0	1
Pirtie	1	0	0	0	1	0
Miller	2	1	0	0	2	2
Atkinson	.1	4	4	3	0	0
Twitchell W,4-12	2.2	1	1	0	2	1
Knowles	1.2	0	0	0	1	2
Bahnsen	0	1	0	0	1	0
Garman S,11	.1	0	0	0	0	0
	9	12	8	6	7	6

Chicago	IP	H	R	ER	BB	SO
Moore	4.1	6	4	3	0	0
McGlothen	.2	0	0	0	2	0
Roberts	2	2	3	3	1	2
Seoane	0	1	1	1	0	0
Sutter L,7-7	1	3	2	2	0	1
Hernandez	1	1	0	0	0	0
	9	13	10	9	3	3

```
Montreal    0 0 0    1 3 2    0 4 0    -10
Chicago     0 3 0    0 5 0    0 0 0    - 8
```

OB: Montreal 5, Chicago 11
E: Speier 2, Cox, Unser, Perez, Scott, Trillo
DP: DeJesus-Biittner (Cromartie)
   Trillo-Sember-Biittner (Carter)
   Cash-Perez (Roberts)
2B: Carter 2, Trillo, Cromartie, Cash
HR: Valentine(22), Kingman(25),
   Parrish(15)
SB: Dawson
SO: Dawson, Speier, Twitchell; Scott, Putman,
   Biittner, Kingman, Trillo, White

BB: Unser, Dawson, Cromartie; Scott 2, White 2(1I),
   Moore, Thompson, Gross
SH: Kelleher, Clines
TIME: 3:20
ATTENDANCE: 8,145 (7,579 paid)
UMPIRES: Jerry Crawford, Doug Harvey, Andy
   Olsen, Jim Quick
SOURCES: Chicago Sun-Times, Tribune; Montreal
   Gazette; Retrosheet

BALANCE	OUT+R+OB=BP=AB+BB+SH+HP+CI
Montreal	27 10 5 42 39 3 0 0 0
Chicago	27 8 11 46 37 7 2 0 0

Who Needs the DH?

184. Teams Total 97 Bases, Drive in 45 Runs, Hit 11 Home Runs in Ten-Inning Game

PHILADELPHIA   at   CHICAGO
(Phillies, 23)   (Cubs, 22)

Thursday, May 17, 1979, Wrigley Field

Pitchers ran for cover and batters couldn't wait to get to the plate as the visiting Phillies slugged it out with the Cubs on a sunny, windy afternoon in Wrigley Field. Chicago unleashed 26 base hits and crossed the plate 22 times, yet it wasn't enough to wear the victory laurels. With "only" 24 hits (coupled with 12 walks and a few errors), Philadelphia managed to prevail, 23–22, in ten innings. In the process, the *two clubs combined for an astonishing 97 total bases,* obliterating the previous major league mark of 85 for a single game (see 7-10-32). They also *combined for the most runs batted in — 45,* another major league record that still stands. In addition, the *two teams clubbed 11 home runs to tie the existing major league standard* (which was finally surpassed in 1995).

Prior to the contest, the Phillies' Mike Schmidt stood on the field and smiled. He was gazing at the flags atop the park which were standing horizontally and pointing out

Kingman had three home runs and two chances for a fourth.

can forget the sarcasm." Mike continued, "I thought I had run the gamut of emotion in that 18–16 game against the Cubs a couple of years ago [see 4-17-76], but this one tops anything I've ever seen. It can only happen in this park."*

The Phillies jumped off to a 7–0 lead in the first on the strength of three home runs. While the team batted around, Schmidt and Bob Boone each clouted three-run shots, and pitcher Randy Lerch added a solo blast. Schmidt's homer was a towering pop up that would have come down at deep short in Veterans Stadium. This day in Wrigley, however, it blew over the left field ivy. Things looked rosy for the Phils, but the Cubs had yet to get their first at-bats.

Chicago responded in the bottom of the first by also batting around and scoring six runs of their own. Dave Kingman's three-run homer was the big blow. After just one inning, Windy City fans had seen 14 hits and 13 runs scored while Schmidt was heard joking with the Cubs' Mike Kelleher that the score of this game would resemble their uniform numbers — 20–20.

The second frame was peculiar in that there were no home runs nor runs scored. Reliever Doug Bird tossed the shutout frame

toward the seats thanks to a 17 to 20 mile-per-hour wind. Mike knew what that meant because he had hit four home runs here three years earlier. He also had hit 31 of his 204 career round-trippers against Cub pitching, 21 in the friendly confines. "Ballplayers often will say that you never can get enough runs to win in this park," said Schmidt, "but they always say it sarcastically. After today, they

Dave Nightingale, "Flags blew an early omen to Schmidt," Chicago Tribune, 18 May 1979, section 6, p. 2, col. 1.

for the Phillies while Donnie Moore, the Cubs' second hurler, held Philadelphia hitless.

Moore's good fortune left him in the third inning as thirteen Phillies stepped to the plate. Donnie was hammered for six runs in the frame and his relief, Willie Hernandez, was tagged for two. Garry Maddox led the assault with a two-run circuit clout.

The Cubs could manage only a single off Bird in their half of the third, and at 15–6, it looked like a "laugher" for the Phillies.

Philadelphia sent eight men to the plate in the fourth, scoring twice on three hits and a walk. That made it 17–6.

After being shut out for two straight innings, the Cubs responded with three runs, a two-run home run by Dave Kingman (his second of the game) and a solo shot by Steve Ontiveros. With the wind strongly blowing out, Cub fans still had hope despite a repulsive 17–9 score.

Ten more Philadelphia batters trounced that hope by adding four more runs in the top of the fifth, making it 21–9. Only two hits were needed, but four walks, an error and two sacrifice flies did the damage. At this point, Phillies shortstop Larry Bowa offered his insight. "When we got up by 12, I figured we could win it if we could hold them under two touchdowns and could block a couple of extra points."* Larry's words would come back to haunt him.

Chicago erupted in the fifth against the Phillies' star reliever, Tug McGraw. Eleven Cubs batted, Bill Buckner hit a grand slam, and Jerry Martin hit a two-run round tripper making it 21–16. The last out was recorded by Philly right-hander Ron Reed who entered the game with a 4–1 log and an 0.43 ERA, but momentum was now on the side of Chicago.

"It's funny," said McGraw later, "... When you're sitting out there in the pen and you see the way things are going, you don't exactly beg to come in the game. And yet, all the time you're saying to yourself: 'Well, I KNOW I could stop all of this foolishness.' So, what happens? I get my chance to stop it, and blowie!"†

Eastwick was the winner and the only hurler to retire the side in order.

The Phillies were held scoreless in the sixth by right-hander Bill Caudill, but the hosts continued their prodigious comeback at the expense of Reed's ERA. Kingman's third home run capped off a three-run rally, and the scoreboard read 21–19. It seemed as if Grover Alexander and Mordecai Brown would have been unable stop the torrent of run scoring. With 40 runs scored, there were still three innings left to play.

Greg Gross's triple and Boone's double nicked Caudill for a run in the seventh, making it 22–19 as fans held their breath in expectation. The visitors were running out of fresh arms, so despite the savagery imposed on Reed, he was left in. Ron recovered from his three-run sixth and held the Cubs scoreless in the seventh.

Chicago's Ray Burris returned the favor by holding Philadelphia without a tally in the top of the eighth, but the Cubs were not so kind to Reed. Five hits added three runs to the home team's total, and tied the game for

*Dave Nightingale, "22 Cub runs one too few to stop Phils," Chicago Tribune, 18 May 1979, section 6, p. 1, col. 6.
†Ibid.

the first time at 22–22. Over the last five innings, Chicago had outscored their guests by 16–7, and the momentum was overwhelmingly on their side. Also during this frame, Kingman had an opportunity to club his fourth home run but flied out to center.

The Cubs now felt confident with their star closer, Bruce Sutter, on the mound. Bruce faced just four batters in the top of the ninth as the Phillies failed to get a hit.

Conversely, with their two best relievers out of the game, the Phillies found themselves at the mercy of the highly erratic Rawly Eastwick with his 8.00 ERA. With a game of this volatility, Eastwick surprised everyone by setting the Cubs down in order for the first time of the day. The battle was now to be decided in extra innings.

Sutter continued his mastery with the first two batters in the tenth. The third batter was Schmidt who had walked four times in the game, twice intentionally. Without the benefit of hindsight, the Cubs elected to pitch to Mike. After running the count full, Sutter delivered a high, inside fastball that Schmidt rocketed into the center field bleachers, giving the Phillies a 23–22 lead.

Eastwick continued his fine relief work by again retiring the Cubs in order in the bottom of the tenth. One of those outs was a strikeout of Kingman, who was making his second attempt at a fourth home run. Shell-shocked Chicago fans sat in disbelief.

After four hours of dazzling baserunning, the participants were incredulous. "I've never seen anything like this one, not even in high school or grammar school," said Phillies pilot Danny Ozark. Veteran reliever Reed noted: "After a game like this, the first thing you do is to check to see if you have any broken bones." "That," added Bowa, "had to be one of the greatest games ever played.... We all knew it was going to be one of those kinds of days. I mean, what the heck, the Cubs had a field-goal kicker warming up on the sidelines for three innings."* Pete Rose quipped, "Hey, what's everybody so excited about? Just another one-run ball game."†

Even the losers were impressed. "What a game!" said Cub manager Herman Franks. "We got nothin' to be ashamed of, the way we kept fighting back. And they didn't give us a thing in those comebacks... we earned them."§

Philadelphia Phillies	AB	R	H	I
Bake McBride rf	8	2	3	1
Larry Bowa ss	8	4	5	1
Pete Rose 1b	7	4	3	4
Mike Schmidt 3b	4	3	2	4
>Del Unser lf	7	1	1	2
Garry Maddox cf	4	3	4	4
Greg Gross pr4,cf	2	1	1	1
Bob Boone c	4	2	3	5
Rudi Meoli 2b	5	0	1	0
Randy Lerch p	1	1	1	1
Doug Bird p1	1	1	0	0
Greg Luzinski ph5	0	0	0	0
Nino Espinosa pr5,ph	1	1	0	0
Tug McGraw p5	0	0	0	0
Ron Reed p5	0	0	0	0
Tim McCarver ph9	1	0	0	0
Rawly Eastwick p9	0	0	0	0
	53	23	24	23

Chicago Cubs	AB	R	H	I
Ivan DeJesus ss	6	4	3	1
Mike Vail rf	5	2	3	1
Ray Burris p7	0	0	0	0
Scot Thompson ph8,rf	2	1	1	0
Bill Buckner 1b	7	2	4	7
Dave Kingman lf	6	4	3	6
>Steve Ontiveros 3b	7	2	1	1
Jerry Martin cf	6	2	3	3
Bruce Sutter p9	0	0	0	0
Barry Foote c	6	1	3	1
Ted Sizemore 2b	4	2	2	1
Bill Caudill p6	0	0	0	0
Bobby Murcer ph7,rf	2	0	1	0
Dennis Lamp p	0	0	0	0
Donnie Moore p1	1	0	1	1
Willie Hernandez p3	1	0	0	0
Steve Dillard ph5,2b	1	2	1	0
Larry Biittner ph7	1	0	0	0
Kelleher 2b8	1	0	0	0
	56	22	26	22

*Dave Nightingale, "22 Cub runs one too few to stop Phils," Chicago Tribune, 18 May 1979, section 6, p. 1, col. 6.
†Jayson Stark, "Phils win on extra point, 23–22," The Philadelphia Inquirer, 18 May 1979, section C, p. 4, col. 5.
§Dave Nightingale, "22 Cub runs one too few to stop Phils," Chicago Tribune, 18 May 1979, section 6, p. 1, col. 6.

Philadelphia	IP	H	R	ER	BB	SO
Lerch	.1	5	5	5	0	0
Bird	3.2	8	4	4	0	2
McGraw	.2	4	7	4	3	1
Reed	3.1	9	6	6	0	0
Eastwick W,1-0	2	0	0	0	0	1
	10	26	22	19	3	4

Chicago	IP	H	R	ER	BB	SO
Lamp	.1	6	6	6	0	0
Moore	2	6	7	7	2	1
Hernandez	2.2	7	8	6	7	1
Caudill	1.1	2	1	1	2	3
Burris	1.2	1	0	0	0	0
Sutter L,1-1	2	2	1	1	1	1
	10	25	23	21	12	6

Philadelphia   7 0 8   2 4 0   1 0 0   1   -23
Chicago   6 0 0   3 7 3   0 3 0   0   -22

OB: Philadelphia 15, Chicago 7
E: Kingman, DeJesus, Schmidt 2
DP: Schmidt-Meoli-Rose (Kingman)
    Bowa-Rose (Biittner)
2B: Bowa 2, Martin, Maddox 2, Rose 2,
    Foote, DeJesus, Boone,
3B: Moore, Gross
HR: Schmidt 2(14), Boone(2), Lerch(1),
    Maddox(6), Buckner(4), Martin(3),
    Kingman 3(12), Ontiveros(1)
SB: Bowa, Meoli
SO: McBride 2, Unser 2, Meoli, Bird;
    DeJesus, Kingman, Ontiveros, …

SO: … Hernandez
BB: Rose, Schmidt 4(2I), Boone 2(2I), Meoli 2, Bird,
    Luzinski, Reed; DeJesus, Kingman, Dillard
SF: Unser, Gross
HP: By Hernandez (Boone)
TIME: 4:03
ATTENDANCE: 14,952
UMPIRES: regular umpires on strike; substitutes
    included Dick Cvanaugh at HP
SOURCES: Chicago Tribune; Philadel-
    phia Bulletin, Inquirer; Retrosheet

BALANCE	OUT	+R	+OB	=BP	=AB	+BB	+SH	+HP	+CI
Philadelphia	30	23	15	68	53	12	2	1	0
Chicago	30	22	7	59	56	3	0	0	0

For statistical buffs there were further interesting notes:

• The slugfest yielded the season's highest single-game totals for each club in runs, hits, home runs, RBIs, and total bases. The Cubs' second best run, hit, and total-base production output also came against Philadelphia later in the year at Chicago.

• Throughout the 1979 campaign the Cubs scored ten or more runs on a dozen occasions. Eleven of those outbursts came in Wrigley Field.

• For the Phillies, this game also represented their top single-game output for doubles, sacrifice flies, total walks, and intentional walks. Their second highest total base harvest (30) of the campaign occurred a day earlier in Chicago giving them a two-game yield of 17 walks, 40 hits, 36 runs, and 78 total bases.

A Tale of Two Cities

185–186. Player Gets a Hit for Different Teams in Different Cities on the Same Day

NEW YORK   at   CHICAGO
(Mets, 7)   (Cubs, 4)

Wednesday, August 4, 1982, Wrigley Field

New York manager George Bamberger was disgusted and fed up with the complaints of malcontent Met players. After this game with Chicago, Bamberger snapped: "I'm sick and tired of listening to these clubhouse lawyers spread their whining and moaning

around to the rest of the team. We have a
bunch of good kids here, and if anybody
doesn't want to play for the New York Mets,
all he has to do is let me know."* Apparently
one to whom he was referring was outfielder
Joel Youngblood. Bamberger proved he was
serious by dealing Youngblood to the Montreal Expos before the game even ended for a
player to be named later (Tom Gorman). The
deal was cut only minutes before Youngblood
drove home two runs with a third inning single in his last at bat with the Mets. It was the
game-winning RBI, and the Mets went on to
win 7–4.

Youngblood traveled over 700 miles to get his second hit of the day.

New York Mets	AB	R	H	I
Wally Backman 2b	5	2	3	1
Ron Gardenhire ss8	0	0	0	0
John Stearns c	4	0	1	1
Joel Youngblood cf	2	0	1	2
Mookie Wilson cf3	3	0	1	0
Mike Jorgensen 1b	5	1	1	0
George Foster lf	4	0	1	1
>Ellis Valentine rf	5	0	1	0
Hubie Brooks 3b	4	1	0	0
Bob Bailor ss	3	1	1	0
Craig Swan p	3	2	2	2
Terry Leach p7	0	0	0	0
Pete Falcone p7	1	0	0	0
	39	7	12	7

Chicago Cubs	AB	R	H	I
Bump Wills 2b	5	1	1	0
Ryne Sandberg 3b	5	1	3	1
>Bill Buckner 1b	5	0	1	1
Leon Durham rf	4	0	1	1
Keith Moreland c	4	0	0	0
Bill Campbell p8	0	0	0	0
Jay Johnstone lf	4	1	2	0
Gary Woods cf	4	0	0	0
Larry Bowa ss	4	0	2	0
Ferguson Jenkins p	1	0	1	1
Steve Henderson ph4	1	0	1	0
Mike Proly p5	0	0	0	0
Willie Hernandez p7	0	0	0	0
Junior Kennedy ph7	0	1	0	0
Jody Davis c8	1	0	0	0
	38	4	12	4

New York	IP	H	R	ER	BB	SO
Swan W,7-4	6	9	3	3	1	0
Leach	0	2	1	1	0	0
Falcone S,2	3	1	0	0	0	0
	9	12	4	4	1	0

Chicago	IP	H	R	ER	BB	SO
Jenkins L,6-13	4	7	5	5	1	5
Proly	2	4	2	2	0	2
Hernandez	1	0	0	0	0	1
Campbell	2	1	0	0	2	3
	9	12	7	7	3	11

New York	0 0 3	2 1 1	0 0 0	- 7
Chicago	0 1 0	0 0 1	2 0 0	- 4

OB: New York 8, Chicago 8
E: Jorgensen
DP: Backman-Bailor-Jorgensen(Moreland)
      Bailor-Jorgensen (Woods)
2B: Jenkins, Backman 2, Henderson, Sandberg
HR: Swan(1)
SB: Sandberg, Brooks 2, Jorgensen, Backman,
      Stearns, Bailor
SO: Backman, Youngblood, Wilson, Foster,
      Valentine 2, Brooks 2, Bailor, Swan,
      Falcone

BB: Stearns, Foster(I), Bailor,
      Kennedy
BK: Campbell
TIME: 2:44
ATTENDANCE: 12,259 (9,237 paid)
UMPIRES: Lannie Harris, Ed Montague,
      Randy Marsh, Harry Wendelstedt
SOURCES: Chicago Sun Times, Tribune;
      DBD; New York Times; Retrosheet

BALANCE	OUT+R+OB=BP=AB+BB+SH+HP+CI
New York	27 7 8 42 39 3 0 0 0
Chicago	27 4 8 39 38 1 0 0 0

*Bob Logan, "Not you, too, Bambi," Chicago Tribune, Sports section, p. 1, col. 1.

MONTREAL   at   PHILADELPHIA
(Expos, 4)   (Phillies, 5)

Wednesday Night, August 4, 1982, Veterans Stadium

Youngblood was seemingly just as pleased with the trade as was his former manager. Being informed of the transaction in the Chicago clubhouse, Joel immediately departed for Philadelphia where his new team was to meet the Phillies later that evening. His impeccable timing enabled him to pack his bags in the locker room, get a cab back to his hotel, pack his belongings there, make another trip back to Wrigley to fetch his glove which he forgot, and board a plane that was just about to depart. He ate dinner while in flight. Once in Philadelphia, a cab ride from the airport directly to Veterans Stadium completed Joel's whirlwind journey. He arrived during the third inning of the Phillies-Expos game, the same frame after which he left the contest in Chicago.

In the sixth, Youngblood entered the game as a Montreal defensive replacement, and subsequently singled in one at bat. Joel thus hit safely off two future Hall of Famers, Ferguson Jenkins in Chicago and Steve Carlton in Philadelphia. Researchers have yet to discover another major leaguer who collected hits for two different teams on the same day, *particularly in two different cities!* Cliff Heathcote and Max Flack were once traded for

Montreal Expos	AB	R	H	I
>Tim Raines lf	5	0	0	0
Jerry White rf	3	0	0	0
Joel Youngblood rf6	1	0	1	0
Andre Dawson cf	4	0	0	0
Al Oliver 1b	3	1	2	0
Gary Carter c	3	1	1	0
Tim Wallach 3b	4	2	2	4
Chris Speier ss	3	0	2	0
Doug Flynn 2b	3	0	0	0
Scott Sanderson p	1	0	0	0
Bryan Little ph7	1	0	0	0
Bryn Smith p7	0	0	0	0
Dan Norman ph9	1	0	0	0
	32	4	8	4

Philadelphia Phillies	AB	R	H	I
Bob Dernier cf	4	1	1	0
Pete Rose 1b	4	1	1	1
Gary Matthews lf	3	1	0	0
Mike Schmidt 3b	4	1	1	0
>Bo Diaz c	4	1	2	0
George Vukovich rf	2	0	1	2
Manny Trillo 2b	3	0	1	2
Ivan DeJesus ss	3	0	0	0
Steve Carlton p	3	0	0	0
	30	5	7	5

Montreal	IP	H	R	ER	BB	SO
Sanderson L,6-9	6	7	5	5	2	4
Smith	2	0	0	0	0	1
	8	7	5	5	2	5

Philadelphia	IP	H	R	ER	BB	SO
Carlton W,15-8	9	8	4	4	4	5

```
Montreal        0 0 0   3 0 0   0 1 0   - 4
Philadelphia    0 0 0   2 0 3   0 0 x   - 5
```

OB: Montreal 6, Philadelphia 3
DP: Diaz-Trillo (Wallach strikeout)
2B: Diaz, Rose
HR: Wallach 2(14)
CS: Oliver
SO: Raines, White, Dawson, Carter, Wallach; Dernier, Schmidt, Diaz, Trillo, DeJesus
BB: Oliver, Carter, Speier, Flynn; Matthews, Vukovich(I)

SH: Sanderson
TIME: 2:14
ATTENDANCE: 36,814
UMPIRES: Dick Stello, John Kibler, Fred Brocklander
SOURCES: Montreal Gazette; Philadelphia Inquirer; Retrosheet

BALANCE	OUT	+R	+OB	=BP	=AB	+BB	+SH	+HP	+CI
Montreal	27	4	6	37	32	4	1	0	0
Philadelphia	24	5	3	32	30	2	0	0	0

----

each other between games of a doubleheader (see 5-30-22), but each failed to hit safely in the opening match.

The Phillies ruined Youngblood's advent by beating the Expos for the third straight night, 5–4. Manny Trillo's clutch single in the sixth and Steve Carlton's 277th major league victory were the keys.

After his second game of the day, Youngblood was diplomatic in referring to his former employer. "There's a lot of confusion over there in New York, and it is a lot easier playing for a club in the pennant race. I wasn't playing over there, so I'm extremely happy to be with Montreal."* According to Expos manager Jim Fanning, Joel would

become the regular Montreal right fielder with Warren Cromartie being benched.

Youngblood's departure marked the beginning of a downward trend for New York. When he left, the Mets were in fifth place, 15 games out. They lost 39 of their last 58 games, sinking to the cellar and finishing 27 games behind league leading St. Louis. Montreal improved little with their acquisition as Youngblood batted only .200 (18 for 90) after hitting .257 (52 for 202) for New York. Joel played another seven seasons in the National League, mostly with San Francisco. He finished his unimpressive, 14-year career in 1989 with a lifetime batting average of .265.

*Peter Pascarelli, "Met, jet, Vet," The Philadelphia Inquirer, section C, p. 4, col. 3.

Rader's Rangers Rally in 15th

187. Team Scores 12 Runs in One Extra Inning

TEXAS   at   OAKLAND
(Rangers, 16)   (Athletics, 4)

Sunday, July 3, 1983, Oakland Coliseum

You'd have thought that Texas manager Doug Rader would have been thrilled with his team's dramatic victory over Oakland. Doug, however, was still fuming in the clubhouse after his Rangers plastered the Athletics, 16–4, with a record-setting 12 runs in the 15th inning. *It was the most runs ever scored by a major league team in an extra inning.*

The reason for the Texas skipper's displeasure was that he had been forced to watch the second half of the contest on the clubhouse television after being ejected in the seventh. In that inning, with two outs and pinch runner Dan Meyer on second, Rick Peters hit a chopper toward the hole between first and second. Ranger first baseman Pete O'Brien

fielded it and tossed to pitcher Charlie Hough covering the bag. The toss was in time, but umpire Bill Kunkel ruled that Hough missed the bag. Adding insult to injury, Meyer, who had moved to third on the play, later scored on a passed ball.

Rader's ejection carried an additional plot. It seems that the Rangers had drafted a college shortstop named Jeff Kunkel a month earlier. Jeff's father, umpire Bill, had said he would likely retire if his son ever made it to the majors. During the argument over the close call at first, Rader reminded umpire Kunkel of his promise. "I'm going to call up your kid tomorrow to get you the hell out of here,"† were among Rader's last words of this game.

†Randy Youngman, "Rngers rout A's with record inning," Dallas Times Herald, 4 July 1983, section B, p. 3, col. 2.

Jones' two doubles in the 15th tied the major league standard.

The Rangers should have won the contest in regulation. They had a 4–2 lead in the bottom of the ninth with two outs and Rickey Henderson on second. But successive singles by Wayne Gross, Carney Lansford and Bill Almon had sent the game into extra innings. Once into overtime, however, the advantage shifted to Texas as the Oakland pitching staff was in sad shape, sporting plenty of overworked arms. In 79 games this season, A's starters had completed only seven games.

Each team had scoring opportunities during the overtime, but neither could cross the plate until the 15th. Here's how the Rangers' record setting inning evolved (run number in parentheses):

• With Oakland's Dave Beard toiling in relief for the second consecutive night, Bucky Dent led off with a walk.

• Buddy Bell lined a single to left.

• Larry Parrish bounced out to the pitcher, advancing both runners.

• George Wright was walked intentionally to load the bases and create a force play at any corner.

• Bobby Jones, a 33-year-old journeyman

minor leaguer, had joined the club eight days earlier when both Ranger left fielders, Billy Sample and Bill Stein, had become hobbled with injuries. It was Jones' first start of the year in the field, having been primarily a DH at Oklahoma City. Nevertheless, Bobby cracked out his fourth hit of the game — a double over the right fielder's head, scoring Dent (1) and Bell (2).

• A wild pitch by Beard enabled Wright (3) to score and Jones to advance to third before Bobby Johnson walked.

• Beard was relieved by Ben Callahan, but it was like pouring gasoline on a fire. Callahan, who had been pounded for seven earned runs in 1⅓ innings on Friday night, was promptly greeted by a Larry Biittner single. That scored Jones (4) as Johnson moved to second.

• Jim Anderson walked, loading the bases again.

• Mickey Rivers hit a routine grounder toward Davey Lopes, but the second baseman threw wildly toward the keystone sack. Biittner (5) and Johnson (6) scored, Anderson moved to third, and Rivers was safe at first on a fielder's choice.

• Batting for the second time in the frame, Dent singled to right, scoring Anderson (7) as Rivers took third.

• Bell singled for the second time in the inning, this one to right-center, driving home Rivers (8) and moving Dent to second. At this point, there was little reason to relieve Callahan. The contest was virtually over, and the A's staff had little left to offer — Chris Codiroli, Tom Bergmeier, and Beard all having hurled in successive games. Even mop-up reliever, utility-man Wayne Gross was unavailable, having left the game for a pinch-runner in the tenth.

• Both runners scored (9 & 10) when Parrish doubled to right-center. Larry's hit marked the ninth consecutive Ranger to reach base.

• The second out came as Wright flied out to left.

• Jones, who had spent 1979 and 1980 playing in Japan, connected for his second double of the frame. This one was hit to right-center and it drove home Parrish (11).

Texas Rangers	AB	R	H	I
Mickey Rivers dh	8	2	2	1
Bucky Dent ss	6	2	2	1
Buddy Bell 3b	6	3	3	3
Larry Parrish rf	8	2	2	3
George Wright cf	7	2	3	0
Bob. Jones lf,1b12,lf14	8	2	5	4
Pete O'Brien 1b	4	0	0	0
Bill Stein ph12	1	0	1	0
Wa. Tolleson pr12,2b	1	0	0	0
Bobby Johnson c14	1	1	1	1
Jim Sundberg c	5	0	1	0
> Lar. Biittner ph14,1b	2	1	1	1
Jim Anderson 2b, lf12,2b14	6	1	0	0
	63	16	21	14

Oakland Athletics	AB	R	H	I
>Rickey Henderson lf	7	1	3	0
Rickey Peters cf	7	0	1	0
Davey Lopes 2b	5	0	1	0
Wayne Gross 1b	5	0	1	1
T. Phillips pr9,ss10	2	1	1	0
Carney Lansford 3b	6	1	2	1
Bill Almon ss,rf10	6	0	3	1
Garry Hancock rf,1b10	7	0	0	0
Mitchell Page dh	3	0	2	0
Jeff Burroughs dh10	3	0	0	0
Bob Kearney c	2	0	0	0
Mike Davis ph7	1	0	0	0
Dan Meyer pr7	0	1	0	0
Mike Heath c8	4	0	0	0
	58	4	14	3

Texas	IP	H	R	ER	BB	SO
Charlie Hough	7.2	7	2	1	6	1
Dave Schmidt	1.1	4	2	2	0	3
Jon Matlack	2.1	2	0	0	0	0
Odell Jones W,3-3	3.2	1	0	0	0	6
	15	14	4	3	6	10

Oakland	IP	H	R	ER	BB	SO
Jeff Jones	6.1	5	2	2	0	3
Steve Baker	1.2	3	2	0	0	1
Chris Codiroli	3	2	0	0	0	1
Tom Bergmeier	1.1	1	0	0	1	0
Dave Beard L,2-1	2	4	5	5	5	1
Ben Callahan	.2	6	7	4	1	0
	15	21	16	11	7	6

Texas	0 0 0	2 0 0	0 1 1
Oakland	0 0 0	0 0 0	1 1 2

	0 0 0	0 0 12	-16
	0 0 0	0 0 0	- 4

OB: Texas 10, Oakland 15

E: Bell, O'Brien, Heath, Henderson, Lopes

DP: Anderson-O'Brien (Gross-batter; base runner Lopes interfered with Anderson)
Lansford-Lopes-Gross(Sundberg)
Bergmeier-Almon-Hancock(Sundberg)
Lansford-Lopes-Hancock(Parrish)

2B: B.Jones 3, Parrish

3B: Wright

HR: Bell(10), Parrish(13), Lansford(4)

SB: Henderson 4(39)

CS: Lansford 2

SO: Dent, Bell, Parrish, B. Jones, O'Brien, Tolleson; Peters 2, Lopes, Phillips, Lansford, Page 2, Heath 3

BB: Dent 2, Bell, Wright(I), Johnson, Biittner(I), Anderson; Henderson, Lopes 2, Lansford, Almon, Page

SF: Bell

WP: Hough, Beard

PB: Sundberg

TIME: 5:19

ATTENDANCE: 20,697

UMPIRES: George Maloney, Bill Kunkel, John Shulock, Derryl Cousins

SOURCES: Dallas Morning News, Times Herald; Oakland Tribune; Retrosheet; San Francisco Chronicle, Examiner

---

BALANCE	OUT+R+OB=BP=AB+BB+SH+HP+CI
Texas	45 16 10 71 63 7 1 0 0
Oakland	45 4 15 64 58 6 0 0 0

Jones' two doubles tied the major league standard by one player in an inning (held by many). The smash also marked the left-hander's fifth hit of the game. For the balance of the season, Bobby collected only nine hits in 61 at-bats.

• Johnson singled to right, scoring Jones (12).

• Biittner terminated the carnage by flying out to left.

Sixteen batters had appeared at the plate, scoring twelve runs on eight hits, four walks, and one error, leaving one left on base. The dozen tallies sent to the baseball dustbin the existing extra-inning mark of 11 first established by the 1928 Yankees.

In the bottom of the 15th, the dazed Athletics submitted meekly as Jeff Burroughs and Mike Heath fanned followed by Rickey Henderson's fly out. It marked the Ranger's seventh consecutive victory over Oakland this year.

With roster limits at 25, each club had strained the limits of its bench. Of the non-pitchers, only Marshall Brant (Oakland) and Billy Sample (Texas) failed to see action.

Sakata Snares Three Jays

188. Three Runners Caught Off Base in One Inning

TORONTO   at   BALTIMORE
(Blue Jays, 4)   (Orioles, 7)

Wednesday Night, August 24, 1983, Memorial Stadium

You won't find the name of Baltimore's Lenn Sakata among baseball record holders, yet it was his mere presence in this game that enabled the Orioles to establish a unique standard, albeit an unofficial one. Stationed behind the plate, the 29-year-old Hawaiian unwittingly became an integral part of a bizarre tenth inning in which *three Toronto Blue Jays were trapped off first base, marking the first such occasion in the twentieth century.* One of the three was eventually tagged out during a rundown and was thus "caught stealing," but the other two were picked off while diving back toward first. Modern record books list only one other game in which three base runners where retired in the same frame without a batted ball being involved. In that contest, all three runners were thrown out by Detroit catcher Les Nunamaker (see 8-03-14).

Embroiled in an extremely tight pennant race, Baltimore held second place only a half-game behind Milwaukee, while Toronto was tied for third, 1.5 games out. The two teams battled for eight frames with Toronto right-hander Jim Clancy holding the upper hand. While the Blue Jays had pushed over three

tallies on eight hits, Baltimore could muster just one run on only two hits. Clancy was still in control in the ninth as he retired two of the first three Orioles. But a walk to the light-hitting Sakata signaled relief help from lefty Dave Geisel. With the game on the line, Baltimore manager Joe Altobelli countered with right-handed Benny Ayala to pinch hit for his second and last catcher, Joe Nolan. Ayala came through with a single as did the next hitter, Al Bumbry. That tied the score at 3-3 but left Altobelli with no backstop for the tenth inning. "I wasn't thinking of a base hit by Ayala," said Altobelli. "I was thinking of a three-run homer."[*]

The Baltimore pilot was then forced to engage in some very creative positioning of his players. Sakata went behind the plate for the first time since he was a nine-year-old Little Leaguer. Gary Roenicke made his inaugural major league appearance at third, and John Lowenstein shifted to second base for the first time in eight seasons. The *Baltimore Sun* suggested the boxscore would have looked more appropriate in Mad magazine.

Tim Stoddard opened the tenth on the mound for the Orioles but ran into immedi-

---

[*]Ray Parrillo, *"Sakata's HR lifts Birds over Jays in 10th,"* Baltimore Sun, *25 August 1983, section C, p. 2, col. 1.*

Martinez failed to retire a batter yet won the game.

Sakata became the catcher of Toronto thieves.

ate trouble. All of Baltimore's desperate shifting seemed moot as Cliff Johnson homered to left center, pushing Toronto back into the lead, 4-3. When the next batter, Barry Bonnell, singled, Altobelli yanked Stoddard and sent in his ace reliever, Tippy Martinez.

Eyeing Sakata behind the plate, Bonnell couldn't wait for the next pitch so he could add an easy steal to his day's numbers. But Martinez anticipated the same, threw over to first, and caught Bonnell leaning the wrong way. Barry was caught in a rundown as he headed for second and was assessed a "caught stealing."

Martinez then walked pinch-hitter Dave Collins but picked him off. Collins felt certain that Martinez was guilty of balking. "You can't even get off the base if they [the umpires] are gonna give him that move," Collins complained. "He'd opened his body up; he was going to the plate."*

The next Toronto batter was Willie Upshaw who beat out an infield single.

Willie was also looking to steal but met the same fate as Collins. "No way he was coming to first," said Upshaw. "I read lefties real good, but I didn't even move."† Thus the top of the tenth ended as Martinez got three outs without retiring a single batter. Oriole pitching coach Ray Miller later explained that the reason Martinez threw over to first so often during the inning was because first baseman Eddie Murray was the only recognizable Oriole in the infield.

Right-hander Joey McGlaughlin had the responsibility of protecting Toronto's one-run lead in the bottom of the tenth, but Cal Ripken celebrated his own 23rd birthday with a leadoff home run. That knotted it again at 4–4. Murray then walked on four pitches and moved to second as Lowenstein grounded out to first. After John Shelby was intentionally passed, Toronto brought on reliever Randy Moffitt. Moffitt was tough on right-handed batters and he overpowered Roenicke with a strikeout. Next up was the weak-hitting

Sakata, but the first-time catcher lined a 1–1 pitch to left that strained to enter the seats in fair territory, giving Baltimore a 7–4 victory, and ending a classic of improbability.

First the defensive catalyst and then the offensive hero, Sakata was thankful after the game. "…I'm glad I didn't have to throw [out baserunners] 'cause I didn't want to give away my secret weapon — the one-hop throw to second."* Sakata never again donned the tools of ignorance in a major league game.

Toronto Blue Jays	AB	R	H	I
Damaso Garcia 2b	5	0	0	0
Lloyd Moseby cf	4	2	2	0
Garth Iorg 3b	4	0	2	1
Cliff Johnson dh	4	1	1	1
Barry Bonnell lf	5	1	2	0
Jesse Barfield rf	4	0	2	0
Dave Collins ph10,rf	0	0	0	0
>Willie Upshaw 1b	5	0	2	0
Buck Martinez c	3	0	0	1
Alfredo Griffin ss	4	0	0	0
	38	4	11	3

Baltimore Orioles	AB	R	H	I
Al Bumbry cf	4	0	1	2
Dan Ford rf	5	0	0	0
Cal Ripken ss	5	1	1	1
Eddie Murray 1b	3	1	0	0
John Lowenstein lf,2b10	5	0	0	0
Ken Singleton dh	1	0	1	0
John Shelby dh8	1	2	1	0
Rich Dauer 2b,3b8	2	0	0	0
Gary Roenicke ph9,3b	2	0	0	0
Todd Cruz 3b	2	1	1	0
Jim Dwyer ph7	0	0	0	0
> Lenn Sakata 2b8,c10	1	2	1	3
Rick Dempsey c	2	0	0	0
Joe Nolan ph7,c	1	0	0	0
Benny Ayala ph9,lf	1	0	1	1
	35	7	7	7

Toronto	IP	H	R	ER	BB	SO
Jim Clancy	8.2	3	3	3	6	2
Dave Geisel	0	2	0	0	0	0
McLaughlin L,7-3	.2	1	3	3	2	1
Randy Moffitt	.1	1	1	1	0	1
	†9.2	7	7	7	8	4

Baltimore	IP	H	R	ER	BB	SO
Scott McGregor	9	8	3	2	2	2
Tim Stoddard	0	2	1	1	0	0
Tip Martinez W,7-3	1	1	0	0	1	0
	10	11	4	3	3	2

Toronto   0 0 1   0 1 0   0 1 0   1   - 4
Baltimore   0 0 1   0 0 0   0 0 2   4   - 7

† *Two outs when winning run scored*

OB: Toronto 9, Baltimore 8
E: T. Cruz 2
2B: T. Cruz
3B: Moseby
HR: Johnson(20), Ripken(18), Sakata(2)
SB: Upshaw(9)
CS: Bonnell
PK: Collins, Upshaw
SO: Bonnell, Griffin; Ford 2, Roenicke 2

BB: Moseby, Johnson, Collins; Murray 2, Singleton 2, Shelby(I) Dauer, Dwyer, Sakata
SF: Iorg, Bumbry, B.Martinez
TIME: 2:54
ATTENDANCE: 25,882
UMPIRES: Russ Goetz, Larry McCoy, Marty Springstead, Durwood Merrill
SOURCES: Baltimore Sun; Globe and Mail (Canada's national newspaper); Retrosheet; Toronto Star; Washington Post

BALANCE	OUT	+R	+OB	=BP	=AB	+BB	+SH	+HP	+CI
Toronto	30	4	9	43	38	3	2	0	0
Baltimore	29	7	8	44	35	8	1	0	0

*Allan Ryan, "Orioles' extra effort beats Jays," Toronto Star, 25 August 1983, section E, p. 1, col. 5.

Search for a Stopper

189. Team Uses Six Pitchers in One Inning

CLEVELAND   at   OAKLAND
(Indians, 13)   (Athletics, 6)

Saturday, September 3, 1983, Oakland Coliseum

Although Oakland didn't hit many home runs this season, they did lead the major leagues in stolen bases; and in the seven-team AL Western Division, only Kansas City had a higher team batting average. It wasn't their offense that had been keeping the Athletics in second place, 11.5 games behind the White Sox, but rather a feeble pitching staff. Only Minnesota and Cleveland absorbed a higher team ERA, and California and Cleveland were the only clubs whose top closer had fewer saves than Oakland's ace, Dave Beard. Despite an innocuous 5–5 log and a team-leading 10 saves, Beard labored under a corpulent 5.37 ERA, not exactly what a manager might look for in a critical situation. The Athletics' team weakness was never more pronounced than in this game when a *record-setting six pitchers hazarded the mound in one inning* while attempting to save a much needed win — and all failed.

Oakland's competition this day was the lowly Cleveland Indians. Last in the AL East, the Tribe also brought up the rear in team batting average, home runs, runs scored and RBIs. It wasn't expected to be a high scoring contest, but the Oakland staff made it such.

Cleveland was first to break into the scoring column on Toby Harrah's bad-hop single in the third inning. Oakland countered with four unearned runs in the fourth on a Dwayne Murphy grand slam (15 rows deep into the center field bleachers) and tacked on a single run in the seventh on Wayne Gross's bunt single.

Oakland starter Mike Warren was unable to hold the 5–1 lead as he departed in the eighth with the bases loaded and no outs. Beard then entered the fray, walking one run home on four pitches and allowing a sacrifice fly for another. Both markers, however, were charged to Warren as the A's held a 5–3 advantage after eight innings.

Beard's wildness continued into the Indians' 45-minute, record-setting ninth:

• Bake McBride walked.

• Pat Tabler walked, and manager Steve Boros made his first trip to the mound to speak with the enigmatic Beard. Having decided to leave Beard in to pitch to the next batter, Boros received vigorous disapproval from 15,196 fans.

Thomas doubled and homered in the ninth.

• Gorman Thomas, batting .195, doubled to left center, driving home McBride, sending Tabler to third and Beard to the showers. It was then 5–4.

• Left-hander Tom Underwood assumed the mound duties for Oakland, and Cleveland countered with a switch-hitting pinch hitter, Chris Bando. Bando singled to center, scoring Tabler, with Thomas stopping at third. It was then tied 5–5, and still there were no outs.

• With left-handed Broderick Perkins as the next scheduled batter, Cleveland manager Pat Corrales elected to use his secret weapon — right-handed Andre Thornton. The club's leading RBI man, Thornton had been on the bench nursing a pulled muscle. Athletics' skipper Boros countered with a right-hander, Ed Farmer, but Thornton singled to drive home Thomas with the lead run (6–5). As Bando rounded second, he became a victim of the right-field rifle of Mike Davis. It was Davis' second assist of the contest and the first out of the inning.

Dave Beard—first in a parade of six Oakland hurlers.

• Farmer, having faced just his first batter while in an Oakland uniform, joined Beard and Underwood in the showers. Curt Young then stopped by the mound just long enough to throw a wild pitch (Thornton to second) and hit a batter (Ron Hassey).

• Manager Boros was wearing a path to the mound as he sent Young packing. The next Oakland victim was Bert Bradley, making his major league debut. Bert was greeted by Alan Bannister with a sharp single to center on which no one could score, so the bases were loaded.

• Harrah cleared the sacks with a double to left center making it 9–5. Oakland fans were losing their faith and began chanting, "We want Gross!" They didn't realize that

Cleveland Indians	AB	R	H	I
Mike Hargrove 1b	2	0	0	1
Carmen Castillo pr8	0	0	0	0
Alan Bannister 2b8	1	1	1	0
Toby Harrah 3b	4	1	2	5
Julio Franco ss	5	0	0	0
Bake McBride dh,rf9	3	2	1	0
Pat Tabler lf	4	2	1	2
Gorman Thomas cf	5	2	2	3
George Vukovich rf	3	1	1	0
Chris Bando ph9	2	0	2	1
Jim Essian c	1	0	0	0
Brod. Perkins ph8,1b	0	1	0	0
Andre Thornton ph9,1b	2	1	2	1
Mike Fischlin 2b	2	1	0	0
> Ron Hassey ph8,c	2	1	1	0
	36	13	13	13

Oakland Athletics	AB	R	H	I
Rickey Henderson lf	3	0	0	0
Bill Almon 1b	5	1	1	0
Mike Heath 3b	3	1	0	0
Wayne Gross ph7,3b	2	0	1	1
Davey Lopes dh	2	1	1	1
>Bob Kearney c	4	1	1	0
Dwayne Murphy cf	4	1	1	4
Donnie Hill ss	4	0	2	0
Mike Davis rf	2	1	0	0
Tony Phillips 2b	3	0	0	0
	32	6	7	6

Cleveland	IP	H	R	ER	BB	SO
Neal Heaton	6.2	5	5	1	6	3
D. Spillner W,2-9	2.1	2	1	1	1	4
	9	7	6	2	7	7

Oakland	IP	H	R	ER	BB	SO
Mike Warren	7	4	3	3	3	3
Dave Beard L,5-5	1	1	3	3	3	0
Tom Underwood	0	1	0	0	0	0
Ed Farmer	.1	1	1	1	0	0
Curt Young	0	0	1	1	0	0
Bert Bradley	.1	3	4	4	1	0
Jeff Jones	.1	3	1	1	0	0
	9	13	13	13	7	3

Cleveland	0 0 1	0 0 0	0 2 10	-13
Oakland	0 0 0	4 0 0	1 0 1	- 6

OB: Cleveland 5, Oakland 8
E: Tabler
DP: Davis-Kearney (Franco liner)
  Fischlin unassisted (Hill liner)
2B: Thomas, Harrah, Tabler, Lopes
HR: Murphy(15), Thomas(19)
SB: Henderson(93), Lopes(20), Davis
  (28)
PK: Henderson
SO: Thomas 2, Essian; Henderson,
  Almon, Heath, Kearney, Murphy,
  Hill, Phillips
BB: Hargrove 2, McBride 2(1I),
  Tabler, Essian, Perkins;
  Henderson 2(1I), Lopes 2(1I),
  Kearney, Davis 2

SH: Phillips
SF: Harrah
HP: By Spillner (Lopes);
  by Young (Hassey)
WP: Young
PB: Essian
TIME: 3:25
ATTENDANCE: 15,196
UMPIRES: Derryl Cousins, Al Clark,
  Bill Kunkel, John Shulock
SOURCES: Cleveland Plain Dealer;
  Oakland Tribune; Retrosheet; San
  Francisco Sunday Examiner &
  Chronicle

BALANCE	OUT+R+OB=BP=AB+BB+SH+HP+CI
Cleveland	27 13 5 45 36 7 1 1 0
Oakland	27 6 8 41 32 7 1 1 0

Wayne Gross, the infielder, who in May had tossed 2⅓ scoreless frames, had a sore shoulder and was unavailable for pitching duty.

• Julio Franco became the second out, but the first batter to be retired, when he grounded out third to first. Bradley thus became somewhat of an Oakland pitching hero, but it didn't last long.

• McBride was intentionally passed.

• Tabler then doubled over Murphy's head; Harrah and McBride both scored making it 11–5. Now, with the game virtually lost, Boros felt pity for his rookie hurler and made one more trip to the mound. In came the sixth Athletics hurler, Jeff Jones.

• Each of the five former Oakland pitchers in this inning had allowed the first batter he faced to reach base safely. Jones joined the club when Thomas welcomed him heartily by driving a pitch over the left field barrier and scoring behind Harrah. That made it 13–5, but Cleveland still wasn't through.

• Bando, who earlier had singled as a pinch hitter, singled again. Unlike Dick Cox (see 9-09-26), however, recent scoring rules awarded Bando just one pinch hit.

• Thornton also had singled earlier as a

pinch hitter, and he too continued the rally with another single.

• Hassey, the 15th batter, mercifully grounded out to end the unsightly Cleveland orgy.

All totaled, manager Boros made seven trips to the mound during the half inning, and each time he was booed lustily. It was heartless treatment for a man celebrating his birthday (47th).

Oakland continued to fall in the standings as the season waned, losing 17 of their last 25 games to finish fourth in the AL West. Cleveland, meanwhile, maintained their last place position in the AL East, finishing 28 games off the pace of the World Champion Baltimore Orioles.

Almost Forever

190. Teams Play 25-Inning Game in Eight Hours, Six Minutes

MILWAUKEE   at   CHICAGO
(Brewers, 6)   (White Sox, 7)

Started: Tuesday Night, May 8, 1984, Comiskey Park
Finished: Wednesday Night, May 9, 1984, Comiskey Park

Theoretically, a baseball game could last forever. Of course one never has, but of more than 115,000 modern major league games, this marathon came closest when measured in time — a mind-numbing eight hours and six minutes. And in terms of innings, only the Boston-Brooklyn duel of May 1, 1920, looms longer.

This legendary game took place on a cold evening in Chicago where the White Sox hosted the Milwaukee Brewers. It started Tuesday night and continued into Wednesday morning, being halted because of a league ruling that no inning could commence after 12:59 A.M. Thus for five hours and 29 minutes, through 17 innings, ten pitchers and 506 pitches, the two clubs struggled only to

leave the field tied at 3–3. Players and patrons then rested, and the battle recommenced Wednesday night prior to a regularly scheduled game.

Looking for a timely conclusion, everyone was disappointed. Three more scoreless frames were played before Milwaukee appeared to clinch it with three in the top of the 21st. But the home team tied it, sending the contest into serious record territory. There was no more scoring until the bottom of the 25th when Harold Baines concluded matters with a one-out, solo home run.

By the time the 753rd pitch had been thrown, a plethora of major league records had been established or tied:

• *Longest game in terms of time — 8:06*

• *Longest night game in terms of innings —*
25 (tied ML mark)
   • *Most at-bats, one club, extra-inning*
game — 95 by Chicago (remains ML record)
   • *Most at-bats, both clubs, extra-inning*
game — 175 (tied ML mark)
   • *Most plate appearances, extra-inning*
game — 104 by Chicago (remains ML record)
   • *Most individual at-bats in an extra-*
inning game — 11 (Cecil Cooper, Rudy
Law, Carlton Fisk, and Julio Cruz tied ML
record)
   • *Most individual plate appearances in an*
extra-inning game — 12 (R.Law, Fisk, and
Harold Baines tied the ML record)
   • *Most innings caught in a game — 25* (Fisk)
In addition, several American League
endurance standards were set and endure:
   • *Longest AL game in terms of innings — 25*
   • *Most plate appearances, both clubs, extra-*
inning game — 198
Don Sutton started for Milwaukee and
shut out the Sox for five frames. In the sixth,
Greg Walker singled with one out and stole
second. Greg Luzinski fouled out, and
Harold Baines hit a foul pop to third which
would have ended the inning had not Randy
Ready dropped it. Baines then walked, and
Tom Paciorek singled home Walker.

Bob Fallon, making just his third major-
league start, pitched six strong innings while
allowing only one hit. Nevertheless, after Fallon walked leadoff batter Ready in the seventh, Salome Barojas was called in to relieve.
Successive singles by Jim Sundberg and
Robin Yount made it 1–1 and sent Barojas to
the showers. Facing Britt Burns, Cecil
Cooper flied out; then Sundberg got caught
in a rundown between third and home on
Ted Simmons' bouncer to the mound. Ben
Oglivie fanned to end the inning.

In the ninth, each team took advantage of
errors to score twice and send the game into
extra innings. Yount led off for the Brewers
with a double. After Cooper grounded out,
Yount stole third and came home with the
lead run on Fisk's throwing error. Simmons
then singled and advanced on a wild pitch.
Oglivie singled home Simmons, making it
3–1, but was caught stealing. Bobby Clark
walked and was also caught stealing.

The closer role for Milwaukee had been
handled by an aging but still effective Rollie
Fingers. Now in the bottom of the ninth,
Fingers started by getting Tom Paciorek to
lift a routine fly to right, but Charlie Moore
dropped it. Vance Law flied out, and pinch-
hitter Jerry Hairston struck out. The game
would have ended right there had it not been
for Moore's error, but the Sox still had
another out. Julio Cruz then doubled
Paciorek home, making it 3–2, and Rudy
Law singled home Cruz to tie it. Fisk
grounded out as the game proceeded into
extra innings.

The next 11 innings were scoreless but not
without opportunity. Milwaukee, who got
their leadoff man aboard in six of the first 11
extra innings, had Jim Gantner on second
with one out in the 13th. With Sundberg
batting, pitcher Al Jones and second baseman
Cruz worked the pickoff play to perfection,
retiring Gantner. Sundberg then singled and
himself went to second on a wild pitch, but
Yount fanned to end the threat.

The sacks became jammed as three of the
first four White Sox batters singled to open
the 14th. Brewer reliever Rick Waits allowed
the last two singles but escaped by fanning
pinch hitter Marc Hill and getting Dave
Stegman on a foul pop to first.

Opening the Milwaukee 16th, Bill
Schroeder and Yount both singled, but
Cooper hit into a force out, and Simmons
grounded into an inning-ending double
play.

Ready doubled leading off the Brewers'
18th and was sacrificed to third. Yount was
intentionally walked before Cooper grounded
into a double play.

The Sox had their best scoring opportunity in the bottom of the same frame when
they placed their first two men on. Paciorek
led off with a single and Vance Law was safe
on a botched sacrifice attempt. Jerry Dybzinski then sacrificed both runners along. After
Cruz fouled out to third, Rudy Law was
intentionally passed, loading the bases. Alas,
Fisk struck out.

Milwaukee finally became reacquainted
with crossing the plate in the 21st. With two
outs and two on, Oglivie seemingly put the

game away with a right field, upper-deck home run giving the Brewers a 6–3 advantage.

Rudy Law led off the bottom of the inning by hitting a routine grounder to third. Ready fielded it cleanly but threw wildly toward first; Law wound up on second. Fisk drove him home with a single to right and also arrived at second when Hill singled. After Stegman whiffed, Baines walked, filling the bases. Paciorek then drove home two mates with his fourth single of the game. Chuck Porter temporarily escaped a loss by retiring Vance Law on a fielder's choice ground out and Dybzinski on a fly ball to center. The teams were again knotted at 6–6.

The marathon came within an eyelash of ending in the bottom of the 23rd. With Stegman on first and one out, Paciorek

The game-winning blow was Baines' first homer in a month.

notched his fifth single, this one to center. Stegman put his head down and motored around second, then toward third. A frantic third-base coach, Jim Leyland, saw the ball momentarily bobbled and motioned for Stegman to continue home with the winning run. But center fielder Rick Manning quickly recovered, and Leyland tried to stop Stegman. In doing so, Stegman stumbled, and the two made faint contact. Milwaukee manager Rene Lachemann argued about the coaching felony with each umpire until he finally found one who saw it—first base ump Ted Hendry. Ted called Stegman out, which of course drew a vehement challenge from Chicago manager Tony LaRussa. LaRussa, an attorney, protested the game, arguing that application of the rule prohibits physically

assisting the runner but does not preclude incidental contact. The decision became critical when the next batter, Vance Law singled, but the Sox were retired as Dybzinski hit into an inning-ending force out. Leyland, when asked about the incident after the game, smiled and motioned toward the manager's office as he said: "You'll have to talk to my lawyer."*

In the Chicago half of the 25th, Stegman led off with his fifth strikeout on a foul bunt. The next hitter, Baines, then drove a ball to the deepest section of the park, 420 feet to the center-field bullpen. It carried over the fence, finally ending the longest game in history. A man of few words who didn't like to talk to the press, Baines had only three words in response to reporter's entreaties to discuss

*Michael Bauman, "Hey, it's no big deal to Seaver," Milwaukee Journal, 10 May 1984, part 3, p. 1, col. 6.

Milwaukee Brewers	AB	R	H	I
Randy Ready 3b	8	1	1	0
Jim Sundberg c	4	0	3	0
Ed Romero pr13	0	0	0	0
Bill Schroeder c13	4	0	2	0
Robin Yount ss	10	1	3	1
>Cecil Cooper dh	11	1	2	0
Ted Simmons 1b	7	2	1	0
Ben Oglivie lf	10	1	2	4
Bobby Clark cf	2	0	1	0
Rick Manning ph12,cf	6	0	2	0
Charlie Moore rf	2	0	0	0
Dion James ph10,rf	2	0	0	0
Mark Brouhard ph17,rf	4	0	1	0
Jim Gantner 2b	10	0	2	0
	80	6	20	5

Chicago White Sox	AB	R	H	I
Rudy Law cf	11	1	4	1
Carlton Fisk c	11	1	3	1
Greg Walker 1b	4	1	2	0
Mike Squires 1b9	2	0	0	0
Marc Hill ph14,1b	4	0	2	0
Rich Dotson pr21	0	1	0	0
Ron Reed p21	1	0	0	0
Floyd Bannister p23	1	0	0	0
Tom Seaver p25	0	0	0	0
Greg Luzinski dh	2	0	0	0
D. Stegman pr8,dh,lf22	8	0	1	0
>Harold Baines rf	10	1	2	1
Ron Kittle lf	1	0	0	0
Tom Paciorek lf4,1b22	9	1	5	3
Vance Law 3b	10	0	1	0
Scott Fletcher ss	3	0	0	0
Jerry Hairston ph9	1	0	0	0
Jerry Dybzinski ss10	6	0	2	0
Julio Cruz 2b	11	1	1	1
	95	7	23	7

Milwaukee	IP	H	R	ER	BB	SO
Don Sutton	7	4	1	0	3	6
Pete Ladd	1	0	0	0	1	0
Rollie Fingers	2	2	2	0	0	2
Tom Tellmann	3.1	3	0	0	1	1
Rick Waits	3.2	3	0	0	0	3
Chk. Porter L,2-1	7.1	11	4	3	2	5
	*24.1	23	7	3	7	17

Chicago	IP	H	R	ER	BB	SO
Bob Fallon	6	1	1	1	3	4
Salome Barojas	0	2	0	0	0	0
Britt Burns	3	3	2	2	3	3
Al Jones	4	4	0	0	1	4
Juan Agosto	7	5	0	0	2	1
Ron Reed	2.2	3	3	3	2	3
Floyd Bannister	1.1	1	0	0	0	1
Tom Seaver W,2-2	1	1	0	0	0	0
	25	20	6	6	11	16

One out when winning run scored

Milwaukee	000	000	102	000	000	000	003	000	0	–	6
Chicago	000	001	002	000	000	000	003	000	1	–	7

OB: Milwaukee 13, Chicago 24
E: Ready 2, Fisk, Moore
DP: Yount-Gantner-Simmons (Dybzinski)
    V. Law-Cruz-Walker (Yount)
    Fletcher-Cruz-Walker (Gantner)
    Fletcher-Walker (Yount)
    Cruz-Hill (Simmons)
    Agosto-Dybzinski-Hill (Cooper)
    Dybzinski-Cruz-Paciorek (Yount)
2B: Yount, Cruz, Baines, Hill, Ready, Fisk
HR: Oglivie(2), Baines(2)
SB: Walker(1), Yount(3), Manning(3)
CS: Oglivie, Clark, James, Brouhard
PK: Gantner
SO: Ready 2, Sundberg, Schroeder, Yount,
    Cooper 2, Oglivie 4, Manning, Moore,
    Gantner 3; Fisk 3, Hill, Luzinski, Stegman 5,
    Kittle, Paciorek 3, Hairston, Cruz 2

BB: Ready 2, Sundberg 2, Yount(I),
    Simmons 3, Clark 2, James; Fisk,
    R. Law(I), Luzinski 2, Baines 2,
    Paciorek(I)
SH: Moore, Ready, Schroeder, V. Law,
    Dybzinski
WP: Burns, Jones
TIME: 8:06
ATTENDANCE: 14,754
UMPIRES: Jim Evans, Greg Kosc, Ted
    Hendry, Drew Coble
SOURCES: BBWS; Chicago Sun-Times,
    Tribune; Milwaukee Journal

BALANCE	OUT	+	R	+	OB	=	BP	=	AB	+	BB	+	SH	+	HP	+	CI
Milwaukee	75		6		13		94		80		11		3		0		0
Chicago	73		7		24		104		95		7		2		0		0

the game-winning blow —"Nope," "Nope," and "Nope."*

METHUSELAH MEMOS

• Tom Seaver made his first relief appearance in eight years. He also started the regularly scheduled contest, pitched 8.1 innings and gained his second winning decision of the night.

• Except for LaMarr Hoyt, Chicago used every player on their 25-man roster.

• Tom Paciorek collected five hits although he didn't enter the game until the fourth inning.

• There were only about 800 fans left in the stadium for the Wednesday morning curfew. It was not reported how many of those returned for the Wednesday night finale.

• Baines' game-winning blast was only his second hit in his last 20 at-bats and his first home run in a month.

Paciorek collected five singles after entering in the fourth.

• In the 22nd, Ron Reed became the first ChiSox pitcher to bat in eight years.

• Bob Fallon, the Chicago left-hander who pitched so proficiently, was shipped back to the minors in a move necessitated by the Sox' immediate need for another starter. (He did not return to Chicago this season and pitched only 16 innings in 1985 before disappearing from the majors.)

• There were no records established by food or drink vendors due to the cold weather. Along with blankets, many fans brought their own thermos bottles; the others were reluctant to take their hands out of their pockets.

Michael Bauman, "Hey, it's no big deal to Seaver," Milwaukee Journal, 10 May 1984, part 3, p. 1, col. 6.

Bobby at Witt's End

191. Pitcher Walks Eight Batters, Strikes Out Ten, Throws Four Wild Pitches, Allows No Hits in Five Innings

TEXAS   at   MILWAUKEE
(Rangers, 7)   (Brewers, 5)

Thursday, April 17, 1986, County Stadium

In this his rookie season, Witt issued 143 walks in 158 innings.

Although no official major league records were established in this game, it was a contest so bizarre as to warrant inclusion in this anthology. Consider the following:

• The two teams managed 21 walks, 21 strikeouts, six wild pitches, four errors, and 346 pitches in this nine-inning affair.

• Texas rookie pitcher Bobby Witt twirled a no-hitter for five innings but was relieved and left trailing 2–0.

• In Witt's five frames, he walked eight Brewers, struck out ten (all swinging), and tossed four wild pitches.

• Bobby's four wild pitches shattered the Rangers' club record and threatened the 74-year-old major-league standard of five (over nine innings). Both of the runs he allowed were scored on wild pitches, and two of those errant tosses were swung at for strikes.

• Witt allowed almost

as many runs as he allowed fair balls. Of the 23 batters Bobby faced, only three put the ball in play in fair territory, and they were all infield grounders. Two foul pop-ups rounded off his five innings of work.

• There were only 12 hits by the two teams combined, yet there were not only twelve runs scored but also 20 runners left on base.

• Milwaukee took a 5–4 lead in the bottom of the eighth but then blew it in the ninth as three relievers issued five walks. The winning run scored, of course, on a wild pitch.

The Brewers opened the scoring in the first on two walks, a double play, and a wild pitch. The Rangers countered in the third on Steve Buechele's solo homer and took the lead in the fourth on a pair of singles surrounding a walk.

The home fifth was a classic in pitching wildness as well as Witt's end. Milwaukee's Rob Deer led off with a walk. After Charlie Moore fouled out, both Mike Felder and Robin Yount also walked, loading the bases. Deer scored, and Felder and Yount advanced on a wild pitch. Witt then fanned Paul Molitor but walked Billy Joe Robidoux to reload the sacks. Witt then struck out Paul Householder.

When the young right-hander returned to the dugout, Texas skipper Bobby Valentine informed him that he was through for the day. With a no-hitter in the making, Witt was visibly upset until Valentine informed him that he had already thrown 107 pitches and would never last nine innings. "I never thought I'd take a pitcher out with a no-

hitter, but..." Valentine said. "His breaking ball was breaking so sharply, Donnie [catcher Slaught] couldn't get in front of it. He was just missing with a lot of pitches."* (Witt had, by then, walked 14 in 8⅓ innings during his first two starts.)

The Rangers tallied once more in the seventh on a pair of singles, two walks, and a wild pitch. Slaught supplied firepower in the eighth with a solo home run giving his club a 4–2 lead, but the Brewers stormed back. After Robidoux walked, Ernest Riles and Jim Gantner singled, making it 4–3. Pinch hitter Ben Oglivie walked to load the bases, and Charlie Moore singled in the tying run. Felder then hit a sacrifice fly to return the advantage to Milwaukee, 5–4.

The ninth was a disaster for Milwaukee as Texas needed little more than a "take" sign to recapture the lead. Oddibe McDowell led off with a walk and stole second as Toby Harrah struck out. Ray Searage then relieved Danny Darwin but issued free passes to both Pete O'Brien and Pete Incaviglia, loading the bases. (It was Incaviglia's first major league walk in 32 at-bats.) Gary Ward forced Incaviglia at second while McDowell scored and O'Brien moved to third. O'Brien scored and Ward advanced to second on the game's sixth wild pitch before Larry Parrish accepted his club's fourth base on balls of the frame. That brought in Mark Clear to relieve Searage. Slaught singled home Ward and sent Parrish to second. Buechele also walked, filling the bases once more before Wilkerson struck out.

Witt's Wildness	1st Inning	2nd Inning	3rd Inning	4th Inning	5th Inning
Bases on Balls	2	0	2	0	4
Strikeouts	1	3	3	1	2
Wild Pitches	1	0	2	0	1

Staggering beneath a woefully ineffective relief effort, the Brewers failed to cross the plate in the last of the ninth and absorbed their fifth consecutive loss. Perhaps this game was an omen as Milwaukee finished in

sixth place in their division and last in "Saves."

The Rangers, meanwhile, finished second in the West despite a staff that issued the most bases on balls.

*Phil Rogers, "Rangers enjoy wild life," Dallas Times Herald, 18 April 1986, section C, p. 5, col. 1.

Texas Rangers	AB	R	H	I
Oddibe McDowell cf	3	1	0	0
Toby Harrah 2b	5	0	1	1
Pete O'Brien 1b	2	2	1	0
Pete Incaviglia rf	4	0	0	0
Gary Ward lf	3	1	0	1
Larry Parrish dh	4	0	0	0
Don Slaught c	5	1	3	3
Steve Buechele 3b	4	2	2	1
>Curt Wilkerson ss	5	0	0	0
	35	7	7	6

Milwaukee Brewers	AB	R	H	I
Mike Felder cf	2	1	1	1
Robin Yount dh	3	0	0	0
Paul Molitor 3b	4	0	0	0
Billy Jo Robidoux 1b	2	1	0	0
>Paul Householder lf	5	0	0	0
Ernest Riles ss	4	1	1	0
Jim Gantner 2b	4	1	2	1
Rob Deer rf	2	1	0	0
Ben Oglivie ph8	0	0	0	0
Rick Manning rf9	0	0	0	0
Charlie Moore c	3	0	1	1
	29	5	5	3

Texas	IP	H	R	ER	BB	SO
Bobby Witt	5	0	2	2	8	10
Ricky Wright	2.1	4	3	3	1	1
Greg Harris W,2-1	1.2	1	0	0	2	0
	9	5	5	5	11	11

Milwaukee	IP	H	R	ER	BB	SO
Juan Nieves	6.1	4	3	3	4	6
Danny Darwin	2	2	2	2	2	3
Ray Searage L,0-1	.1	0	2	2	3	0
Mark Clear	.1	1	0	0	1	1
	9	7	7	7	10	10

```
Texas       0 0 1   1 0 0   1 1 3   - 7
Milwaukee   1 0 0   0 1 0   0 3 0   - 5
```

OB: Texas 11, Milwaukee 9
E: Wilkerson, Riles, Molitor, Incaviglia
DP: Buechele-Harrah-O'Brien(Molitor)
    Incaviglia-Harris-Wilkerson (Felder fly out)
    Moore-Gantner (Parrish SO)
2B: Gantner
HR: Buechele(2), Slaught(2)
SB: Felder(3), McDowell(2)
CS: Ward, Felder
SO: Harrah, Incaviglia 3, Wilkerson,
    Parrish 2, Buechele 2, Ward; Felder,
    Yount, Molitor, Riles, Robidoux,
    Householder 2, Gantner 2, Deer 2

BB: McDowell 2, O'Brien 3, Ward 2, Incaviglia,
    Parrish, Buechele; Felder 2, Yount 2, Molitor,
    Robidoux 3, Deer, Oglivie(I), Moore
SF: Felder
WP: Witt 4, Nieves, Searage
TIME: 3:27
ATTENDANCE: 5,823
UMPIRES: Dan Morrison, Jim McKean,
    Al Clark, John Shulock
SOURCES: BBWS; Dallas Morning News,
    Times Herald; Fort Worth Star-Telegram;
    Milwaukee Journal

BALANCE	OUT	+	R	+	OB	=	BP	=	AB	+	BB	+	SH	+	HP	+	CI
Texas	27		7		11		45		35		10		0		0		0
Milwaukee	27		5		9		41		29		11		1		0		0

April Fools

192. Teams Strike Out
30 Times in Nine-Inning Game

OAKLAND   at   SEATTLE
(Athletics, 7)   (Mariners, 2)

Saturday Night, April 19, 1986, Kingdome

In 1985 the Seattle Mariners had four players who fanned 100 or more times as the club led the American League in strikeouts.

This season they not only again led the Junior Circuit but also established a single-season, league record in the process—1,148,

Rijo struck out more than half of the record number 30.

or an average of more than seven per game. (The 1996 Tigers have since collared the title.) Early in the campaign, the Mariners served notice of their specialty when they combined efforts with the Oakland Athletics to establish *a two-team, nine-inning game, strikeout standard of 30* despite not having a pitcher come to bat. The mark has yet to be surpassed.

This year's version of the Mariners had seven players who hit ten or more home runs, but six of those players fanned more frequently than once every four times at bat. Jim Presley most frustrated the Seattle fans by failing to put the ball in play 172 times, or once for every 3.58 times at-bats. Danny Tartabull, who struck out "only" 157 times, did so every 3.25 times at bat. The team percentage leader in futility, however, was Gorman Thomas, who was fooled once every 3.09 times at bat. Alas, Gorman was released before the season ended and consequently could not amass team-leading numbers.

A record-setting strikeout performance this night was not altogether surprising. Oakland's 20-year-old starter, Jose Rijo, had averaged better than one strikeout per inning in 1985. Seattle's Mark Langston had led the AL in strikeouts as a rookie in 1984, and after incurring an elbow injury in 1985, came back this season to again lead the circuit and average better than one whiff per inning. The hitters too were ripe. In addition to the strikeout savants of Seattle, Oakland also was loaded with free swingers such as Tony Phillips, Mike Davis, Dwayne Murphy, Jose Canseco, Mickey Tettleton, and Dave Kingman.

Despite two strikeouts in the opening frame, Oakland reached Langston for a pair of runs on Tony Phillips' single and Dave Kingman's first round-tripper of the season.

Kingman connected again in the third inning, this time with two mates aboard. Langston had struck out five in three innings but left trailing 5–0.

Bill Swift hurled the next four innings for Seattle. Like his predecessor, Swift also fanned five but allowed single runs in the fourth and sixth. That was more than enough for Rijo, who had struck out 16 through eight innings on a blazing fastball and nasty slider. When Jose took the mound in the ninth, he was within reach of the then all-time strikeout mark of 19. But after Rijo had thrown 158 pitches and allowed the first two batters to reach base, Bill Mooneyham was summoned in relief. It was Mooneyham's major league debut, and he fanned two more Mariners to shatter the old two-team mark of 28 set in 1972 as Oakland won handily, 7–2.

The record-setting performance is outlined in the table below:

BATTER STRIKEOUTS, APRIL 19, 1986

INN	1	2	3	4	5	6	7	8	9
OAK	s-Murphy s-Lansford	s-Bathe	s-Canseco s-Bochte	s-Bathe	c-Canseco	s-Murphy s-Baker	s-Kingman	c-Griffin	s-Phillips
SEA	s-Tartabull c-Thomas	s-Henderson	s-Owen s-Tartabull s-Bradley	s-Calderon s-Thomas c-Presley	s-Yeager	s-Calderon c-Thomas	s-Henderson s-Yeager	s-Tartabull c-Thomas	c-Henderson s-Tartabull

s = swinging; c = called

Seventeen different players struck out, led by Gorman Thomas and Danny Tartabull with four each. Tartabull went down swinging on four occassions while Thomas was called out thrice. Seattle first baseman Alvin Davis became somewhat of a hero by being the only starter not to strike out.

April was a particularly harsh period for Seattle. After their involvement in this benchmark contest, the Mariners went on to establish two more dismal records before the month concluded. On April 29, 20 Mariners went down on strikes from the arm of Roger Clemens, establishing a new nine-inning, major-league mark. The day following, 16 more were retired via the strikeout route for a record smashing 36 whiffs in two games.

Oakland and Seattle each tested three managers this season but to little avail. The Athletics distressed Jackie Moore, Jeff Newman, and Tony LaRussa to finish tied for third at 76–86. Seattle provoked Chuck Cottier, Marty Martinez, and Dick Williams while breathing last place air at 67–95, 25 games out.

Alvin Davis did not strike out.

Oakland Athletics	AB	R	H	I
Tony Phillips 2b,3b9	5	2	4	1
Dwayne Murphy cf	4	0	0	1
Dusty Baker lf	2	1	0	0
Rickey Peters lf7	1	0	0	0
>Dave Kingman dh	5	2	2	5
Jose Canseco rf	3	0	0	0
Carney Lansford 3b,1b9	4	0	0	0
Bruce Bochte 1b	4	0	0	0
Donnie Hill 2b9	0	0	0	0
Alfredo Griffin ss	3	2	1	0
Bill Bathe c	4	0	0	0
	35	7	7	7

Oakland	IP	H	R	ER	BB	SO
Jose Rijo W,1-0	8	5	2	2	4	16
Bill Mooneyham	1	0	0	0	1	2
	9	5	2	2	5	18

Seattle Mariners	AB	R	H	I
>Danny Tartabull 2b	4	0	0	0
Phil Bradley lf	4	0	0	0
Ivan Calderon rf	4	0	2	1
Gorman Thomas dh	4	0	0	0
Alvin Davis 1b	2	1	1	0
Jim Presley 3b	4	0	1	0
Dave Henderson cf	3	0	0	0
Steve Yeager c	3	0	0	0
Ken Phelps ph9	0	0	0	0
Spike Owen ss	3	1	1	0
Al Cowens ph9	1	0	0	1
	32	2	5	2

Seattle	IP	H	R	ER	BB	SO
Ma. Langston L,0-2	3	4	5	5	2	5
Bill Swift	4	3	2	2	2	5
Mike Morgan	1	0	0	0	0	1
Karl Best	1	0	0	0	1	1
	9	7	7	7	5	12

Oakland	2 0 3	1 0 1	0 0 0	- 7
Seattle	0 0 0	0 0 0	0 1 1	- 2

OB: Oakland 6, Seattle 8
E: Langston, Canseco, Owen
2B: Phillips, Owen
HR: Kingman 2(2)
SB: Lansford(1), Griffin(3)
SO: Phillips, Murphy 2, Canseco 2,
     Kingman, Baker, Lansford, Bochte,
     Griffin, Bathe 2; Tartabull 4,
     Bradley, Calderon 2, Thomas 4,
     Presley, Henderson 3, Yeager 2,
     Owen

BB: Murphy, Baker 2, Canseco, Griffin; Tartabull,
     Davis 2, Henderson, Phelps
BK: Rijo
TIME: 3:04
ATTENDANCE: 31,584
UMPIRES: Al Clark, John Shulock, Dan
     Morrison, Jim McKean
SOURCES: BBWS; Oakland Tribune; San
     Francisco Examiner; USA Today

BALANCE	OUT+R+OB=BP=AB+BB+SH+HP+CI							
Oakland	27	7	6	40	35	5	0	0	0
Seattle	27	2	8	37	32	5	0	0	0

Intermission Attracts Pitchers

193. Teams Use 17 Pitchers in 17-Inning Game

PITTSBURGH   at   CHICAGO
(Pirates, 10)   (Cubs, 8)

Started: Sunday, April 20, 1986, Wrigley Field
Completed: Monday. August 11, 1986, Wrigley Field

Suspended games that are completed months after they begin often contain ironic twists of fate. So it was in this contest which started in the early days of the season but wasn't settled until almost four months later. The game winning RBI was delivered by a

Jones fanned eight in four innings.

Lopes had five hits but wasn't in town when the game concluded.

rookie who didn't make his major league debut until more than a month after the curtain rose on this game. The losing pitcher had been on a different team when it all began, and the most prolific hitter in the game was no longer in town. And with it all, the Cubs established *a new major league record by using 10 pitchers in the contest* (later surpassed). In addition, *the two clubs set a National League mark by sending 17 hurlers to the hill* (also later surpassed).

The competitors battled 13 innings to an 8–8 tie on April 20 before the game was called on account of darkness. At that point, both teams were well on their way to record territory. The two staffs had already engaged 13 moundsmen, Chicago employing seven. Noteworthy also was the fact that Chicago's leadoff hitter Davey Lopes, who was later traded in July, had reached base all seven times he batted, and that the Cubs had tied the score with three runs in the bottom of the ninth thanks to Keith Moreland's two out, two-run home run.

During the extended intermission, the Pirates played poorly enough to land in last place, 30 games out. The Cubs hadn't fared

much better, holding the fifth position in a six-team race by the time the two clubs finished their skirmish.

Upon resumption of play, new pitchers took the mound for each squad—Steve Trout for Chicago and Barry Jones for Pittsburgh. No one had crossed the plate since the ninth inning nearly four months earlier, and the futility extended for another three frames although the Cubs did have a golden opportunity to salt away a victory in the 16th. Then, two walks and a single loaded the bases with one out, but Jody Davis watched a third strike go by, and Bob Dernier popped out to third.

In the 17th, the Pirates broke the ice and scored two runs at the expense of the ninth Cub hurler, Frank DiPino. Frank, who had started the season with Houston, relinquished the first tally after Johnny Ray led off the frame with a double. After Jones grounded out, Bobby Bonilla was intentionally passed. Dave Gumpert then replaced DiPino for the Cubs, becoming the 17th hurler to take the mound. Gumpert retired Tony Pena for the second out, but rookie Barry Bonds, pinch-hitting for Jim Morrison, singled to center. Ray scored the go-ahead run and when Dernier overran the ball, Bonilla also tallied.

Jones coasted through the home half of the 17th, striking out the side, and sealing the victory for Pittsburgh. Barry's eight strikeouts over the final four frames highlighted his first win of the campaign. Pittsburgh also won the regularly scheduled game, but the two teams never moved in the standings, finishing fifth and sixth at year's end.

Pittsburgh Pirates	AB	R	H	I
R. J. Reynolds rf,lf7, rf14,lf17	7	1	1	0
Joe Orsulak cf,rf17	7	3	3	0
Johnny Ray 2b	7	2	4	2
Sid Bream 1b	5	2	1	3
Barry Jones p14	1	0	0	0
Steve Kemp lf	4	1	2	1
Mike Brown pr7,rf	2	0	1	0
Bobby Bonilla 1b14	1	1	0	0
Tony Pena c	8	0	1	2
Jim Morrison 3b	6	0	0	0
Barry Bonds ph17,cf	1	0	1	1
Rafael Belliard ss	3	0	1	0
Lee Mazzilli ph11	1	0	0	0
Cecilio Guante p11	0	0	0	0
Mike Diaz ph13	1	0	1	0
Don Robinson p13	0	0	0	0
Pat Clements p13	0	0	0	0
> U. L. Washington ss14	2	0	0	0
Mike Bielecki p	2	0	0	0
Bob Walk p4	2	0	0	0
Jim Winn p9	0	0	0	0
Bill Almon ph11,ss, lf14,3b17	3	0	0	0
	63	10	16	9

Chicago Cubs	AB	R	H	I
Davey Lopes 3b	5	2	5	3
Steve Trout p14	0	0	0	0
Terry Francona ph15	1	0	0	0
Frank DiPino p16	0	0	0	0
Dave Gumpert p17	0	0	0	0
Ron Cey ph17	1	0	0	0
>Shawon Dunston ss	9	0	2	2
Ryne Sandberg 2b	8	0	0	0
Keith Moreland rf	6	1	1	2
Leon Durham 1b	6	0	1	0
Jerry Mumphrey lf	2	0	1	0
Brian Dayett lf4	3	0	0	0
Lee Smith p10	0	0	0	0
Dick Ruthven p11	0	0	0	0
Manny Trillo ph11	1	0	0	0
Rick Sutcliffe p12	0	0	0	0
Chris Speier 3b14	1	0	1	0
Jody Davis c	7	1	1	0
Bob Dernier cf	8	1	2	0
Dennis Eckersley p	2	2	2	1
Gary Matthews ph6	1	0	0	0
Jay Baller p7	0	0	0	0
Matt Keough p7	0	0	0	0
George Frazier p8	0	0	0	0
Thad Bosley ph9,lf	5	1	1	0
	66	8	17	8

Pittsburgh	IP	H	R	ER	BB	SO
Bielecki	3.1	10	5	5	0	0
Walk	4.2	2	2	2	2	2
Winn	2	2	1	1	0	3
Guante	2	1	0	0	2	2
Robinson	0	0	0	0	1	0
Clements	1	0	0	0	0	1
Jones W,1-1	4	2	0	0	3	8
	17	17	8	8	8	16

Chicago	IP	H	R	ER	BB	SO
Eckersley	6	8	6	6	2	5
Baller	.2	3	2	2	1	1
Keough	.1	0	0	0	0	0
Frazier	2	0	0	0	2	1
Smith	1.1	0	0	0	0	1
Ruthven	.2	0	0	0	0	0
Sutcliffe	2	2	0	0	1	4
Trout	2	0	0	0	0	0
DiPino L,1-7	1.1	2	2	1	1	2
Gumpert	.2	1	0	0	0	0
	17	16	10	9	7	14

Pittsburgh	1 0 0	4 1 0	2 0 0	0 0 0	0 0 0	0 2	- 10
Chicago	0 3 0	2 0 0	0 0 3	0 0 0	0 0 0	0 0	- 8

OB: Pittsburgh 10, Chicago 15
E: Almon, Dernier
DP: Dernier-Dunston (Bream)
2B: Orsulak, Dunston, Lopes, Dernier, Ray
3B: Lopes, Bosley
HR: Bream(2), Kemp(1), Moreland(1)
CS: Orsulak, Brown, Lopes, Dunston
SO: Reynolds 3, Orsulak, Ray, Bream, Pena,
    Morrison 2, Mazzilli, Washington, Bielecki,
    Walk, Almon; Cey, Dunston 3, Durham,
    Sandberg 3, Dayett, Trillo, Davis 4, Bosley 2
BB: Reynolds, Orsulak, Ray, Bream, Bonilla(I),
    Morrison(I), Belliard; Lopes 2, Moreland 2,
    Durham 2(1I), Speier, Davis

SF: Bream
WP: Winn
BK: Eckersley, Baller
TIME: 6:09
ATTENDANCE: 18,508
UMPIRES: Bruce Froemming, Randy Marsh,
    Satch Davidson, John Kibler
SOURCES: BBWS; Chicago Tribune; Pittsburgh
    Post Gazette, Press; USA Today

BALANCE	OUT	+R	+OB	=BP	=AB	+BB	+SH	+HP	+CI
Pittsburgh	51	10	10	71	63	7	1	0	0
Chicago	51	8	15	74	66	8	0	0	0

The Rocket Smokes the Mariners

194. Pitcher Strikes Out
20 Batters in Nine-Inning Game

SEATTLE   at   BOSTON
(Mariners, 1)   (Red Sox, 3)

Tuesday Night, April 29, 1986, Fenway Park

In the 111 years of major league baseball, there had been only three pitchers who struck out as many as 19 batters in a nine-inning game. That elite trio were all future Hall of Famers — Steve Carlton, Tom Seaver, and Nolan Ryan. But now there was a new kid on the block, one who would erase the mark of the greats. Roger Clemens, Boston's 23-year-old right-hander, in one of the most awesome pitching performances in major league history, *overpowered the Seattle Mariners this night with 20 strikeouts.*

Clemens had yet to win his 20th major league game, but his delivery, at times, was staggering. During this game, the radar gun clocked his fast ball at an average of 95 mph with peaks on several occasions at 97. The Mariners could put just 10 balls in play, and only two of those were pulled. At one point, Roger tied the American League record of eight straight strikeouts. Seattle's Gorman Thomas, who

Clemens went on to post a 24–4 Cy Young Award season.

blemished the classic with a solo home run, reflected nothing but admiration for the Boston hurler. "When the last out was made, I wanted to tip my hat. He was that good. It's the finest effort you'll ever see."*

Clemens threw 138 pitches, 97 for strikes, and walked no one. He did encounter some early control difficulty, however, for despite striking out six of the first nine batters, Roger went to three-ball counts on five of them. But after the fourth inning, he never ran a count to three balls.

The Boston right-hander had a perfect game brewing into the fourth inning when Spike Owen led off by singling to right on an 0–2 curveball. Clemens punished the Mariners by fanning the next eight batters, before Owen again broke the string by flying out to center.

At the end of five innings, Clemens had struck out 12 Mariners. Through six, he had fanned 14, thrown 92 pitches (60 for strikes), and only four batters had hit balls into play.

In the seventh, with the crowd on their feet and roaring at every pitch, both Phil Bradley and Ken Phelps went down swinging for strikeouts number 15 and 16. The latter established a new personal high for Clemens. But the euphoria was harshly interrupted when Thomas sent a 1–2 pitch into the front row of the center field bleachers. It was the first run of the game, and Clemens was in danger of losing his masterpiece.

Boston retaliated in the bottom of the frame. After the first two batters were retired, Steve Lyons singled and Glenn Hoffman walked. Dwight Evans then homered off the back wall in center giving the Sox a 3–1 advantage. "That picked me up," said Clemens, as if he needed any more incentive.†

The Mariners got their third and final hit in the eighth. Sandwiched between two more strikeouts, Danny Tartabull singled to right center before pinch hitter Al Cowens flied out to center.

The ninth inning was electrified. Owen, owner of one of Seattle's three hits, led off. When he tried to check his swing on a 1–2 pitch and couldn't, that made the 19th notch in Clemens' holster, tying the major league standard. Next was Bradley who had already gone down swinging three times. Phil saw just three pitches (the last one called) and became the record-setting 20th victim. The last batter, Ken Phelps, had also struck out swinging three times, but now made contact and grounded out to shortstop.

ROGER CLEMENS' 20 STRIKEOUTS, APRIL 29, 1986

Inning	1	2	3	4	5	6	7	8	9
Player	s-Owen	s-Presley	c-Henderson	s-Bradley	c-Presley	s-Henderson	s-Bradley	s-Calderon	s-Owen
	s-Bradley	c-Calderon		s-Phelps	c-Thomas	c-Yeager	s-Phelps	s-Henderson	c-Bradley
	s-Phelps			c-Thomas	c-Calderon				

s = swinging; c = called

There have been few clubs in history more prone to being victimized by the strikeout than the 1986 Mariners. In 20 games, they had now whiffed 186 times. At that rate, they would have struck out more than 1500 times, smashing the existing record of 1,203. (They did calm down to amass only 1,148.) Seattle had also struck out 12 times in their previous game for a new major league mark of 32 in consecutive contests. It didn't take them long, however, to break their own record. The following day, April 30, 16 more Mariners went down on strikes for a new standard of 36 in successive games (still stands). Although three-game records are not tracked, Seattle is also the probable record holder with 48.

Sox catcher Rich Gedman, by being on the receiving end of Clemens' phenomenal outing, *broke the American League and tied the major league mark with 20 putouts in a nine-inning game.*

*Dan Shaughnessy, "Clemens fans a record 20," Boston Globe, 30 April 1986, p. 49, col. 1.
†Ibid, p. 50, col. 5.

Red Sox manager John McNamara compared this spectacle to some others he had witnessed. "I saw Catfish Hunter pitch a perfect game, and I saw Mike Witt pitch a perfect game and Tom Seaver pitch some great games, but this was the most awesome display of pitching I've ever seen." All in all, it was quite a night for a young man who had undergone career-threatening, arthroscopic shoulder surgery the previous August.

Seattle Mariners	AB	R	H	I
Spike Owen ss	4	0	1	0
Phil Bradley lf	4	0	0	0
>Ken Phelps 1b	4	0	0	0
Gorman Thomas dh	3	1	1	1
Jim Presley 3b	3	0	0	0
Ivan Calderon rf	3	0	0	0
Danny Tartabull 2b	3	0	1	0
Dave Henderson cf	3	0	0	0
Steve Yeager c	2	0	0	0
Al Cowens ph8	1	0	0	0
Bob Kearney c8	0	0	0	0
	30	1	3	1

Seattle	IP	H	R	ER	BB	SO
Mike Moore L,1-2	7.1	8	3	3	4	4
Matt Young	.1	0	0	0	0	0
Karl Best	.1	0	0	0	0	1
	8	8	3	3	4	5

Seattle	0 0 0	0 0 0	1 0 0	- 1
Boston	0 0 0	0 0 0	3 0 x	- 3

OB: Seattle 2, Boston 7
E: Baylor, Tartabull
DP: Yeager-Tartabull (Baylor SO)
2B: Buckner
HR: Thomas(5), Evans(2)
CS: Rice, Evans
SO: Owen 2, Bradley 4, Phelps 3, Presley 2, Calderon 3, Henderson 3, Thomas, Tartabull, Yeager; Evans, Hoffman, Baylor 2, Barrett

Boston Red Sox	AB	R	H	I
Dwight Evans rf	4	1	2	3
Wade Boggs 3b	3	0	0	0
Bill Buckner dh	4	0	2	0
Jim Rice lf	4	0	1	0
Don Baylor 1b	3	0	1	0
Dave Stapleton 1b9	0	0	0	0
Rich Gedman c	4	0	1	0
>Marty Barrett 2b	3	0	0	0
Steve Lyons cf	3	1	1	0
Glenn Hoffman ss	2	0	0	0
Ed Romero pr7,ss	0	1	0	0
	30	3	8	3

Boston	IP	H	R	ER	BB	SO
R. Clemens W,4-0	9	3	1	1	0	20

BB: Boggs, Baylor, Barrett, Hoffman
TIME: 2:39
ATTENDANCE: 13,414
UMPIRES: Vic Voltaggio, Tim Welke, Dave Phillips, Larry McCoy
SOURCES: BBWS; Boston Globe, Herald; Seattle Times; USA Today

BALANCE	OUT	+R	+OB	=BP	+AB	+BB	+SH	+HP	+CI
Seattle	27	1	2	30	30	0	0	0	0
Boston	24	3	7	34	30	4	0	0	0

Giant Teamwork

195. Fourteen Teammates Get Hits, 13 Score Runs in Nine-Inning Game

SAN DIEGO	at	SAN FRANCISCO
(Padres, 1)		(Giants, 18)

Monday, June 23, 1986, Candlestick Park

It was just like batting practice for San Francisco in their 18–1 romp over San Diego. As a matter of fact, for one inning, the Giants did hit against a Padres' batting-practice hurler. Utility-man Dane Iorg, who had never hurled in the major leagues or any other league since 1972, made his pitching debut in the eighth inning after his club had given up any hope of victory.

The Giants' 18 runs and 21 hits didn't threaten any records, but their offensive *teamwork* did. As the game reached ludicrous proportions, substitutions were made freely, and the replacements continued the barrage. Unmentioned in contemporary newspapers was the fact that *no other team had ever had more than 14 different teammates get hits, nor 13 mates score runs in a nine-inning game*. Both events tied the major league standards.

The Padres set the stage for this carnage by previously depleting their relief staff. Manager Steve Boros desperately tried to coax innings out of starter LaMarr Hoyt despite an unrelenting pounding by the Giants. Hoyt conceded five runs in the opening frame, two in the third, and allowed hits to three of the first four batters in the fourth before Tim Stoddard assumed the mound duties. Stoddard pitched well, but being a reliever, could only be counted on for a few innings. Stoddard left without further damage but the Giants already led 9–1. Mark Thurmond was then called upon to pitch in relief for the first time this season. Mark had also tossed four innings as a starter two days earlier and showed signs of wear as he was

Mike Lacoss — beneficiary of Giant offensive teamwork.

now battered for five runs during the seventh. San Diego then trailed 14–1.

With the outcome apparently sealed, and not wishing to further exhaust his overworked staff, Boros then called on his "utility pitcher," Iorg, to hurl the bottom of the

San Diego Padres	AB	R	H	I
Marvell Wynne cf	4	0	1	1
Tony Gwynn rf	3	0	0	0
Bip Roberts 2b5	1	0	0	0
John Kruk lf,rf5	2	0	0	0
Steve Garvey 1b	2	0	0	0
Carmelo Martinez 1b5	2	0	1	0
Graig Nettles 3b	2	0	0	0
Dane Iorg lf5,p8	2	0	0	0
Terry Kennedy c	2	0	0	0
> Bruce Bochy c5	2	0	0	0
Gary Templeton ss	2	0	0	0
Bob Stoddard p4	0	0	0	0
Mark Thurmond ph7,p	1	0	0	0
Kevin McReynolds lf8	0	0	0	0
Tim Flannery 2b,3b5	2	1	1	0
LaMarr Hoyt p	0	0	0	0
Jerry Royster ss4	2	0	0	0
	29	1	3	1

San Francisco Giants	AB	R	H	I
Randy Kutcher cf	6	2	2	1
Robby Thompson 2b	4	1	1	0
Mike Woodard 2b6	2	2	2	2
Jeff Leonard lf	2	1	1	1
Candy Maldonado lf5	3	1	1	2
Chili Davis rf	2	1	1	0
> J. Youngblood ph4,rf	3	1	1	2
Chris Brown 3b	4	2	3	1
Mike Aldrete 1b	4	1	1	2
Bob Brenly c	4	1	3	2
Harry Spilman ph8,c	1	1	1	0
Jose Uribe ss	2	0	1	1
Luis Quinones ss6	2	2	1	0
Mike LaCoss p	4	2	2	4
	43	18	21	18

San Diego	IP	H	R	ER	BB	SO
Hoyt L,2-4	3.1	13	9	9	0	2
Stoddard	2.2	0	0	0	2	5
Thurmond	1	4	5	3	1	1
Iorg	1	4	4	4	0	1
	8	21	18	16	3	9

San Francisco	IP	H	R	ER	BB	SO
LaCoss W,7-2	9	3	1	1	3	3

San Diego	0 0 1	0 0 0	0 0 0	– 1
San Francisco	5 0 2	2 0 0	5 4 x	–18

OB: San Diego 5, San Francisco 7
E: Roberts, C. Brown
DP: Woodard-Quinones-Aldrete (Iorg)
2B: LaCoss, Youngblood, C. Brown
3B: Maldonado
HR: LaCoss(1), Woodard(1)
SO: Bochy, Thurmond, Royster; Brenly,
Kutcher 2, Thompson, Maldonado,
Leonard, Youngblood, Aldrete 2
BB: Kruk 2, Flannery; Brown, Aldrete,
Uribe(I)

SH: LaCoss, Hoyt
SF: Leonard, Youngblood
WP: Stoddard
TIME: 2:37
ATTENDANCE: 10,604
UMPIRES: Fred Brocklander, Lee Weyer,
Dutch Rennert, Ed Montague
SOURCES: BBWS; San Diego Union;
San Francisco Chronicle; USA Today

BALANCE	OUT	+	R	+	OB	=	BP	=	AB	+	BB	+	SH	+	HP	+	CI
San Diego	27		1		5		33		29		3		1		0		0
San Francisco	24		18		7		49		43		3		3		0		0

eighth. In rapid order, pinch-hitter Harry Spilman singled as did Louis Quinones. Next, Giants pitcher Mike LaCoss capped off a humiliating day for the Padres by blasting his first major-league home run making it 17–1. San Francisco's Randy Kutcher then exposed himself to eternal ridicule by taking a called third strike from Iorg for the first out. Dane's glory was short lived, however, as the very next batter, reserve Mike Woodard, joined LaCoss in smacking his first (and only) major-league home run. Iorg then retired both Candy Maldonado and Joel Youngblood on pop-ups to first, but the Giants had already tied two major-league records while batting in only eight innings.

Philadelphia Extra

196. Team Gets 15 Extra-Base Hits in Nine-Inning Game

CHICAGO   at   PHILADELPHIA
(Cubs, 1)   (Phillies, 19)

Monday Night, June 23, 1986, Veterans Stadium

Anything can happen when the two worst pitching staffs in the league square off, and so it was this night when Philadelphia entertained Chicago at Veterans Stadium. In a shelling the likes of which is normally reserved for Wrigley Field, the Phillies bombed three Cub hurlers for 19 runs on 20 hits, including *15 extra-base blows which established a modern National League record for a nine-inning game.*

Chicago rookie left-hander, Jamie Moyer, was making only his second major-league start. A week earlier, in an auspicious debut, Moyer had chalked up his first big-league victory against these same Phillies when he had them lunging at low-and-away breaking stuff and chopping harmless ground balls. But this night he was quickly and rudely awakened, for by the time Jamie had thrown eight pitches, Philadelphia was already leading 3–0 on a Juan Samuel home run.

"The key to the whole thing, in my own personal opinion," said Mike Schmidt, "is the pitcher that made us look bad with a whole bunch of change-ups — lousy, little ground balls over in Wrigley Field — got in a ballpark where the wind wasn't a factor, and it's an Astroturf field, and he saw a lot of hitters willing to shoot to right field early in the game."*

The second inning saw the Phillies retired in order for the only time in the game. It was also the only frame in which they did not club an extra-base hit.

Moyer struggled again in the third inning when he was reached for a home run, this time a two-run shot by Mike Schmidt. Before the frame ended, George Frazier came on in relief and the Phillies led 6–0.

Samuel led the attack with a double and two home runs.

Frazier tossed a scoreless fourth but collapsed in the fifth when Philadelphia tallied

Chicago Cubs	AB	R	H	I
Shawon Dunston ss	4	0	0	0
Gary Matthews lf	4	0	0	0
Ryne Sandberg 2b	3	0	0	0
Chris Speier 2b8	1	0	0	0
Keith Moreland rf	2	0	0	0
Terry Francona 1b7	1	0	0	0
Ron Cey 3b	4	1	2	0
Leon Durham 1b	3	0	1	1
Dave Martinez cf7	1	0	1	0
>Jerry Mumphrey cf,rf7	4	0	0	0
Steve Lake c	3	0	2	0
Jamie Moyer p	1	0	0	0
George Frazier p3	1	0	0	0
Jay Baller p6	0	0	0	0
	32	1	6	1

Philadelphia Phillies	AB	R	H	I
Ron Roenicke cf,lf6	4	3	2	1
Rick Schu 3b	5	3	4	4
Juan Samuel 2b	5	2	3	6
Luis Aguayo 2b8	1	1	1	1
Mike Schmidt 1b	4	2	2	2
Milt Thompson cf6	2	1	2	2
Von Hayes lf,1b6	3	3	1	0
>Glenn Wilson rf	5	1	2	0
John Russell c	5	1	2	2
Steve Jeltz ss	4	1	0	0
Shane Rawley p	4	1	1	1
	42	19	20	19

Chicago	IP	H	R	ER	BB	SO
Moyer L,1-1	2.2	7	6	6	1	3
Frazier	2.1	6	8	8	4	2
Baller	3	7	5	5	2	2
	8	20	19	19	7	7

Philadelphia	IP	H	R	ER	BB	SO
Rawley W,10-4	9	6	1	1	1	2

*Bill Conlin, "Phils Have Swinging Night," Philadelphia Daily News, *24 June 1986, p. 86, col. 1.*

Chicago   0 0 0   0 0 0   1 0 0   - 1
Phillies   3 0 3   0 6 3   1 3 x   -19

OB: Chicago 6, Philadelphia 8
E: Rawley
DP: Schu-Samuel-Schmidt (Matthews)
2B: Schu 2, Schmidt, Samuel, Wilson 2,
     Russell 2, Cey, Rawley, Roenicke,
     Aguayo
HR: Samuel 2(5), Schmidt(13),
     Thompson(3)
SB: Hayes 3(13)
SO: Matthews, Mumphrey; Hayes, Jeltz,
     Wilson 2, Russell, Rawley 2

BB: Moreland; Roenicke 2, Schu, Hayes 2, Wilson, Jeltz
SH: Hayes, Baller
SF: Rawley
TIME: 2:32
ATTENDANCE: 21,899
UMPIRES: John McSherry, Frank Pulli, Greg Bonin,
     Bill Williams
SOURCES: BBWS; Chicago Tribune; Philadelphia
     Daily News, Inquirer

BALANCE	OUT+R+OB=BP=AB+BB+SH+HP+CI								
Chicago	27	1	6	34	32	1	1	0	0
Philadelphia	24	19	8	51	42	7	2	0	0

six more times, highlighted by another Juan Samuel round-tripper.

When the first two Phillies reached base in the sixth, Jay Baller relieved Frazier. Nothing changed as far as Philadelphia was concerned, however, as they continued to pound the ball and led 15–0 after six.

Chicago's lone tally came in the seventh, and the Phillies responded in kind on a Milt Thompson circuit blast.

Philadelphia closed out the scoring with three more in the eighth, thanks in part to a double by winning hurler Shane Rawley, who needed only 92 pitches to vanquish the Cubs.

In establishing the NL mark, the Phillies batted in only eight rounds, amassing a club record 11 doubles to complement their four home runs. Every Phillie who played, scored, and everyone except Steve Jeltz got at least one hit.

Robbery by Thompson Thwarted

197. Player Caught Stealing Four Times in 12-Inning Game

SAN FRANCISCO   at   CINCINNATI
(Giants, 7)   (Reds, 6)

Friday Night, June 27, 1986, Riverfront Stadium

There have been five players caught stealing twice in the same inning, and many others who have been apprehended three times in one game. But there had never been anyone *thrown out four times in a single contest* until this night when the Giants' larcenous rookie, Robby Thompson, repeatedly tested the arm of Reds catcher Bo Diaz.

In the game, several of Thompson's teammates did have early success against Diaz. Randy Kutcher had stolen third base in the third inning, and with Thompson at bat in

the fourth, pitcher Scott Garrelts and Kutcher combined for a double steal. On that play, Diaz' throw went into left field enabling Garrelts to score and, when left fielder Eric Davis fumbled the ball, Kutcher also tallied. Thompson then singled and, having just watched the previous farce unfold, was off and running. But Diaz anticipated the rookie's action and gunned him down at second base.

In the sixth Thompson singled for the second time driving home a run, but was

Thompson was caught stealing 15 times in 27 attempts during his rookie campaign.

and Dave Parker's three-run home run allowed the Reds to tie it after seven innings, 6–6.

With the score still tied in the ninth, Thompson led off with his third straight single. Representing the lead run, Robby then tried to get himself into scoring position but once again was gunned down by Diaz at second.

Thompson needed a fluke play for his record-setting fourth caught-stealing. With two out in the 11th, he struck out, but John Franco's pitch was wild, enabling Robby to reach first. Franco then atoned for his miscue when he caught Thompson leaning toward second. As Franco threw over to first, Robby decided to sprint for second but was easily caught for the fourth time. "A rough night on the bases," said Thompson. "I wanted to get in the record book, but not like that."*

Despite Thompson's unfortunate baserunning, San Francisco won the game in 12 innings, 7–6, when Mike Aldrete's sacrifice fly scored Chili Davis from third base.

The following table outlines each of Thompson's offensive events, both batting and baserunning:

again victimized while attempting to steal on Diaz' throw to second. Robby's RBI gave the Giants a 6–2 lead, and it didn't appear that he would even get to bat two more times. But an array of failing San Francisco relievers

ROBBY THOMPSON'S DAY OF FRUSTRATION, 6-27-86

Inn	Pitcher	Catcher	Outs	Runners On	Batter	Event
1	Gullickson	Diaz	1	None	Thompson	Fly out to right
3	Gullickson	Diaz	0	Garrelts (3rd) Kutcher (1st)	Thompson	Sac fly to center, RBI
4	Gullickson	Diaz	2	None	Thompson	Single to center
4	Gullickson	Diaz	2	Thompson (1st)	Leonard	Thompson CS (2-6)
6	Willis	Diaz	2	Uribe (3rd)	Thompson	Single thru short, RBI
6	Willis	Diaz	2	Thompson (1st)	Leonard	Thompson CS (2-6)
9	R. Robinson	Diaz	0	None	Thompson	Single to center
9	R. Robinson	Diaz	0	Thompson (1st)	Leonard	Thompson CS (2-4)
11	Franco	Diaz	2	None	Thompson	Strikeout/wild pitch
11	Franco	Diaz	2	Thompson (1st)	Leonard	Thompson CS (1-3-4)

*David Bush, "Giants Beat Reds in 12 Innings," San Francisco Chronicle, *28 June 1986, p. 46, col. 4.*

San Francisco Giants	AB	R	H	I
Randy Kutcher cf	6	2	1	1
Robby Thompson 2b	5	0	3	2
Jeff Leonard lf	6	0	0	0
Chili Davis rf	2	1	0	0
Chris Brown 3b	6	0	2	1
Mike Aldrete 1b	4	0	0	1
>Bob Melvin c	6	1	2	0
Jose Uribe ss	5	1	3	0
Scott Garrelts p	2	2	1	0
Mark Davis p7	0	0	0	0
Jeff Robinson p7	0	0	0	0
Chuck Hensley p7	0	0	0	0
Frank Williams p7	0	0	0	0
Harry Spilman ph8	0	0	0	0
Juan Berenguer p8	0	0	0	0
Candy Maldonado ph11	1	0	0	0
Greg Minton p11	0	0	0	0
	43	7	12	5

Cincinnati Reds	AB	R	H	I
Eddie Milner cf	3	0	1	0
Tracy Jones ph7,lf	1	0	0	0
Pete Rose 1b	3	0	1	0
Tony Perez ph7	1	0	1	0
Tom Browning pr7	0	1	0	0
Ron Robinson p8	0	0	0	0
Max Venable ph9	0	0	0	0
John Franco p10	0	0	0	0
Sal Butera ph11	1	0	0	0
Scott Terry p12	0	0	0	0
Dave Parker rf	6	2	2	3
Eric Davis lf,cf8	4	1	1	0
Buddy Bell 3b	4	0	1	1
>Dave Concepcion ss,1b8	6	1	1	0
Bo Diaz c	4	0	2	2
Ron Oester 2b	4	0	0	0
Bill Gullickson p	1	0	0	0
Wade Rowdon ph5	1	0	0	0
Carl Willis p6	0	0	0	0
Kurt Stillwell ph7,ss	2	1	0	0
	41	6	10	6

San Francisco	IP	H	R	ER	BB	SO
Garrelts	6	7	3	2	3	5
Davis	.1	0	1	1	1	0
J. Robinson	0	1	1	1	0	0
Hensley	0	1	1	1	0	0
Williams	.2	1	0	0	0	1
Berenguer	3	0	0	0	2	4
Minton W,3-4	2	0	0	0	3	2
	12	10	6	5	9	12

Cincinnati	IP	H	R	ER	BB	SO
Gullickson	5	7	5	5	4	3
Willis	2	2	1	0	0	1
R. Robinson	2	2	0	0	2	2
Franco	2	0	0	0	0	1
Terry L,0-2	1	1	1	1	1	0
	12	12	7	6	7	7

```
San Francisco   0 0 2   3 0 1   0 0 0   0 0 1  - 7
Cincinnati      0 1 0   1 0 1   3 0 0   0 0 0  - 6
```

OB: San Francisco 9, Cincinnati 9
E: Uribe, Thompson, Diaz, E. Davis, Rose, Berenguer
DP: Melvin-Brown (Bell SO)
     Garrelts-Uribe-Aldrete (Parker)
     Uribe-Thompson-Aldrete (Bell)
2B: Rose
3B: Concepcion
HR: Parker(15)
SB: E. Davis 2(30), Kutcher 2(2),
     Garrelts(1), Uribe(13), Oester(4)
CS: Milner, Thompson 4, E. Davis
SO: Thompson, Leonard 3, Aldrete,
     Melvin, Garrelts; Rose, Butera,
     Parker 2, Bell, Concepcion, Diaz,
     Oester 2, Gullickson, Stillwell 2

BB: C. Davis 4, Aldrete, Garrelts,
     Spilman; Jones 2(1I), Venable,
     E. Davis 2, Bell, Diaz, Oester,
     Stillwell
SF: Bell, Thompson, Aldrete
WP: Garrelts, Franco
TIME: 4:31
ATTENDANCE: 21,601
UMPIRES: Bill Williams, John McSherry,
     Frank Pulli, Greg Bonin
SOURCES: BBWS; Cincinnati Enquirer;
     San Francisco Chronicle

BALANCE	OUT	+R	+OB	=BP	=AB	+BB	+SH	+HP	+CI
San Francisco	36	7	9	52	43	7	2	0	0
Cincinnati	36	6	9	51	41	9	1	0	0

Before the reader buries Thompson as an abominable baserunner incapable of learning through experience, it should be pointed out that *The San Francisco Chronicle* assigned much of the blame on someone else. It was reported in the Saturday edition that the first three times Robby was apprehended, a slumping Jeff Leonard missed hit-and-run signals. Then, too, perhaps Giants manager Roger Craig should get an assist for persisting in the futile strategy.

In addition to three hits and two RBIs, Thompson also helped save the game for the Giants in the bottom of the ninth. After Tracy Jones drew a one-out walk, pitcher Juan Berenguer tried to pick him off. The ball got by first baseman Aldrete, and as Jones raced around toward third, Thompson retrieved it and made a perfect throw to third which nipped Jones.

Horner Hammers Four Homers

198. Player Hits Four Home Runs in Loss

MONTREAL   at   ATLANTA
(Expos, 11)   (Braves, 8)

Sunday, July 6, 1986, Fulton County Stadium

This day Atlanta Braves captain Bob Horner joined an elite, although expanding, group of sluggers who *homered four times in one game*. Horner thus became the eleventh major leaguer and the ninth since the turn of the century to clout as many, joining fellow Braves Bobby Lowe (1894) and Joe Adcock (1954). He also became the first in 25 years to explode in a nine-inning game. The right-handed swinger did gain the unenviable distinction, however, of being the only slugger this century to hit four in a losing cause as visiting Montreal upended their hosts 11–8. (Ed Delahanty's Phillies also lost in 1896 despite his four round trippers.)

The former Rookie-of-the-Year connected

in the second, fourth, fifth, and ninth. Winning pitcher Tim Burke was the only Expo hurler to retire the 28-year-old Braves clean-up hitter, jamming him into a foul pop in the seventh.

Later in the locker room, Horner claimed that he wasn't worrying too much about hitting a fourth home run in the ninth but did feel that with Montreal leading by three runs, he'd get a good pitch to hit. Bob had been swinging the bat well the past few weeks and felt this day's success was due to a combination of that as well as some good pitches to hit. Horner summarized his prosperity by saying, "I had a good week today!"*

Horner's day of glory unfolded as follows:

BOB HORNER'S FOUR HOME RUN DAY — JULY 6, 1986

Inn	Outs	Pitcher	Runners	Horner's AB	Result
2	0	McGaffigan	None	Solo HR to left	Atlanta led 1-0
4	2	McGaffigan	None	Solo HR to left	Atlanta trailed 4-2
5	2	McGaffigan	Dedmon (2nd) Oberkfell (1st)	3-run HR to left	Atlanta trailed 10-7
7	1	Burke	Moreno (2nd) Oberkfell (1st)	Foul out to first	Atlanta trailed 11-7
9	2	Reardon	None	Solo HR to left-center	Atlanta trailed 11-8

*Earnest Reese, "Horner 'hacks' the Expos for four homers," Atlanta Journal, 7 July 1986, section D, p. 1, col. 4.

Montreal Expos	AB	R	H	I
Mitch Webster lf	6	2	5	3
George Wright cf	6	1	2	1
>Andre Dawson rf	6	1	2	2
Hubie Brooks ss	5	0	2	0
Tim Wallach 3b	2	1	0	0
Andres Galarraga 1b	2	0	0	0
Way. Krenchicki pr5,1b	1	0	1	0
Jeff Reardon p8	0	0	0	0
Mike Fitzgerald c	3	3	1	2
Al Newman 2b	4	3	2	2
Andy McGaffigan p	2	0	1	1
Tim Burke p5	1	0	0	0
Vance Law 1b8	1	0	0	0
	39	11	16	11

Atlanta Braves	AB	R	H	I
Omar Moreno rf	4	0	1	0
Ted Simmons ph8,3b	1	0	0	0
Ken Oberkfell 3b,2b9	5	1	4	1
Dale Murphy cf	5	0	0	0
Bob Horner 1b	5	4	4	6
>Ken Griffey lf	5	0	2	1
Andres Thomas ss	4	0	1	0
Ozzie Virgil c	4	1	1	0
Glenn Hubbard 2b	3	1	1	0
Chris Chambliss ph8	0	0	0	0
Gene Garber p9	0	0	0	0
Zane Smith p	1	0	0	0
Jeff Dedmon p5	0	1	0	0
Billy Sample ph6	1	0	0	0
Paul Assenmacher p7	0	0	0	0
Rafael Ramirez ph8,rf	1	0	0	0
	39	8	14	8

Montreal	IP	H	R	ER	BB	SO
McGaffigan	4.2	8	7	4	0	2
Burke W,6-2	2.2	4	0	0	1	1
Reardon S,19	1.2	2	1	1	0	1
	9	14	8	5	1	4

Atlanta	IP	H	R	ER	BB	SO
Smith L,7-9	4	9	8	8	2	3
Dedmon	2	4	2	2	1	2
Assenmacher	2	2	1	1	2	1
Garber	1	1	0	0	0	0
	9	16	11	11	5	6

Montreal	0 0 1	3 6 0	1 0 0	-11
Atlanta	0 1 0	1 5 0	0 0 1	- 8

OB: Montreal 10, Atlanta 6
E: Horner, Wallach
DP: Brooks-Newman-Galarraga (Murphy)
   Wallach-Newman-Krenchicki(Murphy)
   Oberkfell-Horner (Newman)
2B: Dawson, Webster, Fitzgerald, Wright, Brooks,
   Virgil, Hubbard, Krenchicki
HR: Horner 4(17), Newman(1),
   Dawson(13), Webster(5)
SB: Webster(22), Griffey(1)
CS: Dawson
SO: Wright 2, Dawson, Wallach,
   Galarraga 2; Oberkfell, Murphy,
   Thomas, Ramirez

BB: Wallach 3, Fitzgerald, Newman;
   Chambliss
SH: McGaffigan, Dedmon, Krenchicki
HP: By Dedmon(Galarraga, Fitzgerald)
PB: Virgil
TIME: 3:06
ATTENDANCE: 18,153
UMPIRES: Larry Pancino, Eric Gregg,
   Gerry Davis, Doug Harvey
SOURCES: BBWS; Atlanta Constitution,
   Journal; Montreal Gazette; New
   York Times

BALANCE	OUT+R+OB=BP=AB+BB+SH+HP+CI
Montreal	27 11 10 48 39 5 2 2 0
Atlanta	27 8 6 41 39 1 1 0 0

Horner finished this season with 27 homers and 87 RBIs, but a continuing stormy relationship with Braves owner Ted Turner left him a victim of the baseball owners' collusion. Offered $900,000 from Atlanta but no bids of note from other clubs, Horner instead opted to join the Yakult Swallows for $2.4 million, plus more than a $1 million in endorsements, and numerous personal amenities.

Bob had an awesome collegiate baseball career, being named an All-American as a shortstop-second baseman in both 1977 and 1978. His 56 home runs established a then career NCAA record, and upon graduation from Arizona State he was elected *The Sporting News* 1978 Player of the Year. Horner was drafted by Atlanta and moved directly to the major leagues. He broke in with a bang when he homered off Bert Blyleven in his first game and went on to club 23 round trippers in just 89 contests that summer. Scouts raved about his potential, but in his second year he held out over a contract dispute and played in only 121 games. Still it was enough to smash 33 homers, drive in 98, and bat .314.

Previously, Horner had never hit more than two homers in any game.

In addition to his financial conflicts, a weight problem and injuries took their toll on the baby-faced slugger. Hampered by a left shoulder that once required surgery and two broken bones in his right wrist, Horner played more than 130 games only twice in his career. In 1988, upon his return from a one-year hiatus in Japan, Horner struggled through 60 games with the St. Louis Cardinals. The following spring he called it a career. Bob never quite reached the exalted accomplishment levels predicted of him early in his career and played a total of only ten major-league seasons, hitting .277 with 218 home runs.

This game was also a landmark of another sort for Montreal second baseman Al Newman. In his eight-year major league career, encompassing 2,107 at bats, Newman stroked only one home run. This game witnessed that two-run shot to left in the fourth inning off Zane Smith.

199. Players Hit
Three Grand Slams in One Game

TEXAS   at   BALTIMORE
(Rangers, 13)   (Orioles, 11)

Wednesday Night, August 6, 1986, Memorial Stadium

This was a contest characterized by out-of-control pitchers, long-ball hitting, and abrupt swings in momentum as the Texas Rangers out-slugged the Baltimore Orioles 13–11. In the process, and for the first time in major-league chronicles, *three players socked grand slam home runs in the same game.* And, not only did two Orioles clear the bases in the same inning, but all three of the game's slams were recorded before the end of the fourth stanza. Numerous bizarre twists enabled Baltimore at one point to have regis-

Harrah had four other hits in addition to his grand slam.

tered 11 runs on only four hits. Texas once led by six, then trailed by five before finally emerging victorious.

Baltimore starter Ken Dixon couldn't retire any batters in the second inning as two singles and a pair of walks pushed over one run and left the bases loaded. Toby Harrah then cleared the sacks with a drive over the 360-foot sign in left as Dixon exited trailing 5–0.

The Rangers tacked on another run in the third on a RBI single by Gary Ward, but their often-wild starter, Bobby Witt, couldn't hold the lead. Having allowed no hits through three frames, Witt walked the first three batters in the fourth on just 15 pitches. Larry Sheets then deposited Witt's next offering over the center-field fence reducing the Rangers' lead to 6–4. His first lifetime bases-loaded blast tied the existing two-team grand slam mark (2) for a single game. After the next hitter singled, Witt was headed for the showers.

Jeff Russell picked up where Witt left off by walking the first batter he faced — Rick Dempsey — on four pitches. After Juan Bonilla and Lee Lacy both popped out to second, Fred Lynn drew a walk to re-load the bases. Cal Ripken then sent a ground ball toward third which Steve Buechele couldn't get out of his glove. All runners were safe as another run scored reducing the Ranger lead to 6–5. The next batter, Jim Dwyer, sent a 2–0 pitch deep into center field. The 388-foot towering fly barely cleared the fence for the Orioles' second grand slam of the stanza and the third overall in the game. Dwyer's first career grand slam capped a nine-run uprising for Baltimore as they seized a 9–6

Texas Rangers	AB	R	H	I
Oddibe McDowell cf	6	1	2	0
Scott Fletcher ss	6	0	2	1
>Pete O'Brien 1b	3	1	1	3
Pete Incaviglia rf	5	2	2	0
Ruben Sierra rf9	0	0	0	0
Gary Ward lf	5	2	3	1
Larry Parrish dh	5	1	2	2
Don Slaught c	4	1	0	0
Steve Buechele 3b	4	2	2	2
Toby Harrah 2b	5	3	5	4
	43	13	19	13

Baltimore Orioles	AB	R	H	I
Juan Bonilla 2b	3	1	0	0
Lee Lacy rf	4	1	2	2
Fred Lynn cf	4	1	0	0
Cal Ripken ss	4	2	0	0
Jim Dwyer dh	1	2	1	4
Tom Dodd ph6,dh	1	0	0	0
Juan Beniquez ph9	1	0	1	0
Jim Traber 1b	4	1	0	0
Larry Sheets lf	2	1	1	4
> John Shelby ph7,lf	2	0	0	0
Tom O'Malley 3b	4	1	2	0
Rick Dempsey c	3	1	0	0
	33	11	7	10

Texas	IP	H	R	ER	BB	SO
Bobby Witt	3	2	5	4	7	3
Jeff Russell	.2	1	4	0	2	0
Mike Mason	2.1	1	2	2	1	2
Mi. Williams W,8-3	1	1	0	0	0	1
Dale Mahorcic S,4	2	2	0	0	0	0
	9	7	11	6	10	6

Baltimore	IP	H	R	ER	BB	SO
Ken Dixon	1	3	5	5	3	1
Odell Jones	4	7	1	1	1	3
Brad Havens	.2	0	0	0	1	1
Rich Bordi L,4-2	1.2	6	6	6	0	4
Nate Snell	1.2	3	1	1	0	0
	9	19	13	13	5	9

Texas	0 5 1	0 0 0	0 6 1	-13
Baltimore	0 0 0	9 0 2	0 0 0	-11

OB: Texas 8, Baltimore 5
E: Buechele
DP: Fletcher-Harrah-O'Brien (Lacy)
     Mahorcic-Fletcher-O'Brien (Lynn)
     Ripken-Bonilla-Traber (O'Brien)
     Lacy-Dempsey (Fletcher)
     Dempsey-O'Malley (Slaught)
2B: Incaviglia, Parrish, Harrah
HR: Harrah(4), Sheets(13), Dwyer(8),
     Lacy(11), Buechele(15), O'Brien(16)
SB: McDowell(20)
SO: McDowell 2, Fletcher, Incaviglia, Ward 2,
     Parrish, Slaught 2; Lynn, Traber, Sheets,
     Shelby, O'Malley, Dempsey

BB: O'Brien 3, Slaught, Buechele;
     Bonilla 2, Lacy, Lynn, Ripken,
     Dwyer 2, Traber, Sheets, Dempsey
TIME: 3:42
ATTENDANCE: 19,519
UMPIRES: Don Denkinger, Mike Reilly,
     Drew Coble, Tim McClelland
SOURCES: Baltimore Sun; BBWS; Dallas
     Morning News, Times-Herald; Fort
     Worth Star-Telegram; USA Today;
     Washington Post

BALANCE	OUT+R+OB=BP=AB+BB+SH+HP+CI
Texas	27 13 8 48 43 5 0 0 0
Baltimore	27 11 5 43 33 10 0 0 0

advantage. (It also gave Dwyer 11 RBIs in his last eight official at-bats.) At this point Texas hurlers had thrown 101 pitches, had walked nine, but had given up only three hits.

The Rangers had an opportunity for the game's fourth grand slam in the sixth inning, but Pete Incaviglia fanned with two outs and the bases jammed.

The Orioles padded their margin in the home half of the sixth on a walk followed by a two-run home run by Lee Lacy. The blow extended the lead to 11–6 while relievers Odell Jones, Brad Havens, and Rich Bordi

were holding the Rangers at bay. But in the eighth there was another fateful momentum swing.

Baltimore right-hander Bordi had retired the first four hitters he had faced, three by strikeouts. But leading off the eighth, Steve Buechele broke the streak with a home run to center making it 11–7. Toby Harrah and Oddibe McDowell then both singled before Scott Fletcher struck out. Next, Pete O'Brien unnerved the home crowd by drilling a pitch just inside the right-field foul pole to close the margin to 11–10. With Baltimore ace reliever Don Aase out with a strained back, Bordi lingered on the mound and yielded subsequent singles to Incaviglia and Ward. Nate Snell, the last available Oriole reliever, finally replaced Bordi but immediately relinquished a two-run double to Larry Parrish which restored the lead for Texas, 12–11. Don Slaught terminated the six-run rally by grounding into a double play.

The only other scoring in the game came from the Rangers in the ninth. A double by Harrah and a single by Fletcher added an insurance run while right-hander Dale Mahorcic faced just seven Orioles over the final two innings.

Even the slow, steady drizzle during the game couldn't dampen Texas personnel postgame remarks. "If that's not the greatest Rangers victory, it is tied for first," said man-

ager Bobby Valentine.* Toby Harrah called it the wildest game he'd seen in his 15-year career.

The Orioles' two grand slams in the same inning were not unique; four other clubs had done that, all since 1962. The topsy-turvy contest also marked the fourth occasion that the Baltimore franchise had hit two grand slams in one game. The feat had proven to be no guarantee of victory, however, for this was their second loss in such a game.

For those readers in tune with hexes, gremlins, and other unearthly vibrations, it should be pointed out that during the Rangers' fateful eighth-inning comeback, a black cat ran on to the field and tried several times to jump over the fence into the Orioles' bullpen — but failed each time.

*Phil Rogers, "Rangers Outlast Orioles," Dallas Times-Herald, 7 August 1986, section C, p. 1, col. 6.

Astros and Cubs Empty Benches

200. Teams Use 53 Players in 18-Inning Game

HOUSTON at CHICAGO
(Astros, 8) (Cubs, 7)

Started: Tuesday, September 2, 1986, Wrigley Field
Completed: Wednesday, September 3, 1986, Wrigley Field

Houston manager Hal Lanier was trying to win a division title, but the intentions of Chicago skipper Gene Michael were less evident. Perhaps the third Cub pilot of the season was desperately seeking employment for 1987 by trying to avoid a basement finish, or maybe he was simply attempting to get a look at all of his new September call-ups. Whatever the motives, the two managers went all-out trying to wrestle victory from an extra-inning contest in which a *major league record-setting 53 players saw action*, breaking the previous mark of 51. (The 53 now remains as only the National League record.)

In addition, the 27 Cub participants tied the existing, one-team National League standard (still stands).

The game began on September 2, but was called at 7:13 P.M. because of darkness with the score tied 4–4 after 14 innings. (This was two years prior to the installation of lights in Wrigley Field.) Most of the players felt it should have been postponed much sooner; Chicago's Bob Dernier claimed it was too dark to see the ball as early as 5:00 P.M. Play was then resumed the following day prior to the regularly scheduled contest.

The first substitute didn't see action until

the bottom of the sixth when Chicago's Terry Francona pinch hit for starter Jamie Moyer and grounded out to first. That opened the replacement floodgates.

Two more players entered the contest in the seventh and two in the eighth when Chicago's battery of pitcher Ron Davis and catcher Jody Davis faced Houston batter Glenn Davis. Then, no fewer than 11 new faces appeared in the ninth inning, eight of them Astros. In that ninth frame, Dave Smith and Tony Walker made their entrance for Houston; Chicago countered with Lee Smith and Chico Walker. Center field posed a particularly knotty problem for scorers as seven different players defended the position between the eighth and eleventh frames. *Seven center fielders in one game, by both teams, tied the existing major league mark* (although seven center fielders had previously appeared in a nine-inning contest).

Other bizarre activities also punctuated this press-box nightmare. Chicago's Manny Trillo entered the game in the 11th as a pinch runner for a pitcher, Scott Sanderson, who had been pinch running for pitcher Rick Sutcliffe, who had been hit by a pitch while pinch batting for pitcher Frank DiPino. In addition, *five Chicago pinch runners also established a new major league record for one team.*

Aside from the bewilderment in the press box, the game itself provided plenty of drama. On four different occasions, Houston took the lead only to have Chicago bounce back to tie it each time.

Houston starter Nolan Ryan gave his club the lead in the second on an RBI ground out, but Chicago answered on Chris Speier's solo homer in the third. Glenn Davis led off the Astros' sixth with a circuit clout, and Alan Ashby singled home another, giving the visitors a 3–1 advantage. The Cubs retaliated in the seventh on a two-run home run by Leon Durham. Each team scored once in the ninth, Houston on a RBI double by Denny Walling and Chicago on a sacrifice fly by Jody Davis. It was during this frame that Houston's Davey Lopes, aged 40, stole his 24th base of the campaign, breaking Honus Wagner's record for a player 40 or over.

The first seven extra innings were barren

Hatcher won it with his fourth home run of the season.

for the Astros as they could muster just two baserunners, both on singles. The Cubs, meanwhile, had several golden scoring opportunities. They failed to cross the plate in the 11th despite three walks and a hit batsman because Keith Moreland was thrown out attempting to advance on an apparent wild pitch. In two other frames, the home team left two runners on base.

In the 17th Houston appeared to clinch the victory when they scored three times on a walk, three singles, and a force out. But the Cubs, as they had done three times previously, stormed back. Ryne Sandberg led off with a walk followed by Bob Dernier's double. Moreland then atoned for his earlier baserunning blunder with a dramatic three-run blast to tie the score once again. Two more Cubs singled in the inning, but Danny Darwin retired pinch hitter Mike Martin to squelch the potential game-winning rally.

Chicago's inability to deliver the coup de grâce in the 17th came back to haunt them when Houston's Billy Hatcher stroked a wind-aided homer in the top of the 18th off rookie Greg Maddux. Three harmless fly-ball outs in the home half slammed the door closed on the Cubs as the Astros prevailed 8–7.

Houston went on to win their division, but lost to the Mets in the playoffs. Chicago finished fifth in the East, 37 games out, and both Michael and Lanier were successful enough to be rehired in 1987.

Houston Astros	AB	R	H	I
Davey Lopes cf	5	1	2	0
Charley Kerfeld p9	0	0	0	0
Larry Anderson p9	0	0	0	0
Dave Smith p9	0	0	0	0
Matt Keough p10	2	0	0	0
Bob Knepper p15	0	0	0	0
Bill Doran ph17,2b	2	0	0	0
Jim Pankovits 2b	6	1	1	0
Julio Solano p17	0	0	0	0
> Danny Darwin p17	1	0	0	0
Phil Garner 3b	3	0	1	0
Denny Walling ph7,3b	5	0	2	1
Glenn Davis 1b	4	1	2	1
Dan Driessen 1b9	3	1	2	1
Kevin Bass rf	8	2	3	1
Jose Cruz lf	8	0	1	1
Alan Ashby c	5	1	2	1
Robbie Wine c10	3	0	1	0
Dickie Thon ss	2	0	0	0
Craig Reynolds ph9,ss	5	0	0	0
Nolan Ryan p	3	0	0	1
Aurelio Lopez p8	0	0	0	0
Terry Puhl ph9	1	0	0	0
Tony Walker cf9	0	0	0	0
Ty Gainey cf9	0	0	0	0
Billy Hatcher ph11,cf	4	1	1	1
	70	8	18	8

Chicago Cubs	AB	R	H	I
Dave Martinez cf	4	0	0	0
Lee Smith p9	0	0	0	0
Brian Dayett rf10	5	0	1	0
Ryne Sandberg 2b	7	1	1	0
Jerry Mumphrey lf,cf9	4	0	1	0
> Bob Dernier pr9,cf	5	2	1	0
Keith Moreland rf,1b10	6	2	2	3
Leon Durham 1b	3	1	1	2
Chico Walker pr9	0	0	0	0
Frank DiPino p10	0	0	0	0
Rick Sutcliffe ph11	0	0	0	0
Scott Sanderson pr11	0	0	0	0
Manny Trillo pr11,3b	3	0	0	0
Jody Davis c	6	0	1	1
Greg Maddux pr17,p	0	0	0	0
Chris Speier 3b	3	1	2	1
Guy Hoffman p12	0	0	0	0
Gary Matthews ph14,lf	3	0	1	0
Shawon Dunston ss	7	0	1	0
Jamie Moyer p	1	0	0	0
Terry Francona ph6	1	0	0	0
Ron Davis p7	0	0	0	0
Thad Bosley ph8,lf	4	0	0	0
Steve Trout p15	0	0	0	0
Ron Cey ph16	0	0	0	0
Dave Gumpert p17	0	0	0	0
Mike Martin ph17,c	1	0	0	0
	63	7	12	7

Houston	IP	H	R	ER	BB	SO
Ryan	7	4	3	3	1	5
Lopez	1	0	0	0	0	1
Kerfeld	0	1	1	1	0	0
Anderson	.1	0	0	0	1	0
D. Smith	.2	0	0	0	1	1
Keough	5	1	0	0	3	4
Knepper	2	2	0	0	2	0
Solano	.1	3	3	0	1	0
Darwin W,2-1	1.2	1	0	0	0	1
	18	12	7	4	9	12

Chicago	IP	H	R	ER	BB	SO
Moyer	6	9	3	3	2	2
R. Davis	2	1	0	0	0	0
L. Smith	1	2	1	1	1	1
DiPino	2	0	0	0	0	3
Hoffman	3	1	0	0	0	2
Trout	2	1	0	0	0	1
Gumpert	1	3	3	0	1	1
Maddux L,0-1	1	1	1	1	0	1
	18	18	8	5	4	11

Houston	0 1 0	0 0 2	0 0 1	0 0 0	0 0 0	0 3 1	– 8
Chicago	0 0 1	0 0 0	2 0 1	0 0 0	0 0 0	0 3 0	– 7

OB: Houston 12, Chicago 14
E: Pankovits
DP: Sandberg-Dunston-Durham (Bass)
    Moreland-J.Davis (Thon fly)
2B: Cruz, Lopes, Bass, Moreland,
    Walling, Dernier
HR: Speier(6), G. Davis(27), Durham
    (15), Moreland(9), Hatcher(4)
SB: Speier(2). Lopes(24), Dernier
    (21), C.Walker(1)
CS: Sandberg
SO: Keough, Darwin, G. Davis, Bass,
    Cruz, Ashby, Wine, Thon, Ryan,
    Reynolds, Hatcher; Martinez,
    Dayett, Mumphrey, Durham,
    Trillo, J. Davis, Matthews,
    Dunston 2, Moyer, Bosley 2

BB: Pankovitz 2, G. Davis, Thon; Sandberg,
    Moreland 2(1I), Durham(I), J. Davis,
    Dunston, Speier 2(2I), Cey
SH: Sandberg
SF: J. Davis
HP: By Keough (Sutcliffe)
BK: Moyer
TIME: 5:14
ATTENDANCE: 10,501
UMPIRES: Joe West, John McSherry,
    Bill Williams, Frank Pulli
SOURCES: BBWS; Chicago Tribune;
    Houston Post; USA Today

BALANCE	OUT	+R	+OB	=BP	=AB	+BB	+SH	+HP	+CI
Houston	54	8	12	74	70	4	0	0	0
Chicago	54	7	14	75	63	9	2	1	0

Cubs Slam Astros

201. Players Hit
Three Grand Slams in One Game

HOUSTON   at   CHICAGO
(Astros, 7)   (Cubs, 22)

Wednesday, June 3, 1987, Wrigley Field

It took 110 years before there was a major league game in which three grand slams were hit, but less than one more year before the feat was duplicated. In 1986 (see 8-06-86) an American League contest first harvested the trio; now it was the Senior Circuit's turn.

As they often do, home run winds were blowing out of Wrigley Field this day, kindling a slugfest between the visiting Astros and the host Cubs. Eight balls left the park, *three of them grand slams, tying the major league record* as Chicago ravaged three Astros pitchers for nine walks, 21 hits, and six home runs. Their 22 runs were three more than had ever been scored against Houston in the 26-year history of the franchise. The Cubs further embarrassed their guests by scoring in every frame until Larry Anderson finally strangled them in the eighth. The rout capped a week of plunder against an Astros

staff that in six games had allowed 102 base runners and 58 runs.

Houston got off to an auspicious start when Bill Doran reached Rick Sutcliffe for a two-run homer in the top of the first. But that was not only the Astros' last lead; it also was the last time they were even close.

The Cubs flogged left-hander Bob Knepper for nine earned runs in the home half of the first. Brian Dayett's grand slam to right, Keith Moreland's solo shot, and Ryne Sandberg's three-run homer led the assault. For the game, Dayett reached base all six times he stepped to the plate — on an error, three walks, a double, and his grand slam.

Chicago tacked on a pair in the second and two more in the third, including a solo blast by Andre Dawson, to make it 13–2. Dawson had accounted for four homers and 12 RBIs during the previous two games of the

Batting hero Keith Moreland entered the game hitting .210.

series against the Astros and was now ahead of Roger Maris's 61-homer pace. The Cubs were so relaxed at this point that they pulled the age-old baseball prank of giving Andre the silent treatment after his 19th circuit clout of the season. Sandberg further added, "After the third inning, we stopped looking at (third-base coach John) Vukovich for signs. He was just looking to the outfield. Besides, you're not going to hit-and-run when you're up by 11 runs that early."*

With a huge lead entering the fourth

inning, Sutcliffe committed a pitcher's mortal sin by walking the bases loaded before Billy Hatcher cleared them with a grand slam to left. That made it 13–6. Groping to explain his unexpected wildness, Sutcliffe later said, "Maybe all the rain yesterday shrunk the plate."†

Houston's rejuvenation was short-lived, however, as they tallied just once more in the game, that coming in the fifth. Chicago, meanwhile, added one in the fourth and two in the fifth to lead 16–7. Sutcliffe was barely

*Ivy McLemore, "Cub's fireworks set off angry lecture from Lanier," Houston Post, 4 June 1987, section E, p. 7, col. 3.
†Ibid.

able to withstand the necessary five innings to be eligible for his league leading eighth victory. He faced 27 Astros and 13 of them reached base.

In the home half of the sixth, Moreland connected for his second home run and the game's third grand slam, a ponderous blow to center off right-handed reliever Julio Solano. That gave Keith seven RBIs for the game and the Cubs a formidable 20–7 advantage.

The scoring concluded in the Cubs' seventh when pinch hitter Jim Sundberg poured

salt in the wound by drilling a two-run shot to right making the final score 22–7. Sundberg had been batting for catcher Jody Davis, who had achieved one of the strangest feats in baseball annals. Davis had scored five runs on just one hit (plus four walks) in one official at-bat .

Chicago fans hadn't seen such a glorious display of offense from the home club in years — eight to be exact; not since they scored 22 runs against the Phillies in 1979 and *lost*.

Houston Astros	AB	R	H	I
Billy Hatcher cf	3	2	1	4
Larry Anderson p8	0	0	0	0
Bill Doran 2b	5	1	3	2
Phil Garner 2b8	0	0	0	0
Denny Walling 3b	3	0	0	0
Glenn Davis 1b	5	1	2	0
Kevin Bass rf	4	0	0	0
Jose Cruz lf	4	1	0	0
>Craig Reynolds ss	5	0	1	1
Mark Bailey c	3	1	1	0
Bob Knepper p	1	0	1	0
Dave Meads p2	0	1	0	0
Paul Householder ph5	1	0	0	0
Julio Solano p5	0	0	0	0
Terry Puhl ph8	1	0	0	0
Chuck Jackson cf8	0	0	0	0
	35	7	9	7

Houston	IP	H	R	ER	BB	SO
Knepper L,2-6	1	7	9	9	2	1
Meads	3	7	5	5	3	2
Solano	3	7	8	8	4	2
Anderson	1	0	0	0	0	1
	8	21	22	22	9	6

Houston	2 0 0		4 1 0		0 0 0		- 7
Chicago	9 2 2		1 2 4		2 0 x		-22

OB: Houston 9, Chicago 8
E: Knepper, G. Davis
DP: Reynolds-Doran-G. Davis (Sandberg)
        Sutcliffe-Trillo (Cruz liner)
2B: Dayett, Trillo, G. Davis 2, J. Davis
HR: Doran(6), Dayett(4), Moreland 2(6),
        Sandberg(10), Dawson(19), Hatcher
        (5), Sundberg(2)
SB: Dawson(6)
SO: G. Davis, Bass, Cruz, Reynolds,
        Householder; Dernier, Moreland,
        Dunston, Sutcliffe, Lynch, Noles

Chicago Cubs	AB	R	H	I
Bob Dernier cf	6	1	3	2
Ryne Sandberg 2b	5	4	3	3
Andre Dawson rf	5	2	2	1
Paul Noce ss7	1	0	0	0
Jody Davis c	1	5	1	0
Jim Sundberg ph7,c	1	1	1	2
Brian Dayett lf,rf7	3	3	2	4
Keith Moreland 3b	5	2	3	7
Shawon Dunston ss	5	1	1	0
Dave Martinez lf7	1	0	0	0
Manny Trillo 1b	5	2	3	0
Rick Sutcliffe p	3	1	1	0
Gary Matthews ph5	1	0	1	2
Ed Lynch p6	1	0	0	0
> Dickie Noles p8	1	0	0	0
	44	22	21	21

Chicago	IP	H	R	ER	BB	SO
Sutcliffe W,8-2	5	7	7	7	6	3
Lynch	2	0	0	0	1	2
Noles	2	2	0	0	0	0
	9	9	7	7	7	5

BB: Hatcher, Walling 2, Bass, Cruz, Bailey, Meads;
        Sandberg, Davis 4, Dayett 3, Trillo
SF: Moreland
HP: By Noles (Hatcher)
WP: Meads
TIME: 3:22
ATTENDANCE: 19,725
UMPIRES: Doug Harvey, Dick Stello,
        Eric Gregg, Steve Rippley
SOURCES: BBWS; Chicago Tribune;
        Houston Post; USA Today

BALANCE	OUT+R+OB=BP+AB+BB+SH+HP+CI
Houston	27 7 9 43 35 7 0 1 0
Chicago	24 22 8 54 44 9 1 0 0

Toronto Power Surge

202. Team Hits Ten Home Runs in Eight Innings

BALTIMORE   at   TORONTO
(Orioles, 3)   (Blue Jays, 18)

Monday Night, September 14, 1987, Exhibition Stadium

Throughout baseball history, several major league teams had hit as many as eight home runs in a single game. This night the Toronto Blue Jays shattered that mark when they rocked five different Baltimore hurlers for a *total of ten round trippers* while batting in only eight innings.

This was the year of the home run in the major leagues. Not only did each league clout more than ever before, but five different teams topped 200 circuit blasts. Six other clubs exceeded 190, and in the American League, only Seattle averaged less than one home run per game.

The home team entered this contest tied for first with Detroit while the visitors were struggling to avoid a basement finish. The Orioles were looking forward to the season's end, having lost six straight, ten of 12, and 22 of their last 23 road games. Each club, however, was closing in on the 200-homer mark for the season.

The first inning-and-a-half was uneventful, but then a long-ball volcano erupted. The Jays smacked three home runs in the second, driving Oriole starter Ken Dixon from the hill while taking a 5–0 lead. Ernie Whitt, Rance Mulliniks, and Lloyd Moseby administered the abuse.

Reliever Eric Bell was victimized twice in the third, first by George Bell and secondly by Mulliniks. Both were solo blasts making it 7–1.

Mike Griffin then took the mound for Baltimore and stabilized the Toronto tempest by tossing a homer-less fourth although the Jays did tally another run. Whitt added Griffin's name to the home-run casualty list by opening the fifth with his second round-tripper of the night. That further embarrassed Baltimore as the score mounted to 9–1.

By the time Toronto batted in the sixth, Mike Kinunnen had taken the mound for the Orioles. After the first two Jays were retired, Bell drilled his second homer of the contest and Toronto's seventh. That gave the hosts a 10–2 advantage. Kinunnen was again staggered in the seventh, giving up a walk and

Whitt's three home runs led the Toronto assault.

Baltimore Orioles	AB	R	H	I
Pete Stanicek dh	5	0	0	0
>Billy Ripken 2b	3	1	1	0
Larry Sheets rf	4	1	2	0
Eddie Murray 1b	4	0	3	0
Cal Ripken ss	4	0	2	2
Ron Washington ss8	0	0	0	0
Ray Knight 3b	4	0	0	0
Rene Gonzales 3b8	0	0	0	0
Terry Kennedy c	3	0	0	0
Carl Nichols c8	1	0	1	0
Mike Young lf	4	0	0	0
Mike Hart cf	4	1	2	1
	36	3	11	3

Toronto Blue Jays	AB	R	H	I
Nelson Liriano 2b	4	3	3	1
Lloyd Moseby cf	4	1	1	2
Rob Ducey cf7	2	1	1	3
Tony Fernandez ss	4	0	1	1
> Manny Lee ss7	2	1	1	0
George Bell lf	4	2	2	2
Lou Thornton lf7	1	1	1	0
Ernie Whitt c	5	3	3	5
Greg Myers c8	0	0	0	0
Jesse Barfield rf	5	1	4	0
Rance Mulliniks 3b	3	2	2	3
Kelly Gruber ph7,3b	2	0	0	0
Fred McGriff dh	4	2	1	1
Willie Upshaw 1b	4	1	1	0
	44	18	21	18

Baltimore	IP	H	R	ER	BB	SO
Ken Dixon L,7-10	1.2	5	5	5	1	2
Eric Bell	1.1	2	2	2	0	1
Mike Griffin	2	3	2	2	2	0
Mike Kinunnen	1.2	6	6	6	1	0
Tony Arnold	.2	5	3	3	0	0
Jack O'Connor	.2	0	0	0	0	1
	8	21	18	18	4	4

Toronto	IP	H	R	ER	BB	SO
J. Clancy W,13-10	7	7	2	2	1	6
Mark Eichhorn	1	2	1	1	0	0
Tom Henke	1	2	0	0	0	2
	9	11	3	3	1	8

```
Baltimore   0 0 1   0 0 1   0 1 0   - 3
Toronto     0 5 2   1 1 1   7 1 x   -18
```

OB: Baltimore 7, Toronto 6
DP: C. Ripken-B.Ripken-Murray(Gruber)
    Fernandez-Liriano-Upshaw(Knight)
2B: Murray, C. Ripken, Liriano,
    Barfield
HR: Whitt 3(17), Mulliniks 2(10),
    Moseby(23), G.Bell 2(45), Ducey
    (1), McGriff(19), Hart(4)
SO: Stanicek, Sheets, Knight 2,
    Hart 2, Young 2; Moseby, Ducey,
    McGriff 2

BB: B. Ripken; Liriano 2, McGriff, Upshaw
WP: Clancy
TIME: 3:18
ATTENDANCE: 27,446
UMPIRES: Greg Kosc, Tim Tschida,
    Rocky Roe, Larry Barnett
SOURCES: Baltimore Sun; BBWS; Globe
    and Mail (Canada's national news-
    paper); Toronto Star; USA Today

BALANCE	OUT+R+OB=BP=AB+BB+SH+HP+CI							
Baltimore	27	3	7	37	36	1	0	0	0
Toronto	24	18	6	48	44	4	0	0	0

two singles, the second driving in the 11th Blue Jay run. Canadian Rob Ducey then hit his first major league round-tripper, a three-run shot, making it 14–2. It was also Toronto's record-tying eighth home run. After the next hitter singled, Kinunnen was banished to the showers. (Despite appearances in 48 major league games, Kinunnen retired without a single decision.)

Tony Arnold, the fifth Baltimore pitcher, assumed the mound duties but was promptly greeted by another single and Whitt's third circuit-blast of the night. Whitt thus became only the second Blue Jay to smash a trio in one game. (Otto Velez also did it on May 4, 1980.) That gave Toronto a new major league record of nine home runs and an overwhelming 17–2 lead.

"There's no question I was going up there thinking home run," Whitt said. "It's not often you have a chance to set a major league record."* With three home runs, Whitt

*Larry Millson, "Whitt paces record power surge by Jays," The Globe and Mail, 15 September 1987, section D, p. 1, col. 5.

needed just one more to join a celebrated group of single-game sluggers. Nevertheless, he was replaced by Greg Myers who nearly got to the plate in the bottom of the eighth.

Arnold hopelessly remained on the mound to start the eighth. Leading off was Fred McGriff who needed one more home run to establish the Toronto rookie mark. McGriff got that record when he hammered a ball into the right field seats for his 19th of the season and Toronto's 10th of the game. Previously, the most the Jays had ever hit in one game was five.

Earlier in this mayhem, Baltimore's Mike Hart had hit his fourth, and last, major league home run. That had come in the third frame, so that McGriff's blast brought the *two-team total to 11, equalling another major league mark* accomplished seven other times. (Two teams finally hit 12 home runs in a 1995 contest.)

Toronto's Kelly Gruber also distinguished himself in the contest. Gruber was one of the few Jays who did *not* hit a home run, and in Toronto's seven-run seventh, Gruber, in a manner of speaking, made all three outs. As the second batter in the frame, Kelly grounded into a double play. As the last batter, he flied out to right.

Home runs and Gruber's performance weren't the only bizarre events of this game. At the time, Cal Ripken, Jr., not only had a consecutive-*game* streak in progress, but also an astonishing consecutive-*inning* streak developing. Ripken had played in 8,243 consecutive innings (covering 908 games) before remaining in the dugout after batting in the eighth. The string had dated back to June 4, 1982, and is believed to be the longest of its kind in major league history. On that date, Jim Dwyer pinch-hit for Ripken against Minnesota.

"It had to end sometime and this was the perfect time," said Oriole manager Cal Ripken Sr. "He couldn't hit a 20-run homer… I've been thinking about it for a while. I wanted to take that monkey off his back. Every place we go, somebody has to write an article about the streak. I wanted to get everybody to stop writing about the consecutive inning streak. I wanted to take that burden off his shoulders."*

Despite unleashing 215 homers, Toronto was overtaken by Detroit in the AL East, finishing two games off the pace. Baltimore barely avoided breathing last place air by closing in sixth place, 31 games out.

*Dave Perkins, "Jay's lumber comes to life in once-in-a-lifetime game," Toronto Star, 15 September 1987, section E, p. 3, col. 5.

Mets Win Unassisted

203. Team Records No Assists in Nine-Inning Game

PHILADELPHIA   at   NEW YORK
(Phillies, 1)   (Mets, 5)

Sunday, June 25, 1989, Shea Stadium

The lead story in most of America's sport pages on June 26, 1989, described a restraining order that temporarily saved Pete Rose from a hearing before baseball commissioner A. Bartlett Giamatti on charges of gambling.

The next biggest headlines related another near miss of a no-hitter by Nolan Ryan who was reached safely after two outs in the eighth. (Ryan was eventually chased in the ninth.) But the only baseball event of the

Fernandez led the Mets staff this season with 198 strikeouts in 219 innings, a 2.83 ERA, and a 14–5 log.

preceding day that still carries any significance occurred in an innocuous 5–1 New York Mets victory over the Philadelphia Phillies.

One of the rarest team performances in major league history entails a *club fielding all nine innings of a game without accumulating a single assist*. As far as researchers know, this had occurred only twice since the turn of the century, a period encompassing more than 140,000 games. In 1945, the Cleveland Indians first turned the trick (see 7-04-45) in defeating the Yankees. Almost forty-four years later, on this day, the Mets invoked the same magic formula to trip the Phillies in Shea Stadium. (See also 9-11-95.)

New York starter Sid Fernandez, who had been known as a fly-ball/strikeout pitcher throughout his career, was the winning pitcher. Historically, the left-hander rarely finished what he started, completing only nine of 131 career starts in six previous seasons. True to form, the 26-year-old tossed seven strong innings on 130 pitches, then gave way to reliever Rick Aguilera who completed the aberration. Aguilera struck out four batters over the last two frames.

Philadelphia Phillies	AB	R	H	I
>Lenny Dykstra cf	5	0	0	0
Tommy Herr 2b	3	0	1	0
Von Hayes rf	4	0	0	0
Ricky Jordan 1b	4	1	2	0
Randy Ready lf	3	0	0	0
Dickie Thon ss	4	0	0	0
Steve Jeltz 3b	4	0	4	1
Steve Lake c	3	0	0	0
Curt Ford ph9	1	0	0	0
Terry Mulholland p	1	0	0	0
Eric Bullock ph5	1	0	0	0
Greg A. Harris p5	0	0	0	0
Bob Dernier ph7	0	0	0	0
Larry McWilliams p7	0	0	0	0
Dwayne Murphy ph9	1	0	0	0
	34	1	7	1

New York Mets	AB	R	H	I
Mark Carreon rf	3	0	0	0
Dave Magadan 1b	3	2	1	0
Howard Johnson 3b	3	1	2	0
Kevin McReynolds lf	4	1	2	2
Gregg Jefferies 2b	4	1	3	2
Mookie Wilson cf	4	0	0	0
Barry Lyons c	3	0	0	0
Kevin Elster ss	4	0	1	1
Sid Fernandez p	3	0	0	0
> Rick Aguilera p8	1	0	0	0
	32	5	9	5

Philadelphia	IP	H	R	ER	BB	SO
Mulholland L,0-2	4	6	5	5	3	5
Harris	2	1	0	0	1	1
McWilliams	2	2	0	0	0	1
	8	9	5	5	4	7

New York	IP	H	R	ER	BB	SO
Fernandez W,5-2	7	5	1	1	3	9
Aguilera	2	2	0	0	0	4
	9	7	1	1	3	13

Philadelphia   0 1 0   0 0 0   0 0 0   - 1
New York   1 0 4   0 0 0   0 0 x   - 5

OB: Philadelphia 9, New York 7
E: Jordan
DP: Thon-Herr-Jordan (Jefferies)
2B: Johnson, McReynolds, Jefferies
3B: Jeltz, Jefferies
CS: Carreon
SO: Dykstra, Herr, Jordan, Ready 3,
    Thon 2, Lake, Ford, Mulholland,
    Bullock, Murphy; Carreon,
    Johnson, McReynolds, Wilson,
    Elster, Fernandez 2

BB: Herr, Ready, Dernier; Lyons,
    Carreon, Magadan, Johnson
BK: Fernandez, Aguilera
TIME: 2:52
ATTENDANCE: 47,692
UMPIRES: Terry Tata, Dana DeMuth,
    Bill Hohn, Bruce Froemming
SOURCES: BBWS; DBD; Philadelphia
    Daily News, Inquirer; New York Times

BALANCE	OUT	+R	+OB	=BP	=AB	+BB	+SH	+HP	+CI
Philadelphia	27	1	9	37	34	3	0	0	0
New York	24	5	7	36	32	4	0	0	0

The Phillies hit six fly-balls, six pop-ups, two unassisted ground outs (both to first), and struck out 13 times. The closest New York came to an assist was on the last play of the game when Philadelphia's Lenny Dykstra grounded Aguilera's initial offering between first and second. Dave Magadan, who was aware of the game's oddity, fielded the ball, waived off Aguilera and beat Dykstra to the bag.

The 1989 campaign supported Fernandez' reputation of a fly ball pitcher who needed little help from his infielders. In the 32 games that Sid started, his teammates averaged 7.4 assists, while in the 130 contests he didn't start, the Mets averaged 9.4 assists. Later this season, Fernandez pitched two complete games. In one the Mets contributed just four assists; in the other they tallied but two assists. Of the 72 times New York harvested double-digit assists this year, Fernandez was the starting pitcher on only three occasions.

Henderson's Phantom Runs

204. Player Steals
Five Bases, Scores Four Runs
Without an Official At-Bat

SEATTLE   at   OAKLAND
(Mariners, 14)   (Athletics, 6)

Saturday, July 29, 1989, Oakland Coliseum

Rickey Henderson is probably considered the most productive lead-off hitter of all time. With more home runs than any other player in history from atop the lineup, Henderson exceeded 20 round-trippers in three different seasons. He also possessed a keen eye at the plate, averaging more than 90 walks in each of his first 15 campaigns and was usually among the league leaders in on-base percentage. But the trademark of Henderson's game was his imposing speed once on the basepaths. Still the holder of the modern single-season stolen base mark of 130 set in 1982, he led the American League in that department 11 of 12 seasons between 1980 and 1991. Once on base, Henderson upset pitchers and changed the entire complexion of a game.

Johnson walked Henderson all four times he faced him.

Although he didn't knock any pitches into the seats in this game, Rickey gave an awesome demonstration of his ability to get on base and score. He also lent credence to the adage that "a walk is as good as a hit" when he *stole five bases and scored four runs without an official at-bat.* It is not known if this is the most runs scored in a game without an official at-bat, but it indeed does represent the most steals without an at-bat. These anomalies are not tracked by record keepers, but it is highly unlikely that anyone ever scored more runs under the same circumstances. And, because the single-game stolen base record of six has been treated elsewhere in this book, it is certain that no one ever stole more than five bases without an at-bat. (Three other game accounts in this collection describe players coming to the plate six times in a nine-inning contest without garnering an official at-bat. But none had a stolen base and only one of the players scored two runs.)

Facing Seattle southpaw Randy Johnson in the first, Henderson worked a full count (two foul balls) before walking. He then stole second and third on Johnson's second and third pitches to Carney Lansford and scored when Johnson fumbled Lansford's grounder.

A similar scenario unfolded when Henderson led off the Oakland third with another full-count (all called) walk. As in the first inning, on Johnson's second

Henderson is baseball's all-time stolen base king.

offering to Lansford, Henderson stole second. The third pitch to Lansford was lined to right enabling Henderson to score his second run.

Henderson received his third consecutive base on balls while leading off the fifth. This time, Johnson offered only four pitches, all missing the strike zone. Henderson again stole second, this time on Johnson's first pitch to Lansford, and eventually scored on Jim Presley's throwing error after there were two outs.

In the sixth, again facing Johnson, Henderson drew a two-out walk after another full count. On the first pitch to Lansford, Stan Javier and Henderson combined for a double

steal. Both runners soon scored on Lansford's double. Afterward, all Johnson could say was: "I hope I'm on his [Henderson's] Christmas list."*

Trailing 14–6 entering the ninth, Oakland manager Tony LaRussa made a number of lineup changes. In the shuffle, Mike Gallego moved in to play shortstop for the Athletics and was placed in the lead-off batting position. The move closed one of the more bizarre lines in boxscore annals — R.Henderson 0AB, 4R, 0H, 0RBI.

Henderson's day of personal achievement was sullied by Oakland's loss and some very slovenly pitching by both staffs. The visitors and the hosts each tallied more walks, and

*Frank Blackman, "The A's? Just keep on walking," San Francisco Examiner, 30 July 1989, section C, p. 1, col. 3.

more runs, than they did hits. While Henderson worked four bases on balls, Seattle's Harold Reynolds and Greg Briley each drew three.

Seattle scored all the runs they needed to win in the opening frame as 13 Mariners stepped to the plate collecting six hits, four walks and eight runs. Oakland starter Storm Davis faced only eight batters in 14 minutes, seven of whom scored.

All eight of the game's stolen bases occurred within the first six innings. They

had little effect on the outcome, however, as all were made by runners in Oakland uniforms.

The Athletics brushed aside this unpleasant experience and won not only the American League pennant but the World Series as well. This contest notwithstanding, the Oakland pitching staff excelled during 1989. By season's end no major league club had thrown more shutouts, and they had allowed the fewest hits and had the lowest ERA in the American League.

Seattle Mariners	AB	R	H	I
Harold Reynolds 2b	3	3	1	1
Greg Briley lf	3	2	1	1
Alvin Davis 1b	5	0	3	5
Jeff Leonard dh	6	1	1	0
Darnell Coles rf	6	1	1	2
Mike Kingery cf	5	2	2	0
>Jim Presley 3b	4	2	1	2
Scott Bradley c	4	1	1	1
Omar Vizquel ss	3	2	1	0
	39	14	12	12

Oakland Athletics	AB	R	H	I
Rickey Henderson lf	0	4	0	0
Mike Gallego ss9	0	0	0	0
Dave Parker ph9	1	0	0	0
Carney Lansford 3b	4	0	2	3
Ron Hassey c9	1	0	0	0
Dave Henderson dh	5	0	1	0
>Mark McGwire 1b	3	1	0	0
Terry Steinbach c,3b9	4	0	1	0
Tony Phillips ss,lf9	4	0	1	0
Lance Blankenship rf	4	0	0	0
Glenn Hubbard 2b	4	0	0	0
Stan Javier cf	3	1	0	0
	33	6	5	3

Seattle	IP	H	R	ER	BB	SO
Ran. Johnson W,5-2	6	4	6	3	7	5
Bill Swift S,1	3	1	0	0	0	1
	9	5	6	3	7	6

Oakland	IP	H	R	ER	BB	SO
Storm Davis L,9-5	.1	5	7	7	2	0
Gene Nelson	3.1	5	7	7	5	5
Matt Young	2.1	1	0	0	4	0
Jim Corsi	3	1	0	0	2	2
	9	12	14	14	13	7

Seattle	8 0 2	4 0 0	0 0 0	-14
Oakland	1 0 1	0 2 2	0 0 0	- 6

OB: Seattle 11, Oakland 7
E: Johnson, Presley 2
DP: Swift-Vizquel-A. Davis (Steinbach)
2B: Bradley, A.Davis, Lansford 2
SB: R. Henderson 5(47), Javier(9), Lansford 2(19)
SO: Reynolds, Coles, Kingery, Presley 2, Bradley, Vizquel; D. Henderson 3, Steinbach, Blankenship, Javier
BB: Reynolds 3, Briley 3, A.Davis, Kingery, Presley 2, Bradley, Vizquel 2; R.Henderson 4, Javier, McGwire 2

WP: S. Davis, Johnson, Nelson
TIME: 3:12
ATTENDANCE: 40,734
UMPIRES: Greg Kosc, John Hirschbeck, Derryl Cousins, Vic Voltaggio
SOURCES: BBWS; Oakland Tribune; San Francisco Examiner; Seattle Times

BALANCE	OUT+R+OB=BP=AB+BB+SH+HP+CI
Seattle	27 14 11 52 39 13 0 0 0
Oakland	27 6 7 40 33 7 0 0 0

Hit Parade Opening

205. Team Gets 16 Hits in One Inning; Seven Teammates Get Two Hits Apiece in One Inning

HOUSTON   at   CINCINNATI
(Astros, 2)   (Reds, 18)

Thursday, August 3, 1989, Riverfront Stadium

This was one of those games that was virtually decided before the home team made its first out. As the Phillies did in 1948 (see 8-13-48), Cincinnati blew this game apart before any of their batters were retired. The first seven Reds reached base safely against Astros starter Jim Clancy, and an eighth reached against reliever Bob Forsch. On the 34th Houston pitch, Cincinnati's ninth batter, Tom Browning, finally grounded out to first for the first Cincinnati out. And then the situation grew worse.

After he retired Browning, Forsch was pummelled even harder than Clancy. The next nine batters all hit safely, including the pitcher. Forsch then retired the 19th and 20th hitters of the inning but not before the Reds had crossed the plate 14 times (all earned) on 16 hits and set or tied a string of new records:

New major league records:
- *Most hits in one inning (16)*; previous mark was 14.
- *Most singles in one inning (12)*; previous mark was 11.
- *Most teammates (7) with two or more hits in one inning*; previous mark was 6.

Major league marks tied:
- *By game's end, Cincinnati posted seven players with three or more hits.*
- *Six Reds scored two or more runs in one inning.*

- *Mariano Duncan and Luis Quinones batted three times in one inning.*
- At the time, it was reported that Forsch had also tied the National League benchmark for most consecutive hits (9) allowed by one pitcher. However, Heinie Meine of the Pirates had been reached for ten straight hits on June 23, 1930,* as had Bill Reidy (see 6-02-01).

Following is a blow-by-blow account of the 38-minute, record-shattering half inning (runs in parentheses):
- After a full count by Jim Clancy, Duncan walked and then stole second.
- With the Reds struggling to score runs, Quinones was ordered to bunt. Luis dropped it down the third base line and beat it out for a single; Duncan moved to third on the play. Reds pilot Pete Rose later said: "Today was an example of what makes baseball a great game. You can never tell what will happen. I was playing for one run in the first and had Quinones bunting. Then we end up scoring 14."†
- Eric Davis grounded a single to center scoring Duncan (1) and sending Quinones to second.
- Ken Griffey homered to left-center on a 1–2 count to make it 4–0.
- Rolando Roomes grounded an 0–2 pitch just to the left of second base for a single.
- After fouling off three pitches, Todd

*Bob Fulton, "Records Potpourri," Society for American Baseball Research Records Committee Newsletter, ed. Lyle Spatz, December 1994, p. 4.

†Terry Blount, "It was over long before it was over," Houston Post, 4 August 1989, section C, p. 5, col. 2.

Jamaican Rolando Roomes had four hits in the game including two the first inning.

All seven batters that Clancy faced scored.

Benzinger grounded a single between first and second, sending Roomes to third.

• Jeff Reed lined the first pitch into right driving home Roomes (5). Benzinger went to third, and Forsch replaced Clancy.

• Ron Oester greeted Forsch by slashing a 2–2 pitch on the ground over first for a double; Benzinger scored (6) and Reed went to third. Forsch then wild-pitched Reed home (7) and Oester to third.

• Browning, batting .105, became the Reds' first out when he grounded a 2–0 pitch to first (unassisted). It was a very brief moment of glory for Forsch as the onslaught quickly resumed.

Cincinnati actually improved during their second time through the batting order when *all nine* players got hits.

• Batting for the second time, Duncan popped a double down the right-field line knocking in Oester (8).

• Quinones lined a single to left-center. Duncan stopped at third.

• Davis lined a single to center to drive home Duncan (9) and put Quinones on second.

• Griffey also lined a single to center. Quinones scored (10) and Davis went to third.

• Roomes then beat out an infield single to third. Davis held at third while Griffey moved to second, loading the bases.

• Benzinger cleared the bases with a ground-ball double over first. Davis (11), Griffey (12), and Roomes (13) all tallied.

• On a full count, Reed lined a single to center. Benzinger stopped at third.

• Oester grounded a single between first and second to score Benzinger (14) and move Reed to second. There was still only one out and it was already 14–0.

• Browning grounded a 1–1 pitch between third and short and into left field to finally join the hit parade. Oester could not score, however, leaving the bases jammed.

Sixteen of the first 18 Cincinnati batters had now hit safely, and many of baseball's single-inning benchmarks had already been broken. And, there was still only one out.

Houston Astros	AB	R	H	I
Billy Hatcher lf	4	0	0	0
Gerald Young cf	2	0	0	0
Eric Anthony rf3	2	0	0	0
Bill Doran 2b	3	0	1	0
Terry Puhl 1b7	1	0	0	0
Glenn Davis 1b	2	1	1	1
Harry Spilman 1b4,c7	2	0	0	0
Ken Caminiti 3b	2	1	1	0
Cra. Reynolds 3b4,2b7	2	0	1	0
Rafael Ramirez ss	2	0	1	1
Eric Yelding ss4	2	0	0	0
Mark Davidson rf,cf3	4	0	1	0
>Alex Trevino c,3b7	4	0	1	0
Jim Clancy p	0	0	0	0
Bob Forsch p1	3	0	1	0
Juan Agosto p8	0	0	0	0
	35	2	8	2

Cincinnati Reds	AB	R	H	I
Mariano Duncan ss	4	2	1	1
Jeff Richardson ss6	1	0	0	0
Luis Quinones 3b	6	3	3	0
Eric Davis cf	4	2	3	2
Herm Winningham cf6	2	0	0	0
Ken Griffey lf	5	2	3	4
Dave Collins lf7	1	0	0	0
Rolando Roomes rf	6	3	4	1
>Todd Benzinger 1b	6	3	4	3
Jeff Reed c	5	2	4	3
Joe Oliver c8	0	0	0	0
Ron Oester 2b	5	1	3	2
Tom Browning p	5	0	1	0
	50	18	26	16

Houston	IP	H	R	ER	BB	SO
Clancy L,5-9	0	6	7	7	1	0
Forsch	7	18	10	10	0	3
Agosto	1	2	1	1	0	0
	8	26	18	18	1	3

Cincinnati	IP	H	R	ER	BB	SO
Browning W,9-10	9	8	2	2	0	1

Houston   0 1 0   1 0 0   0 0 0 - 2
Cincinnati 14 0 0   0 0 0   3 1 x -18

OB: Houston 6, Cincinnati 9
E: Forsch
DP: Reynolds-Doran-Spilman (Duncan)
2B: Oester 2, Duncan, Benzinger,
    E. Davis
3B: Ramirez
HR: Griffey(7), G. Davis(24),
    Roomes(7), Reed(3)
SB: Duncan(5)
SO: Young; E. Davis, Griffey, Oester

BB: Duncan
WP: Forsch, Agosto 2
TIME: 2:16
ATTENDANCE: 20,179
UMPIRES: Dutch Rennert, Paul Runge,
    Bob Engel, Tom Hallion
SOURCES: BBWS; Cincinnati Enquirer;
    Houston Post; USA Today

BALANCE	OUT+R+OB=BP+AB+BB+SH+HP+CI							
Houston	27	2	6	35	35	0	0	0	0
Cincinnati	24	18	9	51	50	1	0	0	0

• Duncan, batting for the third time, jumped on Forsch's first offering and hit a shallow fly to left. No runners could advance, and the second out of the inning finally had been made on the 64th pitch.

• Quinones had a chance to get his third hit of the inning but picked on a 1–1 pitch and drove a fly ball to straight-away right to mercifully end the holocaust.

There you have it—14 runs on 12 singles, three doubles, a home run, one walk, one stolen base, and a wild pitch. Twenty batters looked at 67 pitches. Bill Doran, Houston's sparkplug second baseman, reflected the feelings of many of his teammates after the game. "I thought maybe I was still in bed and maybe it was just a nightmare. When it was about 9–0, it was already to the point of being unbelievable, and then it kept getting worse. Thank goodness it just counts as one game. Luckily you don't get a two-game penalty for losing by 16."*

While the Reds were shoving one another to get to the bat rack, Rolando Roomes

*Terry Blount, "It was over long before it was over," Houston Post, 4 August 1989, section C, p. 5, col. 2.

complained that every time he was about to sit down, he had to get up to shake someone else's hand. Once the hits began to fall, no one was looking for a walk. After Duncan's leadoff walk, 13 of the next 19 batters swung at either the first or second pitch.

It wasn't unconscionable malice by Houston management that compelled Forsch to withstand the brunt of this Cincinnati bombardment. Entering this game, the Astros had been trailing first-place San Francisco by only one game and were looking ahead to their important weekend series with the Giants. With an already tired pitching staff, once the game got out of hand early, Forsch was asked to be the designated sacrificial lamb and to pitch as long as he could.

For a hurler who allowed 18 hits and 10 runs, Forsch received an unusual amount of praise. "My hat is off to Bob Forsch, said Reds manager Pete Rose. "He gave up lots of hits and a lot of runs, but he saved their

bullpen for their big series with the Giants. He's a team player."*

Astros reliever Dave Smith said, "Bob went out there and suffered for us. It took a lot of guts to do what he did today."†

Houston manager Art Howe also sang praises for his 39-year-old, 15-year veteran. "When Bob started getting in trouble I walked out there and told him I was sorry, but I had to leave him out there. Bob said it was OK because he felt fine."§ Had Forsch tired, Howe's next middle-relief choices were going to be infielders Craig Reynolds, Eric Yelding, or first baseman Harry Spilman. Actually Forsch pitched respectably after the catastrophic first, allowing only five more hits and no walks until the seventh when he began to tire.

Often lost among the ruins of this historic game is the commendable pitching by Cincinnati's Tom Browning, who needed only 88 pitches to cast aside the Astros.

*Terry Blount, "It was over long before it was over," Houston Post, 4 August 1989, section C, p. 5, col. 2.
†Ibid.
§Ibid.

Turkey-Shoot in Texas

206. Seven Players Hit by Pitch in One Game

KANSAS CITY   at   TEXAS
(Royals, 13)   (Rangers, 2)

Sunday, September 3, 1989, Arlington Stadium

On a 100-degree Texas afternoon, a certain degree of vindictiveness probably accompanied sweaty hands and lack of control to add another painful line to baseball annals. "It was like a turkey shoot out there... You didn't know whether to swing or duck,"* was how Kansas City veteran Frank White described this record-tying game in which *seven batters were hit by pitches*. It marked the

third time this century that seven batsmen had been hit in the same game.

There wasn't much talk about intentionally hitting batters in the first two innings even though three players were plunked, forcing one to leave the game. Texas starter Kevin Brown set the tone for the day when he hit lead-off batter Kevin Seitzer on the left shoulder with just his fourth pitch. He also

*Dick Kaegel, "Royals duke out victory over Rangers," Kansas City Times, 4 September 1989, section D, p. 2, col. 3.

hit Frank White on the left hand in the second inning. At that point, however, the Royals were willing to concede a lack of malice, for Brown was extremely wild. Both batters were hit with two-strike counts, and after hitting White, Brown next walked Seitzer on four pitches, forcing a run home. That earned him a trip to the showers after having thrown 55 pitches while retiring only three batters. Before the top of the second had ended, the visitors had taken advantage of Ranger wildness to harvest a 7–0 lead.

Suspicions arose in the bottom of the second. The Royals' Mark Gubicza, who normally displayed good control, drilled Steve Buechele in the middle of the back. But at the time, there were already two outs and a runner was on first, so the motive of retaliation was questionable.

Rookie Kevin Brown set the tone by hitting two batters in one inning of work.

There were no further controversial situations until the fourth when, with one out, Kansas City's Kurt Stillwell was struck in the right leg with a pitch from Texas reliever Drew Hall. Hall's very next delivery hit George Brett in the right elbow, sending him to the hospital for X-rays. Meanwhile home plate umpire Ted Hendry did nothing. "No pitcher was warned. The one guy [Hall] was wild as heck. I didn't think anybody was

Kansas City Royals	AB	R	H	I
Kevin Seitzer 3b	2	2	0	1
Bill Pecota pr7,ss	1	1	1	0
Kurt Stillwell ss	3	2	1	2
Jeff Schulz lf7	1	0	0	0
George Brett 1b	2	1	1	2
R. Palacios pr4,1b,3b7	3	1	1	1
Bo Jackson dh	4	1	1	3
Bill Buckner ph9	1	0	0	0
Jim Eisenreich cf	5	0	2	3
> Gary Thurman cf7	1	0	0	0
Mike Macfarlane c	4	1	1	0
Bob Boone pr8,c	0	0	0	0
Matt Winters rf	5	1	2	0
Pat Tabler lf,1b7	4	2	2	1
Frank White 2b	0	1	0	0
Brad Wellman 2b2	4	0	1	0
	40	13	13	13

Texas Rangers	AB	R	H	I
>Jack Daugherty lf	4	1	1	1
Rafael Palmeiro 1b	3	0	0	0
Scott Coolbaugh 3b7	1	0	0	0
Harold Baines dh	3	0	1	0
Mike Stanley ph8	0	0	0	0
Ruben Sierra rf	2	0	1	1
Juan Gonzalez pr6,cf	1	0	0	0
Julio Franco 2b	3	0	0	0
Fred Manrique 2b7	1	0	1	0
Pete Incaviglia cf,1b7	4	0	3	0
Jeff Kunkel ss,rf7	2	1	0	0
Thad Bosley ph8,rf	1	0	0	0
Steve Buechele 3b	1	0	0	0
Dean Palmer ss7	2	0	1	0
Chad Kreuter c	4	0	0	0
	32	2	8	2

Kansas City	IP	H	R	ER	BB	SO
M. Gubicza W,14-10	5	5	1	0	0	7
Larry McWilliams	2	1	1	1	1	2
Luis Aquino	2	2	0	0	1	0
	9	8	2	1	2	9

Texas	IP	H	R	ER	BB	SO
Kev. Brown L,11-9	1	4	6	6	1	1
Drew Hall	3	1	1	1	2	1
Darrel Akerfelds	2	3	1	1	1	4
Craig McMurtry	2	4	5	5	1	1
Cecilio Guante	1	1	0	0	0	0
	9	13	13	13	5	7

```
Kansas City   2 5 0   0 1 0   5 0 0   -13
Texas         0 0 1   0 0 0   1 0 0   - 2
```

OB: Kansas City 10, Texas 8
E: Coolbaugh
DP: Seitzer-Wellman-Palacios(Franco)
     Aquino-Palacios-Tabler(Bosley)
     Buechele-Franco-Palmeiro(Macfarlane)
2B: Brett, Incaviglia, Winters, Palmer
HR: Jackson(29)
SO: Stillwell 2, Jackson 2, Winters,
     Macfarlane, Wellman; Daugherty,
     Palmeiro 2, Baines, Sierra, Kunkel,
     Incaviglia, Buechele, Kreuter
BB: Seitzer 2, Stillwell, Jackson(I),
     Tabler; Stanley, Sierra
SF: Daugherty

HP: By Brown (Seitzer, White),
     by Gubicza (Buechele),
     by Hall (Stillwell, Brett),
     by McWilliams (Kunkel),
     by McMurtry (Macfarlane)
PB: Macfarlane, Kreuter
TIME: 3:07
ATTENDANCE: 18,144
UMPIRES: Ted Hendry, Steve Palermo,
     Don Denkinger, Tim Tschida
SOURCES: BBWS; Dallas Morning News,
     Times Herald; Fort Worth Star-
     Telegram; Kansas City Times

BALANCE	OUT+	R+	OB=	BP+	AB+	BB+	SH+	HP+	CI
Kansas City	27	13	10	50	40	5	0	5	0
Texas	27	2	8	37	32	2	1	2	0

throwing at anybody."* Hall, however, had retired the Royals on only six pitches in the third inning.

The Royals put the game out of reach with five runs in the top of the seventh, three of them coming on a Bo Jackson home run.

That gave the visitors a formidable 13–1 margin.

Veteran left-hander Larry McWilliams had made his Kansas City debut when he relieved Gubicza to start the sixth and threw his first pitch behind Ruben Sierra. In the seventh,

*Steve Cameron, "Five hit batters anger Royals," Kansas City Times, 4 September 1989, section D, p. 2, col. 4.

with a 1–2 count on lead-off Ranger Jeff Kunkel, McWilliams drilled the shortstop on the left shoulder. The veteran was rather transparent in expressing his thoughts after the game when he said, "Sometimes, protecting your hitters is part of the job."* But still, no warnings were issued by the umpires.

It didn't take long for the hosts to show their resolve in the "hit parade." The Royals' first batter in the eighth, Mike Macfarlane, stepped in to face Craig McMurtry, the Rangers' fourth hurler. McMurtry's second pitch nailed Macfarlane on the left elbow. It marked the fifth Royal to get hit and Macfarlane rushed toward the mound as both benches emptied for the archetypical wrestling matches.

"It gets stupid after a while," said Macfarlane, who made a clean tackle on McMurtry.

"I thought it was all over with by then and we should be playing out the game... But he definitely threw at me. I'm sorry it happened, but it had to be done."†

Brett, meanwhile, had returned from the hospital and was in the dressing room when he saw the fight break out on television. "I would have felt like I was deserting my teammates if I wasn't out there," Brett said, "so I unwrapped the arm, put my uniform back on and went out... Then I sat in the bullpen the rest of the game, just in case it all started up again."§

The two combatants met nine days later in Kansas City for a three-game series. Despite the hard feelings precipitated in this contest, the hurlers then found love in their hearts, and no one on either side had to absorb any more errant pitches.

*Steve Cameron, "Five hit batters anger Royals," Kansas City Times, 4 September 1989, section D, p. 2, col. 4.
†Ibid.
§Ibid.

Reds Fear the Hawk

207. Player Intentionally Walked Five Times in 16-Inning Game

CINCINNATI   at   CHICAGO
(Reds, 1)   (Cubs, 2)

Tuesday, May 22, 1990, Wrigley Field

During his major league career, Andre Dawson had developed the reputation of an excellent "clutch" hitter. For 15 years, "The Hawk" had terrorized National League pitching, and this season the Cub outfielder was off to a quick start, batting .346, leading the NL in homers and the majors in RBIs. Whether it was his reputation, his early offensive success, or a lack of respect for the batters behind him, the right-handed slugger received few opportunities to swing the bat this day. In eight plate appearances, the visit-

ing Cincinnati Reds *intentionally walked Dawson five times for a new major league record.* It surpassed the previous mark of four, first set by Roger Maris in 1962 and equalled by Garry Templeton in 1985. Rick Wrona and Luis Salazar were also issued intentional free passes, making the *Cubs' team total seven and tying another major league standard.*

The game developed in such a fashion as to invite an abundance of strategy. An 18-mph wind blowing in from center occasionally gusted to gale force, affording little

Dawson was normally a free swinger, walking about once every 17 plate appearences throughout his career.

hope for long balls and shifting the advantage to the pitchers. Runs were scarce, but pinch hitters were plentiful. All ten were unsuccess-ful, and seven struck out. There may even have been more had not each club exhausted its supply of position players long before the final out was made. Despite a scoreless duel for 12 frames, eight intentional bases on balls contributed to the glut of base runners for each team (the Cubs stranded 20). Finally, in the 13th, each team tallied once on a lead-off homer—Cincinnati on Chris Sabo's and Chicago on Salazar's. The Cubs ultimately prevailed in the 16th, 2–1, on Dave Clark's one out, bases loaded single.

Clark got his game winning opportunity because of Dawson's fifth intentional pass. Starting the contest, Lloyd McClendon had batted in the fifth position behind Dawson but had repeatedly failed. After making six straight outs, and stranding nine runners, McClendon was lifted for pinch hitter Clark in the 14th. Clark then struck out but returned for an encore in the 16th when he delivered the game-winning blow.

The extra innings took their toll on the Cub patrons' dinner reservations. The first nine innings consumed only two hours and were without a single substitution. But the extra innings brought on a tidal wave of new players. The final seven frames invited 23 new faces and took an additional two hours and 27 minutes to complete.

ANDRE DAWSON'S PLATE APPEARANCES, MAY 22, 1990

Inn	Pitcher	Outs	Base runners	Dawson's AB	Result
1	Browning	2	Grace (2nd)	Int. BB	McClendon fly out
4	Browning	0	None	Grounded out 6-3	Cubs out in order
6	Browning	2	Sandberg (1st)	Lined out to lf	Third out; no runs
8	Browning	2	Sandberg (3rd)	Int. BB	McClendon ground out
11	Charlton	0	Grace (1st)	Singled to left	Cubs blanked; 3 LOB
12	Birtsas	2	Walton (2nd); Grace (1st)	Int. BB	McClendon forced Dawson out
14	Scudder	2	Sandberg (2nd)	Int. BB	Clark struck out
16	Scudder	1	Sandberg (3rd); Grace (1st)	Int. BB	Clark singled home winning run

The most interesting intentional walk may have come in the 12th. With runners at first and second and two outs, Reds reliever Tim Birtsas went 3–0 to Dawson. Rather than give The Hawk an opportunity to win the game, Cincinnati manager Lou Piniella called for an intentional fourth ball which loaded the bases.

Dawson couldn't understand the Reds' zeal in this game, realizing they were off to a run-away lead in the NL West with a 26–10 record. "He [Piniella] managed like it was the last game of the World Series... [although] he was laughing the last two times they walked me," said the weary walker.*

*Joel Bierig, "Reds intent on Dawson, but Cubs prevail," Chicago Sun-Times, 23 May 1990, p. 118, col. 3.

Cincinnati Reds	AB	R	H	I
Chris Sabo 3b	6	1	1	1
Billy Hatcher cf	6	0	1	0
Paul O'Neill rf	7	0	2	0
Eric Davis lf	6	0	1	0
Hal Morris 1b	4	0	0	0
T. Benzinger ph11,1b	3	0	0	0
Luis Quinones ss	6	0	3	0
Joe Oliver c	4	0	2	0
Herm Winningham pr10	0	0	0	0
> Jeff Reed c10	2	0	0	0
Ron Oester 2b	4	0	0	0
Tom Browning p	3	0	1	0
Barry Larkin ph10	1	0	0	0
Norm Charlton p10	0	0	0	0
Rob Dibble p11	0	0	0	0
Rolando Roomes ph12	1	0	0	0
Tim Layana p12	0	0	0	0
Tim Birtsas p12	0	0	0	0
Randy Myers p13	0	0	0	0
Ken Griffey ph14	1	0	0	0
Scott Scudder p14	0	0	0	0
	54	1	11	1

Chicago Cubs	AB	R	H	I
Jerome Walton cf	7	0	2	0
Ryne Sandberg 2b	7	1	2	0
Mark Grace 1b	7	0	1	0
Andre Dawson rf	3	0	1	0
Lloyd McClendon lf	6	0	0	0
> Dave Clark ph14,lf	2	0	1	1
Luis Salazar 3b	5	1	1	1
Shawon Dunston ss	7	0	2	0
Rick Wrona c	3	0	0	0
Dwight Smith ph11	1	0	0	0
Joe Girardi c12	2	0	0	0
Mike Bielecki p	3	0	0	0
Doug Dascenzo ph10	1	0	0	0
Mitch Williams p11	0	0	0	0
Marvell Wynne ph12	1	0	0	0
Jeff Pico p13	0	0	0	0
Curt Wilkerson ph13	1	0	0	0
Paul Assenmacher p14	0	0	0	0
Domingo Ramos ph15	1	0	0	0
Bill Long p16	0	0	0	0
	57	2	10	2

Cincinnati	IP	H	R	ER	BB	SO
Browning	9	6	0	0	3	4
Charlton	1.1	1	0	0	1	2
Dibble	.2	0	0	0	0	2
Layana	.2	0	0	0	2	2
Birtsas	.1	0	0	0	1	0
Myers	1	1	1	1	0	2
Scudder L,1-1	2.1	2	1	0	4	3
	15.1*	10	2	1	11	15

Chicago	IP	H	R	ER	BB	SO
Bielecki	10	5	0	0	3	8
Williams	2	2	0	0	0	2
Pico	1	2	1	1	0	0
Assenmacher	2	1	0	0	1	0
Long W,2-0	1	1	0	0	0	1
	16	11	1	1	4	11

* One out when winning run scored

```
Cincinnati   0 0 0   0 0 0   0 0 0   0 0 0   1 0 0   0   - 1
Chicago      0 0 0   0 0 0   0 0 0   0 0 0   1 0 0   1   - 2
```

OB: Cincinnati 12, Chicago 20
E: Sabo, Quinones
DP: Sandberg-Dunston-Grace (Morris)
2B: Dunston 2, Hatcher, Oliver, Sandberg
HR: Sabo(8), Salazar(2)
SB: Grace(7), Dawson(5), Walton(8), Quinones(1), Salazar(1)
CS: Sabo, O'Neill
SO: O'Neill 2, Davis 2, Morris, Benzinger, Oliver, Browning 2, Larkin, Roomes; Walton, Sandberg, McClendon, Clark, Dunston, Wrona 2, Smith, Girardi 2, Wynne Bielecki 2, Dascenzo, Wilkerson

BB: Sabo, Davis, Quinones, Oester(I); Walton, Sandberg, Grace, Dawson 5(5I), Salazar 2(1I), Wrona(I)
SH: Oester, Reed
HP: By Bielecki (Hatcher)
WP: Bielecki, Scudder
TIME: 4:27
ATTENDANCE: 29,680
UMPIRES: Tom Hallion, Doug Harvey, Jerry Crawford, Dana DeMuth
SOURCES: BBWS; Chicago Sun-Times, Tribune; Cincinnati Enquirer; USA Today

BALANCE	OUT+R+OB=BP=AB+BB+SH+HP+CI
Cincinnati	48 1 12 61 54 4 2 1 0
Chicago	46 2 20 68 57 11 0 0 0

It Once Was a No-Hitter

208. Pitcher Throws No-Hitter, Loses 4–0

NEW YORK   at   CHICAGO
(Yankees, 0)   (White Sox, 4)

Sunday, July 1, 1990, Comiskey Park

Discounting abbreviated games, there have been several hundred nine-inning no-hitters tossed since the turn of the century. But only rarely, because of walks and/or shoddy fielding, has the victimized club scored a run or two. On four occasions, however, the no-hit team actually scored enough runs to win the game.

First, Houston's Ken Johnson no-hit Cincinnati for nine innings in 1964 but lost, 1–0. In 1967, Baltimore's Steve Barber and Stu Miller combined to no-hit the Tigers yet also lost, 2–1, in nine innings. On this day the anomaly was stretched to the limits of believability as the Yankees' Andy Hawkins entered the eighth inning of a scoreless no-hitter in Chicago and emerged with his no-hitter intact yet with his team trailing 4–0. When New York failed to score in the top of the ninth, the game became *the most lopsided no-hit defeat in history*. (A fourth occasion involved the BoSox' Matt Young losing to Cleveland, 2–1, in nine innings during 1992.)

At the time, Hawkins was credited with a no-hitter, and went into baseball annals as the losing pitcher in a complete-game no-hitter. But a subsequent major league scoring council changed that ruling. In September of 1991, an eight-man committee for "statistical accuracy," chaired by then Commissioner Fay Vincent, decreed that nearly 50 past no-hitters were really not no-hitters. Stricken from the No-Hit Hall of Fame were games called after five, six, seven, eight, or eight and one-half innings for whatever reason. Also eliminated from the no-hit list were the ill-fated who pitched at least nine innings of hitless ball but were reached safely in extra innings. Swept beneath the no-hit pedestal was the Harvey Haddix masterpiece along with 11 other moundsmen who labored at

least nine innings without allowing a safety. Fans are now asked to forget that Hawkins, and later Matt Young, who pitched in completed nine-inning games, were hurling for visiting clubs, and that the winning home team didn't even have an opportunity to bat in the ninth.

Record books presently invite readers to a baffling section on no-hitters. There are lists of no-hitters of less than nine pitched innings; of nine or more pitched innings; and of more than nine innings but broken up in extra innings.

This day's contest marked an historic occasion even before the first pitch was

Hawkins retired after the 1991 campaign.

New York Yankees	AB	R	H	I
Roberto Kelly cf	4	0	0	0
Steve Sax 2b	4	0	0	0
Don Mattingly 1b	4	0	0	0
Steve Balboni dh	4	0	0	0
Wayne Tolleson pr9	0	0	0	0
>Jesse Barfield rf	4	0	1	0
Jim Leyritz lf	3	0	1	0
Mike Blowers 3b	3	0	0	0
Bob Geren c	3	0	1	0
Alvaro Espinoza ss	2	0	1	0
	31	0	4	0

New York	IP	H	R	ER	BB	SO
Andy Hawkins L1-5	8	0	4	0	5	3

Chicago White Sox	AB	R	H	I
Lance Johnson cf	3	1	0	0
Robin Ventura 3b	4	1	0	0
Ivan Calderon dh	3	0	0	0
>Dan Pasqua lf	4	0	0	0
Ron Kittle 1b	3	0	0	0
Steve Lyons 1b8	0	0	0	0
Ron Karkovice c	2	0	0	0
Scott Fletcher 2b	2	0	0	0
Sammy Sosa rf	3	1	0	0
Ozzie Guillen ss	2	1	0	0
	26	4	0	0

Chicago	IP	H	R	ER	BB	SO
Greg Hibbard	7	4	0	0	0	4
Barry Jones W10-1	1	0	0	0	0	1
Scott Radinsky	1	0	0	0	0	0
	9	4	0	0	0	5

New York	0 0 0	0 0 0	0 0 0	- 0
Chicago	0 0 0	0 0 0	0 4 x	- 4

OB: New York 5, Chicago 3
E: Barfield, Leyritz, Blowers,
    Ventura 2
DP: Guillen-Fletcher-Lyons(Barfield)
SB: Sosa
CS: Calderon
SO: Kelly 2, Sax, Balboni, Barfield;
    Pasqua, Kittle 2
BB: Johnson, Calderon, Karkovice,
    Fletcher, Guillen

SH: Espinosa
PB: Geren
TIME: 2:34
ATTENDANCE: 30,642
UMPIRES: Dale Scott, Vic Voltaggio,
    Mike Reilly, Chuck Meriwether
SOURCES: BBWS; Chicago Tribune; New
    York Times; Sporting News; USA Today

BALANCE	OUT+R+OB=BP=AB+BB+SH+HP+CI
New York	27 0 5 32 31 0 1 0 0
Chicago	24 4 3 31 26 5 0 0 0

thrown. Exactly eighty years earlier, Charles Comiskey's White Sox played their first game in this stadium. Now, amid blinding sunshine and swirling winds, several thousand fewer fans paid considerably more than the original 25-cent bleacher admission to witness another celebrated addition to the lore of Comiskey Park I.

Hawkins had entered the game with a disappointing 1–4 record and an ERA bulging at 6.90. Less than a month earlier, the 30-year-old was about to be released, but an injury to another starter, Mike Witt, kept him on the Yankee roster. Big things were not expected of the right-handed journeyman this day. But as the game wore on, Hawkins became very much in control. As Andy sailed into the bottom of the eighth, only three White Sox had reached base — Ron Karkovice and Scott Fletcher had walked in the fifth, and Ivan

Calderon had walked in the seventh. The eighth frame started innocently enough with both Karkovice and Fletcher popping out to second baseman Steve Sax. Here's what then happened:

• Sammy Sosa hit a bouncer to third baseman Mike Blowers who back-handed but dropped the ball and then threw hurriedly to first. Sosa beat the throw amid a cloud of dust generated by his head-first slide. Initially there was some dispute over whether the play constituted a hit or an error, but it was quickly resolved. Later, Blowers readily emphasized it was clearly his error. Sosa then stole second.

• After running the count full, Ozzie Guillen walked.

• Lance Johnson also walked on four straight bad pitches, loading the bases.

• On Hawkins' next pitch, Robin Ventura

lofted what started as a routine fly to rookie Jim Leyritz in left. Leyritz had been listed as a catcher but had played primarily at third with just a few games in the outfield. Fighting the swirling wind, Jim changed direction several times before the ball dropped off the tip of his glove for a two base error. All three runners scored, and Ventura stopped at second. "It was hit right at me," said Leyritz. "It got caught up in the wind, and I couldn't reach it."*

• The next batter, Ivan Calderon, also hit a high fly ball, this one to deep right-center. Jesse Barfield, normally an excellent outfielder, struggled with the sun, gloved the ball but dropped it. Ventura scored, and Calderon ended up on second. "I lost it in the sun coming down," Barfield later said. "The call was right. It was an error."†

• Dan Pasqua finally ended the torment by popping out to shortstop Alvaro Espinoza. It was Hawkins' 37th pitch of the inning.

The Yankees went down in the ninth, despite Ventura's second error, making journeyman reliever Barry Jones the winner and casting Andy Hawkins into a very select fraternity. The 29-year-old was dazed yet gracious following the game, saying that after the last out of a no-hitter he had always dreamed of jumping up and down. "I don't blame Leyritz or Barfield. It was a tough field out there. The wind was blowing everywhere."§

Hard luck followed Hawkins all month. In his next start, he tossed 11 shutout innings and lost. On July 12, he was also the losing pitcher when Chicago's Melido Perez threw a rain-shortened no-hitter (that later also became a non no-hitter).

*Bill Jauss, "Sox's hitless victory a real wonder," Chicago Tribune, 2 July 1990, section 3, p. 6, col. 1.
†Ibid.
§Ibid., col. 4.

Twins Turn Two Triple Plays

209. Team Turns Two Triple Plays in One Game

MINNESOTA   at   BOSTON
(Twins, 0)   (Red Sox, 1)

Tuesday Night, July 17, 1990, Fenway Park

The triple play is not quite the rarity one might assume. As of this writing there have been identified at least 612 of these base-cleansing plays since the birth of the National League in 1876, and 481 since the turn of the century. There had even been five days on which two triple plays had occurred, albeit in different games. On the other hand, there had never been two in the same game — until this contest when fans witnessed not only a pair of triple plays, but saw them accomplished by the same team. The Minnesota Twins, while visiting the Boston Red Sox, and in the midst of a lackluster season, became the first club in major league annals to *execute two triple plays in the same game*. (The most any team has ever collected in an entire season is three.)

On a warm, humid night, Minnesota's Scott Erickson had pitched three perfect innings before loading the bases in the fourth. Wade Boggs walked, Jody Reed doubled and Carlos Quintana also walked. At that point, as he had often done in the past,

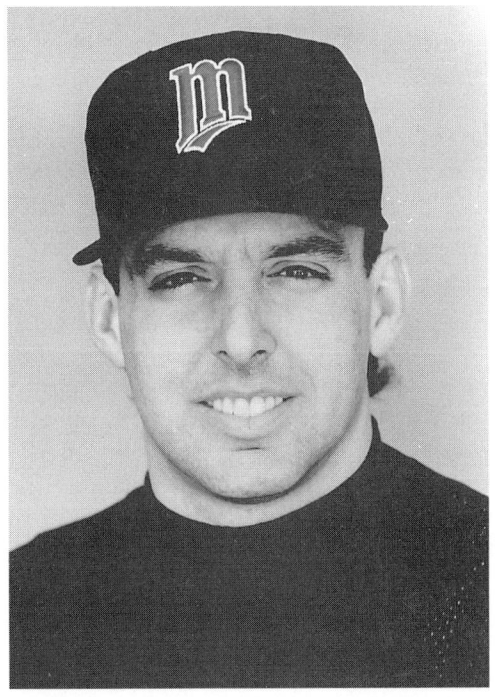

Gary Gaetti started both of the triple plays.

Second baseman Al Newman was the pivot man.

First baseman Kent Hrbek was the triple play anchor.

Minnesota third baseman Gary Gaetti yelled to teammate and second baseman Al Newman, "We're going to turn a triple play."* Boston's Tom Brunansky, himself a former Twin, then smacked a 1–1 pitch sharply on the ground between Gaetti and the third-base bag. Gary had plenty of time to intercept the quick hopper, step on third and throw to Newman, who relayed to Kent Hrbek at first. Brunansky, not a speed merchant, was just nearing the vicinity by the time the third out occurred. Later, Gaetti said he didn't even consider throwing home to cut down the run but had it in his mind to go for three outs.

In the eighth inning, facing Twins reliever John Candelaria, Tim Naehring led off with a double and Boggs walked. Jody Reed then sparked the same 5–4–3 fielding trifecta when he grounded a 1–0 offering sharply to Gaetti. Reed, a much faster runner than Brunansky, stumbled getting out of the batter's box and thus was also out at first by at least a full stride. After this second triple play, the Boston bench, in a gesture of mock

*Jim Caple, "Twins make history, but lose anyway," Saint Paul Pioneer Press, 18 July 1990, section C, p. 1, col. 5.

Minnesota Twins	AB	R	H	I
Shane Mack rf	4	0	0	0
Al Newman 2b	3	0	0	0
Kirby Puckett cf	3	0	0	0
Gary Gaetti 3b	3	0	1	0
Kent Hrbek 1b	3	0	1	0
Dan Gladden lf	3	0	0	0
Carmen Castillo dh	3	0	1	0
Paul Sorrento ph9	1	0	0	0
Junior Ortiz c	4	0	1	0
Greg Gagne ss	3	0	1	0
> John Moses ph9	1	0	0	0
	31	0	5	0

Boston Red Sox	AB	R	H	I
Wade Boggs 3b	2	0	1	0
>Jody Reed 2b	3	0	1	0
Carlos Quintana 1b	2	0	0	0
Tom Brunansky rf	2	0	0	0
Ellis Burks cf	3	0	0	0
Randy Kutcher cf8	0	0	0	0
Mike Greenwell lf	3	1	0	0
Tony Pena c	3	0	1	0
Billy Jo Robidoux dh	3	0	0	0
Tim Naehring ss	3	0	2	1
	24	1	5	1

Minnesota	IP	H	R	ER	BB	SO
Sco. Erickson L,1-2	6	4	1	0	3	4
John Candelaria	2	1	0	0	1	1
	8	5	1	0	4	5

Boston	IP	H	R	ER	BB	SO
Tom Bolton W,3-0	8	5	0	0	4	6
Jeff Reardon S,16	1	0	0	0	0	0
	9	5	0	0	4	6

```
Minnesota   0 0 0   0 0 0   0 0 0   - 0
Boston      0 0 0   0 1 0   0 0 x   - 1
```

OB: Minnesota 9, Boston 4
E: Gagne, Reed, Naehring
DP: Boggs-Reed-Quintana (Newman)
TP: Gaetti-Newman-Hrbek (Brunansky)
    Gaetti-Newman-Hrbek (Reed)
2B: Gaetti, Castillo, Boggs, Reed,
    Naehring
SB: Gladden(18)
CS: Ortiz(2)
SO: Newman, Puckett, Gladden, Ortiz
    2, Castillo; Quintana, Robidoux,
    Brunansky, Burks, Pena

BB: Puckett, Gaetti, Hrbek, Gladden;
    Boggs 2, Quintana, Brunansky(I)
SH: Newman, Reed
TIME: 2:18
ATTENDANCE: 34,113
UMPIRES: Mike Reilly, Chuck Meri-
    wether, Rich Garcia, Dale Scott
SOURCES: BBWS; Boston Globe, Herald;
    Minneapolis Star Tribune; Saint
    Paul Pioneer Press; USA Today

BALANCE	OUT	+	R	+	OB	=	BP	=	AB	+	BB	+	SH	+	HP	+	CI
Minnesota	27		0		9		36		31		4		1		0		0
Boston	24		1		4		29		24		4		1		0		0

Note: Three minor league teams are known to have pulled two triple-plays in the same game—Los Angeles vs. Butte in the Pacific National League (4-23-1903), Kansas City vs. Toledo in the American Association (6-14-1904), and Lodi vs. Fresno in the California League (7-25-78). In a Mexican League (Class AAA) game during 1979, there were three triple-plays executed—two by the Union Leguna Cotton Growers and one by the Ciudad Juarez Indians.

submission, collectively called for a time out to regain their composure. It later was also learned that Boston manager Joe Morgan had put on the hit-and-run sign so the Sox wouldn't hit into a double play.

But surrounding every silver lining there's a cloud, and Boston won the game 1–0 on an unearned run. The lone tally came in the fifth inning when, with two outs, Tim Naehring singled off Erickson to drive home Mike Greenwell. Greenwell had reached base on an error, and Naehring's hit was his first in the majors.

The triple plays were the first turned in the majors this season, in the 1,148th game. At this stage in their club history the Twins had turned 10 triple plays, and Gaetti had started five of them. He, along with Hrbek, had participated defensively in six of the ten. Gaetti is looked upon as somewhat of a triple play specialist, having hit into one himself as well as having fielded in seven others. The all-time triple play overlord, however, is Donie Bush, who between 1908 and 1923 fielded in nine and batted into one.*

The following day, Minnesota came close

Most of the triple play statistics were offered by James A Smith, Jr., a baseball historian and member of the Society for American Baseball Research.

to another defensive record when they pulled off six double plays, falling just short of the single team record of seven (see 8-14-42). Their opponent again was the Red Sox, who contributed four twin (or Twin)-killings themselves *to collaborate on a new nine-inning-game record of 10 double plays.*

Father and Son

210. Father and Son Teammates Get Hits in Same Game

KANSAS CITY   at   SEATTLE
(Royals, 2)   (Mariners, 5)

Friday Night, August 31, 1990, Kingdome

There had been many father and son duos to play major league baseball. But none had done so simultaneously until 1989 when Ken Griffey, Jr., entered the American League as a rookie while his father, of the same name, was still employed by the Cincinnati Reds in the National League. Now, a year later, *for the first time in baseball history, two generations not only played in the same game but also side by side in the field.* In addition, the Griffeys also batted consecutively in the lineup.

Seattle manager Jim Lefebvre, upon acquiring Griffey, Sr., claimed this was no "dog and pony show," and that Ken was actually expected to contribute to the Mariners. Some observers might have thought otherwise, for the 40-year-old, once stellar center fielder for Cincinnati's "Big Red Machine" of the mid–1970s, had officially been released by the Reds a week earlier. He had been batting only

One Ken Griffey going out; one coming in.

Kansas City Royals	AB	R	H	I
Kevin Seitzer 3b	4	0	0	0
Hal McRae cf	4	0	1	0
Danny Tartabull dh	3	0	1	0
Bo Jackson lf	3	1	1	0
Mike Macfarlane c	4	0	1	0
>Jim Eisenreich rf	3	0	0	1
Bill Pecota 1b	3	1	1	1
Frank White 2b	3	0	1	0
Steve Jeltz ss	3	0	0	0
	30	2	6	2

Seattle Mariners	AB	R	H	I
Harold Reynolds 2b	5	0	1	0
>Ken Griffey, Sr. lf	4	1	1	0
Ken Griffey, Jr. cf	4	1	1	0
Alvin Davis dh	2	3	2	1
Pete O'Brien 1b	3	0	0	0
Jay Buhner rf	3	0	2	1
Edgar Martinez 3b	2	0	1	1
Jeff Schaefer 3b	2	0	1	1
Scott Bradley c	4	0	1	0
Omar Vizquel ss	3	0	0	0
	32	5	10	4

Kansas City	IP	H	R	ER	BB	SO
Storm Davis L,7-10	6.2	9	5	4	6	1
Israel Sanchez	1.1	1	0	0	0	0
	8	10	5	4	6	1

Seattle	IP	H	R	ER	BB	SO
Ra. Johnson W,13-8	7.1	5	2	2	2	4
Bill Swift S,3	1.2	1	0	0	0	0
	9	6	2	2	2	4

```
Kansas City   0 2 0    0 0 0    0 0 0   - 2
Seattle       3 0 0    0 1 0    1 0 x   - 5
```

OB: Kansas City 4, Seattle 9
E: Jackson 2, Schaefer
DP: S. Davis-Jeltz-Pecota (Martinez)
      White-Jeltz-Pecota (Griffey Sr.)
      Reynolds-O'Brien (Tartabull)
      Vizquel-Reynolds-O'Brien (Eisenreich)
2B: Buhner, Schaefer
HR: Pecota(4)
SB: Jackson(12)
SO: Tartabull, Macfarlane 2, White;
      Reynolds

BB: Tartabull, Jackson; Griffey Sr., A. Davis 2(11),
      O'Brien, Buhner, Vizquel
SF: Eisenreich
WP: S. Davis, Johnson
TIME: 2:27
ATTENDANCE: 27,166
UMPIRES: Rich Garcia, Steve Palermo, Dale
      Scott, Rocky Roe
SOURCES: BBWS; Kansas City Star; Seattle
      Times; USA Today

BALANCE	OUT	+	R	+	OB	=	BP	=	AB	+	BB	+	SH	+	HP	+	CI
Kansas City	27		2		4		33		30		2		1		0		0
Seattle	24		5		9		38		32		6		0		0		0

.206 (13/63) in this his 18th major league season.

Ken Griffey, Jr., meanwhile, was playing in only his second season, having made his debut with Seattle in 1989 at 19 years of age. Junior was expected to be the star around which this young Mariner club would be built and had been fulfilling those expectations. The morning before this game, he was hitting .306 with 17 homers, 15 stolen bases, and 60 RBIs.

Both father and son were somewhat nervous prior to the game, but that dissolved quickly once the action started. When they first took the field, Junior remembered, "I wanted to cry or something. It just seemed like a father-son game, like we were out play-ing catch in the back yard. But we were actually playing a real game. I just stood there and looked at him (in left). A couple of pitches even went by."*

"I didn't know what to expect," Senior said. "The first time up was like me being a rookie again. After the first pitch I settled down."†

Junior described a dinner bet the two had made concerning who would get the first hit. Senior said that his son didn't have a chance, because the elder knew he would be batting before his son in the lineup. True to his forecast, Senior singled in his first at bat; it was his 2,091st hit in his 7,068th at bat. Not to be outdone, Junior also singled behind his father, his 275th career hit. They both

*Bob Sherwin, "Win adds to M's night," Seattle Times, 1 September 1990, section B, p. 5, col. 4.
†Ibid, p. 1, col. 3.

eventually scored in Seattle's three-run first, which was all the runs the Mariners needed to win. As Junior entered the dugout after scoring the second run, he was hugged by his father.

When the pair returned to their defensive positions in the second inning, fans in the bleachers gave them a standing ovation, to which Senior tipped his hat.

Senior also showed detractors that he could still play defense when, from deep left field, he threw out Bo Jackson trying to stretch a single in the sixth inning. It was a pivotal play and nipped a budding Kansas City rally. Jackson, at the time, was one of the fastest runners in the major leagues.

Two weeks later the father and son accomplished another first. On September 14, they stroked back-to-back home runs in a game against the Angels.

Perhaps inspired by this consanguine relationship, the elder Griffey regained his hitting stroke and completed his partial season in Seattle hitting .377 (29/77). He played with his son again in 1991, although for only 30 games, before retiring with 2,143 lifetime hits and a .296 batting average.

Nixon Swipes Six

211. Player Steals Six Bases in One Game

ATLANTA   at   MONTREAL
(Braves, 6)   (Expos, 7)

Sunday, June 16, 1991, Olympic Stadium

Despite carrying a .348 batting average and leading his team in stolen bases, Atlanta's Otis Nixon had not been scheduled to start this game. But when starting right fielder David Justice became a last-minute scratch due to an upset stomach, Nixon was inserted into the leadoff position. Otis welcomed the opportunity to show his former team they had acted foolishly by trading him to the Braves on April 1.

It didn't take long for Atlanta manager Bobby Cox to suspect he was a genius, for Nixon soon began a Ty Cobb imitation act. As the game's first batter, Otis singled, stole second and third, and scored; he then repeated the sequence in the third frame. Before the contest was over, Nixon had singled three times and had *harvested six stolen bases to set a new National League record and tie the major league mark* established 79 years earlier. (See 9-11-12 and 9-22-12.) Unfortunately for the Braves, however, the host Montreal Expos overcame Nixon's antics and pulled out a 7–6 victory.

With Montreal catcher Mike Fitzgerald behind the plate the entire game, here's how switch-hitter Nixon's day of bounty evolved:

• Nixon led off the game against left-hander Chris Nabholz by lining a 2–1 pitch over second and into center field. After drawing five tosses to first, interspersed in a 3–1 count to Terry Pendleton, Nixon stole second. Pendleton later singled to short and Nixon held at second base. Nixon stole third on a 2–1 pitch to Lonnie Smith and later scored on Ron Gant's double. (Lonnie Smith had been one of four modern shareholders in the NL to steal five bases in one game.)

• Leading off the third inning, Nixon again singled off Nabholz, this time beating out a bunt toward first. On an 0–1 pitch (for strike two) to Pendleton, Otis stole second; and on the very next delivery, stole third.

Atlanta Braves	AB	R	H	I
Otis Nixon rf	5	2	3	0
Terry Pendleton 3b	4	1	1	0
Lonnie Smith lf	5	0	1	1
>Ron Gant cf	5	1	1	1
Jeff Blauser 2b,ss8	4	0	1	1
Brian Hunter 1b	2	0	1	0
Sid Bream ph6,1b	2	1	1	1
Mike Heath c	4	0	1	0
Rafael Belliard ss	3	1	1	0
Greg Olson ph8	1	0	0	0
Mark Lemke 2b8	0	0	0	0
Charlie Liebrandt p	2	0	1	1
Marvin Freeman p5	0	0	0	0
Tommy Gregg ph6	1	0	0	0
Mike Stanton p6	0	0	0	0
Rick Mahler p6	0	0	0	0
David Justice ph8	1	0	0	0
Kent Mercker p8	0	0	0	0
	39	6	12	5

Montreal Expos	AB	R	H	I
Marquis Grissom cf	5	1	0	1
>Delino DeShields 2b	4	2	2	2
Ivan Calderon lf	4	1	3	1
Tim Wallach 3b	4	0	1	1
Dave Martinez rf	4	0	1	0
Mike Fitzgerald c	3	0	0	0
Larry Walker 1b	4	1	1	0
Spike Owen ss	2	1	1	1
Chris Nabholz p	1	0	0	0
Bret Barberie ph4	1	0	0	0
Bill Sampen p5	0	0	0	0
Junior Naboa ph6	1	1	1	0
Doug Platt p7	0	0	0	0
Jeff Fassero p7	0	0	0	0
Eric Bullock ph8	0	0	0	0
Barry Jones p9	0	0	0	0
	33	7	10	6

Atlanta	IP	H	R	ER	BB	SO
Liebrandt	4.1	6	4	3	3	2
Freeman	.2	1	0	0	0	1
Stanton L,2-1	.1	1	2	2	1	1
Mahler	1.2	2	1	1	0	0
Mercker	1	0	0	0	1	1
	8	10	7	6	5	5

Montreal	IP	H	R	ER	BB	SO
Nabholz	4	7	4	3	0	3
Sampen W,4-1	2	3	1	1	0	2
Platt	.2	1	1	1	1	1
Fassero	1.1	0	0	0	0	2
Jones S,4	1	1	0	0	0	3
	9	12	6	5	1	11

Atlanta   2 0 1   1 0 1   1 0 0   — 6
Montreal   0 0 1   1 2 3   0 0 x   — 7

OB: Atlanta 7, Montreal 7
E: Belliard, DeShields, Nabholz
2B: Gant, Blauser, DeShields,
     Calderon, Martinez, Walker, Owen
3B: Liebrandt
HR: Bream(9)
SB: Nixon 6(32), Pendleton(3), Smith (3),
     Grissom 2(33), DeShields(28),
     Martinez(4), Fitzgerald(1)
CS: Pendleton(2), DeShields(12)
PK: Calderon

SO: Pendleton, Smith 3, Gant 3,
     Hunter, Heath, Bream, Justice;
     DeShields, Walker 2, Grissom,
     Martinez
BB: Pendleton; DeShields, Fitzgerald
     Owen 2(1I), Bullock
WP: Mahler
TIME: 3:11
ATTENDANCE: 18,107
UMPIRES: Ed Montague, Ed Rapuano,
     Bruce Froemming, Greg Bonin
SOURCES: Atlanta Constitution/Journal;
     Montreal Gazette; USA Today

BALANCE	OUT+R+OB=BP=AB+BB+SH+HP+CI								
Atlanta	27	6	7	40	39	1	0	0	0
Montreal	24	7	7	38	33	5	0	0	0

Note: Six stolen bases by one player in a game occurred once more before publication of this book. On June 30, 1996, Colorado's Eric Young stole six bases against Los Angeles.

Pendleton later lined out to first, but Smith singled home Nixon.

• With the Braves holding a 4–1 advantage in the fourth, Nixon next stepped to the plate with Charlie Liebrandt at third and two outs. Nabholz finally retired the whirlwind on a 1–1 pitch, getting him to ground out, short to first.

This season Nixon stole 72 bases in 124 games.

Nabholz was the victim of Nixon's first four steals.

• Nixon also made the third out in the Atlanta sixth after the Braves had just regained the lead, 5–4, on Sid Bream's solo homer. With right-hander Bill Sampen on the hill for Montreal, and with teammates at first and second, Nixon lined out to short. It was a crucial out as Montreal captured the lead with their fifth, sixth, and seventh runs in the home half.

• The Braves trailed 7–6 entering the ninth. Facing right-hander Barry Jones and leading off, Nixon lined a 1–1 offering into center for a single representing the Braves' tying run. After drawing four throws to first, Otis stole second on a 1–1 pitch to Pendleton. It was Nixon's fifth steal, but it appeared fruitless as both Pendleton and Smith fanned. Now with two outs, Nixon stole third (uncontested) on the first pitch to Gant, the Atlanta clean-up hitter.

Gant, however, also struck out to end the game.

Like many record performances, this one was accomplished unwittingly. "One writer came up to me and congratulated me, and I didn't know what for," said Nixon later. "To be honest, I would trade all those stolen bases and hits for a win… I thought the record was held by somebody like Rickey Henderson or Vince Coleman. I don't know who this guy [Collins] is."[*] (Hall of Famer Eddie Collins played from 1906 through 1930, collected 3,312 hits and 744 stolen bases. He later coached, managed, became a general manager, and is considered one of the greatest second basemen of all time.)

Nixon also absolved the besieged Montreal back-stop. "Basically, you steal off the pitchers," said Nixon. "You don't steal anything off the catcher."[†]

[*]*I. J. Rosenberg, "Atlanta outfielder's NL record is a steal,"* Atlanta Constitution, *17 June 1991, section D, p. 1, col. 4–5.*
[†]*Ian MacDonald, "Nixon can't steal one from the Expos,"* Montreal Gazette, *17 June 1991, section D, p. 1, col. 5.*

A No-Hit Quartet

212. Four Pitchers
Combine to Throw No-Hitter

BALTIMORE   at   OAKLAND
(Orioles, 2)   (Athletics, 0)

Saturday, July 13, 1991, Oakland Coliseum

It was far from tidy, even a bit strange and confusing, but this day marked the second occasion in major league history that *four teammates combined to toss a no-hitter*. Unlike the first incident (see 9-28-75) which also occurred in the Oakland Coliseum, this teamwork was unplanned. But when Baltimore's starter absorbed a line drive off his pitching hand, manager Johnny Oates was forced to pool his resources.

The Orioles entered this game with the worst staff ERA in the major leagues at 4.90. Their starter, Bob Milacki, had begun the season in the minors and formerly had had little success against his hosts, the Oakland Athletics. In five previous appearances against them, the 26-year-old was 0–2 with a 3.64 ERA, and in his last start, on July 3, Bob had given up six earned runs in 5.1 innings against Detroit. On this day, however, he had excellent command of his fastball and particularly his change-up.

Through the first five frames Oakland had managed only two free passes off Milacki and hadn't come close to getting a hit. Then after retiring Mike Bordick to open the sixth, the right-hander faced Willie Wilson. Willie smashed a line drive up the middle that caught Milacki on the index finger of his right hand, bounced off his left leg, and rolled directly toward first. Teammate Randy Milligan had an easy play to touch the bag for the out, but Milacki was hurt. He walked the next hitter, Dave Henderson, then fanned Jose Canseco to end the inning. With his finger swelling in the dugout, Milacki was examined by the coaching staff. Unable to grip a ball properly, all agreed that despite the no-hitter in progress, Bob's work was finished for the day.

Baseball tradition dictates that players never talk to the pitcher during a no-hitter, but with Milacki out of the game, the dugout was in a state of confusion. The players didn't know who to shun.

It is debatable whether it is more difficult for one, or for four pitchers to complete a no-hitter. Nevertheless, each of the next three relievers faced an exacting assignment, for not only was the no-hitter on the line but the game as well for Baltimore held a scant 2–0 lead.

Mike Flanagan, once a Baltimore starter but now a 39-year-old long-relief man, pitched the seventh. After Harold Baines grounded out, Mark McGwire drove a long fly to right-center field that Mike Devereaux was finally able to chase down. It was only the second ball to threaten the no-hitter. Flanagan then faced two pinch hitters, Vance Law and Terry Steinbach. Law walked and Steinbach made another bid for the first hit when he sent a grounder toward the short-stop side of second. But Cal Ripken ranged far to his left, stretched for the ball nearly behind second base, and threw to first in time for the third out.

Taking the mound for Baltimore in the eighth was a particularly nervous Mark Williamson. In his last appearance in Oakland, Williamson had been mugged, giving up a single, double, triple and homer on six pitches. He had also given up at least one hit in each of his previous 14 appearances. But this time he threw 17 pitches and retired the A's in order with no thrills attached.

The coup de grâce was assigned to Gregg Olson, the Orioles' 25-year-old closer. Dave Henderson, the leadoff batter, stroked a hard

Milacki (left) hurled the first six and was followed by Flanagan (right).

Williamson (left) tossed the eighth; Olson the ninth.

celebration was subdued. Rather than the usual dog pile on the mound for such occasions, catcher Chris Hoiles calmly walked to the hill to shake a composed Olson's hand as he had done many times in normal save situations. Olson later said he didn't feel that he deserved any special credit for simply pitching one inning of the no-hitter. For that matter, neither did Flanagan nor Williamson. If there was a hero, it was Milacki, but he was in the clubhouse waiting to go to the hospital for x-rays on his finger.

"I think it was kind of strange for them," A's manager Tony LaRussa said. "Everybody congratulated different people. Nobody knew who to shake hands with."*

grounder toward the hole between third and short which Ripken back-handed and threw to first, barely beating the runner. Aside from the earlier smash off Milacki's hand and leg, this was the closest the A's came to a safety. Olson then fanned Canseco on four pitches and Baines on five to seal the no-hitter.

After the last out was made, Baltimore's

The crowd too was confused, not knowing whether to stay and cheer or rush out to beat the traffic. It was estimated that at least 10,000 had already left the ballpark before the last pitch was thrown. Nor did the young fans know whose autograph to solicit for posterity.

Baltimore scored the only two runs of the

*Claire Smith, "1 Game/4 Arms = Orioles No-Hitter," New York Times, 14 July 1991, Sports section, p. 1, col. 2.

game while Milacki was still pitching. In the fifth Chito Martinez doubled, took third on an aborted pickoff attempt, and crossed the plate on a single by Chris Hoiles. Mike Devereaux homered to left center in the sixth for the only other tally.

The historic occasion also marked the first Orioles no-hitter since 1969 when Jim Palmer tossed one against the Athletics in Baltimore. Appropriately, Palmer was announcing this contest.

Baltimore Orioles	AB	R	H	I
Mike Devereaux cf	4	1	3	1
Joe Orsulak lf,rf9	4	0	0	0
Cal Ripken ss	4	0	0	0
Sam Horn dh	2	0	0	0
David Segui ph9	1	0	0	0
Randy Milligan 1b	3	0	1	0
Chito Martinez rf	3	1	1	0
Brady Anderson pr9,lf	0	0	0	0
Leo Gomez 3b	4	0	0	0
>Chris Hoiles c	4	0	1	1
Billy Ripken 2b	3	0	0	0
	32	2	6	2

Oakland Athletics	AB	R	H	I
Willie Wilson lf	4	0	0	0
Lance Blankenship 2b9	0	0	0	0
Dave Henderson cf	3	0	0	0
Jose Canseco rf	3	0	0	0
>Harold Baines dh	3	0	0	0
Mark McGwire 1b	3	0	0	0
Jamie Quirk c	2	0	0	0
Vance Law ph7,3b	0	0	0	0
Ernest Riles 3b	2	0	0	0
Terry Steinbach ph7,c	1	0	0	0
Mike Gallego 2b,ss9	3	0	0	0
Mike Bordick ss	2	0	0	0
Rick. Henderson ph8,lf	1	0	0	0
	27	0	0	0

Baltimore	IP	H	R	ER	BB	SO
Bob Milacki W,5-3	6	0	0	0	3	3
Mike Flanagan	1	0	0	0	1	0
Mark Williamson	1	0	0	0	0	0
Gregg Olson S,19	1	0	0	0	0	2
	9	0	0	0	4	5

Oakland	IP	H	R	ER	BB	SO
Eric Show L,0-1	7	5	2	2	1	0
Steve Chitren	.1	1	0	0	0	0
Joe Klink	.2	0	0	0	0	1
Dennis Eckersley	1	0	0	0	2	2
	9	6	2	2	3	3

Baltimore	0 0 0	0 1 1	0 0 0	- 2
Oakland	0 0 0	0 0 0	0 0 0	- 0

OB: Baltimore 6, Oakland 4
E: Show
2B: Martinez
HR: Devereaux(11)
CS: Devereaux(6)
SO: Orsulak, Gomez, Hoiles; Baines, Canseco 3, Gallego
BB: Horn, Milligan, Martinez; Law, D. Henderson, Canseco, Baines

TIME: 2:38
ATTENDANCE: 40,047
UMPIRES: Chuck Meriwether, Jim Joyce, Derryl Cousins, Jim McKean
SOURCES: Baltimore Sun; BBWS; New York Times; Oakland Tribune; San Francisco Examiner

BALANCE	OUT+R+OB=BP=AB+BB+SH+HP+CI								
Baltimore	27	2	6	35	32	3	0	0	0
Oakland	27	0	4	31	27	4	0	0	0

Jays Brewed by Milwaukee

213. Team Gets 31 Hits, 26 Singles in Nine-Inning Game

MILWAUKEE	at	TORONTO
(Brewers, 22)		(Blue Jays, 2)

Friday Night, August 28, 1992, Skydome

This was a night when the Milwaukee Brewer bats wouldn't quit. Inning after inning they pounded away at Toronto offerings until they finally grew weary of swinging and running the bases. By the time the dust had settled, Milwaukee had established a new American League mark and tied the major league record for *most hits in a nine-inning game with 31*. Unlike the only other occasion of 31 hits (see 6-09-01) in the 20th-century, this time there was no fan contribution. In addition, Milwaukee's *26 singles set a new AL standard*, eclipsing the old benchmark of 24. Two other AL records were tied when *nine Brewers gathered two or more hits* (two of the nine didn't even start), and *four teammates amassed four or more safeties*.

The Brewers, in third place, visited the Skydome on August 27 for the first of a four-game series. Although they had lost five straight and were having difficulty scoring runs (less than four runs in nearly half their games this season), they trailed their front-running hosts by just 4½ games. The series was touted as a pivotal match-up for the two pennant contenders. More than 50,000 fans attended the first game which was captured by Toronto, 5–4, as each club harvested a modest total of seven hits.

Another 50,000-plus jammed the stadium for this, the second game, which quickly deteriorated into a blow-out for the visitors. How bad was it? Well, as Jayson Stark, columnist for the *Philadelphia Inquirer* pointed out,* the Brewers collected more hits in this one game than Blue Jays closer Tom Henke had given up all season (26). And, the

first three Brewers each batted three times before all the Blue Jays had come to the plate. Meanwhile, Milwaukee vaulted to a 7–0 lead. Stark also noted that before it ended, the Brewers, who had lost their last 10 road games while averaging 2.5 runs, averaged nearly 2.5 runs *per inning* in this game.

Surprisingly, the bottom of the Milwaukee batting order was more devastating than the top. The number eight and nine hitters, Kevin Seitzer and Scott Fletcher, each chipped in with five hits and combined for eight RBIs and seven runs scored. Hitting from the seven slot, B. J. Surhoff had only

Scott Fletcher—five hits and five RBIs.

*Jayson Stark, "Baseball/Week in Review," Philadelphia Inquirer, 1 September 1992, section D, p. 5, col. 2–3.

two hits but also three walks. The last three Milwaukee hitters thus were on base 15 times; the first three batters reached first "only" 14 times.

No American League team has ever scored in each frame of a nine-inning game, but Milwaukee narrowly missed this day. The only whitewash stanza Toronto pitchers could muster was the fifth when the Brewers still lashed out a pair of singles.

For the altruistic Blue Jays staff this was truely a team effort. So generous were they, that each of the six hurlers gave up at least three runs while permitting *more than* two base runners per inning pitched. Doug Linton was particularly charitable. After retiring the first batter he faced, Linton then fur-

nished six hits and two walks while contributing 33 of the mind-numbing 253 pitches thrown by the Toronto staff. (It is doubtful the Brewers were playing a waiting game, for six of their hits and two of their outs came on first pitches). David Wells nearly performed the impossible when he retired the first two Milwaukee batters he faced in the ninth. His next two offerings to the third hitter were strikes, placing him one pitch away from a perfect frame. But both sides quickly regained their composure, and the next five Brewers hit safely. The benchmark hit was a 20-foot dribbler down the third base line by Jim Gantner.

Here's an inning-by-inning account of the Brewers' astonishing day with the lumber:

MILWAUKEE'S 31 HITS (BY INNING) ON AUGUST 28, 1992

1st	Listach	Molitor(HR)				
2nd	Seitzer(2B)					
3rd	Jaha	Surhoff	Fletcher	Listach	Hamilton	
4th	Yount(2B)	Seitzer	Fletcher	Listach	Hamilton	Molitor
5th	Seitzer	Fletcher				
6th	Vaughn(2B)	Bichette				
7th	Fletcher	Listach	Hamilton	Molitor		
8th	Bichette	Seitzer	Gantner	Hamilton		
9th	Jaha	Surhoff	Seitzer(2B)	Fletcher	Gantner	

single unless noted; 2B = double; HR = home run

The following day Milwaukee again prevailed, 7–2, although they collected only nine hits. Toronto endured, however, to capture

the pennant by four games over this day's adversary and eventually defeated Atlanta in the World Series.

Milwaukee Brewers	AB	R	H	I
Pat Listach ss	6	3	4	1
Jim Gantner 2b7	2	0	2	1
>Darryl Hamilton rf,cf4	7	0	4	5
Paul Molitor dh	7	1	3	4
Greg Vaughn lf	4	1	1	0
Dave Nilsson c6	2	0	0	0
Robin Yount cf	3	2	1	0
Dante Bichette rf4	3	1	2	1
John Jaha 1b	6	3	2	0
B. J. Surhoff c,lf6	4	4	2	1
Kevin Seitzer 3b	7	4	5	3
Scott Fletcher 2b,ss7	6	3	5	5
	57	22	31	21

Toronto Blue Jays	AB	R	H	I
Devon White cf	2	0	0	0
Derek Bell cf5	2	0	1	0
Roberto Alomar 2b	4	0	1	0
Joe Carter rf	2	0	0	0
Pat Tabler rf6	2	0	0	0
Dave Winfield dh	4	0	1	1
John Olerud 1b	4	0	0	0
Candy Maldonado lf	4	0	1	0
Kelly Gruber 3b	2	1	2	0
Tom Quinlin 3b6	2	0	0	0
>Pat Borders c	4	0	2	0
Manny Lee ss	3	1	1	1
	35	2	9	2

Milwaukee	IP	H	R	ER	BB	SO
Cal Eldred W,5-1	7	7	2	2	0	5
Mike Fetters	1	1	0	0	0	1
Doug Henry	1	1	0	0	0	2
	9	9	2	2	0	8

Toronto	IP	H	R	ER	BB	SO
Jimmy Key L,8-12	1.2	3	3	3	3	2
Mike Timlin	1.1	5	4	4	1	1
Doug Linton	.1	6	6	6	2	0
Bob MacDonald	3.2	8	3	3	0	3
Mark Eichhorn	1	4	3	3	1	0
David Wells	1	5	3	3	0	0
	9	31	22	22	7	6

Milwaukee	2 1 4	6 0 1	2 3 3	-22
Toronto	0 0 1	0 0 1	0 0 0	- 2

OB: Milwaukee 16, Toronto 6
E: White (throw)
DP: Fletcher-Listach-Jaha (White)
2B: Vaughn, Yount, Seitzer 2
HR: Molitor(12)
SB: Listach(44)
SO: Listach, Hamilton, Vaughn 2, Jaha,
    Surhoff; White, Carter, Tabler, Winfield,
    Maldonado, Quinlin, Borders, Lee
BB: Hamilton, Vaughn, Yount, Jaha,
    Surhoff 3

SF: Fletcher
WP: Eichhorn
TIME: 3:41
ATTENDANCE: 50,408
UMPIRES: Don Denkinger, John Shulock
    Larry Young, Brian O'Nora
SOURCES: BBWS; Milwaukee Journal,
    Sentinel; Philadelphia Inquirer;
    Toronto Star

BALANCE	OUT+R+OB=BP+AB+BB+SH+HP+CI
Milwaukee	27 22 16 65 57 7 1 0 0
Toronto	27 2 6 35 35 0 0 0 0

Expandable Scorecards Needed

214. Teams Use 54 Players,
Team Uses 11 Pitchers in 16-Inning Game

SEATTLE   at   TEXAS
(Mariners, 4)   (Rangers, 3)

Friday Night, September 25, 1992, Arlington Stadium

On this date, both the Seattle Mariners and the Texas Rangers had long been mathematically eliminated from pennant contention. Only a miraculous finish could have advanced either in the standings, and there seemed to be little reason for heroics by either club. Nevertheless, in what began as a relatively meaningless, season-waning contest, Texas skipper Toby Harrah and Seattle's Bill Plummer turned into a *record-setting extravaganza which saw a total of 54 players take the field.* (That broke the record of 53 — see 9-02-86.) Included in the multitude was the engagement of *11 different Seattle pitchers, establish-* *ing another major league benchmark for hurlers used by one team in a game.* (The previous mark had been 10.) The Rangers engaged 25 players while the Mariners used 29, or every available player on their roster with the exception of pitcher Shawn Barton who was nursing a stiff back. Among the Ranger participants were *four who played the shortstop position,* tying the American League mark.

Amazingly, this game of legions was without substitutions until the bottom of the seventh when Rich DeLucia took the mound for Seattle. The right-hander also issued the game's first walk, opening the floodgates for a

MORNING OF SEPTEMBER 25, 1992				
AL West	**W**	**L**	**GB**	**GR**
Oakland	93	60		9
Minnesota	84	68	8.5	10
Chicago	82	70	10.5	10
Texas	73	80	20	9
Kansas City	68	84	24.5	10
California	67	85	25.5	10
Seattle	58	95	35	9

Vizquel knocked in the winning run.

dozen more to follow. DeLucia's substitution started a procession of players that eventually tallied, among others, 16 pitchers (eight of whom tossed less than one inning), 10 pinch hitters, five pinch runners, and four Texas shortstops (tied AL mark). Only three Mariners batted or fielded from the same position throughout the entire 16-inning game.

With one out and the game tied 3–3 in the bottom of the ninth, both managers began a feverish dredging of their benches. Before the next nine outs transpired, 18 new names found their way into the score book. Four hurlers, eight pinch hitters, two pinch runners, and four defensive replacements encouraged score keepers to seek liquid refreshment.

Remarkably, although there were several rookies in the game, this was not a September purging of the minor league systems. Of

the 54 participants, only two (Seattle's Cris Colon and Dan Smith) had made their major league debuts this month.

For the Rangers, this was a day of frustration. They left 20 runners stranded, 13 in scoring position. A club-record 18 strikeouts helped them leave the bases loaded in the ninth, 10th, and 12th as they registered an 0-for-12 with runners in scoring position from the ninth inning on.

Seattle Mariners	AB	R	H	I
>Omar Vizquel ss	8	1	3	1
Greg Briley dh	4	0	1	0
Henry Cotto ph10,dh	2	0	0	0
Ken Griffey Jr. cf	7	2	2	1
Tino Martinez 1b	6	0	2	1
Jeff Schaefer pr13	0	0	0	0
Mike Blowers 1b13	1	0	0	0
Jay Buhner rf	6	0	1	1
Dann Howitt lf	3	0	0	0
Lance Parrish c10	2	0	1	0
Brett Boone 2b,3b10	7	0	0	0
Dave Valle c	3	0	1	0
Har. Reynolds ph10,2b	3	1	0	0
Rich Amaral 3b	3	0	1	0
Pete O'Brien ph10	1	0	1	0
John Moses pr10,lf	1	0	0	0
Bill Haselman ph14	1	0	1	0
Shane Turner pr14,lf	0	0	0	0
	58	4	14	4

Texas Rangers	AB	R	H	I
David Hulse cf	4	0	1	0
Dickie Thon ph9	0	0	0	0
Jack Daugherty ph9	1	0	0	0
Donald Harris cf10	3	0	0	0
Rafael Palmeiro 1b	7	0	1	0
Jose Canseco rf	7	0	1	0
Juan Gonzalez lf	8	1	3	0
Kevin Reimer dh	7	0	1	0
Dean Palmer 3b	6	1	1	0
Ivan Rodriguez c	7	1	3	1
Jeff Frye 2b	3	0	2	1
Gino Petralli ph10	0	0	0	0
> Monty Fariss 2b11	3	0	1	0
Cris Colon ss	2	0	0	0
Rob Maurer ph7	1	0	1	1
Jeff Huson pr7,ss	0	0	0	0
Brian Downing ph9	0	0	0	0
Al Newman pr9,ss	0	0	0	0
Dan Peltier ph10	1	0	0	0
Mario Diaz ss11	1	0	1	0
	61	3	16	3

Seattle	IP	H	R	ER	BB	SO
Erik Hanson	6	6	2	2	0	7
Rich DeLucia	.2	1	1	1	1	0
Russ Swan	.1	1	0	0	0	1
Mark Grant	1.1	2	0	0	0	1
Eric Gunderson	0	0	0	0	1	0
Jeff Nelson	1.2	1	0	0	3	1
Calvin Jones	.2	1	0	0	1	1
Juan Agosto	.1	0	0	0	0	1
Mike Schooler	.2	2	0	0	1	2
Den. Powell W,4-2	3.1	2	0	0	1	4
Brian Fisher S,1	1	0	0	0	0	0
	16	16	3	3	8	18

Texas	IP	H	R	ER	BB	SO
Jose Guzman	9	8	3	3	1	4
Matt Whiteside	.2	1	0	0	0	0
Kenny Rogers	.2	0	0	0	1	1
Todd Burns	1.2	2	0	0	1	2
Dan Smith L,0-2	4	3	1	1	2	2
	16	14	4	4	5	9

Seattle	2 0 1	0 0 0	0 0 0	0 0 0	0 0 0	1	- 4
Texas	0 2 0	0 0 0	1 0 0	0 0 0	0 0 0	0	- 3

OB: Seattle 12, Texas 20
E: Diaz(1)
DP: Guzman-Huson-Palmeiro (Griffey)
2B: Vizquel, Griffey, T. Martinez 2,
Parrish, O'Brien, Hulse,
Gonzalez, Rodriguez
3B: Griffey
SB: Canseco(6), Reimer(2)
CS: Vizquel(12), Frye(3)
SO: Cotto, Martinez 2, Buhner, Valle,
Parrish, Boone 2, Moses; Harris
2, Palmeiro 2, Canseco, Reimer 3,
Gonzalez 3, Palmer 2, Rodriguez
2, Farris, Colon 2

BB: Cotto(I), Buhner, Howitt, Parrish(I), Reynolds;
Palmeiro (I), Canseco, Reimer, Palmer 2,
Petralli, Downing(I), Diaz(I)
SH: Turner, Rodriguez, Frye
WP: DeLucia
TIME: 5:08
ATTENDANCE: 19,822
UMPIRES: Durwood Merrill, Rick Reed, Tim
McClelland, Drew Coble
SOURCES: BBWS; Dallas Morning News;
Seattle Times

BALANCE	OUT	+	R	+	OB	=	BP	=	AB	+	BB	+	SH	+	HP	+	CI
Seattle	48		4		12		64		58		5		1		0		0
Texas	48		3		20		71		61		8		2		0		0

Seattle shortstop, Omar Vizquel, became the game's hero when he slashed his third hit in the top of the 16th. It drove home Harold Reynolds with the eventual winning run.

Brian Fisher, 30-year-old journeyman reliever, retired the last three Ranger batters to register his first save since 1989 and the final one of his career.

Single-Game Records Fall in Doubleheader

215. Player Hits Four Home Runs, Drives in 12 Runs in Nine-Inning Game; Teams Use 15 Pitchers

ST. LOUIS   at   CINCINNATI
(Cardinals, 13,15)   (Reds, 14,2)

Tuesday Night, September 7, 1993, Riverfront Stadium

In a late season doubleheader between two non-contenders, several longstanding major league benchmarks were broached.

The opener was a 14-13 slugfest, but it wasn't the hitters who broke any records. Instead, the inflated September rosters provided a bounty of pitchers, *15 of whom found their way into the contest, a new major-league mark for a nine-inning game.* The second game witnessed an individual hitting display the likes of which could only be dreamed. As is the case with many of baseball's venerable benchmarks, another unexpected character cast his magical aura over the record book. Mark Whiten, enjoying his finest major league season, albeit far from sensational, erupted for *four home runs and 12 RBIs, tying two of the most esteemed slugging marks in baseball annals.* Whiten also drove home a mate in the opener giving him *13 RBIs in the doubleheader, tying another standard.*

The first game was a wild, see-saw affair, encompassing six lead changes. Cincinnati treated the home town fans to a dramatic victory in the bottom of the ninth with one out on a Reggie Sanders two-run triple. Throughout the contest, pitchers were shuttled in and out as if there were no tomorrow. Six pitchers among the 15 failed to retire even a single batter, and three of the eight (tied the existing NL mark) St. Louis hurlers faced but one hitter. Through the first six frames, only three hurlers saw action. But from the top of the seventh until the bottom of the ninth, the managers wore foot paths to the mound, beckoning a dozen more relievers. The Reds' Rob Dibble was among those who couldn't get anyone out in the first game. He also returned in the nightcap as the final victim of Mark Whiten.

The second game began auspiciously for the switch-hitting Whiten, who blasted a grand slam in his first at-bat. The 26-year-old homered again in the sixth, seventh, and ninth, each time from the left side of the plate. Whiten's second and third circuit clouts came at the expense of Cincinnati hurler Mike Anderson who was making a smashing major-league debut.

As Whiten approached the plate in the ninth, history was just one home run away. "I didn't think about it," he said. "Well, I

Whiten's eruption put him in elite company.

thought about it when I was on the field, but not once I stepped into the box and put the bat on my shoulder."[*]

Cincinnati reliever Rob Dibble was the man who stood between Whiten and the record books. With a 100 mph fastball, Dibble never backed down from a challenge. "I was warming up in the bullpen when he hit the one before that," Dibble said. "I knew I'd probably face him, and I'd give him a chance. I was going to go right after him. I knew it was history."[†] Whiten got one of Dibble's best fastballs right down the heart of the plate and lined it to the deepest part of the park. It was the longest of his four homers.

"I was impressed by that one." Whiten said. "It was the best of the four, I think."[§]

The only time Cincinnati was able to retire Mark was in the fourth when he popped out to Chris Sabo in foul territory.

[*] *The Associated Press, "Baseball History is re-Whiten,"* Norristown Times Herald, *8 September 1993, p. 23, col. 2–6.*
[†] *Ibid.*
[§] *Ibid.*

Whiten, however, demonstrated impeccable timing in making his only out, for it came in his only at-bat without a mate aboard. Here's how his glorious day unfurled:

Inning	Pitcher	Outs	Count	Baserunners	Whiten's Action	Result
1	Luebbers	2	2-0	Maclin (3rd) Ziele (2nd) Perry (1st)	Home Run	4 RBIs 4-0 Cardinals
4	Luebbers	0	—	None	Popped Out	—
6	Anderson	0	First Pitch	Ziele (2nd) Perry (1st)	Home Run	3 RBIs 8-2 Cardinals
7	Anderson	2	2-1	Ziele (2nd) Perry (1st)	Home Run	3 RBIs 12-2 Cardinals
9	Dibble	1	2-0	Perry (1st)	Home Run	2 RBIs 15-2 Cardinals

Whiten was a highly improbable candidate to accomplish such mammoth feats. Consider the following:

• In 1991, not until his 114th major-league at-bat, did he collect his 12th career RBI.

• Home runs were even more scarce for Whiten — he finally collected his fourth career round-tripper in his 75th game, after 228 at-bats. Prior to his heroic game, he hadn't homered in nearly four weeks.

• Before this year, he had never hit more than two home runs in any one game nor hit more than nine in an entire season.

• The press had reported just a week earlier that Whiten would be sent by manager Joe Torre to the Florida Instructional League the following month to work on the "mental approach" to hitting.[*] He was hitting just .251 Tuesday morning.

• It had been more than two years since the Cardinals, as a team, had hit four home runs in one game.

Whiten's post-game interview shed little light on his secret of success. "I don't even have words to explain it, just amazement I guess," said Whiten. "Every time I hit it, I was, like, amazed."[†] Mark's evening of excess swelled his 1993 season totals to 22 homers and 87 RBIs. His second game cannonading also atoned for a costly mistake in the opener when he misplayed Reggie Sanders' liner into a two-run, ninth-inning triple that gave the Reds their opening-game victory.

FIRST GAME

St. Louis Cardinals	AB	R	H	I	Cincinnati Reds	AB	R	H	I
Luis Alicea 2b	6	1	2	1	Jacob Brumfield cf	5	2	3	0
Ozzie Smith ss	5	2	3	1	Hal Morris 1b	3	2	0	1
Gregg Jefferies 1b	6	3	4	2	>Reggie Sanders rf	4	2	2	3
Todd Zeile 3b	3	3	1	3	Chris Sabo 3b	5	2	3	0
>Bernard Gilkey rf,lf8	5	1	2	2	Tim Costo lf	3	2	3	1
Mark Whiten cf	4	1	0	1	Johnny Ruffin p7	0	0	0	0
Lonnie Maclin lf	4	0	1	0	Gary Varsho ph7	1	1	1	0
Stan Royer ph8	1	0	1	2	Dan Wilson c8	1	0	1	2
Tom Pagnozzi c8	0	0	0	0	Joe Oliver c	4	0	2	1
Erik Pappas c,rf8	5	1	3	1	Greg Tubbs pr7	0	1	0	0
Rheal Cormier p	2	0	0	0	Scott Service p8	0	0	0	0

[*] "St. Louis Cardinals," USA Today Baseball Weekly, 8–14 September 1993, p. 18, col. 2.
[†]Associated Press, "Whiten's one-man show one for record books," Philadelphia Daily News, 8 September 1993, p. 64, col. 1.

St. Louis Cardinals	AB	R	H	I
Geronimo Pena ph6	1	0	0	0
Rich Batchelor p6	0	0	0	0
Les Lancaster p7	0	0	0	0
Paul Kilgus p7	0	0	0	0
Rod Brewer ph8	0	0	0	0
Tripp Cromer pr8	1	1	0	0
Steve Dixon p8	0	0	0	0
Mike Perez p8	0	0	0	0
Rob Murphy p9	0	0	0	0
Todd Burns p9	0	0	0	0
	43	13	17	13

Cincinnati Reds	AB	R	H	I
Rob Dibble p8	0	0	0	0
Scott Ruskin p8	0	0	0	0
Jerry Spradlin p8	0	0	0	0
Jack Daugherty ph8	0	0	0	1
Jeff Reardon p9	0	0	0	0
Juan Samuel 2b	3	1	2	4
Jeff Branson ss	5	0	1	0
John Roper p	1	0	0	0
Thomas Howard ph6,lf	2	1	1	0
	37	14	19	13

St. Louis	IP	H	R	ER	BB	SO
Cormier	5	10	5	5	2	3
Batchelor	1	4	4	4	0	0
Lancaster	0	1	0	0	0	0
Kilgus	1	0	0	0	1	1
Dixon	0	0	2	2	2	0
Perez	1.1	3	2	2	0	0
Murphy L,3-6	0	0	1	1	1	0
Burns	0	1	0	0	0	0
	8.1*	19	14	14	6	4

Cincinnati	IP	H	R	ER	BB	SO
Roper	6	8	5	5	3	4
Ruffin	1	3	1	1	0	1
Service	.1	2	3	3	1	0
Dibble	0	1	3	3	2	0
Ruskin	0	1	1	1	1	0
Spradlin	.2	1	0	0	0	1
Reardon W,4-5	1	1	0	0	0	0
	9	17	13	13	7	6

one out when winning run scored

St. Louis	0 0 3	0 2 0	1 7 0	-13
Cincinnati	1 0 3	0 1 2	2 3 2	-14

OB: St. Louis 10, Cincinnati 9
DP: Alicea-Smith-Jefferies (Morris)
    Alicea-Smith-Jefferies (Morris)
2B: Alicea 2, Gilkey, Pappas, Costo,
    Brumfield, Oliver, Samuel,
    Howard
3B: Smith, Sanders
HR: Zeile(13), Samuel(4)
SB: Smith, Jefferies 3, Brumfield 2
CS: Samuel
SO: Alicea 2, Zeile, Whiten, Maclin, Cormier,
    Brumfield, Morris, Sabo, Roper

BB: Smith, Zeile 3, Gilkey, Whiten,
    Brewer, Brumfield, Morris 2,
    Sanders, Samuel(I), Howard
SH: Roper
SF: Daugherty, Sanders, Morris
HP: By Cormier (Samuel)
WP: Dibble, Lancaster
TIME: 3:41
UMPIRES: Harry Wendelstedt, Randy
    Marsh, Jeff Kellogg, Larry Vanover

BALANCE	OUT+R+OB=BP=AB+BB+SH+HP+CI
St. Louis	27 13 10 50 43 7 0 0 0
Cincinnati	25 14 9 48 37 6 4 1 0

SECOND GAME

St. Louis Cardinals	AB	R	H	I
Geronimo Pena 2b	3	1	1	1
Lonnie Maclin lf	4	1	0	1
Bernard Gilkey rf	5	1	1	0
Todd Zeile 3b	2	3	1	0
Stan Royer 3b7	1	0	0	0
Gerald Perry 1b	4	4	3	1
Mark Whiten cf	5	4	4	12
Tom Pagnozzi c	5	0	1	0
>Tripp Cromer ss	5	0	0	0
Bob Tewksbury p	2	1	0	0
	36	15	11	15

Cincinnati Reds	AB	R	H	I
Thomas Howard lf	3	1	0	0
Rob Dibble p8	0	0	0	0
Jacob Brumfield cf	4	1	2	0
Hal Morris 1b	2	0	1	1
Jack Daugherty rf8	1	0	1	0
Chris Sabo 3b	3	0	0	0
Gary Varsho lf8	1	0	0	0
Tim Costo rf,3b8	4	0	1	0
Juan Samuel 2b	4	0	0	0
Dan Wilson c	4	0	0	0
Jeff Branson ss	4	0	1	0

Cincinnati Reds	AB	R	H	I
Larry Luebbers p	1	0	0	0
Greg Tubbs ph5	1	0	0	0
Mike Anderson p6	0	0	0	0
Chris Bushing p7	0	0	0	0
> Brian Dorsett ph7,1b	2	0	1	0
	34	2	7	1

St. Louis	IP	H	R	ER	BB	SO
Tewksbury W,16-8	9	7	2	2	1	4

Cincinnati	IP	H	R	ER	BB	SO
Luebbers L,2-4	5	2	5	5	4	3
Anderson	1.2	6	7	7	2	2
Bushing	.1	0	0	0	0	1
Dibble	2	3	3	3	0	5
	9	11	15	15	6	11

St. Louis	4 0 0	0 1 3	4 1 2	-15
Cincinnati	2 0 0	0 0 0	0 0 0	- 2

OB: St. Louis 2, Cincinnati 7
2B: Brumfield
HR: Pena(3), Whiten 4(22)
SB: Maclin, Brumfield
SO: Pena, Maclin, Gilkey, Royer,
    Perry, Pagnozzi, Cromer 3,
    Tewksbury 2, Morris, Costo,
    Samuel, Wilson
BB: Pena, Zeile 2, Perry,
    Tewksbury 2, Howard
SH: Pena

SF: Maclin, Morris
WP: Luebbers
TIME: 2:17
ATTENDANCE: 22,606
UMPIRES: Randy Marsh, Jeff Kellogg,
    Larry Vanover, Harry Wendelstedt
SOURCES: BBWS; Cincinnati Enquirer;
    Norristown Times Herald; Philadel-
    phia Daily News; St. Louis Post-
    Dispatch; USA Today

BALANCE	OUT	+	R	+	OB	=	BP	=	AB	+	BB	+	SH	+	HP	+	CI
St. Louis	27		15		2		44		36		6		2		0		0
Cincinnati	27		2		7		36		34		1		1		0		0

Pinch Hitters' Parade

216. Teams Use 13 Pinch Hitters in Nine-Inning Game

ATLANTA   at   MONTREAL
(Braves, 18)   (Expos, 5)

Tuesday Night, September 21, 1993, Olympic Stadium

In the waning days of the 1993 campaign, both the Braves and the Expos were enmeshed in tight pennant races. Atlanta was protecting a 2.5 game lead in the Western Division while Montreal was desperately trying to catch Philadelphia in the East, trailing by 4.5 games.

As visitors, Atlanta could think of plenty of places they'd rather be playing. Montreal was on a torrid streak, having won 19 of their last 22 games and, other than the Cardinals, no club had had better success against the Braves.

It looked like more of the same as the Expos jumped off to a 3–1 lead entering the fourth. But the Braves then struck back, hard

Bill Pecota was the fifth consecutive pinch hitter.

and often. Led by Terry Pendleton's three-run home run, Atlanta clobbered Montreal starter Ken Hill for seven more runs.

Pendleton homered again in the fifth, and Fred McGriff contributed a grand slam giving the Braves a commanding 14–3 advantage.

Managing from a new comfort level, Bobby Cox then decided to spell his regulars for the pennant drive. In the sixth, he substituted Raphael Belliard and Deion Sanders, both of whom entered the rout as pinch hitters.

The fact that the Expos tallied twice in the home half of the sixth didn't change Cox's strategy. In the seventh, the Atlanta skipper pinch hit for six batters including the first five. Although it doesn't appear there was any righty-lefty advantage sought by Cox, the pinch hitters and pitchers are referenced as (R) indicating a right-handed batter/pitcher, (L) left-handed, and (B) a switch-hitter. The historic frame emerged as follows:

• Facing 26-year-old Brian Barnes (L),

rookie Chipper Jones (B) pinch hit for Jeff Blauser (R) and walked.

• Tony Tarasco (L), another rookie, swung for Ron Gant (R) and doubled, driving home Jones.

• Veteran Sid Bream (L) batted for Fred McGriff (L) and doubled home Tarasco.

• Still another rookie, Ryan Klesko (L), hit for David Justice (L) and walked.

• Veteran Bill Pecota (R) singled for Pendleton (B), driving home Bream.

• The pinch-hit parade was temporarily interrupted when catcher Greg Olson (R) batted for himself and singled home Klesko.

• Belliard (R), who had pinch hit an inning earlier and stayed in the game, now struck out.

• Atlanta's sixth pinch hitter of the inning, Francisco Cabrera (R), batted for pitcher John Smoltz (R). Cabrera flied out to left for the second out.

• Sanders, who also had pinch hit an inning earlier, grounded out to second ending the Braves' assault.

The bizarre inning saw Atlanta bat around for the third time in the game. This time, however, eight of the nine men who stepped to the plate had originally entered the contest as pinch hitters.

Atlanta's ninth pinch hitter, and the game's 13th, batted in the top of the ninth. Brian Hunter (R) swung for pitcher Marvin Freeman (R) and struck out. By then the Braves had feasted on 213 Expo pitches and tied the Atlanta team record for runs scored (18).

The final tally revealed a new major league record had been set, i.e., *most pinch hitters by both clubs in a nine-inning game—13.* Moreover, three other major league standards were tied, all by Atlanta:

• *Most pinch hitters by one club in a nine-inning game— 9.*

• *Most pinch hitters by one club in an inning— 6.*

• *Most consecutive pinch hitters by one club in an inning— 5.*

Atlanta did manage to win the Western Division pennant by one game but was derailed by Philadelphia in the NL play-offs.

Atlanta Braves	AB	R	H	I
Otis Nixon cf	3	3	1	0
Deion Sanders ph6,cf	2	0	0	0
Jeff Blauser ss	2	1	1	2
Chipper Jones ph7,ss	1	1	1	0
Ron Gant lf	3	2	2	3
Tony Tarasco ph7,rf	2	1	1	1
Fred McGriff 1b	3	2	3	5
Sid Bream ph7,1b	2	1	1	1
David Justice rf	2	1	0	0
Ryan Klesko ph7,lf	1	1	0	0
Terry Pendleton 3b	4	2	2	4
Bill Pecota ph7,3b	2	0	2	1
Greg Olson c	5	1	1	1
Mark Lemke 2b	2	1	0	0
Raph. Belliard ph6,2b	2	0	0	0
John Smoltz p	3	1	1	0
Francisco Cabrera ph7	1	0	0	0
Mike Stanton p7	0	0	0	0
Marvin Freeman p8	0	0	0	0
> Brian Hunter ph9	1	0	0	0
Pete Smith p9	0	0	0	0
	41	18	16	18

Montreal Expos	AB	R	H	I
Delino DeShields 2b	3	0	0	0
> Sean Berry ph6,3b	2	0	0	0
John VanderWal lf,rf6	2	1	0	0
Marquis Grissom cf	3	1	1	0
Lou Frazier lf6	1	0	0	0
Larry Walker rf	3	1	1	2
Rondell White cf6	1	0	0	0
Darrin Fletcher c	3	1	2	1
Joe Siddall c8	1	0	0	0
Will Cordero ss	4	1	1	2
Oreste Marrero 1b	3	0	1	0
Brian Barnes p7	0	0	0	0
Mel Rojas p8	0	0	0	0
Tim Spehr ph8	1	0	0	0
Chris Nabholz p9	0	0	0	0
Mike Lansing 3b,2b7	4	0	2	0
Ken Hill p	0	0	0	0
Butch Henry p4	0	0	0	0
Curtis Pride ph4	1	0	0	0
Gil Heredia p5	0	0	0	0
Jeff Shaw p	0	0	0	0
Cliff Floyd ph6,1b	2	0	0	0
	34	5	8	5

Atlanta	IP	H	R	ER	BB	SO
Smoltz W,15-10	6	8	5	5	2	4
Stanton	1	0	0	0	0	1
Freeman	1	0	0	0	0	1
Smith	1	0	0	0	0	2
	9	8	5	5	2	8

Montreal	IP	H	R	ER	BB	SO
Hill L,9-6	3.2	6	8	4	2	1
Henry	.1	1	0	0	0	0
Heredia	.2	3	6	6	3	1
Shaw	1.1	0	0	0	0	1
Barnes	1	4	4	4	2	1
Rojas	1	1	0	0	0	0
Nabholz	1	1	0	0	0	1
	9	16	18	14	7	5

Atlanta	1 0 0	7 6 0	4 0 0	-18
Montreal	3 0 0	0 0 2	0 0 0	- 5

OB: Atlanta 9, Montreal 5
E: Lansing
DP: DeShields-Cordero-Marrero(Justice)
2B: Nixon, Jones, Gant, Tarasco,
    McGriff, Bream, Fletcher 2
3B: Walker
HR: Cordero(10), McGriff(35),
    Pendleton 2(15&16)
SO: Gant, Lemke, Belliard, Smoltz,
    Hunter; DeShields, Berry 2,
    Frazier, Cordero, Lansing,
    Floyd 2
BB: Nixon, Jones, Gant, Justice 2,
    Klesko, Lemke; VanderWal 2

SH: Smoltz, Hill
SF: Blauser
HP: By Hill (McGriff, Blauser);
    by Heredia (Olson);
    by Shaw (Belliard)
WP: Smoltz 2
TIME: 3:14
ATTENDANCE: 30,585
UMPIRES: Randy Marsh, Ed Rapuano,
    Joe West, Larry Vanover
SOURCES: Atlanta Constitution/Journal;
    BBWS; Montreal Gazette

BALANCE	OUT	+R	+OB	=BP	=AB	+BB	+SH	+HP	+CI
Atlanta	27	18	9	54	41	7	2	4	0
Montreal	27	5	5	37	34	2	1	0	0

Cardinals Couldn't Find Home

217. Team Leaves 16 Runners on Base in Shutout Loss

PHILADELPHIA   at   ST. LOUIS
(Phillies, 4)   (Cardinals, 0)

Tuesday Night, May 24, 1994, Busch Stadium

Being shut out by major league pitching is certainly little reason for a club to be embarrassed. But when the whitewashed team also has been afforded liberal access to the base paths, an elevated level of frustration and humiliation crystallizes.

Four teams since the turn of the century have reached distinguished levels of such frustration by stranding 15 base runners while being shut out. (See 5-22-13, 7-29-31, 8-01-41, and 5-12-75.) As implausible as it may seem, that aberration was magnified still further this day as the St. Louis Cardinals established *a new level of futility by marooning 16 runners on the base paths without scoring a run.* The feat boosted their league-leading left-on-base total to 361 after 43 games.

This was not the story of a wild, fastball pitcher who either struck out or walked most of the batters he faced. Nor was it a game heaped with errors. Instead, four Philadelphia hurlers tossed 184 pitches while issuing a total of eight bases on balls and permitting nine St. Louis safeties. Their ineffectiveness was exceeded only by that of the Cardinal batters, who could not hit safely when it counted most.

As might be expected, several golden opportunities to cross the plate slipped by the Cardinals. Following is an inning-by-inning account of their record-setting day:

ST. LOUIS CARDINALS LEFT-ON-BASE BY INNING, 5-24-94

First	this was the only frame in which St. Louis was retired in order	0H, 0BB, 0LOB
Second	Todd Zeile led off with a double; Bernard Gilkey grounded out; Brian Jordan flied out, moving Zeile to third; Tom Pagnozzi walked but Luis Alicea grounded out	1H, 1BB, 2LOB
Third	with two outs Ozzie Smith singled, but Gregg Jefferies hit into a force out	1H, 0BB, 1LOB
Fourth	with one out Gilkey and Jordan walked; Pagnozzi moved both runners ahead when he grounded out; Alicea was intentionally walked, but Vicente Palacios flied out	0H, 3BB, 3LOB
Fifth	Smith walked after one out; Jefferies singled and Zeile walked, loading the bases; Gilkey grounded into an inning-ending doubleplay	1H, 2BB, 2LOB
Sixth	Jordan and Pagnozzi singled; Alicea was called out on strikes, but pinch hitter Gerald Perry walked to load the bases; Ray Lankford was called out on strikes, and Smith grounded out	2H, 1BB, 3LOB
Seventh	with one out Zeile doubled; Gilkey struck out; Jordan walked, but Pagnozzi grounded out	1H, 1BB, 2LOB
Eighth	Lankford singled after two outs; but Smith grounded out	1H, 0BB, 1LOB
Ninth	Jefferies and Zeile singled; Gilkey forced Jefferies; Jordan struck out, and Pagnozzi flied out	2H, 0BB, 2LOB

St. Louis left-on-base by inning: 0 2 1   3 2 3   2 1 2 = 16

Escaping one threat after another, the charmed Phillies entered the ninth of a scoreless game. On the mound for the Cardinals, in his first inning of work, stood Mike Perez. The 29-year-old right-hander was coming off a superb 1993 campaign in which he worked in 65 games, compiling a 2.48 ERA. This season, however, he had gotten off to a rocky start, having allowed nine earned runs in 13.1 innings.

Philadelphia's Jim Eisenreich led off with a single to left. Ricky Jordan doubled to right-center, driving home Eisenreich with the first run of the game. Milt Thompson walked, and both runners moved up on a sacrifice by Tom Quinlan. Pete Incaviglia then was called upon to pinch hit for Heathcliff Slocumb and responded by blasting the first pitch he saw into the left-field seats, giving the Phillies a 4–0 margin. Bryan Eversgerd relieved Perez and retired the final two batters, but the damage had been done.

Batting in the home half of the ninth, the Cardinals had already left 14 runners aboard. Doug Jones, the Phillies' off-speed closer, was on the mound attempting to seal the victory. Two more Cardinal singles were wasted as

Streak-hitting Pete Incaviglia slammed his fifth homer in seven games.

Philadelphia triumphed, and St. Louis set a new major league benchmark of ignominy.

Philadelphia Phillies	AB	R	H	I
Lenny Dykstra cf	4	0	1	0
>Mickey Morandini 2b	5	0	1	0
Mariano Duncan ss	4	0	0	0
Darren Daulton c	4	0	0	0
Jim Eisenreich rf	3	1	3	0
Ricky Jordan 1b	4	1	2	1
Milt Thompson lf	3	1	1	0
Tom Quinlan 3b	3	0	0	0
Doug West p	1	0	0	0
Tony Longmire ph5	1	0	0	0
Bobby Munoz p5	0	0	0	0
Wes Chamberlain ph7	1	0	0	0
Heathcliff Slocumb p7	0	0	0	0
Pete Incaviglia ph9	1	1	1	3
Doug Jones p9	0	0	0	0
	34	4	9	4

St. Louis Cardinals	AB	R	H	I
Ray Lankford cf	5	0	1	0
Ozzie Smith ss	4	0	1	0
Gregg Jefferies 1b	5	0	2	0
Todd Zeile 3b	4	0	3	0
Bernard Gilkey lf	4	0	0	0
Brian Jordan rf	3	0	1	0
>Tom Pagnozzi c	4	0	1	0
Luis Alicea 2b	3	0	0	0
Vicente Palacios p	2	0	0	0
Gerald Perry ph6	0	0	0	0
Rene Arocha p7	0	0	0	0
Geronimo Pena ph8	1	0	0	0
Mike Perez p9	0	0	0	0
Bryan Eversgerd p9	0	0	0	0
	35	0	9	0

Philadelphia	IP	H	R	ER	BB	SO
West	4	2	0	0	4	2
Munoz	2	3	0	0	3	3
Slocumb W,4-0	2	2	0	0	1	2
Jones	1	2	0	0	0	1
	9	9	0	0	8	8

St. Louis	IP	H	R	ER	BB	SO
Palacios	6	6	0	0	2	6
Arocha	2	0	0	0	0	2
Perez L,1-1	.1	3	4	4	1	0
Eversgerd	.2	0	0	0	0	1
	9	9	4	4	3	9

| Philadelphia | 0 0 0 | 0 0 0 | 0 0 4 | - 4 |
| St. Louis | 0 0 0 | 0 0 0 | 0 0 0 | - 0 |

OB: Philadelphia 7, St. Louis 16
DP: Duncan-Morandini-R.Jordan(Gilkey)
  Smith-Alicea-Jefferies(Thompson)
2B: R. Jordan, Zeile 2
HR: Incaviglia(7)
SO: Morandini, Duncan 3, Daulton,
  R. Jordan, Quinlan 2, Chamberlain;
  Lankford 3, Gilkey, B. Jordan,
  Alicea, Palacios, Pena

BB: Dykstra, Eisenreich, Thompson; Smith, Zeile,
  Gilkey, Alicea(I), B. Jordan 2, Pagnozzi, Perry
SH: Quinlan
TIME: 3:09
ATTENDANCE: 25,618
UMPIRES: Brian Gorman, Steve Rippley, Terry Tata,
  Eric Gregg
SOURCES: BBWS; Philadelphia Daily News,
  Inquirer; St. Louis Post-Dispatch; USA Today

BALANCE	OUT	+R	+OB	=BP	=AB	+BB	+SH	+HP	+CI
Philadelphia	27	4	7	38	34	3	1	0	0
St. Louis	27	0	16	43	35	8	0	0	0

Turbulence in Tiger Stadium

218. Teams Combine for 12 Home Runs in Nine-Inning Game

CHICAGO   at   DETROIT
(White Sox, 14)   (Tigers, 12)

Sunday, May 28, 1995, Tiger Stadium

The National Weather Service claimed there were wind gusts of up to 12 miles-per-hour in Detroit this day, but everyone involved in the home run derby at Tiger Stadium felt that estimate was grossly understated. Taking advantage of mother nature, a cozy ballpark and some generous pitching, an offensive assault unseen in baseball history was unleashed on the record books. In the final tally, several single game, long ball benchmarks were broken or tied:

• Eight different players on the two clubs combined for *a new major league standard of 12 home runs.* The old mark of 11 from both clubs had been achieved eight times. (The eight different players was one shy of the ML benchmark.)

• There were *ten bases-empty circuit blasts,* shattering the previous ML record of seven.

• *Four different players each struck two or more round trippers,* tying the ML benchmark and establishing a new American League mark. This previously had been accomplished only once in a National League contest.

• *Three teammates* (Tigers) *each clouted two or more homers* to tie the ML record for one team.

• In addition, the *two teams combined to set an American League mark with 21 extra-base hits.* (ML and NL record is 24.)

Although the Tigers out-homered their guests seven to five and scored in each of the first six innings, they still lost the 385-pitch marathon. They also became the 41st team in major league history to club seven or more homers in one game, but the first of those to taste defeat.*

---

*Jayson Stark, "Week in Review," The Philadelphia Inquirer, 4 June 1995, section C, p. 7, col. 2.

Along the way, several unlikely candidates contributed to the fusillade. Chicago's Craig Grebeck, who hadn't hit a home run in more than a year, had this to say after blasting the White Sox' third consecutive round tripper in the fourth inning. "I don't hit home runs, but the wind must've been 30 miles per hour."* Grebeck's blast remained his lone home run of the season. Also, Chicago's rookie second baseman Ray Durham had never hit a major league home run, that is until this day when he smashed the first of the three successive Sox homers in the fourth.

Four players each provided two home runs. Chicago catcher Ron Karkovice sent a pair into the seats marking his fifth lifetime multi-homer game, three of which occurred in Tiger Stadium. Three Detroit sluggers also connected twice. Chad Curtis served notice of the day's events by homering to lead off both the first and second innings. Kirk Gibson celebrated his 38th birthday with a pair, giving him six home runs in his last six games. And Cecil Fielder stroked the longest balls of the day with a 450-foot blast into the center field bleachers in the first and then added a 420-foot shot in the second. Each of his blasts were the only ones in the contest with runners on base.

Chicago rookie right-hander James Baldwin started on the mound for the visitors. Baldwin was appearing in his sixth major league game, having been bombarded for 25 hits and 15 runs in 13.1 innings prior to this debacle. But the worst part of his season was just about to begin. The first batter he faced, Curtis, homered. Then he walked Lou Whitaker, and Alan Trammell singled. That set the table for Fielder's first ponderous home run. After four batters, it was 4–0. The Tigers batted around but didn't score again in the opening frame.

Chicago got on the board in the second on Karkovice's sacrifice fly. That made it 4–1. In the home half, Curtis again led off with a homer. Whitaker singled but Trammell fanned. Fielder then repeated his prodigious batting with another tape measure blast giving the home club a 7–1 advantage. That was

Karkovice had his third multi-homer game in Detroit.

all for Baldwin, who departed and was not seen again for the balance of the season. James had thrown 57 pitches to 13 batters and had given up as many home runs as he had gotten outs. Fortunately for Baldwin and the White Sox, the wind was still gusting and the game far from over.

Detroit entrusted their six-run lead to starter David Wells who was not quite up to the challenge. An error, a walk, a hit, a ground out and a sacrifice enabled Chicago to manufacture three runs in the top of the third. The Tigers countered with a run in the bottom half on Trammell's single making it 8–4.

Wells finally succumbed to the long ball in the fourth as Durham, Karkovice, and Grebeck connected successively for solo shots. Gibson answered with a solo blast for the Tigers in the home half. After four, Detroit clung precariously to a 9–7 lead.

The Sox scored a pair in the fifth without a home run. Three doubles and a single tied the score at nine. But it was short-lived satisfaction as Detroit's John Flaherty doubled and was singled home by Lou Whitaker.

*Dan Binkley, "Home Run Derby," Chicago Sun-Times, 29 May 1995, p. 66, col. 1.

The sixth frame saw the teams exchange runs on solo homers by Frank Thomas and Gibson preserving the Tigers' one-run lead at 11–10.

Karkovice tied the score at 11 with his second home run in the top of the seventh. In the bottom half, batterymate Scott Radinsky held the Tigers scoreless for the first time in the game.

With the momentum having swung their way, Chicago pushed across three more runs in the eighth without a homer. The visitors then led 14 to 11. The hosts had just about run out of gas but mustered one more round tripper, a solo blast by Whitaker, in the bottom of the eighth. Whitaker's clout was the record-breaking 12th of the game.

HOME RUNS IN TIGER STADIUM, MAY 28, 1995

Inn	Outs	Team	Batter	Pitcher	Runners On	Count
1	0	Det	C. Curtis	J. Baldwin	None	0-1
1	0	Det	C. Fielder	J. Baldwin	Whitaker (2nd) Trammell (1st)	2-2
2	0	Det	C. Curtis	J. Baldwin	None	2-1
2	1	Det	C. Fielder	J. Baldwin	Whitaker (1st)	3-2
4	0	Chi	R. Durham	D. Wells	None	2-2
4	0	Chi	R. Karkovice	D. Wells	None	2-1
4	0	Chi	C. Grebeck	D. Wells	None	0-0
4	0	Det	K. Gibson	K. McKaskill	None	2-1
6	0	Chi	F. Thomas	J. Doherty	None	2-1
6	0	Det	K. Gibson	R. Dibble	None	3-1
7	1	Chi	R. Karkovice	J. Doherty	None	1-1
8	2	Det	L. Whitaker	S. Radinsky	None	2-2

Having exhausted themselves slugging and running the bases, neither team scored in the final frame. It was a particularly frustrating day for the home team. In addition to losing after blowing a 7–1 lead, they wasted multiple scoring opportunities as evidenced by their 15 runners left on base. Despite 17 hits and eight walks, five of their seven homers came without a mate aboard.

Detroit's Danny Bautista, who struck out once in every four at-bats during this campaign, was apparently anxious to enter the home-run derby. He fanned in five of six plate appearances, tying the major league record for a nine-inning game. His five strikeouts took just 18 pitches.

Chicago White Sox	AB	R	H	I
Paco Martin rf	3	1	0	0
Warren Newson ph5,rf	1	0	0	0
Tim Raines lf	5	2	2	0
>Frank Thomas 1b	5	2	2	2
John Kruk dh	4	2	1	1
Robin Ventura 3b	4	0	1	1
Mike Devereaux cf	5	3	1	2
Ray Durham 2b	5	1	4	3
Ron Karkovice c	3	2	2	4
Craig Grebeck ss	3	1	1	1
Ozzie Guillen ph8,ss	1	0	0	0
	39	14	14	14

Detroit Tigers	AB	R	H	I
Chad Curtis cf	5	3	3	2
Lou Whitaker 2b	4	3	3	2
Alan Trammell ss	6	1	2	1
Cecil Fielder 1b	5	2	2	5
Scott Fletcher pr8,1b	0	0	0	0
Kirk Gibson dh	6	2	4	2
Travis Fryman 3b	4	0	1	0
Bobby Higginson lf	2	0	0	0
Juan Samuel ph7	0	0	0	0
Todd Steverson lf	0	0	0	0
Franklin Stubbs ph9	1	0	0	0
Danny Bautista rf	6	0	1	0
>John Flaherty c	5	1	1	0
	44	12	17	12

Chicago	IP	H	R	ER	BB	SO
James Baldwin	1.1	7	7	7	2	3
Kirk McCaskill	3	5	3	3	2	3
Rob Dibble	1.1	2	1	1	2	2
S. Radinsky W,2-0	2	2	1	1	2	1
R. Hernandez S,8	1.1	1	0	0	0	2
	9	17	12	12	8	11

Detroit	IP	H	R	ER	BB	SO
David Wells	3	7	7	5	1	2
John Doherty	3.2	5	4	4	2	1
Buddy Groom L,1-2	.2	1	3	3	2	1
Mike Henneman	1.2	1	0	0	1	0
	9	14	14	12	6	4

Chicago	0	1	3	3	2	1	1	3	0	-14
Detroit	4	3	1	1	1	1	0	1	0	-12

OB: Chicago 7, Detroit 15
E: Grebeck 2, Wells
DP: Grebeck-Durham-Thomas (Fielder)
 Karkovice-Ventura (Higginson SO)
2B: Raines, Thomas, Kruk, Devereaux,
 Durham 2, Curtis, Gibson, Flaherty
HR: Curtis 2(6), Fielder 2(11), Durham (1),
 Karkovice 2(5), Grebeck (1), Gibson 2(8),
 Thomas (7), Whitaker (1)
SB: Durham (6), Whitaker (2), Gibson 2(5),
 Higginson (3), Fryman (2)
CS: Fryman (1)
SO: Newson, Kruk 2, Ventura; Stubbs, Trammell,
 Fielder, Higginson 2, Bautista 5, Flaherty

BB: Newson 2, Raines, Grebeck, Kruk,
 Thomas(I); Whitaker 2, Flaherty,
 Fryman 2(1I), Higginson 2, Samuel
SF: Karkovice 2, Ventura
HP: By Dibble (Curtis); by Hernandez (Fielder)
TIME: 3:46
ATTENDANCE: 10,813
UMPIRES: Gary Cederstrom, Dave
 Phillips, Rocky Roe, Tim McClelland
SOURCES: BBWS; Chicago Sun-Times,
 Tribune; Detroit News; Philadelphia
 Inquirer; USA Today

BALANCE	OUT+R+OB=BP=AB+BB+SH+HP+CI
Chicago	27 14 7 48 39 6 3 0 0
Detroit	27 12 15 54 44 8 0 2 0

Those who study baseball records are often treated to implausible combinations of events. The context under which this game unfolded offers just such bewilderment, for less than 24 hours earlier these same two teams met in the same stadium with the White Sox prevailing 1–0. Then, the two teams combined for only nine hits, and the winning pitcher was Jason Bere, who had most recently allowed 23 runs in 28 innings.

Cubs High on Coors

219. Fourteen Teammates Get Hits, Nine Score at Least Two Runs in Nine-Inning Game

CHICAGO   at   COLORADO
(Cubs, 26)   (Rockies, 7)

Friday Night, August 18, 1995, Coors Field

No, this game wasn't played in Wrigley Field, although the score would indicate such. Rather, the visitors from Chicago turned the thin air of Denver into a Cubs' Rocky Mountain high by erupting for 27 hits and 26 runs in the new Coors Field.

Chicago's harvest was the most hits and runs by any one club in a game played by the third-year Colorado franchise. In addition, the Cubs tied two major league records and one National League mark:

 • *Nine teammates each scored two or more*

Sammy Sosa contributed four hits.

Anthony Young tossed 19 pitches for the win.

runs, tying the major league standard. (This had been accomplished by nine other teams since the turn of the century.)

• *14 Cubs hit safely in the nine-inning contest*, tying the major league mark (see 6-23-86 and 8-12-48).

• The Cubs also tied the National League benchmark of *26 RBIs*. (The ML mark is 29; see 6-08-50.)

• The major leagues' oldest franchise also increased their record of *scoring 20 or more runs in a game* to 39.

The game began in cloudy, 87-degree weather, with a nine mile-per-hour breeze blowing from right to left. The wind didn't seem to be as much a factor as the barometer, for the game was delayed nearly three hours after the third inning due to rain.

Colorado starter Bret Saberhagen, two-time AL Cy Young Award winner who had joined the Rockies on July 31 of this year in a trade with the Mets, was expected to solidify the Colorado staff and vault the club into the playoffs. But this day would prove

the shortest outing of his 12-year major league career.

The Cubs, desperately clinging to wild-card playoff hopes, had been drubbed by the Rockies the night before, 12–5. This night Chicago wasted little time retaliating as they took advantage of the thin Colorado air and Saberhagen's atypical wildness. The 31-year-old right-hander tossed 67 pitches but retired only one batter while seven Cubs crossed the plate. Hot-hitting Luis Gonzalez led the onslaught with a three-run, opposite-field home run into the left-field bleachers. Every Cub reached base safely during the opening stanza as the Midwesterners jumped out to a 7–0 advantage.

It never got any better for the home assembly. With Colorado trailing 9–1 after three frames, a monstrous thunderstorm chased most of the Rockies' 30th consecutive sellout crowd. The rains finally ended around midnight, but the Cub marauding did not. Chicago picked up where they left off by adding 17 more runs to their bounty. By the game's conclusion at 2:15 A.M., the Cubs had tied their own NL record for runs in a game. Scarcely a few thousand drenched diehards witnessed the conclusion six hours after the first pitch.

Kevin Foster hurled an admirable first three innings for Chicago, allowing only one hit — a home run by Andres Galarraga. But after the long rain delay he was not allowed to return, manager Jim Riggleman cautiously saving him for the stretch drive. Anthony Young picked up the easy victory with one and one-third innings of relief.

After the game, Mark Grace summed up the Cubs' success. "Sabes [Saberhagen] was popping the ball. Bob Feller could have been pitching against us and we would have hit him. It was just our night."*

Early and successful substitutions launched the Cubs into the record books. The 14 Cubs who hit safely included every starter as well as five substitutes. Subs Scott Bullett, Anthony Young, and Todd Haney were among nine Chicago players to score at least twice. Bullett also contributed a career high four RBIs to the record-tying team total.

While Chicago hammered Colorado in this contest, the Rockies went on to lead the National League in virtually every major offensive catagory. Their hitting carried them to the playoffs where they lost in the first round to the eventual world champion Atlanta Braves. Chicago finished third in the NL Central Division.

Chicago Cubs	AB	R	H	I
Brian McRae cf	5	2	3	1
Scott Bullett cf6	2	2	2	4
Shawon Dunston ss	3	0	1	1
Jose Hernandez ss4	4	0	1	2
Mark Grace 1b	6	3	1	2
Sammy Sosa rf	6	4	4	4
Luis Gonzalez lf	6	2	3	6
Larry Casian p7	1	0	0	0
Randy Myers p9	0	0	0	0
Todd Zeile 3b	4	2	3	3
Howard Johnson 3b6	0	0	0	0
> Joe Kmak ph8,3b	2	1	1	0
Rey Sanchez 2b	4	1	1	0
Terry Adams p6	0	0	0	0
Ozzie Timmons lf7	1	0	0	0
Scott Servais c	5	4	3	1
Kevin Foster p	2	1	1	2
Mike Perez p4	0	0	0	0
Anthony Young p4	2	2	2	0
Todd Haney 2b6	1	2	1	0
	54	26	27	26

Colorado Rockies	AB	R	H	I
Eric Young 2b	4	0	0	0
Ellis Burks cf,lf7	4	0	0	0
Dante Bichette lf,rf7	4	1	2	1
Larry Walker rf	3	0	0	0
Jo. Vander Wal rf6,1b	2	0	0	0
Andres Galarraga 1b	3	1	1	1
Mike Kingery cf7	2	1	1	1
Vinny Castilla 3b	5	1	2	0
Joe Girardi c	3	1	1	0
Jayhawk Owens c7	2	1	0	0
Walt Weiss ss	2	0	0	0
Steve Reed p5	0	0	0	0
Mike Munoz p6	0	0	0	0
Bryan Hickerson ph7,p	1	0	1	2
> Darren Holmes p9	1	0	0	0
Bret Saberhagen p	0	0	0	0
Lance Painter p1	0	0	0	0
Jim Tatum ph3	1	0	0	0
David Nied p4	0	0	0	0
Jason Bates ss5	2	1	2	2
	39	7	10	7

Chicago	IP	H	R	ER	BB	SO
Foster	3	1	1	1	2	2
Perez	.2	0	0	0	0	1
Young W,2-4	1.1	3	1	1	0	1
Adams	1.2	6	5	4	2	1
Casian	1.1	0	0	0	1	0
Myers	1	0	0	0	0	0
	9	10	7	6	5	5

Colorado	IP	H	R	ER	BB	SO
Saberhagen L,6-6	.1	5	7	7	2	0
Painter	2.2	5	2	2	0	1
Nied	1.1	6	5	5	1	1
Reed	1.1	5	4	4	1	4
Munoz	1.1	3	4	4	1	0
Hickerson	1	3	4	4	1	0
Holmes	1	0	0	0	0	2
	9	27	26	26	6	8

*Joseph A. Reaves, "Cub's outburst ties modern-day club record," Chicago Tribune, 20 August 1995, section 3, p. 3, col. 6.

| Chicago | 7 0 2 | 0 6 3 | 4 4 0 | -26 |
| Colorado | 0 1 0 | 0 1 2 | 3 0 0 | - 7 |

OB: Chicago 7, Colorado 10
E: Gonzalez, Zeile, Haney; Bichette
DP: Dunston-Sanchez-Grace (Burks)
    Young-Weiss-Galarrago (Gonzalez)
2B: Grace, Servais 2, Foster, Zeile,
    Gonzalez, Bullett; Girardi, Bates
3B: Bullett; Hickerson
HR: Gonzalez(10), Zeile(13),
    Sosa(22); Galarraga(25)
SO: McRae, Dunston, Hernandez, Sosa,
    Casian, Sanchez, Servais 2;
    Young, Burks, Bichette 2, Walker

BB: Grace, Sosa, Zeile, Sanchez,
    Servais, Haney; Young, Burks,
    Bichette, Munoz, Bates
TIME: 3:22 (+2:45 rain delay in 4th)
ATTENDANCE: 48,082
UMPIRES: Gerry Davis, Wally Bell,
    Mike Winters, Terry Tata
SOURCES: BBWS; Chicago Sun-Times,
    Tribune; USA Today

BALANCE	OUT+R+OB=BP=AB+BB+SH+HP+CI
Chicago	27 26 7 60 54 6 0 0 0
Colorado	27 7 10 44 39 5 0 0 0

Robin Rocks the Rangers

220. Player Hits
Two Grand Slams in One Game

CHICAGO   at   TEXAS
(White Sox, 14) (Rangers, 3)

Monday Night, September 4, 1995, The Ballpark in Arlington

Two years earlier Robin Ventura had violated sacred territory when he charged the pitcher's mound at Arlington Stadium to protest a Nolan Ryan fastball. Since then he had been roundly booed by the partisan Texas fans. But this night he evoked a rare standing ovation for a visiting player after he became the *eighth batter to register two grand slams in one game*. It was the first occurrence since Frank Robinson connected twice in 1970, and only the fourth time the feat was accomplished in consecutive innings.

The contest added little drama to the pennant race. With the final standings still 27 games away, the Sox were already mathematically eliminated from the Central Divison crown and needed a miracle of biblical proportion to gain a wild-card berth. The Rangers were still a Western Division and wild-card contender but had just dropped eight of their last ten games to fall to .500 (60–60).

Ventura tied the club mark with 8 RBIs.

Chicago White Sox	AB	R	H	I
Lance Johnson cf	6	2	2	2
Tim Raines lf	4	3	3	0
Mike Cameron rf5	2	0	0	0
Dave Martinez 1b	5	1	1	0
Frank Thomas dh	2	2	0	0
Barry Lyons ph7,dh	2	0	1	0
>Robin Ventura 3b	5	3	3	8
Lyle Mouton rf,lf5	3	2	3	1
Ray Durham 2b	5	0	2	1
Mike LaValliere c	5	0	2	1
Ozzie Guillen ss	5	1	1	1
	44	14	18	14

Texas Rangers	AB	R	H	I
Otis Nixon cf	1	1	0	0
> John Marzano c8	1	0	0	0
Mark McLemore 2b,lf8	4	0	0	0
Will Clark 1b	2	1	0	0
Jeff Frye 2b8	1	0	0	0
Juan Gonzalez dh	3	1	2	2
Luis Ortiz ph8,dh	1	0	0	0
Mickey Tettleton rf	3	0	0	0
Lou Frazier cf8	1	0	0	0
Ivan Rodriguez c	2	0	0	1
Dave Valle 1b8	1	0	1	0
Rusty Greer lf,rf8	4	0	1	0
Mike Pagliarulo 3b	4	0	0	0
Benji Gill ss	3	0	0	0
Sam Horn ph9	0	0	0	0
	31	3	4	3

Chicago	IP	H	R	ER	BB	SO
Jason Bere W,7-11	6	3	3	2	4	5
Scott Radinsky	2	0	0	0	0	1
Rod Bolton	1	1	0	0	1	0
	9	4	3	2	5	6

Texas	IP	H	R	ER	BB	SO
Ke. Gross L,7-14	3.2	8	7	7	3	3
Dennis Cook	.1	3	2	2	0	0
Danny Darwin	4	6	5	5	1	1
Mark Brandenburg	1	1	0	0	1	1
	9	18	14	14	5	5

Chicago	1 1 1	6 4 0	0 1 0	-14
Texas	2 0 0	1 0 0	0 0 0	- 3

OB: Chicago 9, Texas 7
E: Raines, Durham
DP: Valle unassisted (Ventura liner)
2B: Ventura, Mouton 2, LaValliere
3B: Durham, Guillen
HR: Johnson(9), Ventura 2(25);
        Gonzalez(21)
SB: Nixon(36)
CS: Nixon(17)
SO: Raines, Cameron 2, Thomas 2;
        McLemore 2, Gonzalez, Tettleton
        2, Pagliarulo

BB: Martinez, Thomas 2, Ventura, Mouton;
        Nixon 3, Clark, Horn
SF: Rodriguez
HP: By Darwin (Mouton)
TIME: 3:11
ATTENDANCE: 18,036
UMPIRES: Tim McClelland, Rocky Roe,
        Dave Phillips, Gary Cederstrom
SOURCES: BBWS; Chicago Sun-Times, Tribune;
        Dallas Morning News; USA Today

BALANCE	OUT+R+OB=BP=AB+BB+SH+HP+CI							
Chicago	27	14	9	50	44	5	1	1	0
Texas	27	3	7	37	31	5	1	0	0

Chicago held a slim 3–2 lead after three innings, but Texas starter Kevin Gross had struggled mightily. Five Sox hits and two walks through the first three frames were followed by three hits and another base on balls in the fourth. With the score 4–2, two outs, the bases loaded, and left-handed hitting Ventura stepping to the plate, Gross was relieved by left-hander Dennis Cook. The count ran to 2–1 before Ventura connected for his first grand blast, a 423-foot shot over the center field fence.

Danny Darwin replaced Cook on the mound for the Rangers in the fifth. After the first two batters were retired, two singles and another walk to Frank Thomas loaded the bases again for Ventura. Once more the count went to 2–1 before Robin lined a pitch 368 feet down the right field line and into the bleachers. It was Ventura's personal best 25th home run of the season and his seventh career grand slam.

The Chicago hero had several other opportunities in which to break the club RBI mark and threaten the ML record of 12. Leading off the second, he doubled and scored. In the third inning, with two outs and a runner on first, he walked. In the seventh Ventura flied out to right with two outs and no mates aboard. But in the ninth, with runners at the corners and only one out, he lined into a double play.

After the game, Robin called his accomplishment a "freak" thing. "You definitely have to have luck to do that," Ventura said. "You get the opportunity to do that when you bat behind Frank [Thomas] because he walks a lot. I'm sure I'll reflect on it one day. It's nice, but you don't stop playing because you do something."*

*Clarence E. Hill, Jr., "A Grant Night for Ventura," Chicago Sun-Times, 5 September 1995, p. 85, col. 5.

McDowell's Shutout Unassisted

221. Team Records No Assists in Nine-Inning Game

NEW YORK   at   CLEVELAND
(Yankees, 4)   (Indians, 0)

Monday Night, September 11, 1995, Jacobs Field

One of the rarest of baseball's vagaries transpired this evening when Jack McDowell and the New York Yankees *fielded in all nine innings of a game without registering so much as a single assist.* While not as dramatic as a hitter blasting four homers or two grand slams in a single contest, or a pitcher tossing a perfect game, this event is certainly rarer. Since the turn of the century only two other games witnessed such an evasion of defensive teamwork (see 7-4-45 and 6-25-89).

With the campaign drawing to a close, New York was battling for a wild-card position in the playoffs. Cleveland, meanwhile, had long before clinched a first-place berth in their division and was averaging seven runs per game during the past two weeks. Having won their last 14 games at Jacobs Field, the Indians were the dominant team, but the Yankees had McDowell. Nicknamed "Black Jack" for his reputation as a clutch performer, the 1993 Cy Young Award winner had already beaten the Tribe twice this season and had posted a 1.98 ERA over his last seven starts.

The tone of the game was set in the first two innings as McDowell fanned five of the

Outs registered by Yankee fielders, 9-11-95	
McDowell (P)	none
Stanley (C)	8 on strikeouts
Mattingly (1b)	1 pop up; 2 unassisted ground outs
Velarde (2b)	none
Boggs (3b)	4 pop ups (two foul); 1 line drive
Fernandez (ss)	2 pop ups
James (lf)	1 fly ball
G. Williams (lf)	2 fly balls
B. Williams (cf)	3 fly balls; 1 line drive
O'Neill (rf)	2 line drives

first six batters. "I had real good life on the fastball," Jack said. "The balls I left over the plate, they either were fouling back or swinging through, which is a pretty good indication of the velocity I had."† McDowell's fastball was often high and/or rising when the Indians swung. Batter after batter either flied out or popped up. Only two balls were hit on the turf, both going to Don Mattingly at first base for unassisted outs. Yankee third baseman Wade Boggs and shortstop Tony Fernandez didn't have to bend over the entire game, instead limiting themselves to pop ups. Second baseman Randy Velarde never even touched the ball during play.

†Dennis Manoloff, "McDowell quiets Tribe bats again," Cleveland Plain Dealer, 12 September 1995, section D, page 5, col. 3.

McDowell beat the Indians for the third time.

McDowell worked hard for this victory. Only nine Indians swung at his initial offering, forcing him to toss 144 pitches. Surprisingly, with Cleveland trailing 4–0 in the bottom of the ninth, all three batters swung at the first pitch, and all were retired on fly balls.

In addition to the two unassisted putouts made by first baseman Mattingly, there were several other unfulfilled opportunities for assists. The Indians stole second base twice, foiling assists by catcher Mike Stanley. And ironically, three of Cleveland's four hits off McDowell came on ground balls that scooted through the infield.

New York Yankees	AB	R	H	I
Wade Boggs 3b	3	0	0	0
Bernie Williams cf	3	1	2	1
Paul O'Neill rf	4	0	0	0
Darryl Strawberry dh	4	1	1	1
Dion James lf	3	0	1	0
Gerald Williams lf7	1	1	1	0
Don Mattingly 1b	3	0	1	1
Mike Stanley c	3	1	1	0
Tony Fernandez ss	2	0	0	1
>Randy Velarde 2b	4	0	0	0
	30	4	7	4

Cleveland Indians	AB	R	H	I
Kenny Lofton cf	3	0	0	0
Omar Vizquel ss	4	0	0	0
Carlos Baerga 2b	4	0	1	0
Albert Belle lf	4	0	0	0
Eddie Murray dh	4	0	2	0
Jim Thome 3b	3	0	0	0
Manny Ramirez rf	4	0	0	0
>Paul Sorrento 1b	2	0	0	0
Sandy Alomar c	3	0	1	0
	31	0	4	0

New York	IP	H	R	ER	BB	SO
Jack McDowell W,14-10	9	4	0	0	4	8

Cleveland	IP	H	R	ER	BB	SO
D. Martinez L,10-5	7	5	3	3	3	2
Paul Assenmacher	2	2	1	1	0	3
	9	7	4	4	3	5

New York	0 0 1	0 0 2	0 0 1	– 4
Cleveland	0 0 0	0 0 0	0 0 0	– 0

OB: New York 5, Cleveland 8
DP: Baerga-Vizquel-Sorrento (O'Neill)
Martinez-Vizquel-Sorrento(Velarde)
2B: B. Williams, G. Williams
SB: Lofton(36), Baerga(10)
SO: B. Williams, O'Neill, Strawberry, Stanley, Velarde; Baerga, Belle 2, Murray, Thome, Ramirez, Sorrento, Alomar
BB: Boggs, B. Williams, Fernandez; Lofton, Thome, Sorrento 2

SF: Mattingly, Fernandez
HP: By Martinez (Stanley)
WP: McDowell
TIME: 2:52
ATTENDANCE: 41,835
UMPIRES: Vic Voltaggio, Jim Joyce, Dale Scott, Jim McKean
SOURCES: Akron Beacon Journal; BBWS; Cleveland Plain Dealer; New York Times; USA Today

BALANCE	OUT+R+OB=BP=AB+BB+SH+HP+CI
New York	27 4 5 36 30 3 2 1 0
Cleveland	27 0 8 35 31 4 0 0 0

Young Steals Six

222. Player Steals
Six Bases in One Game

LOS ANGELES   at   COLORADO
(Dodgers, 15)   (Rockies, 16)

Sunday, June 30, 1996, Coors Field

Coors Field lived up to its bombastic reputation as the Colorado Rockies climaxed a wild four-game series by rallying in the bottom of the ninth to pull out a 16–15 victory over the Los Angeles Dodgers. Although the two clubs scored 85 runs during the series, the only record established was by Colorado second baseman Eric Young who became the third individual to *steal six bases in one game*. The ex-Dodger thus equaled the mark established by Eddie Collins, who accomplished the feat twice, and later tied by Otis Nixon.

Coors Field, a hitter's delight and pitcher's

Eric Young ran wild on the basepaths.

nightmare, had seen the two teams collect 43 extra base hits during the four games, and the pitchers tagged with a combined ERA of 9.81. This day's Colorado starter, Mark Thompson, felt the full brunt of the park's lofty altitude when he served home runs to Mike Piazza, Eric Karros, and Raul Mondesi on three consecutive pitches in the third inning. The Dodgers' six round-trippers were not enough, however, as the Rockies blasted four of their own. In addition, Colorado engaged a rare Coors Field offensive weapon as they stole 10 bases, nine of them coming off the deliveries of Hideo Nomo, who left after just five frames. Antonio Osuna was the pitching victim of the tenth Colorado theft, while Mike Piazza viewed each one from behind the plate. No Rockies were caught attempting to steal, and their 10 thefts narrowly missed the modern NL record of 11 shared by the 1912 Giants and the 1916 Cardinals. Strange indeed is the fact that in the three previous games of this series, Colorado had not even attempted to steal a base.

Young began his day inauspiciously by grounding out in the first inning. His larcenous feast then started in the third when he singled to center. After Walt Weiss struck out, Young stole second on the first pitch to Ellis Burks, and third on a 2–0 count. Burks eventually walked, bringing to the plate Dante Bichette. On an 0–1 pitch, Young stole home.

After walking in the fourth frame, Eric stole second on a 1–1 offering. He didn't have an opportunity to steal third because Weiss doubled him home on the next pitch.

The 1996 NL stolen base leader pilfered second base in the fifth inning after he was

Los Angeles Dodgers	AB	R	H	I
Chad Fonville lf	5	2	3	0
Delino DeShields 2b	5	2	2	1
Mike Piazza c	6	2	2	2
Eric Karros 1b	5	3	2	2
Raul Mondesi rf	6	3	4	6
>Mike Blowers 3b	4	1	2	0
Todd Hollandsworth cf	4	2	2	3
Greg Gagne ss	4	0	0	0
Hideo Nomo p	3	0	1	1
Juan Castro ph6	1	0	0	0
Chan Ho Park p6	0	0	0	0
Scott Radinsky p7	0	0	0	0
Roger Cedeno ph8	1	0	0	0
Antonio Osuna p8	0	0	0	0
Todd Worrell p9	0	0	0	0
	44	15	18	15

Colorado Rockies	AB	R	H	I
Eric Young 2b	5	3	2	1
Walt Weiss ss	6	2	2	2
Ellis Burks lf	4	3	3	3
Dante Bichette rf	6	2	5	4
Andres Galarraga 1b	5	0	0	0
Vinny Castilla 3b	6	3	3	1
Jayhawk Owens c	4	1	1	0
Jeff Reed ph9	1	0	1	1
>Quinton McCracken cf	6	1	2	1
Mark Thompson p	1	0	0	0
Roger Bailey p3	1	0	0	0
Darren Holmes p5	0	0	0	0
Milt Thompson ph5	1	0	0	0
Steve Reed p6	0	0	0	0
Trenidad Hubbard ph7	1	0	0	0
Curtis Leskanic p8	0	0	0	0
John Vander Wal ph8	1	1	1	2
Bruce Ruffin p9	0	0	0	0
	48	16	20	15

Los Angeles	IP	H	R	ER	BB	SO
Nomo	5	9	9	5	4	9
Park	1	2	1	1	1	0
Radinsky	1	3	2	0	0	2
Osuna	1	2	2	0	0	0
Worrell L,3-4	.2	4	2	2	0	0
	8.2	20	16	8	5	11

Colorado	IP	H	R	ER	BB	SO
Thompson	2.2	8	5	5	3	2
Bailey	2	3	4	4	2	3
Holmes	.1	1	1	1	1	1
S. Reed	2	1	1	1	0	2
Leskanic	1	2	1	1	0	2
Ruffin W,3-2	1	3	3	3	0	2
	9	18	15	15	6	12

Los Angeles   0 0 5   1 4 1   0 1 3   -15
Colorado   0 1 3   4 1 1   2 2 2   -16

OB: Los Angeles 9, Colorado 11
E: Piazza, DeShields, Gagne, Mondesi; Owens
DP: Blowers-DeShields-Karros(Castilla)
2B: Blowers, Nomo; Weiss, Burks, Bichette, McCracken
3B: Mondesi
HR: Piazza(22), Hollandsworth(4), Karros 2(18), Mondesi 2(16); Castilla(17), Bichette(17), Burks(21), Vander Wal(4)
SB: Fonville(5), DeShields(27); Burks(13), Young 6(27), McCracken 2(5), Bichette(13)
SO: Piazza, Karros 2, Mondesi, Blowers 2, Hollandsworth, Gagne 2, Nomo, Castro, Cedeno;

SO: Weiss 2, Bichette, Galarraga 3, Castilla, McCracken, Ma. Thompson, Bailey, Mi. Thompson
BB: Fonville, DeShields, Karros, Blowers 2, Gagne; Young, Burks 2, Galarraga, Owens
SF: Hollandsworth
WP: Nomo; Ruffin
TIME: 4:20
ATTENDANCE: 48,103
UMPIRES: Jerry Layne, Paul Runge, Joe West, Jeffrey Kellogg
SOURCES: BBWS; USA Today, USA Today Baseball Weekly

BALANCE	OUT+	R+	OB=	BP=	AB+	BB+	SH+	HP+CI
Los Angeles	27	15	9	51	44	6	1	0	0
Colorado	26	16	11	53	48	5	0	0	0

safe on a fielder's choice. But he was left stranded when Weiss struck out.

In the seventh frame, Young reached first with two outs on an error by Greg Gagne. He had a few pitches on which to steal, but Weiss singled to deep shortstop on a 1–2 count. Burks then knocked a full count pitch into center field for a single, driving home Young.

The second baseman batted again in the eighth inning with two outs and singled to center. Eric stole second on the first pitch, but his day on the basepaths ended when Weiss grounded out.

The game's six lead changes culminated in the bottom of the ninth as the Rockies used neither its long ball nor baserunning exploits to prevail. Trailing 15–14 with a man on first and two outs, Vinny Castilla singled. Pinch hitter Jeff Reed also singled to tie the contest. Then Quinton McCracken doubled down the first base line to drive home Castilla and seize the victory for Colorado. *Four hours and 20 minutes* had elapsed since the first pitch, *making this the longest nine-inning game on record*. Given the evolution of the game, however, this is a benchmark that is destined to be short-lived. The final tally also disclosed that 13 players had collected two or more hits, and that *runs had been scored in 14 of the 18 half-innings*. The latter tied the major league record.

Mariner Hurlers Treat Green-Well

223. Player Drives in All Nine of His Team's Runs

BOSTON   at   SEATTLE
(Red Sox, 9)   (Mariners, 8)

Monday Night, September 2, 1996, The Kingdome

Veteran Boston outfielder Mike Greenwell, besieged with injuries all season, had managed to play in only 53 of the Red Sox' 138 games to date. In addition to a nagging lower back malady, he had missed nearly two months with a broken ring finger on his left hand. Fortunately for the Red Sox the 33-year-old brought his lunch box to work this Labor Day and practically single-handedly beat the Seattle Mariners. Greenwell's four hits yielded *all nine of his team's runs-batted-in*, including the game winner in the 10th inning. That became the *most RBIs by any one player who accounted for all his team's runs*. Two earlier occurrences (see 6-14-24 and 6-12-38) of players driving home all eight of their club's runs, however, both occurred in nine-inning games. The victory stoked excitement in Boston as it inched the Red Sox closer to a possible wild-card playoff berth; a goal that never came to fruition.

The Red Sox fell behind early, trailing 5–0 after four innings. Then Greenwell took over. He collected four of the team's seven hits and his production was practically flawless. The left-handed swinger made five plate appearances, four of them with men on base. The only out he registered came in the third frame when the bases were empty. Of the eight teammates aboard when he stepped to the plate, Mike drove home seven. The last provided the game-winning run, and the new benchmark.

The fact that no other Boston player drove home a run in is certainly an anomaly, but Greenwell's success was not. A plethora of available baseball statistcs reveal that his performance was much less a surprise than one might expect:

• During his three previous seasons (1993–1995), Greenwell had hit more home runs and had amassed more RBIs against Seattle than against than any other club. This year Mariner arms still were the friendliest

Greenwell feasted on Seattle pitching.

eighth position was his most productive. Despite having only 29 of his at-bats while hitting eighth, he batted .483 and had more home runs and RBIs than from any other batting position.

• During this season Mike hit far better with runners in scoring position (.333) and with two outs (.353) than he did with none on (.261) or no outs (.270). Three of his four successful plate appearances this night came with runners in scoring position, and three came with two outs.

• He also hit nearly 100 points higher (.379 vs. .286) on turf this year than he did on grass, and better on the road (.303) than he did at home (.287). This contest was played on artificial turf and on the road.

Other players have driven in more runs in one game, but none have been their team's sole provider. "It was a storybook night," said free agent Greenwell. "I feel like I still have something to give to this club."* (Mike left Boston after the season and signed to play in Japan.)

Despite his youth, Seattle shortstop Alex Rodriguez knew the score. "It was Greenwell nine and the Mariners eight," he said. "You have to give him a lot of credit."†

toward Mike. In only 20 of his 295 at-bats during 1996, he had more doubles, home runs and RBIs against them than any other staff. He also accumulated his most robust on-base percentage (.522), batting average (.450), and slugging average (.950), while not being struck out by a Mariner pitcher.

• Batting eighth in the lineup this year was nothing new for Greenwell either. Although he usually batted fifth or sixth, the

*Daily News Wire Services, "Greenwell gets all 9 RBI in win," Philadelphia Daily News, 3 September 1996, p. 65, col. 5.
†Ibid.

MIKE GREENWELL'S PRODUCTION, SEPTEMBER 2, 1996

Inning	Outs	Base Runners	Seattle Pitcher	Count	At-bat	Results
3	0	none	Wolcott (rhp)	2-1	flied out to cf	first out
5	2	Naehring(1B)	Wolcott	0-0	HR to deep cf	2 RBI
7	0	Jefferson(3B) O'Leary(2B) Naehring(1B)	Ayala (rhp)	1-0	HR to deep rf	4 RBI
8	2	Vaughn(2B) Tinsley(1B)	Charlton (lhp)	2-0	2B down lf line	2 RBI
10	2	Cordero(2B) Manto(1B)	Carmona (rhp)	2-0	1B down lf line	1 RBI

Boston Red Sox	AB	R	H	I
Darren Bragg cf	5	0	2	0
Jeff Frye 2b	5	0	0	0
John Valentin ss	5	0	0	0
Mo Vaughn 1b	4	1	0	0
Reggie Jefferson dh	2	1	1	0
Will Cordero ph8,dh	1	1	0	0
Troy O'Leary rf	2	1	0	0
Rudy Pemberton ph8,rf	2	0	0	0
Tim Naehring 3b	1	2	0	0
Lee Tinsley pr8	0	1	0	0
Jeff Manto 3b8	0	0	0	0
Mike Greenwell lf	5	2	4	9
Bill Haselman c	3	0	0	0
> Mike Stanley ph8,c	2	0	0	0
	37	9	7	9

Seattle Mariners	AB	R	H	I
Joey Cora 2b	4	1	3	0
>Alex Rodriguez ss	4	1	1	3
Ken Griffey cf	3	2	1	0
Edgar Martinez dh	3	0	0	0
Rich Amaral pr9,dh	0	0	0	0
Jay Buhner rf	3	1	0	0
Paul Sorrento 1b	3	1	1	1
Brian Hunter ph7,1b	0	0	0	1
Doug Strange ph9,3b	1	0	1	0
Mark Whiten lf	5	1	1	1
Dan Wilson c	3	0	0	0
Alex Diaz ph8	1	0	0	0
John Marzano c9	0	0	0	0
Ricky Jordan ph10	1	0	0	0
Dave Hollins 3b,1b10	4	1	2	1
	35	8	10	7

Boston	IP	H	R	ER	BB	SO
Roger Clemens	6	5	5	3	3	4
Reggie Harris	.1	2	3	3	1	0
Kerry Lacy	0	0	0	0	2	0
Vaughn Eshelman	.2	0	0	0	1	0
Mark Brandenburg	.2	0	0	0	1	1
H. Slocumb W,3-5	2.1	3	0	0	2	1
	10	10	8	6	10	6

Seattle	IP	H	R	ER	BB	SO
Bob Wolcott	5.2	2	2	2	2	4
Bobby Ayala	.2	3	4	4	2	2
Rusty Meacham	.2	0	0	0	0	0
Norm Charlton	.2	1	2	2	2	1
Mike Jackson	1.1	0	0	0	0	1
R. Carmona L,6-3	1	1	1	1	2	0
	10	7	9	9	8	8

```
Boston    0 0 0   0 2 0   4 2 0   1   - 9
Seattle   0 0 1   4 0 0   3 0 0   0   - 8
```

OB: Boston 6, Seattle 9
E: Clemens 2, Rodriguez
DP: Frye-Valentin-Vaughn (Whiten)
    Bragg-Frye (Whiten fly to center)
    Slocumb-Valentin-Vaughn(Rodriguez)
    Wolcott-Rodriguez-Sorrento(O'Leary)
2B: Jefferson, Greenwell; Cora
HR: Greenwell 2(6); Rodriguez(35)
CS: Cora 2(5)
SO: Bragg, Frye, Valentin, Vaughn 2, Jefferson,
    Cordero, Haselman; Martinez, Buhner,
    Sorrento 2, Whiten, Hollins

BB: Vaughn, Jefferson, Cordero, O'Leary,
    Naehring 3, Manto; Cora 2, Rodriguez,
    Griffey 2, Martinez 2, Buhner 2, Hunter
SF: Rodriguez, Hollins
TIME: 3:57
ATTENDANCE: 24,470
UMPIRES: Mark Johnson, Larry Young,
    Drew Coble, Ted Barrett
SOURCES: BBWS; Philadelphia Daily
    News; USA Today Baseball Weekly

BALANCE	OUT	+R	+OB	=BP	=AB	+BB	+SH	+HP	+CI
Boston	30	9	6	45	37	8	0	0	0
Seattle	30	8	9	47	35	10	2	0	0

Nine Expo Hurlers Couldn't Tame the Cubs

224. Team Uses Nine Pitchers in a Nine-Inning Game

MONTREAL   at   CHICAGO
(Expos, 3)   (Cubs, 10)

Tuesday Night, September 10, 1996, Wrigley Field

The Montreal Expos were clinging desperately to an opportunity for a wild-card playoff berth that never came to fruition. But the standings this morning showed they had the second best record among the NL division non-leaders, and skipper Felipe Alou was managing as if his job hinged on every pitch. After falling behind early, Alou shuffled pitcher after pitcher to the mound hoping to find someone who could silence the Cub bats. Given the expanded September rosters, Alou had plenty to choose from and *called on nine of his pitchers to establish a new NL record for a nine-inning game.* Only one other major league team, the AL St. Louis Browns (see 10-2-49), used nine hurlers during a nine-inning contest. Unlike the St. Louis caper, however, Montreal's pageantry seemed to be serious and directed toward a victory. Montreal's feat was especially noteworthy because their hosts batted only eight times.

Six of the nine Montreal pitchers toiled just a fraction of an inning. Dave Leiper tossed merely five pitches while Tavo Alvarez and Mel Rojas each threw only two. They were the only three Expo hurlers to escape unscathed by the Cubs. Left-handed starter Omar Daal delivered 30 offerings but didn't make it through the first frame.

Also, hoping to provide an offensive edge, Alou didn't allow any of his nine pitchers to bat. The strategy was unproductive, however, as the Expos gleaned only three runs from 13 hits, leaving nine runners stranded. Chicago, meanwhile, utilized 12 safeties and five walks to win easily, 10–3.

By the close of the season Alou had made more pitching changes than any other manager in the major leagues. Montreal pitchers accumulated 619 appearances in 162 games, or 3.82 per game.

Tavo Alvarez — two pitches to the record books

Montreal Expos	AB	R	H	I
Rondell White cf	5	1	1	0
Mike Lansing 2b	4	0	2	0
>David Segui 1b	5	1	2	1
Moises Alou rf	4	0	1	0
Henry Rodriguez lf	4	0	1	1
F. P. Santangelo 3b,ss8	4	1	2	0
Darrin Fletcher c	4	0	2	0
Tim Spehr c8	0	0	0	0
Mark Grudzielanek ss	4	0	1	1
Rheal Cormier p8	0	0	0	0
Mel Rojas p8	0	0	0	0
Omar Daal p	0	0	0	0
Tavo Alvarez p1	0	0	0	0
Cliff Floyd ph2	1	0	1	0
Barry Manuel p2	0	0	0	0
Dave Silvestri ph4	1	0	0	0
Jeff Juden p4	0	0	0	0
Andy Stankiewicz ph6	1	0	0	0
Dave Veres p6	0	0	0	0
Dave Leiper p7	0	0	0	0
Mike Dyer p7	0	0	0	0
Shane Andrews 3b8	1	0	0	0
	38	3	13	3

Chicago Cubs	AB	R	H	I
Brian McRae cf	4	1	2	1
Ozzie Timmons rf	5	1	1	2
Bob Patterson p8	0	0	0	0
Amaury Telemaco p9	0	0	0	0
Mark Grace 1b	5	2	2	0
Ryne Sandberg 2b	4	2	1	0
Todd Haney 2b9	0	0	0	0
Leo Gomez 3b	1	1	0	0
Jose Hernandez pr7,3b	0	1	0	1
Scott Servais c	3	1	1	2
>Luis Gonzalez lf	4	0	2	2
Rey Sanchez ss	4	1	2	1
Frank Castillo p	1	0	0	0
Larry Casian p5	0	0	0	0
Brant Brown ph5	1	0	0	0
Kent Bottenfield p6	0	0	0	0
Dave Magadan ph7	1	0	1	1
Scott Bullett pr7,rf	0	0	0	0
	33	10	12	10

Montreal	IP	H	R	ER	BB	SO
Daal L,3-3	.2	2	3	3	3	2
Alvarez	.1	0	0	0	0	0
Manuel	2	3	2	2	1	1
Juden	2	1	0	0	0	2
Veres	1	2	2	2	1	0
Leiper	.1	0	0	0	0	0
Dyer	.2	2	1	1	0	0
Cormier	.2	2	2	1	0	0
Rojas	.1	0	0	0	0	0
	8	12	10	9	5	5

Chicago	IP	H	R	ER	BB	SO
Castillo	4	10	3	3	0	0
Casian	1	2	0	0	0	0
Bottenfield W,3-5	2	0	0	0	0	0
Patterson	1	1	0	0	0	1
Telemaco	1	0	0	0	1	0
	9	13	3	3	1	1

Montreal	0 1 0	0 2 0	0 0 0	- 3
Chicago	3 2 0	0 0 0	3 2 x	-10

OB: Montreal 9, Chicago 9
E: Segui, Grudzielanek
DP: Gomez-Sandberg-Grace (Alou)
     Sanchez-Sandberg-Grace (White)
2B: White, Rodriguez
HR: Timmons(5)
SB: Sanchez(7), McRae(35)
SO: Grudzielanek; McRae, Timmons 2,
     Servais 2
BB: Lansing; Sandberg, Gomez 3,
     Servais

SH: Castillo, Gonzalez
SF: McRae, Hernandez, Servais
PB: Spehr
TIME: 3:17
ATTENDANCE: 26,700
UMPIRES: Greg Bonin, Bob Davidson,
     Frank Pulli, Eric Gregg
SOURCES: BBWS; Philadelphia Daily
     News; USA Today Baseball Weekly

BALANCE	OUT	+R	+OB	=BP	=AB	+BB	+SH	+HP	+CI
Montreal	27	3	9	39	38	1	0	0	0
Chicago	24	10	9	43	33	5	5	0	0

The Rocket Soars Again

225. Pitcher Strikes Out
20 Batters in a Nine-Inning Game

BOSTON   at   DETROIT
(Red Sox, 4)   (Tigers, 0)

Wednesday Night, September 18, 1996, Tiger Stadium

Some scribes had just about written off Boston Red Sox fireballer Roger "The Rocket" Clemens. After an injury-shortened 1995 campaign, the big right-hander had begun to show signs of inconsistency, and many felt that all the fastballs and innings pitched had finally reduced his effectiveness. But a late season burst of splendor made the same writers once again shake their heads in admiration as they had so often in the past. What they saw was the three-time Cy Young Award winner tie his own 10-year-old benchmark by *striking out 20 batters in a nine-inning game* (see 4-29-86).

The host Detroit Tigers were the victims of Clemens' brilliance. Entering this contest averaging 7.7 strikeouts per game, the home club not only led the majors in that category but this night tied their own AL season mark of 1,185 whiffs. They were also quickly approaching the ML single-season team record of 1,203 which they surpassed a few days later. Adding further humiliation, the Clemens spectacle also marked Detroit's major-league leading 101st loss of the year.

The Rocket was splendid, allowing only five hits* while walking none. But it was the movement on his split-finger fastball and hard slider that had Detroit swinging at air most of the night. He struck out Travis Fryman four times, Tony Clark three times, and every other Tiger at least once, including pinch hitter Phil Hiatt. Roger tossed 151 pitches, 101 of which were strikes. Of the 32 batters he faced, 23 of them saw a first-pitch

strike. Remarkably, only one batter went down on a three-pitch strikeout—Kimera Bartee in the sixth inning. Every other victim saw at least one called ball.

Clemens had plenty of incentive to be at his best. First, the Red Sox were still in the running for a wild-card playoff berth. On a more emotional level, Roger would become a free agent in a few weeks and was not sure if he would be returning to a Boston uniform. He was also aware that he was chasing an icon, Cy Young, for the club record in lifetime wins (192) and shutouts (38). With this night's performance he tied both marks.

What about fatigue? It never entered Roger's mind. "It was adrenaline," Clemens said. "I knew about the two records. When you're chasing the guy who they named the greatest pitching award after, you don't get tired."† Indeed, The Rocket was clocked at 96 mph in the ninth inning.

The Tiger strikeout pace was nothing short of phenomenal. Through six frames Clemens had registered 15. After eight he had amassed 19. Entering the last inning Roger later claimed that he wasn't certain of the number of strikeouts he had until his catcher Bill Haselman walked to the mound to inform him. But with his teammates standing on the top step of the dugout, Roger knew he was on the verge of something special.

Twenty-year veteran Alan Trammell led off the ninth for Detroit. "I didn't want him to strike me out," Alan said. I was certainly

---

Original scoring credited Detroit with four hits, but later boxscores changed the number to five.
†*Paul Doyle,* The Hartford Courant, *19 September 1996, Online posting, American Online.*

Clemens tied his own record.

aware he had 19, and I've got pride. If he did it, he did it, but I'm trying my best to avoid it."* Trammell popped out. When he did, it marked the first time in the game that consecutive Tigers had been retired *without* a strikeout. The next batter, Ruben Sierra, singled up the middle before Clark flied out to left. Then with two outs and Fryman at the plate, Clemens tossed a wild pitch that sent Sierra to second, threatening the shutout. The Rocket then employed his adrenaline for three final pitches, all strikes, to indelibly etch his name in baseball annals once again. Frequently stoic and calculating, Clemens smiled and looked to the sky with raised fist as his teammates mobbed him.

Buddy Bell, Detroit manager, said that he had witnessed six no-hitters, but none were as dominating as Clemens' performance this night. "I don't think anyone could have

STRIKEOUT VICTIMS OF ROGER CLEMENS, SEPTEMBER 18, 1996

Inning	Clemens' Total Pitches	Strikeout Victim / Count on Which Strikeout Occurred / Swinging or Called		
		Out #1	Out #2	Out #3
1	17		Sierra / 3+2 / S	Clark / 1+2 / S
2	14	Fryman / 2+2 / S	Nieves / 1+2 / C	Nevin / 2+2 / S
3	19		Bartee / 1+2 / S	Higginson / 3+2 / C
4	15		Sierra / 3+2 / C	Clark / 2+2 / S
5	14	Fryman / 1+2 / C	Nieves / 1+2 / S	Nevin / 1+2 / S
6	23	Bartee / 0+2 /S	Higginson / 1+2 / S	Trammell / 3+2 / C
7	12		Clark / 1+2 / S	Fryman / 2+2 / S
8	23	Ausmus / 1+2 / C	Hiatt / 1+2 / S	
9	14			Fryman / 2+2 / S
	151	2 Swinging, 2 Called	6 Swinging, 2 Called	6 Swinging, 2 Called

Boston Red Sox	AB	R	H	I	Detroit Tigers	AB	R	H	I
Jeff Frye 2b	4	0	0	0	Bob Higginson lf,cf9	4	0	0	0
Nomar Garciaparra ss	3	0	0	0	Alan Trammell 2b	4	0	1	0
Mo Vaughn 1b	5	0	1	0	Ruben Sierra dh	4	0	1	0
>Jose Canseco dh	5	0	1	0	Tony Clark 1b	4	0	0	0
John Valentin 3b	4	1	1	0	>Travis Fryman ss	4	0	0	0
Mike Greenwell lf	4	1	2	0	Melvin Nieves rf	3	0	1	0
Lee Tinsley cf8	0	0	0	0	Phil Nevin 3b	3	0	1	0
Rudy Pemberton rf	4	2	3	1	Brad Ausmus c	3	0	1	0
Bill Haselman c	4	0	3	2	Kimera Bartee cf	2	0	0	0
Darren Bragg cf,lf8	3	0	0	0	Phil Hiatt ph8,lf	1	0	0	0
	36	4	11	3		32	0	5	0

*"Bell: Clemens' Ks beat no-hitter," USA Today, *19 September 1996, p. C4, col. 7.*

Boston	IP	H	R	ER	BB	SO
Roger Clemens	9	5	0	0	0	20
W,10-12						

Detroit	IP	H	R	ER	BB	SO
Ju. Thompson L,1-6	4	6	3	3	2	3
C.J. Nitkowski	2	3	0	0	2	0
A.J. Sager	3	2	1	1	0	3
	9	11	4	4	4	6

Boston	0 0 0	3 0 0	0 1 0	- 4
Detroit	0 0 0	0 0 0	0 0 0	- 0

OB: Boston 9, Detroit 5
DP: Fryman-Trammell-Clark (Valentin)
   Nevin-Ausmus (Canseco)
2B: Pemberton 2
SB: Garciaparra(1), Greenwell(4);
   Trammell(6), Ausmus(3)
SO: Frye 2, Garciaparra, Canseco, Greenwell 2;
   Higginson 2, Hiatt, Trammell, Sierra 2,
   Clark 3, Fryman 4, Nieves 2, Nevin 2,
   Ausmus, Bartee 2

BB: Frye, Garciaparra 2, Bragg
WP: Clemens
TIME: 2:56
ATTENDANCE: 8,779
UMPIRES: Tim McClelland, Tim Tschida
   John Shulock, Ed Hickox
SOURCES: America Online; BBWS; USA
   Today; USA Today Baseball Weekly

BALANCE	OUT+R+OB=BP=AB+BB+SH+HP+CI
Boston	27 4 9 40 36 4 0 0 0
Detroit	27 0 5 32 32 0 0 0 0

better stuff than that," the skipper said. "He was absolutely outstanding. He would have done that to a lot of teams tonight."*

This would be The Rocket's last victory for the Red Sox. Roger finished the season at 10–13 with a 3.63 ERA but led the AL in strikeouts (257) and allowed the second lowest batting average (.237). During the off-season, he left his uniform and records in Boston and signed a three-year contract with Toronto.

Details of Clemens' strikeouts are shown in the table on the previous page. It should be noted that sources vary on the number of swinging strikeouts versus those that were called. As this is not an official statistic and is subject to the interpretation of various scorers, it is unlikely to be resolved.

*Karen Allen, "Clemens ties own mark with 20 strikeouts," USA Today, 19 September 1996, p. C1, col. 5.

Fourteen Marlins Contribute

226. Fourteen Teammates
Hit Safely in a Nine-Inning Game

ATLANTA   at   FLORIDA
(Braves, 1)   (Marlins, 12)

Tuesday Night, September 24, 1996, Joe Robbie Stadium

The Florida Marlins did not make efficient use of their 21 hits, but they did produce more than enough runs to defeat the Atlanta Braves, 12–1. In doing so, *14 different Marlins hit safely, tying the major league record for a nine-inning game.* Three other clubs had previously attained this level of offensive teamwork, but Florida was only the second to do so while batting in just eight frames. The other club to do it was the San Francisco

Giants in a game *ten years earlier* (see 6-23-86).

The game itself had no influence on the standings. In the National League East, Atlanta had long since clinched the divisional title, and the Marlins were locked into a third-place finish. Florida's Pat Rapp pitched the first five innings to register the win, while he and each of his starting teammates contributed hits. Entering this game, Pat had only six hits and was batting just .108.

With an 11–1 lead after five innings, Marlins manager John Boles took advantage of his expanded September roster and made liberal substitutions. In addition to Rapp, several of the replacements were extremely unlikely participants in the record-setting event. Relief pitcher Livan Hernandez as well as pinch hitter Josh Booty were making their major league debuts, and both were successful in their first at-bats. Another rookie, outfielder Jerry Brooks, collected just his fourth major league hit and second since 1993. Jesus Tavarez, batting .204 entering this game, and Joe Orsulak, hitting .216, rounded out the party of 14.

The Florida feat was another of baseball's many anomalies. Despite finishing ninth in

Rapp got the win as well as his seventh hit of the season.

the NL in team hits for the season, and closer to the bottom than the top of most offensive categories, the Marlins in one September night fishtailed their way into baseball's logbook.

Atlanta Braves	AB	R	H	I
Luis Polonia lf	5	0	4	0
Jeff Blauser ss	2	0	0	0
Kevin Lomon p5	0	0	0	0
Chipper Jones ph7	0	0	0	0
Joe Borowski p7	0	0	0	0
Carl Schutz p8	0	0	0	0
> Tony Graffanino ph9	1	0	0	0
Andruw Jones cf	4	0	0	0
Ryan Klesko 1b	1	0	1	0
Eddie Perez 1b4	2	0	0	0
Javier Lopez c	3	0	1	0
Joe Ayrault c6	1	0	0	0
Dwight Smith rf	3	1	1	0
Ed Giavanola 3b	3	0	1	1
Mike Mordecai 2b	4	0	1	0
Steve Avery p	0	0	0	0
Brad Woodall p1	1	0	0	0
Raf. Belliard ph5,ss	3	0	1	0
	33	1	10	1

Florida Marlins	AB	R	H	I
Luis Castillo 2b	4	2	3	2
> Craig Grebeck 2b7,3b9	2	0	0	0
Edgar Renteria ss	3	0	1	2
Gary Sheffield rf	4	1	1	0
Jerry Brooks rf6	1	0	1	1
Jeff Conine lf	4	2	2	1
Billy McMillon lf6	1	0	0	0
Devon White cf	3	1	2	3
Jesus Tavarez ph6,cf	2	0	2	0
Greg Colbrunn 1b	3	1	2	0
Joe Orsulak ph6,1b	2	0	1	0
Kurt Abbott 3b	4	1	1	1
Ralph Milliard ph8,2b	0	0	0	0
Charles Johnson c	2	2	2	1
Gregg Zaun c7	2	0	0	0
Pat Rapp p	2	0	1	1
Josh Booty ph5	1	1	1	0
Livan Hernandez p6	1	1	1	0
Bob Natal ph8	1	0	0	0
Jay Powell p9	0	0	0	0
	42	12	21	12

Atlanta	IP	H	R	ER	BB	SO
Avery L,7-9	.2	7	6	6	0	0
Woodall	3.1	7	3	3	0	0
Lomon	2	3	2	2	1	0
Borowski	1	2	1	1	1	0
Schutz	1	2	0	0	1	2
	8	21	12	12	3	2

Florida	IP	H	R	ER	BB	SO
Rapp W,8-16	5	7	1	1	3	2
Hernandez	3	3	0	0	2	2
Powell	1	0	0	0	0	0
	9	10	1	1	5	4

Atlanta	0 0 0	1 0 0	0 0 0	-	1
Florida	6 0 0	3 2 0	1 0 x	-	12

OB: Atlanta 10, Florida 10
E: Polonia
DP: Perez-Belliard-Lomon (Orsulak)
    Renteria-Castillo-Colbrunn
    (Giovanola)
    Castillo-Renteria-Colbrunn (Lopez)
    Abbott-Orsulak (A. Jones)
2B: Smith; Conine, Johnson, White
3B: Castillo
CS: Polonia
SO: Lopez, Smith 2, Mordecai; Zaun,
    Natal

BB: Blauser, C. Jones, Klesko, Smith,
    Giovanola; Renteria, Millard,
    Johnson
SF: Renteria
TIME: 2:35
ATTENDANCE: 18,245
UMPIRES: Brian Gorman, Angel Her-
    nandez, Randy Marsh, Mike Winters
SOURCES: BBWS; Philadelphia Daily
    News; USA Today Baseball Weekly

BALANCE	OUT	+R	+OB	=BP	=AB	+BB	+SH	+HP	+CI
Atlanta	27	1	10	38	33	5	0	0	0
Florida	24	12	10	46	42	3	1	0	0

APPENDIX A:
PERFORMANCE HIGHLIGHTS
(BY GAME)

The following is a master list of all games described in this book. The column on the left gives the entry number in this reference book for each game. The date the game started is shown in the Date column. Following the date may be a /1, /2, or D which signifies the first game, second game, or both games of a doubleheader. One tripleheader is designated by a T. A and N are used to designate American or National League (F is used for one Federal League game). The numbers in parentheses following the cities indicate that that team's runs scored. The Performance Highlights describe only the major records set or tied on that date. Other benchmarks are detailed in the game accounts.

	Date		**Visiting team–Home team: Performance highlights**
1	4-25-01	A	Milwaukee (13)–Detroit (14): Tigers score 10 runs in bottom of ninth to win
2	5-02-01	A	Boston (23)–Philadelphia (12): Boston 19 runs in consecutive innings (1st occurrence); 9 Pilgrims & 13 players score 2+ runs
3	5-05-01	A	Chicago (7)–Milwaukee (21): Roy Patterson faces 57 batters & 53 official ABs in 9-inning game (both ML records)
4	5-23-01	A	Washington (13)–Cleveland (14): Cleveland scores 9 runs after 2 outs, bases empty, (ML record for ninth inning)
5	6-02-01	A	Boston (13)–Milwaukee (2): Boston scores 9 runs after 2 outs, bases empty in 9th; Reidy allows ML record 10 consec. hits
6	6-09-01	N	New York (25)–Cincinnati (13): Most hits (31) by one club; singles (36) & ABs (101 = 57 + 44) by both clubs; teammates with 5+ hits
7	6-21-01	N	Cincinnati (3)–Brooklyn (21): Doc Parker allows 26 hits (ML record), 21 runs (NL record), and 48 official ABs
8	6-24-01	N	Cincinnati (1)–Philadelphia (19): Bill Phillips faces 55 batters & 49 official ABs (both NL records)
9	9-15-01	A	Cleveland (0)–Detroit (21): Jack Bracken allows 24 hits in 7 innings; Detroit wins greatest shutout margin (until 9-16-75)
10	7-08-02	A	Philadelphia (22)–Boston (9): Doc Adkins faces 16 batters (1st occurrence), allows 12 hits in an inning
11	8-05-02	A	Washington (6)–Cleveland (7): Senators bunt successfully 14 times against Otto Hess
12	10-04-02	N	Cincinnati (2)–Pittsburgh (11): Sham game—players smoking, patron money refunded; Rube Vickers ML record 6 passed balls
13	4-21-03	N	New York (2)–Brooklyn (1): Most assists NL, 9-inn. game, both clubs-43 (NY 19, Bro 24)—corrects other claims
14	5-06-03	A	Detroit (9)–Chicago (10): ML record 18 errors in a game—Detroit 6, Chicago 12 (tied one-team mark)

	Date		Visiting team–Home team: Performance highlights

15 5-21-04   A   St. Louis (5)–Boston (3): Bill O'Neill last man to make 6 errors in a game

16 5-30-04 D N   Chicago (4, 5)–Cincinnati (7, 2): Frank Chance gets HBP 3x in first game, and 1x in second game (ML doubleheader record)

17 9-01-06   A   Philadelphia (4)–Boston (1): 24-inning game (longest to date); Coombs faces 89 batters (still AL record) & 18 strikeouts

18 6-28-07   A   Washington (16)–New York (5): Branch Rickey, catcher, allows most (13) stolen bases in a game

19 7-04-08   N   Philadelphia (0)–New York (1): Hooks Wiltse pitches 10-inning, no-hit victory

20 9-26-08 D N   Chicago (5, 3)–Brooklyn (0, 0): Reulbach becomes only pitcher to toss a doubleheader shutout

21 5-27-09   A   Cleveland (5)–St. Louis (2): Most assists (44) in 9-inning game, both clubs — new ML record

22 7-16-09   A   Washington (0)–Detroit (0): Ed Summers tosses 18-inning, (tie game) shutout (first occurrence)

23 8-23-09 /2 N   St. Louis (9)–Brooklyn (1): Bill Bergen throws out 6 runners attempting to steal (tied on 5-12-15 by W.Schang)

24 8-28-09 /1 A   Washington (4)–Chicago (6): Dolly Gray walks 7 in a row and 8 in one inning (both ML records)

25 6-01-10   N   St. Louis (10)–Philadelphia (5): Miller Huggins comes to bat 6 times without an official AB (4 BB, 2 SAC)

26 8-13-10 /2 N   Pittsburgh (8)–Brooklyn (8): Most perfectly tied game

27 5-13-11   N   St. Louis (5)–New York (19): Giants score 7 runs before making their first out of game (record now 9 — 8/13/48)

28 6-07-11   N   New York (9)–Pittsburgh (4): Most assists by one team in a 9-inning game (28)

29 6-18-11   A   Chicago (15)–Detroit (16): Tigers overcome 12-run deficit to win, 16-15 (first occurrence)

30 9-28-11   A   St. Louis (12)–New York (18): Yankees steal 15 bases on 20 attempts in one game (both ML records)

31 5-18-12   A   Detroit (2)–Philadelphia (24): Alan Travers allows 26 H (ties record), 24 R (sets record) in "strike" game

32 6-20-12   N   New York (21)–Boston (12): ML record for runs in 9th (17); NY tied ML mark of most teammates(13) to score at least one run

33 9-11-12   A   Philadelphia (9)–Detroit (7): Eddie Collins steals 6 bases in one game (ML record)

34 9-22-12 /1 A   Philadelphia (8)–St. Louis (2): Collins again steals 6 bases in one game

35 5-22-13   A   New York (0)–St. Louis (7): Highlanders 15 LOB in shutout loss vs Dwight Stone (first occurrence)

36 6-20-13   A   New York (9)–Washington (3): Six teammates (Yankees) HBP in one game — only time this century

37 7-12-13   A   Philadelphia (16)–Detroit (9): Boardwalk Brown walks 15 in 7.2 innings

38 9-14-13   N   New York (0)–Chicago (7): Giants get most hits (14) in a shutout loss (first occurrence); tied 7-10-28

39 10-04-13   A   Boston (9)–Washington (10): Joke game — W. Johnson loses all-time ERA single season record

40 5-30-14 D A   Detroit (2, 0)–St. Louis (1, 2): Only 11 hits combined by both teams in a doubleheader (ML fewest ever)

41 6-16-14   F   Brooklyn (12)–St. Louis (13): 15 runs in 12th inning is the two club, extra-inning ML mark

42 8-03-14   A   New York (1)–Detroit (4): Nunamaker (catcher) throws out three runners in one inning

43 8-24-14 /2 A   Detroit (11)–Washington (0): 7 HBP (both teams) in one game (first occurrence)

44 6-17-15   N   Brooklyn (3)–Chicago (4): Zip Zabel puts in longest relief appearance ever — 18.1 innings

45 6-23-15   A   New York (15)–Philadelphia (7): Bruno Haas walks 16 batters in 9-inning game

46 7-19-15   A   Washington (11)–Cleveland (4): Senators steal 8 bases in one (1st) inning (first occurrence)

47 5-09-16   A   Detroit (16)–Philadelphia (2): Tigers get 18 walks; both clubs get 30 walks in 9-inning game (both ML records)

	Date		Visiting team–Home team: Performance highlights

48 5-26-16   N   New York (12)–Boston (1): Benny Kauff picked off first base three times in a game (only player known)

49 8-13-16 /2   N   Pittsburgh (9)–St. Louis (5): Both clubs, 14 stolen bases in a 5-inning game

50 5-02-17   N   Cincinnati (1)–Chicago (0): Toney and Vaughn both pitch 9-inning no-hitters

51 5-06-17 /2   A   Chicago (0)–St. Louis (3): Chicago sets record for fewest ABs (23) in a 9-inning game

52 5-15-18   A   Chicago (0)–Washington (1): Walter Johnson pitches an 18-inning shutout (second occurrence)

53 7-07-19 /1   N   New York (10)–Philadelphia (5): Phillies "steal" 8 bases in the ninth inning (uncontested)

54 8-16-19   A   Philadelphia (7)–St. Louis (4): Browns get 27 assists (AL record)

55 9-28-19 /1   N   Philadelphia (1)–New York (6): 51-minute game is the fastest ever

56 5-01-20   N   Brooklyn (1)–Boston (1): 26-inning game (most ever played in one game); assorted marks for ABs, PO, assists, chances

57 10-02-20 T   N   Cincinnati (13, 7, 0)–Pittsburgh (4, 3, 6): Only tripleheader of the 20th-century

58 5-30-22 D   N   St. Louis (1, 1)–Chicago (4, 3): Max Flack and Cliff Heathcote traded for one another between doubleheader games

59 8-07-22   N   Pittsburgh (17)–Philadelphia (10): Ten Pirates get 2 hits; five Phillies do the same.

60 8-25-22   N   Philadelphia (23)–Chicago (26): Clubs combine for host of ML records including 51 hits, 49 runs, & 43 RBIs

61 5-11-23   N   St. Louis (14)–Philadelphia (20): Most total bases (79) & most players (23) hit safely by two teams in 9-inning game

62 6-01-23   N   New York (22)–Philadelphia (8): Giants score in each of nine innings (first in 20th-century); most teammates (3) with 5+ hits

63 7-07-23 /1   A   Boston (3)–Cleveland (27): O'Doul faces 16 batters (2nd occurrence), allows 13 runs in one inning (ML record)

64 9-28-23   A   New York (24)–Boston (4): Ehmke faces 16 batters (3rd occurrence), allows 11 runs in one inning

65 6-14-24   N   Cincinnati (6)–New York (8): George Kelly knocks in all 8 of his team's runs

66 9-16-24   N   St. Louis (17)–Brooklyn (3): Bottomley gets 12 RBIs (and 6 hits)

67 5-30-25 /2   N   St. Louis (5)–Pittsburgh (15): Pirates hit 8 triples, both teams combine for 9 (both ML records)

68 6-15-25   A   Cleveland (15)–Philadelphia (17): A's overcome 12-run deficit to win (second occurrence)

69 9-02-25 /2   N   New York (24)–Philadelphia (9): 10 Giants get 2+ hits (ties record), four get 4 hits (set record); 58 team ABs (still record)

70 9-09-26   N   Brooklyn (12)–Philadelphia (6): Dodgers get 6 successful pinch hits

71 9-26-26 D   A   New York (1, 2)–St. Louis (6, 6): Fastest doubleheader ever played — 2 hrs. 7 min.

72 5-24-28 /1   A   New York (9)–Philadelphia (7): 17 future Hall of Famers participate in one game (13 players, 2 managers, 2 umpires)

73 7-10-28 /2   A   Cleveland (0)–Washington (9): Cleveland gets 14 hits off Gaston in shutout loss (ties record set 9-14-13)

74 7-06-29 D   N   St. Louis (6, 28)–Philadelphia (10, 6): 73 hits in doubleheader by both teams; 4 teammates score 4+ runs; 9 teammates score 2+ runs

75 8-04-29 /2   A   Cleveland (14)–New York (6): Indians score 9 runs in the ninth after 2 outs (3rd occurrence)

76 5-12-30   N   New York (14)–Chicago (12): Larry Benton allows 6 homers yet wins (1st occurrence)

77 5-21-30 D   A   New York (7, 1)–Philadelphia (15, 4): Max Bishop walks 8 times in a doubleheader (first time)

78 7-25-30   A   Philadelphia (14)–Cleveland (1): A's pull 2 triple-steals in one game

79 7-07-31   A   Chicago (10)–St. Louis (8): Longest game (12 innings) without a strikeout by either club

80 7-11-31 /1   N   New York (23)–Philadelphia (5): Giants get 58 ABs (ties record)

81 7-12-31 /2   N   Chicago (13)–St. Louis (17): Due to overflow crowd, 23 doubles hit in one game (ML record)

82 7-29-31   A   Cleveland (0)–Washington (6): Senators 15 LOB in shutout loss vs. W. Ferrell (2nd occurrence)

	Date		Visiting team–Home team: Performance highlights
83	6-03-32	A	New York (20)–Philadelphia (13): Gehrig 4 consecutive HRs; AL two-club most total bases (77); ML two-team most extra bases (41)
84	7-10-32	A	Philadelphia (18)–Cleveland (17): Burnett gets 9 hits in 18-inn game; ML record for hits by one(33) & two teams (58)
85	8-13-32 /1	N	Brooklyn (18)–New York (9): Sloppy Thurston allows 6 homers yet wins (2nd occurrence)
86	5-16-33	A	Cleveland (10)–Washington (11): Cecil Travis gets 5 hits in first ML game
87	7-02-33 /1	N	St. Louis (0)–New York (1): Hubbell pitches 18-inning shutout (third occurrence)
88	4-28-34	A	Cleveland (1)–Detroit (4): Goose Goslin hits into 4 double plays (first occurrence)
89	6-13-34	N	Boston (9)–St. Louis (0): Bill Urbanski comes to bat 6x without an official AB (4 BB, 2 SACS), ties record
90	7-08-34 D	A	Philadelph (4, 2)–Boston (7, 7): Max Bishop gets 8 walks in a doubleheader (for second time)
91	8-04-34 /2	N	New York (21)–Philadelphia (4): Mel Ott scores 6 runs in a nine-inning game
92	8-27-35 /1	A	New York (13)–Chicago (10): Two teams combine for 30 LOB (first occurrence)
93	5-24-36	A	New York (25)–Philadelphia (2): Lazzeri 2 grand slams, gets 11 RBIs (AL mark); Chapman reaches base 7 times (ties ML record)
94	7-10-36	N	Philadelphia (9)–Pittsburgh (6): Chuck Klein hits 4 home runs in 10-inning game
95	9-11-36	A	Philadelphia (2)–Chicago (17): Lisenbee allows 26 hits in eight innings; three ChiSox get 5+ hits; both events tie ML records
96	7-25-37 D	A	Washington (16, 15)–St. Louis (10, 5): Mel Almada scores 9 runs in a doubleheader (ML mark)
97	8-14-37 D	A	St. Louis (1, 7)–Detroit (16, 20): Tigers score 36 runs in a doubleheader (ML mark)
98	5-05-38	N	Philadelphia (2)–Chicago (21): Hal Kelleher faces 16 batters in one inning (fourth occurrence)
99	6-12-38 /1	A	St. Louis (3)–Philadelphia (8): Bob Johnson knocks in all 8 of team's runs (second occurrence)
100	6-16-38	A	Boston (12)–St. Louis (8): Jimmie Foxx walks 6 times in nine-inning game
101	6-06-39	N	Cincinnati (3)–New York (17): Giants hit 5 home runs after two outs in an inning
102	6-28-39 D	A	New York (23, 10)–Philadelphia (2, 0): Yankees get 98 ABs, 13 HRs, and 87 total bases in a doubleheader
103	7-04-39 D	A	Boston (17, 18)–Philadelphia (7, 12): Most runs (54) & RBIs (49) by both teams, doubleheader; Jim Tabor hits 2 grand slams in nightcap
104	5-07-41	N	Cincinnati (1)–New York (0): Eddie Joost accepts 19 fielding chances in 9-inning game (ML mark)
105	8-01-41	A	St. Louis (0)–New York (9): Lefty Gomez walks 11 but pitches a shutout; 15 LOB in shutout (third occurrence)
106	5-13-42	N	Chicago (5)–Boston (6): Pitcher Jim Tobin hits 3 home runs (only pitcher to ever do so)
107	8-14-42	A	New York (11)–Philadelphia (2): Yankees turn 7 double plays
108	7-18-43 /1	N	New York (10)–Philadelphia (6): Two teams combine to strand 30 base runners (second occurrence)
109	4-30-44 /1	N	Brooklyn (8)–New York (26): Weintraub 11 RBIs; Ott reaches base 7 times & scores 6 R; Giants 26 RBIs & 17 BB
110	8-10-44	N	Boston (2)–Cincinnati (0): Red Barrett hurls complete game with fewest (58) pitches; remains ML fastest night game (1:15)
111	7-04-45 /1	A	New York (2)–Cleveland (4): Indians get ZERO assists fielding in 9-innings (first occurrence)
112	7-14-46 D	A	Cleveland (10, 4)–Boston (11, 6): First instance of "Boudreau Shift" (in 2nd game); Boudreau gets 5 extra-base hits in first game
113	7-27-46	A	Boston (13)–St. Louis (6): Rudy York hits 2 grand slams in one game
114	5-20-48	A	Boston (4)–Cleveland (13): Indians get 18 walks (second occurrence)
115	7-18-48 /1	A	Chicago (12)–Philadelphia (11): Pat Seerey hits 4 home runs in 11-inning game
116	8-12-48 /2	A	Cleveland (26)–St. Louis (3): 14 different teammates (Indians) get at least 1 hit in a 9-inning game (first occurrence)
117	8-13-48	N	New York (7)–Philadelphia (12): Phillies score 9 runs before making their first out of game (ML record)

	Date		Visiting team–Home team: Performance highlights

118 9-11-49 /1 A Washington (5)–New York (20): Yankees get most (11) BB in one inning, most players (4) with two BB in one inning

119 10-02-49 /1 A Chicago (4)–St. Louis (3): Browns use 9 pitchers in a nine-inning game (ML record)

120 6-08-50 A St. Louis (4)–Boston (29): BoSox tally most runs, RBIs (29), extra-base hits (17), total bases (60) & win by largest margin

121 6-23-50 A New York (9)–Detroit (10): Most home runs (11) in a game by both clubs (later tied 6x), by different (9) players

122 8-31-50 N Boston (3)–Brooklyn (19): Gil Hodges hits 4 home runs

123 5-21-52 N Cincinnati (1)–Brooklyn (19): Dodgers score most runs (15) in 1st inning; most consecutive batters (19) to reach base safely

124 6-15-52 /1 N St. Louis (14)–New York (12): Cardinals overcome 11-0 deficit to win (set NL record)

125 6-29-52 /1 N Chicago (9)–Cincinnati (8): Cubs score 7 runs in ninth after first two batters were out

126 6-18-53 A Detroit (3)–Boston (23): In one inning, BoSox tally 17R, 17RBIs, 23BFP; Stephens gets 3H, White scores 3R (all ML marks)

127 8-30-53 D N Milwaukee (19, 4)–Pittsburgh (4, 5): Braves hit 8 HR in 1st game, 12 in doubleheader (both still NL records)

128 5-02-54 D N New York (6, 9)–St. Louis (10, 7): Musial hits 5 homers in doubleheader

129 7-06-54 A Baltimore (3)–Cleveland (11): Indians score 8 runs before making their first out of game (A record)

130 7-31-54 N Milwaukee (15)–Brooklyn (7): Adcock hits 4 homers and a double, 18 total bases

131 8-08-54 N Cincinnati (7)–Brooklyn (20): Dodgers score 12 runs after 2 outs and nobody on base (ML record)

132 9-12-54 D A New York (1, 2)–Cleveland (4, 3): Greatest attendance for ML game — 86, 563

133 4-23-55 A Chicago (29)–Kansas City (6): Chicago scores 29 runs (second occurrence)

134 5-02-56 N New York (6)–Chicago (5): Teams use 14 pinch hitters and give 11 intentional walks in extra-inn. game (both ML records)

135 5-30-56 D N Milwaukee (9, 11)–Chicago (10, 9): 15 home runs in a doubleheader

136 9-21-56 A New York (7)–Boston (13): 20 Yankees left-on-base in 9-inning game

137 5-13-58 N San Francisco (16)–Los Angeles (9): Five Giants each get 4+ hits

138 4-22-59 A Chicago (20)–Kansas City (6): White Sox get 11 runs on 1 hit in an inning

139 5-26-59 N Pittsburgh (0)–Milwaukee (1): Haddix loses after pitching 12 perfect innings

140 6-10-59 A Cleveland (11)–Baltimore (8): Colavito hits 4 home runs

141 9-22-59 N Los Angeles (10)–St. Louis (11): Dodgers use 9 pinch hitters

142 4-24-60 A Baltimore (9)–New York (15): Yankees score 8 runs before making their first out of game (ties AL record)

143 4-30-61 N San Francisco (14)–Milwaukee (4): Mays hits 4 home runs

144 5-09-61 A Baltimore (13)–Minnesota (5): Gentile hits grand slams in consecutive innings

145 5-09-61 A Cleveland (2)–Chicago (4): Indians tie record for fewest ABs (23) in 9-inning game (second occurrence)

146 9-12-62 A Washington (2)–Baltimore (1): Tom Cheney fans 21 batters in 16-inning game

147 9-30-62 N New York (1)–Chicago (5): Three playing careers end with a triple play

148 7-31-63 /2 A Los Angeles (5)–Cleveland (9): Indians hit four successive HRs off Paul Foytack

149 9-10-63 N San Francisco (2)–New York (4): Jesus, Matty & Felipe Alou (teammates) bat consecutively in the same inning

150 9-27-63 N New York (10)–Houston (3): Astros field an all-rookie lineup

151 5-31-64 /2 N San Francisco (8)–New York (6): Longest NL game (7:23); most NL Ks (36); most ML doubleheader ABs (234)

152 9-12-64 A Kansas City (0)–Baltimore (1): In 9-inn. game, Baltimore gets only 19 official ABs (batted 8 inn), two teams 46 (both ML marks)

153 9-13-64 N St. Louis (15)–Chicago (2): Cardinals score in all 9 innings (2nd occurrence)

154 8-19-65 N Cincinnati (1)–Chicago (0): Jim Maloney throws 10-inning no-hitter (3rd occurrence)

155 9-08-65 A California (5)–Kansas City (3): Bert Campaneris plays all nine fielding positions in a game

	Date		**Visiting team–Home team: Performance highlights**
156	9-09-65	N	Chicago (0)–Los Angeles (1): Nine-inning game in which only 1 hit was made by both clubs combined
157	7-03-66	N	Atlanta (17)–San Francisco (3): Tony Cloninger (pitcher) hits 2 grand slams, gets 9 RBIs
158	4-30-67	A	Detroit (2)–Baltimore (1): Tigers have 14 base runners while being no-hit (ML record)
159	5-17-67	A	Baltimore (12)–Boston (8): Seven different Orioles hit a home run in a game
160	4-15-68	N	New York (0)–Houston (1): 24 innings is longest scoreless tie (still record) & longest night game (later surpassed)
161	5-06-68	A	Detroit (0)–Baltimore (4): Tigers tie record for fewest ABs (23) in 9-inning game (third occurrence)
162	6-24-68	A	Detroit (14)–Cleveland (3): Jim Northrup hits 2 grand slams
163	6-25-68	N	Los Angeles (0)–San Francisco (9): Bobby Bonds hits grand slam in first major league game
164	9-05-69	N	Pittsburgh (9)–Chicago (2): Billy Williams gets all 4 of his team's hits
165	9-10-69	A	Kansas City (4)–California (11): KC Mgr. Joe Gordon uses 27 players in nine-inning game (ML record)
166	4-22-70	N	San Diego (1)–New York (2): Seaver strikes out 10 in a row (and a total of 19)
167	5-21-70	A	Washington (0)–New York (2): Stottlemyre walks 11 in a shutout (second occurrence) but is relieved
168	6-21-70 /2	A	Detroit (9)–Cleveland (8): Cesar Gutierrez gets 7 hits in 7 consecutive plate appearances (extra-inning game)
169	6-26-70	A	Baltimore (12)–Washington (2): Frank Robinson hits 2 grand slams
170	4-13-71	A	Minnesota (3)–Kansas City (5): 7 HBP (both teams) in one game (second occurrence)
171	6-23-71	N	Philadelphia (4)–Cincinnati (0): Rick Wise first pitcher to hit 2 HRs while tossing a no-hitter
172	7-09-71	A	California (0)–Oakland (1): 26 Angels strike out; two clubs combine for 43 Ks (both still ML, extra-inning records)
173	9-14-71 /2	A	Washington (8)–Cleveland (6): Finished Sept 20 in Washington; most pitchers (18) & BB (30), both clubs, extra-inning game
174	8-01-72 D	N	San Diego (9, 11)–Atlanta (0, 7): Nate Colbert hits 5 homers, collects 13 RBIs in a doubleheader
175	9-16-72	N	New York (5)–Chicago (18): As a batter, Glen Beckert leaves 12 runners stranded on base
176	9-19-72	A	Chicago (8)–Oakland (7): Most players (30), second basemen (6), & pinch hitters (10) used by one team in an x-inning game
177	9-11-74	N	St. Louis (4)–New York (3): Longest night game by innings (25), most LOB (45) by two teams (both remain ML records)
178	5-12-75	A	Kansas City (0)–Detroit (5): Kansas City 15 LOB in shutout loss vs Ruhle & Hiller (4th occurrence)
179	7-21-75	N	Houston (6)–New York (2): Joe Torre hits into 4 double plays (2nd occurrence)
180	9-16-75	N	Pittsburgh (22)–Chicago (0): R. Stennett goes 7 for 7 in 9-inning game (first occurrence); largest margin in shutout
181	9-28-75	A	California (0)–Oakland (5): 4 A's pitchers combine for no-hitter (first occurrence)
182	4-17-76	N	Philadelphia (18)–Chicago (16): Mike Schmidt hits 4 home runs; Phils overcome 11 run deficit to win (tied NL mark)
183	9-05-78	N	Montreal (10)–Chicago (8): Two clubs use 45 players in nine-inning game (still record)
184	5-17-79	N	Philadelphia (23)–Chicago (22): Two clubs — most total bases (97), most RBIs (45), & tied HR (11) mark for extra-inning game
185	8-04-82	N	New York (7)–Chicago (4): Joel Youngblood plays for two teams (NY & Mon)
186	8-04-82	N	Montreal (4)–Philadelphia (5) in two different cities on same day and gets a hit in each game
187	7-03-83	A	Texas (16)–Oakland (4): Rangers score ML record 12 runs in an extra inning (15th)
188	8-24-83	A	Toronto (4)–Baltimore (7): Three runners caught off base in one inning (second occurrence)

	Date		Visiting team–Home team: Performance highlights
189	9-03-83	A	Cleveland (13)–Oakland (6): A's use 6 pitchers in one inning
190	5-08-84	A	Milwaukee (6)–Chicago (7): Longest AL game — 25 inn.; longest ML game — 8:06; ties longest ML night game — 25 inn.
191	4-17-86	A	Texas (7)–Milwaukee (5): Bobby Witt wild; relieved although pitching a no-hitter
192	4-19-86	A	Oakland (7)–Seattle (2): Two teams combine for ML record 30 strikeouts in 9-inning game
193	4-20-86	N	Pittsburgh (10)–Chicago (8): NL team record 10 (Cub) pitchers, & 2-team 17 pitchers used in x-inn. game (completed 8-11)
194	4-29-86	A	Seattle (1)–Boston (3): Roger Clemens strikes out ML record 20 batters in 9-inning game
195	6-23-86	N	San Diego (1)–San Francisco (18): 14 Giants gets hits; 13 Giants score runs in 9-inning game — both tie ML record
196	6-23-86	N	Chicago (1)–Philadelphia (19): Phillies get 15 extra-base hits — NL record
197	6-27-86	N	San Francisco (7)–Cincinnati (6): Robby Thompson caught stealing four times in an extra-inning game
198	7-06-86	N	Montreal (11)–Atlanta (8): Bob Horner hits 4 home runs; first to do so in a losing cause (in 20th-century)
199	8-06-86	A	Texas (13)–Baltimore (11): First time 3 grand slams in one game; Sheets & Dwyer (Balt) and Harrah (Tex)
200	9-02-86	N	Houston (8)–Chicago (7): Completed 9-03; NL record 53 players used by both clubs in extra-inning game
201	6-03-87	N	Houston (7)–Chicago (22): Second time 3 grand slams in a game; Dayett & Moreland (Chi) and Hatcher (Hou)
202	9-14-87	A	Baltimore (3)–Toronto (18): Toronto blasts ML record 10 homers in game; Ripken's consecutive-inning streak ends
203	6-25-89	N	Philadelphia (1)–New York (5): Mets get ZERO assists fielding 9 innings (second occurrence)
204	7-29-89	A	Seattle (14)–Oakland (6): Rickey Henderson scores 4 runs without an official AB
205	8-03-89	N	Houston (2)–Cincinnati (18): Reds get most: hits (16), players with 2+ hits (7), singles (12) in an inning
206	9-03-89	A	Kansas City (13)–Texas (2): 7 HBP (both teams) in one game (third occurrence)
207	5-22-90	N	Cincinnati (1)–Chicago (2): Dawson intentionally walked five times (16 innings)
208	7-01-90	A	New York (0)–Chicago (4): Andy Hawkins loses a no-hitter, 4-0
209	7-17-90	A	Minnesota (0)–Boston (1): Twins become first to turn 2 triple plays in one game
210	8-31-90	A	Kansas City (2)–Seattle (5): For the first time: father and son play in same game, on same team; both get hits
211	6-16-91	N	Atlanta (6)–Montreal (7): Otis Nixon ties ML record by stealing 6 bases in one game
212	7-13-91	A	Baltimore (2)–Oakland (0): Four Oriole hurlers combine on a no-hitter (second occurrence)
213	8-28-92	A	Milwaukee (22)–Toronto (2): Milwaukee's 26 singles set modern ML mark; 31 hits set AL mark, tie ML record for 9-inning game
214	9-25-92	A	Seattle (4)–Texas (3): Seattle uses 11 pitchers; two teams use 54 players — both ML records for x-inn. games
215	9-07-93 D	N	St. Louis (13, 15)–Cincinnati (14, 2): (1st) Most pitchers (15), both clubs, 9-inning game; (2nd) Whiten gets 4 HRs & 12 RBIs
216	9-21-93	N	Atlanta (18)–Montreal (5): Most pinch-hitters (13) by both clubs in 9-inn. game; Atlanta (9) ties one-team mark
217	5-24-94	N	Philadelphia (4)–St. Louis (0): Cardinals leave 16 on base while being shut out for a new ML record
218	5-28-95	A	Chicago (14)–Detroit (12): Two teams combine for 12 HRs, ten of which are solo (both ML marks); four players each hit two
219	8-18-95	N	Chicago (26)–Colorado (7): 14 Cubs get hits & nine score 2+ runs (both tie ML marks); Cubs get 26 RBIs (ties NL mark)
220	9-04-95	A	Chicago (14)–Texas (3): Robin Ventura hits two grand slams
221	9-11-95	A	New York (4)–Cleveland (0): Yankees get zero assists while fielding nine innings (third occurrence)
222	6-30-96	N	Los Angeles (15)–Colorado (16): Eric Young steals six bases (fourth occurrence)

Date		Visiting team–Home team: Performance highlights
223 9-02-96	A	Boston (9)–Seattle (8): Greenwell collects all nine of his team's RBIs for a new ML record
224 9-10-96	N	Montreal (3)–Chicago (10): Expos tie ML mark by using nine hurlers in a nine-inning game
225 9-18-96	A	Boston (4)–Detroit (0): Roger Clemens ties his own ML record with 20 strikeouts
226 9-24-96	N	Atlanta (1)–Florida (12): 14 Marlins hit safely to tie the ML benchmark for a nine-inning game

Total: 206 single games,   19 doubleheaders,   1 tripleheader = 247 games

APPENDIX B:
MAJOR LEAGUE RECORDS
AT A GLANCE

This appendix catalogs the major league, record-setting performances described in this book. Only modern major league marks are listed. American or National League records are not listed below but are noted within the game descriptions. Many of these standards were tied in other games that are not covered in this work.

Under the "Games" column are given the entry numbers used in this reference book.

RECORD	GAMES
Assists	
Most by a catcher, nine-inning game: 7	13, 23
Most by a pitcher, extra-inning game: 12	56
Most by one team, nine-inning game: 28	28
Most by both teams, nine-inning game: 44	21
Most by both teams, extra-inning game: 72	56
Fewest by one team, fielding nine innings: 0	111, 203, 221
At-Bats	
Most allowed by one pitcher, nine-inning game: 53	3
Most allowed by one pitcher, extra-inning game: 86	56
Most by one player, in one inning: 3	60, 123, 126, 131, 205
Most by one player, nine-inning game: 7	many games
Most by one player, extra-inning game: 11	56, 84, 177, 190,
Most by one player, game, without a hit: 11	56
Most by one player, doubleheader: 14	151
Most by one team, nine-inning game: 58	69, 80
Most by one team, extra-inning game: 95	190
Most by one team, doubleheader: 119	151
Most by both teams, nine-inning game: 101	6
Most by both teams, extra-inning game: 175	177, 190
Most by both teams, doubleheader: 234	151
Fewest by one team, nine-inning game: 23	51, 145, 161
Fewest by one team, nine-inning game, batting eight innings: 19	152
Fewest by both teams, nine-inning game: 46	152

Attendance

Largest paid crowd for a game and doubleheader: 84, 587   132
Largest total attendance for a game and doubleheader: 86, 563   132

Batters Faced

Most by one pitcher, in one inning: 16   10, 63, 64, 98
Most by one pitcher, nine-inning game: 57   3
Most by one pitcher, extra-inning game: 96   56

Bunts

Most by one team, game: 14   11

Chances

Most by a catcher, extra-inning game: 25   17
Most by a first baseman, extra-inning game: 43   56
Most by a shortstop, nine-inning game: 19   104
Most by one team, extra-inning game: 119   56
Most by one team, outfielders, extra-inning game: 24   56
Fewest by both teams' outfielders, nine-inning game: 2   104

Caught Off Base

Most by one player, game: 3   48
Most by one team, in one inning: 3   188

Caught Stealing

Most by one player, extra-inning game: 4   197
Most by one team, in one inning: 3   42
Most by one team, game: 6   23

Deficits Overcome

Biggest run deficit overcome to victory: 12   29, 68

Double Plays

Most by one team, nine-inning game: 7   107

Doubles

Most by one player, game: 4   1, 112, 120
Most by one team, game: 13   81
Most by both teams, game: 23   81

Errors

Most by one player, extra-inning game: 6   15
Most by one team, nine-inning game: 12   14
Most by both teams, nine-inning game: 18   14

Extra-base Hits

Most by one player, game: 5   112, 130
Most by one team, game: 17   120

Most by both teams, game: 24   81
Most by both teams, doubleheader: 35   81

Game Length by Innings

Longest game: 26   56
Longest game without a strikeout by either side: 12   79
Longest tie game: 26   56
Longest night game: 25   177, 190
Longest 1-0 game: 24   160
Longest shutout game: 24   160
Most innings played in one day, doubleheader: 32   151
Most consecutive innings played, game, no runs: 24   160

Game Length by Time

Longest extra-inning game: 8:06   190
Longest doubleheader: 9:52   151
Shortest nine-inning game: 0:51   55
Shortest nine-inning night game: 1:15   110
Shortest doubleheader: 2:07   71

Grand Slams

Most by one player, consecutive innings: 2   144, 162, 169
Most by one player, game: 2   93, 103, 113, 144, 157, 162,
                                                                           169, 220
Most by one player, first ML game: 1   163
Most by a pitcher, game: 2   157
Most by one team, in one inning: 2   199
Most by one team, game: 2   74, 93, 103, 113, 142, 144,
                                                                           157, 162, 169, 199, 201
Most by both teams, game: 3   199, 201

Ground into double play

Most by one player, game: 4   88, 179

Hit Batsmen

Most by one pitcher, in one inning: 3   36

Hit by Pitch

Most by one player, nine-inning game: 3   16, 36
Most by one player, doubleheader: 4   16
Most by one team, in one inning: 3   36
Most by one team, nine-inning game: 6   36
Most by both teams, nine-inning game: 7   43, 170, 206

Hits

Most by one player, in one inning: 3   126
Most by one player, nine-inning game: 7   180
Most by one player, extra-inning game: 9   84
Most by one player, first major league game: 5   86

Most by one player, one game, consecutively: 7	168, 180
Most by one player, only team hits: 4	164
Most by one player, one day, two different teams: 2	185, 186
Most by one team, in one inning: 16	205
Most by one team, nine-inning game: 31	6, 213
Most by one team, extra-inning game: 33	84
Most by one team, consecutive: 10	5
Most by one team, one game, by pinch hitters: 6	70
Most by one team, while being shut out: 14	38, 73
Most by both teams, nine-inning game: 51	60
Most by both teams, extra-inning game: 58	84
Most by both teams, doubleheader: 73	74
Most teammates, five or more hits, one game: 3	6, 62, 84, 86, 95
Most teammates, four or more hits, nine-inning game: 5	137
Most teammates, three or more hits, nine-inning game: 7	102, 133, 205
Most teammates, two or more hits, nine-inning game: 10	59, 69
Most teammates, two or more hits, in one inning: 7	205
Most teammates, one or more hits, nine-inning game: 14	116, 195, 219, 226
Most players, both teams, five or more hits: 5	84
Most players, both teams, four or more hits, nine-inning game: 5	74, 137
Most players, both teams, hit safely, nine-inning game: 23	61
Fewest by one team, extra-inning game: 0	19, 50, 154
Fewest by both teams, nine-inning game: 1	156
Fewest by both teams, doubleheader: 11	40

Hits Allowed

Most by one pitcher, consecutively: 10	5
Most by one pitcher, in one inning: 12	10
Most by one pitcher, nine inning game: 26	7, 31, 95
Most by one pitcher, nine-inning shutout: 14	38, 73
Most by one pitcher, extra-inning game: 29	84
Most singles by one pitcher, in one inning: 10	91
Most triples by one pitcher, in one inning: 4	31
Most triples by one pitcher, in one game: 6	31
Most home runs by one pitcher, in one inning: 4	76, 148
Most home runs by one pitcher, in one inning, consecutively: 4	148
Most home runs by one pitcher, in one game: 6	76, 85

Home Runs

Most by one player, nine-inning game: 4	83, 122, 130, 140, 143, 198, 215
Most by one player, extra-inning game: 4	94, 115, 182
Most by one player, game, consecutively: 4	83, 140, 182
Most by one player, a pitcher, game: 3	106
Most by one player, doubleheader: 5	128, 174
Most by one team, in one inning: 5	101
Most by one team, in one inning, after two outs: 5	101
Most by one team, in one inning, consecutively: 4	148
Most by one team, game: 10	202
Most by one team, doubleheader: 13	102

Most by both teams, in one inning: 5   121, 159
Most by both teams, game: 12   218
Most by both teams, game, with none on base: 10   218
Most by both teams, doubleheader: 15   135
Most teammates, one or more, game: 7   159
Most teammates, two or more, game: 3   120, 202, 218
Most players, both teams, one or more, game: 9   121, 159
Most players, both teams, two or more, game: 4   218

Innings, Most, in One Game *see* **Game Length by Innings**

Innings Fielded

Most by a catcher, in an extra-inning game: 25   190
Most by non-pitcher/catcher, extra-inning game: 26   56

Innings Pitched

Most by one pitcher, extra-inning game: 26   56
Most by one pitcher, in relief: 18.1   44

Left on Base

Most by one team, nine-inning game: 20   136
Most by one team, nine-inning game, while being shutout: 16   217
Most by one team, extra-inning game: 25   173
Most by both teams, nine-inning game: 30   92, 108
Most by both teams, extra-inning game: 45   177
Fewest by both teams, nine-inning game: 1   156
Fewest by both teams, extra-inning game: 3   50
Most stranded by one batter, game: 12   175

Margin of Victory

Largest, 25   120
Largest, shutout game: 22   180

No-Hit Efforts

Most innings, complete game: 10   19, 50, 154
Most innings by both pitchers: 9   50
Most pitchers combine: 4   181, 212
Most baserunners allowed while pitching: 14   158
Most runs allowed while pitching: 4   208
Most home runs hit while pitching: 2   171

One-Hit Game

Most innings, complete game: 12.2   139

Passed Balls

Most by one catcher, game: 6   12
Most by both teams, game: 6   12

Pinch Hitters

Most by one team, in one inning: 6	216
Most by one team, in one inning, consecutively: 5	216
Most by one team, nine-inning game: 9	141, 216
Most by one team, extra-inning game: 10	176
Most by both teams, nine-inning game: 13	216
Most by both teams, extra-inning game: 14	134, 176

Pinch Runners

Most by one team, extra-inning game: 5	200

Pitchers in a Game

Most by one team, in one inning: 6	189
Most by one team, nine-inning game: 9	119, 224
Most by one team, extra-inning game: 11	214
Most by both teams, nine-inning game: 15	215
Most by both teams, extra-inning game: 18	173

Pitches, Fewest

While completing a nine-inning game: 58	110

Plate Appearances

Most by one player, in one inning: 3	60, 123, 126, 131, 205
Most by one player, nine-inning game: 8	60, 74, 120
Most by one player, nine-inning game, without official AB: 6	25, 89, 100
Most by one player, extra-inning game: 12	177, 190
Most by one player, doubleheader: 14	151
Most by one team, in one inning: 23	126
Most by one team, nine-inning game: 66	60, 74
Most by one team, extra-inning game: 104	190
Most by both teams, nine-inning game: 125	60
Most by both teams, extra-inning game: 202	177
Fewest by one team, nine-inning game, batting nine innings: 27	156
Fewest by both teams, nine-inning game: 53	156

Players at a Position

Most second basemen by one team, extra-inning game: 6	176
Most second basemen by both teams, extra-inning game: 8	176
Most right fielders by one team, extra-inning game: 6	155
Most center fielders by both teams, extra-inning game: 7	200
Most catchers by both teams, extra-inning game: 6	134
Most pitchers by one team, in one inning: 6	189
Most pitchers by one team, nine-inning game: 9	119, 224
Most pitchers by one team, extra-inning game: 11	214
Most pitchers by one team, combining for a no-hit game: 4	181, 212
Most pitchers by both teams, nine-inning game: 15	215
Most pitchers by both teams, extra-inning game: 18	173

Players in a Game

Most by one team, nine-inning game: 27	165
Most by one team, extra-inning game: 30	176
Most by both teams, nine-inning game: 45	183
Most by both teams, extra-inning game: 54	214
Most future Hall-of-Famers in one game: 13	72

Positions by a Player

Most in one game: 9	155

Putouts

Most by a first baseman, extra-inning game: 42	56
Most by a catcher, nine-inning game: 20	166, 194, 225
Most by a catcher, extra-inning game: 22	151

Reached Base

Most by one player, in one inning: 3	123, 126
Most by one player, nine-inning game: 7	60, 93, 109, 180
Most teammates, in one inning: 20	126
Most teammates, in one inning, consecutively: 19	123
Most teammates, in one inning, three times: 3	126

Relatives

Father and Son play in the same game	210
Most brothers, same team, same game: 3	149

Runs Allowed

Most by one pitcher, in one inning: 13	63
Most by one pitcher, in one game: 24	31

Runs Batted In

Most by one player, in one inning: 6	27
Most by one player, in consecutive innings: 8	144, 162, 169
Most by one player, game: 12	66, 215
Most by one player, a pitcher, game: 9	157
Most by one player, accounting for all team runs: 9	223
Most by one player, doubleheader: 13	174, 215
Most by one team, in one inning: 17	126
Most by one team, nine-inning game: 29	120, 133
Most by one team, doubleheader: 34	103
Most by both teams, nine-inning game: 43	60
Most by both teams, extra-inning game: 45	184
Most by both teams, doubleheader: 49	103

Runs Scored

Most by one player, in one inning: 3	126
Most by one player, game: 6	91, 109
Most by one player, doubleheader: 9	96
Most by one team, in one inning: 17	126
Most by one team, in one inning, after two outs: 13	63

Most by one team, in one inning, after two outs, no baserunners: 12   131
Most by one team, in one inning, with only one hit: 11   138
Most by one team, start of game, before first out: 9   117
Most by one team, in the first inning: 15   123
Most by one team, in consecutive innings: 19   2, 126
Most by one team, in ninth inning, after two outs, no baserunners: 9   4, 5
Most by one team, in an extra inning: 12   187
Most by one team, game: 29   120, 133
Most by one team, in shutout victory: 22   180
Most by one team, doubleheader: 36   97
Most teammates, five or more runs: 3   109
Most teammates, four or more runs: 4   74, 120
Most teammates, three or more runs: 7   120
Most teammates, two or more runs: 9   2, 60, 63, 74, 93, 219
Most teammates, two or more runs, in one inning: 6   123, 205
Most teammates, one or more runs: 13   32, 60, 195
Most by pinch hitters, in one inning: 3   70
Most by both teams, game: 49   60
Most by both teams, first inning: 15   123
Most by both teams, ninth inning: 17   32
Most by both teams, in an extra inning: 15   41
Most by both teams, doubleheader: 54   103
Most by both teams, all by way of home runs: 19   121
Most players on both teams, two or more runs: 16   60
Most players on both teams, one or more runs: 22   60
Most innings, scoring by one team, nine-inning game: 9   62, 153
Most innings, scoring by either team, nine-inning game: 14   62, 222
Most innings, scoring ten or more runs, one team, game: 2   60, 74

Scoreless Innings
Most consecutive by one pitcher, one game: 21   56
Most consecutive by both teams, one game: 23   160

Shutout Game
Most by one pitcher, in doubleheader: 2   20
Most hits allowed in: 14   38, 73
Most walks allowed in: 11   105, 167
Most innings by one pitcher: 18   22, 52, 87
Most innings by multiple pitchers: 24   160

Singles
Most by one player, game: 7   84
Most by one team, game: 26   213
Most by one team, in one inning: 12   205
Most by both teams, game: 36   6

Stolen Bases
Most by one player, game: 6   33, 34, 211, 222
Most by one team, in one inning: 8   46, 53
Most by one team, game: 15   30

Most attempted by one team, game: 20	30
Most triple-steals, one team, game: 2	78

Strikeouts

Longest game without strikeout by either team: 12 innings	79
Most by one pitcher, nine-inning game: 20	194, 225
Most by one pitcher, game, consecutively: 10	166
Most by one pitcher, extra-inning game: 21	146
Most by one player, nine-inning game: 5	218
Most by one player, extra-inning game: 6	134, 172
Most by one team, nine-inning game: 20	194
Most by one team, extra-inning game: 26	172
Most by one team, consecutively: 10	166
Most by both teams, nine-inning game: 30	192
Most by both teams, extra-inning game: 43	172

Teams Played For

Most in one day: 2	58, 185, 186

Total Bases

Most by one player, game: 18	130
Most by one player, doubleheader: 22	174
Most by one team, nine-inning game: 60	120
Most by one team, doubleheader: 87	102
Most by both teams, nine-inning game: 79	61
Most by both teams, extra-inning game: 97	184

Triple Plays

Most by one team, nine-inning game: 2	209

Triples

Most by one team, game: 8	67
Most by both teams, game: 9	67

Walks

Most to one player, nine-inning game: 6	100
Most to one player, a pitcher, game: 4	120
Most to one player, doubleheader: 8	77, 90
Most to one player, intentional, game: 5	207
Most teammates, two walks in same inning: 4	118
Most to one team, in one inning: 11	118
Most to one team, in one inning, consecutively: 7	24
Most to one team, nine-inning game: 18	47, 114
Most to one team, nine-inning game, while being shut out: 11	105
Most to one team, intentional, game: 7	134, 207
Most to both teams, nine-inning game: 30	47
Most to both teams, extra-inning game: 30	173
Most to both teams, intentional, game: 11	134

Walks Issued

Most by one pitcher, in one inning: 8	24
Most by one pitcher, in one inning, consecutively: 7	24
Most by one pitcher, nine-inning game: 16	45
Most by one pitcher, nine-inning shutout: 11	105, 167

APPENDIX C: RECORD BOOK ERRATA

As discussed in the introduction, baseball records are an evolving, dynamic system, reflecting the ambition, dedication, and tenacity of the game's researchers. Advances in technology, from microfilm to computer data bases, have also helped shape the efforts of researchers. Each year brings a more reliable reflection of the history of baseball. Current record books are certainly more accurate than previous ones, and those in the future will be even more so.

During the examination of the many reference materials used to complete this work, several dozen necessary additions and deletions to baseball's record books were discovered. All have been made known to the keepers of today's annals, and most have been incorporated. For whatever reason, some have persisted. They are here presented for the scrutiny of interested readers.

BATTERS HIT BY A PITCH, BOTH CLUBS, NINE-INNING GAME

The record for *Most Batters Hit-by-Pitch, Both Clubs, in a Nine-Inning Game* since 1900 is seven. Multiple instances are usually listed. However, one date persists for this record performance that is not credible given the evidence available today. In the second game of a doubleheader, New York at Boston (National League), on August 1, 1903, it is claimed in some record books that seven batters were hit by pitches. Below is a table showing how several contemporary newspapers described the event. *The Sporting Life* account is the only newspaper that declares seven batters hit-by-pitch — with no player names given. All other accounts show only two, and no official league records exist from this period.

Batters hit-by-pitch during the New York–Boston (NL) doubleheader on August 1, 1903				
	1st Game Giants HBP	1st Game Boston HBP	2nd Game Giants HBP	2nd Game Boston HBP
Boston Post	McGann(2) McGraw Gilbert	0	0	Moran
Boston Globe	McGann(2) McGraw Gilbert	0	Warner	0

639

	1st Game Giants HBP	1st Game Boston HBP	2nd Game Giants HBP	2nd Game Boston HBP
Boston Herald	McGann(2) McGraw Gilbert	0	Warner	Moran
NY Herald	4	0	1	1
NY Sun	4	0	1	1
NY Times	McGann(2) McGraw Gilbert	0	1	1
NY Tribune	McGann(2) Gilbert McGraw	0	Warner	Moran
NY World	4	0	?	?
Sporting Life	4	0	4	3
Sporting News	3	0	1	1

? = photocopy unclear

The error of listing this game as having had seven hit batters has also caused some record books to be in error on two related benchmarks:

1. *Most Hit by Pitch, Doubleheader*— The record is shown in some books as 8, the Giants having four batters hit in each game of this day's doubleheader. Most sources show they had only 5 HBP, four in the first game, and one in the second.

2. *Most Hit by Pitch, Doubleheader, Both Clubs*— The record is shown in some books as 11, Giant players having been hit eight times, and Boston players having been hit three times. As stated above, the Giants had only five hit in the two games, and Boston had only one.

MOST PLAYERS, TWO OR MORE RUNS SCORED IN GAME

The modern major league record for *Most Teammates Scoring Two or More Runs in a Game* is nine. This is known to have occurred nine times, although only eight instances are shown in some record books. On May 2, 1901, the Philadelphia Athletics entertained the Boston Pilgrims. In that game, each of the nine Boston players scored two or more runs as the Pilgrims prevailed 23–12. No official league records survive from this era, but following is how each of eight newspapers reported the Boston runs scored:

Boston Pilgrims run scoring on May 2, 1901								
Runs Scored According To These Newspapers:								
Boston Player	Boston Globe	Boston Herald	Boston Post	North American	Phila Inquirer	Phila Press	Public Ledger	Phila Record
Tommy Dowd lf	3	3	3	3	3	3	3	3
Charlie Jones cf	3	3	3	3	3	3	3	3
Chick Stahl cf	3	3	3	3	3	3	3	3

Boston Player	Boston Globe	Boston Herald	Boston Post	North American	Phila Inquirer	Phila Press	Public Ledger	Phila Record
Jimmy Collins 3b	2	2	2	2	2	2	2	2
Buck Freeman 1b	2	2	2	2	2	2	2	2
Freddy Parent ss	4	4	4	4	4	4	4	4
Hobe Ferris 2b	2	2	2	2	2	2	2	2
Lou Criger c	2	2	2	2	2	2	2	2
Ted Lewis p	2	2	2	2	2	2	2	2
Totals	23	23	23	23	23	23	23	23

In addition, an American League mark was set in this contest when four Athletics also scored two or more runs. That made a two-team total of 13 which remains the AL standard, although it was later tied.

MOST HIT-BY-PITCH, DOUBLEHEADER

The major league record holder for *Most Hit-By-Pitch, in a Doubleheader* is listed as Frank Chance with five, on May 30, 1904. Chance, playing for Chicago against the Reds in Cincinnati, did set the record that day for being hit the most times in a doubleheader, but it was four times, not five. He was hit three times in the first game by Jack Harper and once in the second game by Win Kellum. While the National League did not keep official records of batters hit-by-pitch in 1904, newspaper accounts were quite specific in describing each of Chance's at-bats in the doubleheader. (At this time it is uncertain if any other players have been hit four times in a doubleheader.)

Cincinnati Commercial Tribune	"He [Chance] felt three raps off Harper's speed in the morning game, and Kellum hit him on the arm in the afternoon."
Cincinnati Enquirer	"In the forenoon, he [Chance] was given a base three times because he was hit... In the afternoon game, Kellum hit Chance fairly in the short ribs, and on another occasion, narrowly missed him."
Cincinnati Times Star	"Chance was hit four times by the pitchers on Monday — three in the morning, once in the afternoon."
Chicago Chronicle	"Chance is pretty badly banged up, the injury on his head being the most severe. He was hit twice on the left arm and once on the body, and in a day or two he is liable to find himself stiff and sore."

From the above newspapers plus *The Cincinnati Post*, *The Chicago Tribune* and *The Chicago Daily News*, each of Chance's plate appearances can be accounted for. They are as follows:

Morning Game		Afternoon Game	
1st Inning	Hit by a pitch, left on base	1st Inning	Hit by a pitch, scored
4th Inning	Popped out to Kelley (1b)	3rd Inning	Singled, caught stealing
7th Inning	Hit by a pitch, forced at second	6th Inning	Fouled out to Donlin (lf)
9th Inning	Hit by a pitch, scored	8th Inning	Walked, left on base
		9th Inning	Flied out to end the game

MOST INTENTIONAL BASES ON BALLS

Since 1955, when intentional-walk data began being distinguished from other walks, the most instances in a game is listed in some record books as ten, occurring on August 26, 1980, in a game between New York and San Diego. However, research for this book has uncovered a game in which eleven intentional bases on balls were issued. On May 2, 1956, the Giants received seven intentional free passes and the Cubs four. New York's seven intentional walks actually set the one-team standard that was later tied by two other clubs. All of the following data was collected from the official, day-by-day, league records housed in the National Baseball Library, Cooperstown, NY.

BATTERS		Bases on Balls		PITCHERS		Bases on Balls	
Name	Total	Intent		Name	Total	Intent	
New York: Alvin Dark	1	0		New York: Al Worthington	3	1	
Willie Mays	2	2		Don Liddle	1	0	
Dusty Rhodes	1	1		Hoyt Wilhelm	2	2	
Daryl Spencer	1	0		Steve Ridzik	1	0	
Don Mueller	1	1		Marv Grissom	1	0	
Wes Westrum	3	2		Windy McCall	0	0	
Hank Thompson	1	1		Joe Margoneri	1	1	
New York Batters' Total	10	7		Ruben Gomez	0	0	
				New York Pitchers' Total	9	4	
Chicago: Don Hoak	1	0					
Ernie Banks	3	2		Chicago: Russ Meyer	1	1	
Walt Moryn	1	1		Turk Lown	1	0	
Hobie Landrith	1	1		Jim Davis	3	2	
Gale Wade	1	0		Vito Valentinetti	1	0	
Russ Meyer	1	0		Jim Brosnan	4	4	
Pete Whisenant	1	0		Chicago Pitchers' Total	10	7	
Chicago Batters' Total	9	4					
Two-Team Total	**19**	**11**		**Two-Team Total**	**19**	**11**	

MOST ASSISTS, GAME,
NINE INNINGS, BOTH CLUBS

Some record book listings in this category are riddled with errors. Of the three highest single-game claims, all are inaccurate according to official league records. Below is a table showing the three present listings with their claimed number of assists versus the number of assists reflected by official league data. Following the three erroneous dates is a newly discovered assist record, verified by official data. In light of this information, the major league record for assists by both clubs in a nine-inning game is 44 by Cleveland and St. Louis, set on May 27, 1909. The National League record is 43, set by Brooklyn and New York on April 21, 1903.

		CLAIMED RECORD		OFFICIAL LEAGUE DATA	
League	Date	Total	Teams	Total	Teams
A.L.	August 21, 1905	45	New York 23, Chicago 22	41	New York 20, Chicago 21
N.L.	April 21, 1903	44	Brooklyn 23, New York 21	43	Brooklyn 24, New York 19
N.L.	May 15, 1909	44	New York 25, Cincinnati 19	42	New York 25, Cincinnati 17
A.L.	May 27, 1909		Not Listed	44	Cleveland 22, St. Louis 22

OFFICIAL LEAGUE DATA, Game of May 27, 1909

Cleveland	Assists	St. Louis	Assists
Wilbur Good rf	0	Roy Hartzell rf	2
Bill Bradley 3b	1	Art Griggs lf	0
Terry Turner ss	6	Hobe Ferris 3b	2
Nap Lajoie 2b	5	Bobby Wallace ss	4
Bill Hinchman cf	0	Jimmy Williams 2b	2
George Stovall 1b	0	Tom Jones 1b	3
Ted Easterly c	3	John McAleese cf	0
Bris Lord lf	0	Jim Stephens c	3
Addie Joss p	7	Barney Pelty p	6
TOTAL	**22**	**TOTAL**	**22**

MOST CAUGHT STEALING, GAME

The 20th-century record for *Most Runners Caught Stealing* in a game is listed as seven in some record books. This mark is claimed to have occurred on August 23, 1909, in a game between Brooklyn and St. Louis, with Brooklyn catcher Bill Bergen as the sharpshooter who gunned down the base-stealers. Just where this claim originated is unclear, as "caught stealing" was neither an official statistic nor listed in boxscores of the day.

A detailed examination of the play-by-play provided by *The New York Evening Telegram* (August 23, 1909) shows that Bergen caught six baserunners, not seven. Here's how Bergen's day of success unfolded with the number caught stealing in parentheses:

• In the second inning, with one out, St. Louis's Jap Barbeau was caught stealing second, Bergen to McElveen (1). Rube Ellis then walked and also attempted larceny but was gunned down, Bergen to Alperman (2).

• After Jack Bliss and Ed Konetchy had both singled to open the third frame, "Bliss was caught off second on Bergen's fast throw to Alperman." Caught-stealing statistics were not defined in scoring rules until 1951. Historically, when new scoring rules are first stated, they apply to all previous games. This situation, although not the typical caught-stealing assist, nevertheless fulfills the 1951 scoring rule and as such, should be accepted as Bergen's third victim (3).

• With one out in the fourth, Alan Storke was nailed at second while attempting to steal, Bergen to Alperman (4).

• Bergen got a non-stealing assist in the fifth frame. Bliss sacrificed and was thrown out, Bergen to Hummel.

• Bliss found himself on first with two outs in the sixth. For the second time he tested Bergen's arm and failed, Bergen to Alperman (5).

• Bergen caught his sixth thief in the seventh frame. With one out, Steve Evans singled but later was doubled up by Bergen's throw to Alperman (6) when Delahanty fanned.

That was the extent of Bergen's heroics for the day—six runners (not seven) thrown out attempting to steal—still a very fine day's work. However, Bill must now share his remarkable standard with Wally Schang, who tossed out six St. Louis Browns on May 12, 1915. One other instance of six runners being caught stealing on June 18, 1915, was accomplished by three Philadelphia Athletics teammates who shared catching duties that day.

MOST ATTEMPTED
STOLEN BASES, GAME, ONE CLUB

In a bizarre game played in New York on September 28, 1911, the Yankees stole 15 bases against the Browns. This claim is supported by a play-by-play description found in *The New York Evening Telegram*. The same newspaper also describes another five *unsuccessful* thefts by the Yankees, bringing their total attempts in this game to 20. Through some deductive reasoning, one may conclude that their 20 base-stealing attempts is also a 20th-century, major league record.

According to modern record books, no other club has stolen 15 bases in one game since the turn of the century. (Actually the National League record is "only" 11.) If no other team is known to have stolen 15 bases in one game, the only way a club could accumulate 20 or more attempts would be if they were caught stealing six or more times. Three such teams are listed in record books as having been caught stealing six times in this century.

The first club to be caught stealing six times was the St. Louis Cardinals on August 23, 1909. In that game, in addition to their six caught stealing, the Cardinals successfully stole just two bases, giving them only eight total attempts.

Two American League teams are also listed as having been caught stealing six times in one game. On May 12, 1915, the Browns were caught stealing six times by the Athletics. Also in that game, the Browns successfully stole four bases bringing their total attempts to ten. Finally, on June 18, 1915, the White Sox were also caught stealing six times by the Athletics. In that game, the Sox stole five bases, making their total attempts 11.

Thus, the Yankees, on September 28, 1911, distinguished themselves with not only the most stolen bases by one team in one game during this century but also the *Most Stolen Base Attempts*—20, for another major-league record. (Total stolen base attempts are not presently carried in record books.)

MOST STOLEN BASES,
GAME, BOTH CLUBS

A claim is made for the *Most Stolen Bases in a Game (since 1900) by Both Clubs*—16, on June 20, 1912. While newspaper boxscores vary in their accounting, this mark does not withstand the scrutiny of the official daily league records. In that game only 14 bases were stolen by the two teams, nine by the Giants and five by the Braves. The error may have originated with the wire service accounts as the *New York Herald, Sun, Times, Tribune*, and *World* each reported 16 stolen bases. This claim should be eliminated from the record books as it was superseded by the Yankees who stole 15 bases on September 28, 1911. Included below is the official league tally for each participant as well as that from three hometown (Boston) newspapers.

New York Giants	O	P	G	H	Boston Braves	O	P	G	H
Fred Snodgrass cf, 1b	1	1	1	1	Ed McDonald 3b	2	2	2	2
Larry Doyle 2b	0	0	0	0	Vin Campbell cf	1	1	1	1
Tillie Shafer pr, 2b	1	1	1	0	Bill Sweeney 2b	1	1	1	0
Fred Merkle 1b	0	1	1	0	Jay Kirke lf	1	1	1	1
George Burns cf	0	0	0	1	Doc Miller rf	0	0	0	0
Red Murray lf	0	0	0	0	Ben Houser 1b	0	0	0	0
Moose McCormick lf	0	0	0	0	Frank O'Rourke ss	0	0	0	0
Beals Becker rf	1	1	1	2	Johnny Kling c	0	0	0	0

New York Giants	O	P	G	H
Josh Devore rf	4	4	4	2
Buck Herzog 3b	1	1	1	0
Heinie Groh 3b	0	0	0	0
Chief Meyers c	0	0	0	0
Art Wilson pr, c	0	0	1	0
Grover Hartley c	0	0	0	0
Art Fletcher ss	0	1	0	1
Hooks Wiltse p	1	0	1	0
Ernie Shore p	0	0	0	0
Total Stolen Bases	9	10	11	7

Boston Braves	O	P	G	H
Gil Whitehouse c	0	0	0	0
Buster Brown p	0	0	0	0
Ed Donnelly p	0	0	0	0
Brad Hogg p	0	0	0	0
Total Stolen Bases	5	5	5	4

O = Official Day-by-Day League Records
P = *Boston Post*
G = *Boston Globe*
H = *Boston Herald*

ANDY HIGH'S MYSTERIOUS PLATE APPEARANCE

The record for *Most Plate Appearances by One Batter in a Nine-Inning Game* is eight, a mark shared by four players. A fifth player, Andy High of the Cardinals, is also claimed erroneously as having stepped to the plate eight times in the second game of a doubleheader on July 6, 1929. According to official, day-by-day league records, this is impossible. Here's what those records show:

St. Louis = 53 At-Bats + 9 Walks + 2 Sacrifices + 1 Hit Batsman = 65 Batters Faced Pitchers, which balances with St. Louis = 27 Outs + 28 Runs + 10 Left on Base = 65 Batters Faced Pitchers.

Andy High batted in the third position in this game and therefore was the 66th batter. The preceding batter, Eddie Delker, made the final St. Louis out. The original error may have arisen due to the fact that Andy High batted in the second position during the *opening* game of this day's doubleheader.

SECOND GAME, July 6, 1929, ST. LOUIS AT PHILADELPHIA

CARDINALS	Plate Appearances	At-Bats	Walks	Sacrifices	Hit By Pitch
Taylor Douthit cf	8	6	2	0	0
Carey Selph 2b	4	2	1	1	0
Eddie Delker 2b	4	3	1	0	0
Andy High 3b	7	6	0	0	1
Jim Bottomley 1b	7	5	2	0	0
Chick Hafey lf	7	7	0	0	0
Wattie Holm rf	7	5	1	1	0
Jimmie Wilson c	7	6	1	0	0
Charlie Gelbert ss	7	6	1	0	0
Fred Frankhouse p	7	7	0	0	0
Newspaper Totals	65	53	9	2	1
Official League Totals	**65**	**53**	**9**	**2**	**1**

MOST AT-BATS VS. ONE PITCHER,
NINE-INNING GAME

The record for the *Most Official At-Bats Allowed by a National League Pitcher in a Nine-Inning Game* is listed is some record books as 49, shared by Cincinnati teammates Harley Parker and Bill Phillips, in separate 1901 games. Research for this book indicates that Harley "Doc" Parker actually allowed only 48 at-bats in his claim to infamy on June 21, 1901 in Brooklyn. The confusion hinges on an at-bat by Brooklyn's Tom McCreery. In its game description, *The Brooklyn Daily Eagle* described one of McCreery's plate appearances as "McCreery's sacrifice," which would give him *and Parker* one less official at-bat for the game. Official league records for 1901 no longer exist, but of nine newspapers checked, only *The New York Herald* and *Sporting Life* support the error. Neither of their boxscores, however, can balance as presented. Harley Parker should therefore be stricken from a share of this record.

Boxscore Details	Brooklyn Daily Eagle	NY Tribune	NY World	NY Herald	NY Sun	NY Times	Sporting News	Sporting Life	Cincinnati Enquirer
Team ABs	48	48	b	49	b	b	48	49	48
Balanced Box ?	Yes	Yes	c	No	c	c	No	No	No
McCreery's ABs	5	5	b	6	b	b	5	6	5
McCreery SAC ?	Yes	Yes	Yes	b	b	Yes	b	b	Yes
b = None shown in boxscore					*c = Impossible to calculate with available data*				

MOST BATTERS FACING
ONE PITCHER, NINE-INNING GAME

The record for the *Most Batsmen Faced*, or *Most Men Facing Pitcher* in a National League, Nine-Inning Game is listed as 53 by Bill Phillips on June 24, 1901 (second game). In this game, played in Philadelphia, Cincinnati's Phillips actually faced 55 . The error probably stems from either *Sporting Life* or *The Sporting News*, neither of which recorded a pair of sacrifices by the Philadelphia club. But all of the Philadelphia and Cincinnati newspapers reported some combination of sacrifices by the Phillies' Roy Thomas and Bill Hallman. Official National League records for 1901 no longer exist, but of ten newspapers checked, only *The Sporting News* and *Sporting Life* show no sacrifices. An eleventh newspaper, *The Philadelphia Evening Telegraph*, while it had no boxscore, did have a play-by-play for the first inning of this game in which it reported, "Hallman sacrificed."

Boxscore Details	Phila Times	Phila Press	North American Phila	Phila Inquirer	Phila Record	Phila Public Ledger	Cinc Enquirer	Cinc Commer. Tribune	Sporting News	Sporting Life
Phillies ABs	NS	50	48	49	51	49	49	49	49	49
Phillies BB	4	3	4	4	4	4	4	4	4	4
Phillies SH	2	1	3	2	2	2	2	2	NS	NS
Phillies HBP	0	0	0	0	0	0	0	0	0	0
Total faced by Bill Phillips	?	54	55	55	57	55	55	55	?	?
Legend: ABs = at-bats; BB = bases on balls; SH = sacrifice hits; HBP = hit by pitch; NS = not shown										

MOST BATTERS FACING ONE PITCHER, EXTRA-INNING GAME

Each time a batter completes a trip to the plate, he will be charged with a time at bat unless he walks, sacrifices, gets hit by a pitch, or is victim of catcher's interference. Thus, in order to calculate the number of batters a pitcher faces, one only need add all of the aforementioned. Some modern record books list the leader for each league in this category, but below the reader will see several runners-up as well as some numbers that are in disagreement with modern record books. With the exception of the 1906 contest played in Boston, all of the following data was gleaned from official league records. (Official records for 1906 do not list the necessary information to confirm the figures given; instead, it was painstakingly extracted from the newspapers noted.) All games except that by Eddie Rommel were of 20 or more innings.

		Most Batters Faced, by One Pitcher, **Extra-Inning Game**			AB	BB	SAC	HB	**Sources**
NL	96	Leon Cadore	Brooklyn	May 1, 1920	86	5	5	0	Official DBD League Records
	90	Joe Oeschger	Boston	May 1, 1920	85	4	1	0	Official DBD League Records
	89	Bob Smith	Boston	May 17, 1927	71	9	9	0	Official DBD League Records; NY Times
	86	Joe Oeschger	Phila	Apr 30, 1919	75	5	6	0	Official DBD League Records
	83	Burleigh Grimes	Brooklyn	Apr 30, 1919	75	7	1	0	Official DBD League Records
AL	89	Jack Coombs	Phila	Sep 1, 1906	79	6	3	1	Boston Globe, Bos. Herald; North American, Philadelphia Evening Telegraph, Phila. Inquirer, P. Press
	87	Joe Harris	Boston	Sep 1, 1906	82	2	2	1	
	87	Eddie Rommel	Phila	Jul 10, 1932	76	9	2	0	Official DBD League Records
	85	Ted Lyons	Chicago	May 24, 1929	78	2	5	0	Official DBD League Records
	79	George Uhle	Detroit	May 24, 1929	72	3	4	0	Official DBD League Records

MOST AT-BATS VS. ONE PITCHER, EXTRA-INNING GAME

The number of at-bats allowed by a pitcher does not necessarily correspond with the number of batters-faced, although the two usually run parallel. Below are depicted the single-game leaders in this category. All the games specified here were of 20 or more innings except for the 17 innings of relief that Eddie Rommel pitched in 1932. Try to imagine how many pitches these hurlers tossed.

		Most At-Bats vs. One Pitcher, Extra-Inning Game			**Sources**
NL	86	Leon Cadore	Brklyn	May 1, 1920	Official Day-by-Day League Records
	85	Joe Oeschger	Boston	May 1, 1920	Official Day-by-Day League Records
	76	Lefty Tyler	Chic	Jul 17, 1918	Official Day-by-Day League Records; New York Times

Most At-Bats vs. One Pitcher, Extra-Inning Game				Sources
	75	Milt Watson	Phila	Jul 17, 1918	Official Day-by-Day League Records
	75	Burleigh Grimes	Brklyn	Apr 30, 1919	Official Day-by-Day League Records
	75	Joe Oeschger	Phila	Apr 30, 1919	Official Day-by-Day League Records
AL	82	Joe Harris	Boston	Sep 1, 1906	Boston Globe, Bos. Herald; North American, Philadelphia Evening Telegraph, Phila. Inquirer, Phila. Press
	79	Jack Coombs	Phila	Sep 1, 1906	
	78	Ted Lyons	Chic	May 24, 1929	Official Day-by-Day League Records; New York Times
	76	Eddie Rommel	Phila	Jul 10, 1932	Official Day-by-Day League Records

MOST WALKS, BOTH CLUBS, EXTRA-INNING GAME

The American League and Major League record for *Most Bases on Balls by Both Clubs in an Extra-inning Game* is listed as 28, established by Boston and Detroit on September 17, 1920. This benchmark has been surpassed, although it has been unnoticed to date. In a bizarre game started on September 14 and concluded on September 20, 1971, Washington and Cleveland combined for 30 walks and a new major league, *extra-inning* mark. (Although a Detroit-Philadelphia 1916 meeting also produced 30 walks, that was a nine-inning contest.) Each club's totals are confirmed by newspapers of the day as well as by official American League statistics.

Source	Official Day-by-Day Records	Washington Post	Cleveland Plain Dealer	Cleveland Press	New York Times
Walks issued to Washington	19	19	19	19	19
Walks issued to Cleveland	11	11	11	11	11
Total walks issued	30	30	30	30	30

MOST LEFT-ON-BASE, EXTRA-INNING GAME

The American League record for *Most Left on Base in an Extra-inning Game* is listed as 25, set by Kansas City versus Texas on June 6, 1991. The AL benchmark is indeed 25, although it was established many years earlier. In a game started on September 14 and concluded on September 20, 1971, the Washington Senators stranded 25 base runners, which was a new major league standard at the time. This mark is confirmed by official day-by-day league records, *The Washington Post*, *The Cleveland Plain Dealer*, *The Cleveland Press*, *The New York Times*, and scoresheets supplied by Retrosheet. (Kansas City merely tied the AL record in 1991, and the Atlanta Braves later surpassed the mark by stranding 27 runners on May 4, 1973.)

Source	Official Day-by-Day Records	Washington Post	Cleveland Plain Dealer	Cleveland Press	New York Times
Runners left on base by Washington	25	25	25	25	25

MULTIPLE PLAYERS AT A POSITION

Extra-inning games, particularly those occurring in September after rosters become inflated, often include multiple players who field the same position. Managers whose jobs are on the line, or teams in close pennant races, often make liberal use of substitutes. The following games, previously described in this book, witnessed major league marks tied for most players at a particular position. There is little dispute that these events occurred. It is suspected they do not appear in record books simply because they went unnoticed. One of the following benchmarks is for two teams, the other for one club.

Date	Team(s)	Pos	Players who fielded the position	Record set or tied
May 2, 1956	Giants & Cubs	C	6 — (3 Giants) Ray Katt, Wes Westrum, Jim Mangan; (3 Cubs) Hobie Landrith, Elvin Tappe, Harry Chiti	Tied Major League record
Sept 25, 1992	Rangers	SS	4 — Cris Colon, Jeff Huson, Al Newman, Mario Diaz	Tied American League record

MOST TRIPLES ALLOWED
BY ONE PITCHER IN ONE GAME

Record books in 1996 list *Most Triples Allowed in a Game* since the turn of the century as five. The victims were hurlers Barney Pelty of the Browns on April 27, 1907, and Allan Travers of Detroit on May 18, 1912. However, in the infamous "Strike Game" of 1912 played in Philadelphia, Travers allowed *six* triples, not five as carried in modern annals. Although the wire service accounts, including the Detroit newspapers, indicate five Philadelphia triples, official sources as well as hometown newspapers reported six, and named the hitters.

Confirmation can be found in the official, day-by-day league records for the Philadelphia team. They show Travers' opponents, the Athletics, harvesting six three-baggers, and Travers was the only pitcher for Detroit on that day in Philadelphia. In addition, hometown newspapers *The Philadelphia Record*, *The Philadelphia Inquirer*, and *The North American* named the six triples-hitters — McInnis, Strunk, Baker, Murphy, Brown, and Maggert.

The discrepancy surrounds the Athletics' Stuffy McInnis. Most wire-service boxscores omit McInnis as one of the triple hitters, but his official sheet also credits him with a triple on May 18, 1912.

Allan Travers, therefore, should stand alone as having allowed the most triples in one game — 6.

BIBLIOGRAPHY

Books, Articles and Interviews

Alexander, Charles C. *Ty Cobb*. New York: Oxford University Press, 1984. 272 pp., indexed.

The Baseball Encyclopedia. 9th ed. New York: Macmillan, 1993. 2857 pp.

The Baseball Workshop. (Gary Gillette, 619 Wadsworth Ave., Philadelphia, Pa. 19119). Computer data bank of pitch-by-pitch, all games 1984 to present.

Benson, Michael. *Ballparks of North America*. Jefferson, N.C.: McFarland, 1989. 475 pp., indexed.

Carter, Craig, ed. *The Sporting News Complete Baseball Record Book*. St. Louis: The Sporting News, 1995. 500 pp.

Charlton, James, ed. *The Baseball Chronology*. New York: Macmillan, 1991. 707 pp., indexed.

Dewey, Donald, and Nicholas Acocella. *The Biographical History of Baseball*. New York: Carroll & Graf. 1995. 533 pp.

Ferrick, Tom. Personal interview, 7 May 1994.

Gershman, Michael. *The 1992 Baseball Engagement Book*. Boston: Houghton Mifflin, 1991.

Great Moments in Baseball. Lincolnwood, IL: Beekman, 1990. 192 pp., illustrated.

Karst, Gene, and Martin J. Jones, Jr. *Who's Who in Professional Baseball*. New Rochelle, N.Y.: Arlington, 1973. 919 pp.

Lewis, Allen. Personal interview, 29 August 1994.

Lowry, Philip J. *Green Cathedrals*. Reading, Mass.: Addison-Wesley, 1992. 275 pp., indexed.

Mann, Arthur. *Branch Rickey*. Boston: Houghton Mifflin, 1957. 288 pp., indexed.

Nadel, Eric, and Craig R. Wright. *The Man Who Stole First Base*. Dallas: Taylor, 1989. 172 pp., indexed.

Neft, David S., and Richard M. Cohen. *The Sports Encyclopedia: Baseball*. 15th ed. New York: St. Martin's, 1995. 691 pp.

Nemec, David. *Great Baseball Feats, Facts and Firsts*. New York: Plume, 1987. 333 pp.

Okkonen, Marc. *Baseball Memories 1900–1909*. New York: Sterling, 1992. 234 pp., indexed.

_____. *Baseball Uniforms of the 20th Century*. New York: Sterling, 1991. 274 pp., illustrated.

Phillips, Damon. Letter to the author, 20 August 1993.

Reichler, Joseph L. *The Great All-Time Baseball Record Book*. Revised and updated by Ken Samelson. New York: Macmillan, 1993. 592 pp., indexed.

Reichler, Joseph, and Ben Olan. *Baseball's Unforgettable Games*. New York: Ronald, 1960. 362 pp., indexed.

Retrosheet. (David W. Smith, 6 Penncross Circle, Newark, Del. 19702). Computer data bank of play-by-play, many games 1901 to 1983.

Shatzkin, Mike, ed. *The Ballplayers*. New York: Morrow, 1990. 1230 pp., illustrated.

Siwoff, Seymour, ed. *The Book of Baseball Records*. New York: Seymour Siwoff, 1995. 403 pp.

Stout, Steve. "The Greatest Game Ever Pitched." In *The National Pastime*. Cleveland: SABR, 1994, p.4.

Thorn, John, and Pete Palmer, ed. *Total Baseball*. 3rd ed. New York: HarperCollins, 1993. 2362 pp.

Weigand, Jim. *Home Runs by Park, 1900–1959*. Barberton, Oh.: Weigand, 1991-1992. 356 pp.

Newspapers

*The primary sources of information for the game narratives in this book were gleaned
from the following newspapers*

The Akron Beacon Journal
The Atlanta Constitution
The Atlanta Journal
The Boston Globe
The Boston Herald
The Boston Journal
The Boston Post
The Brooklyn Daily Eagle
Chicago American
The Chicago Chronicle
Chicago Daily Journal
Chicago Daily News
The Chicago Evening Post
Chicago Herald American
Chicago Herald Examiner
The Chicago Record-Herald
Chicago Sun Times
Chicago Today
The Chicago Tribune
Daily Mirror (New York)
Daily News (New York)
Daily Times (Chicago)
The Cincinnati Enquirer
The Cincinnati Post
The Cincinnati Times-Star
The Cleveland Leader
Cleveland Plain Dealer
The Cleveland Press
Columbus Ohio State Journal
The Commercial Tribune
    (Cincinnati)
The Dallas Morning News
Dallas Times Herald
The Dayton Daily Herald
The Dayton Daily News
The Detroit Free Press
The Detroit Journal
The Detroit Tribune
The Detroit Times
The Evening Bulletin (Philadel-
    phia)

The Evening News (Detroit)
Evening Public Ledger (Philadel-
    phia)
The Evening Star (Washington)
The Evening Telegraph
    (Philadelphia)
The Evening Times (Philadel-
    phia)
The Evening Wisconsin (Mil-
    waukee)
Fort Worth Star-Telegram
The Gazette (Montreal)
The Gazette Times (Pittsburgh)
The Globe and Mail (Canada)
The Hartford Courant
The Homestead Daily Messen-
    ger (PA)
The Houston Chronicle
The Houston Post
The Inter Ocean (Chicago)
The Kansas City Star
The Kansas City Times
The Kansas City Star &
    Times
Los Angeles Herald-Examiner
Los Angeles Times
The Milwaukee Daily News
The Milwaukee Journal
The Milwaukee Sentinel
The Minneapolis Star
Minneapolis Star Tribune
The Nashville Banner
New York American
New York Evening Post
The New York Herald
New York Herald Tribune
New York Journal American
The New York Press
The New York Times
New York Tribune
New York World Telegram

New York World Telegram and
    The Sun
Norristown Times Herald (PA)
The North American (Philadel-
    phia)
The Oakland Tribune
Philadelphia Daily News
Philadelphia Evening Item
The Philadelphia Inquirer
The Philadelphia Record
The Pittsburgh Dispatch
The Pittsburgh Gazette
The Pittsburgh Leader
The Pittsburgh Post
Pittsburgh Post-Gazette
The Pittsburgh Press
The Pittsburgh Sun Telegraph
The Press (Philadelphia)
Public Ledger (Philadelphia)
St. Louis Globe-Democrat
St. Louis Post-Dispatch
The St. Louis Republic
The St. Louis Star
The St. Louis Times
St. Paul Pioneer Press
The San Diego Union
San Francisco Chronicle
San Francisco Examiner
The Seattle Times
Sporting Life
The Sporting News
The Standard Union (Brooklyn)
The Sun (Baltimore)
The Sun (New York)
The Toronto Star
USA Today
USA Today Baseball Weekly
The Washington Herald
The Washington Post
The Washington Times
The World (New York)

INDEX

References are to entry numbers.